Contemporary Business Mathematics with Canadian Applications

Eighth Edition

S. A. Hummelbrunner
K. Suzanne Coombs
Kwantlen University College

Contributing Author
Bruce Coombs Kwantlen University College

PEARSON
Prentice Hall
Toronto

Library and Archives Canada Cataloguing in Publication

Hummelbrunner, S. A. (Siegfried August)
Contemporary business mathematics with Canadian applications /
S. A. Hummelbrunner, K. Suzanne Coombs. — 8th ed.

Includes index.
ISBN-13: 978-0-13-156467-1
ISBN-10: 0-13-156467-6

1. Business mathematics—Textbooks. I. Coombs, Suzanne II. Title.

HF5691.H85 2007 650.01'513 C2007-900988-3

ISBN-13: 978-0-13-156467-1
ISBN-10: 0-13-156467-6

Editor-in-Chief: Gary Bennett
Executive Editor: Samantha Scully
Executive Marketing Manager: Cas Shields
Developmental Editor: Madhu Ranadive
Production Editor: Cheryl Jackson
Copy Editor: Rodney Rawlings
Proofreader: Betty Robinson
Production Coordinator: Avinash Chandra
Compositor: Integra
Permissions Researcher: Lynn McIntyre
Art Director: Julia Hall
Cover and Interior Design: Anthony Leung
Cover Image: Masterfile

1 2 3 4 5 11 10 09 08 07

Printed and bound in the United States.

PEARSON
Prentice Hall

BRIEF CONTENTS

CONTENTS

PREFACE

INTRODUCTION

Contemporary Business Mathematics is intended for use in introductory mathematics of finance courses in business administration and accounting programs. In a more general application it also provides a comprehensive basis for those who wish to review and extend their understanding of basic business mathematics.

The primary objective of the text is to increase the student's knowledge and skill in the solution of practical financial and mathematical problems encountered in the business community. It also provides a supportive base for mathematical topics in finance, accounting, and marketing.

ORGANIZATION

Contemporary Business Mathematics is a teaching text using the objectives approach. The systematic and sequential development of the material is supported by carefully selected and worked examples. These detailed step-by-step solutions presented in a clear and colourful layout are particularly helpful in allowing students, in either independent studies or in the traditional classroom setting, to carefully monitor their own progress.

Each topic in each chapter is followed by an Exercise containing numerous drill questions and application problems. The Review Exercise, Self-Test, and the Case Studies at the end of each chapter integrate the material studied.

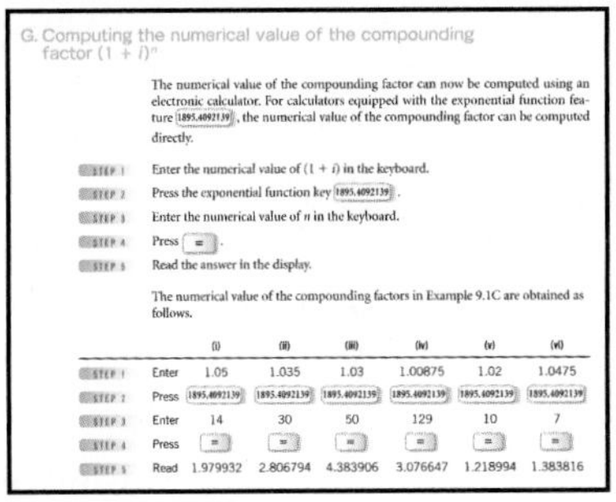

G. Computing the numerical value of the compounding factor $(1 + i)^n$

The numerical value of the compounding factor can now be computed using an electronic calculator. For calculators equipped with the exponential function feature [1895.4092139], the numerical value of the compounding factor can be computed directly.

STEP 1 Enter the numerical value of $(1 + i)$ in the keyboard.

STEP 2 Press the exponential function key [1895.4092139].

STEP 3 Enter the numerical value of n in the keyboard.

STEP 4 Press [=].

STEP 5 Read the answer in the display.

The numerical value of the compounding factors in Example 9.1C are obtained as follows.

		(i)	(ii)	(iii)	(iv)	(v)	(vi)
STEP 1	Enter	1.05	1.035	1.03	1.00875	1.02	1.0475
STEP 2	Press	[1895.4092139]	[1895.4092139]	[1895.4092139]	[1895.4092139]	[1895.4092139]	[1895.4092139]
STEP 3	Enter	14	30	50	129	10	7
STEP 4	Press	[=]	[=]	[=]	[=]	[=]	[=]
STEP 5	Read	1.979932	2.806794	4.383906	3.076647	1.218994	1.383816

The first four chapters and Appendix I (Further Review of Basic Algebra) are intended for students with little or no background in algebra and provide an opportunity to review arithmetic and algebraic processes.

The text is based on Canadian practice, and reflects current trends using available technology—specifically the availability of reasonably priced electronic pocket calculators. Students using this book should have access to electronic calculators having a power function and a natural logarithm function. The use of such calculators eliminates the arithmetic constraints often associated with financial problems and frees the student from reliance on financial tables.

The power function and the natural logarithm function are often needed to determine values that will be used for further computation. Such values should not be rounded and all available digits should be retained. The student is encouraged to use the memory functions of the calculator to retain such values.

When using the memory the student needs to be aware that the number of digits retained in the registers of the calculator is greater than the number of digits displayed. Depending on whether the memory or the displayed digits are used, slight differences may occur. Such differences will undoubtedly be encountered when working through the examples presented in the text. However, they are insignificant and should not be of concern. In most cases the final answers will agree, whichever method is used.

Students are encouraged to use preprogrammed financial calculators, though this is not essential. The use of preprogrammed calculators facilitates the solving of most financial problems and is demonstrated extensively in Chapters 9 to 16.

NEW TO THIS EDITION

In this eighth edition, revisions and updates have been made to the text to reflect current practices in Canada and to better suit the needs of users of this book. Examples and exercises have been updated, rewritten, and expanded. To expand the building-block approach, exercises have been reordered to represent a link with the solved examples. Help references have been added to link selected exercises to solved examples.

Specifically, in Chapter 1 (Review of Arithmetic), examples involving equivalent fractions and percent have been simplified and formatting the calculator has been clarified.

In Chapter 2 (Review of Algebra), new exercises have been added for determining interest rates and to utilize the formulas for discounts, retail pricing, and simple interest. Instructions and explanations have been expanded for the sections on manipulating formulas and solving word problems.

In Chapter 3 (Ratio, Proportion, and Percent), new exercises have been added, and examples, exercises, and solutions have been changed to reflect current prices. Currency conversion rates, index numbers, and personal income tax rates have been updated.

Break-Even and Cost-Volume-Profit Analysis (Chapter 5) has been placed before Trade Discount, Cash Discount, Markup, and Markdown (Chapter 6). This change reflects the continued emphasis on building-block learning. Depreciation has been moved to Appendix C on the Spreadsheet Template Disk, which is included with your text. The presentation of break-even analysis and CVP topics has been expanded to include added solving for various unknowns in basic break-even. Basic break-even has been separated from calculations involving contribution margin and rate. The discussion and exercises on CVP has also been expanded. In Chapter 6, coverage of partial payments and integrated problems has been expanded using the building-block process to explain. Many new exercises have been added in both chapters.

In Chapter 7 (Simple Interest), the section on finding the principal has been clarified and simplified. Again, using the building-block approach, the coverage of equivalent values now includes more simplified solved examples, and many new exercises have been added.

In Chapter 8 (Simple Interest Applications), coverage of promissory notes has been simplified. Additional coverage of home equity lines of credit has been included.

In Chapter 9 (Compound Interest—Future Value and Present Value) and Chapter 10 (Compound Interest—Further Topics), solved examples have been clarified using a step-by-step approach. Updated examples and exercises and comparison questions have been added.

In Chapters 11, 12, and 13, examples and exercises have been updated, and comparison questions and exercises have been added. A new section on Constant-Growth Annuities has been added to Chapter 12.

In Chapter 13, coverage of deferred ordinary annuities and deferred annuities due has been separated with stand-alone sections. Further explanation for perpetuities has been included. Many new exercise questions have been added in all three chapters, as well as additional calculator solutions.

Chapter 14 includes updated information on CMHC mortgage insurance.

In Chapter 15, bond terminology and calculations have been updated and simplified. Bond interest rates in examples and exercises have been updated.

In general, interest rates used reflect the current economic climate in Canada. Calculator tips and solutions have been updated or clarified. Spreadsheet instructions and Internet site references have been updated. *Pitfalls and Pointers* have been included to assist in performing tasks and interpreting word problems, and sections have been rewritten to clarify the explanations. Many more word problems have been added and references to solved examples have been added. All *Business Math News Boxes* and Case Studies have been updated. Examples involving both business and personal situations are included. Where appropriate, the use of six decimal places has been standardized. The pedagogical elements of the previous edition have been retained. In response to requests and suggestions by users of the book, a number of new features for this edition have been included. They are described below.

FEATURES

- A new colourful and student-friendly design has been created for the book, making it more accessible and less intimidating to learners at all levels.
- Any preprogrammed financial calculator may be used, but this edition includes extensive instructions for using the Texas Instruments BA II Plus financial calculator. Equivalent instructions are given in Appendix II for the Sharp EL-733A and the Hewlett Packard 10B financial calculators.

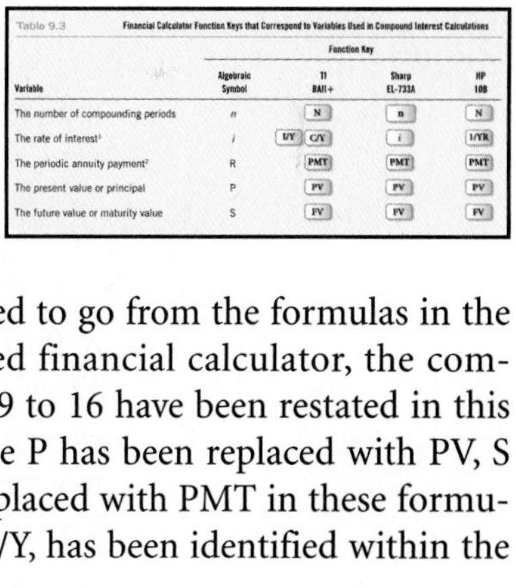

Table 9.3 Financial Calculator Function Keys that Correspond to Variables Used in Compound Interest Calculations

Variable	Algebraic Symbol	Function Key: TI BAII+	Sharp EL-733A	HP 10B
The number of compounding periods	*n*	N	n	N
The rate of interest[1]	*i*	I/Y C/Y	i	I/YR
The periodic annuity payment[2]	R	PMT	PMT	PMT
The present value or principal	P	PV	PV	PV
The future value or maturity value	S	FV	FV	FV

- To reduce the amount of "translation" required to go from the formulas in the text to the keystrokes on the preprogrammed financial calculator, the compounding and annuity formulas in Chapters 9 to 16 have been restated in this edition. From the beginning of Chapter 9, the P has been replaced with PV, S has been replaced with FV, and A has been replaced with PMT in these formulas. In addition, the compounding interval, C/Y, has been identified within the calculator solutions.
- EXCEL NOTES An updated Spreadsheet Template Disk has been developed by Bruce Coombs. It is a CD-ROM that accompanies the text and contains Word files and Excel spreadsheet files. It requires Windows XP or newer versions of Windows to run. The disk contains 24 self-contained tutorials that show how to use one of Excel's special spreadsheet functions to solve business problems. Each tutorial gives a brief description of the

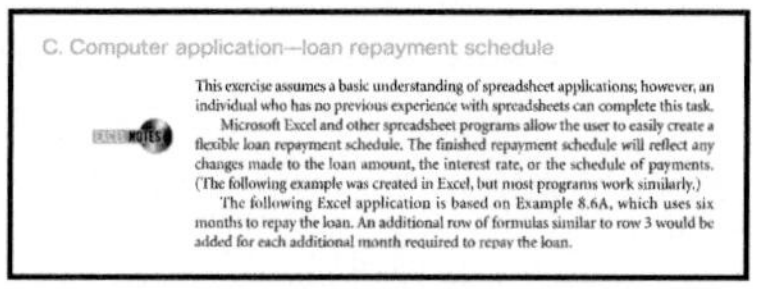

C. Computer application—loan repayment schedule

This exercise assumes a basic understanding of spreadsheet applications; however, an individual who has no previous experience with spreadsheets can complete this task.

Microsoft Excel and other spreadsheet programs allow the user to easily create a flexible loan repayment schedule. The finished repayment schedule will reflect any changes made to the loan amount, the interest rate, or the schedule of payments. (The following example was created in Excel, but most programs work similarly.)

The following Excel application is based on Example 8.6A, which uses six months to repay the loan. An additional row of formulas similar to row 3 would be added for each additional month required to repay the loan.

function, a general example showing how the function might be used, directions for creating a spreadsheet template to use the function, and a list of questions from the text that can be answered using the spreadsheet function. In addition, an Excel file containing ready-to-use examples of each function is included. The student can use these spreadsheets to enter values and obtain immediate results. The Spreadsheet Template Disk also contains spreadsheet templates for the spreadsheet applications described in the text: loan repayment schedules (Chapter 8), accumulation of principal schedules (Chapter 9), amortization schedules (Chapter 14), and sinking fund schedules (Chapter 15). An Excel icon in the text highlights information on the use of Excel to solve problems and the Excel spreadsheet applications, directing students to the spreadsheet template disk.

- A spreadsheet icon in the text highlights the questions in the text that can be solved using an Excel spreadsheet function. Three appendices are also included on the Spreadsheet Template Disk.
- A set of learning objectives is listed at the beginning of each chapter.
- Each chapter opens with a description of a situation familiar to students to emphasize the practical applications of the material to follow.

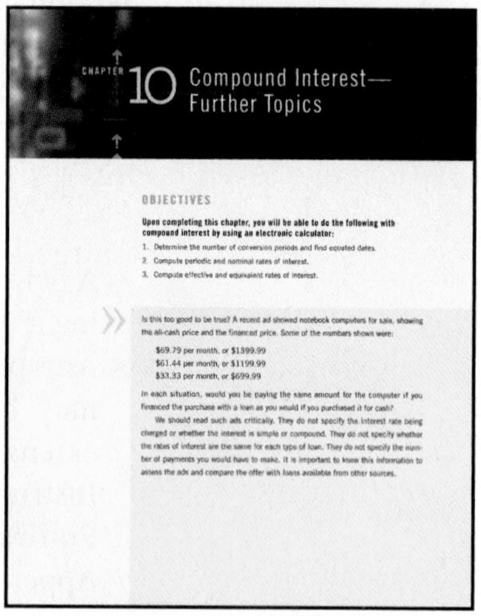
CHAPTER 10 Compound Interest—Further Topics

OBJECTIVES

Upon completing this chapter, you will be able to do the following with compound interest by using an electronic calculator:

1. Determine the number of conversion periods and find equated dates.
2. Compute periodic and nominal rates of interest.
3. Compute effective and equivalent rates of interest.

Is this too good to be true? A recent ad showed notebook computers for sale, showing the all-cash price and the financed price. Some of the numbers shown were:

$69.79 per month, or $1399.99
$61.44 per month, or $1199.99
$33.33 per month, or $699.99

In each situation, would you be paying the same amount for the computer if you financed the purchase with a loan as you would if you purchased it for cash?

We should read such ads critically. They do not specify the interest rate being charged or whether the interest is simple or compound. They do not specify whether the rates of interest are the same for each type of loan. They do not specify the number of payments you would have to make. It is important to know this information to assess the ads and compare the offer with loans available from other sources.

- A *Business Math News Box* is presented in every chapter. This element consists of short excerpts based on material appearing in newspapers, magazines, or websites, followed by a set of questions. These boxes demonstrate how widespread business math applications are in the real world. All of the Business Math News Boxes are new or completely revised in this eighth edition.

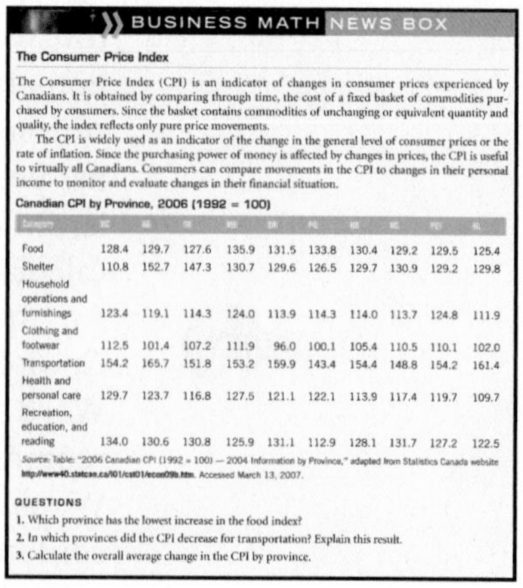
BUSINESS MATH NEWS BOX

The Consumer Price Index

The Consumer Price Index (CPI) is an indicator of changes in consumer prices experienced by Canadians. It is obtained by comparing through time, the cost of a fixed basket of commodities purchased by consumers. Since the basket contains commodities of unchanging or equivalent quantity and quality, the index reflects only pure price movements.

The CPI is widely used as an indicator of the change in the general level of consumer prices or the rate of inflation. Since the purchasing power of money is affected by changes in prices, the CPI is useful to virtually all Canadians. Consumers can compare movements in the CPI to changes in their personal income to monitor and evaluate changes in their financial situation.

Canadian CPI by Province, 2006 (1992 = 100)

[illegible]	[illegible]	[illegible]	[illegible]	[illegible]	[illegible]	[illegible]	[illegible]	[illegible]	[illegible]	[illegible]
Food	128.4	129.7	127.6	135.9	131.5	133.8	130.4	129.2	129.5	125.4
Shelter	110.8	152.7	147.3	130.7	129.6	126.5	129.7	130.9	129.2	129.8
Household operations and furnishings	123.4	119.1	114.3	124.0	113.9	114.3	114.0	113.7	124.8	111.9
Clothing and footwear	112.5	101.4	107.2	111.9	96.0	100.1	105.4	110.5	110.1	102.0
Transportation	154.2	165.7	151.8	153.2	159.9	143.4	154.4	148.8	154.2	161.4
Health and personal care	129.7	123.7	116.8	127.5	121.1	122.1	113.9	117.4	119.7	109.7
Recreation, education, and reading	134.0	130.6	130.8	125.9	131.1	112.9	128.1	131.7	127.2	122.5

Source: Table: "2006 Canadian CPI (1992 = 100) — 2004 Information by Province," adapted from Statistics Canada website http://www40.statcan.ca/l01/cst01/econ09b.htm. Accessed March 13, 2007.

QUESTIONS

1. Which province has the lowest increase in the food index?
2. In which provinces did the CPI decrease for transportation? Explain this result.
3. Calculate the overall average change in the CPI by province.

- The *Pointers and Pitfalls* boxes emphasize good practices, highlight ways to avoid common errors, show how to use a financial calculator efficiently, or give hints for tackling business math situations to reduce math anxiety.

> **POINTERS AND PITFALLS**
>
> You can use the BREAKEVEN function of a financial calculator to determine the break-even point. In this function, FC refers to the total fixed cost for the period, VC refers to the unit variable cost, P refers to the unit price, PFT is the resulting profit, and Q is used to input or calculate the quantity or number of units. For example, for Example 6.1A, press:
>
> 2nd Brkevn FC = 8640.00 Enter ↓
> VC = 30.00 Enter ↓
> P = 50.00 Enter ↓
> PFT = 0 Enter ↓
> CPT Q = 432 units
>
> Any four of the five variables may be entered. You can then compute a value for the fifth variable.

- Numerous Examples with worked-out Solutions are provided throughout the book, offering easy-to-follow, step-by-step instructions.

> **EXAMPLE 1.5C** Teachers with the Northern Manitoba Board of Education are under contract for 200 teaching days per year. They are paid according to the following schedule:
>
> 8% of annual salary on the first day of school
> 4% of annual salary for each of 20 two-week pay periods
> 12% of annual salary at the end of the last pay period in June
>
> Alicia Nowak, a teacher employed by the board, is paid an annual salary of $65 200.
>
> (i) What is Alicia's daily rate of pay?
> (ii) What is Alicia's gross pay
> (a) for the first pay period?
> (b) for the last pay period?
> (c) for all other pay periods?
> (iii) If Alicia takes an unpaid leave of absence for three days during a pay period ending in April, what is her gross pay for that pay period?
>
> **SOLUTION**
>
> (i) Daily rate of pay $= \frac{65\ 200}{200} = \$326.00$
>
> (ii) (a) First gross pay = 0.08 × 65 200.00 = $5216.00
> (b) Last gross pay = 0.12 × 65 200.00 = $7824.00
> (c) All other gross pay = 0.04 × 65 200.00 = $2608.00
>
> (iii) Gross pay for pay period ending in April = $2608.00
> Less 3 days of pay = 3/200 of $65 200.00 = 978.00
> Gross pay $1630.00

- Programmed solutions using the Texas Instruments BA II Plus calculator are offered for all examples in Chapters 9 to 16. Since this calculator display can be pre-set, it is suggested that the learner set the display to show six decimal places to match the mathematical calculations in the body of the text. Both mathematical and calculator solutions for all Exercises, Review Exercises, and Self-Tests are included in the Instructor's Solutions Manual. An icon highlights information on the use of the BA II Plus calculator.

- Key Terms are introduced in the text in boldface type. A Glossary at the end of each chapter lists each term with its definition and a page reference to where the term was first defined in the chapter.

> **11.1 INTRODUCTION TO ANNUITIES**
>
> A. Basic concepts
>
> An **annuity** is a series of payments, usually of equal size, made at periodic intervals. The length of time between the successive payments is called the **payment interval** or **payment period**. The length of time from the beginning of the first payment interval to the end of the last payment interval is called the **term of an annuity**. The size of each of the regular payments is the **periodic rent**, and the sum of the periodic payments in one year is the **annual rent**.

> **GLOSSARY**
>
> Accumulated value of one dollar per period *see* **Accumulation factor for annuities**
>
> Accumulation factor for annuities the factor $\frac{(1+i)^n - 1}{i}$ *(p. 428)*
>
> Annual rent the sum of the periodic payments in one year *(p. 423)*
>
> Annuity a series of payments, usually equal in size, made at equal periodic time intervals *(p. 423)*
>
> Annuity certain an annuity for which the term is fixed *(p. 423)*
>
> Annuity due an annuity in which the periodic payments are made at the beginning of each payment interval *(p. 424)*
>
> Compounding factor for annuities *see* **Accumulation factor for annuities**
>
> Contingent annuity an annuity in which the term is uncertain; that is, either the beginning date of the term or the ending date of the term or both are unknown *(p. 423)*
>
> Deferred annuity an annuity in which the first payment is delayed for a number of payment periods *(p. 424)*
>
> Down payment the portion of the purchase price that is supplied by the purchaser as an initial payment *(p. 441)*
>
> Future value of an annuity the sum of the accumulated values of the periodic payments at the end of the term of the annuity *(p. 427)*
>
> General annuity an annuity in which the conversion (or compounding) period is different from the payment interval *(p. 424)*
>
> Ordinary annuity an annuity in which the payments are made at the end of each payment interval *(p. 424)*

- Main Equations are highlighted in the chapters and repeated in a Summary of Formulas at the ends of the chapters. Each main formula is presented in colour and labelled numerically (with the letter A suffix if equivalent forms of the formula are presented later). By contrast, equivalent formulae are presented in black and labelled with the number of the related main formula followed by the letter B or C.

> NET PRICE FACTOR (NPF) = 100% − % DISCOUNT ——— Formula 5.3A
>
> The resulting relationship between net price and list price may be stated generally.
>
> NET PRICE = NET PRICE FACTOR (NPF) × LIST PRICE ——— Formula 5.4A
>
> The two relationships represented by Formulas 5.3A and 5.4A can be restated in algebraic terms:
>
> Convert the % discount into its decimal equivalent represented by d and express 100% by its decimal equivalent 1.
>
> NET PRICE FACTOR = $1 - d$ ——— Formula 5.3B
>
> Let the list price be represented by L and let the net price be represented by N.
>
> $N = (1 - d)L$ or $N = L(1 - d)$ ——— Formula 5.4B

- A list of the Main Formulas can be found on the study card bound into this text.

- An Exercise set is provided at the end of each section in every chapter. If students choose, they can use the suggested Excel spreadsheet functions to answer those questions marked with the spreadsheet logo. In addition, each chapter contains a Review Exercise set and a Self-Test. If students choose, they can use an Excel spreadsheet function to answer those questions marked with a spreadsheet logo, but they must decide which function to use. Answers to all the odd-numbered Exercises, Review Exercises, and Self-Tests are given at the back of the book. Solutions for questions answered using Excel spreadsheet functions are given in the Instructor's area of the Hummelbrunner/Coombs Companion Website.

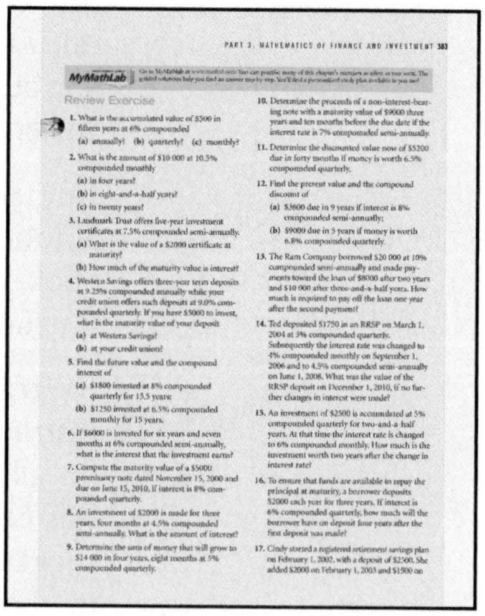

- New to this edition are references to solved Examples from the chapter, which are included at the end of key exercises. Students are directed to specific examples so they can check their work and review fundamental problem types.

- A set of Challenge Problems is provided in each chapter. These problems give users the opportunity to apply the skills learned in the chapter to questions that are pitched at a higher level than the Exercises.

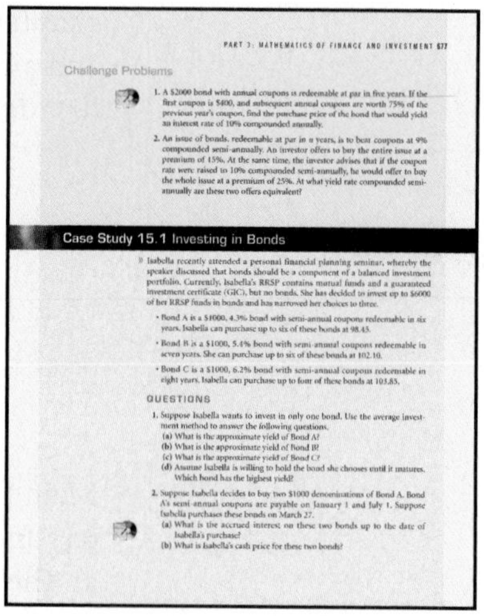

- Thirty-two Case Studies are included in the book, two near the end of each chapter. They present comprehensive realistic scenarios followed by a set of questions and illustrate some of the important types of practical applications of the chapter material. All of the Case Studies are new or completely revised in this eighth edition.

- An updated set of Useful Internet Sites is provided at the end of each chapter, with the URL and a brief description provided for each site. These sites are related to the chapter topic or to companies mentioned in the chapter, or they show how business math is important to the day-to-day operations of companies and industries.

USEFUL INTERNET SITES

www.electronicaccountant.com
Electronic Accountant Free access to news and critical accounting industry information. This site includes Newswire, links and commentary, discussion groups, feature articles, and accounting/tax software exhibit halls.

www.ibc.ca
Insurance Bureau of Canada This site offers an overview of the industry and of recent legal and consumer-related developments and provides significant links to both business and government sites.

SUPPLEMENTS

The following supplements have been carefully prepared to accompany this eighth edition.

- An **Instructor's Resource CD-ROM** has been created for this text. It will include the Solutions Manual in PDF format, a new Instructor's Resource Manual, PowerPoint® Lecture Slides, and Test Generator. Instructions to access each item is given on the CD-ROM. Each supplement is described in more detail below.
- An **Instructor's Solutions Manual** provides complete mathematical and calculator solutions to all the Exercises, Review Exercises, Self-Tests, Business Math News Box questions, Challenge Problems, and Case Studies in the textbook.
- An **Instructor's Resource Manual** includes Chapter Overviews, Suggested Priority of Topics, Chapter Outlines, and centralized information on all the supplements available with the text.
- **PowerPoint® Lecture Slides** present an outline of each chapter in the book, highlighting the major concepts taught. The presentation will include many of the figures and tables from the text and provides the instructor with a visually interesting summary of the entire book.
- A **TestGen**, a special computerized version of the test bank, enables instructors to edit existing questions, add new questions, and generate tests. The Test Generator is organized by chapter, with level of difficulty indicated for each question.
- A **Student's Solutions Manual** provides complete solutions to all the odd-numbered Exercises, Review Exercises, and Self-Test questions in the textbook.
- **Personal Response System Slides** will help gauge students' progress with clicker questions that enable instructors to pose questions, record results, and display those results instantly in the classroom. Questions are provided in PowerPoint® format.
- A **Companion Website** provides students with self-test questions that include Case Studies, Multiple Choice, Fill-in-the-Blank, True/False, and Internet-based Exercises. Hints are included for most of the questions, and immediate feedback is available to assist students to study and test themselves. Did You Know? boxes are available for each chapter and offer interesting practical and mathematical facts. Links to other websites of interest and an Internet search of key business math terms have been updated for the eighth edition. New to this edition is information about web-based calculators and the use of interactive charts and graphs that accompany them. Visit the Hummelbrunner/Coombs website at **www.pearsoned.ca/hummelbrunner** and then click on the *Contemporary Business Mathematics with Canadian Applications*, Eighth Edition, cover.

MYMATHLAB

MyMathLab is a powerful online homework, tutorial, and assessment system tied directly to *Contemporary Business Mathematics*, Eighth Edition. Ideal for use in a lecture, self-paced, or distance-learning course, MyMathLab

- Diagnoses students' weaknesses and creates a personalized study plan based on their test results.
- Provides students with unlimited practice using a database of algorithmically generated exercises correlated to the exercises in the textbook.
- Offers an interactive guided solution and a sample problem with each tutorial exercise, to help students improve their skills independently.
- Includes an interactive eBook that links directly to supplemental multimedia resources such as Excel spreadsheet templates.
- Provides narrated, animated PowerPoints to reinforce core concepts.

Instructors can use MyMathLab to create online homework assignments, quizzes, and tests that are automatically graded and tracked. Instructors can view and manage all students' homework and test results, study plans, and tutorial work in MyMathLab's flexible online Gradebook.

To learn more about how MyMathLab can enhance the use of *Contemporary Business Mathematics*, please contact your Pearson Education Canada Sales and Editorial Representative.

ACKNOWLEDGMENTS

Special thanks must be given to Bruce M. Coombs of Kwantlen University College for his help in creating and updating the Spreadsheet Template Disk and the Companion Website. His encouraging contribution was invaluable. Also, great thanks go to a new author, Sepand Jazzi, also of Kwantlen University College, who contributed the Business Math News Boxes and Case Studies.

We would like to express our thanks to the many people who offered thoughtful suggestions and recommendations for updating and improving the book. We would particularly like to thank the following instructors for providing formal reviews for the eighth edition:

Peter Au, George Brown College
Helen Catania, Centennial College
Hoshiar Gosal, Langara College
Chris Kellman, British Columbia Institute of Technology
Lisa MacKay, Southern Alberta Institute of Technology
Judith I. Palm, Malaspina University-College
Raina Rudko-Buac, Grant MacEwan College
Don St. Jean, George Brown College
Brian Tozer, Conestoga College

We would also like to thank the many people at Pearson Education Canada who helped with the development and production of this book, especially to the production editor, Cheryl Jackson; the production coordinator, Andrea Falkenberg; the copy editor, Rodney Rawlings; the proofreader, Betty Robinson; and to Dorothy Kubsch, who completed a technical check of the entire manuscript. Special thanks to editors Samantha Scully and Madhu Ranadive for their supportive directions.

CHAPTER 1 Review of Arithmetic

Objectives are a "roadmap" showing what will be covered and what is especially important in each chapter.

OBJECTIVES

Upon completing this chapter, you will be able to do the following:

1. Simplify arithmetic expressions using the basic order of operations.
2. Determine equivalent fractions and convert fractions to decimals.
3. Convert percents to common fractions and to decimals, and change decimals and fractions to percents.
4. Through problem solving, compute simple arithmetic and weighted averages.
5. Determine gross earnings for employees remunerated by the payment of salaries, hourly wages, or commissions.
6. Through problem solving, compute GST, sales taxes, and property taxes.

Each chapter opens with a description of a familiar situation, to help you understand the practical applications of the material to follow.

Being able to perform arithmetic calculations is important in business operations. The use of arithmetic expressions, fractions, and percent is common in today's business environment. Competence in problem solving, including calculation of averages, is essential. When you employ people in operating a business, you must determine the amounts to pay them in the form of salaries or wages, and you must deduct and pay payroll taxes such as Canada Pension Plan, Employment Insurance, and employee income taxes. You are responsible for paying your employees and submitting the tax amounts to the federal government. Operating a business also means that you must determine the amount of Goods and Services Tax (GST) to collect on almost everything you sell. The amount you must remit to the federal government, or the refund you are entitled to, is calculated on the basis of the GST you paid when you make purchases of goods and services. By using arithmetic and problem-solving approaches in this chapter, you should be able to determine the amounts owed.

INTRODUCTION

The basics of fraction, decimal, and percent conversions are vital skills for dealing with situations you face, not only as a small business owner, but as a consumer and investor. Although calculators and computers have become common tools for solving business problems, it is still important to understand clearly the process behind the conversions between number forms, the rounding of answers, and the correct order of operations.

1.1 BASICS OF ARITHMETIC

A. The basic order of operations

Boldfaced words are Key Terms that are explained here and defined in the Glossary section at the end of the chapter.

To ensure that arithmetic calculations are performed consistently, we must follow the **order of operations.**

If an arithmetic expression contains brackets as well as any or all of exponents, multiplication, division, addition, and subtraction, we use the following procedure:

1. Perform all operations *inside* a bracket first (the operations inside the bracket must be performed in proper order).
2. Perform exponents.
3. Perform multiplication and division in order as they appear from left to right.
4. Perform addition and subtraction.

Numerous Examples, often with worked-out Solutions, offer you easy-to-follow, step-by-step instructions.

The following "BEDMAS" rule might help you to more easily remember the order of operations:

B	E	D	M	A	S
Brackets	Exponents	Division	Multiplication	Addition	Subtraction

EXAMPLE 1.1A

(i) $(9 - 4) \times 2 = 5 \times 2 = 10$ — work inside the bracket first

(ii) $9 - 4 \times 2 = 9 - 8 = 1$ — do multiplication before subtraction

(iii) $18 \div 6 + 3 \times 2 = 3 + 6 = 9$ — do multiplication and division before adding

(iv) $(13 + 5) \div 6 - 3 = 18 \div 6 - 3 = 3 - 3 = 0$ — work inside the bracket first, then do division before subtraction

(v) $18 \div (6 + 3) \times 2 = 18 \div 9 \times 2 = 2 \times 2 = 4$ — work inside the bracket first, then do division and multiplication in order

(vi) $18 \div (3 \times 2) + 3 = 18 \div 6 + 3 = 3 + 3 = 6$ — work inside the bracket first, then divide before adding

(vii) $8(9 - 4) - 4(12 - 5) = 8(5) - 4(7)$ — work inside the brackets first, then multiply before subtracting
$= 40 - 28$
$= 12$

(viii) $\frac{12 - 4}{6 - 2} = (12 - 4) \div (6 - 2)$ — the fraction line indicates brackets as well as division
$= 8 \div 4$
$= 2$

(ix) $128 \div (2 \times 4)^2 - 3 = 128 \div 8^2 - 3$ — work inside the bracket first, do the exponent, then divide before subtracting
$= 128 \div 64 - 3$
$= 2 - 3$
$= -1$

(x) $128 \div (2 \times 4^2) - 3 = 128 \div (2 \times 16) - 3$ — start inside the bracket and do the exponent first, then multiply, then divide before subtracting
$= 128 \div 32 - 3$
$= 4 - 3$
$= 1$

EXERCISE 1.1

Each section in the chapter ends with an Exercise that allows you to review and apply what you've just learned. And you can find the solutions to the odd-numbered exercises at the back of the text.

A. Simplify each of the following.

1. $12 + 6 \div 3$

2. $(12 + 6) \div 3$

3. $(3 \times 8 - 6) \div 2$

4. $3 \times 8 - 6 \div 2$

5. $(7 + 4) \times 5 - 2$

6. $7 + 4 \times 5 - 2$

7. $5 \times 3 + 2 \times 4$

8. $5(3 + 2) - 12 \div 3$

9. $(3 \times 9 - 3) \div 6$

10. $3 \times (9 - 3) \div 6$

11. $6(7 - 2) - 3(5 - 3)$

12. $8(9 - 6) + 4(6 + 5)$

13. $\frac{16 - 8}{8 - 2}$

14. $\frac{20 - 16}{15 + 9}$

15. $4(8 - 5)^2 - 5(3 + 2^2)$

16. $(3 \times 4 - 2)^2 + (2 - 2 \times 7^2)$

Reference Example 1.1A

References to Examples direct you back to the chapter for help in answering the questions.

1.2 FRACTIONS

A. Common fractions

A **common fraction** is used to show a part of the whole. The fraction ⅔ means two parts out of a whole of three. The number written *above* the dividing line is the *part* and is called the **numerator**. The number written *below* the dividing line is the *whole* and is called the **denominator**. The numbers 2 and 3 are called the **terms of the fraction.**

A **proper fraction** has a numerator that is *less* than the denominator. An **improper fraction** has a numerator that is *greater* than the denominator.

EXAMPLE 1.2A

$\frac{3}{8}$ ← numerator / ← denominator — a proper fraction, since the numerator is less than the denominator

$\frac{6}{5}$ ← numerator / ← denominator — an improper fraction, since the numerator is greater than the denominator

B. Equivalent fractions

Equivalent fractions are obtained by changing the *terms* of a fraction without changing the value of the fraction.

Equivalent fractions in higher terms can be obtained by multiplying both the numerator and the denominator of a fraction by the same number. For any fraction, we can obtain an unlimited number of equivalent fractions in higher terms.

Equivalent fractions in lower terms can be obtained if both the numerator and denominator of a fraction are divisible by the same number or numbers. The process of obtaining such equivalent fractions is called *reducing to lower terms.*

EXAMPLE 1.2B

(i) Convert ¾ into higher terms by multiplying successively by 2, 6, and 25.

SOLUTION

$$\frac{3}{4} = \frac{3 \times 2}{4 \times 2} = \frac{6}{8} = \frac{6 \times 6}{8 \times 6} = \frac{36}{48} = \frac{36 \times 25}{48 \times 25} = \frac{900}{1200}$$

$$\text{Thus } \frac{3}{4} = \frac{6}{8} = \frac{36}{48} = \frac{900}{1200}$$

(ii) Reduce $^{210}/_{252}$ to lower terms.

SOLUTION

$$\frac{210}{252} = \frac{210 \div 2}{252 \div 2} = \frac{105}{126}$$

$$= \frac{105 \div 3}{126 \div 3} = \frac{35}{42}$$

$$= \frac{35 \div 7}{42 \div 7} = \frac{5}{6}$$

The fractions $^{105}/_{126}$, $^{35}/_{42}$, and $^{5}/_{6}$ are lower-term equivalents of $^{210}/_{252}$.

The terms of the fraction $^{5}/_{6}$ cannot be reduced any further. It represents the simplest form of the fraction $^{210}/_{252}$. It is the **fraction in lowest terms.**

C. Converting common fractions into decimal form

Common fractions are converted into decimal form by performing the indicated division to the desired number of decimal places or until the decimal terminates or repeats. We place a dot above a decimal number to show that it repeats. For example, $0.\dot{5}$stands for 0.555. . . .

EXAMPLE 1.2C

(i) $\frac{9}{8} = 9 \div 8 = 1.125$

(ii) $\frac{1}{3} = 1 \div 3 = 0.333333\ldots = 0.\dot{3}$

(iii) $\frac{7}{6} = 7 \div 6 = 1.166666\ldots = 1.1\dot{6}$

D. Converting mixed numbers to decimal form

Mixed numbers consist of a whole number and a fraction, such as $5\frac{3}{4}$. Such numbers represent the *sum* of a whole number and a common fraction and can be converted into decimal form by changing the common fraction into decimal form.

EXAMPLE 1.2D

(i) $5\frac{3}{4} = 5 + \frac{3}{4} = 5 + 0.75 = 5.75$

(ii) $6\frac{2}{3} = 6 + \frac{2}{3} = 6 + 0.666\ldots = 6.6666\ldots = 6.\dot{6}$

(iii) $7\frac{1}{12} = 7 + \frac{1}{12} = 7 + 0.083333\ldots = 7.083333\ldots = 7.08\dot{3}$

E. Rounding

Answers to problems, particularly when obtained with the help of a calculator, often need to be rounded to a desired number of decimal places. In most business problems involving money values, the rounding needs to be done to the nearest cent, that is, to two decimal places.

While different methods of rounding are used, for most business purposes the following procedure is suitable.

1. If the first digit in the group of decimal digits that is to be dropped is the digit 5 or 6 or 7 or 8 or 9, the last digit retained is *increased* by 1.
2. If the first digit in the group of decimal digits that is to be dropped is the digit 0 or 1 or 2 or 3 or 4, the last digit is left *unchanged.*

EXAMPLE 1.2E

Round each of the following to two decimal places.

(i) 7.384 → 7.38 —— drop the digit 4

(ii) 7.385 → 7.39 —— round the digit 8 up to 9

(iii) 12.9448 → 12.94 —— discard 48

(iv) 9.32838 → 9.33 —— round the digit 2 up to 3

(v) 24.8975 → 24.90 —— round the digit 9 up to 0; this requires rounding 89 to 90

(vi) 1.996 → 2.00 — round the second digit 9 up to 0; this requires rounding 1.99 to 2.00

(vii) 3199.99833 → 3200.00 — round the second digit 9 up to 0; this requires rounding 3199.99 to 3200.00

F. Complex fractions

Complex fractions are mathematical expressions containing one or more fractions in the numerator or denominator or both. Certain formulas used in simple interest and simple discount calculations result in complex fractions. When you encounter such fractions, take care to use the order of operations properly.

EXAMPLE 1.2F

(i) $\dfrac{420}{1600 \times \frac{315}{360}} = \dfrac{420}{1600 \times 0.875} = \dfrac{420}{1400} = 0.3$

(ii) $500\left(1 + 0.16 \times \dfrac{225}{365}\right)$

$= 500(1 + 0.098630)$ — multiply 0.16 by 225 and divide by 365

$= 500(1.098630)$ — add inside bracket

$= 549.32$

(iii) $1000\left(1 - 0.18 \times \dfrac{288}{365}\right) = 1000(1 - 0.142027)$

$= 1000(0.857973)$

$= 857.97$

(iv) $\dfrac{824}{1 + 0.15 \times \frac{73}{365}} = \dfrac{824}{1 + 0.03} = \dfrac{824}{1.03} = 800$

(v) $\dfrac{1755}{1 - 0.21 \times \frac{210}{365}} = \dfrac{1755}{1 - 0.120822} = \dfrac{1755}{0.879178} = 1996.18$

Pointers and Pitfalls boxes emphasize good practices, highlight ways to avoid common errors, show how to use a financial calculator efficiently, or give hints for business math situations.

POINTERS AND PITFALLS

When using a calculator to compute business math formulas involving complicated denominators, consider using the reciprocal key ([$\frac{1}{x}$] or [x^{-1}]) to simplify calculations. Start by solving the denominator. Enter the fraction first, then multiply, change the sign, and add. Press the reciprocal key and multiply by the numerator. For example, to calculate part (v) of Example 1.2F above, the following calculator sequence would apply:

$$\frac{1755}{1 - 0.21 \times \frac{210}{365}}$$

210 [÷] 365 [×] 0.21 [±] [+] 1 [=] [$\frac{1}{x}$] [×] 1755 [=]

The result is 1996.18.

EXERCISE 1.2

A spreadsheet icon in the margin highlights a question that can be solved using one of the question-specific Excel spreadsheets contained on the Student CD-ROM.

A. Reduce each of the following fractions to lowest terms.

1. $\frac{24}{36}$ **2.** $\frac{28}{56}$ **3.** $\frac{210}{360}$ **4.** $\frac{330}{360}$

5. $\frac{360}{225}$ **6.** $\frac{360}{315}$ **7.** $\frac{144}{360}$ **8.** $\frac{360}{288}$

9. $\frac{25}{365}$ **10.** $\frac{115}{365}$ **11.** $\frac{365}{73}$ **12.** $\frac{365}{219}$

B. Convert each of the following fractions into decimal form. If appropriate, place a dot above a decimal number to show that it repeats.

1. $\frac{11}{8}$ **2.** $\frac{7}{4}$ **3.** $\frac{5}{3}$ **4.** $\frac{5}{6}$

5. $\frac{11}{6}$ **6.** $\frac{7}{9}$ **7.** $\frac{13}{12}$ **8.** $\frac{19}{15}$

C. Convert each of the following mixed numbers into decimal form.

1. $3\frac{3}{8}$ **2.** $3\frac{2}{5}$ **3.** $8\frac{1}{3}$ **4.** $16\frac{2}{3}$

5. $33\frac{1}{3}$ **6.** $83\frac{1}{3}$ **7.** $7\frac{7}{9}$ **8.** $7\frac{1}{12}$

D. Round each of the following to two decimal places.

1. 5.633 **2.** 17.449 **3.** 18.0046 **4.** 253.4856

5. 57.69875 **6.** 3.09475 **7.** 12.995 **8.** 39.999

E. Simplify each of the following.

1. $\frac{54}{0.12 \times \frac{225}{365}}$ **2.** $\frac{264}{4400 \times \frac{146}{365}}$

3. $620\left(1 + 0.14 \times \frac{45}{365}\right)$ **4.** $375\left(1 + 0.16 \times \frac{292}{365}\right)$

5. $2100\left(1 - 0.135 \times \frac{240}{365}\right)$ **6.** $8500\left(1 - 0.17 \times \frac{216}{365}\right)$

7. $\frac{250\,250}{1 + 0.15 \times \frac{330}{365}}$ **8.** $\frac{2358}{1 + 0.12 \times \frac{146}{365}}$

9. $\frac{3460}{1 - 0.18 \times \frac{270}{365}}$ **10.** $\frac{2901}{1 - 0.165 \times \frac{73}{365}}$

A puzzle icon indicates an exercise or problem that is particularly challenging.

1.3 PERCENT

A. The meaning of percent

Fractions are used to compare the quantity represented by the numerator with the quantity represented by the denominator. The easiest method of comparing the two quantities is to use fractions with denominator 100. The preferred form of writing such fractions is the *percent* form. **Percent** means "per hundred," and the symbol % is used to show "parts of one hundred."

PERCENT means HUNDREDTHS

% means $\frac{\quad}{100}$

Accordingly, any fraction involving "hundredths" may be written as follows:

(i) as a common fraction $\frac{13}{100}$

(ii) as a decimal 0.13

(iii) in percent form 13%

B. Changing percents to common fractions

When speaking or writing, we often use percents in the percent form. However, when computing with percents, we use the corresponding common fraction or decimal fraction. To convert a percent into a common fraction, replace the symbol % by the symbol $\frac{\quad}{100}$. Then reduce the resulting fraction to lowest terms.

EXAMPLE 1.3A

(i) $24\% = \frac{24}{100}$ — replace % by $\frac{\quad}{100}$

$= \frac{6}{25}$ — reduce to lowest terms

(ii) $175\% = \frac{175}{100} = \frac{7 \times 25}{4 \times 25} = \frac{7}{4}$

(iii) $6.25\% = \frac{6.25}{100}$

$= \frac{625}{10\,000}$ — multiply by 100 to change the numerator to a whole number

$= \frac{125}{2000} = \frac{25}{400} = \frac{5}{80}$ — reduce gradually or in one step

$= \frac{1}{16}$

(iv) $0.025\% = \frac{0.025}{100} = \frac{25}{100\,000} = \frac{1}{4000}$

(v) $\frac{1}{4}\% = \frac{\frac{1}{4}}{\frac{100}{1}}$ ——— replace % by $\frac{}{\frac{100}{1}}$

$= \frac{1}{4} \times \frac{1}{100}$ ——— invert and multiply

$= \frac{1}{400}$

(vi) $33\frac{1}{3}\% = \frac{33\frac{1}{3}}{100}$ ——— replace % by $\frac{}{100}$

$= \frac{\frac{100}{3}}{\frac{100}{1}}$ ——— convert the mixed number $33\frac{1}{3}$ into a common fraction

$= \frac{100}{3} \times \frac{1}{100} = \frac{100}{300}$

$= \frac{1}{3}$

(vii) $216\frac{2}{3}\% = \frac{216\frac{2}{3}}{100} = \frac{\frac{650}{3}}{\frac{100}{1}} = \frac{\overset{13}{\cancel{650}}}{3} \times \frac{1}{\underset{2}{\cancel{100}}} = \frac{13}{6}$

Alternatively

$216\frac{2}{3}\% = 200\% + 16\frac{2}{3}\%$ ——— separate the multiple of 100% (i.e., 200%) from the remainder

$= 2 + \frac{\frac{50}{3}}{\frac{100}{1}}$

$= 2 + \frac{50}{3} \times \frac{1}{100}$

$= 2 + \frac{1}{6}$

$= \frac{13}{6}$

C. Changing percents to decimals

Replacing the % symbol by $\overline{100}$ indicates a division by 100. Since division by 100 is performed by moving the decimal point *two places to the left*, changing a percent to a decimal is easy to do. Simply drop the % symbol and move the decimal point two places to the left.

EXAMPLE 1.3B

(i) $52\% = 0.52$ ——— drop the percent symbol and move the decimal point two places to the left

(ii) $175\% = 1.75$

(iii) $6\% = 0.06$

(iv) $0.75\% = 0.0075$

(v) $\frac{1}{4}\% = 0.25\%$ ——— first change the fraction to a decimal

$= 0.0025$ ——— drop the percent symbol and move the decimal point two places to the left

(vi) $\frac{1}{3}\% = 0.\dot{3}\%$ ——— change the fraction to a repeating decimal

$= 0.00\dot{3}$ ——— drop the percent symbol and move the decimal point two places to the left

D. Changing decimals to percents

Changing decimals to percents is the inverse operation of changing percents into decimals. It is accomplished by multiplying the decimal by 100%. Since multiplication by 100 is performed by moving the decimal point *two places to the right*, a decimal is easily changed to a percent. Move the decimal point two places to the right and add the % symbol.

EXAMPLE 1.3C

(i) $0.36 = 0.36(100\%)$ ——— move the decimal point two places to the right and add the % symbol

$= 36\%$

(ii) $1.65 = 165\%$

(iii) $0.075 = 7.5\%$

(iv) $0.4 = 40\%$

(v) $0.001 = 0.1\%$

(vi) $2 = 200\%$

(vii) $0.0005 = 0.05\%$

(viii) $0.\dot{3} = 33.\dot{3}\%$

(ix) $1.1\dot{6} = 116.\dot{6}\%$

(x) $1\frac{5}{6} = 1.8\dot{3} = 183.\dot{3}\%$

E. Changing fractions to percents

When changing a fraction to a percent, it is best to convert the fraction to a decimal and then to change the decimal to a percent.

EXAMPLE 1.3D

(i) $\frac{1}{4} = 0.25$ ——— convert the fraction to a decimal

$= 25\%$ ——— convert the decimal to a percent

(ii) $\frac{7}{8} = 0.875 = 87.5\%$

(iii) $\frac{9}{5} = 1.8 = 180\%$

(iv) $\frac{5}{6} = 0.8\dot{3} = 83.\dot{3}\%$

(v) $\frac{5}{9} = 0.\dot{5} = 55.\dot{5}\%$

(vi) $1\frac{2}{3} = 1.\dot{6} = 166.\dot{6}\%$

EXERCISE 1.3

A. Change each of the following percents into a decimal.

1. 64%	**2.** 300%	**3.** 2.5%	**4.** 0.1%
5. 0.5%	**6.** 85%	**7.** 250%	**8.** 4.8%
9. 450%	**10.** 7.5%	**11.** 0.9%	**12.** 95%
13. 6.25%	**14.** 0.4%	**15.** 99%	**16.** 225%
17. 0.05%	**18.** $8\frac{1}{4}\%$	**19.** $\frac{1}{2}\%$	**20.** $112\frac{1}{2}\%$
21. $9\frac{3}{8}\%$	**22.** $\frac{3}{4}\%$	**23.** $162\frac{1}{2}\%$	**24.** $\frac{2}{5}\%$
25. $\frac{1}{4}\%$	**26.** $187\frac{1}{2}\%$	**27.** $1\frac{3}{4}\%$	**28.** $\frac{1}{40}\%$
29. $137\frac{1}{2}\%$	**30.** $\frac{5}{8}\%$	**31.** 0.875%	**32.** $2\frac{1}{4}\%$
33. $33\frac{1}{3}\%$	**34.** $166\frac{2}{3}\%$	**35.** $16\frac{2}{3}\%$	**36.** $116\frac{2}{3}\%$
37. $183\frac{1}{3}\%$	**38.** $83\frac{1}{3}\%$	**39.** $133\frac{1}{3}\%$	**40.** $66\frac{2}{3}\%$

B. Change each of the following percents into a common fraction in lowest terms.

1. 25%	**2.** $62\frac{1}{2}\%$	**3.** 175%	**4.** 5%
5. $37\frac{1}{2}\%$	**6.** 75%	**7.** 4%	**8.** 225%
9. 8%	**10.** 125%	**11.** 40%	**12.** $87\frac{1}{2}\%$
13. 250%	**14.** 2%	**15.** $12\frac{1}{2}\%$	**16.** 60%
17. 2.25%	**18.** 0.5%	**19.** $\frac{1}{8}\%$	**20.** $33\frac{1}{3}\%$
21. $\frac{3}{4}\%$	**22.** $66\frac{2}{3}\%$	**23.** 6.25%	**24.** 0.25%
25. $16\frac{2}{3}\%$	**26.** 7.5%	**27.** 0.75%	**28.** $\frac{7}{8}\%$
29. 0.1%	**30.** $\frac{3}{5}\%$	**31.** $83\frac{1}{3}\%$	**32.** 2.5%
33. $133\frac{1}{3}\%$	**34.** $183\frac{1}{3}\%$	**35.** $166\frac{2}{3}\%$	**36.** $116\frac{2}{3}\%$

C. Express each of the following as a percent.

1. 3.5	**2.** 0.075	**3.** 0.005	**4.** 0.375
5. 0.025	**6.** 2	**7.** 0.125	**8.** 0.001
9. 0.225	**10.** 0.008	**11.** 1.45	**12.** 0.0225
13. 0.0025	**14.** 0.995	**15.** 0.09	**16.** 3
17. $\frac{3}{4}$	**18.** $\frac{3}{25}$	**19.** $\frac{5}{3}$	**20.** $\frac{7}{200}$
21. $\frac{9}{200}$	**22.** $\frac{5}{8}$	**23.** $\frac{3}{400}$	**24.** $\frac{5}{6}$
25. $\frac{9}{800}$	**26.** $\frac{7}{6}$	**27.** $\frac{3}{8}$	**28.** $\frac{11}{40}$
29. $\frac{4}{3}$	**30.** $\frac{9}{400}$	**31.** $\frac{13}{20}$	**32.** $\frac{4}{5}$

1.4 APPLICATIONS—AVERAGES

A. Basic problems

When calculators are used, the number of decimal places used for intermediate values often determines the accuracy of the final answer. To avoid introducing rounding errors, keep intermediate values unrounded.

EXAMPLE 1.4A

A coffee company received $36\frac{3}{4}$ kilograms of coffee beans at \$240 per kilogram. Sales for the following five days were

$3\frac{5}{8}$ kilograms, $4\frac{3}{4}$ kilograms, $7\frac{2}{3}$ kilograms, $5\frac{1}{2}$ kilograms, and $6\frac{3}{8}$ kilograms.

What was the value of inventory at the end of Day 5?

SOLUTION

$$\begin{aligned}\text{Total sales (in kilograms)} &= 3\tfrac{5}{8} + 4\tfrac{3}{4} + 7\tfrac{2}{3} + 5\tfrac{1}{2} + 6\tfrac{3}{8}\\ &= 3.625 + 4.75 + 7.666667 + 5.5 + 6.375\\ &= 27.916667\end{aligned}$$

$$\text{Inventory (in kilograms)} = 36.75 - 27.916667 = 8.833333$$

$$\text{Value of inventory} = 8.833333 \times 240 = 2119.999992 = \$2120.00$$

EXAMPLE 1.4B

Complete the following excerpt from an invoice.

Quantity	Unit Price	Amount
72	\$0.875	\$_______
45	$66\frac{2}{3}$¢	_______
54	$83\frac{1}{3}$¢	_______
42	$\$1.3\dot{3}$	_______
32	\$1.375	_______
	Total	\$_______

SOLUTION

$$
\begin{aligned}
72 \times \$0.875 &= & \$\ 63.00\\
45 \times 66\tfrac{2}{3}¢ &= 45 \times \$0.\dot{6} & \\
&= 45 \times \$0.666667 = & \$\ 30.00\\
54 \times 83\tfrac{1}{3}¢ &= 54 \times \$0.8\dot{3} & \\
&= 54 \times \$0.833333 = & \$\ 45.00\\
42 \times \$1.3\dot{3} &= 42 \times \$1.\dot{3} = & \$\ 56.00\\
32 \times \$1.375 &= & \$\ 44.00\\
& \text{TOTAL} & \$238.00
\end{aligned}
$$

A calculator icon highlights information on the use of the Texas Instruments BA II Plus calculator.

POINTERS AND PITFALLS

The display on the calculator shows a limited number of decimal places, depending on how the calculator is formatted. By choosing the format function, you can change the setting to show a different number of decimal places. In continuous calculations, the calculator uses unrounded numbers.

To format the calculator to six decimal places:

[2nd] ([Format]) DEC [=] [6] [Enter]

B. Problems involving simple arithmetic average

The **arithmetic average** or **mean** of a set of values is a widely used average found by adding the values in the set and dividing by the number of those values.

EXAMPLE 1.4C

The marks obtained by Byung Kang for the seven tests that make up Section 1 of his Mathematics of Finance course were 82, 68, 88, 72, 78, 96, and 83.

(i) If all tests count equally, what was his average mark for Section 1?

(ii) If his marks for Section 2 and Section 3 of the course were 72.4 and 68.9 respectively and all section marks have equal value, what was his course average?

SOLUTION

(i)
$$
\begin{aligned}
\text{Section average} &= \frac{\text{Sum of the test marks for the section}}{\text{Number of tests}}\\
&= \frac{82 + 68 + 88 + 72 + 78 + 96 + 83}{7}\\
&= \frac{567}{7}\\
&= 81.0
\end{aligned}
$$

(ii)
$$
\begin{aligned}
\text{Course average} &= \frac{\text{Sum of the section marks}}{\text{Number of sections}}\\
&= \frac{81.0 + 72.4 + 68.9}{3}\\
&= \frac{222.3}{3}\\
&= 74.1
\end{aligned}
$$

EXAMPLE 1.4D

Monthly sales of Sheridan Service for last year were:

January	\$13 200	July	\$13 700
February	11 400	August	12 800
March	14 600	September	13 800
April	13 100	October	15 300
May	13 600	November	14 400
June	14 300	December	13 900

What were Sheridan's average monthly sales for the year?

SOLUTION

Total sales = \$164 100

$$\text{Average monthly sales} = \frac{\text{Total sales}}{\text{Number of months}} = \frac{\$164\ 100}{12} = \$13\ 675$$

POINTERS AND PITFALLS

Instead of trying to remember the numbers that you have calculated, you may store them in the calculator. After a calculation has been performed, the unrounded number can be stored and later recalled. The TI BAII Plus has the capability of storing 10 different numbers. To perform a calculation, store, and recall the results, follow the steps below:

To calculate $\frac{1}{3} + \frac{1}{7}$:

1 [÷] 3 [=] Result will show 0.333333 (when set to six decimal places)

To store the results: press [STO] 1

1 [÷] 7 [=] Result will show 0.142857 (when set to six decimal places)

To store the results: press [STO] 2

To recall the results, and to add them together:

[RCL] 1 [+] [RCL] 2 [=] Result will show 0.476190 (rounded to six decimal places)

C. Weighted average

If the items to be included in computing an arithmetic mean are arranged in groups or if the items are not equally important, a **weighted arithmetic average** should be obtained. Multiply each item by the numbers involved or by a weighting factor representing its importance.

EXAMPLE 1.4E

During last season, Fairfield Farms sold strawberries as follows: 800 boxes at \$1.25 per box in the early part of the season; 1600 boxes at \$0.90 per box and 2000 boxes at \$0.75 per box at the height of the season; and 600 boxes at \$1.10 per box during the late season.

(i) What was the average price charged?

(ii) What was the average price per box?

SOLUTION

(i) The average price charged is a simple average of the four different prices charged during the season.

$$\text{Average price} = \frac{1.25 + 0.90 + 0.75 + 1.10}{4} = \frac{4.00}{4} = \$1.00$$

(ii) To obtain the average price per box, the number of boxes sold at each price must be taken into account; that is, a weighted average must be computed.

800 boxes @ $1.25 per box	⟶	$1000.00
1600 boxes @ $0.90 per box	⟶	1440.00
2000 boxes @ $0.75 per box	⟶	1500.00
600 boxes @ $1.10 per box	⟶	660.00
5000 boxes ⟵	TOTALS ⟶	$4600.00

$$\text{Average price per box} = \frac{\text{Total value}}{\text{Number of boxes}} = \frac{\$4600.00}{5000} = \$0.92$$

EXAMPLE 1.4F

The English Tea Shop creates its house brand by mixing 13 kilograms of tea priced at $7.50 per kilogram, 16 kilograms of tea priced at $6.25 per kilogram, and 11 kilograms of tea priced at $5.50 per kilogram. At what price should the store sell its house blend to realize the same revenue it could make by selling the three types of tea separately?

SOLUTION

13 kg @ $7.50 per kg	⟶	$ 97.50
16 kg @ $6.25 per kg	⟶	100.00
11 kg @ $5.50 per kg	⟶	60.50
40 kg ⟵	TOTALS ⟶	$258.00

$$\text{Average value} \frac{\text{Total value}}{\text{Number of units}} = \frac{\$258.00}{40} = \$6.45$$

The house blend should sell for $6.45 per kilogram.

EXAMPLE 1.4G

The credit hours and grades for Dana's first-term courses are listed here.

Course	Credit Hours	Grade
Accounting	5	A
Economics	3	B
English	4	C
Law	2	D
Marketing	4	A
Mathematics	3	A
Elective	2	D

According to the grading system, A's, B's, C's, and D's are worth 4, 3, 2, and 1 quality points respectively. On the basis of this information, determine

(i) Dana's average course grade;

(ii) Dana's grade-point average (average per credit hour).

SOLUTION

(i) The average course grade is the average quality points obtained:

$$\frac{4 + 3 + 2 + 1 + 4 + 4 + 1}{7} = \frac{19}{7} = 2.71$$

(ii) The average obtained in part (i) is misleading since the credit hours of the courses are not equal. The grade-point average is a more appropriate average because it is a weighted average allowing for the number of credit hours per course.

Course	Credit Hours	×	Quality Points	=	Weighted Points
Accounting	5	×	4	=	20
Economics	3	×	3	=	9
English	4	×	2	=	8
Law	2	×	1	=	2
Marketing	4	×	4	=	16
Mathematics	3	×	4	=	12
Elective	2	×	1	=	2
	23	←	Totals	→	69

$$\text{Grade-point average} = \frac{\text{Total weighted points}}{\text{Total credit hours}} = \frac{69}{23} = 3.00$$

EXAMPLE 1.4H

A partnership agreement provides for the distribution of the yearly profit or loss on the basis of the partners' average monthly investment balance. The investment account of one of the partners shows the following entries:

Balance, January 1	$25 750
April 1, withdrawal	3 250
June 1, investment	4 000
November 1, investment	2 000

Determine the partner's average monthly balance in the investment account.

SOLUTION

To determine the average monthly investment, determine the balance in the investment account after each change and weight this balance by the number of months invested.

Date	Change	Balance	×	Invested	=	Value
January 1		25 750	×	3	=	77 250
April 1	−3250	22 500	×	2	=	45 000
June 1	+4000	26 500	×	5	=	132 500
November 1	+2000	28 500	×	2	=	57 000
		Totals		12		311 750

$$\text{Average monthly investment} = \frac{\text{Total weighted value}}{\text{Number of months}} = \frac{\$311\,750}{12} = \$25\,979.17$$

EXAMPLE 1.4I

Several shoe stores in the city carry the same make of shoes. The number of pairs of shoes sold and the price charged by each store are shown below.

Store	Number of Pairs Sold	Price per Pair ($)
A	60	43.10
B	84	38.00
C	108	32.00
D	72	40.50

(i) What was the average number of pairs of shoes sold per store?

(ii) What was the average price per store?

(iii) What was the average sales revenue per store?

(iv) What was the average price per pair of shoes?

SOLUTION

(i) The average number of pairs of shoes sold per store

$$= \frac{60 + 84 + 108 + 72}{4} = \frac{324}{4} = 81$$

(ii) The average price per store

$$= \frac{43.10 + 38.00 + 32.00 + 40.50}{4} = \frac{153.60}{4} = \$38.40$$

(iii) The average sales revenue per store

$$\begin{aligned} 60 \times 43.10 &= \$\ 2\,586.00 \\ 84 \times 38.00 &= \quad 3\,192.00 \\ 108 \times 32.00 &= \quad 3\,456.00 \\ 72 \times 40.50 &= \quad 2\,916.00 \\ &\quad \$12\,150.00 \end{aligned}$$

$$\text{Average} = \frac{\$12\,150.00}{4} = \$3\,037.50$$

(iv) The average price per pair of shoes

$$= \frac{\text{Total sales revenue}}{\text{Total pairs sold}} = \frac{\$12\,150.00}{324} = \$37.50$$

EXERCISE 1.4

A. Answer each of the following questions.

1. Heart Lake Developments sold four lakefront lots for $27 500 per hectare. If the size of the lots in hectares was $3\frac{3}{4}$, $2\frac{2}{3}$, $3\frac{5}{8}$, and $4\frac{5}{6}$ respectively, what was the total sales revenue of the four lots?

2. Five carpenters worked $15\frac{1}{2}$, $13\frac{3}{4}$, $18\frac{1}{2}$, $21\frac{1}{4}$, and $22\frac{3}{4}$ hours respectively. What was the total cost of labour if the carpenters were each paid $12.75 per hour?

3. A piece of property valued at $56 100 is assessed for property tax purposes at $\frac{6}{11}$ of its value. If the property tax rate is $3.75 on each $100 of assessed value, what is the amount of tax levied on the property?

4. A retailer returned 2700 defective items to the manufacturer and received a credit for the retail price of $\$0.8\dot{3}$ or $83\frac{1}{3}$¢ per item less a discount of $\frac{3}{8}$ of the retail price. What was the amount of the credit received by the retailer?

5. Extend the following invoice.

Quantity	Description	Unit Price	$
64	A	$0.75	______
54	B	$83\frac{1}{3}$¢	______
72	C	$0.375	______
42	D	$\$1.3\dot{3}$	______
		Total	______

6. Complete the following inventory sheet.

Item	Quantity	Cost per Unit	Total
1	96	$0.875	______
2	330	$16\frac{2}{3}$¢	______
3	144	$1.75	______
4	240	$\$1.6\dot{6}$	______
		Total	______

An Excel icon highlights information on the use of Excel to solve problems, and directs you to a tutorial or an Excel spreadsheet template on the Student CD-ROM.

EXCEL NOTES

Excel provides the *Simple Arithmetic Average (AVERAGE)* function to calculate the average of a group of numbers. Refer to AVERAGE on the Spreadsheet Template Disk to learn how to use this Excel function.

B. Solve each of the following problems involving an arithmetic average.

1. Records of Montes Service's fuel oil consumption for the last six-month period show that Montes paid 38.5 cents per litre for the first 1100 litres, 41.5 cents per litre for the next 1600 litres, and 42.5 cents per litre for the last delivery of 1400 litres. Determine the average cost of fuel oil per litre for the six-month period.

2. On a trip, a motorist purchased gasoline as follows: 56 litres at 49.0 cents per litre; 64 litres at 60.5 cents per litre; 70 litres at 51.5 cents per litre; and 54 litres at 54.5 cents per litre.
   (a) What was the average number of litres per purchase?
   (b) What was the average cost per litre?
   (c) If the motorist averaged 8.75 km per litre, what was the average cost of gasoline per kilometre?

3. The course credit hours and grades for Bill's fall semester are given below. At his college, an A is worth six quality points, a B four points, a C two points, and a D one point.

Credit hours:	3	5	2	4	4	2
Grade:	B	C	A	C	D	A

   What is Bill's grade-point average?

4. Kim Blair invested $7500 in a business on January 1. She withdrew $900 on March 1, reinvested $1500 on August 1, and withdrew $300 on September 1. What is Kim's average monthly investment balance for the year?

5. Neuer started a systematic investment program by buying $200.00 worth of mutual funds on the first day of every month starting on February 1. When you purchase mutual funds, you purchase units in the fund. Neuer purchased as many units as he could with his $200.00, including fractions of units. Unit prices for the first six months were $10.00, $10.60, $11.25, $9.50, $9.20, and $12.15 respectively.
   (a) What is the simple average of the unit prices?
   (b) What is the total number of units purchased during the first six months (correct to three decimals)?
   (c) What is the average cost of the units purchased?
   (d) What is the value of Neuer's mutual fund holdings on July 31 if the unit price on that date is $11.90?

1.5 APPLICATIONS—PAYROLL

Employees can be remunerated for their services in a variety of ways. The main methods of remuneration are salaries, hourly wage rates, and commission. While the computations involved in preparing a payroll are fairly simple, utmost care is needed to ensure that all calculations are accurate.

A. Salaries

Compensation of employees by **salary** is usually on a monthly or a yearly basis. Monthly salaried personnel get paid either monthly or semi-monthly. Personnel on a yearly salary basis may get paid monthly, semi-monthly, every two weeks, or weekly, or according to special schedules such as those used by some boards of education to pay their teachers. If salary is paid weekly or every two weeks, the year is assumed to consist of exactly 52 weeks.

Calculations of **gross earnings** per pay period is fairly simple. Computing overtime for salaried personnel can be problematic since overtime is usually paid on an hourly basis.

EXAMPLE 1.5A

An employee with an annual salary of $23 296 is paid every two weeks. The regular workweek is 40 hours.

(i) What is the gross pay per pay period?

(ii) What is the hourly rate of pay?

(iii) What are the gross earnings for a pay period in which the employee worked six hours of overtime and is paid one-and-a-half times the regular hourly rate of pay?

SOLUTION

(i) An employee paid every two weeks receives the annual salary over 26 pay periods.

$$\text{Gross pay per two-week period} = \frac{23\,296.00}{26} = \$896.00$$

(ii) Given a 40-hour week, the employee's compensation for two weeks covers 80 hours.

$$\text{Hourly rate of pay} = \frac{896.00}{80} = \$\ 11.20$$

(iii) Regular gross earnings for two-week period $896.00
Overtime pay

6 hours @ $11.20 × 1.5 = 6 × 11.20 × 1.5 = 100.80

Total gross earnings for pay period $996.80

EXAMPLE 1.5B

Mike Paciuc receives a monthly salary of $2080 paid semi-monthly. Mike's regular workweek is 37.5 hours. Any hours worked over 37.5 hours in a week are overtime and are paid at time-and-a-half regular pay. During the first half of October, Mike worked 7.5 hours overtime.

(i) What is Mike's hourly rate of pay?

(ii) What are his gross earnings for the pay period ending October 15?

SOLUTION

(i) When computing the hourly rate of pay for personnel employed on a monthly salary basis, the correct approach requires that the yearly salary be determined first. The hourly rate of pay may then be computed on the basis of 52 weeks per year.

$$\text{Yearly gross earnings} = 2080.00 \times 12 = \$24\,960.00$$

$$\text{Weekly gross earnings} = \frac{24\,960.00}{52} = \$480.00$$

$$\text{Hourly rate of pay} = \frac{480.00}{37.5} = \$12.80$$

(ii) Regular semi-monthly gross earnings $= \frac{2080.00}{2} = \$1040.00$

Overtime pay $= 7.5 \times 12.80 \times 1.5 =$ 144.00

Total gross earnings for pay period $1184.00

EXAMPLE 1.5C

Teachers with the Northern Manitoba Board of Education are under contract for 200 teaching days per year. They are paid according to the following schedule:

8% of annual salary on the first day of school
4% of annual salary for each of 20 two-week pay periods
12% of annual salary at the end of the last pay period in June

Alicia Nowak, a teacher employed by the board, is paid an annual salary of $65 200.

(i) What is Alicia's daily rate of pay?

(ii) What is Alicia's gross pay
(a) for the first pay period?
(b) for the last pay period?
(c) for all other pay periods?

(iii) If Alicia takes an unpaid leave of absence for three days during a pay period ending in April, what is her gross pay for that pay period?

SOLUTION

(i) Daily rate of pay $= \frac{65\ 200}{200} = \$326.00$

(ii) (a) First gross pay $= 0.08 \times 65\ 200.00 = \$5216.00$
(b) Last gross pay $= 0.12 \times 65\ 200.00 = \$7824.00$
(c) All other gross pay $= 0.04 \times 65\ 200.00 = \$2608.00$

(iii) Gross pay for pay period ending in April = $2608.00
Less 3 days of pay = $\frac{3}{200}$ of $65 200.00 = 978.00

Gross pay $1630.00

B. Commission

Persons engaged in the buying and selling functions of a business are often compensated by a **commission**. Of the various types of commission designed to meet the specific circumstances of a particular business, the most commonly encountered are straight commission, graduated (or sliding-scale) commission, and base salary plus commission.

Straight commission is usually calculated as a percent of net sales for a given time period. **Net sales** are the difference between the gross sales for the time period and any sales returns and allowances.

Graduated commission usually involves paying an increasing percent for increasing sales levels during a given time period.

Salary plus commission is a method that guarantees a minimum income per pay period to the salesperson. However, the rate of commission in such cases is either at a lower rate or is not paid until a minimum sales level (called a **quota**) for a time period has been reached.

Sales personnel on commission often have a drawing account with their employer. The salesperson may withdraw funds from such an account in advance to meet business and personal expenses. However, any money advanced is deducted from the commission earned when the salesperson is paid.

EXAMPLE 1.5D

Javier receives a commission of 11.5% on his net sales and is entitled to drawings of up to $1000 per month. During August, Javier's gross sales amounted to $25 540 and sales returns and allowances were $360.

(i) What are Javier's net sales for August?

(ii) How much is his commission for August?

(iii) If Javier drew $1400 in August, what is the amount due to him?

SOLUTION

(i)

Gross sales	$25 540.00
Less sales returns and allowances	360.00
Net sales	$25 180.00

(ii) Commission = 11.5% of net sales
= $0.115 \times 25\ 180.00$
= $2895.70

(iii)

Gross commission earned	$2895.70
Less drawings	1400.00
Amount due	$1495.70

EXAMPLE 1.5E

Valerie works as a salesperson for the local Minutemen Press. She receives a commission of 7.5% on monthly sales up to $8000, 9.25% on the next $7000, and 11% on any additional sales during the month. If Valerie's September sales amounted to $18 750, what is her gross commission for the month?

SOLUTION

Commission on the first $8000.00 = 0.075×8000.00 =	$ 600.00
Commission on the next $7000.00 = 0.0925×7000.00 =	647.50
Commission on sales over $15 000.00 = 0.11×3750.00 =	412.50
Total commission for September	$1660.00

EXAMPLE 1.5F

Ana is employed as a salesclerk in a fabric store. She receives a weekly salary of $575 plus a commission of 6¼% on all weekly sales over the weekly sales quota of $5000. Derek works in the shoe store located next door. He receives a minimum of $500 per week or a commission of 12.5% on all sales for the week, whichever is the greater. If both Ana and Derek had sales of $5960 last week, how much compensation does each receive for the week?

SOLUTION

Ana's compensation

Base salary	\$575.00
Plus commission = $6\frac{1}{4}$% on sales over \$5000.00	
= 0.0625 × 960.00	60.00
Total compensation	\$635.00

Derek's compensation

Minimum weekly pay	\$500.00
Commission = 12.5% of \$5960.00 = 0.125 × 5960.00 =	\$745.00

Since the commission is greater than the guaranteed minimum pay of \$500, Derek's compensation is \$745.

C. Wages

The term **wages** usually applies to compensation paid to *hourly* rated employees. Their gross earnings are calculated by multiplying the number of hours worked by the hourly rate of pay plus any overtime pay. Overtime is most often paid at time-and-a-half the regular hourly rate for any hours exceeding an established number of regular hours per week or per day. The number of regular hours is often established by agreement between the employer and employees. The most common regular workweek is 40 hours. If no agreement exists, federal or provincial employment standards legislation provides for a maximum number of hours per week, such as 44 hours for most employers. Any hours over the set maximum must be paid at least at time-and-a-half of the regular hourly rate.

When overtime is involved, gross earnings can be calculated by either of two methods.

Method A

The most common method, and the easiest for the wage earner to understand, determines total gross earnings by adding overtime pay to the gross pay for a regular workweek.

Method B

In the second method, the overtime excess (or **overtime premium**) is computed separately and added to gross earnings for all hours (including the overtime hours) at the regular rate of pay. Computation of the excess labour cost due to overtime emphasizes the additional expense due to overtime and provides management with information that is useful for cost control.

EXAMPLE 1.5G

Mario is a machinist with Scott Tool and Die and is paid \$14.40 per hour. The regular workweek is 40 hours and overtime is paid at time-and-a-half the regular hourly rate. If Mario worked $46\frac{1}{2}$ hours last week, what were his gross earnings?

SOLUTION

Method A

Gross earnings for a regular workweek = 40 × 14.40	= $576.00
Overtime pay = 6.5 × 14.40 × 1.5	= 140.40
Gross pay	$716.40

Method B

Earnings at the regular hourly rate = 46.5 × 14.40	= $669.60
Overtime premium = $6.5 \times \left(\frac{1}{2} \text{ of } 14.40\right)$ = 6.5 × 7.20 =	46.80
Gross pay	$716.40

EXAMPLE 1.5H

Hasmig works for $8.44 per hour under a union contract that provides for daily overtime for all hours worked over eight hours. Overtime includes hours worked on Saturdays and is paid at time-and-a-half of the regular rate of pay. Hours worked on Sundays or holidays are paid at double the regular rate of pay. Use both methods to determine Hasmig's gross earnings for a week in which she worked the following hours:

Monday	9 hours	Tuesday	10½ hours
Wednesday	7 hours	Thursday	9½ hours
Friday	8 hours	Saturday	6 hours
Sunday	6 hours		

Day	Mon	Tue	Wed	Thu	Fri	Sat	Sun	Total
Regular hours	8	8	7	8	8			39
Overtime at time-and-a-half	1	2.5		1.5		6		11
Overtime at double time							6	6
Total hours worked	9	10.5	7	9.5	8	6	6	56

SOLUTION

Method A

Gross earnings for regular hours = 39 × 8.44 =		$329.16
Overtime pay		
at time-and-a-half = 11 × 8.44 × 1.5	= $139.26	
at double time = 6 × 8.44 × 2	= 101.28	240.54
Total gross pay		$569.70

Method B

Earnings at regular hourly rate = 56 × 8.44 =		$472.64
Overtime pay		
at time-and-a-half = $11\left(\frac{1}{2} \text{ of } \$8.44\right)$		
= 11 × 4.22	= $46.42	
at double time = 6 × 8.44	= 50.64	97.06
Total gross pay		$569.70

EXERCISE 1.5

A. Answer each of the following questions.

1. R. Burton is employed at an annual salary of $22 932 paid semi-monthly. The regular workweek is 36 hours.
   (a) What is the regular salary per pay period?
   (b) What is the hourly rate of pay?
   (c) What is the gross pay for a pay period in which the employee worked 11 hours overtime at time-and-a-half of regular pay?

2. C. Bernal receives a yearly salary of $23 868.00. She is paid bi-weekly and her regular workweek is 37.5 hours.
   (a) What is the gross pay per pay period?
   (b) What is the hourly rate of pay?
   (c) What is the gross pay for a pay period in which she works 8½ hours overtime at time-and-a-half regular pay?

3. Carole is paid a monthly salary of $1101.10. Her regular workweek is 35 hours.
   (a) What is Carole's hourly rate of pay?
   (b) What is Carole's gross pay for May if she worked 7¾ hours overtime during the month at time-and-a-half regular pay?

4. Dimitri receives a semi-monthly salary of $863.20 and works a regular workweek of 40 hours.
   (a) What is Dimitri's hourly rate of pay?
   (b) If Dimitri's gross earnings in one pay period were $990.19, for how many hours of overtime was he paid at time-and-a-half regular pay?

5. An employee of a Board of Education is paid an annual salary in 22 biweekly payments of $1123.00 each. If the employee is under contract for 200 workdays of 7½ hours each,
   (a) what is the hourly rate of pay?
   (b) what is the gross pay for a pay period in which the employee was away for two days at no pay?

6. Geraldine Moog is paid a commission of 9¾% on her net sales and is authorized to draw up to $800 a month. What is the amount due to Geraldine at the end of a month in which she drew $720, had gross sales of $12 660, and sales returns of $131.20?

7. What is a salesperson's commission on net sales of $16 244 if the commission is paid on a sliding scale of 8¼% on the first $6000, 9¾% on the next $6000, and 11.5% on any additional net sales?

8. A sales representative selling auto parts receives a commission of 4.5% on net sales up to $10 000, 6% on the next $5000, and 8% on any further sales. If his gross sales for a month were $24 250 and sales returns were $855, what was his commission for the month?

9. A salesclerk at a local boutique receives a weekly base salary of $225 on a quota of $4500 per week plus a commission of 6½% on sales exceeding the quota.
   (a) What are the gross earnings for a week if sales are $4125?
   (b) What are the gross earnings for a week if sales amount to $6150?

10. A clothing store salesperson is paid a weekly salary of $250 or a commission of 12.5% of his sales, whichever is the greater. What is his salary for a week in which his sales were
(a) $1780?
(b) $2780?

11. For October, Monique Lemay earned a commission of $1884.04 on gross sales of $21 440. If returns and allowances were 5% of gross sales, what is her rate of commission based on net sales?

12. Hans Weissner had gross earnings of $354.30 for last week. Hans earns a base salary of $270 on a weekly quota of $4000. If his sales for the week were $5124, what is his commission rate?

13. Doug Wilson earned a commission of $2036.88 for March. If his rate of commission is 11.25% of net sales, and returns and allowances were 8% of gross sales, what were Doug's gross sales for the month?

14. Corrie Daley had gross earnings of $337.50 for the week. If she receives a base salary of $264 on a quota of $4800 and a commission of 8.75% on sales exceeding the quota, what were Corrie's sales for the week?

15. Carlo Shastri is employed at an hourly rate of $8.42. The regular workweek is 40 hours and overtime is paid at time-and-a-half regular pay. Using the two methods illustrated earlier, compute Carlo's gross earnings for a week in which he worked 47 hours.

16. Kim Van Gelder earns $10.60 per hour. Overtime from Monday to Friday is paid at time-and-a-half regular pay for any hours over $7\frac{1}{2}$ per day. Overtime on weekends is paid at double the regular rate of pay. Last week Kim worked regular hours on Monday, Wednesday, and Friday, 9 hours on Tuesday, $10\frac{1}{2}$ hours on Thursday, and 6 hours on Saturday. Determine Kim's gross wages by each of the two methods.

17. An employee of a repair shop receives a gross pay of $319.44 for a regular workweek of 44 hours. What is the hourly rate of pay?

18. A wage statement shows gross earnings of $361 for 45 hours of work. What is the hourly rate of pay if the regular workweek is 40 hours and overtime is paid at time-and-a-half the regular rate of pay?

1.6 APPLICATIONS—TAXES

A **tax** is defined as a "contribution levied on persons, properties, or businesses to pay for services provided by the government." The taxes we encounter most are the **Provincial Sales Tax (PST)** and the **Goods and Services Tax (GST)**. We also pay *property taxes*, directly (the homeowner pays the municipality) or indirectly (the landlord pays the municipality). PST and GST are expressed as a percent of the value of the items or services purchased, that is, Tax payable = Tax percent (as a decimal) × Value of purchase. Traditionally, property tax rates have been expressed in *mills* (to be explained below).

A. Goods and Services Tax (GST)

The **Goods and Services Tax (GST)** is a federal tax charged on the cost of almost all goods and services. Businesses and organizations carrying out commercial activities in Canada must register with the Canada Revenue Agency (CRA) for the purpose of collecting the GST if their annual revenue from GST taxable goods and services exceeds $30 000. Below that level of revenue, registration is optional.

Effective July 1, 2006, GST taxable goods and services are taxed at 6%. Registered businesses and organizations will charge the 6% GST on taxable sales of goods and services to their customers, and they pay the 6% GST on their business purchases. Depending on the volume of taxable sales, a GST return must be submitted by each registrant to the CRA at selected intervals (monthly, quarterly, annually), showing the amount of tax collected and the amount of tax paid. If the amount of GST collected is more than the amount of GST paid, the difference must be remitted to the CRA. If the amount of GST collected is less than the amount of GST paid, a refund can be claimed. (While most consumers do not have this option, the government has provided GST rebate cheques to Canadians with earnings below a particular annual income level.)

EXAMPLE 1.6A

Suppose you had your car repaired at your local Canadian Tire repair shop. Parts amounted to $165.00 and labour to $246. Since both parts and labour are GST-taxable, what is the amount of GST that Canadian Tire must collect from you?

SOLUTION

The GST taxable amount = 165.00 + 246.00 = $411.00
GST = 6% of $411.00 = 0.06(411.00) = $24.66
Canadian Tire must collect GST of $24.66.

EXAMPLE 1.6B

Canadian Colour Company (CCC) purchased GST-taxable supplies from Kodak Canada worth $35 000 during 2008. CCC used these supplies to provide prints for its customers. CCC's total GST taxable sales for the year were $50 000. How much tax must CCC remit to the Canada Revenue Agency?

SOLUTION

GST collected = 0.06($50 000) = $3000
GST paid = 0.06($35 000) = $2100
GST payable = 3000 − 2100 = $900

B. Provincial Sales Tax (PST)

The **Provincial Sales Tax (PST)** is a provincial tax imposed by all provinces, except Alberta, on the price of most goods. In Ontario, Manitoba, Saskatchewan, and British Columbia, the PST is applied the same way as the GST, that is, as a percent of the retail price. In Quebec and Prince Edward Island, the sales tax is applied after adding the GST to the retail price. Newfoundland, Nova Scotia, and New Brunswick merge their PST with the GST. For these three provinces, the blended sales tax (known as the **Harmonized Sales Tax or HST**) is now 14%.

British Columbia	7%	Ontario	8%
Saskatchewan	7%	Quebec	7.5%
Manitoba	7%	Prince Edward Island	10%
New Brunswick	14% (harmonized with GST)		
Nova Scotia	14% (harmonized with GST)		
Newfoundland	14% (harmonized with GST)		

EXAMPLE 1.6C

Determine the amount of provincial sales tax on an invoice of taxable items totalling $740 before taxes
(i) in Saskatchewan;
(ii) in Quebec.

SOLUTION

(i) In Saskatchewan, the PST = 7% of $740.00 = 0.07(740.00) = $51.80.
(ii) In Quebec, the PST = 7.5% of $740.00 + 7.5% of the GST on $740.00.

Since the GST = 6% of $740.00 = 0.06(740.00) = $44.40, the
PST = 0.075(740.00) + 0.075(44.40) = 55.50 + 3.33 = $58.83.

EXAMPLE 1.6D

In Ontario, restaurant meals are subject to the 6% GST as well as 8% PST on food items and 10% on alcoholic beverages. You take your friend out for dinner and spend $45 on food items and $27 on a bottle of wine. You also tip the waiter 15% of the combined cost of food items and wine. How much do you spend?

SOLUTION

Cost of food items	$45.00
Cost of wine	27.00
Total cost of meal	$72.00

GST = 6% of $72.00 = 0.06(72.00) = $4.32
PST = 8% of $45.00 = 0.08(45.00) = $3.60
= 10% of $27.00 = 0.10(27.00) = $2.70

Total cost including taxes = $72.00 + $4.32 + $3.60 + $2.70 = $82.62
Tip = 15% of $72.00 = 0.15(72.00) = 10.80

Total amount spent = $82.62 + $10.80 = $93.42

C. Property tax

Municipalities raise money by a **property tax**, which is a municipal tax charged on the **assessed value** of real estate, both commercial and residential. Some education taxes are also raised through this method. Traditionally, property taxes have been stated as a *mill rate*, as opposed to as a percent (like the PST and GST). However, some municipalities have started to state the property tax rate as a percent or its decimal equivalent.

A **mill rate** is the amount of tax per $1000 of assessed value of property. Therefore, a mill rate is equivalent to 0.1% of the assessed value of property. The assessed value of a property may be close to its market value, but does not have to be.

$$\text{Property tax} = \text{Mill rate} \times 0.001 \times \text{Assessed value of property}$$

EXAMPLE 1.6E

The municipality of Yellik lists the following mill rates for various local services:

Tax Levy	Mill Rate
General city	3.20
Garbage collection	0.99
Schools	10.51
Capital development	1.20

If a homeowner's property has been assessed at $150 000, determine the property taxes payable.

SOLUTION

Total mill rate = 3.20 + 0.99 + 10.51 + 1.20 = 15.9
Tax payable = Total mill rate × 0.001 × Assessed value
Tax payable = (15.9)(0.001)(150 000) = $2385.00

EXAMPLE 1.6F

The municipality of Verner requires a budget of $450 million to operate next year. Provincial and federal grants, fees, and commercial taxes will cover $250 million, leaving $200 million to be raised by a tax on residential assessments.

(i) Calculate the mill rate required to raise the $200 million if the total assessed residential value for taxation purposes is $5 billion.

(ii) Determine the taxes on a building lot in Verner if it is assessed at $52 800.

SOLUTION

$$\text{(i) Rate} = \frac{\text{Tax revenue required from residential assessments}}{\text{Current assessed value}}$$

$$= \frac{\$200\ 000\ 000}{\$5\ 000\ 000\ 000} = 0.04$$

For each dollar of assessed value on a residential property, each owner must pay 4 cents. Therefore, for each $1000 of assessed value, the mill rate is 0.04 × 1000 = 40.

(ii) Property taxes on the building lot = 40(0.001)(52 800) = $2112.00

EXERCISE 1.6

A. Answer each of the following questions.

1. Cook's Department Store files GST returns monthly. If the figures in the following table represent the store's GST taxable sales and GST is paid on its purchases for the last five months, calculate Cook's monthly GST bills. Determine if Cook's owes the government money or is entitled to a refund.

Month	Sales	Purchases
January	$546 900	$147 832
February	244 000	69 500
March	588 000	866 000
April	650 300	450 000
May	156 800	98 098

2. Riza's Home Income Tax business operates only during tax season. Last season Riza grossed $28 620 including GST. During that season she spent $8000 before GST on her paper and supply purchases. How much does Riza owe the Canada Revenue Agency for GST?

3. "Save the GST" is a popular advertising gimmick. How much would you save on the purchase of a T-shirt with a list price of $15 in an Ontario store during a "Save the GST" promotion?

4. How much would a consumer pay for a T-shirt with a list price of $15 if the purchase was made in Regina, Saskatchewan?

5. During an early season promotion, a weekend ski pass was priced at $84 plus GST and PST at both Blackcomb Mountain, B.C., and Mont Tremblant, Quebec. What is the difference in the total price paid by skiers at the two ski resorts?

6. A retail chain sells snowboards for $625 plus GST and PST. What is the price difference for consumers in Toronto, Ontario, and Calgary, Alberta?

7. Calculate the property taxes on a property assessed at $125 000 if the mill rate is 22.751.

8. The town of Eudora assesses property at market value. How much will the owner of a house valued at $225 000 owe in taxes if this year's mill rate has been set at 19.368?

9. The City of Mississauga sent a semi-annual tax bill to a resident who owns a house assessed at $196 000. If the semi-annual tax bill is $1420.79, what is the annual mill rate in Mississauga?

10. A town has an assessed residential property value of $250 000 000. The town council must meet the following expenditures:

Education	$10 050 000
General purposes	$2 000 000
Recreation	$250 000
Public works	$700 000
Police and fire protection	$850 000

(a) Suppose 80% of the expenditures are charged against residential real estate. Calculate the total property taxes that must be raised.
(b) What is the mill rate?
(c) What is the property tax on a property assessed at $175 000?

BUSINESS MATH NEWS BOX

Property Assessments Surge in Newfoundland

Over the past decade, the Canadian economy has grown rapidly, creating low unemployment and increasing salaries and wages. The country has vast amounts of natural resources—from oil in Alberta to minerals and forests in British Columbia.

Canada has also been labelled as one of the best countries in the world to live in from a quality-of-life perspective. As a result, individuals and businesses have steadily migrated to this country. Therefore, it is no coincidence that Canada's real estate has become red-hot in recent years through a combination of low interest rates and a robust economy.

One of the effects of increased demand for property has been an increase in property values. Property owners in St. John's, Newfoundland, have been shocked by the increase in their property taxes. For example, the City of St. John's Assessment Division is responsible for the assessment of approximately 43 000 accounts to which property taxes apply.

Since 2003, property values have increased an average of 22%, with the mill rate standing at 12.2. This means that at current rates, the city of St. John's is poised to collect $8 000 000 more in municipal taxes.

QUESTIONS

1. Calculate the property tax on property currently worth $150 000.
2. If property values have increased by 22% per year since 2003, calculate the value of property in 2003 worth $150 000 in 2006.
3. If the city collects $8 000 000 more in municipal taxes given the mill rate of 12.2, how much did property values increase?

Source: "Property Assessments Surge in Newfoundland," by Terry Roberts. *The Telegram,* St. John's, Newfoundland, September 7, 2006. Excerpt printed with permission from *The Telegram*.

Business Math News boxes show you how widely business math applications are used in the real world.

MyMathLab reference directs you to online homework and many multimedia learning tools.

powered by CourseCompass™ and MathXL® **MyMathLab** Go to MyMathLab at www.mathxl.com. You can practise many of this chapter's exercises as often as you want. The guided solutions help you find an answer step by step. You'll find a personalized study plan available to you too!

Review Exercise

The Review Exercise provides you with numerous questions that cover all the chapter content. Solutions to the odd-numbered exercises are given at the back of the text.

1. Simplify each of the following.

(a) $32 - 24 \div 8$

(b) $(48 - 18) \div 15 - 10$

(c) $(8 \times 6 - 4) \div (16 - 4 \times 3)$

(d) $9(6 - 2) - 4(3 + 4)$

(e) $\dfrac{108}{0.12 \times \frac{216}{365}}$

(f) $\dfrac{288}{2400 \times \frac{292}{365}}$

(g) $320\left(1 + 0.10 \times \frac{225}{365}\right)$

(h) $1000\left(1 - 0.12 \times \frac{150}{365}\right)$

(i) $\dfrac{660}{1 + 0.14 \times \frac{144}{365}}$

(j) $\dfrac{1120.00}{1 - 0.13 \times \frac{292}{365}}$

2. Change each of the following percents into a decimal.

(a) 185% (b) 7.5% (c) 0.4%

(d) 0.025% (e) $1\frac{1}{4}\%$ (f) $\frac{3}{4}\%$

(g) $162\frac{1}{2}\%$ (h) $11\frac{3}{4}\%$ (i) $8\frac{1}{3}\%$

(j) $83\frac{1}{3}\%$ (k) $266\frac{2}{3}\%$ (l) $10\frac{3}{8}\%$

3. Change each of the following percents into a common fraction in lowest terms.

(a) 50% (b) $37\frac{1}{2}\%$ (c) $16\frac{2}{3}\%$

(d) $166\frac{2}{3}\%$ (e) $\frac{1}{2}\%$ (f) 7.5%

(g) 0.75% (h) $\frac{5}{8}\%$

4. Express each of the following as a percent.

(a) 2.25 (b) 0.02 (c) 0.009

(d) 0.1275 (e) $\frac{5}{4}$ (f) $\frac{11}{8}$

(g) $\frac{5}{200}$ (h) $\frac{7}{25}$

5. Sales of a particular make and size of nails during a day were $4\frac{1}{3}$ kg, $3\frac{3}{4}$ kg, $5\frac{1}{2}$ and $6\frac{5}{8}$ kg.

(a) How many kilograms of nails were sold?

(b) What is the total sales value at $1.20 per kilogram?

(c) What was the average weight per sale?

(d) What was the average sales value per sale?

6. Extend and total the following invoice.

Quantity	Description	Unit Price	Amount
56	Item A	$0.625	
180	Item B	$83\frac{1}{3}$¢	
126	Item C	$\$1.1\dot{6}$	
144	Item D	$1.75	
		Total	

7. The basic pay categories, hourly rates of pay, and the number of employees in each category for the machining department of a company are shown below.

Category	Hourly Pay	No. of Employees
Supervisors	$15.45	2
Machinists	12.20	6
Assistants	9.60	9
Helpers	7.50	13

(a) What is the average rate of pay per category?

(b) What is the average rate of pay per employee?

8. Hélène Gauthier invested $15 000 on January 1 in a partnership. She withdrew $2000 on June 1, withdrew a further $1500 on August 1, and reinvested $4000 on November 1. What was her average monthly investment balance for the year?

Reference Example 1.4H

Referenc[e] Example[s] you bac[k] chapter in answe[r] question

9. Brent DeCosta invested $12 000 in a business on January 1 and an additional $2400 on April 1. He withdrew $1440 on June 1 and invested $2880 on October 1. What was Brent's average monthly investment balance for the year?

10. Maria is paid a semi-monthly salary of $800.80. Her regular workweek is 40 hours. Overtime is paid at time-and-a-half regular pay.

(a) What is Maria's hourly rate of pay?

(b) What is Maria's gross pay if she worked 8½ hours overtime in one pay period?

11. Casey receives an annual salary of $17 472.00, is paid monthly, and works 35 regular hours per week. Overtime is paid at time-and-a-half regular pay.

(a) What is Casey's gross remuneration per pay period?

(b) What is his hourly rate of pay?

(c) How many hours overtime did Casey work during a month for which his gross pay was $1693.60?

12. Tim is employed at an annual salary of $20 292.48. His regular workweek is 36 hours and he is paid semi-monthly.

(a) What is Tim's gross pay per period?

(b) What is his hourly rate of pay?

(c) What is his gross pay for a period in which he worked 12½ hours overtime at time-and-a-half regular pay?

13. Artemis is paid a weekly commission of 4% on net sales of $3000, 8% on the next $1500, and 12.5% on all further sales. Her gross sales for a week were $5580 and sales returns and allowances were $60.

(a) What were her gross earnings for the week?

(b) What was her average hourly rate of pay for the week if she worked 43 hours?

14. Last week June worked 44 hours. She is paid $8.20 per hour for a regular workweek of 37.5 hours and overtime at time-and-a-half regular pay.

(a) What were June's gross wages for last week?

(b) What is the amount of the overtime premium?

15. Vacek is paid a monthly commission on a graduated basis of 7½% on net sales of $7000, 9% on the next $8000, and 11% on any additional sales. If sales for April were $21 500 and sales returns were $325, what were his gross earnings for the month?

16. Margit is paid on a weekly commission basis. She is paid a base salary of $240 on a weekly quota of $8000 and a commission of 4.75% on any sales in excess of the quota.

(a) If Margit's sales for last week were $11 340, what were her gross earnings?

(b) What were Margit's average hourly earnings if she worked 35 hours?

17. Last week Lisa had gross earnings of $321.30. Lisa receives a base salary of $255 and a commission on sales exceeding her quota of $5000. What is her rate of commission if her sales were $6560?

18. Costa earned a gross commission of $2101.05 during July. What were his sales if his rate of commission is 10.5% of net sales and sales returns and allowances for the month were 8% of his gross sales?

19. Edith worked 47 hours during a week for which her gross remuneration was $426.22. Based on a regular workweek of 40 hours and overtime payment at time-and-a-half regular pay, what is Edith's hourly rate of pay?

20. Hong is paid a semi-monthly salary of $682.50. Regular hours are 37½ per week and overtime is paid at time-and-a-half regular pay.

(a) What is Hong's hourly rate of pay?

(b) How many hours overtime did Hong work in a pay period for which his gross pay was $846.30?

21. Silvio's gross earnings for last week were $328.54. His remuneration consists of a base salary of $280 plus a commission of 6% on net sales exceeding his weekly quota of $5000. What were Silvio's gross sales for the week if sales returns and allowances were $136?

22. Sean's gross wages for a week were $541.20. His regular workweek is 40 hours and overtime is paid at time-and-a-half regular pay. What is Sean's regular hourly wage if he worked 47½ hours?

23. Aviva's pay stub shows gross earnings of $349.05 for a week. Her regular rate of pay is $7.80 per hour for a 35-hour week and overtime is paid at time-and-a-half regular pay. How many hours did she work?

24. Ramona's Dry Cleaning shows sales revenue of $76 000 for the year. Ramona's GST-taxable expenses were \$14 960. How much should she remit to the government at the end of the year?

25. When Fred of Fred's Auto Repair tallied up his accounts at the end of the year, he found he had paid GST on parking fees of \$4000, supplies of \$55 000, utilities of \$2000, and miscellaneous eligible costs of \$3300. During this same time, he found he had charged his customers GST on billings that totalled \$75 000 for parts and \$65 650 for labour. How much GST must Fred send to the government?

26. A store located in Kelowna, B.C., sells a computer for \$2625 plus GST and PST. If the same model is sold at the same price in a store in Kenora, Ontario, what is the difference in the prices paid by consumers in the two stores?

27. Some stores in Ontario advertise that the GST is included in the ticket price. If you pay PST on this ticket price, you are paying tax on the tax. Calculate the total tax rate if you purchase a \$100 item under these conditions.

28. Two people living in different communities build houses of the same design on lots of equal size. If the person in Ripley has his house and lot assessed at \$150 000 with a mill rate of 20.051 mills, will his taxes be more or less than the person in Amberly with an assessment of \$135 000 and a mill rate of 22.124 mills?

29. A town has a total residential property assessment of \$975 500 000. It is originally estimated that \$45 567 000 must be raised through residential taxation to meet expenditures.

(a) What mill rate must be set to raise \$45 567 000 in property taxes?

(b) What is the property tax on a property assessed at \$35 000?

(c) The town later finds that it underestimated building costs. An additional \$2 000 000 in taxes must be raised. Find the increase in the mill rate required to meet these additional costs.

(d) How much more will the property taxes be on the property assessed at \$35 000?

Self-Test

You can test your understanding of the chapter content by completing the Self-Test. Again, the solutions to the odd-numbered questions are at the back of the text.

1. Evaluate each of the following.

(a) $4320\left(1 + 0.18 \times \frac{45}{365}\right)$ **(b)** $2160\left(0.15 \times \frac{105}{365}\right)$

(c) $2880\left(1 - 0.12 \times \frac{285}{365}\right)$ **(d)** $\dfrac{410.40}{0.24 \times \frac{135}{365}}$

(e) $\dfrac{5124}{1 - 0.09 \times \frac{270}{365}}$

2. Change each of the following percents into a decimal.

(a) 175% **(b)** $\frac{3}{8}\%$

3. Change each of the following percents into a common fraction in lowest terms.

(a) $2\frac{1}{2}\%$ **(b)** $116\frac{2}{3}\%$

4. Express each of the following as a percent.

(a) 1.125 **(b)** $\frac{9}{400}$

5. The following information is shown in your investment account for last year: balance on January 1 of \$7200; a withdrawal of \$480 on March 1; and deposits of \$600 on August 1 and \$120 on October 1. What was the account's average monthly balance for the year?

6. Extend each of the following and determine the total.

Quantity	Unit Price
72	$1.25
84	$16\frac{2}{3}$¢
40	$0.875
48	$1.33

7. Purchases of an inventory item during the last accounting period were as follows:

No. of Items	Unit Price
5	$9.00
6	$7.00
3	$8.00
6	$6.00

What was the average price per item?

8. Hazzid Realty sold lots for $15 120 per hectare. What is the total sales value if the lot sizes, in hectares, were $5\frac{1}{4}$, $6\frac{1}{3}$, $4\frac{3}{8}$, and $3\frac{5}{6}$?

9. Property valued at $130 000 is assessed at $\frac{2}{13}$ of its value. What is the amount of tax due for this year if the tax rate is $3.25 per $100 of assessed value?

10. A salesperson earned a commission of $806.59 for last week on gross sales of $5880. If returns and allowances were 11.5% of gross sales, what is his rate of commission based on net sales?

11. A.Y. receives an annual salary of $26 478.40. She is paid monthly on a 38-hour workweek. What is the gross pay for a pay period in which she works 8.75 hours overtime at time-and-a-half regular pay?

12. J.B. earns $16.60 an hour with time-and-a-half for hours worked over 8 a day. His hours for a week are 8.25, 8.25, 9.5, 11.5, and 7.25. Determine his gross earnings for that week.

13. A wage earner receives a gross pay of $513.98 for 52.5 hours of work. What is his hourly rate of pay if a regular workweek is 42 hours and overtime is paid at time-and-a-half the regular rate of pay?

14. A salesperson receives a weekly base salary of $200 on a quota of $2500. On the next $2000, she receives a commission of 11%. On any additional sales, the commission rate is 15%. Calculate her gross earnings for a week in which her sales total $6280.

15. C.D. is paid a semi-monthly salary of $780. If her regular workweek is 40 hours, what is her hourly rate of pay?

16. Mahal of Winnipeg, Manitoba, bought a ring for $6400. Since the jeweller is shipping the ring, she must pay a shipping charge of $20. She must also pay PST and GST on the ring. Determine the total purchase price of Mahal's ring.

17. Ilo pays a property tax of $2502.50. In her community the tax rate is 55 mills. What is the assessed value of her property, to the nearest dollar?

18. Suppose you went shopping and bought bulk laundry detergent worth $17.95. You then received a $2.50 trade discount, and had to pay a $1.45 shipping charge. Calculate the final purchase price of the detergent if you lived in Nova Scotia.

Challenge Problems

Challenge Problems give you the opportunity to apply the skills you learned in the chapter at a higher level than the Exercises.

1. A customer in a sporting goods shop gives you a $50 bill for goods totalling $37. He asks that the change he receives include no coins worth $1 or less. Can you give this customer the correct change while meeting his request?

2. Suppose you own a small business with four employees, namely Roberto, Sandra, Petra, and Lee. At the end of the year you have set aside $1800 to divide among them as a bonus. You have two categories in place for your bonus system. An exceptional employee receives one amount and an average employee receives half that amount. You have rated Roberto and Sanda exceptional, and Petra and Lee average employees. How much bonus should each employee receive?

3. Suppose your math grade is based on the results of two tests and one final exam. Each test is worth 30% of your grade and the final exam is worth 40%. If you scored 60% and 50% on your two tests, what mark must you score on the final exam to achieve a grade of 70%?

Case Study 1.1 Business and the GST

Case Studies present comprehensive, realistic scenarios followed by a set of questions, and illustrate some of the important practical applications of the chapter material.

» Businesses providing taxable goods and services in Canada must register to collect GST. As of July 1, 2006, the federal government effectively changed the GST rate from 7% to 6%.

A company must remit its GST collections either on a monthly, quarterly, or annually basis depending on the size of the enterprise and the amount of GST collected per annum. At the end of each fiscal year, registrants must file a return summarizing the collection of GST, GST paid by the registrant (Input Tax Credits), and periodic payments made to the Canada Revenue Agency (CRA). The Agency then uses this information to calculate a business's maximum periodic installment payment for the following year.

However, in order to make it simpler for small businesses with annual revenues of under $30 000, the government gave these businesses the option of registering to collect and remit. If businesses choose not to register, they do not have to charge GST on their services. The disadvantage is that they are then ineligible for a credit on the GST paid on their supplies.

Medium-sized businesses are eligible for a potentially moneymaking option in the form of the Quick Method of Accounting. Intended to simplify GST record keeping for certain types of small businesses, the Quick Method can be used to calculate a company's GST remittance if its annual taxable revenue, including GST, is $200 000 or less. When using the Quick Method, the registrant charges customers 6% GST on sales of goods and services, but does not claim input tax credits on operating expenses and inventory purchases. The GST remittance due is calculated as a percent of the business's combined taxable revenue plus GST collected. Since the percent used in the Quick Method calculation is less than the regular 6%, the business can remit less GST even though the base is larger. Depending on the type of business, the registrant uses either a Quick Method remittance rate of 2.5% or 5%.

The 2.5% rate is for qualifying retailers and wholesalers, including grocery and convenience stores. To qualify, purchases of GST taxable goods for resale must be at least 40% of the registrant's total annual taxable sales. In addition, the remittance rate for the first $30 000 of taxable revenue in a fiscal year is reduced by 1%. This means that the registrant remits 1.5% on the first $30 000 of taxable revenue and 2.5% on the remainder.

The 5% rate is the general rate for service businesses, such as dry cleaners, repair shops, and retailers and wholesalers who do not qualify for the 2.5% remittance rate. The first $30 000 is charged at a rate of 4% and the remainder at 5%.

QUESTIONS

1. Simon operates a GST-registered mobile glass repair service. His service revenue for the year is $28 000. His GST-taxable purchases amounted to $4000. Simon does not use the Quick Method of Accounting for the GST. By calculating the difference between the GST he collected and the GST he paid, determine Simon's GST remittance to the CRA.

2. Courtney operates a souvenir gift shop. Her business is registered for the Quick Method of Accounting for the GST. Her GST-taxable sales were $185 000 for the year. GST taxable purchases of goods for resale were 47% of sales. In addition, Courtney paid GST of $766 on taxable services. Courtney is eligible for the 2.5% method.

(a) Calculate how much less GST Courtney remitted to the CRA when using the Quick Method.

(b) Determine if Simon should take his sister's advice.

3. Steve has been operating Castle Creek Restaurant for the past several years. On the basis of the information that Steve's accountant filed with the CRA during the prior year, Castle Creek Restaurant must make monthly GST payments of $1200 this year. Steve received a copy of the Goods and Services Tax Harmonized Sales Tax (GST/HST) Return. He has asked the accountant for an interpretation, and was provided with this brief explanation:

Line 100 reports amount of GST-taxable revenues.
Line 103 reports amount of GST collected.
Line 106 reports amount of GST paid.
Line 109 reports amount of net GST payable to the CRA.
Line 110 reports amount of GST payments already made to the CRA this year.
Line 113 reports amount of balance to be paid or to be received.

When Steve checked his accounting records, he found the following information for the current fiscal year: GST-taxable revenue of $486 530 and purchases of $239 690. Referring to the form on the next page, help Steve determine the balance of GST to be paid or to be received by calculating each line of this simplified Goods and Services Tax Harmonized Sales Tax (GST/HST) Return.

Sales and other revenue	100	00
NET TAX CALCULATION		
GST and HST amounts collected or collectible	103	
Adjustments	104	
Total GST/HST and adjustments for period (add lines 103 and 104) →	105	
Input tax credits (ITCs) for the current period	106	
Adjustments	107	
Total ITCs and adjustments (add lines 106 and 107) →	108	
Net tax (subtract line 108 from line 105)	109	
OTHER CREDITS IF APPLICABLE		
Installment payments and net tax already remitted	110	
Rebates	111	
Total other credits (add lines 110 and 111) →	112	
Balance (subtract line 112 from line 109)	113	
REFUND CLAIMED	114	
PAYMENT ENCLOSED	115	

Case Study 1.2 How Much Are You Worth?

Eventually, most Canadians will assume the responsibility of purchasing a home. When faced with this choice, financial institutions determine whether this dream is realistic and the size of the loan that can be borrowed. In order to be approved, two key questions are asked to determine net worth. Net worth is calculated as the difference between a person's assets and liabilities. In layperson's terms, this is the difference between what you own and what you owe. Also measured into net worth is a consideration of your potential earnings.

Suppose you have decided to purchase a home, be it a house or condo, and you must borrow some money for the purchase. The next step is to determine whether you have the financial ability to carry the costs of a mortgage and of running the home. The two most widely accepted guidelines used to estimate how much of a home buyer's income can be allocated to housing costs are the Gross Debt Service Ratio and the Total Debt Service Ratio.

The formula for calculating the Gross Debt Service Ratio (GDS) is:

$$\left(\frac{\text{Monthly mortgage payment} + \text{Monthly property taxes} + \text{Monthly heating}}{\text{Gross monthly income}}\right) \times 100\%$$

The GDS ratio should not exceed 32%.

The formula for calculating the Total Debt Service Ratio (TDS) is:

$$\left(\frac{\text{Monthly mortage payment} + \text{Monthly property taxes} + \text{All other monthly debts}}{\text{Gross monthly income}}\right) \times 100\%$$

The TDS should not exceed 40%.

The Wong family have a combined household income of $147 000, and are considering purchasing a condominium. They have tallied up the potential costs of the condo and find that the mortgage will be $1800 per month, property taxes will be $2304 per year, and heating will be about $175 per month on equal billing. The Wongs also have a car loan of $450 per month, which has two more years to run. They find that they pay an average of $8520 per year on their credit cards.

QUESTIONS

The Glossary at the end of each chapter lists each key term with its definition and a page reference to where the term was first defined in the chapter.

1. Calculate the GDS and the TDS for the Wongs. If you were a bank manager, would you recommend the loan for their condo purchase?

2. Suppose the Wongs did not have the car loan and the credit card debt. How would this information affect their GDS and TDS? Would the bank manager's decision be any different?

GLOSSARY

Arithmetic average (mean) average found by adding the values in the set and dividing by the number of those values *(p. 13)*

Assessed value a dollar figure applied to real estate by municipalities to be used in property tax calculations (can be a market value or a value relative to other properties in the same municipality) *(p. 28)*

Commission the term applied to remuneration of sales personnel according to their sales performance *(p. 21)*

Complex fraction a mathematical expression containing one or more fractions in the numerator or the denominator or both *(p. 6)*

Common fraction the division of one whole number by another whole number, expressed by means of a fraction line *(p. 3)*

Denominator the divisor of a fraction (i.e., the number written below the fraction line) *(p. 3)*

Equivalent fractions fractions that have the same value although they consist of different terms *(p. 4)*

Fraction in lowest terms a fraction whose terms cannot be reduced any further (i.e., whose numerator and denominator cannot be evenly divided by the same number except 1) *(p. 4)*

Goods and Services Tax (GST) a federal tax charged on the price of almost all goods and services *(p. 27)*

Graduated commission remuneration paid as an increasing percent for increasing sales levels for a fixed period of time *(p. 21)*

Gross earnings the amount of an employee's remuneration before deductions *(p. 20)*

Harmonized Sales Tax (HST) the merged GST and PST tax used in Newfoundland, Nova Scotia, and New Brunswick *(p. 28)*

Improper fraction a fraction whose numerator is greater than its denominator *(p. 3)*

Mill rate the factor used with the assessed value of real estate to raise property tax revenue, expressed as the amount of tax per $1000 of assessed property value *(p. 29)*

Mixed number a number consisting of a whole number and a fraction, such as $5\frac{1}{2}$ *(p. 5)*

Net sales gross sales less returns and allowances *(p. 21)*

Numerator the dividend of a fraction (i.e., the number written above the fraction line) *(p. 3)*

Order of operations the order in which arithmetic calculations are performed *(p. 2)*

Overtime premium extra labour cost due to overtime *(p. 23)*

Percent (%) a fraction with a denominator of 100 *(p. 8)*

Proper fraction a fraction whose numerator is less than its denominator *(p. 3)*

Property tax a municipal tax charged on the assessed value of real estate, both commercial and residential *(p. 28)*

Provincial Sales Tax (PST) a provincial tax charged on the price of most goods (usually a fixed percent of the cost of a good) *(p. 27)*

Quota a sales level required before the commission percent is paid; usually associated with remuneration by base salary and commission *(p. 22)*

Salary the term usually applied to monthly or annual remuneration of personnel *(p. 19)*

Salary plus commission a method of remunerating sales personnel that guarantees a minimum income per pay period *(p. 22)*

Straight commission remuneration paid as a percent of net sales for a given period *(p. 21)*

Tax a contribution levied on persons, properties, or businesses to pay for services provided by the government *(p. 26)*

Terms of a fraction the numerator and the denominator of a fraction *(p. 3)*

Wages the term usually applied to the remuneration of hourly rated employees *(p. 23)*

Weighted arithmetic average average found by multiplying each item by the weighting factor and totalling the results *(p. 14)*

Useful Internet Sites provide URLs and brief descriptions for sites related to the chapter topic, or for companies mentioned in the chapter.

USEFUL INTERNET SITES

canada.gc.ca

Government of Canada This is the Government of Canada's main Internet site. Links are provided in three main categories: Services for Canadians, Services for Non-Canadians, and Services for Canadian Business.

www.cra-arc.gc.ca

Canada Revenue Agency This Website provides general information about tax, including GST and HST.

www.ctf.ca

Canadian Tax Foundation The Canadian Tax Foundation is an independent tax research organization whose purpose is to provide the public and the government of Canada with the benefit of expert impartial tax research into current problems of taxation and government finance. You can check the site to see what is new in the world of tax and find Canadian tax articles written by several authors.

www.cmhc-schl.gc.ca/en/co/buho/buho_005.cfm

Canada Mortgage and Housing Corporation—How Much Can You Afford? To help you estimate the maximum mortgage you can afford, CMHC has developed this easy-to-use mortgage tool. Just enter the information required and it will calculate the maximum house price you can afford, the maximum mortgage amount you can borrow, and your monthly mortgage payments of principal and interest.

CHAPTER 2

Review of Basic Algebra

OBJECTIVES

Upon completing this chapter, you will be able to do the following:

1. Simplify algebraic expressions using fundamental operations and substitution.
2. Simplify and evaluate powers with positive exponents, negative exponents, and exponent zero.
3. Use an electronic calculator to compute the numerical value of arithmetic expressions involving fractional exponents.
4. Write exponential equations in logarithmic form and use an electronic calculator equipped with a natural logarithm function to determine the value of natural logarithms.
5. Solve basic equations using addition, subtraction, multiplication, and division.
6. Solve equations involving algebraic simplification and formula rearrangement.
7. Solve word problems through creating and solving equations.

In operating her business, Jessie has many daily decisions to make. She must determine how much inventory to buy, what price to set to sell the inventory, how much her expenses will be, and how much money she needs to borrow to keep the business going. Knowledge and competence in algebra are necessary to solve and answer these questions. The skills developed in this chapter will help you in your decisions in business.

INTRODUCTION

An eccentric businessman wants to divide his n gold bars among his four children, so that the first child gets one-half of the bars, the second child gets one-fourth, the third child gets one-fifth, and the fourth child gets seven gold bars. How many gold bars does the eccentric businessman have?

This type of "brain teaser" is an example of the use of basic algebra. We can find the answer by letting the unknown value be represented by a letter (a variable) and applying the laws of algebraic formula manipulation. Many problems in business and finance can be solved by using predetermined formulas. When these formulas are used, we need the skills of algebraic substitution and simplification to solve them.

Many problems do not fit a predetermined formula. We must then use the basics of algebra to create our own equation, and solve it to answer the problem. An equation is a statement of equality between two algebraic expressions. Any equation that has only variables (letter symbols) to the first power is called a linear equation. Linear equations can often be created to represent business problems. When you solve the equation you solve the business problem. When you finish this chapter you should feel comfortable solving linear equations. (And if you have not already solved the brain teaser above, you should be able to figure out that the eccentric businessman has 140 gold bars.)

2.1 SIMPLIFICATION OF ALGEBRAIC EXPRESSIONS

A. Addition and subtraction

1. Simplification Involving Addition and Subtraction

In algebra, only **like terms** may be added or subtracted. This is done by *adding* or *subtracting* the **numerical coefficients** of the like terms according to the rules used for adding and subtracting signed numbers, and *retaining* the common **literal coefficient**. The process of adding and subtracting like terms is called **combining like terms** or **collecting like terms**.

EXAMPLE 2.1A

(i) $6x + 3x + 7x$ ——— all three terms are like terms
$= (6 + 3 + 7)x$ ——— add the numerical coefficients
$= 16x$ ——— retain the common literal coefficient

(ii) $9a - 5a - 7a + 4a$
$= (9 - 5 - 7 + 4)a$
$= a$

(iii) $-5m - (-3m) - (+6m)$
$= -5m + (+3m) + (-6m)$ ——— change the subtraction to addition
$= -5m + 3m - 6m$
$= (-5 + 3 - 6)m$
$= -8m$

(iv) $7x - 4y - 3x - 6y$ — the two sets of like terms are $7x$, $-3x$, and $-4y$, $-6y$, and are collected separately
$= (7 - 3)x + (-4 - 6)y$
$= 4x - 10y$

(v) $5x^2 - 3x - 4 + 2x - 5 + x^2$
$= (5 + 1)x^2 + (-3 + 2)x + (-4 - 5)$
$= 6x^2 - x - 9$

2. Simplification Involving Brackets

When simplifying **algebraic expressions** involving brackets, remove the brackets according to the following rules and collect like terms.

(a) If the brackets are preceded by a (+) sign or no sign, drop the brackets and retain the terms inside the brackets with their signs unchanged: $(-7a + 5b - c)$ becomes $-7a + 5b - c$.

(b) If the brackets are preceded by a (−) sign, drop the brackets and change the sign of every term inside the brackets: $-(-7a + 5b - c)$ becomes $7a - 5b + c$.

EXAMPLE 2.1B

(i) $(7a - 3b) - (4a + 3b)$
$= 7a - 3b - 4a - 3b$ — $(7a - 3b)$ becomes $7a - 3b$; $-(4a + 3b)$ becomes $-4a - 3b$
$= 3a - 6b$

(ii) $-(3x^2 - 8x - 5) + (2x^2 - 5x + 4)$
$= -3x^2 + 8x + 5 + 2x^2 - 5x + 4$
$= -x^2 + 3x + 9$

(iii) $4b - (3a - 4b - c) - (5c + 2b)$
$= 4b - 3a + 4b + c - 5c - 2b$
$= -3a + 6b - 4c$

B. Multiplication

1. Multiplication of Monomials

The product of two or more **monomials** is the product of their numerical coefficients multiplied by the product of their literal coefficients.

EXAMPLE 2.1C

(i) $5(3a)$
$= (5 \times 3)a$ — obtain the product of the numerical coefficients
$= 15a$

(ii) $(-7a)(4b)$
$= (-7 \times 4)(a \times b)$ — obtain the product of the numerical coefficients, −7 and 4, and the product of the literal coefficients, a and b
$= -28ab$

(iii) $(-3)(4x)(-5x)$
$= [(-3)(4)(-5)][(x)(x)]$
$= 60x^2$

2. Multiplication of Monomials with Polynomials

The product of a **polynomial** and a monomial is obtained by multiplying each term of the polynomial by the monomial.

EXAMPLE 2.1D

(i) $5(a-3)$
$= 5(a) + 5(-3)$ — multiply 5 by *a* and 5 by (−3)
$= 5a - 15$

(ii) $-4(3x^2 - 2x - 1)$
$= -4(3x^2) + (-4)(-2x) + (-4)(-1)$ — multiply each term of the trinomial by (−4)
$= (-12x^2) + (+8x) + (+4)$
$= -12x^2 + 8x + 4$

(iii) $3a(4a - 5b - 2c)$
$= (3a)(4a) + (3a)(-5b) + (3a)(-2c)$
$= (12a^2) + (-15ab) + (-6ac)$
$= 12a^2 - 15ab - 6ac$

3. Simplification Involving Brackets and Multiplication

EXAMPLE 2.1E

(i) $3(x-5) - 2(x-7)$
$= 3x - 15 - 2x + 14$ — carry out the multiplication
$= x - 1$ — collect like terms

(ii) $a(3a-1) - 4(2a+3)$
$= 3a^2 - a - 8a - 12$
$= 3a^2 - 9a - 12$

(iii) $5(m-7) - 8(3m-2) - 3(7-3m)$
$= 5m - 35 - 24m + 16 - 21 + 9m$
$= -10m - 40$

(iv) $-4(5a - 3b - 2c) + 5(-2a - 4b + c)$
$= -20a + 12b + 8c - 10a - 20b + 5c$
$= -30a - 8b + 13c$

4. Multiplication of a Polynomial by a Polynomial

The product of two polynomials is obtained by multiplying each term of one polynomial by each term of the other polynomial and collecting like terms.

EXAMPLE 2.1F

(i) $(3a + 2b)(4c - 3d)$
$= 3a(4c - 3d) + 2b(4c - 3d)$ — multiply each term of the first polynomial by the second polynomial
$= 12ac - 9ad + 8bc - 6bd$ — carry out the multiplication

(ii) $(5x - 2)(3x + 4)$
$= 5x(3x + 4) - 2(3x + 4)$
$= 15x^2 + 20x - 6x - 8$
$= 15x^2 + 14x - 8$

C. Division

1. Division of Monomials

The quotient of two monomials is the quotient of their numerical coefficients multiplied by the quotient of their literal coefficients.

EXAMPLE 2.1G

(i) $32ab \div 8b = \left(\frac{32}{8}\right)\left(\frac{ab}{b}\right) = 4a$

(ii) $24x^2 \div (-6x) = \left(\frac{24}{-6}\right)\left(\frac{x^2}{x}\right) = -4x$

2. Division of a Polynomial by a Monomial

To determine the quotient of a polynomial divided by a monomial, divide each term of the polynomial by the monomial.

EXAMPLE 2.1H

(i) $(12a + 8) \div 4 = \frac{12a + 8}{4} = \frac{12a}{4} + \frac{8}{4} = 3a + 2$

(ii) $(18x - 12) \div 6 = \frac{18x - 12}{6} = \frac{18x}{6} - \frac{12}{6} = 3x - 2$

(iii) $(12a^3 - 15a^2 - 9a) \div (-3a)$

$$= \frac{12a^3 - 15a^2 - 9a}{-3a}$$

$$= \frac{12a^3}{-3a} + \frac{-15a^2}{-3a} + \frac{-9a}{-3a}$$

$$= -4a^2 + 5a + 3$$

D. Substitution and evaluation

Evaluating algebraic expressions for given values of the variables requires replacing the variables with the given values. The replacement or substitution of the variables by the given values takes place each time the variables appear in the expression.

EXAMPLE 2.1I

(i) Evaluate $7x - 3y - 5$ for $x = -2, y = 3$

SOLUTION

$7x - 3y - 5$

$= 7(-2) - 3(3) - 5$ ——— replace x by (-2) and y by 3

$= -14 - 9 - 5$

$= -28$

(ii) Evaluate $\dfrac{2NC}{P(n+1)}$ for N = 12, C = 220, P = 1500, n = 15

SOLUTION

$$\frac{2NC}{P(n+1)} = \frac{2(12)(220)}{1500(15+1)} = 0.22$$

(iii) Evaluate $\dfrac{I}{RT}$ for I = 126, R = 0.125, T = $\dfrac{328}{365}$

SOLUTION

$$\frac{I}{RT} = \frac{126}{0.125 \times \frac{328}{365}} = 1121.71$$

(iv) Evaluate P(1 + RT) for P = 900, R = 0.15, T = $\dfrac{244}{365}$

SOLUTION

$$\begin{aligned} P(1 + RT) &= 900\left(1 + 0.15 \times \frac{244}{365}\right) \\ &= 900(1 + 0.100274) \\ &= 900(1.100274) \\ &= 990.25 \end{aligned}$$

(v) Evaluate A(1 − dt) for A = 800, d = 0.135, t = $\dfrac{292}{365}$

SOLUTION

$$\begin{aligned} A(1 - dt) &= 800\left(1 - 0.135 \times \frac{292}{365}\right) \\ &= 800(1 - 0.108) \\ &= 800(0.892) \\ &= 713.60 \end{aligned}$$

(vi) Evaluate $\dfrac{A}{1 + RT}$ for A = 1644, R = 0.16, T = $\dfrac{219}{365}$

SOLUTION

$$\frac{A}{1 + RT} = \frac{1644}{1 + 0.16 \times \frac{219}{365}} = \frac{1644}{1 + 0.096} = \frac{1644}{1.096} = 1500$$

(vii) Evaluate $\dfrac{P}{1 - dt}$ for P = 1000, d = 0.18, t = $\dfrac{335}{365}$

SOLUTION

$$\frac{P}{1 - dt} = \frac{1000}{1 - 0.18 \times \frac{335}{365}} = \frac{1000}{1 - 0.165205} = \frac{1000}{0.834795} = 1197.90$$

EXERCISE 2.1

A. Addition and subtraction. Simplify.

1. $9a + 3a + 7a$

2. $6m - 2m - m$

3. $-4a - 8 + 3a - 2$

4. $2a - 15 - 5a + 1$

5. $2x - 3y - 4x - y$

6. $6p + 2q - 3p - q$

7. $12f - 9v + 2f + 5v$

8. $9c - 8d - 7c + 5d$

9. $x - 0.2x$

10. $x + 0.06x$

11. $x + 0.4x$

12. $x - 0.02x$

13. $x + 0.9x + 0.89x$

14. $3y + 2.81y - 1.76y$

15. $x^2 - 2x - 5 + x - 3 - 2x^2$

16. $3ax - 2x + 1 - 3 + 3x - 4ax$

17. $(2x - 3y) - (x + 4y)$

18. $-(4 - 5a) - (-2 + 3a)$

19. $(12b + 4c + 9) + 8 - (8b + 2c + 15)$

20. $(a^2 - ab + b^2) - (3a^2 + 5ab - 4b^2)$

21. $-(3m^2 - 4m - 5) - (4 - 2m - 2m^2)$

22. $6 - (4x - 3y + 1) - (5x + 2y - 9)$

23. $(7a - 5b) - (-3a + 4b) - 5b$

24. $(3f - f^2 + fg) - (f - 3f^2 - 2fg)$

B. Multiplication and division. Simplify.

1. $3(-4x)$

2. $-7(8a)$

3. $-5x(2a)$

4. $-9a(-3b)$

5. $-x(2x)$

6. $-6m(-4m)$

7. $-4(5x)(-3y)$

8. $2a(-3b)(-4c)(-1)$

9. $-2(x - 2y)$

10. $5(2x - 4)$

11. $a(2x^2 - 3x - 1)$

12. $-6x(4 - 2b - b^2)$

13. $4(5x - 6) - 3(2 - 5x)$

14. $-3(8a - b) - 2(-7a + 9b)$

15. $-3a(5x - 1) + a(5 - 2x) - 3a(x + 1)$

16. $8(3y - 4) - 2(2y - 1) - (1 - y)$

17. $(3x - 1)(x + 2)$

18. $(5m - 2n)(m - 3n)$

19. $(x + y)(x^2 - xy + y^2)$

20. $(a - 1)(a^2 - 2a + 1)$

21. $(5x - 4)(2x - 1) - (x - 7)(3x + 5)$

22. $2(a - 1)(2a - 3) - 3(3a - 2)(a + 1)$

23. $20ab \div 5$

24. $30xy \div (-6x)$

25. $(-12x^2) \div (-3x)$

26. $(-42ab) \div (7ab)$

27. $(20m - 8) \div 2$

28. $(14x - 21) \div (-7)$

29. $(10x^2 - 15x - 30) \div (-5)$

30. $(-a^3 - 4a^2 - 3a) \div (-a)$

C. Substitution and evaluation. Evaluate each of the following for the values given.

1. $3x - 2y - 3$ for $x = -4, y = -5$

2. $\frac{1}{2}(3x^2 - x - 1) - \frac{1}{4}(5 - 2x - x^2)$ for $x = -3$

3. $(pq - vq) - f$ for $p = 12, q = 2000, v = 7, f = 4500$

4. F/C for F = 13 000, C = 0.65

5. $(1 - d_1)(1 - d_2)(1 - d_3)$ for $d_1 = 0.35, d_2 = 0.08, d_3 = 0.02$

6. C + 0.38C + 0.24C for C = 25.00

7. $\frac{\text{RP}(n + 1)}{2\text{N}}$ for R = 0.21, P = 1200, $n = 77$, N = 26

8. $\frac{\text{I}}{\text{P}t}$ for I = 63, P = 840, $t = \frac{219}{365}$

9. $\frac{\text{I}}{rt}$ for I = 198, $r = 0.165$, $t = \frac{146}{365}$

10. $\frac{2\text{NC}}{\text{P}(n + 1)}$ for N = 52, C = 60, P = 1800, $n = 25$

11. $\text{P}(1 + rt)$ for P = 880, $r = 0.12$, $t = \frac{76}{365}$

12. $\text{FV}(1 - rt)$ for FV = 1200, $r = 0.175$, $t = \frac{256}{365}$

13. $\frac{\text{P}}{1 - dt}$ for P = 1253, $d = 0.135$, $t = \frac{284}{365}$

14. $\frac{\text{FV}}{1 + rt}$ for FV = 1752, $r = 0.152$, $t = \frac{228}{365}$

2.2 INTEGRAL EXPONENTS

A. Basic concept and definition

If a number is to be used as a **factor** several times, the mathematical expression can be written more efficiently by using exponents:

$$5 \times 5 \times 5 \times 5 \text{ may be written as } 5^4$$

Note: In the expression 5^4 ——→ 5 is called the **base**
——→ 4 is called the **exponent**
——→ 5^4 is called the **power**

EXAMPLE 2.2A

(i) $7 \times 7 \times 7 \times 7 \times 7 = 7^5$

(ii) $(-4)(-4)(-4) = (-4)^3$

(iii) $(1.01)(1.01)(1.01)(1.01) = (1.01)^4$

(iv) $(a)(a)(a)(a)(a)(a)(a) = a^7$

(v) $(1 + i)(1 + i)(1 + i)(1 + i)(1 + i)(1 + i) = (1 + i)^6$

Definition: When "n" is a positive integer, "a^n" represents the product of "n" equal factors whose value is "a."

$$\boxed{a^n = (a)(a)(a)(a)\ldots(a) \text{ to } n \text{ factors}}$$

a is called the **base**
n is called the **exponent**
a^n is called the **power**

$$\boxed{\text{POWER} = \text{BASE}^{\text{to the EXPONENT}}}$$

Note: If a number is raised to the exponent "1," the power equals the base.

$$5^1 = 5 \text{ and } a^1 = a;$$
$$\text{conversely, } 6 = 6^1 \text{ and } x = x^1.$$

B. Numerical evaluation of powers with positive integral exponents

1. Evaluation When the Base Is a Positive Integer

To evaluate a power, we may rewrite the power in factored form and obtain the product by multiplication.

EXAMPLE 2.2B

(i) 2^5 ——— means that 2 is a factor 5 times
$= (2)(2)(2)(2)(2)$ ——— power rewritten in factored form
$= 32$ ——— product

(ii) $(5)^3$ — 5 is a factor 3 times
$= (5)(5)(5) = 125$

(iii) 1^7 — 1 is a factor 7 times
$= (1)(1)(1)(1)(1)(1)(1)$
$= 1$

(iv) a^n if $a = 4, n = 6$
$a^n = 4^6$
$= (4)(4)(4)(4)(4)(4)$
$= 4096$

2. Evaluation When the Base Is a Negative Integer

If a power has a negative base, the number of equal factors shown by the exponent determines the sign of the product.

(a) If the exponent is an even positive integer, the product is positive.
(b) If the exponent is an odd positive integer, the product is negative.

EXAMPLE 2.2C

(i) $(-4)^3$ — (-4) is a factor 3 times
$= (-4)(-4)(-4)$
$= -64$ — the answer is negative (n is odd)

(ii) $(-2)^8$ — (-2) is a factor 8 times
$= (-2)(-2)(-2)(-2)(-2)(-2)(-2)(-2)$
$= 256$ — the answer is positive (n is even)

Note: -2^8 means $-(2)^8 = -(2)(2)(2)(2)(2)(2)(2)(2) = -256$

(iii) $(-1)^{55}$
$= (-1)(-1)(-1)(-1)\ldots$ to 55 factors
$= -1$

(iv) $3a^n$ for $a = -5, n = 4$
$3a^n = 3(-5)^4$
$= 3(-5)(-5)(-5)(-5)$
$= 3(625)$
$= 1875$

3. Evaluation When the Base Is a Common Fraction or Decimal

EXAMPLE 2.2D

(i) $\left(\frac{3}{2}\right)^5$ — $\frac{3}{2}$ is a factor 5 times
$= \left(\frac{3}{2}\right)\left(\frac{3}{2}\right)\left(\frac{3}{2}\right)\left(\frac{3}{2}\right)\left(\frac{3}{2}\right)$
$= \frac{(3)(3)(3)(3)(3)}{(2)(2)(2)(2)(2)}$
$= \frac{243}{32}$

(ii) $(0.1)^4$ ——— **0.1 is a factor 4 times**

$= (0.1)(0.1)(0.1)(0.1)$

$= 0.0001$

(iii) $\left(-\frac{1}{3}\right)^3$ ——— **$(-\frac{1}{3})$ is a factor 3 times**

$= \left(-\frac{1}{3}\right)\left(-\frac{1}{3}\right)\left(-\frac{1}{3}\right)$

$= \frac{(-1)(-1)(-1)}{(3)(3)(3)}$

$= \frac{-1}{27}$

(iv) $(1.02)^2$

$= (1.02)(1.02)$

$= 1.0404$

(v) $(1 + i)^n$ for $i = 0.03, n = 4$

$(1 + i)^n = (1 + 0.03)^4$

$= (1.03)(1.03)(1.03)(1.03)$

$= 1.12550881$

POINTERS AND PITFALLS

You can use a calculator's *power function* to evaluate powers. On most financial calculators, the power function is represented by y^x. For example, to evaluate $(-1.03)^5$ using the Texas Instruments BAII Plus, use the key sequence

1.03 [±] [y^x] 5 [=]

The answer should be −1.159274.

C. Operations with powers

1. Multiplication of Powers

To multiply powers that have the same base, retain the common base and add the exponents.

$$a^m \times a^n = a^{m+n}$$ ——— **Formula 2.1A**

$$a^m \times a^n \times a^p = a^{m+n+p}$$ ——— **Formula 2.1B**

Notice that Formula 2.1B is an extension of Formula 2.1A.

EXAMPLE 2.2E

(i) $3^5 \times 3^2$
$= 3^{5+2}$ ——— retain the common base 3 and add the exponents 5 and 2
$= 3^7$

(ii) $(-4)^3(-4)^7(-4)^5$
$= (-4)^{3+7+5}$ ——— retain the common base (−4) and add the exponents 3, 7, and 5
$= (-4)^{15}$

(iii) $\left(\frac{1}{8}\right)^5\left(\frac{1}{8}\right) = \left(\frac{1}{8}\right)^{5+1} = \left(\frac{1}{8}\right)^6$

(iv) $(x^3)(x^5)(x) = x^{3+5+1} = x^9$

(v) $(1.06)^{16}(1.06)^{14} = (1.06)^{16+14} = 1.06^{30}$

(vi) $(1+i)(1+i)^5(1+i)^{20} = (1+i)^{1+5+20} = (1+i)^{26}$

2. Division of Powers

To divide powers that have the same base, retain the common base and subtract the exponent of the divisor from the exponent of the dividend.

$$a^m \div a^n = a^{m-n}$$ ——— Formula 2.2

EXAMPLE 2.2F

(i) $2^8 \div 2^5$ ——— retain the common base 2 and subtract the exponent of the divisor, 5, from the exponent of the dividend, 8
$= 2^{8-5}$
$= 2^3$

(ii) $(-10)^8 \div (-10)^7$ ——— retain the common base (−10) and subtract the exponents
$= (-10)^{8-7}$
$= (-10)^1$ or -10

(iii) $\left(-\frac{2}{5}\right)^6 \div \left(-\frac{2}{5}\right)^2 = \left(-\frac{2}{5}\right)^{6-2} = \left(-\frac{2}{5}\right)^4$

(iv) $a^{15} \div a^{10} = a^{15-10} = a^5$

(v) $(1.10)^{24} \div 1.10 = (1.10)^{24-1} = 1.10^{23}$

(vi) $(1+i)^{80} \div (1+i)^{60} = (1+i)^{80-60} = (1+i)^{20}$

3. Raising a Power to a Power

To raise a power to a power, retain the base and multiply the exponents.

$$(a^m)^n = a^{mn}$$ ——— Formula 2.3

EXAMPLE 2.2G

(i) $(3^2)^5$
$= 3^{2\times 5}$ ——— retain the base 3 and multiply the exponents 2 and 5
$= 3^{10}$

(ii) $[(-4)^5]^3$
$= (-4)^{5\times3}$ — retain the base and multiply the exponents
$= (-4)^{15}$

(iii) $\left[\left(\frac{4}{3}\right)^6\right]^{10} = \left(\frac{4}{3}\right)^{6\times10} = \left(\frac{4}{3}\right)^{60}$

(iv) $(a^7)^3 = a^{7\times3} = a^{21}$

(v) $[(1.005)^{50}]^4 = (1.005)^{50\times4} = 1.005^{200}$

(vi) $[(1+i)^{75}]^2 = (1+i)^{75\times2} = (1+i)^{150}$

4. Power of a Product and Power of a Quotient

The power of a product, written in factored form, is the product of the individual factors raised to the exponent.

$$(ab)^m = a^m b^m$$ — Formula 2.4

POINTERS AND PITFALLS

Note that ab^2 is not the same as $(ab)^2$ since ab^2 means $(a)(b)(b)$ while $(ab)^2 = (ab)(ab) = (a)(a)(b)(b) = a^2b^2$.

The power of a quotient is the quotient of the dividend and the divisor raised to the exponent.

$$\left(\frac{a}{b}\right)^m = \frac{a^m}{b^m}$$ — Formula 2.5

EXAMPLE 2.2H

(i) $(2\times3)^5 = 2^5\times3^5$

(ii) $(6\times2^7)^4 = 6^4\times(2^7)^4 = 6^4\times2^{28}$

(iii) $\left(-\frac{5}{7}\right)^3 = \frac{(-5)^3}{7^3}$

(iv) $(a^3b)^4 = (a^3)^4\times b^4 = a^{12}b^4$

(v) $\left[\frac{(1+i)}{i}\right]^3 = \frac{(1+i)^3}{i^3}$

D. Zero exponent

A zero exponent results when using the law of division of powers on powers with equal exponents.

$3^5 \div 3^5$
$= 3^{5-5}$
$= 3^0$

The result may be interpreted as follows.

$$3^5 \div 3^5 = \frac{3^5}{3^5} = \frac{3 \times 3 \times 3 \times 3 \times 3}{3 \times 3 \times 3 \times 3 \times 3} = 1$$

$$\boxed{3^0 = 1}$$

Similarly, $a^6 \div a^6 = a^{6-6} = a^0$

and since $a^6 \div a^6 = \frac{a^6}{a^6} = \frac{(a)(a)(a)(a)(a)(a)}{(a)(a)(a)(a)(a)(a)} = 1$

$$\boxed{a^0 = 1}$$

In general, *any number raised to the exponent zero is 1*, except zero itself. The expression 0^0 has no meaning and is said to be *undefined.*

E. Negative exponents

A negative exponent results when the exponent of the divisor is greater than the exponent of the dividend.

$$\begin{aligned} &4^3 \div 4^5 \\ &= 4^{3-5} \\ &= 4^{-2} \end{aligned}$$

The result may be interpreted as follows.

$$4^3 \div 4^5 = \frac{4^3}{4^5} = \frac{4 \times 4 \times 4}{4 \times 4 \times 4 \times 4 \times 4} = \frac{1}{4 \times 4} = \frac{1}{4^2}$$

$$\boxed{4^{-2} = \frac{1}{4^2}}$$

Similarly, $a^5 \div a^8 = a^{5-8} = a^{-3}$

and since $a^5 \div a^8 = \frac{a^5}{a^8} = \frac{(a)(a)(a)(a)(a)}{(a)(a)(a)(a)(a)(a)(a)(a)}$

$$= \frac{1}{(a)(a)(a)} = \frac{1}{a^3}$$

$$\boxed{a^{-3} = \frac{1}{a^3}}$$

$$\boxed{a^{-m} = \frac{1}{a^m}} \quad \text{Formula 2.6}$$

In general, a base raised to a negative exponent is equivalent to “1” divided by the same base raised to the corresponding positive exponent.

EXAMPLE 2.2I

(i) $2^{-3} = \frac{1}{2^3} = \frac{1}{8}$

(ii) $(-3)^{-2} = \frac{1}{(-3)^2} = \frac{1}{9}$

(iii) $\left(\frac{1}{4}\right)^{-4} = \frac{1}{(\frac{1}{4})^4} = \frac{1}{\frac{1}{256}} = \frac{1}{1} \times \frac{256}{1} = 256$

(iv) $\left(-\frac{3}{5}\right)^{-3} = \frac{1}{(-\frac{3}{5})^3} = \frac{1}{-\frac{27}{125}} = \frac{-125}{27}$

Note: Since $\frac{-125}{27} = \frac{(-5)^3}{3^3} = \left(-\frac{5}{3}\right)^3 = \left(-\frac{3}{5}\right)^{-3}$

$$\left(\frac{y}{x}\right)^{-m} = \left(\frac{x}{y}\right)^{m}$$ **Formula 2.7**

(v) $(-4)^0 = 1$

(vi) $(1.05)^{-2} = \frac{1}{1.05^2} = \frac{1}{1.1025} = 0.9070295$

(vii) $(1 + i)^{-10} = \frac{1}{(1 + i)^{10}}$

(viii) $(1 + i)^{-1} = \frac{1}{1 + i}$

(ix) $(1 + i)^0 = 1$

EXERCISE 2.2

A. Evaluate each of the following.

1. 3^4 **2.** 1^5 **3.** $(-2)^4$ **4.** $(-1)^{12}$

5. $\left(\frac{2}{3}\right)^4$ **6.** $\left(\frac{5}{6}\right)^4$ **7.** $\left(-\frac{1}{4}\right)^3$ **8.** $\left(-\frac{2}{3}\right)^3$

9. $(0.5)^2$ **10.** $(2.2)^6$ **11.** $(-0.1)^3$ **12.** $(-3.2)^5$

13. $(-4)^0$ **14.** m^0 **15.** 3^{-2} **16.** 8^3

17. $(-5)^{-3}$ **18.** $(-3.6)^{-4}$ **19.** $\left(\frac{1}{5}\right)^{-3}$ **20.** $\left(\frac{2}{3}\right)^{-4}$

21. 1.01^{-1} **22.** $(1.05)^0$

B. Simplify.

1. $2^5 \times 2^3$

2. $(-4)^3 \times (-4)$

3. $4^7 \div 4^4$

4. $(-3)^9 \div (-3)^7$

5. $(2^3)^5$

6. $[(-4)^3]^6$

7. $a^4 \times a^{10}$

8. $m^{12} \div m^7$

9. $3^4 \times 3^6 \times 3$

10. $(-1)^3(-1)^7(-1)^5$

11. $\dfrac{6^7 \times 6^3}{6^9}$

12. $\dfrac{(x^4)(x^5)}{x^7}$

13. $\left(\dfrac{3}{5}\right)^4\left(\dfrac{3}{5}\right)^7$

14. $\left(\dfrac{1}{6}\right)^5 \div \left(\dfrac{1}{6}\right)^3$

15. $\left(-\dfrac{3}{2}\right)\left(-\dfrac{3}{2}\right)^6\left(-\dfrac{3}{2}\right)^4$

16. $\left(-\dfrac{3}{4}\right)^8 \div \left(-\dfrac{3}{4}\right)^7$

17. $(1.025^{80})(1.025^{70})$

18. $1.005^{240} \div 1.005^{150}$

19. $[1.04^{20}]^4$

20. $\left[\left(-\dfrac{3}{7}\right)^5\right]^3$

21. $(1+i)^{100}(1+i)^{100}$

22. $(1-r)^2(1-r)^2(1-r)^2$

23. $[(1+i)^{80}]^2$

24. $[(1-r)^{40}]^3$

25. $(ab)^5$

26. $(2xy)^4$

27. $(m^3n)^8$

28. $\left(\dfrac{a^3b^2}{x}\right)^4$

29. $2^3 \times 2^5 \times 2^{-4}$

30. $5^2 \div 5^{-3}$

31. $\left(\dfrac{a}{b}\right)^{-8}$

32. $\left(\dfrac{1+i}{i}\right)^{-n}$

2.3 FRACTIONAL EXPONENTS

A. Radicals

When the product of two or more equal factors is expressed in exponential form, one of the equal factors is called the **root of the product**. The exponent indicates the number of equal factors, that is, the **power of the root**.

For example,

$25 = 5^2$ → 5 is the second power root (square root) of 25
$8 = 2^3$ → 2 is the third power root (cube root) of 8
$81 = 3^4$ → 3 is the fourth (power) root of 81
a^5 → a is the fifth root of a^5
7^n → 7 is the nth root of 7^n
x^n → x is the nth root of x^n

The operational symbol for finding the root of an expression is $\sqrt{}$. This symbol represents the *positive* root only. If the negative root is desired, a minus sign is placed in front of the symbol; that is, the negative root is represented by $-\sqrt{}$.

The power of a root is written at the upper left of the symbol, as in $\sqrt[3]{}$ or $\sqrt[n]{}$.

The indicated root is called a **radical**, the power indicated is called the **index**, and the number under the symbol is called the **radicand.**

In $\sqrt[5]{32}$, the index is 5
the radicand is 32
the radical is $\sqrt[5]{32}$

When the square root is to be found, it is customary to omit the index 2. The symbol $\sqrt{}$ is understood to mean the positive square root of the radicand.

$\sqrt{49}$ means $\sqrt[2]{49}$ or 7

In special cases, like those shown in Example 2.3A, the radicand is an integral power of the root. The root can readily be found by expressing the radicand in exponential form; the index of the root and the exponent are the same.

EXAMPLE 2.3A

(i) $\sqrt{64} = \sqrt{8^2}$ —— the radicand 64 is expressed in exponential form as a square

$= 8$ —— one of the two equal factors 8 is the root

(ii) $\sqrt[5]{32} = \sqrt[5]{2^5}$ —— express the radicand 32 as the fifth power of 2

$= 2$ —— one of the five equal factors 2 is the root

(iii) $\sqrt[3]{0.125} = \sqrt[3]{0.5^3} = 0.5$

In most cases, however, the radicand cannot be easily rewritten in exponential form. The arithmetic determination of the numerical value of these roots is a laborious process. But computating the root is easily accomplished using electronic calculators equipped with a power function.

To use the power function described in the Pointers and Pitfalls box on page 53, first rewrite the radical so it appears in exponential form. Then, as you will see in Formula 2.8 in the next section, $a^{1/n} = \sqrt[n]{a}$. Use the opposite of this formula to rewrite a radical into exponential form: $\sqrt[n]{a} = a^{1/n}$. For example, $\sqrt[5]{32}$ can be written as $32^{1/5}$. Now use the power function. The key sequence is

32 [y^x] [( ] 1 [÷] 5 [ )] [=] The solution is 2.

(Instead of using brackets, you could first calculate 1 ÷ 5, save the result in the calculator's memory, then recall the result from memory after pressing [y^x].)

The problems in Example 2.3B are intended to ensure that students are able to use the power function. They should be done using an electronic calculator.

EXAMPLE 2.3B

(i) $\sqrt{1425} = 37.7492$ —— *Check* $37.7492^2 = 1425$

(ii) $\sqrt[5]{12\,960} = 6.6454$ —— *Check* $6.6454^5 = 12\,960$

(iii) $\sqrt[15]{40\,000} = 2.0268$ —— *Check* $2.0268^{15} = 40\,010$ (due to rounding)

(iv) $\sqrt[20]{1\,048\,576} = 2$ ——— *Check* $2^{20} = 1\,048\,576$

(v) $\sqrt{0.005184} = 0.072$ ——— *Check* $0.072^2 = 0.005184$

(vi) $\sqrt[7]{0.038468} = 0.6279$ ——— *Check* $0.6279^7 = 0.03848$ (due to rounding)

(vii) $\sqrt[45]{1.954213} = 1.015$ ——— *Check* $1.015^{45} = 1.954213$

(viii) $\sqrt[36]{0.022528} = 0.9$ ——— *Check* $0.9^{36} = 0.022528$

(ix) $\sqrt{2^6} = \sqrt{64} = 8$

(x) $\sqrt[3]{5^6} = \sqrt[3]{15\,625} = 25$

Note: Many of the solutions for problems such as those above involve repeating and continuous numbers. In order to standardize, the number of decimal places shown in solutions will be set at six or less. The financial calculator can be set to show a maximum of six decimal places by following the steps:

[2nd] [Format] DEC = 6 [Enter] [2nd] [QUIT]

It is important to note that, even though the calculator display shows six or less decimal places, the complete, non-rounded quantity is used in continuous calculations on the calculator.

EXAMPLE 2.3C

Calculate i in the formula $FV = PV(1 + i)^n$, where $FV = 1102.50$, $PV = 1000.00$, $n = 2$.

SOLUTION

$1102.50 = 1000.00(1 + i)^2$

$(1 + i)^2 = 1.1025$

$(1 + i) = 1.1025^{0.5}$ ——— raise both sides to the power 1/2, that is, 0.5

$(1 + i) = 1.05$

$i = 0.05 = 5\%$

B. Fractional exponents

Radicals may be written in exponential form and fractional exponents may be represented in radical form according to the following definitions.

(a) The exponent is a positive fraction with numerator 1.

$$a^{\frac{1}{n}} = \sqrt[n]{a}$$ ——— Formula 2.8

$$4^{\frac{1}{2}} = \sqrt{4} = 2$$

$$27^{\frac{1}{3}} = \sqrt[3]{27} = \sqrt[3]{3^3} = 3$$

$$625^{\frac{1}{4}} = \sqrt[4]{625} = \sqrt[4]{5^4} = 5$$

(b) The exponent is a negative fraction with numerator 1.

$$a^{-\frac{1}{n}} = \frac{1}{a^{\frac{1}{n}}} = \frac{1}{\sqrt[n]{a}}$$ ——— **Formula 2.9**

$$8^{-\frac{1}{3}} = \frac{1}{8^{\frac{1}{3}}} = \frac{1}{\sqrt[3]{8}} = \frac{1}{\sqrt[3]{2^3}} = \frac{1}{2}$$

$$243^{-\frac{1}{5}} = \frac{1}{243^{\frac{1}{5}}} = \frac{1}{\sqrt[5]{243}} = \frac{1}{\sqrt[5]{3^5}} = \frac{1}{3}$$

(c) The exponent is a positive or negative fraction with numerator other than 1.

$$a^{\frac{m}{n}} = \sqrt[n]{a^m} = (\sqrt[n]{a})^m$$ ——— **Formula 2.10**

$$a^{-\frac{m}{n}} = \frac{1}{a^{\frac{m}{n}}} = \frac{1}{\sqrt[n]{a^m}}$$ ——— **Formula 2.11**

$$16^{\frac{3}{4}} = \sqrt[4]{16^3} = (\sqrt[4]{16})^3 = (\sqrt[4]{2^4})^3 = (2)^3 = 8$$

$$27^{\frac{4}{3}} = \sqrt[3]{27^4} = (\sqrt[3]{27})^4 = (\sqrt[3]{3^3})^4 = (3)^4 = 81$$

$$36^{-\frac{3}{2}} = \frac{1}{(\sqrt[2]{36})^3} = \frac{1}{(\sqrt[2]{6^2})^3} = \frac{1}{6^3} = \frac{1}{216}$$

For calculators, convert fractional exponents into decimals and compute the answer using the power function.

EXAMPLE 2.3D

(i) $36^{\frac{3}{2}} = 36^{1.5} = 216$

(ii) $3^{\frac{5}{4}} = 3^{1.25} = 3.948222$

(iii) $\sqrt[5]{12} = 12^{\frac{1}{5}} = 12^{0.2} = 1.6437518$

(iv) $\sqrt[8]{325^5} = 325^{\frac{5}{8}} = 325^{0.625} = 37.147287$

(v) $\sqrt[6]{1.075} = 1.075^{\frac{1}{6}} = 1.075^{0.166667} = 1.0121264$

EXERCISE 2.3

A. Use an electronic calculator equipped with a power function to compute each of the following, correct to four decimals.

1. $\sqrt{5184}$

2. $\sqrt{205.9225}$

3. $\sqrt[7]{2187}$

4. $\sqrt[10]{1.1046221}$

5. $\sqrt[20]{4.3184}$

6. $\sqrt[16]{0.00001526}$

7. $\sqrt[6]{1.0825}$

8. $\sqrt[12]{1.15}$

B. Compute each of the following.

1. $3025^{\frac{1}{2}}$

2. $2401^{\frac{1}{4}}$

3. $525.21875^{\frac{2}{5}}$

4. $21.6^{\frac{4}{3}}$

5. $\sqrt[12]{1.125^7}$

6. $\sqrt[6]{1.095}$

7. $4^{-\frac{1}{3}}$

8. $1.06^{-\frac{1}{12}}$

9. $\dfrac{1.03^{60} - 1}{0.03}$

10. $\dfrac{1 - 1.05^{-36}}{0.05}$

11. $(1 + 0.08)^{10}$

12. $(1 + 0.045)^{-12}$

13. $26.50\,(1 + 0.043)\left[\dfrac{(1 + 0.043)^{30} - 1}{0.043}\right]$

14. $350.00\,(1 + 0.05)\left[\dfrac{(1 + 0.05)^{20} - 1}{0.05}\right]$

15. $133.00\left[\dfrac{1 - (1 + 0.056)^{-12}}{0.056}\right]$

16. $270.00\left[\dfrac{1 - (1 + 0.035)^{-8}}{0.035}\right]$

17. $5000.00\,(1 + 0.0275)^{-20} + 137.50\left[\dfrac{1 - (1 + 0.0275)^{-20}}{0.0275}\right]$

18. $1000.00\,(1 + 0.03)^{-16} + 300.00\left[\dfrac{1 - (1 + 0.03)^{-16}}{0.03}\right]$

19. $112.55 = 100.00(1 + i)^4$

20. $380.47 = 300.00(1 + i)^{12}$

21. $3036.77 = 2400.00(1 + i)^{6}$

22. $1453.36 = 800.00(1 + i)^{60}$

2.4 LOGARITHMS—BASIC ASPECTS

A. The concept of logarithm

In Section 2.2 and Section 2.3, the exponential form of writing numbers was discussed.

$64 = 2^6$ → the number 64 is represented as a power of 2
$243 = 3^5$ → the number 243 is represented as a power of 3
$10\,000 = 10^4$ → the number 10 000 is represented as a power of 10
$5 = 125^{\frac{1}{3}}$ → the number 5 is represented as a power of 125
$0.001 = 10^{-3}$ → the number 0.001 is represented as a power of 10

In general, when a number is represented as a base raised to an exponent, the exponent is called a logarithm. A **logarithm** is defined as the *exponent* to which a base must be raised to produce a given number.

Accordingly,

$64 = 2^6$ → 6 is the logarithm of 64 to the base 2, written $6 = \log_2 64$
$243 = 3^5$ → 5 is the logarithm of 243 to the base 3, written $5 = \log_3 243$
$10\,000 = 10^4$ → 4 is the logarithm of 10 000 to the base 10, written $4 = \log_{10} 10\,000$
$5 = 125^{\frac{1}{3}}$ → ⅓ is the logarithm of 5 to the base 125, written $\frac{1}{3} = \log_{125} 5$
$0.001 = 10^{-3}$ → −3 is the logarithm of 0.001 to the base 10, written $-3 = \log_{10} 0.001$

In general, if $N = b^y$ (*exponential* form)
then $y = \log_b N$ (*logarithmic* form).

EXAMPLE 2.4A

Write each of the following numbers in exponential form and in logarithmic form using the base indicated.

(i) 32 base 2
(ii) 81 base 3
(iii) 256 base 4
(iv) 100 000 base 10
(v) 6 base 36
(vi) 3 base 27
(vii) 0.0001 base 10
(viii) $\frac{1}{8}$ base 2

SOLUTION

	Exponential Form	Logarithmic Form
(i)	Since $32 = 2\times2\times2\times2\times2$	
	$32 = 2^5$	$5 = \log_2 32$
(ii)	Since $81 = 3\times3\times3\times3$	
	$81 = 3^4$	$4 = \log_3 81$
(iii)	Since $256 = 4\times4\times4\times4$	
	$256 = 4^4$	$4 = \log_4 256$
(iv)	Since $100\,000 = 10\times10\times10\times10\times10$	
	$100\,000 = 10^5$	$5 = \log_{10} 100\,000$
(v)	Since $6 = \sqrt{36}$	
	$6 = 36^{\frac{1}{2}}$	$\frac{1}{2} = \log_{36} 6$
(vi)	Since $3 = \sqrt[3]{27}$	
	$3 = 27^{\frac{1}{3}}$	$\frac{1}{3} = \log_{27} 3$
(vii)	Since $0.0001 = \frac{1}{10\,000} = \frac{1}{10^4}$	
	$0.0001 = 10^{-4}$	$-4 = \log_{10} 0.0001$
(viii)	Since $\frac{1}{8} = \frac{1}{2^3}$	
	$\frac{1}{8} = 2^{-3}$	$-3 = \log_2 \frac{1}{8}$

B. Common logarithms

While the base b may be any positive number other than 1, only the numbers 10 and e are used in practice.

Logarithms with base 10 are called **common logarithms**. Obtained from the exponential function $x = 10^y$, the notation used to represent common logarithms is $y = \log x$. (The base 10 is understood and so is not written.)

By definition then, the common logarithm of a number is the exponent to which the base 10 must be raised to give that number.

$\log 1000 = 3$	since $1000 = 10^3$
$\log 1\,000\,000 = 6$	since $1\,000\,000 = 10^6$
$\log 0.01 = -2$	since $0.01 = 10^{-2}$
$\log 0.0001 = -4$	since $0.0001 = 10^{-4}$
$\log 1 = 0$	since $1 = 10^0$

Historically, common logarithms were used for numerical calculations that were required in problems involving compound interest. However, with the availability of electronic calculators equipped with a power function, the need for common logarithms as a computational tool has disappeared. Accordingly, this text gives no further consideration to common logarithms.

C. Natural logarithms

The most common exponential function is

$$y = e^x$$

where $e = \lim_{n \to \infty} \left(1 + \frac{1}{n}\right)^n = 2.718282$ approximately.

The logarithmic form of this function is $x = \log_e y$ but is always written as $\mathbf{x = \ln y}$ and called the **natural logarithm.**

Electronic calculators equipped with the universal power function are generally equipped as well with the e^x function and the $\ln x$ function (natural logarithm function). This latter function eliminates any need for common logarithms and can be used when solving equations for which the unknown quantity is an exponent. As you will see in Chapters 9 through 16, the natural logarithm function will be used to solve for n, the number of compounding periods, in mathematics of finance applications using the algebraic method.

POINTERS AND PITFALLS

In some calculator models, such as the Texas Instruments BAII Plus, the natural logarithm function is found *directly* by entering the number and pressing the [LN] key. In other calculators, the natural logarithm function is found *indirectly* by entering the number and pressing combinations of keys. For example:

For the Hewlett-Packard 10B calculator, enter the number, then press the keys [■] [2].

For the Sharp EL-733A, enter the number, then press [2nd F] [1/x].

EXAMPLE 2.4B

Use an electronic calculator equipped with the natural logarithm key [LN] to determine the value of each of the following.

(i) ln 2	(ii) ln 3000	(iii) ln 0.5
(iv) ln 1	(v) ln 0.0125	(vi) ln 2.718282

SOLUTION

(i) To evaluate ln 2 (using the Texas Instruments BAII Plus),
1. Key in 2.
2. Press LN.
3. Read the answer in the display.

$\ln 2 = 0.693147$

(ii) To evaluate ln 3000 (using the Sharp EL-733A), key in 3000, press 2nd F, press 1/x, and read the answer in the display.

$\ln 3000 = 8.006368$

(iii) $\ln 0.5 = -0.693147$

(iv) $\ln 1 = 0$

(v) $\ln 0.0125 = -4.382027$

(vi) $\ln 2.718282 = 1$

Note:
1. The natural logarithm of 1 is zero.
2. The natural logarithm of a number greater than 1 is positive, for example, $\ln 2 = 0.693147$.
3. The natural logarithm of a number less than 1 is negative, for example, $\ln 0.5 = -0.693147$.

D. Useful relationships

The following relationships are helpful when using natural logarithms:

1. The logarithm of a product of two or more positive numbers is the sum of the logarithms of the factors.

$$\ln(ab) = \ln a + \ln b$$ **Formula 2.12A**

$$\ln(abc) = \ln a + \ln b + \ln c$$ **Formula 2.12B**

Notice that Formula 2.12B is an extension of Formula 2.12A.

2. The logarithm of the quotient of two positive numbers is equal to the logarithm of the dividend (numerator) minus the logarithm of the divisor (denominator).

$$\ln\left(\frac{a}{b}\right) = \ln a - \ln b$$ **Formula 2.13**

3. The logarithm of a power of a positive number is the exponent of the power multiplied by the logarithm of the number.

$$\ln(a^k) = k(\ln a)$$ **Formula 2.14**

4. (i) $\ln e = 1$ since $e = e^1$

(ii) $\ln 1 = 0$ since $1 = e^0$

EXAMPLE 2.4C

Use an electronic calculator equipped with the natural logarithm function to evaluate each of the following.

(i) $\ln[3(15)(36)]$

(ii) $\ln\left[\left(\frac{5000}{1.045}\right)\right]$

(iii) $\ln[1500(1.05^6)]$

(iv) $\ln[5000(1.045^{-1})]$

(v) $\ln\left[\left(\frac{4000}{1.07^{12}}\right)\right]$

(vi) $\ln[10\,000(1.0125^{-17})]$

(vii) $\ln[1.00e^7]$

(viii) $\ln[2.00e^{-0.6}]$

(ix) $\ln\left[600\left(\frac{1.04^6 - 1}{0.04}\right)\right]$

(x) $\ln\left[\left(\frac{1 - 1.0625^{-12}}{0.0625}\right)\right]$

SOLUTION

(i) $\ln[3(15)(36)] = \ln 3 + \ln 15 + \ln 36$
$= 1.098612 + 2.708050 + 3.583519$
$= 7.390181$

Note: You can verify the answer by first simplifying.
$\ln 3(15)(36) = \ln 1620 = 7.390181$

(ii) $\ln\left[\left(\frac{5000}{1.045}\right)\right] = \ln 5000 - \ln 1.045$
$= 8.517193 - 0.044017$
$= 8.473176$

(iii) $\ln[1500(1.05^6)] = \ln 1500 + \ln 1.05^6$
$= \ln 1500 + 6(\ln 1.05)$
$= 7.313220 + 6(0.048790)$
$= 7.313220 + 0.292741$
$= 7.605961$

(iv) $\ln[5000(1.045^{-1})] = \ln 5000 + \ln 1.045^{-1}$
$= \ln 5000 - 1(\ln 1.045)$
$= 8.517193 - 1(0.044017)$
$= 8.473176$

$$
\begin{aligned}
\text{(v) } \ln\left[\left(\frac{4000}{1.07^{12}}\right)\right] &= \ln 4000 - \ln 1.07^{12} \\
&= 8.294050 - 12(0.067659) \\
&= 8.294050 - 0.811904 \\
&= 7.482146
\end{aligned}
$$

$$
\begin{aligned}
\text{(vi) } \ln[10\,000(1.0125^{-17})] &= \ln 10\,000 - 17(\ln 1.0125) \\
&= 9.210340 - 17(0.0124225) \\
&= 9.210340 - 0.211183 \\
&= 8.999157
\end{aligned}
$$

$$
\begin{aligned}
\text{(vii) } \ln[1.00e^{7}] &= \ln 1.00 + \ln e^{7} \\
&= \ln 1.00 + 7(\ln e) \\
&= 0 + 7(1) \\
&= 7
\end{aligned}
$$

$$
\begin{aligned}
\text{(viii) } \ln[2.00e^{-0.6}] &= \ln 2.00 + \ln e^{-0.6} \\
&= \ln 2.00 - 0.6(\ln e) \\
&= 0.693147 - 0.6 \\
&= 0.093147
\end{aligned}
$$

$$
\begin{aligned}
\text{(ix) } \ln\left[600\left(\frac{1.04^{6} - 1}{0.04}\right)\right] &= \ln 600 + \ln\left(\frac{1.04^{6} - 1}{0.04}\right) \\
&= \ln 600 + \ln(1.04^{6} - 1) - \ln 0.04 \\
&= \ln 600 + \ln(1.265319 - 1) - \ln 0.04 \\
&= \ln 600 + \ln 0.265319 - \ln 0.04 \\
&= 6.396930 - 1.326822 - (-3.218876) \\
&= 6.396930 - 1.326822 + 3.218876 \\
&= 8.288984
\end{aligned}
$$

$$
\begin{aligned}
\text{(x) } \ln\left[\left(\frac{1 - 1.0625^{-12}}{0.0625}\right)\right] &= \ln(1 - 1.0625^{-12}) - \ln 0.0625 \\
&= \ln(1 - 0.483117) - \ln 0.0625 \\
&= \ln 0.516883 - \ln 0.0625 \\
&= -0.659939 - (-2.772589) \\
&= -0.659939 + 2.772589 \\
&= 2.112650
\end{aligned}
$$

EXERCISE 2.4

A. Express each of the following in logarithmic form.

1. $2^9 = 512$

2. $3^7 = 2187$

3. $5^{-3} = \frac{1}{125}$

4. $10^{-5} = 0.00001$

5. $e^{2j} = 18$

6. $e^{-3x} = 12$

B. Write each of the following in exponential form.

1. $\log_2 32 = 5$

2. $\log_3 \frac{1}{81} = -4$

3. $\log_{10} 10 = 1$

4. $\ln e^2 = 2$

C. Use an electronic calculator equipped with a natural logarithm function to evaluate each of the following.

1. $\ln 2$

2. $\ln 200$

3. $\ln 0.105$

4. $\ln[300(1.10^{15})]$

5. $\ln\left(\frac{2000}{1.09^9}\right)$

6. $\ln\left[850\left(\frac{1.01^{-120}}{0.01}\right)\right]$

BUSINESS MATH NEWS BOX

Canadian Housing Affordability

The RBC Economics Research's housing affordability indexes show the proportion of median pre-tax household income required to service the cost of mortgage payments, property taxes, and utilities.

The higher the indexes, the more difficult it is to afford a house.

	Standard Two-Storey House			Standard Condo		
Region	Average Price, 2006 ($)	Qualifying Income ($)	Affordability Index (%)	Average Price, 2006 ($)	Qualifying Income ($)	Affordability Index (%)
Canada	269 785	66 409	39.4	187 414	46 371	27.5
British Columbia	453 923	100 926	62.2	228 986	52 461	32.3
Alberta	274 782	65 247	33.0	176 079	42 587	21.5
Saskatchewan	167 917	46 410	30.5	103 000	29 498	19.4
Manitoba	189 446	52 329	34.2	103 801	29 302	19.1
Ontario	280 896	70 286	37.2	213 966	52 921	28.0
Quebec	205 694	53 382	36.2	163 399	42 269	28.7
Atlantic	157 523	41 860	29.7	140 125	35 975	25.5
Toronto	391 635	92 530	43.9	266 705	63 413	30.1

Montreal	217 867	55 833	36.0	183 704	46 114	29.7
Vancouver	530 111	116 786	68.2	259 202	58 624	34.2
Ottawa	249 060	65 434	30.3	176 569	45 856	21.2
Calgary	325 967	74 935	34.6	197 333	45 783	21.2

Source: "Housing Affordability," RBC Financial Group site, September 2006, **www.rbc.com/economics/market/hi_house.html**, accessed November 4, 2006.

QUESTIONS

1. Why do you think a national average might be misleading for a house buyer?
2. In which region outlined above would you pay the most for a condo?
3. Why do you think there is a major price difference in two-storey house values between British Columbia and Saskatchewan?
4. How much income remains for a family with a household income of $55 836 that purchases an average two-storey house in Montreal?

2.5 SOLVING BASIC EQUATIONS

A. Basic terms and concepts

1. An **equation** is a statement of equality between two algebraic expressions.

$$7x = 35$$
$$3a - 4 = 11 - 2a$$
$$5(2k - 4) = -3(k + 2)$$

2. If an equation contains only one *variable* and the variable occurs with power 1 only, the equation is said to be a **linear** or **first-degree equation** in one unknown. The three equations listed above are linear equations in one unknown.

3. The two expressions that are equated are called the sides or **members of an equation**. Every equation has a left side (left member) and a right side (right member).

   In the equation $3a - 4 = 11 - 2a$,
   $3a - 4$ is the left side (left member) and
   $11 - 2a$ is the right side (right member).

4. The process of finding a replacement value (number) for the variable, which when substituted into the equation makes the two members of the equation equal, is called *solving the equation*. The replacement value that makes the two members equal is called a *solution* or **root of an equation**. A linear or first-degree equation has only one root and the root, when substituted into the equation, is said to *satisfy* the equation.

   The root (solution) of the equation $3a - 4 = 11 - 2a$
   is 3 because when 3 is substituted for a

the left side $3a - 4 = 3(3) - 4 = 9 - 4 = 5$ and
the right side $11 - 2a = 11 - 2(3) = 11 - 6 = 5$.

Thus, for $a = 3$, Left Side = Right Side and 3 satisfies the equation.

5. Equations that have the same root are called **equivalent equations**. Thus,

$$6x + 5 = 4x + 17,\ 6x = 4x + 12,\ 2x = 12, \text{ and } x = 6$$

are equivalent equations because the root of all four equations is 6; that is, when 6 is substituted for x, each of the equations is satisfied.

Equivalent equations are useful in solving equations. They may be obtained

(a) by multiplying or dividing both sides of the equation by a number other than zero; and
(b) by adding or subtracting the same number on both sides of the equation.

6. When solving an equation, the basic aims in choosing the operations that will generate useful equivalent equations are to

(a) isolate the terms containing the variable on one side of the equation (this is achieved by addition or subtraction); and
(b) make the numerical coefficient of the single term containing the variable equal to +1 (this is achieved by multiplication or division).

B. Solving equations using addition

If the same number is added to each side of an equation, the resulting equation is equivalent to the original equation.

	$x - 5 = 4$	original equation
add 3	$x - 5 + 3 = 4 + 3$	equivalent equations
or add 5	$x - 5 + 5 = 4 + 5$	

Addition is used to isolate the term or terms containing the variable when terms that have a negative coefficient appear in the equation.

EXAMPLE 2.5A

(i)	$x - 6 = 4$	
	$x - 6 + 6 = 4 + 6$	add 6 to each side of the equation to eliminate the term −6 on the left side of the equation
	$x = 10$	
(ii)	$-2x = -3 - 3x$	
	$-2x + 3x = -3 - 3x + 3x$	add $3x$ to each side to eliminate the term $-3x$ on the right side
	$x = -3$	
(iii)	$-x - 5 = 8 - 2x$	
	$-x - 5 + 5 = 8 - 2x + 5$	add 5 to eliminate the constant −5 on the left side
	$-x = 13 - 2x$	combine like terms
	$-x + 2x = 13 - 2x + 2x$	add $2x$ to eliminate the term $-2x$ on the right side
	$x = 13$	

C. Solving equations using subtraction

If the same number is subtracted from each side of an equation, the resulting equation is equivalent to the original equation.

	$x + 8 = 9$	original equation
subtract 4	$x + 8 - 4 = 9 - 4$	equivalent equations
or subtract 8	$x + 8 - 8 = 9 - 8$	

Subtraction is used to isolate the term or terms containing the variable when terms having a positive numerical coefficient appear in the equation.

EXAMPLE 2.5B

(i)

$x + 10 = 6$	
$x + 10 - 10 = 6 - 10$	subtract 10 from each side of the equation
$x = -4$	

(ii)

$7x = 9 + 6x$	
$7x - 6x = 9 + 6x - 6x$	subtract $6x$ from each side to eliminate the term $6x$ on the right side
$x = 9$	

(iii)

$6x + 4 = 5x - 3$	
$6x + 4 - 4 = 5x - 3 - 4$	subtract 4 from each side to eliminate the term 4 on the left side
$6x = 5x - 7$	combine like terms
$6x - 5x = 5x - 7 - 5x$	subtract $5x$ from each side of the equation to eliminate the term $5x$ on the right side
$x = -7$	

D. Solving equations using multiplication

If each side of an equation is multiplied by the same non-zero number, the resulting equation is equivalent to the original equation.

	$-3x = 6$	original equation
multiply by 2	$-6x = 12$	equivalent equations
or multiply by -1	$3x = -6$	

Multiplication is used in solving equations containing common fractions to eliminate the denominator or denominators.

EXAMPLE 2.5C

(i)

$\frac{1}{2}x = 3$	original equation
$2\left(\frac{1}{2}x\right) = 2(3)$	multiply each side by 2 to eliminate the denominator
$x = 6$	solution

(ii) $-\frac{1}{4}x = 2$ ——— original equation

$4\left(-\frac{1}{4}x\right) = 4(2)$ ——— multiply each side by 4 to eliminate the denominator

$-1x = 8$

$(-1)(-x) = (-1)(8)$ ——— multiply by (-1) to make the coefficient of the term in x positive

$x = -8$

(iii) $-\frac{1}{7}x = -2$

$(-7)\left(-\frac{1}{7}x\right) = (-7)(-2)$ ——— multiply by (-7) to eliminate the denominator and to make the coefficient of x equal to $+1$

$x = 14$

E. Solving equations using division

If each side of an equation is divided by the same non-zero number, the resulting equation is equivalent to the original equation.

$15x = 45$ ——— original equation

divide by 3 $5x = 15$
or divide by 5 $3x = 9$
or divide by 15 $x = 3$
} ——— equivalent equations

Division is used in solving equations when the numerical coefficient of the single term containing the variable is an integer or a decimal fraction.

EXAMPLE 2.5D

(i) $12x = 36$ ——— original equation

$\frac{12x}{12} = \frac{36}{12}$ ——— divide each side by the numerical coefficient 12

$x = 3$ ——— solution

(ii) $-7x = 42$

$\frac{-7x}{-7} = \frac{42}{-7}$ ——— divide each side by the numerical coefficient -7

$x = -6$

(iii) $0.2x = 3$

$\frac{0.2x}{0.2} = \frac{3}{0.2}$

$x = 15$

(iv) $x - 0.3x = 14$

$0.7x = 14$

$\frac{0.7x}{0.7} = \frac{14}{0.7}$

$x = 20$

F. Using two or more operations to solve equations

When more than one operation is needed to solve an equation, the operations are usually applied as follows.

(a) First, use addition and subtraction to isolate the terms containing the variable on one side of the equation (usually the left side).
(b) Second, after combining like terms, use multiplication and division to make the coefficient of the term containing the variable equal to +1.

EXAMPLE 2.5E

(i) $\left(-\frac{3}{5}\right)x = 12$

$5\left(-\frac{3}{5}\right)x = 5(12)$ — multiply by 5 to eliminate the denominator

$-3x = 60$

$\frac{-3x}{-3} = \frac{60}{-3}$ — divide by −3

$x = -20$

(ii) $7x - 5 = 15 + 3x$

$7x - 5 + 5 = 15 + 3x + 5$ — add 5

$7x = 20 + 3x$ — combine like terms

$7x - 3x = 20 + 3x - 3x$ — subtract $3x$

$4x = 20$

$x = 5$ — divide by 4

(iii) $3x + 9 - 7x = 24 - x - 3$

$9 - 4x = 21 - x$ — combine like terms

$9 - 4x - 9 = 21 - x - 9$

$-4x = 12 - x$

$-4x + x = 12 - x + x$

$-3x = 12$

$x = -4$

G. Checking equations

To check the solution to an equation, substitute the solution into each side of the equation and determine the value of each side.

EXAMPLE 2.5F

(i) For $-\frac{3}{5}x = 12$, the solution shown is $x = -20$.

Check

Left Side $= -\frac{3}{5}x = \left(-\frac{3}{5}\right)(-20) = -3(-4) = 12$

Right Side $= 12$
Since the Left Side = Right Side, −20 is the solution to the equation.

(ii) For $7x - 5 = 15 + 3x$, the solution shown is $x = 5$.

Check
$LS = 7x - 5 = 7(5) - 5 = 35 - 5 = 30$
$RS = 15 + 3x = 15 + 3(5) = 15 + 15 = 30$
Since the LS = RS, 5 is the solution.

(iii) For $3x + 9 - 7x = 24 - x - 3$, the solution shown is $x = -4$.

Check
$LS = 3(-4) + 9 - 7(-4) = -12 + 9 + 28 = 25$
$RS = 24 - (-4) - 3 = 24 + 4 - 3 = 25$
Since LS = RS, -4 is the solution.

EXERCISE 2.5

A. Solve each of the following equations.

1. $15x = 45$ **2.** $-7x = 35$ **3.** $0.9x = 72$

4. $0.02x = 13$ **5.** $\frac{1}{6}x = 3$ **6.** $-\frac{1}{8}x = 7$

7. $\frac{3}{5}x = -21$ **8.** $-\frac{4}{3}x = -32$ **9.** $x - 3 = -7$

10. $-2x = 7 - 3x$ **11.** $x + 6 = -2$ **12.** $3x = 9 + 2x$

13. $4 - x = 9 - 2x$ **14.** $2x + 7 = x - 5$ **15.** $x + 0.6x = 32$

16. $x - 0.3x = 210$ **17.** $x - 0.04x = 192$ **18.** $x + 0.07x = 64.20$

B. Solve each of the following equations and check your solution.

1. $3x + 5 = 7x - 11$ **2.** $5 - 4x = -4 - x$

3. $2 - 3x - 9 = 2x - 7 + 3x$ **4.** $4x - 8 - 9x = 10 + 2x - 4$

5. $3x + 14 = 4x + 9$ **6.** $16x - 12 = 6x - 32$

7. $5 + 3 + 4x = 5x + 12 - 25$ **8.** $-3 + 2x + 5 = 5x - 36 + 14$

2.6 EQUATION SOLVING INVOLVING ALGEBRAIC SIMPLIFICATION

A. Solving linear equations involving the product of integral constants and binomials

To solve this type of equation, multiply first, then simplify.

EXAMPLE 2.6A

(i) $3(2x - 5) = -5(7 - 2x)$

$6x - 15 = -35 + 10x$ ——— expand

$6x - 10x = -35 + 15$ ——— isolate the terms in x

$-4x = -20$

$x = 5$

Check

LS $= 3[2(5) - 5] = 3(10 - 5) = 3(5) = 15$

RS $= -5[7 - 2(5)] = -5(7 - 10) = -5(-3) = 15$

Since LS = RS, 5 is the solution.

(ii) $x - 4(3x - 7) = 3(9 - 5x) - (x - 11)$

$$\begin{aligned} x - 12x + 28 &= 27 - 15x - x + 11 && \text{expand} \\ -11x + 28 &= 38 - 16x && \text{combine like terms} \\ -11x + 16x &= 38 - 28 && \text{isolate the terms in } x \\ 5x &= 10 \\ x &= 2 \end{aligned}$$

Check

$$\begin{aligned} \text{LS} &= 2 - 4[3(2) - 7] \\ &= 2 - 4(6 - 7) \\ &= 2 - 4(-1) \\ &= 2 + 4 \\ &= 6 \end{aligned}$$

$$\begin{aligned} \text{RS} &= 3[9 - 5(2)] - (2 - 11) \\ &= 3(9 - 10) - (-9) \\ &= 3(-1) + 9 \\ &= -3 + 9 \\ &= 6 \end{aligned}$$

Since LS = RS, 2 is the solution.

POINTERS AND PITFALLS

There is a foolproof method of determining the lowest common denominator (LCD) for a given group of fractions:

STEP 1 Divide the given denominators by integers of 2 or greater until they are all reduced to 1. Make sure the integer divides into at least one of the denominators evenly.

STEP 2 Multiply all of the resultant integers (divisors) to find the LCD.

To illustrate, find the LCD for (i) $\frac{4}{5}, \frac{7}{9}, \frac{5}{6}$

(ii) $\frac{3}{4}, \frac{2}{3}, \frac{13}{22}, \frac{11}{15}$

Solution: (i)

	5	9	6	← denominators
$\div 2 =$	5	9	3	← 2 divides into 6 evenly
$\div 3 =$	5	3	1	← 3 divides into 9 and 3 evenly
$\div 3 =$	5	1	1	← 3 divides into 3 evenly
$\div 5 =$	1	1	1	← 5 divides into 5 evenly

LCD $= 2 \times 3 \times 3 \times 5 = 90$

(ii)

	4	3	22	15
$\div 2 =$	2	3	11	15
$\div 2 =$	1	3	11	15
$\div 3 =$	1	1	11	5
$\div 5 =$	1	1	11	1
$\div 11 =$	1	1	1	1

LCD $= 2 \times 2 \times 3 \times 5 \times 11 = 660$

B. Solving linear equations containing common fractions

The best approach when solving equations containing common fractions is to first create an equivalent equation without common fractions. Multiply each term of the equation by the **lowest common denominator (LCD)** of the fractions.

EXAMPLE 2.6B

(i)

$$\frac{4}{5}x - \frac{3}{4} = \frac{7}{12} + \frac{11}{15}x$$ — I.CD = 60

$$60\left(\frac{4}{5}x\right) - 60\left(\frac{3}{4}\right) = 60\left(\frac{7}{12}\right) + 60\left(\frac{11}{15}x\right)$$ — multiply each term by 60

$$12(4x) - 15(3) = 5(7) + 4(11x)$$ — reduce to eliminate the fractions

$$48x - 45 = 35 + 44x$$

$$48x - 44x = 35 + 45$$

$$4x = 80$$

$$x = 20$$

Check

$$LS = \frac{4}{5}(20) - \frac{3}{4} = 16 - 0.75 = 15.25$$

$$RS = \frac{7}{12} + \frac{11}{15}(20) = 0.583333 + 14.666667 = 15.25$$

Since LS = RS, 20 is the solution.

(ii)

$$\frac{5}{8}x - 3 = \frac{3}{4} + \frac{5x}{6}$$ — LCD = 24

$$24\left(\frac{5x}{8}\right) - 24(3) = 24\left(\frac{3}{4}\right) + 24\left(\frac{5x}{6}\right)$$

$$3(5x) - 72 = 6(3) + 4(5x)$$

$$15x - 72 = 18 + 20x$$

$$-5x = 90$$

$$x = -18$$

Check

$$LS = \frac{5}{8}(-18) - 3 = -11.25 - 3 = -14.25$$

$$RS = \frac{3}{4} + \frac{5}{6}(-18) = 0.75 - 15.00 = -14.25$$

Since LS = RS, the solution is −18.

C. Solving linear equations involving fractional constants and multiplication

When solving this type of equation, the best approach is first to eliminate the fractions and then to expand.

EXAMPLE 2.6C

(i) $$\frac{3}{2}(x-2)-\frac{2}{3}(2x-1)=5 \quad \text{——— LCD = 6}$$

$$6\left(\frac{3}{2}\right)(x-2)-6\left(\frac{2}{3}\right)(2x-1)=6(5) \quad \text{——— multiply each side by 6}$$

$$3(3)(x-2)-2(2)(2x-1)=30 \quad \text{——— reduce to eliminate fractions}$$

$$9(x-2)-4(2x-1)=30$$

$$9x-18-8x+4=30$$

$$x-14=30$$

$$x=44$$

Check

$$\text{LS}=\frac{3}{2}(44-2)-\frac{2}{3}(2\times 44-1)=\frac{3}{2}(42)-\frac{2}{3}(87)=63-58=5$$

RS = 5

Since LS = RS, 44 is the solution.

(ii) $$-\frac{3}{5}(4x-1)+\frac{5}{8}(4x-3)=-\frac{11}{10} \quad \text{——— LCD = 40}$$

$$40\left(\frac{-3}{5}\right)(4x-1)+40\left(\frac{5}{8}\right)(4x-3)=40\left(\frac{-11}{10}\right)$$

$$8(-3)(4x-1)+5(5)(4x-3)=4(-11)$$

$$-24(4x-1)+25(4x-3)=-44$$

$$-96x+24+100x-75=-44$$

$$4x-51=-44$$

$$4x=7$$

$$x=\frac{7}{4}$$

Check

$$\text{LS}=-\frac{3}{5}\left[4\left(\frac{7}{4}\right)-1\right]+\frac{5}{8}\left[4\left(\frac{7}{4}\right)-3\right]$$

$$=-\frac{3}{5}(7-1)+\frac{5}{8}(7-3)$$

$$=-\frac{18}{5}+\frac{5}{2}=-\frac{36}{10}+\frac{25}{10}=-\frac{11}{10}$$

$$RS = -\frac{11}{10}$$

Since LS = RS, the solution is $\frac{7}{4}$.

POINTERS AND PITFALLS

When using a lowest common denominator (LCD) to eliminate fractions from an equation involving both fractional constants and multiplication, the LCD must be multiplied by each quantity (on *both* sides of the equation) that is preceded by a + or a − sign *outside of brackets.* (Some students multiply the LCD by each quantity inside *and* outside the brackets, which leads to an answer *much* greater than the correct answer.)

D. Formula rearrangement

Formula rearrangement, also known as **formula manipulation**, is the process of rearranging the terms of an equation. To solve for a particular variable, we want the variable to stand alone on the left side of the equation. If it does not already do so, then we have to rearrange the terms. Developing your skill in rearranging formulas is very important, as it saves a lot of time in memorization. You need only memorize one form of any particular formula. For example, consider the formula $I = Prt$. Once we have memorized this formula, there is no need to memorize equivalent forms as long as we are skilled in formula rearrangement. Thus, for example, we need not "memorize" the form $P = I/rt$.

The key to formula manipulation is the concept of *undoing operations.* Addition and subtraction are *inverse operations* (i.e., they *undo* each other). To move a number that has been added on one side of an equation, subtract the number from both sides of the equation. To move a number that has been subtracted on one side of an equation, add the number to both sides of the equation.

Multiplication and division are also inverse operations. To move a number that has been multiplied on one side of an equation, divide by that number on both sides of the equation. To move a number that has been divided on one side of an equation, multiply by that number on both sides of the equation. Powers and roots are inverses also.

Before you begin formula rearrangement, study the formula to see where the variable you wish to isolate is located and what relationship it has with other variables in the formula. Rearrange the formula so that the variable is isolated on one side of the equal sign, with all other variables on the other side.

EXAMPLE 2.6D

The formula for the perimeter of a rectangle is $P = 2(l + w)$, where l represents length and w represents width. The perimeter of a rectangle is 82 units and the length is 30 units. Solve to find the width.

SOLUTION

$P = 2(l + w)$

$P = 2l + 2w$ ——— multiply to remove brackets

$P - 2l = 2l + 2w - 2l$ ——— to isolate w, subtract $2l$ from both sides

$P - 2l = 2w$

$\frac{P - 2l}{2} = w$ ——— divide both sides by 2

$w = \frac{P - 2l}{2}$ ——— reverse members of the equation

If we know P = 82 and l = 30, then $w = \frac{82 - 2(30)}{2} = \frac{82 - 60}{2} = \frac{22}{2} = 11$

The width of the rectangle is 11 units.

You could have also answered this question by substituting the known values, then solved. It is more logical to rearrange the formula first, then substitute and solve.

EXAMPLE 2.6E

Given $S = P(1 + i)^n$, solve for P.

$\frac{S}{(1 + i)^n} = S(1 + i)^{-n} = P$ ——— divide both sides by $(1 + i)^n$

EXAMPLE 2.6F

Given the formula $S = \frac{n}{2}(2a + d)$, solve for d.

$S = \frac{n}{2}(2a + d)$

$2S = n(2a + d)$ ——— multiply both sides by 2

$\frac{2S}{n} = (2a + d)$ ——— divide both sides by n

$\frac{2S}{n} - 2a = d$ ——— subtract $2a$ from both sides

$d = \frac{2S}{n} - 2a$ ——— reverse members of the equation

EXAMPLE 2.6G

Given $S = P(1 + i)^n$, solve for i.

$S = P(1 + i)^n$

$\frac{S}{P} = (1 + i)^n$ ——— divide both sides by P

$\sqrt[n]{\frac{S}{P}} = 1 + i$ ——— taking a root is the undoing of a power

$\sqrt[n]{\frac{S}{P}} - 1 = i$ ——— subtract 1 from both sides

$i = \sqrt[n]{\frac{S}{P}} - 1$

EXERCISE 2.6

A. Solve each of the following equations and check your solutions.

1. $12x - 4(9x - 20) = 320$

2. $5(x - 4) - 3(2 - 3x) = -54$

3. $3(2x - 5) - 2(2x - 3) = -15$

4. $17 - 3(2x - 7) = 7x - 3(2x - 1)$

5. $4x + 2(2x - 3) = 18$

6. $-3(1 - 11x) + (8x - 15) = 187$

7. $10x - 4(2x - 1) = 32$

8. $-2(x - 4) + 12(3 - 2x) = -8$

B. Solve each of the following equations.

1. $x - \frac{1}{4}x = 15$

2. $x + \frac{5}{8}x = 26$

3. $\frac{2}{3}x - \frac{1}{4} = -\frac{7}{4} - \frac{5}{6}x$

4. $\frac{5}{3} - \frac{2}{5}x = \frac{1}{6}x - \frac{1}{30}$

5. $\frac{3}{4}x + 4 = \frac{113}{24} - \frac{2}{3}x$

6. $2 - \frac{3}{2}x = \frac{2}{3}x + \frac{31}{9}$

C. Solve each of the following equations.

1. $\frac{3}{4}(2x - 1) - \frac{1}{3}(5 - 2x) = -\frac{55}{22}$

2. $\frac{4}{5}(4 - 3x) + \frac{53}{40} = \frac{3}{10}x - \frac{7}{8}(2x - 3)$

3. $\frac{2}{3}(2x - 1) - \frac{3}{4}(3 - 2x) = 2x - \frac{20}{9}$

4. $\frac{4}{3}(3x - 2) - \frac{3}{5}(4x - 3) = \frac{11}{60} + 3x$

D. Solve each of the following equations for the indicated variable.

1. $A = \frac{1}{2}bh$ for h

2. $Q = \frac{p - q}{2}$ for p

3. $F = \frac{9}{5}C + 32$ for C

4. $I = Prt$ for t

5. $A = P(1 + rt)$ for r

6. $P = S(1 + i)^{-n}$ for i

2.7 SOLVING WORD PROBLEMS

One of students' biggest fears is being asked to solve a "word problem." Ironically, word problems are the answer to the "What will I ever need this math for?" question. So think of those dreaded word problems as "practical applications." There are many different types of word problems, from money, to numbers, to mixtures, to when will the train get to the station, to who did the most work. Each type of problem has a specific method of solution, but there is a series of steps that will get you through any word problem. Before you begin the series of steps, read the problem. Then read the problem again. This is not as strange as it seems. The first reading tells you what type of question you are dealing with. It may involve money, or people, or, like the brain teaser at the beginning of this chapter, gold bars. The second reading is done to find out what the question is asking you and what specific information the question is giving you. You can draw a diagram or make a chart if this will help sort out the information in the question. To solve problems by means of an algebraic equation, follow the systematic procedure outlined below.

BEFORE STEP 1 *Read the problem* to determine what type of question you are dealing with. Then *read the problem again* to determine the specific information the question is giving you.

STEP 1 *Introduce the variable* to be used by means of a complete sentence. This ensures a clear understanding and a record of what the variable is intended to represent. The variable is usually the item that you are asked to find—the item you do not know until you solve the problem.

STEP 2 *Translate* the information in the problem statement in terms of the variable. Determine what the words are telling you in relationship to the math. Watch for key words such as "more than" or "less than," "reduced by," and "half of" or "twice."

STEP 3 *Set up* an algebraic equation. This usually means matching the algebraic expressions developed in Step 2 to a specific number. Often one side of the equation represents the total number of items described in the word problem.

STEP 4 *Solve* the equation by rearranging the variables, state a conclusion, and check the conclusion against the problem statement.

EXAMPLE 2.7A A TV set was sold during a sale for \$575. What is the regular selling price of the set if the price of the set was reduced by $\frac{1}{6}$ of the regular price?

SOLUTION

STEP 1 *Introduce the variable.* Let the regular selling price be represented by $\$x$.

STEP 2 *Translate.* The reduction in price is $\$\ \frac{1}{6}x$, and the reduced price is $\$\ (x - \frac{1}{6}x)$.

STEP 3 *Set up an equation.* Since the reduced price is given as \$575,

$$x - \frac{1}{6}x = 575$$

STEP 4 *Solve* the equation, state a conclusion, and check.

$$\frac{5}{6}x = 575$$

$$x = \frac{6(575)}{5}$$

$$x = 690$$

The regular selling price is \$690.

Check	Regular selling price	\$690
	Reduction: $\frac{1}{6}$ of 690	115
	Reduced price	\$575

EXAMPLE 2.7B

The material cost of a product is \$4 less than twice the cost of the direct labour, and the overhead is ⅚ of the direct labour cost. If the total cost of the product is \$157, what is the amount of each of the three elements of cost?

SOLUTION

Three values are needed, and the variable could represent any of the three. However, problems of this type can be solved most easily by representing the proper item by the variable rather than by selecting any of the other items. The *proper* item is the one to which the other item or items are *directly related*. In this problem, direct labour is that item.

Let the cost of direct labour be represented by \$$x$; then the cost of material is \$$(2x - 4)$ and the cost of overhead is \$$\frac{5}{6}x$.

The total cost is \$$(x + 2x - 4 + \frac{5}{6}x)$.

Since the total cost is given as \$157,

$$x + 2x - 4 + \frac{5}{6}x = 157$$
$$3x + \frac{5}{6}x = 161$$
$$18x + 5x = 966$$
$$23x = 966$$
$$x = 42$$

Material cost is \$80, direct labour cost is \$42, and overhead is \$35.

Check	Material cost: $2x - 4 = 2(42) - 4 =$	\$80
	Direct labour cost: $x =$	42
	Overhead cost: $\frac{5}{6}x = \frac{5}{6}(42) =$	35
	Total cost	\$157

EXAMPLE 2.7C

Nalini invested a total of \$24 000 in two mutual funds. Her investment in the Equity Fund is \$4000 less than three times her investment in the Bond Fund. How much did Nalini invest in the Equity Fund?

SOLUTION

Although the amount invested in the Equity Fund is required, it is more convenient to represent her investment in the Bond Fund by the variable since the investment in the Equity Fund is expressed in terms of the investment in the Bond Fund.

Let the amount invested in the Bond Fund be \$$x$; then the amount invested in the Equity Fund is \$$(3x - 4000)$ and the total amount invested is $\$(x + 3x - 4000)$. Since the total amount invested is \$24 000,

$$\begin{aligned} x + 3x - 4000 &= 24\,000 \\ 4x &= 28\,000 \\ x &= 7000 \end{aligned}$$

The amount invested in the Equity Fund is $3x - 4000 = 3(7000) - 4000 = \$17\,000$.

Check		
	Investment in Bond Fund	\$ 7 000
	Investment in Equity Fund	17 000
	Total investment	\$24 000

EXAMPLE 2.7D

The Clarkson Soccer League has set a budget of \$3840 for soccer balls. High-quality game balls cost \$36 each, while lower-quality practice balls cost \$20 each. If 160 balls are to be purchased, how many balls of each type can be purchased to use up exactly the budgeted amount?

SOLUTION

When, as in this case, the items referred to in the problem are not directly related, the variable may represent either item.

Let the number of game balls be represented by x; then the number of practice balls is $(160 - x)$.

Since the prices of the two types of balls differ, the total value of each type of ball must now be represented in terms of x.

The value of x game balls is $\$36x$;
the value of $(160 - x)$ practice balls is $\$20(160 - x)$;
the total value is $\$[36x + 20(160 - x)]$.

Since the total budgeted value is given as \$3840,

$$\begin{aligned} 36x + 20(160 - x) &= 3840 \\ 36x + 3200 - 20x &= 3840 \\ 16x &= 640 \\ x &= 40 \end{aligned}$$

The number of game balls is 40 and the number of practice balls is 120.

Check		
	Number—40 + 120 =	160
	Value—game balls: 36(40) =	\$1440
	practice balls: 20(120) =	\$2400
	Total value	\$3840

EXAMPLE 2.7E

Last year, a repair shop used 1200 small bushings. The shop paid $33\frac{1}{3}$ cents per bushing for the first shipment and $37\frac{1}{2}$ cents per bushing for the second shipment. If the total cost was \$430, how many bushings did the second shipment contain?

SOLUTION

Let the number of bushings in the second shipment be x; then the number of bushings in the first shipment was $1200 - x$. The cost of the second shipment was $\$0.37\frac{1}{2}x$ or $\$\frac{3}{8}x$, and the cost of the first shipment was $\$0.33\frac{1}{3}(1200 - x)$ or $\$\frac{1}{3}(1200 - x)$. The total cost is $\$[\frac{3}{8}x + \frac{1}{3}(1200 - x)]$. Since the total cost is \$430,

$$\frac{3}{8}x + \frac{1}{3}(1200 - x) = 430$$

$$24\left(\frac{3}{8}x\right) + 24\left(\frac{1}{3}\right)(1200 - x) = 24(430)$$

$$3(3x) + 8(1200 - x) = 10\,320$$

$$9x + 9600 - 8x = 10\,320$$

$$x = 720$$

The second shipment consisted of 720 bushings.

Check Total number of bushings: $720 + 480 = 1200$

Total value: $720\left(\frac{3}{8}\right) + 480\left(\frac{1}{3}\right)$

$$= 90(3) + 160(1)$$

$$= 270 + 160$$

$$= \$430$$

POINTERS AND PITFALLS

Translating a Word Problem by Identifying Key Words

What are the key words in the problem and what are they asking you to do?

(a) "And" usually means "add." For example,
"Two times a number and three times a number totals \$10 000"
would be translated as
$2x + 3x = 10\,000$.

(b) "Less than" or "fewer than" usually mean "subtract." For example,
"\$3 less than ten times the amount"
would be translated as
$10x - 3$.

(c) "Reduced by" usually indicates the amount you are to subtract. For example,
"The regular selling price was reduced by 20% to compute the sale price"
would be translated as
$x - 20\%x =$ sales price, where the regular selling price would be x.

(d) "Reduced to" usually indicates the result after a subtraction. For example,
"When a regular selling price of \$589 was reduced to \$441.75, what was the discount?"
would be translated as
$589 - y\% \times 589 = 441.75$.

EXERCISE 2.7

A. For each of the following problems, set up an equation in one unknown and solve.

1. Sears Canada sold a sweater for $49.49. The selling price included a markup of three-fourths of the cost to the department store. What was the cost?

2. S&A Electronics sold a stereo set during a sale for $576. Determine the regular selling price of the set if the price of the set had been reduced by one-third of the original regular selling price.

3. A client at a hair salon paid a total of $37.10 for a haircut. The amount included 6% GST. What was the price of the haircut before the GST was added?

4. Some CDs were put on sale at 40% off. What would be the regular price if the sale price was $11.34?

5. This month's commodity index decreased by one-twelfth of last month's index to 176. What was last month's index?

6. After an increase of one-eighth of his current hourly wage, Jean-Luc receives a new hourly wage of $10.35. How much was his hourly wage before the increase?

7. Tai's sales last week were $140 less than three times Vera's sales. What were Tai's sales if together their sales amounted to $940?

8. A metal pipe 90 centimetres long is cut into two pieces so that the longer piece is 15 centimetres longer than twice the length of the shorter piece. What is the length of the longer piece?

9. Jay purchased tickets for a concert over the Internet. To place the order, a handling charge of $5 per ticket was charged. GST of 6% was also charged on the ticket price and the handling charges. If the total charge for two tickets was $199.28, what was the cost per ticket?

10. Ken and Martina agreed to form a partnership. The partnership agreement requires that Martina invest $2500 more than two-thirds of what Ken is to invest. If the partnership's capital is to be $55 000, how much should Martina invest?

11. A furniture company has been producing 2320 chairs a day working two shifts. The second shift has produced 60 chairs fewer than four-thirds of the number of chairs produced by the first shift. Determine the number of chairs produced by the second shift.

12. An inventory of two types of floodlights showed a total of 60 lights valued at $2580. If Type A cost $40 each while Type B cost $50 each, how many Type B floodlights were in inventory?

13. A machine requires four hours to make a unit of Product A and 3 hours to make a unit of Product B. Last month the machine operated for 200 hours producing a total of 60 units. How many units of Product A were produced?

14. Alick has saved $8.80 in nickels, dimes, and quarters. If he has four nickels fewer than three times the number of dimes and one quarter more than three-fourths the number of dimes, how many coins of each type does Alick have?

15. The local amateur football club spent $1475 on tickets to a professional football game. If the club bought ten more eight-dollar tickets than three times the number of twelve-dollar tickets and three fewer fifteen-dollar tickets than four-fifths the number of twelve-dollar tickets, how many of each type of ticket did the club buy?

16. Giuseppi's Pizza had orders for $539 of pizzas. The prices for each size of pizza were: large $18, medium $15, and small $11. If the number of large pizzas was one less than three times the number of medium pizzas, and the number of small pizzas was one more than twice the number of medium pizzas, how many of each size of pizza were ordered?

Review Exercise

1. Simplify.

(a) $3x - 4y - 3y - 5x$ **(b)** $2x - 0.03x$

(c) $(5a - 4) - (3 - a)$

(d) $-(2x - 3y) - (-4x + y) + (y - x)$

(e) $(5a^2 - 2b - c) - (3c + 2b - 4a^2)$

(f) $-(2x - 3) - (x^2 - 5x + 2)$

2. Simplify.

(a) $3(-5a)$ **(b)** $-7m(-4x)$

(c) $14m \div (-2m)$ **(d)** $(-15a^2b) \div (5a)$

(e) $-6(-3x)(2y)$ **(f)** $4(-3a)(b)(-2c)$

(g) $-4(3x - 5y - 1)$ **(h)** $x(1 - 2x - x^2)$

(i) $(24x - 16) \div (-4)$ **(j)** $(21a^2 - 12a) \div 3a$

(k) $4(2a - 5) - 3(3 - 6a)$

(l) $2a(x - a) - a(3x + 2) - 3a(-5x - 4)$

(m) $(m - 1)(2m - 5)$

(n) $(3a - 2)(a^2 - 2a - 3)$

(o) $3(2x - 4)(x - 1) - 4(x - 3)(5x + 2)$

(p) $-2a(3m - 1)(m - 4)$
$-5a(2m + 3)(2m - 3)$

3. Evaluate each of the following for the values given.

(a) $3xy - 4x - 5y$ for $x = -2, y = 5$

(b) $-5(2a - 3b) - 2(a + 5b)$
for $a = -\frac{1}{4}, b = \frac{2}{3}$

(c) $\frac{2NC}{P(n + 1)}$ for $N = 12, C = 432$,
$P = 1800$, and $n = 35$

(d) $\frac{365I}{RP}$ for $I = 600, R = 0.15, P = 7300$

(e) $A(1 - dt)$ for $A = 720, d = 0.135$, and $t = \frac{280}{360}$

(f) $\frac{S}{1 + RT}$ for $S = 2755, R = 0.17$, and $T = \frac{219}{365}$

4. Simplify.

(a) $(-3)^5$ **(b)** $\left(\frac{2}{3}\right)^4$

(c) $(-5)^0$ **(d)** $(-3)^{-1}$

(e) $\left(\frac{2}{5}\right)^{-4}$ **(f)** $(1.01)^0$

(g) $(-3)^5(-3)^4$ **(h)** $4^7 \div 4^2$

(i) $[(-3)^2]^5$ **(j)** $(m^3)^4$

(k) $\left(\frac{2}{3}\right)^3\left(\frac{2}{3}\right)^7\left(\frac{2}{3}\right)^{-6}$

(l) $\left(-\frac{5}{4}\right)^5 \div \left(-\frac{5}{4}\right)^3$

(m) $(1.03^{50})(1.03^{100})$

(n) $(1 + i)^{180} \div (1 + i)^{100}$

(o) $[(1.05)^{30}]^5$ **(p)** $(-2xy)^4$

(q) $\left(\frac{a^2b}{3}\right)^{-4}$ **(r)** $(1 + i)^{-n}$

5. Use an electronic calculator to compute each of the following.

(a) $\sqrt{0.9216}$ **(b)** $\sqrt[6]{1.075}$

(c) $14.974458^{\frac{1}{40}}$ **(d)** $1.08^{-\frac{5}{12}}$

(e) $\ln 3$ **(f)** $\ln 0.05$

(g) $\ln\left(\frac{5500}{1.10^{16}}\right)$

(h) $\ln\left[375(1.01)\left(\frac{1 - 1.01^{-72}}{0.01}\right)\right]$

6. Solve each of the following equations.

(a) $9x = -63$ **(b)** $0.05x = 44$

(c) $-\frac{1}{7}x = 3$ **(d)** $\frac{5}{6}x = -15$

(e) $x - 8 = -5$ **(f)** $x + 9 = -2$

(g) $x + 0.02x = 255$ **(h)** $x - 0.1x = 36$

(i) $4x - 3 = 9x + 2$

(j) $9x - 6 - 3x = 15 + 4x - 7$

(k) $x - \frac{1}{3}x = 26$ **(l)** $x + \frac{3}{8}x = 77$

7. Solve each of the following equations and check your answers.

(a) $-9(3x - 8) - 8(9 - 7x) = 5 + 4(9x + 11)$

(b) $21x - 4 - 7(5x - 6) = 8x - 4(5x - 7)$

(c) $\frac{5}{7}x + \frac{1}{2} = \frac{5}{14} + \frac{2}{3}x$

(d) $\frac{4x}{3} + 2 = \frac{9}{8} - \frac{x}{6}$

(e) $\frac{7}{5}(6x - 7) - \frac{3}{8}(7x + 15) = 25$

(f) $\frac{5}{9}(7 - 6x) - \frac{3}{4}(3 - 15x) = \frac{1}{12}(3x - 5) - \frac{1}{2}$

(g) $\frac{5}{6}(4x - 3) - \frac{2}{5}(3x + 4) = 5x - \frac{16}{15}(1 - 3x)$

8. Solve each of the following equations for the indicated variable.

(a) $I = Prt$ for r

(b) $S = P(1 + rt)$ for t

(c) $D = \frac{1}{E + F}$ for F

(d) $\frac{W_1}{S_1T_1} = \frac{W_2}{S_2T_2}$ for T_2

(e) $v = \sqrt{2gh}$ for h

9. For each of the following problems, set up an equation and solve.

(a) A company laid off one-sixth of its workforce because of falling sales. If the number of employees after the layoff is 690, how many employees were laid off?

(b) The current average property value is two-sevenths more than last year's average value. What was last year's average property value if the current average is $81 450?

(c) The total amount paid for a banquet, including gratuities of one-twentieth of the price quoted for the banquet, was $2457. How much of the amount paid was gratuities?

(d) A piece of property with a commercial building is acquired by H & A Investments for $184 000. If the land is valued at $2000 less than one-third the value of the building, how much of the amount paid should be assigned to land?

(e) The total average monthly cost of heat, power, and water for Sheridan Service for last year was $2010. If this year's average is expected to increase by one-tenth over last year's average, and heat is $22 more than three-quarters the cost of power while water is $11 less than one-third the cost of power, how much should be budgeted on the average for each month for each item?

(f) Remi Swimming Pools has a promotional budget of $87 500. The budget is to be allocated to direct selling, TV advertising, and newspaper advertising according to a formula. The formula requires that the amount spent on TV advertising be $1000 more than three times the amount spent on newspaper advertising, and that the amount spent on direct selling be three-fourths of the total spent on TV advertising and newspaper advertising combined. How much of the budget should be allocated to direct selling?

(g) A product requires processing on three machines. Processing time on Machine A is three minutes less than four-fifths of the number of minutes on Machine B and processing time on Machine C is five-sixths of the time needed on Machines A and B together. How many minutes processing time is required on Machine C if the total processing time on all three machines is 77 minutes?

(h) Sport Alive sold 72 pairs of ski poles. Superlight poles sell at $30 per pair while ordinary poles sell at $16 per pair. If the total sales value was $1530, how many pairs of each type were sold?

(i) A cash box contains $107 made up of quarters, one-dollar coins, and two-dollar coins. How many quarters are in the box if the number of one-dollar coins is one more than three-fifths of the number of two-dollar coins, and the number of quarters is four times the number of one-dollar coins and two-dollar coins together?

Self-Test

1. Simplify.

(a) $4 - 3x - 6 - 5x$ **(b)** $(5x - 4) - (7x + 5)$

(c) $-2(3a - 4) - 5(2a + 3)$ **(d)** $-6(x - 2)(x + 1)$

2. Evaluate each of the following for the values given.

(a) $2x^2 - 5xy - 4y^2$ for $x = -3, y = 5$

(b) $3(7a - 4b) - 4(5a + 3b)$ for $a = \frac{2}{3}, b = -\frac{3}{4}$

(c) $\frac{2NC}{P(n + 1)}$ for $N = 12, C = 400, P = 2000, n = 24$

(d) $\frac{I}{Pr}$ for $I = 324, P = 5400, r = 0.15$

(e) $S(1 - dt)$ for $S = 1606, d = 0.125, t = \frac{240}{365}$

(f) $\frac{S}{1 + rt}$ for $S = 1566, r = 0.10, t = \frac{292}{365}$

3. Simplify.

(a) $(-2)^3$ **(b)** $\left(\frac{-2}{3}\right)^2$

(c) $(4)^0$ **(d)** $(3)^2(3)^5$

(e) $\left(\frac{4}{3}\right)^{-2}$ **(f)** $(-x^3)^5$

4. Compute each of the following.

(a) $\sqrt[10]{1.35}$ **(b)** $\frac{1 - 1.03^{-40}}{0.03}$

(c) $\ln 1.025$ **(d)** $\ln[3.00e^{-0.2}]$

(e) $\ln\left(\frac{600}{1.06^{11}}\right)$ **(f)** $\ln\left[250\left(\frac{1.07^5 - 1}{0.07}\right)\right]$

5. Solve each of the following equations.

(a) $\frac{1}{81} = \left(\frac{1}{3}\right)^{n-2}$ **(b)** $\frac{5}{2} = 40\left(\frac{1}{2}\right)^{n-1}$

6. Solve each of the following equations.

(a) $-\frac{2}{3}x = 24$ **(b)** $x - 0.06x = 8.46$

(c) $0.2x - 4 = 6 - 0.3x$ **(d)** $(3 - 5x) - (8x - 1) = 43$

(e) $4(8x - 2) - 5(3x + 5) = 18$ **(f)** $x + \frac{3}{10}x + \frac{1}{2} + x + \frac{3}{5}x + 1 = 103$

(g) $x + \frac{4}{5}x - 3 + \frac{5}{6}\left(x + \frac{4}{5}x - 3\right) = 77$

(h) $\frac{2}{3}\left(3x - 1\right) - \frac{3}{4}\left(5x - 3\right) = \frac{9}{8}x - \frac{5}{6}\left(7x - 9\right)$

7. Solve each of the following equations for the indicated variable.

(a) $I = Prt$ for P

(b) $S = \frac{P}{1 - dt}$ for d

8. For each of the following problems, set up an equation and solve.

(a) After reducing the regular selling price by one-fifth, Star Electronics sold a TV set for $192. What was the regular selling price?

(b) The weaving department of a factory occupies 400 square metres more than two times the floor space occupied by the shipping department. The total floor space occupied by both departments is 6700 square metres. Determine the floor space occupied by the weaving department.

(c) A machine requires three hours to make a unit of Product A and five hours to make a unit of Product B. The machine operated for 395 hours producing a total of 95 units. How many units of Product B were produced?

(d) You invested a sum of money in a bank certificate yielding an annual return of one-twelfth of the sum invested. A second sum of money invested in a credit union certificate yields an annual return of one-nineth of the sum invested. The credit union investment is $500 more than two-thirds of the bank investment and the total annual return is $1000. What is the sum of money you invested in the credit union certificate?

Challenge Problems

1. In checking the petty cash a clerk counts "q" quarters, "d" dimes, "n" nickels, and "p" pennies. Later he discovers that x of the nickels were counted as quarters and x of the dimes were counted as pennies. (Assume that x represents the same number of nickels and dimes.) What must the clerk do to correct the original total?

2. Tom and Jerri are planning a 4000-kilometre trip in an automobile with five tires, of which four will be in use at any time. They plan to interchange the tires so that each tire will be used the same number of kilometres. For how many kilometres will each tire be used?

3. A cheque is written for x dollars and y cents. Both x and y are two-digit numbers. In error, the cheque is cashed for y dollars and x cents, with the incorrect amount exceeding the correct amount by $17.82. Which of the following statements is correct?

(a) x cannot exceed 70.

(b) y can equal $2x$.

(c) The amount of the cheque cannot be a multiple of 5.

(d) The incorrect amount can equal twice the correct amount.

(e) The sum of the digits of the correct amount is divisible by 9.

Case Study 2.1 Investing for a Rainy Day

» At the age of 25, Sandi Fulton obtained her university degree and entered the workforce. She sought the opinion of an investment advisor regarding her registered retirement savings plan (RRSP). The main recommendations were to start investing early, to invest often, and to stay invested. This means that someone starting a career needs to consider investing as early as possible.

The advisor provided Sandi with scenarios of investing $100 per month at 8% return at different age ranges and determining the value of her investment at age 65.

Age Started	Total Amount Contributed to Age 65	Total Value of RRSP at Age 65
25	$48 000	$322 108
35	$36 000	$140 855
45	$24 000	$56 900
55	$12 000	$18 012

Source: "RRSP Tips," Clarica site, **www.clarica.com,** accessed November 4, 2006.

Sandi was shown that starting to contribute at a later age, but still wanting to reach a goal of $322 108, would require larger monthly contributions.

Age Started	Monthly Contributions
35	$230
45	$565
55	$1800

Source: "RRSP Tips," Clarica site, **www.clarica.com,** accessed November 4, 2006.

QUESTIONS

1. How much more would Sandi have in her RRSP if she had invested the $100 per month at 25 versus 35 years of age?
2. In order to reach a goal of $322 108, what is the total amount of contributions necessary if Sandi were to begin investing at age 45?
3. If Sandi began her contributions at age 45, how much interest would be earned on the contributions if
   (a) her contributions were $100 per month?
   (b) her contributions were $565 per month?
4. If Sandi's salary is $38 000 per year, calculate the percentage of her monthly salary that would go toward her retirement plan goal of $322 108
   (a) if she began at age 35 and contributed $230.
   (b) if she began at age 45 and contributed $565.
   (c) if she began at age 55 and contributed $1800.

Case Study 2.2 Expenses on the Road

» Shivani Sandhu is a real estate agent's assistant in the Montreal area. The majority of his time involves travelling to different neighbourhoods showing property to potential clients.

Shivani keeps a record of his mileage, meals, and telephone calls. The real estate company reimburses him for these expenses at the end of each month. Shivani is allowed \$0.45 per kilometre for mileage and \$9 per day for telephone calls. In June, his mileage, meals, and telephone expenses totalled \$599.

QUESTIONS

1. Shivani's mileage claim was \$80 more than his claim for telephone calls, and his claim for meals was \$20 less than his mileage claim. How far did Shivani drive in June?
2. The local telephone company has decided to change its billing procedure from a \$24.50 flat rate per month to \$13.30 per month plus a service charge of \$0.35 per local call. How many local calls could Shivani make so that his new monthly telephone bill does not exceed the original June telephone bill?
3. In August, the real estate company indicated that it wanted to increase the mileage allowance to \$0.48 per kilometre and lower the daily payment for telephone calls to \$7.50. What effect would this have had on Shivani's telephone, meals, and mileage reimbursement for June?

SUMMARY OF FORMULAS

Formula 2.1A

$a^m \times a^n = a^{m+n}$ — The rule for multiplying two powers having the same base

Formula 2.1B

$a^m \times a^n \times a^p = a^{m+n+p}$ — The rule for multiplying three or more powers having the same base

Formula 2.2

$a^m \div a^n = a^{m-n}$ — The rule for dividing two powers having the same base

Formula 2.3

$(a^m)^n = a^{mn}$ — The rule for raising a power to a power

Formula 2.4

$(ab)^m = a^m b^m$ — The rule for taking the power of a product

Formula 2.5

$\left(\frac{a}{b}\right)^m = \frac{a^m}{b^m}$ — The rule for taking the power of a quotient

Formula 2.6

$a^{-m} = \frac{1}{a^m}$ — The definition of a negative exponent

Formula 2.7

$\left(\frac{y}{x}\right)^{-m} = \left(\frac{x}{y}\right)^m$ — The rule for a fraction with a negative exponent

Formula 2.8

$a^{\frac{1}{n}} = \sqrt[n]{a}$ — The definition of a fractional exponent with numerator 1

Formula 2.9

$a^{-\frac{1}{n}} = \frac{1}{a^{\frac{1}{n}}} = \frac{1}{\sqrt[n]{a}}$ — The definition of a fractional exponent with numerator −1

Formula 2.10

$a^{\frac{m}{n}} = \sqrt[n]{a^m} = \left(\sqrt[n]{a}\right)^m$ — The definition of a positive fractional exponent

Formula 2.11

$a^{-\frac{m}{n}} = \frac{1}{a^{\frac{m}{n}}} = \frac{1}{\sqrt[n]{a^m}}$ — The definition of a negative fractional exponent

Formula 2.12A

$\ln(ab) = \ln a + \ln b$ — The relationship used to find the logarithm of a product

Formula 2.12B

$\ln(abc) = \ln a + \ln b + \ln c$ — The relationship used to find the logarithm of a product

Formula 2.13

$$\ln\left(\frac{a}{b}\right) = \ln a - \ln b$$

The relationship used to find the logarithm of a quotient

Formula 2.14

$$\ln (a^k) = k(\ln a)$$

The relationship used to find the logarithm of a power

GLOSSARY

Algebraic expression a combination of numbers, variables representing numbers, and symbols indicating an algebraic operation *(p. 43)*

Base one of the equal factors in a power *(p. 49)*

Collecting like terms adding like terms *(p. 42)*

Combining like terms *see* **Collecting like terms**

Common logarithms logarithms with base 10; represented by the notation log x *(p. 62)*

Equation a statement of equality between two algebraic expressions *(p. 68)*

Equivalent equations equations that have the same root *(p. 69)*

Exponent the number of equal factors in a power *(p. 49)*

Factor one of the numbers that, when multiplied with the other number or numbers, yields a given product *(p. 49)*

First-degree equation an equation in which the variable (or variables) appears with power "1" only *(p. 68)*

Formula rearrangement (or formula manipulation) the process of rearranging the terms of an equation *(p. 77)*

Index the power of the root indicated with the radical symbol *(p. 57)*

Least common denominator see **Lowest common denominator**

Like terms terms having the same literal coefficient *(p. 42)*

Linear equation *see* **First-degree equation**

Literal coefficient the part of a term formed with letter symbols *(p. 42)*

Logarithm the exponent to which a base must be raised to produce a given number *(p. 61)*

Lowest common denominator (LCD) the smallest number into which a set of denominators divides without remainders *(p. 75)*

Members of an equation the two sides of an equation; the left member is the left side; the right member is the right side *(p. 68)*

Monomial an algebraic expression consisting of one term *(p. 43)*

Natural logarithms logarithms with base e; represented by the notation ln x *(p. 63)*

Numerical coefficient the part of a term formed with numerals *(p. 42)*

Polynomial an algebraic expression consisting of more than one term *(p. 44)*

Power a mathematical operation indicating the multiplication of a number of equal factors *(p. 49)*

Power of a root the exponent indicating the number of equal factors *(p. 56)*

Radical the indicated root when using the radical symbol for finding a root *(p. 57)*

Radicand the number under the radical symbol *(p. 57)*

Root of an equation the solution (replacement value) that, when substituted for the variable, makes the two sides equal *(p. 68)*

Root of a product one of the equal factors in the product *(p. 56)*

USEFUL INTERNET SITES

www.bmo.com/mutualfunds

Bank of Montreal This Website provides links to pages offering basic information on mutual funds, types of mutual funds, and investment tips.

www.bdc.ca

Business Development Bank of Canada BDC offers financial and consulting services to Canadian small businesses.

strategis.ic.gc.ca

Strategis Strategis is Industry Canada's home page, providing business information and statistics on markets, industries, company sourcing, business partners and alliances, products, international trade, business management, micro-economy, regulations, research laboratories, science and technology, and technology transfer.

CHAPTER 3

Ratio, Proportion, and Percent

OBJECTIVES

Upon completing this chapter, you will be able to do the following:

1. Set up ratios, manipulate ratios, and use ratios to solve allocation problems.
2. Set up proportions, solve proportions, and use proportions to solve problems involving the equivalence of two ratios.
3. Find percents, compute rate percents, and find the base for a rate percent.
4. Solve problems of increase and decrease including finding the rate of increase or decrease and finding the original quantity on which the increase or decrease is based.
5. Solve business problems involving percents.
6. Convert one country's currency to that of another using proportions and currency cross rates tables.
7. Explain how to construct an index number and use the Consumer Price Index to determine the purchasing power of the dollar and to compute real income.
8. Calculate federal income taxes using federal income tax brackets and tax rates.

Every day, in newspapers and magazines, we find articles that spew figures at us. These articles include percent increases, percent decreases, sales figures, ratios, and seemingly unrelated facts. And with information available more quickly than ever from the Internet and all-day news and financial sources, figures are available up to the minute and often presented in a variety of ways. Because they are unavoidable, you *must* be able to sort through the numbers and understand what they mean—or be left behind! When you finish this chapter, you will be able to better understand and work with the numbers you read, see, and hear every day.

INTRODUCTION

Business information is often based on a comparison of related quantities stated in the form of a ratio. When two or more ratios are equivalent, a proportion equating the ratios can be set up. Allocation problems generally involve ratios, and many of the physical, economic, and financial relationships affecting businesses may be stated in the form of ratios or proportions.

The fractional form of a ratio is frequently replaced by the percent form because relative magnitudes are more easily understood as percents. This is done in business reports and articles all the time. Skill in manipulating percents, finding percents, computing rates percent, and dealing with problems of increase and decrease is fundamental to solving many business problems.

3.1 RATIOS

A. Setting up ratios

1. A **ratio** is a comparison of the *relative* values of numbers or quantities and may be written in any of the following ways:
(**a**) by using the word "to," such as in "5 to 2";
(**b**) by using a colon, such as in "5 : 2";
(**c**) as a common fraction, such as "5/2";
(**d**) as a decimal, such as "2.50";
(**e**) as a percent, such as "250%."

2. When comparing more than two numbers or quantities, using the colon is preferred.
To compare the quantities 5 kg, 3 kg, and 2 kg, the ratio is written

5 kg : 3 kg : 2 kg

3. When using a ratio to compare quantities, the unit of measurement is usually dropped.
If three items weigh 5 kg, 3 kg, and 2 kg respectively, their weights are compared by the ratio

5 : 3 : 2

4. The numbers appearing in a ratio are called the **terms of the ratio**. If the terms are in different units, the terms need to be expressed in the same unit of measurement before the units can be dropped.

The ratio of 1 quarter to 1 dollar becomes 25 cents to 100 cents or 25 : 100; the ratio of 3 hours to 40 minutes becomes 180 min : 40 min or 180 : 40.

5. When, as is frequently done, rates are expressed as ratios, ratios drop the units of measurement, even though the terms of the ratio represent different things.

100 km/h becomes 100 : 1
50 m in 5 seconds becomes 50 : 5
$1.49 for 2 items becomes 1.49 : 2

6. Any statement containing a comparison of two or more numbers or quantities can be used to set up a ratio.

EXAMPLE 3.1A

(i) In a company, the work of 40 employees is supervised by five managers.
The ratio of employees to managers is 40 : 5.

(ii) Variable cost is $4000 for a sales volume of $24 000.
The ratio of variable cost to sales volume is 4000 : 24 000.

(iii) The cost of a product is made up of $30 of material, $12 of direct labour, and $27 of overhead.
The elements of cost are in the ratio 30 : 12 : 27.

B. Reducing ratios to lowest terms

When ratios are used to express a comparison, they are usually reduced to *lowest terms*. Since ratios may be expressed as fractions, ratios may be manipulated according to the rules for working with fractions. Thus, the procedure used to reduce ratios to lowest terms is the same as that used to reduce fractions to lowest terms. However, when a ratio is expressed by an improper fraction that reduces to a whole number, the denominator "1" must be written to indicate that two quantities are being compared.

EXAMPLE 3.1B

Reduce each of the following ratios to lowest terms.

(i) 80 : 35 (ii) 48 : 30 : 18

(iii) 225 : 45 (iv) 81 : 54 : 27

SOLUTION

(i) Since each term of the ratio 80 : 35 contains a common factor 5, each term can be reduced.

$$80 : 35 = (16 \times 5) : (7 \times 5) = 16 : 7$$

$$\text{or } \frac{80}{35} = \frac{16 \times 5}{7 \times 5} = \frac{16}{7}$$

(ii) The terms of the ratio 48 : 30 : 18 contain a common factor 6.

$$48 : 30 : 18 = (8 \times 6) : (5 \times 6) : (3 \times 6) = 8 : 5 : 3$$

(iii) $225 : 45 = (45 \times 5) : (45 \times 1) = 5 : 1$

$$\text{or } \frac{225}{45} = \frac{5}{1}$$

(iv) $81 : 54 : 27 = (3 \times 27) : (2 \times 27) : (1 \times 27) = 3 : 2 : 1$

C. Equivalent ratios in higher terms

Equivalent ratios in higher terms may be obtained by *multiplying* each term of a ratio by the same number. Higher-term ratios are used to eliminate decimals from the terms of a ratio.

EXAMPLE 3.1C

State each of the following ratios in higher terms so as to eliminate the decimals from the terms of the ratios.

(i) 2.5 : 3 (ii) 1.25 : 3.75 : 7.5

(iii) $\frac{1.8}{2.7}$ (iv) $\frac{19.25}{2.75}$

SOLUTION

(i) 2.5 : 3 = 25 : 30 —— multiply each term by 10 to eliminate the decimal

= 5 : 6 —— reduce to lowest terms

(ii) 1.25 : 3.75 : 7.5

= 125 : 375 : 750 —— multiply each term by 100 to eliminate the decimals

= (1 × 125) : (3 × 125) : (6 × 125)

= 1 : 3 : 6

(iii) $\frac{1.8}{2.7} = \frac{18}{27} = \frac{2}{3}$

(iv) $\frac{19.25}{2.75} = \frac{1925}{275} = \frac{7 \times 275}{1 \times 275} = \frac{7}{1}$

D. Allocation according to a ratio

Allocation problems require dividing a whole into a number of parts according to a ratio. The number of parts into which the whole is to be divided is the sum of the terms of the ratio.

EXAMPLE 3.1D

Allocate $480 in the ratio 5 : 3.

SOLUTION

The division of $480 in the ratio 5 : 3 may be achieved by dividing the amount of $480 into (5 + 3) or 8 parts.

The value of each part = 480 ÷ 8 = 60.

The first term of the ratio consists of 5 of the 8 parts; that is,

the first term = 5 × 60 = 300 and the second term = 3 × 60 = 180.

$480 is to be divided into $300 and $180.

Alternatively

$480 in the ratio 5 : 3 may be divided by using fractions.

5 of 8 ⟶ $\frac{5}{8} \times 480 = 300$

3 of 8 ⟶ $\frac{3}{8} \times 480 = 180$

EXAMPLE 3.1E

If net income of $72 000 is to be divided among three business partners in the ratio 4 : 3 : 2, how much should each partner receive?

SOLUTION

Divide the net income into 4 + 3 + 2 = 9 parts;
each part has a value of $72 000 ÷ 9 = $8000.

Partner 1 receives 4 of the 9 parts	4 × 8000 = $32 000
Partner 2 receives 3 of the 9 parts	3 × 8000 = 24 000
Partner 3 receives 2 of the 9 parts	2 × 8000 = 16 000
TOTAL	$72 000

Alternatively

Partner 1 receives $\frac{4}{9}$ of 72 000 = $\frac{4}{9}$ × 72 000 = 4 × 8000 = $32 000

Partner 2 receives $\frac{3}{9}$ of 72 000 = $\frac{3}{9}$ × 72 000 = 3 × 8000 = 24 000

Partner 3 receives $\frac{2}{9}$ of 72 000 = $\frac{2}{9}$ × 72 000 = 2 × 8000 = 16 000

TOTAL $72 000

EXAMPLE 3.1F

A business suffered a fire loss of $224 640. It was covered by an insurance policy that stated that any claim was to be paid by three insurance companies in the ratio $\frac{1}{3} : \frac{3}{8} : \frac{5}{12}$. What is the amount that each of the three companies will pay?

SOLUTION

When an amount is to be allocated in a ratio whose terms are fractions, the terms need to be converted into equivalent fractions with the same denominators. The numerators of these fractions may then be used as the ratio by which the amount will be allocated.

STEP 1 Convert the fractions into equivalent fractions with the same denominators.

$$\frac{1}{3} : \frac{3}{8} : \frac{5}{12}$$ — lowest common denominator = 24

$$= \frac{8}{24} : \frac{9}{24} : \frac{10}{24}$$ — equivalent fractions with the same denominators

STEP 2 Allocate according to the ratio formed by the numerators.

The numerators form the ratio 8 : 9 : 10;
the number of parts is 8 + 9 + 10 = 27;
the value of each part is 224 640 ÷ 27 = 8320

First company's share of claim	= 8320 × 8 = $ 66 560
Second company's share of claim	= 8320 × 9 = 74 880
Third company's share of claim	= 8320 × 10 = 83 200
TOTAL	$224 640

EXERCISE 3.1

A. Simplify each of the following ratios.

1. Reduce to lowest terms.

(a) 12 to 32

(b) 84 to 56

(c) 15 to 24 to 39

(d) 21 to 42 to 91

2. Set up a ratio for each of the following and reduce to lowest terms.

(a) 12 dimes to 5 quarters

(b) 15 hours to 3 days

(c) 6 seconds for 50 metres

(d) $72 per dozen

(e) $40 per day for 12 employees for 14 days

(f) 2 percent per month for 24 months for $5000

3. Use equivalent ratios in higher terms to eliminate decimals and fractions from the following ratios.

(a) 1.25 to 4

(b) 2.4 to 8.4

(c) 0.6 to 2.1 to 3.3

(d) 5.75 to 3.50 to 1.25

(e) $\frac{1}{2}$ to $\frac{2}{5}$

(f) $\frac{5}{3}$ to $\frac{7}{5}$

(g) $\frac{3}{8}$ to $\frac{2}{3}$ to $\frac{3}{4}$

(h) $\frac{2}{5}$ to $\frac{4}{7}$ to $\frac{5}{14}$

(i) $\frac{2}{5}$ to $\frac{3}{4}$ to $\frac{5}{16}$

(j) $\frac{3}{7}$ to $\frac{1}{3}$ to $\frac{17}{21}$

(k) $8\frac{5}{8}$ to $11\frac{1}{2}$

(l) $1\frac{3}{4}$ to $3\frac{7}{16}$

(m) $2\frac{1}{5}$ to $4\frac{1}{8}$

(n) $5\frac{1}{4}$ to $5\frac{5}{6}$

B. Set up a ratio for each of the following and reduce the ratio to lowest terms.

1. Deli Delight budgets food costs to account for 40 percent and beverage costs to account for 35 percent of total costs. What is the ratio of food costs to beverage costs?

2. At Bargain Upholstery, commissions amounted to $2500 while sales volume was $87 500 for last month. What is the ratio of commissions to sales volume?

3. A company employs 6 supervisors for 9 office employees and 36 production workers. What is the ratio of supervisors to office employees to production workers?

4. The cost of a unit is made up of \$4.25 direct material cost, \$2.75 direct labour cost, and \$3.25 overhead. What is the ratio that exists between the three elements of cost?

5. The business school at the local college has 8 instructors and 232 students. What is the ratio that exists between the instructors and students?

6. A student spends 20 hours per week in classroom lecture time, 45 hours per week in individual study time, and 5 hours per week travelling to and from school. What is the ratio that exists between the three times?

C. Solve each of the following allocation problems.

1. A dividend of \$3060 is to be distributed among three shareholders in the ratio of shares held. If the three shareholders have nine shares, two shares, and one share respectively, how much does each receive?

2. The cost of operating the Maintenance Department is to be allocated to four production departments based on the floor space each occupies. Department A occupies 1000 m^2; Department B, 600 m^2; Department C, 800 m^2; and Department D, 400 m^2. If the July cost was \$21 000, how much of the cost of operating the Maintenance Department should be allocated to each production department?

3. Insurance cost is to be distributed among manufacturing, selling, and administration in the ratio $\frac{5}{8}$ to $\frac{1}{3}$ to $\frac{1}{6}$. If the total insurance cost was \$9450, how should it be distributed?

4. Executive salaries are charged to three operating divisions on the basis of capital investment in the three divisions. If the investment is \$10.8 million in the Northern Division, \$8.4 million in the Eastern Division, and \$14.4 million in the Western Division, how should executive salaries of \$588 000 be allocated to the three divisions?

5. The cost of warehouse space is allocated to three inventories. Raw materials inventories use one-third of the space, work-in-process inventories use one-sixth of the space, and finished goods inventories use three-eighths of the space. If the total warehouse space is 9.6 million square metres, at a cost of \$11.55 million, how much of the cost should be allocated to each of the inventories?

6. A vehicle dealership has overhead cost of \$480 000. The overhead cost is allocated to new vehicle sales, used vehicle sales, vehicle servicing, and administration. The departments bear overhead cost at $\frac{1}{8}$, $\frac{1}{4}$, $\frac{1}{2}$, and $\frac{1}{16}$ respectively. How much of the overhead cost should be allocated to each of the departments?

EXCEL NOTES

You can use Excel's *Lowest Common Multiplier* (**LCM**) function to convert terms in a ratio that are fractions into equivalent fractions with the same denominator. Refer to **LCM** on the Spreadsheet Template Disk to learn how to use this Excel function.

3.2 PROPORTIONS

A. Solving proportions

When two ratios are equal, they form a **proportion**.

$$2:3 = 4:6$$

$$x:5 = 7:35$$

$$\frac{2}{3} = \frac{8}{x}$$

$$\frac{a}{b} = \frac{c}{d}$$

— are proportions

Note that each proportion consists of *four terms.* These terms form an equation whose sides are common fractions.

If one of the four terms is unknown, the proportions form a linear equation in one variable. The equation can be solved by using the operations discussed in Chapter 2.

EXAMPLE 3.2A

Solve the proportion $2:5 = 8:x$.

SOLUTION

$2:5 = 8:x$ — original form of proportion

$\frac{2}{5} = \frac{8}{x}$ — change the proportion into fractional form

$5x\left(\frac{2}{5}\right) = 5x\left(\frac{8}{x}\right)$ — multiply by the lowest common denominator = $5x$

$$2x = 40$$

$$x = 20$$

Check LS $= \frac{2}{5}$, RS $= \frac{8}{20} = \frac{2}{5}$

Note: The two operations usually applied to solve proportions are multiplication and division. These operations permit the use of a simplified technique called *cross-multiplication* which involves

(a) the multiplication of the numerator of the ratio on the left side with the denominator of the ratio on the right side of the proportion, and

(b) the multiplication of the numerator of the ratio on the right side with the denominator of the ratio on the left side.

When cross-multiplication is used to solve Example 3.2A, the value of x is obtained as follows:

$$\frac{2}{5} \times \frac{8}{x}$$

$x(2) = 5(8)$ — cross-multiply

$$2x = 40$$

$$x = 20$$

EXAMPLE 3.2B

Solve each of the following proportions.

(i) $x : 5 = 7 : 35$ — original proportion

$\frac{x}{5} = \frac{7}{35}$ — in fractional form

$35(x) = 5(7)$ — cross-multiply

$35x = 35$

$x = 1$

(ii) $2\frac{1}{2} : x = 5\frac{1}{2} : 38\frac{1}{2}$

$2.5 : x = 5.5 : 38{:}5$

$\frac{2.5}{x} = \frac{5.5}{38.5}$

$38.5(2.5) = x(5.5)$ — cross-multiply

$96.25 = 5.5x$

$x = \frac{96.25}{5.5}$

$x = 17.5, \text{ or } 17\frac{1}{2}$

(iii) $\frac{5}{6} : \frac{14}{4} = x : \frac{21}{10}$

$\dfrac{\frac{5}{6}}{\frac{14}{4}} = \dfrac{\frac{x}{1}}{\frac{21}{10}}$ — set up in fractional form

$\left(\frac{5}{6}\right)\left(\frac{21}{10}\right) = \left(\frac{x}{1}\right)\left(\frac{14}{4}\right)$ — cross-multiply

$\frac{105}{60} = \frac{14x}{4}$

$(14x)(60) = (105)(4)$

$840x = 420$

$x = 0.5, \text{ or } \frac{1}{2}$

B. Problems involving proportions

Many problems contain information that permits two ratios to be set up. These ratios are in proportion, but one term of one ratio is unknown. In such cases, a letter symbol for the unknown term is used to complete the proportion statement.

To ensure that the proportion is set up correctly, use the following procedure.

STEP 1 Use a complete sentence to *introduce* the *letter* symbol that you will use to represent the missing term.

STEP 2 Set up the *known ratio* on the *left* side of the proportion. Be sure to retain the units or a description of the quantities in the ratio.

STEP 3 Set up the ratio using the *letter symbol* on the *right* side of the proportion. Make certain that the unit or description of the numerator in the ratio on the right side corresponds to the unit or description of the numerator in the ratio on the left side.

EXAMPLE 3.2C Solve each of the following problems involving a proportion.

(i) If five kilograms of sugar cost \$9.20, what is the cost of two kilograms of sugar?

SOLUTION

STEP 1 Introduce the variable.

Let the cost of two kilograms of sugar be $\$x$.

STEP 2 Set up the known ratio retaining the units.

5 kg : \$9.20

STEP 3 Set up the ratio involving the variable.

2 kg : $\$x$

Hence, $\frac{5\text{ kg}}{\$9.20} = \frac{2\text{ kg}}{\$x}$ ——— make certain the units in the numerators and denominators correspond

$$\frac{5}{9.20} = \frac{2}{x}$$

$$x(5) = 9.20(2)$$

$$x = \frac{18.40}{5}$$

$$x = 3.68$$

Two kilograms of sugar cost \$3.68.

(ii) If your car can travel 385 km on 35 L of gasoline, how far can it travel on 24 L?

SOLUTION Let the distance travelled on 24 L be n km;
then the known ratio is 385 km : 35 L;
the second ratio is n km : 24 L.

$$\frac{385\text{ km}}{35\text{ L}} = \frac{n\text{ km}}{24\text{ L}}$$

$$\frac{385}{35} = \frac{n}{24}$$

$$n = \frac{385 \times 24}{35}$$

$$n = 264$$

The car can travel 264 km on 24 L.

(iii) Past experience shows that a process requires \$17.50 worth of material for every \$12 spent on labour. How much should be budgeted for material if the budget for labour is \$17 760?

SOLUTION

Let the material budget be $\$k$.

The known ratio is $\dfrac{\$17.50 \text{ material}}{\$12 \text{ labour}}$;

the second ratio is $\dfrac{\$k \text{ material}}{\$17\,760 \text{ labour}}$.

$$\frac{\$17.50 \text{ material}}{\$12 \text{ labour}} = \frac{\$k \text{ material}}{\$17\,760 \text{ labour}}$$

$$\frac{17.50}{12} = \frac{k}{17\,760}$$

$$k = \frac{17.50 \times 17\,760}{12}$$

$$k = 25\,900$$

The material budget should be \$25 900.

EXAMPLE 3.2D

Two contractors agreed to share revenue from a job in the ratio 2 : 3. Contractor A, who received the smaller amount, made a profit of \$480 on the job. If contractor A's profit compared to revenue is in the ratio 3 : 8, determine

(i) contractor A's revenue;

(ii) the total revenue of the job.

SOLUTION

(i) Let $\$x$ represent contractor A's revenue.

Then $\dfrac{\text{A's profit}}{\text{A's revenue}} = \dfrac{3}{8}$ ——— known ratio

and $\dfrac{\text{A's profit}}{\text{A's revenue}} = \dfrac{\$480}{\$x}$ ——— second ratio

$$\frac{3}{8} = \frac{480}{x}$$

$$3x = 480 \times 8$$

$$x = \frac{480 \times 8}{3}$$

$$x = 1280$$

Contractor A's revenue from the job is \$1280.

(ii) Let $y represent contractor B's revenue.

$$\text{Then } \frac{\text{A's revenue}}{\text{B's revenue}} = \frac{2}{3} \text{ ——— known ratio}$$

$$\text{and } \frac{\text{A's revenue}}{\text{B's revenue}} = \frac{\$1280}{\$y} \text{ ——— second ratio}$$

$$\frac{2}{3} = \frac{1280}{y}$$

$$2y = 1280 \times 3$$

$$y = \frac{1280 \times 3}{2}$$

$$y = 1920$$

Total revenue $= x + y = 1280 + 1920 = 3200$
Total revenue on the job is $3200.

Alternatively
Let total revenue be $z.

$$\text{Then } \frac{\text{A's revenue}}{\text{Total revenue}} = \frac{2}{5} = \frac{\$1280}{\$z}$$

$$\frac{2}{5} = \frac{1280}{z}$$

$$2z = 1280 \times 5$$

$$z = 3200$$

EXERCISE 3.2

A. Find the unknown term in the following proportions.

1. $3 : n = 15 : 20$

2. $n : 7 = 24 : 42$

3. $3 : 8 = 21 : x$

4. $7 : 5 = x : 45$

5. $1.32 : 1.11 = 8.8 : k$

6. $2.17 : 1.61 = k : 4.6$

7. $m : 3.4 = 2.04 : 2.89$

8. $3.15 : m = 1.4 : 1.8$

9. $t : \frac{3}{4} = \frac{7}{8} : \frac{15}{16}$

10. $\frac{3}{4} : t = \frac{5}{8} : \frac{4}{9}$

11. $\frac{9}{8} : \frac{3}{5} = t : \frac{8}{15}$

12. $\frac{16}{7} : \frac{4}{9} = \frac{15}{14} : t$

B. Use proportions to solve each of the following problems.

1. Le Point Bookbindery pays a dividend of $1.25 per share every three months. How many months would it take to earn dividends amounting to $8.75 per share?

2. The community of Oakcrest sets a property tax rate of $28 per $1000 assessed valuation. What is the assessment if a tax of $854 is paid on a property?

3. A car requires 9 litres of gasoline for 72 kilometres. At the same rate of gasoline consumption, how far can the car travel if the gas tank holds 75 litres?

4. A manufacturing process requires $85 supervision cost for every 64 labour hours. At the same rate, how much supervision cost should be budgeted for 16 000 labour hours?

5. Suhami Chadhuri has a two-fifths interest in a partnership. She sold five-sixths of her interest for $3000.
(a) What was the total amount of Ms. Chadhuri's interest before selling?
(b) What is the value of the partnership?

6. Five-eighths of Jesse Black's inventory was destroyed by fire. He sold the remaining part, which was slightly damaged, for one-third of its value and received $1300.
(a) What was the value of the destroyed part of the inventory?
(b) What was the value of the inventory before the fire?

7. Last year, net profits of Herd Inc. were two-sevenths of revenue. If the company declared a dividend of $12 800 and five-ninths of the net profit was retained in the company, what was last year's revenue?

8. Material cost of a fan belt is five-eighths of total cost, and labour cost is one-third of material cost. If labour cost is $15, what is the total cost of the fan belt?

3.3 THE BASIC PERCENTAGE PROBLEM

A. Computing percentages

To find percentages, multiply a number by a percent.

$$50\% \text{ of } 60 = 0.50 \times 60 = 30$$

Note: 50% is called the *rate*;
60 is called the *base* or *original number*;
30 is called the *percentage* or *new number*.

PERCENTAGE = RATE × BASE ——— **Formula 3.1A**

or

NEW NUMBER = RATE × ORIGINAL NUMBER

To determine a percentage of a given number, change the percent to a decimal fraction or a common fraction and then multiply by the given number.

EXAMPLE 3.3A

(i) $80\% \text{ of } 400 = 0.80 \times 400 = 320$ — convert the percent into a decimal and multiply

(ii) $5\% \text{ of } 1200 = 0.05 \times 1200 = 60$

(iii) $240\% \text{ of } 15 = 2.40 \times 15 = 36$

(iv) $1.8\% \text{ of } \$600 = 0.018 \times 600 = \$10.80$

(v) $33\frac{1}{3}\% \text{ of } \$45.60 = \frac{1}{3} \times 45.60 = \$15.20$

(vi) $0.25\% \text{ of } \$8000 = 0.0025 \times 8000 = \$20$

(vii) $\frac{3}{8}\% \text{ of } \$1800 = 0.375\% \text{ of } \$1800 = 0.00375 \times 1800 = \$6.75$

B. Computation with commonly used percents

Many of the more commonly used percents can be converted into fractions. These are easy to use when computing manually. The most commonly used percents and their fractional equivalents are listed in Table 3.1.

Table 3.1 **Commonly Used Percents and Their Fractional Equivalents**

(i)	(ii)	(iii)	(iv)	(v)
$25\% = \frac{1}{4}$	$16\frac{2}{3}\% = \frac{1}{6}$	$12\frac{1}{2}\% = \frac{1}{8}$	$20\% = \frac{1}{5}$	$8\frac{1}{3}\% = \frac{1}{12}$
$50\% = \frac{1}{2}$	$33\frac{1}{3}\% = \frac{1}{3}$	$37\frac{1}{2}\% = \frac{3}{8}$	$40\% = \frac{2}{5}$	$6\frac{2}{3}\% = \frac{1}{15}$
$75\% = \frac{3}{4}$	$66\frac{2}{3}\% = \frac{2}{3}$	$62\frac{1}{2}\% = \frac{5}{8}$	$60\% = \frac{3}{5}$	$6\frac{1}{4}\% = \frac{1}{16}$
	$83\frac{1}{3}\% = \frac{5}{6}$	$87\frac{1}{2}\% = \frac{7}{8}$	$80\% = \frac{4}{5}$	

EXAMPLE 3.3B

(i) $25\% \text{ of } 32 = \frac{1}{4} \times 32 = 8$

(ii) $33\frac{1}{3}\% \text{ of } 150 = \frac{1}{3} \times 150 = 50$

(iii) $87\frac{1}{2}\% \text{ of } 96 = \frac{7}{8} \times 96 = 7 \times 12 = 84$

(iv) $83\frac{1}{3}\% \text{ of } 48 = \frac{5}{6} \times 48 = 5 \times 8 = 40$

(v) $116\frac{2}{3}\%$ of 240 $= \left(100\% + 16\frac{2}{3}\%\right)$ of 240

$$= \left(1 + \frac{1}{6}\right)(240)$$

$$= \frac{7}{6} \times 240$$

$$= 7 \times 40$$

$$= 280$$

(vi) 275% of 64 $= \left(2 + \frac{3}{4}\right)(64)$

$$= \frac{11}{4} \times 64$$

$$= 11 \times 16$$

$$= 176$$

POINTERS AND PITFALLS

Using the 1% Method

Percentages can be computed by determining 1% of the given number and then figuring the value of the given percent. While this method can be used to compute any percentage, it is particularly useful when dealing with *small* percents.

EXAMPLE 3.3C Use the 1% method to determine each of the following percentages.

(i) 3% of \$1800

SOLUTION

1% of \$1800 = \$18

3% of \$1800 = 3 × 18 = \$54

(ii) $\frac{1}{2}\%$ of \$960

SOLUTION

1% of \$960 = \$9.60

$\frac{1}{2}\%$ of \$960 $= \frac{1}{2} \times 9.60 =$ \$4.80

(iii) $\frac{5}{8}\%$ of \$4440

SOLUTION

1% of \$4440 = \$44.40

$\frac{1}{8}\%$ of \$4440 $= \frac{1}{8} \times 44.40 =$ \$5.55

$\frac{5}{8}\%$ of \$4440 $= 5 \times 5.55 =$ \$27.75

(iv) $2\frac{1}{4}\%$ of \$36 500

SOLUTION

$$\begin{aligned}
1\% \text{ of } \$36\,500 &= \$365.00 \\
2\% \text{ of } \$36\,500 &= 2 \times 365.00 = \$730.00 \\
\frac{1}{4}\% \text{ of } \$36\,500 &= \frac{1}{4} \times 365.00 = \underline{\quad 91.25} \\
2\tfrac{1}{4}\% \text{ of } 36\,500 &= \$821.25
\end{aligned}$$

C. Finding a rate percent

Finding a rate means *comparing* two numbers. This comparison involves a **ratio** that is usually written in the form of a common fraction. When the common fraction is converted to a percent, a rate percent results.

When setting up the ratio, the base (or original number) is always the denominator of the fraction, and the percentage (or new number) is always the numerator.

$$\text{RATE} = \frac{\text{PERCENTAGE}}{\text{BASE}} \text{ or } \frac{\text{NEW NUMBER}}{\text{ORIGINAL NUMBER}}$$ ——— **Formula 3.1B**

The problem statement indicating that a rate percent is to be found is usually in the form
(a)"What percent of x is y?"or
(b)"y is what percent of x?"

This means that y is to be compared to x and requires the setting up of the ratio $y:x$ or the fraction $\frac{y}{x}$ where x is the base (or original number) while y is the percentage (or new number).

EXAMPLE 3.3D

Answer each of the following questions.

(i) What percent of 15 is 6?

SOLUTION

$$\text{Rate} = \frac{6}{15}$$ ——— percentage (or new number) / base (or original number)

$$= 0.40$$
$$= 40\%$$

(ii) 90 is what percent of 72?

SOLUTION

$$\text{Rate} = \frac{90}{72}$$ ——— original number

$$= 1.25$$
$$= 125\%$$

(iii) What percent of \$112.50 is \$292.50?

SOLUTION

$$\text{Rate} = \frac{292.50}{112.50} = 2.60 = 260\%$$

D. Finding the base

A great number of business problems involve the relationship from Formula 3.1A,

$$\text{PERCENTAGE} = \text{BASE} \times \text{RATE}$$
$$(\text{or NEW NUMBER} = \text{RATE} \times \text{ORIGINAL NUMBER})$$

Since three variables are involved, three different problems may be solved using this relationship:

(a) finding the percentage (see Sections A and B)
(b) finding the rate percent (see Section C)
(c) finding the base (see Section D)

Of the three, the problem of finding the rate percent is the most easily recognized. However, confusion often arises in deciding whether the percentage or the base needs to be found. In such cases it is useful to represent the unknown value by a variable and set up an equation.

EXAMPLE 3.3E

Solve each of the following problems by setting up an equation.

(i) What number is 25% of 84?

SOLUTION

Introduce a variable for the unknown value and write the statement in equation form.

What number is 25% of 84

↓ ↓ ↓ ↓

$$x = 25\% \text{ of } 84$$

$$x = \frac{1}{4} \times 84$$ ——— change the percent to a fraction or a decimal

$$x = 21$$

The number is 21.

(ii) 60% of what number is 42?

SOLUTION

60% of what number is 42

↓ ↓ ↓

$$60\% \text{ of } x = 42$$

$$0.6x = 42$$

$$x = \frac{42}{0.6}$$

$$x = 70$$

The number is 70.

(iii) How much is $16\frac{2}{3}\%$ of \$144?

SOLUTION

$x = 16\frac{2}{3}\%$ of 144

$$x = \frac{1}{6} \times 144$$

$$x = 24$$

The amount is \$24.

(iv) \$160 is 250% of what amount?

SOLUTION

160 = 250% of x

$160 = 2.5x$

$$x = \frac{160}{2.5}$$

$$x = 64$$

The amount is \$64.

POINTERS AND PITFALLS

You can calculate the percent of increase over a base with your business calculator. The function is labelled [Δ96].

Press [2nd] [Δ96].

OLD is shown on the display. Enter the original value and press [Enter] [↓].

NEW is shown on the display. Enter the next number and press [Enter] [↓].

%CH is shown on the display. Press [CPT].

Example: OLD = 150; NEW = 180; %CH = 20.0.

Press [2nd] [QUIT] to close the worksheet.

Note: Any two of the three values can be entered into the calculator. If the NEW number is greater than the OLD number, the resulting %CH will be a positive number. If the OLD number is greater than the NEW number, the resulting %CH will be a negative number. The fourth input required by the calculator is #PD, indicating how many periods the number changes by the percent indicated. The default for this is 1.

E. Applications

EXAMPLE 3.3F

Solve each of the following problems.

(i) Variable cost on monthly sales of $48 600 amounted to $30 375. What is the variable cost rate based on sales volume?

SOLUTION

$$\text{Rate} = \frac{\text{Variable cost}}{\text{Sales volume}} \quad \text{—— base for the comparison}$$

$$= \frac{30\ 375}{48\ 600}$$
$$= 0.625$$
$$= 62.5\%$$

The variable cost is 62.5% of sales volume.

(ii) What is the annual dividend on a preferred share paying 11.5% on a par value of $20?

SOLUTION

Let the annual dividend be $$x$.
Since the annual dividend is 11.5% of $20,

$$x = 11.5\% \text{ of } 20$$
$$x = 0.115 \times 20$$
$$x = 2.30$$

The annual dividend is $2.30.

(iii) What was the amount of October sales if November sales of $14 352 were 115% of October sales?

SOLUTION

Let October sales be represented by $$x$.
Since November sales equal 115% of October sales,

$$14\ 352 = 115\% \text{ of } x$$
$$14\ 352 = 1.15x$$
$$x = \frac{14\ 352}{1.15}$$
$$x = 12\ 480$$

October sales amounted to $12 480.

(iv) The 14% blended sales tax charged on the regular selling price of a computer sold in Halifax, Nova Scotia amounted to $187.60. What was the total cost of the computer?

SOLUTION

Let the regular selling price be $$x$.
Since the sales tax is 14% of the regular selling price,

$$187.60 = 14\% \text{ of } x$$
$$187.60 = 0.14x$$
$$x = \frac{187.60}{0.14}$$
$$x = 1340$$

The regular selling price is	\$1340.00
Add 14% of \$1340	187.60
TOTAL COST	\$1527.60

The total cost of the computer was \$1527.60.

EXERCISE 3.3

A. Compute each of the following.

1. 40% of 90
2. 0.1% of 950
3. 250% of 120
4. 7% of 800
5. 3% of 600
6. 15% of 240
7. 0.5% of 1200
8. 300% of 80
9. 0.02% of 2500
10. $\frac{1}{2}$% of 500
11. $\frac{1}{4}$% of 800
12. 0.05% of 9000
13. 0.075% of 10 000
14. $\frac{7}{8}$% of 3600
15. 2.5% of 700
16. 0.025% of 40 000

B. Use fractional equivalents to compute each of the following.

1. $33\frac{1}{3}$% of \$48
2. $137\frac{1}{2}$% of \$400
3. $162\frac{1}{2}$% of \$1200
4. $66\frac{2}{3}$% of \$72
5. $37\frac{1}{2}$% of \$24
6. 175% of \$1600
7. 125% of \$160
8. $12\frac{1}{2}$% of \$168
9. $83\frac{1}{3}$% of \$720
10. $166\frac{2}{3}$% of \$90
11. $116\frac{2}{3}$% of \$42
12. $16\frac{2}{3}$% of \$54
13. 75% of \$180
14. $183\frac{1}{3}$% of \$24
15. $133\frac{1}{3}$% of \$45
16. 25% of \$440

C. Find the rate percent for each of the following.

1. original amount 60; new amount 36
2. original amount 72; new amount 54
3. base \$800; percentage \$920

4. base \$140; percentage \$490

5. new amount \$6; original amount \$120

6. new amount \$11; original amount \$440

7. percentage \$132; base \$22

8. percentage \$30; base \$45

9. new amount \$150; base \$90

10. percentage \$39; original amount \$18

D. Answer each of the following questions.

1. \$60 is 30% of what amount?
2. \$36 is what percent of \$15?
3. What is 0.1% of \$3600?
4. 150% of what amount is \$270?
5. $\frac{1}{2}$% of \$612 is what amount?
6. 250% of what amount is \$300?
7. 80 is 40% of what amount?
8. \$120 is what percent of \$60?
9. What is $\frac{1}{8}$% of \$880?
10. \$180 is what percent of \$450?
11. \$600 is 250% of what amount?
12. What percent of \$70 is \$350?
13. \$90 is 30% of what amount?
14. 350% of what amount is \$1050?

E. Answer each of the following questions.

1. The price of a carpet was reduced by 40%. If the original price was \$70, what was the amount by which the price was reduced?

2. Labour content in the production of an article is $37\frac{1}{2}$% of total cost. How much is the labour cost if the total cost is \$72?

3. If waste is normally 6% of the material used in a production process, how much of \$25 000 worth of material will be wasted?

4. If total deductions on a yearly salary of \$18 600 amounted to $16\frac{2}{3}$%, how much was deducted?

5. If the actual sales of \$40 500 for last month were 90% of the budgeted sales, how much was the sales budget for the month?

6. The Canada Pension Plan premium deducted from an employee's wages was \$53.46. If the premium rate is 4.95% of gross wages, how much were the employee's gross wages?

7. A property was sold for 300% of what the vendors originally paid. If the vendors sold the property for \$180 000, how much did they originally pay for the property?

8. Gerry's four sons were to share equally in a prize, receiving \$28 each. How much was the total prize?

9. Shari's portion of the proceeds of a business was $\frac{1}{2}$%. If the proceeds were \$1200, how much would she receive?

10. Mei Jung paid \$18 toward a dinner that cost a total of \$45. What percent of the total was her portion?

3.4 PROBLEMS INVOLVING INCREASE OR DECREASE

A. Percent change

Problems involving a *change* (an increase or a decrease) are identifiable by such phrases as

"is 20% *more than*," "is 40% *less than*,"
"is *increased by* 150%," "is *decreased by* 30%."

The amount of change is to be added for an increase to or subtracted for a decrease from the *original number* (*base*) and is usually stated as a percent of the original number.

The existing relationship may be stated as

$$\text{ORIGINAL NUMBER} \begin{array}{l} + \text{ INCREASE} \\ - \text{ DECREASE} \end{array} = \text{NEW NUMBER}$$

——— **Formula 3.2**

where the change (the increase or decrease) is understood to be a *percent of the original number*.

EXAMPLE 3.4A

Answer each of the following questions.

(i) 36 increased by 25% is what number?

SOLUTION

The original number is 36;
the change (increase) is 25% of 36. ——— **in such problems the change is a percent of the original number**
Since the original number is known,
let x represent the new number.

$$36 + 25\% \text{ of } 36 = x$$
$$36 + \frac{1}{4} \times 36 = x$$
$$36 + 9 = x$$
$$x = 45$$

The number is 45.

(ii) What number is 40% less than 75?

SOLUTION

The change (decrease) is 40% of 75.
The original number is 75.
Let x represent the new number.

$$75 - 40\% \text{ of } 75 = x$$
$$75 - 0.40 \times 75 = x$$
$$75 - 30 = x$$
$$x = 45$$

The number is 45.

(iii) How much is \$160 increased by 250%?

SOLUTION

The increase is 250% of \$160 and the original number is \$160.
Let the new amount be \$$x$.

$$\begin{aligned} 160 + 250\% \text{ of } 160 &= x \\ 160 + 2.50 \times 160 &= x \\ 160 + 400 &= x \\ x &= 560 \end{aligned}$$

The amount is \$560.

B. Finding the rate of increase or decrease

This type of problem is indicated by such phrases as

(a) "20 is what percent *more than* 15?" or
(b) "What percent *less than* 96 is 72?"

In (a), the increase, which is the difference between 15, the original number, and 20, the number after the increase, is to be compared to the original number, 15.

$$\text{The rate of increase} = \frac{5}{15} = \frac{1}{3} = 33\tfrac{1}{3}\%$$

In (b), the decrease, which is the difference between 96, the number before the decrease (the original number), and 72, the number after the decrease, is to be expressed as a percent of the original number.

$$\text{The rate of decrease} = \frac{24}{96} = \frac{1}{4} = 25\%$$

In more generalized form, the problem statement is:

$$\text{"}y \text{ is what percent } \begin{Bmatrix} \text{more} \\ \text{less} \end{Bmatrix} \text{ than } x\text{?"}$$

This means the difference between x, the number before the change (the original number), and y, the number after the change, is to be expressed as a percent of the original number.

$$\text{RATE OF CHANGE} = \frac{\text{AMOUNT OF CHANGE}}{\text{ORIGINAL NUMBER}}$$

Formula 3.3

EXAMPLE 3.4B

Answer each of the following questions.

(i) \$425 is what percent more than \$125?

SOLUTION

The amount before the change (the original number) is \$125.
The change (increase) = 425 − 125 = \$300.

$$\text{The rate of increase} = \frac{\text{Amount of increase}}{\text{Original amount}}$$

$$= \frac{300}{125} = 2.40 = 240\%$$

(ii) What percent less than \$210 is \$175?

SOLUTION

The amount before the decrease is \$210.
The decrease is 210 − 175 = \$35.

$$\text{The rate of decrease} = \frac{35}{210} = \frac{1}{6} = 16\tfrac{2}{3}\%$$

C. Finding the original amount

If the quantity *after* the change has taken place is known, the quantity *before* the change (the original quantity) may be found by using the relationship stated in Formula 3.2.

EXAMPLE 3.4C

Answer each of the following questions.

(i) 88 is 60% more than what number?

SOLUTION

88 is the number after the increase; the number before the increase is unknown. Let the original number be x; then the increase is 60% of x.

$$x + 60\% \text{ of } x = 88 \qquad \text{——— using Formula 3.2}$$
$$x + 0.6x = 88$$
$$1.6x = 88$$
$$x = \frac{88}{1.6}$$
$$x = 55$$

The original number is 55.

(ii) 75 is 40% less than what number?

SOLUTION

75 is the number after the decrease.
Let the original number be x;
then the decrease is 40% of x.

$$x - 40\% \text{ of } x = 75$$
$$x - 0.4x = 75$$
$$0.6x = 75$$
$$x = \frac{75}{0.6}$$
$$x = 125$$

The original number is 125.

(iii) What sum of money increased by 175% amounts to $143?

SOLUTION

$143 is the amount after the increase.
Let the original sum of money be $$x$;
then the increase is 175% of x.

$$x + 175\% \text{ of } x = 143$$
$$x + 1.75x = 143$$
$$2.75x = 143$$
$$x = \frac{143}{2.75}$$
$$x = 52$$

The original amount is $52.

(iv) What sum of money when diminished by $33\frac{1}{3}\%$ is $48?

SOLUTION

$48 is the amount after the decrease.
Let the original sum of money be $$x$;
then the decrease is $33\frac{1}{3}\%$ of x.

$$x - 33\tfrac{1}{3}\% \text{ of } x = 48$$
$$x - \frac{1}{3}x = 48, \quad \text{or} \quad x - 0.333333x = 48$$
$$\frac{2}{3}x = 48, \quad \text{or} \quad 0.666667x = 48$$
$$x = \frac{48 \times 3}{2}, \quad \text{or} \quad x = \frac{48}{0.666667}$$
$$x = 72$$

The original sum of money is $72.

EXERCISE 3.4

A. Answer each of the following questions.

1. What is 120 increased by 40%?

2. What is 900 decreased by 20%?

3. How much is $1200 decreased by 5%?

4. How much is $24 increased by 200%?

5. What number is $83\frac{1}{3}\%$ more than 48?

6. What amount is $16\frac{2}{3}\%$ less than $66?

B. Find the rate of change for each of the following.

1. What percent more than 30 is 45?

2. What percent less than $90 is $72?

3. The amount of $240 is what percent more than $80?

4. The amount of \$110 is what percent less than \$165?

5. What percent less than \$300 is \$294?

6. The amount of \$2025 is what percent more than \$2000?

C. Solve each of the following equations.

1. $x + 40\%$ of $x = 28$
2. $x - 20\%$ of $x = 240$
3. $x - 5\%$ of $x = 418$
4. $x + 7\%$ of $x = 214$
5. $x + 16\frac{2}{3}\%$ of $x = 42$
6. $x - 33\frac{1}{3}\%$ of $x = 54$
7. $x + 150\%$ of $x = 75$
8. $x + 200\%$ of $x = 36$

D. Answer each of the following questions.

1. The number 24 is 25% less than what number?
2. The number 605 is $37\frac{1}{2}\%$ more than what number?
3. What amount increased by 150% will equal \$325?
4. What sum of money decreased by $16\frac{2}{3}\%$ will equal \$800?
5. After deducting 5% from a sum of money, the remainder is \$4.18. What was the original sum of money?
6. After an increase of 7%, the new amount was \$749. What was the original amount?

3.5 PROBLEMS INVOLVING PERCENT

A. Summary of useful relationships

Problems involving percents abound in the field of business. The terminology used varies depending on the situation. However, most problems can be solved by means of the two basic relationships

$$\text{RATE} \times \text{ORIGINAL AMOUNT} = \text{NEW AMOUNT}$$ — **Formula 3.1A**

and

$$\text{ORIGINAL NUMBER} \begin{matrix} + \text{ INCREASE} \\ - \text{ DECREASE} \end{matrix} = \text{NEW AMOUNT}$$ — **Formula 3.2**

or, in the case of finding a rate percent, by means of the formulas

$$\text{RATE} = \frac{\text{NEW AMOUNT}}{\text{ORIGINAL AMOUNT}}$$ — **Formula 3.1B**

and

$$\text{RATE OF CHANGE} = \frac{\text{AMOUNT OF CHANGE}}{\text{ORIGINAL AMOUNT}}$$ — **Formula 3.3**

B. Problems involving the computation of a rate percent

EXAMPLE 3.5A

Solve each of the following problems.

(i) Material content in a lighting fixture is \$40. If the total cost of the fixture is \$48, what percent of cost is the material cost?

SOLUTION

$$\frac{\text{Material cost}}{\text{Total cost}} = \frac{40}{48} = \frac{5}{6} = 83\tfrac{1}{3}\%$$

(ii) A cash discount of \$3.60 was allowed on an invoice of \$120. What was the rate of discount?

SOLUTION

$$\text{The rate of discount} = \frac{\text{Amount of discount}}{\text{Invoice amount}}$$

$$= \frac{3.60}{120.00} = \frac{360}{12\,000} = \frac{3}{100} = 3\%$$

(iii) What percent increase did Nirel Walker receive if her bi-weekly salary rose from \$800 to \$920?

SOLUTION

Salary before the increase (original salary) is \$800;
the raise is 920 − 800 = \$120.

$$\text{The rate of increase} = \frac{\text{Amount of increase}}{\text{Original salary}}$$

$$= \frac{120}{800} = 0.15 = 15\%$$

(iv) Expenditures for a government program were reduced from \$75 000 to \$60 000. What percent change does this represent?

SOLUTION

Expenditure before the change is \$75 000;
the change (decrease) = 75 000 − 60 000 = \$15 000.

$$\text{The rate of change} = \frac{\text{Amount of change}}{\text{Original amount}}$$

$$= \frac{15\,000}{75\,000} = 0.20 = 20\%$$

Expenditures were reduced by 20%.

C. Problems involving the basic percentage relationship

EXAMPLE 3.5B

Solve each of the following problems.

(i) An electronic calculator marked \$39.95 in a bookstore is subject to 6% GST (Goods and Services Tax) and 8% PST (Provincial Sales Tax). What will it cost you to buy the calculator?

SOLUTION

$$\begin{aligned} \text{Cash price} &= \text{Marked price} + \text{GST} + \text{PST} \\ &= 39.95 + 6\% \text{ of } 39.95 + 8\% \text{ of } 39.95 \\ &= 39.95 + 0.06(39.95) + 0.08(39.95) \\ &= 39.95 + 2.40 + 3.20 \\ &= 45.55 \end{aligned}$$

The calculator will cost \$45.55.

(ii) Sales for this year are budgeted at $112\frac{1}{2}\%$ of last year's sales of \$360 000. What is the sales budget for this year?

SOLUTION

$$\begin{aligned} \text{This year's sales} &= 112\tfrac{1}{2}\% \text{ of } 360\,000 \\ &= 1.125 \times 360\,000 \\ &= 405\,000 \end{aligned}$$

Budgeted sales for this year are \$405 000.

(iii) A commission of \$300 was paid to a broker's agent for the sale of a bond. If the commission was $\frac{3}{4}\%$ of the sales value of the bond, how much was the bond sold for?

SOLUTION

$$\text{The commission paid} = \frac{3}{4}\% \text{ of the bond sale}$$

$$\begin{aligned} 300 &= \frac{3}{4}\% \text{ of } x \\ 300 &= 0.75\% \text{ of } x \\ 300 &= 0.0075x \\ x &= 40\,000 \end{aligned}$$

The bond was sold for \$40 000.

(iv) On the basis of past experience, Simcoe District Credit Union estimates uncollectible loans at $1\frac{1}{4}\%$ of the total loan balances outstanding. If, at the end of March, the loans account shows a balance of \$3 248 000, how much should the credit union have in reserve for uncollectible loans at the end of March?

SOLUTION

The provision for uncollectible loans = $1\frac{1}{4}\%$ of \$3 248 000

1% of \$3 248 000 ⟶ \$32 480

$\frac{1}{4}$ of 1% of \$3 248 000 ⟶ 8 120

$1\frac{1}{4}\%$ of \$3 248 000 ⟶ \$40 600

The credit union should have a reserve of \$40 600 for uncollectible loans at the end of March.

(v) The Consumer Price Index in July of this year was 225 or 180% of the index ten years ago. What was the index ten years ago?

SOLUTION

This year's index = 180% of the index ten years ago

$$225 = 180\% \text{ of } x$$
$$225 = 1.80x$$
$$x = \frac{225}{1.8}$$
$$x = 125$$

The index ten years ago was 125.

D. Problems of increase or decrease

EXAMPLE 3.5C

Solve each of the following problems.

(i) Daily car loadings for August were 5% more than for July. If August car loadings were 76 020, what were the July car loadings?

SOLUTION

Because July is earlier than August, its car loadings are the original number and are not known. Let them be represented by x.

$$x + 5\% \text{ of } x = 76\,020$$
$$x + 0.05x = 76\,020$$
$$1.05x = 76\,020$$
$$x = \frac{76\,020}{1.05}$$
$$x = 72\,400$$

Car loadings in July numbered 72 400.

(ii) The trading price of shares of Northern Gold Mines dropped 40% to \$7.20. Determine the trading price before the drop.

SOLUTION

The trading price before the drop is the original value and is not known. Let it be $\$x$.

$$x - 40\% \text{ of } x = 7.20$$
$$x - 0.4x = 7.20$$
$$0.6x = 7.20$$
$$x = \frac{7.20}{0.6}$$
$$x = 12.00$$

The trading price before the drop was \$12.00.

(iii) Dorian Guy sold his house for \$149 500. If he sold the house for $187\frac{1}{2}\%$ more than what he paid for it, how much did he gain?

SOLUTION

The base for the percent gain is the original amount paid for the house. Since this amount is not known, let it be \$$x$.

Original Amount Paid + Gain = Selling Price

$$x + 187\tfrac{1}{2}\% \text{ of } x = 149\,500$$
$$x + 1.875x = 149\,500$$
$$2.875x = 149\,500$$
$$x = \frac{149\,500}{2.875}$$
$$x = 52\,000$$

The amount originally paid was \$52 000.
Gain = 149 500 − 52 000 = \$97 500.

(iv) The amount paid for an article, including 6% Goods and Services Tax, was \$99.64. How much was the marked price of the article?

SOLUTION

The unknown marked price, represented by \$$x$, is the base for the sales tax.

Marked Price + GST = Amount Paid

$$x + 6\% \text{ of } x = 99.64$$
$$x + 0.06x = 99.64$$
$$1.06x = 99.64$$
$$x = \frac{99.64}{1.06}$$
$$x = 94.00$$

The marked price of the article was \$94.

(v) After taking off a discount of 5%, a retailer settled an invoice by paying \$532.00. How much was the amount of the discount?

SOLUTION

The unknown amount of the invoice, represented by \$$x$, is the base for the discount.

Amount of Invoice − Discount = Amount Paid

$$x - 5\% \text{ of } x = 532$$
$$x - 0.05x = 532$$
$$0.95x = 532$$
$$x = 560$$

Discount = 5% of 560 = 0.05×560 = \$28.

BUSINESS MATH NEWS BOX

National Salary Comparisons

How much you are worth in the job market can be critical to not being underpaid. Successful salary negotiations can be accomplished by having accurate information. In today's electronic age, the Internet offers a variety of Websites focusing on salary information.

The following are three popular job functions along with the respective salaries by major metropolitan location.

Controller

Responsible for directing an organization's accounting functions. These functions include establishing and maintaining the organization's accounting principles, practices, and procedures. Prepares financial reports and presents findings and recommendations to top management.

Branch Manager

Oversees the daily activities of the branch office. Provides guidance on more complex issues. Familiar with a variety of the field's concepts, practices, and procedures. Relies on extensive experience and judgment to plan and accomplish goals.

Marketing Manager

Develops and implements strategic marketing plan for an organization. Generally manages a group of marketing professionals. Typically reports to an executive.

October 2006 Salary Comparison (Averages)

Job Description	Vancouver	Calgary	Toronto	Montreal	National
Controller	$107 211	$100 109	$108 068	$103 652	$96 775
Bank branch manager	62 149	58 032	62 646	60 086	56 099
Marketing manager	94 575	88 310	95 331	91 436	85 369

Source: CanWest MediaWorks. Available Salary.com, **http://www.salary.com,** accessed November 4, 2006.

QUESTIONS

1. Assuming that an employee works a 40-hour week, calculate the hourly rate of each job function by location.
2. Calculate the dollar and percent difference by which each job function in different cities varies from the national average.
3. What might account for the salary differences from the national average?

EXERCISE 3.5

A. Solve each of the following problems.

1. Of FasDelivery's 1200 employees, $2\frac{1}{4}\%$ did not report to work last Friday due to an outbreak of the flu. How many employees were absent?
2. A storekeeper bought merchandise for $1575. If she sells the merchandise at $33\frac{1}{3}\%$ above cost, how much gross profit does she make?
3. A clerk whose salary was $280 per week was given a raise of $35 per week. What percent increase did the clerk receive?
4. Your hydro bill for March is $174.40. If you pay after the due date, a late payment penalty of $8.72 is added. What is the percent penalty?
5. A sales representative receives a commission of $16\frac{2}{3}\%$ on all sales. How much must his weekly sales be so that he will make a commission of $720 per week?
6. HRH Collection Agency retains a collection fee of 25% of any amounts collected. How much did the agency collect on a bad debt if the agency forwarded $2490 to a client?
7. A commercial building is insured under a fire policy that has a face value of 80% of the building's appraised value. The annual insurance premium is $\frac{3}{8}\%$ of the face value of the policy and the premium for one year amounts to $675.
   (a) What is the face value of the policy?
   (b) What is the appraised value of the building?
8. A residential property is assessed for tax purposes at 40% of its market value. The residential property tax rate is $3\frac{1}{3}\%$ of the assessed value and the tax is $1200.
   (a) What is the assessed value of the property?
   (b) What is the market value of the property?

B. Solve each of the following problems.

1. A merchant bought an article for $7.92. How much did the article sell for if he sold it at an increase of $83\frac{1}{3}\%$?
2. A retail outlet is offered a discount of $2\frac{1}{2}\%$ for payment in cash of an invoice of $840. If it accepted the offer, how much was the cash payment?
3. A bicycle shop reduced its selling price on a bicycle by $33\frac{1}{3}\%$. If the regular selling price was $195, what was the reduced price?
4. From August 2003 to June 2006, the price of gasoline increased 42%. If the price in 2003 was 75.6 cents per litre, what was the price per litre in 2006?
5. The 14% blended sales tax on a pair of shoes amounted to $10.36. What was the total cost of the shoes?
6. Ms. Daisy pays $37\frac{1}{2}\%$ of her monthly gross salary as rent on a townhouse. If the monthly rent is $660, what is her monthly salary?
7. The annual interest on a bond is $4\frac{1}{2}\%$ of its face value and amounts to $225. What is the face value of the bond?

8. A brokerage house charges a fee of $2\frac{1}{4}\%$. If its fee on a stock purchase was \$432, what was the amount of the purchase?

9. Profit last quarter decreased from \$6540 in the previous quarter to \$1090. What was the percent decrease in profit?

10. A wage earner's hourly rate of pay was increased from \$11.50 to \$11.96. What was the percent raise?

11. A property purchased for \$42 000 is now appraised at \$178 500. What is the percent gain in the value of the property?

12. The Bank of Montreal reduced its annual lending rate from 6% to 5.75%. What is the percent reduction in the lending rate?

13. After a reduction of $33\frac{1}{3}\%$ of the marked price, a fan was sold for \$64.46. What was the marked price?

14. A special purpose index has increased 125% during the last ten years. If the index is now 279, what was the index ten years ago?

15. After a cash discount of 5%, an invoice was settled by a payment of \$646. What was the invoice amount?

16. Sales in May increased $16\frac{2}{3}\%$ over April sales. If May sales amounted to \$24 535, what were April sales?

17. The working capital at the end of the third quarter was 75% higher than at the end of the second quarter. What was the amount of working capital at the end of the second quarter if the working capital at the end of the third quarter was \$78 400?

18. After real estate fees of 8% had been deducted from the proceeds of a property sale, the vendor of the property received \$88 090. What was the amount of the real estate fee?

19. A company's employee compensation expense for August, consisting of the gross pay plus 4% vacation pay based on gross pay, was \$23 400. How much was the amount of vacation pay expense?

20. In Vancouver, a car was sold for \$16 074.25 including 6% GST and 7% PST. How much was the provincial sales tax on the car?

3.6 APPLICATIONS—CURRENCY CONVERSIONS

One practical application of proportions is currency conversion. To perform currency conversions, we use exchange rates. An **exchange rate** is the value of one nation's currency expressed in terms of another nation's currency. In other words, the exchange rate tells us how much of one currency we need in order to buy one unit of another currency. By using proportions and exchange rate tables (sometimes called *currency cross rate* tables), we can convert easily from one currency to another.

A. Using proportions

Suppose we were told that the U.S. dollar is worth $1.115 Canadian today. How would we calculate the exchange rates between the Canadian dollar and the U.S. dollar? Since there are two currencies involved, we can express the exchange rate in two different ways.

First, we can set up the exchange rate converting U.S. dollars to Canadian dollars. To do so, set up the ratio:

$$\frac{\text{Canadian dollars}}{\text{U.S. dollars}} = \frac{\$1.115}{\$1.00} = 1.115$$

1.115 is the exchange rate for converting U.S. dollars to Canadian dollars

To convert U.S. dollars to Canadian dollars, multiply the number of U.S. dollars by 1.115. Thus, to convert US$10 to Canadian dollars, calculate: $\$10.00 \times 1.115 = \$11.15$.

Second, we can set up the exchange rate converting Canadian dollars to U.S. dollars. To do so, set up the ratio:

$$\frac{\text{U.S. dollars}}{\text{Canadian dollars}} = \frac{\$1.00}{\$1.115} = 0.8969$$

0.8969 is the exchange rate for converting Canadian dollars to U.S. dollars

To convert Canadian dollars to U.S. dollars, multiply the number of Canadian dollars by 0.8969. Thus, to convert C$10 to U.S. dollars, calculate: $\$10.00 \times 0.8969 = \$8.97$.

In general, if we know the exchange rate from currency A to currency B (ratio B/A), then we can find the exchange rate from currency B to currency A by taking the reciprocal of the original ratio (i.e., A/B).

If both rates are known, choosing which exchange rate to use can be confusing. The best way to choose the exchange rate is to express the exchange rate as a proportion of two currencies so that the wanted currency is in the numerator of the known ratio.

EXAMPLE 3.6A

Suppose you wanted to convert C$150 into U.S. dollars. You read in the newspaper that one U.S. dollar is worth 1.115 Canadian dollars, and that one Canadian dollar is worth 0.8969 U.S. dollars. How much would you receive in U.S. dollars?

SOLUTION

Let the number of U.S. dollars be x. The wanted currency is U.S. dollars.

Known ratio $\qquad \dfrac{\text{US}\$0.8969}{\text{C}\$1}$

Second ratio $\qquad \dfrac{\text{US}\$x}{\text{C}\$150}$

Proportion $\frac{\text{US\$0.8969}}{\text{C\$1}} = \frac{\text{US\$}x}{\text{C\$150}}$

$$\frac{0.8969}{1} = \frac{x}{150}$$

Then cross-multiply:

$$x = 0.8969(150)$$
$$x = 134.54$$

Therefore, C$150 is worth US$134.54.

EXAMPLE 3.6B While travelling in the United States, you filled your gas tank with 16.6 U.S. gallons of gas at a cost of US$45.82.

(i) How much did the fillup cost you in Canadian funds if one Canadian dollar cost 0.88 U.S. dollars?

SOLUTION Let the amount in Canadian dollars be x.

$$\frac{\text{C\$ }1}{\text{US\$ }0.88} = \frac{\text{C\$ }x}{\text{US\$ }45.82}$$

$$\frac{1}{0.88} = \frac{x}{45.82}$$

$$1(45.82) = x(0.88)$$

$$x = \frac{45.82}{0.88}$$

$$x = 52.07$$

The fillup cost $52.07 in Canadian funds.

(ii) What was the cost of gas per litre in Canadian funds, if one U.S. gallon is equivalent to 3.6 litres?

SOLUTION Since 1 U.S. gallon = 3.6 litres,

16.6 U.S. gallons = 3.6(16.6) = 59.76 litres

From (i), US$45.82 = C$52.07

$$\text{Cost per litre} = \frac{52.07}{59.76} = \text{C\$0.8713}$$

The cost per litre in Canadian funds was $0.8713.

B. Using cross rate tables

Cross rate tables are commonly found in newspapers and business and travel magazines. They show the exchange rates between a number of currencies. One example is shown in Table 3.2. Notice that exchange rates are often given to more decimal places than the usual two places for dollars and cents. To convert currency A into currency B, first find currency A in the column headings (along the top of the table). Then find currency B in the row headings (along the left side of the table). The exchange rate is the number where the column and row intersect. For instance, from the table, the exchange rate to convert Canadian dollars to U.S. dollars is 0.8969.

EXAMPLE 3.6C Convert $55 Canadian into Swiss francs.

SOLUTION First, to find the exchange rate from Canadian dollars to Swiss francs, locate the Canadian dollar column in the table. Move down the Canadian dollar column until you come to the Swiss franc row. The exchange rate is 1.0963.

$$\text{Conversion} = 55.00 \times 1.0963$$
$$= 60.2965 \text{ Swiss francs}$$

Table 3.2 **Currency Cross Rates** 1 unit of Currency

	Canadian Dollar	U.S. Dollar	British Pound	Euro	Japanese Yen	Swiss Franc
Candian Dollar	—	1.1150	2.0614	1.4246	0.0097	0.9121
U.S. Dollar	0.8969	—	1.8488	1.2777	0.0087	0.8181
British Pound	0.4851	0.5409	—	0.6911	0.0047	0.4425
Euro	0.7020	0.7827	1.4470	—	0.0068	0.6403
Japanese Yen	102.70	114.51	211.71	146.31	—	93.68
Swiss Franc	1.0963	1.2224	2.2600	1.5618	0.0107	—

EXAMPLE 3.6D Suppose you are taking a trip from Canada to France, and then to Japan. Convert C$100 to Euros, then convert the Euros to Japanese yen. Use the exchange rates in Table 3.2.

SOLUTION

(i) From the table, the exchange rate for Canadian dollars to Euros is 0.7020.

$$\text{Conversion} = 100 \times 0.7020$$
$$= 70.2 \text{ Euros}$$

(ii) From the table, the exchange rate for Euros to Japanese yen is 146.31.

$$\text{Conversion} = 70.2 \times 146.31$$
$$= 10\,270.962 \text{ Japanese yen}$$

You can check this answer by converting C$100 to Japanese yen. However, the answers may differ slightly due to rounding.

EXERCISE 3.6

A. Answer each of the following questions.

1. How many U.S. dollars can you buy for C$750 if one Canadian dollar is worth US$0.9026?
2. How many Canadian dollars can you buy for US$750 if one Canadian dollar is worth US$0.9026?
3. Suppose the exchange rate was US$0.89 for each Canadian dollar. What is the price, in Canadian dollars, of a flight to Florida costing US$299?
4. What is the price of gasoline per litre in Canadian dollars if a U.S. gallon of gasoline costs US$2.74? One U.S. dollar is worth C$1.14 and one U.S. gallon is equivalent to 3.8 litres.

B. Use Table 3.2 to make each of the following conversions.

1. Convert US$350 to Canadian dollars.
2. Convert C$200 to Euros.
3. Convert US$175 to Swiss francs.
4. Convert 250 British pounds to Japanese yen.
5. Convert $550 Euros to Canadian dollars.

3.7 APPLICATIONS—INDEX NUMBERS

A. The nature of index numbers

An **index number** results when you compare two values of the same thing measured at different points in time. The comparison of the two values is stated as a ratio, then expressed as a percent. When the percent symbol is dropped, the result is called an index number.

EXAMPLE 3.7A The price of a textbook was $90 in 2005 and $105 in 2008. Compare the two prices to create an index number.

SOLUTION The change in price over the time period 2005 to 2008 can be measured in relative terms by writing the ratio

$$\frac{\text{Price in 2008}}{\text{Price in 2005}} = \frac{105}{90} = 1.1\dot{6} = 116.\dot{6}\%$$

An index number can now be created by dropping the percent symbol. The price index is $116.\dot{6}$.

To construct an index number, you must select one of the two values as the denominator of the ratio. The point in time at which the denominator was measured is called the **base period**. In Example 3.7A, 2005 was chosen as the base period. The chronologically earlier time period is usually used as the base period.

The index for the base period is always 100. The difference between an index number and 100 indicates the relative change that has taken place. For Example 3.7A, the index number $116.\dot{6}$ indicates that the price of the book in 2008 was $16.\dot{6}\%$ higher than in 2005.

Indexes provide an easy way of expressing changes that occur in daily business. Converting data to indexes makes working with very large or small numbers easier and provides a basis for many types of analysis. Indexes are used in comparing and analyzing economic data and have become a widely accepted tool for measuring changes in business activity. Two of the more common indexes frequently mentioned in the media are the Consumer Price Index (CPI) and the Toronto Stock Exchange S&P/TSX Composite Index.

B. The Consumer Price Index and its uses

The **Consumer Price Index** (**CPI**) is the most widely accepted indicator of changes in the overall price level of goods and services. In Canada, a fixed "basket" or collection of goods and services is used to represent all Canadian goods and services. The prices of the items in this collection are monitored and are used to represent the price change of all goods and services. The CPI is currently based on 1992 price levels and is published monthly by Statistics Canada. For example, the 2004 CPI of 124.6 indicated that the price level increased 24.6% from 1992 (the base year) to 2004.

You can use the Consumer Price Index to determine the *purchasing power of the Canadian dollar* and to compute *real income.*

The **purchasing power of the dollar** is the reciprocal of the CPI, that is,

$$\text{Purchasing power of the dollar} = \frac{\$1}{\text{Consumer Price Index}}(100)$$

EXAMPLE 3.7B

The CPI was 122.3 for 2003 and 124.6 for 2004. Determine the purchasing power of the Canadian dollar for the two years, and interpret the meaning of the results.

SOLUTION

Purchasing power of the dollar for 2003

$$= \frac{\$1}{122.3}(100) = 0.817661$$

Purchasing power of the dollar for 2004

$$= \frac{\$1}{124.6}(100) = 0.802568$$

This means the dollar in 2003 could purchase only 81.8% of what it could purchase in 1992 (the base year). In 2004, the dollar could purchase even less (about 80.3% of what it could purchase in 1992).

The CPI can be used to eliminate the effect of inflation on income by adjusting **nominal income** (income stated in current dollars) to **real income** (income stated in base-period dollars).

$$\text{REAL INCOME} = \frac{\text{INCOME IN CURRENT DOLLARS}}{\text{CONSUMER PRICE INDEX}}(100) \qquad \textbf{Formula 3.4}$$

EXAMPLE 3.7C

Heather's income was $40 000 in 1992, $46 000 in 2002, and $49 000 in 2004. The Canadian CPI was 119.0 in 2002 and 124.6 in 2004. The CPI base year is 1992.

(i) Determine Heather's real income in 2002 and 2004.

(ii) Should Heather be happy about her increases in wages from 1992 to 2004?

SOLUTION

(i) $$\text{Real income in 2002} = \frac{\text{Nominal income}}{\text{CPI in 2002}}(100)$$
$$= \frac{\$46\,000}{119.0}(100) = \$38\,655.46$$

$$\text{Real income in 2004} = \frac{\text{Nominal income}}{\text{CPI in 2004}}(100)$$
$$= \frac{\$49\,000}{124.6}(100) = \$39\,325.84$$

(ii) To compare nominal income with real income, it is useful to determine income changes in absolute and relative terms.

While Heather's income in 2002 increased 15.0% over her 1992 income, her purchasing power, reflected by her 2002 real income, actually decreased by 3.4% over the ten-year period. From 1992 to 2004, her nominal income increased by 22.5% over her 1992 income. Her real income decreased 1.7%, indicating that real income decreased somewhat during the period 1992 to 2004.

Year	1992	2002	2004
Nominal income	$40 000	$46 000	$49 000
Simple price index	$\frac{40\,000}{40\,000}(100)$	$\frac{46\,000}{40\,000}(100)$	$\frac{49\,000}{40\,000}(100)$
	= 100.00	= 115.0	122.5
Absolute ($) increase		$6000	$9000
Relative (%) increase		15%	22.5%
Real income	$40 000	$38 655	$39 326
Simple price index	$\frac{40\,000}{40\,000}(100)$	$\frac{38\,655}{40\,000}(100)$	$\frac{39\,326}{40\,000}(100)$
	= 100.00	= 96.6	= 98.3
Absolute ($) increase (decrease)		($1345)	($674)
Relative (%) increase (decrease)		(3.4%)	(1.7%)

EXERCISE 3.7

A. Solve each of the following problems.

1. Using 2003 as the base period, compute a simple price index for each of the following commodities. Interpret your results.

Commodity	Price in 2003	Price in 2004
Bread (loaf)	$1.49	$1.54
Bus pass	$105.00	$110.00
Clothing	$1475.00	$1400.00

2. Using 2000 as the base period, compute a series of simple price indexes for the price of gold for the period 2000 to 2005. Interpret your results.

	2000	2001	2002	2003	2004	2005
Price per ounce	$274.45	$276.50	$347.20	$416.25	$435.60	$513.00

B. Solve each of the following problems.

1. The Consumer Price Index for 2000 was 113.5 and for 2004 it was 124.6.
   (a) Determine the purchasing power of the dollar in 2000 and 2004 relative to the base year 1992.
   (b) Compute the purchasing power of the dollar in 2004 relative to 2000.

2. Kim's annual incomes for 1992, 1996, 2000, and 2004 were $33 000, $36 000, $38 000, and $41 000 respectively. Given that the Consumer Price Index for the four years was 100.0, 105.9, 113.5, and 124.6 respectively, compute Kim's real income for 1996, 2000, and 2004.

3. Tamara earned $34 000 in 1995. If the Consumer Price Index in 1995 was 104.2 and in 2004 it was 124.6, what did Tamara have to earn in 2004 just to keep up with inflation?

4. The S&P/TSX 60 Stock Index was 947.50 on March 31, 2005 and 789.35 on March 31, 2006. Josh holds an investment portfolio representative of the 35 stocks in the index. If the value of the portfolio on March 31, 2005 was $214 450, what was the value of the portfolio on March 31, 2006?

3.8 APPLICATIONS—PERSONAL INCOME TAXES

Personal income taxes are taxes imposed by the federal and provincial governments on the earned income of residents of Canada. The federal government collects and refunds income taxes based on the income you calculate on your income tax return each year.

Federal tax rates currently vary from 15.25% to 29% of taxable income. The tax rates increase as your income increases. The 2006 federal income tax brackets and tax rates are shown in Table 3.3.

The income tax brackets are adjusted annually for changes in the Consumer Price Index (CPI) in excess of 3%. If the CPI increases by less than 3% during a year, there is no increase in the tax brackets.

Table 3.3 **2006 Federal Income Tax Brackets and Tax Rates**

Taxable Income (income tax brackets)	Tax Rates
\$36 378 or less	15.25%
\$36 378 to \$72 756	\$5548 plus 22% of income over \$36 378
\$72 756 to \$118 285	\$13 551 plus 26% of income over \$72 756
Over \$118 285	\$25 388 plus 29% of income over \$118 285

The **marginal tax rate** is the rate at which your next dollar of earned income is taxed. Your marginal tax rate increases when your earnings increase and you move from a lower tax bracket to a higher tax bracket. It decreases if your earnings decline and you move into a lower tax bracket. Due to the variety of provincial tax rates and surtaxes, the combined federal-provincial marginal tax rates vary from province to province.

EXAMPLE 3.8A

Use the tax brackets and rates in Table 3.3 to compute the federal tax for Jim, Kulvir, and Lee, who are declaring taxable income respectively of

(i) \$31 000

(ii) \$62 000

(iii) \$93 000

SOLUTION

(i) Federal tax for Jim = 15.25% of \$31 000
= 0.1525(31 000)
= \$4727.50

(ii) Federal tax for Kulvir = \$5548 + 22% of (\$62 000 − \$36 378)
= 5548 + 0.22(25 622)
= 5548 + 5636.84
= \$11 184.84

(iii) Federal tax for Lee = \$13 551 + 26% of (\$93 000 − \$72 756)
= 13 551 + 0.26(20 244)
= 13 551 + 5263.44
= \$18 814.40

Therefore, Jim, Kulvir, and Lee must report federal tax of \$4727.50, \$11 184.84, and \$18 814.40 respectively.

Taxpayer	Taxable Income \$	Increase in Income \$	Federal Tax \$	Increase in Federal Tax \$
Jim	31 000		4 727.50	
Kulvir	62 000	31 000 (100%)	11 184.84	6 457.34 (137%)
Lee	93 000	62 000 (200%)	18 814.40	14 086.90 (298%)

For an increase in income of 100%, the federal tax increases 137%. For an increase in income of 200%, the federal tax increases 298%.

EXERCISE 3.8

A. Use the 2006 federal income tax brackets and rates in Table 3.3 to answer each of the following questions.

1. Victor calculated his 2006 taxable income to be \$49 450. How much federal income tax should he report?

2. Sonja reported a taxable income of \$86 300 on her 2006 income tax return. How much federal income tax should she report?

3. How much federal income tax should Aman report if she earned taxable income of \$32 920 and \$7700 from her two jobs?

4. In early 2006, Mei Ling's gross pay increased from \$70 000 per year to \$77 000 per year.

(a) What was the annual percent increase in Mei Ling's pay before federal income taxes?

(b) What was the annual percent increase in Mei Ling's pay after federal income taxes were deducted?

Review Exercise

1. Set up ratios to compare each of the following sets of quantities. Reduce each ratio to its lowest terms.

(a) twenty-five dimes and three dollars
(b) five hours to 50 min
(c) \$6.75 for thirty litres of gasoline
(d) \$21 for three-and-a-half hours
(e) 1440 words for 120 lines for 6 pages
(f) 90 kg for 24 ha (hectares) for 18 weeks

2. Solve each of the following proportions.

(a) $5 : n = 35 : 21$ **(b)** $10 : 6 = 30 : x$
(c) $1.15 : 0.85\,5 = k : 1.19$
(d) $3.60 : m = 10.8 : 8.10$
(e) $\frac{5}{7} : \frac{15}{14} = \frac{6}{5} : t$ **(f)** $y : \frac{9}{8} = \frac{5}{4} : \frac{45}{64}$

3. Compute each of the following.

(a) 150% of 140 **(b)** 3% of 240
(c) $9\frac{3}{4}$% of 2000 **(d)** 0.9% of 400

4. Use fractional equivalents to compute each of the following.

(a) $66\frac{2}{3}$% of \$168 **(b)** $37\frac{1}{2}$% of \$2480
(c) 125% of \$924 **(d)** $183\frac{1}{3}$% of \$720

5. Use the 1% method to determine each of the following.

(a) $\frac{1}{4}$% of \$2664 **(b)** $\frac{5}{8}$% of \$1328
(c) $1\frac{2}{3}$% of \$5400 **(d)** $2\frac{1}{5}$% of \$1260

6. Answer each of the following questions.

(a) What is the rate percent if the base is 88 and the percentage is 55?
(b) 63 is what percent of 36?
(c) What is $\frac{3}{4}$% of \$64?
(d) 450% of \$5 is what amount?
(e) \$245 is $87\frac{1}{2}$% of what amount?
(f) $2\frac{1}{4}$% of what amount is \$9.90?
(g) What percent of \$62.50 is \$1.25?
(h) \$30 is what percent of \$6?
(i) $166\frac{2}{3}$% of what amount is \$220?
(j) \$1.35 is $\frac{1}{3}$% of what amount?

7. Answer each of the following questions.

(a) How much is \$8 increased by 125%?
(b) What amount is $2\frac{1}{4}$% less than \$2000?
(c) What percent less than \$120 is \$100?
(d) \$975 is what percent more than \$150?
(e) \$98 is 75% more than what amount?
(f) After a reduction of 15%, the amount paid for a CD player was \$289. What was the price before the reduction?
(g) What sum of money increased by 250% will amount to \$490?

8. D, E, and F own a business jointly and share profits and losses in the same proportion as their investments. How much of a profit of \$4500 will each receive if their investments are \$4000, \$6000, and \$5000 respectively?

9. Departments A, B, and C occupy floor space of 80 m², 140 m², and 160 m² respectively. If the total rental cost for the floor space is \$11 400 per month, how much of the rental cost should each department pay?

10. Four beneficiaries are to divide an estate of \$189 000 in the ratio $\frac{1}{3} : \frac{1}{4} : \frac{3}{8} : \frac{1}{24}$. How much should each receive?

11. Three insurance companies have insured a building in the ratio $\frac{1}{2}$ to $\frac{1}{3}$ to $\frac{2}{5}$. How much of a fire loss of \$185 000 should each company pay?

12. A hot water tank with a capacity of 220 L can be heated in twenty minutes. At the same rate, how many minutes will it take to heat a tank containing 176 L?

13. If the variable cost amounts to \$130 000 when sales are \$250 000, what will the variable cost be when sales are \$350 000?

14. Gross profit for April was two-fifths of net sales, and net income was two-sevenths of gross profit. Net income was $4200.

(a) What was the gross profit for April?

(b) What were net sales for April?

15. In a college, $\frac{4}{9}$ of all employees are faculty and the ratio of the faculty to support staff is 5 : 4. How many people does the college employ if the support staff numbers 192?

16. In the last municipal election, $62\frac{1}{2}\%$ of the population of 94 800 was eligible to vote. Of those eligible, $33\frac{1}{3}\%$ voted.

(a) What was the number of eligible voters?

(b) How many voted?

17. An investment portfolio of $150 000 consists of the following: $37\frac{1}{2}\%$ in bonds, $56\frac{1}{4}\%$ in common stock, and the remainder in preferred shares. How much money is invested in each type of investment security?

18. A sales representative's orders for May were $16\frac{2}{3}\%$ less than her April orders, which amounted to $51 120.

(a) How much were the sales rep's orders in May?

(b) By what amount did her orders decrease?

19. The appraised value of a property has increased $233\frac{1}{3}\%$ since it was purchased by the present owner. The purchase price of the property was $120 000, its appraised value at that time.

(a) How much is the current appraised value?

(b) How much would the owner gain by selling at the appraised value?

20. The direct material cost of manufacturing a product is $103.95, direct labour cost is $46.20, and overhead is $57.75.

(a) What is the percent content of each element of cost in the product?

(b) What is the overhead percent rate based on direct labour?

21. Inspection of a production run of 2400 items showed that 180 items did not meet specifications. Of the 180 that did not pass inspection, 150 could be reworked. The remainder had to be scrapped.

(a) What percent of the production run did not pass inspection?

(b) What percent of the items that did not meet specifications had to be scrapped?

22. The price of a stock a week ago was $56.25 per share. Today the price per share is $51.75.

(a) What is the percent change in price?

(b) What is the new price as a percent of the old price?

23. A wage earner's hourly rate of pay increased from $6.30 to $16.80 during the last decade.

(a) What was the percent change in the hourly rate of pay?

(b) What is the current rate of pay as a percent of the rate a decade ago?

24. A firm's bad debts of $7875 were $2\frac{1}{4}\%$ of sales. What were the firm's sales?

25. A ski shop lists ski boots at 240% of cost. If the ski shop prices the DX2 Model at $396, what was the cost of the ski boots to the shop?

26. A property owner listed his property for 160% more than he paid for it. The owner eventually accepted an offer $12\frac{1}{2}\%$ below his asking price and sold the property for $191 100. How much did the owner pay for the property?

27. A marina listed a yacht at $33\frac{1}{3}\%$ above cost. At the end of the season, the list price was reduced by 22.5% and the yacht was sold for $15 500. What was the cost of the yacht to the marina?

28. A & E Holdings' profit and loss statement showed a net income of $9\frac{3}{4}\%$ of revenue or $29 250. Twenty percent of net income was paid in corporation tax and 75% of the net income after tax was paid out as dividends to Alice and Emile, who hold shares in the ratio 5 to 3.

(a) What was the revenue of A & E Holdings?

(b) How much was the after-tax income?

(c) How much was paid out in dividends?

(d) What percent of net income did Alice receive as a dividend?

29. A farm was offered for sale at 350% above cost. The farm was finally sold for \$330 000 at $8\frac{1}{3}\%$ below the asking price.

(a) What was the original cost of the farm to the owner?

(b) How much gain did the owner realize?

(c) What percent of the original cost does this gain represent?

30. Suppose it costs C\$250.69 to purchase US\$218.10.

(a) What is the exchange rate?

(b) How many U.S. dollars will you receive if you convert C\$725 into U.S. dollars?

31. Media Marketing of Atlanta, Georgia, offers a three-day accommodation coupon for a Hilton Head resort in South Carolina at a promotion price of C\$216. If the exchange rate is C\$1.15 per U.S. dollar, what is the value of the coupon in U.S. dollars?

32. Suppose the Consumer Price Index in 2004 is 124.6, with 1992 as the base year.

(a) What is the purchasing power of the dollar in 2004 compared to 1992?

(b) What is the real income, relative to 1992, of a wage earner whose income amounted to \$62 900 in 2004?

33. Abeni calculated her 2006 taxable income to be \$83 450. How much federal income tax should she report if she is in the tax bracket where tax is \$13 551 plus 26% of income over \$72 756?

34. Matt's gross pay had been \$68 000 per year, when he received an increase of \$6000 per year.

(a) What was the annual percent increase in Matt's pay before federal income taxes?

(b) What was the annual percent increase in Matt's pay after federal income taxes were deducted?

Self-Test

1. Compute each of the following.

(a) 125% of \$280 **(b)** $\frac{3}{8}\%$ of \$20 280

(c) $83\frac{1}{3}\%$ of \$174 **(d)** $1\frac{1}{4}\%$ of \$1056

2. Solve each of the following proportions.

(a) $65 : 39 = x : 12$ **(b)** $\frac{7}{6} : \frac{35}{12} = \frac{6}{5} : x$

3. The results of a market survey indicate that 24 respondents preferred Brand X, 36 preferred Brand Y, and 20 had no preference. What percent of the sample preferred Brand Y?

4. Departments A, B, and C occupy floor space of 40 m^2, 80 m^2, and 300 m^2 respectively. If the total rental for the space is \$25 200 per month, how much rent should Department B pay?

5. Past experience shows that the clientele of a restaurant spends \$9.60 on beverages for every \$12 spent on food. If it is expected that food sales will amount to \$12 500 for a month, how much should be budgeted for beverage sales?

6. After a reduction of $16\frac{2}{3}\%$ off the marked price, a pair of boots sold for \$60. What was the marked price?

7. A bonus is to be divided among four employees in the ratio $\frac{1}{2} : \frac{1}{3} : \frac{1}{5} : \frac{1}{6}$. What is each employee's share of a bonus of $40 500?

8. Jorjanna Fawcett's hourly rate of pay was increased from $11 to $12.54. What was the percent raise?

9. A bicycle was sold for $287.50. The selling price included 15% blended sales tax. Find the amount of sales tax on the bike.

10. A microwave oven originally advertised at $220 is reduced to $209 during a sale. By what percent was the price reduced?

11. A special consumer index has increased 100% during the last 10 years. If the index is now 360, what was it 10 years ago?

12. Mr. Braid owned $\frac{3}{8}$ of a store. He sold $\frac{2}{3}$ of his interest in the store for $18 000. What was the value of the store?

13. Suppose it cost C$0.9022 to purchase one Australian dollar.
    (a) How much would it cost in Australian dollars to purchase one Canadian dollar?
    (b) How many Australian dollars would you need to buy 500 Canadian dollars?

14. If one Canadian dollar is equivalent to US$0.7250, how much do you need in Canadian funds to buy US$800.00?

15. What is the purchasing power of the dollar relative to the base year of 1992 if the Consumer Price Index is 113.6?

16. Suppose a taxpayer is in the tax bracket where federal income tax is calculated as $5548 plus 22% of income over $36 378. How much federal income tax must he report if he earns $48 750?

Challenge Problems

1. Two consecutive price reductions of the same percent reduced the price of an item from $25 to $16. By what percent was the price reduced each time?

2. Suppose you own a fast-food outlet and buy 100 kilograms of potatoes that are 99% water. After leaving them outside for a few days, you are told that they are now only 98% water. Assuming that they have simply lost some water, how much do the potatoes now weigh?

3. Luis ordered four pairs of black socks and some additional pairs of blue socks from a clothing catalogue. The price of the black socks per pair was twice that of the blue. When the order was filled, it was found that the number of pairs of the two colours had been interchanged. This increased the bill by 50% (before taxes and delivery charges). Find the ratio of the number of pairs of black socks to the number of pairs of blue socks in Luis's original order.

4. Following a 10% decrease in her annual salary, what percent increase would an employee need to receive in future to get back to her original salary level?

Case Study 3.1 The Business of Taxes

» Camille operates a child care service from her home. Her gross business income for 2005 amounted to $42 350. Her tax-deductible business expenses consisted of the following:

Advertising	$1700
Dues, memberships, subscriptions	520
Motor vehicle expenses	1115
Supplies	582
Meals and entertainment	495
Other expenses	437

Camille can also deduct home expenses, such as utilities, property taxes, house insurance, mortgage interest, and maintenance for the business use of a workspace in her home. The amount that may be deducted is a proportion of the total annual home expenses allocated to the workspace on a reasonable basis, such as area or number of rooms. Camille's eligible home expenses for the year were:

Heat	$3750
Power	2480
Water	610
House insurance	1420
Maintenance	1930
Mortgage interest	6630
Property taxes	3260
Other expenses	690

The house covers 345 square metres and consists of eight rooms. Camille uses one room with an area of 45 square metres as her business office.

QUESTIONS

1. What portion of her eligible home expenses may Camille claim as tax-deductible expenses if the expenses are allocated on the basis of:
   (a) area? **(b)** number of rooms?

2. What is her net business income if Camille allocates home expenses on the basis of area?

3. For most individuals, Basic Federal Income Tax equals the federal tax calculated according to Table 3.3 less non-refundable tax credits. What is Camille's Basic Federal Income Tax if she reports a non-refundable tax credit of $8430?
   Note: Federal tax is reduced by 15.25% of total non-refundable tax credits.

4. What percent of Camille's business income is Basic Federal Income Tax?

5. What percent of Camille's taxable income is Basic Federal Income Tax?

Case Study 3.2 Trip of a Lifetime

» Franco and Pho-Lynn had been planning their honeymoon to Europe. Both felt that travelling right after their wedding would be the perfect time and perhaps the only opportunity to take an extended trip before starting a family.

A major part of their planning focused on the financial costs they would incur over the 21 days of their trip. Their plan was to spend five days in Switzerland, six days in Germany, and ten days in England.

Franco and Pho-Lynn budgeted C$1500 each for the multi-destination round-trip airfare. They would leave Edmonton, land in Zurich, and return from London, England. Research over the Internet indicated that they could each comfortably live on the following amounts in the local currencies (including transportation, food, accommodation, and miscellaneous expenditures):

Switzerland	230 Swiss francs/day
Germany	200 Euros/day
England	100 pounds/day

QUESTIONS

1. The currency cross rates in Table 3.2 were in effect when Franco and Pho-Lynn were planning their trip. Using these rates, what is the expected total cost of this trip for each traveller in Canadian dollars?

2. What would be the total cost in U.S. dollars for each traveller if Franco and Pho-Lynn were American citizens planning the same trip? Assume the round-trip airfare from Chicago to London, England and from Zurich, Switzerland to Chicago costs each of them US$1050.

SUMMARY OF FORMULAS

Formula 3.1A

$$\text{PERCENTAGE} = \text{RATE} \times \text{BASE}$$

or

$$\text{NEW NUMBER} = \text{RATE} \times \text{ORIGINAL NUMBER}$$

The basic percentage relationship

Formula 3.1B

$$\text{RATE} = \frac{\text{PERCENTAGE}}{\text{BASE}} \quad \text{or} \quad \frac{\text{NEW NUMBER}}{\text{ORIGINAL NUMBER}}$$

Formula for finding the rate percent when comparing a number (the percentage) to another number (the base or original number)

Formula 3.2

$$\text{ORIGINAL NUMBER} \begin{array}{l} + \text{ INCREASE} \\ - \text{ DECREASE} \end{array} = \text{NEW NUMBER}$$

The relationship to use with problems of increase or decrease (problems of change)

Formula 3.3

$$\text{RATE OF CHANGE} = \frac{\text{AMOUNT OF CHANGE}}{\text{ORIGINAL NUMBER}}$$

Formula for finding the rate of change (rate of increase or decrease)

Formula 3.4

$$\text{REAL INCOME} = \frac{\text{INCOME IN CURRENT DOLLARS}}{\text{CONSUMER PRICE INDEX}}$$

Formula for eliminating the effect of inflation on income

GLOSSARY

Base period in an index, the period of time against which comparisons are made. The base period is arbitrarily selected, but it always has an index number of 100 *(p. 132)*

Consumer Price Index (CPI) the index that shows the price change for a sample of goods and services that is used to indicate the price change for all goods and services *(p. 132)*

Equivalent ratios in higher terms ratios obtained by multiplying each term of a ratio by the same number *(p. 97)*

Exchange rate the value of one nation's currency expressed in terms of another's currency *(p. 127)*

Index number expresses the relative change in the value of an item at different points in time. One of the points in time is a base period, which is always defined to have a value of 100 *(p. 131)*

Marginal tax rate rate at which your next dollar of earned income is taxed. Marginal tax rates tend to increase as earnings increase *(p. 135)*

Nominal income income stated in current dollars *(p. 133)*

Personal income tax taxes imposed by the federal and provincial governments on the earned income of Canadian residents *(p. 134)*

Proportion a statement of equality between two ratios *(p. 102)*

Purchasing power of the dollar the reciprocal of the Consumer Price Index *(p. 132)*

Ratio a comparison by division of the relative values of numbers or quantities *(p. 96)*

Real income income stated in base-period dollars *(p. 133)*

Terms of a ratio the numbers appearing in a ratio *(p. 96)*

USEFUL INTERNET SITES

www.taxpayer.com
Canadian Taxpayers Federation The CTF, a federally incorporated, non-profit, non-partisan organization, acts as a watchdog on government spending and taxation.

www.cnnfn.com/markets/currencies
Foreign Currency Exchange Rates The Cable News Network (CNN) site provides current currency exchange rates on its financial page.

www.globeinvestor.com
The Globe and Mail This Canadian newspaper's site provides price, performance, and index benchmark data on securities trading on North American stock exchanges.

www.statcan.ca
Statistics Canada This government Website for Canadian statistics contains a lengthy and informative discussion of the Consumer Price Index.

CHAPTER 4 Linear Systems

OBJECTIVES

Upon completing this chapter, you will be able to do the following:

1. Solve linear systems consisting of two simultaneous equations in two variables using algebraic elimination.
2. Graph linear equalities in two variables.
3. Graph linear systems consisting of two linear relations in two variables.
4. Solve problems by setting up systems of linear equations in two variables.

Most manufacturing companies produce more than one product. In deciding the quantities of each product to produce, management has to take into account the combination of production levels that will make the most efficient use of labour, materials, and transportation, and produce the highest level of profit. Most companies have so many factors to consider that they need sophisticated methods of evaluation. However, many situations like this can be simplified and solved. Suppose you were in the business of producing children's toys. If you cannot produce all the items because of limited budget or limited manufacturing capacity, you would need to consider the relative profitability of each item to determine which combination of items to produce. You can define the variables, set up a system of linear equations, and solve the system by algebraic or graphical methods to decide how to best allocate your resources.

INTRODUCTION

In many types of problems, the relationship between two or more variables can be represented by setting up linear equations. Algebraic as well as graphic techniques are available to solve such problems.

4.1 ALGEBRAIC SOLUTION OF SYSTEMS OF LINEAR EQUATIONS IN TWO VARIABLES

A. Basic concept

Any linear system that consists of two equations in two variables can be solved algebraically or graphically.

Solving a system of two equations requires finding a pair of values for the two variables that satisfies both of the equations. The value of one of the two variables can be determined by first reducing the system of equations to one equation in one variable and solving this equation. The value of the variable obtained is then substituted into one of the original equations to find the value of the second variable.

Algebraic and graphic solutions of systems of linear equations in two variables are used extensively when doing break-even analysis. Break-even analysis is explored further in Chapter 6.

B. Solving a system of two linear equations by algebraic elimination

If the coefficients of one variable are the same in both equations, the system can be reduced to one equation by addition or subtraction as follows.

(a) If the coefficients of one variable are numerically equal but opposite in sign, addition will eliminate the variable.

(b) If the coefficients of one variable are numerically equal and have the same sign, subtraction can eliminate the variable. Alternatively, one equation can be multiplied by -1; addition can then be used.

EXAMPLE 4.1A

Solve each of the following systems of equations.

(i) $x + y = 1$
$x - y = 7$

(ii) $5x + 4y = 7$
$3x - 4y = 17$

(iii) $x - 3y = 2$
$4x - 3y = -10$

SOLUTION

(i) $x + y = 1$ ——— equation ①
$x - y = 7$ ——— equation ②
$2x = 8$ ——— add ① and ② to eliminate y
$x = 4$ ——— *Note*: The coefficient of y in ① is 1; the coefficient of y in ② is -1. Since the coefficients are the same but opposite in sign, adding the two equations will eliminate the term in y.

$4 + y = 1$ — substitute the value of x in ①
$y = -3$
$\boxed{x = 4, y = -3}$ — solution

Check
in ① LS $= 4 + (-3) = 4 - 3 = 1$
RS $= 1$
in ② LS $= 4 - (-3) = 4 + 3 = 7$
RS $= 7$

(ii) $5x + 4y = 7$ — equation ①
$3x - 4y = 17$ — equation ②
$8x = 24$ — add ① and ② to eliminate y
$x = 3$
$5(3) + 4y = 7$ — substitute 3 for x in ①
$15 + 4y = 7$
$4y = -8$
$y = -2$
$\boxed{x = 3, y = -2}$ — solution

Check
in ① LS $= 5(3) + 4(-2) = 15 - 8 = 7$
RS $= 7$
in ② LS $= 3(3) - 4(-2) = 9 + 8 = 17$
RS $= 17$

(iii) $x - 3y = 2$ — ①
$4x - 3y = -10$ — ②
$x - 3y = 2$ — ①
$-4x + 3y = 10$ — ② multiplied by -1 to set up addition
$-3x = 12$ — add
$x = -4$
$-4 - 3y = 2$ — substitute -4 for x in ①
$-3y = 6$
$y = -2$
$\boxed{x = -4, y = -2}$ — solution

Check
in ① LS $= -4 - 3(-2) = -4 + 6 = 2$
RS $= 2$
in ② LS $= 4(-4) - 3(-2) = -16 + 6 = -10$
RS $= -10$

C. Solving a system of two linear equations when the coefficients are not numerically equal

Sometimes numerical equality of one pair of coefficients must be *created* before addition or subtraction can be used to eliminate a variable. This equality is usually achieved by multiplying one or both equations by a number or numbers that make the coefficients of the variable to be eliminated numerically equal.

EXAMPLE 4.1B

Solve each of the following systems of equations.

(i) $x - 3y = -12$
$3x + y = -6$

(ii) $x + 4y = 18$
$2x + 5y = 24$

(iii) $6x - 5y + 70 = 0$
$4x = 3y - 44$

SOLUTION

(i) $x - 3y = -12$ ——— ①
$3x + y = -6$ ——— ②

To eliminate the term in y, multiply equation ② by 3.

$x - 3y = -12$ ——— ①
$9x + 3y = -18$ ——— ② multiplied by 3
$10x = -30$ ——— add
$x = -3$
$-3 - 3y = -12$ ——— substitute -3 for x in ①
$-3y = -9$
$y = 3$

$\boxed{x = -3, y = 3}$ ——— solution

(ii) $x + 4y = 18$ ——— ①
$2x + 5y = 24$ ——— ②

To eliminate the term in x, multiply ① by 2.

$2x + 8y = 36$ ——— ① multiplied by 2
$-2x - 5y = -24$ ——— ② multiplied by -1 to set up addition
$3y = 12$ ——— add
$y = 4$
$x + 4(4) = 18$ ——— substitute 4 for y in ①
$x + 16 = 18$
$x = 2$

$\boxed{x = 2, y = 4}$ ——— solution

(iii) $6x - 5y + 70 = 0$ ——— ①
$4x = 3y - 44$ ——— ②

Rearrange the two equations in the same order.

$6x - 5y = -70$ ——— ①
$4x - 3y = -44$ ——— ②

To eliminate the term in y, multiply ① by 3 and ② by -5.

$18x - 15y = -210$ ——— ① multiplied by 3

$-20x + 15y = 220$ ——— ② multiplied by -5

$-2x = 10$ ——— add

$x = -5$

$6(-5) - 5y = -70$ ——— substitute -5 for x in ①

$-30 - 5y = -70$

$-5y = -40$

$y = 8$

$\boxed{x = -5, y = 8}$ ——— solution

D. Solving linear systems in two variables involving fractions

When one or both equations contain decimals or common fractions, it is best to eliminate the decimals or fractions by multiplying; then solve the system as shown in the previous examples.

EXAMPLE 4.1C Solve each of the following systems of equations.

(i) $1.5x + 0.8y = 1.2$
$0.7x + 1.2y = -4.4$

(ii) $\dfrac{5x}{6} + \dfrac{3y}{8} = -1$
$\dfrac{2x}{3} - \dfrac{3y}{4} = -5$

SOLUTION

(i) $1.5x + 0.8y = 1.2$ ——— ①

$0.7x + 1.2y = -4.4$ ——— ②

To eliminate the decimals, multiply each equation by 10.

$15x + 8y = 12$ ——— ③

$7x + 12y = -44$ ——— ④

To eliminate the term in y, multiply ③ by 3 and ④ by 2.

$45x + 24y = 36$ ——— ③ multiplied by 3

$14x + 24y = -88$ ——— ④ multiplied by 2

$31x = 124$ ——— subtract

$x = 4$

$15(4) + 8y = 12$ ——— substitute 4 for x in ③

$60 + 8y = 12$

$8y = -48$

$y = -6$

$\boxed{x = 4, y = -6}$ ——— solution

(ii) $\dfrac{5x}{6} + \dfrac{3y}{8} = -1$ ——— ①

$\dfrac{2x}{3} + \dfrac{3y}{4} = -5$ ——— ②

To eliminate the fractions, multiply ① by 24 and ② by 12.

$$\frac{24(5x)}{6} + \frac{24(3y)}{8} = 24(-1) \quad \text{——— ① multiplied by 24}$$

$$4(5x) + 3(3y) = -24$$

$$20x + 9y = -24 \quad \text{——— ③}$$

$$\frac{12(2x)}{3} + \frac{12(3y)}{4} = 12(-5) \quad \text{——— ② multiplied by 12}$$

$$4(2x) - 3(3y) = -60$$

$$8x - 9y = -60 \quad \text{——— ④}$$

To eliminate the term in y, add ③ and ④.

$$20x + 9y = -24 \quad \text{——— ③}$$

$$8x - 9y = -60 \quad \text{——— ④}$$

$$28x = -84$$

$$x = -3$$

$$20(-3) + 9y = -24 \quad \text{——— substitute } -3 \text{ for } x \text{ in ③}$$

$$-60 + 9y = -24$$

$$9y = 36$$

$$y = 4$$

$$\boxed{x = -3, y = 4} \quad \text{——— solution}$$

POINTERS AND PITFALLS

When removing decimals or fractions from linear systems in two variables, remember that each equation can, if necessary, be multiplied by a *different quantity.*

For example,

(i) Solve $1.2x + 3.5y = 50$ ——— multiply by *10* to eliminate decimals
$2.26x - 0.70y = 6.5$ ——— multiply by *100* to eliminate decimals

(ii) Refer to Example 4.1C (ii). In this example, the first equation is multiplied by a lowest common denominator (LCD) of *24* to eliminate fractions, while the second equation is multiplied by an LCD of *12* to eliminate fractions.

EXERCISE 4.1

A. Solve each of the following systems of equations and check your solutions.

1. $x + y = -9$
$x - y = -7$

2. $x + 5y = 0$
$x + 2y = 6$

3. $5x + 2y = 74$
$7x - 2y = 46$

4. $2x + 9y = -13$
$2x - 3y = 23$

5. $y = 3x + 12$
$x = -y$

6. $3x = 10 - 2y$
$5y = 3x - 38$

B. Solve each of the following systems of equations and check your solutions.

1. $4x + y = -13$
$x - 5y = -19$

2. $6x + 3y = 24$
$2x + 9y = -8$

3. $7x - 5y = -22$
$4x + 3y = 5$

4. $8x + 9y = 129$
$6x + 7y = 99$

5. $12y = 5x + 16$
$6x + 10y - 54 = 0$

6. $3x - 8y + 44 = 0$
$7x = 12y - 56$

C. Solve each of the following systems of equations.

1. $0.4x + 1.5y = 16.8$
$1.1x - 0.9y = 6.0$

2. $6.5x + 3.5y = 128$
$2.5x + 4.5y = 106$

3. $2.4x + 1.6y = 7.60$
$3.8x + 0.6y = 7.20$

4. $2.25x + 0.75y = 2.25$
$1.25x + 1.75y = 2.05$

5. $\frac{3x}{4} - \frac{2y}{3} = \frac{-13}{6}$
$\frac{4x}{5} + \frac{3y}{4} = \frac{123}{10}$

6. $\frac{9x}{5} + \frac{5y}{4} = \frac{47}{10}$
$\frac{2x}{9} + \frac{3y}{8} = \frac{5}{36}$

7. $\frac{x}{3} + \frac{2y}{5} = \frac{7}{15}$
$\frac{3x}{2} - \frac{7y}{3} = -1$

8. $\frac{x}{4} + \frac{3y}{7} = \frac{-2}{21}$
$\frac{2x}{3} + \frac{3y}{2} = \frac{-7}{36}$

4.2 GRAPHING LINEAR EQUATIONS

A. Graphing in a system of rectangular coordinates

A system of rectangular coordinates, as shown in Figure 4.1 below, consists of two straight lines that intersect at right angles in a plane. The *horizontal* line is called the **X axis** while the *vertical* line is called the **Y axis**. The point of intersection of the two axes is called the **origin**.

FIGURE 4.1 Rectangular Coordinates

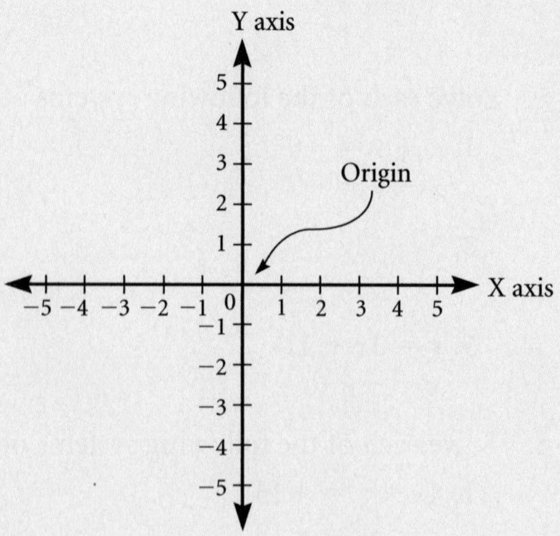

The two axes are used as number lines. By agreement, on the X axis the numbers are positive to the right of the origin and negative to the left. On the Y axis the numbers are positive above the origin and negative below the origin.

The position of any point relative to the pair of axes is defined by an **ordered pair of numbers** (x, y) such that the first number (the x value or ***x* coordinate**) always represents the directed distance of the point from the Y axis. The second number (the y value or ***y* coordinate**) always represents the directed distance of the point from the X axis.

The origin is identified by the ordered pair (0, 0); that is, the coordinates of the origin are (0, 0) since the distance of the point from either axis is zero.

As shown in Figure 4.2, the point marked A is identified by the coordinates (4, 3). That is, the directed distance of the point is four units to the right of the Y axis (its x value or x coordinate is +4), and the directed distance of the point is three units above the X axis (its y coordinate is +3). Note that the point may be found by counting four units to the right along the X axis and then moving three units up parallel to the Y axis.

FIGURE 4.2 Locating a Point

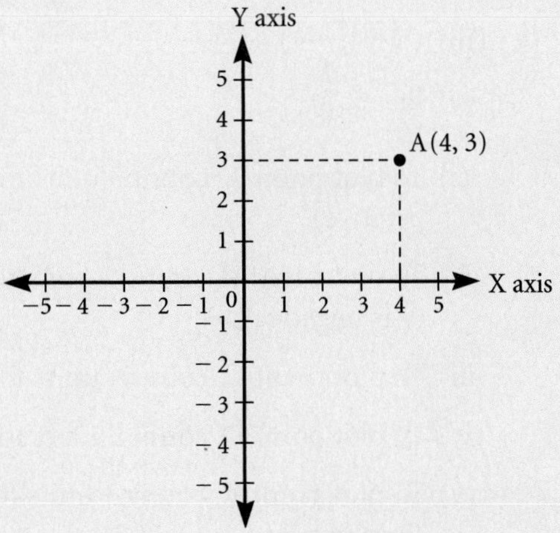

EXAMPLE 4.2A

Determine the coordinates of the points A, B, C, D, E, F, G, and H as marked in the following diagram.

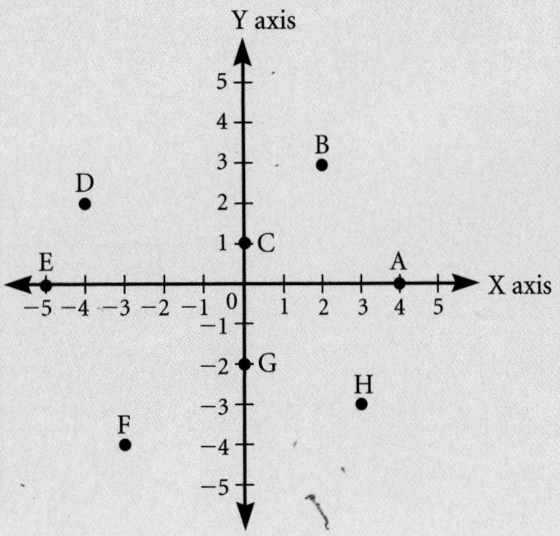

SOLUTION

POINT	COORDINATES	
A	(4, 0)	4 units to the right of the origin ($x = 4$) on the X axis ($y = 0$)
B	(2, 3)	2 units to the right ($x = 2$) and 3 units up ($y = 3$)
C	(0, 1)	on the Y axis ($x = 0$) 1 unit up ($y = 1$)
D	(−4, 2)	4 units to the left ($x = -4$) and 2 units up ($y = 2$)
E	(−5, 0)	5 units to the left ($x = -5$) on the X axis ($y = 0$)
F	(−3, −4)	3 units to the left ($x = -3$) and 4 units down ($y = -4$)
G	(0, −2)	on the Y axis ($x = 0$) 2 units down ($y = -2$)
H	(3, −3)	3 units to the right ($x = 3$) and 3 units down ($y = -3$)

To draw the graphs of linear relations, you must plot two or more points in a set of rectangular axes. To *plot* point (x, y), count the number of units represented by x along the X axis (to the right if x is positive, to the left if x is negative) and then count the number of units represented by y up or down (up if y is positive, down if y is negative).

EXAMPLE 4.2B

Plot the following points in a set of rectangular axes.

(i) A(−3, 4) (ii) B(2, −4)

(iii) C(−4, −4) (iv) D(3, 3)

(v) E(−3, 0) (vi) F(0, −2)

SOLUTION

(i) To plot point A, count 3 units to the left (x is negative) and 4 units up (y is positive).

(ii) To plot point B, count 2 units to the right (x is positive) and 4 units down (y is negative).

(iii) To plot point C, count 4 units to the left and 4 units down.

(iv) To plot point D, count 3 units to the right and 3 units up.

(v) To plot point E, count 3 units to the left and mark the point on the X axis since $y = 0$.

(vi) To plot point F, count 2 units down and mark the point on the Y axis since $x = 0$.

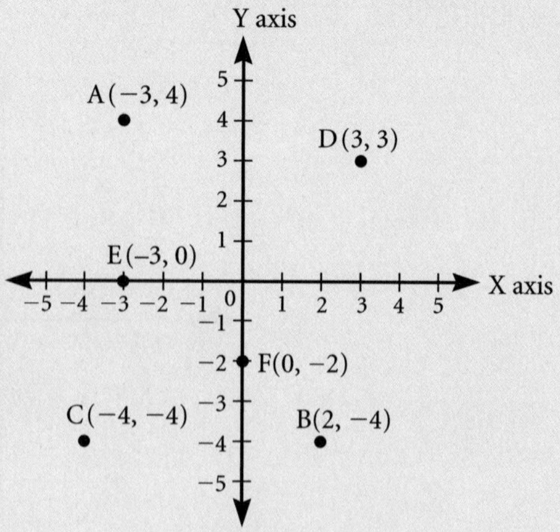

B. Constructing a table of values

To graph linear equations, plot a set of points whose coordinates *satisfy* the equation and then join the points.

A suitable set of points may be obtained by constructing a table of values. Substitute arbitrarily chosen values of x or y in the equation and compute the value of the second variable. The chosen value and the corresponding computed value form an ordered pair (x, y). A listing of such ordered pairs forms a table of values.

EXAMPLE 4.2C

Construct a table of values for

(i) $x = 2y$ for integral values of y from $y = +3$ to $y = -3$;

(ii) $y = 2x - 3$ for integral values of x from $x = -2$ to $x = +4$.

SOLUTION

(i) To obtain the desired ordered pairs, substitute assumed values of y into the equation $x = 2y$.

$y = +3 \qquad x = 2(3) = 6$
$y = +2 \qquad x = 2(2) = 4$
$y = +1 \qquad x = 2(1) = 2$
$y = 0 \qquad x = 2(0) = 0$
$y = -1 \qquad x = 2(-1) = -2$
$y = -2 \qquad x = 2(-2) = -4$
$y = -3 \qquad x = 2(-3) = -6$

Listing the obtained ordered pairs gives the following table of values.

Table of values

x	6	4	2	0	−2	−4	−6	corresponding computed *x* values
y	3	2	1	0	−1	−2	−3	chosen *y* values

(ii) To obtain the desired ordered pairs, substitute assumed values of x into the equation $y = 2x - 3$.

$x = -2 \qquad y = 2(-2) - 3 = -4 - 3 = -7$
$x = -1 \qquad y = 2(-1) - 3 = -2 - 3 = -5$
$x = 0 \qquad y = 2(0) - 3 = 0 - 3 = -3$
$x = 1 \qquad y = 2(1) - 3 = 2 - 3 = -1$
$x = 2 \qquad y = 2(2) - 3 = 4 - 3 = +1$
$x = 3 \qquad y = 2(3) - 3 = 6 - 3 = +3$
$x = 4 \qquad y = 2(4) - 3 = 8 - 3 = +5$

Table of values

x	−2	−1	0	1	2	3	4
y	−7	−5	−3	−1	1	3	5

chosen *x* values
corresponding computed *y* values

Guidelines for constructing a table of values:

(1) Values may be chosen arbitrarily for either x or y.
(2) The values chosen are usually integers.
(3) Integers that yield an integer for the computed value are preferred.

C. Graphing linear equations

To graph a linear equation, you need a minimum of two points. A third point is useful for checking purposes. To graph linear equations,

(1) *construct* a table of values consisting of at least two (preferably three) ordered pairs (x, y);
(2) *plot* the points in a system of rectangular axes;
(3) *join* the points by a straight line.

EXAMPLE 4.2D

Graph each of the following equations.

(i) $x + y = 4$
(ii) $x - y = 5$
(iii) $x = y$
(iv) $y = -2x$
(v) $y = 2x + 100$ for all values of x from $x = 0$ to $x = 200$

SOLUTION

(i) Equation: $x + y = 4$

Table of values

x	0	4	2
y	4	0	2

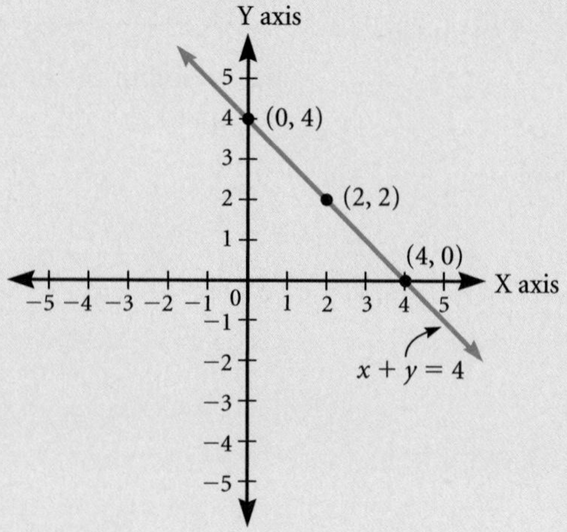

(ii) Equation: $x - y = 5$

Table of values

x	0	5	3
y	−5	0	−2

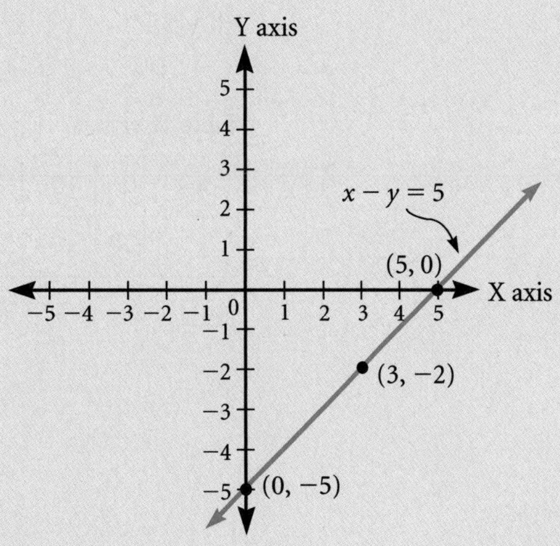

(iii) Equation: $x = y$

Table of values

x	0	3	−3
y	0	3	−3

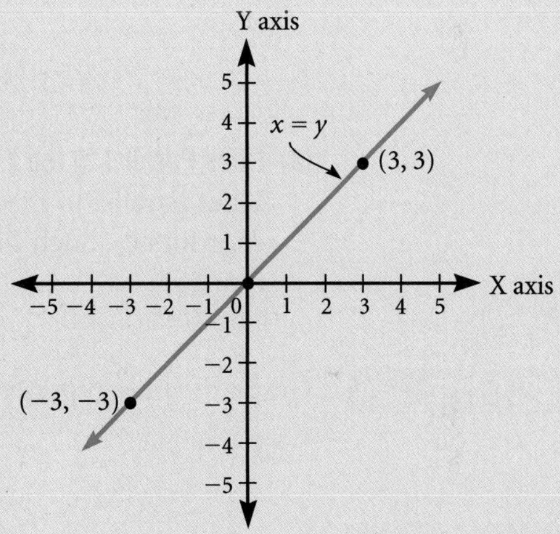

(iv) Equation: $y = -2x$

Table of values

x	0	2	−2
y	0	−4	4

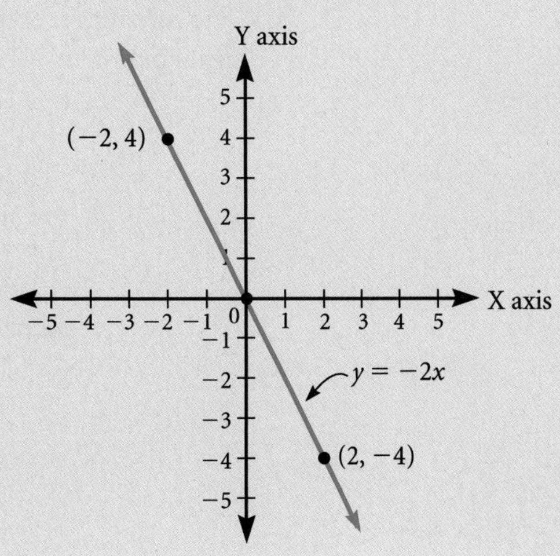

(v) Equation: $y = 2x + 100$ for all values of x from $x = 0$ to $x = 200$

Table of values

x	0	100	200
y	100	300	500

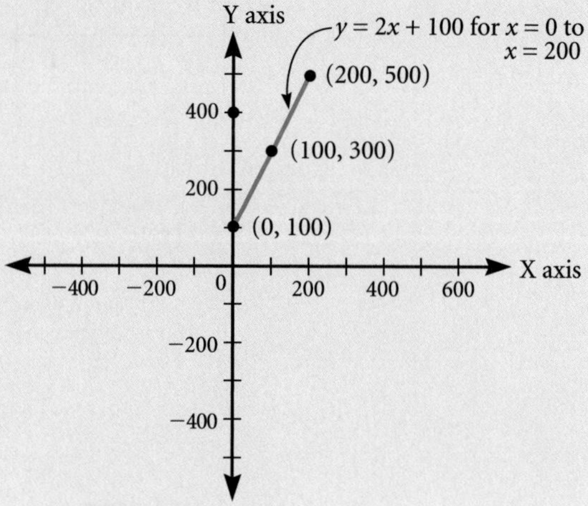

D. Special cases—lines parallel to the axes

(a) Lines Parallel to the X Axis

Lines parallel to the X axis are formed by sets of points that all have the *same* y coordinates. Such lines are defined by the equation $y = b$ where b is any real number.

EXAMPLE 4.2E

Graph the lines represented by

(i) $y = 3$ (ii) $y = -3$

SOLUTION

(i) The line represented by $y = 3$ is a line parallel to the X axis and three units above it.

(ii) The line represented by $y = -3$ is a line parallel to the X axis and three units below it.

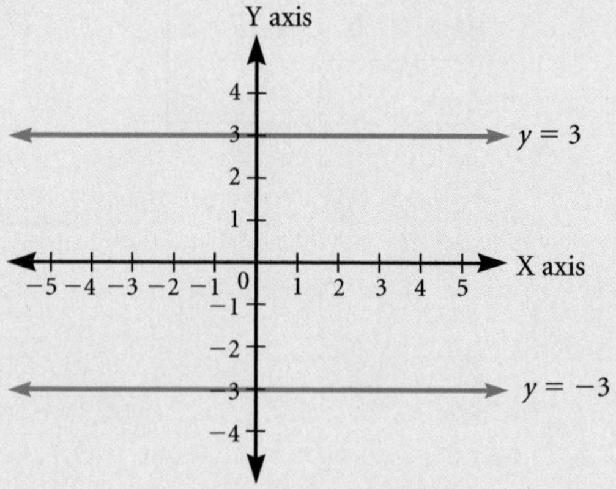

(b) Lines Parallel to the Y Axis

Lines parallel to the Y axis are formed by sets of points that all have the same x coordinates. Such lines are defined by the equation $x = a$ where a is any real number.

EXAMPLE 4.2F

Graph the lines represented by

(i) $x = 3$ (ii) $x = -3$

SOLUTION

(i) The line represented by $x = 3$ is a line parallel to the Y axis and three units to the right of it.

(ii) The line represented by $x = -3$ is a line parallel to the Y axis and three units to the left of it.

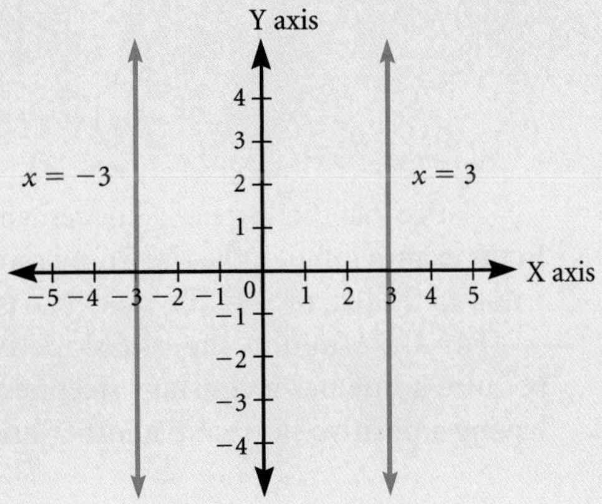

(c) The Axes

X axis The y coordinates of the set of points forming the X axis are zero. Thus the equation $y = 0$ represents the X axis.

Y axis The x coordinates of the set of points forming the Y axis are zero. Thus the equation $x = 0$ represents the Y axis.

E. The slope-y-intercept form of a linear equation

Every line has two important characteristics: its steepness, called the **slope**, and a point where the line intersects with the Y axis, called the ***y*-intercept**.

In more technical terms, **slope** is the ratio of the *rise* of a line to its *run*. The **rise** of a line is the distance along the Y axis between two points on a line. The **run** of a line is the distance along the X axis between the same two points on the line.

As shown in Figure 4.3, point A(1, 3) and point B(2, 1) lie on the line $2x + y = 5$. The *rise* between point A and point B is -2, since you must move 2 units down, parallel to the Y axis, when you move from point A to point B. The *run* between point A and point B is $+ 1$, since you must move 1 unit to the right, parallel to the X axis, when you move from point A to point B. The ratio $^{rise}/_{run}$ is $^{-2}/_{1}$, or -2.

FIGURE 4.3

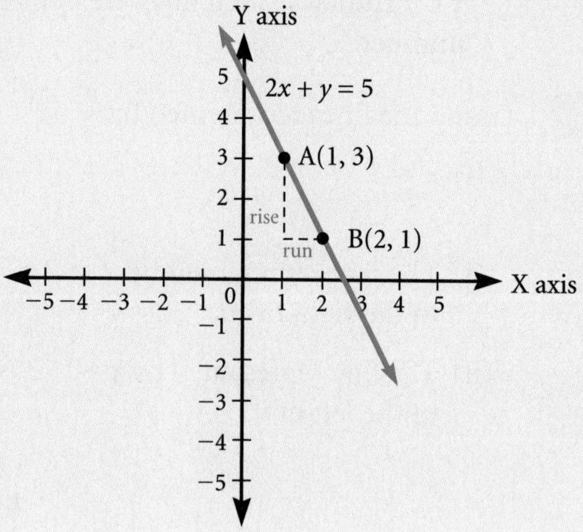

Notice that the slope of a line remains the same if you go from point B to point A. In the example above, the rise from point B to point A is 2 units up, or + 2. The run is 1 unit to the left, or −1. The ratio $^{rise}/_{run}$ is $^{-2}/_{1}$, or −2, the same as was shown earlier.

For any straight line, the slope is the same for *any* two points on the line because a line has a constant steepness. Figure 4.4 shows an example of one line having a positive slope and another line having a negative slope.

FIGURE 4.4

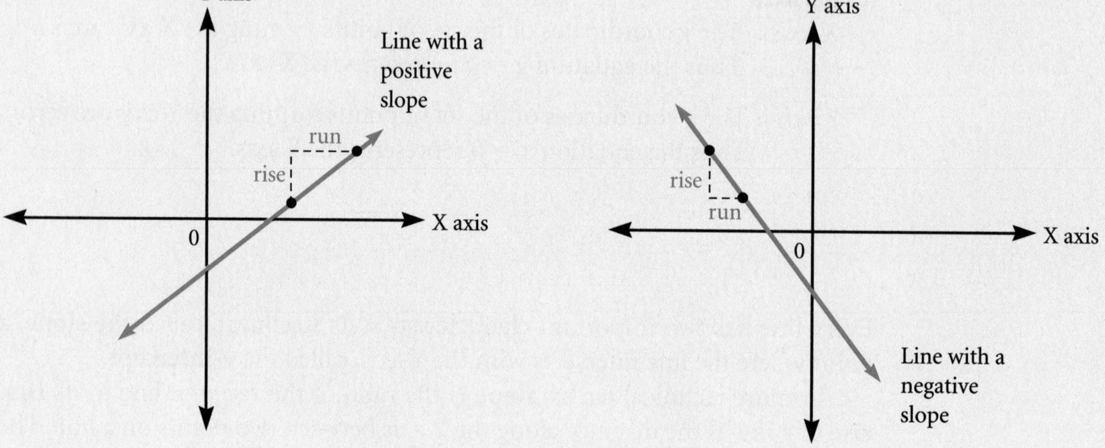

We know from Figure 4.3 that the slope of the line representing $2x + y = 5$ is −2. By rearranging the terms of this equation, we see that the equation of this line can be written $y = -2x + 5$. We say the line's equation is in the form $y = mx + b$. When a linear equation is in this form, it is easy to see that m, the coefficient of x, represents the slope of the line, which is −2 (or $^{-2}/_{1}$ or $^{2}/_{-1}$).

By substituting $x = 0$ into $y = -2x + 5$, we find that $y = 5$. You can see that the line $y = -2x + 5$ crosses the Y axis at the point (0, 5) in Figure 4.3. In the linear equation $y = mx + b$, b is the y-intercept of the line.

The **slope-*y*-intercept form of a linear equation** is a linear equation expressed in the form $y = mx + b$.

$$y = mx + b \quad \text{Formula 4.1}$$

In any equation in the form $y = mx + b$, m is the slope and b is the y-intercept.

EXAMPLE 4.2G

Using algebra, find the slope and y-intercept of each of the following equations.

(i) $y = \frac{2}{3}x - 7$ (ii) $3x + 4y = -2$

SOLUTION

(i) $y = \frac{2}{3}x - 7$ is already in the form $y = mx + b$.

Thus, slope $= \frac{2}{3}$, since $m = \frac{2}{3}$ in the equation $y = \frac{2}{3}x - 7$.

The y-intercept $= -7$, since $b = -7$ in the equation $y = \frac{2}{3}x - 7$

(ii) $3x + 4y = -2$ must be expressed in the form $y = mx + b$.

$-3x + 3x + 4y = -3x - 2$ ——— add $-3x$ to each side

$4y = -3x - 2$ ——— simplify

$y = -\frac{3}{4}x - \frac{1}{2}$ ——— slope-y-intercept form

Thus, slope $= -\frac{3}{4}$, since $m = -\frac{3}{4}$ in the equation $y = -\frac{3}{4}x - \frac{1}{2}$.

The y-intercept $= -\frac{1}{2}$, since $b = -\frac{1}{2}$ in the equation $y = -\frac{3}{4}x - \frac{1}{2}$.

Once you have found m and b, you can use the slope and y-intercept to graph a linear equation.

1. Graph the y-intercept, which is the point $(0, b)$.
2. Find another point on the line by using the slope. Beginning at the y-intercept, move up (if positive) or down (if negative) by the number of units in the rise (the numerator of the slope). Then move right (if positive) or left (if negative) by the number of units in the run (the denominator of the slope), and mark this point.
3. Draw a line through the point you just marked and the y-intercept to represent the linear equation.

EXAMPLE 4.2H

Given the linear equation $6x + 2y = 8$,

(i) rearrange the equation into the slope-y-intercept form;
(ii) determine the values of m and b;
(iii) graph the equation.

SOLUTION

(i)
$$6x + 2y = 8$$
$$-6x + 6x + 2y = -6x + 8 \quad \text{——— add } -6x \text{ to each side}$$
$$2y = -6x + 8 \quad \text{——— simplify}$$
$$y = -3x + 4 \quad \text{——— slope-}y\text{-intercept form}$$

(ii) $m = -3, b = 4$

(iii) Since $b = 4$, the y-intercept is 4, which is represented by the point (0, 4). Since $m = -3$ (or $-3/1$), plot a second point on the graph by beginning at the point (0, 4) and moving 3 units down and 1 unit to the right. (You could also move 3 units up and 1 unit to the left if you consider $m = -3$ to be $m = 3/-1$.) Draw the line that passes through these two points, as shown below.

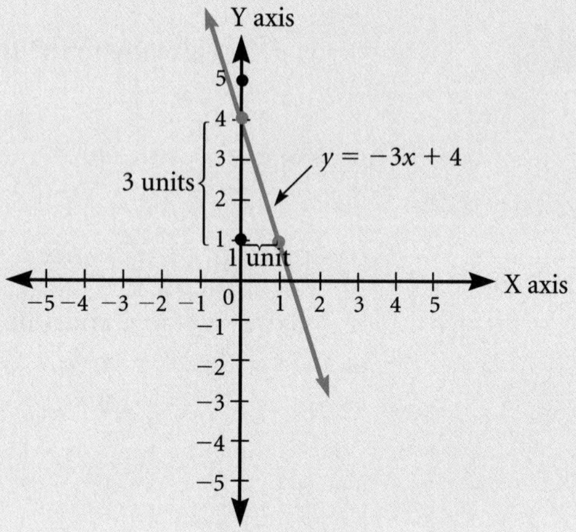

EXAMPLE 4.2I

Graph the equation $x - 2y + 400 = 0$ for all values of x from $x = 0$ to $x = 400$.

SOLUTION

Rearrange the equation into the slope-y-intercept form:

$$-x + x - 2y + 400 - 400 = 0 - x - 400 \quad \text{——— add } -x - 400 \text{ to each side}$$
$$-2y = -x - 400 \quad \text{——— simplify}$$
$$y = \frac{1}{2}x + 200$$
$$m = \frac{1}{2}, \; b = 200$$

Since $b = 200$, the y-intercept is 200, which is represented by the point (0, 200). Since $m = 1/2$, the slope is $1/2$. To make plotting points easier, convert $m = 1/2$ to the equivalent slope $m = 100/200$. Plot a second point on the graph by beginning at the point (0, 200) and moving 100 units up and 200 units to the right.

Draw the line through that point starting at (0, 200) and extend the line to the point where $x = 400$. The graph should indicate that for the last point, $x = 400$ and $y = 400$.

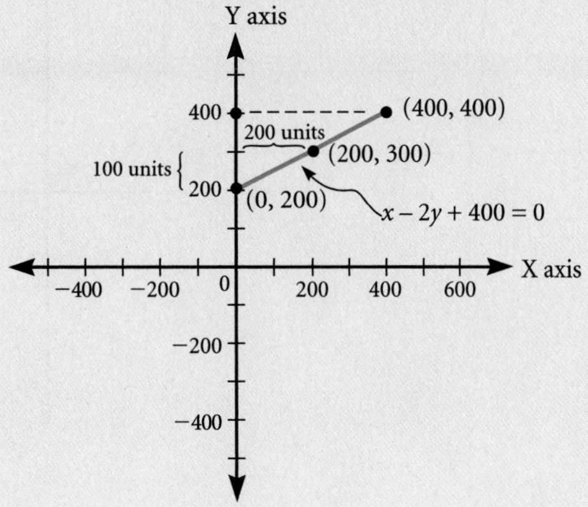

F. Special cases of the slope-*y*-intercept form of a linear equation

1. Lines Parallel to the X Axis

Recall from Section 4.2D that lines parallel to the X axis are defined by the equation $y = b$, where b is any real number. Since there is no mx in the equation $y = b$, the linear equation $y = b$ represents a line parallel to the X axis that crosses the Y axis at point $(0, b)$ and has a slope of 0.

FIGURE 4.5

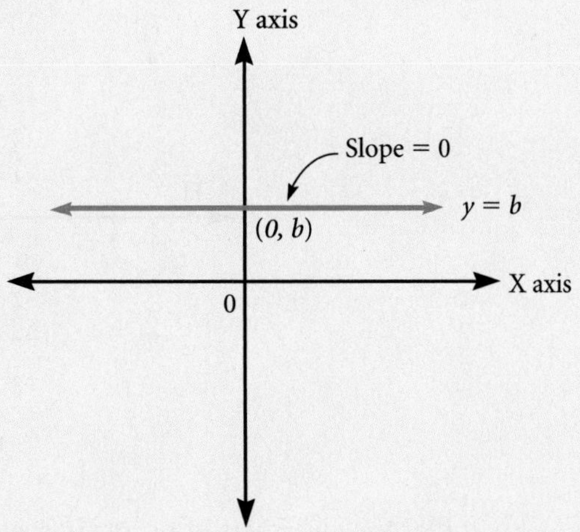

2. Lines Parallel to the Y Axis

Recall from Section 4.2D that lines parallel to the Y axis are defined by the equation $x = a$, where a is any real number. Since there is no y in the equation $x = a$, it cannot be expressed in the form $y = mx + b$. The equation $x = a$ represents a line parallel to the Y axis that crosses the X axis at point $(a, 0)$. Its slope is undefined.

FIGURE 4.6

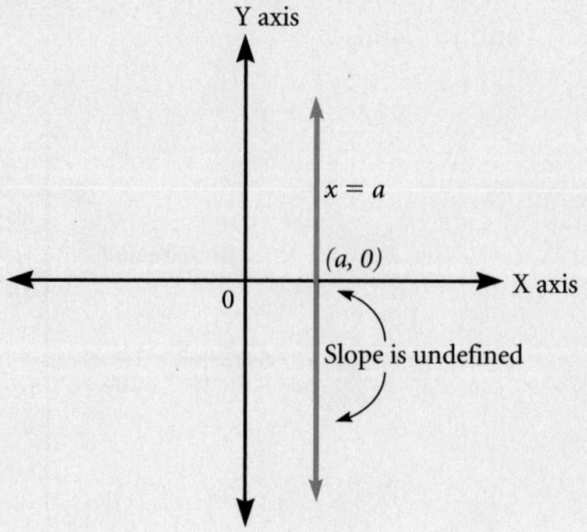

EXERCISE 4.2

A. Do each of the following.

1. Write the coordinates of the points A, B, C, D, E, F, G, and H marked in the diagram below.

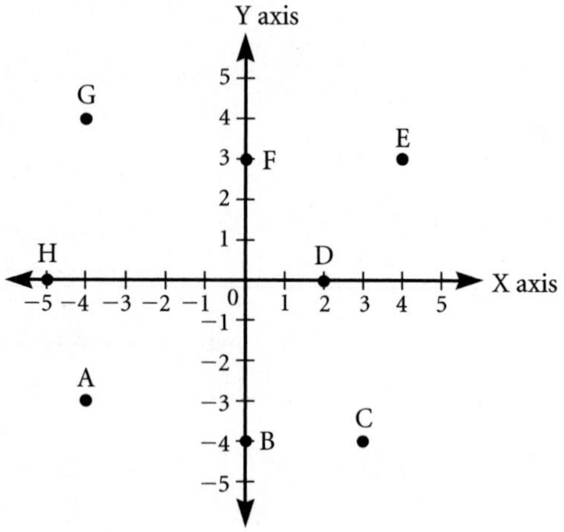

2. Plot the given sets of points in a system of rectangular axes.

a. A(−4, −5), B(3, −2), C(−3, 5), D(0, −4), E(4, 1), F(−2, 0)
b. K(4, −2), L(−3, 2), M(0, 4), N(−2, −4), P(0, −5), Q(−3, 0)

3. Construct a table of values for each of the following equations as shown.

a. $x = y - 2$ for integral values of y from -3 to $+5$
b. $y = 2x - 1$ for integral values of x from $+3$ to -2

c. $y = 2x$ for integral values of x from $+3$ to -3
d. $x = -y$ for integral values of y from $+5$ to -5

4. Using algebra, find the slope and y-intercept of the lines represented by each of the following equations.

a. $4x + 5y = 11$ **b.** $2y - 5x = 10$
c. $1 - \frac{1}{2}y = 2x$ **d.** $3y + 6 = 0$
e. $\sqrt{2x - y} = 3$ **f.** $0.15x + 0.3y - 0.12 = 0$
g. $2 - \frac{1}{2}x = 0$ **h.** $(x - 2)(y + 1) - xy = 2$

B. Graph each of the following equations.

1. $x - y = 3$ **2.** $x + 2y = 4$
3. $y = -x$ **4.** $x = 2y$
5. $3x - 4y = 12$ **6.** $2x + 3y = 6$
7. $y = -4$ **8.** $x = 5$
9. $y = 2x - 3$ **10.** $y = -3x + 9$

C. Graph each of the following equations for all of the values of x indicated.

1. $y = 3x + 20$ for $x = 0$ to $x = 40$

2. $y = -\frac{2}{5}x + 40$ for $x = 0$ to $x = 100$

3. $3x + 4y = 1200$ for $x = 0$ to $x = 400$

4. $3y - 12x - 2400 = 0$ for $x = 0$ to $x = 300$

4.3 GRAPHING LINEAR SYSTEMS OF EQUATIONS IN TWO UNKNOWNS

Systems that consist of two linear equations in two variables may be solved by drawing the graph of each equation. The graph of the system (or solution) is the point where the two lines representing the equations intersect.

EXAMPLE 4.3A Graph the linear system $x + y = 5$ and $x - y = 3$.

SOLUTION

Table of values for $x + y = 5$

x	0	5	2
y	5	0	3

Table of values for $x - y = 3$

x	0	3	2
y	−3	0	−1

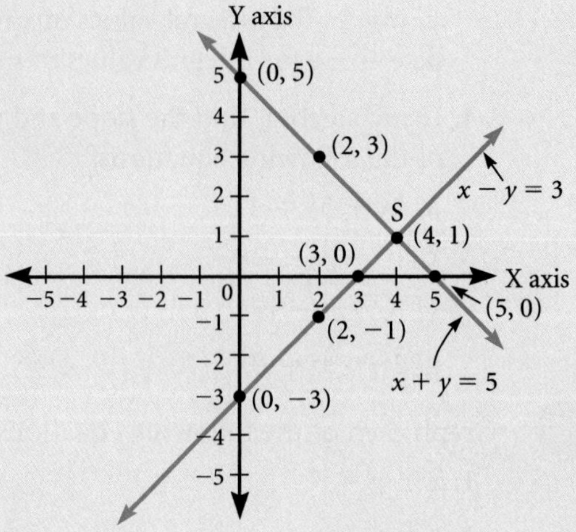

The graph of the system is S, the point of intersection of the two lines, whose coordinates apparently are (4, 1). The coordinates (4, 1) satisfy the equation of either line and are called the *solution* of the system.

EXAMPLE 4.3B Graph the system $x = -2y$ and $y = 3$.

SOLUTION

Table of values for $x = -2y$

x	0	−4	4
y	0	2	−2

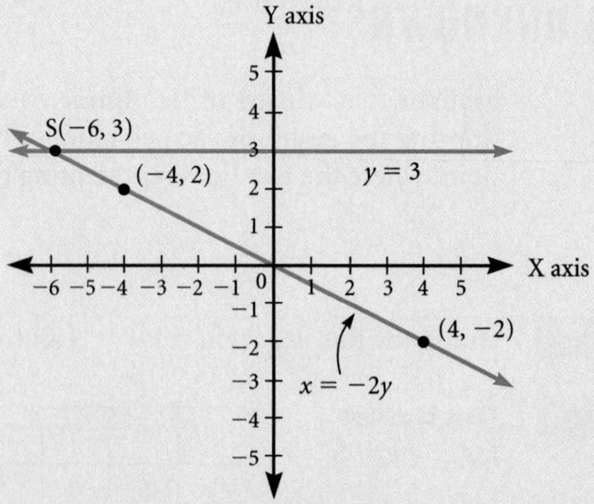

The graph of $y = 3$ is a line parallel to the X axis three units above it. The graph of the system is S, the point of intersection of the two lines. The coordinates of S are apparently $(-6, 3)$ and represent the solution of the system.

EXAMPLE 4.3C

Graph the system $x = y$ and $x - 2y + 2000 = 0$ for all values of x from $x = 0$ to $x = 4000$.

SOLUTION

Table of values for $x = y$

x	0	2000	4000
y	0	2000	4000

or use $m = 1, b = 0$.

Table of values for $x - 2y + 2000 = 0$

x	0	2000	4000
y	1000	2000	3000

or use $m = \frac{1}{2}, b = 1000$.

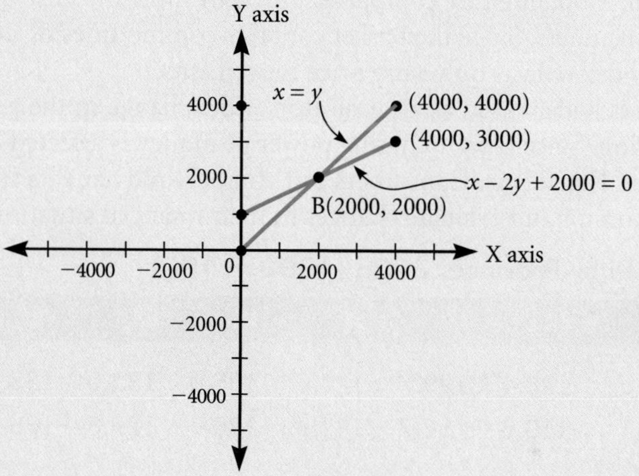

The graph of $x = y$ for all values of x from $x = 0$ to $x = 4000$ is the line joining the points (0, 0) and (4000, 4000). The graph of $x - 2y + 2000 = 0$ for all values of x from $x = 0$ to $x = 4000$ is the line joining the points (0, 1000) and (4000, 3000).

The graph of the system is B, the point of intersection of the two lines. The coordinates of B are apparently (2000, 2000) and represent the solution of the system.

EXERCISE 4.3

A. Solve each of the following linear systems graphically.

1. $x + y = 4$ and $x - y = -4$

2. $x - y = 3$ and $x + y = 5$

3. $x = 2y - 1$ and $y = 4 - 3x$

4. $2x + 3y = 10$ and $3x - 4y = -2$

5. $3x - 4y = 18$ and $2y = -3x$

6. $4x = -5y$ and $2x + y = 6$

7. $5x - 2y = 20$ and $y = 5$

8. $3y = -5x$ and $x = -3$

B. Graph each of the following systems of equations for all values of x indicated.

1. $y - 4x = 0$ and $y - 2x - 10\,000 = 0$ for $x = 0$ to $x = 10\,000$
2. $4x + 2y = 200$ for $x = 0$ to $x = 50$ and $x + 2y = 80$ for $x = 0$ to $x = 80$
3. $3x + 3y = 2400$ and $x = 500$ for $x = 0$ to $x = 800$
4. $2y = 5x$ and $y = 5000$ for $x = 0$ to $x = 8000$

BUSINESS MATH NEWS BOX

The Consumer Price Index

The Consumer Price Index (CPI) is an indicator of changes in consumer prices experienced by Canadians. It is obtained by comparing through time, the cost of a fixed basket of commodities purchased by consumers. Since the basket contains commodities of unchanging or equivalent quantity and quality, the index reflects only pure price movements.

The CPI is widely used as an indicator of the change in the general level of consumer prices or the rate of inflation. Since the purchasing power of money is affected by changes in prices, the CPI is useful to virtually all Canadians. Consumers can compare movements in the CPI to changes in their personal income to monitor and evaluate changes in their financial situation.

Canadian CPI by Province, 2006 (1992 = 100)

Category	BC	AB	SK	MB	ON	PQ	NB	NS	PEI	NL
Food	128.4	129.7	127.6	135.9	131.5	133.8	130.4	129.2	129.5	125.4
Shelter	110.8	152.7	147.3	130.7	129.6	126.5	129.7	130.9	129.2	129.8
Household operations and furnishings	123.4	119.1	114.3	124.0	113.9	114.3	114.0	113.7	124.8	111.9
Clothing and footwear	112.5	101.4	107.2	111.9	96.0	100.1	105.4	110.5	110.1	102.0
Transportation	154.2	165.7	151.8	153.2	159.9	143.4	154.4	148.8	154.2	161.4
Health and personal care	129.7	123.7	116.8	127.5	121.1	122.1	113.9	117.4	119.7	109.7
Recreation, education, and reading	134.0	130.6	130.8	125.9	131.1	112.9	128.1	131.7	127.2	122.5

Source: Table: "2006 Canadian CPI (1992 = 100) — 2004 Information by Province," adapted from Statistics Canada website **http://www40.statcan.ca/l01/cst01/econ09b.htm**. Accessed March 13, 2007.

QUESTIONS

1. Which province has the lowest increase in the food index?
2. In which provinces did the CPI decrease for transportation? Explain this result.
3. Calculate the overall average change in the CPI by province.

4.4 PROBLEM SOLVING

A. Problems leading to one equation in two variables

In many problems, the relationship between two or more variables can be represented by setting up linear equations. To find the solution to such problems, there must be as many equations as there are variables.

In the case of problems involving two variables, two equations are needed to obtain a solution. If only one equation can be set up, you can represent the relationship between the two variables graphically.

EXAMPLE 4.4A

A manufacturer processes two types of products through the Finishing Department. Each unit of Product A needs 20 time units in Finishing while each unit of Product B needs 30 time units. Per day, 1200 time units are available. Set up an equation that describes the relationship between the number of units of each product that can be processed daily in Finishing. Graph the relationship.

SOLUTION

Let the number of units of Product A that can be processed daily be represented by x, and let the number of units of Product B be represented by y. Then the number of time units required per day for Product A is $20x$ and the number of time units for Product B is $30y$. The total number of time units per day needed by both products is $20x + 30y$. Since 1200 time units are available,

$20x + 30y = 1200$

Table of values

x	60	0	30
y	0	40	20

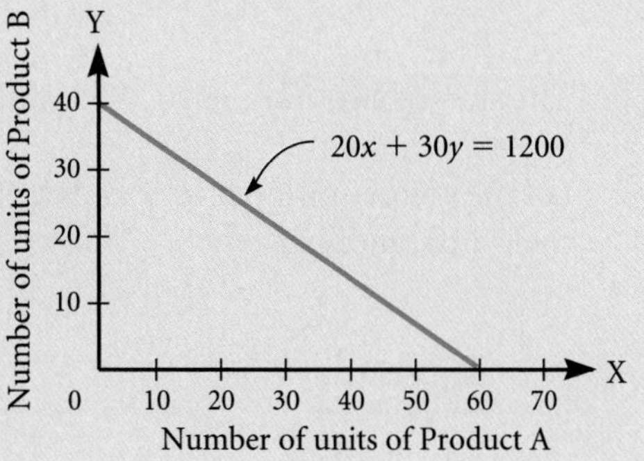

EXAMPLE 4.4B

The Olympic Swim Club rents pool facilities from the city at $2000 per month. Coaching fees and other expenses amount to $40 per swimmer per month. Set up an equation that describes the relationship between the number of swimmers and the total monthly cost of operating the swim club. Graph the relationship.

SOLUTION

Let the number of swimmers be represented by x, and let the total monthly cost be represented by $\$y$. Then the monthly coaching fees and expenses are $\$40x$ and total monthly costs amount to $\$(2000 + 40x)$.

$y = 2000 + 40x$

Table of values

x	0	50	100
y	2000	4000	6000

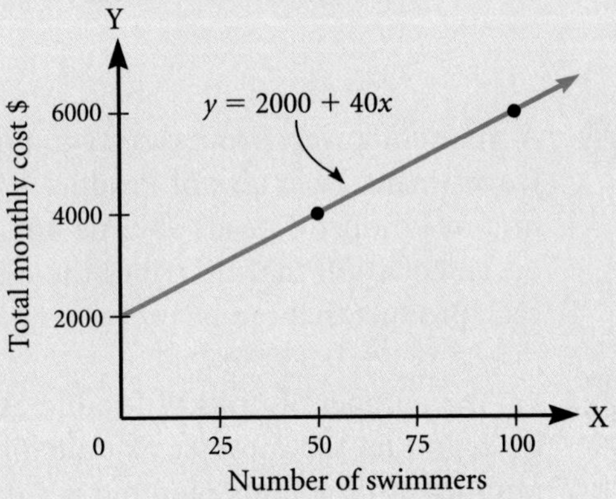

B. Problems leading to systems of equations

The problems in Chapter 2 were solved by using one variable, expressing all the information in terms of that variable, and setting up one equation. To solve many problems, using more than one variable and setting up a system of equations is necessary.

EXAMPLE 4.4C

The sum of two numbers is 64 and their difference is 10. Find the two numbers.

SOLUTION

Let the greater number be x and the smaller number be y. Their sum is $x + y$ and their difference is $x - y$.

$$x + y = 64 \quad \text{①}$$
$$x - y = 10 \quad \text{②}$$
$$2x = 74$$
$$x = 37$$
$$37 + y = 64$$
$$y = 27$$

The larger number is 37 and the smaller number is 27.

Check
Sum, $37 + 27 = 64$
Difference, $37 - 27 = 10$

EXAMPLE 4.4D

Kim invested a total of \$24 000 in two mutual funds. Her investment in the Equity Fund is \$4000 less than three times her investment in the Bond Fund. How much did Kim invest in the Equity Fund?

SOLUTION

Let the amount invested in the Bond Fund be $\$x$; let the amount invested in the Equity Fund be $\$y$; the total amount invested is

$$x + y = 24\,000 \quad \text{——— ①}$$

\$4000 less than three times the investment in the Bond Fund is

$$y = 3x - 4000 \quad \text{——— ②}$$

Substitute ② in ①

$$\begin{aligned} x + 3x - 4000 &= 24\,000 \\ 4x &= 28\,000 \\ x &= 7000 \\ y &= 3(7000) - 4000 \\ y &= 17\,000 \end{aligned}$$

The amount invested in the Equity Fund is \$17 000.

EXAMPLE 4.4E

The Clarkson Soccer League has set a budget of \$3840 for soccer balls. High-quality game balls cost \$36 each while lower-quality practice balls cost \$20 each. If 160 balls are to be purchased, how many balls of each type can be purchased to exactly use up the budgeted amount?

SOLUTION

Let the number of game balls be x;
let the number of practice balls be y;
then the total number of balls is $x + y$.

$$x + y = 160 \quad \text{——— ①}$$

The value of the x game balls is $\$36x$;
the value of the y practice balls is $\$20y$;
the total value of the balls is $\$(36x + 20y)$.

$$\begin{aligned} 36x + 20y &= 3840 && \text{——— ②} \\ -20x - 20y &= -3200 && \text{——— ① multiplied by } -20 \\ \hline 16x &= 640 && \text{——— add} \\ x &= 40 \\ 40 + y &= 160 && \text{——— substitute in ①} \\ y &= 120 \end{aligned}$$

Forty game balls and 120 practice balls can be bought.

EXAMPLE 4.4F

The Dutch Nook sells two brands of coffee—one for \$7.90 per kilogram, the other for \$9.40 per kilogram. If the store owner mixes 20 kilograms and intends to sell the mixture for \$8.50 per kilogram, how many kilograms of each brand should she use to make the same revenue as if the two brands were sold unmixed?

SOLUTION

Let the number of kilograms of coffee sold for \$7.90 be x;
let the number of kilograms of coffee sold for \$9.40 be y;
then the number of kilograms of coffee in the mixture is $x + y$.

$$x + y = 20 \quad \text{——— ① weight relationship}$$

The value of coffee in the mixture selling for \$7.90 is \$7.90x;
the value of coffee in the mixture selling for \$9.40 is \$9.40y;
the total value of the mixture is \$(7.90x + 9.40y). Since each kilogram of mixture is to be sold at \$8.50, the value is \$8.50(20), or \$170.

$7.90x + 9.40y = 170.00$	② value relationship
$79x + 94y = 1700.0$	② multiplied by 10
$79x + 79y = 1580.0$	① multiplied by 79
$15y = 120.00$	subtract
$y = 8$	
$x + 8 = 20$	substitute in ①
$x = 12$	

The store owner should mix 12 kilograms of coffee selling for \$7.90 per kilogram with 8 kilograms of coffee selling for \$9.40 per kilogram.

Check
Weight: $12 + 8 = 20$ kg
Value: $12 \times 7.90 + 8 \times 9.40 = 94.80 + 75.20 = \$170.00$

EXERCISE 4.4

A. Set up an equation that describes the relationship between the two variables in each of the following. Graph that relationship.

1. A manufacturer makes two types of products. Profit on Product A is \$30 per unit while profit on Product B is \$40 per unit. Budgeted monthly profit is \$6000.
2. Nakia Company manufactures two products. Product 1 requires three hours of machine time per unit while Product 2 requires four hours of machine time per unit. There are 120 hours of machine time available per week.
3. U-Save-Bucks tax consulting service rents space at \$200 per week and pays the accounting personnel \$4 per completed tax return.
4. Raimi is offered a position as a sales representative. The job pays a salary of \$500 per month plus a commission of 10% on all sales.

B. Set up a system of simultaneous equations to solve each of the following problems.

1. The sum of two numbers is 24. If twice the larger number is three more than three times the smaller number, what are the two numbers?
2. The difference between seven times a number and four times a second number is 12. The sum of three-fourths of the first number and two-thirds of the second number is 21. Find the two numbers.

3. Loblaws sells two brands of Jam. Brand X sells for \$2.25 per jar while the No-Name brand sells for \$1.75 per jar. If 140 jars were sold for a total of \$290, how many jars of each brand were sold?

4. Nancy's sales last week were \$140 less than three times Andrea's sales. Together they sold \$940. Determine how much each person sold last week.

5. Kaya and Fred agree to form a partnership. The partnership agreement requires that Fred invest \$2500 more than two-thirds of what Kaya is to invest. If the total investment in the partnership is to be \$55 000, how much should each partner invest?

6. A Brush with Wood has been producing 2320 chairs a day working two shifts. The second shift has produced 60 chairs fewer than four-thirds of the number of chairs produced by the first shift. Determine the number of chairs each shift has produced.

7. An inventory of two types of floodlights showed a total of 60 lights valued at \$2580. If Type A cost \$40 each while Type B cost \$50 each, how many of each type of floodlight were in inventory?

8. A machine requires four hours to make a unit of Product A and three hours to make a unit of Product B. Last month the machine operated for 200 hours producing a total of 60 units. How many units of each type of product did it produce?

9. Marysia has saved \$85.75 in quarters and loonies. If she has one quarter more than three-fourths the number of loonies, how many coins of each type does Marysia have?

10. The local amateur football club spent \$675 on tickets to a professional football game. If the club bought three fewer fifteen-dollar tickets than four-fifths the number of twelve-dollar tickets, how many tickets of each type did the club buy?

Review Exercise

1. Using algebra, find the slope and y-intercept of the line represented by each of the following equations.
   (a) $7x + 3y = 6$ (b) $10y = 5x$
   (c) $\frac{2y - 3x}{2} = 4$ (d) $1.8x + 0.3y - 3 = 0$
   (e) $\frac{1}{3}x = -2$ (f) $11x - 33y = 99$
   (g) $xy - (x + 4)(y - 1) = 8$
   (h) $2.5y - 12.5 = 0$

2. Graph each of the following.
   (a) $2x - y = 6$ (b) $3x + 4y = 0$
   (c) $5x + 2y = 10$ (d) $y = -3$
   (e) $5y = -3x + 15$ (f) $5x - 4y = 0$
   (g) $x = -2$ (h) $3y = -4x - 12$

3. Graphically solve each of the following.
   (a) $3x + y = 6$ and $x - y = 2$
   (b) $x + 4y = -8$ and $3x + 4y = 0$
   (c) $5x = 3y$ and $y = -5$
   (d) $2x + 6y = 8$ and $x = -2$
   (e) $y = 3x - 2$ and $y = 3$
   (f) $y = -2x$ and $x = 4$
   (g) $x = -2$ and $3x + 4y = 12$
   (h) $y = -2$ and $5x + 3y = 15$

4. Solve each of the following systems of equations.
   (a) $3x + 2y = -1$, $5x + 3y = -2$ (b) $4x - 5y = 25$, $3x + 2y = 13$
   (c) $y = -10x$, $3y = 29 - x$ (d) $2y = 3x + 17$, $3x = 11 - 5y$
   (e) $2x - 3y = 13$, $3x - 2y = 12$ (f) $2x = 3y - 11$, $y = 13 + 3x$
   (g) $2a - 3b - 14 = 0$, $a + b - 2 = 0$ (h) $a + c = -10$, $8a + 4c = 0$
   (i) $3b - 3c = -15$, $-2b + 4c = 14$ (j) $48a - 32b = 128$, $16a + 48b = 32$
   (k) $0.5m + 0.3n = 54$, $0.3m + 0.7n = 74$ (l) $\frac{3}{4}m + \frac{5}{8}n = \frac{3}{4}$, $\frac{5}{6}n + \frac{2}{3}m = \frac{7}{9}$

5. Write an equation describing the relationship between the two variables in each of the following problems and graph the relationship.
   (a) Sun 'N' Ski Travel pays for radio advertising at the fixed rate of \$1000 per week plus \$75 per announcement during the week.
   (b) The Bi-Products Company markets two products. Each unit of Product A requires five units of labour while each unit of Product B requires two units of labour. Two hundred units of labour are available per time period.

6. Set up a system of equations to solve each of the following problems.
   (a) Find two numbers such that the sum of six times the first number and five times the second number is 93 and the difference between three-quarters of the first number and two-thirds of the second number is zero.
   (b) The college theatre collected \$1300 from the sale of 450 tickets. If the tickets were sold for \$2.50 and \$3.50 respectively, how many tickets were sold at each price?
   (c) A jacket and two pairs of pants together cost \$175. The jacket is valued at three times the price of one pair of pants. What is the value of the jacket?
   (d) Three cases of White Bordeaux and five cases of Red Bordeaux together cost \$438. Each case of Red Bordeaux costs \$6 less than twice the cost of a case of White Bordeaux. Determine the cost of a case of each type.

Self-Test

1. Using algebra, find the slope and y-intercept of the line represented by each of the following questions.
   (a) $4y + 11 = y$
   (b) $\frac{2}{3}x - \frac{1}{9}y = 1$
   (c) $x + 3y = 0$
   (d) $-6y - 18 = 0$
   (e) $13 - \frac{1}{2}x = 0$
   (f) $ax + by = c$

2. Graphically solve each of the following systems of equations.
   (a) $y = -x - 2$ and $x - y = 4$
   (b) $3x = -2y$ and $x = 2$

3. Graph each of the following systems of equations for all values of x indicated.
   (a) $-x = -55 + y$ and $y = 30$ for $x = 0$ to $x = 55$
   (b) $x = 125$ and $3x + 2y + 600 = 0$ for $x = 0$ to $x = 200$

4. Solve each of the following systems of equations.
   (a) $6x + 5y = 9$
   $4x - 3y = 25$
   (b) $12 - 7x = 4y$
   $6 - 2y = 3x$
   (c) $0.2a + 0.3b = 0$
   $0.7a - 0.2b = 250$
   (d) $\frac{4}{3}b - \frac{3}{5}c = -\frac{17}{3}$
   $\frac{5}{6}b + \frac{4}{9}c = \frac{5}{9}$

5. Erica Lottsbriner invests \$12 000 so that part earns interest at 4% per annum and part at 6% per annum. If the total annual interest on the investment is \$560, how much has Erica invested at each rate?

6. Eyad and Rahia divide a profit of \$12 700. If Eyad is to receive \$2200 more than two-fifths of Rahia's share, how much will Rahia receive?

Challenge Problems

1. Terry invested a total of \$4500. A portion was invested at 4% and the rest was invested at 6%. The amount of Terry's annual return on each portion is the same. Find the average rate of interest Terry earned on the \$4500.

2. In September, Polar Bay Wines had a net revenue of \$574.56 from the sale of 3216 new wine bottles less the refund paid for 1824 returned bottles. In October, net revenue was \$944.88 from the sale of 5208 bottles less the refund paid on 2232 returned bottles. How much did Polar Bay Wines charge per new wine bottle and how much was the refund for each returned bottle?

3. Ezhno, the owner of AAA College Painting, pays wages totalling \$29 760 for a 40-hour work week to a crew consisting of 16 painters and 24 helpers. To keep their jobs, the painters accepted a wage cut of 10% and the helpers a wage cut of 8%. The wage cut reduces Ezhno's weekly payroll by \$2688. What hourly rates of pay does Ezhno pay after the wage cut?

Case Study 4.1 Finding the Right Combination

» Amarjit was preparing his annual tax return when he realized that he had a $28 500 unused RRSP contribution limit. Through discussion with his financial advisor, Amarjit realized that he had not fully contributed to his RRSP in past years.

The advisor suggested that Amarjit borrow funds through an RRSP loan to take advantage of his unused contribution limit, as she believed that his RRSP's growth rate would be higher than the interest paid on the loan.

Amarjit agreed to this idea, and contemplated being more aggressive with his investments. He asked his advisor to discuss investments in the stock market.

The advisor suggested to him that while investing in the stock market had the potential for higher gains, there was also the possibility of losing money. Investing in equities (stocks) was riskier than his current conservative portfolio of bank savings accounts, treasury bills, and guaranteed investment certificates (GICs).

Details of several leading Canadian companies were provided to Amarjit to consider investing in:

Company	Latest Selling Price per Share	52-Week High/Low Price
Goldcorp	$26.36	$45.99/$20.57
TELUS	$62.90	$64.74/$42.62
International Forest Products	$6.65	$8.11/$6.01
Bank of Montreal	$67.60	$70.24/$56.00

QUESTIONS

1. What is the cost of borrowing if Amarjit borrows $28 500 and repays it over a four-year period?
2. How many shares of each stock would he get if he used the $28 500 and invested equally in all four companies?
3. Suppose Amarjit decided to only buy shares in TELUS and Goldcorp. How many shares of each would he get if used the $28 500 and bought three times as many shares of TELUS as he bought of Goldcorp?
4. Suppose Amarjit decided to only buy shares in International Forest Products and the Bank of Montreal. How many shares of each company would he get if he used the $28 500 and bought two shares of the Bank of Montreal for every three shares of International Forest Products?

Case Study 4.2 What to Produce?

» The Tiny Tikes Toy Company produces play sets and swinging apparatus for children three to eight years of age. The company has developed many different designs, and through experience and testing has decided to produce two designs that were popular with daycare and recreation centres.

Both models consist of prefabricated material and require assembly by the purchaser. The first model, the Jungle Jackie, can be produced for $260 and sold for $450. The second model, the Eagle's Nest, can be produced for $315 and sold for $510.

The company's senior accountant says, "We used a lot of the budget for this year on design and testing, so we really have to watch what we spend on production. The most we can spend to produce Jungle Jackies and Eagle's Nests is $650 500 per month. It's up to the sales manager to decide which models to produce and sell."

The sales manager says, "Let's use the full plant capacity to produce as many Jungle Jackies and Eagle's Nests as we can. The kids are screaming for these things! We can sell all we produce. Let's get as many of these items out there as soon as possible!" The plant's capacity is 2100 units per month.

QUESTIONS

1. Which of the two designs has the greatest percent gross profit per unit based on cost? (Gross profit is the difference between selling price and cost.)
2. (a) Assume Tiny Tikes Toy Company decides to produce as many Jungle Jackies and Eagle's Nests as possible, given the plant's capacity. How many of each model would be produced in one month if the entire $650 500 per month were spent on production?
   (b) What gross profit would be earned when these quantities of Jungle Jackies and Eagle's Nests are sold?
3. A business student from the local college has a summer job in the accounting department of Tiny Tikes Toy Company. She wonders whether it would be possible to produce a different number of Jungle Jackies and Eagle's Nests that would generate greater gross profits. She plays with the numbers for a while and discovers the combination of 2000 Jungle Jackies and 100 Eagle's Nests would do just that.
   (a) Assume that the student is correct and that all the Jungle Jackies and Eagle's Nests produced can be sold. What is the production cost of the combination discovered by the student?
   (b) What gross profit would be earned when these quantities of Jungle Jackies and Eagle's Nests are sold?
   (c) How much more gross profit could be earned if this combination of 2100 units were produced rather than the combination of units calculated in Question 2?

SUMMARY OF FORMULAS

Formula 4.1

$y = mx + b$ Slope-y-intercept form of a linear equation

GLOSSARY

Ordered pair of numbers the coordinates of a point (x, y) *(p. 151)*

Origin the point of intersection of the two axes in a system of rectangular coordinates *(p. 150)*

Rise vertical distance (distance along Y axis) between two points on a line or line segment *(p. 157)*

Run horizontal distance (distance along X axis) between two points on a line or line segment *(p. 157)*

Slope measure of the steepness of a line; it is the ratio of the rise of a line to its run *(p. 157)*

Slope-y-intercept form of a linear equation a linear equation expressed in the form $y = mx + b$ *(p. 159)*

X axis the horizontal reference line in a system of rectangular coordinates *(p. 150)*

x coordinate the first number in an ordered pair of numbers. It describes the position of a point relative to the axes or the directed distance of a point from the vertical axis (Y axis). *(p. 151)*

Y axis the vertical reference line in a system of rectangular coordinates *(p. 150)*

y coordinate the second number in an ordered pair of numbers. It describes the position of a point relative to the axes or the directed distance of a point from the horizontal axis (X axis). *(p. 151)*

y-intercept the y coordinate of the point of intersection of a line and the Y axis *(p. 157)*

USEFUL INTERNET SITES

www.nationalpost.com/financialpost

Financial Post *The Financial Post*, one of Canada's leading business newspapers, provides valuable financial information. Use this site to find information about corporations and their stocks, mutual funds, and articles on the latest financial topics.

www.accountnetguide.com

Morochove's AccountNetGuide This site lists hundreds of useful accounting and finance links, including financial software resources and tax tips with a Canadian emphasis.

CHAPTER 5 Trade Discount, Cash Discount, Markup, and Markdown

OBJECTIVES

Upon completing this chapter, you will be able to do the following:

1. Solve problems involving trade discounts.
2. Calculate equivalent single rates of discount for discount series and solve problems involving discount series.
3. Apply the three most commonly used methods of cash discount.
4. Solve problems involving markup based on either cost or selling price.
5. Solve problems involving markdown.
6. Solve integrated problems involving discounts, markup, and markdown.

Suppose you are the owner of a bicycle manufacturing company. You purchase your raw materials from suppliers, who offer their goods to you at a list, or catalogue, price. You might receive a trade discount if you pay for the materials promptly or if you purchase the materials in bulk. When you sell your bicycles to bicycle retailers, you offer your bicycles at a list, or catalogue, price, and you might offer a discount for prompt payment or bulk purchases. As you can see, we need to be careful, since the same terms are used by different companies to represent different dollar amounts.

INTRODUCTION

A product typically passes through a number of stages of the *merchandising chain* on its way from being a raw material to a finished product purchased by the consumer.

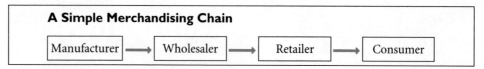

A Simple Merchandising Chain

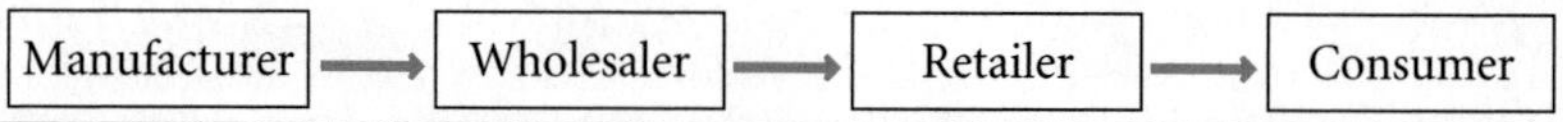

A simple merchandising chain may include manufacturers, wholesalers, and retailers, all of whom must make a profit on the product to remain in business. As the product is purchased and resold along the chain, each merchandiser adds a *markup* above their cost to buy the merchandise, which increases the price of the product. Sometimes a merchandiser sets a *list price*, and then offers a discount from that price in order to sell more of their product or to encourage prompt payment for the product. When the product is sold to the consumer, the regular selling price may be *marked down* to a sale price in response to competitors' prices or other economic conditions.

This chapter deals with trade discount, cash discount, markup, and markdown. These may apply to any of the stages within the merchandising chain.

As you make your way through the merchandising chain, you will find many of the same terms used to represent different things, depending on where you are in the chain. As shown in Figure 5.1, the terms *markup*, *list price*, and *trade discount* are used throughout the merchandising chain.

If you are a manufacturer or supplier, you might mark up an item to create a list, or catalogue, price. If you want to sell the item to a wholesaler for less than that list price, you might offer a trade discount or a series of trade discounts. The wholesaler would add a markup to create a list price at which it offers the item to the retailer. The wholesaler might offer the retailer a trade discount to sell the item for less than the list price. The retailer would then add a markup and offer the item

FIGURE 5.1 Terminology Used in the Merchandising Chain

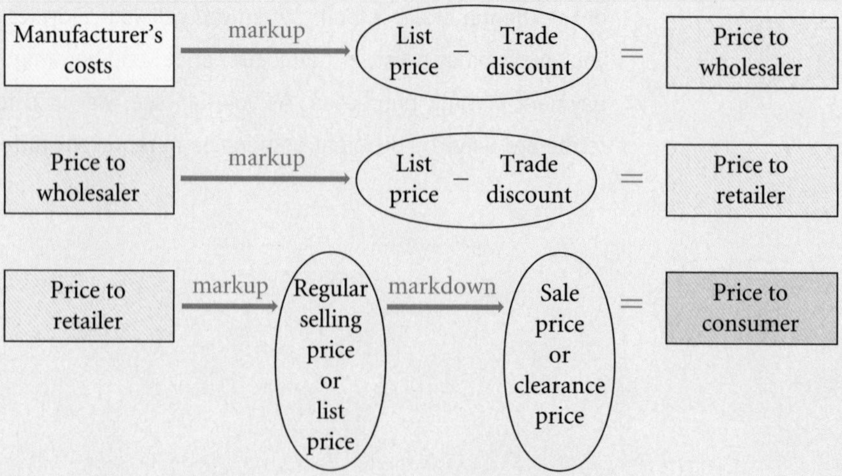

to the consumer at a regular selling price, or list price. The retailer might then offer a markdown on the item to sell the item for less than the regular selling price.

For any particular situation, first identify where you are in the merchandising chain. You will then be able to understand and apply these terms correctly.

5.1 TRADE DISCOUNTS

A. Computing discount amount, discount rate, net price, and list price

The merchandising chain is made up of manufacturers, distributors, wholesalers, and retailers. Merchandise is usually bought and sold among these members of the chain on credit terms. The prices quoted to other members often involve *trade discounts*. A **trade discount** is a reduction of a catalogue or **list price** or **manufacturer's suggested retail price (MSRP)** and is usually stated as a percent of the list price or MSRP. For example, an item with a list price of $35 may be sold at a trade discount of 40%.

Trade discounts are used by manufacturers, wholesalers, and distributors as pricing tools for a number of reasons. The most important reasons are

(a) to facilitate the establishment of price differentials for different groups of customers;.
(b) to facilitate the communication of changes in prices;
(c) to reduce the cost of making changes in prices in published catalogues.

When computing trade discounts, keep in mind that the **rate of discount** is based on the list price.

$$\text{AMOUNT OF DISCOUNT} = \text{RATE OF DISCOUNT} \times \text{LIST PRICE}$$ ——— **Formula 5.1A**

The amount of discount is then subtracted from the list price. The remainder is the **net price**.

$$\text{NET PRICE} = \text{LIST PRICE} - \text{AMOUNT OF DISCOUNT}$$ ——— **Formula 5.2**

To compute the amount of the discount and the net price when the list price and discount rate are known, apply Formula 5.1A to determine the amount of the trade discount, then apply Formula 5.2 to calculate the net price.

EXAMPLE 5.1A

An item listed at $80 is subject to a trade discount of 25%. Compute

(i) the amount of discount;

(ii) the net price.

SOLUTION

(i) Amount of trade discount = Rate of discount × List price
= (0.25)(80.00) = \$20.00

(ii) Net price = List price − Trade discount
= 80.00 − 20.00 = \$60.00

To compute the list price and net price when the discount rate and discount amount are known, rearrange Formula 5.1A to determine the list price, then rearrange Formula 5.2 to determine the net price.

$$\text{LIST PRICE} = \frac{\text{AMOUNT OF DISCOUNT}}{\text{RATE OF DISCOUNT}}$$ **Formula 5.1B**

EXAMPLE 5.1B

The 30% discount on a tennis racket amounts to \$28.98.
Compute

(i) the list price;

(ii) the net price.

SOLUTION

(i) $\text{List price} = \frac{\text{Amount of discount}}{\text{Rate of discount}} = \frac{28.98}{0.30} = \$96.60$

(ii) Net price = List price − Amount of discount
= 96.60 − 28.98 = \$67.62

Since the rate of trade discount is based on a list price, computing a rate of discount involves comparing the amount of discount to the list price.

$$\text{RATE OF TRADE DISCOUNT} = \frac{\text{AMOUNT OF DISCOUNT}}{\text{LIST PRICE}}$$ **Formula 5.1C**

EXAMPLE 5.1C

Find the rate of discount for

(i) skis listed at \$280 less a discount of \$67.20;

(ii) ski gloves listed at \$36.80 whose net price is \$23.92;

(iii) ski sweaters whose net price is \$55.68 after a discount of \$40.32.

SOLUTION

(i) $\text{Rate of discount} = \frac{\text{Amount of discount}}{\text{List price}} = \frac{67.20}{280.00} = 0.24 = 24\%$

(ii) Since Net price = List price − Amount of discount (Formula 5.2),
Amount of discount = List price − Net price = 36.80 − 23.92 = \$12.88

$\text{Rate of discount} = \frac{\text{Amount of discount}}{\text{List price}} = \frac{12.88}{36.80} = 0.35 = 35\%$

(iii) Since Net price = List price − Amount of discount (Formula 5.2),
List price = Net price + Amount of discount = 55.68 + 40.32 = \$96.00

$\text{Rate of discount} = \frac{\text{Amount of discount}}{\text{List price}} = \frac{40.32}{96.00} = 0.42 = 42\%$

B. The net price factor approach

Instead of computing the amount of discount and then deducting this amount from the list price, the net price can be found by using the more efficient net factor approach developed in the following illustration.

Referring back to Example 5.1A, the solution can be restated as follows:

List price	\$80.00
Less trade discount 25% of 80.00	20.00
Net price	\$60.00

Since the discount is given as a percent of the list price, the three dollar values may be stated as percents of list price:

List price	\$80.00	⟶	100% of list price
Less trade discount	20.00	⟶	25% of list price
Net price	\$60.00	⟶	75% of list price

Note: The resulting "75%" is called the **net price factor** or **net factor** (in abbreviated form **NPF**) and is obtained by deducting the 25% discount from 100%.

$$\text{NET PRICE FACTOR (NPF)} = 100\% - \%\ \text{DISCOUNT}$$ Formula 5.3A

The resulting relationship between net price and list price may be stated generally.

$$\text{NET PRICE} = \text{NET PRICE FACTOR (NPF)} \times \text{LIST PRICE}$$ Formula 5.4A

The two relationships represented by Formulas 5.3A and 5.4A can be restated in algebraic terms:

Convert the % discount into its decimal equivalent represented by d and express 100% by its decimal equivalent 1.

$$\text{NET PRICE FACTOR} = 1 - d$$ Formula 5.3B

Let the list price be represented by L and let the net price be represented by N.

$$N = (1 - d)L \quad \text{or} \quad N = L(1 - d)$$ Formula 5.4B

EXAMPLE 5.1D

Find the net price for

(i) list price \$36.00 less 15%;

(ii) list price \$86.85 less $33\frac{1}{3}\%$.

SOLUTION

(i) Net price = Net price factor × List price — using Formula 5.4A
= (100% − 15%)(36.00) — using Formula 5.3A
= (85%)(36) — subtract
= (0.85)(36) — convert the percent into a decimal
= \$30.60

(ii) Net price $= (100\% - 33\tfrac{1}{3}\%)(86.85)$ —— using Formula 5.3A

$= (66\tfrac{2}{3}\%)(86.85)$

$= (0.666667)(86.85)$ —— use a sufficient number of decimals

$= \$57.90$

EXAMPLE 5.1E

A manufacturer can cover its cost and make a reasonable profit if it sells an article for $63.70. At what price should the article be listed so that a discount of 30% can be allowed?

SOLUTION

Let the list price be represented by $L. The net price factor is $1 - d = 100\% - 30\% = 70\% = 0.70$ and the net price is $63.70.

$63.70 = 0.70L$ —— using Formula 5.4A

$$L = \frac{63.70}{0.70} = \$91.00$$

The article should be listed at $91.

C. Discount series

A manufacturer may offer two or more **discounts** to different members of the merchandising chain. If a list price is subject to two or more discounts, these discounts are called a **discount series**. For example, a chain member closest to the consumer might be offered additional discounts, if there are fewer chain members who must make a profit on an item. If the manufacturer wants to encourage large-volume orders or early orders of seasonal items, it may offer additional discounts. For example, a manufacturer might offer a store a 5% discount on orders over 1000 items and an additional discount of 6% for ordering Christmas items in April. It may also offer additional discounts to compensate for advertising, promotion, and service costs handled by merchandising chain members.

When computing the net price, the discounts making up the discount series are applied to the list price successively. The net price resulting from the first discount becomes the list price for the second discount; the net price resulting from the second discount becomes the list price for the third discount; and so on. In fact, finding the net price when a list price is subject to a discount series consists of solving as many discount problems as there are discounts in the discount series.

EXAMPLE 5.1F

An item listed at $150 is subject to the discount series 20%, 10%, 5%. Determine the net price.

SOLUTION

List price	$150.00	Problem 1
Less first discount 20% of 150.00	30.00	
Net price after first discount	$120.00	Problem 2
Less second discount 10% of 120.00	12.00	
Net price after second discount	$108.00	Problem 3
Less third discount 5% of 108.00	5.40	
Net price	$102.60	

Because the solution to Example 5.1F consists of three problems involving a simple discount, the net price factor approach can be used to solve it or any problem involving a series of discounts.

Problem 1 Net price after the first discount
= NPF for 20% discount × Original list price
= (1 − 0.20)(150.00)
= (0.80)(150.00)
= \$120.00

Problem 2 Net price after the second discount
= NPF for 10% discount × Net price after the first discount
= (1 − 0.10)(120.00)
= (0.90)(120.00)
= (0.90)(0.80)(150.00)
= \$108.00

Problem 3 Net price after the third discount
= (1 − 0.05)(108.00)
= (0.95)(108.00)
= (0.95)(0.90)(0.80)(150.00)
= \$102.60

The final net price of \$102.60 is obtained from
(0.95)(0.90)(0.80)(150.00)
= (0.80)(0.90)(0.95)(150.00) ——— **the order of the factors may be rearranged**
= NPF for 20% × NPF for 10% × NPF for 5% × Original list price
= Product of the NPFs for the discounts in the discount series × Original list price
= Net price factor for the discount series × Original list price

This result may be generalized to find the net price for a list price subject to a discount series.

$$\text{NPF FOR THE DISCOUNT SERIES} = \text{NPF FOR THE FIRST DISCOUNT} \times \text{NPF FOR THE SECOND DISCOUNT} \times \ldots \times \text{NPF FOR THE LAST DISCOUNT}$$ ——— **Formula 5.5A**

$$\text{NET PRICE} = \text{NPF FOR THE DISCOUNT SERIES} \times \text{LIST PRICE}$$ ——— **Formula 5.6A**

The two relationships represented by Formulas 5.5A and 5.6A can be restated in algebraic terms:

Let the net price be represented by N,
the original list price by L,
the first rate of discount by d_1,
the second rate of discount by d_2,
the third rate of discount by d_3, and
the last rate of discount by d_n.

Then Formula 5.5A can be shown as

$$\text{NPF FOR A DISCOUNT SERIES} = (1 - d_1)(1 - d_2)(1 - d_3)\ldots(1 - d_n)$$ —— Formula 5.5B

and Formula 5.6A can be shown as

$$\text{NET PRICE} = (1 - d_1)(1 - d_2)(1 - d_3)\ldots(1 - d_n)L$$ —— Formula 5.6B

D. Single equivalent rates of discount

For every discount series, a **single equivalent rate of discount** exists.

SINGLE EQUIVALENT RATE OF DISCOUNT FOR A DISCOUNT SERIES

$$= 1 - \text{NPF FOR THE DISCOUNT SERIES}$$

$$= 1 - [(1 - d_1)(1 - d_2)(1 - d_3)\ldots(1 - d_n)]$$ —— Formula 5.7

EXAMPLE 5.1G

A manufacturer sells skidoos to dealers at a list price of $2100 less 40%, 10%, 5%. Determine

(i) the amount of discount;

(ii) the single rate of discount.

SOLUTION

(i) Net price = NPF × List price

$$= (1 - 0.40)(1 - 0.10)(1 - 0.05)(2100.00)$$
$$= (0.60)(0.90)(0.95)(2100.00)$$
$$= \$1077.30$$

Amount of discount = List price − Net price

$$= 2100.00 - 1077.30 = \$1022.70$$

(ii) $$\text{Single equivalent rate of discount} = \frac{\text{Amount of discount}}{\text{List price}} = \frac{1022.70}{2100.00} = 0.487 = 48.7\%$$

Note: Taking off a single discount of 48.7% has the *same* effect as using the discount series 40%, 10%, 5%. That is, the single discount of 48.7% is equivalent to the discount series 40%, 10%, 5%. Caution: The sum of the discounts in the series, 40% + 10% + 5% or 55%, is *not* equivalent to the single discount.

You can find the single equivalent rate of discount by choosing a suitable list price and computing first the amount of discount and then the rate of discount.

EXAMPLE 5.1H

Find the single equivalent rate of discount for the discount series 30%, 8%, 2%.

SOLUTION

Assume a list price of $1000.

Net price = NPF for the series × List price

$$= (0.70)(0.92)(0.98)(1000.00)$$
$$= (0.63112)(1000.00)$$
$$= \$631.12$$

Amount of discount = 1000.00 − 631.12 = $368.88

$$\text{Single equivalent rate of discount} = \frac{368.88}{1000.00} = 0.36888 = 36.888\%$$

Note: The net price factor for the series = (0.70)(0.92)(0.98) = 0.63112, and 1 − 0.63112 = 0.36888. Therefore, you can find the single equivalent rate of discount by subtracting the net price factor for the series from 1.

Note: When computing or using single equivalent rates of discount, use a sufficient number of decimals to ensure an acceptable degree of accuracy.

EXAMPLE 5.1I

Determine the amount of discount for a $625 list price subject to the discount series 40%, 12.5%, 8⅓%, 2%.

SOLUTION

Single equivalent rate of discount

$= 1 - (1 - 0.40)(1 - 0.125)(1 - 0.08\dot{3})(1 - 0.02)$ ——using Formula 5.7

$= 1 - (0.60)(0.875)(0.91\dot{6})(0.98)$

$= 1 - 0.471625$

$= 0.528375$

$= 52.8375\%$

Amount of discount = Rate of discount × List price

= (0.528375)(625.00)

= $330.23

POINTERS AND PITFALLS

The single equivalent rate of discount is not simply the sum of the individual discounts. Proper application of Formula 5.7 will always result in a single equivalent discount rate that is less than the sum of the individual discounts. You can use this fact to check whether the single equivalent discount rate you calculate is reasonable.

EXAMPLE 5.1J

The local hardware store has listed a power saw for $136 less 30%. A department store in a nearby shopping mall lists the same model for $126 less 20%, less an additional 15%. What additional rate of discount must the hardware store give to meet the department store price?

SOLUTION

Hardware store net price = 136.00(0.70)	$95.20
Department store price = 126.00(0.80)(0.85)	85.68
Additional discount needed	$ 9.52

$$\text{Additional rate of discount needed} = \frac{9.52}{95.20} = 0.10 = 10\%$$

EXAMPLE 5.1K

Redden Distributors bought a shipment of camcorders at a net price of $477.36 each, after discounts of 15%, 10%, 4%. What is the list price?

SOLUTION

Let the list price be $L.

The net price factor is (0.85)(0.90)(0.96) ——using Formula 5.5A

The net price is \$477.36.

$477.36 = L(0.85)(0.90)(0.96)$

$$L = \frac{477.36}{(0.85)(0.90)(0.96)} = \$650.00$$

The camcorders were listed at \$650.

EXERCISE 5.1

A. Find the missing values (represented by question marks) for each of the following questions.

	Rate of Discount	List Price	Amount of Discount	Net Price
1.	45%	\$ 24.60	?	?
2.	$16\frac{2}{3}\%$	\$184.98	?	?
3.	?	\$ 76.95	?	\$ 51.30
4.	?	\$724.80	?	\$616.08
5.	?	?	\$37.89	\$214.71
6.	?	?	\$19.93	\$976.57
7.	62.5%	?	\$83.35	?
8.	1.5%	?	\$13.53	?
9.	37.5%	?	?	\$ 84.35
10.	22.5%	?	?	\$121.29

B. Find the missing values (represented by question marks) for each of the following questions.

	Rate of Discount	List Price	Net Price	Single Equivalent Rate of Discount
1.	25%, 10%	\$ 44.80	?	?
2.	$33\frac{1}{3}\%$, 5%	\$126.90	?	?
3.	40%, 12.5%, 2%	\$268.00	?	?
4.	20%, $16\frac{2}{3}\%$, 3%	\$ 72.78	?	?
5.	35%, $33\frac{1}{3}\%$, 10%	?	\$617.50	?
6.	20%, 20%, 10%	?	\$ 53.28	?

C. Answer each of the following questions.

1. An item with a list price of \$125.64 is offered at a discount of 37.5%. What is the net price?

2. An item with a list price of \$49.98 is offered at a discount of $16\frac{2}{3}\%$. What is the net price?

3. A mountain bike listed for \$975 is sold for \$820. What rate of discount was allowed?

4. A washer-dryer combination listed at \$1136 has a net price of \$760. What is the rate of discount?

5. A 17.5% discount on a flat-screen TV amounts to $560. What is the list price?

6. Golf World sells a set of golf clubs for $762.50 below suggested retail price. Golf World claims that this represents a 62.5% discount. What is the suggested retail price (or list price)?

7. A $16\frac{2}{3}\%$ discount allowed on a silk shirt amounted to $14.82. What was the net price?

8. A store advertises a discount of $44.75 on a screwdriver set. If the discount is 25%, for how much were the sets of screwdrivers sold?

9. The net price of a freezer after a discount of $16\frac{2}{3}\%$ is $355. What is the list price?

10. The net price of an article is $63.31. What is the suggested retail price (the list price) if a discount of 35% was allowed?

11. Compute the equivalent single rate of discount for each of the following discount series.
(a) 30%, 12.5%
(b) $33\frac{1}{3}\%$, 20%, 3%

12. Determine the equivalent single rate of discount for each of the following series of discounts.
(a) $16\frac{2}{3}\%$, 7.5%
(b) 25%, $8\frac{1}{3}\%$, 2%

13. An outdoor furniture set is listed for $599 less 30%, 20%, 5%.
(a) What is the net price?
(b) What is the total amount of discount allowed?
(c) What is the exact single rate of discount that was allowed?

14. A power saw is listed for $174 less $16\frac{2}{3}\%$, 10%, 8%.
(a) What is the net price?
(b) What is the total amount of discount allowed?
(c) What is the exact single rate of discount that was allowed?

15. A compressor is listed for $786.20 less 36%, 10%, 2%.
(a) What is the net price?
(b) What is the total amount of discount allowed?
(c) What is the exact single rate of discount that was allowed?

16. A tractor is listed for $1293.44 less $18\frac{1}{3}\%$, $9\frac{1}{9}\%$, 3%.
(a) What is the net price?
(b) What is the total amount of discount allowed?
(c) What is the exact single rate of discount that was allowed?

17. An item listed by a wholesaler for $750 less 20%, 5%, 2% is reduced at a clearance sale to $474.81. What additional rate of discount was offered?

18. An office desk listed at $440 less 25%, 15% is offered at a further reduced price of $274.89. What additional rate of discount was offered?

19. An electronic game listed at $180 less 30%, 12.5%, 5% is offered at a further reduced price of $99.50. What additional rate of discount was offered?

20. A computer listed at $1260 less $33\frac{1}{3}$%, $16\frac{2}{3}$% is offered at a clearance price of $682.50. What additional rate of discount was offered?

21. Arrow Manufacturing offers discounts of 25%, 12.5%, 4% on a line of products. For how much should an item be listed if it is to be sold for $113.40?

22. What is the list price of an article that is subject to discounts of $33\frac{1}{3}$%, 10%, 2% if the net price is $564.48?

23. A distributor lists an item for $85 less 20%. To improve lagging sales, the net price of the item is reduced to $57.80. What additional rate of discount does the distributor offer?

24. A hat is listed for $66 less 40%. The net price of the hat is further reduced to $35.64. What additional rate of discount is offered?

25. Galaxy Jewellers sells diamond necklaces for $299 less 25%. Brilliants Jewellers offers the same necklace for $350 less 35%, 10%. What additional rate of discount must Galaxy offer to meet the competitor's price?

26. Polar Bay Wines advertises California Juice listed at $125 per bucket at a discount of 24%. A nearby competitor offers the same type of juice for $87.40 per bucket. What additional rate of discount must Polar Bay Wines give to meet the competitor's price?

5.2 PAYMENT TERMS AND CASH DISCOUNTS

A. Basic concepts

Manufacturers, wholesalers, distributors, and retailers usually sell amongst each other goods on credit rather than for cash. An invoice for the goods is sent, and the seller specifies **payment terms** on the invoice. These payment terms indicate when the invoice amount is due for payment and how much is to be paid. The business selling the goods can offer a **cash discount** to encourage prompt payment. This discount reduces the amount to be paid, and is based on the original amount of the invoice, the discount rate, and the timing of the payment or payments.

All payment terms have three things in common:

1. The **rate of discount** is stated as a percent of the net amount of the invoice. The net amount of the invoice is the amount after trade discounts are deducted.
2. The **discount period** is stated, indicating the time period when the cash discount can be applied.
3. The **credit period** is stated, indicating the time period when the invoice must be paid.

If payment is not made during the stated discount period, the net amount of the invoice is to be paid by the end of the credit period. The end of the credit period is called the *due date*, and is either stipulated by the payment terms or implied by the prevailing business practice. If payment is not made by the due date, the account is considered to be overdue and may be subject to a late payment fee or interest charges.

Cash discounts are offered in a variety of ways. The three most commonly used methods are

1. ordinary dating;
2. end-of-the-month dating;
3. receipt-of-goods dating.

The mathematics of working with cash discounts is similar to that used in working with trade discounts.

B. Ordinary dating

The most frequently used method of offering a cash discount is **ordinary dating,** and the most commonly used payment terms are *2/10, n/30* (read "two ten, net thirty").

This payment term means that if payment is made *within* ten days of the date of the invoice, a discount of 2% may be deducted from the net amount of the invoice. Otherwise, payment of the net amount of the invoice is due within 30 days. (See Figure 5.2.)

FIGURE 5.2 **Interpretation of Payment Terms**

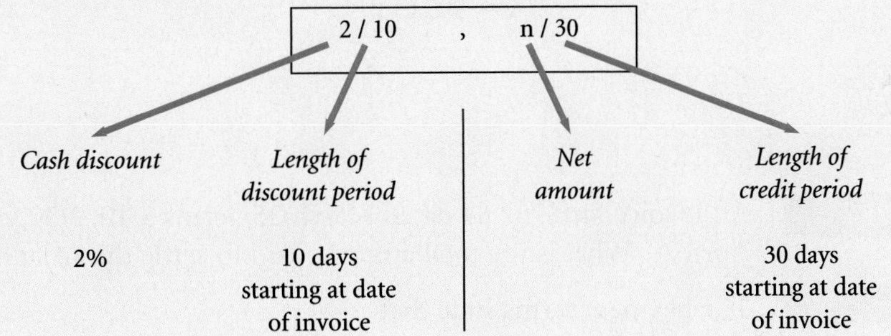

EXAMPLE 5.2A Determine the payment needed to settle an invoice with a net amount of $950 dated September 22, terms 2/10, n/30, if the invoice is paid

(i) on October 10;

(ii) on October 1.

SOLUTION The terms of the invoice indicate a credit period of 30 days and state that a 2% discount may be deducted from the invoice net amount of $950 if the invoice is paid within ten days of the invoice date of September 22. The applicable time periods and dates are shown in Figure 5.3.

FIGURE 5.3 Discount and Credit Periods—Example 5.3A, Ordinary Dating

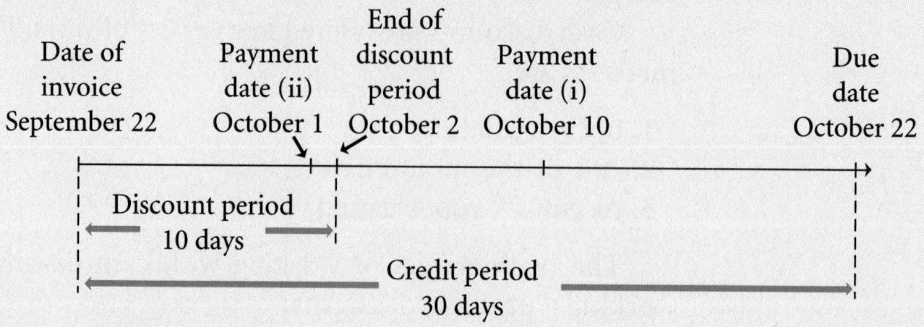

Ten days after September 22 is October 2. The discount period ends October 2.

(i) Payment on October 10 is beyond the last day for taking the discount. The discount cannot be taken. The full amount of the invoice of $950 must be paid.

(ii) October 1 is within the discount period; the 2% discount can be taken.

$$\begin{aligned}\text{Amount paid} &= \text{Net amount} - 2\% \text{ of the net amount}\\ &= 950.00 - 0.02(950.00)\\ &= 950.00 - 19.00\\ &= \$931.00\end{aligned}$$

Alternatively: Using the net price factor approach,

$$\begin{aligned}\text{Amount paid} &= \text{NPF for a 2\% discount} \times \text{Net amount}\\ &= (1 - 0.02)(950.00)\\ &= 0.98(950.00)\\ &= \$931.00\end{aligned}$$

EXAMPLE 5.2B

An invoice for $752.84 dated March 25, terms 5/10, 2/30, n/60, is paid in full on April 20. What is the total amount paid to settle the account?

SOLUTION

The payment terms state that

(i) a 5% discount may be taken within ten days of the invoice date (up to April 4); or

(ii) a 2% discount may be taken within 30 days of the invoice date (after April 4 but no later than April 24); or

(iii) the net amount is due within 60 days of the invoice date if advantage is not taken of the cash discounts offered.

The 5% cash discount is *not* allowed; payment on April 20 is after the end of the discount period for the 5% discount. However, the 2% discount *is* allowed, since payment on April 20 is within the 30 day period for the 2% discount.

Amount paid = 0.98(752.84) = $737.78 (See Figure 5.4.)

FIGURE 5.4 Discount and Credit Periods—Example 5.2B, Ordinary Dating

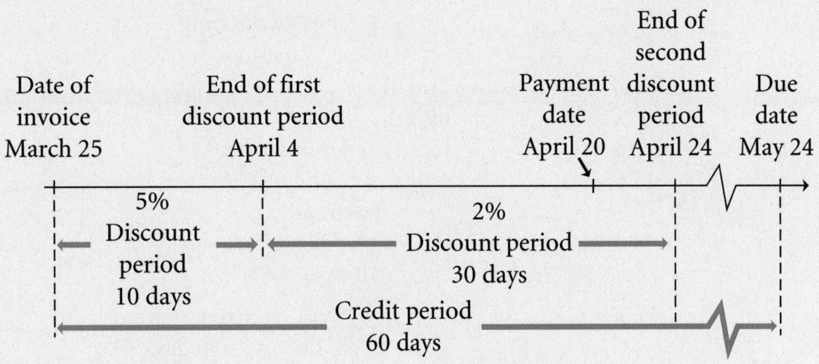

EXAMPLE 5.2C Three invoices with terms 5/10, 3/20, and n/60 are paid on November 15. The invoices are for $645 dated September 30, $706 dated October 26, and $586 dated November 7. What is the total amount paid?

SOLUTION

Invoice Dated	End of Discount Period For 5%	End of Discount Period For 3%	Discount Allowed	Amount Paid	
Sept. 30	Oct. 10	Oct. 20	None		$ 645.00
Oct. 26	Nov. 5	Nov. 15	3%	0.97(706.00)	684.82
Nov. 7	Nov. 17	Nov. 27	5%	0.95(586.00)	556.70
				Amount paid	$1886.52

C. End-of-the-month dating

End-of-the-month dating is shown in the terms of payment by the abbreviation E.O.M. (*end of month*), as in "2/10, n/30 E.O.M." The abbreviation means that the discount may be taken within the stipulated number of days following the end of the month shown in the invoice date. It has the effect of shifting the invoice date to the last day of the month.

Commonly, in end-of-the-month dating, the credit period (such as n/30) is not stated. In our example, "2/10, n/30 E.O.M." would be written "2/10 E.O.M." In this case, it is understood that the end of the credit period (the due date) is *twenty* days after the last day for taking the discount.

EXAMPLE 5.2D An invoice for $1233.95 dated July 16, terms 2/10 E.O.M., is paid on August 10. What is the amount paid?

SOLUTION The abbreviation E.O.M. means that the invoice is to be treated as if the invoice date were July 31. Therefore, the last day for taking the discount is August 10.

Amount paid = 0.98(1233.95) = $1209.27 (See Figure 5.5.)

FIGURE 5.5 **Discount and Credit Periods—Example 5.2D, End-of-the-Month Dating**

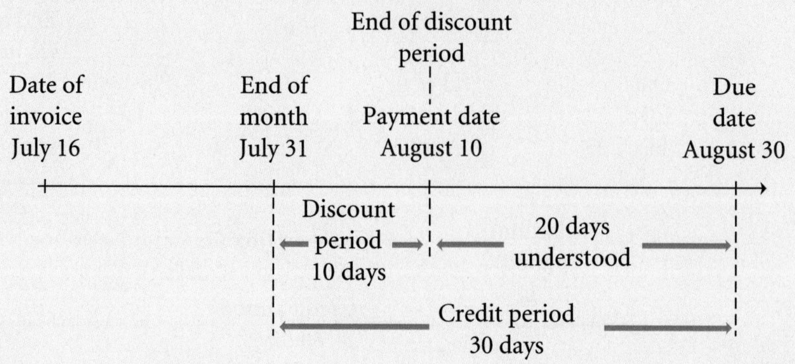

D. Receipt-of-goods dating

When the abbreviation R.O.G. (*receipt of goods*) appears in the terms of payment, as in "2/10, n/30 R.O.G.," the last day for taking the discount is the stipulated number of days after the date the merchandise is received rather than the invoice date. This method, known as **receipt-of-goods dating,** of offering a cash discount is used when the transportation of the goods takes a long time, as in the case of long-distance overland shipments by rail or truck, or shipments by boat.

EXAMPLE 5.2E

Hansa Import Distributors has received an invoice of $8465 dated May 10, terms 3/10, n/30 R.O.G., for a shipment of cuckoo clocks that arrived on July 15. What is the last day for taking the cash discount and how much is to be paid if the discount is taken?

SOLUTION

The last day for taking the discount is ten days after receipt of the shipment, that is, July 25.

Amount paid $= 0.97(8465.00) = \$8211.05$ (See Figure 5.6.)

FIGURE 5.6 **Discount and Credit Periods—Example 5.2E, Receipt-of-Goods Dating**

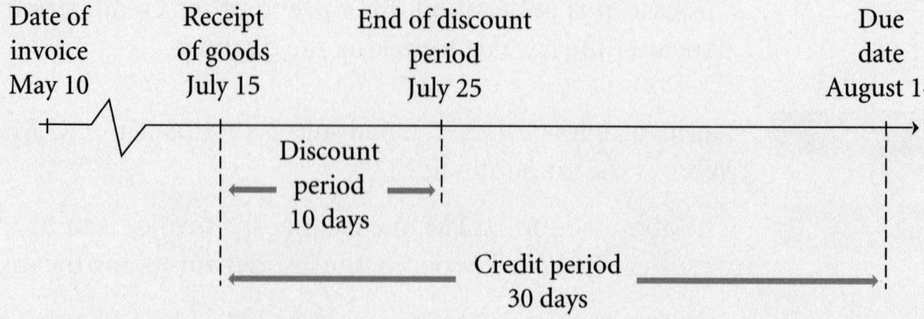

E. Partial payments and additional problems

The problem of a cash discount for a **partial payment** arises when a business pays *part* of an invoice within the discount period. In such cases, the purchaser is entitled to the cash discount on the partial amount paid. Each time a partial payment is made, separate the invoice into different parts, then determine whether the discount applies to each individual part.

EXAMPLE 5.2F

George Brown Inc. has received an invoice of \$2780 dated August 18, terms 2/10 E.O.M. What payment must be made on September 10 to reduce the debt

(i) by \$1000?

(ii) to \$1000?

SOLUTION

Since the terms of payment involve end-of-month dating, the last day for taking the cash discount is September 10. The discount of 2% may be taken off the partial payment.

(i) Reducing the debt by \$1000 requires paying \$1000 less the discount.

Amount paid = 1000(0.98) = \$980

Even though less than \$1000 has been paid, the debt still owing has been reduced by \$1000. This amount must be subtracted from the balance before the payment to determine the amount owing after the payment. The balance of the debt still owing is now \$2780.00 − \$1000.00 = \$1780.00.

(ii) Reducing the debt to \$1000 requires separating the debt into two parts, the first debt being \$2780 − \$1000, that is, \$1780. Then, determine whether or not the \$1780 is eligible for the discount. Since the first payment is made within the discount period, the discount is to be applied.

Amount paid = 1780.00(0.98) = \$1744.40

The balance of the debt still owing in this case is now \$2780 − \$1780 = \$1000.

EXAMPLE 5.2G

Applewood Supplies received a payment of \$807.50 from Main Street Service on October 10 on an invoice of \$2231.75 dated September 15, terms 5/10 E.O.M.

(i) For how much should Applewood credit Main Street Service's account for the payment?

(ii) How much does Main Street Service still owe on the invoice?

SOLUTION

Since the payment terms involve end-of-month dating, the payment is within the discount period. Main Street Service is entitled to the 5% discount on the partial payment. The amount of \$807.50 represents a partial payment already reduced by 5%.

Let the credit allowed be x.

Amount paid = NPF × Credit allowed

$$807.50 = 0.95x$$

$$x = \frac{807.50}{0.95} = \$850.00$$

(i) Applewood should credit the account of Main Street Service with $850.

(ii) Main Street Service still owes ($2231.75 − 850.00) = $1381.75.

EXAMPLE 5.2H

Thrifty Furniture sells family room furniture consisting of a couch, loveseat, and two tables for a package price of $2495 if the purchase is financed. The company also advertises "no interest for one year." Diana buys the furniture and pays $2395.20 in cash at the time of the purchase.

(i) How much was the discount for paying cash?

(ii) What was the rate of discount on the cash purchase?

SOLUTION

Since the payment was in cash at the time of purchase, Thrifty Furniture did allow a discount. The question then arises, "Is this actually no interest for one year?"

List price − Amount paid = Discount

$2495.00 − 2395.20 = $99.80

(i) Thrifty Furniture allowed a discount of $99.80.

$$\text{Discount rate} = \frac{99.80}{2495.00} = 4\%$$

(ii) Thrifty Furniture allowed a 4% discount rate for this cash payment.

EXERCISE 5.2

A. Determine the amount paid to settle each of the following eight invoices on the date indicated.

	Invoice Amount	Payment Terms	Date of Invoice	Date Goods Received	Date Paid
1.	$ 640.00	2/10, n/30	Aug. 10	Aug. 11	Sept. 9
2.	$1520.00	3/15, n/60	Sept. 24	Sept. 27	Oct. 8
3.	$ 783.95	3/10, 1/20, n/60	May 18	May 20	June 5
4.	$1486.25	5/10, 2/30, n/60	June 28	June 30	July 8
5.	$1160.00	2/10 E.O.M.	Mar. 22	Mar. 29	April 10
6.	$ 920.00	3/15 E.O.M.	Oct. 20	Oct. 30	Nov. 12
7.	$4675.00	2/10 R.O.G.	April 15	May 28	June 5
8.	$2899.65	4/20 R.O.G.	July 17	Sept. 21	Oct. 10

B. Determine the missing values for each of the following six invoices. Assume that a partial payment was made on each of the invoices by the last day for taking the cash discount.

	Invoice Amount	Payment Terms	Amount of Credit for Payment	Net Payment Received	Invoice Balance Due
1.	$1450.00	3/10, n/30	$ 600.00	?	?
2.	$3126.54	2/10 E.O.M.	$2000.00	?	?
3.	$ 964.50	5/20 R.O.G.	?	?	$400.00
4.	$1789.95	4/15, n/60	?	?	$789.95
5.	$1620.00	3/20 E.O.M.	?	$ 785.70	?
6.	$2338.36	2/10 R.O.G.	?	$1311.59	?

C. Answer the following questions.

1. Canadian Wheel received an invoice dated May 13 with terms 2/10, n/30. The amount stated on the invoice was $2499.
(a) What is the last day for taking the cash discount?
(b) What is the amount due if the invoice is paid on the last day for taking the discount?

2. An invoice was received for $6200 dated June 21 with terms 2/10, n/30.
(a) What is the last day for taking the cash discount?
(b) What is the amount due if the invoice is paid on the last day for taking the discount?

3. Triton Company received an invoice for $842 dated March 9 with terms 5/10, 2/20, n/60.
(a) If the invoice is paid on March 19, how much is to be paid?
(b) If the invoice is paid on March 27, how much is to be paid?
(c) If the invoice is paid on April 3, how much is to be paid?

4. Manual Company received an invoice for $2412 dated January 22 with terms 3/15, 1/30, n/60.
(a) If the invoice is paid on January 31, how much is to be paid?
(b) If the invoice is paid on February 20, how much is to be paid?
(c) If the invoice is paid on March 22, how much is to be paid?

5. What amount must be remitted if invoices dated July 25 for $929, August 10 for $763, and August 29 for $864, all with terms 3/15 E.O.M., are paid together on September 12?

6. The following invoices, all with terms 5/10, 2/30, n/60, were paid together on May 15. Invoice No. 234 dated March 30 is for $394.45; Invoice No. 356 dated April 15 is for $595.50; and Invoice No. 788 dated May 10 is for $865.20. What amount was remitted?

7. An invoice for $5275 dated November 12, terms 4/10 E.O.M., was received on November 14. What payment must be made on December 10 to reduce the debt to $3000?

8. What amount will reduce the amount due on an invoice of $1940 by $740 if the terms of the invoice are 5/10, n/30 and the payment was made during the discount period?

9. Santucci Appliances received an invoice dated August 12 with terms 3/10 E.O.M. for the items listed below:

5 GE refrigerators at $980 each less 25%, 5%;

4 Inglis dishwashers at $696 each less $16\frac{2}{3}\%$, 12.5%, 4%.

(a) What is the last day for taking the cash discount?
(b) What is the amount due if the invoice is paid on the last day for taking the discount?
(c) What is the amount of the cash discount if a partial payment is made such that a balance of $2000 remains outstanding on the invoice?

10. Import Exclusives Ltd. received an invoice dated May 20 from Dansk Specialties of Copenhagen with terms 5/20 R.O.G. for:

100 teak trays at $34.30 each;
25 teak icebuckets at $63.60 each;
40 teak salad bowls at $54.50 each.

All items are subject to trade discounts of $33\frac{1}{3}\%$, $7\frac{1}{2}\%$, 5%.

(a) If the shipment was received on June 28, what is the last day of the discount period?
(b) What is the amount due if the invoice is paid in full on July 15?
(c) If a partial payment only is made on the last day of the discount period, what amount is due to reduce the outstanding balance to $2500?

11. Sheridan Service received an invoice dated September 25 from Wolfedale Automotive. The invoice amount was $2540.95, and the payment terms were 3/10, 1/20, n/30. Sheridan Service made a payment on October 5 to reduce the balance due by $1200, made a second payment on October 15 to reduce the balance to $600, and paid the remaining balance on October 25.
(a) How much did Sheridan Service pay on October 5?
(b) How much did it pay on October 15?
(c) What was the amount of the final payment on October 25?

12. The Ski Shop received an invoice for $9600 dated August 11, terms 5/10, 2/30, n/90, for a shipment of skis. The Ski Shop made two partial payments.
(a) How much was paid on August 20 to reduce the unpaid balance to $7000?
(b) How much was paid on September 10 to reduce the outstanding balance by $3000?
(c) What is the remaining balance on September 10?

13. Jelinek Sports received a cheque for $1867.25 in partial payment of an invoice owed by The Ski Shop. The invoice was for $5325 with terms 3/20 E.O.M. dated September 15, and the cheque was received on October 18.
(a) By how much should Jelinek Sports credit the account of The Ski Shop?
(b) How much does The Ski Shop still owe Jelinek?

14. Darrigo Grape received an invoice for $13 780 dated September 28, terms 5/20 R.O.G., from Nappa Vineyards for a carload of grape juice received October 20. Darrigo made a partial payment of $5966 on November 8.
(a) By how much did Darrigo reduce the amount due on the invoice?
(b) How much does Darrigo still owe?

15. Highway One Gas sells gas for vehicles at $1.12 per litre. Louis purchases 50 litres of gas for his car. He pays for the purchase in cash, paying a total of $54.04.
    (a) How much did he save by paying cash?
    (b) What was the rate of discount on the cash purchase?

16. Deals on Wheels advertises a vehicle at $26 465. Marina buys the vehicle, paying $24 877.10 in cash.
    (a) How much did she save by paying cash?
    (b) What was the rate of discount on the cash purchase?

5.3 MARKUP

A. Basic concepts and calculations

The primary purpose of operating a business is to generate profits. Businesses engaged in merchandising generate profits through their buying and selling activities. The amount of profit depends on many factors, one of which is the pricing of goods. The selling price must cover

1. the cost of buying the goods;
2. the operating expenses (or overhead) of the business;
3. the profit required by the owner to stay in business.

SELLING PRICE = COST OF BUYING + EXPENSES + PROFIT

$$S = C + E + P$$ —— **Formula 5.8A**

EXAMPLE 5.3A

Main Street Service buys a certain type of battery at a cost of $84 each. Operating expenses of the business are 25% of cost and the owner requires a profit of 10% of cost. For how much should Main Street sell this type of battery?

SOLUTION

Selling price = Cost of buying + Expenses + Profit
= 84.00 + 25% of 84.00 + 10% of 84.00
= 84.00 + 0.25(84.00) + 0.10(84.00)
= 84.00 + 21.00 + 8.40
= $113.40

Main Street should sell the batteries for $113.40 to cover the cost of buying, the operating expenses, and the required profit.

In Example 5.3A, the selling price is $113.40 while the cost is $84. The difference between selling price and cost = 113.40 − 84.00 = $29.40. This difference covers operating expenses of $21 and a profit of $8.40 and is known as the **markup, margin,** or **gross profit.**

MARKUP = EXPENSES + PROFIT

$M = E + P$ ——————————— **Formula 5.9**

Using this relationship between markup, expenses, and profit, the relationship stated in Formula 5.8A becomes

SELLING PRICE = COST OF BUYING + MARKUP

$S = C + M$ ——————————— **Formula 5.8B**

Figure 5.7 illustrates the relationships among cost of buying (C), markup (M), operating expenses (E), profit (P), and selling price (S) established in Formulas 5.8A, 5.8B, and 5.9.

FIGURE 5.7

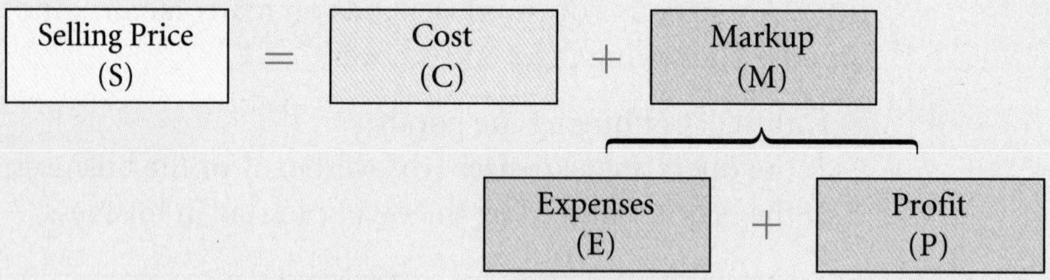

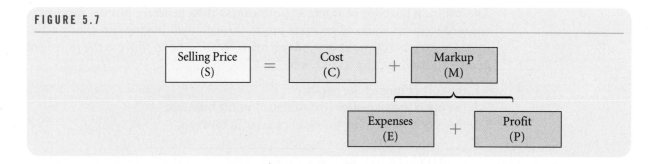

EXAMPLE 5.3B

Frisson Business Machines bought two types of electronic calculators for resale. Model A costs $42 and sells for $56.50. Model B costs $78 and sells for $95. Business overhead is 24% of cost. For each model, determine

(i) the markup (or gross profit);

(ii) the operating expenses (or overhead);

(iii) the profit.

SOLUTION

	Model A	**Model B**	
(i)	$C + M = S$	$C + M = S$	using Formula 5.8B
	$42.00 + M = 56.50$	$78.00 + M = 95.00$	
	$M = 56.50 - 42.00$	$M = 95.00 - 78.00$	
	$M = 14.50$	$M = 17.00$	
	The markup on Model A is $14.50.	The markup on Model B is $17	
(ii)	Expenses (or overhead)	Expenses (or overhead)	
	= 24% of 42.00	= 24% of 78.00	
	= 0.24(42.00)	= 0.24(78.00)	
	= 10.08	= 18.72	
	Overhead for Model A is $10.08.	Overhead for Model B is $18.72.	

(iii)

Model A	Model B
$E + P = M$	$E + P = M$ —— **Formula 5.9**
$10.08 + P = 14.50$	$18.72 + P = 17.00$
$P = 14.50 - 10.08$	$P = 17.00 - 18.72$
$P = 4.42$	$P = -1.72$
Profit on Model A is \$4.42.	Profit on Model B is –\$1.72, that is, a loss of \$1.72.

EXAMPLE 5.3C

A ski shop bought 100 pairs of skis for \$105 per pair and sold 60 pairs for the regular selling price of \$295 per pair. The remaining skis were sold during a clearance sale for \$180 per pair. Overhead is 40% of the regular selling price. Determine

(i) the markup, the overhead, and the profit per pair of skis sold at the regular selling price;

(ii) the markup, the overhead, and the profit per pair of skis sold during the clearance sale;

(iii) the total profit realized.

SOLUTION

(i) *At regular selling price*	(ii) *At clearance price*
Markup	**Markup**
$C + M = S$	$C + M = S$
$105.00 + M = 295.00$	$105.00 + M = 180.00$
$M = \$190.00$	$M = \$75.00$
Overhead	**Overhead**
$E = 40\%$ of regular selling price	$E = 40\%$ of regular selling price
$= 0.40(295.00)$	$= 0.40(295.00)$
$= \$118.00$	$= \$118.00$
Profit	**Profit**
$E + P = M$	$E + P = M$
$118.00 + P = 190.00$	$118.00 + P = 75.00$
$P = \$72.00$	$P = -\$43.00$

(iii) Profit from sale of 60 pairs

at regular selling price $= 60(72.00)$	\$4320.00
Profit from sale of 40 pairs during clearance sale $= 40(-43.00)$	-1720.00
Total profit	\$2600.00

B. Rate of markup

A markup may be stated in one of two ways:

1. As a percent of cost; or
2. As a percent of selling price.

The method used is usually determined by the way in which a business keeps its records. Since most manufacturers keep their records in terms of cost, they usually calculate markup as a percent of cost. Since most department stores and other retailers keep their records in terms of selling price, they usually calculate markup as a percent of selling price.

Computing the rate of markup involves comparing the amount of markup to a base amount. Depending on the method used, the base amount is either the cost or the selling price. Since the two methods produce different results, great care must be taken to note whether the markup is based on the cost or on the selling price.

$$\text{RATE OF MARKUP BASED ON COST} = \frac{\text{MARKUP}}{\text{COST}} = \frac{M}{C}$$ ——— **Formula 5.10**

$$\text{RATE OF MARKUP BASED ON SELLING PRICE} = \frac{\text{MARKUP}}{\text{SELLING PRICE}} = \frac{M}{S}$$ ——— **Formula 5.11**

EXAMPLE 5.3D

Compute (a) the missing value (cost, selling price, or markup), (b) the rate of markup based on cost, and (c) the rate of markup based on selling price for each of the following:

(i) cost, \$60; selling price, \$75

(ii) cost, \$48; markup, \$16

(iii) selling price, \$88; markup, \$33

(iv) cost, \$8; markup, \$8

(v) selling price, \$24; markup, \$18

SOLUTION

	(a) Missing Value	(b) Rate of Markup Based on Cost	(c) Rate of Markup Based on Selling Price
(i)	Markup = 75.00 − 60.00 = \$15.00	$\frac{15}{60} = 0.25 = 25\%$	$\frac{15}{75} = 0.20 = 20\%$
(ii)	Selling price = 48.00 + 16.00 = \$64.00	$\frac{16}{48} = \frac{1}{3} = 33\frac{1}{3}\%$	$\frac{16}{64} = 0.25 = 25\%$

(iii)	Cost $= 88.00 - 33.00$ $= \$55.00$	$\frac{33}{55} = 0.60 = 60\%$	$\frac{33}{88} = 0.375 = 37.5\%$
(iv)	Selling price $= 8.00 + 8.00$ $= \$16.00$	$\frac{8}{8} = 1.00 = 100\%$	$\frac{8}{16} = 0.50 = 50\%$
(v)	Cost $= 24.00 - 18.00$ $= \$6.00$	$\frac{18}{6} = 3.00 = 300\%$	$\frac{18}{24} = 0.75 = 75\%$

C. Finding the cost or the selling price

When the rate of markup is given and either the cost or the selling price is known, the missing value can be found using Formula 5.8B.

COST + MARKUP = SELLING PRICE $\qquad$ C + M = S

When using this formula, pay special attention to the base of the markup, that is, whether it is based on cost or based on selling price.

EXAMPLE 5.3E What is the selling price of an article costing $72 if the markup is

(i) 40% of cost?

(ii) 40% of the selling price?

SOLUTION

(i)

$$C + M = S \quad \text{——— using Formula 5.8B}$$
$$C + 40\% \text{ of } C = S \quad \text{——— replacing M by 40\% of C is the crucial step in the solution}$$
$$72.00 + 0.40(72.00) = S$$
$$72.00 + 28.80 = S$$
$$S = 100.80$$

When the markup is 40% based on cost, the selling price is $100.80.

(ii)

$$C + M = S$$
$$C + 40\% \text{ of } S = S$$
$$72.00 + 0.40S = S$$
$$72.00 = S - 0.40S$$
$$72.00 = 0.60S$$
$$S = \frac{72.00}{0.60}$$
$$S = 120.00$$

When the markup is 40% based on selling price, the selling price is $120.00.

Note: In problems of this type, replace M by *X*% of C or *X*% of S before using specific numbers. This approach is used in the preceding problem and in the following worked examples.

EXAMPLE 5.3F

What is the cost of an article selling for $65 if the markup is

(i) 30% of selling price?

(ii) 30% of cost?

SOLUTION

(i)

$$C + M = S$$
$$C + 30\% \text{ of } S = S \quad \text{——— replace M by 30\% of S}$$
$$C + 0.30(65.00) = 65.00$$
$$C + 19.50 = 65.00$$
$$C = 65.00 - 19.50$$
$$C = 45.50$$

When the markup is 30% based on selling price, the cost is $45.50.

(ii)

$$C + M = S$$
$$C + 30\% \text{ of } C = S \quad \text{——— replace M by 30\% of C}$$
$$C + 0.30C = 65.00$$
$$1.30C = 65.00$$
$$C = \frac{65.00}{1.30}$$
$$C = 50.00$$

If the markup is 30% based on cost, the cost is $50.

EXAMPLE 5.3G

The Beaver Ski Shop sells ski vests for $98. The markup based on cost is 75%.

(i) What did the Beaver Ski Shop pay for each vest?

(ii) What is the rate of markup based on the selling price?

SOLUTION

(i)

$$C + M = S$$
$$C + 75\% \text{ of } C = S$$
$$C + 0.75C = 98.00$$
$$1.75C = 98.00$$
$$C = 56.00$$

The Beaver Ski Shop paid $56 for each vest.

(ii)

$$\text{Rate of markup based on selling price} = \frac{\text{Markup}}{\text{Selling price}}$$
$$= \frac{98.00 - 56.00}{98.00}$$
$$= \frac{42.00}{98.00} = 0.428571 = 42.86\%$$

EXAMPLE 5.3H

Main Street Service bought four Michelin tires from a wholesaler for $343 and sold the tires at a markup of 30% of the selling price.

(i) For how much were the tires sold?

(ii) What is the rate of markup based on cost?

SOLUTION

(i)
$$\begin{aligned} C + M &= S \\ C + 30\% \text{ of } S &= S \\ 343.00 + 0.30S &= S \\ 343.00 &= 0.70S \\ S &= 490.00 \end{aligned}$$

Main Street Service sold the tires for $490.

(ii)
$$\text{Rate of markup based on cost} = \frac{\text{Markup}}{\text{Cost}} = \frac{490.00 - 343.00}{343.00} = \frac{147.00}{343.00} = 0.428571 = 42.86\%$$

EXAMPLE 5.3I

The markup, or gross profit, on each of two separate articles is $25.80. If the rate of markup for Article A is 40% of cost while the rate of markup for Article B is 40% of the selling price, determine the cost and the selling price of each.

SOLUTION

For Article A

$$\begin{aligned} \text{Markup (or gross profit)} &= 40\% \text{ of cost} \\ 25.80 &= 0.40C \\ C &= 64.50 \end{aligned}$$

The cost of Article A is $64.50.
The selling price is 64.50 + 25.80 = $90.30.

For Article B

$$\begin{aligned} \text{Markup (or gross profit)} &= 40\% \text{ of selling price} \\ 25.80 &= 0.40S \\ S &= 64.50 \end{aligned}$$

The selling price of Article B is $64.50.
The cost = 64.50 − 25.80 = $38.70.

EXERCISE 5.3

A. For each of the following six questions, determine

(a) the amount of markup;
(b) the amount of overhead;
(c) the profit or loss realized on the sale;
(d) the rate of markup based on cost;
(e) the rate of markup based on selling price.

	Cost	Selling Price	Overhead
1.	\$24.00	\$30.00	16% of cost
2.	\$72.00	\$96.00	15% of selling price
3.	\$52.50	\$87.50	36% of selling price
4.	\$42.45	\$67.92	60% of cost
5.	\$27.00	\$37.50	34% of selling price
6.	\$36.00	\$42.30	21% of cost

B. For each of the following twelve questions, compute the missing values represented by the question marks.

				Rate of Markup Based On:	
	Cost	Selling Price	Markup	Cost	Selling Price
1.	\$25.00	\$ 31.25	?	?	?
2.	\$63.00	\$ 84.00	?	?	?
3.	\$64.00	?	\$38.40	?	?
4.	?	\$162.00	\$27.00	?	?
5.	\$54.25	?	?	40%	?
6.	?	\$ 94.50	?	?	30%
7.	?	\$ 66.36	?	50%	?
8.	?	\$133.25	?	$66\frac{2}{3}\%$	?
9.	\$31.24	?	?	?	60%
10.	\$87.74	?	?	?	$33\frac{1}{3}\%$
11.	?	?	\$22.26	?	$16\frac{2}{3}\%$
12.	?	?	\$90.75	125%	?

C. Answer each of the following questions.

1. Giuseppe's buys supplies to make pizzas for \$4. Operating expenses of the business are 110% of the cost and the profit made is 130% of cost. What is the regular selling price of each pizza?

2. Neptune Dive Shop sells snorkelling equipment for \$50. Their cost is \$25 and their operation expenses are 30% of regular selling price. How much profit will they make on each sale?

3. Mi Casa imports pottery from Mexico. Their operation expenses are 260% of the cost of buying and the profit is 110% of the cost of buying. They sell a vase for \$14.10. What is their cost for each piece?

4. Windsor Hardware buys outdoor lights for \$5 per dozen less 20%, 20%. The store's overhead is 45% of cost and the required profit is 15% of cost. For how much per dozen should the lights be sold?

5. A merchant buys an item listed at \$96 less $33\frac{1}{3}\%$ from a distributor. Overhead is 32% of cost and profit is 27.5% of cost. For how much should the item be retailed?

6. Tennis racquets were purchased for \$55 less 40% (for purchasing more than 100 items), and less a further 25% (for purchasing the racquets in October). They were sold for \$54.45.

(a) What is the markup as a percent of cost?
(b) What is the markup as a percent of selling price?

7. A dealer bought personal computers for $1240 less 50%, 10%. They were sold for $1395.
(a) What was the markup as a percent of cost?
(b) What was the markup as a percent of selling price?

8. The Bargain Bookstore marks up textbooks by $3.42 per textbook. The store's markup is 15% of cost.
(a) For how much did the bookstore buy each textbook?
(b) What is the selling price of each textbook?
(c) What is the rate of markup based on the selling price?

9. An appliance store sells electric kettles at a markup of 18% of the selling price. The store's margin on a particular model is $6.57.
(a) For how much does the store sell the kettles?
(b) What was the cost of the kettles to the store?
(c) What is the rate of markup based on cost?

10. The markup on an item selling for $74.55 is 40% of cost.
(a) What is the cost of the item?
(b) What is the rate of markup based on the selling price?

11. Sheridan Service sells oil at a markup of 40% of the selling price. If Sheridan paid $0.99 per litre of oil,
(a) what is the selling price per litre?
(b) what is the rate of markup based on cost?

12. The Ski Shop purchased ski poles for $12.80 per pair. The poles are marked up 60% of the selling price.
(a) For how much does The Ski Shop sell a pair of ski poles?
(b) What is the rate of markup based on cost?

13. Neal's Photographic Supplies sells a Pentax camera for $444.98. The markup is 90% of cost.
(a) How much does the store pay for this camera?
(b) What is the rate of markup based on selling price?

14. The Cookery buys sets of cookware for $45 and marks them up at $33\frac{1}{3}\%$ of cost.
(a) What is the selling price of the cookware sets?
(b) What is the rate of markup based on selling price?

15. The Leather Factory buys bags for $84 and marks them up at 40% of selling price.
(a) What is the selling price of the bags?
(b) What is the rate of markup based on cost?

16. Boxes of candles are sold for $3.24. The store's markup based on selling price is $16\frac{2}{3}\%$.
(a) What is the cost of the boxes of candles?
(b) What is the rate of markup based on cost?

17. It's About Time sells clocks for $23.10. The store's markup based on cost is 37.5%.
(**a**) What is the cost of the clocks?
(**b**) What is the rate of markup based on selling price?

18. A car accessory is sold for $42.90. The store's markup based on cost is 50%.
(**a**) What is the cost of the car accessory?
(**b**) What is the rate of markup based on selling price?

5.4 MARKDOWN

A. Pricing strategies

The pricing relationship, Selling price = Cost + Expense + Profit, or (S = C + E + P), plays an important role in pricing. It describes how large a markup is needed to cover overhead and a reasonable profit, and how large a markdown can be tolerated. One pricing strategy is to set a selling price based on the business' "internal" factors—actual costs and expenses, and a desired profit level. However, pricing decisions must often be based on "external" market factors—competitors' prices, consumers' sensitivity to a high price, economic conditions that affect interest rates and income available for purchases, and so on. Often, selling prices must be marked down more than anticipated in response to market conditions, leading to less-than-desired profit levels. Use the pricing relationship S = C + E + P as a guide to determine the effect of markdown decisions on the operations of a business.

The cost of buying an article plus the overhead represents the **total cost**, or handling cost, of the article.

TOTAL COST = COST OF BUYING + EXPENSES

If an article is sold at a price that *equals* the total cost, the business makes no profit nor does it suffer a loss. This price is called the break-even point and is discussed in Chapter 6. Any business, of course, prefers to sell at a price that is at least the break-even price. If the price is insufficient to recover the total cost, the business will suffer an operating loss. If the price does not even cover the cost of buying the item, the business suffers an absolute loss. To determine the profit or loss, the following accounting relationship is used.

PROFIT = SELLING PRICE − TOTAL COST

PROFIT = REVENUE − TOTAL COST

B. Basic concepts and calculations

A **markdown** is a reduction in the price of an article sold to the consumer. Markdowns are used for a variety of purposes, such as sales promotions, meeting competitors' prices, reducing excess inventories, clearing out seasonal merchandise, and selling off discontinued items. A markdown, unlike a markup, is always stated as a percent of the price to be reduced and is computed as if it were a discount.

FIGURE 5.8

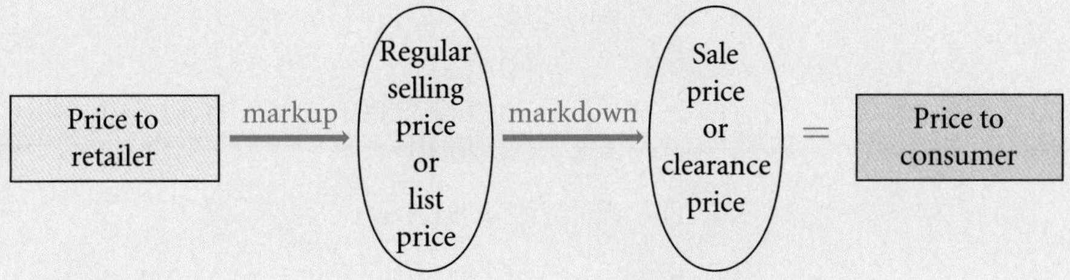

While markdowns are simple to calculate, the rather wide variety of terms used to identify both the price to be reduced (such as *regular selling price, selling price, list price, marked price, price tag*) and the reduced price (such as *sale price* or *clearance price*) introduces an element of confusion. In this text, we use **regular selling price** to describe the price to be reduced and **sale price** to describe the reduced price.

In general,

SALE PRICE = REGULAR SELLING PRICE − MARKDOWN

However, since the markdown is a percent of the regular selling price, the net price factor approach used with discounts is applicable (see Formula 5.4A).

SALE PRICE = NPF × REGULAR SELLING PRICE
where NPF = 100% − % markdown

EXAMPLE 5.4A

The Cook Nook paid $115.24 for a set of dishes. Expenses are 18% of selling price and the required profit is 15% of selling price. During an inventory sale, the set of dishes was marked down 30%.

(i) What was the regular selling price?

(ii) What was the sale price?

(iii) What was the operating profit or loss?

SOLUTION

(i) Selling price = Cost + Expenses + Profit

$$S = C + 18\% \text{ of } S + 15\% \text{ of } S$$
$$S = C + 0.18S + 0.15S$$
$$S = 115.24 + 0.33S$$
$$0.67S = 115.24$$
$$S = \frac{115.24}{0.67} = \$172.00$$

The regular selling price is $172.

(ii) Sale price = Regular selling price − Markdown
= S − 30% of S
= S − 0.30S
= 0.70S
= 0.70(172.00)
= $120.40

The sale price is $120.40.

(iii) Total cost = Cost of buying + Expenses
= C + 18% of S
= 115.24 + 0.18(172.00)
= 115.24 + 30.96
= $146.20

Profit = Revenue − Total cost
= 120.40 − 146.20
= −$25.80

The dishes were sold at an operating loss of $25.80.

EXAMPLE 5.4B

Lund Sporting Goods sold a bicycle regularly priced at $195 for $144.30.

(i) What is the amount of markdown?

(ii) What is the rate of markdown?

SOLUTION

(i) Markdown = Regular selling price − Sale price
= 195.00 − 144.30
= $50.70

(ii) $\text{Rate of markdown} = \dfrac{\text{Markdown}}{\text{Regular selling price}}$

$= \dfrac{50.70}{195.00} = 0.26 = 26\%$

EXAMPLE 5.4C

During its annual Midnight Madness Sale, The Ski Shop sold a pair of ski boots, regularly priced at $245, at a discount of 40%. The boots cost $96 and expenses are 26% of the regular selling price.

(i) For how much were the ski boots sold?

(ii) What was the total cost of the ski boots?

(iii) What operating profit or loss was made on the sale?

SOLUTION

(i) Sale price = 0.60(245.00) = $147.00

(ii) Total cost = Cost of buying + Expenses
= 96.00 + 0.26(245.00)
= 96.00 + 63.70
= $159.70

(iii) Profit = Revenue − Total cost
= 147.00 − 159.70
= −$12.70 (a loss)

Since the total cost was higher than the revenue received from the sale of the ski boots, The Ski Shop had an operating loss of $12.70.

EXAMPLE 5.4D

The Winemaker sells Okanagan concentrate for $22.50. The store's overhead expenses are 50% of cost and the owners require a profit of 30% of cost.

(i) For how much does The Winemaker buy the concentrate?

(ii) What is the price needed to cover all of the costs and expenses?

(iii) What is the highest rate of markdown at which the store will still break even?

(iv) What is the highest rate of discount that can be advertised without incurring an absolute loss?

SOLUTION

(i)
$$S = C + E + P$$
$$S = C + 50\% \text{ of } C + 30\% \text{ of } C$$
$$S = C + 0.50C + 0.30C$$
$$22.50 = 1.80C$$
$$C = \frac{22.50}{1.80} = \$12.50$$

The Winemaker buys the concentrate for $12.50.

(ii) Total cost = C + 50% of C
= 1.50C
= 1.50(12.50)
= $18.75

The price needed to cover costs and expenses is $18.75.

(iii) To break even, the maximum markdown is 22.50 − 18.75 = $3.75.

$$\text{Rate of markdown} = \frac{3.75}{22.50} = 0.166667 = 16\tfrac{2}{3}\%$$

The highest rate of markdown to break even is $16\frac{2}{3}\%$.

(iv) The lowest price at which the concentrate can be offered for sale without incurring an absolute loss is the cost at which the concentrate was purchased, that is, $12.50. The maximum amount of discount is 22.50 − 12.50 = $10.00.

$$\text{Rate of discount} = \frac{10.00}{22.50} = 0.444444 = 44\tfrac{4}{9}\%$$

The maximum rate of discount that can be advertised without incurring an absolute loss is $44\frac{4}{9}\%$.

EXERCISE 5.4

A. Compute the values represented by question marks for each of the following six questions.

	Regular Selling Price	Markdown	Sale Price	Cost (C)	Overhead	Total Cost	Operating Profit (Loss)
1.	$85.00	40%	?	$ 42.00	20% of S	?	?
2.	?	$33\frac{1}{3}$%	$ 42.00	$ 34.44	12% of S	?	?
3.	?	35%	$ 62.66	?	25% of S	$54.75	?
4.	$72.80	$12\frac{1}{2}$%	?	$ 54.75	20% of C	?	?
5.	?	25%	$120.00	$105.00	? of S	?	($4.20)
6.	$92.40	$16\frac{2}{3}$%	?	?	15% of C	?	$8.46

B.

1. The Music Store paid $14.95 for a DVD. Expenses are 21% of selling price and the required profit is 11% of selling price. During an inventory sale, the DVD was marked down 20%.
(**a**) What was the regular selling price?
(**b**) What was the sale price?
(**c**) What was the operating profit or loss?

Reference Example 5.4A

2. A retail store paid $44 for a microwave oven. Expenses are 27% of selling price and the required profit is 18% of selling price. During an inventory sale, the microwave was marked down 40%.
(**a**) What was the regular selling price?
(**b**) What was the sale price?
(**c**) What was the operating profit or loss?

3. A sports drink was offered for sale at $1.99 at West Store. At East Store, the regular selling price of a similar sports drink was $2.49. What rate of markdown would East Store have to offer to sell the drink at the same price as West Store?

Reference Example 5.4B

4. An eyeglass company sells frames for $279. If they wanted to offer the lower price of $239, what rate of markdown would they have to offer?

5. A seminar was advertised at a price of $125 per person. If the tickets were purchased at least two weeks in advance, the price would be lowered to $105 per person. What rate of markdown has been offered?

6. A seven-day Mexican cruise was advertised at a price of $1299 per person based on double occupancy. If the cruise was booked two months in advance, the price would be lowered to $935 per person. What rate of markdown has been offered?

7. Luigi's Restaurant offered a "buy one get one half off" sale for the midweek period. The "one half off" referred to the lesser-priced dinner. A customer ordered a steak dinner, with a regular price of $19, and a chicken dinner, with a regular price of $14.
(**a**) What was the overall markdown at which the dinners were sold?
(**b**) What was the overall rate of markdown at which the dinners were sold?

8. A lakeside resort offered a midweek package at \$199 per night for two people. The package included accommodation in a one-bedroom suite, which regularly sold for \$225, breakfast for two, regularly priced at \$12 per person, and a 25% discount on spa services, a value of \$20 per person.
  (a) What was the overall markdown at which the packages were sold?
  (b) What was the overall rate of markdown at which the packages were sold?

9. Par Putters Company sells golf balls for \$29 per dozen. The store's overhead expenses are 43% of cost and the owners require a profit of 20% of cost.
  (a) For how much does Par Putters Company buy the golf balls?
  (b) What is the price needed to cover all of the costs and expenses?
  (c) What is the highest rate of markdown at which the store will still break even?
  (d) What is the highest rate of discount that can be advertised without incurring an absolute loss? Reference Example 5.4D

10. Get-Aways Company sells sightseeing tours for the Ottawa valley for C\$3849 per person. Overhead expenses for the company are 31% of cost and the target profit is 17% of cost.
  (a) How much does Get-Aways Company pay for the tours?
  (b) What is the lowest price they can offer while still covering all of the costs and expenses?
  (c) What is the highest rate of markdown at which the company will still break even?

5.5 INTEGRATED PROBLEMS

Many businesses encounter complex situations where discounts, markups, and markdowns are involved. In order to determine desired profits, prices must be set carefully. To determine the appropriate price, each complex situation must be separated into the different steps and calculations needed, and a solution determined for each part before an overall solution can be determined.

EXAMPLE 5.5A

Solomon ski bindings purchased for \$57.75 were marked up 45% of the selling price. When the binding was discontinued, it was marked down 40%. What was the sale price of the binding?

SOLUTION

Consider the given information step by step. The following computations are necessary to determine the sale price.

STEP 1

First determine the regular selling price S.

$$C + M = S$$
$$C + 45\% \text{ of } S = S$$
$$57.75 + 0.45S = S$$
$$57.75 = 0.55S$$
$$S = \$105.00$$

The regular selling price is \$105.

STEP 2 Next, determine the sale price.

$$\begin{aligned}\text{Sale price} &= \text{Regular selling price} - \text{Markdown}\\ &= 105.00 - 40\% \text{ of } 105.00\\ &= 105.00 - 42.00\\ &= \$63.00\end{aligned}$$

Alternatively:

$$\begin{aligned}\text{Sale price} &= \text{NPF} \times \text{Regular selling price}\\ &= 0.60 \times 105.00\\ &= \$63.00\end{aligned}$$

The sale price is $63.

EXAMPLE 5.5B Canadian Car Company has just introduced its latest model, the Cheetah, marketed as fast, quiet, and efficient. Andretti's Cars, the local dealer, purchased one of the cars for $27 685 less 30%. Andretti's marks all vehicles at a list or sticker price that allows them to offer a discount of 20% and maintain a markup based on cost of 25%. During its annual midsummer sale, the car was advertised at $27 995. Determine the cost, the regular price, the normal selling price, and the midsummer sale markdown rate.

SOLUTION To solve this problem, start with a step-by-step approach. The following computations are necessary to determine the profit.

STEP 1 The cost C (or purchase price) to the store;

STEP 2 The selling price S required to maintain the markup based on cost;

STEP 3 The list price L from which the 20% discount is offered;

STEP 4 The midsummer sale markdown rate.

Step-by-Step Computations

STEP 1

$$\text{Cost} = \text{NPF} \times \text{Manufacturer's list price}$$

$$\text{Cost} = (0.70)(27\,685.00) = \$19\,379.50$$

STEP 2 Let the normal selling price be S.

$$\begin{aligned}S &= C + \text{Markup}\\ S &= C + 25\% \text{ of } C\\ S &= C + 0.25C\\ S &= 1.25(19\,379.50)\\ S &= \$24\,224.38\end{aligned}$$

The normal selling price is $24 224.38.

STEP 3 List price − Discount = Normal selling price

Let the regular price be L.

$$L - 20\% \text{ of } L = 24\,224.38$$
$$L - 0.20L = 24\,224.38$$
$$0.80L = 24\,224.38$$
$$L = \frac{24\,224.38}{0.80} = \$30\,280.48$$

The list price was $30 280.48.

STEP 4

$$\text{Markdown} = \text{List price} - \text{Midsummer sale price}$$
$$= 30\,280.48 - 27\,995.00$$
$$= 2285.48$$
$$\text{Markdown rate} = \frac{2285.48}{30\,280.48} = 7.55\%$$

The markdown rate was 7.55%.

EXAMPLE 5.5C

Big Sound Electronics bought stereo equipment at a cost of $960 less 30%, 15%. Big Sound marks all merchandise at a list price that allows the store to offer a discount of 20% while still making its usual profit of 15% of regular selling price. Overhead is 25% of regular selling price. During its annual Boxing Week sale, the usual discount of 20% was replaced by a markdown of 45%. What operating profit or loss was made when the equipment was sold?

SOLUTION

Complex problems of this type are best solved by a systematic approach. Consider the given information step by step. The following computations are necessary to determine the profit.

STEP 1 The cost C (or purchase price) to the store;

STEP 2 The regular selling price S required to cover cost, expenses, and the usual profit;

STEP 3 The list price L from which the 20% discount is offered;

STEP 4 The Boxing Week sale price;

STEP 5 The total cost (cost and expenses);

STEP 6 The resulting operating profit or loss.

Step-by-Step Computations

STEP 1 Cost = NPF × List price = (0.70)(0.85)(960.00) = $571.20

STEP 2 Let the regular selling price be S.

$$S = C + E + P$$
$$S = C + 25\% \text{ of } S + 15\% \text{ of } S$$
$$S = C + 0.25S + 0.15S$$
$$S = 571.20 + 0.40S$$
$$0.60S = 571.20$$
$$S = \frac{571.20}{0.60} = \$952.00$$

The regular selling price is $952.

STEP 3

List price − Discount = Regular selling price
Let the List price be L.

$$L - 20\% \text{ of } L = 952.00$$
$$L - 0.20L = 952.00$$
$$0.80L = 952.00$$
$$L = \frac{952.00}{0.80} = \$1190.00$$

The list price was $1190.

STEP 4

$$\text{Boxing Week sale price} = \text{List price} - \text{Markdown}$$
$$= 1190.00 - 45\% \text{ of } 1190.00$$
$$= 1190.00 - 0.45(1190.00)$$
$$= 1190.00 - 535.50$$
$$= \$654.50$$

STEP 5

$$\text{Total cost} = \text{Cost of buying} + \text{Expenses}$$
$$= C + 25\% \text{ of } S$$
$$= 571.20 + 0.25(952.00)$$
$$= 571.20 + 238.00$$
$$= \$809.20$$

STEP 6

$$\text{Profit} = \text{Sale price} - \text{Total cost}$$
$$= 654.50 - 809.20$$
$$= -\$154.70$$

The equipment was sold at an operating loss of $154.70.

EXAMPLE 5.5D

Magder's Furniture Emporium bought a dining room suite that must be retailed for $5250 to cover the cost, overhead expenses of 50% of the cost, and a normal net profit of 25% of the cost. The suite is marked at a list price so that the store can allow a 20% discount and still receive the required regular selling price.

When the suite remained unsold, the store owner decided to mark the suite down for an inventory clearance sale. To arrive at the rate of markdown, the owner decided that the store's profit would have to be no less than 10% of the normal net profit and that part of the markdown would be covered by reducing the commission paid to the salesperson. The normal commission (which accounts for 40% of the overhead) was reduced by $33\frac{1}{3}\%$.

What is the maximum rate of markdown that can be advertised instead of the usual 20%?

SOLUTION

STEP 1

Determine the cost C.
Let the regular selling price be S.

$$S = C + E + P$$
$$S = C + 50\% \text{ of } C + 25\% \text{ of } C$$
$$S = C + 0.50C + 0.25C$$
$$5250.00 = 1.75C$$
$$C = \frac{5250.00}{1.75} = \$3000.00$$

STEP 2 Determine the list price L.

Let the list price be \$L.

$$\text{List price} - \text{Discount} = \text{Regular selling price}$$
$$L - 20\% \text{ of } L = 5250.00$$
$$L - 0.20L = 5250.00$$
$$0.80L = 5250.00$$
$$L = \frac{5250.00}{0.80} = \$6562.50$$

STEP 3 Determine the required profit.

$$\text{Normal net profit} = 25\% \text{ of cost}$$
$$= 0.25(3000.00)$$
$$= \$750.00$$
$$\text{Required net profit} = 10\% \text{ of normal net profit}$$
$$= 0.10(750.00)$$
$$= \$75.00$$

STEP 4 Determine the amount of overhead expense to be recovered.

$$\text{Normal overhead expense} = 50\% \text{ of cost}$$
$$= 0.50(3000.00)$$
$$= \$1500.00$$
$$\text{Normal commission} = 40\% \text{ of normal overhead expense}$$
$$= 0.40(1500.00)$$
$$= \$600.00$$
$$\text{Reduction in commission} = 33\tfrac{1}{3}\% \text{ of normal commission}$$
$$= 33\tfrac{1}{3}\%(600.00)$$
$$= \$200.00$$
$$\text{Overhead expense to be recovered} = 1500.00 - 200.00 = \$1300.00$$

STEP 5 Determine the inventory clearance price.

$$\text{Inventory clearance price} = \text{Cost} + \text{Overhead} + \text{Profit}$$
$$= 3000.00 + 1300.00 + 75.00$$
$$= \$4375.00$$

STEP 6 Determine the amount of markdown.

$$\text{Markdown} = \text{List price} - \text{Inventory clearance price}$$
$$= 6562.50 - 4375.00$$
$$= \$2187.50$$

STEP 7 Determine the rate of markdown.

$$\text{Rate of markdown} = \frac{\text{Amount of markdown}}{\text{List price}}$$
$$= \frac{2187.50}{6562.50}$$
$$= 0.333333$$
$$= 33\tfrac{1}{3}\%$$

Instead of the usual 20%, the store can advertise a markdown of $33\frac{1}{3}\%$.

EXERCISE 5.5

A. Answer each of the following questions.

1. A cookware set that cost a dealer \$440 less 55%, 25% is marked up 180% of cost. For quick sale, the cookware was reduced 45%.
   (a) What is the sale price?
   (b) What rate of markup based on cost was realized?

Reference Example 5.5A

2. A gas barbecue cost a retailer \$420 less 33⅓%, 20%, 5%. It carries a regular selling price on its price tag at a markup of 60% of the regular selling price. During the end-of-season sale, the barbecue is marked down 45%.
   (a) What is the end-of-season sale price?
   (b) What rate of markup based on cost will be realized during the sale?

3. The Stereo Shop sold a radio regularly priced at \$125 for \$75. The cost of the radio was \$120 less 33⅓%, 15%. The store's overhead expense is 12% of the regular selling price.
   (a) What was the rate of markdown at which the radio was sold?
   (b) What was the operating profit or loss?
   (c) What rate of markup based on cost was realized?
   (d) What was the rate of markup based on the sale price?

4. An automatic dishwasher cost a dealer \$620 less 37½%, 4%. It is regularly priced at \$558. The dealer's overhead expense is 15% of the regular selling price and the dishwasher was cleared out for \$432.45.
   (a) What was the rate of markdown at which the dishwasher was sold?
   (b) What is the regular markup based on selling price?
   (c) What was the operating profit or loss?
   (d) What rate of markup based on cost was realized?

5. A hardware store paid \$33.45 for a set of cookware. Overhead expense is 15% of the regular selling price and profit is 10% of the regular selling price. During a clearance sale, the set was sold at a markdown of 15%. What was the operating profit or loss on the sale?

6. Aldo's Shoes bought a shipment of 200 pairs of women's shoes for \$42 per pair. The store sold 120 pairs at the regular selling price of \$125 per pair, 60 pairs at a clearance sale at a discount of 40%, and the remaining pairs during an inventory sale at a price that equals cost plus overhead (i.e., a break-even price). The store's overhead is 50% of cost.
   (a) What was the price at which the shoes were sold during the clearance sale?
   (b) What was the selling price during the inventory sale?
   (c) What was the total profit realized on the shipment?
   (d) What was the average rate of markup based on cost that was realized on the shipment?

Reference Example 5.5B

7. The Pottery bought 600 pans auctioned off en bloc for \$4950. This means that each pan has the same cost. On inspection, the pans were classified as normal quality, seconds, or substandard. The 360 normal-quality pans

were sold at a markup of 80% of cost, the 190 pans classified as seconds were sold at a markup of 20% of cost, and the remaining pans classified as substandard were sold at 80% of their cost.

(a) What was the unit price at which each of the three classifications was sold?

(b) If overhead is $33\frac{1}{3}$% of cost, what was the amount of profit realized on the purchase?

(c) What was the average rate of markup based on the selling price at which the pans were sold?

8. A clothing store buys shorts for $24 less 40% for buying over 50 pairs, and less a further $16\frac{2}{3}$% for buying last season's style. The shorts are marked up to cover overhead expenses of 25% of cost and a profit of 33⅓% of cost.
   (a) What is the regular selling price of the shorts?
   (b) What is the maximum amount of markdown to break even?
   (c) What is the rate of markdown if the shorts are sold at the break-even price?

9. Furniture City bought chairs for $75 less 33⅓%, 20%, 10%. The store's overhead is 75% of cost and net profit is 25% of cost.
   (a) What is the regular selling price of the chairs?
   (b) At what price can the chairs be put on sale so that the store incurs an operating loss of no more than 33⅓% of the overhead?
   (c) What is the maximum rate of markdown at which the chairs can be offered for sale in part (b)?

10. Bargain City clothing store purchased raincoats for $36.75. The store requires a markup of 30% of the sale price. What regular selling price should be marked on the raincoats if the store wants to offer a 25% discount without reducing its markup?

11. A jewellery store paid $36.40 for a watch. Store expenses are 24% of regular selling price and the normal net profit is 20% of regular selling price. During a Special Bargain Day Sale, the watch was sold at a discount of 30%. What operating profit or loss was realized on the sale?

12. The Outdoor Shop buys tents for $264 less 25% for buying more than 20 tents. The store operates on a markup of 33⅓% of the sale price and advertises that all merchandise is sold at a discount of 20% of the regular selling price. What is the regular selling price of the tents?

13. The Blast bought stereo equipment listed at $900 less 60%, 16⅔%. Expenses are 45% of the regular selling price and net profit is 15% of the regular selling price. The store decided to change the regular selling price so that it could advertise a 37.5% discount while still maintaining its usual markup. During the annual inventory sale, the unsold equipment was marked down 55% of the new regular selling price. What operating profit or loss was realized on the equipment sold during the sale?

14. Lund's Pro Shop purchased sets of golf clubs for $500 less 40%, 16⅔%. Expenses are 20% of the regular selling price and the required profit is

17.5% of the regular selling price. The store decided to change the regular selling price so that it could offer a 36% discount without affecting its margin. At the end of the season, the unsold sets were advertised at a discount of 54% of the new regular selling price. What operating profit or loss was realized on the sets sold at the end of the season?

15. Big Boy Appliances bought self-cleaning ovens for \$900 less 33⅓%, 5%. Expenses are 15% of the regular selling price and profit is 9% of the regular selling price. For competitive reasons, the store marks all merchandise with a new regular selling price so that a discount of 25% can be advertised without affecting the margin. To promote sales, the ovens were marked down 40%. What operating profit or loss did the store make on the ovens sold during the sales promotion?

16. Blue Lake Marina sells a make of cruiser for \$16 800. This regular selling price covers overhead of 15% of cost and a normal net profit of 10% of cost. The cruisers were marked with a new regular selling price so that the marina can offer a 20% discount while still maintaining its regular gross profit. At the end of the boating season, the cruiser was marked down. The marina made 25% of its usual profit and reduced the usual commission paid to the sales personnel by 33⅓%. The normal commission accounts for 50% of the normal overhead. What was the rate of markdown?

BUSINESS MATH NEWS BOX

The 2006 National Hockey League Salary Cap

From coast to coast, Canada loves its hockey. Millions of fans flock to arenas every season to cheer on their favorite team, dreaming of the day when their team will hoist the Stanley Cup.

There are currently six Canadian teams in the 30-team National Hockey League (NHL); Toronto Maple Leafs, Montreal Canadiens, Ottawa Senators, Edmonton Oilers, Calgary Flames, and Vancouver Canucks.

However, during the 2004/2005 season, NHL owners locked out the players for the first time in league history. The major cause for the lockout was a disagreement between team owners and players regarding player contracts and salaries.

The players felt that the owners were greedy, believing that owners did not want to share in league profits. On the other hand, the owners felt they could no longer afford the spiraling players' salaries. Owners believed that if a salary limit were not put into action, unprofitable franchises would be in financial ruins within a few years.

After a full season of no hockey, owners and players came to a settlement. It was decided that all teams in the NHL would have a salary cap to limit the escalating salaries. Under the salary cap agreement, it was established that no team could spend more than US$39 million for players' salaries. The $39 million NHL salary cap was based on estimated total league revenues of US$1.8 billion.

Recently, the NHL Commissioner, Gary Bettman, announced that the NHL's salary cap could rise as much as 12% to US$44 million in the 2006/2007 season because total league revenues had increased.

Sources: National Hockey League Fans' Association website. "Salary-Cap views prompted impasse." Downloaded February 9, 2007. David Pollack, *San Jose Mercury News*, September 16, 2004. **www.nhlfa.com/news/nr09_16_04.asp;** CBC website. "NHL Salary Cap expected to rise." Downloaded February 9, 2007. *CBC Sports.* December 20, 2005. **www.cbc.ca/sports/story/2005/12/15/nhl051215.html#skip300x250;** USA Today website. *Salaries Database.* Downloaded February 9, 2007. **http://asp.usatoday.com/sports/hockey/nhl/salaries/teamdetail.aspx?year=2003-04&team=28;** Larry DiTore and Sophie Caronello. Bloomberg News, "NHL's Salary Cap May Rise 12 Percent on Higher League Revenue," June 6, 2006. (New York).

QUESTIONS

1. What is total payroll for all 30 teams during the 2005/2006 season?
2. If league revenues remain at $1.8 billion, yet each team increases its salary cap to $44 million, how much profit is earned by the NHL? What is the value of profit as a percentage of league revenues?
3. The Toronto Maple Leafs have a 22-man roster. Ten of their high profile players have been signed. Based on a league cap of $44 million, calculate the average salary for the remaining 12 players.

Player	Annual Salary (in $ Millions)
Mats Sundin	$7.60
Bryan McCabe	$7.15
Pavel Kubina	$5.00
Tomas Kaberle	$4.25
Mike Peca	$2.50
Hal Gill	$2.05
Andrew Raycroft	$1.80
Darcy Tucker	$1.60
Jeff O'Neill	$1.50
Chad Kilger	$1.20

powered by CourseCompass™ and MathXL®
MyMathLab
Go to MyMathLab at www.mathxl.com. You can practise many of this chapter's exercises as often as you want. The guided solutions help you find an answer step by step. You'll find a personalized study plan available to you too!

Review Exercise

1. A toolbox is listed for $56 less 25%, 20%, 5%.

(a) What is the net price of the toolbox?

(b) What is the amount of discount?

(c) What is the single rate of discount that was allowed?

2. Compute the rate of discount allowed on a lawnmower that lists for $168 and is sold for $105.

3. Determine the single rate of discount equivalent to the discount series 35%, 12%, 5%.

4. A 40% discount allowed on an article amounts to $1.44. What is the net price?

5. Baton Construction Supplies has been selling wheelbarrows for $112 less 15%. What additional discount percent must the company offer to meet a competitor's price of $80.92?

6. A freezer was sold during a clearance sale for $387.50. If the freezer was sold at a discount of 16⅔%, what was the list price?

7. The net price of a snow shovel is $20.40 after discounts of 20%, 15%. What is the list price?

8. On May 18, an invoice dated May 17 for $4000 less 20%, 15%, terms 5/10 E.O.M., was received by Aldo Distributors.

(a) What is the last day of the discount period?

(b) What is the amount due if the invoice is paid within the discount period?

9. Air Yukon received a shipment of plastic trays on September 2. The invoice amounting to $25 630 was dated August 15, terms 2/10, n/30 R.O.G. What is the last day for taking the cash discount and how much is to be paid if the discount is taken?

10. What amount must be remitted if the following invoices, all with terms 5/10, 2/30, n/60, are paid together on December 8?
Invoice No. 312 dated November 2 for $923.00
Invoice No. 429 dated November 14 for $784.00
Invoice No. 563 dated November 30 for $873.00

11. Delta Furnishings received an invoice dated May 10 for a shipment of goods received June 21. The invoice was for $8400.00 less 33⅓%, 12½% with terms 3/20 R.O.G. How much must Delta pay on July 9 to reduce its debt

(a) by $2000?

(b) to $2000?

12. The Peel Trading Company received an invoice dated September 20 for $16 000 less 25%, 20%, terms 5/10, 2/30, n/60. Peel made a payment on September 30 to reduce the debt to $5000 and a payment on October 20 to reduce the debt by $3000.

(a) What amount must Peel remit to pay the balance of the debt at the end of the credit period?

(b) What is the total amount paid by Peel?

13. Emco Ltd. received an invoice dated May 5 for $4000 less 15%, 7½%, terms 3/15 E.O.M. A cheque for $1595.65 was mailed by Emco on June 15 as part payment of the invoice.

(a) By how much did Emco reduce the amount due on the invoice?

(b) How much does Emco still owe?

14. Homeward Hardware buys cat litter for $6 less 20% per bag. The store's overhead is 45% of cost and the owner requires a profit of 20% of cost.

(a) For how much should the bags be sold?

(b) What is the amount of markup included in the selling price?

(c) What is the rate of markup based on selling price?

(d) What is the rate of markup based on cost?

(e) What is the break-even price?

(f) What operating profit or loss is made if a bag is sold for $6?

15. A retail store realizes a markup of $31.50 if it sells an article at a markup of 35% of the selling price.

(a) What is the regular selling price?

(b) What is the cost?

(c) What is the rate of markup based on cost?

(d) If overhead expense is 28% of cost, what is the break-even price?

(e) If the article is sold at a markdown of 24%, what is the operating profit or loss?

16. Using a markup of 35% of cost, a store priced a book at $8.91.

(a) What was the cost of the book?

(b) What is the markup as a percent of selling price?

17. A bicycle helmet costing $54.25 was marked up to realize a markup of 30% of the regular selling price.

(a) What was the regular selling price?

(b) What was the markup as a percent of cost?

18. A bedroom suite that cost a dealer $1800 less 37.5%, 18% carries a price tag with a regular selling price at a markup of 120% of cost. For quick sale, the bedroom suite was marked down 40%.

(a) What was the sale price?

(b) What rate of markup based on cost was realized?

19. Gino's purchased men's suits for $195 less 33⅓%. The store operates at a normal markup of 35% of regular selling price. The owner marks all merchandise with new regular selling prices so that the store can offer a 16⅔% discount while maintaining the same gross profit. What is the new regular selling price?

20. An appliance store sold GE coffeemakers for $22.95 during a promotional sale. The store bought the coffeemakers for $36 less 40%, 15%. Overhead is 25% of the regular selling price.

(a) If the store's markup is 40% of the regular selling price, what was the rate of markdown?

(b) What operating profit or loss was made during the sale?

(c) What rate of markup based on cost was realized?

21. Billington's buys shirts for $21 less 25%, 20%. The shirts are priced at a regular selling price to cover expenses of 20% of regular selling price and a profit of 17% of regular selling price. For a special weekend sale, shirts were marked down 20%.

(a) What was the operating profit or loss on the shirts sold during the weekend sale?

(b) What rate of markup was realized based on cost?

22. A jewellery store paid a unit price of $250 less 40%, 16⅔%, 8% for a shipment of designer watches. The store's overhead is 65% of cost and the normal profit is 55% of cost.

(a) What is the regular selling price of the watches?

(b) What must the sale price be for the store to break even?

(c) What is the rate of markdown to sell the watches at the break-even price?

23. Sight and Sound bought large-screen colour TV sets for $1080.00 less 33⅓%, 8⅓%. Overhead is 18% of regular selling price and required profit is 15⅓% of regular selling price. The TV sets were marked at a new regular selling price so that the store was able to advertise a discount of 25% while still maintaining its margin. To clear the inventory, the remaining TV sets were marked down 37½%.

(a) What operating profit or loss is realized at the clearance price?

(b) What is the realized rate of markup based on cost?

24. Ward Machinery lists a log splitter at $1860 less 33⅓%, 15%. To meet competition, Ward wants to reduce its net price to $922.25. What additional percent discount must Ward allow?

25. West End Appliances bought bread makers for $180 less 40%, 16⅔%, 10%. The store's overhead is 45% of regular selling price and the profit required is 21¼% of regular selling price.

(a) What is the break-even price?

(b) What is the maximum rate of markdown that the store can offer to break even?

(c) What is the realized rate of markup based on cost if the bread makers are sold at the break-even price?

26. A merchant realizes a markup of $42 by selling an item at a markup of 37.5% of cost.

(a) What is the regular selling price?

(b) What is the rate of markup based on the regular selling price?

(c) If the merchant's overhead expenses are 17.5% of the regular selling price, what is the break-even price?

(d) If the article is reduced for sale to $121.66, what is the rate of markdown?

27. The Knit Shoppe bought 250 sweaters for $3100; 50 sweaters were sold at a markup of 150% of cost and 120 sweaters at a markup of 75% of cost; 60 of the sweaters were sold during a clearance sale for $15 each and the remaining sweaters were disposed of at 20% below cost. Assume all sweaters had the same cost.

(a) What was the amount of markup realized on the purchase?

(b) What was the percent markup realized based on cost?

(c) What was the gross profit realized based on selling price?

Self-Test

1. Determine the net price of an article listed at $590 less 37.5%, 12.5%, 8⅓%.

2. What rate of discount has been allowed if an item that lists for $270 is sold for $168.75?

3. Compute the single discount percent equivalent to the discount series 40%, 10%, 8⅓%.

4. Discount Electronics lists an article for $1020 less 25% and 15%. A competitor carries the same article for $927 less 25%. What further discount (correct to the nearest 1/10 of 1%) must the competitor allow so that its net price is the same as Discount's?

5. What amount must be remitted if the following invoices, all with terms 4/10, 2/30, n/60, are paid on May 10?
   $850 less 20%, 10% dated March 21
   $960 less 30%, 16⅔% dated April 10
   $1040 less 33⅓%, 25%, 5% dated April 30

6. An invoice for $3200, dated March 20, terms 3/10 E.O.M., was received March 23. What payment must be made on April 10 to reduce the debt to $1200?

7. On January 15, Sheridan Service received an invoice dated January 14, terms 4/10 E.O.M., for $2592. On February 9, Sheridan Service mailed a cheque for $1392 in partial payment of the invoice. By how much did Sheridan Service reduce its debt?

8. What is the regular selling price of an item purchased for $1270 if the markup is 20% of the regular selling price?

9. The regular selling price of merchandise sold in a store includes a markup of 40% based on the regular selling price. During a sale, an item that cost the store $180 was marked down 20%. For how much was the item sold?

10. The net price of an article is $727.20 after discounts of 20% and 10% have been allowed. What was the list price?

11. An item that cost the dealer $350 less 35%, 12.5% carries a regular selling price on the tag at a markup of 150% of cost. For quick sale, the item was reduced 30%. What was the sale price?

12. Find the cost of an item sold for $1904 to realize a markup of 40% based on cost.

13. An article cost $900 and sold for $2520. What was the percent markup based on cost?

14. A markup of $90 is made on a sale. If the markup was 45% based on selling price, what was the cost?

15. An appliance shop reduces the price of an appliance for quick sale from $1560 to $1195. Compute the markdown correct to the nearest $\frac{1}{100}$ of 1%.

16. An invoice shows a net price of $552.44 after discounts of $33\frac{1}{3}$%, 20%, $8\frac{1}{3}$%. What was the list price?

17. A retailer buys an appliance for $1480 less 25%, 15%. The store marks the merchandise at a regular selling price to cover expenses of 40% of the regular selling price and a net profit of 10% of the regular selling price. During a clearance sale, the appliance was sold at a markdown of 45%. What was the operating profit or loss?

18. Discount Electronics buys stereos for $830 less 37.5%, 12.5%. Expenses are 20% of the regular selling price and the required profit is 15% of the regular selling price. All merchandise is marked with a new regular selling price so that the store can advertise a discount of 30% while still maintaining its regular markup. During the annual clearance sale, the new regular selling price of unsold items is marked down 50%. What operating profit or loss does the store make on items sold during the sale?

Challenge Problems

1. Rose Bowl Florists buys and sells roses only by the complete dozen. The owner buys 12 dozen fresh roses daily for $117. He knows that 10% of the roses will wilt before they can be sold. What price per dozen must Rose Bowl Florists charge for its saleable roses to realize a 55% markup based on selling price?

2. A merchant bought some goods at a discount of 25% of the list price. She wants to mark them at a regular selling price so that she can give a discount of 20% of the regular selling price and still make a markup of 25% of the sale price.
   (a) At what percent of the list price should she mark the regular selling price of the goods?
   (b) Suppose the merchant decides she must make a markup of 25% of the cost price. At what percent of the list price should she mark the regular selling price of the goods?

3. On April 13, a stereo store received a new sound system with a list price of $2500 from the manufacturer. The stereo store received a trade discount of 25%. The invoice, with terms 2/10, n/30, arrived on the same day as the sound system. The owner of the store marked up the sound system by 60% of the invoice amount (before cash discount) to cover overhead and profits. The owner paid the invoice on April 20. How much extra profit will be made on the sale, as a percent of the regular selling price, due to the early payment of the invoice?

Case Study 5.1 Planning for Production

» Ethan Baxter has decided to expand his garden supply manufacturing business. He has an available factory site that is presently costing him $65 000 per year in taxes and maintenance. Ethan has made a deal with Stellar Supply Company to provide him with the necessary material to produce 1400 garden sprinklers. Stellar has agreed to supply the material for $7200 less 2% for quantity discount. Ethan's shop steward has informed him that labour costs will amount to $11 500 to make the sprinklers.

QUESTIONS

1. Ethan expects that it will take three months to produce the garden sprinklers, and he intends to market them at $35.99 per sprinkler. How many sprinklers must Ethan sell to break even?
2. What is the break-even point as a percent of capacity?
3. If Ethan sells all 1400 sprinklers, how much profit can he expect to make assuming the costs listed above?
4. Ethan has been informed that the union has negotiated a 3.5% wage increase.
   (a) What effect will the wage increase have on the break-even point?
   (b) What effect will the wage increase have on Ethan's profit if 1400 units are sold?

Case Study 5.2 Calculating Car Costs

» Abraham is concerned about the high-cost gasoline that his current car consumes. He is considering purchasing a new car. He realizes that he must take into account the purchase price of the new car as well as the savings in gasoline costs to determine when he would be saving money by having a new car.

Abraham has designed a mathematical formula to calculate the number of years he must drive the new car. He uses the following variables in his formula:

y = the number of years Abraham must own the new car

m = the gasoline used by the current car, measured in kilometres per litre

n = the gasoline used by the new car, measured in kilometres per litre

c = the net cost of the new car (purchase price of the new car minus trade-in value of the old car)

d = the average number of kilometres driven per year

p = the price of gasoline per litre

x = the number of years to break even

Abraham has decided the "current car–new car" relationship might be expressed as follows:

Cost of gasoline for current car during break-even period = Cost of gasoline for new car during break-even period + Net cost of new car

QUESTIONS

1. Using the variables defined by Abraham, what is the expression for each side of the "current car–new car" relationship?
2. What is the general formula for the break-even period for the "current car–new car" relationship?
3. What is the break-even period if Abraham's current car has a trade-in value of $6500 and gets 9 km/L? Gasoline prices in Abraham's neighbourhood average $0.95/L. Assume Abraham drives an average of 35 000 kilometres per year.
4. Assume that the price of gasoline can vary by 25% from the price of $0.95/L.
   (a) How does the break-even period change when the price of gasoline declines by 25%?
   (b) How does the break-even period change when the price of gasoline increases by 25%?
5. What is the expected break-even period if Abraham buys a car costing $23 000 with an expected gas consumption of 18 km/L if the average price is
   (a) $0.95/L?
   (b) $1.05/L?
   (c) $1.10/L?
6. What assumptions did you make when you solved these problems? What cost factors have not been considered?

SUMMARY OF FORMULAS

Formula 5.1A

$$\text{AMOUNT OF DISCOUNT} = \text{RATE OF DISCOUNT} \times \text{LIST PRICE}$$

Finding the amount of discount when the list price is known

Formula 5.1B

$$\text{LIST PRICE} = \frac{\text{AMOUNT OF DISCOUNT}}{\text{RATE OF DISCOUNT}}$$

Finding the list price when the amount of discount is known

Formula 5.1C

$$\text{RATE OF DISCOUNT} = \frac{\text{AMOUNT OF DISCOUNT}}{\text{LIST PRICE}}$$

Finding the rate of discount when the amount of discount is known

Formula 5.2

$$\text{NET PRICE} = \text{LIST PRICE} - \text{AMOUNT OF DISCOUNT}$$

Finding the net amount when the amount of discount is known

Formula 5.3A

$$\text{NET PRICE FACTOR (NPF)} = 100\% - \%\ \text{DISCOUNT}$$

Finding the net price factor (NPF)

Formula 5.3B

$$\text{NET PRICE FACTOR (NPF)} = (1 - d)$$

where d = rate of discount in decimal form

Restatement of Formula 5.3A in algebraic terms

Formula 5.4A

$$\text{NET PRICE} = \text{NET PRICE FACTOR (NPF)} \times \text{LIST PRICE}$$

Finding the net amount directly without computing the amount of discount

Formula 5.4B

$$N = (1 - d)L \text{ or } N = L(1 - d)$$

Restatement of Formula 5.4A in algebraic terms

Formula 5.5A

$$\text{NET PRICE FACTOR (NPF) FOR THE DISCOUNT SERIES} = \text{NPF FOR THE FIRST DISCOUNT} \times \text{NPF FOR THE SECOND DISCOUNT} \times \ldots \times \text{NPF FOR THE LAST DISCOUNT}$$

Formula 5.5B

$$\text{NPF FOR A DISCOUNT SERIES} = (1 - d_1)(1 - d_2)(1 - d_3) \ldots (1 - d_n)$$

Restatement of Formula 5.5A in algebraic terms

Formula 5.6A

$$\text{NET PRICE} = \text{NET PRICE FACTOR FOR THE DISCOUNT SERIES} \times \text{LIST PRICE}$$

Finding the net amount directly when a list price is subject to a series of discounts

Formula 5.6B

$$\text{NET PRICE} = (1 - d_1)(1 - d_2)(1 - d_3) \ldots (1 - d_n)L$$

Restatement of Formula 5.6A in algebraic terms

Formula 5.7

SINGLE EQUIVALENT RATE OF DISCOUNT FOR A DISCOUNT SERIES

$$= 1 - \text{NPF FOR THE DISCOUNT SERIES}$$

$$= 1 - [(1 - d_1)(1 - d_2)(1 - d_3) \ldots (1 - d_n)]$$

Finding the single rate of discount that has the same effect as a given series of discounts

Formula 5.8A

$$\text{SELLING PRICE} = \text{COST OF BUYING} + \text{EXPENSES} + \text{PROFIT}$$

or

$$S = C + E + P$$

Basic relationship between selling price, cost of buying, operating expenses (or overhead), and profit

Formula 5.8B

$$\text{SELLING PRICE} = \text{COST OF BUYING} + \text{MARKUP}$$

or

$$S = C + M$$

Formula 5.9

$$\text{MARKUP} = \text{EXPENSES} + \text{PROFIT}$$

or

$$M = E + P$$

Basic relationship between markup, cost of buying, operating expenses (or overhead), and profit

Formula 5.10

$$\text{RATE OF MARKUP BASED ON COST} = \frac{\text{MARKUP}}{\text{COST}} = \frac{M}{C}$$

Finding the rate of markup as a percent of cost

Formula 5.11

$$\text{RATE OF MARKUP BASED ON SELLING PRICE} = \frac{\text{MARKUP}}{\text{SELLING PRICE}} = \frac{M}{S}$$

Finding the rate of markup as a percent of selling price

GLOSSARY

Cash discount a reduction in the amount of an invoice, usually to encourage prompt payment of the invoice *(p. 188)*

Credit period the time period at the end of which an invoice has to be paid *(p. 188)*

Discount a reduction from the original price *(p. 182)*

Discount period the time period during which a cash discount applies *(p. 188)*

Discount series two or more discounts taken off a list price in succession *(p. 182)*

End-of-month dating payment terms based on the last day of the month in which the invoice is dated *(p. 191)*

Gross profit *see* **Markup**

List price price printed in a catalogue or in a list of prices *(p. 179)*

Manufacturer's suggested retail price (MSRP) catalogue or list price that is reduced by a trade discount *(p. 179)*

Margin *see* **Markup**

Markdown a reduction in the price of an article sold to the consumer *(p. 206)*

Markup the difference between the cost of merchandise and the selling price *(p. 197)*

Net factor *see* **Net price factor (NPF)**

Net price the difference between a list price and the amount of discount *(p. 179)*

Net price factor (NPF) the difference between 100% and a percent discount—the net price expressed as a fraction of the list price *(p. 181)*

Ordinary dating payment terms based on the date of an invoice *(p. 189)*

Partial payment part payment of an invoice *(p. 193)*

Payment terms a statement of the conditions under which a cash discount may be taken *(p. 188)*

Rate of discount a reduction in price expressed as a percent of the original price *(p. 179, 188)*

Receipt-of-goods dating payment terms based on the date the merchandise is received *(p. 192)*

Regular selling price the price of an article sold to the consumer before any markdown is applied *(p. 207)*

Sale price the price of an article sold to the consumer after a markdown has been applied *(p. 207)*

Single equivalent rate of discount the single rate of discount that has the same effect as a specific series of discounts *(p. 184)*

Total cost the cost at which merchandise is purchased plus the overhead *(p. 206)*

Trade discount a reduction of a catalogue or list price *(p. 179)*

USEFUL INTERNET SITES

www.electronicaccountant.com

Electronic Accountant Free access to news and critical accounting industry information. This site includes Newswire, links and commentary, discussion groups, feature articles, and accounting/tax software exhibit halls.

www.ibc.ca

Insurance Bureau of Canada This site offers an overview of the industry and of recent legal and consumer-related developments and provides significant links to both business and government sites.

CHAPTER 6

Break-Even and Cost-Volume-Profit Analysis

OBJECTIVES

Upon completing this chapter, you will be able to do the following:

1. Compute break-even values using cost-volume-profit relationships.
2. Compute break-even values using contribution margin and contribution rate.
3. Construct and interpret cost-volume-profit charts.
4. Compute the effects of changes to cost, volume, and profit.

Determining how many items you need, just to cover costs, is an important technique in many business situations. Through analysis of the relationships among costs, volumes, and profits, you can calculate the number of units you need to sell, the price to charge, and the costs you may incur in operating a business. Understanding the relationships among costs, volumes, and profits allows you to determine the effect of changes to these on quantities and profits.

INTRODUCTION

One of the main concerns to owners and management in operating a business is profitability. To achieve or maintain a desired level of profitability, managers must make decisions that determine product quantity, total revenue, and total cost.

Cost-volume-profit analysis is a valuable tool in evaluating the potential effects of decisions on profitability. In this type of analysis, computations involving **break-even analysis** may be involved. Further calculations may be performed to determine the effect of changes in one or more components. This technique is **sensitivity analysis.**

Appendix I on the CD-ROM at the back of this text contains an introduction to linear programming, which is a useful mathematical tool in making decisions regarding product mix to maximize total profit.

6.1 BREAK-EVEN ANALYSIS AND COST-VOLUME-PROFIT RELATIONSHIPS

Eric is planning to set up a business to make and sell wooden birdhouses. He would sell these through family and friends, and display and sell them at craft fairs. He had always been interested in making unique items out of wood, even from scraps of wood, and had also always been interested in operating his own business. Since his friends and family had already placed orders for his items, he had determined that there was further demand for these wooden birdhouses. He had been offered the use of a workshop for only $400 a month. The low rent had been negotiated based on the agreement that he would clean up the workshop each week. For supplies and materials, Eric estimated that he would have to spend $10 to make each birdhouse. He also estimated that he could sell each of them for $30. If he worked hard, he could make 500 birdhouses in a year. After purchasing a heavy duty sander and saw, along with his other tools, he was ready to get started.

To determine how much profit he would make, Eric calculated his income on the basis of different numbers of birdhouses sold, summarizing the information in the chart shown below.

Number of Birdhouses	0	100	200	300	400	500
Revenue	0	3 000	6 000	9 000	12 000	15 000
Material and supplies	0	1 000	2 000	3 000	4 000	5 000
Workshop costs	400	400	400	400	400	400
Total cost	400	1 400	2 400	3 400	4 400	5 400
Net income (Revenue − Total cost)	−400	1 600	3 600	5 600	7 600	9 600

To proceed, Eric took all the above information to his friend Ravi, a business student. Eric wanted to know if there was a way of determining how many birdhouses he needed to make and sell in order to cover his expenses. He also wanted to know how to determine the effects on the net income of changes in the price per birdhouse, the cost of materials, and other costs.

Ravi pointed out that he would analyze the situation using "break-even analysis." Ravi needed to determine which costs were fixed and which were variable to the number of birdhouses made and sold. He would use all the information, and then make changes to one part to determine the effect.

A primary function of accounting is the collection of cost and revenue data. These data are then used to examine the existing relationships between cost behaviour and revenue behaviour.

Any analysis, whether algebraic or graphic, makes certain assumptions about the behaviour of costs and revenue. In its simplest form, cost-volume-profit analysis makes the following assumptions:

Cost-Volume-Profit Assumptions

1. Revenue per unit of output (price) is constant. Total revenue varies directly with volume.
2. Costs can be classified as either fixed or variable.
3. **Fixed costs** remain constant over the time period considered for all levels of output. Examples of costs in this category are rent, amortization, property taxes, and supervision and management salaries. Since fixed costs are constant in total, they can be averaged over various numbers of units. When this is calculated, the fixed costs appear to vary per unit of output. Fixed costs per unit of output decrease as volume increases because the total cost is spread out over more units.
4. **Variable costs** are constant per unit of output regardless of volume. They increase or decrease in total amount as volume fluctuates. Examples of costs in this category are direct material costs, direct labour costs, and sales commissions.

With the above assumptions, the real world is viewed in a simplified manner. In most actual situations, fixed costs are not constant across all levels of output; instead, they tend to change in step fashion. Also, per-unit variable costs are not always constant; they are often influenced by economies of scale. Finally, most of the time, costs cannot be rigidly classified as fixed or variable; many costs are semi-variable, with both a fixed and a variable component. However, for purposes of an uncomplicated introductory analysis, these assumptions are useful.

The break-even approach to cost-volume-profit analysis focuses on profitability. When total costs are subtracted from total revenue, the result is net income.

$$\text{TOTAL REVENUE} - \text{TOTAL COST} = \text{NET INCOME}$$

The approach is specifically concerned with identifying the level of output at which the business neither makes a profit nor sustains a loss—that is, the level of output at which

$$\text{NET INCOME} = 0$$

This level of output is called the **break-even point** and is obtained from the relationship

$$\text{TOTAL REVENUE} = \text{TOTAL COST}$$

Total revenue is determined when the quantity of units sold is multiplied by the selling price for a unit.

$$\text{TOTAL REVENUE} = \text{VOLUME (in units)} \times \text{PRICE}$$

The amount of total cost is separated into the amount of fixed cost and the amount of variable cost.

$$\text{TOTAL COST} = \text{FIXED COST} + \text{TOTAL VARIABLE COST}$$

Also, when the quantity of units sold is multiplied by the variable cost for a unit, the result is the total variable cost.

$$\text{TOTAL VARIABLE COST} = \text{VOLUME (in units)} \times \text{VARIABLE COST PER UNIT}$$

Thus, the relationship is determined as follows:

$$(\text{VOLUME} \times \text{PRICE}) - (\text{VOLUME} \times \text{VARIABLE COST PER UNIT}) - \text{FIXED COST} = \text{PROFIT}$$ **Formula 6.1**

Therefore, using Formula 6.1,

$(P \times X) - (VC \times X) - FC = PFT$ where the volume in units is X.

In Eric's birdhouse business, we identify the following:

$$P = 30.00$$
$$VC = 10.00$$
$$FC = 400.00$$

At the break-even point, let the volume in units be X.

We calculate the break-even point in units as

$$(30.00X) - (10.00X) - 400.00 = 0$$
$$(30.00 - 10.00)X - 400.00 = 0$$
$$20.00X = 400.00$$
$$X = 20$$

Therefore, Eric will break even when he sells 20 birdhouses. At that point, his revenues will exactly cover his expenses.

It is also important to determine the amount of revenue, or total sales dollars, needed to break even.

We view the break-even point as the point at which the total revenue equals the total costs. When Eric sells 20 birdhouses, his total costs are

$$(\$10 \times 20) + \$400 = \$600$$

To cover all of his costs, in order to break even, the revenues needed are ($20 \times \$30$), or \$600.

Break-Even Analysis—Case 1

EXAMPLE 6.1A

Market research for a new product indicates that the product can be sold at $50 per unit. Cost analysis provides the following information.

Fixed cost per period = $8640
Variable cost per unit = $30
Production capacity per period = 900 units

Perform a break-even analysis. Provide:

(i) an algebraic statement of the total revenue and the total cost;

(ii) computation of the break-even point in units;

(iii) computation of the break-even point in dollars.

SOLUTION

(i) Let the volume in units be X.

(a) Total revenue, TR = Volume × Price

$$\text{TR} = (X)(50.00)$$
$$\text{TR} = 50.00X$$

(b) Total variable cost = Volume × Variable cost per unit

$$\text{TVC} = (X)(30.00)$$
$$\text{TVC} = 30.00X$$

Total cost, TC = Fixed cost + Total variable cost

$$\text{TC} = 8640.00 + 30.00X$$

(ii) Substituting into the break-even formula:

$$50.00X - (30.00X + 8640.00) = 0$$
$$50.00X - 30.00X - 8640.00 = 0$$
$$20.00X - 8640.00 = 0$$
$$20.00X = 8640.00$$
$$X = 432$$

(iii) The total revenue needed to break even would be
$50.00 \times 432 = \$21\,600.00$

Proven by:
$(50.00 \times 432) - (30.00 \times 432) - 8640.00 = 0$

Break-Even Analysis—Case 2

When the sales and variable costs are only available in total dollars, not in the form of dollars per unit, a relationship between sales and variable costs can be determined. Note that, in the given information, the net income is not zero. This indicates that the given sales amount does not represent a break-even point.

To determine the break-even point in sales dollars, assume that the price per unit is $1. You can then calculate the variable cost per unit by dividing the total variable costs by the total sales. The break-even point can then be calculated.

EXAMPLE 6.1B

The following information is available about the operations of the King Corporation for the current years.

Sales		\$40 000
Fixed costs	\$12 600	
Variable costs	16 000	
Total cost		28 600
Net income		\$11 400

Capacity is a sales volume of \$60 000.

Perform a break-even analysis. Provide

(i) an algebraic statement of
  (a) the revenue function;
  (b) the cost function;

(ii) computation of
  (a) the break-even point in sales dollars;
  (b) the break-even point as a percent of capacity.

SOLUTION

(i) When the data are in terms of total dollars rather than units, express the functions in terms of sales volume.
Let X represent the number of units sold.

(a) Assuming that the price per unit is \$1, the revenue function, TR, is expressed as $\$1 \times X$.

(b) Since variable costs are directly related to sales volume, they can be expressed as a percent of sales volume.

In this example, total variable costs are \$16 000 for a sales volume of \$40 000.

$$\frac{\text{Total variable cost}}{\text{Total revenue}} = \frac{16\ 000}{40\ 000} = 0.40 = 40\%$$

This means that when the price per unit is \$1, the variable cost per unit is \$0.40.

Total variable cost $= \$0.40 \times$ Number of units $= 0.40X$

The total cost function is TC $= 0.40X + 12\ 600.00$

or TC $= 0.40X + 12\ 600.00$

(ii) The break-even point is given by

$$1.00X = 0.40X + 12\ 600.00$$
$$0.60X = 12\ 600.00$$
$$X = 21\ 000.00$$

(a) The break-even volume in dollars is \$21 000.

(b) The break-even point as a percent of capacity is $\frac{21\ 000.00}{60\ 000.00} = 0.35 = 35\%$.

EXAMPLE 6.1C

Nia and Jody are putting together a plan for a student skiing trip for their class. The trip would involve two days of ski passes, with a one-night stay in a local hotel, and round-trip bus transportation to the ski resort. The cost of a two-day ski pass is $99. They estimate the hotel stay would cost $49 per night per person. To rent the bus and to pay for the driver's time, the cost would be $1000 for the two days. The bus can hold a maximum of 40 people, excluding the driver.

If they sell only 25 tickets, how much must they charge each person for the trip?

SOLUTION

$X = 25$
$\text{VC} = 99.00 + 49.00 = \$148.00$
$\text{FC} = 1000.00$

Substituting into the formula:

Let the price per unit be P.

$$(\text{P} \times 25) - (148.00 \times 25) - 1000.00 = 0$$
$$(\text{P} \times 25) - 3\,700.00 - 1000.00 = 0$$
$$(\text{P} \times 25) = 4\,700.00$$
$$\text{P} = \frac{4\,700.00}{25}$$
$$\text{P} = \$188.00$$

They must charge $188 per person to break even.

EXAMPLE 6.1D

Galaxy Caterers provides dinners for events at a price of $87.50 per contract. The average variable cost for a contract is $62.50. They catered 112 contracts last month, and expect that this will be the average for each month in the future. The company is wishing to expand, but their kitchen and food preparation space is limited. The owner has located several possible new locations to rent and needs to determine how much extra space she can afford and still stay profitable.

What is the most they can spend on rent and other fixed costs in order to break even?

SOLUTION

$\text{P} = 87.50$
$\text{VC} = 62.50$
$X = 112$

Let the fixed cost be FC.

Substituting into the formula:

$$(87.50 \times 112) - (62.50 \times 112) - \text{FC} = 0$$
$$9800.00 - 7000.00 = \text{FC}$$
$$\text{FC} = 2800.00$$

Therefore, they must pay no more than $2800 in fixed costs to break even.

EXAMPLE 6.1E

Helene and Michel have approached their Uncle Henri for a loan to set up a business. They wish to deliver bouquets of flowers to the people and businesses in their neighbourhood. Uncle Henri has asked them to estimate their revenue and their costs and do a break-even analysis. They need to lease a delivery van, at \$900 per month including insurance. The cost of advertising would be \$300 per month. If they price the bouquets at \$35 each, they estimate that they can sell 80 units per month.

What is the most they can spend to purchase each bouquet of flowers to break even?

SOLUTION

$P = 35.00$
$FC = 900.00 + 300.00 = 1200.00$
$X = 80$

Let the cost of each bouquet be VC.

Substituting into the formula:

$$
\begin{aligned}
(35.00 \times 80) - (VC \times 80) - 1200.00 &= 0 \\
2800.00 - (VC \times 80) &= 1200.00 \\
-(VC \times 80) &= -1600.00 \\
VC &= 20
\end{aligned}
$$

Therefore, they must pay no more than \$20 to purchase each bouquet of flowers to break even.

POINTERS AND PITFALLS

You can use the BREAKEVEN function of a financial calculator to determine the break-even point. In this function, FC refers to the total fixed cost for the period, VC refers to the unit variable cost, P refers to the unit price, PFT is the resulting profit, and Q is used to input or calculate the quantity or number of units. For example, for Example 6.1A, press:

2nd **Brkevn** FC = 8640.00 **Enter** ↓

VC = 30.00 **Enter** ↓

P = 50.00 **Enter** ↓

PFT = 0 **Enter** ↓

CPT Q = 432 units

Any four of the five variables may be entered. You can then compute a value for the fifth variable.

EXERCISE 6.1

A. For each of the following, perform a break-even analysis showing

(a) an algebraic statement of

(i) the revenue function,

(ii) the cost function;

(b) computation of the break-even point

(i) in units,

(ii) in sales dollars,

(iii) as a percent of capacity.

1. Engineering estimates show that the variable cost of manufacturing a new product will be \$35 per unit. Based on market research, the selling price of the product is to be \$120 per unit and variable selling expense is expected to be \$15 per unit. The fixed costs applicable to the new product are estimated to be \$2800 per period and capacity per period is 100 units.

2. A firm manufactures a product that sells for \$12 per unit. Variable cost per unit is \$8 and fixed cost per period is \$1200. Capacity per period is 1000 units.

3. The neighbourhood bookstore sells novels for \$6.95 per unit. The cost to purchase one book is \$3.95. The store has fixed costs per month of \$1800. The store estimates that they can sell 1000 books every month.

4. Tara makes and sells hats for children and adults. She is able to sell the hats for \$18 per unit. Materials for the hats cost \$4 each. She has fixed costs per month of \$280, and estimates that she can make and sell 80 hats each month.

B. **1.** Bargain Toys has just acquired the rights to merchandise the latest video game. They can purchase these games for \$16. If they advertise the games, at a cost of \$630 per month, and sell them for \$30 each, how many games do they need to sell each month to break even? Reference Example 6.1A

2. Old-Tyme Fashions specializes in hats modelled after fashions from the past. It purchases these hats for \$42 each. It can provide a custom service to print the new owner's name on the hatband. The printing machine costs \$243 per month to rent. If Old-Tyme sells the hats at a price of \$69 each, how many does it need to sell to break even?

3. The operating budget for Packard Machinery Company shows a net income of \$469 300. To achieve this, the company is targeting sales of \$740 000, variable costs of \$259 000, and fixed costs of \$11 700. Based on this information, what is the total revenue at the break-even point? Reference Example 6.1B

4. The Scarlet Letter bookstore has \$85 000 of sales, variable costs of \$36 550, and fixed costs of \$27 360. What would their sales have to be to break even?

5. Parma is considering the expansion of her picture-framing camera business to include the printing of oversize pictures from CDs. She would need to lease equipment, at a cost of \$417 per month. To process the pictures, she estimates that she would have supplies expenses of \$3 per picture. If she can sell 60 pictures per month, what price should she charge to break even? Reference Example 6.1C

6. Jay and his friends have set up a baseball tournament. He can rent a baseball field for a daily charge of \$200 and equipment for \$150 per day. If he hires independent umpires, he would need to pay \$280 for the day. He would arrange to have caps made for each player at a cost of \$4 each. If John can get 90 people to participate, what would he have to charge each of them to recover his costs?

7. John wants to earn money this summer by maintaining gardens and lawns. He would have variable costs for each job of \$2 for supplies. To be competitive, he can charge \$22 per job, and would be able to maintain at least 80 jobs.
   (a) To break even, what is the most he could pay for equipment?
   (b) If John wanted to make \$900, what is the most he could pay to purchase his equipment? Reference Example 6.1D

8. Melinda and Morris sell soda at ball games. They charge \$2 per can of soda. The cost to purchase the soda is \$0.60 per can. They estimate that they can sell at least 200 cans at each game.
   (a) To break even, what is the most that they can pay in fixed costs?
   (b) If they sell 300 cans during a game, how much can they pay in fixed costs?

9. Woody Woodworks makes and sells cedar planter boxes, charging \$35 for each box. Woody had purchased tools costing \$756 to make the planter boxes. Wood and other supplies cost \$8 per box if the boxes are unfinished. An additional amount for supplies would be spent if the boxes were painted.
   (a) To break even, how many unfinished boxes must he sell?
   (b) A special order from the City of Langdale for 100 boxes at \$30 per box has been negotiated. They want the boxes to be painted. To make a profit of \$12 per box, how much can be spent on additional painting supplies? Reference Example 6.1E

10. Little Hands Daycare charges \$40 per day per child. Fixed expenses include \$120 per day for wages and \$300 per day for space rental and insurance. The daycare can take in up to 20 children each day and is expected to be full.
   (a) To break even, what is the most that can be spent on supplies per child per day?
   (b) To achieve a profit of \$200 per day, what is the amount that can be spent on supplies per child per day?

6.2 CONTRIBUTION AND CONTRIBUTION MARGIN

As an alternative to using the break-even relationship Total revenue = Total cost, we can use the concept of contribution margin to determine break-even volume.

For Eric's birdhouse project, each additional birdhouse sold increases the revenue by \$30. However, at the same time, costs increase by the variable cost (material and supplies) of \$10 per birdhouse. As a result the profit increases by the difference, which is $30 - 10 = \$20$. This difference of \$20, which is the selling price per unit less the variable cost per unit, is the **contribution margin** per unit.

If Eric sells zero units, revenue is \$0 and variable cost is \$0. Total cost then equals fixed cost, which is \$400. His net income (which is Revenue − Total cost) is –\$400 (a loss); that is, his loss equals the fixed cost.

If Eric sells one birdhouse, revenue increases by \$30; total cost increases by \$10 to \$410; net income = 30 − 410 = −\$380 (a loss). The sale of one unit decreases the loss by \$20; that is, the contribution margin of \$20 has absorbed \$20 in fixed costs.

If Eric sells 10 birdhouses, total revenue = 10(30) = \$300; variable costs = 10(10) = 100 and total costs = 400 + 100 = \$500; the loss = 300 − 500 = −\$200. The reduction in loss is \$200. This reduction in loss represents the contribution margin for 10 units, which has absorbed \$200 in fixed costs.

The break-even volume is reached when the accumulated contribution margin of a number of units covers the fixed costs. In Eric's case, this happens when 20 units are sold, since 20(20) = \$400.

The contribution margin of \$20 expressed as a fraction of the unit selling price is $\frac{20}{30} = 0.333 = 33\frac{1}{3}\%$. This is called the **contribution rate.**

The contribution margin approach is attractive to businesspeople, because it looks at how much the sale of each additional unit (or how each additional sales dollar) contributes to the absorption of fixed costs and increases net income.

In general,

$$\text{CONTRIBUTION MARGIN PER UNIT} = \text{SELLING PRICE PER UNIT} - \text{VARIABLE COST PER UNIT}$$ — **Formula 6.2**

$$\text{CONTRIBUTION RATE} = \frac{\text{UNIT CONTRIBUTION MARGIN}}{\text{UNIT SELLING PRICE}}$$ — **Formula 6.3**

$$\text{BREAK-EVEN VOLUME} = \frac{\text{FIXED COST}}{\text{UNIT CONTRIBUTION MARGIN}}$$ — **Formula 6.4**

EXAMPLE 6.2A

Use contribution margin per unit to determine the contribution rate and the break-even volume for Example 6.1A.

SOLUTION

Fixed cost = \$8640.00;
Selling price per unit = \$50.00;
Variable cost per unit = \$30.00.
Contribution margin per unit = 50.00 − 30.00 = \$20.00.

$$\text{Contribution rate} = \frac{20}{50} = 0.40 = 40\%$$

$$\text{Break-even volume} = \frac{\text{FIXED COST}}{\text{CONTRIBUTION MARGIN}} = \frac{\$8640}{\$20} = 432.$$

Break-even volume is 432 units.

EXAMPLE 6.2B

Use contribution margin per unit to determine the contribution rate and the break-even volume for Example 6.1B.

SOLUTION

Fixed cost = \$12 600;
when the sales volume is given in total dollars, the selling price per unit = \$1;
contribution margin in total = \$40 000 − \$16 000 = \$24 000

$$\text{Contribution rate} = \frac{\$0.60}{\$1} = 60\%$$

$$\text{Break-even volume} = \frac{12\,600}{0.60} = 21\,000.$$

Break-even volume is a sales volume of \$21 000.

EXERCISE 6.2

A. For each of the following, perform a break-even analysis showing computation of the

(a) contribution margin;
(b) contribution rate;
(c) break-even point in units;
(d) break-even point in sales dollars.

1. Rubber and Steel Company is planning to manufacture a new product. The variable costs will be \$61 per unit and the fixed costs are estimated to be \$5904. To be competitive, the selling price of the product is to be \$150 per unit. Variable selling expense is expected to be \$17 per unit. Reference Example 6.2A

2. Rosemary is planning to make fancy multi-tiered wedding cakes for the next wedding season. To make the cakes, she must invest \$834 in some special baking pans and tools. To get started, she needs to spend \$1800 to advertise in the newspaper. She estimates that supplies and materials for each cake will cost \$60. She is planning to set the price for each cake at \$499.

3. To pay for his academic fees, Tarek, a college student, is selling a computer accessory to other students. His cost to purchase each piece is \$53, and he is planning to sell the accessories for \$99 each. Fixed costs for advertising amount to \$500.

4. Lorne is considering working for Part-Time Painters. He would operate as an independent painter, but the jobs would be given to him by the company. In the company's advertisements, \$100 would be charged for each room painted. The painter would then receive 80% of the amount billed. For each job, the painter would supply paint and brushes, at a cost of \$38. Each painter must have his or her own ladders, drop cloths, and other tools, at a cost of \$720.

5. The following data pertain to the operating budget of Jones Tent Manufacturing.

Sales		$1 020 000
Fixed cost	$160 000	
Total variable cost	581 400	
Total cost		741 400
Net income		$278 600

Reference Example 6.2B

6. Furry Friends Food Manufacturing has compiled the following estimates for operations.

Sales		$765 000
Fixed cost	$152 100	
Total variable cost	497 250	
Total cost		649 350
Net income		$115 650

B.

1. A watchmaker charges $19.99 to replace the battery and clean watches. Variable costs include the battery and cost $7. Specialized tools costing $346 had to be purchased. How many watches need to be cleaned to break even?

Reference Example 6.2A

2. A vehicle accessory shop is considering buying a new style of wheels for $168 and selling them at $369.60 for each wheel. Fixed costs related to this new style of wheel amount to $2465. It is estimated that 16 wheels per month could be sold. How much profit will the accessory shop make each month?

3. Slicks Mechanics provide oil changes for vehicles for $21.99. For each vehicle, the cost of oil is $6.59 to the shop. Fixed costs for this type of service are $2602.60. How many oil changes need to be completed to break even?

4. Rover's Friends provides dog washing services. For each dog, supplies cost $3 and wages are $5. To provide this service, a special room and equipment are needed, at a cost of $300 per month. Rover's Friends maintains an average of 30 dogs washed each month. What must they charge as a price for the dog washing service in order to break even?

5. MacDonald Elementary School needs to raise money for new playground equipment. The students will be selling chocolate bars for $3 each. The chocolate bars will be purchased for $1.25 each. The school budgets $140 for flyers to be distributed to the houses in the school neighbourhood. How many chocolate bars must they sell to break even? How much money will they make if they achieve their target of selling 1000 chocolate bars?

6. Tina, an entrepreneurial business student, wants to set up a business completing tax forms for other students. Her price would be $50 for each job. Fixed expenses include $395 for the purchase of tax software, which Tina would purchase. Tina would hire some accounting students to complete the forms, paying them for two hours at $12 per hour for each job. She would also have paper and supplies costs of $5 per job. How many jobs would she have to generate before she starts to make a profit?

7. The following data pertain to the operating budget of Matt Manufacturing:

Sales		$720 000
Fixed cost	$220 000	
Total variable cost	324 000	
Total cost		544 000
Net income		$176 000

Reference Example 6.2B

8. Harrow Seed and Fertilizer has compiled the following estimates for operations:

Sales		$240 000
Fixed cost	$43 200	
Total variable cost	96 000	
Total cost		139 200
Net income		$100 800

6.3 BREAK-EVEN CHARTS

The behaviour of revenue and the behaviour of costs may be represented graphically by straight-line diagrams. These are shown in Figures 6.1 and 6.2, which portray Eric's birdhouse revenue and costs. Figures 6.3 and 6.4 are general representations of revenue and cost behaviour.

FIGURE 6.1 Eric's Birdhouse Revenue

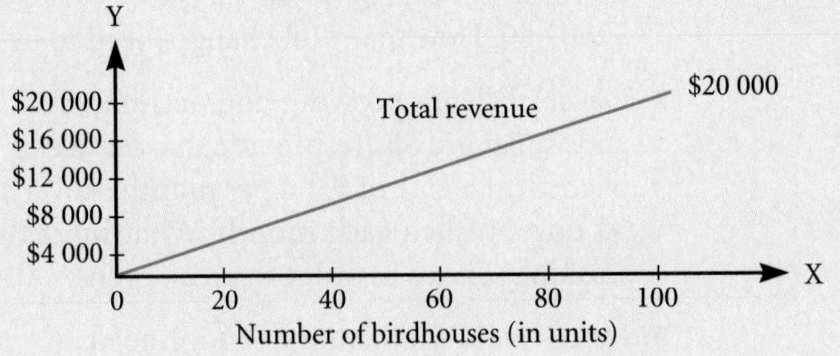

FIGURE 6.2 Eric's Birdhouse Costs

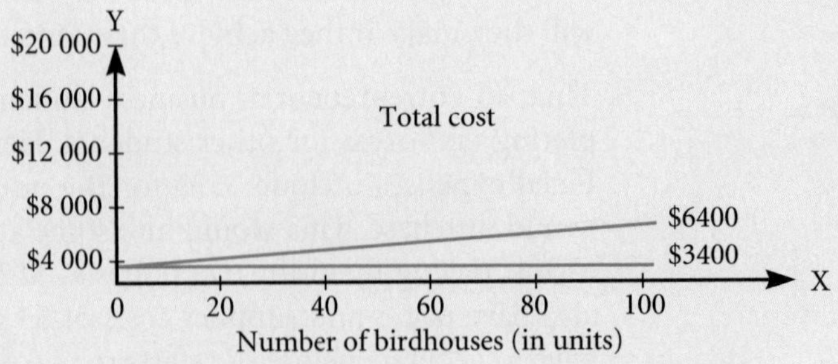

FIGURE 6.3 **Revenue Behaviour**

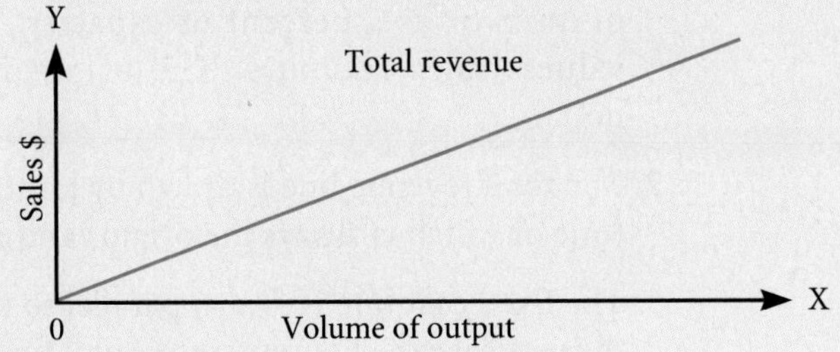

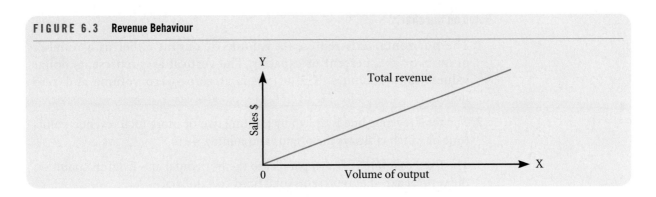

FIGURE 6.4 **Cost Behaviour**

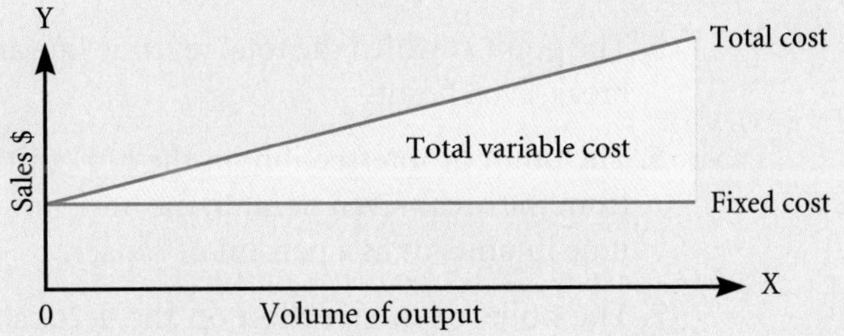

The break-even approach to cost-volume-profit analysis focuses on profitability. The relationship between revenue and costs at different levels of output may be portrayed graphically by showing revenue behaviour (Figure 6.3) and cost behaviour (Figure 6.4) on the same graph. The resulting graph shows the break-even point and is known as a **break-even chart** (Figure 6.5).

FIGURE 6.5 **Break-Even Chart**

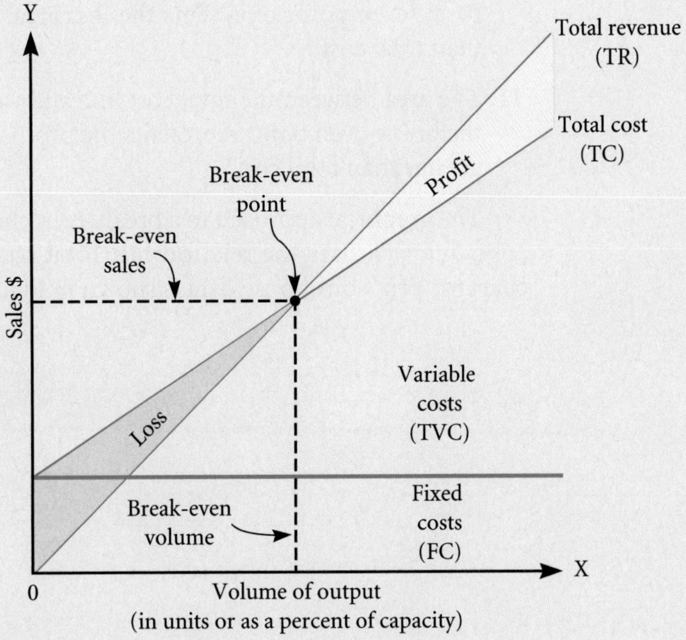

Notes on the charts

1. The horizontal axis represents volume of output either as a number of units or as a percent of capacity. The vertical axis represents dollar values (sales revenue). The origin is at zero—zero volume and zero dollars.
2. The total revenue line is drawn by plotting two or more total revenue points (one of which is always the origin) and joining them.
3. The fixed cost line is drawn parallel to the horizontal axis from the point on the vertical axis that represents total fixed cost dollars.
4. The total cost line is drawn by plotting two or more total cost points (one of which is always the point at which the fixed cost line starts on the vertical axis) and joining them.
5. The point at which the total revenue line and the total cost line intersect is the break-even point.
6. The point of intersection on the horizontal axis of the perpendicular drawn from the break-even point to the horizontal axis indicates the break-even volume in units or as a percent of capacity.
7. The point of intersection on the vertical axis of the perpendicular drawn from the break-even point to the vertical axis indicates the break-even volume in dollars ("Sales $").
8. The area between the horizontal axis and the fixed cost line represents the fixed cost in dollars.
9. The area between the fixed cost line and the total cost line represents the total variable cost in dollars for all levels of operations.
10. The area between the total revenue line and the total cost line to the left of the break-even point represents the loss area, that is, where total revenue is less than total cost.
11. The area between the total cost line and the total revenue line to the right of the break-even point represents the profit area, that is, where total revenue is greater than total cost.

The graphical approach to a break-even chart is complemented by an algebraic approach that uses the relationship Total revenue = Total cost. The break-even chart for Eric's birdhouse data is shown in Figure 6.6.

FIGURE 6.6 Break-Even Chart for Eric's Birdhouse Data

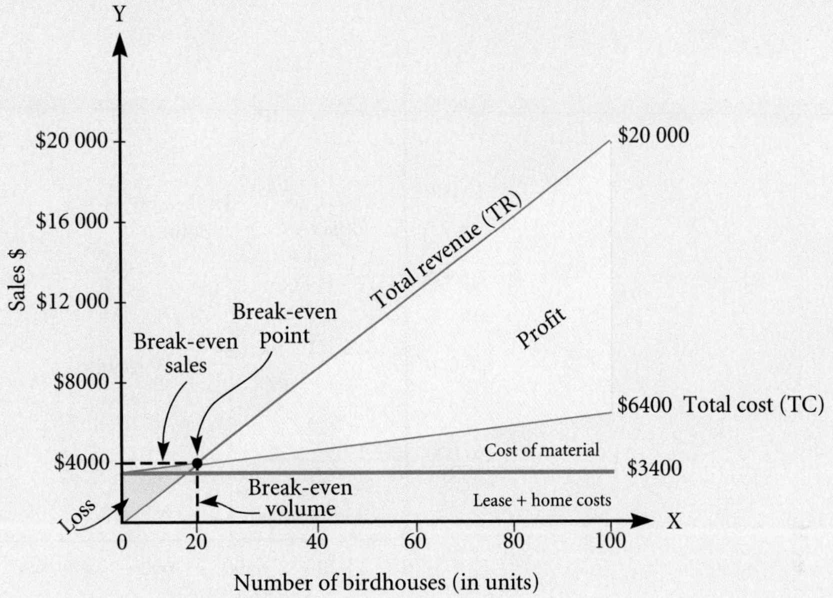

For Eric's business, the break-even point may be calculated by using the relationship

Total revenue = Total cost

Number of birdhouses × Price per birdhouse = (Number of birdhouses × Cost per birdhouse) + Lease cost + Home costs

$$\text{Number of birdhouses} \times 200 = (\text{Number of birdhouses} \times 30) + 1200 + 2200$$

$$(200 - 30) \times \text{Number of birdhouses} = 3400$$

$$170 \times \text{Number of birdhouses} = 3400$$

$$\text{Numbers of birdhouses to break even} = \frac{3400}{170} = 20$$

For Example 6.1A, use the information from Case 1 on page 233.

You can draw the break-even chart by graphing the **revenue function**, TR = 50X, and the **cost function**, TC = 8640 + 30X.

Since capacity is 900 units, the horizontal scale needs to allow for X values up to 900. The vertical scale must allow for maximum sales dollars of (900)(50) = 45 000.

Graphing the Revenue Function, TR = 50*X*

To graph the revenue function, assume at least two values of X and compute the corresponding value of TR.

For $X = 0$, TR = (50)(0) = 0 ⟶ Graph point (0, 0)
For $X = 900$, TR = (50)(900) = 45 000 ⟶ Graph point (900, 45 000)

FIGURE 6.7 Break-Even Chart for Case 1, Example 6.1A

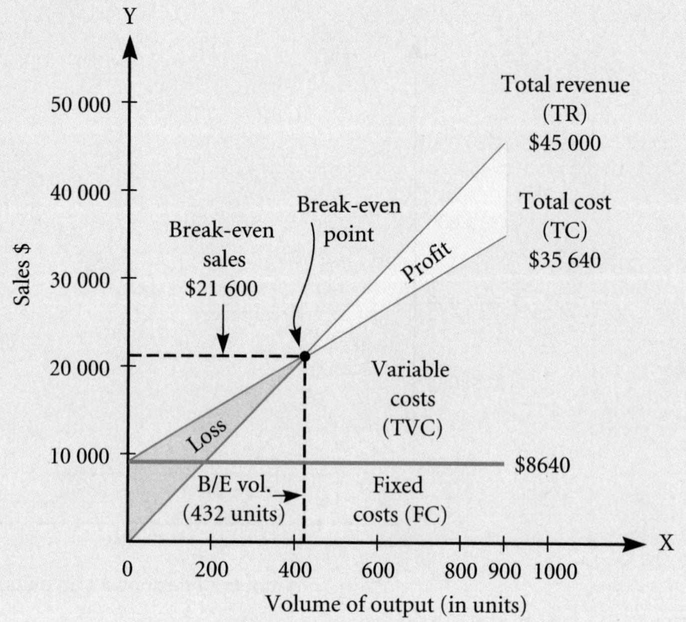

While any value of X may be used, the two values selected are the preferred values. They represent the two extreme values (minimum and maximum volume) for the example.

Graphing the Cost Function, $TC = 8640 + 30X$

Assume two values of X and compute the corresponding value of TC.

For $X = 0$, $TC = 8640 + 30(0) = 8640$ ⟶ Graph point (0, 8640)

For $X = 900$, $TC = 8640 + 30(900)$
$= 8640 + 27\,000 = 35\,640$ ⟶ Graph point (900, 35 640)

For Example 6.1B, use the information from Case 2 on page 233. Provide a detailed break-even chart.

When the accounting data are in terms of total dollars, the horizontal axis represents output in terms of percent of sales capacity. Subdivide the horizontal scale to allow percent sales levels up to 100%. The vertical scale must allow for the maximum sales level of $60 000.

Graphing the Revenue Function, $TR = x$

To graph the revenue function, assume at least two sales volume levels expressed as a percent of capacity.

For $x = 0$, $TR = 0$ ⟶ Graph point (0, 0)

For $x = 60\,000$, $TR = 60\,000$ ⟶ Graph point (60 000, 60 000)

The line joining the two points represents the revenue function.

Graphing the Cost Function, TC = 12 600 + 0.40*x*

Assume two sales volume levels and compute TC.

For $x = 0$, TC = 12 600 + 0.40(0)
= 12 600 ⟶ Graph point (0, 12 600)

For $x = 60\,000$, TC = 12 600 + 0.40(60 000)
= 12 600 + 24 000
= 36 600 ⟶ Graph point (60 000, 36 600)

FIGURE 6.8 Break-Even Chart for Case 2, Example 6.1B

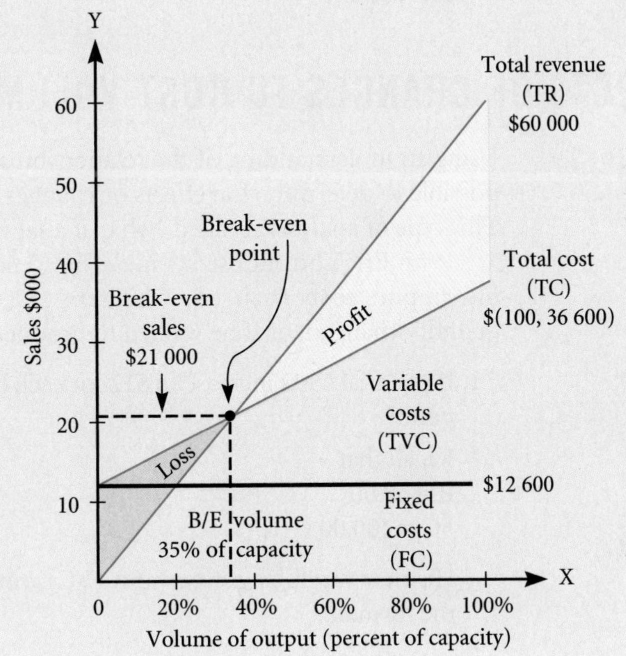

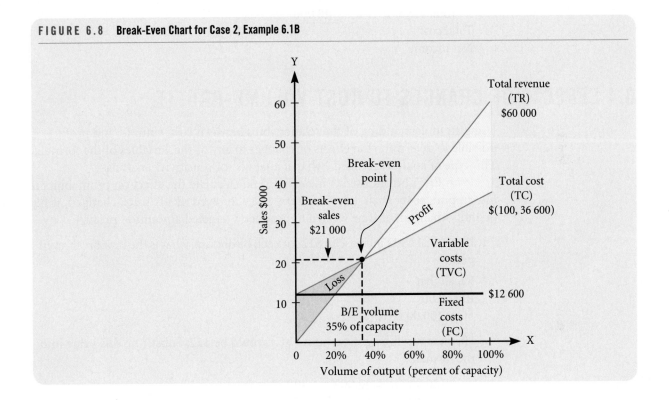

EXERCISE 6.3

A. For each of the following, perform a break-even analysis showing a detailed break-even chart.

1. Engineering estimates show that the variable cost of manufacturing a new product will be $35 per unit. Based on market research, the selling price of the product is to be $120 per unit and variable selling expense is expected to be $15 per unit. The fixed costs applicable to the new product are estimated to be $2800 per period and capacity per period is 100 units.

2. A firm manufactures a product that sells for $12 per unit. Variable cost per unit is $8 and fixed cost per period is $1200. Capacity per period is 1000 units.

3. The following data pertain to the operating budget of Matt Manufacturing.

Sales		$720 000
Fixed cost	$220 000	
Total variable cost	324 000	
Total cost		544 000
Net income		$176 000

4. Harrow Seed and Fertilizer has compiled the following estimates for operations.

Sales		$120 000
Fixed cost	$43 200	
Total variable cost	48 000	
Total cost		91 200
Net income		$ 28 800

6.4 EFFECTS OF CHANGES TO COST-VOLUME-PROFIT

Using an understanding of the relationships between cost, volume, and profit, it is possible to determine the effects of changes to any of the variables of the formula. This type of analysis is called "what-if analysis" or sensitivity analysis.

With Eric's birdhouse business, he could calculate the effect on profitability if his supplies costs changed, if his rent costs changed, if his price changed, if his quantity changed, or if he wished to produce a targeted amount of profit.

1. If material costs increase to $12 for each birdhouse, what is the new break-even point?

Recall that
P = 30.00
FC = 400.00

His new variable cost per unit (VC) would be $12. Substitute this value into the formula.

$$(30.00X) - (12.00X) - 400.00 = 0$$
$$(30.00 - 12.00)X - 400.00 = 0$$
$$18.00X = 400.00$$
$$X = 22.2$$

Therefore, to break even, he would have to produce 23 birdhouses.

2. Exclusive of the change in (1), if the rental cost decreased to $300 and he sold 50 birdhouses, what would be the resulting profit?

Let the profit be PFT.
Substitute the new values into the formula.

$$\text{PFT} = (30.00 \times 50) - (10.00 \times 50) - (300.00)$$
$$\text{PFT} = (30.00 - 10.00) \times 50 - 300.00$$
$$\text{PFT} = 20.00 \times 50 - 300.00$$
$$\text{PFT} = 1000 - 300$$
$$\text{PFT} = 700$$

Therefore, he would realize a profit of $700.

EXERCISE 6.4

1. Ingrid is planning to expand her business by taking on a new product. She can purchase the new product at a cost of \$8. In order to market this new product, she would need to spend \$984 on advertising each month. The suggested retail price for the product is \$14, but she is not sure if she should price her product at this amount. Answer each of the following *independent* questions.
   (a) If she chooses a price of \$14, how many units does she need to sell to break even?
   (b) If she chooses a price of \$12, how many units does she need to sell to break even?
   (c) If she spends \$1500 on advertising, and keeps the price at \$14, how many units does she need to sell to break even?
   (d) If she estimates that she can sell 300 units, when she spends \$1500 for advertising, what is the lowest price she should charge and still break even?

2. Time-For-Us has set up a booth in a shopping mall to sell calendars during the holiday season. They can purchase the calendars for \$2.69 each. They plan to set the unit price at \$9.99. During the time they are in business, they must rent equipment for \$190 per day, and pay wages of \$321 per day. Answer each of the following *independent* questions.
   (a) How many calendars must they sell each day to break even?
   (b) If they decrease the wages to \$240.70 per day, how many must they sell each day to break even?
   (c) If they put the calendars "on sale" at 25% off, what would be their profit if they sold 120 units in a day?
   (d) On the last day that they plan to be in the mall, they have 200 calendars remaining on hand. If the wages for the day are \$222, what is the lowest price they can charge for each calendar and still break even for that day?

3. Sub Stop, selling sandwiches, is located on a busy corner near many other businesses. Their busiest time is during the mid-day period. Rent for the location is \$900 per month and wages amount to \$2500 per month. Variable costs consist of supplies and sandwich ingredients that cost \$2.20 per sub sandwich. The subs are to be sold at a price of \$5.69 each. Answer each of the following *independent* questions.
   (a) How many sandwiches must they sell to break even?
   (b) If they increase variable costs by \$0.20 per sandwich, how many sandwiches must they sell to break even?
   (c) If the rent increases by 10%, what would their profit be if they sold 1600 units?
   (d) If the sandwich price was reduced by \$0.20, how many sandwiches must they sell to make \$1000 profit?

4. A news stand sells Local Business magazines. The cost to purchase the magazines is the list price of \$5 less a discount of 25%. Fixed costs, including rent on the display space, are \$190 per week. The usual price for

the magazines is the list price. Answer each of the following *independent* questions.

(a) If the desired profit is $100, how many magazines must they sell each week?

(b) If the purchase discount is 20% of the list price, how many magazines must they sell each week to achieve a desired profit of $150?

(c) If they put the magazines "on sale" at 10% off, how much would the profit be if they sold 300 units in a week?

(d) If the cost to purchase the magazines is 30% off the list price, and 200 magazines are sold, what is the lowest price they can charge for each magazine and still break even?

BUSINESS MATH NEWS BOX

World's Largest Passenger Ship Christened

The world's largest cruise ship is so immense that even its captain hasn't finished exploring it. "I'm still discovering things," Bill Wright said as he walked around the bridge of Royal Caribbean's newly built *Freedom of the Seas* while it was docked in Bayonne.

Freedom of the Seas is 72 metres tall and 339 metres long with 15 passenger decks.

Standing upright on its bow, it would be taller than the Eiffel tower. The ship comes in at 160 000 gross registered tons, a standard measurement of carrying capacity (equal to 145 150 tonnes).

Built by Norwegian shipbuilder Aker Yards ASA, the ship cost US$800 million and can carry more than 4000 passengers. The world's previous largest ship, the *Queen Mary 2*, can carry about 3000 people and is 151 400 gross registered tons. (*Titanic*'s gross registered tonnage was 46 329.)

If you want to sail on the new ship, it won't be cheap. Prices for seven-day voyages range from US$1900 per couple for an interior room during the low season to nearly $2500 for the same-size cabin with a balcony during high season.

A three-level dining room seats 2140. There are more than 2000 deck chairs and an ice-skating rink. The fitness centre measures 900 square metres and includes a boxing ring. The spa provides luxuries from teeth whitening to massages, and a 13th-floor deck offers a rock climbing wall and a big wave pool with simulated surfing.

Source: Associated Press, "World's Largest Passenger Ship Christened," *Times-Colonist* (Victoria, BC), May 13, 2006, p. D.2.

QUESTIONS

1. Calculate the difference between the *Freedom of the Seas* and the *Queen Mary 2* on the basis of
   (a) weight
   (b) length
   (c) passenger capacity
2. Suppose the ship makes four high season trips and three low season trips during a year. Also assume a 90% capacity during high season and 70% capacity during low season. Calculate annual revenues for this ship.
3. Using the same assumptions as above, and if variable costs are 60% of revenues and fixed cost is assumed to be the cost of the ship, calculate when the ship will break even.

Review Exercise

1. The lighting division of Universal Electric Company plans to introduce a new street light based on the following accounting information:

Fixed costs per period are $3136; variable cost per unit is $157; selling price per unit is $185; and capacity per period is 320 units.

(a) Compute
  (i) the contribution margin;
  (ii) the contribution rate.

(b) Compute the break-even point
  (i) in units;
  (ii) as a percent of capacity;
  (iii) in dollars.

(c) Draw a detailed break-even chart.

(d) For each of the following *independent* situations, determine the break-even point as a percent of capacity:
  (i) fixed costs are reduced to $2688;
  (ii) fixed costs increase to $4588 and variable costs are reduced to 80% of the selling price;
  (iii) the selling price is reduced to $171.

2. The following information is available from the accounting records of Eva Corporation:

Fixed costs per period are $4800. Sales volume for the last period was $19 360 and variable costs were $13 552. Capacity per period is a sales volume of $32 000.

(a) Compute
  (i) the contribution margin;
  (ii) the contribution rate.

(b) Compute the break-even point
  (i) in dollars;
  (ii) as a percent of capacity.

(c) Draw a detailed break-even chart.

(d) For each of the following *independent* situations, determine the break-even point:
  (i) fixed costs are decreased by $600;
  (ii) fixed costs are increased to $5670 and variable costs are changed to 55% of sales.

3. The operating budget of the Bea Company contains the following information:

Sales at 80% of capacity		$400 000
Fixed costs	$105 000	
Variable costs	260 000	
Total costs		365 000
Net income		$ 35 000

(a) Compute
  (i) the contribution margin;
  (ii) the contribution rate.

(b) Compute the break-even point
  (i) as a percent of capacity;
  (ii) in dollars.

(c) Draw a detailed break-even chart.

(d) Determine the break-even point in dollars if fixed costs are reduced by $11 200 while variable costs are changed to 72% of sales.

4. A manufacturer of major appliances provides the following information about the operations of the refrigeration division:

Fixed costs per period are $26 880; variable costs per unit are $360; selling price per unit is $640; and capacity is 150 units.

(a) Compute
  (i) the contribution margin;
  (ii) the contribution rate.

(b) Compute the break-even point
  (i) in units;
  (ii) as a percent of capacity;
  (iii) in dollars.

(c) Determine the break-even point in dollars if fixed costs are increased to $32 200.

(d) Determine the break-even point as a percent of capacity if fixed costs are reduced to $23 808 while variable costs are increased to 60% of sales.

5. Alicia works in a restaurant that has monthly costs of $1500 for rent, $2000 for salaries, and $1700 for other expenses.

On the menu, the restaurant has entrees that sell for $9.99 each. On average, it costs $3.50 in food and materials to serve each of these entrees. How many do they need to sell to break even?

6. Quickprint Services operates several franchises, where they print brochures, business cards, and stationery. They plan to sell 80 jobs next week, at an average cost of $52 each. Their weekly expenses are $1840.
   (a) How much must they charge for each job to break even?
   (b) If they wish to make a profit of $1200, what price do they have to charge?
   (c) If they sell 90 jobs, how much profit will they realize?
   (d) If they sell 100 jobs through a special promotion, what is the minimum price they could charge to break even?

Self-Test

1. The Superior CD Company sells CDs for $10 each. Manufacturing cost is $2.60 per CD; marketing costs are $2.40 per CD; and royalty payments are 20% of the selling price. The fixed cost of preparing the CDs is $18 000. Capacity is 15 000 CDs.
   (a) Compute
      (i) the contribution margin;
      (ii) the contribution rate.
   (b) Compute the break-even point
      (i) in units;
      (ii) in dollars;
      (iii) as a percent of capacity.
   (c) Draw a detailed break-even chart.
   (d) Determine the break-even point in units if fixed costs are increased by $1600 while manufacturing cost is reduced by $0.50 per CD.
   (e) Determine the break-even point in units if the selling price is increased by 10% while fixed costs are increased by $2900.

2. The management of Lambda Corporation has received the following forecast for the next year.

Sales revenue		$600 000
Fixed costs	$275 000	
Variable costs	270 000	
Total costs		545 000
Net income		$ 55 000

   Capacity is a sales volume of $800 000.
   (a) Compute
      (i) the contribution margin;
      (ii) the contribution rate.
   (b) Compute the break-even point
      (i) in dollars;
      (ii) as a percent of capacity.
   (c) Determine the break-even volume in dollars if fixed costs are increased by $40 000 while variable costs are held to 40% of sales.

Challenge Problem

1. An aluminium company uses a highly mechanized production process to produce brackets for the automotive industry. The company's profit function in millions of dollars for x million brackets is $P = 0.7x + 24.5$. The cost function is $C = 0.9x + 24.5$. Find the break-even point in millions of units.

Case Study 6.1 Focusing on Prices

» Edward's Electronics is a small electronics store selling a variety of electronics equipment. It has a small but progressive camera department. Since Edward's does not sell very many cameras during the year, it only has a small number in stock. Edward's has just ordered six of the new digital cameras from Nikon. Edward's owner has been told that the cost of each camera will be \$170, with terms 2/15, n/30. The Manufacturer's Suggested Retail Price (MSRP) of each camera is \$400. Edward's owner calculates that the overhead is 15% of the MSRP and that the desired profit is 18% of the MSRP.

Zellers has a large camera shop in its store in the mall in this same town. It has ordered 70 of these same cameras from Nikon. Zellers has been offered both a cash discount and a quantity discount off the list price of \$170. The cash discount is 3/20, n/45, while the quantity discount is 3.5%. Zellers estimates its overhead is 25% of the MSRP and it would like to make a profit of 35% of the MSRP.

QUESTIONS

1. What is the cost per camera (ignoring taxes) for Edward's Electronics and for Zellers?

2. For each store, what is the minimum selling price required to cover cost, overhead, and desired profits?

3. If Edward's and Zellers sell the camera at the MSRP, how much extra profit will each store make
   (a) in dollars?
   (b) as a percent of MSRP?

4. What rate of a markdown from MSRP can Edward's offer to cover its overhead and make its originally intended profit?

Case Study 6.2 Putting a Price on Furniture

» Superior Sofa Company manufactures a variety of upscale sofas. Superior has found that there is confusion surrounding the term *list price*. For instance, there is the list price at which Superior offers its product to the furniture retailers. These retailers expect to receive a discount on this list price, because either they pay their bills early, they order large quantities, or they offer a prestigious location for selling

Superior's sofas. In addition, Superior also has a list price or Manufacturer's Suggested Retail Price (MSRP) at which it would like to see its product sold. Superior feels that this MSRP is a fair price in comparison with competing products and will provide a good return to both Superior Sofa and the retailer. Most retailers, of course, would like to advertise the list price (MSRP) less a discount, so that consumers will feel that they are getting a bargain. To resolve this problem, Superior has decided to offer its sofas to retail outlets at the MSRP and offer a larger trade discount.

Putting its new policy into practice, Superior has offered its newest sofa to Johnston's Furniture Store for a list price (MSRP) of $1400, less a trade discount of 35%. Johnston's will now advertise the sofa as $1400 less 15%.

QUESTIONS

1. For how much did Johnston's purchase the sofa?
2. What is Johnston's selling price?
3. If Johnston's sells at the price calculated in Question 2, what will be the rate of markup on the basis of cost?
4. Johnston's discovers that Becker Furniture, across town, is advertising a similar sofa for $1000. By what additional percent must Johnston's mark down its sofa to match this price?
5. If Johnston's marks down its sofa to match the Becker Furniture advertised price, what rate of markup on the basis of cost will Johnston's make?

SUMMARY OF FORMULAS

Formula 6.1

$$\text{PROFIT} = (\text{VOLUME} \times \text{PRICE}) - (\text{VOLUME} \times \text{VARIABLE COST PER UNIT}) - \text{FIXED COST}$$

Formula for finding profit when separating fixed and variable costs

Formula 6.2

$$\text{CONTRIBUTION MARGIN PER UNIT} = \text{SELLING PRICE PER UNIT} - \text{VARIABLE COST PER UNIT}$$

Formula for finding contribution margin per unit

Formula 6.3

$$\text{CONTRIBUTION RATE} = \frac{\text{UNIT CONTRIBUTION MARGIN}}{\text{UNIT SELLING PRICE}}$$

Formula for finding contribution rate

Formula 6.4

$$\text{BREAK-EVEN VOLUME} = \frac{\text{FIXED COST}}{\text{UNIT CONTRIBUTION MARGIN}}$$

Formula for finding break-even volume based on unit contribution margin

GLOSSARY

Break-even analysis a method of determining the level of output at which a business neither makes a profit nor sustains a loss *(p. 230)*

Break-even chart a graphical representation of cost-volume-profit relationships used to identify the break-even point *(p. 243)*

Break-even point the level of output at which net income is zero *(p. 231)*

Contribution margin difference between unit selling price and unit variable cost *(p. 238)*

Contribution rate contribution margin per unit expressed as a fraction of the unit selling price *(p. 239)*

Cost function an algebraic expression stating the relationship between cost and volume *(p. 245)*

Cost-volume-profit analysis a tool used to evaluate the potential effect of decisions on profitability *(p. 230)*

Fixed costs costs that remain constant for the time period for all levels of output considered *(p. 231)*

Revenue function an algebraic expression representing the behaviour of revenue *(p. 245)*

Sensitivity analysis calculations performed to determine the effect of changes in one or more components of analysis *(p. 230)*

Variable costs costs that are constant per unit of output regardless of volume; they fluctuate in total amount as volume fluctuates *(p. 231)*

USEFUL INTERNET SITES

www.icb.org/english/registration/index.asp

Institute for Canadian Bankers (ICB) The ICB provides training for the financial services industry. To determine whether you are ready to take ICB courses, this site features a mathematics self-test that you can complete and have scored automatically. After you finish this business mathematics course, you should be ready to tackle an ICB course of your choice.

www.toolkit.cch.com/text/p06_7530.asp

Break-Even Analysis This informative article on break-even analysis, including a detailed example, is hosted on the CCH Business Owner's Toolkit site.

www.bized.ac.uk

Biz/ed This Website for the Institute of Learning and Research Technology at the University of Bristol provides aids and tools to be used in business education. Included are news articles, practice questions, and virtual learning, in topics ranging from general business to accounting and economics.

CHAPTER 7

Simple Interest

OBJECTIVES

Upon completing this chapter, you will be able to do the following:

1. Compute the amount of simple interest using the formula $I = Prt$.
2. Compute the principal, interest rate, or time using variations of the formula $I = Prt$.
3. Compute the maturity value (future value) using the formula $S = P(1 + rt)$.
4. Compute the principal (present value) using the formula $P = \frac{S}{1 + rt}$
5. Compute equivalent or dated values for specified focal dates.

Every day in business, money is borrowed for short periods of time. Businesses lend money when they extend credit to customers or clients, or when they make short-term investments. Businesses borrow money when they purchase on credit from vendors, use a line of credit from a financial institution, or utilize credit cards to make a purchase. With these loans, interest must be considered.

INTRODUCTION

Transactions in business often involve the daily borrowing or loaning of money. To compensate the lenders for the use of their money, interest is paid. The amount of interest paid is based on three factors: the amount of money borrowed, the rate of interest at which it is borrowed, and the time period for which it is borrowed.

7.1 FINDING THE AMOUNT OF SIMPLE INTEREST

A. Basic concepts and formula

Interest is the rent charged for the use of money. The amount of **simple interest** is determined by the relationship

Interest = Principal × Rate × Time

$$I = Prt$$ — **Formula 7.1A**

where I is the amount of interest earned, measured in dollars and cents;
P is the principal sum of money earning the interest, measured in dollars and cents;
r is the simple annual (yearly or **nominal**) **rate** of interest, expressed as a percent, which can be converted into a decimal;
t is the **interest period** in years.

Simple interest is often used in business, through short-term loans to and from financial institutions, vendors, and customers.

POINTERS AND PITFALLS

To use the TI BA II Plus financial calculator to determine the number of days between two dates, choose the DATE worksheet by pressing **2nd** **DATE**. The first date, DT1, is usually the earlier date. The date format can be set to show the U.S. format, mm/dd/yy, or the European format, dd/mm/yy. When the U.S. format is used, enter the date by choosing the one- or two-digit number representing the month, followed by a period, and then enter two digits for the day and the last two digits for the year. Only one period is entered between the month and the day. Press **Enter** to save the data. To move to the next label, press the down arrow. The second date, DT2, is usually the later date. Enter the second date in the same manner as the first date, with one or two digits for the number of the month, a period, two digits for the day, and two digits for the year. Following the second date is the "days between dates" calculation. Press the down arrow to access this part of the worksheet. To show the exact days, press **CPT** (Compute) to instruct the calculator to perform the calculation. When the first date precedes the second date, the days between dates will appear as a positive number. If the second date is entered as the earlier date, the days between dates will appear as a negative number. The fourth label within the worksheet sets the calculator to show the actual number of days between the dates indicated, including adjustments for leap years. Set this label to ACT by pressing **2nd** **SET**.

For example, to determine the number of days between April 23, 2009, and July 21, 2009, press

2nd	DATE	DT1	04.2309	Enter	↓
		DT2	07.2109	Enter	↓
CPT		DBD			Result is 89

Note that the month is entered first, with one or two digits, followed by a period; the day is entered using two digits; and then the year is entered using two digits.

If only one of the dates and the desired days between the dates are entered, it is possible to determine the second date.

EXCEL NOTES If you choose, you can use Excel's Coupon Days, or days between dates (COUPDAYSNC) function, to find the number of days between two dates. Refer to COUPDAYSNC on the Spreadsheet Template Disk to learn how.

You can also use Excel's Accrued Interest (ACCRINT) function to compute the amount of interest when the time is given in days. Refer to ACCRINT on the Spreadsheet Template Disk to learn how.

B. Matching *r* and *t*

While the time may be stated in days, months, or years, the rate of interest is generally stated as a yearly charge, often followed by "per annum" or "p.a." In using the simple interest formula, it is imperative that the time t correspond to the interest rate r. Time expressed in months or days often needs to be converted into years. The number of days between two dates can be determined manually or by using the DATE function on a business calculator. Manual techniques are outlined in a section on the CD accompanying the text.

EXAMPLE 7.1A

State r and t for each of the following:

(i) rate 4%; time 3 years;

(ii) rate 6.5% p.a. (per annum); time 18 months;

(iii) rate 5.25% p.a.; time 243 days.

SOLUTION

(i) The annual rate $r = 4\% = 0.04$
The time in years $t = 3$

(ii) The annual rate $r = 6.5\% = 0.065$
The time in years $t = \dfrac{18}{12}$

Note: To convert months into years, divide by 12.

(iii) The annual rate $r = 5.25\% = 0.0525$
The time in years $t = \dfrac{243}{365}$

Note: To convert days into years, divide by 365.

C. Computing the amount of interest

When the principal, rate, and time are known, the amount of interest can be determined by the formula $I = Prt$.

EXAMPLE 7.1B

Compute the amount of interest for

(i) \$3600 at 6.25% p.a. (per annum) for 3 years;

(ii) \$5240 at 4.5% p.a. for 16 months;

(iii) \$1923.60 at 3% p.a. for 215 days.

SOLUTION

(i) $P = \$3600.00; \quad r = 6.25\% = 0.0625; \quad t = 3$

$I = Prt = (3600.00)(0.0625)(3) = \$675.00$

(ii) $P = \$5240.00; \quad r = 4.5\% = 0.045; \quad t = 16 \text{ months} = \frac{16}{12}$

$$I = Prt = (5240.00)(0.045)\left(\frac{16}{12}\right) = \$314.40$$

(iii) $P = \$1923.60; \quad r = 3\% = 0.03; \quad t = 215 \text{ days} = \frac{215}{365}$

$$I = Prt = (1923.60)(0.03)\left(\frac{215}{365}\right) = \$33.99$$

EXAMPLE 7.1C

Compute the amount of interest on \$785.95 borrowed at 18% p.a. from January 30, 2009, until March 21, 2009.

SOLUTION

Number of days = 50

$$P = 785.95; \quad r = 18\% = 0.18; \quad t = \frac{50}{365}$$

$$I = (785.95)(0.18)\left(\frac{50}{365}\right) = \$19.38$$

EXAMPLE 7.1D

Compute the amount of interest on \$1240 earning 6% p.a. from September 30, 2009, to May 16, 2010.

SOLUTION

The starting date is September 30, 2009 (DT1). The ending date is May 16, 2010 (DT2).

Days between dates (DBD) = 228

$$P = 1240.00; \quad r = 6\% = 0.06; \quad t = \frac{228}{365}$$

$$I = (1240.00)(0.06)\left(\frac{228}{365}\right) = \$46.47$$

EXERCISE 7.1

A. State *r* and *t* for each of the following:

1. rate is $3\frac{1}{2}\%$; time is $1\frac{1}{4}$ years
2. rate is $9\frac{3}{4}\%$; time is 21 months
3. rate is 8.25%; time is 183 days
4. rate is $5\frac{1}{2}\%$; time is 332 days

B. Compute the amount of interest for each of the following:

1. \$5000 at $9\frac{3}{4}\%$ for $2\frac{1}{4}$ years
2. \$645 at $6\frac{1}{4}\%$ for $1\frac{3}{4}$ years
3. \$1755 at 4.65% for 14 months
4. \$1651.43 at 4.9% for 9 months
5. \$980 at 11.5% for 244 days
6. \$1697.23 at 3.4% for 163 days
7. \$275 at 9.25% from November 30, 2009 to May 5, 2010
8. \$1090.60 at 7.8% from October 12, 2011 to April 24, 2012
9. \$424.23 at $8\frac{3}{4}\%$ from April 4, 2010 to November 4, 2010
10. \$1713.09 at 4.4% from August 30, 2010 to March 30, 2011
11. \$629.99 at 6.9% from June 16, 2009 to January 24, 2010
12. \$17 000 at 15.6% from November 12, 2008 to July 31, 2009

C.

1. On April 1, 2009, Faircloud Variety Company deposited \$24 000 into a savings account earning simple interest of 1.5%. Interest is paid to the account at the end of every calendar quarter. How much interest was paid to Faircloud's account on June 30, 2009?
2. Leah deposited \$1500 into a savings account that earned simple interest of 2.25% on July 17, 2009. How much interest was earned and paid into Leah's account on December 1, 2009?
3. Kenneth borrowed \$6100 to buy a car. If interest was charged on the loan at 9.7%, how much interest would he have to pay in 30 days?
4. Lin Yan borrowed \$1800 from her parents to finance a vacation. If interest was charged on the loan at 7.2%, how much interest would she have to pay in 100 days?

7.2 FINDING THE PRINCIPAL, RATE, OR TIME

A. Formulas derived from the simple interest formula

The simple interest formula I = Prt contains the four variables I, P, r, and t. If any three of the four are given, the value of the unknown variable can be computed by substituting the known values in the formula or by solving for the unknown variable first and then substituting in the resulting derived formula.

The three derived formulas are

(i) To find the principal P,

$$P = \frac{I}{rt}$$ ——— **Formula 7.1B**

(ii) To find the rate of interest r,

$$r = \frac{I}{Pt}$$ ——— **Formula 7.1C**

(iii) To find the time period t,

$$t = \frac{I}{Pr}$$ ——— **Formula 7.1D**

Note:

(a) In Formula 7.1C, if the time period t is expressed in years, the value of r represents an annual rate of interest in decimal form.

(b) In Formula 7.1D, if the rate of interest r is an annual rate, the value of t represents years in decimal form.

POINTERS AND PITFALLS

This diagram is a useful aid in remembering the various forms of the simple interest formula I = Prt.

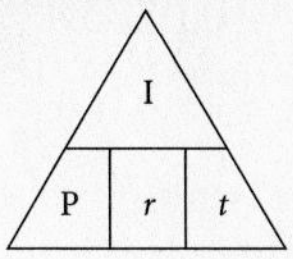

B. Finding the principal

When the amount of interest, the rate of interest, and the time period are known, the principal can be determined.

EXAMPLE 7.2A What principal will earn interest of \$18.20 at 3.25% in 8 months?

SOLUTION $I = 18.20; \quad r = 3.25\%; \quad t = \frac{8}{12}$

(i) Using the formula I = Prt,

$$18.20 = (P)(0.0325)\left(\frac{8}{12}\right)$$ ——— **by substitution**

$$18.20 = (P)(0.021667) \quad \text{———— } (0.0325)\left(\frac{8}{12}\right)$$

$$P = \frac{18.20}{0.021667} \quad \text{———— divide 18.20 by the coefficient of P}$$

$$= \$840.00$$

(ii) Using the derived formula $P = \frac{I}{rt}$,

$$P = \frac{18.20}{(0.0325)\left(\frac{8}{12}\right)} \quad \text{———— by substitution}$$

$$= \frac{18.20}{0.021667} = \$840.00$$

EXAMPLE 7.2B Determine the amount of money that must be invested for 245 days at 5.75% to earn $42.46.

SOLUTION $I = 42.46; \quad r = 5.75\% = 0.0575; \quad t = \frac{245}{365}$

(i) Using the formula $I = Prt$,

$$42.46 = (P)(0.0575)\left(\frac{245}{365}\right)$$

$$42.46 = (P)(0.038596)$$

$$P = \frac{42.46}{0.038596} = \$1100.11$$

(ii) Using the derived formula $P = \frac{I}{rt}$,

$$P = \frac{42.46}{(0.0575)\left(\frac{245}{365}\right)} = \$1100.11$$

C. Finding the rate

When the amount of interest, the principal, and the time period are known, the rate of interest can be determined.

EXAMPLE 7.2C Find the annual rate of interest required for $744 to earn $75.95 in 14 months.

SOLUTION $I = 75.95; \quad P = 744.00; \quad t = \frac{14}{12}$

(i) Using the formula $I = Prt$,

$$75.95 = (744)(r)\left(\frac{14}{12}\right)$$

$$75.95 = (868)(r)$$

$$r = \frac{75.95}{868} = 0.0875 = 8.75\% \quad \text{———— convert to a percent}$$

(ii) Using the derived formula $r = \frac{I}{Pt}$,

$$r = \frac{75.95}{(744.00)\left(\frac{14}{12}\right)}$$

$$= \frac{75.95}{868.00} = 0.0875 = 8.75\%$$

D. Finding the time

When the amount of interest, the principal, and the rate of interest are known, the time period can be determined.

EXAMPLE 7.2D

Find the number of years required for \$745 to earn \$178.80 simple interest at 8% p.a.

SOLUTION

$I = 178.80$; $P = 745.00$; $r = 8\% = 0.08$

(i) Using the formula $I = Prt$,

$$178.80 = (745.00)(0.08)(t)$$
$$178.80 = (59.60)(t)$$
$$t = \frac{178.80}{59.60}$$
$$= 3.00 \text{ (years)}$$

(ii) Using the derived formula $t = \frac{I}{Pr}$,

$$t = \frac{178.80}{(745.00)(0.08)}$$
$$= 3.00 \text{ (years)}$$

Note: The value of t in the formula $I = Prt$ will be in years. If the time period is to be stated in months or in days, it is necessary to multiply the initial value of t by 12 for months or 365 for days.

EXAMPLE 7.2E

Determine the number of months required for a deposit of \$1320 to earn \$16.50 interest at 3.75%.

SOLUTION

$I = 16.50$; $P = 1320.00$; $r = 3.75\% = 0.0375$

(i) Using the formula $I = Prt$,

$$16.50 = (1320.00)(0.0375)(t)$$
$$16.50 = (49.50)(t)$$
$$t = \frac{16.50}{49.50}$$
$$= 0.333333 \text{ years}$$
$$= (0.333333)(12) \text{ months}$$
$$= 4 \text{ months}$$

(ii) Using the derived formula $t = \frac{I}{Pr}$,

$$t = \frac{16.50}{(1320.00)(0.0375)} \text{ years}$$
$$= \frac{16.50}{49.50} \text{ years} = \frac{1}{3} \text{ years}$$
$$= 4 \text{ months}$$

EXAMPLE 7.2F

For how many days would a loan of \$1500 be outstanding to earn interest of \$36.16 at 5.5% p.a.?

SOLUTION

$I = 36.16$; $P = 1500.00$; $r = 5.5\% = 0.055$

(i) Using the formula $I = Prt$,

$$36.16 = (1500.00)(0.055)(t)$$
$$36.16 = (82.50)(t)$$
$$t = \frac{36.16}{82.50}$$
$$= 0.438303 \text{ years}$$
$$= (0.438303)(365) \text{ days}$$
$$= 160 \text{ days}$$

(ii) Using the derived formula $t = \frac{I}{Pr}$,

$$t = \frac{36.16}{(1500.00)(0.055)} \text{ years}$$
$$= \frac{36.16}{82.50} \text{ years}$$
$$= 0.438303 \text{ years}$$
$$= (0.438303)(365) \text{ days} = 159.98 \text{ days}$$
$$= 160 \text{ days}$$

EXERCISE 7.2

A. Determine the missing value for each of the following.

	Interest	Principal	Rate	Time
1.	\$ 67.83	?	9.5%	7 months
2.	\$106.25	?	4.25%	250 days
3.	\$215.00	\$2400.00	?	10 months
4.	\$ 53.40	\$ 750.00	?	315 days
5.	\$ 36.17	\$ 954.00	3.25%	? (months)
6.	\$ 52.64	\$1295.80	9.75%	? (months)
7.	\$ 7.14	\$ 344.75	5.25%	? (days)
8.	\$ 68.96	\$ 830.30	10.75%	? (days)

B. Find the value indicated for each of the following:

1. Find the principal that will earn $148.32 at 6.75% in 8 months.

2. Determine the deposit that must be made to earn $39.27 in 225 days at 2.75%.

3. A loan of $880 can be repaid in 15 months by paying the principal sum borrowed plus $104.50 interest. What was the rate of interest charged?

4. Joan borrowed $650 and is to repay the balance plus interest of $23.70 in seven months. What was the rate of interest charged?

5. At what rate of interest will $1387 earn $63.84 in 200 days?

6. A deposit of $2400 will earn $22.74 in 91 days at what rate of interest?

7. In how many months will $1290 earn $100.51 interest at $8\frac{1}{2}\%$?

8. Interest of $20.95 is earned at 3.15% on a deposit of $2660 in how many months?

9. Determine the number of days it will take $564 to earn $15.09 at $7\frac{3}{4}\%$.

10. How many days will it take $1200 to earn $12.22 interest at 16.9%?

11. What principal will earn $39.96 from June 18, 2009 to December 15, 2009 at 9.25%?

12. What rate of interest is required for $740.48 to earn $42.49 interest from September 10, 2011 to March 4, 2012?

13. Philip wants to supplement his pension by $2000 per month with income from his investments. His investments pay him monthly and earn 6% p.a. What value of investments must Philip have in his portfolio to generate enough interest to give him his desired income?

14. Bunny's Antiques received $88.47 interest on a 120-day term deposit of $7800. At what rate of interest was the term deposit invested?

15. Anne's Dress Shop borrowed $3200 to buy material. The loan was paid off seven months later by a lump-sum payment that included $168 of interest. What was the simple rate of interest at which the money was borrowed?

16. Mac's credit card statement included $360 in cash advances and $3.20 in interest charges. The interest rate on the statement was 13.5%. For how many days was Mac charged interest?

17. Bill filed his income tax return with the Canada Revenue Agency (CRA) after the April 30 deadline. He calculated that he owed the CRA $3448, but did not include a payment for this amount when he sent in his tax return. The CRA's Notice of Assessment indicated agreement with Bill's tax calculation. It also showed that the balance due was $3827.66, which included a 10% late-filing penalty and interest at 9% p.a. For how many days was Bill charged interest?

18. On August 15, 2010, Low Rider Automotive established a line of credit at its bank, with interest at 8.75% p.a. This line of credit was used to purchase

$5000 of inventory and supplies. Low Rider paid $5113.87 to satisfy the incurred debt. On what date did Low Rider Automotive honour the line of credit?

7.3 COMPUTING FUTURE VALUE (MATURITY VALUE)

A. Basic concept

When you borrow money, you are obligated to repay both the sum borrowed (the principal) and any interest due. Therefore, the **future value of a sum of money** (or **maturity value**) is the value obtained by adding the original principal and the interest due.

FUTURE VALUE (OR MATURITY VALUE) = PRINCIPAL + INTEREST

$$S = P + I$$ — Formula 7.2

EXAMPLE 7.3A Determine the future value (maturity value), principal, or interest as indicated.

(i) The principal is $2200 and the interest is $240. Find the future value (maturity value).

SOLUTION

$P = 2200.00; \quad I = 240.00$

$$\begin{aligned} S &= P + I \\ &= 2200.00 + 240.00 \\ &= \$2440.00 \end{aligned}$$

The future value is $2440.

(ii) The principal is $850 and the future value (maturity value) is $920. Compute the amount of interest.

SOLUTION

$P = 850.00; \quad S = 920.00$

$$\begin{aligned} S &= P + I \\ I &= S - P \\ I &= 920.00 - 850.00 \\ I &= \$70.00 \end{aligned}$$

The amount of interest is $70.

(iii) The future value (maturity value) is $430 and the interest is $40. Compute the principal.

SOLUTION

$S = 430.00; \quad I = 40.00$

$$\begin{aligned} S &= P + I \\ P &= S - I \\ P &= 430.00 - 40.00 \\ P &= \$390.00 \end{aligned}$$

The principal is $390.

B. The future value formula $S = P(1 + rt)$

To obtain the future value (maturity value) formula for simple interest, the formulas $I = Prt$ and $S = P + I$ are combined.

$S = P + I$

$S = P + Prt$ ——— substitute Prt for I

$S = P(1 + rt)$ ——— take out the common factor P

$$S = P(1 + rt)$$ ——— Formula 7.3A

EXAMPLE 7.3B Find the future value (maturity value) of an investment of $720 earning 4% p.a. for 146 days.

SOLUTION $P = 720.00;\quad r = 4\% = 0.04;\quad t = \frac{146}{365}$

$$\begin{aligned} S &= P(1 + rt) \\ &= (720.00)\left[1 + (0.04)\left(\frac{146}{365}\right)\right] \\ &= (720.00)\,(1 + 0.016) \\ &= (720.00)\,(1.016) \\ &= \$731.52 \end{aligned}$$

The future value of the investment is $731.52.

EXAMPLE 7.3C Find the maturity value of a deposit of $1250 invested at 2.75% p.a. from October 15, 2009 to May 1, 2010.

SOLUTION The time period in days = 198

$P = 1250.00;\quad r = 2.75\% = 0.0275;\quad t = \frac{198}{365}$

$$\begin{aligned} S &= P(1 + rt) \\ &= (1250.00)\left[1 + (0.0275)\left(\frac{198}{365}\right)\right] \\ &= (1250.00)\,(1 + 0.014918) \\ &= (1250.00)\,(1.014918) \\ &= \$1268.65 \end{aligned}$$

The maturity value of the deposit is $1268.65.

EXERCISE 7.3

A. Use the future value (maturity value) formula to answer each of the following.

1. Find the future value of $480 at $3\frac{1}{2}\%$ for 220 days.
2. Find the future value of $1100 invested at 6.75% for 360 days.
3. Find the maturity value of $732 invested at 9.8% from May 20, 2010 to November 23, 2010.
4. Find the maturity value of $775 invested at 6.25% from March 1, 2009 to October 20, 2009.
5. Compute the future value of $820 over nine months at $4\frac{3}{4}\%$.
6. Compute the future value of $570 over seven months at $5\frac{1}{2}\%$.
7. What payment is required to pay off a loan of $1200 at 7% fourteen months later?
8. What payment is required to pay off a loan of $2000 at 6% eighteen months later?

B.

1. Paul invested $2500 in a 180-day term deposit at 3.45% p.a. What is the maturity value of the deposit?
2. Suzette invested $800 in a 210-day term deposit at 2.75% p.a. What is the maturity value of the deposit?
3. Jack signed a two-year loan of $12 000 at 7.5% p.a. How much will he owe at maturity?
4. Hao Lin borrowed $8000 at 8.55% p.a. for fifteen months. How much will he owe at maturity?
5. On September 30, 2010, Red Flag Inn invested $26 750 in a short-term investment of 215 days. An investment of this length earns 1.3% p.a. How much will the investment be worth at maturity?
6. Jo-Mar Consulting invested $17 200 on July 18, 2009 into a short-term investment of 150 days. The investment would earn 1.85% p.a. How much will the investment be worth at maturity?
7. Speedy Courier invested $13 500 in a 270-day term deposit. What is the maturity value if the rate of interest is 3.65%?
8. Diamond Drilling invested $40 000 in a 240-day term deposit earning interest at 2.43%. What is the maturity value of the investment?
9. Mishu wants to invest an inheritance of $50 000 for one year. His credit union offers 3.95% for a one-year term or 3.85% for a six-month term.
   (a) How much will Mishu receive after one year if he invests at the one-year rate?
   (b) How much will Mishu receive after one year if he invested for six months at a time at 3.85% each time?
   (c) What would the one-year rate have to be to yield the same amount of interest as the investment described in part (b)?

10. Prairie Grains Cooperative wants to invest \$45 000 in a short-term deposit. The bank offers 1.3% interest for a one-year term and 1.1% for a six-month term.

(a) How much would Prairie Grains receive if the \$45 000 is invested for one year?
(b) How much would Prairie Grains receive at the end of one year if the \$45 000 is invested for six months and then the principal and interest earned is reinvested for another six months?
(c) What would the one-year rate have to be to yield the same amount of interest as the investment described in part (b)?

7.4 FINDING THE PRINCIPAL (PRESENT VALUE)

A. Finding the principal when the maturity value (future value) is known

When the maturity value, the rate, and the time are given, calculation of the principal utilizes the formula $S = P(1 + rt)$.

When interest is paid for the use of money, the value of any sum of money subject to interest changes with time. This change is called the **time value of money**. The **present value** of an amount at any given time is the principal needed to grow to that amount at a given rate of interest over a given period of time.

Since the problem of finding the present value is equivalent to finding the principal when the future value, rate, and time are given, the future value formula $S = P(1 + rt)$ applies. However, because the problem of finding the present value of an amount is one of the frequently recurring problems in financial analysis, it is useful to solve the future value formula for P to obtain the present value formula.

$$S = P(1 + rt)$$ ——— starting with the future value formula

$$\frac{S}{(1 + rt)} = \frac{P(1 + rt)}{(1 + rt)}$$ ——— divide both sides by $(1 + rt)$

$$\frac{S}{(1 + rt)} = P$$ ——— reduce the fraction $\frac{(1 + rt)}{(1 + rt)}$ to 1

This is the present value formula for simple interest.

$$P = \frac{S}{(1 + rt)}$$ ——— Formula 7.3B

EXAMPLE 7.4A Compute the value of an investment eight months before the maturity date that earns interest at 6% p.a. and has a maturity value of $884.

FIGURE 7.1 Time Graph for Example 7.4A

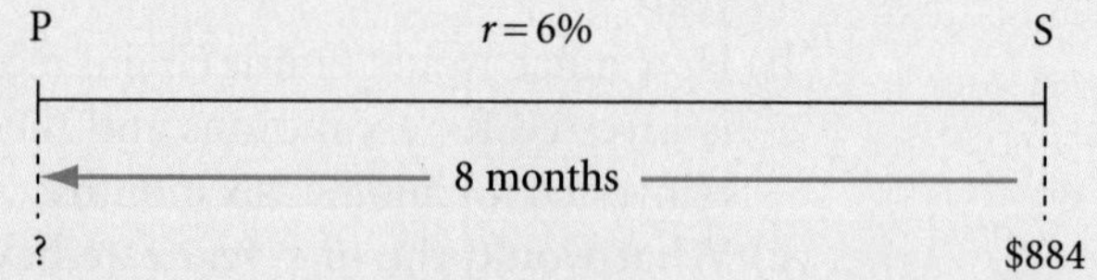

SOLUTION $S = 884.00$; $r = 6\% = 0.06$; $t = \frac{8}{12}$

$$P = \frac{S}{(1 + rt)}$$ — use the present value formula when S is known

$$P = \frac{884.00}{1 + (0.06)\left(\frac{8}{12}\right)}$$ — using Formula 7.3B

$$P = \frac{884.00}{1.04}$$

$$= \$850.00$$

The present value of the investment is $850.00

EXAMPLE 7.4B What sum of money must be invested on January 31, 2008 to amount to $7700 on August 18, 2008 at 10% p.a.?

SOLUTION The time period in days = 200.

$$P = \frac{S}{(1 + rt)}$$ — use the present value formula when S is known

$S = 7700.00$; $r = 10\% = 0.10$; $t = \frac{200}{365}$

$$P = \frac{7700.00}{1 + (0.10)\left(\frac{200}{365}\right)}$$

$$P = \frac{7700.00}{1.054795}$$

$$= \$7300.00$$

Note:

1. The total interest earned is $7700 − $7300 = $400.
2. The daily amount of interest is $\frac{\$400}{200} = \$2$.

To illustrate the concept of the time value of money, Example 7.4B is represented on the time graph shown in Figure 7.2.

FIGURE 7.2 Time Graph for Example 7.4B

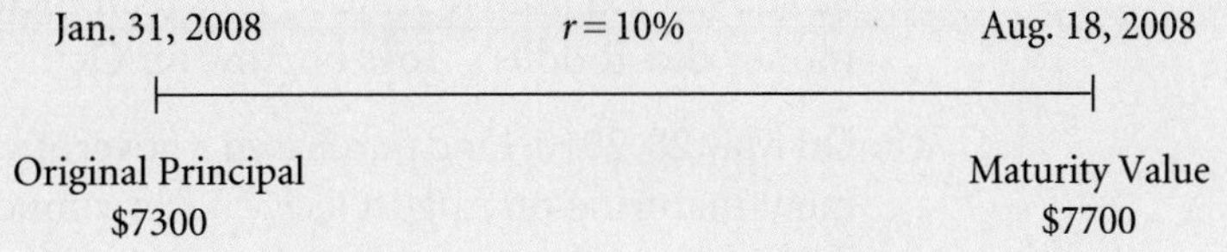

The original principal of $7300 will grow to $7700 at 10% in 200 days. Interest of $400 will be earned in those 200 days, indicating that the original principal will grow by $2 each day. The value of the investment changes day by day. On January 31, 2008, the $7300 principal is known as the present value of the August 18, 2008 $7700.

EXERCISE 7.4

A. Find the principal and the missing value in each of the following.

	Present Value (Principal)	Interest Amount	Future Value (Maturity Value)	Interest Rate	Time
1.	?	?	$ 279.30	4%	15 months
2.	?	$117.30	$ 729.30	?	20 months
3.	?	$ 29.67	?	8.6%	8 months
4.	?	$ 27.11	?	9.5%	240 days
5.	?	$ 84.24	$2109.24	5.2%	?
6.	?	?	$1035.38	7.5%	275 days

B. Solve each of the following.

1. What principal will have a future value of $1241.86 at 3.9% in five months?
2. What amount of money will accumulate to $480.57 in 93 days at 4.6%?
3. Determine the present value of a debt of $1760 due in four months if interest at 9¾% is allowed.
4. Compute the present value of a debt of $708.13 eighty days before it is due if money is worth 5.3%.
5. Compute the amount of money that, deposited in an account on April 1, 2009, will grow to $657.58 by September 10, 2009 at 4.75% p.a.
6. The annual Deerfield Golf Club membership fees of $1750 are due on March 1, 2010. Club management offers a reduction of membership fees of 18.9% p.a. to members who pay the dues by September 1, 2009. How much must a member pay on September 1 if she chooses to take advantage of the club management's offer?
7. You are the accountant for Peel Credit Union. The lawyer for a member has sent a cheque for $7345.64 in full settlement of the member's loan balance including interest at 6.25% for 11 months. How much of the payment is interest?

8. On March 15, 2009, Ben bought a government-guaranteed short-term investment maturing on September 12, 2009. How much did Ben pay for the investment if he will receive $10 000 on September 12, 2009 and interest is 5.06%?

9. On October 29, 2009, Toddlers' Toys borrowed money with a promise to pay $23 520.18 on March 5, 2010. This loan included interest at 6.5%. How much money did Toddlers' Toys borrow on October 29?

10. On May 28, 2010, Ling purchased a government-guaranteed short-term investment maturing on August 4, 2010. How much did Ling pay for the investment if $10 000 will be received on August 4, 2010, and interest is 1.35% p.a.?

BUSINESS MATH NEWS BOX

The iPod, iTune and Macintosh

Apple Computer Inc. is a publicly traded company that trades its shares on the NASDAQ stock exchange. Investors buy and sell Apple stock based on the expectation that the company has long-term projection of increased revenues, net income, and profit. Investors compare current revenue, net income, and profit results with the previous year's results. If the comparisons are within the expectations of investors, then the stock price increases. The future looks bright for Apple Inc. The iPod music player and the Macintosh personal computer are pioneering products that have propelled the company to financial success. In addition, Apple's online music store iTunes now accounts for a significant portion of legal Internet music downloads.

Apple Inc. provided investors with its 2006 second quarter results. Financial highlights are as follows:

- Sales increased 34% to US$4.36 billion, compared with growth that averaged 65% in the prior five periods.
- Net income rose to US$410 million, or US$0.47 cents a share, from US$290 million (US$0.34 cents) a year earlier.
- Profits rose 41%, and are estimated to be within a range of US$0.39 cents to US$0.43 cents.

Other relevant information in which investors were interested:

- Shipments of iPod music players fell to 8.5 million units from 14 million.
- Macintosh shipments dropped to 1.1 million from 1.25 million.
- Apple is also generating revenue from the iTunes online music store. More than one billion songs have been sold at US$0.99 cents each since iTunes opened in 2003.
- More than 15 million videos were sold at US$1.99 each since Apple began selling videos online.

Due to this news release, Apple's stock price increased by US$1.28 to US$66.93 on the NASDAQ stock exchange.

Sources: Connie Guglielmo. Bloomberg News, "Apple's 2nd-Qtr Profit Rises; Ipod, Macintosh Shipments Slow," April 19, 2006. (New York); Apple report Q2 2006 results. **http://www.apple.com/investor**.

QUESTIONS

1. Calculate the percentage increase of Apple shares if the stock increased by $1.28 to $66.93. What was the initial price of the stock?
2. If the average price of an iPod is US$300 and a Mac is US$2000, calculate the revenues generated by Apple in the first half of this year.
3. Calculate how much revenue has been generated by video sales.

7.5 COMPUTING EQUIVALENT VALUES

A. Dated values

If an amount of money is subject to a rate of interest, it will grow over time. Thus, the value of the amount of money changes with time. This change is known as the time value of money. For example, if you invested $1000 today at 4% p.a. simple interest, your investment has a value of $1000 today, $1010 in three months, $1020 in six months, and $1040 in one year.

The value of the original amount at any particular time is a **dated value**, or **equivalent value**, of that amount. The dated value combines the original sum with the interest earned up to the dated value date. Each dated value at a different time is equivalent to the original amount of money. The table below shows four dated values for $1000 invested at 4% p.a. The longer the time is from today, the greater is the dated value. This is so because interest has been earned on the principal over a longer time period.

Time	Dated Value
Today	$1000.00
3 months from today	$1010.00
6 months from today	$1020.00
1 year from today	$1040.00

Timberwest Company owes Abco Inc. $500 and payment is due today. Timberwest asks for an extension of four months to pay off the obligation. How much should they expect to pay in four months' time if money is worth 6%?

Since Abco could invest the $500 at 6% p.a., Timberwest should be prepared to pay the dated value. This dated value includes interest for the additional four-month time period. It represents the amount to which the $500 will grow in four months (the future value) and is found using Formula 7.3A.

$$S = P(1 + rt)$$

$$= 500.00\left[1 + (0.06)\left(\frac{4}{12}\right)\right]$$

$$= 500.00\,(1 + 0.02)$$

$$= \$510.00$$

In addition, Red Rock Construction owes Abco Inc. $824, due to be paid six months from now. Suppose Red Rock Construction offers to pay the debt today. How much should Red Rock Construction pay Abco Inc. if money is worth 6%?

Since Abco Inc. could invest the payment at 6%, the payment should be the sum of money that will grow to $824 in six months earning 6% p.a. interest. By definition, this amount of money is the present value of the $824. The present value represents today's dated value of the \$824 and is found using Formula 7.3B.

$$P = \frac{S}{1 + rt}$$

$$= \frac{824.00}{1 + (0.06)\left(\frac{6}{12}\right)}$$

$$= \frac{824.00}{1 + 0.03}$$

$$= \$800.00$$

Because of the time value of money, sums of money given at different times are not directly comparable. For example, imagine you are given a choice between \$2000 today and \$2200 one year from now. It does not automatically follow, from the point of view of investing money, that either the larger amount of money or the chronologically earlier amount of money is preferable.

To make a rational choice, we must allow for the rate of interest money can earn and choose a comparison date or **focal date** to obtain the dated values of the amounts of money at a specific time.

Equivalent values on the same date are directly comparable and may be obtained for simple interest by using either the maturity value (future value) formula, Formula 7.3A, $S = P(1 + rt)$, or the present value formula, Formula 7.3B,

$$P = \frac{S}{1 + rt}$$

B. Choosing the appropriate formula

The choice of which formula to use for computing dated values depends on the due date of the sum of money relative to the selected focal (or comparison) date.

(a) If the due date falls before the focal date, use the future value (maturity value) formula.

FIGURE 7.3 When to Use the Future Value (or Maturity Value) Formula

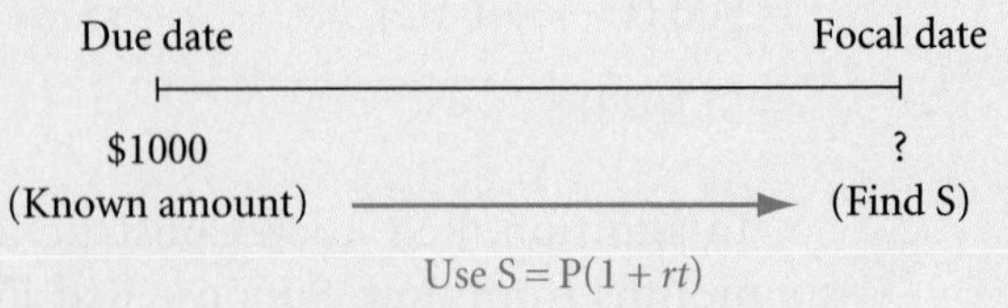

Explanation of Figure 7.3: We are looking for a future value relative to the given value. This future value will be higher than the known value by the interest that accumulates on the known value from the due date to the focal date. Because this is a future value problem (note that the arrow points to the right), the future value (or maturity value) formula $S = P(1 + rt)$ applies.

(b) If the due date falls after the focal date, use the present value formula.

FIGURE 7.4 When to Use the Present Value Formula

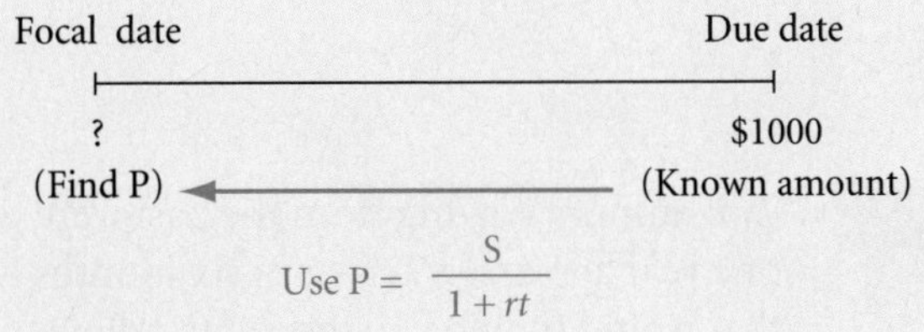

Explanation of Figure 7.4: We are looking for an earlier value relative to the given value. This earlier value will be less than the given value by the interest that would accumulate on the unknown earlier value from the focal date to the due date. We are, in fact, looking for the principal that will grow to the given value. Because this is a present value problem (note that the arrow points to the left), the present value formula $P = \frac{S}{1 + rt}$ is appropriate.

C. Finding the equivalent single payment

EXAMPLE 7.5A

A debt can be paid off by payments of \$872 one year from now and \$1180 two years from now. Determine the single payment now that would fully repay the debt. Allow for simple interest at 9% p.a.

SOLUTION

See Figure 7.5 for the graphic representation of the dated values. Refer to Figures 7.3 and 7.4 to determine which formula is appropriate.

FIGURE 7.5 Graphical Representation of the Dated Values

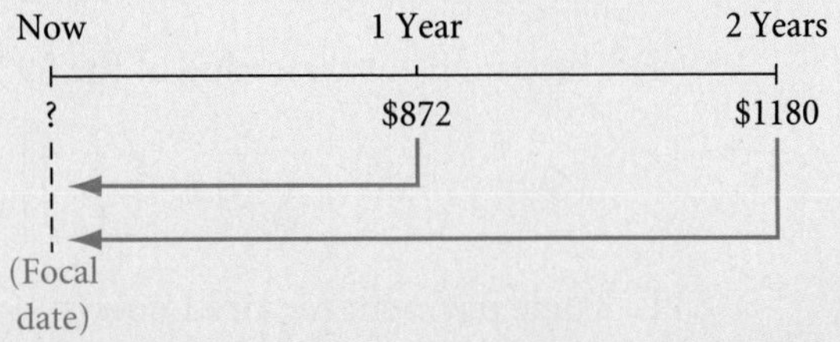

Since the focal date is *earlier* relative to the dates for the given sums of money (the arrows point to the left), the present value formula $P = \frac{S}{1 + rt}$ is appropriate.

(i) The dated (present) value of the \$872.00 at the focal date:

$$P = \frac{872.00}{1 + (0.09)(1)} = \frac{872.00}{1.09} = \$800.00$$

(ii) The dated (present) value of the $1180.00 at the focal date

$$P = \frac{1180.00}{1 + (0.09)(2)} = \frac{1180.00}{1.18} = \$1000.00$$

(iii) Single payment required now = 800.00 + 1000.00 = $1800.00

EXAMPLE 7.5B

Two amounts owing from the past were to be paid today. One debt was $620 from one year ago and $925 from six months ago. Determine the single payment today that would fully repay the debts. Allow for simple interest at 12% p.a.

SOLUTION

See Figure 7.6 for the graphic representation of the dated values. Refer to Figures 7.3 and 7.4 to determine which formula is appropriate.

FIGURE 7.6 Graphical Representation of the Dated Values

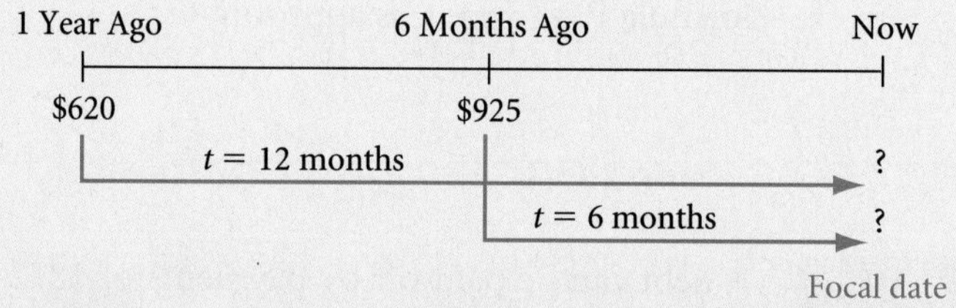

Since the focal date is *future* relative to the dates for the given sums of money (the arrows point to the right), the future value formula $S = P(1 + rt)$ is appropriate.

(i) The dated (future) value of the $620 at the focal date:

$$S = 620.00\left[1 + (0.12)\left(\frac{12}{12}\right)\right] = \$694.40$$

(ii) The dated (future) value of the $925 at the focal date:

$$S = 925.00\left[1 + (0.12)\left(\frac{6}{12}\right)\right] = \$980.50$$

(iii) Single payment required now = 694.40 + 980.50 = $1674.90

EXAMPLE 7.5C

You are owed payments of $400 due today, $500 due in five months, and $618 due in one year. You have been approached to accept a single payment nine months from now with interest allowed at 12% p.a. How much will the single payment be?

SOLUTION

FIGURE 7.7 **Graphical Representation of the Dated Values**

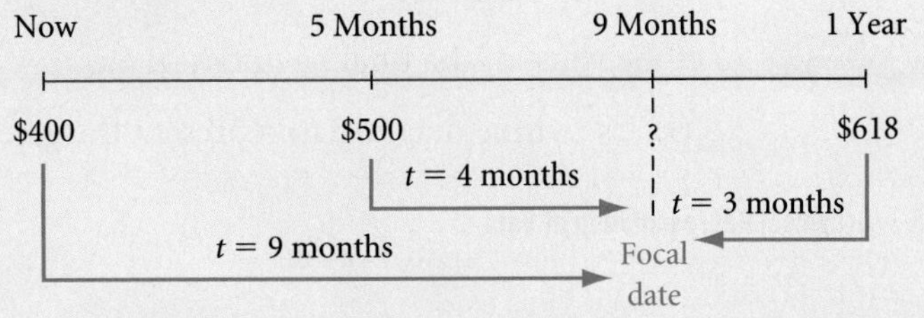

Since the focal date is in the *future* relative to the \$400 now and the \$500 five months from now (the arrows point to the right), the future value formula $S = P(1 + rt)$ is appropriate for these two amounts. However, since the focal date is *earlier* relative to the \$618 one year from now (the arrow points to the left), the present value formula $P = \frac{S}{1 + rt}$ is appropriate for this amount.

(i) The dated (future) value of \$400 at the focal date:

$$P = 400.00; \quad r = 12\% = 0.12; \quad t = \frac{9}{12}$$

$$S = 400\left[1 + (0.12)\left(\frac{9}{12}\right)\right] = 400(1 + 0.09) = 400(1.09) = \$436.00$$

(ii) The dated (future) value of \$500 at the focal date:

$$P = 500.00; \quad r = 12\% = 0.12; \quad t = \frac{4}{12}$$

$$S = 500\left[1 + (0.12)\left(\frac{4}{12}\right)\right] = 500(1 + 0.04) = 500(1.04) = \$520.00$$

(iii) The dated (present) value of \$618 at the focal date:

$$S = 618.00; \quad r = 12\% = 0.12; \quad t = \frac{3}{12}$$

$$P = \frac{618.00}{1 + (0.12)\left(\frac{3}{12}\right)}$$

$$= \frac{618.00}{1 + 0.03}$$

$$= \frac{618.00}{1.03} = \$600.00$$

(iv) The single payment to be made nine months from now will be = 436.00 + 520.00 + 600.00 = \$1556.00.

EXAMPLE 7.5D

Scheduled payments of $400 due now and $700 due in five months are to be settled by a payment of $500 in three months and a final payment in eight months. Determine the amount of the final payment at 6% p.a., using eight months from now as the focal date.

SOLUTION

Let the value of the final payment be $x.

(i) Use a time diagram to represent the given data.

FIGURE 7.8 Graphical Representation of Data

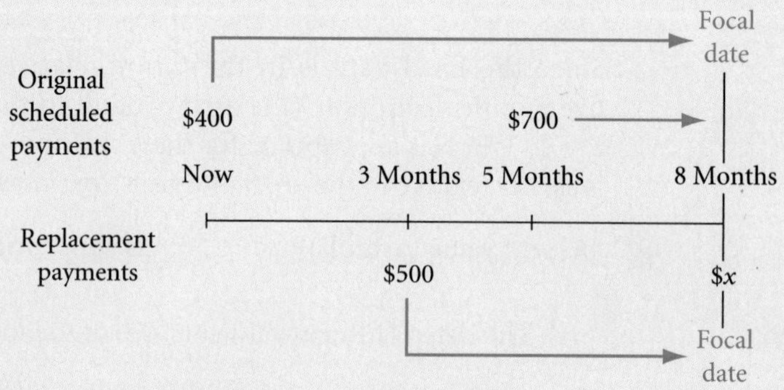

(ii) Dated value of the original scheduled payments:

(a) The value at the focal date of the $400 payment due eight months before the focal date is found by using the future value formula.

$$S = 400\left[1 + (0.06)\left(\frac{8}{12}\right)\right] = 400(1 + 0.04) = 400(1.04) = \$416.00$$

(b) The value at the focal date of the $700 payment due three months before the focal date is found by using the future value formula.

$$S = 700\left[1 + (0.06)\left(\frac{3}{12}\right)\right]$$

$$= 700(1 + 0.015)$$

$$= 700(1.015)$$

$$= \$710.50$$

(iii) Dated value of the replacement payments:

(a) The value at the focal date of the $500 payment made five months before the focal date is found by using the future value formula.

$$S = 500\left[1 + (0.06)\left(\frac{5}{12}\right)\right]$$

$$= 500(1 + 0.025)$$

$$= 500(1.025)$$

$$= \$512.50$$

(b) The value at the focal date of the final payment is $\$x$ (no adjustment for interest is necessary for an amount of money located at the focal date).

(iv) The **equation of values** at the focal date is now set up by matching the dated values of the original debts to the dated values of the replacement payments.

$$500\left[1 + (0.06)\left(\frac{5}{12}\right)\right] + x = 400\left[1 + (0.06)\left(\frac{8}{12}\right)\right] + 700\left[1 + (0.06)\left(\frac{3}{12}\right)\right]$$

$$512.50 + x = 416.00 + 710.50$$

$$512.50 + x = 1126.50$$

$$x = 1126.50 - 512.50$$

$$x = 614.00$$

The final payment to be made in eight months is \$614.

D. Finding the value of two or more equivalent payments

The equivalent values (the dated value of the original scheduled payments) obtained when using simple interest formulas are influenced by the choice of focal date. Choose a focal date on the basis of the date when an equivalent value must be calculated. When two or more equivalent values must be calculated, choose one of the dates for which an equivalent value must be calculated.

EXAMPLE 7.5E

Jeremy had two equal outstanding loans, one from 63 days ago and one from 105 days ago. He repaid both loans today with the single amount of \$3700. If interest is 9% on the loans, what was the size of the equal amounts borrowed?

SOLUTION

Let the value of each of the equal loans be $\$x$.

(i) Use a time diagram to represent the given data.

FIGURE 7.9 **Graphical Representation of Data**

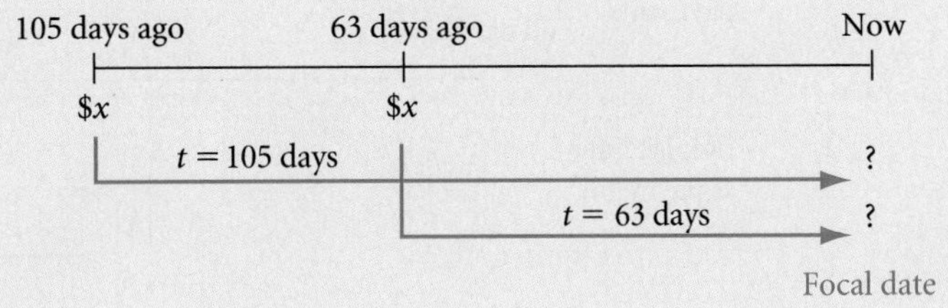

(ii) Dated value of the original scheduled payments:

(a) The value at the focal date of the first $x payment due 105 days before the focal date is found by using the future value formula.

$$S = x\left[1 + (0.09)\left(\frac{105}{365}\right)\right] = x(1 + 0.025890) = 1.025890x$$

(b) The value at the focal date of the second $x payment due 63 days before the focal date is found by using the future value formula.

$$S = x\left[1 + (0.09)\left(\frac{63}{365}\right)\right] = x(1 + 0.015534) = 1.015534x$$

(iii) Dated value of the replacement payments:

(a) The value at the focal date of the repayment is $3700 on the focal date.

(b) The value at the focal date of the two equal payments is

$$1.025890x + 1.015534x = 2.041424x$$

(iv) The equation of values at the focal date is now set up by matching the dated values of the original debts to the dated values of the replacement payments.

THE SUM OF THE DATED VALUES OF THE REPLACEMENT PAYMENTS = THE SUM OF THE DATED VALUES OF THE ORIGINAL SCHEDULED PAYMENTS

$$3700 = 2.041424x$$

$$x = \frac{3700.00}{2.041424}$$

$$x = 1812.46$$

Each of the two equal loans had been $1812.46.

EXAMPLE 7.5F

Clarkson Developments was supposed to pay Majestic Flooring $2000 sixty days ago and $1800 in thirty days. Majestic Flooring agreed to accept three equal payments due today, 60 days from today, and 120 days from today. Compute the size of the equal payments at 10% p.a. Use today as the focal date.

SOLUTION

Let the size of the equal payments be $x.

(i) Graphical representation of data:

FIGURE 7.10 Graphical Representation of Data

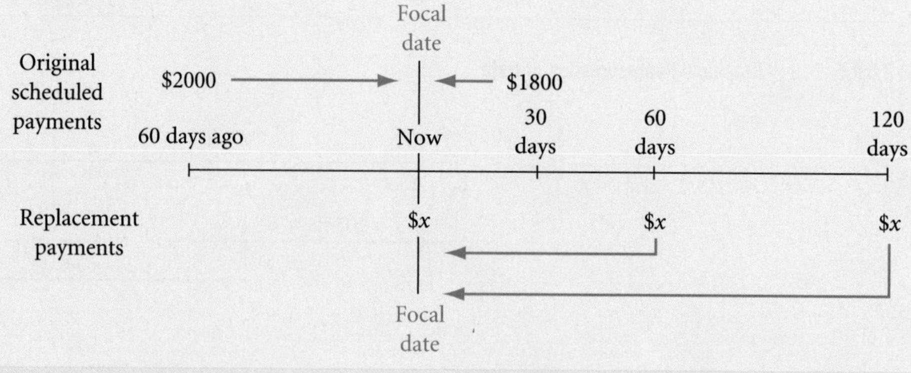

(ii) Dated value of the original scheduled payments at the focal date:

(a) Because the \$2000 payment is due 60 days before the focal date, the future value formula is appropriate.

$$S = 2000\left[1 + (0.10)\left(\frac{60}{365}\right)\right] = 2000(1 + 0.016438) = \$2032.88$$

(b) Because the \$1800 payment is due 30 days after the focal date, the present value formula is appropriate.

$$P = \frac{1800.00}{1 + (0.10)\left(\frac{30}{365}\right)} = \frac{1800.00}{1 + 0.008219} = \$1785.33$$

(iii) Dated value of the replacement payments at the focal date:

(a) Since the first payment is to be made at the focal date, its value is $\$x$.
(b) Because the second payment is to be made 60 days after the focal date, the present value formula is appropriate.

$$P = \frac{x}{1 + (0.10)\left(\frac{60}{365}\right)} = \frac{x}{1 + 0.016438} = \frac{1(x)}{1.016438} = \$0.983828x$$

(c) Because the third payment is to be made 120 days after the focal date, the present value formula is appropriate.

$$P = \frac{x}{1 + (0.10)\left(\frac{120}{365}\right)} = \frac{x}{1 + 0.032877}$$

$$= \frac{1(x)}{1.0032877} = \$0.968170x$$

(iv) The equation of values (dated value of the replacement payments = dated value of the original scheduled payments):

$$x + 0.983828x + 0.968170x = 2032.88 + 1785.33$$

$$2.951998x = 3818.21$$

$$x = \frac{3818.21}{2.951998}$$

$$x = \$1293.43$$

The size of each of the three equal payments is \$1293.43.

EXAMPLE 7.5G

Two debts, one of \$4000 due in three months with interest at 8% and the other of \$3000 due in eighteen months with interest at 10%, are to be discharged by making two equal payments. What is the size of the equal payments if the first is due one year from now, the second two years from now, money is worth 12%, and the chosen focal date is one year from now?

SOLUTION Let the size of the equal payments be $x.

(i) Graphical representation of data:

FIGURE 7.11 Graphical Representation of Data

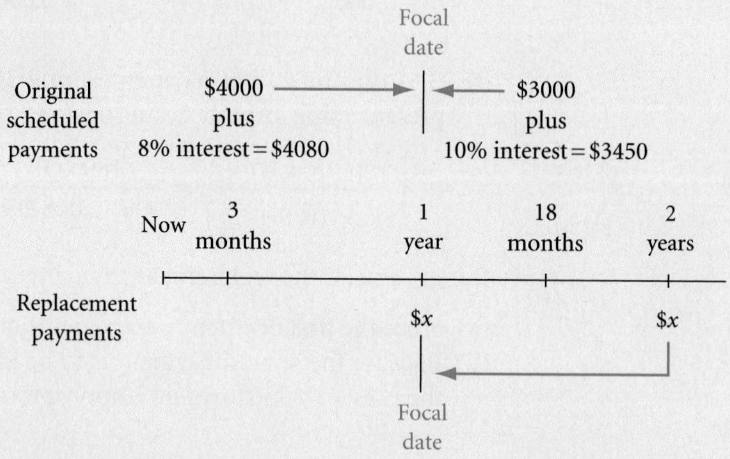

(ii) Maturity value of the original debts:
Since the two original debts are interest-bearing, their maturity values need to be determined first so that the principal and interest of these original debts are discharged by the two equal payments.

(a) For the $4000 debt: P = 4000; $r = 8\% = 0.08$; $t = \frac{3}{12}$

$$\text{Maturity value, S} = 4000\left[1 + (0.08)\left(\frac{3}{12}\right)\right] = 4000(1.02) = \$4080$$

(b) For the $3000 debt: P = 3000; $r = 10\% = 0.10$; $t = \frac{18}{12}$

$$\text{Maturity value, S} = 3000\left[1 + (0.10)\left(\frac{18}{12}\right)\right] = 3000(1.15) = \$3450$$

(iii) Dated value of the money value of the original payments at 12%:

(a) Because the maturity value of $4080 is due nine months before the focal date, the future value formula is appropriate.

$$S = 4080\left[1 + (0.12)\left(\frac{9}{12}\right)\right] = 4080(1.09) = \$4447.20$$

(b) Because the maturity value of $3450 is due six months after the focal date, the present value formula is appropriate.

$$P = \frac{3450}{1 + (0.12)\left(\frac{6}{12}\right)} = \frac{3450}{1.06} = \$3254.72$$

(iv) Dated value of the replacement payments:

(a) Since the first replacement payment is made at the focal date, its value is $x.

(b) Because the second replacement payment is made 12 months after the focal date, the present value formula is appropriate.

$$P = \frac{x}{1 + (0.12)\left(\frac{12}{12}\right)} = \frac{x}{1.12} = 0.892857x$$

(v) The equation of values:

$$x + 0.892857x = 4447.20 + 3254.72$$

$$1.892857x = 7701.92$$

$$x = \frac{7701.92}{1.892857}$$

$$x = \$4068.94$$

The size of the equal payments is $4068.94.

E. Loan repayments

Loans by financial institutions to individuals are usually repaid by **blended payments**, which are equal periodic payments that include payment of interest and repayment of principal. To repay the loan, the sum of the present values of the periodic payments must equal the original principal. The concept of equivalent values is used to determine the size of the blended payments.

EXAMPLE 7.5H

A loan of $2000 made at 8.5% p.a. is to be repaid in four equal payments due at the end of the next four quarters respectively. Determine the size of the quarterly payments if the agreed focal date is the date of the loan.

SOLUTION

Let the size of the equal quarterly payments be represented by $x.

(i) Graphical representation of data:

FIGURE 7.12 Graphical Representation of Data

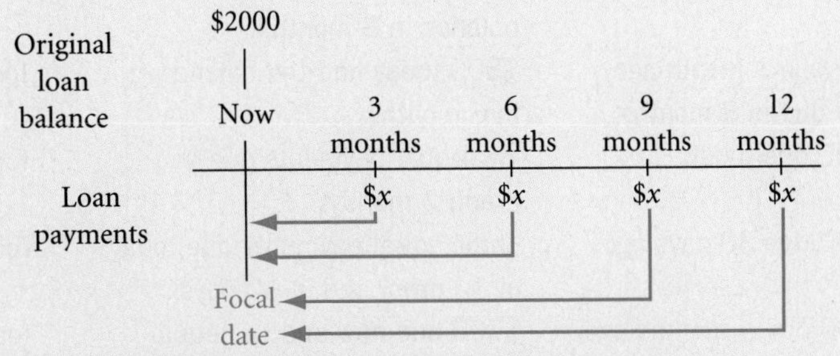

(ii) Dated value of the loan balance at the focal date is $2000.

(iii) Dated value of the loan payments at the focal date:
The payments are due three, six, nine, and twelve months after the focal date respectively. Their values are

$$\text{(a) } P_1 = \frac{x}{1 + (0.085)\left(\frac{3}{12}\right)} = \frac{x}{1 + 0.02125} = \frac{1(x)}{1.02125} = 0.979192x$$

$$\text{(b) } P_2 = \frac{x}{1 + (0.085)\left(\frac{6}{12}\right)} = \frac{x}{1 + 0.0425} = \frac{1(x)}{1.0425} = 0.959233x$$

$$\text{(c) } P_3 = \frac{x}{1 + (0.085)\left(\frac{9}{12}\right)} = \frac{x}{1 + 0.06375} = \frac{1(x)}{1.06375} = 0.940071x$$

$$\text{(d) } P_4 = \frac{x}{1 + (0.085)\left(\frac{12}{12}\right)} = \frac{x}{1 + 0.085} = \frac{1(x)}{1.085} = 0.921659x$$

$$\text{(iv) } 0.979192x + 0.959233x + 0.940071x + 0.921659x = 2000.00$$
$$3.800155x = 2000.00$$
$$x = 526.29$$

The size of the quarterly payment is \$526.29.

EXERCISE 7.5

A. Find the equivalent replacement payments indicated for each of the following scheduled payments.

	Original Scheduled Payments	Replacement Payments	Focal Date	Rate
1.	\$800 due today	In full	4 months from today	11%
2.	\$1200 due 4 months ago	In full	Today	6%
3.	\$600 due in 2 months	In full	7 months from today	7%
4.	\$1000 due in 8 months	In full	2 months from today	10%
5.	\$500 due 4 months ago, \$600 due in 2 months	In full	Today	5%
6.	\$800 due today, \$700 due in 2 months	In full	4 months from today	9%
7.	\$2000 due today	\$1200 in 4 months and the balance in 8 months	Today	6%
8.	\$400 due 1 month ago, \$600 due in 3 months	\$500 today and the balance in 6 months	Today	8%
9.	\$1500 due today	Two equal payments due in 2 and 7 months	Today	10%
10.	\$1800 due 30 days ago	Three equal payments due today, in 30 days, and in 60 days	Today	9%
11.	\$1500 due 4 months ago, \$1200 due in 8 months with 10% interest	\$700 due now and two equal payments due in 6 months and in 12 months	Today	5%
12.	\$2000 due in 6 months with interest at 8%, \$1600 due in 2 years with interest at 7%	Three equal payments due in 6, 12, and 18 months respectively	1 year from today	11%

B. Solve each of the following problems.

1. Scheduled debt payments of $600 each are due three months and six months from now respectively. If interest at 10% is allowed, what single payment today is required to settle the two scheduled payments? Reference Example 7.5A

2. Debt payments are due of $700 in two months and $800 in five months. If interest at 8.3% is allowed, what single payment today is required to settle the two scheduled payments?

3. A loan payment of $1000 was due 60 days ago and another payment of $1200 is due 30 days from now. What single payment 90 days from now will pay off the two obligations if interest is to be 8% and the agreed focal date is 90 days from now? Reference Example 7.5B

4. A loan payment of $2200 was due 91 days ago and another payment of $1800 is due 45 days from now. What single payment 75 days from now will pay off the two obligations if interest is to be 9% and the agreed focal date is 75 days from now?

5. Jay was due to make loan payments of $500 four months ago, $800 today, and $400 in three months. He has agreed instead to make a single payment one month from today. If money is worth 10.5% and the agreed focal date is one month from today, what is the size of the replacement payment? Reference Example 7.5C

6. Jane was due to make loan payments of $1200 six months ago, $1500 one month ago, and $700 in two months. Instead, she is to make a single payment today. If money is worth 9.8% and the agreed focal date is today, what is the size of the replacement payment?

7. Loan payments of $400 due 95 days ago and $700 due today are to be repaid by a payment of $600 30 days from today and the balance in 125 days. If money is worth 6% and the agreed focal date is 125 days from today, what is the size of the final payment? Reference Example 7.5D

8. Loan payments of $4000 due 200 days ago and $6000 due 63 days ago are to be replaced by a payment of $5000 today and the balance 92 days from today. If money is worth 8.3% and the agreed focal date is 92 days from today, what is the size of the final payment?

9. Dan borrowed $1100 today and is to repay the loan in two equal payments, one in four months and one in six months. If interest is 8.5% on the loan, what is the size of the equal payments if a focal date of today is used? Reference Example 7.5E

10. When Ruby borrowed $2300, she agreed to repay the loan in two equal payments, to be made 90 days and 135 days from the day the money was borrowed. If interest is 9.25% on the loan, what is the size of the equal payments if a focal date of today is used?

11. Ruben repaid $800, paying back two equal outstanding loans from seven months ago and five months ago. If interest is 11% on the loans, and the agreed focal date is today, what was the size of the equal amount borrowed?

12. Judy received a payment of $2950 and paid back two equal outstanding loans from 45 days ago and 190 days ago. If interest is 12.5% on the loans, and the agreed focal date is today, what was the size of the equal amounts borrowed?

13. Jessica should have made two payments of $800 each. The first was due 60 days ago and the second payment was due 30 days ago. The two original scheduled payments are to be settled by two equal payments to be made today and 60 days from now respectively. If interest allowed is 7.25% and the agreed focal date is today, what is the size of the equal payments?

14. Krista borrowed $14 000. The loan is to be repaid by three equal payments due in 120, 240, and 260 days from now respectively. Determine the size of the equal payments at 7% with a focal date of today. Reference Example 7.5F

15. Jerry borrowed $4000. The loan is to be repaid by three equal payments due in four, eight, and twelve months from now respectively. Determine the size of the equal payments at 8.5% with a focal date of today.

16. On March 1, Bear Mountain Tours borrowed $1500. Three equal payments are required, on April 30, June 20, and August 10, and a final payment of $400 on September 30 of the same year. If the focal date is September 30, what is the amount of the equal payments at 6.75%?

17. Two debt payments, of $1900 due today and $1200 due with interest at 9% nine months from now, are to be settled by two equal payments due in three and six months respectively. Determine the amount of the equal payments if money is worth 7% and the focal date is today. Reference Example 7.5G

18. Wayne's Windows should have made a payment of $1200 to Shane's Woodcraft one year ago. They are also scheduled to pay $1500 due with interest of 8% in nine months. Shane's Woodcraft agreed to accept three equal payments due today, six months from now, and one year from now at 9.5%. Determine the amount of the equal payments if the focal date is one year from today.

powered by CourseCompass™ and MathXL® MyMathLab Go to MyMathLab at www.mathxl.com. You can practise many of this chapter's exercises as often as you want. The guided solutions help you find an answer step by step. You'll find a personalized study plan available to you too!

Review Exercise

1. Determine the number of days from

(a) April 25, 2009 to October 14, 2009;

(b) July 30, 2011 to February 29, 2012.

2. Compute the amount of interest for

(a) \$1975.00 at 5.5% for 215 days;

(b) \$844.65 at 8.25% from May 30, 2009 to January 4, 2010.

3. What principal will earn

(a) \$34.80 interest at 5% in 219 days?

(b) \$34.40 interest at 9.75% from October 30, 2009 to June 1, 2010?

4. Answer each of the following.

(a) What was the rate of interest if the interest on a loan of \$675 for 284 days was \$39.39?

(b) How many days will it take for \$2075 to earn \$124.29 interest at $8\frac{1}{4}$% p.a.?

(c) If \$680 is worth \$698.70 after three months, what interest rate was charged?

(d) How many months will it take \$750 to grow to \$795.00 at 7.2% p.a.?

5. Solve each of the following.

(a) What principal will have a maturity value of \$785.96 at 10% in 175 days?

(b) What is the present value of \$6300.00 due in 16 months at 7.75%?

6. What principal will earn \$24.87 at 4.75% in 156 days?

7. What sum of money will earn \$148.57 from September 1, 2009 to April 30, 2010 at 7.5%?

8. At what rate of interest must a principal of \$1545 be invested to earn interest of \$58.93 in 150 days?

9. At what rate of interest will \$1500 grow to \$1562.04 from June 1, 2009 to December 1, 2009?

10. In how many months will \$2500 earn \$51.04 interest at 3.5%?

11. In how many days will \$3100 grow to \$3195.72 at 5.75%?

12. Compute the accumulated value of \$4200 at 4.5% after 11 months.

13. What is the amount to which \$1550 will grow from June 10, 2009 to December 15, 2009 at 6.5%?

14. What amount of money will accumulate to \$1516.80 in eight months at 8%?

15. What principal will amount to \$3367.28 if invested at 9% from November 1, 2011 to May 31, 2012?

16. What is the present value of \$3780 due in nine months if interest is 5%?

17. Compute the present value on June 1, 2009 of \$1785 due on October 15, 2009 if interest is 7.5%.

18. Payments of \$1750 and \$1600 are due four months from now and nine months from now respectively. What single payment is required to pay off the two scheduled payments today if interest is 9% and the focal date is today?

19. A loan payment of \$1450 was due 45 days ago and a payment of \$1200 is due in 60 days. What single payment made 30 days from now is required to settle the two payments if interest is 7% and the focal date is 30 days from now?

20. Scheduled payments of \$800 due two months ago and \$1200 due in one month are to be repaid by a payment of \$1000 today and the balance in three months. What is the amount of the final payment if interest is 7.75% and the focal date is one month from now?

21. An obligation of \$10 000 is to be repaid by equal payments due in 60 days, 120 days, and 180 days. What is the amount of the equal payments if money is worth 6.5% and the focal date is today?

22. Payments of \$4000 each due in four, nine, and eleven months from now are to be settled by three equal payments due today, six months from now, and twelve months from now. What is the amount of the equal payments if interest is 7.35% and the agreed focal date is today?

23. A loan of $5000 due in one year is to be repaid by three equal payments due today, six months from now, and one year from now. What is the amount of the equal payments if interest is 6.5% and the focal date is today?

24. Three debts, the first for $1000 due two months ago, the second for $1200 due in two months, and the third for $1400 due in four months, are to be paid by a single payment today. How much is the single payment if money is worth 8.25% p.a. and the focal date is today?

25. Loan payments of $700 due three months ago and of $1000 due today are to be paid by a payment of $800 in two months and a final payment in five months. If 9% interest is allowed, and the focal date is five months from now, what is the amount of the final payment?

26. A loan of $5000 is to be repaid in three equal installments due 60, 120, and 180 days after the date of the loan. If the focal date is the date of the loan and interest is 6.9% p.a., compute the amount of the installments.

27. Three loan payments, the first for $2000 due three months ago, the second for $1400 with interest of 7.5% due in nine months, and the third for $1200 with interest of 5.75% due in sixteen months, are to be paid in three equal installments due today, four months from now, and one year from now. If money is worth 8.5% and the focal date is today, determine the amount of the equal payments. (Compute the maturity values of the original debts first.)

28. A loan of $7000 is to be settled by four equal payments due today, and one year, two years, and three years from now. Determine the amount of the equal payments if money is worth 5.75% and the focal date is today.

Self-Test

1. Compute the amount of interest earned by $1290 at 3.5% p.a. in 173 days.
2. In how many months will $8500 grow to $8818.75 at 5% p.a.?
3. What interest rate is paid if the interest on a loan of $2500 for six months is $81.25?
4. What principal will have a maturity value of $10 000 at 8.25% p.a. in three months?
5. What is the amount to which $6000 will grow at 3.75% p.a. in ten months?
6. What principal will earn $67.14 interest at 6.25% for 82 days?
7. What is the present value of $4400 due at 3.25% p.a. in 243 days?
8. What rate of interest is paid if the interest on a loan of $2500 is $96.06 from November 14, 2009 to May 20, 2010?
9. How many days will it take for $8500 to earn $689.72 at 8.25% p.a.?
10. What principal will earn $55.99 interest at 9.75% p.a. from February 4, 2008 to July 6, 2008?
11. What amount invested will accumulate to $7500 at 3.75% p.a. in 88 days?
12. Compute the amount of interest on $835 at 7.5% p.a. from October 8, 2011 to August 4, 2012.

13. A loan of $3320 is to be repaid by three equal payments due in 92 days, 235 days, and 326 days. Determine the amount of the equal payments at 8.75% p.a. with a focal date of today.

14. Loan payments of $1725 due today, $510 due in 75 days, and $655 due in 323 days are to be combined into a single payment to be made 115 days from now. What is that single payment if money is worth 8.5% p.a. and the focal date is 115 days from now?

15. Scheduled payments of $1010 due five months ago and $1280 due today are to be repaid by a payment of $615 in four months and the balance in seven months. If money is worth 7.75% p.a. and the focal date is in seven months, what is the amount of the final payment?

16. A payment of $1310 due five months ago and a second payment of $1225 with interest at 12% p.a. due in three months are to be settled by two equal payments due now and seven months from now. Compute the amount of the equal payments at 6.5%, with the focal date now.

Challenge Problems

1. Nora borrows $37 500 on September 28, 2011 at 7% p.a. simple interest, to be repaid on October 31, 2012. She has the option of making payments toward the loan before the due date. Nora pays $6350 on February 17, 2012, $8250 on July 2, 2012, and $7500 on October 1, 2012. Compute the payment required to pay off the debt on the focal date of October 31, 2012.

2. A supplier will give Shark Unibase Company a discount of 2% if an invoice is paid 60 days before its due date. Suppose Shark wants to take advantage of this discount but needs to borrow the money. It plans to pay back the loan in 60 days. What is the highest annual simple interest rate at which Shark Unibase can borrow the money and still save by paying the invoice 60 days before its due date?

Case Study 7.1 Short-Term Loans

» Skyline Sports stocked and sold seasonal sporting equipment for hiking and skiing. Due to a spell of warm weather during the ski season, sales of skiing and snowboarding equipment had not been as high as expected. Since Skyline Sports had already purchased the equipment from their suppliers, payment was due. Aaron Baxter, the manager, was trying to borrow the cash to make the payment of $14 600. At the company's bank, he would be able to obtain a one-month loan for the full amount, at 6.95% per annum simple interest. At a second bank, he would have three months to pay, with interest at 7.3%.

Later that same day, in talking with his suppliers, Aaron learned that they were willing to finance the purchases at 8.15% per annum if he signed a promissory note. Three equal payments would then be due, two months, four months, and six months from now.

QUESTIONS

1. What are the maturity values of the two different bank loans?
2. What equal payments would have to be made to the supplier?
3. As of today's date, compute the equivalent values of each of the three options. Which option should Aaron choose?

Case Study 7.2 Cost of Financing Pay Now or Pay Later

» Along with licensing, the purchase of auto insurance for vehicles is required in Canada. Benefits of auto insurance are as follows:

- Safeguards the investment in the automobile.
- Pays for medical expenses in case of an accident.
- Covers losses caused by uninsured or underinsured drivers.
- Compensates for damage due to theft, vandalism, or natural disasters.

Quick Courier Service is about to purchase insurance on its new delivery van. Taylor, the manager, has the company's insurance agent outline three payment plans to provide coverage for the next 12 months.

Plan One requires that the full year's premium of $4000 be paid at the beginning of the year.

Plan Two allows payment of the annual premium in two installments. The first installment would have to be paid immediately and would amount to one-half of the annual premium, plus a $60 service charge. The second installment would be paid in six months' time, and would amount to the remaining half of the premium.

Plan Three allows for twelve equal monthly payments of $355 each. These payments would be made on the same date within each month, starting immediately.

Quick Courier Service pays its insurance using Plan One. However, the company realizes that it is missing out on interest it could have earned on this money when it pays the full year's premium at the beginning of the policy term. Taylor considers this to be the "cost" of paying its bill in one lump sum. Taylor is interested in knowing the cost of its insurance payment options.

QUESTIONS

1. Suppose Quick Courier Service could earn 4% p.a. simple interest on its money over the next year. Assume the first premium payment is due today (the first day of the insurance policy term) and the focal date is today. Ignoring all taxes, compute the cost to Quick Courier Service of paying the insurance using each of the three payment plans.

2. Suppose Quick Courier Service expects to earn 2.5% p.a. simple interest on any money it invests in the first three months of this year, and 1.8% p.a. simple interest on any money it invests during the rest of this year. Assume the focal date is today. Which option—Plan One, Plan Two, or Plan Three—will have the least cost for the company?
3. Examine a vehicle insurance policy of your own or of a family member. Calculate what you could earn on your money at today's rates of interest. What is the cost of this insurance policy if you pay the annual premium at the beginning of the policy term? Make the focal date the first day of the policy term.

SUMMARY OF FORMULAS

Formula 7.1A

$I = Prt$

Finding the amount of interest when the principal, the rate, and the time are known

Formula 7.1B

$$P = \frac{I}{rt}$$

Finding the principal directly when the amount of interest, the rate of interest, and the time are known

Formula 7.1C

$$r = \frac{I}{Pt}$$

Finding the rate of interest directly when the amount of interest, the principal, and the time are known

Formula 7.1D

$$t = \frac{I}{Pr}$$

Finding the time directly when the amount of interest, the principal, and the rate of interest are known

Formula 7.2

$S = P + I$

Finding the future value (maturity value) when the principal and the amount of interest are known

Formula 7.3A

$S = P(1 + rt)$

Finding the future value (maturity value) at simple interest directly when the principal, rate of interest, and time are known

Formula 7.3B

$$P = \frac{S}{1 + rt}$$

Finding the present value at simple interest when the future value (maturity value), the rate of interest, and the time are known

GLOSSARY

Blended payments equal periodic payments that include payment of interest and repayment of principal, usually paid by individuals to financial institutions *(p. 283)*

Dated value the value of a sum of money at a specific time relative to its due date, including interest *(p. 273)*

Equation of values the equation obtained when matching the dated values of the original payments at an agreed focal date to the dated values of the replacement payments at the same focal date *(p. 279)*

Equivalent value see **Dated value**

Focal date a specific time chosen to compare the time value of one or more dated sums of money *(p. 274)*

Future value of a sum of money the value obtained when the amount of interest is added to the original principal *(p. 266)*

Interest rent paid for the use of money *(p. 257)*

Interest period the time period for which interest is charged *(p. 257)*

Maturity value see **Future value of a sum of money**

Nominal rate the yearly or annual rate of interest charged on the principal of a loan *(p. 257)*

Present value the principal that grows to a given future value (maturity value) over a given period of time at a given rate of interest *(p. 269)*

Simple interest interest calculated on the original principal by the formula $I = Prt$, and paid only when the principal is repaid *(p. 257)*

Time value of money a concept of money value that allows for a change in the value of a sum of money over time if the sum of money is subject to a rate of interest *(p. 269)*

USEFUL INTERNET SITES

www.cis-pec.gc.ca
Canada Investment and Savings (CIS) CIS is a special operating agency of the Department of Finance that markets and manages savings and investment products for Canadians. Their site provides information on products, including Canada Savings Bonds, as well as rates, savings programs, and publications.

www.tsx.com
Toronto Stock Exchange (TSX) Visit this site to see the latest market trends, get quotes, and read about the market data services offered.

www.m-x.ca/accueil_en.php
Montreal Stock Exchange Visit this site to see companies traded on the exchange, its history, mission, operations, and FAQs.

www.standardandpoors.com
Standard and Poor's Standard and Poor's research services provide data, analysis, and economic forecasts, and analyze economic events and trends in business and government around the globe to help people make informed business decisions.

CHAPTER 8 Simple Interest Applications

OBJECTIVES

Upon completing this chapter, you will be able to do the following:

1. Identify and define promissory notes and their related terms.
2. Compute the maturity value of interest-bearing promissory notes.
3. Compute the present value of promissory notes and treasury bills.
4. Compute interest and balances for demand loans.
5. Compute interest and balances for lines of credit and credit card loans.
6. Construct repayment schedules for loans using blended payments.

A business often needs to borrow money for periods of less than one year. It may need to pay for products purchased or for work done by employees now, but will not collect the money owed to it until some time in the future. A business may need to replace higher-interest-rate loans, such as credit card debts, with lower-interest-rate loans, such as a bank loan or line of credit. Financial institutions are making it easier for businesses and individuals to borrow money, and are making it more convenient to repay what is borrowed. In addition to the traditional promissory notes, demand loans and lines of credit are being made available for use.

INTRODUCTION

Businesses often encounter situations that involve the application of simple interest. Simple interest calculation is usually restricted to financial instruments subject to time periods of less than one year. In this chapter we apply simple interest to short-term promissory notes, treasury bills, lines of credit, credit card loans, and demand loans.

8.1 PROMISSORY NOTES—BASIC CONCEPTS AND COMPUTATIONS

A. Nature of promissory notes and illustration

A **promissory note** is a written promise by one party to pay a certain sum of money, with or without interest, at a specific date or on demand, to another party. (See Figure 8.1.)

FIGURE 8.1 Promissory Note

$650.00 MISSISSAUGA, ONTARIO OCTOBER 30, 2010

FOUR MONTHS after date I promise to pay to the order of

CREDIT VALLEY NURSERY

SIX-HUNDRED-FIFTY and 00/100 ······························ Dollars

at SHERIDAN CREDIT UNION LIMITED for value received

with interest at 7.25% per annum.

Signed D. Peel

This is an **interest-bearing promissory note** because it is a note subject to the rate of interest stated on the face of the note.

B. Related terms explained

The following information is directly available in the promissory note (see items a, b, c, d, e, f below) or can be determined (see items g, h, i, j).

(a) The **maker** of the note is the party making the promise to pay. —— **(D. Peel)**

(b) The **payee** of the note is the party to whom the promise to pay is made. —— **(Credit Valley Nursery)**

(c) The **face value** of the note is the sum of money (principal) specified. —— **($650.00)**

(d) The **rate of interest** is stated as a simple annual rate based on the face value. —— **(7.25%)**

(e) The **date of issue** or **issue date** is the date on which the note was made. — (October 30, 2010)

(f) The **term** of the promissory note is the length of time before the note matures (becomes payable). — (four months)

(g) The **due date** or **date of maturity** is the date on which the note is to be paid. — (See Subsection C)

(h) The **interest period** is the time period from the date of issue to the legal due date. — (See Subsection C)

(i) The **amount of interest** is payable together with the face value on the legal due date. — (See Subsection C)

(j) The **maturity value** is the amount payable on the due date (face value plus interest). — (See Subsection C)

The Canadian law relating to promissory notes adds **three days of grace** to the term of the note to obtain the **legal due date** (Bills of Exchange Act, Section 41). This is to allow for the situation of the repayment date falling on a statutory holiday. In this case, without three days of grace, you would either have to pay the note early, or take a penalty for paying three days late. Therefore, three days are added to the due date of a promissory note. Interest must be paid for those three days of grace, but there is no late payment penalty and your credit rating remains good. Today, with electronic banking, you can arrange to pay your note at any time, even on the weekend, so you may not need the three days of grace. If you decide not to include the three days of grace, write "No Grace Days" on the note when you negotiate the loan.

C. Computed values

EXAMPLE 8.1A

For the promissory note illustrated in Figure 8.1, determine
(i) the due date;
(ii) the interest period;
(iii) the amount of interest;
(iv) the maturity value.

SOLUTION

(i) *Finding the due date*

Add three days of grace to the term of the note to obtain the legal due date. Since calendar months vary in length, the month in which the term ends does not necessarily have a date that corresponds to the date of issue. In such cases, the last day of the month is used as the end of the term of the note. Three days of grace are added to that date to determine the legal due date. (Throughout this chapter, we have included three days of grace in the exercises. However, as we pointed out earlier, electronic banking has reduced the need for three days of grace.)

With reference to the promissory note in Figure 8.1,

- the date of issue is October 30, 2010;
- the term of the note is four months;
- the month in which the term ends is February 2011;

- the end of the term is February 28 (since February has no day corresponding to day 30, the last day of the month is used to establish the end of the term of the note);
- the legal due date (adding 3 days) is March 3.

(ii) *Determining the interest period*
If the note bears interest, the interest period covers the number of days from the date of issue of the note to the legal due date.

October 30 to March 3 = 124 days

(iii) *Computing the amount of interest*
The interest payable on the note is the simple interest based on the face value of the note for the interest period at the stated rate. It is found using the simple interest formula:

$$I = Prt \qquad \text{Formula 7.1A}$$

$$I = (650.00)(0.0725)\left(\frac{124}{365}\right) = \$16.01$$

(iv) *Finding the maturity value of the note*
The maturity value of the promissory note is the total amount payable at the legal due date.
Face value + Interest = 650.00 + 16.01 = \$666.01

EXCEL NOTES

In Excel, use the following functions to do these calculations:

COUPDAYSNC	Days between dates
ACCRINTM	Accrued interest
YIELDDISC	Simple interest yields
ACCRINTM	Accrued interest to maturity

EXERCISE 8.1

A. Determine each of the items listed from the information provided in the promissory note below.

> \$530.00   OAKVILLE, ONTARIO   DECEMBER 30, 2010
>
> FIVE MONTHS after date I promise to pay
>
> to the order of JANE WELTON
>
> FIVE-HUNDRED-THIRTY and 00/100 ······················ Dollars
>
> at SHERIDAN CENTRAL BANK for value received
>
> with interest at 6.5% per annum.
>
> Signed *E. Salt*

1. Date issued
2. Legal due date
3. Face value
4. Interest rate
5. Interest period (days)
6. Amount of interest
7. Maturity value

B. For each of the following notes, determine

(a) the legal due date; (b) the interest period (in days);

(c) the amount of interest; (d) the maturity value.

1. The face value of a five-month, 6% note dated September 30, 2011 is \$840.
2. A note for \$760 dated March 20, 2010, with interest at 5% per annum, is issued for 120 days.
3. A 60-day, 6.5% note for \$1250 is issued January 31, 2008.
4. A four-month, 5.25% note for \$2000 is issued July 31, 2009.

8.2 MATURITY VALUE OF INTEREST-BEARING PROMISSORY NOTES

A. Using the formula S = P(1 + *rt*)

Since the maturity value of a promissory note is the principal (face value) plus the interest accumulated to the legal due date, the future value formula for simple interest will determine the maturity value directly.

$$\boxed{S = P(1 + rt)}$$ —— **Formula 7.3A**

S = maturity value of the promissory note;
P = the face value of the note;
r = the rate of interest on the note;
t = the interest period (the number of days between the *date of issue* and the *legal due date*).

B. Worked examples

EXAMPLE 8.2A Find the maturity value of an \$800, six-month note with interest at 7.5% dated May 31, 2010.

SOLUTION The date of issue is May 31, 2010;
the term of the note is six months;
the term ends November 30, 2010;
the legal due date is December 3, 2010;
the interest period (May 31 to December 3) has 186 days.

$$P = 800.00; \quad r = 0.075; \quad t = \frac{186}{365}$$

$$S = 800.00\left[1 + (0.075)\left(\frac{186}{365}\right)\right] = 800.00(1 + 0.038219) = \$830.58$$

EXAMPLE 8.2B

Determine the maturity value of a 90-day, $750 note dated December 15, 2011, with interest at 8%.

SOLUTION

The date of issue is December 15, 2011;
the term is 90 days;
the term ends March 14, 2012 (from 90 days take away 17 days remaining in December, 31 days for January, 29 days for February, 2012 being a leap year, which leaves 13 days for March);
the legal due date (adding the three days of grace) is March 17;
the interest period (December 15 to March 17) has 93 days.

$$P = 750.00; \quad r = 0.08; \quad t = \frac{93}{365}$$

$$S = 750.00\left[1 + (0.08)\left(\frac{93}{365}\right)\right] = 750.00(1 + 0.020384) = \$765.29$$

EXERCISE 8.2

A. Use the future value formula to compute the maturity value of each of the following promissory notes.

1. A four-month, 5.25% note for $620 is issued May 25, 2009.
2. A $350 note is issued on October 30, 2011 at 4.5% for 90 days.
3. A 150-day note for $820 with interest at 5% is dated June 28, 2010.
4. A seven-month, $575 note dated November 1, 2011 earns interest at 7.5%.
5. A five-month, 6.18% note for $835 is issued January 24, 2010.
6. A $230 note is issued on July 18, 2011 at 7.5% for 101 days.
7. A 92-day note for $10 200 with interest at 8.05% is dated August 22, 2010.
8. A ten-month, $5650 note dated September 1, 2011 earns interest at 3.8%.

8.3 PRESENT VALUE OF PROMISSORY NOTES

A. Finding the face value

The face value (or principal) of promissory notes can be obtained by solving the future value formula $S = P(1 + rt)$ for P, that is, by using the present value formula

$$P = \frac{S}{1 + rt} \qquad \text{Formula 7.3B}$$

P = the face value (or present value) of the note at the date of issue;
S = the maturity value;
r = the rate of interest;
t = the interest period.

EXAMPLE 8.3A A five-month note dated January 31, 2011 and bearing interest at 8% p.a. (per annum, i.e., per year) has a maturity value of \$558.11. Find the face value of the note.

SOLUTION

FIGURE 8.2 Graphical Representation of Data

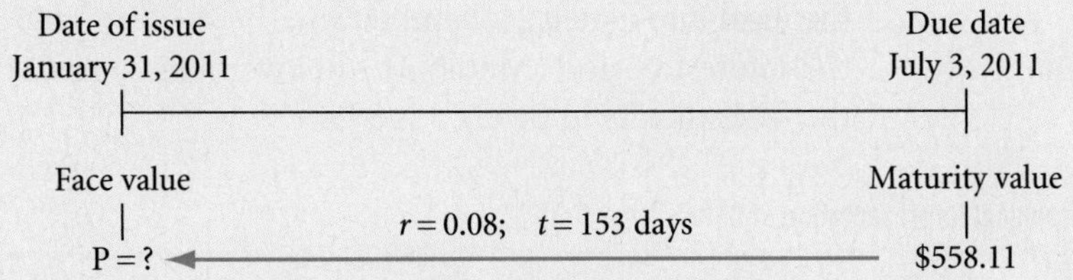

The term of the note ends June 30;
the legal due date is July 3;
the interest period (January 31 to July 3) has 153 days.

$$S = 558.11; \quad r = 0.08; \quad t = \frac{153}{365}$$

$$P = \frac{558.11}{1 + (0.08)\left(\frac{153}{365}\right)} = \frac{558.11}{1 + 0.033534} = \$540.00$$

B. Present value of promissory notes

The present value of a promissory note is its value any time before the due date, allowing for the rate money is worth, the time between the present date and its date of maturity, and its maturity value.

The first step in determining the present value is to ascertain whether the note is an interest-bearing or a non-interest-bearing note.

If the rate of interest is stated, the promissory note is an interest-bearing note. The face value of the note is the principal amount borrowed. To determine the present value of an interest-bearing note, two steps are required:

1. First, the maturity value of the note must be calculated, using the stated interest rate.
2. Next, the present value of the note must be calculated, using the **rate money is worth.**

If there is no rate of interest stated, the promissory note is a non-interest-bearing note. Interest on money borrowed may be implied, but is not stated. The face value of the note is the amount to be repaid at maturity. To determine the present value of a non-interest-bearing note, use the rate at which money is worth. The present value can be computed in one step.

Because the two rates are likely to be *different*, take care in using them.

EXAMPLE 8.3B A seven-month note for \$1500 is issued on March 31, 2010, bearing interest at 9%. Compute the present value of the note on the date of issue if money is worth 7%.

SOLUTION

(i) First, determine the *maturity value* of the note. Use the date of issue as the focal date.
The term of the note ends October 31;
the legal due date is November 3;
the interest period (March 31 to November 3) has 217 days;
the interest rate to be used is 9%.

FIGURE 8.3 Graphical Representation of Data

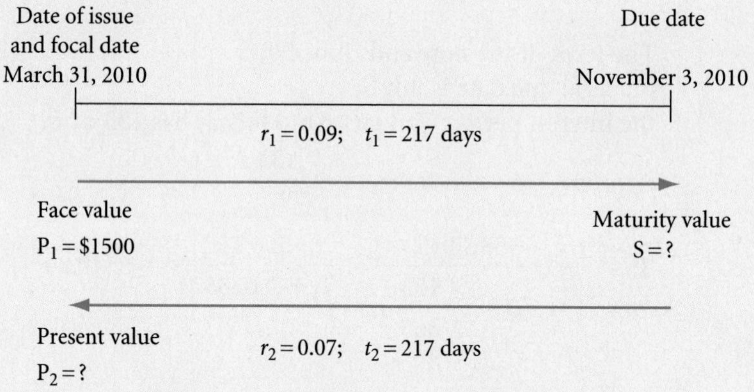

$$P_1 = 1500.00; \quad r_1 = 0.09; \quad t_1 = \frac{217}{365}$$

$$S = 1500\left[1 + (0.09)\left(\frac{217}{365}\right)\right] = 1500(1 + 0.053507) = \$1580.26$$

(ii) Second, use the maturity value found in part (i) to determine the *present value* at the specified date.
The focal date (date of issue) is March 31;
the legal due date is November 3;
the interest period (March 31 to November 3) has 217 days;
the interest rate to be used is 7%.

$$S = 1580.26; \quad r_2 = 0.07; \quad t_2 = \frac{217}{365}$$

$$P_2 = \frac{1580.26}{1 + (0.07)\left(\frac{217}{365}\right)} = \frac{1580.26}{1 + 0.041616} = \$1517.12$$

Note: The present value at the date of issue is more than the face value of the note, because the interest rate on the note (9%) is more than the rate money is worth (7%).

EXAMPLE 8.3C A 180-day note for \$2000 with interest at 7% is dated September 18, 2010. Compute the value of the note on December 1, 2010 if money is worth 5%.

SOLUTION

FIGURE 8.4 Graphical Representation of Data

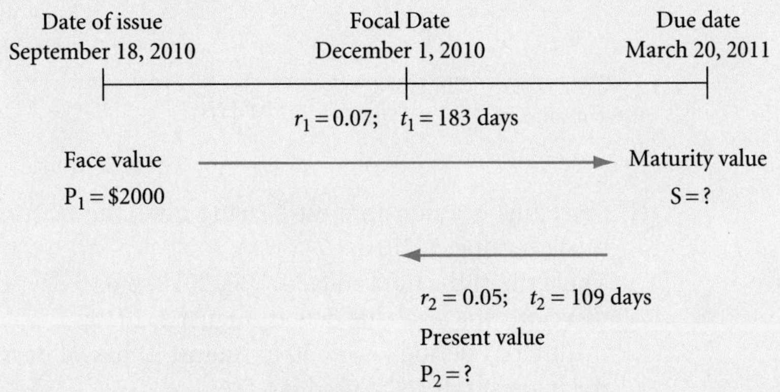

(i) *Compute the maturity value of the note.*
The term of the note is 180 days plus 3 days of grace;
therefore, the term ends March 20, 2011;
the interest rate to be used is 7%.

$$P_1 = 2000; \quad r_1 = 0.07; \quad t_1 = \frac{183}{365}$$

$$S = 2000\left[1 + (0.07)\left(\frac{183}{365}\right)\right] = 2000(1 + 0.035096) = \$2070.19$$

(ii) *Compute the present value.*
The focal date is December 1, 2010;
the interest period (December 1, 2010 to March 20, 2011) has 109 days:
the interest rate to be used is 5%.

$$S = 2070.19; \quad r_2 = 0.05; \quad t_2 = \frac{109}{365}$$

$$P_2 = \frac{2070.19}{\left[1 + (0.05)\left(\frac{109}{365}\right)\right]} = \frac{2070.19}{(1 + 0.014932)} = \$2039.73$$

EXAMPLE 8.3D Compute the present value on the date of issue of a non-interest-bearing \$950, three-month promissory note dated April 30, 2010 if money is worth 6.5%.

SOLUTION

FIGURE 8.5 Graphical Representation of Data

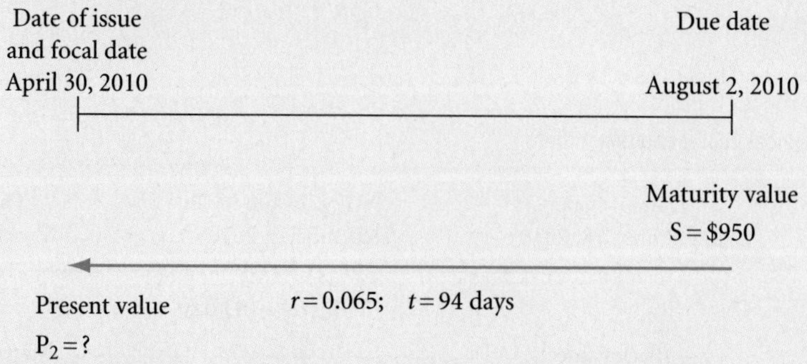

(i) Since this is a non-interest-bearing note, the maturity value of the note is the face value, $950.
The term of the note ends July 30, 2010, plus 3 days of grace;
therefore, the legal due date is August 2, 2010;
the interest period (April 30 to August 2) has 94 days;
the interest rate to be used is 6.5%.

$$S = 950; \quad r = 0.065; \quad t = \frac{94}{365}$$

$$P = \frac{950}{\left[1 + (0.065)\left(\frac{94}{365}\right)\right]} = \frac{950}{(1 + 0.016740)} = \$934.36$$

EXAMPLE 8.3E

Henry purchased a large-screen TV at a local store that had advertised, "No payment until 2009." He signed the contract on March 14, 2008, agreeing to pay $1995 on January 2, 2009. If money is worth 11%, what is the value of the note on the day of signing?

SOLUTION

Between March 14, 2008 and January 2, 2009 are 294 days;
the maturity value of the contract is its face value, $1995.00.

FIGURE 8.6 Graphical Representation of Data

$$S = 1995.00; \quad r = 0.11; \quad t = \frac{294}{365}$$

$$P = \frac{1995.00}{\left[1 + (0.11)\left(\frac{294}{365}\right)\right]} = \frac{1995.00}{(1 + 0.088603)} = \$1832.62$$

C. Present value of treasury bills

Treasury bills (or **T-bills**) are promissory notes issued by the federal government and most provincial governments to meet short-term financing requirements.

Government of Canada T-bills are for terms of 91 days, 182 days, and 364 days. There are no days of grace with T-bills. T-bills are auctioned by the Bank of Canada on behalf of the federal government. They are available in denominations of \$1000, \$5000, \$25 000, \$100 000, and \$1 000 000. T-bills are bought at the auction mainly by chartered banks and investment dealers for resale to other investors, such as smaller financial institutions, corporations, mutual funds, and individuals.

T-bills are promissory notes that do not carry an interest rate. The issuing government guarantees payment of the face value at maturity. The investor purchases T-bills at a discounted price reflecting a rate of return that is determined by current market conditions. The discounted price is determined by computing the present value of the T-bills.

EXAMPLE 8.3F

An investment dealer bought a 91-day Canada T-bill to yield an annual rate of return of 4.21%.

(i) What was the price paid by the investment dealer for a T-bill with a face value of \$100 000?

(ii) The investment dealer resold the \$100 000 T-bill the same day to an investor to yield 4.06%. What was the investment dealer's profit on the transaction?

SOLUTION

(i) *Find the purchase price, P_1.*

The maturity value is the face value of the T-bill, \$100 000.00; the discount period has 91 days (no days of grace are allowed on T-bills).

$$S = 100\,000.00; \quad r_1 = 0.0421; \quad t_1 = \frac{91}{365}$$

$$P_1 = \frac{S}{1 + r_1 t_1} = \frac{100\,000.00}{1 + 0.0421\left(\frac{91}{365}\right)} = \frac{100\,000.00}{1 + 0.010496} = \$98\,961.29$$

The investment dealer paid \$98 961.29 for a \$100 000 T-bill.

(ii) *Find the resale price, P_2.*

$$S = 100\,000.00; \quad r_2 = 0.0406; \quad t_2 = \frac{91}{365}$$

$$P_2 = \frac{100\,000.00}{1 + 0.0406\left(\frac{91}{365}\right)} = \frac{100\,000.00}{1 + 0.010122} = \$98\,997.92$$

Investment dealer's profit = Resale price – Price paid by dealer

$= P_2 - P_1$

$= 98\,997.92 - 98\,961.29 = \$36.63$

The investment dealer's profit on the transaction was \$36.63.

EXAMPLE 8.3G

An investor purchased \$250 000 in 364-day T-bills 315 days before maturity to yield 3.38%. He sold the T-bills 120 days later to yield 3.72%.

(i) How much did the investor pay for the T-bills?
(ii) For how much did the investor sell the T-bills?
(iii) What rate of return did the investor realize on the investment?

SOLUTION

(i) *Find the purchase price of the T-bills, P_1.*

$$S = 250\,000.00; \quad r_1 = 0.0338; \quad t_1 = \frac{315}{365}$$

$$P_1 = \frac{250\,000.00}{1 + 0.0338\left(\frac{315}{365}\right)} = \frac{250\,000.00}{1 + 0.029170} = \$242\,914.23$$

The investor sold the T-bills for \$242 914.23.

(ii) *Find the selling price of the T-bills, P_2.*
The time to maturity at the date of sale is 195 days (315−120).

$$S = 250\,000.00; \quad r_2 = 0.0372; \quad t_2 = \frac{195}{365}$$

$$P_2 = \frac{250\,000.00}{1 + 0.0372\left(\frac{195}{365}\right)} = \frac{250\,000.00}{1 + 0.019874} = \$245\,128.33$$

The investor sold the T-bills for \$245 128.33.

(iii) The investment of \$242 914.23 grew to \$245 128.33 in 120 days.
To compute the rate of return, use the future value formula (Formula 7.3A).

$$P = 242\,914.23; \quad S = 245\,128.33; \quad t = \frac{120}{365}$$

$$S = P(1 + rt)$$

$$245\,128.33 = 242\,914.23\left[1 + r\left(\frac{120}{365}\right)\right]$$

$$\frac{245\,128.33}{242\,914.23} = 1 + \left(\frac{120}{365}\right)r$$

$$1.009115 = 1 + 0.328767r$$

$$0.009115 = 0.328767r$$

$$\frac{0.009115}{0.328767} = r$$

$$r = 0.027724 = 2.77\%$$

The investor realized a rate of return of about 2.77%.

Alternatively:
The gain realized represents the interest.

$$I = 245\,128.33 - 242\,914.23 = \$2214.10$$

Using the formula $r = \frac{I}{Pt}$,

$$r = \frac{2214.10}{242\,914.23\left(\frac{120}{365}\right)} = \frac{2214.10}{79\,862.21} = 0.027724 = 2.77\%.$$

EXERCISE 8.3

A. Compute the face value of each of the following promissory notes.

1. A six-month note dated April 9, 2009, with interest at 4% has a maturity value of $510.19.
2. The maturity value of a 150-day, 5% note dated March 25, 2010 is $1531.44.

B. Find the present value, on the date indicated, of each of the following promissory notes.

1. A non-interest-bearing note for $1500 issued August 10, 2010 for three months if money is worth 7.5%, on the date of issue;
2. A non-interest-bearing note for $750 issued February 2, 2012 for 180 days if money is worth 6.25%, on June 1, 2012;
3. A 60-day, 9% note for $1600 issued October 28 if money is worth 7%, on November 30;
4. A four-month note for $930 dated April 1 with interest at 6.5% if money is worth 8%, on June 20.

C. Answer each of the following questions.

1. What is the price of a 91-day, $100 000 Government of Canada treasury bill that yields 3.83% per annum?
2. An investment dealer bought a 182-day Government of Canada treasury bill at the price required to yield an annual rate of return of 4.02%.
   (a) What was the price paid by the investment dealer if the T-bill has a face value of $1 000 000?
   (b) Later the same day, the investment dealer sold this T-bill to a large corporation to yield 3.88%. What was the investment dealer's profit on this transaction?
3. An investment dealer acquired a $5000, 91-day Province of Alberta treasury bill on its date of issue at a price of $4966.20. What was the annual rate of return?
4. On June 2 you bought for $24 767.75 a $25 000 Province of New Brunswick treasury bill maturing October 7. What was the discount rate at which you bought the treasury bill?
5. An investor purchased a 91-day, $100 000 T-bill on its issue date for $99 326.85. After holding it for 42 days, she sold the T-bill for a yield of 2.72%.
   (a) What was the original yield of the T-bill?
   (b) For what price was the T-bill sold?
   (c) What rate of return (per annum) did the investor realize while holding this T-bill?

6. On April 1, \$25 000 364-day treasury bills were auctioned off to yield 2.92%.
   (a) What is the price of each \$25 000 T-bill on April 1?
   (b) What is the yield rate on August 15 if the market price is \$24 377.64?
   (c) Calculate the market value of each \$25 000 T-bill on October 1 if the rate of return on that date is 4.545%.
   (d) What is the rate of return realized if a \$25 000 T-bill purchased on April 1 is sold on November 20 at a market rate of 4.625%?

8.4 DEMAND LOANS

A. Nature of demand loans

A **demand loan** is a loan for which repayment, in full or in part, may be required at any time, or made at any time. The financial instrument representing a demand loan is called a **demand note.**

When borrowing on a demand note, the borrower receives the full face value of the note. The lender may demand payment of the loan in full or in part at any time. Conversely, the borrower may repay all of the loan or any part at any time without notice and without interest penalty. Interest, based on the unpaid balance, is usually payable monthly. The interest rate on such loans is normally not fixed for the duration of the loan but fluctuates with market conditions. Thus the total interest cost cannot be predicted with certainty. Note that the method of counting days is to count the first day but not the last.

B. Examples

EXAMPLE 8.4A

Rose 'n' Blooms borrowed \$1200 from the Royal Bank on a demand note. It agreed to repay the loan in six equal monthly installments (each payment is made at the end of the month) and also authorized the bank to collect interest monthly from its bank account at 6% p.a. calculated on the unpaid balance. What will the loan cost?

SOLUTION

$$\text{Monthly payment of principal} = \frac{1200.00}{6} = \$200.00$$

$$\text{Monthly rate of interest} = \frac{6\%}{12} = 0.5\% = 0.005$$

Month	Loan Amount Owing During Month		Interest Collected for Month	
1	\$1200.00	Original	\$ 6.00	(1200)(0.005)
2	\$1000.00	1200 – 200	\$ 5.00	(1000)(0.005)
3	\$ 800.00	1000 – 200	\$ 4.00	(800)(0.005)
4	\$ 600.00	800 – 200	\$ 3.00	(600)(0.005)
5	\$ 400.00	600 – 200	\$ 2.00	(400)(0.005)
6	\$ 200.00	400 – 200	\$ 1.00	(200)(0.005)
	Total interest cost	→	\$21.00	

EXAMPLE 8.4B

On August 17, 2010 Sheridan Toy Company borrowed \$30 000 from Peel Credit Union on a demand note to finance its inventory. Interest on the loan, calculated on the daily balance, is charged against the borrower's current account on the 17th of each month while the loan is in force. The company makes a payment of \$5000 on September 24, makes a further payment of \$10 000 on October 20, and pays the balance on December 10. The interest on demand loans on August 17 was 6% p.a. The rate was changed to 7% effective October 1, to 8.5% effective November 1, and to 8% effective December 1. Determine the cost of financing the loan.

SOLUTION

Date	Interest Period	Principal	Rate	Interest Due	
Sept. 17	Aug. 17–Sept. 17	\$30 000.00	6.0%	\$152.88	— $(30\,000)(0.06)\left(\frac{31}{365}\right)$
Oct. 17	Sept. 17–Sept. 24	\$30 000.00	6.0%	34.52	— $(30\,000)(0.06)\left(\frac{7}{365}\right)$
	Sept. 24–Sept. 30*	\$25 000.00	6.0%	28.77	— $(25\,000)(0.06)\left(\frac{7}{365}\right)$
	Oct. 1–Oct. 17	\$25 000.00	7.0%	76.71	— $(25\,000)(0.07)\left(\frac{16}{365}\right)$
				\$292.88	
Nov. 17	Oct. 17–Oct. 20	\$25 000.00	7.0%	\$ 14.38	— $(25\,000)(0.07)\left(\frac{3}{365}\right)$
	Oct. 20–Oct. 31*	\$15 000.00	7.0%	34.52	— $(15\,000)(0.07)\left(\frac{12}{365}\right)$
	Nov. 1–Nov. 17	\$15 000.00	8.5%	55.89	— $(15\,000)(0.85)\left(\frac{16}{365}\right)$
				\$104.79	
Dec. 10	Nov. 17–Nov. 30*	\$15 000.00	8.5%	\$ 48.90	— $(15\,000)(0.85)\left(\frac{14}{365}\right)$
	Dec. 1–Dec. 10	\$15 000.00	8.0%	29.59	— $(15\,000)(0.8)\left(\frac{9}{365}\right)$
				\$ 78.49	
	Total cost of financing →			\$476.16	

*Inclusive

C. Partial payments

Demand loans and similar debts are sometimes paid off by a series of **partial payments**. The commonly used approach to dealing with this type of loan repayment is the **declining balance approach**, requiring that each partial payment be applied first to the accumulated interest. Any remainder is then used to reduce the outstanding principal. Thus, interest is always calculated on the unpaid balance and the new unpaid balance is determined after each partial payment.

The following step-by-step procedure is useful in dealing with such problems:

(a) Compute the interest due to the date of the partial payment.

(b) Compare the interest due computed in part (a) with the partial payment received, and do part (c) if the partial payment is *greater than* the interest due or do part (d) if the partial payment is *less than* the interest due.

(c) *Partial payment greater than interest due:*
   (i) Deduct the interest due from the partial payment.
   (ii) Deduct the remainder in part (i) from the principal balance to obtain the new unpaid balance.

(d) *Partial payment less than interest due:*
   In this case, the partial payment is not large enough to cover the interest due.
   (i) Deduct the partial payment from the interest due to determine the unpaid interest due at the date of the principal payment.
   (ii) Keep a record of this balance and apply any future partial payments to this unpaid interest first.

EXAMPLE 8.4C

On April 20, 2011, Bruce borrowed $4000 at 5% on a note requiring payment of principal and interest on demand. Bruce paid $600 on May 10 and $1200 on July 15. What payment is required on September 30 to pay the note in full?

SOLUTION

April 20			
Original loan balance		$4000.00	
May 10			
Deduct			
First partial payment	$ 600.00		
Less interest			
April 20–May 10	10.96		$(4000)(0.05)\left(\frac{20}{365}\right)$
		589.04	
Unpaid balance		$3410.96	
July 15			
Deduct			
Second partial payment	$1200.00		
Less interest			
May 10–July 15	30.84		$(3410.96)(0.05)\left(\frac{66}{365}\right)$
		1169.16	
Unpaid balance		$2241.80	
September 30			
Add			
Interest			
July 15–Sept. 30		23.65	$(2241.80)(0.05)\left(\frac{77}{365}\right)$
Payment required to pay the note in full		$2265.45	

POINTERS AND PITFALLS

When determining the number of days in any given time period between interest rate changes or between two partial payments, remember to always count the first day and omit the last day. As well, keep in mind that

(a) The date on which there is a change in the interest rate is counted as the first day at the new interest rate.

(b) The date on which a partial payment is made is counted as the first day at the new outstanding principal balance.

EXAMPLE 8.4D

The Provincial Bank lent \$20 000 to the owner of the Purple Pelican on April 1, 2010 for commercial improvements. The loan was secured by a demand note subject to a variable rate of interest. This rate was 7% on April 1. The rate of interest was raised to 9% effective August 1 and reduced to 8% effective November 1. Partial payments, applied to the loan by the declining balance method, were made as follows: June 10, \$1000; September 20, \$400; November 15, \$1200. How much interest is due to the Provincial Bank on December 31?

SOLUTION

April 1				
Original loan balance			\$20 000.00	
June 10				
Deduct				
First partial payment		\$1000.00		
Less interest				
April 1–June 10		268.49		$(20\,000)(0.07)\left(\frac{70}{365}\right)$
			731.51	
Unpaid loan balance			\$19 268.49	
September 20				
Deduct				
Second partial payment		\$ 400.00		
Less interest				
June 10–Sept. 20:				
June 10–July 31 (inclusive)	\$192.16			$(19\,268.49)(0.07)\left(\frac{52}{365}\right)$
Aug. 1–Sept. 20	237.56	429.72		$(19\,268.49)(0.09)\left(\frac{50}{365}\right)$
Unpaid interest to Sept. 20		\$ 29.72		
Unpaid loan balance			\$19 268.49	
November 15				
Deduct				
Third partial payment		\$1200.00		

Less interest				
Unpaid interest to				
Sept. 20 →	\$ 29.72			**(see above)**
Sept. 20–Oct. 31 → (inclusive)	199.55			$(19\,268.49)(0.09)\left(\frac{42}{365}\right)$
Nov. 1–Nov. 15 →	59.13			$(19\,268.49)(0.08)\left(\frac{42}{365}\right)$
		288.40		
			911.60	
Unpaid loan balance →			\$18 356.89	
December 31				
Interest due				
Nov. 15–Dec. 31 →			\$ 185.08	$-(18\,356.89)(0.08)\left(\frac{42}{365}\right)$

EXERCISE 8.4

A. Determine the total interest cost for each of the following loans.

1. On June 15, 2009, Jean-Luc borrowed \$2500 from his bank secured by a demand note. He agreed to repay the loan in five equal monthly installments and authorized the bank to collect the interest monthly from his bank account at 6.0% per annum calculated on the unpaid balance.

2. James TV & Stereo borrowed \$1800 from the Teachers' Credit Union. The loan was to be repaid in six equal monthly payments, plus interest of 7.5% per annum calculated on the unpaid balance.

3. Jamie borrowed \$900 from the Essex District Credit Union. The loan agreement provided for repayment of the loan in four equal monthly payments plus interest at 12% per annum calculated on the unpaid balance.

4. Erindale Automotive borrowed \$8000 from the Bank of Montreal on a demand note on May 10. Interest on the loan, calculated on the daily balance, is charged to Erindale's current account on the 10th of each month. Erindale made a payment of \$2000 on July 20, a payment of \$3000 on October 1, and repaid the balance on December 1. The rate of interest on the loan on May 10 was 8% per annum. The rate was changed to 9.5% on August 1 and to 8.5% on October 1.

5. The Tomac Swim Club arranged short-term financing of \$12 500 on July 20 with the Bank of Commerce and secured the loan with a demand note. The club repaid the loan by payments of \$6000 on September 15, \$3000 on November 10, and the balance on December 30. Interest, calculated on the daily balance and charged to the club's current account on the last day of each month, was at 9.5% per annum on July 20. The rate was changed to 8.5% effective September 1 and to 9% effective December 1.

B. Answer each of the following.

1. On March 10, Fat Tires Ltd. borrowed $10 000 with an interest rate of 5.5%. The loan was repaid in full on November 15, with payments of $2500 on June 30 and $4000 on September 4. What was the final payment?
2. Automotive Excellence Inc. borrowed $20 000 on August 12 with an interest rate of 6.75% per annum. On November 1 $7500 was repaid, and on December 15 $9000 was repaid. Automotive Excellence paid the balance of the loan on February 20. What was the final payment?
3. A loan of $6000 made at 11% per annum on March 10 is repaid in full on November 15. Payments were made of $2000 on June 30 and $2500 on September 5. What was the final payment?
4. D. Slipp borrowed $15 000 on August 12. She paid $6000 on November 1, $5000 on December 15, and the balance on February 20. The rate of interest on the loan was 10.5%. How much did she pay on February 20?
5. The Continental Bank made a loan of $20 000 on March 25 to Dr. Hirsch to purchase equipment for her office. The loan was secured by a demand loan subject to a variable rate of interest that was 7% on March 25. The rate of interest was raised to 8.5% effective July 1 and to 9.5% effective September 1. Dr. Hirsch made partial payments on the loan as follows: $600 on May 15; $800 on June 30; and $400 on October 10. The terms of the note require payment of any accrued interest on October 31. How much must Dr. Hirsch pay on October 31?
6. Dirk Ward borrowed $12 000 for investment purposes on May 10 on a demand note providing for a variable rate of interest and payment of any accrued interest on December 31. He paid $300 on June 25, $150 on September 20, and $200 on November 5. How much is the accrued interest on December 31 if the rate of interest was 7.5% on May 10, 6% effective August 1, and 5% effective November 1?

8.5 LINES OF CREDIT AND CREDIT CARD LOANS

A **line of credit** is a pre-approved loan agreement between a financial institution and a borrower. The borrower may withdraw money, up to an agreed maximum, at any time. Interest is charged only on the amount withdrawn from the line of credit. A minimum repayment may be required each month. The borrower may repay any additional amount at any time without further penalty. The rate of interest charged for money borrowed on a line of credit is often lower than the rate of interest charged on most credit cards. The interest rate can change over time.

A **credit card** is a plastic card entitling the bearer to a revolving line of credit with a pre-established credit limit. Interest rates are set by the credit card issuers, vary considerably, and can be changed at any time. Generally, interest rates charged on credit cards are higher than rates charged on loans made by financial institutions. Some credit card issuers require an annual fee to be paid by the user. When the bearer withdraws cash by presenting the credit card, a cash advance fee is usually charged. Depending on the issuer of the credit card, the cash advance fee may be deducted directly from the cash advance at the time the money is received or it may be posted to the account on the day the cash is received. Interest on the cash advance is calculated starting from the day the money is withdrawn. The bearer of the credit card, with an authorizing signature, may make purchases instead of using cash to pay.

An **unsecured line of credit** is a line of credit with no assets promised to the lender to cover non-payment of the loan. Since no security is offered to the lender, the limit of an unsecured line of credit depends on the individual's credit rating and past relationship with the lender.

A **secured line of credit** is a line of credit with assets promised to the lender to cover non-payment of the loan. For example, homeowners might pledge the value of their home, that is, their home equity, to secure a line of credit. In general, the limit of a secured line of credit is higher than the limit of an unsecured one. Furthermore, the interest rate of a secured line of credit is lower than the interest rate of an unsecured one.

Lines of credit secured by home equity are becoming quite popular and are used by some borrowers as an alternative to mortgages. Home equity lines of credit (HELOC) provide access to larger credit limits.

EXAMPLE 8.5A

Suppose your business has secured a line of credit and receives the following statement of account for the month of February.

Date	Transaction Description	Deposit	Withdrawal	Balance
Feb. 01	Balance			–600.00
04	Cheque 262		500.00	–1100.00
10	Deposit	2050.00		950.00
16	Cheque 263		240.00	710.00
20	Cheque 264		1000.00	–290.00
22	Cheque 265		80.00	–370.00
27	Cheque 266		150.00	–520.00
28	Interest earned	?		
	Line of credit interest		?	
	Overdraft interest		?	
	Service charge		?	

Note: "–" indicates a negative balance.

The limit on your line of credit is \$1000. You receive daily interest of 1.5% p.a. on positive balances and pay daily interest of 7% p.a. on *negative (line of credit) balances.* Overdraft interest is 18% p.a. on the daily amount exceeding your line of credit limit. There is a service charge of \$5 for each transaction causing an overdraft or adding to an overdraft.

Determine

(i) the amount of interest earned;
(ii) the amount of interest charged on the line of credit;
(iii) the amount of interest charged on overdrafts;

(iv) the amount of the service charge;
(v) the account balance on February 28.

SOLUTION

(i) Interest earned (on positive balances):
February 10 to February 15 inclusive: 6 days at 1.5% on \$950.00

$$I = 950.00(0.015)\left(\frac{6}{365}\right) = \$0.23$$

February 16 to February 19 inclusive: 4 days at 1.5% on \$710.00

$$I = 710.00(0.015)\left(\frac{4}{365}\right) = \$0.12$$

Total interest earned = 0.23 + 0.12 = \$0.35

(ii) Line of credit interest charged (on negative balances up to \$1000.00):
February 1 to February 3 inclusive: 3 days at 7% on \$600.00

$$I = 600.00(0.07)\left(\frac{3}{365}\right) = \$0.35$$

February 4 to February 9 inclusive: 6 days at 7% on \$1000.00

$$I = 1100.00(0.07)\left(\frac{6}{365}\right) = \$1.27$$

February 20 to February 21 inclusive: 2 days at 7% on \$290.00

$$I = 290.00(0.07)\left(\frac{2}{365}\right) = \$0.11$$

February 22 to February 26 inclusive: 5 days at 7% on \$370.00

$$I = 370.00(0.07)\left(\frac{5}{365}\right) = \$0.35$$

February 27 to February 28 inclusive: 2 days at 7% on \$520.00

$$I = 520.00(0.07)\left(\frac{2}{365}\right) = \$0.20$$

Total line of credit interest charged
= 0.35 + 1.27 + 0.11 + 0.35 + 0.20 = \$2.28

(iii) Since your line of credit limit is \$1000.00, overdraft interest is charged on the amount in excess of a negative balance of \$1000.00. You were in overdraft from February 4 to February 9 inclusive in the amount of \$100.00.

$$\text{Overdraft interest} = 100.00\ (0.18)\left(\frac{6}{365}\right) = \$0.30$$

(iv) You had one transaction causing an overdraft or adding to an overdraft.
Service charge = 1(5.00) = \$5.00

(v) The account balance on February 28
= −520.00 + 0.35 − 2.28 − 0.30 − 5.00 = −\$527.23

EXAMPLE 8.5B

You have applied for and received a credit card. The interest rate charged is 18.9% per annum. You note the following transactions for the month of September.

September 6	Purchased textbooks and supplies for a total of $250.
September 10	Withdrew $100 as a cash advance through your credit card.
September 30	Received the credit card statement, showing a minimum balance owing of $25. A payment date of October 10 is stated on the statement.

(i) Compute the amount of interest charged on the cash advance from September 10 until September 30.
(ii) You decide to pay the amount owing, in full, on October 1. How much must you pay?
(iii) Instead of paying the full amount, you decide to pay the minimum, $25, on October 1. What would be the balance owing after the payment?
(iv) If there are no further transactions during October, how much is owing at the end of October?

SOLUTION

(i) Interest charged (on cash advance):
September 10 to September 30 inclusive: $100 at 18.9% for 21 days.

$$I = 100.00(0.189)\left(\frac{21}{365}\right) = \$1.09$$

(ii) $250.00 + 100.00 + 1.09 = $351.09

(iii) $351.09 − 25.00 = $326.09

(iv)
$$I = 326.09(0.189)\left(\frac{31}{365}\right) = \$5.23$$

$326.09 + 5.23 = $331.32
At the end of October $331.32 is owing.

EXERCISE 8.5

A. Determine the missing information for each of the following lines of credit.

1. Suppose you have a line of credit and receive the following statement for the month of March.

Date	Transaction Description	Deposit	Withdrawal	Balance
Feb. 28	Balance			−527.71
Mar. 02	Cheque 264		600.00	−1127.71
05	Cheque 265		300.00	−1427.71
10	Deposit	2000.00		572.29
16	Cheque 266		265.00	307.29

B. Construction of loan repayment schedules illustrated

EXAMPLE 8.6A

Great Lakes Marina borrowed $1600 from Sheridan Credit Union at 9% p.a. and agreed to repay the loan in monthly installments of $300 each, such payments to cover interest due and repayment of principal. Use the design shown in Figure 8.8 to construct a complete repayment schedule including the totalling of columns ③, ④, and ⑤ ("Amount Paid," "Interest Paid," and "Principal Repaid").

SOLUTION

See Figure 8.9 and the explanatory notes that follow.

FIGURE 8.9 **Loan Repayment Schedule for Example 8.6A**

① Payment Number	② Balance Before Payment	③ Amount Paid (1)	④ Interest Paid (2)	⑤ Principal Repaid (3)	⑥ Payment After Balance (4)
0					1600.00 (5)
1	1600.00	300.00	12.00 (6)	288.00 (7)	1312.00 (8)
2	1312.00	300.00	9.84 (9)	290.16 (10)	1021.84 (11)
3	1021.84	300.00	7.66	292.34	729.50
4	729.50	300.00	5.47	294.53	434.97
5	434.97	300.00	3.26	296.74	138.23 (12)
6	138.23	139.27 (15)	1.04 (14)	138.23 (13)	0.00
Totals (16)		1639.27 (18)	39.27 (19)	1600.00 (17)	

Notes:

(1) The Amount Paid shown in column ③ is the agreed-upon monthly payment of $300.

(2) The Interest Paid shown in column ④ is at 9% per annum. This figure is converted into a periodic (monthly) rate of $\frac{9\%}{12}$ (0.75% per month) to facilitate the computation of the monthly amount of interest paid. (See notes (6) and (9).)

(3) The amount of Principal Repaid each month shown in column ⑤ is found by subtracting the Interest Paid for the month (column ④) from the Amount Paid for the month (column ③). (See notes (7) and (10).)

(4) The Balance After Payment for a month shown in column ⑥ is found by subtracting the Principal Repaid for the month (column ⑤) from the Balance Before Payment for the month (column ②) *or* from the previous Balance After Payment figure (column ⑥). (See notes (8) and (11).)

(5) The original loan balance of $1600 is introduced as the starting amount for the schedule and is the only amount shown in Line 0.

(6) Interest paid in Payment Number 1
$= 0.75\%$ of $1600.00 = (0.0075)(1600.00) = \$12.00$

(7) Principal repaid by Payment Number 1
$= 300.00 - 12.00 = \$288.00$

(8) Balance after Payment Number 1
= 1600.00 − 288.00 = $1312.00

(9) Interest paid in Payment Number 2
= 0.75% of 1312.00 = (0.0075)(1312.00) = $9.84

(10) Principal repaid by Payment Number 2
= 300.00 − 9.84 = $290.16

(11) Balance after Payment Number 2
= 1312.00 − 290.16 = $1021.84

(12) The Balance after Payment Number 5 of $138.23 is smaller than the regular monthly payment of $300. The next payment need only be sufficient to pay the outstanding balance of $138.23 plus the interest due. (See notes (13), (14), and (15).)

(13) Principal repaid in Payment Number 6 must be $138.23 to pay off the outstanding loan balance.

(14) Interest paid in Payment Number 6 is the interest due on $138.23
= 0.75% of 138.23 = (0.0075)(138.23) = $1.04.

(15) Amount paid in Payment Number 6
= 138.23 + 1.04 = $139.27.

(16) The Totals of columns ③, ④, and ⑤ serve as a check of the arithmetic accuracy of the payment schedule. (See notes (17), (18), and (19).)

(17) Principal Repaid, the total of column 5, must equal the original loan balance of $1600.

(18) Amount Paid, the total of column ③, must equal the total of all the payments made (five payments of $300 each plus the final payment of $139.27).

(19) Interest paid, the total of column ④, must be the difference between the totals of columns ④ and ⑤ = 1639.27 − 1600.00 = $39.27.

C. Computer application—loan repayment schedule

EXCEL NOTES

This exercise assumes a basic understanding of spreadsheet applications; however, an individual who has no previous experience with spreadsheets can complete this task.

Microsoft Excel and other spreadsheet programs allow the user to easily create a flexible loan repayment schedule. The finished repayment schedule will reflect any changes made to the loan amount, the interest rate, or the schedule of payments. (The following example was created in Excel, but most programs work similarly.)

The following Excel application is based on Example 8.6A, which uses six months to repay the loan. An additional row of formulas similar to row 3 would be added for each additional month required to repay the loan.

STEP 1 Enter the labels shown in Figure 8.10 in row 1 and in column A.

STEP 2 Enter the numbers shown in row 2.

STEP 3 Enter only the formulas shown in row 3 and row 9. Make sure that the entry includes the dollar sign ($) as shown in the figure.

FIGURE 8.10

Workbook 1

	A	B	C	D	E	F	G
1	Payment	Balance before payment	Amount paid	Interest paid	Principal repaid	Balance	
2	0					1600.00	300.00
3	1	= F2	= G2	= G4*B3	= C3–D3	= B3–E3	
4	2	= F3	= G2	= G4*B4	= C4–D4	= B4–E4	= 0.09/12
5	3	= F4	= G2	= G4*B5	= C5–D5	= B5–E5	
6	4	= F5	= G2	= G4*B6	= C6–D6	= B6–E6	
7	5	= F6	= G2	= G4*B7	= C7–D7	= B7–E7	
8	6	= F7	= D8+E8	= G4*B8	= B8	= B8–E8	
9	Totals		= SUM(C3:C8)	= SUM(D3:D8)	= SUM(E3:E8)		

STEP 4 The formulas that are entered in row 3 can be copied through the remaining rows.
(a) Select and copy the formulas in row 3.
(b) Select cells C4 to C8, and select Paste.
(c) The formulas are now active in all the cells.

STEP 5 To ensure readability of the spreadsheet, format the numbers to display as two decimal places, and widen the columns to display the full labels.

This spreadsheet can now be used to reflect changes in aspects of the loan and display the effects quickly. Put a new principal amount in cell F2 and a new interest rate in cell G4. The interest rate must be divided by 12 to convert the annual interest rate to a monthly rate. For example, new annual interest rate of 5% would be entered as $\frac{0.05}{12}$.

EXCEL NOTES

A copy of this spreadsheet, called Template 2, appears on the Spreadsheet Template Disk.

EXERCISE 8.6

A. Use the design shown in Figure 8.8 to construct a complete repayment schedule including the totalling of the Amount Paid, Interest Paid, and Principal Repaid columns for each of the following loans.

1. Carla borrowed $1200 from the Royal Bank at 8.5% per annum calculated on the monthly unpaid balance. She agreed to repay the loan in blended payments of $180 per month.
2. Blended payments on a $3400 loan were $800 per month. Interest was charged at 7.75% per annum calculated on the monthly unpaid balance.
3. On March 15, Julio borrowed $900 from Sheridan Credit Union at 7.5% per annum calculated on the daily balance. He gave the Credit Union six cheques

for $135 dated the 15th of each of the next six months starting April 15 and a cheque dated October 15 for the remaining balance to cover payment of interest and repayment of principal.

4. On February 8, Manuel borrowed $700 from his uncle at 6% per annum calculated on the daily balance. He gave his uncle seven cheques for $100 dated the 8th of each of the next seven months starting March 8 and a cheque dated September 8 for the remaining balance to cover payment of interest and repayment of principal.

BUSINESS MATH NEWS BOX

It Keeps Getting Easier to Fall into the Debt Trap

Canadians' love affair with debt continues unabated. The ratio of consumer credit and mortgage debt to personal disposable income rose to a new high of 100.1% in the second quarter of this year, Statistics Canada reported last week. This means we owe more than $1 in debt for every dollar of income we earn. As long as interest rates stay low, most people seem to be handling the higher debt loads in relative comfort. However, there are some casualties. The number of consumer bankruptcies in Canada rose 8% to 49 730 in the first seven months of 2003. Canadians' personal debt loads—which now average $22 697 for every man, woman, and child in the country—will keep escalating. Stanley Kershman is a bankruptcy lawyer in Ottawa who's spent 25 years helping people and companies get back on their feet. He just finished acting for the bankrupt Ottawa Senators hockey team. "Marketers will find more innovative ways to lend people money," he says. "Furniture stores such as Leon's and The Brick used to advertise buying on store credit and paying no interest for six months. "The interest-free period grew to 12 months and now it's 16 months. They're spreading out the payments longer and longer to make it more attractive for people to buy." In a similar trend, Visa and MasterCard issuers once required payments of 3% of the balance owing to keep an account in good standing. Now the minimum payment is slipping to 2%.

Source: Ellen Roseman, "It Keeps Getting Easier to Fall into the Debt Trap," *Toronto Star*, October 1, 2003, p. C.03. Reprinted with Permission of Torstar Syndication Services.

QUESTIONS

1. Estimate the value of Canadian consumer credit card debt in Canada, given that the Canadian population is approximately 32 million.
2. Given the information above, calculate the number of bankruptcies at the beginning of 2003.
3. A credit card has a $3000 balance with an interest rate of 18.9% per annum compounded monthly. If the credit card holder pays $100 per month toward the debt, calculate how long it will take to pay off this debt.
4. Calculate the interest paid on a $3000 credit card balance given monthly payments made over seven years. Assume interest is at 18.9% per annum compounded monthly.

Review Exercise

1. A four-month promissory note for $1600 dated June 30 bears interest at 6.5%.
   (a) What is the due date of the note?
   (b) What is the amount of interest payable at the due date?
   (c) What is the maturity value of the note?

2. Determine the maturity value of a 120-day note for $1250 dated May 23 and bearing interest at 5.75%.

3. Compute the face value of a 120-day note dated September 10 bearing interest at 6.75% whose maturity value is $1534.12.

4. The maturity value of a seven-month promissory note issued July 31, 2009 is $3275. What is the present value of the note on the date of issue if interest is 7.75%?

5. Compute the maturity value of a 150-day, 6% promissory note with a face value of $5000 dated August 5.

6. What is the face value of a three-month promissory note dated November 30, 2011, with interest at 4.5 percent if its maturity value is $950.89?

7. A 90-day, $800 promissory note was issued July 31 with interest at 8%. What is the value of the note on October 20?

8. On June 1, 2010, a four-month promissory note for $1850 with interest at 5% was issued. Compute the proceeds of the note on August 28, 2010, if money is worth 6.5%.

9. Determine the value of a $1300 non-interest-bearing note four months before its maturity date of July 13, 2010, if money is worth 7%.

10. Compute the proceeds of a five-month, $7000 promissory note dated September 6, 2009, with interest at 5.5% if the note is paid on November 28, 2009, when money is worth 6.5%.

11. An investment dealer paid $24 256.25 to acquire a $25 000, 182-day Government of Canada treasury bill at the weekly auction. What was the rate of return on this T-bill?

12. Government of Alberta 364-day T-bills with a face value of $1 000 000 were purchased on April 7 for $971 578. The T-bills were sold on May 16 for $983 500.
    (a) What was the market yield rate on April 7?
    (b) What was the yield rate on May 16?
    (c) What was the rate of return realized?

13. Mel's Photography borrowed $15 000 on March 10 on a demand note. The loan was repaid by payments of $4000 on June 20, $3000 on September 1, and the balance on November 15. Interest, calculated on the daily balance and charged to Mel's Photography current account on the last day of each month, was at 5.5% on March 10 but was changed to 6.25% effective June 1 and to 6% effective October 1. How much did the loan cost?

14. Quick Print Press borrowed $20 000 from the Provincial Bank on May 25 at 7.5% and secured the loan by signing a promissory note subject to a variable rate of interest. Quick Print made partial payments of $5000 on July 10 and $8000 on September 15. The rate of interest was increased to 8% effective August 1 and to 8.5% effective October 1. What payment must Quick Print make on October 31 if, under the terms of the loan agreement, any interest accrued as of October 31 is to be paid on October 31?

15. Muriel has a line of credit with a limit of $10 000. She owed $8195 on July 1. Principal withdrawals for the period July 1 to November 30 were $3000 on August 20 and $600 on October 25. The line of credit agreement requires regular payments of $300 on the 15th day of each month. Muriel has made all required payments. Interest (including overdraft interest) is charged to the account on the last day of each month. The interest rate was 8% on July 1, but was changed to 7.5% effective

September 15. Overdraft interest is 16% for any balance in excess of $10 000.

(a) Calculate the interest charges on July 31, August 31, September 30, October 31, and November 30.

(b) Calculate the account balance on November 30.

16. You borrowed $3000 at 9% per annum calculated on the unpaid monthly balance and agreed to repay the principal together with interest in monthly payments of $500 each. Construct a complete repayment schedule.

Self-Test

1. For the following promissory note, determine the amount of interest due at maturity.

> $565.00 TORONTO, ONTARIO JANUARY 10, 2008
>
> FIVE MONTHS after date we promise to pay to the order of
>
> WILSON LUMBER COMPANY
>
> EXACTLY FIVE-HUNDRED-SIXTY-FIVE and 00/100 --------------- Dollars
>
> at WILSON LUMBER COMPANY for value received
>
> with interest at 8.25% per annum.
>
> Due ______________ (seal) ______________
>
> (seal) ______________

2. Find the maturity value of a $1140, 7.75%, 120-day note dated February 19, 2010.

3. Determine the face value of a four-month promissory note dated May 20, 2011, with interest at 7.5% p.a. if the maturity value of the note is $1190.03.

4. Find the present value of a non-interest-bearing seven-month promissory note for $1800 dated August 7, 2011, on December 20, 2011, if money is then worth 6%.

5. A 180-day note dated September 14, 2010 is made at 5.25% for $1665. What is the present value of the note on October 18, 2010, if money is worth 6.5%?

6. What is the price of a 91-day, $25 000 Government of Canada treasury bill that yields 3.28% per annum?

7. An investor purchased a 182-day, $100 000 T-bill on its issue date. It yielded 3.85%. The investor held the T-bill for 67 days, then sold it for $98 853.84.

(a) What was the original price of the T-bill?

(b) When the T-bill was sold, what was its yield?

8. The owner of Jane's Boutique borrowed $6000 from Halton Community Credit Union on June 5, 2010. The loan was secured by a demand note with

interest calculated on the daily balance and charged to the store's account on the 5th day of each month. The loan was repaid by payments of $1500 on July 15, $2000 on October 10, and $2500 on December 30. The rate of interest charged by the credit union was 8.5% on June 5. The rate was changed to 9.5% effective July 1 and to 10% effective October 1. Determine the total interest cost on the loan.

9. Herb's Restaurant borrowed $24 000 on March 1, 2009 on a demand note providing for a variable rate of interest. While repayment of principal is open, any accrued interest is to be paid on November 30. Payments on the loan were made as follows: $600 on April 15, $400 on July 20, and $400 on October 10. The rate of interest was 7% on March 1 but was changed to 8.5% effective August 1 and to 7.5% effective November 1. Using the declining balance method to record the partial payments, determine the accrued interest on November 30.

10. Jing has a line of credit from her local bank with a limit of $10 000. On March 1, 2010, she owed $7265. From March 1 to June 30, she withdrew principal amounts of $3000 on April 10 and $500 on June 20. According to the line of credit agreement, Jing must make a regular payment of $200 on the 15th of each month. She has made these payments. Interest (including overdraft interest) is charged to the account on the last day of each month. On March 1, the interest rate was 9%, but it was changed to 8.5% effective May 15. Overdraft interest is 18% for any balance in excess of $10 000.

(a) Calculate the interest charges on March 31, April 30, May 31, and June 30.

(b) What is the account balance on June 30?

11. Use the design shown in Figure 8.8 to construct a complete repayment schedule, including the totalling of the "Amount Paid," "Interest Paid," and "Principal Repaid" columns, for a loan of $4000 repaid in monthly installments of $750 each including interest of 6.5% per annum calculated on the unpaid balance.

Challenge Problems

1. Mike Kornas signed a 12-month, 11% p.a. simple interest promissory note for $12 000 with MacDonald's Furniture. After 100 days, MacDonald's Furniture sold the note to the Royal Bank at a rate of 13% p.a. Royal Bank resold the note to Friendly Finance Company 25 days later at a rate of 9% p.a. Find the gain or loss on this note for each company and bank involved.

2. A father wanted to show his son what it might be like to borrow money from a financial institution. When his son asked if he could borrow $120, the father lent him the money and set up the following arrangements. He charged his son $6 for the loan of $120. The son therefore received $114 and agreed to pay his father 12 installments of $10 a month, beginning one month from today, until the loan was repaid. Find the approximate rate of simple interest the father charged on this loan.

Case Study 8.1 The Business of Borrowing

» Bits and Bytes Computer Store agrees to purchase some new computer monitors costing $3500 plus 6% GST. Farid Kamlani, the store's owner, was informed that if he paid cash on receipt of the goods he could take a cash discount of 4.5% of the invoice price before GST. GST would then be added to the new invoice price. Farid would like to take advantage of this discount, but his store is short of cash right now. A number of customers are expected to pay their invoices in the next 30 to 60 days.

Farid went to his bank manager to negotiate a short-term loan to pay for the monitors when they arrive and take advantage of the cash discount. The bank manager suggested a 60-day promissory note bearing interest at 6.5%. Farid agreed to the note and suggested that the three days of grace should be added to provide him more repayment flexibility.

QUESTIONS

1. What is the maturity value of the 60-day promissory note using three days of grace for the goods including GST?
2. Suppose Farid decides he does not need the three days of grace. What effect would this have on the maturity value of the note?
3. Farid later discussed his situation with a friend, who suggested that Farid could have negotiated a short-term loan for 60 days instead of using a promissory note. What is the highest annual simple interest rate at which Farid could have borrowed the money and still saved by taking the cash discount?

Case Study 8.2 Debt Consolidation

» Shannon and Duncan Fisher were concerned about their level of debt. They had borrowed from their bank to purchase their house, car, and computer. For these three loans, the Fishers must make regular monthly payments. The couple also owe $6000 to MasterCard and $2500 to Visa. Shannon and Duncan decided to meet with a consumer credit counsellor to gain control of their debts.

The counsellor explained to them the details of their loans and credit card debts. Shannon and Duncan were shocked to discover that whereas their computer and car loans had an interest rate of 10.5% p.a., their credit cards had an interest rate of 19.5% p.a. The counsellor pointed out that the interest rate on their three loans was reasonable. However, because the interest rate on the credit cards was so high, she advised Shannon and Duncan to borrow money at a lower interest rate and pay off the credit card debts.

The credit counsellor suggested that they should consider obtaining a line of credit. She explained that the rate of interest on the line of credit would likely be a few percentage points higher than the prime rate, but much lower than the rate of interest charged on credit card balances. Shannon and Duncan would have to make a minimum payment every month, similar to that of a credit card. The payment would then be applied to pay all the interest and a portion of the principal balance owing on the line of credit. The line of credit would allow them to make monthly payments higher than the minimum so that they could pay as much toward the principal balance as they could afford. Due to the much lower interest rate on a line of credit as compared to a typical credit card, the money they would save on interest each month could be paid toward the principal. A line of credit appealed to Shannon and Duncan, as it helped them feel more in control of their finances and gave them the resolve to pay off their credit card debts.

Shannon and Duncan then met with their bank manager and were approved for a \$15 000 line of credit. Immediately, they paid off the \$6000 owed to MasterCard and the \$2500 owed to Visa with money from the line of credit. They then decided to pay off the line of credit over the next ten months by making monthly payments equal to one-tenth of the original line of credit balance plus the simple interest owed on the remaining line of credit balance. The simple interest rate on the line of credit is expected to be 6.25% over the next ten months. Shannon and Duncan agreed to cut up their credit cards and not charge any more purchases until they had paid off their line of credit.

QUESTIONS

1. Suppose Shannon and Duncan pay off their credit cards with their line of credit on April 20. They will make their monthly payments on the 20th of each month, beginning in May. Create a schedule showing their monthly payments for the next ten months. How much interest will they pay using this repayment plan?

2. Suppose Shannon and Duncan had not gotten a line of credit but kept their credit cards. They decided not to make any more credit card purchases. Instead, they made monthly payments equal to one-tenth of the original credit card balance plus the simple interest owed on the remaining credit card balance. They will make their monthly payments on the 20th of each month, beginning in May. Create a schedule showing their monthly payments for the next ten months. How much interest would they have paid using this repayment plan?

3. How much money did Shannon and Duncan save on interest by getting the line of credit?

4. What are the requirements for obtaining a line of credit from your financial institution?

SUMMARY OF FORMULAS

Formula 7.1A

$I = Prt$ — **Finding the amount of interest on promissory notes**

Formula 7.3A

$S = P(1 + rt)$ — **Finding the maturity value of promissory notes directly**

Formula 7.3B

$$P = \frac{S}{1 + rt}$$

Finding the present value of promissory notes or treasury bills given the maturity value

GLOSSARY

Amortization schedule see **Loan repayment schedule**

Amount of interest interest, in dollars and cents, payable to the payee on the legal due date *(p. 295)*

Blended payment the usual method of repaying a personal consumer loan by a fixed periodic (monthly) payment that covers payment of interest and repayment of principal *(p. 316)*

Credit card a card entitling the bearer to a revolving line of credit with a pre-approved credit limit *(p. 311)*

Date of issue the date on which a promissory note is made *(p. 295)*

Date of maturity *see* **Legal due date**

Declining balance approach the commonly used approach to applying partial payments to demand loans whereby each partial payment is first applied to pay the interest due and then applied to the outstanding principal *(p. 307)*

Demand loan a loan for which repayment in full or in part may be required at any time or made at any time *(p. 306)*

Demand note the financial instrument representing a demand loan *(p. 306)*

Due date *see* **Legal due date**

Face value the sum of money specified on the promissory note *(p. 294)*

Interest-bearing promissory note a note subject to the rate of interest stated on the note *(p. 294)*

Interest period the time, in days, from the date of issue to the legal due date for promissory notes *(p. 295)*

Issue date *see* **Date of issue**

Legal due date the date on which the promissory note is to be paid; it includes three days of grace unless "No Grace Days" is written on the promissory note *(p. 295)*

Line of credit a pre-approved loan amount issued by a financial institution for use by an individual or business at any time for any purpose; interest is charged only for the time money is borrowed on the line of credit; a minimum monthly payment is required (similar to a credit card); the interest rate can change over time *(p. 311)*

Loan repayment schedule a detailed statement of installment payments, interest cost, repayment of principal, and outstanding balance of principal for an installment plan *(p. 316)*

Maker the party making the promise to pay by signing the promissory note *(p. 294)*

Maturity value the amount (face value plus interest) that must be paid on the legal due date to honour the note *(p. 295)*

Partial payments a series of payments on a debt *(p. 307)*

Payee the party to whom the promise to pay is made *(p. 294)*

Promissory note a written promise to pay a specified sum of money after a specified period of time or on demand, with or without interest as specified *(p. 294)*

Rate money is worth the prevailing rate of interest *(p. 299)*

Rate of interest the simple annual rate of interest based on the face value *(p. 294)*

Secured line of credit a line of credit with assets pledged as security *(p. 312)*

T-bills *see* **Treasury bills**

Term (of a promissory note) the time period for which the note was written (in days or months) *(p. 295)*

Three days of grace the number of days added to the term of a note in Canada to determine its legal due date *(p. 295)*

Treasury bills promissory notes issued at a discount from their face values by the federal government and most provincial governments to meet short-term financing requirements (the maturity value of treasury bills is the same as their face value) *(p. 303)*

Unsecured line of credit a line of credit in which no assets are pledged by the borrower to the lender to cover non-payment of the line of credit *(p. 312)*

USEFUL INTERNET SITES

www.royalbank.com

Royal Bank Visit the "Daily Numbers" area of this site for current interest rates on investment products. This site also provides links to detailed rate schedules for mortgages, T-bills, personal accounts, and RRSPs.

www.bankofcanada.ca/en/rates/exchange.html

Bank of Canada Current T-bill rates are posted on this section of the Bank of Canada site. A link to selected historical interest rates is also provided.

www.bankrate.com

Bankrate.com Go to "Calculators" and select "Credit Cards" to determine what it really costs to pay the minimum payment on your credit card. (This is a U.S. site. Some of the interest rates displayed will not be applicable in Canada.)

CHAPTER 9 Compound Interest—Future Value and Present Value

OBJECTIVES

Upon completing this chapter, you will be able to do the following:

1. Calculate interest rates and the number of compounding periods.
2. Compute future (maturity) values of investments.
3. Compute present values of future sums of money.
4. Discount long-term promissory notes.
5. Solve problems involving equivalent values.

The world of computerized banking and investing uses compound interest extensively. With compound interest, you earn interest on a principal, and the interest is then added to form a new principal. You then earn interest on this new higher principal. This is what is meant by the expression "earning interest on interest."

To calculate compound interest, and to decide which interest terms are best for you, you need to understand how compound interest works. When you need to calculate compound interest amounts for all sorts of interest rates and time periods, calculators and computers make the job easy. To calculate compound interest amounts using formulas, an understanding of exponents is required.

INTRODUCTION

Under the compound interest method, interest is added periodically to the principal. As we did with simple interest, we use compound interest calculations to determine future values and present values. The compound interest formulas contain the compounding factor $(1 + i)^n$. The calculations are not difficult if you use electronic calculators equipped with an exponential function, especially if they are financial calculators preprogrammed with the ability to calculate future value and present value for compound interest.

9.1 BASIC CONCEPTS AND COMPUTATIONS

A. Basic procedure for computing compound interest

The term **compound interest** refers to a procedure for computing interest whereby the interest for a specified time period is added to the original principal. The resulting amount becomes the new principal for the next time period. The interest earned in earlier periods earns interest in future periods.

The compound interest method is generally used to calculate interest for long-term investments. The amount of compound interest for the first interest period is the same as the amount of simple interest, but for further interest periods the amount of compound interest becomes increasingly greater than the amount of simple interest.

The basic procedure for computing compound interest and the effect of compounding is illustrated in Table 9.1. The table also provides a comparison of

Table 9.1 **Compound Interest versus Simple Interest for a Principal of $10 000 Invested at 10% per Annum for 6 Years**

		At Compound Interest		At Simple Interest	
Year		Interest Computation	Amount	Interest Computation	Amount
	Original principal		$10 000.00		$10 000.00
1	Add interest	(0.10)(10 000.00)	1 000.00	(0.10)(10 000.00)	1 000.00
	Amount end Year 1		11 000.00		11 000.00
2	Add interest	(0.10)(11 000.00)	1 100.00	(0.10)(10 000.00)	1 000.00
	Amount end Year 2		12 100.00		12 000.00
3	Add interest	(0.10)(12 100.00)	1 210.00	(0.10)(10 000.00)	1 000.00
	Amount end Year 3		13 310.00		13 000.00
4	Add interest	(0.10)(13 310.00)	1 331.00	(0.10)(10 000.00)	1 000.00
	Amount end Year 4		14 641.00		14 000.00
5	Add interest	(0.10)(14 641.00)	1 464.10	(0.10)(10 000.00)	1 000.00
	Amount end Year 5		16 105.10		15 000.00
6	Add interest	(0.10)(16 105.10)	1 610.51	(0.10)(10 000.00)	1 000.00
	Amount end Year 6		$17 715.61		$16 000.00

compound interest and simple interest for an original principal of $10 000 invested at 10% per annum for six years.

The method of computation used in Table 9.1 represents the step-by-step approach used in maintaining a compound interest record, such as a savings account. Note that the amount of interest is determined for each interest period on the basis of the previous balance and is then added to that balance.

Note the following about the end results after six years:

	At compound interest	*At simple interest*
Amount after six years	$17 715.61	$16 000.00
Less original principal	10 000.00	10 000.00
Amount of interest	$ 7 715.61	$ 6 000.00

In this case, the compound interest exceeds the simple interest by $1715.61. This difference represents the amount of interest earned by interest added to the principal at the end of each compounding period.

B. Computer application—accumulation of principal using a spreadsheet

Table 9.1 displays the manual calculations for the accumulation of a principal of $10 000 earning compound interest at 10% per annum for six years. Microsoft Excel and other spreadsheet programs can be used to create a file that will immediately display the results of a change in the principal, interest rate, or number of years of accumulation.

EXCEL NOTES

The following steps are general instructions for creating a file to calculate the compound interest data in Table 9.1. The formulas in the spreadsheet file were created using Excel; however, most spreadsheet programs work similarly.

Although this exercise assumes a basic understanding of spreadsheet applications, someone without previous spreadsheet experience will be able to complete this task.

STEP 1 Enter the labels shown in Figure 9.1 in row 1.

STEP 2 Enter the principal in cell B2. Do not type in the dollar sign or a comma.

STEP 3 Enter only the formulas shown in cells C2, D2, and B3. Make sure that the formula entry includes the dollar ($) sign as shown in Figure 9.1. Use Copy and Paste to enter the remainder of the formulas shown.

STEP 4 The formulas that were entered in Step 3 can be copied through the remaining cells.

(a) Select and Copy the formulas in cells C2 and D2.

(b) Select cells C3 to C7, and Paste.

FIGURE 9.1

Workbook 1

	A	B	C	D	E
1	Year	Amount, beginning of year	Interest	Amount, end of year	0.10
2	1	10000	= B2*E1	= B2+C2	
3	2	= D2	= B3*E1	= B3+C3	
4	3	= D3	= B4*E1	= B4+C4	
5	4	= D4	= B5*E1	= B5+C5	
6	5	= D5	= B6*E1	= B6+C6	
7	6	= D6	= B7*E1	= B7+C7	

(c) Select and Copy the formula in cell B3.
(d) Select cells B4 to B7, and Paste.
(e) The formulas are now active in all the cells.

STEP 5

To ensure readability of the spreadsheet, format the numbers to display as two decimal places, and widen the columns to display the full labels.

This spreadsheet can now be used to reflect changes in aspects of the investment. You will be able to input the changes and see the effects quickly. Use cell B2 for a new principal amount and cell E1 for a new interest rate.

C. The future value formula for compound interest

Creating a compound interest table is useful, and serves many purposes, but can be time-consuming. As in calculating simple interest, the **future value**, **maturity value**, or **amount** of a loan or investment can be found by using the future value formula.

For *simple interest*, the future value formula is $S = P(1 + rt)$, Formula 7.3A.
For *compound interest*, the formula for the future value is

$$S = P(1 + i)^n$$ restated as:

$$FV = PV(1 + i)^n$$ **Formula 9.1A**

S or FV = the future or maturity value;
P or PV = the original principal;
i = the periodic rate of interest;
n = the number of compounding periods for the term of the loan or investment.

The results of Table 9.1 could have been obtained by using the two future value formulas.

For simple interest: P = 10 000.00; $r = 0.10$; $t = 6$

$$\begin{aligned} S = P(1 + rt) &= 10\,000.00[1 + (0.10)(6)] \\ &= 10\,000.00(1 + 0.60) \\ &= 10\,000.00(1.60) \\ &= \$16\,000.00 \end{aligned}$$

For compound interest: PV = 10 000.00; $i = 0.10$; $n = 6$

$$\begin{aligned} FV = PV(1 + i)^n &= 10\,000.00(1 + 0.10)^6 \\ &= 10\,000.00(1.10)^6 \\ &= 10\,000.00(1.10)(1.10)(1.10)(1.10)(1.10)(1.10) \\ &= 10\,000.00(1.771561) \\ &= \$17\,715.61 \end{aligned}$$

When using the compound interest formula, determining the factor $(1 + i)^n$ is the main computational problem. The value of this factor, called the **compounding factor** or **accumulation factor**, depends on the values of i and n.

D. Determining the periodic rate of interest

The value of i, the **periodic rate of interest**, is determined from the stated rate of interest to be used in the compounding situation. The stated rate is called the **nominal rate of interest**. Since the nominal rate of interest is usually stated as an annual rate, the value of i depends on the **compounding** (or **conversion**) **frequency** per year. The value of i is obtained by dividing the nominal annual rate by the number of **compounding** (or **conversion**) **periods** per year.

The compounding (conversion) periods commonly used in business and finance cover a number of months, usually an exact divisor of 12, and are listed in Table 9.2.

Table 9.2 **Commonly Used Compounding Frequencies and Conversion Periods**

Compounding (Conversion) Frequency	Length of Compounding (Conversion) Period	Number of Compounding (Conversion) Periods per Year
Annual	12 months (1 year)	1
Semi-annual	6 months	2
Quarterly	3 months	4
Monthly	1 month	12

The relationship between the periodic rate of interest and the nominal annual rate of interest can be stated in the form of a formula.

$$\text{PERIODIC RATE OF INTEREST, } i = \frac{\text{NOMINAL (ANNUAL) RATE}}{\text{NUMBER OF COMPOUNDING (CONVERSION) PERIODS PER YEAR}}$$

Therefore,

$$i = \frac{j}{m} \qquad \text{Formula 9.2}$$

where i = periodic rate of interest
j = nominal annual rate of interest
m = number of compounding (conversion) periods per year

EXAMPLE 9.1A

Determine the periodic rate of interest i for
(i) 5% p.a. compounded annually;
(ii) 7% p.a. compounded semi-annually;
(iii) 12% p.a. compounded quarterly;
(iv) 10.5% p.a. compounded monthly.

SOLUTION

	(i)	(ii)	(iii)	(iv)
The nominal annual rate j	5%	7%	12%	10.5%
The compounding (conversion) frequency	annually	semi-annually	quarterly	monthly
The length of the compounding (conversion) period	12 months	6 months	3 months	1 month
The number of compounding (conversion) periods per year m	1	2	4	12
The periodic rate of interest $i = \frac{j}{m}$	$\frac{5\%}{1}$ = 5.0%	$\frac{7\%}{2}$ = 3.5%	$\frac{12\%}{4}$ = 3.0%	$\frac{10.5\%}{12}$ = 0.875%

E. Determining the number of compounding (conversion) periods in the term of an investment or loan

To find the number of compounding (conversion) periods in the term of an investment or a loan, multiply the number of years in the term by the number of compounding periods per year.

EXAMPLE 9.1B

Determine the number of compounding periods when
(i) compounding annually for 14 years;
(ii) compounding semi-annually for 15 years;
(iii) compounding quarterly for 12.5 years;
(iv) compounding monthly for 10.75 years;
(v) compounding quarterly for 30 months;
(vi) compounding semi-annually for 42 months.

SOLUTION

	Term (in years)	Compounding Frequency	Number of Compounding Periods per Year, m	Number of Compounding Periods in Term, n
(i)	14	annually	1	14(1) = 14
(ii)	15	semi-annually	2	15(2) = 30
(iii)	12.5	quarterly	4	12.5(4) = 50
(iv)	10.75	monthly	12	10.75(12) = 129
(v)	$\frac{30}{12} = 2.5$	quarterly	4	2.5(4) = 10
(vi)	$\frac{42}{12} = 3.5$	semi-annually	2	3.5(2) = 7

POINTERS AND PITFALLS

Many students have difficulty determining the value of m when compounding is stated as "quarterly." This term means that interest is compounded every quarter of a year. Since there are four quarters in a year, m then becomes 4, each quarter of a year being 3 months in length. The value of m is never 3.

F. Setting up the compounding factor $(1 + i)^n$

The *compounding (accumulation) factor* $(1 + i)^n$ can be set up by first determining i and n and then substituting i and n in the general form of the factor, $(1 + i)^n$.

EXAMPLE 9.1C

Set up the compounding factor $(1 + i)^n$ *for*
(i) 5% p.a. compounded annually for 14 years;
(ii) 7% p.a. compounded semi-annually for 15 years;
(iii) 12% p.a. compounded quarterly for 12.5 years;
(iv) 10.5% p.a. compounded monthly for 10.75 years;

(v) 8% p.a. compounded quarterly for 30 months;
(vi) 9.5% p.a. compounded semi-annually for 42 months.

SOLUTION

	i	m	n	$(1+i)^n$
(i)	5% = 0.05	1	14(1) = 14	$(1+0.05)^{14} = 1.05^{14}$
(ii)	3.5% = 0.035	2	15(2) = 30	$(1+0.035)^{30} = 1.035^{30}$
(iii)	3.0% = 0.03	4	12.5(4) = 50	$(1+0.03)^{50} = 1.03^{50}$
(iv)	0.875% = 0.00875	12	10.75(12) = 129	$(1+0.00875)^{129} = 1.00875^{129}$
(v)	2% = 0.02	4	30/12 = 10	$(1+0.02)^{10} = 1.02^{10}$
(vi)	4.75% = 0.0475	2	42/12 = 7	$(1+0.0475)^{7} = 1.0475^{7}$

G. Computing the numerical value of the compounding factor $(1+i)^n$

The numerical value of the compounding factor can now be computed using an electronic calculator. For calculators equipped with the exponential function feature y^x, the numerical value of the compounding factor can be computed directly.

STEP 1 Enter the numerical value of $(1+i)$ in the keyboard.

STEP 2 Press the exponential function key y^x.

STEP 3 Enter the numerical value of n in the keyboard.

STEP 4 Press =.

STEP 5 Read the answer in the display.

The numerical value of the compounding factors in Example 9.1C are obtained as follows.

		(i)	(ii)	(iii)	(iv)	(v)	(vi)
STEP 1	Enter	1.05	1.035	1.03	1.00875	1.02	1.0475
STEP 2	Press	y^x	y^x	y^x	y^x	y^x	y^x
STEP 3	Enter	14	30	50	129	10	7
STEP 4	Press	=	=	=	=	=	=
STEP 5	Read	1.979932	2.806794	4.383906	3.076647	1.218994	1.383816

Note: Do not be concerned if your calculator shows a difference in the last decimal. There is no error. It reflects the precision of the calculator and the number of decimal places formatted to show on the display of the calculator.

With the increasing availability of inexpensive electronic calculators, the two traditional methods of determining the compounding factor $(1 + i)^n$—logarithms and tables—are rapidly falling into disuse. Neither method is used in this text.

EXERCISE 9.1

A. Determine m, i, and n for each of the following.

1. 12% compounded annually for 5 years
2. 7.4% compounded semi-annually for 8 years
3. 5.5% compounded quarterly for 9 years
4. 7% compounded monthly for 4 years
5. 11.5% compounded semi-annually for 13.5 years
6. 4.8% compounded quarterly for $5\frac{3}{4}$ years
7. 8% compounded monthly for 12.5 years
8. 10.75% compounded quarterly for 3 years, 9 months
9. 12.25% compounded semi-annually for 54 months
10. 8.1% compounded monthly for 15.5 years

B. Set up and compute the compounding factor $(1 + i)^n$ for each of the questions in part A.

C. Answer each of the following questions.

1. For a sum of money invested at 10% compounded quarterly for 12 years, state
   (a) the number of compounding periods;
   (b) the periodic rate of interest;
   (c) the compounding factor $(1 + i)^n$;
   (d) the numerical value of the compounding factor.
2. For each of the following periodic rates of interest, determine the nominal annual compounding rate.
   (a) $i = 2\%$; compounding is quarterly
   (b) $i = 0.75\%$; compounding is monthly
   (c) $i = 5.5\%$; compounding is semi-annually
   (d) $i = 9.75\%$; compounding is annually

9.2 USING THE FORMULA FOR THE FUTURE VALUE OF A COMPOUND AMOUNT $FV = PV(1 + i)^n$

A. Finding the future value (maturity value) of an investment

EXAMPLE 9.2A

Find the amount to which \$6000 will grow if invested at 10% per annum compounded quarterly for five years.

SOLUTION

The original principal PV = 6000.00;
the nominal annual rate $j = 10\%$;
the number of compounding periods per year $m = 4$;
the quarterly rate of interest $i = \frac{10\%}{4} = 2.5\% = 0.025$;
the number of compounding periods (quarters) $n = (5)(4) = 20$.

$$\begin{aligned} FV &= PV(1+i)^n && \text{using Formula 9.1A} \\ &= 6000.00(1+0.025)^{20} && \text{substituting for P, } i, n \\ &= 6000.00(1.025)^{20} && \text{exponential form of factor} \\ &= 6000.00(1.638616) && \text{using a calculator} \\ &= \$9831.70 \end{aligned}$$

EXAMPLE 9.2B

What is the future value after 78 months of \$2500 invested at 5.25% p.a. compounded semi-annually?

SOLUTION

The original principal PV = 2500.00;
the nominal annual rate $j = 5.25$;
the number of compounding periods per year $m = 2$;
the semi-annual rate of interest $i = \frac{5.25\%}{2} = 2.625\% = 0.02625$;
the number of compounding periods (each period is six months)
$n = \left(\frac{78}{12}\right)(2) = (6.5)(2) = 13$.

$$\begin{aligned} FV &= PV(1+i)^n \\ &= 2500.00(1+0.02625)^{13} \\ &= 2500.00(1.02625)^{13} \\ &= 2500.00(1.400526) \\ &= \$3501.32 \end{aligned}$$

EXAMPLE 9.2C

Accumulate a deposit of \$1750 made into a registered retirement savings plan from March 1, 1995 to December 1, 2010 at 4.4% p.a. compounded quarterly.

SOLUTION

The original principal PV = 1750.00; $j = 4.4\%$; $m = 4$;
the quarterly rate of interest $i = \frac{4.4\%}{4} = 1.1\% = 0.011$;

the time period from March 1, 1995 to December 1, 2010 contains 15 years and 9 months, or 15.75 years: $n = (15.75)(4) = 63$.

$$\begin{aligned} FV &= PV(1+i)^n \\ &= 1750.00(1+0.011)^{63} \\ &= 1750.00(1.011)^{63} \\ &= 1750.00(1.992154) \\ &= \$3486.27 \end{aligned}$$

B. Using preprogrammed financial calculators

Compound interest calculations, which can become complex, are performed frequently and repeatedly. Doing the calculations algebraically can enhance your understanding and appreciation of the theory, but it can also be time-consuming, laborious, and subject to mechanical errors. Using preprogrammed financial calculators can save time and reduce or eliminate mechanical errors, assuming they are set up properly and numerical sign conventions are observed when entering data and interpreting results.

Different models of financial calculators vary in their operation and labelling of the function keys and faceplate. Appendix II, entitled "Instructions and Tips for Three Preprogrammed Financial Calculator Models," highlights the relevant variations for students using Texas Instruments' BAII Plus, Sharp's EL-733A, and Hewlett-Packard's 10B calculators. (Note that Appendix II is intended to help you use one of these three calculators, and merely supplements the instruction booklet that came with your calculator. Refer to the instruction booklet for your particular model to become familiar with your calculator.)

Specific function keys on preprogrammed financial calculators correspond to the five variables used in compound interest calculations. Function keys used for the calculator models presented in Appendix II are shown in Table 9.3.

The function keys are used to enter the numerical values of the known variables into the appropriate preprogrammed calculator registers. The data may be entered in any order. The answer is then displayed by using a computation key or by depressing the key representing the unknown variable, depending on the calculator model.

Before entering the numerical data to complete compound interest calculations, it is important to verify that your calculator has been set up correctly to ensure error-free operation. There are a number of items to check during this "pre-calculation" phase. Specifically, does the calculator require a mode change within a register to match the text presentation? Does the calculator have to be in the financial mode? Are the decimal places set to the correct number to ensure the required accuracy?

Further checks must be made when entering data during the "calculation" phase. For example, have the function key registers been cleared? What numerical data require a minus sign to avoid errors in operation and incorrect answers? How can the data entered be confirmed? Responses to these queries in the "pre-calculation" and "calculation" phases for three preprogrammed financial calculators are given in Appendix II, along with general information.

Table 9.3 **Financial Calculator Function Keys that Correspond to Variables Used in Compound Interest Calculations**

Variable	Algebraic Symbol	Function Key: TI BAII+	Function Key: Sharp EL-733A	Function Key: HP 10B
The number of compounding periods	n	N	n	N
The rate of interest[1]	i	I/Y C/Y	i	1/YR
The periodic annuity payment[2]	R	PMT	PMT	PMT
The present value or principal	P	PV	PV	PV
The future value or maturity value	S	FV	FV	FV

Notes: 1. The periodic rate of interest is entered as a percent and not as a decimal equivalent (as it is when using the algebraic method to solve compound interest problems). For example, 8% is entered as "8" not ".08". With some calculators, the rate of interest is the periodic rate. In the case of the BAII Plus, the rate of interest entered is the rate per year (nominal rate).

2. The periodic annuity payment function key PMT is used only for annuity calculations, which are introduced in Chapter 11.

Instructions in this text are given for the Texas Instruments BAII Plus calculator. Refer to Appendix II for instructions for setting up and using the Sharp EL-733A and Hewlett-Packard 10B calculators.

Using the Texas Instruments BAII Plus to Solve Compound Interest Problems

Follow the steps below to compute the future value of a sum of money using the formula $FV = PV(1 + i)^n$ and a Texas Instruments BAII Plus calculator. Compare your result with Example 9.2A.

Pre-calculation Phase (Initial Setup)

STEP 1 The P/Y register, and behind it the C/Y register, must be set to match the calculator's performance to the text presentation. The P/Y register is used to represent the number of regular payments per year. If the text of the question does not discuss regular payments per year, this should be set to equal the C/Y in the calculator. The C/Y register is used to represent the number of compounding periods per year, that is, the compounding frequency. The description of the compounding frequency is usually contained within the phrase that describes the nominal interest rate. An example would be "8% p.a. compounded quarterly." This means that the nominal, or annual, interest rate of 8% is compounded four times each year at 8%/4, or 2%, each period. The compounding frequency of 4 is entered into the C/Y register within the calculator.

Key in	*Press*	*Display shows*	
	2nd (P/Y)	P/Y = 12	checks the P/Y register
4	ENTER	P/Y = 4	changes the value to "4"
	↓	C/Y = 4	changed automatically to match the P/Y
	2nd (QUIT)	0	returns to the standard calculation mode

STEP 2 Verify that the decimal format is set to the number you require. A setting of "9" represents a floating decimal point format. The default setting is "2."

Key in	*Press*	*Display shows*	
	2nd (Format)	DEC = 2	checks the decimal format
6	ENTER	DEC = 6	changes to "6"
	2nd (QUIT)	0	returns to the standard calculation mode

This calculator is ready for financial calculations in its standard mode.

Calculation Phase

STEP 3 Always clear the function key registers before beginning compound interest calculations.

Key in	*Press*	*Display shows*	
	2nd (CLR TVM)	0	clears the function key registers

STEP 4 To solve Example 9.2A in which P = 6000, i = 2.5%, and n = 20, use the following procedure. Remember that i represents the interest rate per compounding period, and n represents the number of times that interest is compounded. To enter the accurate information into the calculator, you must determine the nominal interest rate for the year, and enter this information into the I/Y register. In this example, the interest rate per year is 10%. The compounding frequency, denoted by the phrase "compounded quarterly," is four times per year. This must be entered into the C/Y register. Also, notice that 6000 is entered as a negative number since it is cash paid out for an investment. This "cash flow sign convention" is explained below.

If you follow this convention, your calculation will be error-free, and the answer will be accurate and interpreted consistently.

Key in	*Press*	*Display shows*	
	2nd (P/Y)	P/Y = 12	checks the P/Y register
4	ENTER	P/Y = 4	changes the value to "4"
	↓	C/Y = 4	changed automatically to match the P/Y
	2nd (QUIT)	0	returns to the standard calculation mode
6000	± PV	PV = −6000	this enters the present value P (principal) with the correct sign convention
10	I/Y	I/Y = 10	this enters the periodic interest rate as a percent
20	N	N = 20	this enters the number of compounding periods *n*
	CPT FV	FV = 9831.698642	this computes and displays the unknown future value S

The future value is $9831.70.

Cash Flow Sign Convention for Entering Numerical Data

The Texas Instruments BAII Plus calculator follows the established convention of treating cash inflows (cash received) as positive numbers and cash outflows (cash paid out) as negative numbers. In the calculation above, the present value was considered to be cash paid out for an investment and so the present value of 6000 was entered as a negative number. The resulting future value was considered to be cash received from the investment and so had a positive value. Note that if the present value had been entered as a positive value, then the future value would have been displayed as a negative number. The *numerical* value would have been correct but the result would have been a negative number. "Error 5" is displayed when calculating i or n if both the present value and future value are entered using the same sign. Therefore, to avoid errors, always enter the present value as a negative number for compound interest calculations. Enter all other values as positive numbers. This topic is discussed further in Appendix II and throughout this text as required.

EXCEL NOTES

Excel has a ***Future Value (FV)*** function you can use to calculate the future value of an investment subject to compound interest. Refer to **FV** on the Spreadsheet Template Disk to learn how to use this Excel function.

C. Finding the future value when n is a fractional value

The value of n in the compounding factor $(1 + i)^n$ is not restricted to integral values; n may take any fractional value. The future value can be determined by means of the formula $FV = PV(1 + i)^n$ whether the time period contains an integral number of conversion periods or not.

EXAMPLE 9.2D

Find the accumulated value of \$1000 invested for two years and nine months at 10% p.a. compounded annually.

SOLUTION

The entire time period is 2 years and 9 months; the number of whole conversion periods is 2; the fractional conversion period is $\frac{9}{12}$ of a year.

$PV = 1000.00$; $I/Y = 10$; $C/Y = 1$; $i = 10\% = 0.10$; $n = 2\frac{9}{12} = 2.75$

$FV = 1000.00(1.10)^{2.75} = 1000.00(1.299660) = \$1299.66$

Programmed Solution

(Set P/Y, C/Y = 1) [2nd] (CLR TVM) 1000 [±] [PV] 10 [I/Y]

2.75 [N] [CPT] [FV] [1299.660393]

EXAMPLE 9.2E

Determine the compound amount of \$400 invested at 6% p.a. compounded quarterly for three years and five months.

SOLUTION

$PV = 400.00$; $i = 1.5\% = 0.015$

$$n = \left(3\frac{5}{12}\right)(4) = \left(\frac{41}{12}\right)(4) = \frac{41}{3} = 13\frac{2}{3} = 13.666667$$

$FV = 400.00(1.015)^{13.666667} = 400.00(1.225658) = \$490.26$

Programmed Solution

(Set P/Y, C/Y = 4) [2nd] (CLR TVM) 400 [±] [PV] 6 [I/Y]

13.666667 [N] [CPT] [FV] [490.263134]

EXAMPLE 9.2F

A debt of \$3500 dated August 31, 2009 is payable together with interest at 9% p.a. compounded quarterly on June 30, 2012. Determine the amount to be paid.

SOLUTION

$PV = 3500.00$; $I/Y = 9$; $C/Y = 4$; $i = \frac{9\%}{4} = 2.25\% = 0.0225$; the time period August 31, 2009 to June 30, 2012 contains 2 years and 10 months; the number of quarters $n = 11.333333$.

$$\begin{aligned} FV &= 3500.00(1.0225)^{11.333333} \\ &= 3500.00(1.286819) \\ &= \$4503.87 \end{aligned}$$

Programmed Solution

(Set P/Y, C/Y = 4) [2nd] (CLR TVM) 3500 [±] [PV] 9 [I/Y]

11.333333 [N] [CPT] [FV] [4503.867756]

D. Applications involving changes in interest rate or principal

EXAMPLE 9.2G A deposit of \$2000 earns interest at 6% p.a. compounded monthly for four years. At that time, the interest rate changes to 7% p.a. compounded quarterly. What is the value of the deposit three years after the change in the rate of interest?

SOLUTION The data given can be represented on a time diagram as shown in Figure 9.2.

FIGURE 9.2 Graphical Representation of Data

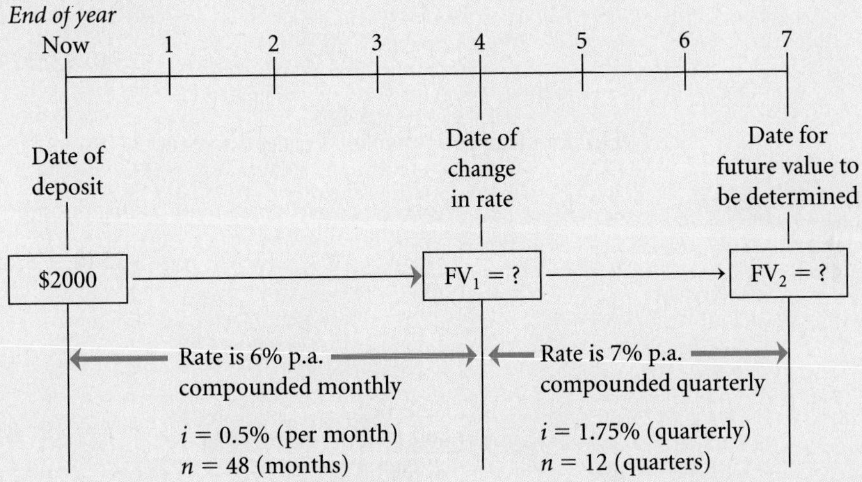

Separate the entire problem into the time periods where different interest rates apply.

STEP 1 Determine the accumulated value of the original deposit at the time the interest rate changes, that is, after four years.

$$PV = 2000.00;\ I/Y = 6;\ C/Y = 12;\ i = \frac{6\%}{12} = 0.5\% = 0.005;\ n = 48$$

$$FV_1 = 2000.00\ (1 + 0.005)^{48} = 2000.00(1.270489) = \$2540.98$$

STEP 2 Use the accumulated value after four years as the new principal and calculate its accumulated value three years later using the new rate of interest.

$$PV = 2540.98;\ I/Y = 7;\ C/Y = 4;\ i = \frac{7\%}{4} = 1.75\% = 0.0175;\ n = 12$$

$$FV_2 = 2540.98\ (1 + 0.0175)^{12} = 2540.98(1.231439) = \$3129.06$$

Solution By Preprogrammed Calculator
Keys are applicable to the Texas Instruments BAII Plus calculator (this is the case throughout the rest of this chapter).

STEP 1

Key in	Press	Display shows
	2nd (P/Y)	
12	ENTER	P/Y = 12
	↓	C/Y = 12
	2nd (QUIT)	0
	2nd (CLR TVM)	0
2000	± PV	−2000
6	I/Y	6
48	N	48
	CPT FV	2540.978322 — answer to Step 1 (FV_1 = 2540.978322)

Do *not* clear your display. Proceed to Step 2.

STEP 2

Key in	Press	Display shows
	± PV	−2540.978322 – this step enters the new principal and the proper sign convention, since this amount is reinvested (a cash outflow)
	2nd (P/Y)	P/Y = 12
4	ENTER	P/Y = 4
	↓	C/Y = 4
	2nd (QUIT)	0
7	I/Y	7
12	N	12
	CPT FV	3129.060604 — final answer (FV_2 = \$3129.06)

EXAMPLE 9.2H A debt of \$500 accumulates interest at 8% p.a. compounded quarterly from April 1, 2008 to July 1, 2009, and 9% p.a. compounded monthly thereafter. Determine the accumulated value of the debt on December 1, 2010.

SOLUTION

STEP 1 Determine the accumulated value of the debt on July 1, 2009.

$PV = 500.00;\ I/Y = 8;\ C/Y = 4;\ i = \frac{8\%}{4} = 2\% = 0.02;$

the period April 1, 2008 to July 1, 2009 contains 15 months: $n = 5$

$FV_1 = 500.00(1.02)^5 = 500.00(1.104081) = \$552.04$

STEP 2 Use the result of Step 1 as new principal and find its accumulated value on December 1, 2010.

$PV = 552.04$; $I/Y = 9$; $P/Y = 12$; $i = \frac{9\%}{12} = 0.75\% = 0.0075$;

the period July 1, 2009 to December 1, 2010 contains 17 months: $n = 17$

$FV_2 = 552.04(1.0075)^{17} = 552.04(1.135445) = \$626.81$

Programmed Solution

STEP 1 (Set P/Y, C/Y= 4) [2nd] (CLR TVM) 500 [±] [PV] 8 [I/Y] 5 [N] [CPT] [FV]

Result: [552.040402]

STEP 2 552.040402 [±] [PV] (Set P/Y, C/Y= 12) 9 [I/Y] 17 [N] [CPT] [FV]

Result: [626.811268]

EXAMPLE 9.2I Jay opened a registered retirement savings plan with his credit union on February 1, 2007, with a deposit of \$2000. He added \$1900 on February 1, 2008 and another \$1700 on February 1, 2011. What will his account amount to on August 1, 2017, if the plan earns a fixed rate of interest of 7% p.a. compounded semi-annually?

SOLUTION

FIGURE 9.3 Graphical Representation of Data

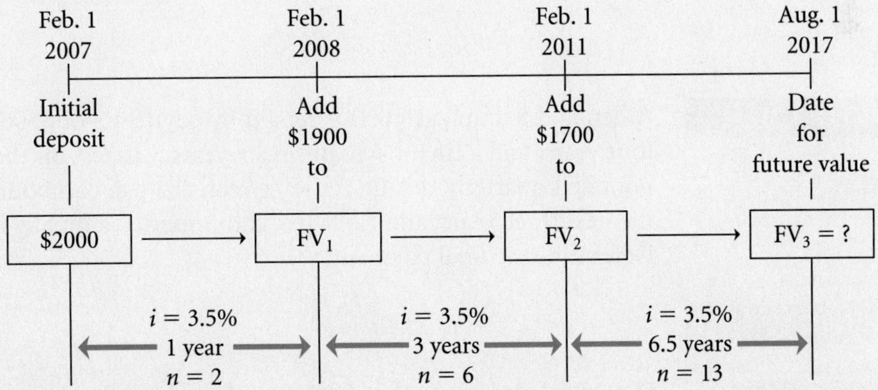

STEP 1 Determine the future value, FV_1, of the initial deposit on February 1, 2008.

$PV = 2000.00$; $I/Y = 7$; $C/Y = 2$; $i = \frac{7\%}{2} = 3.5\% = 0.035$;

the period February 1, 2007 to February 1, 2008 contains 1 year: $n = 2$

$FV_1 = 2000.00(1.035)^2 = 2000.00(1.071225) = \$2142.45$

STEP 2 Add the deposit of \$1900 to the amount of \$2142.45 to obtain the new principal as of February 1, 2008, and determine its future value, FV_2, on February 1, 2011.

$PV = 2142.45 + 1900.00 = 4042.45; i = 0.035;$
the period February 1, 2008 to February 1, 2011 contains 3 years: $n = 6$
$FV_2 = 4042.45(1.035)^6 = 4042.45(1.229255) = \$4969.20$

STEP 3 Add the deposit of \$1700 to the amount of \$4969.20 to obtain the new principal as of February 1, 2011, and determine its future value, FV_3, on August 1, 2017.

$PV = 4969.20 + 1700.00 = 6669.20; i = 0.035;$
the period February 1, 2011 to August 1, 2017 contains 6.5 years: $n = 13$
$FV_3 = 6669.20(1.035)^{13} = 6669.20(1.563956) = \$10\,430.34$

Programmed Solution

STEP 1 (Set P/Y, C/Y=2) [2nd] (CLRTVM)2000 [±] [PV] 7 [I/Y] 2 [N] [CPT] [FV]

Result: [2142.45]

STEP 2 [+] 1900 [=] [4042.65] [±] [PV] 6 [N] [CPT] [FV]

Result: [4969.203194]

STEP 3 [+] 1700 [=] [6669.20] [±] [PV] 13 [N] [CPT] [FV]

Result: [10430.34075]

Note: There is no need to key in the interest rate in Steps 2 and 3—it is already programmed from Step 1.

EXAMPLE 9.2J

A demand loan of \$10 000 is repaid by payments of \$5000 in one year, \$6000 in four years, and a final payment in six years. Interest on the loan is 10% p.a. compounded quarterly during the first year, 8% p.a. compounded semi-annually for the next three years, and 7.5% p.a. compounded annually for the remaining years. Determine the final payment.

SOLUTION

STEP 1 Determine the accumulated value of the debt at the time of the first payment.

$PV = 10\,000.00; I/Y = 10; C/Y = 4; i = \frac{10\%}{4} = 2.5\% = 0.025; n = 4$

$FV_1 = 10\,000.00(1.025)^4 = 10\,000.00(1.103813) = \$11\,038.13$

STEP 2 Subtract the payment of \$5000 from the accumulated value of \$11 038.13 to obtain the debt balance. Now determine its accumulated value at the time of the second payment three years later.

FIGURE 9.4 Graphical Representation of Data

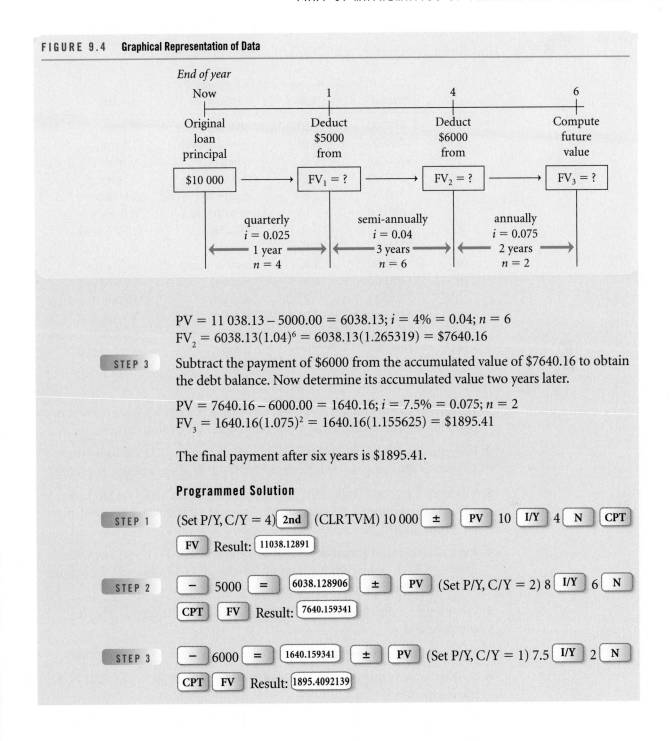

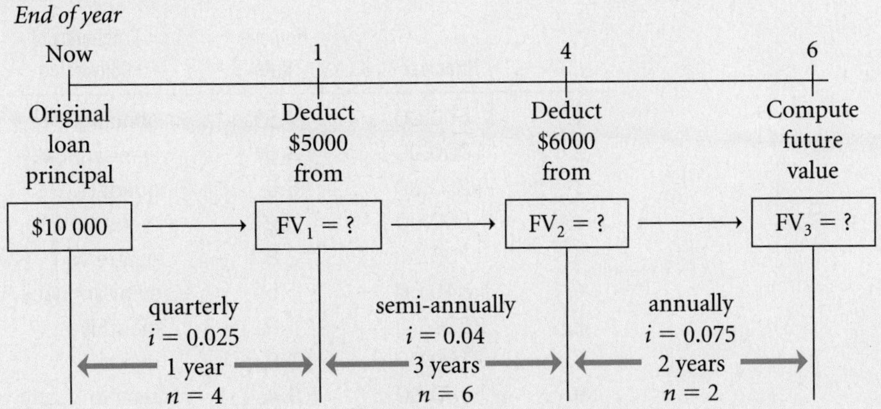

$PV = 11\,038.13 - 5000.00 = 6038.13; i = 4\% = 0.04; n = 6$

$FV_2 = 6038.13(1.04)^6 = 6038.13(1.265319) = \$7640.16$

STEP 3 Subtract the payment of \$6000 from the accumulated value of \$7640.16 to obtain the debt balance. Now determine its accumulated value two years later.

$PV = 7640.16 - 6000.00 = 1640.16; i = 7.5\% = 0.075; n = 2$

$FV_3 = 1640.16(1.075)^2 = 1640.16(1.155625) = \$1895.41$

The final payment after six years is \$1895.41.

Programmed Solution

STEP 1 (Set P/Y, C/Y = 4) [2nd] (CLR TVM) 10 000 [±] [PV] 10 [I/Y] 4 [N] [CPT] [FV] Result: [11038.12891]

STEP 2 [−] 5000 [=] [6038.128906] [±] [PV] (Set P/Y, C/Y = 2) 8 [I/Y] 6 [N] [CPT] [FV] Result: [7640.159341]

STEP 3 [−] 6000 [=] [1640.159341] [±] [PV] (Set P/Y, C/Y = 1) 7.5 [I/Y] 2 [N] [CPT] [FV] Result: [1895.4092139]

EXERCISE 9.2

EXCEL NOTES

If you choose, you can use Excel's ***Future Value (FV)*** function to calculate the future value of an investment subject to compound interest. Refer to **FV** on the Spreadsheet Template Disk to learn how to use this Excel function.

A. Find the future value for each of the investments in the table below.

	Principal	Nominal Rate	Frequency of Conversion	Time
1.	$ 400.00	7.5%	annually	8 years
2.	1000.00	3.5	semi-annually	12 years
3.	1250.00	6.5	quarterly	9 years
4.	500.00	12	monthly	3 years
5.	1700.00	8	quarterly	14.75 years
6.	840.00	5.5	semi-annually	8.5 years
7.	2500.00	8	monthly	12.25 years
8.	150.00	10.8	quarterly	27 months
9.	480.00	9.4	semi-annually	42 months
10.	1400.00	4.8	monthly	18.75 years
11.	2500.00	7	annually	7 years, 6 months
12.	400.00	9	quarterly	3 years, 8 months
13.	1300.00	5	semi-annually	9 years, 3 months
14.	4500.00	3.5	monthly	7.5 months

B. Answer each of the following questions.

1. What is the maturity value of a five-year term deposit of $5000 at 6.5% compounded semi-annually? How much interest did the deposit earn?

2. How much will a registered retirement savings deposit of $1500 be worth in 15 years at 8% compounded quarterly? How much of the amount is interest?

3. You made a registered retirement savings plan deposit of $1000 on December 1, 2008 at a fixed rate of 5.5% compounded monthly. If you withdraw the deposit on August 1, 2015, how much will you receive?

4. Ray's parents made a trust deposit of $500 on October 31, 1990 to be withdrawn on Ray's eighteenth birthday on July 31, 2008. To what will the deposit amount on that date at 7% compounded quarterly?

5. What is the accumulated value of $100 invested for eight years at 9% p.a. compounded

(a) annually? **(b)** semi-annually? **(c)** quarterly? **(d)** monthly?

6. To what future value will a principal of $500.00 amount in five years at 7.5% p.a. compounded

(a) annually? **(b)** semi-annually? **(c)** quarterly? **(d)** monthly?

7. What is the future value of and the amount of compound interest for $100 invested at 8% compounded quarterly for

(a) 5 years? **(b)** 10 years? **(c)** 20 years?

8. Find the future value of and the compound interest on $500 invested at 4.5% compounded monthly for

(a) 3.5 years; **(b)** 6 years; **(c)** 11.5 years.

9. A demand loan for $5000 with interest at 9.75% compounded semi-annually is repaid after five years, ten months. What is the amount of interest paid?

10. Suppose $4000 is invested for four years, eight months at 8.5% compounded annually. What is the compounded amount?

11. Determine the maturity value of a $600 promissory note dated August 1, 2004 and due on June 1, 2009, if interest is 5% p.a. compounded semi-annually.

12. Find the maturity value of a promissory note for $3200 dated March 31, 2006 and due on August 31, 2012, if interest is 7% compounded quarterly.

13. A debt of $8000 is payable in seven years, five months. Determine the accumulated value of the debt at 10.8% p.a. compounded annually.

14. A $6000 investment matures in three years, eleven months. Find the maturity value if interest is 9% p.a. compounded quarterly.

15. The Canadian Consumer Price Index was approximately 98.5 (base year 1992) at the beginning of 1991. If inflation continued at an average annual rate of 3%, what would the index have been at the beginning of 2008?

16. Peel Credit Union expects an average annual growth rate of 20% for the next five years. If the assets of the credit union currently amount to $2.5 million, what will the forecasted assets be in five years?

17. A local bank offers $5000 five-year certificates at 6.75% compounded semi-annually. Your credit union makes the same type of deposit available at 6.5% compounded monthly.
    (a) Which investment gives more interest over the five years?
    (b) What is the difference in the amount of interest?

18. The Continental Bank advertises capital savings at 4.25% compounded semi-annually while TD Canada Trust offers premium savings at 4% compounded monthly. Suppose you have $1000 to invest for two years.
    (a) Which deposit will earn more interest?
    (b) What is the difference in the amount of interest?

C. Answer each of the following questions.

1. A deposit of $2000 earns interest at 3% p.a. compounded quarterly. After two-and-a-half years, the interest rate is changed to 2.75% compounded monthly. How much is the account worth after six years?

2. An investment of $2500 earns interest at 4.5% p.a. compounded monthly for three years. At that time the interest rate is changed to 5% compounded quarterly. How much will the accumulated value be one-and-a-half years after the change?

3. A debt of $800 accumulates interest at 10% compounded semi-annually from February 1, 2008 to August 1, 2010, and 11% compounded quarterly thereafter. Determine the accumulated value of the debt on November 1, 2013.

4. Accumulate \$1300 at 8.5% p.a. compounded monthly from March 1, 2006 to July 1, 2008, and thereafter at 8% p.a. compounded quarterly. What is the amount on April 1, 2011?

5. Patrice opened an RRSP deposit account on December 1, 2002, with a deposit of \$1000. He added \$1000 on July 1, 2004 and \$1000 on November 1, 2006. How much is in his account on January 1, 2010, if the deposit earns 6% p.a. compounded monthly?

6. Terri started an RRSP on March 1, 2000, with a deposit of \$2000. She added \$1800 on December 1, 2002 and \$1700 on September 1, 2004. What is the accumulated value of her account on December 1, 2011, if interest is 7.5% compounded quarterly?

7. A debt of \$4000 is repaid by payments of \$1500 in nine months, \$2000 in 18 months, and a final payment in 27 months. If interest was 10% compounded quarterly, what was the amount of the final payment?

8. Sheridan Service has a line of credit loan with the bank. The initial loan balance was \$6000. Payments of \$2000 and \$3000 were made after four months and nine months respectively. At the end of one year, Sheridan Service borrowed an additional \$4000. Six months later, the line of credit loan was converted into a collateral mortgage loan. What was the amount of the mortgage loan if the line of credit interest was 9% compounded monthly?

9. A demand loan of \$3000 is repaid by payments of \$1500 after two years, \$1500 after four years, and a final payment after seven years. Interest is 9% compounded quarterly for the first year, 10% compounded semi-annually for the next three years, and 10% compounded monthly thereafter. What is the size of the final payment?

10. A variable rate demand loan showed an initial balance of \$12 000, payments of \$5000 after eighteen months, \$4000 after thirty months, and a final payment after five years. Interest was 11% compounded semi-annually for the first two years and 12% compounded monthly for the remaining time. What was the size of the final payment?

11. Joan borrowed \$15 000 to buy a car. She repaid \$2000 two months later and \$5000 seven months later. After twelve months, she borrowed an additional \$4000, and repaid \$3000 after 16 months. She paid the entire balance, including the interest, after 24 months. Interest was 7% compounded monthly for the first year and 7.5% compounded monthly for the remaining time. What was the size of the final payment?

12. A variable rate demand loan showed an initial balance of \$9000, payments of \$2500 after six months, \$2500 after 21 months, and a final payment after four years. Interest was 8% compounded quarterly for the first 21 months and 7.75% compounded monthly for the remaining time. What was the size of the final payment?

9.3 PRESENT VALUE AND COMPOUND DISCOUNT

A. The present value concept and related terms

EXAMPLE 9.3A Find the principal that will amount in six years to \$17 715.61 at 10% p.a. compounded annually.

SOLUTION The problem may be graphically represented as shown in Figure 9.5.

FIGURE 9.5 Graphical Representation of Data

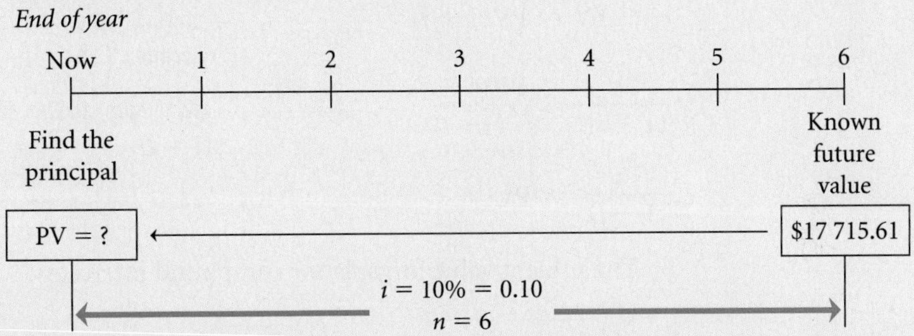

This problem is the inverse of the problem used to illustrate the meaning of compound interest. Instead of knowing the value of the principal and finding its future value, we know that the future value is \$17 715.61. What we want to determine is the value of the principal.

To solve the problem, we use the future value formula $FV = PV(1 + i)^n$ and substitute the known values.

$$FV = 17\,715.61;\ I/Y = 10;\ C/Y = 1;\ i = \frac{10\%}{1} = 10\% = 0.10;\ n = 6$$

$17\,715.61 = PV(1.10)^6$ ——— by substituting in $FV = PV(1 + i)^n$

$17\,715.61 = PV(1.771561)$ ——— computing $(1.10)^6$

$PV = \dfrac{17\,715.61}{1.771561}$ ——— solve for PV by dividing both sides by 1.771561

$PV = \$10\,000.00$

The principal that will grow to \$17 715.61 in six years at 10% p.a. compounded annually is \$10 000.

This principal is called the **present value** or **discounted value** or **proceeds** of the known future amount.

The difference between the known future amount of \$17 715.61 and the computed present value (principal) of \$10 000 is the **compound discount** and represents the compound interest accumulating on the computed present value.

The process of computing the present value or discounted value or proceeds is called **discounting.**

B. The present value formula

With compound interest, the present value of an amount at a given time is defined as the principal that will grow to the given amount if compounded at a given periodic rate of interest over a given number of conversion periods.

Since the problem of finding the present value is equivalent to finding the principal when the future value, the periodic rate of interest, and the number of conversion periods are given, the formula for the future value formula, $FV = PV(1 + i)^n$, applies.

However, because the problem of finding the present value of an amount is frequently encountered in financial analysis, it is useful to solve the future value formula for PV to obtain the present value formula.

$$FV = PV(1 + i)^n$$ — start with the future value formula, Formula 9.1A

$$\frac{FV}{(1 + i)^n} = \frac{PV(1 + i)^n}{(1+ i)^n}$$ — divide both sides by the compounding factor $(1 + i)^n$

$$\frac{FV}{(1 + i)^n} = PV$$ — reduce the fraction $\frac{(1+i)^n}{(1+i)^n}$ to 1

The present value formula for compound interest is:

$$PV = \frac{FV}{(1 + i)^n}$$ — Formula 9.1B

EXAMPLE 9.3B

Find the present value of \$6836.56 due in nine years at 6% p.a. compounded quarterly.

SOLUTION

$FV = 6836.56;\ I/Y = 6;\ P/Y = 4;\ i = \frac{6\%}{4} = 1.5\% = 0.015;\ n = 36$

$$PV = \frac{FV}{(1 + i)^n}$$ — using the present value formula

$$= \frac{6836.56}{(1 + 0.015)^{36}}$$ — by substitution

$$= \frac{6836.56}{1.709140}$$

$$= \$4000.00$$

Note: The division of 6836.56 by 1.709140, like any division, may be changed to a multiplication by using the reciprocal of the divisor.

$$\frac{6836.56}{1.709140}$$ — the division to be changed into a multiplication

$$= 6836.56\left(\frac{1}{1.709140}\right)$$ — the reciprocal of the divisor 1.709140 is found by dividing 1 by 1.709140

$$= 6836.56(0.585090)$$ — computed value of the reciprocal

$$= \$4000.00$$

For calculators equipped with the reciprocal function key [1/x], converting the division into a multiplication is easily accomplished by first computing the compounding factor and then using the [1/x] key to obtain the reciprocal.

EXAMPLE 9.3C

What principal will amount to $5000 seven years from today if interest is 9% p.a. compounded monthly?

SOLUTION

Finding the principal that amounts to a future sum of money is equivalent to finding the present value.

FV = 5000.00; I/Y = 9; C/Y = 12; $i = \frac{9\%}{12} = 0.75\% = 0.0075$; $n = 84$

$$\text{PV} = \frac{5000.00}{(1.0075)^{84}} \quad \text{——— using Formula 9.1B}$$

$$= \frac{5000.00}{1.873202} \quad \text{——— computing the factor } (1.0075)^{84}$$

$$= 5000.00(0.533845) \quad \text{——— using the reciprocal function key}$$

$$= \$2669.23$$

Using the reciprocal of the divisor to change division into multiplication is reflected in the practice of stating the present value formula with a negative exponent.

$$\frac{1}{a^n} = a^{-n} \quad \text{——— negative exponent rule}$$

$$\frac{1}{(1+i)^n} = (1+i)^{-n}$$

$$\frac{\text{FV}}{(1+i)^n} = \text{FV}(1+i)^{-n}$$

Formula 9.1B, the present value formula, can be restated in multiplication form using a negative exponent.

$$\boxed{\text{PV} = \text{FV}(1+i)^{-n}} \quad \text{——— Formula 9.1C}$$

The factor $(1 + i)^{-n}$ is called the **discount factor** and is the reciprocal of the compounding factor $(1 + i)^n$.

C. Using preprogrammed financial calculators to find present value

As explained in Section 9.2B, preprogrammed calculators provide quick solutions to compound interest calculations. Three of the four variables are entered and the value of the fourth variable is retrieved.

To solve Example 9.3C, in which FV = 5000, $i = 0.75\%$, $n = 84$, and PV is to be determined, use the following procedure. (Remember that the interest rate for the year, 9%, must be entered into the calculator as I/Y.)

Key in	*Press*	*Display shows*	
	2nd (CLR TVM)	0	clears the function key registers
	2nd (P/Y)	0	checks the P/Y register
12	ENTER	P/Y = 12	changes the value to "12"
	↓	C/Y = 12	changed automatically to match the P/Y
	2nd (QUIT)	0	returns to the standard calculation mode
5000	FV	5000	enters the future value amount FV
9	I/Y	9	enters the nominal interest rate
84	N	84	enters the number of compounding periods n
	CPT PV	−2669.226329	retrieves the unknown principal (present value) PV, an investment or cash outflow as indicated by the negative sign

The principal is $2669.23.

EXCEL NOTES

Excel has a ***Present Value (PV)*** function you can use to calculate the present value of an investment subject to compound interest. Refer to **PV** on the Spreadsheet Template Disk to learn how to use this Excel function.

D. Finding the present value when *n* is a fractional value

When PV is to be determined, use Formula 9.1A, $FV = PV(1 + i)^n$, or Formula 9.1B, $PV = \frac{FV}{(1 + i)^n}$, or Formula 9.1C, $PV = FV(1 + i)^{-n}$, where n is a fractional value representing the *entire* time period and FV is a known value.

EXAMPLE 9.3D

Find the present value of \$2000 due in three years and eight months if money is worth 8% p.a. compounded quarterly.

SOLUTION

FV = 2000.00; I/Y = 8; P/Y = 4; $i = \frac{8\%}{4} = 2\% = 0.02$;

$n = \left(3\frac{8}{12}\right)(4) = 14\frac{2}{3} = 14.666667$

$$PV = \frac{FV}{(1+i)^n}$$ — using Formula 9.1B

$$= \frac{2000.00}{(1+0.02)^{14.666667}}$$ — use as many decimals as are available in your calculator

$$= 2000.00(0.747936)$$ — multiply by the reciprocal

$$= \$1495.87$$

Programmed Solution

(Set P/Y, C/Y = 4) [2nd] (CLR TVM) 2000 [FV] 8 [I/Y]

14.666667 [N] [CPT] [PV] [-1495.871001]

EXAMPLE 9.3E

Determine the principal that will accumulate to \$2387.18 from September 1, 2008 to April 1, 2012 at 5% p.a. compounded semi-annually.

SOLUTION

Finding the principal that will grow to the given amount of \$2387.18 is equivalent to finding the present value or discounted value of this amount.

The time period September 1, 2008 to April 1, 2012 contains three years and seven months; that is, it consists of seven whole conversion periods of six months each and a fractional conversion period of one month.

Use $PV = \frac{FV}{(1+i)^n}$

FV = 2387.18; I/Y = 5; P/Y = 2; $i = \frac{5\%}{2} = 2.5\% = 0.025$;

$n = \left(3\frac{7}{12}\right)(2) = 7\frac{1}{6} = 7.166667$

$$PV = \frac{2387.18}{(1.025)^{7.166667}}$$

$$= \frac{2387.18}{1.193588}$$

$$= 2387.18(0.837810)$$

$$= \$2000.00$$

Programmed Solution

(Set P/Y = 2) [2nd] (CLR TVM) 2387.18 [FV] 5 [I/Y]

7.166667 [N] [CPT] [PV] [-2000.003696]

EXERCISE 9.3

EXCEL NOTES

If you choose, you can use Excel's ***Present Value (PV)*** function to calculate the present value of an investment subject to compound interest. Refer to **PV** on the Spreadsheet Template Disk to learn how to use this Excel function.

A. Find the present value of each of the following amounts.

	Amount	Nominal Rate	Frequency of Conversion	Time
1.	$1000.00	8%	quarterly	7 years
2.	1500.00	6.5	semi-annually	10 years
3.	600.00	8	monthly	6 years
4.	350.00	7.5	annually	8 years
5.	1200.00	9	monthly	12 years
6.	3000.00	12.25	semi-annually	5 years, 6 months
7.	900.00	6.4	quarterly	9 years, 3 months
8.	500.00	8.4	monthly	15 years
9.	1500.00	4.5	annually	15 years, 9 months
10.	900.00	5.5	semi-annually	8 years, 10 months
11.	6400.00	7	quarterly	5 years, 7 months
12.	7200.00	6	monthly	21.5 months

B. Answer each of the following questions.

1. Find the present value and the compound discount of $1600 due four-and-a-half years from now if money is worth 4% compounded semi-annually.
2. Find the present value and the compound discount of $2500 due in six years, three months, if interest is 6% compounded quarterly.
3. Find the principal that will amount to $1250 in five years at 10% p.a. compounded quarterly.
4. What sum of money will grow to $2000 in seven years at 9% compounded monthly?
5. A debt of $5000 is due November 1, 2015. What is the value of the obligation on February 1, 2009, if money is worth 7% compounded quarterly?
6. How much would you have to deposit in an account today to have $3000 in a five-year term deposit at maturity if interest is 7.75% compounded annually?
7. What is the principal that will grow to $3000 in eight years, eight months at 9% compounded semi-annually?
8. Find the sum of money that accumulates to $1600 at 5% compounded quarterly in six years, four months.

9. You have the choice of receiving \$100 000 now or \$60 000 now and another \$60 000 five years from now. In terms of today's dollar, which choice is better and by how much? Money is worth 6% compounded annually.

10. In winning the lottery you have the choice of receiving \$50 000 now or \$20 000 now and \$35 000 two years from now. In terms of today's dollar, which choice is better and by how much? Money is worth 4.25% compounded annually.

11. Joe is negotiating the purchase of a sound system. He can either pay \$2000 now or pay \$100 now and \$2200 in eighteen months. Which option is better if money is worth 8% compounded monthly?

12. Jane is purchasing a membership in a fitness centre. She can pay either \$350 now or pay \$130 now, \$150 in twelve months, and \$170 in fifteen months. Which option is better if money is worth 7.5% compounded monthly?

9.4 APPLICATION—DISCOUNTING NEGOTIABLE FINANCIAL INSTRUMENTS AT COMPOUND INTEREST

A. Discounting long-term promissory notes

Long-term promissory notes (written for a term longer than one year) are usually subject to compound interest. Long-term promissory notes are negotiable and can be bought and sold (*discounted*) at any time before maturity. The principles involved in discounting long-term promissory notes are similar to those used in discounting short-term promissory notes by the simple discount method *except* that no requirement exists to add three days of grace in determining the legal due date of a long-term promissory note.

The discounted value (or proceeds) of a long-term promissory note is the present value at the date of discount of the maturity value of the note. It is found using the present value formula $PV = \frac{FV}{(1+i)^n}$ or $PV = FV(1+i)^{-n}$.

For non-interest-bearing notes, the maturity value is the face value. However, for interest-bearing promissory notes, the maturity value must be determined first by using the future value formula $FV = PV(1+i)^n$.

Like promissory notes, long-term bonds promise to pay a specific face value at a specified future point in time. In addition, there is a promise to periodically pay a specified amount of interest. Long-term bonds will be covered in detail in Chapter 15.

B. Discounting non-interest-bearing promissory notes

Since the face value of a non-interest-bearing note is also its maturity value, the proceeds of a non-interest-bearing note are the present value of its face value at the date of discount.

EXAMPLE 9.4A

Determine the proceeds of a non-interest-bearing note for $1500 discounted two-and-a-quarter years before its due date at 9% p.a. compounded monthly.

SOLUTION

The maturity value FV = 1500.00;

the rate of discount I/Y = 9; P/Y, C/Y = 12; $i = \frac{9\%}{12} = 0.75\% = 0.0075$;

the number of conversion periods $n = (2.25)(12) = 27$.

$$\begin{aligned} PV &= FV(1+i)^{-n} \quad \text{——— using restated Formula 9.1C} \\ &= 1500.00(1+0.0075)^{-27} \\ &= 1500.00\left(\frac{1}{1.223535}\right) \\ &= 1500.00(0.817304) \\ &= \$1225.96 \end{aligned}$$

Programmed Solution

(Set P/Y, C/Y = 12) [2nd] (CLR TVM) 1500 [FV] 9 [I/Y] 27 [N] [CPT] [PV]

[-1225.955705]

EXAMPLE 9.4B

A four-year, non-interest-bearing promissory note for $6000 dated August 31, 2008 was discounted on October 31, 2009 at 6% p.a. compounded quarterly. Determine the proceeds of the note.

SOLUTION

The due date of the note is August 31, 2012; the discount period October 31, 2009 to August 31, 2012 contains 2 years and 10 months.

FV = 6000.00; I/Y = 6; C/Y = 4; $i = \frac{6\%}{4} = 1.5\% = 0.015$;

$$n = \left(2\frac{10}{12}\right)(4) = 11\frac{1}{3} = 11.333333$$

$$\begin{aligned} PV &= FV(1+i)^{-n} \\ &= 6000.00(1+0.015)^{-11.333333} \\ &= 6000.00(0.844731) \\ &= \$5068.38 \end{aligned}$$

Programmed Solution

(Set P/Y, C/Y = 4) [2nd] (CLR TVM) 6000 [FV] 6 [I/Y] 11.333333 [N] [CPT]

[PV] [-5068.383399]

C. Discounting interest-bearing promissory notes

The proceeds of an interest-bearing note are equal to the present value at the date of discount of the value of the note at maturity. Therefore, the maturity value of an interest-bearing promissory note must be determined before finding the discounted value.

EXAMPLE 9.4C

Determine the proceeds of a promissory note for $3600 with interest at 6% p.a. compounded quarterly, issued September 1, 2008, due on June 1, 2014, and discounted on December 1, 2010 at 8% p.a. compounded semi-annually.

SOLUTION

STEP 1 Find the maturity value of the note using Formula 9.1A, FV 5 PV(1 1 i)n.

$PV = 3600.00$; $I/Y = 6$; $P/Y, C/Y = 4$; $i = \frac{6\%}{4} = 1.5\% = 0.015$; the interest period,

September 1, 2008 to June 1, 2014, contains 5 years and 9 months:
$n = (5\frac{9}{12})(4) = 23.$

$$\begin{aligned} FV &= 3600.00(1 + 0.015)^{23} \\ &= 3600.00(1.408377) \\ &= \$5070.16 \end{aligned}$$

STEP 2 Find the present value at the date of discount of the maturity value found in Step 1 using $PV = FV(1 + i)^{-n}$.

$FV = 5070.16$; $I/Y = 8$; $P/Y, C/Y = 2$; $i = \frac{8\%}{2} = 4\% = 0.04$;

the discount period, December 1, 2010 to June 1, 2014, contains 3 years and 6 months: $n = (3\frac{6}{12})(2) = 7.$

$$\begin{aligned} PV &= 5070.16(1 + 0.04)^{-7} \\ &= 5070.16(0.759918) \\ &= \$3852.90 \end{aligned}$$

The proceeds of the note on December 1, 2010 are $3852.90. The method and the data are represented graphically in Figure 9.6.

FIGURE 9.6 Graphical Representation of Method and Data

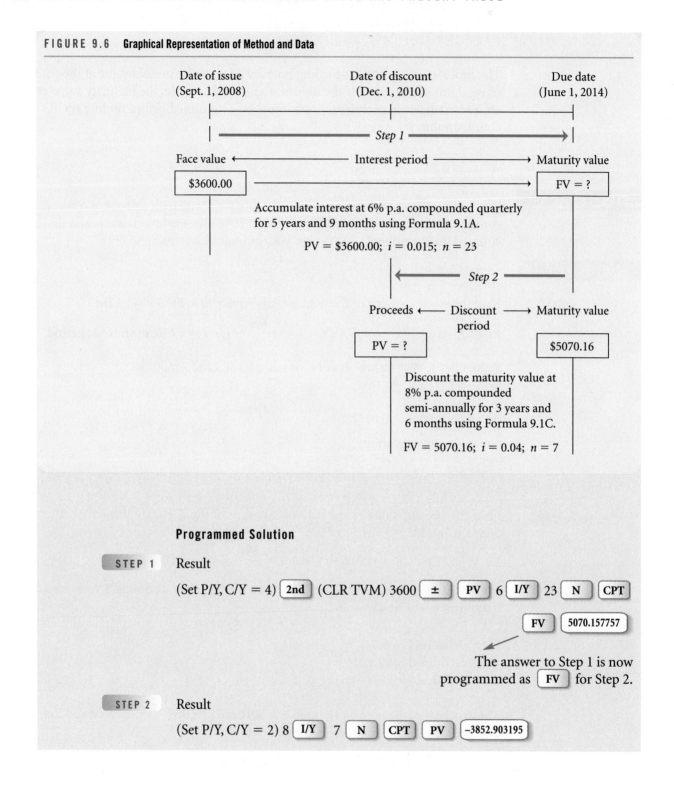

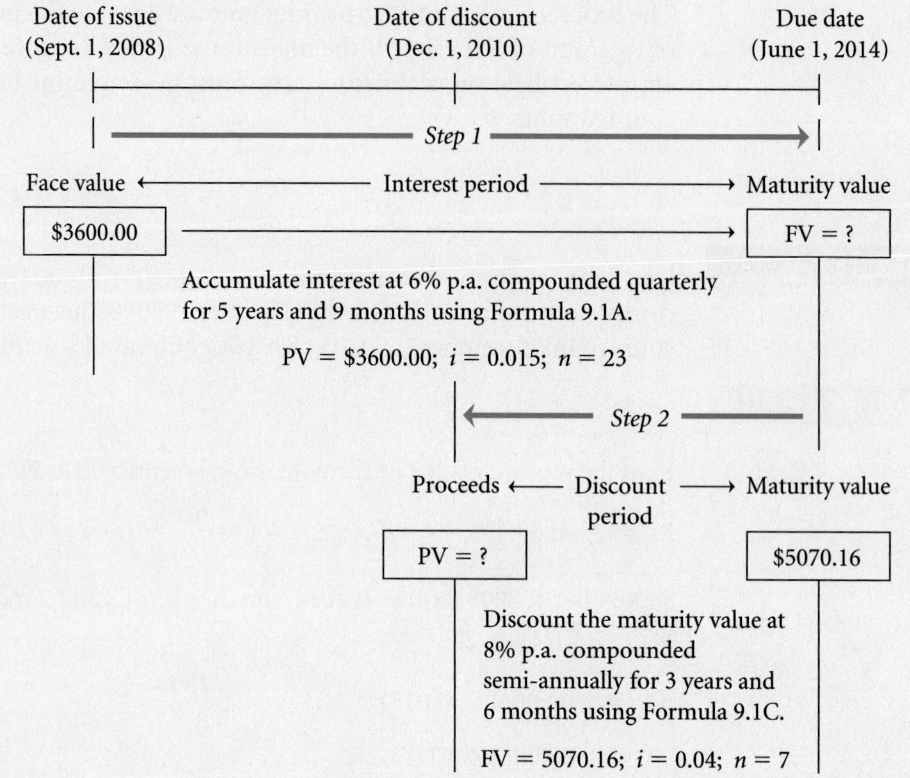

Programmed Solution

STEP 1 Result

(Set P/Y, C/Y = 4) 2nd (CLR TVM) 3600 ± PV 6 I/Y 23 N CPT FV 5070.157757

The answer to Step 1 is now programmed as FV for Step 2.

STEP 2 Result

(Set P/Y, C/Y = 2) 8 I/Y 7 N CPT PV −3852.903195

EXAMPLE 9.4D

A five-year note for $8000 bearing interest at 6% p.a. compounded monthly is discounted two years and five months before the due date at 5% p.a. compounded semi-annually. Determine the proceeds of the note.

SOLUTION

STEP 1 Find the maturity value using $FV = PV(1 + i)^n$.

$PV = 8000.00$; $I/Y = 6$; $P/Y, C/Y = 12$; $i = \frac{6\%}{12} = 0.5\% = 0.005$; $n = 60$

$$\begin{aligned} FV &= 8000.00(1.005)^{60} \\ &= 8000.00(1.348850) \\ &= \$10\,790.80 \end{aligned}$$

STEP 2 Find the present value of the maturity value found in Step 1 using $PV = FV(1 + i)^{-n}$.

$FV = 10\,790.80$; $I/Y = 5$; $P/Y = 2$; $i = \frac{5\%}{2} = 2.5\% = 0.025$;

$$n = \left(\frac{29}{12}\right)(2) = 4.833333$$

$$\begin{aligned} PV &= 10\,790.80(1.025)^{-4.833333} \\ &= 10\,790.80(0.887499) \\ &= \$9576.83 \end{aligned}$$

Programmed Solution

STEP 1 (Set P/Y, C/Y = 12) [2nd] (CLR TVM) 8000 [±] [PV] 6 [I/Y] 60 [N] [CPT] [FV] [10790.80122]

STEP 2 (Set P/Y, C/Y = 2) 5 [I/Y] 4.833333 [N] [CPT] [PV] [-9576.82776]

EXERCISE 9.4

EXCEL NOTES

If you choose, you can use Excel's ***Future Value (FV)*** or ***Present Value (PV)*** functions to answer the questions below. Refer to **FV** and **PV** on the Spreadsheet Template Disk to learn how to use these Excel functions.

A. Find the proceeds and the compound discount for each of the long-term promissory notes shown in the table below. Note that the first six are non-interest-bearing promissory notes.

	Face Value	Date of Issue	Term	Int. Rate	Frequency of Conversion	Date of Discount	Discount Rate	Frequency of Conversion
1.	$2000.00	30-06-2010	5 years	—	—	31-12-2012	5%	semi-annually
2.	700.00	01-04-2008	10 years	—	—	01-07-2013	10	quarterly
3.	5000.00	01-04-2008	10 years	—	—	01-08-2013	5	annually
4.	900.00	31-08-2009	8 years	—	—	30-06-2014	4	quarterly
5.	3200.00	31-03-2010	6 years	—	—	31-10-2013	8	quarterly
6.	1450.00	01-10-2007	9 years	—	—	01-12-2012	6	semi-annually
7.	780.00	30-09-2007	10 years	8%	annually	30-04-2011	8	quarterly
8.	2100.00	01-02-2006	12 years	6	monthly	01-07-2013	7	semi-annually
9.	1850.00	01-11-2012	5 years	10	quarterly	01-10-2014	9	semi-annually
10.	3400.00	31-01-2009	7 years	9	monthly	31-12-2013	7.5	quarterly
11.	1500.00	31-05-2009	8 years	7	annually	31-05-2014	8	semi-annually
12.	4000.00	30-09-2011	4 years	5	semi-annually	31-03-2013	4	quarterly
13.	800.00	01-02-2010	7.75 years	9	quarterly	01-11-2015	9	monthly
14.	2200.00	31-10-2009	8.25 years	6	monthly	31-01-2012	7	quarterly

B. Find the proceeds of each of the following promissory notes.

1. A non-interest-bearing promissory note for $6000, discounted 54 months before its due date at 6% compounded quarterly.

2. A $4200, non-interest-bearing note due August 1, 2014 discounted on March 1, 2010 at 7.5% compounded monthly.

3. A promissory note with a maturity value of $1800 due on September 30, 2011 discounted at 8.5% compounded semi-annually on March 31, 2008.

4. A fifteen-year promissory note discounted after six years at 9% compounded quarterly with a maturity value of $7500.

5. A five-year promissory note for $3000 with interest at 8% compounded semi-annually, discounted 21 months before maturity at 9% compounded quarterly.

6. A $5000, seven-year note bearing interest at 8.0% compounded quarterly, discounted two-and-a-half years after the date of issue at 6.0% compounded monthly.

7. A six-year, $900 note bearing interest at 10% compounded quarterly, issued June 1, 2007, discounted on December 1, 2012 to yield 8.5% compounded semi-annually.

8. A ten-year promissory note dated April 1, 2003, with a face value of $1300 bearing interest at 7% compounded semi-annually, discounted seven years later when money was worth 9% compounded quarterly.

C. Solve each of the following problems.

1. Determine the proceeds of an investment with a maturity value of $10 000 if discounted at 9% compounded monthly 22.5 months before the date of maturity.

2. Compute the discounted value of $7000 due in three years, five months if money is worth 8% compounded quarterly.

3. Find the discounted value of $3800 due in six years, eight months if interest is 7.5% compounded annually.

4. Calculate the proceeds of $5500 due in seven years, eight months discounted at 4.5% compounded semi-annually.

5. A four-year non-interest-bearing promissory note for $3750 is discounted 32 months after the date of issue at 5.5% compounded semi-annually. Find the proceeds of the note.

6. A seven-year non-interest-bearing note for $5200 is discounted three years, eight months before its due date at 9% compounded quarterly. Find the proceeds of the note.

7. A non-interest-bearing eight-year note for $4500 issued August 1, 2006 is discounted April 1, 2010 at 6.5% compounded annually. Find the compound discount.

8. A $2800 promissory note issued without interest for five years on September 30, 2008 is discounted on July 31, 2011 at 8% compounded quarterly. Find the compound discount.

9. A six-year note for $1750 issued on December 1, 2009, with interest at 6.5% compounded annually, is discounted on March 1, 2012 at 7% compounded semi-annually. What are the proceeds of the note?

10. A ten-year note for $1200 bearing interest at 6% compounded monthly is discounted at 8% compounded quarterly three years, ten months after the date of issue. Find the proceeds of the note.

11. Four years, seven months before its due date, a seven-year note for $2650 bearing interest at 9% compounded quarterly is discounted at 8% compounded semi-annually. Find the compound discount.

12. On April 15, 2014, a ten-year note dated June 15, 2009 is discounted at 10% compounded quarterly. If the face value of the note is $4000 and interest is 8% compounded quarterly, find the compound discount.

BUSINESS MATH NEWS BOX

Payday Loan Firm Charged "Criminal" Rates

A B.C. Supreme Court judge says a B.C. payday loan company was charging "criminal" rates of interest to clients borrowing to make it through to their next paycheque.

In the first class-action civil ruling of its kind in Canada, the multimillion-dollar decision is expected to create a ripple effect for payday loan companies across the country.

Justice Brenda Brown has ruled the processing fees and late fees charged by the A OK Payday Loans Inc. were interest.

The court heard during the trial in April that A OK charges a 21% interest rate and a processing fee of $9.50 for every $50 borrowed.

There is a $75 fee if a cheque is returned and if the borrower wants to put off a loan payment, A OK charges $25 for every $100 deferred.

"I accept the plaintiff's submission that if processing fees and late fees are interest, and their payment results in payments at a criminal rate, then A OK has necessarily received interest at a criminal rate," Brown said in a written ruling released Monday.

An expert testified that with fees added in, the interest rate was well above the 60% annual rate allowed under the Criminal Code.

Paul Bennett, the lawyer for the representative plaintiff Doris Kilroy, said they're very pleased with the ruling.

"This is the first decision in Canada that has been rendered in a class proceeding with respect to the fees charged to payday loan companies," he said.

Source: "Payday Loan Firm Charged 'Criminal' Rates, Judge Says," *Times-Colonist,* August 15, 2006, p. B.9 Copyright by the *Canadian Press.*

QUESTIONS

1. Suppose $1000 is borrowed for six months, and all processing fees are deducted when the cash is borrowed. Calculate the monthly payments required to pay back this amount. Assume a 60% rate of interest compounded monthly.
2. If $500 is borrowed for three months and payment is due at the end of this period and includes all processing fees, calculate the rate of interest if compounding is assumed to be monthly.
3. Assuming that the rate of interest is 60% per annum compounded quarterly, calculate the lump-sum final payment required in one month to pay off a $700 loan. Assume all processing fees are deducted when the transaction occurs.

9.5 EQUIVALENT VALUES

A. Equations of value

Because of the time value of money, amounts of money have different values at different times, as explained in Chapter 7. When sums of money fall due or are payable at different times, they are not directly comparable. To make such sums of money comparable, a point in time—the **comparison date** or **focal date**—must be chosen. Allowance must be made for interest from the due dates of the sums of money to the selected focal date; that is, the dated values of the sums of money must be determined.

Any point in time may be chosen as the focal date; the choice does not affect the final answers. It is advisable, however, to choose a date on which an amount is unknown. The choice of date determines which formula is to be used. For compound interest, equations of value need to be set up.

Which formula is appropriate depends on the position of the due dates relative to the focal date. The following rules apply:

(a) If an amount in the future of, or after, the focal date is to be determined, use the future value formula, $FV = PV(1 + i)^n$ (see Figure 9.7).

(b) If an amount in the past of, or before, the focal date is to be determined, use the present value formula, $PV = FV(1 + i)^{-n}$ (see Figure 9.8).

B. Finding the equivalent single payment

Equivalent values are the dated values of an original sum of money.

EXAMPLE 9.5A

\$4000 is due for payment three years from now. If money is worth 9% p.a. compounded semi-annually, determine the equivalent value

(i) seven years from now; (ii) now.

SOLUTION

(i) Using "seven years from now" as the focal date, the method and the data can be represented graphically as shown in Figure 9.7.

FIGURE 9.7 Graphical Representation of Method and Data

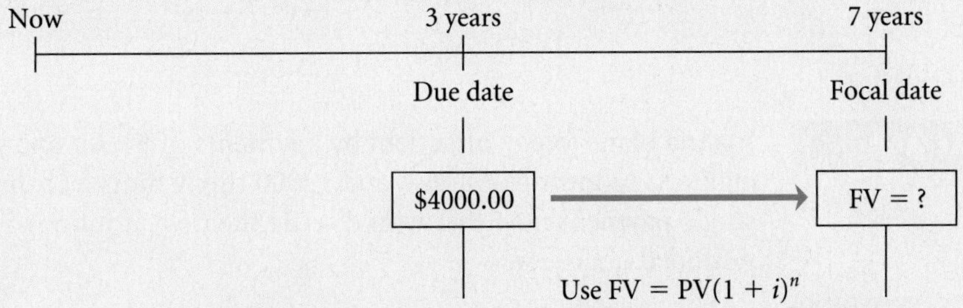

Since the due date falls *before* the focal date, use the future value formula.

$PV = 4000.00$; $I/Y = 9$; $P/Y, C/Y = 2$; $i = \dfrac{9\%}{2} = 0.045$; $n = 4(2) = 8$

$FV = 4000.00(1 + 0.045)^8 = 4000.00(1.422101) = \$5688.40$

The equivalent value of the \$4000 seven years from now is \$5688.40.

(ii) Using "now" as the focal date, the method and the data can be represented graphically as shown in Figure 9.8.

FIGURE 9.8 **Graphical Representation of Method and Data**

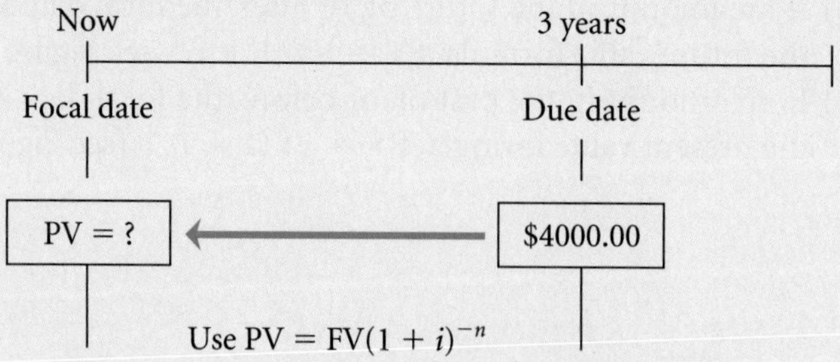

Since the due date falls *after* the focal date, use the present value formula.

$FV = 4000.00; i = \frac{9\%}{2} = 0.045; n = 3(2) = 6$

$PV = 4000.00(1 + 0.045)^{-6} = 4000.00(0.767896) = \$3071.58$

The equivalent value of the $4000.00 now is $3017.58.

Programmed Solution

(i) (Set P/Y, C/Y = 2) [2nd] (CLR TVM) 4000 [±] [PV] 9 [I/Y]

8 [N] [CPT] [FV] [5688.402451]

(ii) [2nd] (CLR TVM) 4000 [FV] 9 [I/Y] 6 [N] [CPT] [PV] [-3071.582953]

EXAMPLE 9.5B

Joanna plans to pay off a debt by payments of $1600 one year from now, $1800 eighteen months from now, and $2000 thirty months from now. Determine the single payment now that would settle the debt if money is worth 8% p.a. compounded quarterly.

SOLUTION

While any date may be selected as the focal date, a logical choice for the focal date is the time designated "now," since the single payment "now" is wanted. As is shown in Figure 9.9, the due dates of the three scheduled payments are after the focal date. Therefore, the present value formula $PV = FV(1 + i)^{-n}$ is appropriate for finding the equivalent values of each of the three scheduled payments.

The equivalents of the three scheduled payments at the selected focal date are

$PV_1 = 1600.00(1 + 0.02)^{-4} = 1600.00(0.923845) = \$1478.15$

$PV_2 = 1800.00(1 + 0.02)^{-6} = 1800.00(0.887971) = \$1598.35$

$PV_3 = 2000.00(1 + 0.02)^{-10} = 2000.00(0.820348) = \$1640.70$

The equivalent single payment to settle the debt now is $4717.20.

FIGURE 9.9 Graphical Representation of Method and Data

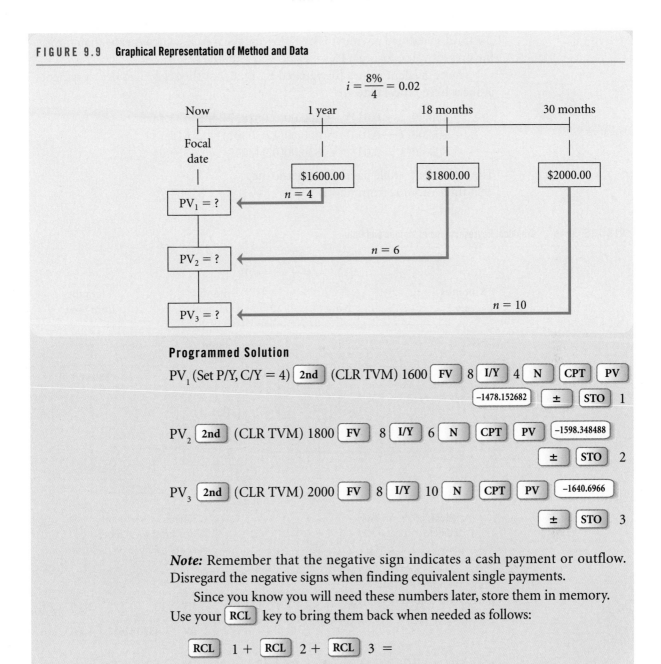

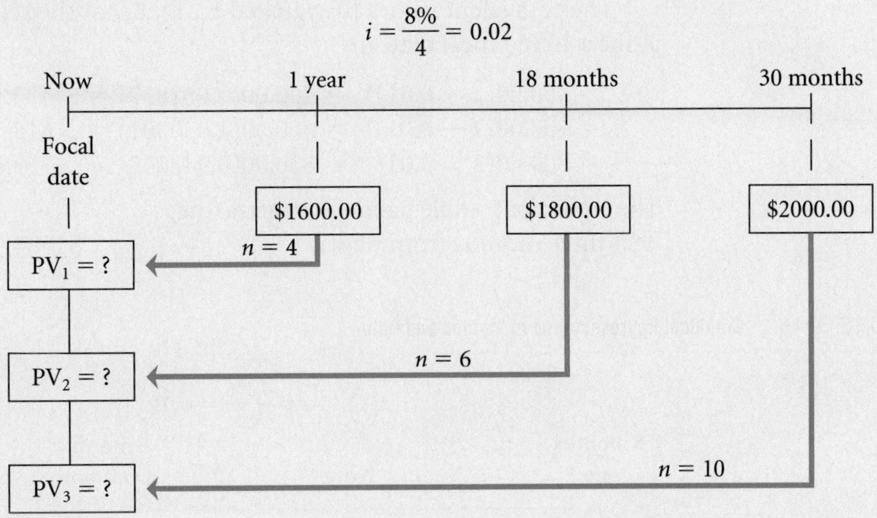

Programmed Solution

PV_1 (Set P/Y, C/Y = 4) [2nd] (CLR TVM) 1600 [FV] 8 [I/Y] 4 [N] [CPT] [PV] [−1478.152682] [±] [STO] 1

PV_2 [2nd] (CLR TVM) 1800 [FV] 8 [I/Y] 6 [N] [CPT] [PV] [−1598.348488] [±] [STO] 2

PV_3 [2nd] (CLR TVM) 2000 [FV] 8 [I/Y] 10 [N] [CPT] [PV] [−1640.6966] [±] [STO] 3

Note: Remember that the negative sign indicates a cash payment or outflow. Disregard the negative signs when finding equivalent single payments.

Since you know you will need these numbers later, store them in memory. Use your [RCL] key to bring them back when needed as follows:

[RCL] 1 + [RCL] 2 + [RCL] 3 =

1478.152682 + 1598.348488 + 1640.6966 = 4717.19777 = $4717.20

EXAMPLE 9.5C

Debt payments of $400 due five months ago, $600 due today, and $800 due in nine months are to be combined into one payment due three months from today at 12% p.a. compounded monthly.

SOLUTION

The logical choice for the focal date is "3 months from now," the date when the equivalent single payment is to be made.

As shown in Figure 9.10, the first two scheduled payments are due before the focal date; the future value formula $FV = PV(1 + i)^n$ should be used. However, the third scheduled payment is due *after* the focal date, which means that, for it, the present value formula $PV = FV(1 + i)^{-n}$ applies.

The equivalent values (designated E_1, E_2, E_3) of the scheduled debt payments at the selected focal date are

$$E_1 = 400.00(1 + 0.01)^8 = 400.00(1.082857) = \$\ 433.14$$
$$E_2 = 600.00(1 + 0.01)^3 = 600.00(1.030301) = 618.18$$
$$E_3 = 800.00(1 + 0.01)^{-6} = 800.00(0.942045) = 753.64$$

The equivalent single payment to settle the debt three months from now is $1804.96

FIGURE 9.10 Graphical Representation of Method and Data

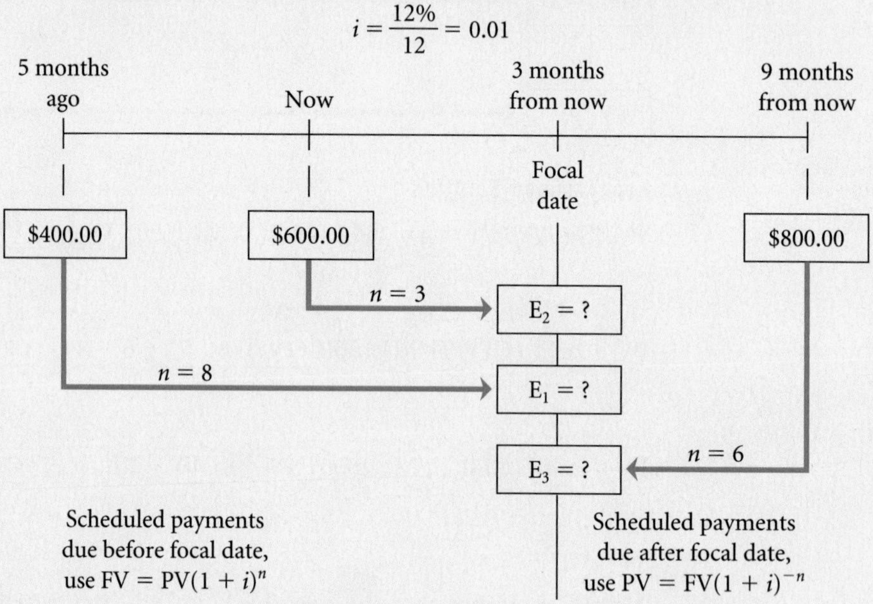

Programmed Solution

E_1 (Set P/Y, C/Y = 12) 2nd (CLR TVM) 400 ± PV 12 I/Y 8 N CPT FV 433.142682 STO 1

E_2 2nd (CLR TVM) 600 ± PV 12 I/Y 3 N CPT FV 618.1806 STO 2

E_3 2nd (CLR TVM) 800 FV 12 I/Y 6 N CPT PV −753.636188 ± STO 3

Remember to treat this payment as a positive amount.

RCL 1 + RCL 2 + RCL 3

433.142682 + 618.1806 + 753.636188 = 1804.959470 = $1804.96

EXAMPLE 9.5D

Payments of \$500 are due at the end of each of the next five years. Determine the equivalent single payment five years from now (just after the last scheduled payment is due) if money is worth 10% p.a. compounded annually.

SOLUTION

Select as the focal date "five years from now."

Let the equivalent single payment be represented by E and the dated values of the first four scheduled payments be represented by E_1, E_2, E_3, E_4 as indicated in Figure 9.11. Then the following equation of values can be set up.

$$
\begin{aligned}
E &= 500.00 + E_4 + E_3 + E_2 + E_1 \\
&= 500.00 + 500.00(1.1) + 500.00(1.1)^2 + 500.00(1.1)^3 + 500.00(1.1)^4 \\
&= 500.00[1 + (1.1) + (1.1)^2 + (1.1)^3 + (1.1)^4] \\
&= 500.00(1 + 1.1 + 1.21 + 1.331 + 1.4641) \\
&= 500.00(6.1051) \\
&= \$3052.55
\end{aligned}
$$

The equivalent single payment after five years is \$3052.55.

FIGURE 9.11 Graphical Representation of Method and Data

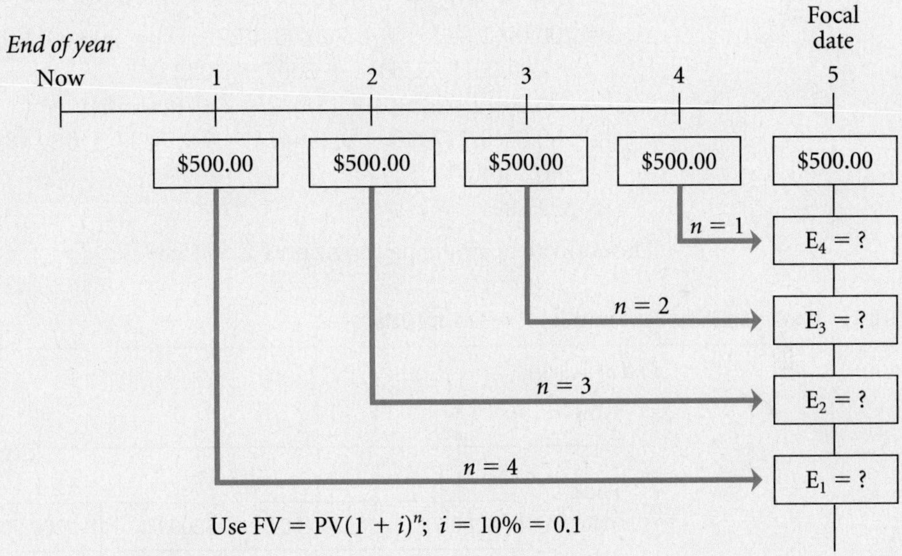

Programmed Solution

(Set P/Y, C/Y =1) E_1 [2nd] (CLR TVM) 500 [±] [PV] 10 [I/Y] 4 [N]

[CPT] [FV] [732.05] [STO] 1

E_2 [2nd] (CLR TVM) 500 [±] [PV] 10 [I/Y] 3 [N]

[CPT] [FV] [665.50] [STO] 2

E_3 [2nd] (CLR TVM) 500 [±] [PV] 10 [I/Y] 2 [N]

[CPT] [FV] [605.00] [STO] 3

E_4 [2nd] (CLR TVM) 500 [±] [PV] 10 [I/Y] 1 [N] [CPT] [FV] 550.00 [STO] 4

[RCL] 1 + [RCL] 2 + [RCL] 3 + [RCL] 4 + 500 =

or

732.05 + 665.50 + 605.00 + 550.00 + 500.00 = \$3052.55

EXAMPLE 9.5E

Payments of \$200 are due at the end of each of the next five quarters. Determine the equivalent single payment that will settle the debt now if interest is 9% p.a. compounded quarterly.

SOLUTION

Select as the focal date "now."

Let the equivalent single payment be represented by E and the dated values of the five scheduled payments by E_1, E_2, E_3, E_4, E_5 respectively as shown in Figure 9.12.

Then the following equation of values can be set up.

$$\begin{aligned}E &= E_1 + E_2 + E_3 + E_4 + E_5\\ &= 200.00(1.0225)^{-1} + 200.00(1.0225)^{-2} + 200.00(1.0225)^{-3}\\ &\quad + 200.00(1.0225)^{-4} + 200.00(1.0225)^{-5}\\ &= 200.00[(1.0225)^{-1} + (1.0225)^{-2} + (1.0225)^{-3} + (1.0225)^{-4} + (1.0225)^{-5}]\\ &= 200.00(0.977995 + 0.956474 + 0.935427 + 0.914843 + 0.894712)\\ &= 200.00(4.679452)\\ &= \$935.89\end{aligned}$$

The equivalent single payment now is \$935.89.

FIGURE 9.12 Graphical Representation of Method and Data

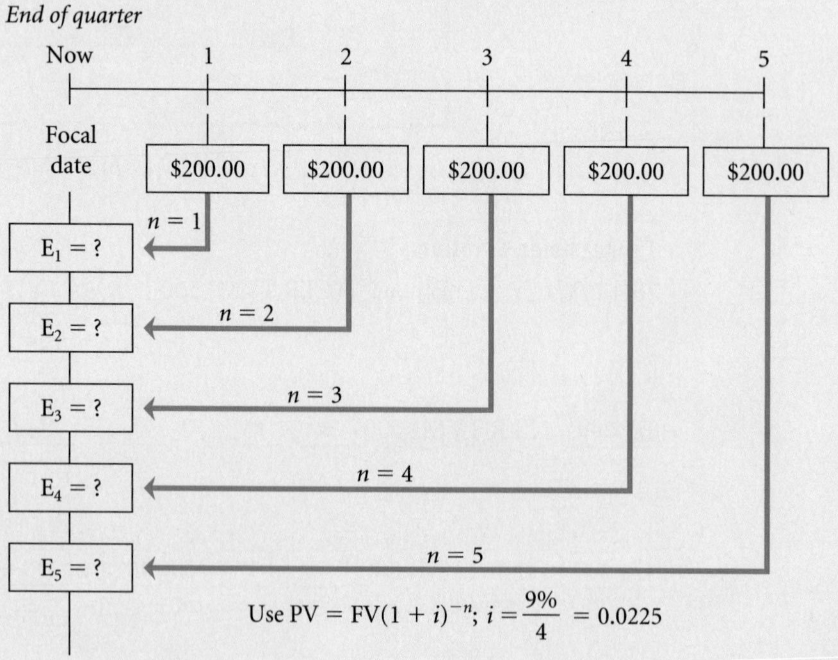

Programmed Solution

(Set P/Y, C/Y = 4) E_1 2nd (CLR TVM) 200 FV 9 I/Y 1 N

CPT PV -195.599022 ± STO 1

E_2 2nd (CLR TVM) 200 FV 9 I/Y 2 N

CPT PV -191.294887 ± STO 2

E_3 2nd (CLR TVM) 200 PV 9 I/Y 3 N CPT PV

-187.085464 ± STO 3

E_4 2nd (CLR TVM) 200 FV 9 I/Y 4 N CPT PV

-182.968669 ± STO 4

E_5 2nd (CLR TVM) 200 PV 9 I/Y 5 N CPT PV

-178.942464 ± STO 5

Remember to treat these payments as positive amounts.

RCL 1 + RCL 2 + RCL 3 + RCL 4 + RCL 5 =

195.599022 + 191.294887 + 187.085464 + 182.968669 + 178.942464 =
935.890506 = \$935.89

C. Finding the value of two or more equivalent replacement payments

When two or more equivalent replacement payments are needed, an equation of values matching the dated values of the original scheduled payments against the dated values of the proposed replacement payments on a selected focal date should be set up. This procedure is similar to the one used for simple interest in Chapter 7.

EXAMPLE 9.5F

Scheduled debt payments of \$1000 due today and \$2000 due one year from now are to be settled by a payment of \$1500 three months from now and a final payment eighteen months from now. Determine the size of the final payment if interest is 10% p.a. compounded quarterly.

SOLUTION

Let the size of the final payment be \$$x$. The logical focal date is the date of the final payment.

As shown in Figure 9.13, the two original scheduled debt payments and the first replacement payment are due before the selected focal date. The future value formula $FV = PV(1 + i)^n$ applies. Because the final payment is dated on the focal date, its dated value is \$$x$.

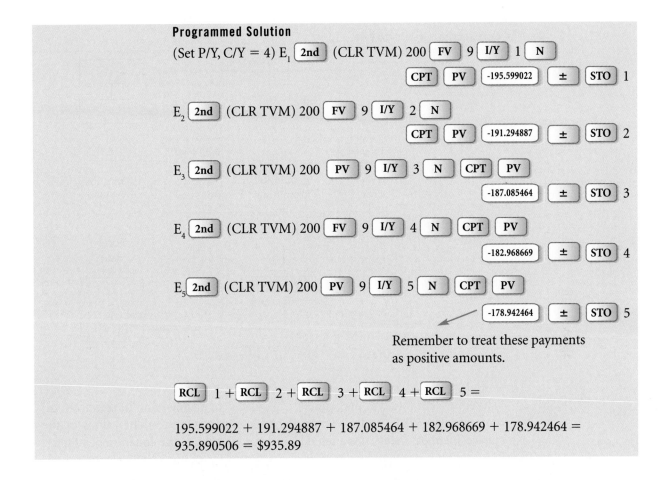

FIGURE 9.13 **Graphical Representation of Method and Data**

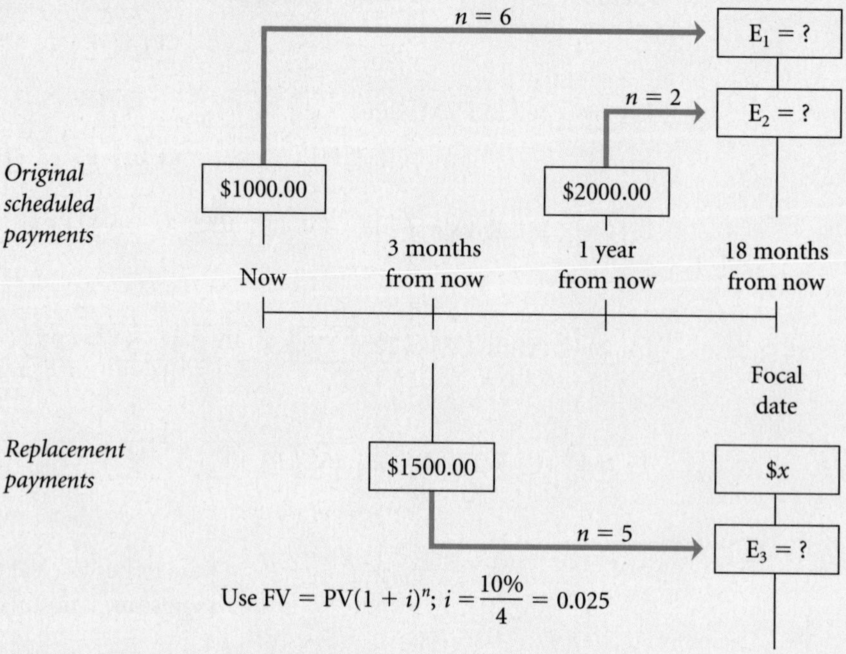

The equivalent values of the original scheduled debt payments at the selected focal date, designated E_1 and E_2, are matched against the equivalent values of the replacement payments, designated E_3 and x, giving rise to the equation of values.

$$E_1 + E_2 = x + E_3$$
$$1000.00(1.025)^6 + 2000.00(1.025)^2 = x + 1500.00(1.025)^5$$
$$1000.00(1.159693) + 2000.00(1.050625) = x + 1500.00(1.131408)$$
$$1159.69 + 2101.25 = x + 1697.11$$
$$x = 1563.83$$

The final payment is $1563.83.

Programmed Solution

E_1 (Set P/Y, C/Y = 4) [2nd] (CLR TVM) 1000 [±] [PV] 10 [I/Y] 6 [N] [CPT] [FV] [1159.693418] [STO] 1

E_2 [2nd] (CLR TVM) 2000 [±] [PV] 10 [I/Y] 2 [N] [CPT] [FV] [2101.25] [STO] 2

E_3 [2nd] (CLR TVM) 1500 [±] [PV] 10 [I/Y] 5 [N] [CPT] [FV] [1697.11239] [STO] 3

[RCL] 1 + [RCL] 2 − [RCL] 3 = x

$$1159.693418 + 2101.25 = x + 1697.112319$$
$$x = 1563.831099$$

EXAMPLE 9.5G

What is the size of the equal payments that must be made at the end of each of the next five years to settle a debt of \$5000 due in five years if money is worth 9% p.a. compounded annually?

SOLUTION

Select as the focal date "five years from now." Let the equal payments be represented by \$x and let the dated values of the first four payments be represented by E_1, E_2, E_3, and E_4 respectively as shown in Figure 9.14.

Then the equation of values may be set up.

$$5000.00 = x + E_4 + E_3 + E_2 + E_1$$
$$5000.00 = x + x(1.09) + x(1.09)^2 + x(1.09)^3 + x(1.09)^4$$
$$5000.00 = x[1 + (1.09) + (1.09)^2 + (1.09)^3 + (1.09)^4]$$
$$5000.00 = x(1 + 1.09 + 1.1881 + 1.295029 + 1.411582)$$
$$5000.00 = 5.984711x$$
$$x = \$835.46$$

The size of the equal payments is \$835.46.

FIGURE 9.14 Graphical Representation of Method and Data

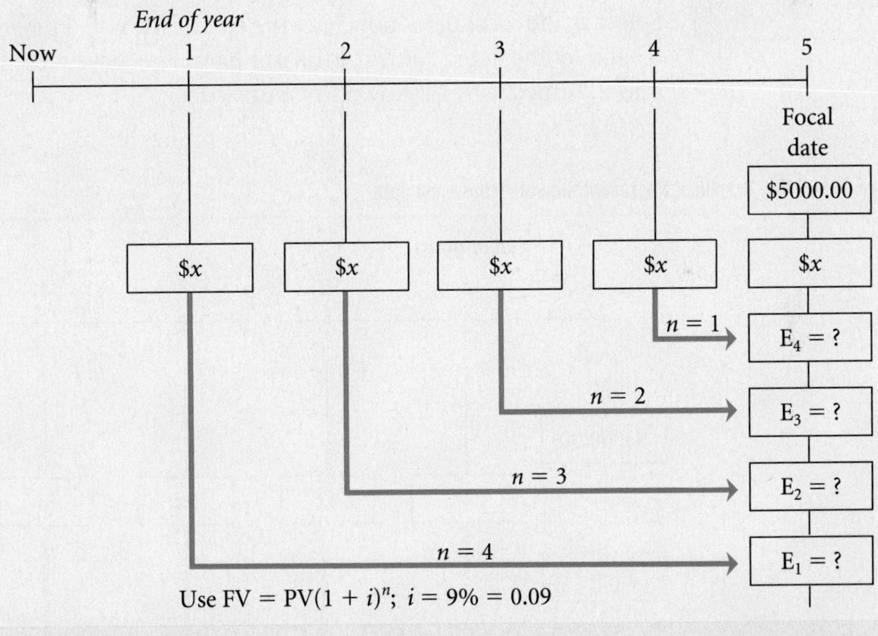

Programmed Solution

(Set P/Y, C/Y = 1) E_1 [2nd] (CLR TVM) 1 [±] [PV] 9 [I/Y] 4 [N] [CPT] [FV] [1.411582] [STO] 1

E_2 [2nd] (CLR TVM) 1 [±] [PV] 9 [I/Y] 3 [N] [CPT] [FV] [1.295029] [STO] 2

E_3 [2nd] (CLR TVM) 1 [±] [PV] 9 [I/Y] 2 [N] [CPT] [FV]

[1.1881] [STO] 3

E_4 [2nd] (CLR TVM) 1 [±] [PV] 9 [I/Y] 1 [N] [CPT] [FV]

[1.09] [STO] 4

[RCL] 1 + [RCL] 2 + [RCL] 3 + [RCL] 4 + 1 = 5.984711 [STO] 5

or

$$1.411582x + 1.295029x + 1.1881x + 1.09x + x = \$5000.00$$
$$5.984711x = \$5000.00$$
$$x = \$835.46 \quad (5000 \div [RCL]\ 5 =)$$

EXAMPLE 9.5H

What is the size of the equal payments that must be made at the end of each of the next five quarters to settle a debt of $3000 due now if money is worth 12% p.a. compounded quarterly?

SOLUTION

Select as the focal date "now." Let the size of the equal payments be represented by $x and let the dated values of the five payments be represented by E_1, E_2, E_3, E_4, and E_5 respectively as shown in Figure 9.15.

FIGURE 9.15 **Graphical Representation of Method and Data**

$$\text{Use PV} = \text{FV}(1 + i)^{-n}; \ i = \frac{12\%}{4} = 0.03$$

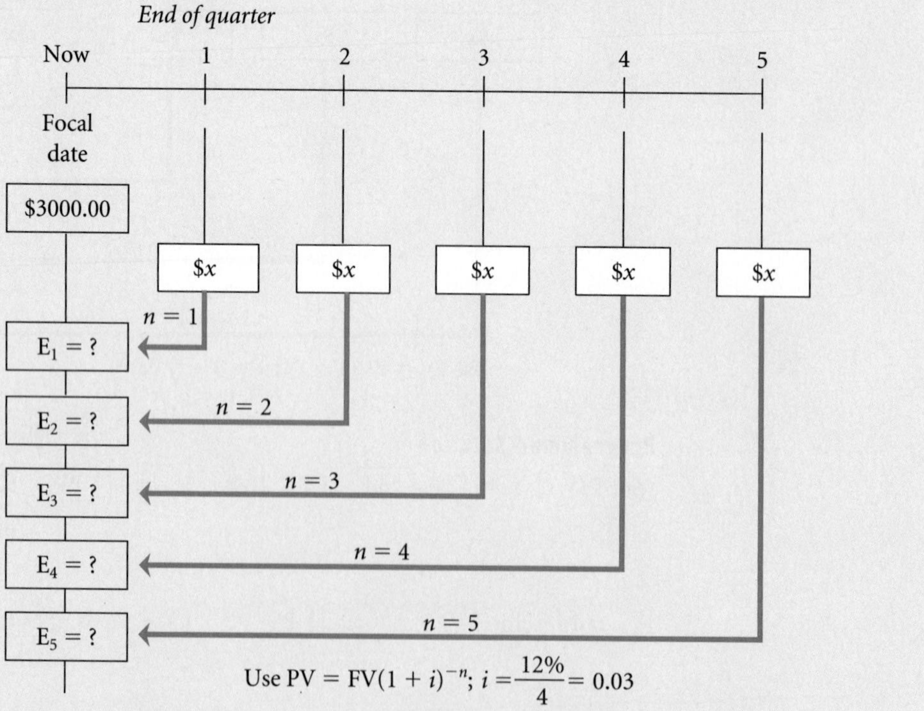

Then the equation of values may be set up.

$3000.00 = E_1 + E_2 + E_3 + E_4 + E_5$

$3000.00 = x(1.03)^{-1} + x(1.03)^{-2} + x(1.03)^{-3} + x(1.03)^{-4} + x(1.03)^{-5}$

$3000.00 = x[(1.03)^{-1} + (1.03)^{-2} + (1.03)^{-3} + (1.03)^{-4} + (1.03)^{-5}]$

$3000.00 = x(0.970874 + 0.942596 + 0.915142 + 0.888487 + 0.862609)$

$3000.00 = 4.579707x$

$$x = \frac{3000.00}{4.579707}$$

$x = \$655.06$

The size of the equal payments is $655.06.

Programmed Solution

(Set P/Y = 4) E_1 2nd (CLR TVM) 1 FV 12 I/Y 1 N CPT PV -0.970874 ± STO 1

E_2 2nd (CLR TVM) 1 FV 12 I/Y 2 N CPT PV -0.942596 ± STO 2

E_3 2nd (CLR TVM) 1 FV 12 I/Y 3 N CPT PV -0.915142 ± STO 3

E_4 2nd (CLR TVM) 1 FV 12 I/Y 4 N CPT PV -0.888487 ± STO 4

E_5 2nd (CLR TVM) 1 FV 12 I/Y 5 N CPT PV -0.862609 ± STO 5

Remember to treat these payments as positive amounts.

RCL 1 + RCL 2 + RCL 3 + RCL 4 + RCL 5 = 4.594707 STO 6

$0.970874x + 0.942596x + 0.915142x + 0.888487x + 0.862609x = \$3000.00$

$4.579707x = \$3000.00$

$x = \$655.06$ (3000 ÷ RCL 6 =)

EXAMPLE 9.5I

Scheduled debt payments of $750 due seven months ago, $600 due two months ago, and $900 due in five months are to be settled by two equal replacement payments due now and three months from now respectively. Determine the size of the equal replacement payments at 9% p.a. compounded monthly.

SOLUTION

Let the size of the equal replacement payments be represented by $x and choose "now" as the focal date.

I/Y= 9; P/Y, C/Y = 12; $i = \frac{9\%}{12} = 0.0075$

Figure 9.16 shows the method and data.

FIGURE 9.16 Graphical Representation of Method and Data

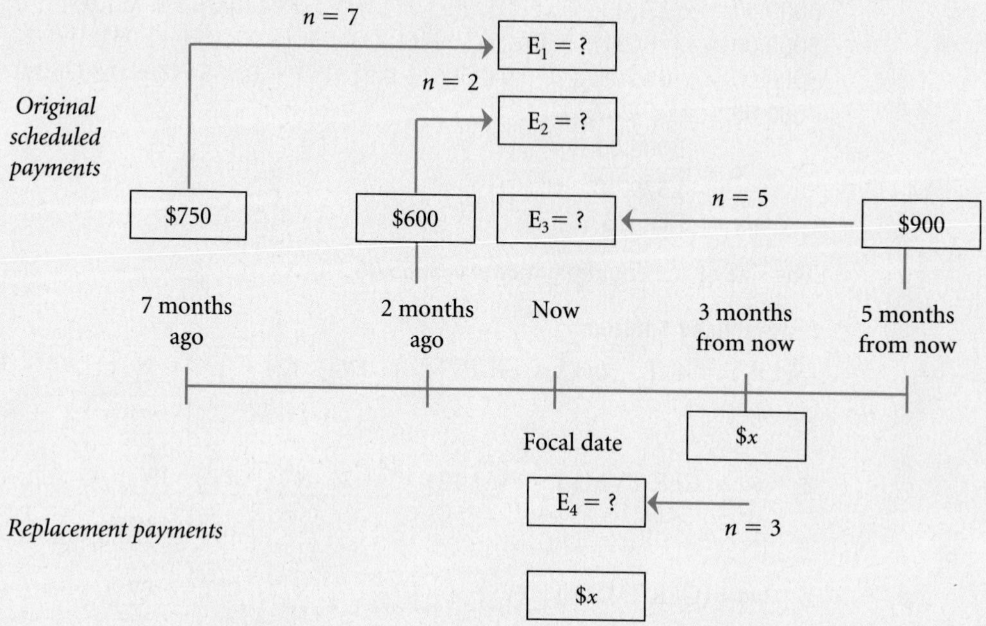

STEP 1 DATED VALUES OF SCHEDULED PAYMENTS

First, consider the dated values of the original scheduled debt payments at the chosen focal date.

The due dates of the debt payments of \$750 and \$600 are seven months and two months respectively before the focal date. Their dated values at the focal date are $750.00(1.0075)^7$ and $600.00(1.0075)^2$, represented by E_1 and E_2 respectively.

The due date of the scheduled payment of \$900 is five months after the focal date. Its dated value is $900.00(1.0075)^{-5}$, shown as E_3.

STEP 2 DATED VALUES OF REPLACEMENT PAYMENTS

Second, consider the dated values of the replacement payments at the selected focal date.

The first replacement payment due at the focal date is \$$x$. The second replacement payment is due three months after the focal date. Its dated value is $x(1.0075)^{-3}$, shown as E_4.

STEP 3 EQUATION OF DATED VALUES

Now equate the dated values of the replacement payments with the dated values of the original scheduled debt payments to set up the equation of values.

$$x + x(1.0075)^{-3} = 750.00(1.0075)^7 + 600.00(1.0075)^2 + 900.00(1.0075)^{-5}$$
$$x + 0.977833x = 750.00(1.053696) + 600.00(1.015056) + 900.00(0.963329)$$
$$1.977833x = 790.27 + 609.03 + 867.00$$

$1.977833x = 2266.30$

$$x = \frac{2266.30}{1.9778333}$$

$x = \$1145.85$

The size of the two equal payments is \$1145.85.

For E_1 and E_2, use $FV = PV(1 + i)^n$; $i = \frac{9\%}{12} = 0.0075$

For E_3 and E_4, use or $PV = FV(1 + i)^{-n}$; $i = \frac{9\%}{12} = 0.0075$

Programmed Solution

$x + x(1.0075)^{-3}$

(Set P/Y, C/Y = 12) [2nd] (CLR TVM) 1 [FV] 9 [I/Y] 3 [N] [CPT] [PV]

[-0.977833] [±] [STO] 1 (E_4)

$x + 0.977833x$

$750(1.0075)^7$

[2nd] (CLR TVM) 750 [±] [PV] 9 [I/Y] 7 [N] [CPT] [FV]

[790.272095] [STO] 2 (E_1)

$600(1.0075)^2$

[2nd] (CLR TVM) 600 [±] [PV] 9 [I/Y] 2 [N] [CPT] [FV]

[609.03375] [STO] 3 (E_2)

$900(1.0075)^{-5}$

[2nd] (CLR TVM) 900 [FV] 9 [I/Y] 5 [N] [CPT] [PV]

[–866.996283] [±] [STO] 4 (E_3)

1 + [RCL] 1 = [STO] 5 [RCL] 2 + [RCL] 3 + [RCL] 4 = [STO] 6

or $x + (E_4) = (E_1) + (E_2) + (E_3)$

$x + 0.977833x = 790.272095 + 609.03375 + 866.996283$

$1.977833x = 2266.302128$

$x = 1145.85$ ([RCL] 6 ÷ [RCL] 5 =)

Note: In $x(1.0075)^{-3}$, [FV] is not known. To obtain the factor $(1.0075)^{-3}$, use

[FV] = 1.

EXAMPLE 9.5J

Two scheduled payments, one of \$4000 due in three months with interest at 9% compounded quarterly and the other of \$3000 due in eighteen months with interest at 8.5% compounded semi-annually, are to be discharged by making two equal replacement payments. What is the size of the equal replacement payments if the first is due one year from now, the second two years from now, and money is now worth 10% compounded monthly?

SOLUTION

Let the size of the equal replacement payments be represented by \$$x$. Choose "one year from now" as the focal date.

Figure 9.17 illustrates the problem.

FIGURE 9.17 Graphical Representation of Method and Data

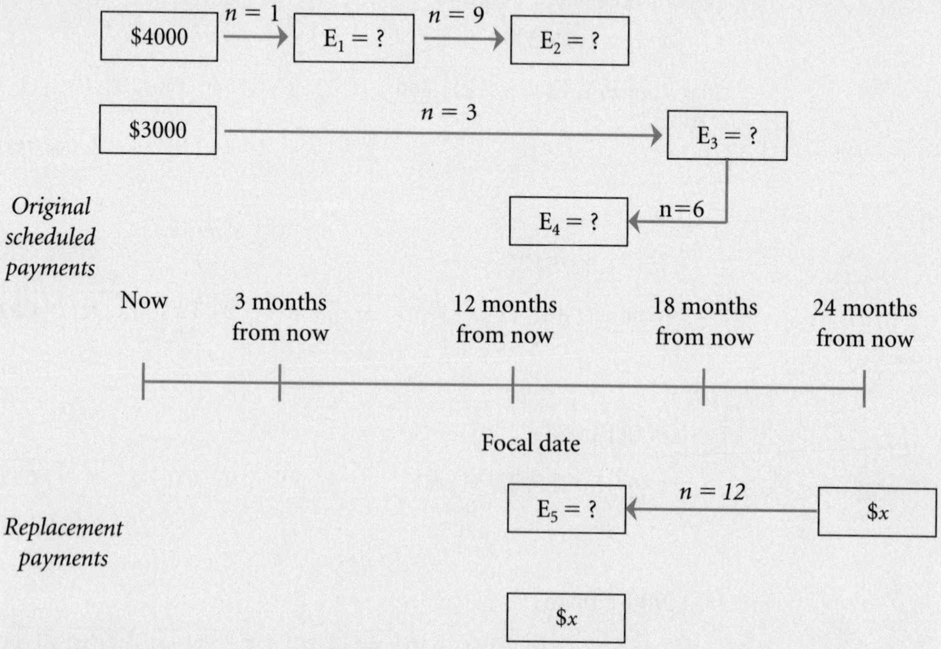

STEP 1 MATURITY VALUES OF SCHEDULED PAYMENTS

Since the two scheduled payments are interest-bearing, first determine their maturity value.

The maturity value of \$4000 due in three months at 9% compounded quarterly $= 4000(1.0225)^1 = \$4090.00$, shown as E_1.

The maturity value of \$3000 due in eighteen months at 8.5% compounded semi-annually $= 3000(1.0425)^3 = 3000(1.1329955) = \$3398.99$, shown as E_3.

STEP 2 DATED VALUES OF SCHEDULED PAYMENTS

Now determine the dated values of the two maturity values at the selected focal date subject to 10% compounded monthly.

The first scheduled payment matures nine months *before* the selected focal date. Its dated value $= 4090.00(1.008333)^9 = 4090.00(1.077549) = \$4407.18$, shown as E_2.

The second scheduled payment matures six months *after* the selected focal date. Its dated value = $3398.99(1.008333)^{-6} = 3398.99(0.951427) = \$3233.89$, shown as E_4.

STEP 3 DATED VALUES OF REPLACEMENTS PAYMENTS

The dated values of the two replacement payments at the selected focal date are $\$x$ and $\$x(1.008333)^{-12}$, shown as E_5.

STEP 4 EQUATION OF VALUES

Therefore, the equation of values is

$$x + x(1.008333)^{-12} = 4407.18 + 3233.89$$

$$x + 0.905212x = 7641.07$$

$$x = \frac{7641.07}{1.905212}$$

$$x = \$4010.61$$

The size of the two equal replacement payments is \$4010.61.

For E_1 use $FV = PV(1 + i)^n$; $i = \frac{9\%}{4} = 0.0225$

For E_3 use $FV = PV(1 + i)^n$; $i = \frac{8.5\%}{2} = 0.0425$

For E_2 use $FV = PV(1 + i)^n$; $i = \frac{10\%}{12} = 0.008333$

For E_4 and E_5, use $PV = \frac{FV}{(1 + i)^n}$ or $PV = FV(1 + i)^{-n}$; $i = \frac{10\%}{12} = 0.008333$

Programmed Solution

Maturity value of \$4000

(Set P/Y, C/Y = 4) 2nd (CLR TVM) 4000 ± PV 9 I/Y 1 N CPT FV 4090 STO 1

Maturity value of \$3000

(Set P/Y, C/Y = 2) 2nd (CLR TVM)3000 ± PV 8.5 I/Y 3 N CPT FV 3398.98656 STO 2

$x + x(1.008333)^{-12}$

(Set P/Y, C/Y = 12) 2nd (CLR TVM) 1 FV 10 I/Y 12 N CPT PV -0.9052124 ± STO 3

This gives $x + 0.905212x$.

2nd (CLR TVM) 4090 ± PV 10 I/Y 9 N CPT FV 4407.176326 STO 4

[2nd] (CLR TVM) 3398.986547 [FV] 10 [I/Y] 6 [N] [CPT] [PV]

[-3233.885954] [±] [STO] 5

1 + [RCL] 3 = [STO] 6

[RCL] 4 + [RCL] 5 = [STO] 7

$$x + 0.905212x = 4407.176326 + 3233.885594$$
$$1.905212x = 7641.062280$$
$$x = 4010.61$$ ([RCL] 7 ÷ [RCL] 6 =)

EXERCISE 9.5

EXCEL NOTES

If you choose, you can use Excel's ***Future Value (FV)*** or ***Present Value (PV)*** functions to answer the questions below. Refer to **FV** and **PV** on the Spreadsheet Template Disk to learn how to use these Excel functions.

A. Find the equivalent single replacement payment on the given focal date for each of the following eight situations.

	Scheduled Payments	Int. Rate	Frequency of Conversion	Focal Date
1.	\$5000.00 due in 2 years	6%	monthly	5 years from now
2.	\$1600.00 due in 18 months	8%	quarterly	42 months from now
3.	\$3400.00 due in 4 years	10%	semi-annually	1 year from now
4.	\$2700.00 due in 60 months	7%	quarterly	6 months from now
5.	\$800.00 due in 6 months and \$700.00 due in 15 months	9.5%	monthly	2 years from now
6.	\$1000.00 due in 9 months and \$1200.00 due in 18 months	8.8%	quarterly	3 years from now
7.	\$400.00 due in 3 years and \$600.00 due in 5 years	11%	semi-annually	now
8.	\$2000.00 due in 20 months and \$1500.00 due in 40 months	10.5%	monthly	9 months from now

B. Solve each of the following problems.

1. A loan of \$4000 is due in five years. If money is worth 7% compounded annually, find the equivalent payment that would settle the debt
(a) now; **(b)** in 2 years; **(c)** in 5 years; **(d)** in 10 years.

2. A debt payment of \$5500 is due in 27 months. If money is worth 8.4% p.a. compounded quarterly, what is the equivalent payment
(a) now? **(b)** 15 months from now?
(c) 27 months from now? **(d)** 36 months from now?

3. A debt can be paid by payments of $2000 scheduled today, $2000 scheduled in three years, and $2000 scheduled in six years. What single payment would settle the debt four years from now if money is worth 10% compounded semi-annually?
Reference Example 9.5A

4. Scheduled payments of $600, $800, and $1200 are due in one year, three years, and six years respectively. What is the equivalent single replacement payment two-and-a-half years from now if interest is 7.5% compounded monthly?

5. Scheduled payments of $400 due today and $700 due with interest at 4.5% compounded monthly in eight months are to be settled by a payment of $500 six months from now and a final payment in fifteen months. Determine the size of the final payment if money is worth 6% compounded monthly.

6. Scheduled payments of $1200 due one year ago and $1000 due six months ago are to be replaced by a payment of $800 now, a second payment of $1000 nine months from now, and a final payment eighteen months from now. What is the size of the final payment if interest is 10.8% compounded quarterly?

7. Two debts—the first of $800 due six months ago and the second of $1400 borrowed one year ago for a term of three years at 6.5% compounded annually—are to be replaced by a single payment one year from now. Determine the size of the replacement payment if interest is 7.5% compounded quarterly and the focal date is one year from now.

8. Scheduled payments of $2000 due now and $2000 due in four years are to be replaced by a payment of $2000 due in two years and a second payment due in seven years. Determine the size of the second payment if interest is 10.5% compounded annually and the focal date is seven years from now.

9. Scheduled loan payments of $1500 due in six months and $1900 due in 21 months are rescheduled as a payment of $2000 due in three years and a second payment due in 45 months. Determine the size of the second payment if interest is 7% compounded quarterly and the focal date is 45 months from now.
Reference Example 9.5C

10. An obligation of $8000 due one year ago is to be settled by four equal payments due at the beginning of each year, with the first payment now. What is the size of the equal payments if interest is 8% compounded semi-annually?
Reference Example 9.5D

11. A loan of $3000 borrowed today is to be repaid in three equal installments due in one year, three years, and five years respectively. What is the size of the equal installments if money is worth 7.2% compounded monthly?

12. Scheduled payments of $500 each are due at the end of each of the next five years. If money is worth 11% compounded annually, what is the single equivalent replacement payment
(a) five years from now? **(b)** now?

13. What is the size of the equal payments that must be made at the end of each of the next four years to settle a debt of $3000 subject to interest at 10% p.a. compounded annually
(a) due four years from now? **(b)** due now?
Reference Example 9.5E

14. Scheduled payments of $800 due two years ago and $1000 due in five years are to be replaced by two equal payments. The first replacement payment is due in four years and the second payment is due in eight years. Determine the size of the two replacement payments if interest is 12% compounded semi-annually and the focal date is four years from now.

15. Loan payments of $3000 due one year ago and $2500 due in four years are to be rescheduled by two equal payments. The first replacement payment is due now and the second payment is due in six years. Determine the size of the two replacement payments if interest is 6.9% compounded monthly and the focal date is now. Reference Example 9.5I

16. A payment of $500 is due in six months with interest at 12% compounded quarterly. A second payment of $800 is due in 18 months with interest at 10% compounded semi-annually. These two payments are to be replaced by a single payment nine months from now. Determine the size of the replacement payment if interest is 9% compounded monthly and the focal date is nine months from now.

17. Scheduled payments of $900 due in three months with interest at 11% compounded quarterly and $800 due in thirty months with interest at 11% compounded quarterly are to be replaced by two equal payments. The first replacement payment is due today and the second payment is due in three years. Determine the size of the two replacement payments if interest is 9% compounded monthly and the focal date is today. Reference Example 9.5J

18. Scheduled payments of $1400 due today and $1600 due with interest at 11.5% compounded annually in five years are to be replaced by two equal payments. The first replacement payment is due in 18 months and the second payment is due in four years. Determine the size of the two replacement payments if interest is 11% compounded quarterly and the focal date is 18 months from now.

powered by CourseCompass™ and MathXL®
MyMathLab
Go to MyMathLab at www.mathxl.com. You can practise many of this chapter's exercises as often as you want. The guided solutions help you find an answer step by step. You'll find a personalized study plan available to you too!

Review Exercise

1. What is the accumulated value of $500 in fifteen years at 6% compounded

(a) annually? **(b)** quarterly? **(c)** monthly?

2. What is the amount of $10 000 at 10.5% compounded monthly

(a) in four years?

(b) in eight-and-a-half years?

(c) in twenty years?

3. Landmark Trust offers five-year investment certificates at 7.5% compounded semi-annually.

(a) What is the value of a $2000 certificate at maturity?

(b) How much of the maturity value is interest?

4. Western Savings offers three-year term deposits at 9.25% compounded annually while your credit union offers such deposits at 9.0% compounded quarterly. If you have $5000 to invest, what is the maturity value of your deposit

(a) at Western Savings?

(b) at your credit union?

5. Find the future value and the compound interest of

(a) $1800 invested at 8% compounded quarterly for 15.5 years;

(b) $1250 invested at 6.5% compounded monthly for 15 years.

6. If $6000 is invested for six years and seven months at 6% compounded semi-annually, what is the interest that the investment earns?

7. Compute the maturity value of a $5000 promissory note dated November 15, 2000 and due on June 15, 2010, if interest is 8% compounded quarterly.

8. An investment of $2000 is made for three years, four months at 4.5% compounded semi-annually. What is the amount of interest?

9. Determine the sum of money that will grow to $14 000 in four years, eight months at 5% compounded quarterly.

10. Determine the proceeds of a non-interest-bearing note with a maturity value of $9000 three years and ten months before the due date if the interest rate is 7% compounded semi-annually.

11. Determine the discounted value now of $5200 due in forty months if money is worth 6.5% compounded quarterly.

12. Find the present value and the compound discount of

(a) $3600 due in 9 years if interest is 8% compounded semi-annually;

(b) $9000 due in 5 years if money is worth 6.8% compounded quarterly.

13. The Ram Company borrowed $20 000 at 10% compounded semi-annually and made payments toward the loan of $8000 after two years and $10 000 after three-and-a-half years. How much is required to pay off the loan one year after the second payment?

14. Ted deposited $1750 in an RRSP on March 1, 2004 at 3% compounded quarterly. Subsequently the interest rate was changed to 4% compounded monthly on September 1, 2006 and to 4.5% compounded semi-annually on June 1, 2008. What was the value of the RRSP deposit on December 1, 2010, if no further changes in interest were made?

15. An investment of $2500 is accumulated at 5% compounded quarterly for two-and-a-half years. At that time the interest rate is changed to 6% compounded monthly. How much is the investment worth two years after the change in interest rate?

16. To ensure that funds are available to repay the principal at maturity, a borrower deposits $2000 each year for three years. If interest is 6% compounded quarterly, how much will the borrower have on deposit four years after the first deposit was made?

17. Cindy started a registered retirement savings plan on February 1, 2002, with a deposit of $2500. She added $2000 on February 1, 2003 and $1500 on

February 1, 2008. What is the accumulated value of her RRSP account on August 1, 2012, if interest is 5% compounded quarterly?

18. A demand loan of $8000 is repaid by payments of $3000 after fifteen months, $4000 after thirty months, and a final payment after four years. If interest was 8% for the first two years and 9% for the remaining time, and compounding is quarterly, what is the size of the final payment?

19. A non-interest-bearing note for $1500 is due on June 30, 2012. The note is discounted at 10% compounded quarterly on September 30, 2008. What are the proceeds of the note?

20. Find the present value and the compound discount of $4000 due in seven years and six months if interest is 8.8% compounded quarterly.

21. Find the principal that will accumulate to $6000 in fifteen years at 5% compounded monthly.

22. Find the proceeds of a non-interest-bearing promissory note for $75 000 discounted 42 months before maturity at 6.5% compounded semi-annually.

23. A ten-year promissory note for $1750 dated May 1, 2003 bearing interest at 4% compounded semi-annually is discounted on August 1, 2009 to yield 6% compounded quarterly. Determine the proceeds of the note.

24. A seven-year, $10 000 promissory note bearing interest at 8% compounded quarterly is discounted four years after the date of issue at 7% compounded semi-annually. What are the proceeds of the note?

25. A $40 000, 15-year promissory note dated June 1, 2000, bearing interest at 12% compounded semi-annually is discounted on September 1, 2008 at 11% compounded quarterly. What are the proceeds of the note?

26. A fifteen-year promissory note for $16 500 bearing interest at 12% compounded semi-annually is discounted at 9% compounded monthly three years and four months after the date of issue. Compute the proceeds of the note.

27. An eight-year promissory note for $20 000 dated May 2, 2007, bearing interest at 10% compounded quarterly, is discounted on September 2, 2009 at 9.5% compounded semi-annually. Determine the proceeds of the note.

28. Three years and five months after its date of issue, a six-year promissory note for $3300 bearing interest at 7.5% compounded monthly is discounted at 7% compounded semi-annually. Find the proceeds of the note.

29. A sum of money has a value of $3000 eighteen months from now. If money is worth 6% compounded monthly, what is its equivalent value

(a) now? **(b)** one year from now?

(c) three years from now?

30. Payments of $1000, $1200, and $1500 are due in six months, eighteen months, and thirty months from now, respectively. What is the equivalent single payment two years from now if money is worth 9.6% compounded quarterly?

31. An obligation of $10 000 is due one year from now with interest at 10% compounded semi-annually. The obligation is to be settled by a payment of $6000 in six months and a final payment in fifteen months. What is the size of the second payment if interest is now 9% compounded monthly?

32. Waldon Toys owes $3000 due in two years with interest at 11% compounded semi-annually and $2500 due in fifteen months at 9% compounded quarterly. If the company wants to discharge these debts by making two equal payments, the first one now and the second eighteen months from now, what is the size of the two payments if money is now worth 8.4% compounded monthly?

33. Debt payments of $400 due today, $500 due in eighteen months, and $900 due in three years are to be combined into a single payment due two years from now. What is the size of the single payment if interest is 8% p.a. compounded quarterly?

34. Debt payments of \$2600 due one year ago and \$2400 due two years from now are to be replaced by two equal payments due one year from now and four years from now respectively. What is the size of the equal payments if money is worth 9.6% p.a. compounded semi-annually?

35. A loan of \$7000 taken out two years ago is to be repaid by three equal installments due now, two years from now, and three years from now, respectively. What is the size of the equal installments if interest on the debt is 12% p.a. compounded monthly?

Self-Test

1. What sum of money invested at 4% compounded quarterly will grow to \$3300 in 11 years?

2. Find the compound interest earned by \$1300 invested at 7.5% compounded monthly for seven years.

3. Determine the compounding factor for a sum of money invested for 14.5 years at 7% compounded semi-annually.

4. Determine the maturity value of \$1400 due in 71 months compounded annually at 7.75%.

5. Five years after Anne deposited \$3600 in a savings account that earned interest at 4.8% compounded monthly, the rate of interest was changed to 6% compounded semi-annually. How much was in the account twelve years after the deposit was made?

6. A debt can be repaid by payments of \$4000 today, \$4000 in five years, and \$3000 in six years. What single payment would settle the debt one year from now if money is worth 7% compounded semi-annually?

7. A \$10 200 debt will accumulate for five years at 11.6% compounded semi-annually. For how much will the debt sell three years after it was incurred if the buyer of the debt charges 10% compounded quarterly?

8. What is the present value of \$5900 payable in 15 years if the current interest rate is 7.5% compounded semi-annually?

9. Determine the compound discount on \$8800 due in 7.5 years if interest is 9.6% compounded monthly.

10. Two debt payments, the first for \$800 due today and the second for \$600 due in nine months with interest at 10.5% compounded monthly, are to be settled by a payment of \$800 six months from now and a final payment in 24 months. Determine the size of the final payment if money is now worth 9.5% compounded quarterly.

11. A note dated July 1, 1998 promises to pay \$8000 with interest at 7% compounded quarterly on January 1, 2007. Find the proceeds from the sale of the note on July 1, 2002 if money is then worth 8% compounded semi-annually.

12. Adam borrowed \$5000 at 10% compounded semi-annually. He repaid \$2000 after two years and \$2500 after three years. How much will he owe after five years?

13. A debt of $7000 due today is to be settled by three equal payments due three months from now, 15 months from now, and 27 months from now, respectively. What is the size of the equal payments at 11% compounded quarterly?

14. Seven years and two months after its date of issue, an eleven-year promissory note for $8200 bearing interest at 13.5% compounded monthly is discounted at 10.5% compounded semi-annually. Find the proceeds of the note.

15. Compute the proceeds of a non-interest-bearing note for $1100 three years and seven months before the due date if money is worth 7.5% compounded annually.

Challenge Problems

1. Jean-Guy Renoir wanted to leave some money to his grandchildren in his will. He decided that they should each receive the same amount of money when they each turn 21. When he died, his grandchildren were 19, 16, and 13, respectively. How much will they each receive when they turn 21 if Jean-Guy left a lump sum of $50 000 to be shared among them equally? Assume the interest rate will remain at 7.75% p.a. compounded semi-annually from the time of Jean-Guy's death until the youngest grandchild turns 21.

2. Miranda has $1000 to invest. She has narrowed her options to two four-year certificates, A and B. Certificate A pays interest at 8% p.a. compounded semi-annually the first year, 8% p.a. compounded quarterly the second year, 8% p.a. compounded monthly the third year, and 8% p.a. compounded daily the fourth year. Certificate B pays 8% p.a. compounded daily the first year, 8% p.a. compounded monthly the second year, 8% p.a. compounded quarterly the third year, and 8% p.a. compounded semi-annually the fourth year.
   (a) What is the value of each certificate at the end of the four years?
   (b) How do the values of certificates A and B compare with the value of a third certificate that pays interest at 7% compounded daily for the full four-year term?

Case Study 9.1 Your Best Interest

» Regan received a bonus from her employer and decided to deposit the bonus into a savings account at her bank. Her personal banking representative explained to her that there were four different savings accounts that she should consider. All of them pay compound interest.

The Daily Interest Savings Account has an interest rate of 1.50%; compound interest is calculated on the minimum balance in the account each day and is paid monthly. The Monthly Interest Savings Account has an interest rate of 2.00%; compound interest is calculated on the minimum balance in the account during the month and is paid monthly. The Investment Savings Account has an interest rate of 2.50%; compound interest is calculated on the minimum monthly balance and paid monthly, but only when the balance remains above $10 000 for the whole month. If the balance drops below $5000 at any time during the month, no interest is paid for that month. Compound interest on the Basic Savings Account is calculated on the minimum balance in the account during the six-month periods ending April 30 and October 31, and is paid on those dates. The Basic Savings Account has an interest rate of 2.80%.

The personal banking representative advised Regan that she should also consider the number of transactions made in the account each month or year when choosing an account. She thanked the representative and went home to consider her options.

QUESTIONS

1. Suppose Regan's bonus was $9000 and she planned to invest the money immediately in a bank account for one year. Assume that the bank's interest rates will remain the same throughout the year.
   (a) For each of the bank's four savings accounts, how much interest would Regan earn in one year's time?
   (b) Which savings account would pay the most interest?

2. Suppose Regan's bonus was $12 000 and she planned to leave the money in a savings account for one year. Assume that the bank's interest rates will remain the same throughout the year.
   (a) For each of the bank's four savings accounts, how much interest would Regan earn in one year's time if she left the money in the account for one year?
   (b) Which savings account would pay the most interest?
   (c) Suppose Regan knew she would have to withdraw $3500 after ten months. Which savings account would pay the most interest?

3. Suppose Regan had $12 000 to put into a savings account. She planned to leave the money in the account for one year, then withdraw $5000. She would then leave the remaining balance in the account for one more year. Which savings account would pay the most interest over the two-year period? Assume that the bank's interest rates will stay the same over the next two years.

4. For the savings accounts at your bank, credit union, or trust company, find the features and interest rates offered for each. If you had $3500 to deposit for one year, which account would you choose?

Case Study 9.2 Planning Ahead

» Precision Machining Corporation has been growing steadily over the past decade. Demand for the company's products continues to rise, so management has decided to expand their production facility; $2 800 000 has been set aside for this over the next four years.

Management has developed two different plans for expanding over the next four years, Plan A and Plan B. Plan A would require equal amounts of $750 000 one year from now, two years from now, three years from now, and four years from now. Plan B would require $300 000 now, $700 000 one year from now, $900 000 two years from now, and $975 000 four years from now.

The company has decided to fund the expansion with only the $2 800 000 and any interest it can earn on it. Before deciding which plan to use, the company asks its treasurer to predict the rates of interest it can earn on the $2 800 000. The treasurer expects that Precision Machining Corporation can invest the $2 800 000 and earn interest at a rate of 4.5% p.a. compounded semi-annually during Year 1, 5.0% p.a. compounded semi-annually during Years 2 and 3, and 5.5% p.a. compounded semi-annually during Year 4. The company can withdraw part of the money from this investment at any time without penalty.

QUESTIONS

1. **(a)** Could Precision Machining Corporation meet the cash requirement of Plan A by investing the $2 800 000 as described above? (Use "now" as the focal date.)

(b) What is the exact difference between the cash required and the cash available from the investment?

2. **(a)** Could Precision Machining Corporation meet the cash requirements of Plan B by investing the $2 800 000 as described above? (Use "now" as the focal date.)

(b) What is the difference between the cash required and the cash available from the investment?

3. **(a)** Suppose Plan A was changed so that it required equal amounts of $750 000 now, one year from now, two years from now, and four years from now. Could Precision Machining Corporation meet the cash requirements of the new Plan A by investing the $2 800 000 as described above? (Use "now" as the focal date.)

(b) What is the difference between the cash required and the cash available from the investment?

4. Suppose the treasurer found another way to invest the $2 800 000 that earned interest at a rate of 4.9% compounded quarterly for the next five years.

(a) Could the company meet the cash requirements of the original Plan A with this new investment? (Show all your calculations.)

(b) Could the company meet the cash requirements of Plan B with this new investment? (Show all your calculations.)

(c) If the company could meet the cash requirements of both plans, which plan would the treasurer recommend? In other words, which plan would have the lower present value?

SUMMARY OF FORMULAS

Formula 9.1A

$S = P(1 + i)^n$ — **Finding the future value (or maturity value) when the original principal, the rate of interest, and the time period are known**

restated as

$FV = PV(1 + i)^n$

Formula 9.1B

$$P = \frac{S}{(1 + i)^n}$$

Finding the present value (or principal or proceeds or discounted value) when the future value, the rate of interest, and the time period are known

restated as

$$PV = \frac{FV}{(1 + i)^n}$$

Formula 9.1C

$P = S(1 + i)^{-n}$ — **Finding the present value by means of the discount factor (the reciprocal of the compounding factor)**

restated as

$PV = FV(1 + i)^{-n}$

Formula 9.2

$$i = \frac{j}{m}$$

Finding the periodic rate of interest

GLOSSARY

Accumulation factor *see* **Compounding factor**

Amount *see* **Future value**

Comparison date *see* **Focal date**

Compound discount the difference between a given future amount and its present value (or proceeds or discounted value) at a specified time *(p. 351)*

Compound interest a procedure for computing interest whereby interest earned during an interest period is added onto the principal at the end of the interest period *(p. 329)*

Compounding factor the factor $(1 + i)^n$ found in compound interest formulas *(p. 332)*

Compounding frequency the number of times interest is compounded during a given time period (usually one year) *(p. 332)*

Compounding period the time between two successive interest dates *(p. 332)*

Conversion frequency *see* **Compounding frequency**

Conversion period *see* **Compounding period**

Discount factor the factor $(1 + i)^{-n}$; the reciprocal of the compounding factor *(p. 353)*

Discounted value *see* **Present value**

Discounting the process of computing the present value (or proceeds or discounted value) of a future sum of money *(p. 351)*

Equivalent values the dated values of an original sum of money *(p. 365)*

Focal date a specific date chosen to compare the time values of one or more dated sums of money *(p. 364)*

Future value the sum of money to which a principal will grow at compound interest in a specific number of compounding or conversion periods at a specified periodic rate of interest *(p. 331)*

Maturity value *see* **Future value**

Nominal rate of interest the stated rate at which the compounding is done one or more times per year; usually stated as an annual rate *(p. 332)*

Periodic rate of interest value of interest is obtained by dividing the nominal annual rate by the number of compounding periods per year *(p. 332)*

Present value the principal at any time that will grow at compound interest to a given future value over a given number of compounding periods at a given rate of interest *(p. 351)*

Proceeds *see* **Present value**

USEFUL INTERNET SITES

www.globefund.com

Globefund.com This popular site for mutual fund information and analysis is hosted by the *Globe and Mail* Website.

www.fin.gc.ca/fin-eng.html

Department of Finance This site has information on the preparation of the federal government's budget that shows what is happening to taxes, as well as information related to interest rates and the economy.

www.cannex.com

CANNEX This site has a large list of comparative interest rates for GICs and term deposits offered by financial institutions in Canada, the United States, Australia, and New Zealand.

CHAPTER 10

Compound Interest—Further Topics

OBJECTIVES

Upon completing this chapter, you will be able to do the following with compound interest by using an electronic calculator:

1. Determine the number of conversion periods and find equated dates.
2. Compute periodic and nominal rates of interest.
3. Compute effective and equivalent rates of interest.

Is this too good to be true? A recent ad showed notebook computers for sale, showing the all-cash price and the financed price. Some of the numbers shown were:

$69.79 per month, or $1399.99
$61.44 per month, or $1199.99
$33.33 per month, or $699.99

In each situation, would you be paying the same amount for the computer if you financed the purchase with a loan as you would if you purchased it for cash?

We should read such ads critically. They do not specify the interest rate being charged or whether the interest is simple or compound. They do not specify whether the rates of interest are the same for each type of loan. They do not specify the number of payments you would have to make. It is important to know this information to assess the ads and compare the offer with loans available from other sources.

INTRODUCTION

In the previous chapter, we considered future value and present value when using compound interest. In this chapter, we will look at other aspects of compound interest, including finding the number of conversion periods, and computing equated dates and equivalent and effective rates of interest.

For these calculations we can either manipulate the formulas or use electronic calculators. In this and the following chapters, we will use calculators.

We can save time on our calculations by using the memory of the calculator when working with these functions. Of course, we might get slightly different results if we use memory rather than rekeying the displayed digits, because the number of digits retained in memory is almost always greater than the number of digits displayed. However, the differences are so small that we can ignore them. For the worked examples in this text, we have used the memory whenever it was convenient to do so.

10.1 FINDING n AND RELATED PROBLEMS

A. Finding the number of conversion periods

If the principal PV, the future value FV, and the periodic rate of interest i are known, the number of conversion periods n can be determined by substituting the known values in Formula 9.1A and solving for n.

$$FV = PV(1 + i)^n$$ —— Formula 9.1A

EXCEL NOTES

You can use Excel's ***Number of Compounding Periods (NPER)*** function to find the number of conversion periods. Refer to **NPER** on the Spreadsheet Template Disk to learn how to use this Excel function.

EXAMPLE 10.1A In how many years will \$2000.00 grow to \$2440.38 at 4% compounded quarterly?

SOLUTION $PV = 2000.00$; $FV = 2440.38$; $I/Y = 4$; $P/Y = 4$; $i = \frac{4\%}{4} = 1\% = 0.01$

$2440.38 = 2000.00(1.01)^n$ —— substituting in Formula 9.1A

$(1.01)^n = 1.22019$

$n \ln 1.01 = \ln 1.22019$ —— solve for n using the natural logarithm

$0.009950n = 0.199007$ —— obtain the numerical values using the LN key

$$n = \frac{0.199007}{0.009950} = 19.999998 = 20 \text{ (quarters)}$$

$$\text{Number of years} = \frac{20}{4} = 5$$

Programmed Solution

You can use preprogrammed financial calculators to find n by the same procedure previously used to find FV, PV.

(Set P/Y, C/Y = 4) 2nd (CLR TVM) 2000 ± PV

2440.38 FV 4 I/Y CPT N 19.999997

At 10% compounded quarterly, \$2000 will grow to \$2440.38 in 20 quarters or five years.

Note: Another way to solve Example 10.1A is first to rearrange Formula 9.1A to solve for n:

$$FV = PV(1 + i)^n$$

$$(1 + i)^n = \frac{FV}{PV}$$

$$n \ln(1 + i) = \ln\left(\frac{FV}{PV}\right)$$

$$n = \frac{\ln\left(\frac{FV}{PV}\right)}{\ln(1 + i)}$$

Recall that the total number of conversion periods is n. To convert to years if compounding semi-annually, divide n by 2; if compounding quarterly, divide by 4; if compounding monthly, divide by 12; and if compounding daily, divide by 365. Remember, you do not have to memorize this equation if you understand the principles of formula rearrangement.

EXAMPLE 10.1B

How long does it take for money to double
(i) at 5% p.a.?
(ii) at 10% p.a.?

SOLUTION

While neither PV nor FV is given, any sum of money may be used as principal. For this calculation, a convenient value for the principal is \$1.00.

PV = 1.00; FV = 2.00; I/Y = 5; P/Y = 1

(i) At 5% p.a., $i = 5\% = 0.05$

$$2 = 1(1.05)^n$$

$$1.05^n = 2$$

$$n \ln 1.05 = \ln 2$$

$$0.048790n = 0.693147$$

$$n = 14.206699 \text{ (years)}$$

Programmed Solution

(Set P/Y, C/Y = 1) 2nd (CLR TVM) 1 ± PV 2 FV 5 I/Y

CPT N 14.206699 (years)

At 5% p.a., money doubles in approximately 14 years and 3 months.

(ii) At 10% p.a., I/Y = 10; P/Y = 1; $i = 10\% = 0.10$

$$2 = 1(1 + 0.10)^n$$
$$1.10^n = 2$$
$$n \ln 1.10 = \ln 2$$
$$0.095310n = 0.693147$$
$$n = 7.272541 \text{ (years)}$$

Programmed Solution

[2nd] (CLR TVM) 1 [±] [PV] 2 [FV]

10 [I/Y] [CPT] [N] [7.272541] (years)

At 10% p.a., money doubles in approximately 7 years and 4 months.

POINTERS AND PITFALLS

The Rule of 70

Did you know that there is a quick way to estimate the number of conversion periods needed to double an amount of money? It is known as the *Rule of 70*. According to this rule, the number of conversion periods required to double money is 70 divided by the periodic rate of interest *i*.

Suppose we want to estimate how long it will take to double money if the interest rate is 10% compounded semi-annually. Applying the Rule of 70, we find it will take about 7 years (that is 70/5 half-year conversion periods). By comparison, if we calculate the time using the standard formulas, we get a result of about 7.103 years (i.e., about 14.207 half-year conversion periods).

EXAMPLE 10.1C How long will it take for money to triple at 6% compounded monthly?

SOLUTION Let PV = 1; then FV = 3; I/Y = 6; P/Y = 12; $i = \frac{6\%}{12} = 0.5\% = 0.005$

$$3 = 1(1.005)^n$$
$$1.005^n = 3$$
$$n \ln 1.005 = \ln 3$$
$$0.004988n = 1.098612$$
$$n = 220.271 \text{ (months)}$$

Programmed Solution

(Set P/Y, C/Y = 12) [2nd] (CLR TVM) 1 [±] [PV] 3 [FV]

6 [I/Y] [CPT] [N] [220.271307] (months)

At 6% compounded monthly, money triples in approximately 18 years and 4 months.

B. Equated date

In Chapter 9, Section 9.5, we considered the concept of *equivalence* of values when using the compound interest method. In solving problems of equivalence, the unknown value was the size of a payment at the selected focal date. While we often need to find the size of the payment, occasionally we need to find the focal date or the interest rate instead.

The **equated date** is the date on which a single sum of money is equal to the sum of two or more dated sums of money. To find an equated date, an equation of values can be set up by the same technique used in Section 9.5. However, solving the equation for n requires the same technique as used in Section 10.1A. Since this method involves the use of logarithms, you can solve the problem using an electronic calculator as long as the calculator is equipped with the natural logarithm function (LN key).

You may also use a financial calculator that is preprogrammed with the time value of money (TVM) worksheet. After entering all of the relevant data into the calculator, press CPT N. Note that the units of N calculated are in the compounding period. For example, if you are compounding quarterly, your answer for N is in quarters. If you wish to determine a specific date to solve your problem, use the DATE worksheet within the calculator. An explanation of how to use this worksheet is included on the CD attached to this text.

EXCEL NOTES

EXAMPLE 10.1D

A financial obligation requires the payment of \$2000 in 6 months, \$3000 in 15 months, and \$5000 in 24 months. When can the obligation be discharged by the single payment equal to the sum of the required payments if money is worth 9% p.a. compounded monthly?

SOLUTION

The single payment equal to the sum of the required payments is \$2000 plus \$3000 plus \$5000, or \$10 000. Select as the focal date "now." Let the number of compounding periods from the focal date to the equated date be represented by n. Since the compounding is done monthly, n will be a number of months, I/Y = 9, P/Y = 12, and $i + \frac{9}{12}\% = 0.75\% = 0.0075$. The method and data are shown graphically in Figure 10.1.

Let E_1, E_2, and E_3 represent the equivalent values of the original payments at the focal date as shown in Figure 10.1.

Let E_4 represent the equivalent value of the single payment of \$10 000 at the focal date.

The equation of values can now be set up.

$$E_4 = E_1 + E_2 + E_3$$

$$10\,000.00(1.0075)^{-n} = 2000.00(1.0075)^{-6} + 3000.00(1.0075)^{-15} + 5000.00(1.0075)^{-24}$$

$$10\,000.00(1.0075)^{-n} = 2000.00(0.956158) + 3000.00(0.893973) + 5000.00(0.835831)$$

$$10\,000.00(1.0075)^{-n} = 1912.32 + 2681.92 + 4179.16$$

$$10\,000.00(1.0075)^{-n} = 8773.40$$

$$(1.0075)^{-n} = \frac{8773.40}{10\,000.00}$$

$$(1.0075)^{-n} = 0.87734$$
$$-n(\ln 1.0075)^{-n} = \ln 0.87734$$
$$-n(0.007472)^{-n} = -0.130861$$
$$n = \frac{0.130861}{0.007472}$$
$$n = 17.513477$$

The equated date is about 17.5 months from now.

FIGURE 10.1 Graphical Representation of Method and Data

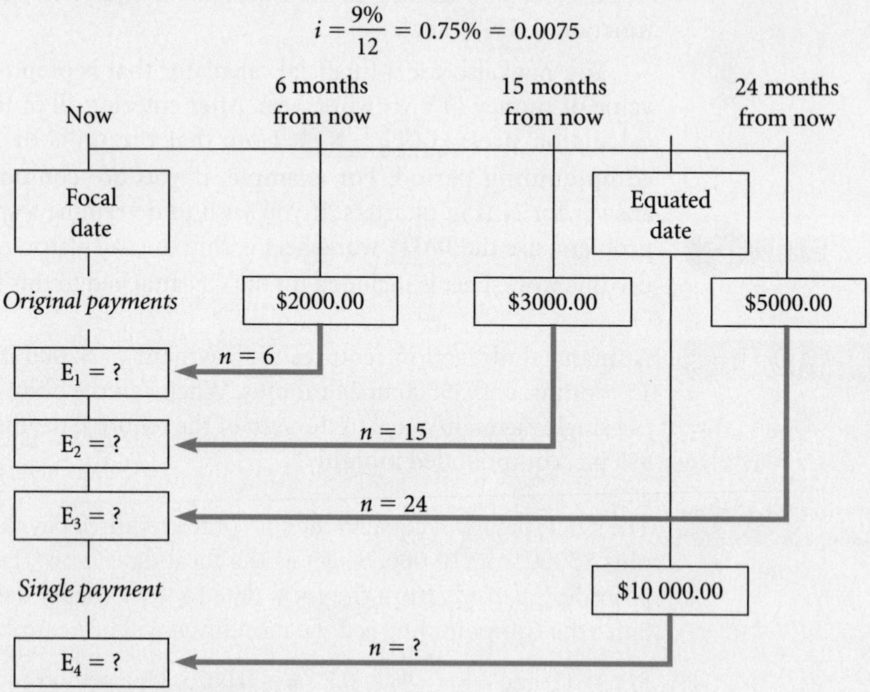

Programmed Solution

First simplify the equation $E_4 = E_1 + E_2 + E_3$.

$10\,000(1.0075)^{-n} = 2000.00(1.0075)^{-6} + 3000(1.0075)^{-15} + 5000(1.0075)^{-24}$

$2000(1.0075)^{-6}$

(Set P/Y, C/Y = 12) 2nd (CLR TVM) 2000 FV

9 I/Y 6 N CPT PV -1912.316036 ± STO 1

$3000(1.0075)^{-15}$

2nd (CLR TVM) 3000 FV 9 I/Y 15 N

CPT PV -2681.917614 ± STO 2

$5000(1.0075)^{-24}$

2nd (CLR TVM) 5000 FV 9 I/Y

24 N CPT PV -4179.15702 ± STO 3

RCL 1 + RCL 2 + RCL 3 =

or

$10\,000(1.0075)^{-n} = 1912.316036 + 2681.917614 + 4179.15702$

Remember to remove the negative (cash outflow) signs.

$10\,000(1.0075)^{-n} = 8773.39067$

Now solve the simplified equation:

$10\,000(1.0075)^{-n} = 8773.39067$

in which FV = 10 000; PV = 8773.39067; $i = 0.75\%$

2nd (CLR TVM) 10 000 FV 8773.39067

± PV 9 I/Y CPT N 17.513581

The equated date is approximately 17.5 months from now.

While the definition of equated date requires that the single sum of money be equal to the sum of the dated sums of money considered, the method used in solving the problem can be applied to problems in which the single sum of money does not equal the sum of the dated sums of money considered.

EXAMPLE 10.1E

A loan is to be repaid by three equal payments of $1500 due now, two years from now, and four years from now, respectively. When can the obligation be paid off by a single payment of $5010 if interest is 10% compounded annually?

SOLUTION

Select as the focal date "now." Let the number of compounding periods from the focal date to the equated date be represented by n. Since the compounding is done annually, n will be a number of years, I/Y = 10, P/Y = 1, and $i = 10\% = 0.10$.

Let E_1, E_2, and E_3 represent the equivalent values of the original payments at the focal date.

$$E_1 = 1500.00 = 1500.00$$
$$E_2 = 1500.00(1.10)^{-2} = 1500.00(0.826446) = 1239.67$$
$$E_3 = 1500.00(1.10)^{-4} = 1500.00(0.683014) = \underline{1024.52}$$
$$E_1 + E_2 + E_3 = \underline{\underline{3764.19}}$$

Let E_4 represent the equivalent value of the single payment of $5010 at the focal date.

$$E_4 = 5010.00(1.10)^{-n}$$
$$E_4 = E_1 + E_2 + E_3$$
$$5010.00(1.10)^{-n} = 3764.19$$
$$(1.10)^{-n} = 0.751335$$
$$-n(\ln 1.10) = \ln 0.751335$$
$$-0.095310n = -0.285903$$
$$n = 3$$

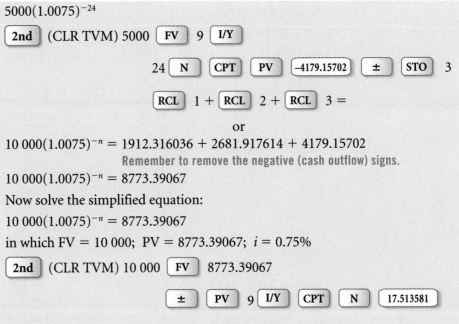

Programmed Solution

$E_4 = E_1 + E_2 + E_3$
$5010.00(1.10)^{-n} = 1500.00 + 1500(1.10)^{-2} + 1500(1.10)^{-4}$
$1500(1.10)^{-2}$
(Set P/Y, C/Y = 1) [2nd] (CLR TVM) 1500 [FV] 10 [I/Y]
2 [N] [CPT] [PV] [-1239.669421] [±] [STO] 1

$1500(1.10)^{-4}$
[2nd] (CLR TVM)1500 [FV] 10 [I/Y] 4 [N]
[CPT] [PV] [-1024.520183] [±] [STO] 2
[RCL] 1 + [RCL] 2 =

$5010.00(1.10)^{-n} = 1500.00 + 1239.67 + 1024.52$
$5010.00(1.10)^{-n} = 3764.19$
[2nd] (CLR TVM) 5010 [FV] 3764.19 [±] [PV]
10 [I/Y] [CPT] [N] [2.999713]

The single payment should be made three years from now.

EXAMPLE 10.1F

A loan of \$2000 taken out today is to be repaid by a payment of \$1200 in six months and a final payment of \$1000.00. If interest is 12% compounded monthly, when should the final payment be made?

SOLUTION

Let the focal point be "now"; I/Y = 12; P/Y = 12; $i = \frac{12\%}{12} = 1.0\% = 0.01$.

$$\begin{aligned}
2000.00 &= 1200.00(1.01)^{-6} + 1000.00(1.01)^{-n} \\
2000.00 &= 1200.00(0.942045) + 1000.00(1.01)^{-n} \\
2000.00 &= 1130.45 + 1000.00(1.01)^{-n} \\
869.55 &= 1000.00(1.01)^{-n} \\
(1.01)^{-n} &= 0.86955 \\
-n(\ln 1.01) &= \ln 0.86955 \\
-0.009950n &= -0.139779 \\
n &= 14.0478 \text{ (months)}
\end{aligned}$$

Programmed Solution

$2000.00 = 1200.00(1.01)^{-6} + 1000(1.01)^{-n}$
$1200.00(1.01)^{-6}$
(Set P/Y, C/Y = 12) [2nd] (CLR TVM) 1200 [FV] 12 [I/Y]
6 [N] [CPT] [PV] [-1130.454282]

$2000.00 = 1130.454282 + 1000(1.01)^{-n}$
$869.545717 = 1000(1.01)^{-n}$
869.545717 [±] [PV] 1000 [FV] 12 [I/Y]
[CPT] [N] [14.048213] (months)

$n = 427$ *days* ——— $\left(\frac{14.048213}{12}\right)(365)$

The final payment should be made in 427 days.

EXERCISE 10.1

EXCEL NOTES

If you choose, you can use Excel's ***Number of Compounding Periods (NPER)*** function to answer the questions indicated below. Refer to **NPER** on the Spreadsheet Template Disk to learn how to use this Excel function.

A.

1. Determine the number of compounding periods for each of the following six investments.

	Principal	Future Value	Interest Rate	Frequency of Conversion
(a)	$2600.00	$6437.50	7%	annually
(b)	1240.00	1638.40	4	quarterly
(c)	560.00	1350.00	9	monthly
(d)	3480.00	4762.60	8	semi-annually
(e)	950.00	1900.00	7.5	quarterly
(f)	1300.00	3900.00	6	semi-annually

2. Find the equated date at which the original payments are equivalent to the single payment for each of the following four sets of payments.

	Original Payments	Interest Rate	Frequency of Conversion	Single Payment
(a)	$400 due in 9 months and $700 due in 21 months	12%	quarterly	$1256.86
(b)	$1200 due today and $2000 due in 5 years	8	semi-annually	3808.70
(c)	$1000 due 8 months ago, $1200 due in 6 months, and $1500 due in 16 months	9	monthly	3600.00
(d)	$600 due in 2 years, $800 due in 3.5 years, and $900 due in 5 years	10	quarterly	1800.00

B.

Answer each of the following questions.

1. How long will it take $400 to accumulate to $760 at 7% p.a. compounded semi-annually?

2. In how many days will $580 grow to $600 at 4.5% p.a. compounded monthly?

3. In how many years will money quadruple at 8% compounded quarterly?

4. In how many months will money triple at 9% compounded semi-annually?

5. If an investment of $800 earned interest of $320 at 6% compounded monthly, for how many years was the money invested?

6. A loan of $2000 was repaid together with interest of $604.35. If interest was 8% compounded quarterly, for how many months was the loan taken out?

7. If you borrowed $1000 on May 1, 2009, at 10% compounded semi-annually and interest on the loan amounts to $157.63, on what date is the loan due?

8. A promissory note for $600 dated May 15, 2008 requires an interest payment of $150 at maturity. If interest is at 9% compounded monthly, determine the due date of the note.

9. A non-interest-bearing promissory note for $1500 was discounted at 5% p.a. compounded quarterly. If the proceeds of the note were $1375.07, how many months before the due date was the note discounted?

10. A five-year, $1000 note bearing interest at 9% compounded annually was discounted at 12% compounded semi-annually yielding proceeds of $1416.56. How many months before the due date was the discount date?

11. A contract requires payments of $4000 today, $5000 in three years, and $6000 in five years. When can the contract be fulfilled by a single payment equal to the sum of the required payments if money is worth 9% p.a. compounded monthly?

12. A financial obligation requires the payment of $500 in nine months, $700 in fifteen months, and $600 in 27 months. When can the obligation be discharged by a single payment of $1600 if interest is 10% compounded quarterly?

13. When Brenda bought Sheridan Service from Ken, she agreed to make three payments of $6000 each in one year, three years, and five years respectively. Because of initial cash flow difficulties, Brenda offered to pay $8000 in two years and a second payment of $10 000 at a later date. When should she make the second payment if interest is 9.75% compounded semi-annually?

14. Leo sold a property and is to receive $3000 in six months, $4000 in 24 months, and $5000 in 36 months. The deal was renegotiated after nine months at which time Leo received a payment of $7000; he was to receive a further payment of $6000 later. When should Leo receive the second payment if money is worth 11% compounded quarterly?

10.2 FINDING *i* AND RELATED PROBLEMS

A. Finding the periodic rate *i* and the nominal annual rate of interest *j*

If the original principal PV, the future value FV, and the number of conversion periods n are known, the periodic rate of interest (conversion rate) i can be determined by substituting in Formula 9.1A, $FV = PV(1 + i)^n$, and solving for i. The nominal annual rate of interest j can then be found by multiplying i by the number of conversion periods per year m.

EXAMPLE 10.2A What is the annual compounding rate if \$200 accumulates to \$318.77 in eight years?

SOLUTION PV = 200.00; FV = 318.77; C/Y(m) = 1; $n = 8$

$$318.77 = 200.00(1 + i)^8 \quad \text{———— } i \text{ is an } \textit{annual} \text{ rate}$$
$$(1 + i)^8 = 1.59385$$
$$[(1 + i)^8]^{\frac{1}{8}} = 1.59385^{0.125} \quad \text{———— raise each side to the power } \frac{1}{8}$$
$$1 + i = 1.59385^{0.125}$$
$$1 + i = 1.060000$$
$$i = 0.06000$$
$$i = 6.0\% \quad \text{———— the desired annual rate}$$

The annual compounding rate is 6.0%.

Programmed Solution

You can use preprogrammed financial calculators to find i by the same procedure used previously to determine FV or PV. That is, select the compound interest mode, enter the given variables FV, PV, and N, and retrieve the fourth variable I/Y.

(Set P/Y, C/Y = 1) [2nd] (CLR TVM) 200 [±] [PV] 318.77 [FV]

8 [N] [CPT] [I/Y] [6.000016] (annual)

Note: As we emphasized in Chapter 2, it is important to know how to rearrange the terms of an equation. For instance, another way to solve Example 10.2A is first to rearrange Formula 9.1A to solve for i:

$$FV = PV(1 + i)^n$$
$$(1 + i)^n = \frac{FV}{PV}$$
$$1 + i = \left(\frac{FV}{PV}\right)^{\frac{1}{n}}$$
$$i = \left(\frac{FV}{PV}\right)^{\frac{1}{n}} - 1$$

Recall that i is the periodic rate of interest. If interest is calculated m times per year, then the nominal annual rate of interest $j = m(i)$.

Remember, you do not have to memorize this equation if you understand the principles of formula rearrangement.

Note: In the financial calculator that you use, you must determine whether the interest rate to be entered represents i, the periodic rate of interest, or j, the nominal rate of interest. In the BAII Plus calculator the [I/Y] to be used equates to j in the formula. Thus, the variables in the formula $i = j/m$ can be translated into i = [I/Y] / [C/Y] for use in the calculator. The value of I/Y obtained from the calculator is to be expressed as the nominal rate. For example, if C/Y = 4, or quarterly, and the calculator determines that I/Y = 8.5, then the rate is expressed as 8.5% p.a. compounded quarterly.

EXAMPLE 10.2B

Find the nominal annual rate of interest compounded quarterly if \$1200 accumulates to \$2064.51 in five years.

SOLUTION

PV = 1200.00 FV = 2064.51; C/Y(m) = 4; n = 20; m = 4

$2064.51 = 1200.00(1+i)^{20}$ ——— i is a *quarterly* rate

$(1+i)^{20} = 1.720425$

$1+i = 1.720425^{0.05}$ ——— raise both side to the power $\frac{1}{20}$, that is, 0.05

$1+i = 1.027500$

$i = 0.027500$

$i = 2.75\%$

The quarterly compounding rate is 2.75%.

Nominal rate = 2.75% × 4 = 11% compounded quarterly.

Programmed Solution

(Set P/Y, C/Y = 4) [2nd] (CLR TVM) 1200 [±] [PV]

2064.51 [FV] 20 [N] [CPT] [I/Y] [11.00]

The nominal annual rate of interest is 11.0% per annum compounded quarterly. The periodic rate of interest would be $i = j/m$ = 11.0%/4 = 2.75% per quarter.

EXAMPLE 10.2C

At what nominal rate of interest compounded quarterly will money double in four years?

SOLUTION

While neither PV nor FV are given, any sum of money may be used as principal. For this calculation, a convenient value for the principal is \$1.00.

PV = 1; FV = 2; C/Y(m) = 4; n = 16; m = 4

$2 = 1(1+i)^{16}$ ——— i is a *quarterly* rate

$(1+i)^{16} = 2$

$1+i = 2^{\frac{1}{16}}$

$1+i = 2^{0.0625}$

$1+i = 1.044274$

$i = 0.044274$

$i = 4.4274\%$

Nominal rate = 4.4274% × 4 = 17.71% compounded quarterly.

Programmed Solution

(Set P/Y, C/Y= 4) [2nd] (CLR TVM) 1 [±] [PV] 2 [FV] 16 [N]

[CPT] [I/Y] [17.709513]

The nominal annual rate is 17.709513% per annum compounded quarterly. The quarterly rate is 17.709513%/4 = 4.427%.

EXAMPLE 10.2D

Suppose $1000 earns interest of $93.81 in one year.

(i) What is the nominal annual rate of interest compounded annually?
(ii) What is the nominal annual rate of interest compounded monthly?

SOLUTION

(i) PV = 1000.00; I = 93.81; FV = PV + I = 1093.81; C/Y(m) = 1; n = 1

$$1093.81 = 1000.00(1 + i)^1 \quad \text{———— } i \text{ is an } annual \text{ rate } (m = 1)$$
$$1 + i = 1.09381$$
$$i = 0.09381$$
$$i = 9.381\%$$

Programmed Solution

(Set P/Y, C/Y= 1) [2nd] (CLR TVM) 1000 [±] [PV]

1093.81 [FV] 1 [N] [CPT] [I/Y] [9.381]

The annual rate of interest is 9.381%.

Notice that both the nominal rate and the periodic rate of interest are 9.381%, since interest is compounded annually.

(ii) P/Y = 12

$$1093.81 = 1000.00\,(1 + i)^{12} \quad \text{———— } i \text{ is a } monthly \text{ rate } (m = 12)$$
$$(1 + i)^{12} = 1.09381$$
$$1 + i = 1.09381^{\frac{1}{12}}$$
$$1 + i = 1.09381^{0.083333}$$
$$1 + i = 1.007500$$
$$i = 0.007500$$
$$i = 0.75\%$$

Nominal rate = 0.75% × 12 = 9.0% compounded quarterly

Programmed Solution

(Set P/Y, C/Y = 12) [2nd] (CLR TVM) 1000 [±] [PV]

1093.81 [FV] 12 [N] [CPT] [I/Y] [9.000286]

The nominal annual rate of interest compounded monthly is 9% p.a. The periodic rate of interest is 9%/12 = 0.75% per month.

EXCEL NOTES

You can use Excel's ***Compound Interest Rate per Period (RATE)*** function to find the periodic rate of interest i. Refer to **RATE** on the Spreadsheet Template Disk to learn how to use this Excel function.

EXERCISE 10.2

A. Answer each of the following.

Find the nominal annual rate of interest for each of the following investments.

	Principal	Future Value	Time Due	Frequency of Conversion
1.	$1400.00	$1905.21	7 years	annually
2.	2350.00	3850.00	5 years	quarterly
3.	690.00	1225.00	6 years	monthly
4.	1240.00	2595.12	12 years	semi-annually
5.	3160.00	5000.00	4 years, 9 months	quarterly
6.	900.00	1200.00	3 years, 8 months	monthly

B. Solve each of the following.

1. What is the nominal annual rate of interest compounded quarterly at which $420 will accumulate to $1000 in nine years and six months?

2. A principal of $2000 compounded monthly amounts to $2800 in 7.25 years. What is the nominal annual rate of interest?

3. At what nominal annual rate of interest will money double itself in
(a) six years, nine months if compounded quarterly?
(b) nine years, two months if compounded monthly?

4. What is the nominal annual rate of interest at which money will triple itself in 12 years
(a) if compounded annually?
(b) if compounded semi-annually?

5. Yin Li deposited $800 into a savings account that compounded interest monthly. What nominal annual rate compounded monthly was earned on the investment if the balance was $952.75 in five years?

6. An investment of $4000 earned interest semi-annually. If the balance after $6\frac{1}{2}$ years was $6000, what nominal annual rate compounded semi-annually was charged?

7. Surinder borrowed $1200 and agreed to pay $1400 in settlement of the debt in three years, three months. What annual nominal rate compounded quarterly was charged on the debt?

8. A debt of $600 was to be repaid in 15 months. If $750.14 was repaid, what was the nominal rate compounded monthly that was charged?

10.3 EFFECTIVE AND EQUIVALENT INTEREST RATES

A. Effective rate of interest

In Example 10.2D, compounding at an annual rate of interest of 9.381% has the same effect as compounding at 9.0% p.a. compounded monthly since, in both cases, the interest amounts to $93.81.

The annually compounded rate of 9.381% is called the **effective rate of interest.** This rate is defined as the rate of interest compounded annually that yields the same amount of interest as a nominal annual rate of interest compounded a number of times per year other than one.

Converting nominal rates of interest to effective rates is the method used for comparing nominal rates of interest. Since the effective rates of interest are the equivalent rates of interest compounded annually, they may be obtained for any set of nominal rates by computing the accumulated value of $1 after one year for each of the nominal rates under consideration.

Effective Rates Using the BAII Plus

The BAII Plus is programmed in the **2nd** function to quickly and efficiently calculate effective interest rates by inputting the nominal rate and the number of compounds. You can also calculate the nominal rate if you know the effective rate.

To go from nominal to effective the process is:

1. **2nd** (ICONV) (2-key).
2. Enter the nominal rate, NOM =
3. Arrow down to C/Y= and enter the number of times interest compounds in a year.
4. Arrow up to EFF= and press **CPT** .

To go from effective to nominal the process is:

1. **2nd** (ICONV).
2. Arrow down to EFF= and enter the effective rate.
3. Arrow down to C/Y= and enter the compounding number relating to the nominal rate you are converting to.
4. Arrow down to NOM= and press **CPT** .

Equivalent Rates Using the BAII Plus

The BAII Plus can be used to calculate equivalent interest rates by using the effective rate as a constant to make equivalent calculations.

The process is:

1. **2nd** (ICONV).
2. Enter any nominal rate, NOM =
3. Arrow down to C/Y= and enter the compounds relating to the nominal rate entered in Step 2.
4. Arrow up to EFF= and press **CPT** .
5. Arrow down and change C/Y= to the compounds you want to convert to.
6. Arrow down to NOM= and press **CPT** .
7. Repeat the process as many times as required to calculate all equivalent rates you are interested in.

EXAMPLE 10.3A

Assume you are given a choice of a term deposit paying 7.2% compounded monthly or an investment certificate paying 7.25% compounded semi-annually. Which rate offers the higher rate of return?

SOLUTION

The investment certificate offers the higher nominal rate of return while the term deposit offers the higher compounding frequency. Because of the different compounding frequencies, the two nominal rates are not directly comparable. To determine which nominal rate offers the higher rate of return, we need to determine the effective rates for the two given rates.

For the term deposit

I/Y = 7.2; P/Y = 12; $i = 0.6\% = 0.006$; $m = 12$;
the accumulated value of $1 after one year,
$\text{FV} = 1(1.006)^{12} = 1.074424$

The decimal fraction 0.074424 is the interest earned in one year and represents the effective rate of interest = 7.44242%.

For the investment certificate

I/Y = 7.25; P/Y = 2; $i = 3.625\% = 0.03625$; $m = 2$;
the accumulated value of $1 after one year,
$\text{FV} = 1(1.03625)^2 = 1.073814$

The decimal fraction 0.073814 represents the effective rate of interest = 7.3814%.

Since the term deposit has the higher effective rate, it offers the higher rate of return.

Programmed Solution

For the term deposit

$(1 + i)^{12} = (1.0006)^{12} = 1.0744242$

(Set P/Y, C/Y = 12) [2nd] (CLR TVM) 1 [±] [PV] 7.2 [I/Y]

12 [N] [CPT] [FV] [1.074424]

Alternatively:

[2nd] (IConv) Nom = 7.2; C/Y = 12; Eff = [CPT] 7.4424

For the investment certificate

$(1 + i)^2 = (1.03625)^2 = 1.073814$

(Set P/Y, C/Y = 2) [2nd] (CLR TVM) 1 [±] [PV] 7.25 [I/Y]

2 [N] [CPT] [FV] [1.073814]

Alternatively:

[2nd] (IConv) Nom = 7.25; C/Y = 2; Eff = [CPT] 7.3814

The nominal annual rate is 7.4424% for the term deposit and 7.3814% for the investment certificate.

EXAMPLE 10.3B

How much better is a rate of 8.4% compounded monthly than 8.4% compounded quarterly?

SOLUTION

For 8.4% compounded monthly

I/Y = 8.4; P/Y = 12; $i = 0.7\% = 0.007$; $m = 12$;
the accumulated value of \$1 after one year,
$FV = 1(1.007)^{12} = 1.087311$

The decimal fraction 0.087311 is the interest earned in one year and represents the effective rate of interest = 8.7311%.

For 8.4% compounded quarterly

I/Y = 8.4; P/Y = 4; $i = 2.1\% = 0.021$; $m = 4$;
the accumulated value of \$1 after one year,
$FV = 1(1.021)^4 = 1.086683$

The decimal fraction 0.086683 represents the effective rate of interest = 8.6683%.

Difference = 8.7311% − 8.6683% = 0.0628%.

Programmed Solution

For 8.4% compounded monthly

$(1 + i)^{12} = (1.007)^{12} = 1.087311$

(Set P/Y, C/Y = 12) [2nd] (CLR TVM) 1 [±] [PV] 8.4 [I/Y] 12 [N] [CPT] [FV] [1.087311]

Alternatively:

[2nd] (IConv) Nom = 8.4; C/Y = 12; Eff = [CPT] 8.7311

For 8.4% compounded quarterly

$(1 + i)^4 = (1.021)^4 = 1.086683$

(Set P/Y, C/Y = 4) [2nd] (CLR TVM) 1 [±] [PV] 8.4 [I/Y] 4 [N] [CPT] [FV] [1.086683]

Alternatively:

[2nd] (IConv) Nom = 8.4; C/Y = 4; Eff = [CPT] 8.6683

The effective rate is 8.7311% with 8.4% compounded monthly and 8.6683% for 8.4% compounded quarterly.

The effective rates of interest can also be determined by using Formula 10.1 obtained from the method of calculation used in Examples 10.3A and 10.3B.

The formula is obtained as follows:

Let the nominal annual rate of interest be compounded m times per year and let the interest rate per conversion period be i.
Then the accumulated amount after one year is $FV_1 = PV(1 + i)^m$.
Let the corresponding effective annual rate of interest be f.
Then the accumulated amount after one year is $FV_1 = PV(1 + f)^1$.

$PV(1 + f)^1 = PV(1 + i)^m$ —— the amounts are equal by definition
$1 + f = (1 + i)^m$ —— divide both sides by PV

$$f = (1 + i)^m - 1$$ —— Formula 10.1

EXAMPLE 10.3C Determine the effective rate of interest corresponding to 9% p.a. compounded

(i) monthly;
(ii) quarterly;
(iii) semi-annually;
(iv) annually;
(v) daily.

SOLUTION

(i) $i = \left(\frac{9\%}{12}\right) = 0.0075; \quad m = 12$

$$\begin{aligned} f &= (1 + i)^m - 1 \quad \text{—— using Formula 10.1} \\ &= (1 + 0.0075)^{12} - 1 \\ &= 1.093807 - 1 \\ &= 0.093807 \\ &= 9.381\% \end{aligned}$$

(ii) $i = \left(\frac{9\%}{4}\right) = 0.0225; \quad m = 4$

$$\begin{aligned} f &= (1.0225)^4 - 1 \\ &= 1.093083 - 1 \\ &= 0.093083 \\ &= 9.308\% \end{aligned}$$

(iii) $i = \left(\frac{9\%}{2}\right) = 0.045; \quad m = 2$

$$\begin{aligned} f &= (1.045)^2 - 1 \\ &= 1.092025 - 1 \\ &= 9.2025\% \end{aligned}$$

(iv) $i = 9\% = 0.09; \quad m = 1$

$$\begin{aligned} f &= (1.09)^1 - 1 \\ &= 9.000\% \end{aligned}$$

(v) $i = \left(\frac{9\%}{365}\right) = 0.000246; \quad m = 365$

$$\begin{aligned} f &= (1.000246)^{365} - 1 \\ &= 1.094162 - 1 \\ &= 9.416\% \end{aligned}$$

Summary of Results

For a nominal annual rate of 9% p.a., effective rates are

when compounding annually ($m = 1$)	$f = 9.000\%$
when compounding semi-annually ($m = 2$)	$f = 9.2025\%$
when compounding quarterly ($m = 4$)	$f = 9.308\%$
when compounding monthly ($m = 12$)	$f = 9.381\%$
when compounding daily ($m = 365$)	$f = 9.416\%$

Programmed Solution

For 9% compounded monthly

$(1 + i)^{12} = (1.0075)^{12} = 1.093807$

(Set P/Y, C/Y = 12) [2nd] (CLR TVM) 1 [±] [PV] 9 [I/Y]

12 [N] [CPT] [FV] [1.093807]

Alternatively:

[2nd] (IConv) Nom = 9; C/Y = 12; Eff = [CPT] 9.3807

For 9% compounded quarterly

$(1 + i)^4 = (1.0225)^4 = 1.093083$

(Set P/Y, C/Y = 4) [2nd] (CLR TVM) 1 [±] [PV] 9 [I/Y]

4 [N] [CPT] [FV] [1.093083]

Alternatively:

[2nd] (IConv) Nom = 9; C/Y = 4; Eff = [CPT] 9.3083

For 9% compounded semi-annually

$(1 + i)^2 = (1.045)^2 = 1.092025$

(Set P/Y, C/Y = 2) [2nd] (CLR TVM) 1 [±] [PV] 9 [I/Y]

2 [N] [CPT] [FV] [1.092025]

Alternatively:

[2nd] (IConv) Nom = 9; C/Y = 2; Eff = [CPT] 9.2025

For 9% compounded annually

$(1 + i)^1 = (1.09)^1 = 1.09$

(Set P/Y, C/Y = 1) [2nd] (CLR TVM) 1 [±] [PV] 9 [I/Y]

1 [N] [CPT] [FV] [1.09]

Alternatively:

2nd (IConv) Nom = 9; C/Y = 1; Eff = CPT 9

For 9% compounded daily

$(1 + i)^{365} = (1.000246)^{365} = 1.094162$

(Set P/Y, C/Y = 365) 2nd (CLR TVM) 1 ± PV 9 I/Y

365 N CPT FV 1.094162

Alternatively:

2nd (IConv) Nom = 9; C/Y = 365; Eff = CPT 9.4162

POINTERS AND PITFALLS

For nominal annual interest rates and effective rates, the following two points are always true:

1. The nominal annual rate is the effective rate of interest *only* if the number of conversion periods per year is 1, that is, if compounding annually.
2. For a given nominal annual rate, the effective rate of interest increases as the number of conversion periods per year increases.

EXAMPLE 10.3D

You have money to invest in interest-earning deposits. You have determined that suitable deposits are available at your bank paying 6.5% p.a. compounded semi-annually, at a local trust company paying 6.625% compounded annually, and at your credit union paying 6.45% p.a. compounded monthly. What institution offers the best rate of interest?

SOLUTION

Since the methods of conversion differ, the interest rates are not directly comparable. To make the rates comparable, determine the effective rates of interest corresponding to the nominal annual rates.

For the bank:

$$i = \left(\frac{6.5\%}{2}\right) = 0.0325; \quad m = 2$$

$$f = (1 + 0.0325)^2 - 1 = 1.066056 - 1 = 0.066056 = 6.606\%$$

For the trust company:

$$i = 6.625 = 0.06625; \quad m = 1$$

$$f = i = 6.625\%$$

For the credit union:

$$i = \left(\frac{6.45\%}{12}\right) = 0.005375; \quad m = 12$$

$$f = (1.005375)^{12} - 1 = 1.066441 - 1 = 0.066441 = 6.644\%$$

While the nominal rate offered by the credit union is lowest, the corresponding effective rate of interest is highest due to the higher frequency of conversion. The rate offered by the credit union is best.

Programmed Solution

For the bank:

6.5% compounded semi-annually:

$(1 + i)^2 = (1.032500)^2 = 1.066056$

(Set P/Y, C/Y = 2) [2nd] (CLR TVM) 1 [±] [PV] 6.5 [I/Y]

2 [N] [CPT] [FV] [1.066056]

Alternatively:

[2nd] (IConv) Nom = 6.5; C/Y = 2; Eff = [CPT] 6.6056

For the trust company:

6.625% compounded annually:

$(1 + i)^1 = (1.06625)^1 = 1.06625$

(Set P/Y, C/Y = 1) [2nd] (CLR TVM) 1 [±] [PV] 6.625 [I/Y]

1 [N] [CPT] [FV] [1.06625]

Alternatively:

[2nd] (IConv) Nom = 6.625; C/Y = 1; Eff = [CPT] 6.625

For the credit union:

6.45% compounded monthly:

$(1 + i)^{12} = (1.005375)^{12} = 1.066441$

(Set P/Y, C/Y = 12) [2nd] (CLR TVM) 1 [±] [PV] 6.45 [I/Y]

12 [N] [CPT] [FV] [1.066441]

Alternatively:

[2nd] (IConv) Nom = 6.45; C/Y = 12; Eff = [CPT] 6.6441

B. Equivalent rates

Notice that in Example 10.2D, two different nominal annual rates of interest (9.381% compounded annually and 9% compounded monthly) produced the same future value ($1093.81) for a given principal ($1000.00) after one year. Interest rates that increase a given principal to the same future value over the same period of time are called **equivalent rates**—9.381% compounded annually and 9% compounded monthly are equivalent rates.

EXAMPLE 10.3E

Find the future value after one year of $100 accumulated at

(i) 12.55% compounded annually;
(ii) 12.18% compounded semi-annually;
(iii) 12.00% compounded quarterly;
(iv) 11.88% compounded monthly.

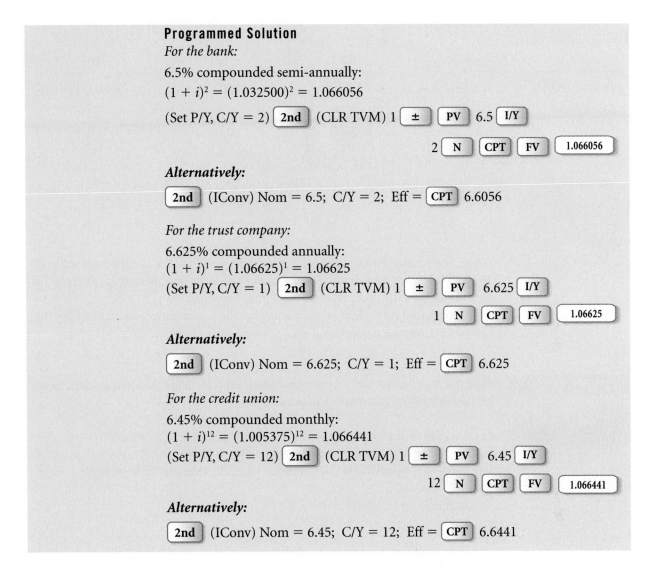

SOLUTION

	(i)	(ii)	(iii)	(iv)
Principal (PV)	100.00	100.00	100.00	100.00
Nominal rate	12.55%	12.18%	12.00%	11.88%
i	0.1255	0.0609	0.03	0.0099
n	1	2	4	12
Future value (FV)	$100.00(1.1255)^1$ $= 100.00(1.1255)$ $= \$112.55$	$100.00(1.0609)^2$ $= 100.00(1.125509)$ $= \$112.55$	$100.00(1.03)^4$ $= 100.00(1.125509)$ $= \$112.55$	$100.00(1.0099)^{12}$ $= 100.00(1.125487)$ $= \$112.55$

Note: The four different nominal annual rates produce the same future value of \$112.55 for the same principal of \$100 over the same time period of one year. By definition, the four nominal rates are equivalent rates.

We can find equivalent rates by equating the accumulated values of \$1 for the rates under consideration based on a selected time period, usually one year.

EXAMPLE 10.3F

Find the nominal annual rate compounded semi-annually that is equivalent to an annual rate of 6% compounded annually.

SOLUTION

Let the semi-annual rate of interest be represented by i; P/Y = 2.
For PV = 1, $n = 2$, the accumulated value $FV_1 = (1 + i)^2$.
For the given nominal rate compounded annually the accumulated value $FV_2 = (1 + 0.06)^1$.
By definition, to be equivalent, $FV_1 = FV_2$.

$$(1 + i)^2 = 1.06$$
$$1 + i = 1.06^{0.5}$$
$$1 + i = 1.029563$$
$$i = 0.029563 \text{ ——— semi-annual rate}$$

Nominal rate = 2.9563% × 2 = 5.9126% compounded semi-annually.

Programmed Solution

$$1\,(1 + i)^2 = 1.06$$
(1 ↓ PV; 1.06 ↓ FV)

(Set P/Y, C/Y = 2) [2nd] (CLR TVM) 1 [±] [PV] 1.06 [FV]

2 [N] [CPT] [I/Y] [5.912603]

Alternatively:

[2nd] (IConv) Eff = 6.0; C/Y = 2; Nom = [CPT] 5.912603

The nominal annual rate compounded semi-annually is 5.91%.

The periodic rate is 5.912603%/2 = 2.956301% per semi-annual period.

EXAMPLE 10.3G

What nominal annual rate compounded quarterly is equivalent to 8.4% p.a. compounded monthly?

SOLUTION

Let the quarterly rate be i; PV = 1; $n = 4$.
The accumulated value of \$1 after one year $FV_1 = (1 + i)^4$.

For the given rate I/Y = 8.4; P/Y = 12; $i = \frac{8.4\%}{12} = 0.7\% = 0.007$; $n = 12$.

The accumulated value of \$1 after one year $FV_2 = (1.007)^{12}$.
To be equivalent, $FV_1 = FV_2$.

$$(1 + i)^4 = (1.007)^{12}$$
$$1 + i = (1.007)^3$$
$$1 + i = 1.021147$$
$$i = 0.021147 \text{ — quarterly rate}$$

Programmed Solution

(Set P/Y, C/Y = 12) [2nd] (CLR TVM) 1 [±] [PV] 8.4 [I/Y]

12 [N] [CPT] [FV] [1.087311]

(Set P/Y, C/Y = 4) [2nd] (CLR TVM) 1 [±] [PV] 1.087311 [FV]

4 [N] [CPT] [I/Y] 8.458937%

Alternatively:

[2nd] (IConv) Nom = 8.4; C/Y = 12; Eff = [CPT] 8.7311

C/Y = 4; Nom = [CPT] 8.458937

The nominal annual rate compounded quarterly is 8.46%. The periodic rate is 2.11473% per quarterly period.

EXAMPLE 10.3H

Peel Credit Union offers premium savings deposits at 8% interest paid semi-annually. The board of directors wants to change to monthly payment of interest. What nominal annual rate compounded monthly should the board set to maintain the same yield?

SOLUTION

Let the monthly rate be i; P/Y = 12; $n = 12$; PV = 1.
The accumulated value of \$1 after one year $FV_1 = (1 + i)^{12}$.
For the existing rate, P/Y = 2; $n = 2$, $i = 0.04$.
The accumulated value of \$1 in one year $FV_2 = (1.04)^2$.
To maintain the same yield the two rates must be equivalent.

$$(1 + i)^{12} = (1.04)^2$$
$$1 + i = (1.04)^{\frac{1}{6}}$$
$$1 + i = 1.006558$$
$$i = 0.006558 \text{ — monthly rate}$$

Nominal rate = 0.6558% × 12 = 7.87% compounded monthly.

Programmed Solution

$(1 + i)^{12} = (1.04)^2$

$(1.04)^2$

(Set P/Y, C/Y = 2) [2nd] (CLR TVM) 1 [±] [PV] 8 [I/Y]

2 [N] [CPT] [FV] [1.0816]

$1(1 + i)^{12} = 1.0816$

(Set P/Y, C/Y = 12) [2nd] (CLR TVM) 1 [±] [PV] 1.0816 [FV]

12 [N] [CPT] [I/Y] [7.869836]

Alternatively:

[2nd] (IConv) Nom = 8.0; C/Y = 2; Eff = [CPT] 8.16

C/Y = 12; Nom = [CPT] 7.869836

The nominal rate compounded monthly is 7.87%. The periodic rate is 7.869836%/12 = 0.6558% per monthly period.

EXERCISE 10.3

EXCEL NOTES

If you choose, you can use Excel's ***Effective Annual Interest Rate (EFFECT)*** or ***RATE*** functions to answer the questions indicated below. Refer to **EFFECT** or **RATE** on the Spreadsheet Template Disk to learn how to use these functions.

A. Answer each of the following.

1. Find the nominal rate of interest compounded annually equivalent to each of the following.
   (a) 12.5% compounded semi-annually
   (b) 6% compounded monthly
   (c) 7.2% compounded quarterly
   (d) 10.2% compounded monthly

2. Compute the effective annual rate of interest for each of the following.
   (a) 9.5% compounded semi-annually
   (b) 10.5% compounded quarterly
   (c) 5.0% compounded monthly
   (d) 7.2% compounded monthly
   (e) 3.6% compounded quarterly
   (f) 8.2% compounded semi-annually

3. Find the nominal annual rate compounded
   (a) quarterly that is equivalent to 9% compounded semi-annually
   (b) monthly that is equivalent to 6.5% compounded quarterly
   (c) monthly that is equivalent to 7.5% compounded semi-annually
   (d) semi-annually that is equivalent to 4.25% compounded quarterly

B. Solve each of the following.

1. What is the effective annual rate of interest if \$100 grows to \$150 in six years compounded quarterly?

2. What is the effective annual rate of interest if \$450 grows to \$750 in three years, five months compounded monthly?

3. If \$1100 accumulates to \$1350 in four years, six months compounded semi-annually, what is the effective annual rate of interest?

4. An amount of \$2300 earns \$500 interest in three years, two months. What is the effective annual rate if interest compounds monthly?

5. Find the nominal annual rate of interest compounded quarterly that is equal to an effective rate of 9.25%.

6. What nominal annual rate of interest compounded semi-annually is equivalent to an effective rate of 6.37%?

7. If the effective rate of interest on an investment is 6.4%, what is the nominal rate of interest compounded monthly?

8. What is the nominal rate of interest compounded quarterly if the effective rate of interest on an investment is 5.3%?

9. The Central Bank pays 7.5% compounded semi-annually on certain types of deposits. If interest is compounded monthly, what nominal rate of interest will maintain the same effective rate of interest?

10. The treasurer of National Credit Union proposes changing the method of compounding interest on premium savings accounts to daily compounding. If the current rate is 6% compounded quarterly, what nominal rate should the treasurer suggest to the board of directors to maintain the same effective rate of interest?

11. Sofia made a deposit of \$600 into a bank account that earns interest at 3.5% compounded monthly. The deposit earns interest at that rate for five years.
    (a) Find the balance of the account at the end of the period.
    (b) How much interest is earned?
    (c) What is the effective rate of interest?

12. Ying invested \$5000 into an account earning 2.75% interest compounding daily for two years.
    (a) Find the balance of the account at the end of the period.
    (b) How much interest is earned?
    (c) What is the effective rate of interest?

13. An RRSP earns interest at 4.25% compounded quarterly. An amount of \$1200 is invested into the RRSP and earned interest for ten years.
    (a) Find the balance of the account at the end of the period.
    (b) How much interest is earned?
    (c) What is the effective rate of interest?

14. Josef invested $1750 into an RRSP that earned interest at 5% compounded semi-annually for eight years.
   (a) Find the balance of the account at the end of the period.
   (b) How much interest is earned?
   (c) What is the effective rate of interest?

BUSINESS MATH NEWS BOX

How to Maximize Savings for a Child's Education

You can tell when school has started when the nights are cooler and parents' wallets are emptier.

Looking longer term toward college funding, there are two main ways to save. The first is the Registered Education Savings Plan, or RESP. The other way is simply to put money away, either in your name or in an account in your name "in-trust" for your child or grandchild.

The advantage to the RESP is that the government will put in one dollar for every five dollars you put in, up to a maximum government grant (CESG) of $400 per year per child. That's based on a $2000 contribution from you, although you are allowed to put in up to $4000 per year.

The money invested inside an RESP grows tax deferred. The original capital can be withdrawn tax free at any time, but the investment income and the grant are taxable to the student beneficiary, when withdrawn. This assumes that the beneficiary enrolls in some form of post-secondary education. This could be technical or community college, university, or a number of other full-time courses of study.

If the beneficiary (or any of the beneficiaries, in a family plan RESP) does not attend a qualifying course of study, then the income and grant become taxable to the subscriber (the adult who set up the plan). There is also a 20% surcharge, above the regular income taxes, which really just makes up for the grant money and the time all of the money was allowed to grow tax-deferred.

The bottom line is that the RESP is likely the best means of accumulating money for post-secondary education, at least to the extent of $2000 a year per child.

Source: "How to Maximize Savings for a Child's Education" by David Christianson. *Winnipeg Free Press*, August 25, 2006, p. B.4. Edited excerpt reprinted with permission.

QUESTIONS

1. Assume the Wong family contributes $2000 per year over a 16-year period to an RESP plan earning 4.85% interest compounded semi-annually.
   a. Calculate the value the plan would have at the start of the 17th year.
   b. Calculate the value of annual contributions of $2000 into a non-RESP plan over a 16-year period at 4.85% interest compounded semi-annually.
   c. Determine the difference in plan values of the RESP plan from those of the non-RESP plan.

2. Assume that $1000 was contributed at the beginning of each year into an RESP plan for 10 years.
   a. If the rate of interest was 4% per annum compounded annually for the first 5 years, and 5.2% compounded quarterly for the last 5 years, calculate the amount of the plan.
   b. If the tax rate is 40% and the student uses this amount for a four-year degree, calculate the monthly value that can be used by the student.

Review Exercise

1. At what nominal rate of interest compounded monthly will $400 earn $100 interest in four years?

2. At what nominal rate of interest compounded quarterly will $300 earn $80 interest in six years?

3. Find the equated date at which payments of $500 due six months ago and $600 due today could be settled by a payment of $1300 if interest is 9% compounded monthly.

4. Find the equated date at which two payments of $600 due four months ago and $400 due today could be settled by a payment of $1100 if interest is 7.25% compounded semi-annually.

5. In what period of time will money triple at 10% compounded semi-annually?

6. In how many years will money double at 8% compounded monthly?

7. What nominal rate of interest compounded monthly is equivalent to an effective rate of 6.2%?

8. What nominal rate of interest compounded quarterly is equivalent to an effective rate of 5.99%?

9. Find the nominal annual rate of interest

(a) at which $2500 will grow to $4000 in eight years compounded quarterly;

(b) at which money will double in five years compounded semi-annually;

(c) if the effective annual rate of interest is 9.2% and compounding is done monthly;

(d) that is equivalent to 8% compounded quarterly.

10. Find the nominal annual rate of interest

(a) at which $1500 will grow to $1800 in four years compounded monthly;

(b) at which money will double in seven years compounded quarterly;

(c) if the effective annual rate of interest is 7.75% and compounding is done monthly;

(d) that is equivalent to 6% compounded quarterly.

11. Compute the effective annual rate of interest

(a) for 4.5% compounded monthly;

(b) at which $2000 will grow to $3000 in seven years compounded quarterly.

12. Compute the effective annual rate of interest

(a) for 6% compounded monthly;

(b) at which $1100 will grow to $2000 in seven years compounded monthly.

13. What is the nominal annual rate of interest compounded monthly that is equivalent to 8.5% compounded quarterly?

14. What is the nominal annual rate of interest compounded quarterly that is equivalent to an effective annual rate of 5%?

15. Patrick had $2000 to invest. Which of the following options should he choose?

(a) 4% compounded annually

(b) 3.75% compounded semi-annually

(c) 3.5% compounded quarterly

(d) 3.25% compounded monthly

16. **(a)** How many years will it take for $7500 to accumulate to $9517.39 at 3% compounded semi-annually?

(b) Over what period of time will money triple at 9% compounded quarterly?

(c) How many years will it take for a loan of $10 000 to amount to $13 684 at 10.5% compounded monthly?

17. Matt had agreed to make two payments—a payment of $2000 due in nine months and a payment of $1500 in a year. If Matt makes a payment of $1800 now, when should he make a second payment of $1700 if money is worth 8% compounded quarterly?

18. A four-year, \$3200 promissory note with interest at 7% compounded monthly was discounted at 9% compounded quarterly yielding proceeds of \$3870.31. How many months before the due date was the discount date?

19. A financial obligation requires the payment of \$2000 now, \$2500 in six months, and \$4000 in one year. When will a single payment of \$9000 discharge the obligation if interest is 6% compounded monthly?

20. Girard owes two debt payments—a payment of \$5000 due in six months and a payment of \$6000 due in fifteen months. If Girard makes a payment of \$5000 now, when should he make a second payment of \$6000 if money is worth 11% compounded semi-annually?

21. Payment of a debt of \$10 000 incurred on December 1, 2008, with interest at 9.5% compounded semi-annually is due on December 1, 2011. If a payment of \$7500 is made on December 1, 2010, on what date should a second payment of \$7500 be made if money is worth 12% compounded quarterly?

22. A seven-year, \$1500 promissory note with interest at 10.5% compounded semi-annually was discounted at 12% compounded quarterly yielding proceeds of \$2150. How many months before the due date was the discount date?

Self-Test

1. A ten-year, \$9200 promissory note with interest at 6% compounded monthly is discounted at 5% compounded semi-annually yielding proceeds of \$12 915.60. How many months before the due date was the date of discount?

2. An amount of \$1400 was invested for 71 months, maturing to \$2177.36. What annually compounded rate was earned?

3. Determine the effective annual rate of interest equivalent to 5.4% compounded monthly.

4. How many months from now can a payment of \$1000 due twelve months ago and a payment of \$400 due six months from now be settled by a payment of \$1746.56 if interest is 10.2% compounded monthly?

5. At what nominal rate of interest compounded semi-annually will \$6900 earn \$3000 interest in five years?

6. In how many years will money double at 7.2% compounded quarterly?

7. What is the nominal rate of interest compounded semi-annually that is equivalent to an effective rate of 10.25%?

8. Seven years and two months after its date of issue, an eleven-year promissory note for \$8200 bearing interest at 13.5% compounded monthly is discounted to yield \$24 253.31. What semi-annually compounded nominal discount rate was used?

9. A non-interest-bearing note for \$1100 is discounted three years and seven months before the due date. What annually compounded rate of interest yields proceeds of \$848.88?

Challenge Problems

1. Olga deposited $800 in an investment certificate paying 9% compounded semi-annually. On the same day, her sister Ursula deposited $600 in an account paying 7% compounded semi-annually. To the nearest day, when will the future value of Olga's investment be equal to twice the future value of Ursula's investment?
2. A financial institution is advertising a new three-year investment certificate. The interest rate is 7.5% compounded quarterly the first year, 6.5% compounded monthly the second year, and 6% compounded daily the third year. What nominal rate of interest compounded semi-annually for three years would a competing institution have to offer to match the interest produced by this investment certificate?

Case Study 10.1 Choosing a Credit Card

» Jane Zhao is deciding which credit card to apply for. She has just received advertising from several large credit card companies, some of which feature low introductory rates. She has estimated that, based on her good credit rating, she could apply for any of the credit cards being offered.

Credit card A has a $33 annual fee and advertises the relatively low interest rate of 9.5%. A $5 fee is charged for each cash advance, plus the applicable interest charges.

Credit card B has no annual fee and advertises a 17.5% interest rate on purchases and cash advances.

Credit card C advertises an introductory promotional interest rate of 3.9% on cash advances and balance transfers for the first six months, if you make your minimum monthly payments on time. The regular annual interest rate is 18.50% on purchases and cash advances.

For all three credit cards, interest will not be assessed if the monthly statement amount is paid in full by the payment due date and no cash advances have been taken during the billing period. If the new balance is not paid in full, interest will be charged (1) on the outstanding balance from the statement closing date and (2) on future purchases from the day the purchases are posted to the account. On cash advance transactions, interest is always charged from the date the cash advance is taken.

Currently, Jane has a credit card with a major Canadian department store. For this card, D, there is an outstanding balance of $1000. Its annual interest rate is 27.5%. If she receives one of the other three cards, she would transfer the department store credit card balance to the new card.

QUESTIONS

1. Jane maintains an average daily balance of $1500 for the first year, based solely on purchases and balance transfers. For each of the four credit cards,
   (a) calculate the interest charge and fees that she would have to pay over a twelve-month period;
   (b) determine the effective annual rate of interest over the first twelve-month period; and
   (c) decide which credit card she should choose.

2. If the introductory interest rate fell to 2.5% for credit card C, and the regular annual interest rate rose to 19.50% on purchases, what would be the effective annual rate of interest over the twelve-month period?

3. If you have a credit card, how do its rates and conditions compare with those of the cards described above?

Case Study 10.2 Comparing Car Loans

» After reading consumer car guides and receiving advice from family and friends, Aysha has chosen the new car she wants to purchase. She now wants to research her financing options to choose the best way to pay for the car.

Aysha knows that with taxes, licence, delivery, and dealer preparation fees, her car will cost $17 850. She has saved $7500 toward the purchase price but must borrow the rest. She has narrowed her financing choices to three options: dealer financing, credit union financing, and bank financing.

(i) The car dealer has offered 48-month financing at 8.5% compounded monthly.
(ii) The credit union has offered 36-month financing at 9.0% compounded quarterly. It has also offered 48-month financing at 9.3% compounded quarterly.
(iii) The bank has offered 36-month financing at 8.8% compounded semi-annually. It has also offered 48-month financing at 9.1% compounded semi-annually.

Aysha desires the financing option that offers the best interest rate. However, she also wants to explore the financing options that allow her to pay off her car loan more quickly.

QUESTIONS

1. Aysha wants to compare the 48-month car loan options offered by the car dealer, the credit union, and the bank.

    (a) What is the effective annual rate of interest for each 48-month option?
    (b) How much interest will Aysha save by choosing the best option as against the worst option?

2. Suppose Aysha wants to try to pay off her car loan within three years.

    (a) What is the effective annual rate of interest for both of the 36-month options?
    (b) How much interest will Aysha save by choosing the better option?

3. If you wanted to get a car loan today, what are the rates of interest for 36-month and 48-month terms? Are car dealers currently offering better interest rates than the banks or credit unions? If so, why?

SUMMARY OF FORMULAS

Formula 9.1A

$FV = PV(1 + i)^n$ — **Finding the future value of a sum of money when *n* is a fractional value using the exact method**

Formula 9.1B

$$PV = \frac{FV}{(1 + i)^n}$$

Finding the present value (discounted value or proceeds) when *n* is a fractional value using the exact method

Formula 9.1C

$PV = FV(1 + i)^{-n}$

Formula 10.1

$f = (1 + i)^m - 1$ — **Finding the effective rate of interest *f* for a nominal annual rate compounded *m* times per year**

GLOSSARY

Effective rate of interest the annual rate of interest that yields the same amount of interest per year as a nominal rate compounded a number of times per year *(p. 405)*

Equated date the date on which a single sum of money is equal to the sum of two or more dated sums of money *(p. 395)*

Equivalent rates interest rates that accumulate a given principal to the same future value over the same period of time *(p. 411)*

USEFUL INTERNET SITES

mathforum.org/dr.math

The Rule of 70 Visit the "Ask Dr. Math" site to read about how to use the Rule of 70 or ask other math-related questions.

www.rate.net

Rate.net Rate.net tracks over 11 000 financial institutions in 175 markets nationwide. The site analyzes interest rate performance and financial stability.

www.money.canoe.ca

Credit Card Rates To compare credit card rates and terms for major Canadian financial institutions and department stores, visit this (independent) Website and click on "Rates," then "Credit Cards."

CHAPTER 11 Ordinary Simple Annuities

OBJECTIVES

Upon completing this chapter, you will be able to do the following:

1. Distinguish between types of annuities based on term, payment date, and conversion period.
2. Compute the future value (or accumulated value) FV for ordinary simple annuities.
3. Compute the present value (or discounted value) PV for ordinary simple annuities.
4. Compute the payment PMT for ordinary simple annuities.
5. Compute the number of periods N for ordinary simple annuities.
6. Compute the interest rate I/Y for ordinary simple annuities.

In many business situations, we have seen the use of simple and compound interest and their calculations involving present value and future value. In other situations, we pay or receive regular, equal amounts of money, possibly for payment of rent, insurance, car loans, student loans, and mortgages. We may also receive regular, equal amounts of money, such as wages, salaries, and pensions. These are all examples of annuities. The same principles apply to all of the examples above. Annuity formulas and calculations enable us to answer questions such as "How much money will I have in five years if I deposit $100 per month into a savings account?" and "If I make regular payments toward the purchase of a car, how much am I really paying for it?"

INTRODUCTION

An annuity is a series of payments, usually of equal size, made at periodic time intervals. The word *annuity* implies yearly payments but the term applies to all periodic payment plans, the most frequent of which require annual, semi-annual, quarterly, or monthly payments. Practical applications of annuities are widely encountered in the finances of both businesses and individuals. Various types of annuities are identified based on the term of an annuity, the date of payment, and the length of the conversion period. In this chapter, we will deal with ordinary simple annuities, and calculate the future value, present value, payment amount, number of periods, or the interest rate.

11.1 INTRODUCTION TO ANNUITIES

A. Basic concepts

An **annuity** is a series of payments, usually of equal size, made at periodic intervals. The length of time between the successive payments is called the **payment interval** or **payment period**. The length of time from the beginning of the first payment interval to the end of the last payment interval is called the **term of an annuity**. The size of each of the regular payments is the **periodic rent,** and the sum of the periodic payments in one year is the **annual rent.**

B. Types of annuities

Several time variables affect annuities, and annuities are classified according to the time variable considered. The term of the annuity can be fixed or can be indefinite. Annuities are classified based on this differentiation.

Annuities certain are annuities for which the term is fixed, that is, for which both the beginning date and ending date are known. Typical examples of annuities certain include rental payments for real estate, lease payments on equipment, installment payments on loans, mortgage payments, and interest payments on bonds and debentures.

Contingent annuities are annuities for which the beginning date or the ending date or both are uncertain. Life insurance premiums and pension payments or payments from an RRSP converted into a life annuity are typical examples of contingent annuities. The ending date is unknown for these annuities since they terminate with the death of the recipient. Some contingent annuities are the result of clauses in wills, where the beginning date of periodic payments to a beneficiary is unknown, or of payments from a trust fund for the remaining life of a surviving spouse, since neither the beginning date nor the ending date is known.

A special type of annuity is the **perpetuity**, an annuity for which the payments continue forever. Perpetuities result when the size of the period rent is equal to or less than the periodic interest earned by a fund, such as a scholarship fund or an endowment fund to a university.

Variations in the date of payment are another way to classify annuities certain. If payments are made at the end of each payment period, we are dealing with an **ordinary annuity**. If, on the other hand, payments are made at the beginning of each payment period, we are dealing with an **annuity due**.

Typical examples of ordinary annuities are installment payments on loans, mortgage payments, and interest payments on bonds and debentures. Rent payments on real estate and lease payments on equipment rentals are examples of annuities due.

Deferring the first payment for a specified period of time gives rise to a **deferred annuity**. This type may be either an ordinary annuity or an annuity due, depending on whether the future payments are at the beginning or at the end of each payment interval.

A third time variable used to classify annuities is the length of the conversion period relative to the payment period. We distinguish between simple annuities and general annuities, depending on whether the conversion period coincides with the payment interval.

A **simple annuity** is an annuity in which the conversion period coincides with the payment interval. An example is when there are monthly payments on a loan for which the interest is compounded monthly. Since the compound interest period is the same as the payment period, this is a simple annuity, and P/Y and C/Y are equal.

A **general annuity** is an annuity in which the conversion period and the payment interval do not coincide. Typically, mortgages on homes are compounded semi-annually but repaid by monthly payments. Often, lending institutions offer the borrower the option of making weekly or bi-weekly payments. This is an example of a general annuity, since the conversion period is different from the payment period.

We will introduce ordinary simple annuities in this chapter. In Chapter 12, we will introduce ordinary general annuities. Other annuities, such as annuities due, deferred annuities, and perpetuities, will be introduced in Chapter 13.

EXAMPLE 11.1A

Classify each of the following annuities by

(i) term; (ii) date of payment; (iii) conversion period.

(a) Deposits of $150 earning interest at 12% compounded quarterly are made at the beginning of each quarter for four years.

SOLUTION

(i) annuity certain (the term is fixed: four years)

(ii) annuity due (payments are made at the beginning of each quarter)

(iii) simple annuity (the quarterly conversion period equals the quarterly payment period)

(b) Payments of $200 are made at the end of each month for five years. Interest is 9% compounded semi-annually.

SOLUTION

(i) annuity certain (the term is fixed: five years)

(ii) ordinary annuity (payments are made at the end of each month)

(iii) general annuity (semi-annual conversion period does not match the monthly payment period)

(c) A fund of $10 000 is deposited in a trust account earning interest compounded annually. Starting five years from the date of deposit, the interest earned for the year is to be paid out as a scholarship.

SOLUTION

(i) perpetuity (the payments can go on forever)

(ii) deferred annuity (the first payment is deferred for five years)

(iii) simple annuity (the annual conversion period equals the annual interest period)

(d) In his will, Dr. Chu directed that part of his estate be invested in a trust fund earning interest compounded quarterly. His surviving wife was to be paid, for the remainder of her life, $2000 at the end of every three months starting three months after his death.

SOLUTION

(i) contingent annuity (both the starting date and the ending date are uncertain)

(ii) ordinary annuity (payments at the end of every three months)

(iii) simple annuity (the quarterly conversion period equals the quarterly payment period)

EXERCISE 11.1

A. Classify each of the following by (a) term; (b) date of payment; (c) conversion period.

1. Payments of $50 are made at the beginning of each month for five years at 5% compounded semi-annually.
2. Deposits of $500 are made at the end of each quarter for nine years earning interest at 7% compounded quarterly.
3. A fund with an initial deposit of $50 000 is set up to provide annual scholarships to eligible business students in an amount not exceeding the annual interest earned by the fund. Scholarship payments are to begin three years from the date of deposit. Interest earned by the fund is compounded semi-annually.
4. The Saskatoon Board of Education introduced a long-term disability plan for its employees. The plan provides for monthly payments equal to 90% of regular salary starting one month after the beginning of the disability. Assume that the plan is subject to monthly compounding.
5. Gary invested $10 000 in an account paying interest compounded monthly with the provision that equal monthly payments be made to him from the account for fifteen years at the beginning of each month starting ten years from the date of deposit.
6. Ms. Baka set up a trust fund earning interest compounded semi-annually to provide equal monthly support payments for her surviving husband starting one month after her death.

11.2 ORDINARY SIMPLE ANNUITY—FINDING FUTURE VALUE FV

A. Future value of a series of payments—basic computation

EXAMPLE 11.2A Deposits of \$2000, \$4000, \$5000, \$1000, and \$3000 were made at the end of each of five consecutive years respectively at 6% compounded annually. Find the future value just after the last deposit was made.

SOLUTION The series of deposits can be represented on a time graph as shown:

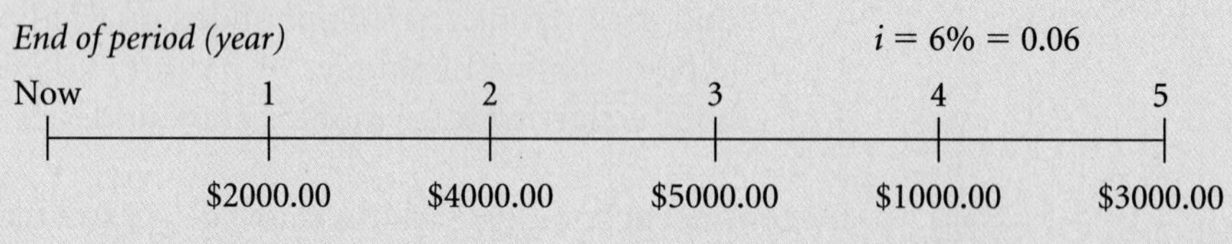

To find the future value of the series of deposits, we need to determine the combined value of the five deposits, including interest, at the focal point five years from now. This can be done using Formula 9.1A, $FV = PV(1 + i)^n$. A graphical representation of the method and data is shown in Figure 11.1 below.

FIGURE 11.1 Graphical Representation of Method and Data

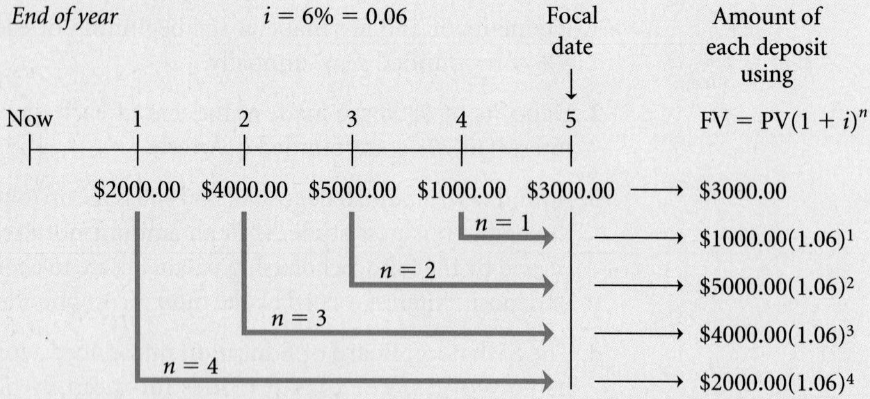

Explanations regarding the amount of each deposit:
The deposit of \$3000 has just been made and has a value of \$3000 at the focal date. The deposit of \$1000 has been in for one year ($n = 1$) and has earned interest for one year at the focal date. Similarly, the deposit of \$5000 has been in for two years ($n = 2$), the deposit of \$4000 for three years ($n = 3$), and the deposit of \$2000.00 for four years ($n = 4$).

The problem can now be solved by computing the future value of the individual deposits and adding.

Deposit 5	3000.00	=	\$3 000.00
Deposit 4	$1000.00(1.06)^1 = 1000.00(1.06)$	=	1 060.00
Deposit 3	$5000.00(1.06)^2 = 5000.00(1.1236)$	=	5 618.00
Deposit 2	$4000.00(1.06)^3 = 4000.00(1.191016)$	=	4 764.06
Deposit 1	$2000.00(1.06)^4 = 2000.00(1.262477)$	=	2 524.95
	TOTAL	=	\$16 967.01

EXAMPLE 11.2B

Find the future value of five deposits of \$3000 each made at the end of each of five consecutive years respectively at 6% compounded annually, just after the last deposit has been made.

SOLUTION

This example is basically the same as Example 11.2A except that all deposits are equal in size. The problem can be solved in the same way.

While the approach to solving the problem is fundamentally the same as in Example 11.2A, the fact that the deposits are *equal in size* permits a useful mathematical simplification. The equal deposit of \$3000 can be taken out as a common factor and the individual compounding factors can be added. This method avoids computing the amount of each individual deposit. In other words, it avoids computing separately $3000.00(1)$, $3000.00(1.06)^1$, $3000.00(1.06)^2$, and so on.

FIGURE 11.2 **Graphical Representation of Method and Data**

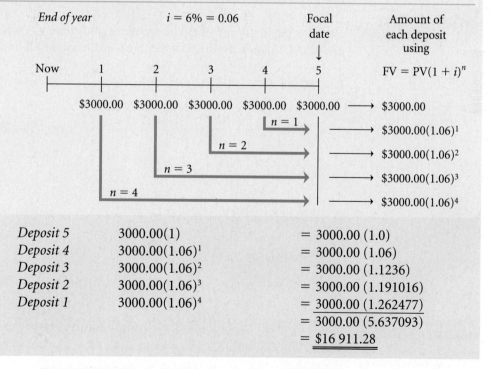

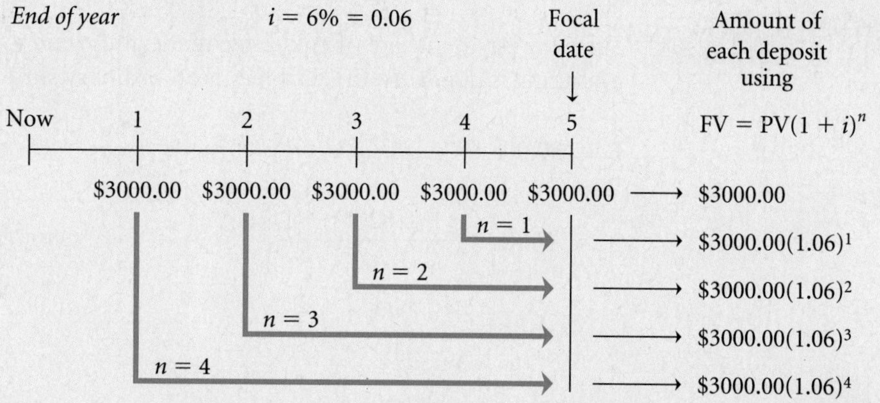

Deposit 5	$3000.00(1)$	$= 3000.00\ (1.0)$
Deposit 4	$3000.00(1.06)^1$	$= 3000.00\ (1.06)$
Deposit 3	$3000.00(1.06)^2$	$= 3000.00\ (1.1236)$
Deposit 2	$3000.00(1.06)^3$	$= 3000.00\ (1.191016)$
Deposit 1	$3000.00(1.06)^4$	$= 3000.00\ (1.262477)$
		$= 3000.00\ (5.637093)$
		$= \$16\,911.28$

Since the deposits in Example 11.2B are equal in size and are made at the end of each period and the payment interval is the same as the compounding period (one year), the problem is an ordinary simple annuity. Finding the sum of the accumulated values of the individual payments at the end of the term of the annuity is defined as finding the **future value of an annuity**.

B. Formula for finding the future value of an ordinary simple annuity

Because annuities are geometric progressions, the following formula has been developed for finding the accumulated value of this type of series of payments.

$$S_n = R\left[\frac{(1+i)^n - 1}{i}\right]$$ ——— Formula 11.1 ——— future value of an ordinary simple annuity

where S_n = the future value (accumulated value) of an ordinary simple annuity;
R = the size of the periodic payment (rent);
i = the interest rate per conversion period;
n = the number of periodic payments (which for simple annuities is also the number of conversion periods).

The factor $\frac{(1+i)^n - 1}{i}$ is called the **compounding** or **accumulation factor for annuities** or the **accumulated value of one dollar per period.**

EXAMPLE 11.2C

Find the accumulated value of quarterly payments of $50 made at the end of each quarter for ten years just after the last payment has been made if interest is 8% compounded quarterly.

SOLUTION

Since the payments are of equal size made at the end of each quarter and compounding is quarterly, the problem is an ordinary simple annuity.

$R = 50.00$; I/Y = 8; P/Y, C/Y = 4; $i = \frac{8\%}{4} = 2\% = 0.02$; $n = 10(4) = 40$

$$S_n = 50.00\left[\frac{(1+0.02)^{40} - 1}{0.02}\right]$$ ——— substituting in Formula 11.1

$$= 50.00\left(\frac{2.208040 - 1}{0.02}\right)$$

$$= 50.00\left(\frac{1.208040}{0.02}\right)$$

$$= 50.00(60.401983)$$

$$= \$3020.10$$

EXAMPLE 11.2D

You deposit $10 at the end of each month for five years in an account paying 6% compounded monthly.

(i) What will be the balance in your account at the end of the five-year term?

(ii) How much of the balance will you have contributed?

(iii) How much is interest?

SOLUTION

(i) R = 10.00; I/Y = 6; P/Y = 12; $i = \frac{6\%}{12} = 0.5\% = 0.005$; $n = 60$

$$
\begin{aligned}
S_n &= 10.00\left[\frac{(1+i)^n - 1}{i}\right] \\
&= 10.00\left[\frac{1.005^{60} - 1}{0.005}\right] \\
&= 10.00\left[\frac{(1.348850 - 1)}{0.005}\right] \\
&= 10.00(69.770031) \\
&= \$697.70
\end{aligned}
$$

(ii) Your contribution is $10 per month for 60 months, or 10.00(60) = $600.

(iii) Since your contribution is $600, the interest earned is 697.70 – 600.00 = $97.70.

C. Restatement of the ordinary simple annuity formula

The algebraic symbols used in the ordinary simple annuity formula correspond to the calculator keys of four preprogrammed financial calculators. To make it easier to relate annuity formulas directly to the symbols used on financial calculator keys and in spreadsheet software such as Excel, we will make the following changes to restate this and upcoming annuity formulas:

1. Replace A_n with PV_n as the symbol for Present Value;
2. Replace S_n with FV_n as the symbol for Future Value;
3. Replace R with PMT as the symbol for Periodic Payment.

From now on

Formula 11.1, $S_n = R\left[\frac{(1+i)^n - 1}{i}\right]$ will be presented as $FV_n = PMT\left[\frac{(1+i)^n - 1}{i}\right]$

D. Using preprogrammed financial calculators

In the same way that you can for compound interest calculations, you can use preprogrammed financial calculators to solve annuity problems efficiently by entering given values and retrieving the answer.

Specific function keys on preprogrammed financial calculators correspond to the five variables used in ordinary simple annuity calculations. Different models of financial calculators vary in their operation and labelling of the function keys. Appendix II, "Instructions and Tips for Three Preprogrammed Financial

Calculator Models," highlights the relevant variations for students using Texas Instruments' BAII Plus, Sharp's EL-733A, and Hewlett-Packard's 10BII calculators. The function keys used for the calculator models presented in Appendix II are shown in Table 11.1.

Table 11.1 Financial Calculator Function Keys That Correspond to Variables Used in Ordinary Simple Annuity Calculations

		Function Key		
Variable	**Algebraic Symbol**	**TI BAII+**	**Sharp EL-733A**	**HP 10BII**
The number of compounding periods	n	N	n	N
The periodic rate of interest[1]	i	I/Y + C/Y	i	I/Yr + P/YR
The periodic annuity payment	PMT or R	PMT	PMT	PMT
The present value or principal	PV or A_n	PV	PV	PV
The future value or maturity value	FV or S_n	FV	FV	FV

Note: The periodic rate of interest is entered as a percent and not as a decimal equivalent. For example, 8% is entered as "8" not ".08."

Instructions in this text are given for the Texas Instruments BAII Plus calculator. Refer to Appendix II for instructions for using the Sharp EL-733A and Hewlett-Packard 10BII calculators.

To begin an ordinary simple annuity calculation, previous data must be cleared. The following key sequence resets all entries to the defaults for each field: 2nd CLR TVM.

The number of payments per year must be determined. Enter this number as the P/Y. If the number of payments per year is specified as "monthly," follow the sequence 2nd P/Y 12 Enter 2nd QUIT. Substitute the number for the appropriate number of payments per year in each case. The most common frequencies are monthly, quarterly, semi-annually, or annually. Enter the given values in any order. Pressing CPT followed by the key representing the unknown variable then retrieves the value of the unknown variable.

Note: This assumes that the calculator is in the "END" mode. This is the default. To check, look at the upper right corner of the display screen. If no letters are shown in that corner, you are in the END mode. If the letters BGN are there, you must switch modes:

2nd BGN (PMT key)

2nd SET (END will now appear.)

2nd QUIT (Back to standard calculator—upper-right corner now blank.)

When performing an annuity calculation, usually only one of either the present value PV *or* the future value FV is involved. To avoid incorrect answers, the present value PV should be set to zero when determining the future value FV and vice versa. In addition, recall that the Texas Instruments BAII Plus calculator follows the established convention of treating cash inflows (cash received) as positive numbers and cash outflows (cash paid out) as negative numbers. Since periodic annuity payments are considered to be cash outflows, always enter the periodic payment as a negative number. Also, continue to always enter the present value as a negative number (if the present value is other than 0) to ensure your result has a positive value.

To solve Example 11.2D, in which PMT = 10.00, I/Y = 6; P/Y = 12, and $n = 60$, use the following procedure.

	Key in	Press	Display shows	
(Set P/Y, C/Y = 12)	0	PV	0	a precaution to avoid incorrect answers
	10	± PMT	10	this enters the periodic payment PMT
	6.0	I/Y	6.0	this enters the interest rate per year
	60	N	60	this enters the number of payments *n*
	CPT	FV	697.700305	this retrieves the wanted amount FV

The future value is $697.70.

E. Applications

EXAMPLE 11.2E

Jim set up a savings plan with Interior Trust whereby he deposits $300 at the end of each quarter for eight years. The amount in his account at that time will become a term deposit withdrawable after a further five years. Interest throughout the total time period is 5% compounded quarterly.

(i) How much will be in Jim's account just after he makes his last deposit?
(ii) What will be the balance of his account when he can withdraw the deposit?
(iii) How much of the total at the time of withdrawal did Jim contribute?
(iv) How much is the interest earned?

SOLUTION

As Figure 11.3 shows, problems of this type may be solved in stages. The first stage involves finding the future value of an *ordinary annuity*. This amount becomes the principal for the second stage, which involves finding the future value of a *single* sum of money invested for five years.

(i) PMT = 300.00; I/Y = 5; P/Y, C/Y = 4; $i = \frac{5\%}{4} = 1.25\% = 0.0125$; $n = 8(4) = 32$

$$FV_1 = 300.00\left[\frac{(1.0125^{32} - 1)}{0.0125}\right] \text{ ——— Formula 11.1}$$

$$= 300.00\left[\frac{(1.488131 - 1)}{0.0125}\right]$$

$$= 300.00(39.050441)$$

$$= \$11\,715.13$$

(ii) $PV = FV_1 = 11\,715.13$; $i = 0.0125$; $n = 5(4) = 20$

$$FV_2 = 11\,715.13(1.0125)^{20} \text{ ——— Formula 9.1A}$$

$$= 11\,715.13(1.282037)$$

$$= \$15\,019.23$$

FIGURE 11.3 Graphical Representation of Method and Data

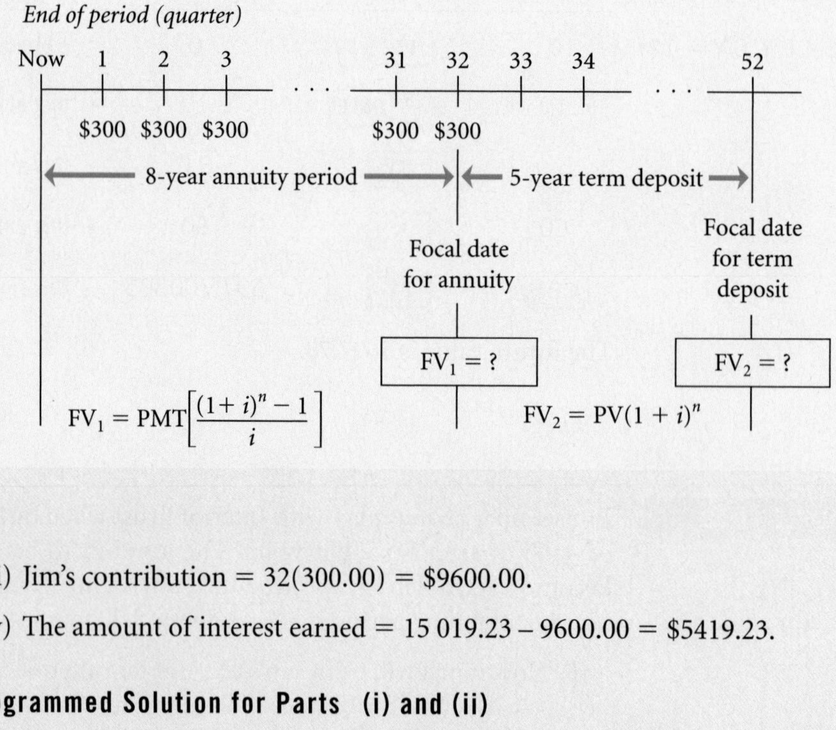

(iii) Jim's contribution = 32(300.00) = $9600.00.

(iv) The amount of interest earned = 15 019.23 – 9600.00 = $5419.23.

Programmed Solution for Parts (i) and (ii)

(i) (Set P/Y, C/Y = 4) 0 [PV] 300 [±] [PMT]

5.0 [I/Y] 32 [N] [CPT] [FV] 11715.13221

(ii) 11 715.13221 [±] [PV] 0 [PMT]

5.0 [I/Y] 20 [N] [CPT] [FV] 15019.23566

EXAMPLE 11.2F

The Gordons saved for the purchase of their dream home by making deposits of \$1000 per year for ten consecutive years in an account with Cooperative Trust in Saskatoon. The account earned interest at 5.75% compounded annually. At the end of the ten-year contribution period, the deposit was left for a further six years earning interest at 5.5% compounded semi-annually.

(i) What down payment were the Gordons able to make on their house?
(ii) How much of the down payment was interest?

SOLUTION

STEP 1

(i) Find the amount in the account at the end of the term of the ordinary annuity formed by the yearly deposits.

PMT = 1000.00; I/Y = 5.75; P/Y = 1; $i = 5.75\% = 0.0575$; $n = 10$

$$\begin{aligned} FV_1 &= 1000.00\left[\frac{(1.0575^{10} - 1)}{0.0575}\right] \\ &= 1000.00\left[\frac{1.749056 - 1}{0.0575}\right] \\ &= 1000.00(13.027064) \\ &= \$13\,027.06 \end{aligned}$$

STEP 2

Then compute the accumulated value of FV_1 in six years.

PV = FV_1 = 13 027.06; I/Y = 5.5; P/Y = 2; $i = \frac{5.5\%}{2} = 2.75\% = 0.0275$; $n = 12$

$$\begin{aligned} FV_2 &= 13\,027.06(1.0275)^{12} \\ &= 13\,027.06(1.384784) \\ &= \$18\,039.66 \end{aligned}$$

The Gordons made a down payment of \$18 039.66.

(ii) Since the Gordons contributed (1000.00)(10) = \$10 000.00, the amount of interest in the down payment is \$8039.66.

Programmed Solution for Part (i)

(Set P/Y, C/Y = 1) 0 [PV] 1000 [±] [PMT]
5.75 [I/Y] 10 [N] [CPT] [FV] [13027.06408]

(Set P/Y, C/Y = 2) 13 027.06408 [±] [PV]
0 [PMT] 5.5 [I/Y] 12 [N] [CPT] [FV] [18039.66698]

EXAMPLE 11.2G

Marisa has contributed \$1500 per year for the last twelve years into an RRSP deposit account with her bank in Windsor. Interest earned by these deposits was 4.5% compounded annually for the first eight years and 5.5% compounded annually for the last four years. Five years after the last deposit, she converted her

RRSP into a registered retirement income fund (RRIF). How much was the beginning balance in the RRIF if interest for those five years remained at 5.5%?

SOLUTION

As Figure 11.4 shows, the problem may be divided into two simple annuities. The first simple annuity covers the deposits for the first eight years; the second simple annuity covers the next four payments.

STEP 1 The focal date for the first annuity is at the end of Year 8 (focal date 1). The accumulated value (future value) of this simple annuity is computed using Formula 11.1.

$$
\begin{aligned}
FV_1 &= 1500.00\left[\frac{(1.045^8 - 1)}{0.045}\right] \\
&= 1500.00\left[\frac{1.422101 - 1}{0.045}\right] \\
&= 1500.00(9.380014) \\
&= \$14070.02
\end{aligned}
$$

STEP 2 FV_1 then accumulates for nine years (to the end of Year 17) at 5.5% to obtain FV_4 at the focal date for the beginning balance in the RRIF (focal date 3).

$$
\begin{aligned}
FV_4 &= 14\,070.02(1.055)^9 \\
&= 14\,070.02(1.619094) \\
&= \$22\,780.69
\end{aligned}
$$

FIGURE 11.4 Graphical Representation of Method and Data

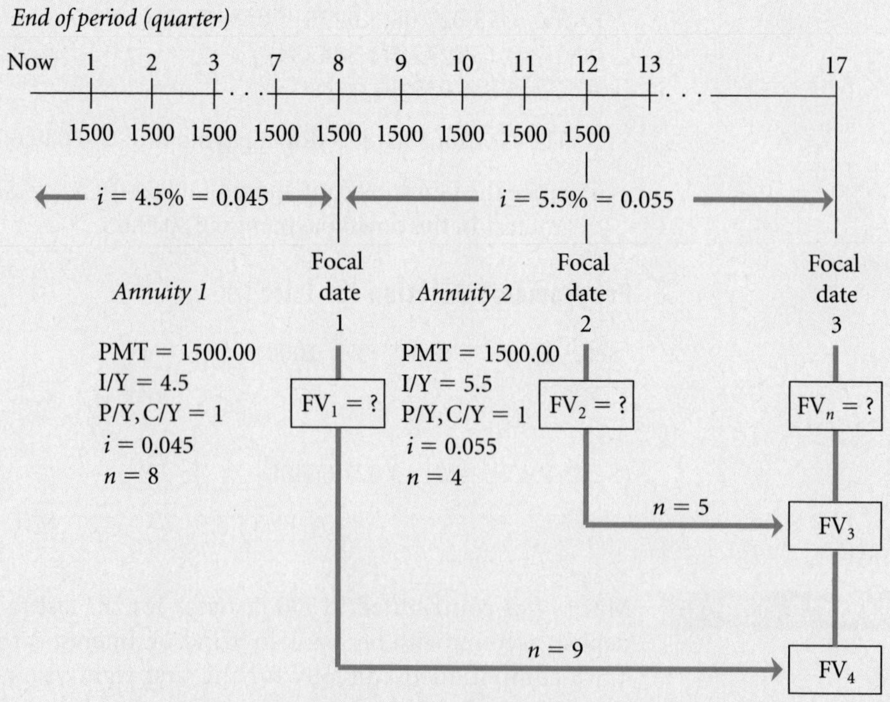

STEP 3 The focal date for the second simple annuity is at the end of Year 12 (focal date 2).

$$FV_2 = 1500.00\left[\frac{(1.055^4 - 1)}{0.055}\right]$$

$$= 1500.00\left[\frac{1.238825 - 1}{0.055}\right]$$

$$= 1500.00(4.342266)$$

$$= \$6513.40$$

STEP 4 FV_2 then accumulates for five years (to the end of Year 17) to obtain FV_3 at focal date 3.

$$FV_3 = 6513.40(1.055)^5$$

$$= 6513.40(1.306960)$$

$$= \$8512.75$$

STEP 5 The beginning balance FV_n in the RRIF is then obtained by adding FV_3 and FV_4.

$$FV_n = 8512.75 + 22\,780.69$$

$$= \$31\,293.44$$

Programmed Solution

FV_1

(Set P/Y, C/Y = 1) 0 [PV] 1500 [±] [PMT]

4.5 [I/Y] 8 [N] [CPT] [FV] [14070.02043]

FV_4

14 070.02043 [±] [PV] 0 [PMT]

5.5 [I/Y] 9 [N] [CPT] [FV] [22780.6895] [STO1]

FV_2

0 [PV] 1500 [±] [PMT] 5.5 [I/Y] 4 [N] [CPT] [FV] [6513.399563]

FV_3

6513.399563 [±] [PV] 0 [PMT]

5.5 [I/Y] 5 [N] [CPT] [FV] [8512.752734] [STO2]

[RCL] 1 + [RCL] 2 = 31 293.44

$FV_n = FV_3 + FV_4 = 8512.75 + 22\,780.69 = \$31\,293.44$

EXERCISE 11.2

EXCEL NOTES

If you choose, you can use Excel's ***Future Value (FV)*** function to answer the questions indicated below. Refer to **FV** on the Spreadsheet Template Disk to learn how to use this Excel function.

A. Find the future value of the ordinary simple annuity for each of the following six series of payments.

	Periodic Payment	Payment Interval	Term	Interest Rate	Conversion Period
1.	\$1500	1 quarter	$7\frac{1}{2}$ years	5%	quarterly
2.	20	1 month	6.75 years	6	monthly
3.	700	6 months	20 years	7	semi-annually
4.	10	1 month	15 years	9	monthly
5.	320	3 months	8 years, 9 months	10.4	quarterly
6.	2000	$\frac{1}{2}$ year	11 years, 6 months	8.8	semi-annually

B. Answer each of the following questions.

1. Find the accumulated value of payments of \$200 made at the end of every three months for twelve years if money is worth 5% compounded quarterly.

Reference Example 11.2C

2. What will deposits of \$60 made at the end of each month amount to after six years if interest is 4.8% compounded monthly?

3. How much interest is included in the future value of an ordinary simple annuity of \$1500 paid every six months at 7% compounded semi-annually if the term of the annuity is fifteen years?

4. Jane Allison made ordinary annuity payments of \$15 per month for sixteen years earning 9% compounded monthly. How much interest is included in the future value of the annuity?

5. Saving for his retirement 25 years from now, Jimmy Olsen set up a savings plan whereby he will deposit \$25 at the end of each month for the next 15 years. Interest is 3.6% compounded monthly.

(a) How much money will be in Mr. Olsen's account on the date of his retirement?

(b) How much will Mr. Olsen contribute?

(c) How much is interest?

Reference Example 11.2E

6. Mr. and Mrs. Wolf have each contributed \$1000 per year for the last ten years into RRSP accounts earning 6% compounded annually. Suppose they leave their accumulated contributions for another five years in the RRSP at the same rate of interest.

(a) How much will Mr. and Mrs. Wolf have in total in their RRSP accounts?

(b) How much did the Wolfs contribute?

(c) How much will be interest?

7. Cam saved \$250 each month for the last five years while he was working. Since he has now gone back to school, his income is lower and he cannot

continue to save this amount during the time he is studying. He plans to continue with his studies for four years and not withdraw any money from his savings account. Money is worth 4.5% compounded monthly.
(a) How much will Cam have in total in his savings account?
(b) How much did he contribute?
(c) How much will be interest?

8. Scott has saved $560 per quarter for the last three years in a savings account earning 5.20% compounded quarterly. He plans to leave the accumulated savings for seven years in the savings account at the same rate of interest.
(a) How much will Scott have in total in his savings account?
(b) How much did he contribute?
(c) How much will be interest?

9. Ms. Pitt has made quarterly payments of $1375 at the end of each quarter into an RRSP for the last seven years earning interest at 7% compounded quarterly. If she leaves the accumulated money in the RRSP for another three years at 8% compounded semi-annually, how much will she be able to transfer at the end of the three years into a registered retirement income fund?

Reference Example 11.2G

10. For the last six years Joe Borelli has made deposits of $300 at the end of every six months earning interest at 5% compounded semi-annually. If he leaves the accumulated balance in an account earning 6% compounded quarterly, what will the balance be in Joe's account at the end of another ten years?

11.3 ORDINARY SIMPLE ANNUITY—FINDING PRESENT VALUE PV

A. Present value of series of payments—basic computation

EXAMPLE 11.3A Find the single sum of money whose value now is equivalent to payments of $2000, $4000, $5000, $1000, and $3000 made at the end of each of five consecutive years respectively at 6% compounded annually.

SOLUTION The series of payments can be represented on a time graph.

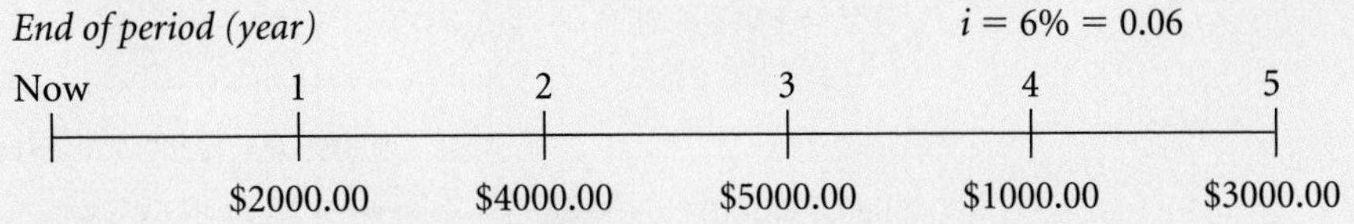

To find the present value of the series of payments, we need to determine the combined present value of the five payments at the focal point "now." This can be done using Formula 9.1C, $PV = FV(1 + i)^{-n}$. A graphical representation of the method and data is shown in Figure 11.5.

The solution to the problem can be completed by computing the present value of the individual payments and adding.

FIGURE 11.5 Graphical Representation of Method and Data

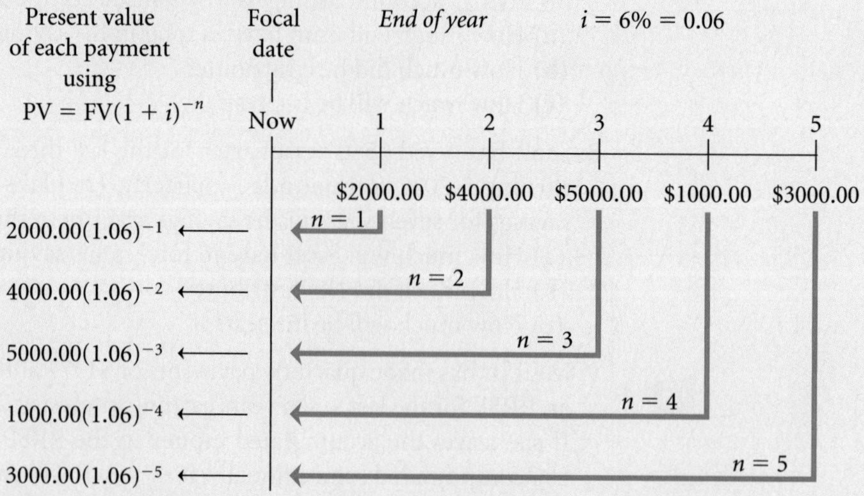

Payment 1	$2000.00(1.06)^{-1}$	=	$2000.00(0.943396)$	=	$ 1 886.79
Payment 2	$4000.00(1.06)^{-2}$	=	$4000.00(0.889996)$	=	3 559.99
Payment 3	$5000.00(1.06)^{-3}$	=	$5000.00(0.839619)$	=	4 198.10
Payment 4	$1000.00(1.06)^{-4}$	=	$1000.00(0.792094)$	=	792.09
Payment 5	$3000.00(1.06)^{-5}$	=	$3000.00(0.747258)$	=	2 241.77
			TOTAL		$12 678.74

EXAMPLE 11.3B Find the present value of five payments of $3000 made at the end of each of five consecutive years respectively if money is worth 6% compounded annually.

SOLUTION This example is basically the same as Example 11.3A except that all payments are equal in size.

FIGURE 11.6 Graphical Representation of Method and Data

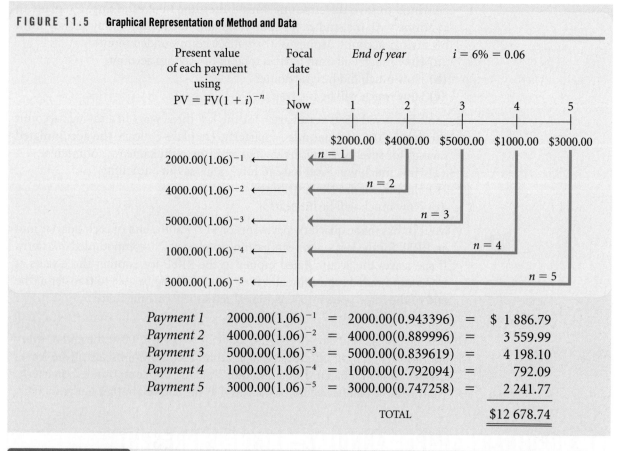

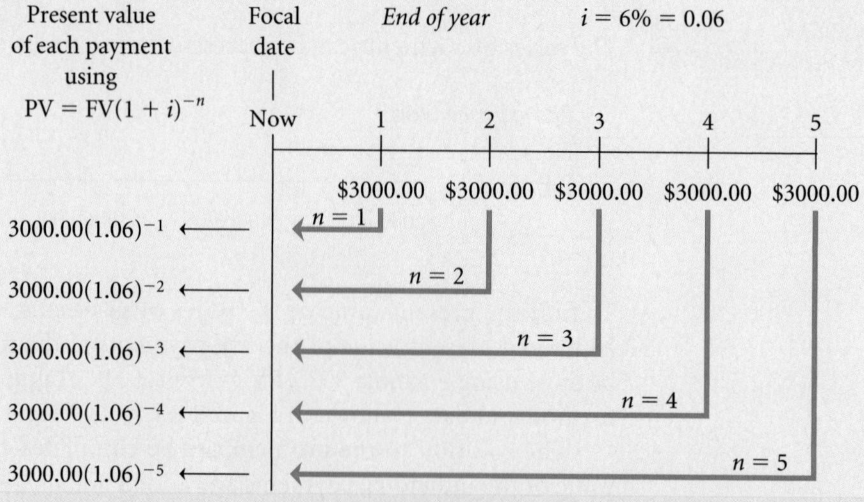

While the approach to solving the problem is fundamentally the same as in Example 11.3A, the fact that the payments are equal in size permits the same mathematical simplification used for Example 11.2B. The equal payment of \$3000 can be taken out as a common factor and the individual discount factors can be added.

Payment 1	$3000.00(1.06)^{-1}$	=	3000.00 (0.943396)
Payment 2	$3000.00(1.06)^{-2}$	=	3000.00 (0.889996)
Payment 3	$3000.00(1.06)^{-3}$	=	3000.00 (0.839619)
Payment 4	$3000.00(1.06)^{-4}$	=	3000.00 (0.792094)
Payment 5	$3000.00(1.06)^{-5}$	=	3000.00 (0.747258)
		=	3000.00 (4.212363)
		=	\$12 637.09

Since the payments in Example 11.3B are equal in size and are made at the end of each period, and the payment period is the same as the compounding period (one year), the problem is an ordinary simple annuity. Finding the sum of the present values of the individual payments at the beginning of the term of an annuity is defined as finding the present value of an annuity. It is useful to carry the mathematical simplification beyond simply taking out the common factor 3000.00.

B. Formula for finding the present value of an ordinary simple annuity

Because annuities are geometric progressions, the following formula for finding the present value of an ordinary simple annuity has been developed.

$$A_n = R\left[\frac{1-(1+i)^{-n}}{i}\right]$$

Formula 11.2 — **present value of an ordinary simple annuity**

where A_n = the present value (discounted value) of an ordinary simple annuity;
R = the size of the periodic payment (rent);
i = the interest rate per conversion period;
n = the number of periodic payments (which for simple annuities equals the number of conversion periods).

The factor $\frac{1-(1+i)^{-n}}{i}$ is called the present value factor or discount factor for annuities or the discounted value of one dollar per period.

EXAMPLE 11.3C

Find the present value at the beginning of the first payment period of payments of \$50 made at the end of each quarter for ten years, if interest is 8% compounded quarterly.

SOLUTION

Because the payments are of equal size made at the end of each quarter and compounding is quarterly, the problem is an ordinary simple annuity. Since the focal date is the beginning of the term of the annuity, the formula for finding the present value of an ordinary simple annuity applies.

$$R = 50.00;\ \ I/Y = 8;\ \ P/Y, C/Y = 4;\ \ i = \frac{8\%}{4} = 0.02;\ n = 10(4) = 40$$

$$A_n = 50.00\left[\frac{1-(1+0.02)^{-40}}{0.02}\right] \text{ ——— substituting in Formula 11.2}$$

$$= 50.00\left[\frac{1-0.452890}{0.02}\right]$$

$$= 50.00\left[\frac{0.547110}{0.02}\right]$$

$$= 50.00(27.355480)$$

$$= \$1367.77$$

EXAMPLE 11.3D

Suppose you want to withdraw \$100 at the end of each month for five years from an account paying 4.5% compounded monthly.

(i) How much must you have on deposit at the beginning of the month in which the first withdrawal is made at the end of the month?

(ii) How much will you receive in total?

(iii) How much of what you will receive is interest?

SOLUTION

(i) $R = 100.00;\ I/Y = 4.5;\ P/Y, C/Y = 12;\ i = \frac{4.5\%}{12} = 0.375\% = 0.00375;\ n = 60$

$$A_n = R\left[\frac{1-(1+i)^{-n}}{i}\right]$$

$$= 100.00\left[\frac{1-(1.00375)^{-60}}{0.00375}\right]$$

$$= 100.00\left[\frac{(1-0.798852)}{0.00375}\right]$$

$$= 100.00\left(\frac{0.201148}{0.00375}\right)$$

$$= 100(53.639381)$$

$$= \$5363.94$$

(ii) Total receipts will be \$100 per month for 60 months or \$6000.

(iii) Since the initial balance must be \$5363.94, the interest received will be 6000.00 – 5363.94 = \$636.06.

C. Restatement of the ordinary simple annuity formula

To make it easier to relate annuity formulas directly to the symbols used on financial calculator keys and in spreadsheet software such as Excel, we will make the changes noted on page 439 to restate Formula 11.2. From now on

Formula 11.2, $A_n = R\left[\frac{1-(1+i)^{-n}}{i}\right]$, will be presented as

$$PV_n = PMT\left[\frac{1-(1+i)^{-n}}{i}\right]$$

D. Present value using preprogrammed financial calculators

Refer to Appendix II for instructions for using the Sharp EL-733A and Hewlett-Packard 10B calculators to perform annuity calculations. The instructions given in this text are for the Texas Instruments BAII Plus calculator.

To find the present value of the ordinary simple annuity in Example 11.3D, in which R or PMT = 100.00, I/Y = 4.5, P/Y, C/Y = 12, and n = 60, proceed as follows.

	Key in	Press	Display shows	
(Set P/Y, C/Y = 12)	0	FV	0	a precaution
	100	± PMT	100	
	4.5	I/Y	4.5	
	60	N	60	
	CPT	PV	5363.938035	pressing the PV key retrieves the unknown present value PV_n

You must have $5363.94 on deposit.

E. Applications

When buying a home or vehicle, most people do not have enough money saved to pay the entire price. However, a small initial payment, called a **down payment**, is often accepted in the meantime. A mortgage loan from a financial institution is needed to supply the balance of the purchase price. The larger the down payment, the lesser the amount that needs to be borrowed. Based on the amount borrowed, the rate of interest, and the time to repay, the payments are determined. The amount of the loan is the *present value of the future periodic payments.*

The *cash value* is the price of the property at the date of purchase and represents the dated value of all payments at that date.

CASH VALUE = DOWN PAYMENT + PRESENT VALUE OF THE PERIODIC PAYMENTS

EXAMPLE 11.3E

Mr. and Mrs. Hong bought a vacation property, paying $3000 as a down payment and making further payments of $1000 every six months for twelve years. If interest is 7% compounded semi-annually, what was the cash value of the property?

SOLUTION

Since the first ongoing payment is due at the end of the first six-month period and compounding is semi-annual, the present value of the periodic payments is the present value of an ordinary simple annuity.

$$PMT = 1000.00;\ I/Y = 7;\ P/Y, C/Y = 2;\ i = \frac{7\%}{2} = 3.5\% = 0.035;\ n = 12(2) = 24$$

$$\begin{aligned}
PV_n &= 1000.00\left[\frac{(1 - 1.035^{-24})}{0.035}\right] \\
&= 1000.00\left[\frac{(1 - 0.437957)}{0.035}\right] \\
&= 1000.00\left(\frac{0.562043}{0.035}\right) \\
&= 1000.00(16.058368) \\
&= \$16\,058.37
\end{aligned}$$

Programmed Solution

(Set P/Y, C/Y = 2) 0 [FV] 1000 [±] [PMT]

7.0 [I/Y] 24 [N] [CPT] [PV] [16058.3676]

The cash value = 3000.00 + 16 058.37 = $19 058.37.

EXAMPLE 11.3F

Armand Rice expects to retire in seven years and would like to receive $500 per month for ten years starting at the end of the first month after his retirement. To achieve this goal, he deposited part of the proceeds of $50 000 from the sale of a property into a fund earning 10.5% compounded monthly.

(i) How much must be in the fund at the date of his retirement?

(ii) How much of the proceeds did he deposit in the fund?

(iii) How much does he expect to receive from the fund?

(iv) How much of what he will receive is interest?

SOLUTION

As Figure 11.7 shows, problems of this type should be solved in stages. The first step involves finding the present value of an annuity. This sum of money becomes the future amount for the second step, which involves finding the present value of that future amount at the date of deposit.

FIGURE 11.7 Graphical Representation of Method and Data

End of period (month) I/Y = 10.5; P/Y, C/Y= 12; $i = \frac{10.5\%}{12} = 0.875\% = 0.00875$

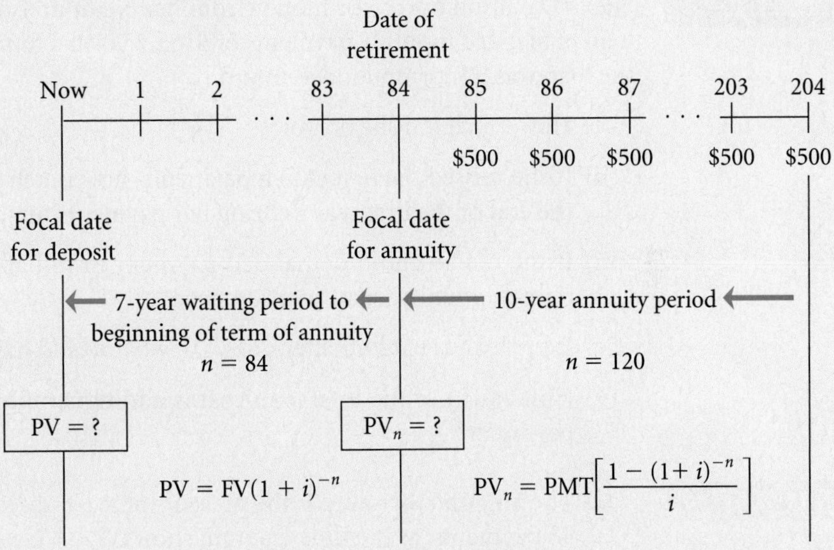

(i) PMT = 500.00; I/Y = 10.5; P/Y, C/Y = 12; $i = \frac{10.5\%}{12} = 0.875\% = 0.00875$;

n=120

$$PV_n = 500.00\left[\frac{(1 - 1.00875^{-120})}{0.00875}\right]$$

$$PV_n = 500.00\left[\frac{(1 - 0.35154)}{0.00875}\right]$$

$$= 500.00(74.109758)$$

$$= \$37\,054.88$$

(ii) $FV = PV_n = 37\,054.88$; $i = 0.00875$; $n = 84$

$$PV = 37\,054.88(1.00875)^{-84}$$
$$= 37\,054.88(0.481041)$$
$$= \$17\,824.91$$

(iii) He expects to receive 500.00(120) = $60 000.00.

(iv) Interest received will be 60 000.00 – 17 824.91 = $42 175.09.

Programmed Solution for Parts (i) and (ii)

(i) (Set P/Y, C/Y = 12) 0 [FV] 500 [±] [PMT]

10.5 [I/Y] 120 [N] [CPT] [PV] [37054.87916]

(ii) 37 054.87916 [FV] 0 [PMT]

10.5 [I/Y] 84 [N] [CPT] [PV] [–17824.9119]

EXAMPLE 11.3G

Sheila Davidson borrowed money from her credit union and agreed to repay the loan in blended monthly payments of \$161.75 over a four-year period. Interest on the loan was 9% compounded monthly.

(i) How much did she borrow?

(ii) If she missed the first eleven payments, how much would she have to pay at the end of the first year to bring her payments up to date?

(iii) If the credit union demanded payment in full after one year, how much money would Sheila Davidson need?

(iv) If the loan is paid off after one year, what would have been its total cost?

(v) How much of the total loan cost is additional interest paid on the missed payments?

SOLUTION

(i) The amount borrowed is the present value (or discounted value) of the 48 payments, as the time diagram shows.

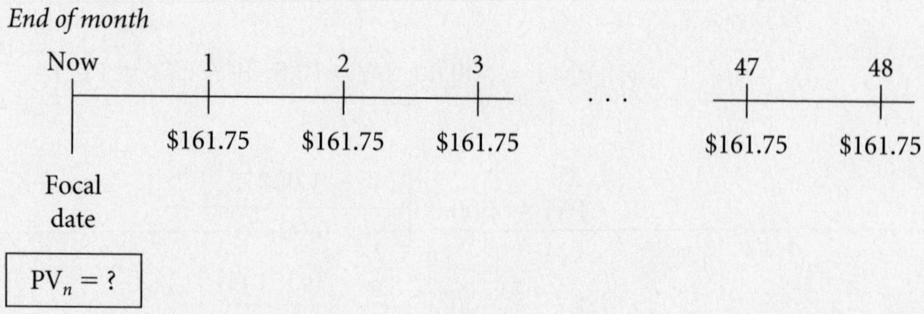

$$\text{PMT} = 161.75;\ \text{I/Y} = 9;\ \text{P/Y, C/Y} = 12;\ i = \frac{9\%}{12} = 0.75\% = 0.0075;$$

$$n = 4(12) = 48$$

$$PV_n = 161.75\left[\frac{(1 - 1.0075^{-48})}{0.0075}\right] \qquad \text{using Formula 11.2}$$

$$= 161.75\left[\frac{1 - 0.698614}{0.0075}\right]$$

$$= 161.75(40.184782)$$

$$= \$6499.89$$

Programmed Solution

(Set P/Y, C/Y = 12) 0 (FV) 161.75 (±) (PMT)

9.0 (I/Y) 48 (N) (CPT) (PV) 6499.88847

(ii) As the diagram below shows, Sheila Davidson must pay the accumulated value of the first twelve payments to bring her payments up to date after one year.

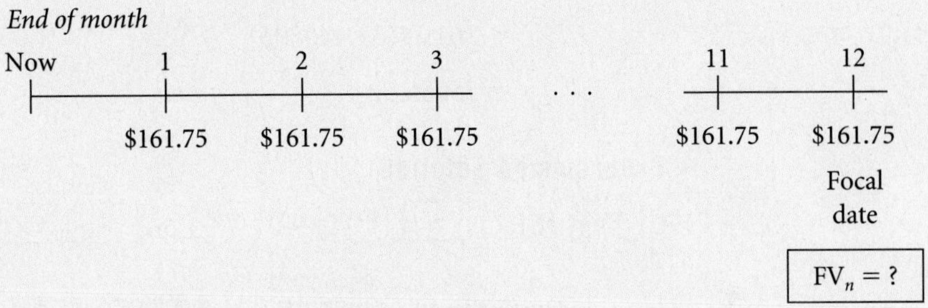

PMT = 161.75; $i = 0.0075$; $n = 12$

$$FV_n = 161.75\left[\frac{(1.0075^{12} - 1)}{0.0075}\right]$$ ——— using Formula 11.1

$$= 161.75\left[\frac{1.093807 - 1}{0.0075}\right]$$

$$= 161.75(12.507586)$$

$$= \$2023.10$$

Programmed Solution

0 (PV) 161.75 (±) (PMT) 9.0 (I/Y) 12 (N) (CPT) (FV) 2023.102093

(iii) The sum of money required to pay off the loan in full is the sum of the accumulated values of the first 12 payments plus the discounted values of the remaining 36 payments.

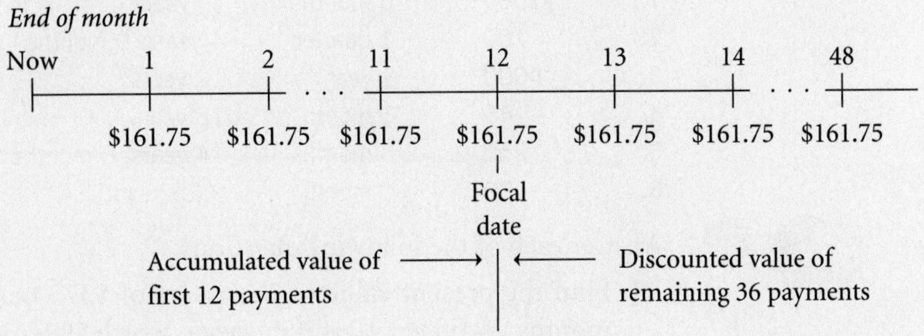

The accumulated value of the first 12 payments, as computed in part (ii) above, is \$2023.10. The discounted value of the remaining payments is found using Formula 11.2.

$$\text{PMT} = 161.75; \quad i = 0.0075; \quad n = 36$$

$$\text{PV}_n = 161.75\left[\frac{(1 - 1.0075^{-36})}{0.0075}\right]$$

$$= 161.75\left[\frac{1 - 0.764149}{0.0075}\right]$$

$$= 161.75(31.446805)$$

$$= \$5086.52$$

Programmed Solution

0 [FV] 161.75 [±] [PMT] 9.0 [I/Y] 36 [N] [CPT] [PV] [5086.520749]

The amount of money needed is 5086.52 + 2023.10 = \$7109.62.

(iv) The total cost of the loan if paid off after one year is 7109.62 – 6499.89 = \$609.73.

(v) To bring the payments up to date, \$2023.10 is needed. Since the normal amount paid during the first year would have been 161.75(12) = \$1941.00, the additional interest paid is 2023.10 – 1941.00 = \$82.10.

EXERCISE 11.3

EXCEL NOTES

If you choose, you can use ***Excel's Present Value (PV)*** function to answer the questions indicated below. Refer to **PV** on the Spreadsheet Template Disk to learn how to use this Excel function.

A. Determine the present value of the ordinary simple annuity for each of the following series of payments.

	Periodic Payment	Payment Interval	Term	Interest Rate	Compounding Period
1.	\$1600	6 months	$3\frac{1}{2}$ years	8.5%	semi-annually
2.	700	1 quarter	4 years, 9 months	5	quarterly
3.	4000	1 year	12 years	7.5	annually
4.	45	1 month	18 years	6.6	monthly
5.	250	3 months	14 years, 3 months	4.4	quarterly
6.	80	1 month	9.25 years	7.2	monthly

B. Answer each of the following questions.

1. Find the present value of payments of \$375 made at the end of every six months for fifteen years if money is worth 7% compounded semi-annually.

2. What is the discounted value of payments of $60 made at the end of each month for nine years if interest is 4.5% compounded monthly?

3. You want to receive $600 at the end of every three months for five years. Interest is 7.6% compounded quarterly.
(a) How much would you have to deposit at the beginning of the five-year period?
(b) How much of what you receive is interest?

4. An installment contract for the purchase of a car requires payments of $252.17 at the end of each month for the next three years. Suppose interest is 8.4% p.a. compounded monthly.
(a) What is the amount financed?
(b) How much is the interest cost?

5. For home entertainment equipment, Ted paid $400 down and signed an installment contract that required payments of $69.33 at the end of each month for three years. Suppose interest is 10.8% compounded monthly.
(a) What was the cash price of the equipment?
(b) How much was the cost of financing?

6. Elynor bought a vacation property for $2500 down and quarterly mortgage payments of $550.41 at the end of each quarter for five years. Interest is 8% compounded quarterly.
(a) What was the purchase price of the property?
(b) How much interest will Elynor pay?

7. Ed intends to retire in eight years. To supplement his pension he would like to receive $450 every three months for fifteen years. If he is to receive the first payment three months after his retirement and interest is 5% p.a. compounded quarterly, how much must he invest today to achieve his goal? Reference Example 11.3F

8. Planning for their son's college education, Vivien and Adrian Marsh opened an account paying 6.3% compounded monthly. If ordinary annuity payments of $200 per month are to be paid out of the account for three years starting seven years from now, how much did the Marshes deposit?

9. Joel and Jacquie each have a savings account that they will deposit money into today. From his account, Joel is planning to withdraw $50 at the end of each month for the next five years, starting one month from today. From her account, Jacquie is planning to wait three years, then withdraw $50 per month for the next five years. If the savings accounts pay interest at 3.6% compounded monthly, who needs to deposit more today and by how much?

10. Diane and Mike are planning to purchase a new plasma TV. They are debating whether it is better to pay $150 at the end of each month for eighteen months, starting now, or to take advantage of the store's offer of no payment for one year. They would then pay $180 at the end of each of eighteen months after the first payment. Which option results in the lower cost to purchase the TV if the interest rate on the loan is 13.56% compounded monthly?

11. Kimiko signed a mortgage requiring payments of $234.60 at the end of every month for six years at 7.2% compounded monthly.
(**a**) How much was the original mortgage balance?
(**b**) If Kimiko missed the first five payments, how much would she have to pay after six months to bring the mortgage payments up to date?
(**c**) How much would Kimiko have to pay after six months to pay off the mortgage?
(**d**) If the mortgage were paid off after six months, what would the total interest cost be?
(**e**) How much of the total interest cost is additional interest because of the missed payments?
Reference Example 11.3G

12. Field Construction agreed to lease payments of $642.79 on construction equipment to be made at the end of each month for three years. Financing is at 9% compounded monthly.
(**a**) What is the value of the original lease contract?
(**b**) If, due to delays, the first eight payments were deferred, how much money would be needed after nine months to bring the lease payments up to date?
(**c**) How much money would be required to pay off the lease after nine months?
(**d**) If the lease were paid off after nine months, what would the total interest be?
(**e**) How much of the total interest would be due to deferring the first eight payments?

BUSINESS MATH NEWS BOX

Get Rich, DRIP by DRIP

A lot of investors don't realize it, but if they DRIPped, they could find themselves awash in cash years down the road.

DRIPs—dividend reinvestment plans—enable you to take a particular corporation's dividends and use the money to buy more of its stock. If that wasn't brilliant enough, investors typically don't have to pay a commission on the reinvested dividends, unlike when they make their initial share purchase.

When the company's dividends are paid out, the proceeds are immediately used to buy shares in the company. This eliminates the temptation to try to time the market.

Lou Caci, an investment executive at ScotiaMcLeod in Winnipeg, says some companies will allow you to buy their shares through a DRIP at a discount of between 3% and 5% from the current market price. If, for example, your dividend comes in and the stock is trading at $20, you may be able to purchase shares for as little as $19 each. "It's kind of like a member's privilege. The deal is only available to shareholders," he says.

So if you decide you'd like to dip into a DRIP, just how much money will you have to reinvest in your favourite stocks? Dividends tend to average between 1% and 3% per year of the value of a stock, with blue-chip companies typically sitting at the upper end of the range. It might not seem like much in the short term, but over the long run the financial benefits can be substantial.

Source: "Get Rich, DRIP by DRIP: Enjoy Them While They Last," Geoff Kirbyson, *Winnipeg Free Press*, June 26, 2006, p. A.29. Edited excerpt reprinted with permission.

QUESTIONS

1. You purchase 1000 shares of a stock each year for five years. Assume that in the first year the stock price is $20 per share and the shares increase in price by 1% per year.
   a. What is the value of your investment in five years?
   b. If the same company provides annual dividends equal to 3% of stock price, calculate the amount of dividends that an investor will attain over this five-year period.
   c. If a company provided a DRIP that allows investors to attain a discount of 5% on the stock price, calculate the value of the investment after five years.

11.4 ORDINARY SIMPLE ANNUITIES—FINDING THE PERIODIC PAYMENT PMT

A. Finding the periodic payment PMT when the future value of an annuity is known

If the future value of an annuity FV_n, the number of conversion periods n, and the conversion rate i are known, you can find the periodic payment PMT by substituting the given values in the appropriate future value formula.

For ordinary simple annuities, use Formula 11.1.

$$FV_n = PMT\left[\frac{(1+i)^n - 1}{i}\right]$$ —— **Formula 11.1**

When using a preprogrammed financial calculator, you can find PMT by entering the five known values (FV, N, I/Y, P/Y, and C/Y) and pressing CPT PMT.

Recall that the PMT amount will be negative since payments are considered to be cash outflows.

EXAMPLE 11.4A What deposit made at the end of each quarter will accumulate to $10 000 in four years at 4% compounded quarterly?

SOLUTION $FV_n = 10\,000.00$; I/Y = 4; P/Y, C/Y = 4; $i = \frac{4\%}{4} = 1.0\% = 0.01$; $n = 16$

$$10\,000.00 = PMT\left(\frac{1.01^{16} - 1}{0.01}\right)$$ —— substituting in Formula 11.1

$$10\,000.00 = PMT\left(\frac{1.172579 - 1}{0.01}\right)$$

$$10\,000.00 = PMT(17.25786)$$

$$PMT = \frac{10\,000.00}{17.25786}$$

$$PMT = \$579.45$$

As we have emphasized throughout this book, beginning in Chapter 2, understanding how to rearrange terms in a formula is a very important skill. By knowing how to do this, you avoid having to memorize equivalent forms of the same formula.

When using a scientific calculator, you can find PMT by first rearranging the terms of the future value formulas as shown below. Then substitute the three known values (FV, n, and i) into the rearranged formula and use the calculator to solve for PMT.

$$FV_n = PMT\left[\frac{(1+i)^n - 1}{i}\right]$$ ——— Formula 11.1

$$PMT = \frac{FV_n}{\left[\frac{(1+i)^n - 1}{i}\right]}$$ ——— divide both sides by $\left[\frac{(1+i)^n - 1}{i}\right]$

$$PMT = \frac{FV_n i}{(1+i)^n - 1}$$ ——— dividing by a fraction is the same as inverting the fraction and multiplying

$FV_n = 10\,000.00$; $i = 0.01$; $n = 16$

$$PMT = \frac{10\,000.00(0.01)}{1.01^{16} - 1}$$ ——— substituting in rearranged Formula 11.1

$PMT = \$579.45$

EXAMPLE 11.4B

If you want to have \$5000 on deposit in your bank account in three years, how much must you deposit at the end of each month if interest is 4.5% compounded monthly?

SOLUTION

$FV_n = 5000.00$; $I/Y = 4.5$; $P/Y, C/Y = 12$; $i = 0.375\%$; $n = 36$

(Set P/Y = 12) [2nd] (CLR TVM) 0 [PV] 5000 [FV]

4.5 [I/Y] 36 [N] [CPT] [PMT] [-129.984622]

The monthly deposit required is \$129.98.

B. Finding the periodic payment PMT when the present value of an annuity is known

If the present value of an annuity PV_n, the number of conversion periods n, and the conversion rate i are known, you can find the periodic payment PMT by substituting the given values in the appropriate present value formula.

For ordinary simple annuities, use Formula 11.2.

$$PV_n = PMT\left[\frac{1 - (1+i)^{-n}}{i}\right]$$ ——— **Formula 11.2**

When using a scientific calculator, you can find PMT by first rearranging the terms of the present value formulas above. Then substitute the three known values (PV, n, and i) into the rearranged formula and solve for PMT.

When using a preprogrammed financial calculator, you can find PMT by entering the five known values (PV, N, P/Y, C/Y, and I/Y) and pressing CPT PMT.

EXAMPLE 11.4C

What semi-annual payment at the end of each six-month period is required to pay off a loan of $8000 in ten years if interest is 10% compounded semi-annually?

SOLUTION

$PV_n = 8000.00$; I/Y = 10; P/Y, C/Y = 2; $i = \frac{10\%}{2} = 5\% = 0.05$; $n = 10(2) = 20$

$$8000.00 = \text{PMT}\left(\frac{1 - 1.05^{-20}}{0.05}\right)$$ — substituting in Formula 11.2

$$8000.00 = \text{PMT}\left(\frac{1 - 0.376889}{0.05}\right)$$

$$8000.00 = \text{PMT}(12.462210)$$

$$\text{PMT} = \frac{8000.00}{12.462210}$$

$$\text{PMT} = \$641.94$$

Alternatively:

You can first rearrange the terms of Formula 11.2 to solve for PMT.

$$PV_n = \text{PMT}\left[\frac{1 - (1 + i)^{-n}}{i}\right]$$ — Formula 11.2

$$\text{PMT} = \frac{PV_n}{\left[\frac{1 - (1 + i)^{-n}}{i}\right]}$$ — divide both sides by $\left[\frac{1 - (1 + i)^{-n}}{i}\right]$

$$\text{PMT} = \frac{PV_n\, i}{1 - (1 + i)^{-n}}$$ — divide by a fraction is the same as inverting the fraction and multiplying

$PV_n = 8000.00$; $i = 0.05$; $n = 20$

$$\text{PMT} = \frac{8000.00(0.05)}{1 - 1.05^{-20}}$$

$$\text{PMT} = \$641.94$$

EXAMPLE 11.4D

Derek bought a new car valued at \$9500.00. He paid \$2000 down and financed the remainder over five years at 9% compounded monthly. How much must Derek pay at the end of each month?

SOLUTION

$PV_n = 9500.00 - 2000.00 = 7500.00$; I/Y = 9; P/Y, C/Y = 12; $i = \frac{9\%}{12} = 0.75\%$; $n = 60$

(Set P/Y = 12) 0 [FV] 7500 [±] [PV]

9 [I/Y] 60 [N] [CPT] [PMT] 155.687664

Derek's monthly payment is \$155.69.

C. Applications

EXAMPLE 11.4E

Taylor Marche, now age 37, expects to retire at age 62. To plan for her retirement, she intends to deposit \$1500.00 at the end of each of the next 25 years in a registered retirement savings plan. After her last contribution, she intends to convert the existing balance into a registered retirement income fund from which she expects to make 20 equal annual withdrawals. If she makes the first withdrawal one year after her last contribution and interest is 6.5% compounded annually, how much is the size of the annual retirement withdrawal?

SOLUTION

As the following time diagram shows, the problem can be broken down into two steps.

STEP 1 Compute the *accumulated* value FV_n of the 25 annual deposits of \$1500.00 into the RRSP.

PMT = 1500.00; I/Y = 6.5; P/Y = 1; $i = 6.5\% = 0.065$; $n = 25$

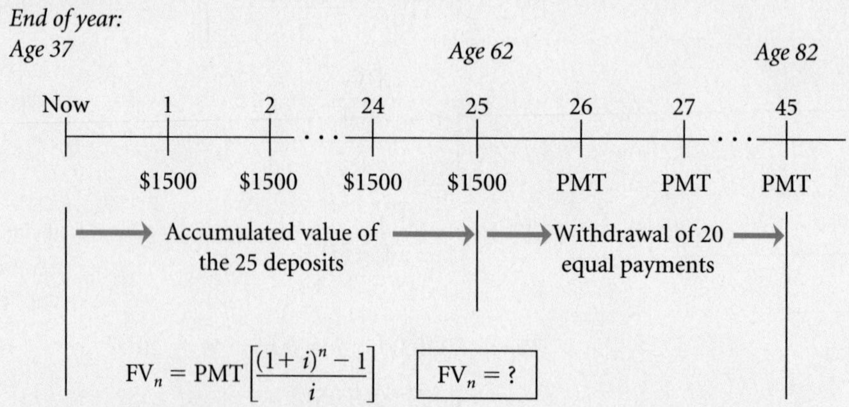

$$FV_n = 1500.00\left(\frac{1.065^{25} - 1}{0.065}\right) \quad \text{substituting in Formula 11.1}$$

$$= 1500.00(58.887679)$$

$$= \$88\,331.52$$

STEP 2 Compute the annual payment that can be withdrawn from the RRIF that has an initial balance of $88 331.52.

$PV_n = 88\,331.52;\quad i = 0.065;\quad n = 20$

$$88\,331.52 = \text{PMT}\left(\frac{1 - 1.065^{-20}}{0.065}\right) \qquad \text{using Formula 11.2}$$

$$88\,331.52 = \text{PMT}\,(11.018507)$$

$$\text{PMT} = \$8016.65$$

Programmed Solution

STEP 1 (Set P/Y, C/Y = 1) 0 [PV] 1500 [±] [PMT] 6.5 [I/Y] 25 [N] [CPT] [FV] [88331.51788]

STEP 2 88 331.518 [±] [PV] 0 [FV] 6.5 [I/Y] 20 [N] [CPT] [PMT] [8016.650159]

The sum of money that Taylor can withdraw each year is $8016.65.

EXERCISE 11.4

EXCEL NOTES

If you choose, you can use Excel's ***Payment (PMT)*** function to answer all of the questions below. Refer to **PMT** on the Spreadsheet Template Disk to learn how to use this Excel function.

A. For each of the following ten ordinary annuities, determine the size of the periodic rent.

	Future Value	Present Value	Payment Period	Term of Annuity	Interest Rate	Conversion Period
1.	$15 000		6 months	7 years, 6 mos.	5.5%	semi-annually
2.	6 000		1 quarter	9 years, 9 mos.	8	quarterly
3.		$12 000	12 months	15 years	4.5	annually
4.		7 000	6 months	12.5 years	7.5	semi-annually
5.	8 000		3 months	6 years	6.8	quarterly
6.		20 000	1 month	20 years	12	monthly
7.	45 000		1 month	10 years	9	monthly
8.		35 000	1 quarter	15 years	4	quarterly
9.		20 000	6 months	8 years	7	semi-annually
10.	16 500		3 months	15 years	5.75	quarterly

B. Answer each of the following questions.

1. What deposit made at the end of each quarter for fifteen years will accumulate to $20 000 at 6% compounded quarterly? Reference Example 11.4B
2. What payment is required at the end of each month for five years to repay a loan of $8000 at 8.4% compounded monthly?

3. A contract can be fulfilled by making an immediate payment of $7500 or equal payments at the end of every six months for ten years. What is the size of the semi-annual payments at 9.6% compounded semi-annually?

4. What payment made at the end of each month for eighteen years will amount to $16 000 at 9.6% compounded monthly?

5. What payment is required at the end of each month for twelve years to repay a $32 000 mortgage if interest is 6.5% compounded monthly?

6. How much must be deposited at the end of each quarter for nine years to accumulate to $11 000 at 4% compounded quarterly?

7. What payment made at the end of every six months for fifteen years will accumulate to $18 000 at 5% compounded semi-annually?

8. How much does a depositor have to save at the end of every three months for seven years to accumulate $3500 if interest is 3.75% compounded quarterly?

9. How much would you have to pay into an account at the end of every six months to accumulate $10 000 in eight years if interest is 3% compounded semi-annually?

10. Ontario Credit Union entered a lease contract valued at $7200. The contract provides for payments at the end of each quarter for three years. If interest is 6.5% compounded quarterly, what is the size of the quarterly payment?

11. Hunan bought a car priced at $15 300 for 15% down and equal monthly payments for four years. If interest is 8% compounded monthly, what is the size of the monthly payment? Reference Example 11.4D

12. Ruben bought a boat valued at $16 500 on the installment plan requiring a $2000 down payment and equal monthly payments for five years. If the first payment is due one month after the date of purchase and interest is 7.5% compounded monthly, what is the size of the monthly payment?

13. Olivia bought a car priced at $10 600 for 10% down and the balance in equal monthly payments over four years at 7.2% compounded monthly. How much does Olivia have to pay at the end of each month?

14. The Watsons bought a rental property valued at $50 000 by paying 20% down and mortgaging the balance over twenty-five years through equal payments at the end of each quarter at 10% compounded quarterly. What was the size of the quarterly payments?

15. Jie purchased a computer priced at $949.99, financing it by paying $75.12 on the date of purchase, and signing a contract to pay equal monthly payments over the next fifteen months. If the terms of the contract state that interest is calculated at 10.4% compounded monthly, how much does Jie have to pay at the end of each month?

16. George plans to deposit $1200 at the end of every six months for fifteen years into an RRSP account. After the last deposit, he intends to convert the

existing balance into an RRIF and withdraw equal amounts at the end of every six months for twenty years. If interest is expected to be 7.5% compounded semi-annually, how much will George be able to collect every six months?

Reference Example 11.4E

17. Starting three months after her grandson Robin's birth, Mrs. Devine made deposits of $60 into a trust fund every three months until Robin was twenty-one years old. The trust fund provides for equal withdrawals at the end of each quarter for four years, beginning three months after the last deposit. If interest is 4.75% compounded quarterly, how much will Robin receive every three months?

18. On the day of his daughter's birth, Mr. Dodd deposited $2000 in a trust fund with his credit union at 5% compounded quarterly. Following her eighteenth birthday, the daughter is to receive equal payments at the end of each month for four years while she is at college. If interest is to be 6% compounded monthly after the daughter's eighteenth birthday, how much will she receive every month?

19. Equal payments are to be made into a fund at the end of each month for fifteen years with interest at 9% compounded monthly. After the last payment, the fund is to be invested for seven years at 10% compounded quarterly and have a maturity value of $20 000. What is the size of the monthly payment?

20. Mr. Talbot received a retirement bonus of $18 000, which he deposited in an RRSP. He intends to leave the money for fourteen years, then transfer the balance into an RRIF and make equal withdrawals at the end of every six months for twenty years. If interest is 6.5% compounded semi-annually, what will be the size of each withdrawal?

21. When his aunt died, Ariel inherited $30 000. The terms of the will stated that he was to place the money into a savings account for eight years, and then withdraw equal amounts at the end of each month for ten years. If interest is 4.37% compounded monthly, what will be the size of each withdrawal?

11.5 FINDING THE TERM *n* OF AN ANNUITY

A. Finding the term *n* when the future value of an annuity is known

If the future value of an annuity FV_n, the periodic payment PMT, and the conversion rate i are known, you can find the term of the annuity n by substituting the given values in the appropriate future value formula.

For ordinary simple annuities, use Formula 11.1.

$$FV_n = PMT\left[\frac{(1+i)^n - 1}{i}\right]$$ ——— **Formula 11.1**

EXAMPLE 11.5A How long will it take for \$200 deposited at the end of each quarter to amount to \$5726.70 at 6% compounded quarterly?

SOLUTION $FV_n = 5726.70$; I/Y = 6; P/Y, C/Y = 4; $i = \frac{6\%}{4} = 1.5\% = 0.015$; PMT = 200.00

$$5726.70 = 200.00\left(\frac{1.015^n - 1}{0.015}\right) \quad \text{——— substituting in Formula 11.1}$$

$$28.6335 = \frac{1.015^n - 1}{0.015} \quad \text{——— divide both sides by 200.00}$$

$$0.429503 = 1.015^n - 1 \quad \text{——— multiply both sides by 0.015}$$

$$1.015^n = 1.429503 \quad \text{——— add 1 to both sides}$$

$$n \ln 1.015 = \ln 1.429503 \quad \text{——— solve for } n \text{ using natural logarithms}$$

$$0.014889n = 0.357327$$

$$n = \frac{0.357327}{0.014889}$$

$$n = 24 \text{ (quarters)}$$

It will take 24 quarters or six years for \$200 per quarter to grow to \$5726.70.

Alternatively:

You can first rearrange the terms of Formula 11.1 to solve for n.

$$FV_n = PMT\left[\frac{(1+i)^n - 1}{i}\right] \quad \text{——— Formula 11.1}$$

$$\frac{FV_n}{PMT} = \frac{(1+i)^n - 1}{i} \quad \text{——— divide both sides by PMT}$$

$$(1+i)^n = \left(\frac{FV_n i}{PMT}\right) + 1 \quad \text{——— multiply both sides by } i \text{ and add 1 to both sides}$$

$$n \ln(1+i) = \ln[(FV_n i/PMT) + 1] \quad \text{——— solve for } n \text{ using natural logarithms}$$

$$n = \frac{\ln[(FV_n i/PMT) + 1]}{\ln(1+i)} \quad \text{——— divide both sides by } \ln(1+i)$$

$FV_n = 5726.70$; $i = 0.015$; PMT = 200.00

$$n = \frac{\ln[5726.70 \times 0.015/200.00 + 1]}{\ln 1.015}$$

$$n = \frac{0.357327}{0.014889}$$

$$n = 24 \text{ (quarters)}$$

POINTERS AND PITFALLS

For annuity problems in which the period of investment or loan repayment must be determined, once n has been calculated, simply divide n by m to calculate the period of investment or loan repayment in years. To illustrate, the solution in Example 11.5A is $n = 24$. Since $m = 4$ (the question states "at the end of each quarter"), the period of investment is n / m, or $24 / 4 = 6$ years.

EXAMPLE 11.5B

In how many months will your bank account grow to \$3000 if you deposit \$150 at the end of each month and the account earns 9% compounded monthly?

SOLUTION

$FV_n = 3000.00$; PMT = 150.00; I/Y = 9; P/Y, C/Y = 12; $i = \frac{9\%}{12} = 0.75\%$

(Set P/Y, C/Y = 12) 0 [PV] 3000 [FV]

150 [±] [PMT] 9 [I/Y] [CPT] [N] 18.7047

It will take about 19 months to accumulate \$3000.00.

Interpretation of Result

When FV_n, PMT, and i are known, it is unlikely that n will be a whole number. The fractional time period of 0.7 month indicates that the accumulated value of 18 deposits of \$150 will be less than \$3000, while the accumulated value of 19 deposits will be more than \$3000. This point can be verified by computing FV_{18} and FV_{19}.

$$FV_{18} = 150.00\left(\frac{1.0075^{18} - 1}{0.0075}\right) = 150.00(19.194718) = \$2879.21$$

$$FV_{19} = 150.00\left(\frac{1.0075^{19} - 1}{0.0075}\right) = 150.00(20.338679) = \$3050.80$$

The definition of an annuity does not provide for making payments at unequal time intervals. The appropriate answer to problems in which n is a fractional value is a whole number. The usual approach is to round upward so that in this case $n = 19$.

Rounding upward implies that the deposit made at the end of the nineteenth month is smaller than the usual deposit of \$150.00. The method of computing the size of the final deposit or payment when the term of the annuity is a fractional value rounded upward is considered in Chapter 14.

B. Finding the term n when the present value of an annuity is known

If the present value PV_n, the periodic payment PMT, and the conversion rate i are known, you can find the term of the annuity n by substituting the given values in the present value formula.

$$PV_n = PMT\left[\frac{1 + (1 + i)^{-n}}{i}\right]$$ ——— **Formula 11.2**

When using a scientific calculator, you can find n by first rearranging the terms of the present value formulas above. Then substitute the three known values (PV, PMT, and i) into the rearranged formula and solve for n.

When using a preprogrammed financial calculator, you can find n by entering the five known values (PV, PMT, P/Y, C/Y, and I/Y) and pressing **CPT** **N**.

Note: When using the Texas Instruments BAII Plus financial calculator, you *must* enter *either* the PV or PMT as a negative amount, *but not both.* Due to the sign conventions used by this calculator, entering *both* PV and PMT as negative amounts or as positive amounts will lead to an *incorrect* final answer. The calculator does *not* indicate that the answer is incorrect or that an entry error was made. (This has not been an issue until now because either PV or PMT was 0 in all the examples we discussed.) To avoid incorrect answers, *always* enter the PV amount as a negative number and the PMT amount as a positive number when FV = 0 and you are calculating n. However, if PV = 0, enter PMT as a negative number and FV as a positive number. The examples in this text follow these rules. Refer to Appendix II to check whether this step is necessary if you use the Sharp EL-733A or the Hewlett-Packard 10B calculator.

EXAMPLE 11.5C

How many quarterly payments of \$600 are required to repay a loan of \$5400 at 6% compounded quarterly?

SOLUTION

$PV_n = 5400.00$; $PMT = 600.00$; $I/Y = 6$; $P/Y, C/Y = 4$; $i = \frac{6\%}{4} = 1.5\% = 0.015$

$$5400.00 = 600.00\left(\frac{1 - 1.015^{-n}}{0.015}\right)$$ ——— substituting in Formula 11.2

$$9.00 = \frac{1 - 1.015^{-n}}{0.015}$$ ——— divide both sides by 600.00

$$0.135 = 1 - 1.015^{-n}$$ ——— multiply both sides by 0.015

$$1.015^{-n} = 0.865$$

$$-n \ln 1.015 = \ln 0.865$$ ——— solve for n using natural logarithms

$$-0.014889n = -0.145026$$

$$n = \frac{-0.145026}{-0.014889}$$

$$n = 9.740726$$

$$n = 10 \text{ quarters}$$

To repay the loan, 10 quarterly payments are required.

Alternatively:

You can first rearrange the terms of Formula 11.2 to solve for n.

$$PV_n = PMT\left[\frac{1 - (1 + i)^{-n}}{i}\right]$$ ——— Formula 11.2

$$\frac{PV_n}{PMT} = \frac{1-(1+i)^{-n}}{i}$$ —— divide both sides by PMT

$$\left(\frac{PV_n i}{PMT}\right) - 1 = -(1+i)^{-n}$$ —— multiply both sides by *i* and subtract 1 from both sides

$$(1+i)^{-n} = 1 - \left(\frac{PV_n i}{PMT}\right)$$ —— multiply both sides by −1

$$-n\ln(1+i) = \ln\left[1 - \left(\frac{PV_n i}{PMT}\right)\right]$$ —— solve for *n* using natural logarithms

$$n = \frac{\ln\left[1 - \left(\frac{PV_n i}{PMT}\right)\right]}{-\ln(1+i)}$$ —— divide both sides by −ln(1+*i*)

$PV_n = 5400.00$; $PMT = 600.00$; $i = 0.015$

$$n = \frac{\ln\left[1 - \frac{(5400.00)(0.015)}{600.00}\right]}{-\ln(1.015)}$$ —— substituting in rearranged Formula 11.2

$$n = \frac{-0.145026}{-0.014889}$$

$$n = 9.740718$$

$$n = 10 \text{ quarters}$$

EXAMPLE 11.5D

On his retirement, Art received a bonus of $8000 from his employer. Taking advantage of the existing tax legislation, he invested the money in an annuity that provides for semi-annual payments of $1200 at the end of every six months. If interest is 6.25% compounded semi-annually, how long will the annuity exist?

SOLUTION

$PV_n = 8000.00$; PMT = 1200.00; I/Y = 6.25; P/Y, C/Y = 2; $i = \frac{6.25\%}{2} = 3.125\%$

(Set P/Y, C/Y = 2) 0 [FV] 8000 [±] [PV]

1200 [PMT] 6.25 [I/Y] [CPT] [N] 7.59188

↑ half-year periods

The annuity will be in existence for four years. Art will receive seven half-yearly payments of $1200 and a final payment that will be less than $1200.

EXERCISE 11.5

EXCEL NOTES

If you choose, you can use Excel's ***Number of Compounding Periods (NPER)*** function to answer all of the questions below. Refer to **NPER** on the Spreadsheet Template Disk to learn how to use this Excel function.

A. Find the term of each of the following ten ordinary annuities. (State your answer in years and months.)

	Future Value	Present Value	Periodic Rent	Payment Interval	Interest Rate	Conversion Period
1.	$20 000		$ 800	1 year	7.5%	annually
2.	17 000		35	1 month	9	monthly
3.		$14 500	190	1 month	5.25	monthly
4.		5 000	300	3 months	4	quarterly
5.	3 600		175	6 months	7.4	semi-annually
6.		9 500	740	1 quarter	5.2	quarterly
7.		21 400	1660	6 months	4.5	semi-annually
8.	13 600		140	3 months	8	quarterly
9.	7 200		90	1 month	3.75	monthly
10.		9 700	315	3 months	11	quarterly

B. Answer each of the following questions.

1. How long would it take you to save $4500 by making deposits of $50 at the end of every month into a savings account earning 6% compounded monthly?

Reference Example 11.5A

2. How long will it take to save $5000 by making deposits of $60 at the end of every month into an account earning interest at 6% monthly?

3. Suppose $646.56 is deposited at the end of every six months into an account earning 6.5% compounded semi-annually. If the balance in the account four years after the last deposit is to be $20 000, how many deposits are needed?

4. For how long can $1000 be withdrawn at the end of each month from an account containing $36 000 if interest is 6.4% compounded monthly?

5. In what period of time could you pay back a loan of $3600 by making payments of $96 at the end of each month if interest is 10.5% compounded monthly?

Reference Example 11.5C

6. For how long will Amir have to make payments of $300 at the end of every three months to repay a loan of $5000 if interest is 7% compounded quarterly?

7. Josie borrowed $8000 compounded monthly to help finance her education. She contracted to repay the loan in monthly payments of

$300 each. If the payments are due at the end of each month and interest is 4% compounded monthly, how long will Josie have to make monthly payments?

8. A mortgage of $26 500 is to be repaid by making payments of $1560 at the end of every six months. If interest is 7% compounded semi-annually, what is the term of the mortgage?

9. A car loan of $12 000 is to be repaid with end-of-month payments of $292.96. If interest is 8% compounded monthly, how long is the term of the loan?

10. A deposit of $4000 is made today. For how long can $500 be withdrawn from the account at the end of every three months starting three months from now if interest is 4% compounded quarterly? Reference Example 11.5D

11. Lauren deposited $12 000 today. He plans to withdraw $1100 every six months. For how long can he withdraw from the account starting six months from now if interest is 3.9% compounded semi-annually?

12. Cathy placed $7000 into a savings account. For how long can $800 be withdrawn from the account at the end of every month starting one month from now if interest is 4.58% compounded monthly?

13. Rae deposited $5741, the earnings from her part-time job, into a savings account. If she withdraws $650 at the end of each month, how long will the money last if interest is 5.15% compounded monthly?

14. Kaye deposited $6000 into a savings account today. For how long can $730 be withdrawn from the account at the end of every three months starting three months from now if interest is 3.9% compounded quarterly?

11.6 FINDING THE PERIODIC RATE OF INTEREST *i* USING PREPROGRAMMED FINANCIAL CALCULATORS

A. Finding the periodic rate of interest *i* for simple annuities

Preprogrammed financial calculators are especially helpful when solving for the conversion rate i. Determining i without a financial calculator is extremely time-consuming. However, it *can* be done by hand, as illustrated in Appendix B on the CD-ROM.

When the future value or present value, the periodic payment PMT, and the term n of an annuity are known, the periodic rate of interest i can be found by entering the three known values into a preprogrammed financial calculator. (Remember, if both PV and PMT are non-zero, enter PV only as a negative amount.) For ordinary simple annuities, retrieve the answer by pressing CPT I/Y . This represents the nominal annual rate of interest j. By dividing j by the number of compounding periods per year m, you can obtain the periodic interest rate i.

EXAMPLE 11.6A

Compute the nominal annual rate of interest at which \$100 deposited at the end of each month for ten years will amount to \$15 000.

SOLUTION

$FV_n = 15\,000.00$; $PMT = 100.00$; $P/Y, C/Y = 12$; $n = 120$; $m = 12$

(Set P/Y, C/Y = 12) 0 [PV] 15 000 [FV] 100 [±] [PMT]

120 [N] [CPT] [I/Y] [4.350057]

Allow several seconds for the computation.

The nominal annual rate of interest is approximately 4.35% compounded monthly. The monthly conversion rate is approximately 4.350057/12 = 0.362505 per month.

EXAMPLE 11.6B

A loan of \$6000 is paid off over five years by monthly payments of \$120.23. What is the nominal annual rate of interest on the loan?

SOLUTION

$PV_n = 6000.00$; $PMT = 120.23$; $n = 60$; $P/Y, C/Y = 12$

(Set P/Y, C/Y = 12) 0 [FV] 6000 [±] [PV] 120.23 [PMT]

60 [N] [CPT] [I/Y] [7.500810]

Allow several seconds for the computation.

The nominal annual rate of interest is approximately 7.5% compounded monthly. The monthly compounding rate is approximately 7.500810/12 = 0.625067%.

EXERCISE 11.6

A. Compute the nominal annual rate of interest for each of the following eight ordinary simple annuities.

	Future Value	Present Value	Periodic Rent	Payment Interval	Term	Conversion Period
1.	\$ 9 000		\$ 230.47	3 months	8 years	quarterly
2.	4 800		68.36	1 month	5 years	monthly
3.		\$ 7 400	119.06	1 month	7 years	monthly
4.		6 980	800.00	6 months	5 years	semi-annually
5.	70 000		1014.73	1 year	25 years	annually
6.		42 000	528.00	1 month	10 years	monthly
7.		28 700	2015.00	6 months	15 years	semi-annually
8.	36 000		584.10	3 months	12 years	quarterly

B. Answer each of the following questions.

1. Compute the nominal annual rate of interest at which $350 paid at the end of every three months for six years accumulates to $12 239.76.

Reference Example 11.6A

2. Katrina contributed $2500 at the end of every year into an RRSP for ten years. What nominal annual rate of interest will the RRSP earn if the balance in Katrina's account just after she made her last contribution was $33 600?

3. What nominal annual rate of interest compounded monthly was paid if contributions of $250 made into an RRSP at the end of every month amounted to $35 000 after ten years?

4. Compute the nominal annual rate of interest compounded monthly at which $400 paid at the end of the month for eight years accumulates to $45 000.

5. What is the nominal annual rate of interest if a four-year loan of $6000 is repaid by end-of-month payments of $144.23?

6. Rita converted an RRSP balance of $119 875.67 into an RRIF that will pay her $1800 at the end of every month for nine years. What is the nominal annual rate of interest?

7. A car valued at $11 400 can be purchased for 10% down and end-of-month payments of $286.21 for three-and-a-half years. What is the effective annual cost of financing?

8. Property worth $50 000 can be purchased for 20% down and mortgage payments of $1000 at the end of each quarter for 25 years. What effective annual rate of interest is charged?

9. What is the nominal annual rate of interest compounded quarterly if a loan of $21 500 is repaid in seven years by payments of $1000 made at the end of every three months?

10. A property worth $35 000 is purchased for 10% down and payments of $2100 at the end of every six months for twelve years. What is the effective annual rate of interest?

Review Exercise

1. Payments of $360 are made into a fund at the end of every three months for twelve years. The fund earns interest at 7% compounded quarterly.
   (a) What will be the balance in the fund after twelve years?
   (b) How much of the balance is deposits?
   (c) How much of the balance is interest?

2. A trust fund is set up to make payments of $950 at the end of each month for seven-and-a-half years. Interest on the fund is 7.8% compounded monthly.
   (a) How much money must be deposited into the fund?
   (b) How much will be paid out of the fund?
   (c) How much interest is earned by the fund?

3. How much interest is included in the accumulated value of $75.90 paid at the end of each month for four years if interest is 9% compounded monthly?

4. If a loan was repaid by payments of $320 at the end of each quarter in five years at 8% compounded quarterly, how much money had been borrowed?

5. How long will it take to build up a fund of $10 000 by saving $300 at the end of every six months at 4.5% compounded semi-annually?

6. What is the term of a mortgage of $35 000 repaid by end-of-month payments of $475 if interest is 7.5% compounded monthly?

7. Suppose you would like to have $10 000 in your savings account and interest is 8% compounded quarterly. How much must you deposit every three months for five years if the deposits are made at the end of each quarter?

8. Equal sums of money are withdrawn monthly from a fund of $20 000 for fifteen years. If interest is 9% compounded monthly, what is the size of each withdrawal if the withdrawal is made at the end of each month?

9. If you contribute $1500 into an RRSP at the end of every six months for twelve years and interest on the deposits is 8% compounded semi-annually, how much would the balance in the RRSP be seven years after the last contribution?

10. Doris purchased a piano with $300 down and end-of-month payments of $124 for two-and-a-half years at 9% compounded monthly. What was the purchase price of the piano?

11. A contract valued at $11 500 requires payment of $1450 at the end of every six months. If interest is 10.5% compounded semi-annually, what is the term of the contract?

12. What nominal annual rate of interest is paid on RRSP contributions of $1100 made at the end of each quarter for fifteen years if the balance just after the last contribution is $106 000?

13. What nominal annual rate of interest was charged on a loan of $5600 repaid in end-of-month installments of $121.85 in four-and-a-half years?

14. Glenn has made contributions of $250 at the end of every three months into an RRSP for ten years. Interest for the first four years was 4% compounded quarterly. Since then the interest rate has been 5% compounded quarterly. How much will Glenn have in his RRSP three years after the last contribution?

15. Avi expects to retire in twelve years. Beginning one month after his retirement he would like to receive $500 per month for twenty years. How much must he deposit into a fund today to be able to do so if the rate of interest on the deposit is 6% compounded monthly?

16. A contract is signed requiring payments of $750 at the end of every three months for eight years. How much is the cash value of the contract if money is worth 9% compounded quarterly?

17. The amount of $10 000 is put into a five-year term deposit paying 7.5% compounded semi-annually. After five years the deposit is converted

into an ordinary annuity of equal semi-annual payments of \$2000 each. If interest remains the same, what is the term of the annuity?

18. Mirielle has deposited \$125 at the end of each month for 15 years at 7.5% compounded monthly. After her last deposit she converted the balance into an ordinary annuity paying \$1200 every three months for twelve years. If interest on the annuity is compounded quarterly, what is the effective annual rate of interest paid by the annuity?

19. A contract is signed requiring payments of \$750 at the end of every three months for eight years. How much is the cash value of the contract if money is worth 10.5% compounded quarterly?

20. A savings plan requiring deposits of \$400 at the end of each quarter for twenty years provides for a lump-sum payment of \$92 000 just after the last deposit has been made.
   (a) What is the effective annual rate of interest on the savings plan?
   (b) If, instead of the lump sum, monthly ordinary annuity payments of \$1350 may be accepted at the same nominal rate of interest (correct to two decimals) but compounded monthly, what is the term of the annuity?

Self-Test

1. You won \$100 000 in a lottery and you want to set some of that sum aside for ten years. After ten years, you would like to receive \$2400 at the end of every three months for eight years. How much of your winnings must you set aside if interest is 5.5% compounded quarterly?

2. A sum of money is deposited at the end of every month for ten years at 7.5% compounded monthly. After the last deposit, interest for the account is to be 6% compounded quarterly and the account is to be paid out by quarterly payments of \$4800 over six years. What is the size of the monthly deposit?

3. Compute the nominal annual rate of interest compounded semi-annually on a loan of \$48 000 repaid in installments of \$4000 at the end of every six months in ten years.

4. A loan of \$14 400 is to be repaid in end-of-the-quarter payments of \$600. How many payments are required to repay the loan at 10.5% compounded quarterly?

5. The amount of \$57 426 is invested at 6% compounded monthly for six years. After the initial six-year period, the balance in the fund is converted into an annuity due paying \$3600 at the end of every three months. If interest on the annuity is 5.9% compounded quarterly, what is the term of the annuity in months?

6. A loan was repaid in seven years by end-of-month payments of \$450. If interest was 12% compounded monthly, how much interest was paid?

7. Ms. Simms made deposits of \$540 at the end of every three months into a savings account. For the first five years interest was 5% compounded quarterly. Since then the rate of interest has been 5.5% compounded quarterly. How much is the account balance after thirteen years?

8. How much interest is included in the accumulated value of \$3200 paid at the end of every six months for four years if the interest rate is 6.5% compounded semi-annually?

9. What is the size of deposits made at the end of each period that will accumulate to \$67 200 after eight years at 6.5% compounded semi-annually?

Challenge Problems

1. After winning some money at a casino, Tony is considering purchasing an annuity that promises to pay him $300 at the end of each month for 12 months, then $350 at the end of each month for 24 months, and then $375 at the end of each month for 36 months. If the first payment is due at the end of the first month and interest is 7.5% compounded monthly over the life of the annuity, find Tony's purchase price.
2. On March 1, 2008, Yves decided to save for a new truck. He deposited $500 at the end of every three months in a bank account earning interest at 5% compounded quarterly. He made his first deposit on June 1, 2008. On June 1, 2010, Yves decided that he needed the money to go to college, so on September 1, 2010, he stopped making deposits and started withdrawing $300 at the end of each quarter until December 1, 2011. How much is left in his account after the last withdrawal if his bank account interest rate changed to 6.5% compounded quarterly on March 1, 2011?

Case Study 11.1 Saving for Your Dream

» Andrea Shertov dreams of spending an extended holiday in Thailand. If she can save enough money, she wants to have six months to travel with friends. She has done some research and determined that she would need approximately $1800 in Canadian currency per month to achieve her dream.

At her current salary, she plans to save $150 at the end of each month, investing it at 2.8% interest compounded monthly. She hopes to be able to take this trip three years from now.

QUESTIONS

1. If Andrea saves $150 per month for three years, will she have enough to pay for her trip?
2. If Andrea saves the $150 per month, and earns an interest rate of 4.6% compounded monthly, will she have enough to pay for her trip?
3. If Andrea saves $300 per month for three years, with interest at 5.5% compounded monthly, how much will she have in her vacation investment account?

Case Study 11.2 Getting the Picture

» Suzanne had a summer job working in the business office of Blast-It TV and Stereo, a local chain of home electronics stores. When Michael Jacobssen, the owner of the chain, heard she had completed one year of business courses, he asked Suzanne to calculate the profitability of two new large-screen TVs. He plans to offer a special payment plan for the two new models to attract customers to his stores. He wants to heavily promote the more profitable TV.

When Michael gave Suzanne the information about the two TVs, he told her to ignore all taxes when making her calculations. The cost of TV A to the company is $1950 and the cost of TV B to the company is $2160, after all trade discounts have been taken. The company plans to sell TV A for a $500 down payment and $230 per month for twelve months, beginning one month from the date of the purchase. The company plans to sell TV B for a $100 down payment and $260 per month for eighteen months, beginning one month from the date of purchase. The monthly payments for both TVs reflect an interest rate of 15.5% compounded monthly.

Michael wants Suzanne to calculate the profit of TV A and TV B as a percent of the TV's cost to the company. To calculate profit, Michael deducts overhead (which he calculates as 15% of cost) and the cost of the item from the selling price of the item. When he sells items that are paid for at a later time, he calculates the selling price as the *cash value* of the item. (Remember that cash value equals the down payment plus the present value of the periodic payments.)

Suzanne realized that she could calculate the profitability of each TV by using her knowledge of ordinary annuities. She went to work on her assignment to provide Michael with the information he requested.

QUESTIONS

1. **(a)** What is the cash value of TV A? Round your answer to the nearest dollar.
(b) What is the cash value of TV B? Round your answer to the nearest dollar.

2. **(a)** Given Michael's system of calculations, how much overhead should be assigned to TV A?
(b) How much overhead should be assigned to TV B?

3. **(a)** According to Michael's system of calculations, what is the profit of TV A as a percent of its cost?
(b) What is the profit of TV B as a percent of its cost?
(c) Which TV should Suzanne recommend be more heavily promoted?

4. Three months later, due to Blast-It's successful sales of TV A and TV B, the suppliers of each model gave the company new volume discounts. For TV A, Blast-It received a discount of 9% off its current cost, and for TV B one of 6%. The special payment plans for TV A and TV B will stay the same. Under these new conditions, which TV should Suzanne recommend be more heavily promoted?

SUMMARY OF FORMULAS

Formula 9.1A

$FV = PV(1 + i)^n$

Finding the future value of a compound amount (maturity value) when the original principal, the rate of interest, and the time period are known

Formula 9.1C

$PV = FV(1 + i)^{-n}$

Finding the present value by means of the discount factor (the reciprocal of the compounding factor)

Formula 10.1

$f = (1 + i)^m - 1$

Finding the effective rate of interest *f* for a nominal annual rate compounded *m* times per year

Formula 11.1

$$S_n = R\left[\frac{(1 + i)^n - 1}{i}\right]$$

Finding the future value (accumulated value) of an ordinary simple annuity

restated as

$$FV_n = PMT\left[\frac{(1 + i)^n - 1}{i}\right]$$

Formula 11.2

$$A_n = R\left[\frac{1 - (1 + i)^{-n}}{i}\right]$$

Finding the present value (discounted value) of an ordinary simple annuity

restated as

$$PV_n = PMT\left[\frac{1 - (1 + i)^{-n}}{i}\right]$$

GLOSSARY

Accumulated value of one dollar per period *see* **Accumulation factor for annuities**

Accumulation factor for annuities the factor $\frac{(1 + i)^n - 1}{i}$ *(p. 428)*

Annual rent the sum of the periodic payments in one year *(p. 423)*

Annuity a series of payments, usually equal in size, made at equal periodic time intervals *(p. 423)*

Annuity certain an annuity for which the term is fixed *(p. 423)*

Annuity due an annuity in which the periodic payments are made at the beginning of each payment interval *(p. 424)*

Compounding factor for annuities *see* **Accumulation factor for annuities**

Contingent annuity an annuity in which the term is uncertain; that is, either the beginning date of the term or the ending date of the term or both are unknown *(p. 423)*

Deferred annuity an annuity in which the first payment is delayed for a number of payment periods *(p. 424)*

Down payment the portion of the purchase price that is supplied by the purchaser as an initial payment *(p. 441)*

Future value of an annuity the sum of the accumulated values of the periodic payments at the end of the term of the annuity *(p. 427)*

General annuity an annuity in which the conversion (or compounding) period is different from the payment interval *(p. 424)*

Ordinary annuity an annuity in which the payments are made at the end of each payment interval *(p. 424)*

Payment interval the length of time between successive payments *(p. 423)*

Payment period *see* **Payment interval**

Periodic rent the size of the regular periodic payment *(p. 423)*

Perpetuity an annuity for which the payments continue forever *(p. 423)*

Simple annuity an annuity in which the conversion period is the same as the payment interval *(p. 424)*

Term of an annuity the length of time from the beginning of the first payment interval to the end of the last payment interval *(p. 423)*

USEFUL INTERNET SITES

www.gordonpape.com

Building Wealth on the Net Visit Buildwealth.ca to read Gordon Pape's latest financial advice or subscribe to the Internet Wealth Builder. Pape is one of Canada's best-known and highly regarded investment advisors.

www.nmfn.com/tn/learnctr--lifeevents--longevity

The Longevity Game Click on "Learning Centre/The Longevity Game" to predict your life expectancy with this game on Northwestern Mutual Life Insurance Company's site. Life expectancy is used to calculate life insurance rates.

www.money.msn.ca

RRSP This Canadian site provides information on advantages and disadvantages of RRSPs, including a calculator to determine tax savings. Some U.S. news is included.

CHAPTER 12 Ordinary General Annuities

OBJECTIVES

Upon completing this chapter, you will be able to do the following:

1. Compute the future value (or accumulated value) for ordinary general annuities.
2. Compute the present value (or discounted value) for ordinary general annuities.
3. Compute the payment for ordinary general annuities.
4. Compute the number of periods for ordinary general annuities.
5. Compute the interest rate for ordinary general annuities.

We often encounter situations where the frequency of the payment in an annuity is not the same as the frequency of the compounding when interest is applied. In these cases, we are dealing with a general annuity. When the payment is made at the end of the period, we have an ordinary general annuity. It is necessary to understand these annuities so that we can make informed decisions about different payment options. When considering borrowing money to buy a car, or negotiating a mortgage, we must determine when it is best for us to make the payments and how much we can afford. The timing of the payments is crucial in planning our cash flow.

INTRODUCTION

In Chapter 11, we calculated the present value, future value, payment, term, and interest rate for ordinary simple annuities. In this chapter, we will calculate the present value, future value, payment, term, and interest rate for ordinary general annuities. We will analyze the relationship between the payment interval and the interest conversion period. We will introduce new formulas to calculate the future value and the present value of an ordinary general annuity. We will rearrange these formulas to determine the payment, term, and interest rate for these annuities. We will also use preprogrammed calculators as an alternative to determining the results.

12.1 ORDINARY GENERAL ANNUITIES—FINDING THE FUTURE VALUE

A. Basic concepts and computation

Chapter 11 considered ordinary simple annuities in detail. Simple annuities are a special case in which the payment interval and the interest conversion period are the same length. However, interest is often compounded more or less frequently than payments are made. In Canada, for example, residential mortgages are usually compounded semi-annually while payments are made monthly.

Annuities in which the length of the interest conversion period is different from the length of the payment interval are called *general annuities.*

The basic method of solving problems involving interest uses equivalent sets of financial obligations at a selected focal date. Thus, when dealing with any kind of annuity, including general annuities, the essential tool is an equation of value. This basic approach is used to make the basic computations and develop useful formulas.

EXAMPLE 12.1A

What is the accumulated value of $100 deposited at the end of every six months for three years if interest is 4% compounded annually?

SOLUTION

Since the payments are made semi-annually while the compounding is done annually, this annuity is classified as a general annuity. Furthermore, since the payments are at the end of each payment interval, the annuity is an ordinary general annuity. While the difference in the length of the payment period compared to the length of the compounding period introduces a mathematical complication, the basic approach to finding the amount of the ordinary general annuity is the same as that used in finding the amount of an ordinary simple annuity.

The basic solution and data for the problem are shown graphically in Figure 12.1. Since deposits are made at the end of every six months for three years, there are six deposits of \$100 at the times indicated. Because interest is compounded annually, I/Y = 4%, P/Y = 2, C/Y = 1, $i = 4\% = 0.04$, and there are three conversion periods.

FIGURE 12.1 Graphical Representation of Method and Data

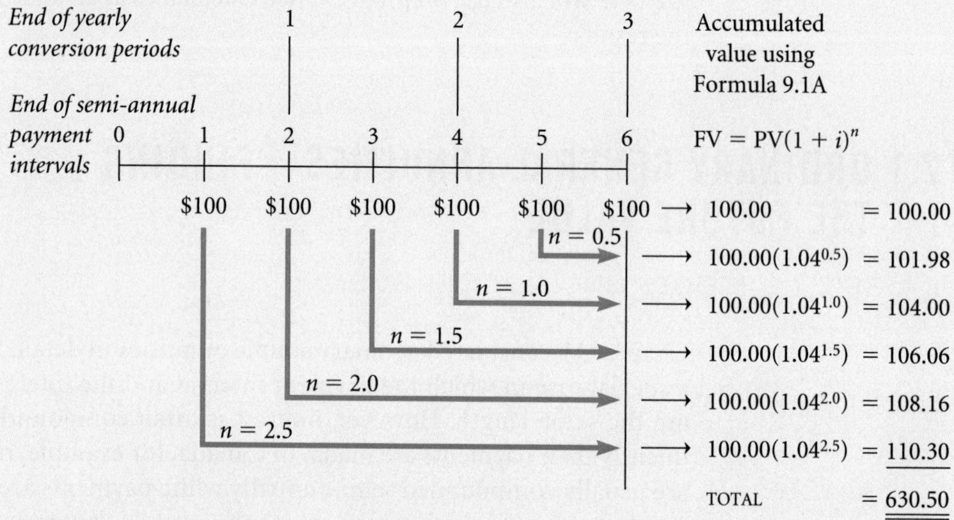

The focal point is at the end of Year 3. The last deposit is made at the focal date and has a value of \$100 on that date. The fifth deposit is made after 2.5 years and, in terms of conversion periods, has accumulated for a half conversion period ($n = 0.5$); its accumulated value is $100.00(1.04^{0.5}) = \$101.98$ at the focal date.

The fourth deposit made after two years has accumulated for one conversion period ($n = 1.0$); its accumulated value at the focal date is $100.00(1.04^{1.0}) = \$104.00$. Similarly, the accumulated value of the third deposit is $100.00(1.04^{1.5}) = \$106.06$, while the accumulated value of the second deposit is $100.00(1.04^{2.0}) = \$108.16$. Finally, the accumulated value of the first deposit is $100.00(1.04^{2.5}) = \$110.30$. The total accumulated value after three years is \$630.50.

EXAMPLE 12.1B

What is the accumulated value of deposits of \$100 made at the end of each year for four years if interest is 4% compounded quarterly?

SOLUTION

Since the deposits are made at the end of every year for four years, there are four payments of \$100.00 at the times shown in Figure 12.2. Since interest is compounded quarterly, I/Y = 4, P/Y, C/Y = 4, $i = \frac{4}{4}\% = 1\% = 0.01\%$, and there are $4(4) = 16$ conversion periods.

FIGURE 12.2 Graphical Representation of Method and Data

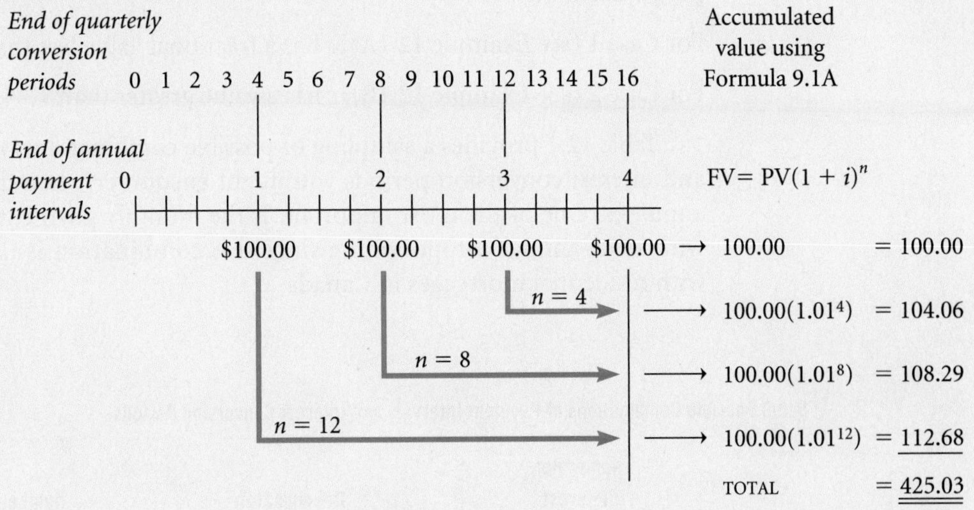

The focal point is the end of Year 4. The last payment is made at the focal point and has a value of $100 at that date. The third payment is made after three years and, in terms of conversion periods, has accumulated for four conversion periods ($n = 4$); its accumulated value is $100.00(1.01^4) = \$104.06$. The second deposit has accumulated for 8 conversion periods ($n = 8$); its accumulated value is 100.00(1.018) = $108.29. The first deposit has accumulated for 12 conversion periods ($n = 12$); its accumulated value is 100.00(1.0112) = $112.68. The total accumulated value of the deposits after four years is $425.03.

B. Relationship between payment interval and interest conversion period

Examples 12.1A and 12.1B illustrate the two possible cases of ordinary general annuities.

CASE 1 The interest conversion period is *longer* than the payment period; each payment interval contains only a fraction of one conversion period.

CASE 2 The interest conversion period is *shorter* than the payment period; each payment period contains more than one conversion period.

The number of interest conversion periods per payment interval, designated by the letter c, can be determined from the following ratio.

$$c = \frac{\text{THE NUMBER OF INTEREST CONVERSION PERIODS PER YEAR}}{\text{THE NUMBER OF PAYMENT PERIODS PER YEAR}}$$

In dealing with general annuities it is important to understand clearly the relationship between the *payment interval* and the number of *interest conversion periods* per payment interval.

For Case 1 (see Example 12.1A), c has a fractional value less than 1.

For Case 2 (see Example 12.1B), c has a value greater than 1.

Table 12.1 provides a sampling of possible combinations of payment intervals and interest conversion periods you might encounter when dealing with general annuities. One of the most important is the monthly payment interval combined with semi-annual compounding since this combination is usually encountered with residential mortgages in Canada.

Table 12.1 **Some Possible Combinations of Payment Intervals and Interest Conversion Periods**

Numerator: Interest Conversion Period	Denominator: Payment Interval	Number of Interest Conversion Periods per Payment Interval
monthly	semi-annually	$c = \frac{12}{2} = 6$
monthly	quarterly	$c = \frac{12}{4} = 3$
quarterly	annually	$c = \frac{4}{1} = 4$
annually	semi-annually	$c = \frac{1}{2} = 0.5$
annually	quarterly	$c = \frac{1}{4} = 0.25$
semi-annually	monthly	$c = \frac{2}{12} = \frac{1}{6}$
quarterly	monthly	$c = \frac{4}{12} = \frac{1}{3}$
annually	monthly	$c = \frac{1}{12}$

C. Computing the effective rate of interest per payment period

In Chapter 10 you were introduced to the concept of the effective rate of interest. It was defined as the nominal rate of interest compounded annually and represented by the symbol f. It can readily be determined from the periodic rate of interest i by means of Formula 10.1, $f = (1 + i)^m - 1$, where m is the number of compounding periods per year.

When dealing with general annuities, it is useful to utilize the **equivalent rate of interest per payment period**. Depending on the length of the payment interval, the equivalent interest rate per payment period may be a monthly, quarterly, semi-annual, or annual rate. It can be obtained from the periodic rate of interest i by a formula identical in nature to Formula 10.1.

To avoid confusion, we will distinguish the equivalent rate of interest per payment period from the effective annual rate of interest f by using the symbol p for the equivalent rate of interest per payment period. It can be determined by means of Formula 12.1 that

$$p = (1+i)^c - 1 \qquad \text{———— Formula 12.1}$$

$$\text{where } c = \frac{\text{THE NUMBER OF INTEREST CONVERSION PERIODS PER YEAR}}{\text{THE NUMBER OF PAYMENT PERIODS PER YEAR}}$$

Note: Formula 12.1 is the same as Formula 10.1 except that f is replaced by p, and m is replaced by c. Also note that when the payment interval is one year, $p = f$.

POINTERS AND PITFALLS

Formula 12.1, which is $p = (1+i)^c - 1$, is useful in calculating the equivalent interest rate per rent payment period in general annuity problems, while Formula 10.1, which is the effective rate formula $f = (1+i)^m - 1$, is useful in making conversions between compound rates of interest and corresponding effective rates of interest.

When using an electronic calculator equipped with a universal power key, the given periodic rate of interest i can be easily converted into the equivalent rate of interest per payment period.

EXAMPLE 12.1C

Jean receives annuity payments at the end of every six months. If she deposits these payments in an account earning interest at 9% compounded monthly, what is the semi-annually compounded rate of interest?

SOLUTION

Since the payments are made at the end of every six months while interest is compounded monthly,

$$c = \frac{\text{THE NUMBER OF INTEREST CONVERSION PERIODS PER YEAR}}{\text{THE NUMBER OF PAYMENT PERIODS PER YEAR}} = \frac{12}{2} = 6$$

$$i = \frac{9\%}{12} = 0.75\% = 0.0075$$

$p = (1 + i)^c - 1$

$p = 1.0075^6 - 1$

$p = 1.045852 - 1$

$p = 0.045852 = 4.5852\%$

The rate of interest is 4.5852% per semi-annual period.

EXAMPLE 12.1D

Peel Credit Union pays 6% compounded quarterly on its Premium Savings Accounts. If Roland Catchpole deposits $25 in his account at the end of every month, what is the monthly compounded rate of interest?

SOLUTION

Since the payments are made at the end of every month while interest is compounded quarterly,

$$c = \frac{4}{12} = \frac{1}{3}; \qquad i = \frac{6\%}{4} = 1.5\% = 0.015$$

$p = 1.015^{\frac{1}{3}} - 1$

$p = 1.004975 - 1$

$p = 0.004975 = 0.4975\%$

The rate of interest is 0.4975% per month.

D. Future value of an ordinary general annuity using the equivalent rate of interest per payment period

Determining the equivalent rate per payment period p allows us to convert the ordinary general annuity problem into an ordinary simple annuity problem. To be consistent with the symbols previously used for developing formulas for ordinary simple annuities, we will use the following notation:

FV_{nc} = the future value (or accumulated value) of an ordinary general annuity;
PMT = the size of the periodic payment;
n = the number of periodic payments;
c = the number of interest conversion periods per payment interval;
i = the interest rate per interest conversion period;
p = the equivalent rate of interest per payment period.

Substituting p for i in Formula 11.1, we obtain

$$FV_{nc} = PMT\left[\frac{(1 + p)^n - 1}{p}\right] \text{ where } p = (1 + i)^c - 1 \qquad \textbf{Formula 12.2}$$

EXAMPLE 12.1E

Determine the accumulated value after ten years of payments of \$2000 made at the end of each year if interest is 6% compounded monthly.

SOLUTION

This problem is an ordinary general annuity.

$$\text{PMT} = 2000.00; \quad n = 10; \quad c = 12; \quad i = \frac{6\%}{12} = 0.5\% = 0.005$$

The equivalent annual rate

$$p = 1.005^{12} - 1 = 1.061678 - 1 = 0.061678 = 6.1678\%$$

The given ordinary general annuity can be converted into an ordinary simple annuity.

$$\text{PMT} = 2000.00; \quad n = 10; \quad p = 0.061678$$

$$\text{FV}_{nc} = 2000.00\left(\frac{1.061678^{10} - 1}{0.061678}\right) \text{ ——— substituting in Formula 12.2}$$

$$= 2000.00(13.285114)$$

$$= \$26\,570.23$$

The accumulated value after ten years is about \$26 570.23.

EXAMPLE 12.1F

Crestview Farms set aside \$1250 at the end of each month for the purchase of a combine. How much money will be available after five years if interest is 6.0% compounded semi-annually?

SOLUTION

This problem involves an ordinary general annuity.

$$\text{PMT} = 1250.00; \quad n = 5(12) = 60; \quad c = \frac{2}{12} = \frac{1}{6}; \quad i = \frac{6.0\%}{2} = 3.0\% = 0.03$$

The equivalent monthly rate of interest

$$p = 1.03^{\frac{1}{6}} - 1 = 1.004939 - 1 = 0.004939 = 0.4939\%$$

$$\text{FV}_{nc} = 1250.00\left(\frac{1.004939^{60} - 1}{0.004939}\right) \text{ ——— substituting in Formula 12.2}$$

$$= 1250(69.638936)$$

$$= \$87\,048.67$$

After five years, the amount available is \$87 048.67.

E. Using preprogrammed calculators to find the future value of an ordinary general annuity

The use of p rather than i as the rate of interest is the only difference in the programmed solution for the general annuity compared to the programmed solution for a simple annuity.

When using preprogrammed calculators, such as the BAII Plus, the calculator must be set for the number of payment periods per year P/Y and the number of interest compounding periods per year C/Y. To set the calculator for Example 12.1G, follow these steps:

2nd P/Y 2 Enter ↓ C/Y 4 Enter 2nd QUIT

To show the nominal interest rate per year, I/Y needs to be entered. In this example, the number is 6, indicating 6%.

Remember also that n denotes the number of payments made. In this example, there are 20 payments (10 years × P/Y of 2).

Note: This assumes the calculator is in the default setting "END."

Note that each time the P/Y is changed, the C/Y automatically changes to match the P/Y. To make the C/Y different from the P/Y, it must be re-entered separately, after the P/Y may have been changed.

EXAMPLE 12.1G

Find the future value of $2500 deposited at the end of every six months for ten years if interest is 6% compounded quarterly.

SOLUTION

$\text{PMT} = 2500.00;\quad n = 2(10) = 20;\quad \text{P/Y} = 2;\quad \text{C/Y} = 4;\quad c = \frac{4}{2} = 2;$

$\text{I/Y} = 6;\quad i = \frac{6\%}{4} = 1.5\% = 0.015$

To use the formula:

STEP 1 Convert i into the equivalent semi-annual rate of interest.

$p = 1.015^2 - 1 = 1.030225 - 1 = 0.030225 = 3.0225\%$

STEP 2 Using p as the interest rate per payment period, determine the amount of the ordinary annuity.

To use the calculator:

(Set P/Y = 2; C/Y = 4)

Key in	*Press*	*Display shows*	
6	I/Y	6	
0	PV	0	
2500	± PMT	−2500	
20	N	20	the number of payments
CPT	FV	67329.89319	

The amount on deposit after ten years will be $67 329.89.

EXAMPLE 12.1H

Determine the accumulated value of payments of $1250 made at the end of each quarter for eight years if interest is 5.5% compounded annually.

SOLUTION

$\text{PMT} = 1250.00;\quad n = 8(4) = 32;\quad \text{P/Y} = 4;\quad \text{C/Y} = 1;\quad c = \frac{1}{4} = 0.25;$

$\text{I/Y} = 5.5;\quad i = 5.5\% = 0.055$

To use the formula:

$p = 1.055^{0.25} - 1 = 1.013475 - 1 = 0.013475 = 1.3475\%$

To use the calculator:

(Set P/Y = 4; C/Y = 1) 5.5 [I/Y] 0 [PV]

1250 [±] [PMT] 32 [N] [CPT] [FV] [49599.22016]

The accumulated value of the payments is $49 599.22.

EXERCISE 12.1

EXCEL NOTES

If you choose, you can use Excel's ***Future Value (FV)*** function to answer the questions indicated below. Refer to **FV** on the Spreadsheet Template Disk to learn how to use this Excel function.

A. Find the future value of each of the following eight ordinary annuities.

	Periodic Payment	Payment Interval	Term	Interest Rate	Conversion Period
1.	$2500	6 months	7 years	8%	quarterly
2.	900	3 months	5 years	6	monthly
3.	72	1 month	15 years	3	semi-annually
4.	225	3 months	10 years	5	annually
5.	1750	6 months	12 years	7	annually
6.	680	1 month	3 years	9	annually
7.	7500	1 year	4 years	6	quarterly
8.	143	1 month	9 years	4	quarterly

B. Answer each of the following questions.

1. Find the future value of payments of $425 made at the end of every three months for nine years if interest is 9% compounded monthly.

Reference Example 12.1B

2. What is the accumulated value of deposits of $1500 made at the end of every six months for six years if interest is 6% compounded quarterly?

3. How much will deposits of $15 made at the end of each month amount to after ten years if interest is 5% compounded quarterly? Reference Example 12.1D

4. What is the future value of payments of $250 made at the end of every three months in fifteen years if interest is 7.5% compounded annually?

5. Mr. Tomas has contributed $1000 at the end of each year into an RRSP paying 6% compounded quarterly.
   (a) How much will Mr. Tomas have in the RRSP after ten years?
   (b) After ten years, how much of the amount is interest?

6. Alexa Sanchez saves $5 at the end of each month and deposits the money in an account paying 4% compounded quarterly.
   (a) How much will she accumulate in 25 years?
   (b) How much of the accumulated amount is interest?

7. Edwin Ng has made deposits of $500 into his savings account at the end of every three months for ten years. If interest is 4.5% compounded semi-annually and if he leaves the accumulated balance for another five years, what will be the balance in his account then?

8. Mrs. Cook has made deposits of \$950 at the end of every six months for fifteen years. If interest is 3% compounded monthly, how much will Mrs. Cook have accumulated ten years after the last deposit?

9. For the last four years, Joely has authorized the payroll department at her work to deduct \$30 per week to be placed into an RRSP account. If interest is 5.17% compounded monthly, how much will Joely have accumulated in her RRSP?

10. Clark's younger brother has saved \$18 per month from his paper route for the last two years. If interest is 4% compounded quarterly, how much will he have accumulated in his savings account?

12.2 ORDINARY GENERAL ANNUITIES—FINDING THE PRESENT VALUE PV

A. Present value of an ordinary general annuity using the equivalent rate of interest per payment period

As with the future value of an ordinary general annuity, we can convert the given periodic rate of interest i into the effective rate of interest per payment period.

$p = (1 + i)^c - 1$

The use of p converts the ordinary general annuity problem into an ordinary simple annuity problem.

Substituting p for i in Formula 11.2, we obtain

$$PV_{nc} = PMT\left[\frac{1 - (1 + p)^{-n}}{p}\right] \qquad \text{Formula 12.3}$$

EXAMPLE 12.2A A loan is repaid by making payments of \$2000 at the end of every six months for twelve years. If interest on the loan is 8% compounded quarterly, what was the principal of the loan?

SOLUTION PMT = 2000.00; $n = 12(2) = 24$; P/Y = 2; C/Y = 4; $c = \frac{4}{2} = 2$;

I/Y = 8; $i = \frac{8\%}{4} = 2\% = 0.02$

The equivalent semi-annual rate of interest

$p = 1.02^2 - 1 = 1.0404 - 1 = 0.0404 = 4.04\%$

$$PV_{nc} = 2000.00\left(\frac{1 - 1.0404^{-24}}{0.0404}\right) \qquad \text{substituting in Formula 12.3}$$

$= 2000.00(15.184713)$

$= \$30\ 369.43$

The loan principal was \$30 369.43.

EXAMPLE 12.2B

A second mortgage requires payments of \$370 at the end of each month for fifteen years. If interest is 11% compounded semi-annually, what was the amount borrowed?

SOLUTION

PMT = 370.00; $n = 15(12) = 180$; P/Y = 12; C/Y = 2; $c = \frac{2}{12} = \frac{1}{6}$;

I/Y = 11; $i = \frac{11\%}{2} = 5.5\% = 0.055$

The effective monthly rate of interest

$$p = 1.055^{\frac{1}{6}} - 1 = 1.008963 - 1 = 0.008963 = 0.8963\%$$

$$PV_{nc} = 370.00\left(\frac{1 - 1.008963^{-180}}{0.008963}\right)$$ ——— substituting in Formula 12.3

$$= 370.00(89.180057)$$

$$= \$32\,996.62$$

The amount borrowed was \$32 996.62.

B. Using preprogrammed calculators to find the present value of an ordinary general annuity

STEP 1 Set P/Y as the number of payment periods per year.

STEP 2 Set C/Y as the number of compounding periods per year and I/Y as the nominal interest rate.

STEP 3 Determine the present value of the ordinary general annuity.

EXAMPLE 12.2C

A contract is fulfilled by making payments of \$8500 at the end of every year for fifteen years. If interest is 7% compounded quarterly, what is the cash price of the contract?

SOLUTION

PMT = 8500.00; $n = 15$; P/Y = 1; C/Y = 4; $c = 4$; I/Y = 7

$i = \frac{7\%}{4} = 1.75\% = 0.0175$

(Set P/Y = 1; C/Y = 4) 7 [I/Y] 0 [FV] 8500 [±] [PMT]

15 [N] [CPT] [PV] [76516.37862]

The cash price of the contract is \$76 516.38.

EXAMPLE 12.2D

A 25-year mortgage on a house requires payments of \$619.94 at the end of each month. If interest is 9.5% compounded semi-annually, what was the mortgage principal?

SOLUTION

PMT = 619.94; $n = 25(12) = 300$; P/Y = 12; C/Y = 2; $c = \frac{2}{12} = \frac{1}{6}$;

I/Y = 9.5; $i = \frac{9.5\%}{2} = 4.75\% = 0.0475$

(Set P/Y = 12; C/Y = 2) 9.5 [I/Y] 0 [FV] 619.94 [±] [PMT]

300 [N] [CPT] [PV] [72000.01223]

The mortgage principal was $72 000.01.

EXERCISE 12.2

EXCEL NOTES

If you choose, you can use Excel's ***Present Value (PV)*** function to answer the questions indicated below. Refer to **PV** on the Spreadsheet Template Disk to learn how to use this Excel function.

A. Find the present value of the following eight ordinary annuities.

	Periodic Payment	Payment Interval	Term	Interest Rate	Conversion Period
1.	$1400	3 months	12 years	6%	monthly
2.	6000	1 year	9 years	10	quarterly
3.	3000	3 months	4 years	6	annually
4.	200	1 month	2 years	5	semi-annually
5.	95	1 month	5 years	4.5	annually
6.	975	6 months	8 years	8	annually
7.	1890	6 months	15 years	7	quarterly
8.	155	1 month	10 years	8	quarterly

B. Answer each of the following questions.

1. Find the present value of payments of $250 made at the end of every three months for twelve years if money is worth 3% compounded monthly.

Reference Example 12.2A

2. What is the discounted value of $1560 paid at the end of each year for nine years if interest is 6% compounded quarterly?

3. What cash payment is equivalent to making payments of $825 at the end of every three months for 16 years if interest is 7% compounded semi-annually?

Reference Example 12.2B

4. What is the principal from which $175 can be withdrawn at the end of each month for twenty years if interest is 5% compounded quarterly?

5. A property was purchased for $5000 down and payments of $2500 at the end of every six months for six years. Interest is 6% compounded monthly.
(**a**) What was the purchase price of the property?
(**b**) How much is the cost of financing?

6. A car was purchased for $1500 down and payments of $265 at the end of each month for four years. Interest is 9% compounded quarterly.
(**a**) What was the purchase price of the car?
(**b**) How much interest will be paid?

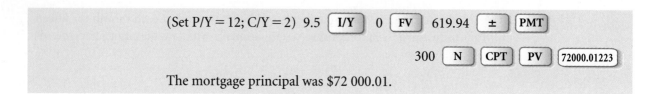

7. Payments of $715.59 are made at the end of each month to repay a 25-year mortgage. If interest is 10% compounded semi-annually, what is the original mortgage principal?

8. A 15-year mortgage is amortized by making payments of $1031.61 at the end of every three months. If interest is 8.25% compounded annually, what was the original mortgage balance?

9. Mac Dale purchased a retirement annuity paying $1200 every three months for twenty years. If the first payment is due three months after his retirement and interest is 6.6% compounded monthly, how much did Mr. Dale invest in the annuity?

10. For her daughter's education, Georgina Harcourt has invested an inheritance in a fund paying 5.2% compounded quarterly. If ordinary annuity payments of $178 per month are to be made out of the fund for eight years, how much was the inheritance?

11. As a settlement for an insurance claim, Craig was offered one of two choices. He could either accept a lump-sum amount of $5000 now, or accept quarterly payments of $145 for the next ten years. If the money is placed into a trust fund earning 3.95% compounded semi-annually, which is the better option and by how much?

12. Carl Hightop, a popular basketball player, has been offered a two-year salary deal. He can either accept $2 000 000 now or accept monthly amounts of $100 000 payable at the end of each month. If money can be invested at 5.7% compounded quarterly, which option is the better option for Carl and by how much?

12.3 ORDINARY GENERAL ANNUITIES—FINDING THE PERIODIC PAYMENT PMT

A. Finding the periodic payment PMT when the future value of a general annuity is known

If the future value of an annuity FV_{nc}, the number of conversion periods n, and the conversion rate i are known, you can find the periodic payment PMT by substituting the given values in the future value Formula 12.2.

$$FV_{nc} = PMT\left[\frac{(1 + p)^n - 1}{p}\right] \text{ where } p = (1 + i)^c - 1 \qquad \textbf{Formula 12.2}$$

As we have emphasized throughout this book, beginning in Chapter 2, understanding how to rearrange terms in a formula is a very important skill. By knowing how to do this, you avoid having to memorize equivalent forms of the same formula.

When using a scientific calculator, you can find PMT by first rearranging the terms of the future value formulas as shown below. Then substitute the three known values (FV, n, and i) into the rearranged formula and use the calculator to solve for PMT.

$$FV_{nc} = PMT\left[\frac{(1+p)^n - 1}{p}\right]$$ —— Formula 12.2

$$PMT = \frac{FV_{nc}}{\left[\frac{(1+p)^n - 1}{p}\right]}$$ —— divide both sides by $\left[\frac{(1+p)^n - 1}{p}\right]$

$$PMT = \frac{FV_{nc}\,p}{(1+p)^n - 1}$$ —— Formula 12.2A: dividing by a fraction is the same as inverting the fraction and multiplying

When using a preprogrammed financial calculator, you can find PMT by entering the five known values (FV, N, I/Y, P/Y, and C/Y) and pressing CPT PMT.

Recall that the PMT amount will be negative since payments are considered to be cash outflows.

EXAMPLE 12.3A

What sum of money must be deposited at the end of every three months into an account paying 6% compounded monthly to accumulate to $25 000 in ten years?

SOLUTION

$FV_{nc} = 25\,000.00$; $n = 10(4) = 40$; P/Y = 4; C/Y = 12; $c = \frac{12}{4} = 3$;

I/Y = 6; $i = 0.5\% = 0.005$

The effective quarterly rate of interest

$$p = 1.005^3 - 1 = 1.015075 - 1 = 0.015075 = 1.5075\%$$

$$25\,000.00 = PMT\left(\frac{1.015075^{40} - 1}{0.015075}\right)$$ —— substituting in Formula 12.2

$$25\,000.00 = PMT(54.354225)$$

$$PMT = \frac{25\,000.00}{54.354225}$$

$$PMT = \$459.95$$

Using Formula 12.2A, which is Formula 12.2 rearranged,

$$PMT = \frac{FV_{nc}p}{(1+p)^n - 1}$$

$$PMT = \frac{25\,000.000(0.015075)}{1.015075^{40} - 1}$$ —— substituting in Formula 12.2A

$$PMT = \$459.95$$

Programmed Solution

(Set P/Y = 4; C/Y = 12) 2nd (CLR TVM) 6 I/Y 0 PV

25 000 FV 40 N CPT PMT -459.945847

The required quarterly deposit is $459.95.

B. Finding the periodic payment PMT when the present value of a general annuity is known

If the present value of a general annuity PV_{nc}, the number of conversion periods n, and the conversion rate i are known, you can find the periodic payment PMT by substituting the given values in the present value Formula 12.3.

$$PV_{nc} = PMT\left[\frac{1 - (1 + p)^{-n}}{p}\right] \quad \text{—— Formula 12.3}$$

When using a scientific calculator, you can find PMT by first rearranging the terms of the present value formulas. Then substitute the three known values (PV, n, and i) into the rearranged formula and solve for PMT.

$$PV_{nc} = PMT\left[\frac{1 - (1 + p)^{-n}}{p}\right] \quad \text{—— Formula 12.3}$$

$$PMT = \frac{PV_{nc}}{\left[\frac{1 - (1 + p)^{-n}}{p}\right]} \quad \text{—— divide both sides by } \left[\frac{1 - (1 + p)^{-n}}{p}\right]$$

$$PMT = \frac{PV_{nc}p}{1 - (1 + p)^{-n}} \quad \text{—— Formula 12.3A: dividing by a fraction is the same as inverting the fraction and multiplying}$$

When using a preprogrammed financial calculator, you can find PMT by entering the five known values (PV, N, I/Y, P/Y, and C/Y) and pressing CPT PMT.

EXAMPLE 12.3B

Mr. and Mrs. White applied to their credit union for a first mortgage of \$60 000 to buy a house. The mortgage is to be amortized over 25 years and interest on the mortgage is 8.5% compounded semi-annually. What is the size of the monthly payment if payments are made at the end of each month?

SOLUTION

$PV_{nc} = 60\,000.00$; $n = 25(12) = 300$; $P/Y = 12$; $C/Y = 2$; $c = \frac{2}{12} = \frac{1}{6}$;

$I/Y = 8.5$; $i = \frac{8.5\%}{2} = 4.25\% = 0.0425$

The effective monthly rate of interest

$$p = 1.0425^{\frac{1}{6}} - 1 = 1.006961 - 1 = 0.006961 = 0.6961\%$$

$$60\,000.00 = PMT\left(\frac{1 - 1.006961^{-300}}{0.006961}\right) \quad \text{—— substituting in Formula 12.3}$$

$$60\,000.00 = PMT(125.72819)$$

$$PMT = \frac{60\,000.00}{125.72819}$$

$$PMT = \$477.22$$

Programmed Solution

(Set P/Y = 12; C/Y = 2) 8.5 [I/Y] 0 [FV] 60 000 [±] [PV]

300 [N] [CPT] [PMT] [477.218111]

The monthly payment due at the end of each month is $477.22.

EXERCISE 12.3

EXCEL NOTES

If you choose, you can use Excel's ***Payment (PMT)*** function to answer all of the questions below. Refer to **PMT** on the Spreadsheet Template Disk to learn how to use this Excel function.

A. For each of the following ten ordinary general annuities, determine the size of the periodic rent.

	Future Value	Present Value	Payment Period	Term of Annuity	Interest Rate	Conversion Period
1.	$15 000		6 months	7 years, 6 mos	5.5%	annually
2.	6 000		1 quarter	9 years, 9 mos	8	monthly
3.		$12 000	12 months	15 years	4.5	semi-annually
4.		7 000	6 months	12.5 years	7.5	quarterly
5.	8 000		3 months	6 years	6.8	semi-annually
6.		20 000	3 months	20 years	12	monthly
7.	45 000		6 months	10 years	9	quarterly
8.	35 000		1 year	15 years	4	quarterly
9.	20 000		1 month	8 years	7	semi-annually
10.	16 500		3 months	15 years	5.75	annually

B. Answer each of the following questions.

1. What payment made at the end of each quarter for fifteen years will accumulate to $12 000 at 6% compounded monthly? Reference Example 12.3A

2. What payment is required at the end of each month for five years to repay a loan of $6000 at 7% compounded semi-annually?

3. A contract can be fulfilled by making an immediate payment of $9500 or equal payments at the end of every six months for eight years. What is the size of the semi-annual payments at 7.4% compounded quarterly?

4. What payment made at the end of each year for eighteen years will amount to $16 000 at 4.2% compounded monthly?

5. What payment is required at the end of each month for fifteen years to amortize a $32 000 mortgage if interest is 9.5% compounded semi-annually?

Reference Example 12.3B

6. How much must be deposited at the end of each quarter for ten years to accumulate to $12 000 at 6% compounded monthly?

7. What payment made at the end of every three months for twenty years will accumulate to \$20 000 at 7% compounded semi-annually?

8. Derrick bought a car priced at \$9300 for 15% down and equal monthly payments for four years. If interest is 8% compounded semi-annually, what is the size of the monthly payment?

9. Equal payments are to be made at the end of each month for fifteen years with interest at 9% compounded quarterly. After the last payment, the fund is to be invested for seven years at 10% compounded quarterly and have a maturity value of \$20 000. What is the size of the monthly payment?

10. To finance the development of a new product, a company borrowed \$30 000 at 7% compounded monthly. If the loan is to be repaid in equal quarterly payments over seven years and the first payment is due three months after the date of the loan, what is the size of the quarterly payment?

12.4 ORDINARY GENERAL ANNUITIES—FINDING THE TERM n

A. Finding the term n when the future value of a general annuity is known

If the future value of an annuity FV_{nc}, the periodic payment PMT, and the conversion rate i are known, you can find the term of the annuity n by substituting the given values in the future value Formula 12.2.

$$FV_{nc} = PMT\left[\frac{(1+p)^n - 1}{p}\right] \quad \text{where } p = (1+i)^c - 1$$ ——— **Formula 12.2**

When using a scientific calculator, you can find n by first rearranging the terms of the future value Formula 12.2. Then substitute the three known values (FV, PMT, and p) into the rearranged formula and solve for n.

$$FV_{nc} = PMT\left[\frac{(1+p)^n - 1}{p}\right]$$ ——— Formula 12.2

$$\frac{FV_{nc}}{PMT} = \frac{(1+p)^n - 1}{p}$$ ——— divide both sides by PMT

$$(1+p)^n = \left(\frac{FV_{nc}p}{PMT}\right) + 1$$ ——— multiply both sides by p and add 1 to both sides

$$n\ln(1+p) = \ln[(FV_{nc}p/PMT) + 1]$$ ——— solve for n using natural logarithms

$$n = \frac{\ln[FV_{nc}p/PMT + 1]}{\ln(1+p)}$$ ——— Formula 12.2B: divide both sides by $\ln(1+p)$

When using a preprogrammed financial calculator, you can find n by entering the five known values (FV, PMT, I/Y, P/Y, and C/Y) and pressing CPT N.

EXAMPLE 12.4A What period of time is required for $125 deposited at the end of each month at 11% compounded quarterly to grow to $15 000?

SOLUTION $FV_{nc} = 15\,000.00$; $PMT = 125.00$; $P/Y = 12$; $C/Y = 4$;

$$c = \frac{4}{12} = \frac{1}{3}; \quad I/Y = 11; \quad i = \frac{11\%}{4} = 2.75\% = 0.0275$$

The effective monthly rate of interest

$$p = 1.0275^{\frac{1}{3}} - 1 = 1.009084 - 1 = 0.009084 = 0.9084\%$$

$$15\,000.00 = 125.00\left(\frac{1.009084^n - 1}{0.009084}\right) \quad \text{——— using Formula 12.2}$$

$$120.00 = \frac{(1.009084^n - 1)}{0.009084}$$

$$1.090068 = 1.009084^n - 1$$

$$1.009084^n = 2.090068$$

$$n \ln 1.009084 = \ln 2.090068$$

$$n(0.009043) = 0.737197$$

$$n = \frac{0.737197}{0.009043}$$

$$n = 81.522227$$

$$n = 82 \text{ months approximately}$$

With a preprogrammed calculator, the procedure is

(Set P/Y = 12; C/Y = 4) 11 [I/Y] 0 [PV] 15 000 [FV]

125 [±] [PMT] [CPT] [N] [81.522240]

It will take about 82 months to accumulate $15 000.

B. Finding the term n when the present value of a general annuity is known

If the present value PV_{nc}, the periodic payment PMT, and the conversion rate i are known, you can find the term of the annuity n by substituting the given values in the present value Formula 12.3.

$$PV_{nc} = PMT\left[\frac{1 - (1 + p)^{-n}}{p}\right] \quad \text{——— Formula 12.3}$$

Alternatively, you can first rearrange the terms of Formula 12.3 to solve for n.

$$\frac{PV_{nc}}{PMT} = \frac{1 - (1 + p)^{-n}}{p} \quad \text{——— divide both sides by PMT}$$

$$\left(\frac{PV_{nc}p}{PMT}\right) = 1 - (1 + p)^{-n} \quad \text{——— multiply both sides by } i \text{ and subtract 1 from both sides}$$

$$(1 + p)^{-n} = 1 - \left(\frac{PV_{nc}p}{PMT}\right)$$ multiply both sides by –1

$$-n \ln(1 + p) = \ln\left[1 - \left(\frac{PV_{nc}p}{PMT}\right)\right]$$ solve for n using natural logarithms

$$n = \frac{\ln\left[1 - \left(\frac{PV_{nc}p}{PMT}\right)\right]}{-\ln(1 + p)}$$ Formula 12.3B: divide both sides by –ln(1 + p)

When using a scientific calculator, you can find n by first rearranging the terms of the present value formulas above. Then substitute the three known values (PV, PMT, and i) into the rearranged formula and solve for n.

When using a preprogrammed financial calculator, you can find n by entering the five known values (PV, PMT, I/Y, P/Y, and C/Y) and pressing **CPT** **N**.

Note: When using the Texas Instruments BAII Plus financial calculator, you *must* enter *either* the PV or PMT as a negative amount, *but not both*. Due to the sign conventions used by this calculator, entering *both* PV and PMT as negative amounts or as positive amounts will lead to an *incorrect* final answer. The calculator does *not* indicate that the answer is incorrect or that an entry error was made. (This has not been an issue until now because either PV or PMT was 0 in all the examples we discussed.) To avoid incorrect answers, *always* enter the PV amount as a negative number and the PMT amount as a positive number when FV = 0 and you are calculating N. However, if PV = 0, enter PMT as a negative number and FV as a positive number. The examples in this text follow these rules. Refer to Appendix II to check whether this step is necessary if you use the Sharp EL-733A or the Hewlett-Packard 10BII calculator.

EXAMPLE 12.4B

A business valued at \$96 000 is bought for a down payment of 25% and payments of \$4000 at the end of every three months. If interest is 9% compounded monthly, for how long will payments have to be made?

SOLUTION

$PV_{nc} = 96\,000.00(0.75) = 72\,000.00$; $PMT = 4000.00$;

$P/Y = 4$; $C/Y = 12$; $c = \frac{12}{4} = 3$; $I/Y = 9$; $i = \frac{9\%}{12} = 0.75\% = 0.0075$

The effective quarterly rate of interest

$p = 1.0075^3 - 1 = 1.022669 - 1 = 0.022669 = 2.2669\%$

$$72\,000.00 = 4000.00\left(\frac{1 - 1.022669^{-n}}{0.022669}\right)$$ using Formula 12.3

$$0.408046 = 1 - 1.022669^{-n}$$
$$1.022669^{-n} = 0.591954$$
$$-n \ln 1.022669 = \ln 0.591954$$
$$-n(0.022416) = -0.524326$$
$$n = 23.390585 \text{ (quarters)}$$

Programmed Solution

(Set P/Y = 4; C/Y = 12) 9 [I/Y] 0 [FV] 72 000

[±] [PV] 4000 [PMT] [CPT] [N] [23.390604]

Payments will have to be made for 24 quarters or six years.

EXERCISE 12.4

EXCEL NOTES

If you choose, you can use Excel's ***Number of Compounding Periods (NPER)*** function to answer all of the questions below. Refer to **NPER** on the Spreadsheet Template Disk to learn how to use this Excel function.

A. Find the term of each of the following ten ordinary general annuities. (State your answer in years and months.)

	Future Value	Present Value	Periodic Rent	Payment Interval	Interest Rate	Compounding Period
1.	$20 000		$ 800	1 year	7.5%	semi-annually
2.	17 000		35	3 months	9	monthly
3.		$14 500	190	1 month	5.25	quarterly
4.		5 000	300	3 months	4	semi-annually
5.	36 000		175	6 months	7.4	annually
6.		9 500	740	1 quarter	5.2	monthly
7.		21 400	1660	6 months	4.5	monthly
8.	13 600		140	6 months	8	quarterly
9.	72 000		90	1 month	3.75	semi-annually
10.		11 700	315	3 months	11	annually

B. Answer each of the following questions.

1. How long would it take you to save $5000 by making deposits of $100 at the end of every month into a savings account earning 6% compounded quarterly?

Reference Example 12.4A

2. How long will it take to save $15 000 by making deposits of $90 at the end of every month into an account earning interest at 4% compounded quarterly?
3. In what period of time could you pay back a loan of $3000 by making monthly payments of $90 if interest is 10.5% compounded semi-annually?

Reference Example 12.4B

4. For how long will Jack have to make payments of $350 at the end of every three months to repay a loan of $6000 if interest is 9% compounded monthly?
5. Mirsad is saving $500 at the end of each month. How soon can he retire if he wants to have a retirement fund of $120 000 and interest is 5.4% compounded quarterly?
6. For how long must contributions of $2000 be made at the end of each year to accumulate to $100 000 at 6% compounded quarterly?
7. For how long can $800 be withdrawn at the end of each month from an account originally containing $16 000, if interest is 6.8% compounded semi-annually?

8. A mortgage of $120 000 is to be repaid by making payments of $750 at the end of each month. If interest is 5.75% compounded semi-annually, what is the term of the mortgage?

9. Suppose $370.37 is deposited at the end of every three months into an account earning 6.5% compounded semi-annually. If the balance in the account is to be $20 000, how many deposits are needed?

10. Mr. Deneau accumulated $100 000 in an RRSP. He converted the RRSP into an RRIF and started to withdraw $4500 at the end of every three months from the fund. If interest is 6.75% compounded monthly, for how long can Mr. Deneau make withdrawals?

12.5 ORDINARY GENERAL ANNUITIES—FINDING THE PERIODIC INTEREST RATE *i*

A. Finding the periodic rate of interest *i* using preprogrammed financial calculators

EXCEL NOTES

Preprogrammed financial calculators are especially helpful when solving for the conversion rate *i*. Determining *i* without a financial calculator is extremely time-consuming. However, it *can* be done by hand, as illustrated in Appendix B on the CD-ROM.

BUSINESS MATH NEWS BOX

University of Windsor Enters Bond Market

The University of Windsor took a first-time trip to the financial markets and issued $108.3 million in bonds to fund major construction projects—creating the largest debenture in its 43-year history as a public institution.

The first project to benefit from the infusion of cash will be a new school of engineering worth $53 million. The university expects to pay for the new digs for aspiring engineers with government funding, fundraising dollars, and some of the borrowed money.

The university will pay an interest rate of 5.37% to the bond's investors over 40 years. Of the $108.3 million, $29 million will be used to pay off the school's existing debt. Another $14 million will be placed in a sinking fund that will be used to help pay off the bond's principal in 2046.

The balance will be invested and interest will be earned on the money until it is needed for capital projects, Paul said.

The decision to issue bonds came earlier this year as the school's board of governors considered its options to raise the cash for capital projects. A bond is essentially a loan. The purchaser of a bond is lending money to the issuer—in this case the university. The purchaser is paid a certain rate of interest at fixed intervals, plus the original investment when the bond matures.

Source: "University of Windsor enters bond market: $108M to help finance projects," by Roseann Danese, *The Windsor Star,* June 29, 2006. Material reprinted with the express permission of: "Windsor Star Group Inc.," a CanWest Partnership.

QUESTIONS

1. Calculate the interest provided to investors if the coupon rate is 5.37% paid semi-annually.
2. Calculate the amount remaining after all plans for the $108 million bond have been satisfied.
3. **a.** If a sinking fund is created with this remaining amount, earning 4.2% p.a. compounded quarterly, calculate the future value after 40 years.

   b. What amount is required to add to this sinking fund on a quarterly basis in order to satisfy the loan repayment?

When the future value or present value, the periodic payment PMT, and the term n of a general annuity are known, retrieve the value of I/Y by pressing CPT I/Y.

EXAMPLE 12.5A

Irina deposited $150 in a savings account at the end of each month for 60 months. If the accumulated value of the deposits was $10 000 and interest was compounded semi-annually, what was the nominal annual rate of interest?

SOLUTION

FV = 10 000.00; PMT = 150.00; $n = 60$; P/Y = 12; C/Y = 2; $c = \frac{2}{12} = \frac{1}{6}$

(Set P/Y = 12; C/Y = 2) 0 PV 10 000 FV

150 ± PMT 60 N CPT I/Y 4.255410

The nominal annual rate of interest is 4.26% p.a. compounded semi-annually.

EXAMPLE 12.5B

Compute the nominal annual rate of interest compounded monthly at which $500 paid at the end of every three months for ten years will eliminate a debt of $16 000.

SOLUTION

PV = 16 000.00; PMT = 500.00; $n = 40$; P/Y = 4; C/Y = 12; $c = \frac{12}{4} = 3$

(Set P/Y = 4; C/Y = 12) 0 FV 16 000 PV

500 ± PMT 40 N CPT I/Y 4.528237

The nominal annual rate is 4.53% p.a. compounded monthly.

EXERCISE 12.5

A. For each of the following eight ordinary general annuities, determine the nominal annual rate of interest.

	Future Value	Present Value	Periodic Payment	Payment Interval	Term	Conversion Period
1.	$39 200		$2 300	1 year	12 years	monthly
2.		$ 9 600	1 220	6 months	5 years	monthly
3.		62 400	2 600	6 months	25 years	annually
4.	55 500		75	1 month	20 years	semi-annually
5.	6 400		200	6 months	9 years	monthly
6.	25 000		790	1 year	15 years	quarterly
7.		7 500	420	3 months	5 years	monthly
8.		60 000	450	1 month	25 years	semi-annually

B. Answer each of the following questions.

1. What is the nominal annual rate of interest compounded quarterly if deposits of $253 made each month for 3½ years accumulate to $11 600?

Reference Example 12.5A

2. Victoria saved $416 every six months for eight years. What nominal rate of interest compounded annually is earned if the savings account amounts to $7720 in eight years?

3. What is the nominal annual rate of interest compounded semi-annually if a four-year loan of $6000 is repaid by monthly payments of $144.23?

Reference Example 12.5B

4. A car valued at $11 400 can be purchased for 10% down and monthly payments of $286.21 for three-and-a-half years. What is the nominal rate of interest compounded annually?

5. A property worth $50 000 can be purchased for 20% down and quarterly mortgage payments of $1000 for 25 years. What nominal rate of interest compounded monthly is charged?

6. A vacation property valued at $25 000 was bought for fifteen payments of $2200 due at the end of every six months. What nominal annual rate of interest compounded annually was charged?

7. Compute the nominal annual rate of interest compounded monthly at which $400 paid at the end of every three months for eight years accumulates to $20 000.

8. What is the nominal annual rate of interest compounded quarterly if a loan of $21 500 is repaid in seven years by payments of $2000 made at the end of every six months?

9. If Paige has accumulated $4850 by saving $120 every month for 3 years, what nominal annual rate of interest compounded quarterly has been earned?

10. Deanna wants to save $3500 in two years by depositing $420 every three months into a savings account. What nominal rate of interest compounded annually does her savings have to earn?

11. A mortgage of \$27 500 is repaid by making payments of \$280 at the end of each month for fifteen years. What is the nominal annual rate of interest compounded semi-annually?

12. A property worth \$35 000 is purchased for 10% down and semi-annual payments of \$2100 for twelve years. What is the effective annual rate of interest if interest is compounded quarterly?

12.6 CONSTANT-GROWTH ANNUITIES

The annuities we have considered so far have the common feature of periodic payments that are equal in size. **Constant-growth annuities** differ from these fixed-payment-size annuities in that the periodic payments change (usually grow) at a constant rate. The assumption of constant growth is often used in sales forecasting and long-term financial planning. It is consistent with the indexing of pensions and is also present in federal tax policies.

The types of constant-growth annuities parallel the types of fixed payment annuities considered in Chapter 11 and the previous sections of Chapter 12. However, we will deal only with ordinary simple constant-growth annuities.

With ordinary simple constant-growth annuities, the computations may involve determining the size of any periodic payment, the total amount of the periodic payments, the future value and present value of the stream of periodic payments, the amount of interest earned by the periodic payments, and the size of the first payment if either the present value or the future value is known. We will also consider in this section the special case when the constant growth rate equals the periodic rate of interest.

A. Future value of an ordinary simple constant-growth annuity

To compute the future value of a series of payments growing at a constant rate, the approach is similar to that used in Example 11.2B.

In general, if the first payment is represented by PMT and the constant rate of growth by k, the constant growth factor for the annuity payments is $(1+k)$ and the size of the successive payments is as follows:

$$\begin{aligned}
&\text{1st payment} &&= \text{PMT}\\
&\text{2nd payment} &&= \text{PMT}(1+k)\\
&\text{3rd payment} &&= \text{PMT}(1+k)^2\\
&\text{4th payment} &&= \text{PMT}(1+k)^3\\
&\quad\downarrow && \quad\downarrow\\
&\quad\downarrow && \quad\downarrow\\
&\text{10th payment} &&= \text{PMT}(1+k)^9
\end{aligned}$$

$$\text{SIZE OF THE } n\text{TH PAYMENT} = \text{PMT}(1+k)^{n-1}$$ ——— **Formula 12.4**

The periodic constant-growth payments form an ordinary simple annuity in which PMT is the size of the first payment, k is the periodic compounding rate, and n is the number of payments.

SUM OF THE PERIODIC CONSTANT-GROWTH PAYMENTS $= \text{PMT}\dfrac{(1+k)^n - 1}{k}$ ——— **Formula 12.5**

Note: Formula 12.5 is the same as Formula 11.1 except that i has been replaced by k.

The formula for finding the future value of an ordinary simple constant-growth annuity is similar in structure to future value Formula 11.1.

$$\text{FV} = \text{PMT}\frac{(1+i)^n - (1+k)^n}{i-k}$$ ——— **Formula 12.6**

where FV = the future (accumulated) value of an ordinary simple constant-growth annuity;
PMT = the size of the first annuity payment;
i = the interest rate per conversion period;
k = the constant growth rate of the annuity payments;
n = the number of conversion periods.

The factor $\dfrac{(1+i)^n - (1+k)^n}{i-k}$ is the compounding factor for constant-growth annuities. If $k = 0$, which means there is no growth in the periodic payments, the factor becomes the compounding factor used in Formula 11.1. Formula 11.1 is, in fact, a special case of Formula 12.6—the "zero-growth case."

EXAMPLE 12.6A

Five deposits increasing at a constant rate of 2% are made at the end of each of four successive years respectively. The size of the first deposit is \$3000 and the fund earns interest at 6% compounded annually.

(i) What is the size of the last deposit?

(ii) How much was deposited in total?

(iii) What is the accumulated value of the deposits?

(iv) What is the interest earned by the deposits?

SOLUTION

The situation is pictured in Figure 12.3.

FIGURE 12.3 **End of period (year) $i = 6\% = 0.06$**

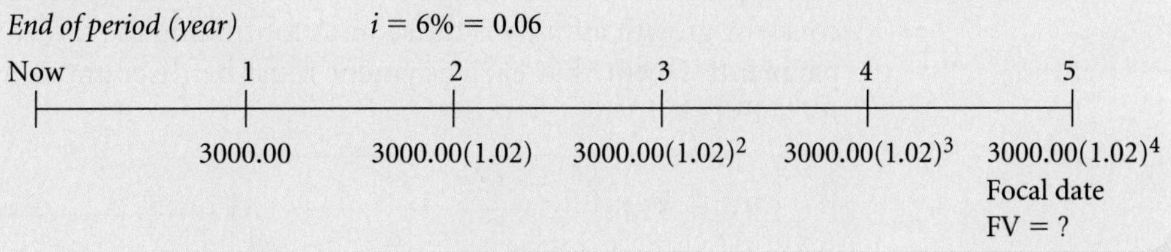

(i) PMT = 3000.00; $k = 2\% = 0.02$; $n = 5$

Size of the 5th payment

$= \text{PMT}(1 + k)^{n-1}$ ——— using Formula 12.4

$= 3000.00(1.02)^4$

$= 3000.00(1.082432)$

$= \$3247.30$

(ii) PMT = 3000.00; $k = 2\% = 0.02$; $n = 5$

Sum of the constant-growth deposits

$$= \text{PMT}\left[\frac{(1 + k)^n - 1}{k}\right] \text{ ——— using Formula 12.5}$$

$$= 3000.00\left[\frac{(1.02)^5 - 1}{0.02}\right]$$

$$= 3000.00\left[\frac{1.010408 - 1}{0.02}\right]$$

$$= 3000.00(5.20404)$$

$$= \$15\ 612.12$$

(iii) PMT = 3000.00; $k = 2\% = 0.02$; $n = 5$; $i = 6\% = 0.06$

Sum of the constant-growth deposits

$$\text{FV} = \text{PMT}\left[\frac{(1 + i)^n - (1 + k)^n}{i - k}\right] \text{ ——— using Formula 12.6}$$

$$= 3000.00\left[\frac{(1.06)^5 - (1.02)^5}{0.06 - 0.02}\right]$$

$$= 3000.00\left[\frac{1.338226 - 1.104081}{0.02}\right]$$

$$= 3000.00(5.853620)$$

$$= \$17\ 560.86$$

(iv) The interest earned by the deposits

$= 17\ 560.86 - 15\ 612.12 = \$1948.74.$

B. Present value of an ordinary simple constant-growth annuity

The approach to determining the present value of a series of payments forming a constant-growth annuity is the same as for finding the future value of the series of payments except that each payment must be discounted using Formula 9.1C, $\text{PV} = \text{FV}(1 + i)^{-n}$.

$$\text{PV} = \text{PMT}\left[\frac{1 - (1 + k)^n(1 + i)^{-n}}{i - k}\right] \text{ ——— Formula 12.7}$$

where PV = the present (discounted) value of an ordinary simple constant-growth annuity;
PMT = the size of the first annuity payment;
i = the interest rate per conversion period;
k = the constant growth rate of the annuity payments;
n = the number of conversion periods.

The factor $\left[\frac{(1-(1+k)^n(1+i)^{-n}}{i-k}\right]$ is the discount factor for constant-growth annuities. If $k = 0$, which means there is no growth in the periodic payments, the factor becomes the discount factor used in Formula 11.2. Formula 11.2 is, in fact, a special case of formula 12.7—the "zero-growth case."

Constant-growth annuity formulas are not part of the programming of most financial calculators. Problems involving constant-growth annuities can be solved by substituting in the appropriate formulas as shown in Examples 12.6A and 12.6B.

EXAMPLE 12.6B Use Formula 12.7 to calculate the present value of the deposits in Example 12.6A.

SOLUTION PMT = 3000.00; $k = 2\% = 0.02$; $n = 5$; $i = 6\% = 0.06$;

$$PV = 3000.00\left[\frac{1-(1.02)^5(1.06)^{-5}}{0.06-0.02}\right]$$ ——— using Formula 12.7

$$PV = 3000.00\left[\frac{1-(1.104081)(0.747258)}{0.04}\right]$$

$$PV = 3000.00(4.374165)$$

$$PV = \$13\ 122.50$$

When the constant-growth rate of the annuity payments and the number of conversion periods are the same, Formula 12.8 is used to calculate future value of an ordinary simple constant-growth annuity.

$$FV = n(PMT)(1+i)^{n-1}$$ ——— Formula 12.8

When the constant-growth rate of the annuity payments and the number of conversion periods are the same, Formula 12.9 is used to calculate present value of an ordinary simple constant-growth annuity.

$$PV = n(PMT)(1+i)^{-1}$$ ——— Formula 12.9

EXERCISE 12.6

A. Answer each of the following questions.

1. You plan to make twenty-five periodic deposits into your RRSP starting with $500 and increasing thereafter by 3%.
   (a) What will be the size of the twenty-fifth deposit?
   (b) What will be the total amount deposited?

2. Sally has accumulated a sizeable balance in her investment fund. She wants to make annual withdrawals for fifteen years starting with $5000 and decreasing (negative growth) by 5% thereafter.
   (a) What will be the size of the fifteenth withdrawal? (***Hint:*** Let $k = -5\%$.)
   (b) What will be the total amount withdrawn?

3. Twenty semi-annual deposits are made earning interest of 5% compounded semi-annually. The size of the first deposit is $1200 and the deposits increase at 1.5% thereafter.
   (a) Determine the total amount deposited.
   (b) How much was the accumulated value of the deposits just after the last deposit was made?
   (c) What is the size of the twelfth deposit?
   (d) What is the amount of interest included in the accumulated value?

4. Withdrawals increasing at a constant rate of 4% are made quarterly for six years from an account earning 6% compounded quarterly.
   (a) What must be the balance in the account to permit the withdrawals if the first withdrawal is $1500?
   (b) What is the size of the last withdrawal?
   (c) What is the total amount withdrawn?
   (d) How much interest is included in the withdrawals?

B. Solve each of the following.

1. Lucy won a large sum in the lottery. She invested part of her winnings into a fund earning 6% compounded monthly. She has arranged a systematic withdrawal plan that provides for 120 monthly payments increasing at a constant rate of 0.5% per payment. The first payment of $400 is due one month after she set up the fund. How much interest is included in the payments?

Reference Example 12.6A

2. Trent has opened an RRSP account by making an initial deposit of $1500. He intends to make semi-annual deposits for 30 years increasing at a constant rate of 3.5%. How much of the accumulated value just after the last deposit was made is interest if interest is 7% compounded semi-annually?

Reference Example 12.6B

3. Shelby paid \$150 000 for a 10-year indexed annuity in which the monthly payments received at the end of each month diminish by 0.6% per payment. What is the total amount received by Shelby if interest is 7.2% compounded monthly?

4. Cecile intends to make end-of-the-year payments growing by 8% per payment for 12 years. If the payments earn 7% compounded annually, what is the size of the last payment if the accumulated value of the payments is \$250 000?

Review Exercise

1. Payments of \$375 made every three months are accumulated at 3% compounded monthly. What is their future value after eight years if the payments are made at the end of every three months?

2. What is the accumulated value after twelve years of monthly deposits of \$145 earning interest at 5% compounded semi-annually if the deposits are made at the end of each month?

3. What single cash payment is equivalent to payments of \$3500 every six months at 7% compounded quarterly if the payments are made at the end of every six months for fifteen years?

4. What is the principal invested at 6.5% compounded semi-annually from which monthly withdrawals of \$240 can be made at the end of each month for twenty-five years?

5. Contributions of \$500 are made at the end of every three months into an RRSP. What is the accumulated balance after twenty years if interest is 6% compounded semi-annually?

6. A 25-year mortgage is amortized by payments of \$761.50 made at the end of each month. If interest is 9.5% compounded semi-annually, what is the mortgage principal?

7. Kristan wants to accumulate \$18 000 into an account earning 7.5% compounded semi-annually. How much must she deposit
   (a) at the end of each month for ten years?
   (b) at the end of each year for eight years?

8. What sum of money can be withdrawn from a fund of \$15 750 invested at 4.25% compounded semi-annually
   (a) at the end of every month for twelve years?
   (b) at the end of each year for fifteen years?

9. How long will it take for payments of \$350 to accumulate to \$12 000 at 3% compounded monthly if made
   (a) at the end of every three months?
   (b) at the end of every six months?

10. A \$92 000 mortgage with a 25-year term is repaid by making payments at the end of each month. If interest is 5.8% compounded semi-annually, how much are the payments?

11. A debt of \$14 000 is repaid by making payments of \$1500. If interest is 9% compounded monthly, for how long will payments have to be made
    (a) at the end of every six months?
    (b) at the end of each year?

12. What is the nominal rate of interest compounded monthly at which payments of \$200 made at the end of every three months accumulate to \$9200 in eight years?

13. A debt of \$2290 is repaid by making payments of \$198. If interest is 16.95% compounded monthly, for how long will quarterly payments have to be made?

14. A \$60 000 mortgage with a 25-year term is repaid by making monthly payments of \$480. What is the nominal annual rate of interest compounded semi-annually on the mortgage?

15. Marc invested a bonus of \$6000 in an RRSP earning 4.9% compounded semi-annually for twenty years. At the end of the twenty years, he rolled the RRSP balance over into an RRIF paying \$2000 at the end of each quarter starting three months after the date of rollover. If interest on the RRIF is 4.3% compounded monthly, for how long will Marc receive quarterly payments?

16. Satwinder deposited \$145 at the end of each month for fifteen years at 7.5% compounded monthly. After her last deposit she converted the balance into an ordinary annuity paying \$1200 every three months for twelve years. If interest on the annuity is compounded semi-annually, what is the nominal rate of interest paid by the annuity?

17. Mrs. Jolly contributes $222 at the end of every three months to an RRSP. Interest on the account is 6% compounded monthly.

(a) What will the balance in the account be after eleven years?

(b) How much of the balance will be interest?

(c) If Mrs. Jolly converts the balance after eleven years into an RRIF paying 5% compounded monthly and makes equal quarterly withdrawals for twelve years starting three months after the conversion into her RRIF, what is the size of the quarterly withdrawal?

(d) What is the combined interest earned by the RRSP and the RRIF?

18. How much must be contributed into an RRSP at the end of each year for twenty-five years to accumulate to $100 000 if interest is 8% compounded quarterly?

19. For how long must $75 be deposited at the end of each month to accumulate to $9500 at 6.5% compounded quarterly?

20. A $70 000 mortgage is amortized by making monthly payments of $534.95. If interest is 7.2% compounded semi-annually, what is the term of the mortgage?

21. Toby has opened an RRSP account by making an initial deposit of $1200. She intends to make quarterly deposits for twenty years increasing at a constant rate of 1.5%. How much of the accumulated value just after the last deposit was made is interest if interest is 7% compounded quarterly?

22. Harry paid $250 000 for a fifteen-year indexed annuity in which the monthly payments received at the end of each month increase by 0.7% per payment. What is the total amount received by Harry if interest is 8.4% compounded monthly?

Self-Test

1. Monthly deposits of $480 were made at the end of each month for eight years. If interest is 4.5% compounded semi-annually, what amount can be withdrawn immediately after the last deposit?

2. A loan was repaid in five years by end-of-quarter payments of $1200 at 9.5% compounded semi-annually. How much interest was paid?

3. A loan of $6000 was repaid by quarterly payments of $450. If interest was 12% compounded monthly, how long did it take to pay back the loan?

4. A mortgage of $95 000 is to be amortized by monthly payments over twenty-five years. If the payments are made at the end of each month and interest is 8.5% compounded semi-annually, what is the size of the monthly payments?

5. The amount of $46 200 is invested at 9.5% compounded quarterly for four years. After four years the balance in the fund is converted into an annuity. If interest on the annuity is 6.5% compounded semi-annually and payments are made at the end of every three months for seven years, what is the size of the payments?

6. A $45 000 mortgage is repaid in twenty years by making monthly payments of $387.72. What is the nominal annual rate of interest compounded semi-annually?

7. For how long would you have to deposit $491 at the end of every three months to accumulate $20 000 at 6.0% compounded monthly?

8. What is the size of monthly deposits that will accumulate to $67 200 after eight years at 6.5% compounded semi-annually?

9. Eva contributed $200 every month for five years into an RRSP earning 4.3% compounded quarterly. Six years after the last contribution, she converted the RRSP into an annuity that is to pay her monthly for thirty years. If the first payment is due one month after the conversion into the annuity and interest on the annuity is 5.4% compounded semi-annually, how much will Eva receive every month?

10. Joy would like to receive $6000 at the end of every three months for ten years after her retirement. If she retires now and interest is 6.5% compounded semi-annually, how much must she deposit into an account?

11. Mira has opened a registered retirement income fund (RRIF) with a starting balance of $250 000. Beginning six months later, she plans to make semi-annual withdrawals from the RRIF for twenty years. The withdrawals will increase at a constant rate of 1.75%. If the RRIF earns 8% compounded semi-annually, how much is the amount of interest included in the total withdrawals?

Challenge Problems

1. After winning some money at a casino, Tony is considering purchasing an annuity that promises to pay him $300 at the end of each month for 12 months, then $350 at the end of each month for 24 months, and then $375 at the end of each month for 36 months. If the first payment is due at the end of the first month and interest is 7.5% compounded annually over the life of the annuity, find Tony's purchase price.

2. A loan of $5600 is to be repaid at 9% compounded annually by making ten payments at the end of each quarter. Each of the last six payments is two times the amount of each of the first four payments. What is the size of each payment?

Case Study 12.1 Vehicle Cash-Back Incentives

» Karim Soltan is shopping for a new vehicle, and has noticed that many vehicle manufacturers are offering special deals to sell off the current year's vehicles before the new models arrive. Karim's local Ford dealership is advertising 3.9% financing for a full 48 months (i.e., 3.9% compounded monthly) or up to $4000 cash back on selected vehicles.

The vehicle that Karim wants to purchase costs $24 600 including taxes, delivery, licence, and dealer preparation. This vehicle qualifies for $1800 cash back if Karim pays cash for the vehicle. Karim has a good credit rating and knows that he could arrange a vehicle loan at his bank for the full price of any vehicle he chooses. His other option is to take the dealer financing offered at 3.9% for 48 months.

Karim wants to know which option requires the lower monthly payment. He knows he can use annuity formulas to calculate the monthly payments.

QUESTIONS

1. Suppose Karim buys the vehicle on July 1. What monthly payment must Karim make if he chooses the dealer's 3.9% financing option and pays off the loan over 48 months? (Assume he makes each monthly payment at the end of the month and his first payment is due on July 31.)

2. Suppose the bank offers Karim a 48-month loan with the interest compounded monthly and the payments due at the end of each month. If Karim accepts the bank loan, he can get $1800 cash back on this vehicle.

   Karim works out a method to calculate the bank rate of interest required to make bank financing the same cost as dealer financing. First, calculate the monthly rate of interest that would make the monthly bank payments equal to the monthly dealer payments. Then calculate the effective rate of interest represented by the monthly compounded rate. If the financing from the bank is at a lower rate of interest compounded monthly, choose the bank financing. The reason is that the monthly payments for the bank's financing would be lower than the monthly payments for the dealer's 3.9% financing.

   (a) How much money would Karim have to borrow from the bank to pay cash for this vehicle?

   (b) Using the method above, calculate the effective annual rate of interest and the nominal annual rate of interest required to make the monthly payments for bank financing exactly the same as for dealer financing.

3. Suppose Karim decides to explore the costs of financing a more expensive vehicle. The more expensive vehicle costs $34 900 in total and qualifies for the 3.9% dealer financing for 48 months or $2500 cash back. What is the highest effective annual rate of interest at which Karim should borrow from the bank instead of using the dealer's 3.9% financing?

Case Study 12.2 Fiscal Fitness

» Rosalinda is planning to open Fitness Quest, a new health and fitness club. She must decide what to charge for each type of membership and what payment options to offer.

Rosalinda plans to offer two types of memberships. General membership allows members to use all facilities, and it provides a simple locker room. Premium membership allows members to use all facilities, and it provides towels, shower supplies, and a sauna. When members pay for their annual membership when they join, the fee is $550 for the General membership and $700 for the Premium membership.

QUESTIONS

1. Rosalinda wants to offer members the option of paying their annual membership fees in twelve equal monthly installments. The first installment would be due on the day of joining.
   (a) To the nearest dollar, how much should Rosalinda charge General members monthly if she wants to make interest of 17.5% compounded monthly?
   (b) To the nearest dollar, how much should she charge Fitness Quest members monthly if she wants to make interest of 21% compounded monthly?
2. Rosalinda knows that many of the Fitness Quest members will be executives whose companies will pay for their memberships. Many companies prefer to make quarterly payments for annual memberships. For this reason, Rosalinda decides to offer a quarterly payment option. The first installment would be due on the day of joining. To the nearest dollar, how much should Rosalinda charge Fitness Quest members quarterly if she wants to make interest of 21% compounded monthly?
3. As an opening special, Rosalinda wants to offer all members who join during the opening week three free months of membership. To calculate the nominal rate of interest she would earn on these opening special memberships, Rosalinda will add the payments made for the year for a membership, then spread the total payments equally over fifteen months as if the payment period were fifteen months. She would then calculate the nominal rate of interest earned on these new monthly payments over the fifteen-month membership period.
   (a) What is the nominal rate of interest earned on the opening special for the General membership with the monthly payment option?
   (b) What is the nominal rate of interest earned on the opening special for the Premium membership with the monthly payment option?
   (c) What is the nominal rate of interest earned on the opening special for the Premium membership with the quarterly payment option?

SUMMARY OF FORMULAS

Formula 12.1

$$p = (1 + i)^c - 1$$

Finding the equivalent rate of interest per payment period p for a nominal annual rate of interest compounded c times per payment interval

Formula 12.2

$$FV_{nc} = PMT\left[\frac{(1+p)^n - 1}{p}\right]$$

Finding the future value of an ordinary general annuity using the effective rate of interest per payment period

where $p = (1 + i)^c - 1$

Formula 12.2A

$$PMT = \frac{FV_{nc}p}{(1+p)^n - 1}$$

Finding the payment of an ordinary general annuity using the effective rate of interest per payment period when the future value is known

Formula 12.2B

$$n = \frac{\ln[FV_n p/PMT + 1]}{\ln(1+p)}$$

Finding the number of payments of an ordinary general annuity using the effective rate of interest per payment period when the future value is known

Formula 12.3

$$PV_{nc} = PMT\left[\frac{1 - (1+p)^{-n}}{p}\right]$$

Finding the present value of an ordinary general annuity using the effective rate of interest per payment period

Formula 12.3A

$$PMT = \frac{PV_{nc}p}{1 - (1+p)^{-n}}$$

Finding the payment of an ordinary general annuity using the effective rate of interest per payment period when the present value is known

Formula 12.3B

$$n = \frac{\ln[1 - (PV_n p/PMT)]}{-\ln(1+p)}$$

Finding the number of payments of an ordinary general annuity using the effective rate of interest per payment period when the present value is known

Formula 12.4

$$\text{SIZE OF THE } n\text{TH PAYMENT} = PMT(1+k)^{n-1}$$

Finding the size of the nth payment of a constant-growth annuity

Formula 12.5

$$\text{SUM OF THE PERIODIC CONSTANT-GROWTH PAYMENTS} = \frac{PMT\,(1+k)^{n-1}}{k}$$

Finding the sum of the periodic payments of a constant-growth annuity.

Formula 12.6

$$FV = PMT\frac{(1+i)^n - (1+k)^n}{i-k}$$

Finding the future value of an ordinary simple constant-growth annuity

Formula 12.7

$$PV = PMT\left[\frac{1-(1+k)^n(1+i)^{-n}}{i-k}\right]$$

Finding the present value of a series of payments forming a constant-growth annuity

Formula 12.8

$$FV = n\,(PMT)(1+i)^{n-1}$$

Finding the future value of an ordinary simple constant-growth annuity when the constant-growth rate and the number of conversion periods are the same

Formula 12.9

$$PV = n\,(PMT)(1+i)^{-1}$$

Finding the present value of an ordinary simple constant-growth annuity when the constant-growth rate and the number of conversion periods are the same

GLOSSARY

Constant-growth annuity an annuity in which the payments change by the same percentage from one period to the next *(p. 494)*

Equivalent rate of interest per payment period the rate of interest earned during the payment period that yields the same amount of interest as a nominal annual rate compounded *c* times per year, where *c* is the number of payment periods per year *(p. 475)*

USEFUL INTERNET SITES

www.money.canoe.ca
RRIF: Savings Find current information and rates of return on RRIFs from several financial institutions and financial services providers on the Canoe Money site.

www.fidelity.ca
Growth Calculator Click on "Investor Centre," "Education/Planning," "Calculators," and then "Growth Calculator." This interactive chart on the Fidelity Investments site allows you to calculate both simple and compound earnings on investment capital by entering values for a series of variables.

www.butterworths.ca
The Bottom Line A monthly Canadian magazine for finance professionals. Click on "The Bottom Line."

CHAPTER 13

Annuities Due, Deferred Annuities, and Perpetuities

OBJECTIVES

Upon completing this chapter, you will be able to do the following:

1. Compute the future value, present value, periodic payment, term, and interest rate for simple annuities due.
2. Compute the future value, present value, periodic payment, term, and interest rate for general annuities due.
3. Compute the future value, present value, periodic payment, term, and interest rate for ordinary deferred annuities.
4. Compute the future value, present value, periodic payment, term, and interest rate for deferred annuities due.
5. Compute the present value, periodic payment, and interest rate for ordinary perpetuities, perpetuities due, and deferred perpetuities.

When you pay rent on an apartment, a house or a commercial space, your rent is due at the beginning of the month. This series of regular, equal payments paid at the beginning of the period represents a type of annuity called an annuity due. The payment schedule for an annuity due differs from that of an ordinary annuity (which we discussed in Chapters 11 and 12) where payments were due at the end of each period.

In some situations, a series of regular, equal payments may not begin until some future time. These payment situations are known as deferred annuities. For example, if you won a large amount of money today and you wanted a series of regular, equal payments to begin five years from now, you would set up a deferred annuity. Both ordinary annuities and annuities due can be deferred.

INTRODUCTION

In the previous chapters, we considered ordinary annuities, both simple and general, in which the payments are made at the end of each payment period.

In this chapter we will consider other annuities resulting from variations in the payment dates and the length of time that the payments continue. These include annuities due (in which payments are made at the beginning of the period), deferred annuities (in which the first payment is made after the first or several payment intervals have been completed), and perpetuities (in which payments continue indefinitely).

13.1 SIMPLE ANNUITIES DUE

A. Future value of a simple annuity due

An **annuity due** is an annuity in which the periodic payments are made at the beginning of each payment interval. The future value of an annuity due is closely related to the future value of an ordinary annuity. This same close relationship also holds for the present value.

EXAMPLE 13.1A Find the accumulated value (future value) at the end date of the last payment period of deposits of \$3000 each made at the beginning of five consecutive years respectively with interest at 6% compounded annually.

SOLUTION As for any problem involving a series of payments, the method of solution and the data can be shown on a time diagram.

FIGURE 13.1 Graphical Representation of Method and Data

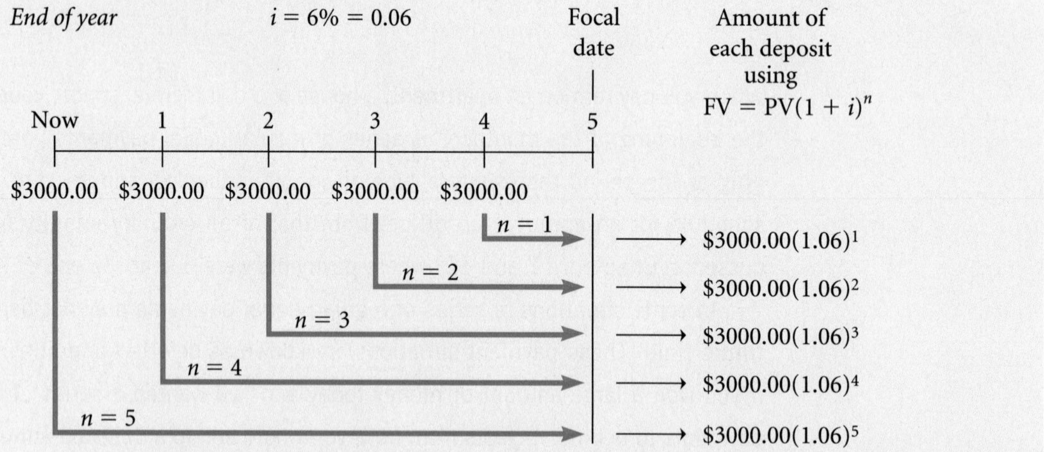

As shown in Figure 13.1, the first deposit is located at the beginning of Year 1, which is the same as "now"; the second deposit is located at the beginning of Year 2, which is the same as the end of Year 1; the third at the beginning of Year 3; the fourth at the beginning of Year 4; and the fifth and last deposit at the beginning of Year 5, which is also the beginning of the last payment period. The focal date, however, is located at the *end* of the last payment period.

The accumulated values of the individual deposits are obtained by using Formula 9.1A, $FV = PV(1 + i)^n$. Finding the combined total of the five accumulated values is made easier by taking out the common factors 3000.00 and 1.06 as follows:

$$
\begin{array}{ll}
\textit{Deposit 5} & 3000.00(1.06)^1 = \\
\textit{Deposit 4} & 3000.00(1.06)^2 = \\
\textit{Deposit 3} & 3000.00(1.06)^3 = \\
\textit{Deposit 2} & 3000.00(1.06)^4 = \\
\textit{Deposit 1} & 3000.00(1.06)^5 =
\end{array}
3000.00(1.06)\begin{bmatrix}(1.0)\\(1.06)\\(1.06)^2\\(1.06)^3\\(1.06)^4\end{bmatrix}
= 3000.00(1.06)\begin{bmatrix}(1.0)\\(1.06)\\(1.1236)\\(1.191016)\\(1.262477)\end{bmatrix}
$$

$$
\begin{aligned}
&= 3000.00(1.06)(5.637093)\\
&= 16\,911.28(1.06)\\
&= \$17\,925.96
\end{aligned}
$$

Note: This example is the same as Example 11.2B except that the deposits are made at the beginning of each payment period rather than at the end. The answer to Example 11.2B was \$16 911.28. We could have obtained the answer to Example 13.1A simply by multiplying \$16 911.28 by 1.06. It appears that the future value of the annuity due can be obtained by multiplying the future value of the ordinary annuity by the factor $(1 + i)$.

The general notation for simple annuities due is the same as for ordinary simple annuities except that the accumulated value (future value) of the annuity due is represented by the symbol FV_n(due).

The formula for the future value of a simple annuity due is:

$$S_n(\text{due}) = R(1 + i)\left[\frac{(1 + i)^n - 1}{i}\right]$$

restated as

$$FV_n(\text{due}) = PMT(1 + i)\left[\frac{(1 + i)^n - 1}{i}\right]$$

Formula 13.1

Note: Formula 13.1, the future value of a simple annuity due, differs from Formula 11.1, the future value of an ordinary simple annuity, only by the factor $(1 + i)$.

$$\text{FUTURE VALUE OF A SIMPLE ANNUITY DUE} = (1 + i) \times \text{FUTURE VALUE OF THE ORDINARY SIMPLE ANNUITY}$$

The relationship between an annuity due and the corresponding ordinary annuity is graphically illustrated in the comparison of the line diagrams.

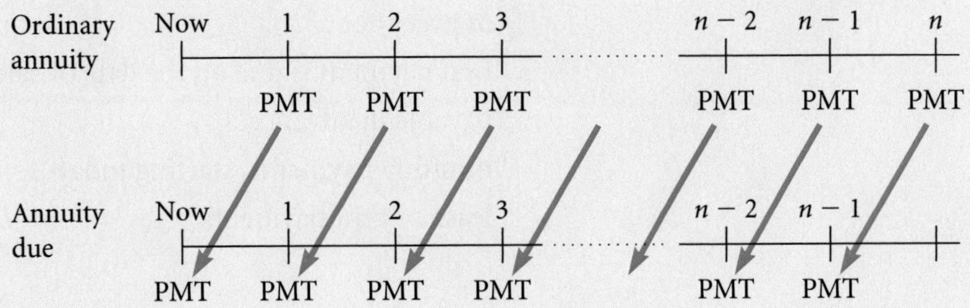

The two line graphs show the shift of the payments by one period. In an annuity due, every payment earns interest for one more period than in an ordinary annuity and this explains the factor $(1 + i)$.

EXAMPLE 13.1B

You deposit \$100 at the beginning of each month for five years in an account paying 4.2% compounded monthly.

(i) What will the balance in your account be at the end of five years?
(ii) How much of the balance will you have contributed?
(iii) How much of the balance will be interest?

SOLUTION

(i) PMT = 100.00; P/Y = 12; C/Y = 12; I/Y = 4.2;

$$i = \frac{4.2\%}{12} = 0.35\% = 0.0035; \quad n = 5(12) = 60$$

$$\begin{aligned} FV_n(\text{due}) &= 100.00(1.0035)\left(\frac{1.0035^{60} - 1}{0.0035}\right) \\ &= 100.00(1.0035)(66.635949) \\ &= 6663.5949(1.0035) \\ &= \$6686.92 \end{aligned}$$

(ii) Your contribution is (100.00)(60) = \$6000.00.

(iii) The interest earned = 6686.92 − 6000.00 = \$686.92.

POINTERS AND PITFALLS

To distinguish between problems dealing with ordinary annuities and annuities due, look for key words or phrases that signal one type of annuity or the other.

Ordinary annuities:	"payments (or deposits) made at the *end* of each (or every) ..." "monthly payments, starting one month from today ..." "interest payments"
Annuities due:	"payments (or deposits) made at the *beginning* of each (or every) ..." "first payment is due on the date of sale (or signing)" "payable in advance" "monthly payments, starting today ..." "lease or rent payments"

B. Present value of a simple annuity due

EXAMPLE 13.1C Find the present value of five payments of \$3000 each made at the beginning of each of five consecutive years respectively if money is worth 6% compounded annually.

SOLUTION As Figure 13.2 shows, the present value of the individual payments is obtained using Formula 9.1C, $PV = FV(1 + i)^{-n}$. The sum of the individual present values is easier to find when the common factor 3000.00 is taken out.

FIGURE 13.2 **Graphical Representation of Method and Data**

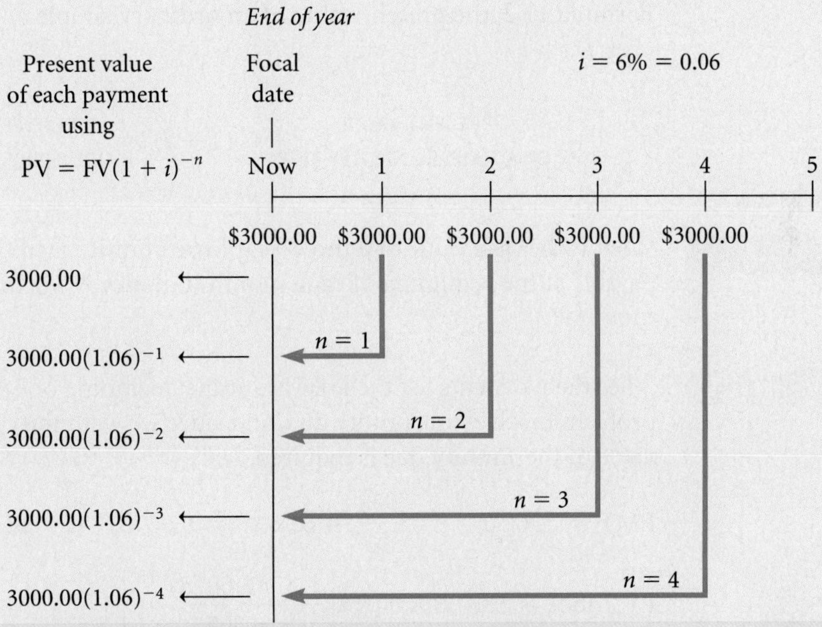

$$\begin{array}{ll} \textit{Payment 1} & 3000.00(1.06)^{0} \\ \textit{Payment 2} & 3000.00(1.06)^{-1} \\ \textit{Payment 3} & 3000.00(1.06)^{-2} \\ \textit{Payment 4} & 3000.00(1.06)^{-3} \\ \textit{Payment 5} & 3000.00(1.06)^{-4} \end{array} = 3000.00 \begin{bmatrix} (1.0) \\ (1.06)^{-1} \\ (1.06)^{-2} \\ (1.06)^{-3} \\ (1.06)^{-4} \end{bmatrix} = 3000.00 \begin{bmatrix} (1.000000) \\ (0.943396) \\ (0.889996) \\ (0.839619) \\ (0.792094) \end{bmatrix}$$

$$= 3000.00 \quad (4.465105)$$

$$= \$13\,395.32$$

Example 13.1C is the same as Example 11.3B, except that the payments are made at the beginning of each payment period. The answer to Example 11.3B was \$12 637.09. If this amount is multiplied by 1.06, the result is \$13 395.32, the answer to Example 13.1C.

This result implies that we could have obtained the present value of the annuity due in Example 13.1C by multiplying the present value of the ordinary annuity in Example 11.3B by the factor 1.06, which is the factor $(1 + i)$.

The present value of an annuity due is represented by the symbol PV_n(due). The formula for the present value of a simple annuity due is:

$$A_n(\text{due}) = R(1 + i)\left[\frac{1 - (1 + i)^{-n}}{i}\right]$$

restated as — **Formula 13.2**

$$PV_n(\text{due}) = PMT(1 + i)\left[\frac{1 - (1 + i)^{-n}}{i}\right]$$

Note: Formula 13.2, the present value of a simple annuity due, differs from Formula 11.2, the present value of an ordinary simple annuity, only by the factor $(1 + i)$.

$$\text{PRESENT VALUE OF A SIMPLE ANNUITY DUE} = (1 + i) \times \text{PRESENT VALUE OF THE ORDINARY SIMPLE ANNUITY}$$

EXAMPLE 13.1D

What is the cash value of a three-year lease of office facilities renting for \$536.50 payable at the beginning of each month if money is worth 9% compounded monthly?

SOLUTION

Since the payments for the lease are at the beginning of each payment period, the problem involves an annuity due, and since we want the cash value, the present value of the annuity due is required.

$$PMT = 536.50; \quad i = \frac{9\%}{12} = 0.75\% = 0.0075; \quad n = 3(12) = 36$$

$$PV_n(\text{due}) = 536.50(1.0075)\left[\frac{1 - (1.0075)^{-36}}{0.0075}\right]$$

$$= 536.50(1.0075)(31.446805)$$

$$= 16\,871.21(1.0075)$$

$$= \$16\,997.74$$

The cash value of the lease is \$16 997.74.

C. Using preprogrammed financial calculators

The future value or the present value of an annuity due can easily be determined by using a preprogrammed financial calculator. One method is to begin by finding the corresponding value for an ordinary simple annuity and multiply it by $(1 + i)$. If you are using the Texas Instruments BAII Plus, set the calculator in "BGN" mode (since annuity due payments are made at the beginning of each payment period), then solve for the unknown variable the same way as you do for ordinary simple annuities. Using the Texas Instruments BAII Plus, follow this key sequence to set the calculator in "BGN" mode:

Key in	*Press*	*Display shows*	
2nd	(BGN)	END *or* BGN	checks the mode
2nd	(SET)	BGN	if previously in "END" mode. BGN will appear in the upper-right corner of the display.
		or END	if previously in "BGN" mode. The display will be blank. Press 2nd (SET) again so that BGN appears in the display.
2nd	(QUIT)		returns to the standard calculation mode

Refer to Appendix II for instruction for annuity due calculations if you are using the Sharp EL-733A or the Hewlett-Packard 10BII calculator.

EXAMPLE 13.1E

Payments of $425 are to be made at the beginning of each quarter for 10 years. If money is worth 6% compounded quarterly, determine

(i) the accumulated value of the payments;
(ii) the present value of the payments.

SOLUTION

(i) PMT = 425; I/Y = 6; P/Y, C/Y = 4; $i = \dfrac{6\%}{4} = 1.5\%$; $n = 40$

Using the Texas Instruments BAII Plus, ensure the calculator is in "BGN" mode, and then follow this key sequence to retrieve the *future value* of an annuity due.

(Set P/Y = 4) 0 PV 425 ± PMT 6.0 I/Y

40 N CPT FV 23409.81274

The accumulated value of the annuity due is $23 409.81.

(ii) Using the Texas Instruments BA II Plus, ensure the calculator is in "BGN" mode, and then follow this key sequence to retrieve the *present value* of an annuity due.

0 FV 425 ± PMT 6.0 I/Y 40 N CPT PV 12904.94772

The present value of the annuity due is $12 904.95.

EXAMPLE 13.1F

Frank deposited monthly receipts of $250 at the beginning of each month into a savings account paying 4.5% compounded monthly for four years. Frank made no further deposits after four years but left the money in the account.

(i) What will the balance be twelve full years after he made the first deposit?
(ii) How much in total was deposited?
(iii) How much interest will have been earned?

SOLUTION

This problem involves two time periods, which must be separated and calculated individually. The time periods are the four years when deposits are being made on a regular basis, and the remaining time period of 12 − 4 = 8 years when no further deposits are being made but the balance is earning interest.

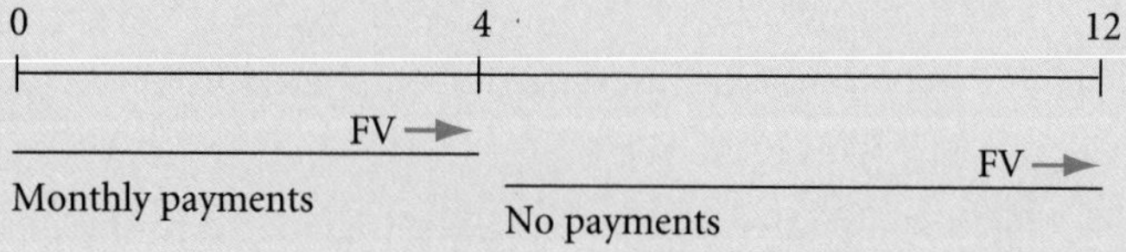

(i) First determine the balance at the end of four years. This problem involves finding the future value of a simple annuity due.

$$\text{PMT} = 250.00;\ \text{I/Y} = 4.5;\ \text{P/Y, C/Y} = 12;\ i = \frac{4.5\%}{12} = 0.375\%;\ n = 48$$

$$\begin{aligned} \text{FV}_n(\text{due}) &= 250.00(1.00375)\left(\frac{1.00375^{48} - 1}{0.00375}\right) \\ &= 250.00(1.00375)(52.483834) \\ &= 13\ 120.96(1.00375) \\ &= \$13\ 170.16 \end{aligned}$$

Now accumulate $13 170.16 for another eight years.

$$\text{PV} = 13\ 170.16;\quad i = 0.00375;\quad n = 8(12) = 96$$

$$\begin{aligned} \text{FV} &= 13\ 170.16(1.00375)^{96} \quad \text{—— substituting in Formula 9.1A} \\ &= 13\ 170.16(1.432365) \\ &= \$18\ 864.47 \end{aligned}$$

Programmed Solution

("BGN" mode) (Set P/Y = 12) 0 [PV] 250 [±] [PMT]
4.5 [I/Y] 48 [N] [CPT] [FV] [13170.16209]

13 170.16209 [±] [PV] 0 [PMT] 4.5 [I/Y]
96 [N] [CPT] [FV] [18864.47466]

The balance in the account after twelve years is $18 864.47.

(ii) The total deposited is 250.00(48) = $12 000.00.

(iii) Interest in the balance is 18 864.47 − 12 000.00 = $6864.47.

D. Finding the periodic payment PMT of a simple annuity due

If the future value of an annuity FV_n(due), the number of conversion periods n, and the conversion rate i are known, you can find the periodic payment PMT by substituting the given values in the future value Formula 13.1.

$$FV_n(\text{due}) = PMT(1 + i)\left[\frac{(1 + i)^n - 1}{i}\right] \qquad \text{——— Formula 13.1}$$

If the present value of an annuity PV_n(due), the number of conversion periods n, and the conversion rate i are known, you can find the periodic payment PMT by substituting the given values in the present value Formula 13.2.

$$PV_n(\text{due}) = PMT(1 + i)\left[\frac{1 - (1 + i)^{-n}}{i}\right] \qquad \text{——— Formula 13.2}$$

When using a scientific calculator, you can find PMT by first rearranging the terms of the above formulas. Then substitute the three known values (FV(due) or PV(due), n, and i) into the appropriate rearranged formula and solve for PMT.

When using a preprogrammed financial calculator, you can find PMT by entering the five known values (FV(due) or PV(due), N, I/Y, P/Y, and C/Y) and pressing CPT PMT .

EXAMPLE 13.1G

What semi-annual payment must be made into a fund at the beginning of every six months to accumulate to \$9600 in ten years at 7% compounded semi-annually?

SOLUTION

$FV_n(\text{due}) = 9600.00;\quad i = \frac{7\%}{2} = 3.5\% = 0.035\%;$ P/Y, C/Y = 2; I/Y = 7

$n = 10(2) = 20$

$$9600.00 = PMT(1.035)\left(\frac{1.035^{20} - 1}{0.035}\right) \qquad \text{——— substituting in Formula 12.1}$$

$$9600.00 = PMT(1.035)(28.279682)$$

$$9600.00 = PMT(29.269471)$$

$$PMT = \frac{9600.00}{29.269471}$$

$$PMT = \$327.99$$

Programmed Solution

("BGN" mode) 0 PV 9600 FV 7 I/Y 20 N CPT PMT -327.986799

The semi-annual payment is \$327.99.

EXAMPLE 13.1H

What monthly rent payment at the beginning of each month for four years is required to fulfill a lease contract worth $7000 if money is worth 7.5% compounded monthly?

SOLUTION

$PV_n(\text{due}) = 7000.00; \quad P/Y = 12; \quad C/Y = 12; \quad I/Y = 7.5;$

$i = \frac{7.5\%}{12} = 0.625\% = 0.00625; \quad n = 4(12) = 48$

$$7000.00 = PMT(1.00625)\left(\frac{1 - 1.00625^{-48}}{0.00625}\right)$$ ——— **substituting in Formula 13.2**

$$7000.00 = PMT(1.00625)(41.358371)$$

$$7000.00 = PMT(41.616861)$$

$$PMT = \frac{7000.00}{41.616861}$$

$$PMT = \$168.20$$

Programmed Solution

("BGN" mode) (Set P/Y = 12; C/Y = 12) 0 [FV] 7000 [±] [PV]

7.5 [I/Y] 48 [N] [CPT] [PMT] [168.201057]

The monthly rent payment due at the beginning of each month is $168.20.

EXAMPLE 13.1I

How much will you have to deposit into an account at the beginning of every three months for twelve years if you want to have a balance of $100 000 twenty years from now and interest is 8% compounded quarterly?

SOLUTION

First, find the balance that you must have in the account at the end of the term of the annuity (after twelve years).

$FV = 100\,000.00; \quad P/Y = 4; \quad C/Y = 4; \quad I/Y = 8; \quad i = \frac{8\%}{4} = 2\% = 0.02;$

$n = 8(4) = 32$

$$PV = 100\,000.00(1.02)^{-32}$$

$$= 100\,000.00(0.530633)$$

$$= \$53\,063.33$$

Next, find the quarterly payment needed at the beginning of each quarter to accumulate to $53 063.33.

$FV_n(\text{due}) = 53\,063.33; \quad P/Y = 4; \quad C/Y = 4; \quad I/Y = 8; \quad i = \frac{8\%}{4} = 0.02;$

$n = 12(4) = 48$

$$53\,063.33 = \text{PMT}(1.02)\left(\frac{1.02^{48} - 1}{0.02}\right)$$

$$53\,063.33 = \text{PMT}(1.02)(79.353519)$$

$$53\,063.33 = \text{PMT}(80.940590)$$

$$\text{PMT} = \frac{53\,063.33}{80.940590}$$

$$\text{PMT} = 53\,063.33(0.012355)$$

$$\text{PMT} = \$\,655.58$$

Programmed Solution

(Set P/Y = 4; C/Y = 4) 0 [PMT] 100 000 [FV]

8 [I/Y] 32 [N] [CPT] [PV] [-53063.33035]

("BGN" mode) [±] 53 063.33035 [FV] 0 [PV]

8 [I/Y] 48 [N] [CPT] [PMT] [-655.583689]

The quarterly deposit at the beginning of each payment period is $655.58.

E. Finding the term n of a simple annuity due

If the future value of an annuity FV_n(due), the periodic payment PMT, and the conversion rate i are known, you can find the term of the annuity n by substituting the given values in the future value Formula 13.1.

$$FV_n(\text{due}) = \text{PMT}(1 + i)\left[\frac{(1 + i)^n - 1}{i}\right] \quad \text{——— Formula 13.1}$$

If the present value PV_n(due), the periodic payment PMT, and the conversion rate i are known, you can find the term of the annuity due n by substituting the given values in the present value Formula 13.2.

$$PV_n(\text{due}) = \text{PMT}(1 + i)\left[\frac{1 - (1 + i)^{-n}}{i}\right] \quad \text{——— Formula 13.2}$$

When using a scientific calculator, you can find n by first rearranging the terms of the appropriate formula above. Then substitute the three known values (FV(due) or PV(due), PMT, and i) into the rearranged formula and solve for n.

When using a preprogrammed financial calculator, you can find n by entering the five known values (PV, PMT, I/Y, P/Y, and C/Y) and pressing [CPT] [N].

EXAMPLE 13.1J

Over what length of time will $75 deposited at the beginning of each month grow to $5000 at 4.5% compounded monthly?

SOLUTION

$FV_n(\text{due}) = 5000.00;\quad PMT = 75.00;\quad P/Y = 12;\quad C/Y = 12;\quad I/Y = 4.5;$

$$i = \frac{4.5\%}{12} = 0.375\%; = 0.00375$$

$$5000.00 = 75.00(1.00375)\left(\frac{1.00375^n - 1}{0.00375}\right) \text{ ——— substituting in Formula 12.1}$$

$$5000.00 = 20\,075.00(1.00375^n - 1)$$

$$\frac{5000.00}{20\,075.00} = 1.00375^n - 1$$

$$0.249066 + 1 = 1.00375^n$$

$$n \ln 1.00375 = \ln 1.249066$$

$$n\,(0.003743) = 0.222396$$

$$n = \frac{0.222396}{0.003743}$$

$$n = 59.416748$$

As discussed in Example 11.5, n should be rounded upward.

$$n = 60 \text{ (months)}$$

Programmed Solution

("BGN" mode)(Set P/Y = 12; C/Y = 12) 0 [PV] 5000 [FV]

75 [±] [PMT] 4.5 [I/Y] [CPT] [N] [59.416748]

It will take 60 months or five years to accumulate $5000.

EXAMPLE 13.1K

Surrey Credit Union intends to accumulate a building fund of $150 000 by depositing $4125 at the beginning of every three months at 7% compounded quarterly. How long will it take for the fund to reach the desired amount?

SOLUTION

$FV_n(\text{due}) = 150\ 00.00;\quad PMT = 4125.00;\quad P/Y = 4;\quad C/Y = 4;\quad I/Y = 7;$

$$i = \frac{7\%}{4} = 1.75\%$$

Programmed Solution

("BGN" mode) (Set P/Y = 4; C/Y = 4) 150 000 [FV]

4125 [±] [PMT] 7 [I/Y] [CPT] [N] [28.000210]

It will take 28 quarters or seven years to build up the fund.

EXAMPLE 13.1L

For how long can you withdraw $480 at the beginning of every three months from a fund of $9000 if interest is 10% compounded quarterly?

SOLUTION

$PV_n(\text{due}) = 9000.00$; $PMT = 480.00$; $P/Y = 4$; $C/Y = 4$; $I/Y = 10$;

$$i = \frac{10\%}{4} = 2.5\% = 0.025$$

$$9000.00 = 480.00(1.025)\frac{1 - 1.025^{-n}}{0.025}$$ —— **substituting in Formula 13.2**

$$\begin{aligned}
9000.00 &= 19\,680.00(1 - 1.025^{-n}) \\
\frac{9000.00}{19\,680.00} &= 1 - 1.025^{-n} \\
0.457317 &= 1 - 1.025^{-n} \\
1.025^{-n} &= 1 - 0.457317 \\
1.025^{-n} &= 0.542683 \\
-n \ln 1.025 &= \ln 0.542683 \\
-n(0.024693) &= -0.611230 \\
n &= \frac{0.611230}{0.024693} \\
n &= 24.753561 \\
n &= 25 \text{ (quarters)}
\end{aligned}$$

Programmed Solution

(Set P/Y = 4; C/Y = 4) ("BGN" mode) 9000 [±] [PV]

0 [FV] 480 [PMT] 10 [I/Y] [CPT] [N] [24.753560]

Withdrawals of $480 can be made for 25 quarters or six years and three months. (The last withdrawal will be less than $480.)

EXAMPLE 13.1M

A lease contract valued at $7800 is to be fulfilled by rental payments of $180 due at the beginning of each month. If money is worth 9% compounded monthly, what should the term of the lease be?

SOLUTION

$PV_n(\text{due}) = 7800.00$; $PMT = 180.00$; $P/Y = 12$; $C/Y = 12$; $I/Y = 9$;

$$i = \frac{9\%}{12} = 0.75\%$$

Programmed Solution

("BGN" mode) (Set P/Y = 12; C/Y = 12) 0 [FV] 7800 [±] [PV]

180 [PMT] 9 [I/Y] [CPT] [N] [52.123125]

The term of the lease should be 53 months, or four years and five months.

F. Finding the periodic rate of interest of a simple annuity due

Preprogrammed financial calculators are especially helpful when solving for the conversion rate i. Determining i without a financial calculator is extremely time-consuming. However, it *can* be done by hand, as illustrated in Appendix II on the CD-ROM.

When the future value or present value, the periodic payment PMT, and the term n of an annuity due are known, the periodic rate of interest i can be found by entering the five known values into a preprogrammed financial calculator. (Remember, if both PV and PMT are non-zero, enter PV *only* as a negative amount.) For simple annuities due, retrieve the answer by being in "BGN" mode and pressing [CPT] [I/Y]. This is the nominal annual rate of interest.

EXAMPLE 13.1N

Compute the nominal annual rate of interest at which $100 deposited at the beginning of each month for ten years will amount to $15 000.

SOLUTION

$FV_n(\text{due}) = 15\,000$; $PMT = 100.00$; $P/Y = 12$; $C/Y = 12$; $n = 120$; $m = 12$

("BGN" mode) (Set P/Y = 12; C/Y = 12) 0 [PV] 15 000 [FV]

100 [±] [PMT] 120 [N] [CPT] [I/Y] [4.282801]

↑ Allow several seconds for the computation.

The nominal annual rate of interest is 4.28% compounded monthly.
The monthly conversion rate is 4.282801/12 = 0.356900%.

EXAMPLE 13.1O

A lease agreement valued at $7500 requires payment of $450 at the beginning of every quarter for five years. What is the nominal annual rate of interest charged?

SOLUTION

$PV_n(\text{due}) = 7500.00$; $PMT = 450.00$; $P/Y = 4$; $C/Y = 4$; $n = 20$; $m = 4$

("BGN" mode) (Set P/Y = 4; C/Y = 4) 0 [FV] 7500 [±] [PV]

450.00 [PMT] 20 [N] [CPT] [I/Y] [8.032647]

↑ Allow several seconds for the computation.

The nominal annual rate of interest is 8.03% compounded quarterly.
The quarterly compounding rate is 8.032647/4 = 2.008162%.

EXERCISE 13.1

EXCEL NOTES

If you choose, you can use Excel's ***Present Value (PV)*** function or ***Future Value (FV)*** function to answer the questions indicated below. Refer to **PV** and **FV** on the Spreadsheet Template Disk to learn how to use these Excel functions.

A. Find the future value and the present value of each of the following six simple annuities due.

	Periodic Payment	Payment Interval	Term	Interest Rate	Conversion Period
1.	$3000	3 months	8 years	8%	quarterly
2.	750	1 month	5 years	7.2	monthly
3.	2000	6 months	12 years	5.6	semi-annually
4.	450	3 months	15 years	4.4	quarterly
5.	65	1 month	20 years	9	monthly
6.	160	1 month	15 years	6	monthly

B. Find the periodic payment for each of the following four simple annuities due.

	Future Value	Present Value	Payment Period	Term	Interest Rate	Conversion Period
1.	$20 000		3 months	15 years	6%	quarterly
2.		$12 000	1 year	8 years	7	annually
3.		$18 500	6 months	12 years	3	semi-annually
4.	9 400		1 month	5 years	12	monthly

C. Find the length of the term for each of the following four simple annuities due.

	Future Value	Present Value	Periodic Payment	Payment Period	Interest Rate	Conversion Period
1.	$ 5 300		$ 35	1 month	6%	monthly
2.		$8 400	440	3 months	7	quarterly
3.		6 450	1 120	1 year	10	annually
4.	15 400		396	6 months	5	semi-annually

D. Compute the nominal annual rate of interest for each of the following four simple annuities due.

	Future Value	Present Value	Periodic Rent	Payment Interval	Term	Compounding Period
1.	$70 000		$1 014.73	1 year	25 years	annually
2.		$42 000	528.00	1 month	10 years	monthly
3.		28 700	2 015.00	6 months	15 years	semi-annually
4.	36 000		584.10	3 months	12 years	quarterly

E. Answer each of the following questions.

1. Find the accumulated value of an annuity due of $300 payable at the beginning of every month for seven years at 6% compounded monthly.

Reference Example 13.1A

2. Determine the accumulated value after twelve years of deposits of $360 made at the beginning of every three months and earning interest at 7% compounded quarterly.

3. Until he retires sixteen years from now, Mr. Lait plans to deposit \$300 at the beginning of every three months in an account paying interest at 5% compounded quarterly.
   (a) What will be the balance in his account when he retires?
   (b) How much of the balance will be interest?

4. Joanna contributes \$750 at the beginning of every six months into an RRSP paying interest at 8% compounded semi-annually.
   (a) How much will her RRSP deposits amount to in twenty years?
   (b) How much of the amount will be interest?

5. Find the present value of payments of \$2500 made at the beginning of every six months for ten years if money is worth 9.5% compounded semi-annually.

Reference Example 13.1C

6. What is the discounted value of deposits of \$240 made at the beginning of every three months for seven years if money is worth 8.8% compounded quarterly?

7. A washer-dryer combination can be purchased from a department store by making monthly credit card payments of \$52.50 for two-and-a-half years. The first payment is due on the date of sale and interest is 21% compounded monthly.
   (a) What is the purchase price?
   (b) How much will be paid in installments?
   (c) How much is the cost of financing?

8. Diane Wallace bought a living-room suite on credit, signing an installment contract with a finance company that requires monthly payments of \$62.25 for three years. The first payment is made on the date of signing and interest is 24% compounded monthly.
   (a) What was the cash price?
   (b) How much will Diane pay in total?
   (c) How much of what she pays will be interest?

9. The monthly premium on a three-year insurance policy is \$64 payable in advance. What is the cash value at the beginning of the policy if money is worth 4.8% compounded monthly?

10. The monthly rent payment on office space is \$535 payable in advance. What equivalent yearly payment made in advance would satisfy the lease if interest is 6.6% compounded monthly?

11. Claude made semi-annually deposits of \$3100 at the beginning of a six-month period into a fund earning 6.8% compounded semi-annually for nine years. No further deposits were made.
    (a) How much will be in the account fifteen years after the first deposit?
    (b) How much in total was deposited?
    (c) How much interest will have been earned?

Reference Example 13.1F

12. For Carly's education, her grandmother deposited \$30 at the beginning of every month for seven years. Interest was earned at 4.85% compounded monthly.
    (a) How much will be in the account eighteen years after the first deposit?
    (b) How much in total was deposited?
    (c) How much interest will have been earned?

13. How much does a depositor have to save at the beginning of every three months for nine years to accumulate \$35 000 if interest is 8% compounded quarterly?

Reference Example 13.1G

14. If Gary accumulated \$5700 in his savings account over five years, how much did he deposit at the beginning of every month if interest is 4.32% compounded monthly?

15. Elspeth McNab purchased a boat valued at \$12 500 on the installment plan requiring equal monthly payments for four years. If the first payment is due on the date of purchase and interest is 7.5% compounded monthly, what is the size of the monthly payment?

Reference Example 13.1H

16. Payments on a seven-year lease valued at \$12 200 are to be made at the beginning of each month during the last five years of the lease. If interest is 9% compounded monthly, what is the size of the monthly payments?

17. Julia deposited \$1500 in an RRSP at the beginning of every six months for twenty years. The money earned interest at 6.25% compounded semi-annually. After twenty years, she converted the RRSP into an RRIF from which she wants to withdraw equal amounts at the beginning of each month for fifteen years. If interest on the RRIF is 6.6% compounded monthly, how much does she receive each month?

Reference Example 13.1I

18. Mr. Clark wants to receive payments of \$900 at the beginning of every three months for twenty years starting on the date of his retirement. If he retires in twenty-five years, how much must he deposit in an account at the beginning of every three months if interest on the account is 5.25% compounded quarterly?

19. Tom is saving \$600 at the beginning of each month. How soon can he retire if he wants to have a retirement fund of \$120 000 and interest is 5.4% compounded monthly?

Reference Example 13.1J

20. Ali deposits \$450 at the beginning of every three months. He wants to build up his account so that he can withdraw \$1000 every three months starting three months after the last deposit. If he wants to make the withdrawals for fifteen years and interest is 10% compounded quarterly, for how long must Ali make the quarterly deposits?

21. If you save \$75 at the beginning of every month for ten years, for how long can you withdraw \$260 at the beginning of each month starting ten years from now, assuming that interest is 6% compounded monthly?

22. Quarterly payments of \$1445 are to be made at the beginning of every three months on a lease valued at \$25 000. What should the term of the lease be if money is worth 8% compounded quarterly?

23. What nominal annual rate of interest was paid if contributions of \$250 made into an RRSP at the beginning of every three months amounted to \$14 559 after ten years?

Reference Example 13.1N

24. An insurance policy provides a benefit of \$250 000 twenty years from now. Alternatively, the policy pays \$4220 at the beginning of each year for twenty years. What is the effective annual rate of interest paid?

25. A vacation property valued at \$25 000 was bought for fifteen payments of \$2200 due at the beginning of every six months. What nominal annual rate of interest was charged?

26. A vehicle can purchased by paying \$27 000 now, or it can be leased by paying \$725 per month for the next four years, with the first payment due on the day of signing the lease. What nominal annual rate of interest charged on the lease?

13.2 GENERAL ANNUITIES DUE

A. Future value of a general annuity due

As with a simple annuity due, the future value of a **general annuity due** is greater than the future value of the corresponding ordinary general annuity by the interest on it for one payment period.

Since the interest on a general annuity for one payment period is $(1 + i)^c$, or $(1 + p)$,

PRESENT VALUE OF A GENERAL ANNUITY DUE $= (1 + p) \times$ PRESENT VALUE OF THE CORRESPONDING ORDINARY GENERAL ANNUITY

Thus, for the future value of a general annuity due use Formula 13.3:

$$S_{nc}(\text{due}) = R(1 + p)\left[\frac{(1 + p)^n - 1}{p}\right]$$

restated as

$$FV_{nc}(\text{due}) = PMT(1 + p)\left[\frac{(1 + p)^n - 1}{p}\right]$$ — **Formula 13.3**

where $p = (1 + i)^c - 1$

EXAMPLE 13.2A What is the accumulated value after five years of payments of \$20 000 made at the beginning of each year if interest is 7% compounded quarterly?

SOLUTION

PMT = 20 000.00; $n = 5$; $c = 4$; P/Y = 1; C/Y = 4; I/Y = 7

$$i = \frac{7\%}{4} = 1.75\% = 0.0175$$

The effective annual rate of interest

$$p = 1.0175^4 - 1 = 1.071859 - 1 = 0.071859 = 7.1859\%$$

$$FV_{nc}(\text{due}) = 20\,000.00(1.071859)\left(\frac{1.071859^5 - 1}{0.071859}\right)$$ — **substituting in Formula 13.3**

$$= 20\,000.00(1.071859)(5.772109)$$
$$= 20\,000.00(6.186888)$$
$$= \$123\,737.75$$

Programmed Solution

("BGN" mode) (Set P/Y = 1; C/Y = 4) 7 [I/Y] 0 [PV]

20 000 [±] [PMT] 5 [N] [CPT] [FV] [123737.7535]

The accumulated value after five years is $123 737.75.

B. Present value of a general annuity due

For a general annuity due, the present value is greater than the present value of the corresponding ordinary general annuity by the interest on it for one payment period.

THE PRESENT VALUE OF A GENERAL ANNUITY DUE = $(1 + p) \times$ THE PRESENT VALUE OF THE CORRESPONDING ORDINARY GENERAL ANNUITY

Thus, for the present value of a general annuity due use Formula 13.4. Using the effective rate of interest per payment period,

$$A_{nc}(\text{due}) = R(1 + p)\left[\frac{1 - (1 + p)^{-n}}{p}\right]$$

restated as

$$PV_{nc}(\text{due}) = PMT(1 + p)\left[\frac{1 - (1 + p)^{-n}}{p}\right]$$

where $p = (1 + i)^c - 1$

—— **Formula 13.4**

EXAMPLE 13.2B A three-year lease requires payments of $1600 at the beginning of every three months. If money is worth 9.0% compounded monthly, what is the cash value of the lease?

SOLUTION

$PMT = 1600.00;\ n = 3(4) = 12;\ P/Y = 4;\ C/Y = 12;\ c = \frac{12}{4} = 3;\ I/Y = 9;$

$i = \frac{9.0\%}{12} = 0.75\% = 0.0075$

The effective quarterly rate of interest

$p = 1.0075^3 - 1 = 1.022669 - 1 = 0.022669 = 2.2669\%$

$$\begin{aligned} PV_{nc}(\text{due}) &= 1600.00(1.022669)\left(\frac{1 - 1.022669^{-12}}{0.022669}\right) \\ &= 1600.00(1.022669)(10.404043) \\ &= 1600.00(10.639894) \\ &= \$17\,023.83 \end{aligned}$$

—— substituting in Formula 13.4

Programmed Solution

("BGN" mode)(Set P/Y = 4; C/Y = 12) 9 [I/Y] 0 [FV]

1600.00 [±] [PMT] 12 [N] [CPT] [PV] [17023.83049]

The cash value of the lease is \$17 023.83.

C. Finding the periodic payment PMT of a general annuity due

If the future value of an annuity FV_{nc}(due), the number of conversion periods n, and the conversion rate i are known, you can find the periodic payment PMT by substituting the given values in the future value formula.

$$FV_{nc}(\text{due}) = PMT(1 + p)\left[\frac{(1 + p)^n - 1}{p}\right]$$

where $p = (1 + i)^c - 1$

—— **Formula 13.3**

If the present value of an annuity PV_{nc}(due), the number of conversion periods n, and the conversion rate i are known, you can find the periodic payment PMT by substituting the given values in the present value formula.

$$PV_{nc}(\text{due}) = PMT(1 + p)\left[\frac{1 - (1 + p)^{-n}}{p}\right]$$

where $p = (1 + i)^c - 1$

—— **Formula 13.4**

When using a scientific calculator, you can find PMT by first rearranging the terms of the appropriate formulas above. Then substitute the three known values (FV_{nc}(due), PV_{nc}(due), n, and i) into the rearranged formula and solve for PMT.

When using a preprogrammed financial calculator, you can find PMT by entering the five known values (FV_{nc}(due) or PV_{nc}(due), N, I/Y, P/Y, and C/Y) and pressing [CPT] [PMT].

EXAMPLE 13.2C

What deposit made at the beginning of each month will accumulate to \$18 000 at 5% compounded quarterly at the end of eight years?

SOLUTION

$FV_{nc}(\text{due}) = 18\,000.00;\; n = 8(12) = 96;\; P/Y = 12;\; C/Y = 4;\; c = \frac{4}{12} = \frac{1}{3}$

$I/Y = 5;\quad i = \frac{5\%}{4} = 1.25\% = 0.0125\%$

The effective monthly rate of interest

$p = 1.0125^{\frac{1}{3}} - 1 = 1.004149 - 1 = 0.004149 = 0.4149\%$

$18\,000.00 = PMT(1.004149)\left(\frac{1.004149^{96} - 1}{0.004149}\right)$ —— substituting in Formula 13.3

$18\,000.00 = PMT(1.004149)(117.638106)$

$18\,000.00 = PMT(118.126236)$

$PMT = \frac{18\,000.00}{118.126236}$

$PMT = \$152.38$

Programmed Solution

("BGN" mode) (Set P/Y = 12; C/Y = 4) 5 [I/Y] 0 [PV]

18 000 [FV] 96 [N] [CPT] [PMT] -152.379359

The monthly deposit is \$152.38.

EXAMPLE 13.2D

What monthly payment must be made at the beginning of each month on a five-year lease valued at \$100 000 if interest is 10% compounded semi-annually?

SOLUTION

$PV_{nc}(\text{due}) = 100\,000.00;\ n = 5(12) = 60;\ P/Y = 12;\ C/Y = 2;\ c = \frac{2}{12} = \frac{1}{6};$

$I/Y = 10;\ i = \frac{10\%}{2} = 5\% = 0.05$

The effective monthly rate of interest

$p = 1.05^{\frac{1}{6}} - 1 = 1.008165 - 1 = 0.008165 = 0.8165\%$

$10\,000.00 = PMT(1.008165)\left(\frac{1 - 1.008165^{-60}}{0.008165}\right)$ ———— substituting in Formula 13.4

$100\,000.00 = PMT(1.008165)(47.286470)$

$100\,000.00 = PMT(47.672557)$

$PMT = \frac{100\,000.00}{47.672557}$

$PMT = \$2097.64$

Programmed Solution

("BGN" mode) (Set P/Y = 12; C/Y = 2) 10 [I/Y] 0 [FV]

100 000 [±] [PV] 60 [N] [CPT] [PMT] 2097.642904

The monthly payment due at the beginning of each month is \$2097.64.

D. Finding the term *n* of a general annuity due

If the future value of an annuity FV_{nc}(due), the periodic payment PMT, and the conversion rate i are known, you can find the term of the annuity n by substituting the given values in the future value Formula 13.3.

$$FV_{nc}(\text{due}) = PMT(1 + p)\left[\frac{(1 + p)^n - 1}{p}\right]$$

where $p = (1 + i)^c - 1$

—— **Formula 13.3**

If the present value PV_{nc}(due), the periodic payment PMT, and the conversion rate i are known, you can find the term of the annuity n by substituting the given values in the present value Formula 13.4.

$$PV_{nc}(\text{due}) = PMT(1 + p)\left[\frac{1 - (1 + p)^{-n}}{p}\right]$$

where $p = (1 + i)^c - 1$

—— **Formula 13.4**

When using a scientific calculator, you can find n by first rearranging the terms of the appropriate formula. Then substitute the three known values (FV_{nc}(due) or PV_{nc}(due), PMT, and i) into the rearranged formula and solve for n.

When using a preprogrammed financial calculator, you can find n by entering the five known values (FV_{nc}(due) or PV_{nc}(due), PMT, I/Y, P/Y, and C/Y) and pressing CPT N.

EXAMPLE 13.2E

Ted Davis wants to accumulate \$140 000 in an RRSP by making annual contributions of \$5500 at the beginning of each year. If interest on the RRSP is 11% compounded quarterly, for how long will Ted have to make contributions?

SOLUTION

FV_{nc}(due) = 140 000.00; PMT = 5500.00; P/Y = 1; C/Y = 4; $c = 4$;

I/Y = 11; $i = \frac{11\%}{4} = 2.75\% = 0.0275$

The effective annual rate of interest

$p = 1.0275^4 - 1 = 1.114621 - 1 = 0.114621 = 11.4621\%$

$$140\,000.000 = 5500.00(1.114621)\left(\frac{1.114621^n - 1}{0.114621}\right)$$ —— using Formula 13.3

$$140\,000.00 = 53\,484.118(1.114621^n - 1)$$
$$2.617600 = 1.114621^n - 1$$
$$1.114621^n = 3.617600$$
$$n \ln 1.114621 = \ln 3.617600$$

$$n(0.108515) = 1.285811$$

$$n = \frac{1.285811}{0.108515}$$

$$n = 11.849188$$

$$n = 12 \text{ years (approximately)}$$

Programmed Solution

("BGN" mode) (Set P/Y = 1; C/Y = 4) 11 [I/Y] 0 [PV]

5500 [±] [PMT] 140 000 [FV] [CPT] [N] [11.849188]

Ted will have to contribute for about twelve years.

EXAMPLE 13.2F

Ted Davis, having reached his goal of a \$140 000 balance in his RRSP, immediately converts it into an RRIF and withdraws from it \$1650 at the beginning of each month. If interest continues at 5.75% compounded quarterly, for how long can he make withdrawals?

SOLUTION

$PV_{nc}(\text{due}) = 140\,000.00$; PMT = 1650.00; P/Y = 12; C/Y = 4; $c = \frac{4}{12} = \frac{1}{3}$;

I/Y = 5.75; $i = \frac{5.75\%}{4} = 1.4375\% = 0.014375$

The effective monthly rate of interest

$$p = 1.014375^{\frac{1}{3}} - 1 = 1.004769 - 1 = 0.004769 = 0.4769\%$$

$$140\,000.00 = 1650.00(1.004769)\left(\frac{1 - 1.004769^{-n}}{0.004769)}\right)$$ — using Formula 13.4

$$140\,000.00 = 347\,642.59(1 - 1.004769^{-n})$$

$$0.402712 = 1 - 1.004769^{-n}$$

$$1.004769^{-n} = 0.597288$$

$$-n \ln 1.004769 = \ln 0.597288$$

$$-n(0.004758) = -0.515357$$

$$n = 108.32388$$

$$n = 109 \text{ months (approximately)}$$

Programmed Solution

("BGN" mode) (Set P/Y = 12; C/Y = 4) 5.75 [I/Y] 0 [FV]

140 000 [±] [PV] 1650 [PMT] [CPT] [N] [108.323882]

Ted will be able to make withdrawals for 109 months, or nine years and one month.

E. Finding the rate of interest of a general annuity due

When the future value or present value, the periodic payment PMT, and the term n of a general annuity due are known, you can find the nominal interest rate by entering the given values into a preprogrammed calculator. Retrieve the value of I/Y by being in "BGN" mode and pressing CPT I/Y.

EXAMPLE 13.2G

Compute the nominal annual rate of interest compounded monthly at which \$500 deposited at the beginning of every three months for ten years will amount to \$30 000.

SOLUTION

$FV_{nc}(\text{due}) = 30\,000.00;\quad PMT = 500.00;\quad n = 40;\quad P/Y = 4;\quad C/Y = 12;$

$$c = \frac{12}{4} = 3$$

Programmed Solution

("BGN" mode) (Set P/Y = 4; C/Y = 12) 0 PV 30 000 FV

500 ± PMT 40 N CPT I/Y 7.484516

The nominal annual rate is 7.48% compounded monthly.

EXERCISE 13.2

EXCEL NOTES

If you choose, you can use Excel's ***Present Value (PV)*** function or ***Future Value (FV)*** function to answer the questions indicated below. Refer to **PV** and **FV** on the Spreadsheet Template Disk to learn how to use these Excel functions.

A. For each of the following four annuities due, determine the unknown value represented by the question mark.

	Future Value FV_{nc}(due)	Present Value PV_{nc}(due)	Periodic Payment PMT	Payment Interval	Term	Nominal Rate of Interest	Conversion Period
1.	?		\$1500	6 months	10 years	5%	quarterly
2.	?		175	1 month	7 years	7	semi-annually
3.		?	650	3 months	6 years	12	monthly
4.		?	93	1 month	4 years	4	quarterly

B. Find the periodic payment for each of the following four annuities due.

	Future Value	Present Value	Payment Period	Term	Interest Rate	Conversion Period
1.	\$16 500		1 year	10 years	4%	quarterly
2.	9 200		3 months	5 years	5	semi-annually
3.		\$10 000	3 months	3 years	6	monthly
4.		24 300	1 month	20 years	9	semi-annually

C. Find the length of the term for each of the following four annuities due.

	Future Value	Present Value	Periodic Payment	Payment Period	Interest Rate	Conversion Period
1.	$32 000		$450	6 months	7.5%	monthly
2.	7 500		150	3 months	11	annually
3.		$12 500	860	3 months	9	monthly
4.		45 000	540	1 month	4	semi-annually

D. For each of the following four annuities due, determine the nominal annual rate of interest.

	Future Value	Present Value	Periodic Payment	Payment Interval	Term	Conversion Period
1.	$ 6 400		$200	6 months	9 years	monthly
2.	25 000		790	1 year	15 years	quarterly
3.		$ 7 500	420	3 months	5 years	monthly
4.		60 000	450	1 month	25 years	semi-annually

E. Answer each of the following questions.

1. Bomac Steel sets aside $5000 at the beginning of every six months in a fund to replace equipment. If interest is 6% compounded quarterly, how much will be in the fund after five years? Reference Example 13.2A

2. Jamie Dean contributes $125 at the beginning of each month into an RRSP paying interest at 6.5% compounded semi-annually. What will be the accumulated balance in the RRSP at the end of 25 years?

3. What is the cash value of a lease requiring payments of $750 at the beginning of each month for three years if interest is 8% compounded quarterly? Reference Example 13.2B

4. Gerald and Marysia bought a property by making semi-annual payments of $2500 for seven years. If the first payment is due on the date of purchase and interest is 9% compounded quarterly, what is the purchase price of the property?

5. How much would you have to pay into an account at the beginning of every six months to accumulate $10 000 in eight years if interest is 7% compounded quarterly? Reference Example 13.2C

6. Teachers' Credit Union entered a lease contract valued at $5400. The contract provides for payments at the beginning of each month for three years. If interest is 5.5% compounded quarterly, what is the size of the monthly payment?

7. Sarah Ling has saved $85 000. If she decides to withdraw $3000 at the beginning of every three months and interest is 6.125% compounded annually, for how long can she make withdrawals? Reference Example 13.2F

8. For how long must contributions of $1600 be made at the beginning of each year to accumulate to $96 000 at 10% compounded quarterly?

9. What is the nominal annual rate of interest compounded annually on a lease valued at $21 600 if payments of $680 are made at the beginning of each month for three years? Reference Example 13.2G

10. An insurance policy provides for a lump-sum benefit of $50 000 fifteen years from now. Alternatively, payments of $1700 may be received at the beginning of each of the next fifteen years. What is the effective annual rate of interest if interest is compounded quarterly?

BUSINESS MATH NEWS BOX

Pay Off the Mortgage, or Top Up the RRSP?

The Vuongs have been happily married for more than a year. Now Danielle and her husband Vu own a bungalow in Toronto, and like many Canadian first-time homeowners, the Vuongs borrowed from their RRSPs for the down payment.

In fact, they each borrowed the personal maximum of $20 000 allowed under the federal government's Home Buyers Plan, which means they have an interest-free loan for up to 17 years.

On the not-so-bright side: the Vuongs have no registered retirement savings left.

Now they're faced with a dilemma—pay off the zero-interest RRSP loan as soon as they can, or use their spare cash to chip away at their $265 000 mortgage.

The answer to their big question is to focus on several goals at once.

The Vuongs are ahead of many couples—they have no consumer debt, and they're already paying their mortgage biweekly to get rid of it faster. But how do they work toward all their goals when there is only a limited amount of funds to do it all?

Once the $1700 monthly mortgage bill and other costs are paid, Danielle figures they have about $700 left over, though she admits "We have never added things up."

They spend their money on vacations, lindy hop dancing, and repairs and renovations on the house such as the chimney, a grounded electrical system, and air conditioning. They own their car outright, and earn a combined $120 000 annual salary, of which Danielle brings in one-quarter but has multiple tax write-offs for her business.

The Vuongs should consider developing a financial plan that factors in monthly payments of about $500, said Tom Zaks, an investment adviser at RBC Dominion Securities Inc. That money should build back their RRSPs and build an emergency fund of about three months' gross salary, he added.

Source: Theresa Ebden, "Pay Off the Mortgage, or Top Up the RRSP?," *The Globe and Mail*, October 9, 2006, p. B.10. Reprinted with permission of the author.

QUESTIONS

1. Calculate the monthly payments required to pay off each of the $20 000 RRSP loans over a 17-year period.
2. If the family pays off the $265 000 mortgage by paying $1700 per month, calculate the mortgage rate. Assume the amortization period is over 25 years.
3. Given that the family earns a combined annual salary of $120 000 and their average tax rate is 30%, calculate the amount the family will have remaining after paying off the mortgage and the RRSP loan.

13.3 ORDINARY DEFERRED ANNUITIES

A. Computation of an ordinary simple deferred annuity

A **deferred annuity** is one in which the first payment is made at a time *later* than the end of the first payment interval. The time period from the time referred to as "now" to the starting point of the term of the annuity is called the **period of deferment.** The number of compounding periods in the period of deferment is designated by the letter symbol *d*. The future value of a deferred ordinary simple annuity (designated by the symbol FV_n(defer)) is the accumulated value of the periodic payments at the end of the term of the annuity.

EXAMPLE 13.3A

Deposits of \$500 are due to be made at the end of each year for ten years. If the deposits are deferred for four years and interest is 6% compounded annually, what is the accumulated value of the deferred annuity?

SOLUTION

Since the deposits are not made during the first four years, there is no balance, and no interest is earned. During the following ten years, deposits are made, the balance increases, and interest is earned.

FIGURE 13.3 Graphical Representation of Method and Data

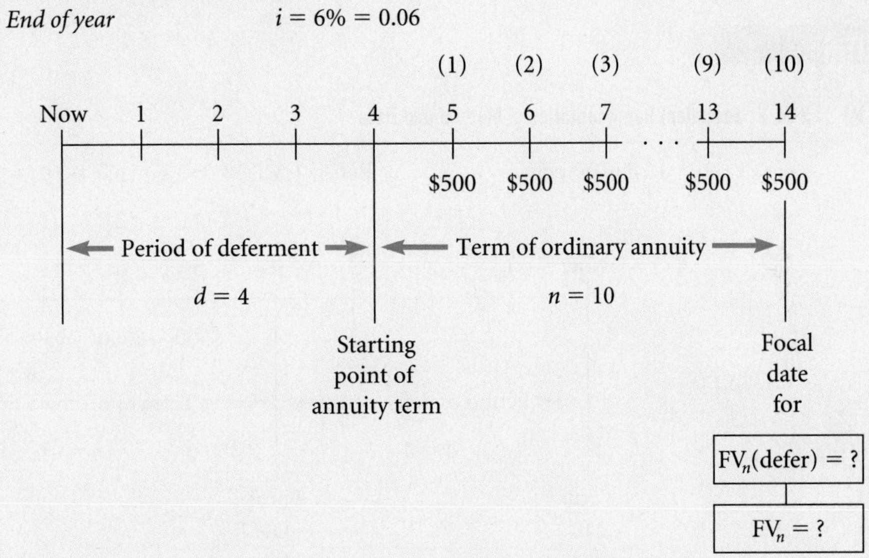

PMT = 500.00; P/Y = 1; C/Y = 1; I/Y = 6; $i = 6\% = 0.06$; $n = 10$; $d = 4$

$$FV_n(\text{defer}) = FV_n = 500.00\left(\frac{1.06^{10} - 1}{0.06}\right) \text{ — using Formula 11.1}$$

$$= 500.00(13.180795)$$

$$= \$6590.40$$

Programmed Solution

("END" mode) (Set P/Y = 1; C/Y = 1) 0 [PV] 500 [±] [PMT]

10 [N] 6 [I/Y] [CPT] [FV] [6590.397471]

Note: The period of deferment does *not* affect the solution to the problem of finding the future value of a deferred annuity: $FV_n(\text{defer}) = FV_n$. Therefore, the problem of finding the future value of a deferred annuity is identical to the problem of finding the future value of an annuity. No further consideration is given in this text to the problem of finding the future value of a deferred annuity.

The present value of a deferred annuity is the discounted value of the periodic payment at the beginning of the period of deferment.

The present value of a deferred simple annuity is designated by the symbol PV_n (defer).

The present value of a deferred general annuity is designated by the symbol PV_{nc}(defer).

EXAMPLE 13.3B

Payments of \$500 are due at the end of each year for ten years. If the annuity is deferred for four years and interest is 6% compounded annually, determine the present value of the deferred annuity.

SOLUTION

FIGURE 13.4 Graphical Representation of Method and Data

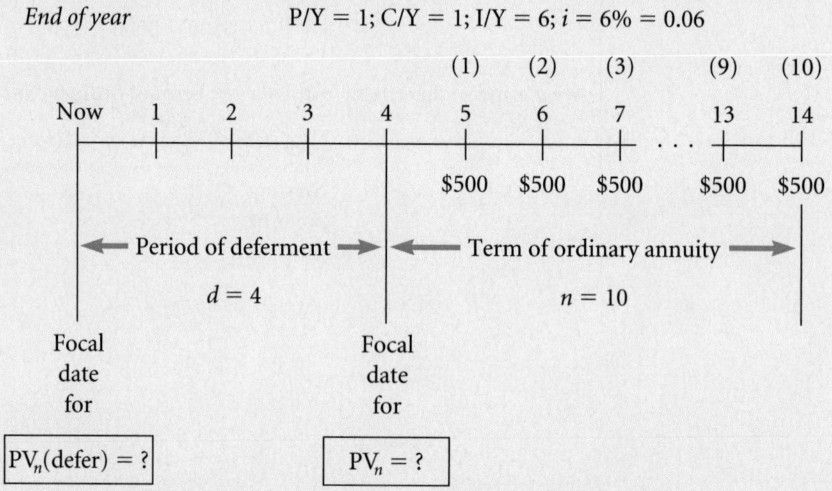

The problem of finding the present value of a deferred annuity can be divided into two smaller problems. We have used this approach in solving Example 11.3F in Chapter 11. We use it again in this problem to find the present value of the deferred annuity.

First, find the present value of the ordinary annuity (focal date at the beginning of the term of the annuity).

$$PV_n = 500.00\left(\frac{1 - 1.06^{10}}{0.06)}\right) \quad \text{—— using Formula 11.2}$$

$$= 500.00(7.360087)$$

$$= \$3680.04$$

Second, find the present value of PV_n at the focal date "now."

$$PV_n(\text{defer}) = PV = 3680.04(1.06^{-4}) \quad \text{—— using Formula 9.1C}$$

$$= 3680.04(0.792094)$$

$$= \$2914.94$$

Programmed Solution

(Set P/Y = 1; C/Y = 1) 0 [FV] 500 [±] [PMT]

6 [I/Y] 10 [N] [CPT] [PV] [3680.043526]

0 [PMT] 3680.043526 [FV] 6 [I/Y] 4 [N] [CPT] [PV] [-2914.939157]

You can find the periodic payment PMT for deferred annuities by first determining the future value of the known present value at the end of the period of deferment. Then substitute in the appropriate annuity formula.

EXAMPLE 13.3C

Find the size of the payment required at the end of every three months to repay a five-year loan of $25 000 if the payments are deferred for two years and interest is 6% compounded quarterly.

SOLUTION

The payments form a deferred ordinary annuity

$PV_n(\text{defer}) = 25\,000.00;\ P/Y = 4;\ C/Y = 4;\ I/Y = 6;\ i = \frac{6\%}{4} = 1.5\% = 0.015;$

$n = 5(4) = 20;\ d = 2(4) = 8$

Value of $25 000.00 at the end of the period of deferment

$$\begin{aligned} FV &= 25\,000.00(1.015)^8 \quad \text{—— using Formula 9.1A} \\ &= 25\,000.00(1.126493) \\ &= \$28\,162.32 \end{aligned}$$

$$28\,162.32 = PMT\left(\frac{1 - 1.015^{-20}}{0.015}\right) \quad \text{—— subtituting in Formula 11.2}$$

$$28\,162.32 = (17.168639)PMT$$

$$PMT = \frac{28\,162.32}{17.168639}$$

$$PMT = \$1640.34$$

Programmed Solution

(Set P/Y = 4; C/Y = 4) [2nd] (CLR TVM) 25 000 [±] [PV]

6 [I/Y] 8 [N] [CPT] [FV] [28162.31466]

28162.31466 [±] [PV] 0 [FV] 6 [I/Y] 20 [N] [CPT] [PMT] [-1640.334742]

The size of the required payment is $1640.33.

You can find the term for deferred ordinary annuities by the same approach used to determine the periodic payment PMT.

EXAMPLE 13.3D

For how long can you pay \$500 at the end of each month out of a fund of \$10 000, deposited today at 10.5% compounded monthly, if the payments are deferred for nine years?

SOLUTION

The payments form a deferred ordinary annuity.

$PV_n(\text{defer}) = 10\,000.00$; $PMT = 500.00$; $P/Y = 12$; $C/Y = 12$; $I/Y = 10.5$;

$i = \frac{10.5\%}{12} = 0.875\% = 0.00875$; $d = 9(12) = 108$

The value of the \$10 000.00 at the end of the period of deferment,

$$\begin{aligned} FV &= 10\,000.00(1.00875)^{108} \\ &= 10\,000.00(2.562260) \\ &= 25\,622.60 \end{aligned}$$

$$\begin{aligned} 25\,622.60 &= 500.00\left(\frac{1-1.00875^{-n}}{0.00875}\right) \\ 25\,622.60 &= 57\,142.857(1-1.00875^{-n}) \\ \frac{25\,622.60}{57\,142.857} &= 1-1.00875^{-n} \\ 0.448400 &= 1-1.00875^{-n} \\ 1.00875^{-n} &= 0.551605 \\ -n\ln 1.00875 &= \ln 0.551605 \\ -n(0.008712) &= -0.594924 \\ n &= \frac{0.594924}{0.008712} \\ n &= 68.288334 \\ n &= 69 \text{ (months)} \end{aligned}$$

Programmed Solution

(Set P/Y = 12; C/Y = 12) 0 [PMT] 10 000 [±] [PV]

10.5 [I/Y] 108 [N] [CPT] [FV] [25622.59753]

[±] 25 622.59753 [PV] 0 [FV] 10.5 [I/Y]

500 [PMT] [CPT] [N] [68.288332]

Payments can be made for 69 months, or five years and nine months.

EXAMPLE 13.3E

Mr. Dhaliwal wants to receive payments of \$800 at the end of each month for ten years after his retirement in seven years. If he invests \$50 000 now to earn 6% compounded monthly until he retires, what monthly compounded nominal rate of interest must he earn after he retires?

SOLUTION

First, the accumulated value of the investment at retirement, after the first seven years, must be determined. The period of deferment is 7 years.

$PV_n = 50\,000.00$; PMT = 0; P/Y = 12; C/Y = 12; $i = \frac{6\%}{12} = 0.5\% = 0.005$;
$d = 7(12) = 84$

$$FV_n = 50\,000.00(1.005^{84})$$
$$= 50\,000(1.520370)$$
$$= \$76\,018.48$$

Next, for the period of ten years after retirement, the monthly payments form an ordinary annuity.

$PV_n = 76018.48$; PMT = 800.00; P/Y = 12; C/Y = 12; $n = 10(12) = 120$

Programmed Solution

(Set P/Y = 12; C/Y = 12) 50 000.00 [±] [PV] 0 [PMT] 6 [I/Y]

84 [N] [CPT] [FV] [76018.4818]

76 018.4818 [±] [PV] 0 [FV] 800 [PMT]

120 [N] [CPT] [I/Y] [4.830216]

Mr. Dhaliwal's investments must earn 4.83% compounded monthly.

B. Computation of an ordinary general deferred annuity

The same principles apply to an ordinary general deferred annuity as apply to an ordinary simple deferred annuity.

EXAMPLE 13.3F

Payments of $1000 are due at the end of each year for five years. If the payments are deferred for three years and interest is 10% compounded quarterly, what is the present value of the deferred payments?

SOLUTION

STEP 1

Find the present value of the ordinary general annuity.

PMT = 1000.00; $n = 5$; P/Y = 1; C/Y = 4; $c = 4$; I/Y = 10;
$i = \frac{10\%}{4} = 2.5\% = 0.025$

The effective annual rate of interest

$p = 1.025^4 - 1 = 1.103813 - 1 = 0.103813 = 10.3813\%$

$$PV_{nc} = 1000.00\left(\frac{1 - 1.103813^{-5}}{0.103813}\right)$$ ——— substituting in Formula 12.3

$$= 1000.00(3.754149)$$
$$= \$3754.15$$

Programmed Solution

(Set P/Y = 1; C/Y = 4) 1000 [±] [PMT] 0 [FV] 10 [I/Y]

5 [N] [CPT] [3754.148977]

STEP 2 Find the present value of PV_{nc} at the beginning of the period of deferment.

FV = 3754.15 is the present value of the general annuity PV_{nc};

$d = 3$ is the number of deferred payment intervals;

$p = 10.38129\%$ is the effective rate of interest per payment interval.

$$\begin{aligned} PV_{nc}(\text{defer}) = PV &= 3754.15(1.103813^{-3}) \quad \text{——— substituting in Formula 9.1C} \\ &= 3754.15(0.743556) \\ &= \$2791.42 \end{aligned}$$

Programmed Solution

3754.15 [FV] 10 [I/Y] 0 [PMT] 3 [N] [CPT] [PV] [-2791.420326]

The present value of the deferred payments is \$2791.42.

EXAMPLE 13.3G

Mr. Kovacs deposited a retirement bonus of \$31 500 in an income averaging annuity paying \$375 at the end of each month. If payments are deferred for nine months and interest is 6% compounded quarterly, for what period of time will Mr. Kovacs receive annuity payments?

SOLUTION

PV_{nc} (defer) = 31 500.00; PMT = 375.00; $d = 9$; P/Y = 12; C/Y = 4;

$c = \frac{4}{12} = \frac{1}{3}$; I/Y = 6; $i = \frac{6\%}{4} = 1.5\% = 0.015$

The effective monthly rate of interest

$$p = 1.015^{\frac{1}{3}} - 1 = 1.004975 - 1 = 0.004975 = 0.4975\%$$

First find the accumulated value at the end of the period of deferment

$$\begin{aligned} FV &= 31\,500.00(1.004975)^9 \\ &= 31\,500.00(1.045678) \\ &= 32\,938.87 \end{aligned}$$

Programmed Solution

(Set P/Y = 12; C/Y = 4) 6 [I/Y] 0 [PMT]

31 500 [±] [PV] 9 [N] [CPT] [FV] [32938.86881]

Then find the number of payments for an ordinary annuity with a present value of \$32 938.87.

$$\begin{aligned} 32\,938.87 &= 375.00\left(\frac{1 - 1.004975^{-n}}{0.004975)}\right). \\ 32\,938.87 &= 75\,373.854(1 - 1.004975^{-n}) \\ 0.437007 &= 1 - 1.004975^{-n} \\ 1.00497^{-n} &= 0.562993 \\ -n \ln 1.00497 &= \ln 0.562993 \\ -n(0.004963) &= -0.574487 \end{aligned}$$

$$n = \frac{0.574487}{0.004963}$$
$$n = 115.75639$$
$$n = 116 \text{ months}$$

Programmed Solution

32 938.869 [±] [PV] 0 [FV] 6 [I/Y] 375 [PMT] [CPT] [N] [115.757250]

Mr. Kovacs will receive payments for 116 months, or nine years and eight months.

EXAMPLE 13.3H

A contract that has a cash value of \$36 000 requires payments at the end of every three months for six years. If the payments are deferred for three years and interest is 9% compounded semi-annually, what is the size of the quarterly payments?

SOLUTION

$PV_{nc}(\text{defer}) = 36\,000.00$; $n = 6(4) = 24$; $d = 3(4) = 12$; $P/Y = 4$; $C/Y = 2$;

$c = \frac{2}{4} = 0.5$; $I/Y = 9$; $i = \frac{9\%}{2} = 4.5\% = 0.045$

The effective quarterly rate of interest

$p = 1.045^{0.5} - 1 = 1.022252 - 1 = 0.022252 = 2.2252\%$

First determine the accumulated value of the deposit at the end of the period of deferment.

$$FV = 36\,000.00(1.022252)^{12}$$ ——— substituting in Formula 9.1A
$$= 36\,000.00(1.302260)$$
$$= \$46\,881.36$$

Programmed Solution

(Set P/Y = 4; C/Y = 2) 9 [I/Y] 0 [PMT] 36 000 [±] [PV]

12 [N] [CPT] [FV] [46881.36449]

Now determine the periodic payment for the ordinary general annuity whose present value is \$46 881.36.

$$46\,881.36 = PMT\left(\frac{1 - 1.022252^{-24}}{0.022252}\right)$$ — substituting in Formula 12.3
$$46\,881.36 = PMT(18.440075)$$
$$PMT = \frac{46\,881.36}{18.440075}$$
$$PMT = \$2542.36$$

Programmed Solution

46 881.36 [±] [PV] 0 [FV] 9 [I/Y] 24 [N] [CPT] [PMT] [2542.363174]

The required quarterly payment is \$2542.36.

EXERCISE 13.3

EXCEL NOTES

If you choose, you can use Excel's ***Present Value (PV)*** function to answer the questions indicated below. Refer to **PV** on the Spreadsheet Template Disk to learn how to use this Excel function.

A. Find the present value of each of the following five ordinary deferred annuities.

	Periodic Payment	Made At:	Payment Period	Period of Deferment	Term	Interest Rate	Conversion Period
1.	$ 45.00	end	1 month	5 years	7 years	12%	monthly
2.	125.00	end	6 months	8 years	15 years	7	semi-annually
3.	2125.00	end	1 month	12 years	20 years	10.5	monthly
4.	720.00	end	3 months	4 years	10 years	12	monthly
5.	1500.00	end	1 month	2 years	3 years	5	semi-annually

B. Answer each of the following questions.

1. Calvin Jones bought his neighbour's farm for $10 000 down and payments of $5000 at the end of every three months for ten years. If the payments are deferred for two years and interest is 8% compounded quarterly, what was the purchase price of the farm?

Reference Example 13.3B

2. Mrs. Bell expects to retire in seven years and would like to receive $800 at the end of each month for ten years following the date of her retirement. How much must Mrs. Bell deposit today in an account paying 7.5% compounded semi-annually to receive the monthly payments?

3. The Omega Venture Group needs to borrow to finance a project. Repayment of the loan involves payments of $8500 at the end of every three months for eight years. No payments are to be made during the development period of three years. Interest is 9% compounded quarterly.
   (a) How much should the Group borrow?
   (b) What amount will be repaid?
   (c) How much of that amount will be interest?

4. What sum of money invested now will provide payments of $1200 at the end of every three months for six years if the payments are deferred for nine years and interest is 10% compounded quarterly?

5. An annuity with a cash value of $14 500 earns 7% compounded semi-annually. End-of-period semi-annual payments are deferred for seven years, and then continue for ten years. How much is the amount of each payment?

Reference Example 13.3C

6. A deposit of $20 000 is made for a twenty-year term. After the term expires, equal withdrawals are to be made for twelve years at the end of every six months. What is the size of the semi-annual withdrawal if interest is 4.75% compounded semi-annually?

7. Mr. Talbot received a bonus of $18 000, which he deposited in an RRSP. He intends to leave the money for fourteen years, then transfer the balance into an RRIF and make equal withdrawals at the end of every six months for twenty years. If interest is 6.5% compounded semi-annually, what will be the size of each withdrawal?

8. Josie won $8000 in an essay-writing contest. The money was deposited into a savings account earning 4.2% compounded monthly. She intends to leave the money for five-and-a-half years, then withdraw amounts at the end of each month for the next four years while she studies to become an entrepreneur. What will be the size of each withdrawal?

9. An annuity with a cash value of $8800 pays $325 at the end of every month. If the annuity earns 6% compounded monthly, and payments begin three years from now, how long will the payments last? Reference Example 13.3D

10. A deposit of $4000 is made today for a five-year period. For how long can $500 be withdrawn from the account at the end of every three months starting three months after the end of the five-year term if interest is 4% compounded quarterly?

11. For how long can $1000 be withdrawn at the end of each month from an account containing $16 000, if the withdrawals are deferred for six years and interest is 7.2% compounded monthly?

12. Greg borrowed $6500 at 6.4% compounded monthly to help finance his education. He contracted to repay the loan in monthly payments of $300 each. If the payments are due at the end of each month and the payments are deferred for four years, for how long will Greg have to make monthly payments?

13. Samantha wants to be able to withdraw $500 at the end of each month for two years while she travels, starting three years from now. If she invests $10 000 now to earn 4.68% compounded monthly until she begins to travel, what monthly compounded nominal rate of interest must she earn after she starts to travel?

Reference Example 13.3E

14. Paul is in the process of purchasing a new sound system for his car. The cash price is $1500, or he can sign a contract to "buy now and pay later." During the first year, the loan charges interest at 12.4% compounded monthly. The terms of the contract state that he would start making payments at the end of the month that is twelve months from now, paying $114 per month for eighteen months to fulfill the contract.
   (a) What monthly compounded nominal rate of interest would he be paying during the time he would be making payments?
   (b) How much extra would Paul be paying to "buy now and pay later?"

15. Thomas is planning to withdraw $8000 from a savings account at the end of each quarter for four years. If the payments are deferred for five years and interest is 5.34% compounded semi-annually, what amount has to be invested now into the savings account? Reference Example 13.3F

16. Asa has invested money from the settlement of an insurance claim. She plans to withdraw $600 from her savings account at the end of each month for four years. If the payments are deferred for two years and interest is 6% compounded quarterly, what was the amount of the insurance settlement?

17. Arianne borrowed $6200 to buy a vehicle to drive to school. She plans to study for three years, and then start her career using her education. Interest is charged on the loan at 7.64% compounded annually. If she starts making month-end payments of $230 when she begins working, how many payments will she have to make? Reference Example 13.3G

18. Jean inherited \$25 000, where the terms of the inheritance state that she is to receive \$1500 at the end of each quarter, starting in three years, until the money is completely withdrawn. If the money is placed in a savings account earning 2.75% compounded monthly, how long will the inheritance last?

19. Amir invested \$12 000 in a three-year term investment earning 4.48% compounded semi-annually. He then invested the money in an investment earning 3.82% compounded semi-annually. How many quarterly \$1000 withdrawals can he make?

20. On the day of his daughter's birth, Mr. Dornan deposited \$2000 in a trust fund with his credit union at 5% compounded quarterly. Following her eighteenth birthday, the daughter is to receive equal payments at the end of each month for four years while she is at college. If interest is to be 6% compounded monthly after the daughter's eighteenth birthday, how much will she receive every month?

21. An annuity purchased for \$9000 makes month-end payments for seven years and earns interest at 5% quarterly. If payments are deferred for three years, how much is each payment? Reference Example 13.3H

22. Ed Ainsley borrowed \$10 000 from his uncle to finance his postgraduate studies. The loan agreement calls for equal payments at the end of each month for ten years. The payments are deferred for four years and interest is 8% compounded semi-annually. What is the size of the monthly payments?

13.4 DEFERRED ANNUITIES DUE

A. Computation of a simple deferred annuity due

The same principles apply to a simple deferred annuity due as apply to a simple annuity due.

EXAMPLE 13.4A

Mei Willis would like to receive annuity payments of \$2000 at the beginning of each quarter for seven years. The annuity is to start five years from now and interest is 5% compounded quarterly.

(i) How much must Mei invest today?
(ii) How much will Mei receive from the annuity?
(iii) How much of what she receives will be interest?

SOLUTION

(i) First, find the present value of the annuity due (the focal point is five years from now).

(i) PMT = 2000.00; P/Y = 4; C/Y = 4; I/Y = 5; $i = \frac{5\%}{4} = 1.25\% = 0.0125$;

$n = 7(4) = 28$

$$
\begin{aligned}
PV_n(\text{due}) &= 2000.00(1.0125)\left[\frac{1 - 1.0125^{-28}}{1.0125}\right] \\
&= 2000.00(1.0125)(23.502518) \\
&= 47\,005.035(1.0125) \\
&= \$47\,592.60
\end{aligned}
$$

Second, determine the present value of \$47 592.60 (the focal point is "now").

FV = 47 592.60; $i = 1.25\%$; $n = 5(4) = 20$

$$\begin{aligned} PV &= 47\,592.60(1.0125)^{-20} \\ &= 47\,592.60(0.780009) \\ &= \$37\,122.63 \end{aligned}$$

Programmed Solution

("BGN" mode) (Set P/Y = 4; C/Y = 4) 0 [FV] 2000 [±] [PMT]

5 [I/Y] 28 [N] [CPT] [PV] [47592.5985]

47 592.5985 [FV] 0 [PMT] 5 [I/Y] 20 [N] [CPT] [PV] [-37122.63367]

Mei will have to invest \$37 122.63.

(ii) Mei will receive 28(2000.00) = \$56 000.00.
(iii) Interest will be 56 000.00 − 37 122.63 = \$18 877.37.

EXAMPLE 13.4B

\$2000 is to be withdrawn from a fund at the beginning of every three months for twelve years starting ten years from now. If interest is 10% compounded quarterly, what must be the balance in the fund today to permit the withdrawals?

SOLUTION

The withdrawals form an annuity due.

PMT = 2000.00; P/Y = 4; C/Y = 4; I/Y = 10; $i = \frac{10\%}{4} = 2.5\% = 0.025$;
$n = 12(4) = 48$

The period of deferment is 10 years, so $d = (10)(4) = 40$.

$$\begin{aligned} PV_n(\text{due}) &= 2000.00(1.025)\left[\frac{1 - (1.025)^{-48}}{0.025}\right] \\ &= 2000(1.025)(27.773154) \\ &= 56\,934.97 \end{aligned}$$

$$\begin{aligned} PV_n(\text{defer}) &= 56\,934.97(1.025)^{-40} \\ &= 56\,934.97(0.372431) \\ &= 21\,204.33 \end{aligned}$$

Programmed Solution

("BGN" mode) (Set P/Y = 4; C/Y = 4) 0 [FV] 2000 [±] [PMT]

10 [I/Y] 48 [N] [CPT] [PV] [56934.9651]

56 934.9651 [FV] 0 [PMT] 10 [I/Y] 40 [N] [CPT] [PV] [-21204.32456]

The balance in the fund today must be \$21 204.33.

EXAMPLE 13.4C

What payment can be made at the beginning of each month for six years if \$5000 is invested today at 12% compounded monthly and the payments are deferred for ten years?

SOLUTION

The payments form a deferred annuity due.

$PV_n(\text{defer}) = 5000.00$; $P/Y = 12$; $C/Y = 12$; $I/Y = 12$; $i = \frac{12\%}{12} = 1\% = 0.01$;

$n = 6(12) = 72$; $d = 10(12) = 120$

Value of the \$5000 at the end of the period of deferment,

$$\begin{aligned} FV &= 5000.00(1.01)^{120} \\ &= 5000.00(3.300387) \\ &= \$16\,501.94 \end{aligned}$$

$$16\,501.94 = PMT(1.01)\left(\frac{(1 - 1.01^{-72})}{0.01}\right)$$ —— substituting in Formula 13.2

$$16\,501.94 = PMT(1.01)(51.150392)$$

$$16\,501.94 = (51.661896)\,PMT$$

$$PMT = \frac{16\,501.94}{51.661896}$$

$$PMT = \$319.42$$

Programmed Solution

(Set P/Y = 12; C/Y = 12) 0 [PMT] 5000 [±] [PV]

12 [I/Y] 120 [N] [CPT] [FV] [16501.93447]

("BGN" mode) 16 501.93447 [±] [PV] 0 [FV]

12 [I/Y] 72 [N] [CPT] [PMT] [319.421778]

The monthly payment is \$319.42.

EXAMPLE 13.4D

What payment can be received at the beginning of each month for fifteen years if \$10 000 is deposited in a fund ten years before the first payment is made and interest is 6% compounded monthly?

SOLUTION

First, find the accumulated value of the initial deposit at the beginning of the term of the annuity due ten years after the deposit.

$PV = 10\,000.00$; $P/Y = 12$; $C/Y = 12$; $I/Y = 6$; $i = \frac{6\%}{12} = 0.5\% = 0.005$;

$n = 10(12) = 120$

$$\begin{aligned} FV &= 10\,000(1.005)^{120} \\ &= 10\,000.00(1.819397) \\ &= \$18\,193.97 \end{aligned}$$

Now determine the monthly withdrawal that can be made at the beginning of each month from the initial balance of $18 193.97.

$PV_n(\text{due}) = 18\,193.87; \quad i = 0.5\%; \quad n = 15(12) = 180$

$$18\,193.97 = \text{PMT}(1.005)\left[\frac{1 - (1.005)^{-180}}{0.005}\right]$$

$$18\,193.97 = \text{PMT}(1.005)(118.503515)$$

$$\text{PMT} = \frac{18\,193.97}{119.096032}$$

$$\text{PMT} = \$152.77$$

Programmed Solution

(Set P/Y = 12; C/Y =12) 0 PMT 10 000 ± PV

6 I/Y 120 N CPT FV 18193.96734

("BGN" mode) 18 193.96734 ± PV 0 FV

6 I/Y 180 N CPT PMT 152.767200

A payment of $152.77 can be made at the beginning of each month.

EXAMPLE 13.4E

A scholarship of $2000 per year is to be paid at the beginning of each year from a scholarship fund of $15 000 invested at 7% compounded annually. How long will the scholarship be paid if payments are deferred for five years?

SOLUTION

The annual payments form a deferred annuity due.

$PV_n(\text{defer}) = 15\,000.00; \quad \text{PMT} = 2000.00; \quad \text{P/Y} = 1; \quad \text{C/Y} = 1; \quad \text{I/Y} = 7;$
$i = 7\% = 0.07; \quad d = 5$

The value of the $15 000 at the end of the period of deferment,

$$\begin{aligned} \text{FV} &= 15\,000.00(1.07)^5 \\ &= 15\,000.00(1.402552) \\ &= 21\,038.28 \end{aligned}$$

$$21\,038.28 = 2000.00(1.07)\left(\frac{1 - 1.07^{-n}}{0.07}\right)$$

$$21\,038.28 = 30\,571.43(1 - 1.07^{-n})$$

$$0.688168 = 1 - 1.07^{-n}$$

$$1.07^{-n} = 0.311832$$

$$-n \ln 1.07 = \ln 0.311832$$

$$-0.067659n = -1.165291$$

$$n = \frac{1.165291}{0.067659}$$

$n = 17.223$

$n = 18$ years (approximately)

Programmed Solution

(Set P/Y = 1; C/Y = 1) 0 [PMT] 15 000 [±] [PV]

7 [I/Y] 5 [N] [CPT] [FV] 21038.27596

("BGN" mode) 21 038.27596 [±] [PV] 0 [FV]

7 [I/Y] 2000 [PMT] [CPT] [N] 17.223081

The scholarship fund will provide 17 payments of \$2000 and a final payment of less than \$2000.

B. Computation of a general deferred annuity due

The same principles apply to a general deferred annuity due as apply to a simple annuity due.

EXAMPLE 13.4F

Tom Casey wants to withdraw \$925 at the beginning of each quarter for twelve years. If the withdrawals are to begin ten years from now and interest is 4.5% compounded monthly, how much must Tom deposit today to be able to make the withdrawals?

SOLUTION

PMT = 925.00; $n = 12(4) = 48$; $d = 10(4) = 40$; P/Y = 4; C/Y = 12;

I/Y = 4.5; $c = \dfrac{12}{4} = 3$; $i = \dfrac{4.5\%}{12} = 0.375\% = 0.00375$

The effective quarterly rate of interest

$p = 1.00375^3 - 1 = 1.011292 - 1 = 0.011292 = 1.1292\%$

STEP 1 Find the present value of the general annuity due.

$$PV_{nc}(\text{due}) = 925.00(1.011292)\left(\frac{1 - 1.011292^{-48}}{0.011292}\right) \text{——substituting in Formula 13.4}$$

$$= 925.00(1.011292)(36.898160)$$

$$= \$34\,516.21$$

Programmed Solution

(Set P/Y = 4; C/Y = 12) ("BGN" mode) 4.5 [I/Y] 0 [FV]

925 [±] [PMT] 48 [N] [CPT] [PV] 34516.21131

STEP 2

Find the present value of PV_{nc}(due) at the beginning of the period of deferment.

FV = 34 516.21 is the present value of the general annuity PV_{nc}(due)
d = 40 is the number of deferred payment intervals
p = 1.1292% is the effective rate of interest per payment interval

$PV_{nc}(\text{defer}) = PV = 34\,516.21(1.011292)^{-40}$ ——— **substituting in Formula 9.1C**
$= 34\,516.21(0.638165)$
$= \$22\,027.04$

Programmed Solution

34 516.21131 [FV] 4.5 [I/Y] 0 [PMT] 40 [N] [CPT] [PV] [-22027.03920]

Tom must deposit $22 027.04 to make the withdrawals. (A small difference in the results is due to rounding.)

EXAMPLE 13.4G

A lease contract that has a cash value of $64 000 requires payments at the beginning of each month for seven years. If the payments are deferred for two years and interest is 8% compounded quarterly, what is the size of the monthly payment?

SOLUTION

$PV_{nc}(\text{defer}) = 64\,000.00$; $n = 7(12) = 84$; P/Y = 12; C/Y = 4;

$d = 2(12) = 24$; $c = \frac{4}{12} = \frac{1}{3}$; I/Y = 8; $i = \frac{8\%}{4} = 2\% = 0.02$

The effective monthly rate of interest

$P = 1.02^{\frac{1}{3}} - 1 = 1.006623 - 1 = 0.6623\%$

First determine the accumulated value of the cash value at the end of the period of deferment.

$FV = 64\,000.00(1.006623)^{24}$
$= 64\,000.00(1.171659)$
$= \$74\,986.20$

Programmed Solution

(Set P/Y = 12; C/Y = 4) 8 [I/Y] 0 [PMT]

64 000 [±] [PV] 24 [N] [CPT] [FV] [74986.20038]

Now determine the periodic payment for the general annuity due whose present value is $74 986.20.

$$74\,986.20 = PMT(1.006623)\left(\frac{1 - 1.006623^{-84}}{0.006623)}\right)$$

$$74\,986.20 = PMT(1.006623)(64.267570)$$

$$74\,986.20 = PMT(64.693195)$$

$$PMT = \$1159.10$$

Programmed Solution

("BGN" mode) 74 986.20 [±] [PV] 0 [FV]

8 [I/Y] 84 [N] [CPT] [PMT] [1159.104917]

The monthly payment is \$1159.10.

EXAMPLE 13.4H

By age 65, Janice Berstein had accumulated \$120 000 in an RRSP by making yearly contributions over a period of years. At age 69, she converted the existing balance into an RRIF from which she started to withdraw \$2000 per month. If the first withdrawal was on the date of conversion and interest on the account is 6.5% compounded quarterly, for how long will Janice Berstein receive annuity payments?

SOLUTION

PV_{nc} (defer) = 120 000.00; PMT = 2000.00; $d = 4(12) = 48$

P/Y = 12; C/Y = 4; $c = \frac{4}{12} = \frac{1}{3}$; I/Y = 6.5; $i = \frac{6.5\%}{4} = 1.625 = 0.01625$

The effective monthly rate of interest

$$p = 1.01625^{\frac{1}{3}} - 1 = 1.005388 - 1 = 0.005388 = 0.5388\%$$

Since payments are at the beginning of each month, the problem involves a deferred general annuity due.

First find the accumulated value at the end of the period of deferment.

$$\begin{aligned} FV &= 120\,000.00(1.005388)^{48} \\ &= 120\,000.00(1.294222) \\ &= \$155\,306.70 \end{aligned}$$

Programmed Solution

(Set P/Y = 12; C/Y = 4) 6.5 [I/Y] 0 [PMT]

120 000 [±] [PV] 48 [N] [CPT] [FV] [155306.6971]

Then find the number of payments for an annuity due with a present value of \$155 306.70.

$$\begin{aligned} 155\,306.78 &= 2000.00(1.005388)\left(\frac{1 - 1.005388^{-n}}{0.0053888}\right) \\ 155\,306.78 &= 373\,222.81(1 - 1.005388^{-n}) \\ 0.416124 &= 1 - 1.005388^{-n} \\ 1.005388^{-n} &= 0.583876 \\ -n \ln 1.005388 &= \ln 0.583876 \\ -n(0.005373) &= -0.538066 \\ n &= 100.141 \\ n &= 101 \text{ months} \end{aligned}$$

Programmed Solution

("BGN" mode) 155 306.6971 [±] [PV] 0 [FV]

6.5 [I/Y] 2000 [PMT] [CPT] [N] [100.139798]

Janice Berstein will receive payments for 101 months, or eight years and five months.

EXERCISE 13.4

EXCEL NOTES

If you choose, you can use Excel's ***Present Value (PV)*** function to answer the questions indicated below. Refer to **PV** on the Spreadsheet Template Disk to learn how to use this Excel function.

A. Find the present value of each of the following five deferred annuities due.

	Periodic Payment	Made At:	Payment Period	Period of Deferment	Term	Interest Rate	Conversion Period
1.	$850	beginning	1 year	3 years	10 years	7.5%	annually
2.	720	beginning	3 months	6 years	12 years	4	quarterly
3.	85	beginning	1 month	20 years	15 years	6	monthly
4.	145	beginning	6 months	3 years	5 years	8	quarterly
5.	225	beginning	3 months	6 years	8 years	9	annually

B. Answer each of the following questions.

1. Dana Kenyon intends to retire in twelve years and would like to receive $2400 every six months for fifteen years starting on the date of her retirement. How much must Dana deposit in an account today if interest is 6.5% compounded semi-annually? Reference Example 13.4A

2. Arlene and Mario Dumont want to set up a fund to finance their daughter's university education. They want to be able to withdraw $400 from the fund at the beginning of each month for four years. Their daughter enters university in seven-and-a-half years and interest is 6% compounded monthly.

(a) How much must the Dumonts deposit in the fund today?
(b) What will be the amount of the total withdrawals?
(c) How much of the amount withdrawn will be interest?

3. Edmonton Pizza borrowed money to redesign their restaurants. Payments of $1600 would be made at the beginning of each month for two years, starting in eighteen months. Interest on the loan is 7.12% compounded monthly.

(a) How much must the company borrow today?
(b) What will be the amount of the total payments?
(c) How much of the amount paid will be interest?

4. An investment in a lease offers returns of $2500 per month due at the beginning of each month for five years. What investment is justified if the returns are deferred for two years and the interest required is 12% compounded monthly?

5. From his savings account, Samuel planned to withdraw amounts at the beginning of every three months for five years starting three years from now. If he started with $7200, and the account earned 9% compounded quarterly, what is the amount of each withdrawal? Reference Example 13.4C

6. To finance the development of a new product, a company borrowed $50 000 at 7% compounded quarterly. If the loan is to be repaid in equal quarterly payments over seven years and the first payment is due three years after the date of the loan, what is the size of the quarterly payment?

7. Mike borrowed $14 000 at 6.5% compounded semi-annually. If the loan is to be repaid in equal semi-annual payments over three years and the first payment is due four years after the date of the loan, what is the size of the semi-annual payment?

8. Matt's Machine Shop purchased a computer to use in tuning engines. To finance the purchase, the company borrowed $12 000 at 8% compounded monthly. To repay the loan, equal monthly payments are made over five years, with the first payment due one year after the date of the loan. What is the size of each monthly payment?

9. An RRIF with a beginning balance of $21 000 earns interest at 10% compounded quarterly. If withdrawals of $3485 are made at the beginning of every three months, starting eight years from now, how long will the RRIF last?

Reference Example 13.4E

10. Mrs. Woo paid $24 000 into a retirement fund paying interest at 11% compounded semi-annually. If she retires in seventeen years, for how long can Mrs. Woo withdraw $10 000 from the fund at the beginning of every six months? Assume that the first withdrawal is on the date of retirement.

11. A lease valued at $32 000 requires payments of $4000 every three months. If the first payment is due three years after the lease was signed and interest is 12% compounded quarterly, what is the term of the lease?

12. For his business, Nicholas leased equipment valued at $23 000. The terms of the lease required payments of $1800 every month. If the first payment is due nine months after the lease was signed and interest is 11% compounded monthly, what is the term of the lease?

13. The sale of a property provides for payments of $2000 due at the beginning of every three months for five years. If the payments are deferred for two years and interest is 9% compounded monthly, what is the cash value of the property?

Reference Example 13.4F

14. Annuity payments of $735 due at the beginning of every month for three years are deferred for two years. If interest is 6% compounded quarterly, how much must be invested today?

15. An annuity pays $6000 at the beginning of every year for twelve years. If the payments are deferred for seven years and interest is 4.38% compounded monthly, what is the cash value of the property?

16. The proceeds of a property sale were invested for six years, then transferred into an annuity paying $4000 at the beginning of every month for twenty

years. If interest is 4.88% compounded quarterly, how much was received from the property sale?

17. Sarah has just inherited a $12 650 annuity from her grandmother. The annuity earns interest at 6% quarterly and makes payments at the beginning of every six months for four years. If the payments begin in two years, what is the amount of each payment? Reference Example 13.4G

18. Dr. Young bought $18 000 worth of equipment from Medical Supply Company. The purchase agreement requires equal payments every six months for eight years. If the first payment is due two years after the date of purchase and interest is 7% compounded quarterly, what is the size of the payments?

19. A business borrows $250 000 to finance an expansion. The loan agreement requires equal payments every three months for nine years. If the first payment is due two years after the date of purchase and interest is 8.3% compounded monthly, what is the size of the payments?

20. Tina purchases a new computer by financing it on the "no payment until next year" plan. The cash price of the computer is $1384. The financing agreement requires equal payments every month for two years. If the first payment is due one year after the date of purchase and interest is 29.6% compounded annually, what is the size of the payments?

21. Mrs. McCarthy has paid a single premium of $22 750 for an annuity, with the understanding that she will receive $385 at the beginning of each month. How long will the annuity last if it earns 5% compounded semi-annually, and the first payment period starts one year from now? Reference Example 13.4H

22. Bhupinder, who has just had his fifty-fifth birthday, invested $3740 on that day for his retirement. The investment earns 8% compounded monthly. For how long will he be able to withdraw $1100 at the beginning of each year, starting on his sixty-fifth birthday?

23. A property development agreement valued at $45 000 requires annual lease payments of $15 000. The first payment is due five years after the date of the agreement and interest is 11% compounded semi-annually. For how long will payments be made?

24. A retirement bonus of $23 600 is invested in an annuity deferred for twelve years. The annuity provides payments of $4000 due at the beginning of every six months. If interest is 10% compounded annually, for how long will annuity payments be made?

13.5 PERPETUITIES

A. Basic concepts

A **perpetuity** is an annuity in which the periodic payments begin on a fixed date and continue indefinitely. Interest payments on permanently invested sums of money are prime examples of perpetuities. Dividends on preferred shares fall into this category assuming that the issuing corporation has an indefinite life. Scholarships paid perpetually from an endowment fit the definition of perpetuity.

Since there is no end to the term, it is *not* possible to determine the future value of a perpetuity. However, the present value of a perpetuity *is* a definite value. This section deals with the present value of simple perpetuities.

B. Present value of ordinary perpetuities

We will use the following symbols when dealing with perpetuities:

A = the present value of the perpetuity;
R = the periodic rent (or perpetuity payment);
i = the rate of interest per conversion period;
p = the effective rate of interest per payment period.

FIGURE 13.5 Graphical Representation of an Ordinary Perpetuity

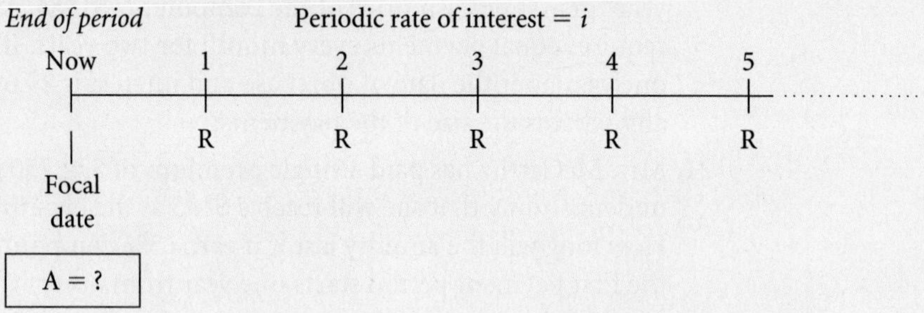

The **perpetuity payment** R is the interest earned by the present value of the perpetuity in one interest period.

When N is determined, the present value of an ordinary simple annuity was calculated using the formula

$$PV_n = PMT\left[\frac{1-(1+i)^{-n}}{i}\right]$$

As N in the formula increases and approaches infinity, the factor $(1 + i)^{-n}$ approaches 0.

Thus, the formula for finding the present value of an ordinary simple perpetuity is:

$$A = \frac{R}{i}$$

restated as

$$PV = \frac{PMT}{i}$$

Formula 13.5

Remember that the i represents the periodic interest rate, calculated as the nominal interest rate divided by the number of conversion periods per year. That is, in the terms of the financial calculator, this represents the I/Y divided by the C/Y.

For an ordinary general perpetuity, the payment R (or PMT) is the interest earned by the present value of the perpetuity in one payment interval. That is,

$$R = pA \text{ or } PMT = pPV$$

Thus, the formula for finding the present value of an ordinary general perpetuity is:

$$A = \frac{R}{p}$$

restated as

$$PV = \frac{PMT}{p}$$

where $p = (1 + i)^c - 1$ ——— **Formula 13.6**

where

p = the effective rate of interest per payment interval;
c = the number of conversion periods per payment period.

EXAMPLE 13.5A

What sum of money invested today at 10% compounded annually will provide a scholarship of $1500 at the end of every year?

SOLUTION

$PMT = 1500.00; \quad i = 10\% = 0.10$

$$PV = \frac{1500.00}{0.10} = \$15\,000.00$$ ——— substituting in Formula 13.5

EXAMPLE 13.5B

The maintenance cost for Northern Railroad of a crossing with a provincial highway is $2000 at the end of each month. Proposed construction of an overpass would eliminate the monthly maintenance cost. If money is worth 12% compounded monthly, how much should Northern be willing to contribute toward the cost of construction?

SOLUTION

The monthly maintenance expense payments form an *ordinary simple perpetuity*.

$PMT = 2000.00; \quad i = \frac{12\%}{12} = 0.01$

$$PV = \frac{2000.00}{0.01} = \$200\,000.00$$

Northern should be willing to contribute $200 000 toward construction.

EXAMPLE 13.5C

What sum of money invested today at 8% compounded quarterly will provide for payments of \$2500 to be paid at the end of each year indefinitely?

SOLUTION

Since the payments are to continue indefinitely, the payments form a perpetuity. Furthermore, since the payments are made at the end of each payment interval and the interest conversion period is not the same length as the payment interval, the problem involves an *ordinary general perpetuity.*

$$\text{PMT} = 2500.00; \quad c = 4; \quad i = \frac{8\%}{4} = 2\% = 0.02$$

The effective annual rate of interest

$$p = 1.02^4 - 1 = 1.082432 - 1 = 0.082432 = 8.2432\%$$

$$\text{PV} = \frac{2500.00}{0.082432} = \$30\,327.95$$ — substituting in Formula 13.6

The required sum of money is \$30 327.95.

EXAMPLE 13.5D

A will gives an endowment of \$50 000 to a university with the provision that a scholarship be paid at the end of each year indefinitely. If the money is invested at 11% compounded annually, how much is the annual scholarship?

SOLUTION

$$\text{PV} = 50\,000.00; \quad i = 11\% = 0.11$$

By rearranging the terms of Formula 13.5, we get the equation PMT = PVi.

$$\text{PMT} = \text{PV}i = 50\,000.00(0.11) = \$5500.00$$

The annual scholarship is \$5500.

EXAMPLE 13.5E

The alumni of Peel College collected \$32 000 to provide a fund for ongoing bursaries. If the money is invested at 7% compounded annually, what is the size of the bursary that can be paid every six months?

SOLUTION

$$\text{PV} = 32\,000.00; \quad c = \frac{1}{2}; \quad i = 7\% = 0.07$$

The effective semi-annual rate of interest

$$p = 1.07^{0.5} - 1 = 1.034408 - 1 = 0.034408 = 3.4408\%$$

By rearranging the terms of Formual 13.6, we get the equation PMT = pPV.

$$\text{PMT} = p\text{PV} = 0.034408(32\,000.00) = \$1101.06$$

The size of the bursary is \$1101.06.

C. Present value of perpetuities due

A perpetuity due differs from an ordinary perpetuity only in that the first payment is made at the focal date. Therefore, a simple perpetuity due may be treated as consisting of an immediate payment R followed by an ordinary perpetuity. The formula for finding the present value of a simple perpetuity due is:

$$A(\text{due}) = R + \frac{R}{i}$$

restated as

$$PV(\text{due}) = PMT + \frac{PMT}{i}$$

Formula 13.7

A general perpetuity due can also be treated as consisting of an immediate payment R followed by an ordinary general perpetuity. Using the symbol A(due) for the present value, the formula for finding the present value of a general perpetuity due is:

$$A(\text{due}) = R + \frac{R}{p}$$

restated as

$$PV(\text{due}) = PMT + \frac{PMT}{p}$$

where $p = (1 + i)^c - 1$

Formula 13.8

EXAMPLE 13.5F

A tract of land is leased in perpetuity at $1250 due at the beginning of each month. If money is worth 7.5% compounded monthly, what is the present value of the lease?

SOLUTION

$$PMT = 1250.00; \quad i = \frac{7.5\%}{12} = 0.625\% = 0.00625$$

$$PV = 1250.00 + \frac{1250.00}{0.00625} \quad \text{substituting in Formula 13.7}$$

$$= 1250.00 + 200\,000.00$$

$$= \$201\,250.00$$

EXAMPLE 13.5G

What is the present value of perpetuity payments of $750 made at the beginning of each month if interest is 8.5% compounded semi-annually?

SOLUTION

$$PMT = 750.00; \quad c = \frac{2}{12} = \frac{1}{6}; \quad i = \frac{8.5\%}{2} = 4.25\% = 0.0425$$

The effective semi-annual rate of interest

$$p = 1.0425^{\frac{1}{6}} - 1 = 1.006961 - 1 = 0.006961 = 0.6961\%$$

$$PV(\text{due}) = 750.00 + \frac{750.00}{0.006961} = \$108\,491.59 \quad \text{substituting in Formula 13.8}$$

The present value of the perpetuity is $108 491.59.

EXAMPLE 13.5H

How much money must be invested today in a fund earning 5.5% compounded annually to pay annual scholarships of \$2000 starting

(i) one year from now?
(ii) immediately?
(iii) four years from now?

SOLUTION

PMT = 2000.00; $i = 5.5\% = 0.055$

(i) The annual scholarship payments form an ordinary perpetuity.

$$PV = \frac{2000.00}{0.055} = \$36\,363.64$$

The required sum of money is \$36 363.64.

(ii) The annual scholarship payments form a perpetuity due.

$$PV = 2000.00 + \frac{2000.00}{0.055}$$
$$= 2000.00 + 36\,363.64$$
$$= \$38\,363.64$$

The required sum of money is \$38 363.64.

(iii) The annual scholarship payments form an ordinary perpetuity deferred for three years. The first payment is at the end of the fourth year.

$$PV(defer) = PV(1.055^{-3})$$
$$= 36\,363.64(0.851614)$$
$$= \$30\,967.77$$

The required sum of money is \$30 967.77.

EXAMPLE 13.5I

What sum of money invested today in a fund earning 6.6% compounded monthly will provide perpetuity payments of \$395 every three months starting

(i) immediately?
(ii) three months from now?
(iii) one year from now?

SOLUTION

$$PMT = 395.00; \quad c = \frac{12}{4} = 3; \quad i = \frac{6.6\%}{12} = 0.55\% = 0.0055$$

The effective quarterly rate of interest

$$p = 1.0055^3 - 1 = 1.016591 - 1 = 0.016591 = 1.6591\%$$

(i) Because the perpetuity payments are at the beginning of each payment interval, they form a *perpetuity due*.

$$PV(due) = 395.00 + \frac{395.00}{0.016591} = 395.00 + 23\,808.23 = \$24\,203.23$$

The required sum of money is \$24 203.23.

(ii) Since the first payment is three months from now, the perpetuity payments form an *ordinary perpetuity*.

$$PV = \frac{395.00}{0.016591} = \$23\ 808.23$$

The required sum of money is \$23 808.23.

(iii) If you consider that the payments are deferred for one year, they form a *deferred perpetuity due*.

$$\begin{aligned} PV(defer) &= PV(due) \times (1.0055)^{-12} \\ &= 24\ 203.23(0.936300) \\ &= \$22\ 661.49 \end{aligned}$$

The required sum of money is \$22 661.49.

Perpetuities Using a BAII Plus

Perpetuities can be treated like any other annuity on the BAII Plus. While technically there are two missing variables, present value and payments can be calculated using arbitrary values for time and future value. The suggested values to use are a time of 300 years when calculating the value of N and 0 for the future value. Using these values will allow the BAII Plus to mimic perpetuity and allow you to calculate perpetuity values the same way as you would any other annuity.

The process would be:

1. Set the calculator to beginning or end.
2. Set P/Y and C/Y.
3. Input the variables you know.
4. Compute the variable you want to know (present value or payments).

Note: When you are using this method, the answer may be marginally different from the formula due to rounding.

EXERCISE 13.5

A. Find the present value of each of the following eight perpetuities.

	Perpetuity Payment	Made At:	Payment Interval	Interest Rate	Conversion Period
1.	\$1250	end	3 months	6.8%	quarterly
2.	3420	end	1 year	8.3	annually
3.	5600	end	6 months	12	monthly
4.	380	end	3 months	8	semi-annually
5.	985	beginning	6 months	4.5	semi-annually
6.	125	beginning	1 month	5.25	monthly
7.	2150	beginning	3 months	9	monthly
8.	7250	beginning	1 month	10	quarterly

B. Answer each of the following questions.

1. The Xorex Company pays a dividend of $4.25 every three months per preferred share. What is the expected market price per share if money is worth 8% compounded semi-annually? Reference Example 13.5A

2. Transcontinental Pipelines is considering a technical process that is expected to reduce annual maintenance costs by $85 000. What is the maximum amount of money that could be invested in the process to be economically feasible if interest is 7% compounded quarterly?

3. What is the size of the scholarship that can be paid at the end of every six months from a fund of $25 000 if interest is 6.75% compounded quarterly? Reference Example 13.5D

4. Alain Rich wants to set up a scholarship fund for his alma mater. The annual scholarship payment is to be $2500 with the first such payment due four years after his deposit into the fund. If the fund pays 7.25% compounded annually, how much must Mr. Rich deposit?

5. A rental property provides a monthly income of $1150 due at the beginning of every month. What is the cash value of the property if money is worth 6.6% compounded monthly?

6. A rental property provides a net income of $4200 at the beginning of every three months. What is the cash value of the property if money is worth 9% compounded monthly?

7. Municipal Hydro offers to acquire a right-of-way from a property owner who receives annual lease payments of $2225 due in advance. What is a fair offer if money is worth 5.5% compounded quarterly? Reference Example 13.5F

8. The faculty of Eastern College collected $1400 for the purpose of setting up a memorial fund from which an annual award is to be made to a qualifying student. If the money is invested at 7% compounded annually and the first annual award payment is to be made five years after the money was deposited, what is the size of the annual award payment?

9. Barbara Katzman bought an income property for $28 000 three years ago. She has held the property for the three years without renting it. If she rents the property out now, what should be the size of the monthly rent payment due in advance if money is worth 6% compounded monthly?

10. What monthly lease payment due in advance should be charged for a tract of land valued at $35 000 if the agreed interest is 8.5% compounded semi-annually?

Review Exercise

1. Find the future value and the present value of semi-annual payments of $540 for seven-and-a-half years if interest is 9.0% compounded semi-annually and the payments are made
   (a) at the end of every six months;
   (b) at the beginning of every six months.

2. Determine the future value and the present value of monthly payments of $50 each for eight years at 6% compounded monthly if
   (a) the payments form an annuity due;
   (b) the payments form an ordinary annuity.

3. Robert Deed deposited $100 in a trust account on the day of his son's birth and every three months thereafter. If interest paid is 7% compounded quarterly, what will the balance in the trust account be before the deposit is made on the son's twenty-first birthday?

4. Jim Wong makes deposits of $225 at the beginning of every three months. Interest earned by the deposits is 3% compounded quarterly.
   (a) What will the balance in Jim's account be after eight years?
   (b) How much of the balance will Jim have contributed?
   (c) How much of the balance is interest?

5. Home entertainment equipment can be purchased by making monthly payments of $82 for three-and-a-half years. The first payment is due at the time of purchase and the financing cost is 16.5% compounded monthly.
   (a) What is the purchase price?
   (b) How much will be paid in installments?
   (c) How much is the cost of financing?

6. How long will it take to build up a fund of $10 000 by saving $300 at the beginning of every six months at 4.5% compounded semi-annually?

7. How long will it take to accumulate $18 000 at 6% compounded monthly if $125 is deposited in an account at the beginning of every month?

8. For how long must $1000 be deposited at the beginning of every year to accumulate to $180 000 twelve years after the end of the year in which the last deposit was made if interest is 7.5% compounded annually?

9. Kelly Farms bought a tractor priced at $10 500 on February 1. Kelly agreed to make monthly payments of $475 beginning December 1 of the same year. For how long will Kelly Farms have to make these payments if interest is 10.5% compounded monthly?

10. Okanagan Vineyards borrowed $75 000 on a five-year promissory note. It agreed to make payments of $6000 every three months starting on the date of maturity. If interest is 8.5% compounded quarterly, for how long will the company have to make the payments?

11. At what nominal annual rate of interest compounded semi-annually will $1700 deposited at the beginning of every six months accumulate to $40 000 in nine years?

12. What is the effective annual rate of interest charged on a four-year lease valued at $9600 if payments of $235 are made at the beginning of each month for the four years?

13. Suppose you would like to have $10 000 in your savings account and interest is 8% compounded quarterly. How much must you deposit every three months for five years if the deposits are made
    (a) at the end of each quarter?
    (b) at the beginning of each quarter?

14. Equal sums of money are withdrawn monthly from a fund of $20 000 for fifteen years. If interest is 9% compounded monthly, what is the size of each withdrawal
    (a) if the withdrawal is made at the beginning of each month?
    (b) if the withdrawal is made at the end of each month?

15. Mrs. Bean contributes $450 at the beginning of every three months to an RRSP. Interest on the account is 6% compounded quarterly.

(a) What will the balance in the account be after seven years?

(b) How much of the balance will be interest?

(c) If Mrs. Bean converts the balance after seven years into an RRIF paying 5% compounded quarterly and makes equal quarterly withdrawals for twelve years starting three months after the conversion into the RRIF, what is the size of the quarterly withdrawal?

(d) What is the combined interest earned by the RRSP and the RRIF?

16. Art will receive monthly payments of $850 from a trust account starting on the date of his retirement and continuing for twenty years. Interest is 10.5% compounded monthly.

(a) What is the balance in the trust account on the date of Art's retirement?

(b) How much interest will be included in the payments Art receives?

(c) If Art made equal monthly deposits at the beginning of each month for fifteen years before his retirement, how much did he deposit each month?

17. Alicia Sisko invested a retirement bonus of $12 500 in an RRSP paying 5.95% compounded semi-annually for ten years. At the end of ten years, she rolled the RRSP balance over into an RRIF paying $500 at the beginning of each month starting with the date of rollover. If interest on the RRIF is 5.94% compounded monthly, for how long will Alicia receive monthly payments?

18. Mrs. Ball deposits $550 at the beginning of every three months. Starting three months after the last deposit, she intends to withdraw $3500 every three months for fourteen years. If interest is 8% compounded quarterly, for how long must Mrs. Ball make deposits?

19. Terry saves $50 at the beginning of each month for sixteen years. Beginning one month after his last deposit, he intends to withdraw $375 per month. If interest is 6% compounded monthly, for how long can Terry make withdrawals?

20. Payments of $375 made every three months are accumulated at 3.75% compounded monthly. What is their amount after eight years if the payments are made

(a) at the end of every three months?

(b) at the beginning of every three months?

21. What is the accumulated value after twelve years of monthly deposits of $145 earning interest at 5% compounded semi-annually if the deposits are made

(a) at the end of each month?

(b) at the beginning of each month?

22. If you save $25 at the beginning of each month and interest is 4% compounded quarterly, how much will you accumulate in thirty years?

23. A property was purchased for quarterly payments of $1350 for ten years. If the first payment was made on the date of purchase and interest is 5.5% compounded annually, what was the purchase price of the property?

24. How much must be deposited into an account to accumulate to $32 000 at 7% compounded semi-annually

(a) at the beginning of each month for twenty years?

(b) at the end of each year for fifteen years?

25. Kelly Associates are the makers of a ten-year $75 000 promissory note bearing interest at 8% compounded semi-annually. To pay off the note on its due date, the company is making payments at the beginning of every three months into a fund paying 7.5% compounded monthly. What is the size of the quarterly payments?

26. A church congregation has raised $37 625 for future outreach work. If the money is invested in a fund paying 7% compounded quarterly, what annual payment can be made for ten years from the fund to its mission if the first payment is to be made four years from the date of investment in the fund?

27. What sum of money can be withdrawn from a fund of $16 750 invested at 6.5% compounded semi-annually

(a) at the end of every three months for twelve years?

(b) at the beginning of each year for twenty years?

(c) at the end of each month for fifteen years but deferred for ten years?

(d) at the beginning of every three months for twelve years but deferred for twenty years?

(e) at the end of each month in perpetuity?

(f) at the beginning of each year in perpetuity?

28. In what period of time will payments of $450 accumulate to $20 000 at 6% compounded monthly if made

(a) at the end of every three months?

(b) at the beginning of every six months?

29. Over what period of time will RRSP contributions of $1350 made at the beginning of each year amount to $125 000 if interest is 7% compounded quarterly?

30. A lease contract valued at $50 000 requires semi-annual payments of $5200. If the first payment is due at the date of signing the contract and interest is 9% compounded monthly, what is the term of the lease?

31. A debt of $20 000 is repaid by making payments of $3500. If interest is 9% compounded monthly, for how long will payments have to be made

(a) at the end of every six months?

(b) at the beginning of each year?

(c) at the end of every three months with payments deferred for five years?

(d) at the beginning of every six months with payments deferred for three years?

32. What is the nominal rate of interest compounded quarterly at which payments of $400 made at the beginning of every six months accumulate to $8400 in eight years?

33. A contract is signed requiring payments of $750 at the end of every three months for eight years.

(a) How much is the cash value of the contract if money is worth 10.5% compounded quarterly?

(b) If the first three payments are missed, how much would have to be paid after one year to bring the contract up to date?

(c) If, because of the missed payments, the contract has to be paid out at the end of one year, how much money is needed?

(d) How much of the total interest paid is due to the missed payments?

34. Anne received $45 000 from her mother's estate. She wants to set aside part of her inheritance for her retirement nine years from now. At that time she would like to receive a pension supplement of $600 at the end of each month for twenty-five years. If the first payment is due one month after her retirement and interest is 6.5% compounded monthly, how much must Anne set aside?

35. Frank invested a retirement bonus of $15 000 in an income averaging annuity paying 6% compounded monthly. He withdraws the money in equal monthly amounts over five years. If the first withdrawal is made nine months after the deposit, what is the size of each withdrawal?

36. Aaron deposited $900 every six months for twenty years into a fund paying 5.5% compounded semi-annually. Five years after the last deposit he converted the existing balance in the fund into an ordinary annuity paying him equal monthly payments for fifteen years. If interest on the annuity is 6% compounded monthly, what is the size of the monthly payment he will receive?

37. Sally contributed $500 every six months for fourteen years into an RRSP earning interest at 6.5%

compounded semi-annually. Seven years after the last contribution, Sally converted the RRSP into an RRIF that is to pay her equal quarterly amounts for sixteen years. If the first payment is due three months after the conversion into the RRIF and interest on the RRIF is 7% compounded quarterly, how much will Sally receive every three months?

38. Wendy deposited $500 into an RRSP every three months for twenty-five years. Upon her retirement she converted the RRSP balance into an RRIF that is to pay her equal quarterly amounts for twenty years. If the first payment is due three months after her retirement and interest is 9% compounded quarterly, how much will Wendy receive every three months?

39. Ty received a separation payment of $25 000 at age thirty-five. He invested that sum of money at 5.5% compounded semi-annually until he was sixty-five. At that time he converted the existing balance into an ordinary annuity paying $6000 every three months with interest at 6% compounded quarterly. For how long will the annuity run?

40. Mr. Maxwell intends to retire in ten years and wishes to receive $4800 every three months for twenty years starting on the date of his retirement. How much must he deposit now to receive the quarterly payments from an account paying 6% compounded quarterly?

41. Tomac Swim Club bought electronic timing equipment on a contract requiring monthly payments of $725 for three years beginning eighteen months after the date of purchase. What was the cash value of the equipment if interest is 7.5% compounded monthly?

42. What sum of money invested today in a retirement fund will permit withdrawals of $800 at the end of each month for twenty years if interest is 5.75% compounded semi-annually and the payments are deferred for fifteen years?

43. A lease requires semi-annual payments of $6000 for five years. If the first payment is due in four years and interest is 9% compounded monthly, what is the cash value of the lease?

44. A debt of $40 000 is to be repaid in installments due at the end of each month for seven years. If the payments are deferred for three years and interest is 7% compounded quarterly, what is the size of the monthly payments?

45. Redden Ogilvie bought his parents' farm for $200 000. The transfer agreement requires Redden to make quarterly payments for twenty years. If the first payment is due in five years and the rate of interest is 10% compounded annually, what is the size of the quarterly payments?

46. An annuity provides payments of $4500 at the end of every three months. The annuity is bought for $33 500 and payments are deferred for twelve years. If interest is 12% compounded monthly, for how long will payments be received?

47. A retirement bonus of $25 000 is invested in an income-averaging annuity paying $1400 every three months. If the interest is 11.5% compounded semi-annually and the first payment is due in one year, for how long will payments be received?

48. $8000 was invested at a fixed rate of 5.95% compounded semi-annually for seven years. After seven years, the fund was converted into an ordinary annuity paying $450 per month. If interest on the annuity was 6.6% compounded monthly, what was the term of the annuity?

49. What single cash payment made now is equivalent to payments of $3500 every six months at 8% compounded quarterly if the payments are made

(a) at the end of every six months for fifteen years?

(b) at the beginning of every six months for ten years?

(c) at the end of every six months for eight years but deferred for four years?

(d) at the beginning of every six months for nine years but deferred for three years?

(e) at the end of every six months in perpetuity?

(f) at the beginning of every six months in perpetuity?

50. What is the principal invested at 4.75% compounded semi-annually from which monthly withdrawals of $240 can be made

(a) at the end of each month for twenty-five years?

(b) at the beginning of each month for fifteen years?

(c) at the end of each month for twenty years but deferred for ten years?

(d) at the beginning of each month for fifteen years but deferred for twelve years?

(e) at the end of each month in perpetuity?

(f) at the beginning of each month in perpetuity?

51. An income property is estimated to net $1750 per month continually. If money is worth 6.6% compounded monthly, what is the cash price of the property?

52. Preferred shares of Western Oil paying a quarterly dividend are to be offered at $55.65 per share. If money is worth 9% compounded semi-annually, what is the minimum quarterly dividend to make investment in such shares economically feasible?

53. The semi-annual dividend per preferred share issued by InterCity Trust is $7.50. If comparable investments yield 14% compounded quarterly, what should be the selling price of these shares?

54. Western Pipelines pays $8000 at the beginning of each year for using a tract of land. What should the company offer the property owner as a purchase price if interest is 9.5% compounded annually?

55. A fund to provide an annual scholarship of $4000 is to be set up. If the first payment is due in three years and interest is 11% compounded quarterly, what sum of money must be deposited in the scholarship fund today?

Self-Test

1. Payments of $1080 are made into a fund at the beginning of every three months for eleven years. If the fund earns interest at 9.5% compounded quarterly, how much will the balance in the fund be after eleven years?

2. Find the present value of payments of $960 made at the beginning of every month for seven years if money is worth 6% compounded monthly.

3. Tim bought a boat valued at $10 104 on the installment plan. He made equal semi-annual payments for five years. If the first payment is due on the date of purchase and interest is 10.5% compounded semi-annually, what is the size of the semi-annual payments?

4. Sara Eng wants to withdraw $3000 at the beginning of every three months for thirty years starting at the date of her retirement. If she retires in twenty years and interest is 10% compounded quarterly, how much must Ms. Eng deposit into an account every month for the next twenty years starting now?

5. J.J. deposited $1680 at the beginning of every six months for eight years into a fund paying 5.5% compounded semi-annually. Fifteen years after the first deposit, he converted the existing balance into an annuity paying him equal monthly payments for twenty years. If the payments are made at the end of

each month and interest is 6% compounded monthly, what is the size of the monthly payments?

6. The amount of \$57 426 is invested at 6% compounded monthly for six years. After the initial six-year period, the balance in the fund is converted into an annuity due paying \$3600 every three months. If interest on the annuity is 5.9% compounded quarterly, what is the term of the annuity in months?

7. What is the nominal annual rate of interest charged on a lease valued at \$3840 if payments of \$200 are made at the beginning of every three months for six years?

8. Deposits of \$1400 made at the beginning of every three months amount to \$40 000 after six years. What is the effective annual rate of interest earned by the deposits if interest is compounded quarterly?

9. A lease requires monthly payments of \$950 due in advance. If interest is 12% compounded quarterly and the term of the lease is five years, what is the cash value of the lease?

10. Sally Smedley and Roberto Jones bought their neighbour's farm for \$30 000 down and payments of \$6000 at the end of every six months for six years. What is the purchase price of the farm if the semi-annual payments are deferred for four years and interest is 8.5% compounded semi-annually?

11. Eden would like to receive \$3000 at the end of every six months for seven years after her retirement. If she retires ten years from now and interest is 6.5% compounded semi-annually, how much must she deposit into an account every six months starting now?

12. Ken acquired his sister's share of their business by agreeing to make payments of \$4000 at the end of each year for twelve years. If the payments are deferred for three years and money is worth 5% compounded quarterly, what is the cash value of the sister's share of the business?

13. The amount of \$46 200 is invested at 9.5% compounded quarterly for four years. After four years the balance in the fund is converted into an annuity. If interest on the annuity is 6.5% compounded semi-annually and payments are made at the end of every six months for seven years, what is the size of the payments?

14. What sum of money must be deposited in a trust fund to provide a scholarship of \$960 payable at the end of each month if interest is 7.5% compounded monthly?

15. A bank pays a quarterly dividend of \$0.75 per share. If comparable investments yield 13.5% compounded monthly, what is the sales value of the shares?

16. Western Pipelines pays \$480 at the beginning of every half-year for using a tract of land. What should the company offer the property owner as a purchase price if interest is 11% compounded semi-annually?

17. Carla plans to invest in a property that after three years will yield $1200 at the end of each month indefinitely. How much should Carla be willing to pay if an alternative investment yields 9% compounded monthly?

18. Mr. Smart wants to set up an annual scholarship of $3000. If the first payment is to be made in five years and interest is 7.0% compounded annually, how much must Mr. Smart pay into the scholarship fund?

Challenge Problems

1. A regular deposit of $100 is made at the beginning of each year for twenty years. Simple interest is calculated at i % per year for the twenty years. At the end of the twenty-year period, the total interest in the account is $840. Suppose that interest of i % compounded annually had been paid instead. How much interest would have been in the account at the end of the twenty years?

2. Herman has agreed to repay a debt by using the following repayment schedule. Starting today, he will make $100 payments at the beginning of each month for the next two-and-a-half years. He will then pay nothing for the next two years. Finally, after four-and-a-half years, he will make $200 payments at the beginning of each month for one year, which will pay off his debt completely. For the first four-and-a-half years, the interest on the debt is 9% compounded monthly. For the final year, the interest is lowered to 8.5% compounded monthly. Find the size of Herman's debt. Round your answer to the nearest dollar.

Case Study 13.1 Planning for College

» Victor and Jasmine Gonzalez were discussing how to plan for their three young sons' university education. Stephen turned twelve years old in April, Jack turned nine in January, and Danny turned seven in March. Although university was still a long way off for the boys, Victor and Jasmine wanted to ensure enough funds were available for their studies.

Victor and Jasmine decided to provide each son with a monthly allowance that would cover tuition and some living expenses. Because they were uncertain about the boys' finding summer jobs in the future, Victor and Jasmine decided their sons would receive the allowance at the beginning of each month for four years. The parents also assumed that the costs of education would continue to increase.

Stephen would receive an allowance of $1000 per month starting September 1 of the year he turns eighteen.

Jack would receive an allowance that is 8% more than Stephen's allowance. He would also receive it at the beginning of September 1 of the year he turns eighteen.

Danny would receive an allowance that is 10% more than Jack's at the beginning of September of the year he turns eighteen.

Victor and Jasmine visited their local bank manager to fund the investment that would compensate the boys' allowances for university. The bank manager suggested an investment paying interest of 5.5% compounded monthly from now until the three boys had each completed their four years of education. Victor and Jasmine thought this sounded reasonable. So on June 1, a week after talking with the bank manager, they deposited the sum of money necessary to finance their sons' postsecondary educations.

QUESTIONS

1. How much allowance will each of the boys receive per month based on their parents' assumptions of price increases?
2. **a.** How much money must Victor and Jasmine invest for each son on June 1 in order to provide them the desired allowance?
   b. Create a timeline of events for each of the sons.
   c. What is the total amount invested on June 1?

Case Study 13.2 Setting Up Scholarships

» King's Cross University College recently launched a fundraising campaign for three new student bursaries. The Student Awards Committee of the college has been working with three community organizations to create and fund these bursaries: Friends of Education, Environmental Betterment Foundation, and Community Service Club. These organizations are all convinced that the best way to fund the bursaries is to make one large donation to the college. The donation would be invested so that it would grow over time, and regular, annual bursaries would be paid out indefinitely.

Friends of Education has agreed to donate a sum of money on September 1 that would allow its annual bursary of $1900 to be awarded immediately on September 1, and has agreed to allow the college to choose the best local student to receive its bursary every year.

Environmental Betterment Foundation would like to earn some interest on its September 1 donation before awarding its first bursary on December 1, three months later. The Foundation has agreed to award one bursary of $2100 per year. It will choose the recipient from all applications received.

Community Service Club will make its donation on September 1, but it wants to award its bursary of $1000 per year starting September 1 next year. This will give the club time to develop the criteria used to choose the recipient of the bursary.

QUESTIONS

1. What sum of money must Friends of Education invest on September 1 if its donation is expected to earn 7.2% compounded semi-annually?
2. What sum of money must Environmental Betterment Foundation invest on September 1 if its donation is expected to earn 7.5% compounded quarterly?
3. What sum of money must Community Service Club invest on September 1 this year if its donation is expected to earn 6.6% compounded monthly?

SUMMARY OF FORMULAS

Formula 13.1

$$S_n(\text{due}) = R(1 + i)\left[\frac{(1 + i)^n - 1}{i}\right]$$

restated as

$$FV_n(\text{due}) = PMT(1 + i)\left[\frac{(1 + i)^n - 1}{i}\right]$$

Finding the future value of a simple annuity due

Formula 13.2

$$A_n(\text{due}) = R(1 + i)\left[\frac{1 - (1 + i)^{-n}}{i}\right]$$

restated as

$$PV_n(\text{due}) = PMT(1 + i)\left[\frac{1 - (1 + i)^{-n}}{i}\right]$$

Finding the present value of a simple annuity due

Formula 13.3

$$S_{nc}(\text{due}) = R(1 + p)\left[\frac{(1 + p)^n - 1}{p}\right]$$

restated as

$$FV_{nc}(\text{due}) = PMT(1 + p)\left[\frac{(1 + p)^n - 1}{p}\right]$$

where $p = (l + i)^c - 1$

Finding the future value of a general annuity due using the effective rate of interest per payment period

Formula 13.4

$$A_{nc}(\text{due}) = R(1 + p)\left[\frac{1 - (1 + p)^{-n}}{p}\right]$$

restated as

$$PV_{nc}(\text{due}) = PMT(1 + p)\left[\frac{1 - (1 + p)^{-n}}{p}\right]$$

where $p = (l + i)^c - 1$

Finding the present value of a general annuity due using the effective rate of interest per payment period

Formula 13.5

$$A = \frac{R}{i}$$

restated as

$$PV = \frac{PMT}{i}$$

Finding the present value of an ordinary simple perpetuity

Formula 13.6

$$A = \frac{R}{p}$$

restated as

$$PV = \frac{PMT}{p}$$

where $p = (1 + i)^c - 1$

Finding the present value of an ordinary general perpetuity

Formual 13.7

$$A(due) = R + \frac{R}{i}$$

restated as

$$PV(due) = PMT + \frac{PMT}{i}$$

Finding the present value of a simple perpetuity due

Formual 13.8

$$A(due) = R + \frac{R}{p}$$

restated as

$$PV(due) = PMT + \frac{PMT}{p}$$

Finding the present value of a general perpetuity due

where $p = (l + i)^c - 1$

GLOSSARY

Annuity due an annuity in which the periodic payments are made at the beginning of each payment interval *(p. 508)*

Deferred annuity an annuity in which the first payment is made at a time later than the end of the first payment interval *(p. 532)*

General annuity due a general annuity in which the payments are made at the beginning of each payment interval *(p. 524)*

Period of deferment the period from the time referred to as "now" to the starting point of the term of the annuity *(p. 532)*

Perpetuity an annuity in which the periodic payments begin at a fixed date and continue indefinitely *(p. 551)*

Perpetuity payment the interest earned by the present value of the perpetuity in one interest period *(p. 552)*

USEFUL INTERNET SITES

www.tdcanadatrust.com/mutualfunds/edu_planning.jsp

RESPs Visit the Toronto-Dominion Bank's financial planning centre to read general information and FAQs about RESPs (Registered Education Savings Plans) and the products that TD Bank offers.

www.smartmoney.com

SmartMoney.com SmartMoney has daily stock and mutual fund recommendations, hourly market updates, personal finance investing research tools and advice, and up-to-the-minute stock and mutual fund quotes and charts.

www.forbes.com

***Forbes* Magazine** This site provides access to articles on current financial business issues, as well as tools for mutual funds, stocks, and personal finances.

CHAPTER 14

Amortization of Loans, Including Residential Mortgages

OBJECTIVES

Upon completing this chapter, you will be able to do the following:

1. Perform computations associated with amortization of debts involving simple annuities, including the size of the periodic payments, outstanding balance, interest due, and principal repaid, and construct complete or partial amortization schedules.
2. Perform computations associated with the amortization of debts involving general annuities, and construct complete or partial amortization schedules.
3. Find the size of the final payment when all payments except the final payment are equal in size.
4. Compute the effective interest rate for fixed-rate residential mortgages.
5. Compute the periodic payments for fixed-rate mortgages and for demand mortgages.
6. Distinguish between regular mortgage payments and rounded mortgage payments.
7. Create statements for various types of residential mortgages.

When budgeting for the future, businesses often consider various loan terms. If you know the interest rate, you might want to calculate what the loan will cost over various time periods. You can do this by using the formulas for annuities that you are already very familiar with. By knowing the size of your equal loan payments, you can make an informed decision about which loan terms to arrange.

One of the largest loans most of us will ever have is a mortgage on a house or a condominium. Given the payment amounts, we can calculate the amount of each payment that goes toward principal and the amount that goes toward interest. This information can help us decide what we can afford to buy and how quickly we can pay off the mortgage.

INTRODUCTION

Amortization of loans refers to the repayment of interest-bearing debts by a series of payments, usually equal in size, made at equal intervals of time. The periodic payments, when equal in size, form an annuity whose present value is equivalent to the original loan principal. Mortgages and many consumer loans are repaid by this method. An amortization schedule shows the allocation of each payment to first cover the interest due and then reduce the principal.

14.1 AMORTIZATION INVOLVING SIMPLE ANNUITIES

A. Finding the periodic payment

What is **amortization**? An interest-bearing debt is *amortized* if both principal and interest are repaid by a series of equal payments made at equal intervals of time.

The basic problem in amortizing a debt is finding the size of the periodic payment. If the payment interval and the interest conversion period are equal in length, the problem involves finding the periodic payment for a simple annuity. Since debts are generally repaid by making payments at the end of the payment interval, the method and formula for ordinary simple annuities apply.

$$PV_n = PMT\left[\frac{1-(1+i)^{-n}}{i}\right] \qquad \text{———— Formula 11.2}$$

EXAMPLE 14.1A

A debt of $5000 with interest at 9% compounded annually is to be repaid by equal payments at the end of each year for six years. What is the size of the annual payments?

SOLUTION

FIGURE 14.1 **Graphical Representation of Method and Data**

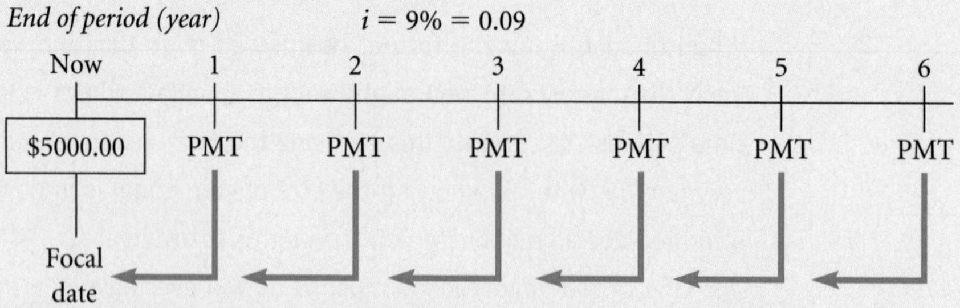

As Figure 14.1 shows, the equal annual payments (designated by PMT) form an ordinary simple annuity in which

$PV_n = 5000.00$; $n = 6$; P/Y = 1; C/Y = 1; I/Y = 9; $i = 9\% = 0.09$

Using "now" as the focal date, you can find the value of the annual payment PMT using Formula 11.2.

$$5000.00 = \text{PMT}\left(\frac{1 - 1.09^{-6}}{0.09}\right) \text{ ——— using Formula 11.2}$$

$$5000.00 = \text{PMT}(4.485919)$$

$$\text{PMT} = \$1114.60$$

Programmed Solution

("END" mode) (Set P/Y = 1; C/Y = 1) 0 [FV] 5000 [±] [PV] 9 [I/Y]

6 [N] [CPT] [PMT] [1114.598916]

The annual payment is $1114.60.

EXAMPLE 14.1B

A loan of $8000 made at 6% compounded monthly is amortized over five years by making equal monthly payments.

(i) What is the size of the monthly payment?
(ii) What is the total amount paid to amortize the loan?
(iii) What is the cost of financing?

SOLUTION

(i) $PV_n = 8000.00$; $n = 5(12) = 60$; $P/Y = 12$; $C/Y = 12$; $I/Y = 6$;

$$i = \frac{6\%}{12} = 0.5\%$$

$$8000.00 = \text{PMT}\left(\frac{1 - 1.005^{-60}}{0.005}\right) \text{ ——— using Formula 11.2}$$

$$8000.00 = \text{PMT}(51.725561)$$

$$\text{PMT} = \$154.66$$

Programmed Solution

("END" mode) (Set P/Y = 12; C/Y = 12) 0 [FV] 8000 [±] [PV] 6 [I/Y]

60 [N] [CPT] [PMT] [154.662412]

(i) The monthly payment is $154.66.
(ii) The total amount paid is 60(154.66) = $9279.60.
(iii) The cost of financing is 9279.60 − 8000.00 = $1279.60.

B. Amortization schedules

As previously discussed in Section 8.6, **amortization schedules** show in detail how a debt is repaid. Such schedules normally show the payment number (or payment date), the amount paid, the interest paid, the principal repaid, and the outstanding debt balance.

1. Amortization Schedule When All Payments Are Equal (Blended Payments)

When all payments are equal, you must first determine the size of the periodic payment, as shown in Examples 14.1A and 14.1B, then construct the amortization schedule.

EXAMPLE 14.1C

A debt of $5000 is amortized by making equal payments at the end of every three months for two years. If interest is 8% compounded quarterly, construct an amortization schedule, as in Example 14.1C.

SOLUTION

STEP 1 Determine the size of the quarterly payments.

$PV_n = 5000.00;\ n = 4(2) = 8;\ P/Y = 4;\ C/Y = 4;\ I/Y = 8;\ i = \frac{8\%}{4} = 2.0\%$

$$5000.00 = PMT\left(\frac{1 - 1.02^{-8}}{0.02}\right)$$

$$5000.00 = PMT(7.325481)$$

$$PMT = \$682.55$$

Programmed Solution

("END" mode) (Set P/Y = 4; C/Y = 4) 0 [FV] 5000 [±] [PV] 8 [I/Y]

8 [N] [CPT] [PMT] [682.548996]

STEP 2 Construct the amortization schedule as shown below.

Payment Number	Amount Paid	Interest Paid $i = 0.02$	Principal Repaid	Outstanding Principal Balance
0				5000.00
1	682.55	100.00	582.55	4417.45
2	682.55	88.35	594.20	3823.25
3	682.55	76.47	606.08	3217.17
4	682.55	64.34	618.21	2598.96
5	682.55	51.98	630.57	1968.39
6	682.55	39.37	643.18	1325.21
7	682.55	26.50	656.05	669.16
8	682.54	13.38	669.16	0.00
TOTAL	5460.39	460.39	5000.00	

Explanations regarding the construction of the amortization schedule

1. Payment 0 is used to introduce the initial balance of the loan.
2. The interest included in the first payment is the periodic interest rate i multiplied by the period's beginning balance, $0.02 \times 5000.00 = \$100.00$. Since the amount paid is $682.55, the amount available for repayment of principal is

682.55 – 100.00 = \$582.55. The outstanding principal balance after the first payment is 5000.00 – 582.55 = \$4417.45.

3. The interest included in the second payment is 0.02 × 4417.45 = \$88.35. Since the amount paid is \$682.55, the amount available for repayment of principal is 682.55 − 88.35 = \$594.20. The outstanding principal is 4417.45 − 594.20 = \$3823.25.
4. Computation of interest, principal repaid, and outstanding balance for Payments 3 to 7 are made in a similar manner.
5. The last payment of \$682.54 is slightly different from the other payments as a result of rounding in the amount paid or the interest paid. To allow for such rounding errors, the last payment is computed by adding the interest due in the last payment (0.02 × 669.16 = \$13.38) to the outstanding balance: 669.16 + 13.38 = \$682.54.
6. The three totals provide useful information and can be used as a check on the accuracy of the schedule.
   (a) The total principal repaid must equal the original outstanding balance;
   (b) The total amount paid is the periodic payment times the number of such payments plus/minus any adjustment in the last payment:
   682.55 × 8 − 0.01 = 5460.40 − 0.01 = \$5460.39;
   (c) The total interest paid is the difference between the amount paid and the original principal, 5460.39 − 5000.00 = \$460.39.

Programmed Solution

The amortization schedule can also be built by using the Amortization function within the preprogrammed financial calculator. Using the Texas Instruments BAII Plus, follow these steps:

1. Enter all of the information within the TVM function and compute the payment, PMT, as above.
2. Press **2nd** **AMORT** to start the function.
3. On the calculator display, P1 refers to the number of the first period of the range to be specified. For example, to obtain data for periods 2 through 5, P1 would be entered as "2." Remember to press the **Enter** key to enter new data.
4. Press the down arrow **↓** to move to the next cell. P2 refers to the number of the last period of the range to be specified. For example, to obtain data for periods 2 through 5, P2 would be entered as "5." Note that, to obtain information for just one period, both P1 and P2 must be entered, as the same number. For example, to obtain data for period 1, both P1 and P2 must be entered as "1," specifying "from" period 1 and "to" period 1.
5. Press the down arrow **↓** to move to the next cell. BAL is automatically calculated as the loan balance at the end of the period specified in P2. In the amortization schedule above, when period 1 is specified, the BAL calculated is –4417.45. The outstanding balance appears as a negative number because the PV was entered as a negative number.

6. Press the down arrow [↓] to move to the next cell. PRN is automatically calculated as the portion of the principal that was repaid. In the amortization schedule on page 572, the PRN is calculated as 582.55.
7. Press the down arrow [↓] to move to the next cell. INT is automatically calculated as the portion of the period's payment that was interest on the loan. In the amortization schedule on page 572, the INT is calculated as 100.00.

   With each method described, the results may be slightly different due to when and where rounding takes place.

2. Amortization Schedule When All Payments Except the Final Payment are Equal

When the size of the periodic payment is determined by agreement, usually because it is a convenient round figure rather than a computed blended payment, the size of the final payment will probably be different from the preceding agreed-upon payments. This final payment is obtained in the amortization schedule by adding the interest due on the outstanding balance to the outstanding balance.

This type of loan repayment schedule has been illustrated and explained in Section 8.6. The following example is included for review.

EXAMPLE 14.1D

Bronco Repairs borrowed \$15 000 from National Credit Union at 10% compounded quarterly. The loan agreement requires payment of \$2500 at the end of every three months. Construct an amortization schedule.

SOLUTION

$$i = \frac{10\%}{4} = 2.5\% = 0.025$$

Payment Number	Amount Paid	Interest Paid $i = 0.025$	Principal Repaid	Outstanding Principal Balance
0				15 000.00
1	2 500.00	375.00	2 125.00	12 875.00
2	2 500.00	321.88	2 178.12	10 696.88
3	2 500.00	267.42	2 232.58	8 464.30
4	2 500.00	211.61	2 288.39	6 175.91
5	2 500.00	154.40	2 345.60	3 830.31
6	2 500.00	95.76	2 404.24	1 426.07
7	1 461.72	35.65	1 426.07	0.00
TOTAL	16 461.72	1461.72	15 000.00	

Note: After Payment 6, the outstanding principal is less than the agreed-upon payment. When this happens, the final payment will be the outstanding balance plus the interest due on the outstanding balance.

$$1426.07 + (1426.07 \times 0.025) = 1426.07 + 35.65 = \$1461.72$$

C. Finding the outstanding principal balance

For various reasons, such as early partial repayment or early full repayment or refinancing, either the borrower or the lender needs to know the outstanding balance at a certain time. This can be done by checking the amortization schedule, if available, or by direct mathematical computation. This computation is also useful for checking the accuracy of the schedule as it is developed.

1. Finding the Outstanding Principal When All Payments Are Equal

EXAMPLE 14.1E

For Example 14.1C, compute the outstanding balance just after the third payment has been made.

SOLUTION

The loan history showing the quarterly payments of \$682.55 can be represented on a time diagram as shown in Figure 14.2.

FIGURE 14.2 Graphical Representation of Loan Payments

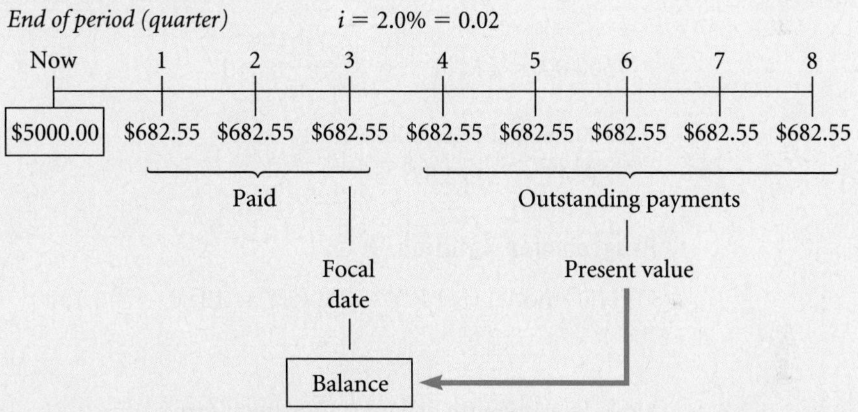

In the same way in which the original loan balance of \$5000 equals the present value of the number of payments that are necessary to amortize the loan, the outstanding balance at the end of any payment interval just after a payment has been made is the present value of the remaining outstanding payments.

$$\text{OUTSTANDING BALANCE} = \text{PRESENT VALUE OF THE OUTSTANDING PAYMENTS}$$

To answer this problem, use Formula 11.2. Since three of the eight payments have been made, five payments remain outstanding.

$\text{PMT} = 682.55;\quad n = 5;\quad \text{P/Y} = 4;\quad \text{I/Y} = 8;\quad i = 2.0\% = 0.02$

$$PV_3 = 682.55\left(\frac{1 - 1.02^{-5}}{0.02}\right) \text{ ——— using Formula 11.2}$$

$$= 682.55(4.713460)$$

$$= \$3217.17$$

Programmed Solution

("END" mode) (Set P/Y = 4; C/Y = 4) 0 [FV] 682.55 [±] [PMT] 8 [I/Y]

5 [N] [CPT] [PV] [3217.171788]

The outstanding balance after the third payment is $3217.17.

Note: Any minor difference in the amortization schedule is due to rounding.

EXAMPLE 14.1F

You borrow $7500 from a finance company at 13.5% compounded monthly with the agreement to make monthly payments. If the loan is amortized over five years, what is the loan balance after two years?

SOLUTION

First determine the size of the monthly payment.

$PV_n = 7500.00$; $n = 5(12) = 60$; $P/Y = 12$; $C/Y = 12$; $I/Y = 13.5$;

$$i = \frac{13.5\%}{12} = 1.125\% = 0.01125$$

$$7500.00 = PMT\left(\frac{1 - 1.01125^{-60}}{0.01125}\right)$$

$$7500.00 = PMT(43.459657)$$

$$PMT = \$172.57$$

Programmed Solution

("END" mode) (Set P/Y = 12; C/Y = 12) 0 [FV] 7500 [±] [PV] 13.5 [I/Y]

60 [N] [CPT] [PMT] [172.573845]

Now determine the balance after two years.

After two years, 24 of the 60 payments have been made; 36 payments remain outstanding.

$PMT = 172.57$; $n = 36$; $i = 1.125\%$

$$PV_{24} = 172.57\left(\frac{1 - 1.01125^{-36}}{0.01125}\right)$$

$$= 172.57(29.467851)$$

$$= \$5085.27$$

Programmed Solution

("END" mode) (Set P/Y = 12; C/Y = 12) 172.57 [±] [PMT] 0 [FV]

13.5 [I/Y] 36 [N] [CPT] [PV] [5085.267094]

The outstanding balance after two years is $5085.27.

The method used in Examples 14.1E and 14.1F is called the **prospective method** of finding the outstanding balance, because it considers the future prospects of the debt—the payments that remain outstanding.

Alternatively, the outstanding balance can be found by the **retrospective method**, which considers the payments that have been made. This method finds the outstanding balance by deducting the accumulated value of the payments that have been made from the accumulated value of the original debt.

OUTSTANDING BALANCE = ACCUMULATED VALUE OF THE ORIGINAL DEBT − ACCUMULATED VALUE OF THE PAYMENTS MADE

For Example 14.1E

The accumulated value of the original debt at the end of three payment intervals

$$\begin{aligned} FV &= 5000.00(1.02^3) \quad \text{——— using Formula 9.1A} \\ &= 5000.00(1.061208) \\ &= 5306.04 \end{aligned}$$

The accumulated value of the payments made

$$\begin{aligned} FV_3 &= 682.55\left(\frac{1.02^3 - 1}{0.02}\right) \\ &= 682.55(3.060400) \\ &= \$2088.88 \end{aligned}$$

Programmed Solution

("END" mode) (Set P/Y = 4; C/Y = 4) [2nd] (CLR TVM) 5000 [±] [PV]

8 [I/Y] 3 [N] [CPT] [FV] [5306.04]

0 [PV] 682.55 [±] [PMT] 8 [I/Y] 3 [N] [CPT] [FV] [2088.87602]

The outstanding balance is 5306.04 − 2088.88 = \$3217.16.

For Example 14.1F

The accumulated value of the debt after two years (24 payments)

$$\begin{aligned} FV &= 7500.00(1.01125^{24}) \\ &= 7500.00(1.307991) \\ &= \$9809.93 \end{aligned}$$

The accumulated value of the 24 payments made

$$\begin{aligned} FV_{24} &= 172.57\left(\frac{1.01125^{24} - 1}{0.01125}\right) \\ &= 172.57(27.376998) \\ &= \$4724.45 \end{aligned}$$

Programmed Solution

("END" mode) (Set P/Y = 12; C/Y = 12) [2nd] (CLR TVM) 7500 [±] [PV]

13.5 [I/Y] 24 [N] [CPT] [FV] [9809.934198]

0 [PV] 172.57 [±] [PMT] 13.5 [I/Y] 24 [N] [CPT] [FV] [4724.448528]

The outstanding balance is 9809.93 − 4724.45 = $5085.48.

Note: The different balances produced by the two methods—$5085.48 versus $5085.27—are a result of rounding in the payment.

Because the prospective method is more direct, it is preferred when finding the outstanding balance of loans repaid by installments that are all equal.

2. Finding the Outstanding Balance When All Payments Except the Final Payment are Equal

When the last payment is different from the other payments, the retrospective method for finding the outstanding balance is preferable.

EXAMPLE 14.1G

For Example 14.1D, compute the outstanding balance after four payments.

SOLUTION

The accumulated value of the original debt after four payments

$$\begin{aligned} FV &= 15\,000.00(1.025^4) \\ &= 15\,000.00(1.103813) \\ &= \$16\,557.19 \end{aligned}$$

The accumulated value of the four payments

$$\begin{aligned} FV &= 2500.00\left(\frac{1.025^4 - 1}{0.025}\right) \\ &= 2500.00(4.152516) \\ &= \$10\,381.29 \end{aligned}$$

Programmed Solution

("END" mode) (Set P/Y = 4; C/Y = 4) [2nd] (CLR TVM) 15 000 [±] [PV] 10

[I/Y] 4 [N] [CPT] [FV] [16557.19336]

0 [PV] 2500 [±] [PMT] 10 [I/Y] 4 [N] [CPT] [FV] [10381.28906]

The outstanding balance is 16 557.19 − 10 381.29 = $6175.90.

EXAMPLE 14.1H

A debt of $25 000 with interest at 11% compounded semi-annually is amortized by making payments of $2000 at the end of every six months. Determine the outstanding balance after five years.

SOLUTION

$PV_n = PV = 25000.00$; $P/Y = 2$; $C/Y = 2$; $I/Y = 11$; $i = \frac{11\%}{2} = 5.5\% = 0.055$

The accumulated value of the original principal after five years

$$\begin{aligned} FV &= 25\,000.00(1.055^{10}) \\ &= 25\,000.00(1.708145) \\ &= \$42\,703.61 \end{aligned}$$

The accumulated value of the first ten payments

$$\begin{aligned} FV_{10} &= 2000.00\left(\frac{1.055^{10} - 1}{0.055}\right) \\ &= 2000.00(12.875354) \\ &= \$25\,750.71 \end{aligned}$$

Programmed Solution

("END" mode) (Set P/Y = 2; C/Y = 2) [2nd] (CLR TVM) 25 000 [±] [PV] 11 [I/Y] 10 [N] [CPT] [FV] [42703.61146]

0 [PV] 2000 [±] [PMT] 11 [I/Y] 10 [N] [CPT] [FV] [25750.70758]

The outstanding balance after five years is 42 703.61 − 25 750.71 = $16 952.90.

D. Finding the interest paid and the principal repaid; constructing partial amortization schedules

Apart from computing the outstanding balance at any one time, all the other information contained in an amortization schedule, such as interest paid and principal repaid, can also be computed.

EXAMPLE 14.1I

For Example 14.1C, compute

(i) the interest paid in the fifth payment period;
(ii) the principal repaid in the fifth payment period.

SOLUTION

(i) The interest due for any given payment period is based on the outstanding balance at the beginning of the period. This balance is the same as the outstanding balance at the end of the previous payment period.

To find the interest paid by the fifth payment, we need to know the outstanding balance after the fourth payment.

$$\begin{aligned} PV_4 &= 682.55\left(\frac{1 - 1.02^{-4}}{0.02}\right) \\ &= 682.55(3.807729) \\ &= \$2598.97 \end{aligned}$$

Programmed Solution

("END" mode) (Set P/Y = 4; C/Y = 4) 0 [FV] 682.55 [±] [PMT] 8 [I/Y]

4 [N] [CPT] [PV] [2598.965223]

Interest for Payment Period 5 is 2598.97(0.02) = \$51.98.

(ii) Principal repaid = Amount paid − Interest paid
= 682.55 − 51.98
= \$630.57

EXCEL NOTES

You can use Excel's ***Cumulative Interest Paid Between Two Periods (CUMIPMT)*** *and* ***Cumulative Principal Paid Between Two Periods (CUMPRINC)*** functions to answer questions like these. Refer to **CUMIPMT** and **CUMPRINC** on the Spreadsheet Template Disk to learn how to use these Excel functions.

EXAMPLE 14.1J

Jackie Kim borrowed \$6000 from her trust company at 9% compounded monthly. She was to repay the loan with monthly payments over five years.

(i) What is the interest included in the 20th payment?

(ii) What is the principal repaid in the 36th payment period?

(iii) Construct a partial amortization schedule showing the details of the first three payments, the 20th payment, the 36th payment, and the last three payments, and determine the totals of amount paid, interest paid, and principal repaid.

SOLUTION

$PV_n = 6000.00$; $n = 5(12) = 60$; P/Y = 12; C/Y = 12; I/Y = 9;

$$i = \frac{9\%}{12} = 0.75\% = 0.0075$$

$$6000.00 = PMT\left(\frac{1-1.0075^{-60}}{0.0075}\right)$$

$$6000.00 = PMT(48.173374)$$
$$PMT = \$124.55$$

Programmed Solution

("END" mode) (Set P/Y = 12; C/Y = 12) 0 [FV] 6000 [±] [PV] 9 [I/Y]

60 [N] [CPT] [PMT] [124.550131]

(i) The outstanding balance after the 19th payment

$$PV_{19} = 124.55\left(\frac{1-1.0075^{-41}}{0.0075}\right)$$
$$= 124.55(35.183064)$$
$$= \$4382.05$$

Programmed Solution

0 [FV] 124.55 [±] [PMT] 9 [I/Y] 41 [N] [CPT] [PV] [4382.050802]

The interest included in the 20th payment is 4382.05(0.0075) = \$32.87.

(ii) The outstanding balance after the 35th payment

$$PV_{35} = 124.55\left(\frac{1-1.0075^{-25}}{0.0075}\right)$$
$$= 124.55(22.718755)$$
$$= \$2829.62$$

Programmed Solution

0 [FV] 124.55 [±] [PMT] 9 [I/Y] 25 [N] [CPT] [PV] [2829.620994]

The interest included in Payment 36 is 2829.62(0.0075) = \$21.22.
The principal repaid by Payment 36 is 124.55 – 21.22 = \$103.33.

(iii) We can develop the first three payments of the amortization schedule in the usual way. To show the details of the 20th payment, we need to know the outstanding balance after 19 payments (computed in part (i)). For the 36th payment, we need to know the outstanding balance after 35 payments (computed in part (ii)). Since there are 60 payments, the last three payments are Payments 58, 59, and 60. To show the details of these payments, we must determine the outstanding balance after Payment 57.

$$PV_{57} = 124.55\left(\frac{1-1.0075^{-3}}{0.0075}\right)$$
$$= 124.55(2.955556)$$
$$= \$368.11$$

Programmed Solution

0 [FV] 124.55 [±] [PMT] 9 [I/Y] 3 [N] [CPT] [PV] [368.114529]

Partial amortization schedule

Payment Number	Amount Paid	Interest Paid $i = 0.0075$	Principal Repaid	Outstanding Principal Balance
0				6000.00
1	124.55	45.00	79.55	5920.45
2	124.55	44.40	80.15	5840.30
3	124.55	43.80	80.75	5759.55
•	•	•	•	•
•	•	•	•	•

(continued)

Payment Number	Amount Paid	Interest Paid $i = 0.0075$	Principal Repaid	Outstanding Principal Balance
19	•	•	•	4382.05
20	124.55	32.87	91.68	4290.37
•	•	•	•	•
•	•	•	•	•
35	•	•	•	2829.62
36	124.55	21.22	103.33	2726.29
•	•	•	•	•
•	•	•	•	•
57	•	•	•	368.11
58	124.55	2.76	121.79	246.32
59	124.55	1.85	122.70	123.62
60	124.55	0.93	123.62	0.00
TOTAL	7473.00	1473.00	6000.00	

Note: The total principal repaid must be \$6000; the total amount paid is 124.55(60) = \$7473; the total interest paid is 7473 – 6000 = \$1473.

EXAMPLE 14.1K

The Erin Construction Company borrowed \$75 000 at 14% compounded quarterly to buy construction equipment. Payments of \$3500 are to be made at the end of every three months.

(i) Determine the principal repaid in the 16th payment.

(ii) Construct a partial amortization schedule showing the details of the first three payments, the 16th payment, the last three payments, and the totals.

SOLUTION

(i) Since the quarterly payments are not computed blended payments, the last payment will probably be different from the preceding equal payments. Use the retrospective method for finding the outstanding balance.

PV = 75 000.00; PMT = 3500.00; P/Y = 4; C/Y = 4; I/Y = 14;

$$i = \frac{14\%}{4} = 3.5\% = 0.035$$

The accumulated value of the original principal after the 15th payment

$$\begin{aligned} FV &= 75\,000.00(1.035^{15}) \\ &= 75\,000.00(1.675349) \\ &= \$125\,651.16 \end{aligned}$$

Programmed Solution

("END" mode) (Set P/Y = 4; C/Y = 4) [2nd] (CLR TVM) 75 000 [±] [PV] 14 [I/Y] 15 [N] [CPT] [FV] [125651.1623]

The accumulated value of the first 15 payments

$$FV_{15} = 3500.00\left(\frac{1.035^{15} - 1}{0.035}\right)$$
$$= 3500.00(19.295681)$$
$$= \$67\,534.88$$

Programmed Solution

0 [PV] 3500 [±] [PMT] 14 [I/Y] 15 [N] [CPT] [FV] [67534.88308]

The outstanding principal after the 15th payment
= 125 651.16 – 67 534.88
= $58 116.28

The interest included in the 16th payment is 58 116.28(0.035) = $2034.07.
The principal repaid by the 16th payment is 3500.00 – 2034.07 = $1465.93.

(ii) To show details of the last three payments, we need to know the number of payments required to amortize the loan principal.

$PV_n = 75\,000.00$; $PMT = 3500.00$; $i = 3.5\%$

$$75\,000.00 = 3500.00\left(\frac{1 - 1.035^{-n}}{0.035}\right)$$
$$0.75 = 1 - 1.035^{-n}$$
$$1.035^{-n} = 0.25$$
$$-n \ln 1.035 = \ln 0.25$$
$$-n(0.034401) = -1.386294$$
$$n = 40.297584$$

Programmed Solution

0 [FV] 75 000 [±] [PV] 3500 [PMT] 14 [I/Y] [CPT] [N] [40.2975834]

Forty-one payments (40 payments of $3500.00 each plus a final payment) are required. This means the amortization schedule should show details of Payments 39, 40, and 41. To do so, we need to know the outstanding balance after 38 payments.

The accumulated value of the original loan principal after 38 payments

$$FV = 75\,000.00(1.035^{38})$$
$$= 75\,000.00(3.696011)$$
$$= \$277\,200.85$$

Programmed Solution

[2nd] (CLR TVM) 75 000 [±] [PV] 14 [I/Y] 38 [N] [CPT] [FV]

[277200.8486]

The accumulated value of the first 38 payments

$$FV_{38} = 3500.00\left(\frac{1.035^{38} - 1}{0.035}\right)$$

$$= 3500.00(77.028895)$$

$$= \$269\,601.13$$

Programmed Solution

0 PV 3500 ± PMT 14 I/Y 38 N CPT FV 269601.1315

The outstanding balance after the 38th payment
= 277 200.85 − 269 601.13
= $7599.72

Partial amortization schedule

Payment Number	Amount Paid	Interest Paid $i = 0.035$	Principal Repaid	Outstanding Principal Balance
0				75 000.00
1	3 500.00	2 625.00	875.00	74 125.00
2	3 500.00	2 594.38	905.62	73 219.38
3	3 500.00	2 562.68	937.32	72 282.06
•	•	•	•	•
•	•	•	•	•
•	•	•	•	•
15	•	•	•	58 116.28
16	3 500.00	2 034.07	1 465.93	56 650.35
•	•	•	•	•
•	•	•	•	•
•	•	•	•	•
38	•	•	•	7 599.72
39	3 500.00	265.99	3 234.01	4 365.71
40	3 500.00	152.80	3 347.20	1 018.51
41	1 054.16	35.65	1 018.51	0.00
TOTAL	141 054.16	66 054.16	75 000.00	

E. Computer application—amortization schedule

The amortization schedule in Example 14.1C displays the manual calculations for the repayment of $5000 with quarterly payments and interest at 8% compounded quarterly. Microsoft Excel and other spreadsheet programs can be used to create a file that will immediately display the results of a change in the principal, interest rate, or amount paid.

Following are general instructions for creating a file to calculate the amortization schedule in Example 14.1C. The formulas in the spreadsheet file were created using Excel; however, most spreadsheet software works in a similar manner.

This exercise assumes a basic understanding of spreadsheet applications, but an individual who has no previous experience with spreadsheets will be able to complete it.

STEP 1 Enter the labels shown in Figure 14.3 in row 1 and in column A.

FIGURE 14.3

Workbook 1

	A	B	C	D	E	F
1	Payment Number	Amount Paid	Interest Paid	Principal Repaid	Outstanding Principal Balance	
2	0				5000.00	682.55
3	1	= F2	= F4*E2	= B3−C3	= E2−D3	
4	2	= F2	= F4*E3	= B4−C4	= E3−D4	= 0.08/4
5	3	= F2	= F4*E4	= B5−C5	= E4−D5	
6	4	= F2	= F4*E5	= B6−C6	= E5−D6	
7	5	= F2	= F4*E6	= B7−C7	= E6−D7	
8	6	= F2	= F4*E7	= B8−C8	= E7−D8	
9	7	= F2	= F4*E8	= B9−C9	= E8−D9	
10	8	= C10+D10	= F4*E9	= E9	= E9−D10	
11	Totals	= SUM(B3:B10)	= SUM(C3:C10)	= SUM(D3:D10)		

STEP 2 Enter the principal in cell E2. Do not type in the dollar sign or a comma.

STEP 3 Enter only the formulas shown in cells B3, C3, D3, and E3. Make sure that the formula entry includes the dollar ($) signs as shown in the figure.

STEP 4 The formulas that were entered in Step 3 can be copied through the remaining cells.

(a) Select and Copy the formulas in cells B3, C3, D3, and E3.
(b) Select cells B4 to E9 and Paste.
(c) The formulas are now active in all the cells.

Alternatively, to copy formulas in Excel you can use the Fill handle, dragging it down the desired range through consecutive cells.

STEP 5 Enter the formulas shown in cells B10, C10, D10, and E10.

STEP 6 Enter the formula shown in cell B11, and then use Copy and Paste to enter the formulas in cells C11 and D11.

STEP 7 To ensure readability of the spreadsheet, format the numbers to display with two decimal places, and widen the columns to display the full labels.

This spreadsheet can now be used to reflect changes in aspects of the loan and create a new amortization schedule. Use cell E2 for new principal amounts and cell F4 for new interest rates.

EXERCISE 14.1

EXCEL NOTES

If you choose, you can use Excel's **CUMIPMT**, **CUMPRINC**, **NPER**, **PMT**, or **PV** functions or **Template4** to answer the questions indicated below. Refer to the Spreadsheet Template Disk to find **Template4** or to learn how to use these Excel functions.

A. For each of the following four debts amortized by equal payments made at the end of each payment interval, compute (a) the size of the periodic payments; (b) the outstanding principal at the time indicated; (c) the interest paid; and (d) the principal repaid by the payment following the time indicated for finding the outstanding principal.

	Debt Principal	Repayment Period	Payment Interval	Interest Rate	Conversion Period	Outstanding Principal Required After:
1.	$12 000	8 years	3 months	10%	quarterly	20th payment
2.	8 000	5 years	1 month	12	monthly	30th payment
3.	15 000	10 years	6 months	8	semi-annually	15th payment
4.	9 600	7 years	3 months	6	quarterly	12th payment

B. For each of the following four debts repaid by periodic payments as shown, compute (a) the number of payments required to amortize the debts; (b) the outstanding principal at the time indicated.

	Debt Principal	Debt Payment	Payment Interval	Interest Rate	Conversion Period	Outstanding Principal Required After:
1.	$12 000	$ 750	3 months	8%	quarterly	16th payment
2.	7 800	175	1 month	12	monthly	24th payment
3.	21 000	2000	6 months	9	semi-annually	10th payment
4.	15 000	800	3 months	6	quarterly	12th payment

C. Answer each of the following questions.

1. Mr. and Mrs. Good purchased a ski chalet for $36 000. They paid $4000 down and agreed to make equal payments at the end of every three months for fifteen years. Interest is 8% compounded quarterly. Reference Example 14.1B

(a) What size payment are the Goods making every three months?
(b) How much will they owe after ten years?
(c) How much will they have paid in total after fifteen years?
(d) How much interest will they pay in total?

2. A contractor's price for a new building was $96 000. Slade Inc., the buyers of the building, paid $12 000 down and financed the balance by making equal

payments at the end of every six months for twelve years. Interest is 12% compounded semi-annually.
(a) What is the size of the semi-annual payment?
(b) How much will Slade Inc. owe after eight years?
(c) What is the total cost of the building for Slade Inc.?
(d) What is the total interest included in the payments?

3. Sam's Auto Repairs Inc. borrowed $5500 to be repaid by end-of-month payments over four years. Interest on the loan is 9% compounded monthly.
(a) What is the size of the periodic payment?
(b) What is the outstanding principal after the thirteenth payment?
(c) What is the interest paid in the fourteenth payment?
(d) How much principal is repaid in the fourteenth payment?

Reference Example 14.1H

4. To start their business, Ming and Ling borrowed $24 000 to be repaid by semi-annual payments over twelve years. Interest on the loan is 7% compounded semi-annually.
(a) What is the size of the periodic payment?
(b) What is the outstanding principal after the seventh payment?
(c) What is the interest paid in the eighth payment?
(d) How much principal is repaid in the eighth payment?

5. A loan of $10 000 with interest at 10% compounded annually is to be amortized by equal payments at the end of each year for seven years. Find the size of the annual payments and construct an amortization schedule showing the total paid and the cost of financing.

6. A loan of $8000 is repaid by equal payments made at the end of every three months for two years. If interest is 7% compounded quarterly, find the size of the quarterly payments and construct an amortization schedule showing the total paid and the total cost of the loan.

7. Hansco borrowed $9200 paying interest at 13% compounded annually. If the loan is repaid by payments of $2000 made at the end of each year, construct an amortization schedule showing the total paid and the total interest paid.

8. Pinto Brothers are repaying a loan of $14 500 by making payments of $2600 at the end of every six months. If interest is 7% compounded semi-annually, construct an amortization schedule showing the total paid and the total cost of the loan.

9. For Question 5, calculate the interest included in the fourth payment. Verify your answer by checking the amortization schedule.

10. For Question 6, calculate the principal repaid in the fifth payment period. Verify your answer by checking the amortization schedule.

11. For Question 7, calculate the principal repaid in the fourth payment period. Verify your answer by checking the amortization schedule.

12. For Question 8, calculate the interest included in the fifth payment. Verify your answer by checking the amortization schedule.

13. Apex Corporation borrowed \$85 000 at 8% compounded quarterly for eight years to buy a warehouse. Equal payments are made at the end of every three months.

(a) Determine the size of the quarterly payments.
(b) Compute the interest included in the 16th payment.
(c) Determine the principal repaid in the 20th payment period.
(d) Construct a partial amortization schedule showing details of the first three payments, the last three payments, and totals. Reference Example 14.1J

14. Mr. Brabham borrowed \$7500 at 15% compounded monthly. He agreed to repay the loan in equal monthly payments over five years.

(a) What is the size of the monthly payment?
(b) How much of the 25th payment is interest?
(c) What is the principal repaid in the 40th payment period?
(d) Prepare a partial amortization schedule showing details of the first three payments, the last three payments, and totals.

15. Thornhill Equipment Co. borrowed \$24 000 at 11% compounded semi-annually. It is to repay the loan by payments of \$2500 at the end of every six months.

(a) How many payments are required to repay the loan?
(b) How much of the sixth payment is interest?
(c) How much of the principal will be repaid in the tenth payment period?
(d) Construct a partial amortization schedule showing details of the first three payments, the last three payments, and totals.

16. Locust Inc. owes \$16 000 to be repaid by monthly payments of \$475. Interest is 6% compounded monthly.

(a) How many payments will Locust Inc. have to make?
(b) How much interest is included in the 18th payment?
(c) How much of the principal will be repaid in the 30th payment period?
(d) Construct a partial amortization schedule showing details of the first three payments, the last three payments, and totals.

14.2 AMORTIZATION INVOLVING GENERAL ANNUITIES

A. Finding the periodic payment and constructing amortization schedules

If the length of the payment interval is different from the length of the interest conversion period, the equal debt payments form a general annuity. The amortization of such debts involves the same principles and methods discussed in Section 14.1 except that general annuity formulas are applicable. Provided that the payments are made at the end of the payment intervals, use Formula 12.5.

$$PV_{nc} = PMT\left[\frac{1-(1+p)^{-n}}{p}\right]$$

where $p = (1+i)^c - 1$

Formula 12.5

EXAMPLE 14.2A A debt of \$30 000 with interest at 12% compounded quarterly is to be repaid by equal payments at the end of each year for seven years.

(i) Compute the size of the yearly payments.
(ii) Construct an amortization schedule.

SOLUTION (i) $PV_{nc} = 30\,000.00$; $n = 7$; $P/Y = 1$; $C/Y = 4$; $c = 4$; $I/Y = 12$;

$$i = \frac{12\%}{4} = 3\% = 0.03$$

$$p = 1.03^4 - 1 = 1.125509 - 1 = 0.125509 = 12.5509\%$$

$$30\,000.00 = PMT\left(\frac{1 - 1.125509^{-7}}{0.125509}\right)$$

$$30\,000.00 = PMT(4.485127)$$

$$PMT = \$6688.77$$

Programmed Solution

("END" mode) (Set P/Y = 1; C/Y = 4) 0 [FV] 30 000 [±] [PV] 12 [I/Y]

7 [N] [CPT] [PMT] [6688.77031]

(ii) *Amortization schedule*

Payment Number	Amount Paid	Interest Paid $p = 0.125509$	Principal Repaid	Outstanding Principal Balance
0				30 000.00
1	6 688.77	3 765.26	2 923.51	27 076.49
2	6 688.77	3 398.34	3 290.43	23 786.06
3	6 688.77	2 985.36	3 703.41	20 082.65
4	6 688.77	2 520.55	4 168.22	15 914.43
5	6 688.77	1 997.40	4 691.37	11 223.06
6	6 688.77	1 408.59	5 280.18	5 942.88
7	6 688.76	745.88	5 942.88	0.00
TOTAL	46 821.38	16 821.38	30 000.00	

B. Finding the outstanding principal

1. Finding the Outstanding Principal When All Payments Are Equal

When all payments are equal, the prospective method used in Section 14.1 is the more direct method when finding the outstanding principal at any point during the repayment of the loan.

EXAMPLE 14.2B

For Example 14.2A, compute the outstanding balance after three payments.

SOLUTION

The outstanding balance after three payments is the present value of the remaining four payments.

$$\text{PMT} = 6688.77; \quad n = 4; \quad c = 4; \quad i = 3\%; \quad p = 12.5509\%$$

$$\begin{aligned}\text{PV}_{nc} &= 6688.77\left(\frac{1 - 1.125509^{-4}}{0.125509}\right)\\ &= 6688.77(3.002443)\\ &= \$20\,082.65\end{aligned}$$

Programmed Solution

("END" mode) (Set P/Y = 1; C/Y = 4) 0 [FV] 6688.77 [±] [PMT] 12 [I/Y]

4 [N] [CPT] [PV] [20082.65134]

The outstanding balance after three payments is $20 082.65.

EXAMPLE 14.2C

A $25 000 mortgage amortized by monthly payments over twenty years is renewable after five years.

(i) If interest is 6.5% compounded semi-annually, what is the outstanding balance at the end of the five-year term?
(ii) If the mortgage is renewed for a further three-year term at 6% compounded semi-annually, what is the size of the new monthly payment?
(iii) What is the payout figure at the end of the three-year term?

SOLUTION

(i) $\text{PV}_{nc} = 25\,000.00$; $n = 20(12) = 240$; P/Y = 12; C/Y = 2; I/Y = 6.5;

$$c = \frac{2}{12} = \frac{1}{6}; \quad i = \frac{6.5\%}{2} = 3.25\% = 0.0325;$$

$$p = 1.0325^{\frac{1}{6}} - 1 = 1.005345 - 1 = 0.005345 = 0.5345$$

$$25\,000.00 = \text{PMT}\left[\frac{1 - (1.005345)^{-240}}{0.005345}\right]$$

$$25\,000.00 = \text{PMT}(135.043813)$$

$$\text{PMT} = \$185.13$$

The number of outstanding payments after five years is 15(12)=180.

$$\begin{aligned}\text{PV}_{nc} &= 185.13\left[\frac{1 - (1.005345)^{-180}}{0.005345}\right]\\ &= 185.13(115.424194)\\ &= \$21\,368.48\end{aligned}$$

Programmed Solution

("END" mode) (Set P/Y = 12; C/Y = 2) 0 [FV] 25 000 [±] [PV]

6.5 [I/Y] 240 [N] [CPT] [PMT] 185.125104

0 [FV] 185.13 [±] [PMT] 6.5 [I/Y] 180 [N] [CPT] [PV] 21368.48105

The outstanding balance after five years is $21 368.48.

(ii) After the five-year term is up, the outstanding balance of $21 368.48 is to be amortized over the remaining fifteen years.

$PV_{nc} = 21\,368.48;\quad n = 15(12) = 180;\quad P/Y = 12;\quad C/Y = 2;\quad I/Y = 6;$

$c = \frac{1}{6};\quad i = \frac{8\%}{2} = 4\% = 0.04;$

$p = 1.03^{\frac{1}{6}} - 1 = 1.004939 - 1 = 0.004939 = 0.4939\%$

$$21\,368.48 = PMT\left[\frac{1 - (1.004939)^{-180}}{0.004939}\right]$$

$$21\,368.48 = PMT(119.064232)$$

$$PMT = \$179.47$$

Programmed Solution

("END" mode) (Set P/Y = 12; C/Y = 2) 0 [FV] 21 368.48 [±] [PV]

6 [I/Y] 180 [N] [CPT] [PMT] 179.470187

The monthly payment for the three-year term will be $179.47.

(iii) At the end of the three-year term, the number of outstanding payments is 144.

$$PV_{nc} = 179.47\left[\frac{1 - (1.004939)^{-144}}{0.004939}\right]$$

$$= 179.47(102.876118)$$

$$= \$18\,463.18$$

Programmed Solution

("END" mode) (Set P/Y = 12; C/Y = 2) 0 [FV] 179.47 [±] [PMT] 6 [I/Y]

144 [N] [CPT] [PV] 18463.17693

The outstanding balance at the end of the three-year term will be $18 463.18.

2. Finding the Outstanding Balance When All Payments Except the Final Payment Are Equal

When the final payment is different from the preceding payments, use the retrospective method for finding the outstanding balance. Since this method requires finding the future value of an ordinary general annuity, Formula 12.2 applies.

$$FV_{nc} = PMT\left[\frac{(1 + p)^n - 1}{p}\right] \quad \text{where } p = (1 + i)^c - 1$$ —— **Formula 12.2**

EXAMPLE 14.2D

A loan of $12 000 with interest at 12% compounded monthly and amortized by payments of $700 at the end of every three months is repaid in full after three years. What is the payout figure just after the last regular payment?

SOLUTION

Accumulate the value of the original principal after three years.

$$PV = 12\,000.00; \quad n = 3(12) = 36; \quad i = \frac{12\%}{12} = 1\% = 0.01$$

$$\begin{aligned} FV &= 12\,000.00(1.01^{36}) \\ &= 12\,000.00(1.430769) \\ &= \$17\,169.23 \end{aligned}$$

Programmed Solution

("END" mode) (Set P/Y = 12; C/Y = 12) [2nd] (CLR TVM) 12 000 [±] [PV]

12 [I/Y] 36 [N] [CPT] [FV] [17169.2254]

Accumulate the value of the twelve payments made.

$$PMT = 700.00; \ n = 3(4) = 12; \ P/Y = 4; \ C/Y = 12; \ I/Y = 12; c = \frac{12}{4} = 3;$$

$$i = 1\%$$

$$p = 1.01^3 - 1 = 1.030301 - 1 = 0.030301 = 3.0301\%$$

$$\begin{aligned} FV_{nc} &= 700.00\left(\frac{1.030301^{12} - 1}{0.030301}\right) \\ &= 700.00(14.216322) \\ &= \$9951.43 \end{aligned}$$

Programmed Solution

("END" mode) (Set P/Y = 4; C/Y = 12) 0 [PV] 700 [±] [PMT] 12 [I/Y]

12 [N] [CPT] [FV] [9951.425646]

The outstanding balance after three years is 17 169.23 − 9951.43 = $7217.80. The payout figure after three years is $7217.80.

Alternative Programmed Solution

(Set P/Y = 4; C/Y = 12) 12 000 [±] [PV] 700 [PMT] 12 [I/Y]

12 [N] [CPT] [FV] [7217.799757]

C. Finding the interest paid and the principal repaid; constructing partial amortization schedules

EXAMPLE 14.2E

Mr. and Mrs. Poh took out a $40 000, 25-year mortgage renewable after five years. The mortgage bears interest at 9.5% compounded semi-annually and is amortized by equal monthly payments.

(i) What is the interest included in the 13th payment?
(ii) How much of the principal is repaid by the 13th payment?
(iii) What is the total interest cost during the first year?
(iv) What is the total interest cost during the fifth year?
(v) What will be the total interest paid by the Pohs during the initial five-year term?

SOLUTION

(i) First find the size of the monthly payment.

$PV_{nc} = 40\,000.00$; $n = 300$; $P/Y = 12$; $C/Y = 2$; $I/Y = 9.5$;

$c = \frac{1}{6}$; $i = 4.75\%$

$$p = 1.0475^{\frac{1}{6}} - 1 = 1.007764 - 1 = 0.007764 = 0.7764\%$$

$$40\,000.00 = PMT\left(\frac{1 - 1.007764^{-300}}{0.007764}\right)$$

$$40\,000.00 = PMT(116.140291)$$

$$PMT = \$344.41$$

Programmed Solution

("END" mode) (Set P/Y = 12; C/Y = 2) 0 [FV] 40 000 [±] [PV] 9.5 [I/Y] 300 [N] [CPT] [PMT] [344.411053]

Now find the outstanding balance after one year.

$PMT = 344.41$; $p = 0.7764\%$

The number of outstanding payments after one year $n = 288$.

$$PV_{nc} = PMT\left(\frac{1 - 1.007764^{-288}}{0.007764}\right)$$

$$= 344.41(114.90953)$$

$$= \$\,39\,576.05$$

Programmed Solution

0 [FV] 344.41 [±] [PMT] 9.5 [I/Y] 288 [N] [CPT] [PV] [39576.05454]

The resulting difference in the present value amount is due to rounding of the payment.

The interest in the 13th payment is 39 576.05(0.007764) = \$307.28.

(ii) The principal repaid in the 13th payment is 344.41 − 307.28 = \$37.13.

(iii) The total amount paid during the first year is 344.41(12) = \$4132.92
The total principal repaid is 40 000.00 − 39 576.05 = 423.95
The total cost of interest for the first year = \$3708.97

(iv) After four years, $n = 300 - 48 = 252$.

$$PV_{nc} = 344.41\left(\frac{1 - 1.007764^{-252}}{0.007764}\right)$$

$$= 344.41(110.45204)$$

$$= \$38\,040.79$$

Programmed Solution

("END" mode) (Set P/Y = 12; C/Y = 2) 0 [FV] 344.41 [±] [PMT]
9.5 [I/Y] 252 [N] [CPT] [PV] [38040.84291]

After five years, $n = 300 - 60 = 240$.

$$PV_{nc} = 344.41\left(\frac{1 - 1.007764^{-240}}{0.007764}\right)$$

$$= 344.41(108.66827)$$

$$= \$37\,426.44$$

Programmed Solution

("END" mode) (Set P/Y = 12; C/Y = 2) 0 [FV] 344.41 [±] [PMT]
9.5 [I/Y] 240 [N] [CPT] [PV] [37426.49132]

The total amount paid during the fifth year is 344.41(12) = \$4132.92
The total principal repaid in Year 5 is 38 040.84 − 37 426.49 = 614.35
The total cost of interest in Year 5 = \$3518.57

(v) The total amount paid during the first five years is 344.41(60) = \$20 664.60
The total principal repaid is 40 000.00 − 37 426.49 = 2 573.51
The total cost of interest for the first five years = \$18 091.09

EXAMPLE 14.2F

Confederated Venture Company financed a project by borrowing \$120 000 at 7% compounded annually and is repaying the loan at the rate of \$7000 due at the end of every three months.

(i) Compute the interest paid and the principal repaid by the tenth payment.
(ii) Construct a partial amortization schedule showing the first three payments, the tenth payment, the last three payments, and the totals.

SOLUTION

(i) Accumulate the value of the original loan after nine payments.

$$PV = 120\,000.00;\ n = 9;\ P/Y = 4;\ C/Y = 1;\ I/Y = 7;\ c = \frac{1}{4} = 0.25;$$

$$i = 7\% = 0.07;$$

$$p = 1.07^{0.25} - 1 = 1.017059 - 1 = 0.017059 = 1.7059\%$$

$$\begin{aligned} FV &= 120\,000.00(1.017059^9) \\ &= 120\,000.00(1.16443) \\ &= \$139\,731.61 \end{aligned}$$

Programmed Solution

("END" mode) (Set P/Y = 4; C/Y = 1) [2nd] (CLR TVM) 120 000 [±] [PV] 7 [I/Y] 9 [N] [CPT] [FV] [139731.6366]

Accumulate the value of the first nine payments.

$$PMT = 7000.00;\quad n = 9$$

$$\begin{aligned} FV_{nc} &= 7000.00\left(\frac{1.017059^9 - 1}{0.017059}\right) \\ &= 7000.00(9.639186) \\ &= \$67\,474.30 \end{aligned}$$

Programmed Solution

("END" mode) (Set P/Y = 4; C/Y = 1) 0 [PV] 7000 [±] [PMT] 7 [I/Y] 9 [N] [CPT] [FV] [67474.30606]

The outstanding balance after nine payments is 139 731.64 − 67 474.31 = \$72 257.33.

The interest included in the tenth payment is 72 257.33(0.017059) = \$1232.60.

The principal repaid by the tenth payment is 7000.00 − 1232.60 = \$5767.40.

(ii) To show the details of the last three payments, we need to know the number of payments required to amoritize the loan.

PV_{nc} = 120 000.00; PMT = 7000.00; p = 1.7059%

$$120\,000.00 = 7000.00\left(\frac{1 - 1.017059^{-n}}{0.017059}\right)$$

$$0.292432 = 1 - 1.017059^{-n}$$

$$1.017059^{-n} = 0.707568$$

$$-n \ln 1.017059 = \ln 0.707568$$

$$-n(0.016915) = -0.345921$$

$$n = 20.450975 \text{ (There may be a difference due to rounding.)}$$

Programmed Solution

("END" mode) (Set P/Y = 4; C/Y = 1) 0 [FV] 120 000 [±] [PV]

7000 [PMT] 7 [I/Y] [CPT] [N] [20.450975]

Twenty-one payments (20 payments of $7000 plus a final payment) are required. This means the amortization schedule needs to show details of Payments 19, 20, and 21. To do so, we need to know the outstanding balance after 18 payments. Accumulate the value of the original principal after 18 payments.

$$FV = 120\,000.00(1.017059^{18})$$
$$= 120\,000.00(1.355898)$$
$$= \$162\,707.75$$

Programmed Solution

("END" mode) (Set P/Y = 4; C/Y = 1) [2nd] (CLR TVM) 120 000 [±]

[PV] 7 [I/Y] 18 [N] [CPT] [FV] [162707.7523]

Accumulate the value of the first 18 payments.

$$FV_{nc} = 7000.00\left(\frac{1.017059^{18} - 1}{0.017059}\right)$$
$$= 7000.00(20.863348)$$
$$= \$146\,4043.43$$

Programmed Solution

("END" mode) (Set P/Y = 4; C/Y = 1) 0 [PV] 7000 [±] [PMT]

7 [I/Y] 18 [N] [CPT] [FV] [146043.4329]

The outstanding balance after 18 payments is 162 707.75 − 146 043.43 = $16 664.32.

Partial amortization schedule

Payment Number	Amount Paid	Interest Paid $p = 0.017059$	Principal Repaid	Outstanding Principal Balance
0				120 000.00
1	7 000.00	2 047.02	4 952.98	115 047.02
2	7 000.00	1 962.53	5 037.47	110 009.55
3	7 000.00	1 876.60	5 123.40	104 886.15
•	•	•	•	•
•	•	•	•	•
9	•	•	•	72 257.33
10	7 000.00	1 232.60	5 767.40	66 489.93
•	•	•	•	•
•	•	•	•	•
•	•	•	•	•
18	•	•	•	16 664.32
19	7 000.00	284.27	6 715.73	9 948.59
20	7 000.00	169.71	6 830.29	3 118.30
21	3 171.49	53.19	3 118.30	0.00
TOTAL	143 171.49	23 171.49	120 000.00	

As an alternative, use the calculator's Amortization function. Instructions on its use are available on the CD-ROM accompanying this book.

D. Computer application—Amortization schedule

EXCEL NOTES

As shown in Section 14.1E, amortization schedules can be created using spreadsheet programs like Excel. Refer to Section 14.1E for instructions for creating amortization schedules in spreadsheets. Using those instructions and the formulas shown in Figure 14.4 below, you can create the amortization schedule for the debt in Example 14.2A.

FIGURE 14.4

Workbook 1

	A	B	C	D	E	F
1	Payment Number	Amount Paid	Interest Paid	Principal Repaid	Outstanding Principal Balance	
2	0				30000.00	6688.77
3	1	= F2	= F4*E2	= B3−C3	= E2−D3	
4	2	= F2	= F4*E3	= B4−C4	= E3−D4	0.1255088
5	3	= F2	= F4*E4	= B5−C5	= E4−D5	
6	4	= F2	= F4*E5	= B6−C6	= E5−D6	
7	5	= F2	= F4*E6	= B7−C7	= E6−D7	
8	6	= F2	= F4*E7	= B8−C8	= E7−D8	
9	7	= C9+D9	= F4*E8	= E8	= E8−D9	
10	Totals	= SUM(B3:B9)	= SUM(C3:C9)	= SUM(D3:D9)		

EXERCISE 14.2

EXCEL NOTES

If you choose, you can use Excel's **CUMIPMT**, **CUMPRINC**, **EFFECT**, **NPER**, **PMT**, or **PV** functions or **Template4** to answer the questions indicated below. Refer to the Spreadsheet Template Disk to find **Template4** or to learn how to use these Excel functions.

A. For each of the following four loans amortized by equal payments made at the end of each payment interval, compute: (a) the size of the periodic payments; (b) the outstanding principal at the time indicated; (c) the interest paid; and (d) the principal repaid by the payment following the time indicated for finding the outstanding principal.

	Debt Principal	Repayment Period	Payment Interval	Interest Rate	Conversion Period	Outstanding Principal Required After:
1.	$36 000	20 years	6 months	8%	quarterly	25th payment
2.	15 000	10 years	3 months	12	monthly	15th payment
3.	8 500	5 years	1 month	6	semi-annually	30th payment
4.	9 600	7 years	3 months	9	semi-annually	10th payment

B. For each of the following four loans repaid by periodic payments as indicated, compute: (a) the number of payments required to amortize the debts; and (b) the outstanding principal at the time indicated.

	Debt Principal	Debt Repayment	Payment Interval	Interest Rate	Conversion Period	Outstanding Principal Required After:
1.	$ 6 000	$ 400	3 months	6%	monthly	10th payment
2.	8 400	1200	6 months	10	quarterly	5th payment
3.	23 500	1800	3 months	7	annually	14th payment
4.	18 200	430	1 month	8	semi-annually	48th payment

C. Answer each of the following questions.

1. A debt of $45 000 is repaid over fifteen years with semi-annual payments. Interest is 9% compounded monthly.
(a) What is the size of the periodic payments?
(b) What is the outstanding principal after the eleventh payment?
(c) What is the interest paid in the twelfth payment?
(d) How much principal is repaid in the twelfth payment? Reference Example 14.2E

2. A debt of $60 000 is repaid over twenty-five years with monthly payments. Interest is 7% compounded semi-annually.
(a) What is the size of the periodic payments?
(b) What is the outstanding principal after the 119th payment?
(c) What is the interest paid in the 120th payment?
(d) How much principal is repaid in the 120th payment?

3. A $36 000 mortgage amortized by monthly payments over twenty-five years is renewable after three years.
  (a) If interest is 7% compounded semi-annually, what is the size of each monthly payment?
  (b) What is the mortgage balance at the end of the three-year term?
  (c) How much interest will have been paid during the first three years?
  (d) If the mortgage is renewed for a further three-year term at 9% compounded semi-annually, what will be the size of the monthly payments for the renewal period?

4. Fink and Associates bought a property valued at $80 000 for $15 000 down and a mortgage amortized over fifteen years. The firm makes equal payments due at the end of every three months. Interest on the mortgage is 6.5% compounded annually and the mortgage is renewable after five years.
  (a) What is the size of each quarterly payment?
  (b) What is the outstanding principal at the end of the five-year term?
  (c) What is the cost of the mortgage for the first five years?
  (d) If the mortgage is renewed for a further five years at 9% compounded semi-annually, what will be the size of each quarterly payment?

5. A loan of $10 000 with interest at 10% compounded quarterly is repaid by payments of $950 made at the end of every six months.
  (a) How many payments will be required to amortize the loan?
  (b) If the loan is repaid in full after six years, what is the payout figure?
  (c) If paid out, what is the total cost of the loan?

6. The owner of the Blue Goose Motel borrowed $12 500 at 12% compounded semi-annually and agreed to repay the loan by making payments of $700 at the end of every three months.
  (a) How many payments will be needed to repay the loan?
  (b) How much will be owed at the end of five years?
  (c) How much of the payments made at the end of five years will be interest?

7. A loan of $16 000 with interest at 9% compounded quarterly is repaid in seven years by equal payments made at the end of each year. Find the size of the annual payments and construct an amortization schedule showing the total paid and the total interest.
Reference Example 14.2E

8. A debt of $12 500 with interest at 7% compounded semi-annually is repaid by payments of $1900 made at the end of every three months. Construct an amortization schedule showing the total paid and the total cost of the debt.

9. For Question 7, calculate the interest included in the fifth payment period. Verify your answer by checking the amortization schedule.

10. For Question 8, compute the principal repaid in the sixth payment period. Verify your answer by checking the amortization schedule.

11. A $40 000 mortgage amortized by monthly payments over 25 years is renewable after five years.

(a) If interest is 8.5% compounded semi-annually, what is the size of each monthly payment?

(b) Find the total interest paid during the first year.

(c) Compute the interest included in the 48th payment.

(d) If the mortgage is renewed after five years at 10.5% compounded semi-annually, what is the size of the monthly payment for the renewal period?

(e) Construct a partial amortization schedule showing details of the first three payments for each of the two five-year terms.

12. A debt of $32 000 is repaid by payments of $2950 made at the end of every six months. Interest is 12% compounded quarterly.

(a) What is the number of payments needed to retire the debt?

(b) What is the cost of the debt for the first five years?

(c) What is the interest paid in the tenth payment period?

(d) Construct a partial amortization schedule showing details of the first three payments, the last three payments, and totals.

14.3 FINDING THE SIZE OF THE FINAL PAYMENT

A. Three methods for computing the final payment

When all payments except the final payment are equal, three methods are available to compute the size of the final payment.

METHOD 1 Compute the value of the term n and determine the present value of the outstanding fractional payment. If the final payment is made at the end of the payment interval, add interest for one payment interval to the present value.

METHOD 2 Use the retrospective method to compute the outstanding principal after the last of the equal payments. If the final payment is made at the end of the payment interval, add to the outstanding principal the interest for one payment interval.

METHOD 3 Assume all payments to be equal, compute the overpayment, and subtract the overpayment from the size of the equal payments. This method must not be used when the payments are made at the beginning of the payment interval.

EXAMPLE 14.3A For Example 14.1D, compute the size of the final payment using each of the three methods. Compare the results with the size of the payment shown in the amortization schedule.

SOLUTION

METHOD 1 PV = 15 000.00; PMT = 2500.00; P/Y = 4; C/Y = 4; I/Y = 10; $i = 2.5\%$

$$15\,000.00 = 2500.00\left(\frac{1 - 1.025^{-n}}{0.025}\right)$$

$$6.00 = \frac{1 - 1.025^{-n}}{0.025}$$
$$0.15 = 1 - 1.025^{-n}$$
$$1.025^{-n} = 0.85$$
$$-n \ln 1.025 = \ln 0.85$$
$$-n(0.024693) = -0.162519$$
$$n = 6.581684$$

Programmed Solution

("END" mode) (Set P/Y = 4; C/Y = 4) 0 [FV] 15 000 [±] [PV] 2500 [PMT]
10 [I/Y] [CPT] [N] [6.581682]

PMT = 2500.00; $i = 2.5\%$; $n = 0.581684$

$$PV_n = 2500.00\left(\frac{1 - 1.025^{-0.581684}}{0.025}\right)$$
$$= 2500.00(0.570426)$$
$$= \$1426.06$$

Programmed Solution

0 [FV] 2500 [±] [PMT] 10 [I/Y] 0.581684 [N] [CPT] [PV] [1426.058892]

Interest for one interval is 1426.06(0.025) = \$35.65.
Final payment is 1426.06 + 35.65 = \$1461.71.

METHOD 2 Compute the value of n as done in Method 1.
Since $n = 6.581684$, the number of equal payments is 6.
The accumulated value of the original principal after six payments

$$FV = 15\,000.00(1.025^6)$$
$$= 15\,000.00(1.159693)$$
$$= \$17\,395.40$$

Programmed Solution

("END" mode) (Set P/Y = 4; C/Y = 4) [2nd] (CLR TVM) 15 000 [±] [PV]
10 [I/Y] 6 [N] [CPT] [FV] [17395.40127]

The accumulated value of the first six payments

$$FV_6 = 2500.00\left(\frac{1.025^6 - 1}{0.025}\right)$$
$$= 2500.00(6.387737)$$
$$= \$15\,969.34$$

Programmed Solution

0 [PV] 2500 [±] [PMT] 10 [I/Y] 6 [N] [CPT] [FV] [15969.34182]

The outstanding balance after six payments is 17 395.40 − 15 969.34 = $1426.06.
The final payment = outstanding balance + interest for one period
= the accumulated value of $1426.06 for one year
= 1426.06(1.025)
= $1461.71

METHOD 3 Compute the value of n as done in Method 1.
Since $n = 6.581684$, the number of assumed full payments is 7.
The accumulated value of the original principal after seven payments

$$\begin{aligned} FV &= 15\,000.00(1.025^7) \\ &= 15\,000.00(1.188686) \\ &= \$17\,830.29 \end{aligned}$$

Programmed Solution

("END" mode) (Set P/Y = 4; C/Y = 4) [2nd] (CLR TVM) 15 000 [±] [PV]
10 [I/Y] 7 [N] [CPT] [FV] [17830.28631]

The accumulated value of seven payments

$$\begin{aligned} FV_7 &= 2500.00\left(\frac{1.025^7 - 1}{0.025}\right) \\ &= 2500.00(7.547430) \\ &= \$18\,868.58 \end{aligned}$$

Programmed Solution

0 [PV] 2500 [±] [PMT] 10 [I/Y] 7 [N] [CPT] [FV] [18868.57537]

Since the accumulated value of seven payments is greater than the accumulated value of the original principal, there is an overpayment.

18 868.58 − 17 830.29 = $1038.29

The size of the final payment is 2500.00 − 1038.29 = $1461.71.

Note:

1. For all three methods, you must determine the term n using the methods shown in Chapters 11 and 12.
2. When using a scientific calculator, Method 1 is preferable, because it is the most direct method. It is the method used in Subsection B below.

POINTERS AND PITFALLS

When dealing with loan repayment problems in which the size of the final payment must be determined, once n has been calculated, the size of the final payment *cannot* be calculated by simply multiplying the periodic pay (PMT) by the decimal portion of n (i.e., the non-integral part of n). For example, if you had done it *incorrectly*, the final rent payment in Example 14.3A would have shown as 0.586488 × \$2500.00 = \$1454.21 Using the *correct* method, the value for the size of the final rent payment in Example 14.3A, Method 1 is \$1461.71. The difference is due to interest on the outstanding balance of the loan for the final payment period.

B. Applications

EXAMPLE 14.3B

On his retirement, Art received a bonus of \$8000 from his employer. Taking advantage of the existing tax legislation, he invested his money in an annuity that provides for payments of \$1200 at the end of every six months. If interest is 6.25% compounded semi-annually, determine the size of the final payment. (See Chapter 11, Example 11.5D.)

SOLUTION

To start, the number of payments must be determined.

$PV_n = 8000.00$; PMT = 1200.00; P/Y = 2; C/Y = 2; I/Y = 6.25;

$$i = \frac{6.25\%}{2} = 3.125\%$$

$$8000.00 = 1200.00\left(\frac{1 - 1.03125^{-n}}{0.03125}\right)$$

$$0.208333 = 1 - 1.03125^{-n}$$

$$1.03125^{-n} = 0.791667$$

$$-n \ln 1.03125 = \ln 0.791667$$

$$-n(0.030772) = -0.233615$$

$$n = 7.59188 \text{ (half-year periods)}$$

The annuity will be in existence for four years. Art will receive seven payments of \$1200.00 and final payment that will be less than \$1200.00

PMT = 1200.00; $i = 3.125\%$; $n = 0.59188$

$$PV_n = 1200.00\left(\frac{1 - 1.03125^{-0.59188}}{0.03125}\right)$$

$$= 1200.00(0.577545)$$

$$= \$693.05$$

The final step is to determine the interest for that final period, and add it to the beginning-of-period balance to determine the final payment.

The final payment including the interest for one payment interval is 693.06(1.03125) = \$714.72.

Programmed Solution

("END" mode) (Set P/Y = 2; C/Y = 2) 0 [FV] 8000 [±] [PV] 1200 [PMT]

6.25 [I/Y] [CPT] [N] 7.591884

0 [FV] 1200 [±] [PMT] 6.25 [I/Y] 0.591884 [N]

[CPT] [PV] 693.057863

EXAMPLE 14.3C

A lease contract valued at \$7800 is to be fulfilled by payments of \$180 due at the beginning of each month. If money is worth 9% compounded monthly, determine the size of the final lease payment. (See Chapter 13, Example 13.1O.)

SOLUTION

$PV_n(\text{due}) = 7800.00;\quad PMT = 180.00;\quad P/Y = 12;\quad C/Y = 12;\quad I/Y = 9;$

$i = \frac{9\%}{12} = 0.75\%$

$n = 52.123125$ (see solution to Example 13.1O)

Present value of the final payment

$PMT = 180.00;\quad i = 0.75\%;\quad n = 0.123125$

$$\begin{aligned} PV_n(\text{due}) &= 180.00(1.0075)\left(\frac{1 - 1.0075^{-0.123125}}{0.0075}\right) \qquad \text{Formula 12.2} \\ &= 180.00(1.0075)(0.122609) \\ &= 180.00(0.123529) \\ &= \$22.24 \end{aligned}$$

Programmed Solution

("BGN" mode) (Set P/Y = 12; C/Y = 12) 0 [FV] 180 [PMT] 9 [I/Y] 7800 [±]

[PV] [CPT] [N] 52.123125

("BGN" mode) 0 [FV] 180 [±] [PMT] 9 [I/Y] 0.123125 [N]

[CPT] [PV] 22.235252

Since the payment is made at the beginning of the last payment interval, no interest is added. The final payment is \$22.24.

EXAMPLE 14.3D

Payments of \$500 deferred for nine years are received at the end of each month from a fund of \$10 000 deposited at 10.5% compounded monthly. Determine the size of the final payment. (See Chapter 13, Example 13.3E.)

SOLUTION

$PV_n(\text{defer}) = 10\,000.00$; PMT $= 500.00$; $d = 9(12) = 108$; P/Y $= 12$; C/Y $= 12$;

I/Y $= 10.5$; $i = \dfrac{10.5\%}{12} = 0.875\%$

$n = 68.288334$ (see solution to Example 13.3E)

Present value of the final payment

PMT $= 500.00$; $i = 0.875\%$; $n = 0.288334$

$$PV_n = 500.00\left(\frac{1 - 1.00875^{-0.288334}}{0.00875}\right)$$
$$= 500.00(0.286720)$$
$$= \$143.36$$

Programmed Solution

("END" mode) (Set P/Y = 12; C/Y = 12) 0 [FV] 500 [±] [PMT] 10.5 [I/Y]

0.288334 [N] [CPT] [PV] [143.359793]

The size of the final payment is 143.36(1.00875) = \$144.61.

EXAMPLE 14.3E

A business valued at \$96 000 is purchased for a down payment of 25% and payments of \$4000.00 at the end of every three months. If interest is 9% compounded monthly, what is the size of the final payment? (See Chapter 12, Example 12.4B.)

SOLUTION

$PV_{nc} = 96\,000.00(0.75) = 72\,000.00$; PMT $= 4000.00$; P/Y $= 4$; C/Y $= 12$;

I/Y $= 9$; $c = \dfrac{12}{4} = 3$; $i = \dfrac{9\%}{12} = 0.75\% = 0.0075$; $p = 1.0075^3 - 1 = 2.2669\%$;

$n = 23.390585$ (see solution to Example 12.4B)

Present value of the final payment

PMT $= 4000.00$; $p = 2.2669\%$; $n = 0.390585$

$$PV_n = 4000.00\left(\frac{1 - 1.022669^{-0.390585}}{0.022669}\right)$$
$$= 4000.00(0.384538)$$
$$= \$1538.15$$

Programmed Solution

("END" mode) (Set P/Y = 4; C/Y = 12) 0 [FV] 4000 [±] [PMT]

9 [I/Y] 0.390585 [N] [CPT] [PV] [1538.151278]

The final payment is 1538.15(1.022669) = \$1573.02.

EXAMPLE 14.3F

Ted Davis, having reached his goal of a $140 000 balance in his RRSP, converts it into an RRIF and withdraws from it $1650 at the beginning of each month. If interest is 5.75% compounded quarterly, what is the size of the final withdrawal? (See Chapter 13, Example 13.2G.)

SOLUTION

$PV_{nc} = 140\,000.00$; $PMT = 1650.00$; $P/Y = 12$; $C/Y = 4$; $I/Y = 5.75$;

$$c = \frac{4}{12} = \frac{1}{3}; \quad i = \frac{5.75\%}{4} = 1.4375\% = 0.014375;$$

$$p = 1.014375^{\frac{1}{3}} - 1 = 1.004769 - 1 = 0.4769\%$$

$n = 108.32388$ (see solution to Example 13.2G)

Present value of final payment

$PMT = 1650.00$; $p = 0.47689\%$; $n = 0.32388$

$$PV_n = 1650.00(1.004769)\left(\frac{1 - 1.004769^{-0.32395}}{0.004769}\right)$$

$$= 1650.00(1.004769)(0.322861)$$

$$= 1650.00(0.324401)$$

$$= \$535.26$$

Programmed Solution

("BGN" mode) (Set P/Y = 12; C/Y = 4) 0 [PV] 1650 [±] [PMT] 5.75 [I/Y]

0.32388 [N] [CPT] [PV] [535.261739]

Since the payment is at the beginning of the last payment interval, it is $535.26.

EXERCISE 14.3

EXCEL NOTES

If you choose, you can use Excel's **NPER** or **PV** function to answer the questions indicated below. Refer to the Spreadsheet Template Disk to learn how to use these Excel functions.

A. For each of the following six loans, compute the size of the final payment.

	Principal	Periodic Payment	Payment Interval	Payment Made At:	Interest Rate	Conversion Period
1.	$17 500	$1100	3 months	end	9%	quarterly
2.	7 800	775	6 months	beginning	7	semi-annually
3.	9 300	580	3 months	beginning	7	quarterly
4.	15 400	1600	6 months	end	8	quarterly
5.	29 500	1650	3 months	end	9	monthly
6.	17 300	425	1 month	beginning	6	quarterly

B. Answer each of the following questions.

1. A loan of $7200 is repaid by payments of $360 at the end of every three months. Interest is 11% compounded quarterly.
(a) How many payments are required to repay the debt?
(b) What is the size of the final payment? Reference Example 14.3B

2. Seanna O'Brien receives pension payments of $3200 at the end of every six months from a retirement fund of $50 000. The fund earns 7% compounded semi-annually.
(a) How many payments will Seanna receive?
(b) What is the size of the final pension payment?

3. A loan of $35 000 is repaid by payments of $925 at the end of every month. Interest is 12% compounded monthly.
(a) How many payments are required to repay the debt?
(b) What is the size of the final payment?

4. An annuity with a cash value of $10 500 pays $900 at the beginning of every three months. The investment earns 11% semi-annually.
(a) How many payments will be paid?
(b) What is the size of the final annuity payment?

5. Payments of $1200 are made out of a fund of $25 000 at the end of every three months. If interest is 6% compounded monthly, what is the size of the final payment?

6. A debt of $30 000 is repaid in monthly installments of $550. If interest is 8% compounded quarterly, what is the size of the final payment?

7. A lease valued at $20 000 requires payments of $1000 every three months due in advance. If money is worth 7% compounded quarterly, what is the size of the final lease payment? Reference Example 14.3C

8. Eduardo Martinez has saved $125 000. If he withdraws $1250 at the beginning of every month and interest is 10.5% compounded monthly, what is the size of the last withdrawal?

9. Equipment priced at $42 000 was purchased on a contract requiring payments of $5000 at the beginning of every six months. If interest is 9% compounded quarterly, what is the size of the final payment?

10. Noreen Leung has agreed to purchase her partner's share in the business by making payments of $1100 every three months. The agreed transfer value is $16 500 and interest is 10% compounded annually. If the first payment is due at the date of the agreement, what is the size of the final payment?

11. David Jones has paid $16 000 for a retirement annuity from which he will receive $1375 at the end of every three months. The payments are deferred for ten years and interest is 10% compounded quarterly.
(a) How many payments will David receive?
(b) What is the size of the final payment?

(c) How much will David receive in total?
(d) How much of what he receives will be interest? Reference Example 14.3D

12. A contract valued at $27 500 requires payments of $6000 every six months. The first payment is due in four years and interest is 11% compounded semi-annually.
(a) How many payments are required?
(b) What is the size of the last payment?
(c) How much will be paid in total?
(d) How much of what is paid is interest?

14.4 RESIDENTIAL MORTGAGES IN CANADA

A. Basic concepts and definitions

A **residential mortgage** is a claim to a residential property given by a borrower to a lender as security for the repayment of a loan. It is often the largest amount of money ever borrowed by an individual. The borrower is called the **mortgagor;** the lender is called the **mortgagee.** The **mortgage contract** spells out the obligations of the borrower and the rights of the lender, including the lender's rights in case of default in payment by the borrower. If the borrower is unable to make the mortgage payments, the lender ultimately has the right to dispose of the property under *power of sale* provisions.

To secure legal claim against a residential property, the lender must register the mortgage against the property at the provincial government's land titles office. A **first mortgage** is the first legal claim against a residential property if the mortgage payments cannot be made and the property must be sold. **Equity** in a property is the difference between the property's market value and the total debts, or mortgages, registered against the property. It is possible to have a **second mortgage** on a residential property that is backed by equity in the property, even if there is a first mortgage already registered against the property. If the borrower defaults on the mortgage payments and the property must be sold, the first mortgagee gets paid before the second mortgagee. For this reason, second mortgages are considered riskier investments than first mortgages. They command higher interest rates than first mortgages to compensate for this risk. Home improvement loans, home equity loans, or home equity lines of credit (HELOCs) are often secured by second mortgages. It is even possible to obtain *third mortgages* against residential properties. Third mortgages rank behind first and second mortgages. Thus, they command even higher interest rates.

Financial institutions offer two types of mortgages—fixed-rate mortgages and demand (or variable-rate) mortgages. A **fixed-rate mortgage** is a mortgage for which the rate of interest is fixed for a specific period of time. A **demand** (or **variable-rate**) **mortgage** is a mortgage for which the rate of interest changes as money market conditions change. The interest rate change is usually related to the change in a bank's prime lending rate. Both types of mortgage are usually repaid by equal payments that blend principal and interest. Payments are often required to be made monthly, but some lenders are more flexible and allow semi-monthly, bi-weekly, and even weekly payments.

For all types of mortgages, the amortization period is a part of the mortgage agreement. The amortization period is used to calculate the amount of the blended payments. The most common amortization period is twenty-five years for fixed-rate mortgages and twenty years for demand mortgages. Other amortization periods, such as thirty, fifteen, or ten years, may be used at the discretion of the lender or the borrower.

The *term* of the mortgage specifies the period of time for which the interest rate is fixed. By definition, only fixed-rate mortgages have terms. The term ranges from six months to five years. Longer terms, such as seven and ten years, are becoming available more frequently.

For fixed-rate mortgages, Canadian law dictates that interest must be calculated semi-annually or annually, not in advance. In this context, "not in advance" means that interest is calculated at the end of each six-month or twelve-month period, not at the beginning. It is Canadian practice to calculate fixed-rate mortgage interest semi-annually, not in advance.

Fixed-rate mortgages can be either open or closed. Closed mortgages restrict the borrower's ability to increase payments, make lump-sum payments, change the term of the mortgage, or transfer the mortgage to another lender without penalty. Most closed mortgages contain some prepayment privileges. For example, some mortgages allow a lump-sum payment each year of up to 10% or 15% of the original mortgage principal, usually on the anniversary date of the mortgage. Some lenders permit increases in the periodic payments up to 10% or 15% once each calendar year. Changes in the term or transfers are usually subject to prohibitive penalties.

Open mortgages allow prepayment or repayment of the mortgage at any time without penalty. They are available from most lenders for terms of up to two years. However, interest rates on open mortgages are significantly higher than interest rates on closed mortgages. For a six-month term, the usual charge (i.e., the premium) for an open mortgage is an interest rate at least 0.5% (i.e., 50 basis points) higher than for a closed mortgage. For one-year and two-year terms, the interest rate is usually at least 1.0% (i.e., 100 basis points) higher.

As we stated above, a demand (or variable-rate) mortgage is a mortgage for which the rate of interest changes over time. Interest is calculated on a daily basis. Therefore, demand mortgages are not subject to the legal restriction of compounding semi-annually, not in advance. Demand mortgages also do not have a fixed term, because the interest rate may fluctuate.

B. CMHC mortgages

Fixed-rate mortgages and demand mortgages are usually available from financial institutions for up to 75% of the value of a property (calculated as the lesser of the purchase price and the appraised value of a property). This means the borrower needs to have at least a 25% down payment for the purchase of a residential property or at least 25% equity in a property. To borrow beyond the 75% level, the mortgage must be insured by the Canada Mortgage and Housing Corporation (CMHC).

Canada Mortgage and Housing Corporation (CMHC) is the corporation of the federal government that administers the National Housing Act (NHA) and provides mortgage insurance to lenders. CMHC acts as the insurer for the lender in the event that the borrower defaults on the mortgage payments. Anyone buying a home as a principal residence can qualify as an eligible borrower under certain conditions.

CMHC borrowers must qualify to determine how much they can pay by meeting the two affordability rules:

- First affordability rule: monthly housing costs as a percentage of the gross household monthly income. The maximum **Gross Debt Service (GDS) ratio,** including heating costs, is 32%. (Recall from Chapter 1 that the GDS ratio is the percent of your gross annual income required to cover housing costs such as mortgage payments, property taxes, and heating costs.)
- Second affordability rule: monthly debt load as a percentage of the gross monthly income. The maximum **Total Debt Service (TDS) ratio** is 40%. (Recall from Chapter 1 that the TDS ratio is the percent of your gross annual income required to cover housing costs *and* all other debts and obligations, such as a car loan or lease.)

Although the usual amortization period is twenty-five years, extended amortization periods have recently been introduced, such as thirty and thirty-five years, to further facilitate home ownership.

There is no maximum on the amount of the mortgage loan available, but if the mortgage is insured by CMHC, home buyers may borrow up to 95% of the purchase price. The borrower must pay the insurance premium to CMHC as a single lump-sum or as an amount added to the mortgage payment.

CMHC insurance premiums depend on the ratio determined when the amount of the financing required is compared to the maximum home price. For example, a home buyer purchasing a $200 000 home with a $40 000 or 20% down payment needs to borrow $160 000 or 80% of the maximum home price.

The current insurance premiums are as follows:

Up to and including 65%	0.50% of loan amount
Up to and including 75%	0.65% of loan amount
Up to and including 80%	1.00% of loan amount
Up to and including 85%	1.75% of loan amount
Up to and including 90%	2.00% of loan amount
Between 90.01 and 95%	2.75% of loan amount

EXAMPLE 14.4A

The Wongs want to purchase a home in Vancouver with a CMHC-approved mortgage. They have qualified under the affordability rules, and the house that they have chosen is valued at $450 000. They have saved enough to meet the 5% down payment rule, and will have to pay mortgage loan insurance at 2.75% of the mortgage balance. According to the CMHC terms and conditions, determine the maximum initial mortgage balance if the Wongs want the insurance premium added to the maximum allowable loan balance.

SOLUTION

The maximum CMHC loan balance = 95% of \$450 000 = \$427 500;
the insurance premium = 2.75% of \$427 500 = \$11 756.25;
the maximum initial mortgage balance = \$427 500.00 + \$11 756.25 = \$439 256.25.

C. Computing the effective rate of interest for fixed-rate mortgages

For residential mortgages, Canadian legislation requires the rate of interest charged by the lender to be calculated annually or semi-annually, not in advance. The fixed rates advertised, posted, or quoted by lenders are usually nominal annual rates. To meet the legislated requirements, the applicable nominal annual rate of interest must be converted into the equivalent effective rate of interest per payment period.

This is done as explained in Section 12.1A by using Formula 12.1.

$$p = (1 + i)^c - 1$$

where p = the effective rate of interest per payment period

where i = the rate per conversion period

$$c = \frac{\text{THE NUMBER OF INTEREST CONVERSION PERIODS PER YEAR}}{\text{THE NUMBER OF PAYMENT PERIODS PER YEAR}}$$

Note that when using the BAII Plus financial calculator, this means that the c in the formula above can be derived by dividing the C/Y by the P/Y.

The prevailing practice is semi-annual compounding and monthly payment for most mortgages. For most mortgages (with semi-annual compounding and monthly payment),

$$c = \frac{2 \text{ (compounding periods per year)}}{12 \text{ (payments per year)}} = \frac{1}{6}$$

EXAMPLE 14.4B

Suppose a financial institution posted the interest rates for closed mortgages shown below. The interest is compounded semi-annually and the mortgages require monthly payments.

Term	Interest Rate
6 months	5.25%
1 year	5.50%
2 years	6.50%
3 years	7.00%
4 years	7.25%
5 years	7.50%

Compute the effective rate of interest per payment period for each term.

SOLUTION

$c = \frac{1}{6}$; $p = (1 + i)^{\frac{1}{6}} - 1$

For the six-month term, $i = \frac{5.25\%}{2} = 2.625\% = 0.02625$

$$p = (1 + 0.02625)^{\frac{1}{6}} - 1$$
$$= 1.004328 - 1$$
$$= 1.004328\text{, or } 0.4328\%$$

For the one year term, $i = \frac{5.50\%}{2} = 2.75\% = 0.0275$

$$p = (1.0275)^{\frac{1}{6}} - 1 = 0.004532 = 0.4532\%$$

You can obtain the effective rates using a preprogrammed financial calculator by using the function keys as follows:

("END" mode) (Set P/Y = 1; C/Y = 1) [2nd] (CLR TVM) 1 [±] [PV]

$\frac{1}{6} = 0.166667$ [N] (enter applicable interest rate)

[I/Y] [CPT] [FV] [Display Shows (1 + p)]

For the two-year term, $i = 3.25\% = 0.0325$; $p = (1.0325^{\frac{1}{6}}) - 1 = 0.005345 = 0.5345\%$

[2nd] (CLR TVM) 1 [±] [PV] 0.166667 [N]

3.25 [I/Y] [CPT] [FV] [1.005345]

$p = 0.5345\%$

(Note that if you perform these calculations in succession, you do not have to key in PV and N each time.)

For the three-year term, $i = 3.5\% = 0.035$; $p = (1.035^{\frac{1}{6}}) - 1$
$= 0.00575 = 0.575\%$

[2nd] (CLR TVM) 1 [±] [PV] 0.166667 [N]

3.5 [I/Y] [CPT] [FV] [1.005750]

$p = 0.5750\%$

For the four-year term, $i = 3.625\% = 0.03625$; $p = (1.03625^{\frac{1}{6}}) - 1$
$= 0.00592 = 0.5952\%$

[2nd] (CLR TVM) 1 [±] [PV] 0.166667 [N]

3.625 [I/Y] [CPT] [FV] [1.005952]

$p = 0.5952\%$

For the five-year term, $i = 3.75\% = 0.0375$; $p = (1.0375^{\frac{1}{6}}) - 1$
$= 0.00615 = 0.6155\%$

2nd (CLR TVM) 1 ± PV 0.166667 N

3.75 I/Y CPT FV 1.006155

$p = 0.6155\%$

D. Computing mortgage payments and balances

Blended residential mortgage payments are ordinary general annuities. Therefore, Formula 12.3 applies.

$$PV_{nc} = PMT\left[\frac{1-(1+p)^{-n}}{p}\right], \text{ where } p = (1+i)^c - 1$$ ——Formula 11.5

The periodic payment PMT is calculated using the method shown in Section 12.3.

EXAMPLE 14.4C

A mortgage for \$120 000 is amortized over 25 years. Interest is 7.5% p.a., compounded semi-annually, for a five-year term and payments are monthly.

(i) Compute the monthly payment.
(ii) Compute the balance at the end of the five-year term.
(iii) Compute the monthly payment if the mortgage is renewed for a four-year term at 7.0% compounded semi-annually.

SOLUTION

(i) When computing the monthly payment, n is the total number of payments in the amortization period. The term for which the rate of interest is fixed (in this case, five years) does *not* enter into this calculation.

$PV_{nc} = 120\,000.00$; $n = 12(25) = 300$; $P/Y = 12$; $C/Y = 2$;

$I/Y = 7.5$; $i = \frac{7.5\%}{2} = 3.75\%$; $c = \frac{1}{6}$

We must first compute the effective monthly rate of interest.

$p = (1.0375)^{\frac{1}{6}} - 1 = 1.006155 - 1 = 0.006155 = 0.06155\%$

$$120\,000.00 = PMT\left(\frac{1-(1.006155)^{-300}}{0.006155}\right)$$ —— using Formula 12.3

$120\,000.00 = PMT\,(136.695138)$

$PMT = \$877.87$

Programmed Solution

("END" mode) (Set P/Y = 12; C/Y = 2) 0 FV 120 000 ± PV 7.5 I/Y

300 N CPT PMT 877.865900

The monthly payment for the original five-year term is \$877.87.

(ii) The balance at the end of the five-year term is the present value of the outstanding payments. After five years, 60 of the required 300 payments have been made; 240 payments remain outstanding. Note that the payment has been rounded to the nearest cent.

PMT = 877.87; $n = 240$; $p = 0.6155\%$

$$PV_{nc} = 877.87\left(\frac{1 - (1.006155)^{-240}}{0.006155}\right) \quad \text{——— using Formula 11.5}$$

$$= 877.87(125.218804)$$

$$= \$109\,925.83$$

Programmed Solution

0 (FV) 877.87 (±) (PMT) 240 (N) 7.5 (I/Y) (CPT) (PV) 109925.8315

The mortgage balance at the end of the first five-year term is $109 925.83.

(iii) For the renewed term, the starting principal is the balance at the end of the five-year term. The amortization period is the number of years remaining after the initial term. We must recalculate p for the new interest rate.

$PV_{nc} = 109\,925.83$; $n = 12(20) = 240$; I/Y = 7; $i = 3.5\%$

$$p = (1.035)^{\frac{1}{6}} - 1 = 1.00575 - 1 = 0.00575 = 0.575\%$$

$$109\,925.83 = PMT\left(\frac{1 - (1.00575)^{-240}}{0.00575}\right)$$

$$109\,925.83 = PMT(129.986504)$$

$$PMT = \$845.67$$

Programmed Solution

0 (FV) 109 925.83 (±) (PV) 7 (I/Y)

240 (N) (CPT) (PMT) 845.671102

The monthly payment for the renewed four-year term is $845.67.

E. Rounded payments

Mortgage payments are sometimes rounded up to an exact cent or dollar value (such as to the next cent, the next dollar, or the next ten dollars). The payment calculation of $845.671102 might be rounded up to $845.68 or $850 or even $900. Rounded payments up to a higher value will result in a lower balance at the end of the term. In the final renewal term, rounding will affect the size of the final payment.

EXAMPLE 14.4D

A mortgage balance of \$17 321.50 is renewed for the remaining amortization period of three years at 8% compounded semi-annually.

(i) Compute the size of the monthly payments.
(ii) Determine the size of the last payment if the payments computed in part (i) have been rounded up to the next cent.
(iii) Determine the size of the last payment if the payments computed in part (i) have been rounded up to the next ten dollars.

SOLUTION

(i) $PV_{nc} = 17\,321.50$; $n = 12(3) = 36$; $P/Y = 12$; $C/Y = 2$; $I/Y = 8$;

$i = 4\%$; $c = \frac{1}{6}$

$$p = (1.04)^{\frac{1}{6}} - 1 = 1.006558 - 1 = 0.6558\%$$

$$17\,321.50 = PMT\left(\frac{1 - (1.006558)^{-36}}{0.006558}\right)$$

$$17\,321.05 = PMT\,(31.973037)$$

$$PMT = \$541.75$$

Programmed Solution

("END" mode) (Set P/Y = 12; C/Y = 2) 0 [FV] 17 321.50 [±] [PV] 8 [I/Y]

36 [N] [CPT] [PMT] [541.75335]

The monthly payment is \$541.75.

(ii) If payments are rounded up to \$541.76, the last payment will be less than a full payment. To calculate the size of the last payment we need to determine the number of payments of \$541.76 that are required to amortize the loan balance.

$PV_{nc} = 17\,321.50$; $PMT = 541.76$; $p = 0.6558\%$

$$17\,321.50 = 541.76\left(\frac{1 - (1.006558)^{-n}}{0.006558}\right)$$

$$0.209683 = 1 - 1.006558^{-n}$$

$$1.006558^{-n} = 0.790317$$

$$-n(\ln 1.006558) = \ln 0.790317$$

$$-n(0.006537) = -0.235321$$

$$n = 35.999502$$

Programmed Solution

0 [FV] 17 321.50 [±] [PV] 8 [I/Y]

541.76 [PMT] [CPT] [N] [35.999502]

There will be 35 payments of \$541.76 and a final payment smaller than \$541.76. We need to determine the balance after the 35th payment.

$$\text{PMT} = 541.76; \quad n = 0.999502; \quad p = 0.6558\%$$

$$\begin{aligned}\text{PV}_{nc} &= 541.76\left(\frac{1 - (1.006558)^{-0.999502}}{0.006558}\right)\\ &= 541.76(0.992991)\\ &= \$537.96\end{aligned}$$

Programmed Solution

0 [FV] 541.76 [±] [PMT] 8 [I/Y] 0.999502 [N]

[CPT] [PV] [537.963017]

The final payment includes interest on the balance of \$537.96.
Final payment = 537.96(1.006558) = \$541.49.

(iii) If payments are rounded to \$550, the last payment will be less than \$550. To calculate the size of the last payment we need to determine the number of payments of \$550 that are required to amortize the loan balance.

$$\text{PV}_{nc} = 17\,321.50; \quad \text{PMT} = 550.00; \quad p = 0.6558\%$$

$$\begin{aligned}17\,321.50 &= 550.00\left(\frac{1 - (1.006558)^{-n}}{0.006558}\right)\\ 0.206541 &= 1 - 1.006558^{-n}\\ 1.006558^{-n} &= 0.793459\\ -n(\ln 1.006558) &= \ln 0.793459\\ -n(0.006537) &= -0.231354\\ n &= 35.392625\end{aligned}$$

Programmed Solution

0 [FV] 17 321.50 [±] [PV] 8 [I/Y] 550 [PMT] [CPT] [N] [35.392625]

There will be 35 payments of \$550 and a final payment smaller than \$550. We need to determine the balance after the 35th payment.

$$\text{PMT} = 550.00; \quad n = 0.392625; \quad p = 0.6558\%$$

$$\begin{aligned}\text{PV}_{nc} &= 550.00\left(\frac{1 - (1.006558)^{-0.392625}}{0.006558}\right)\\ &= 550.00(0.390842)\\ &= \$214.96\end{aligned}$$

Programmed Solution

0 [FV] 550.00 [±] [PMT] 8 [I/Y] 0.392625 [N]

[CPT] [PV] [214.963019]

The final payment includes interest on the balance of \$214.96.
Final payment = 214.96(1.006558) = \$216.37.

BUSINESS MATH NEWS BOX

How to Have a Million-Dollar Baby

If you're about to experience the miracle of birth in your household, consider doing this—get your spouse and all the grandparents together in one room and shake out everybody's pockets and purses to come up with \$7000. That's a stretch, I know—but if you can find \$7000 and put it in a non-registered investment when your new child is born, your baby will retire a millionaire.

Sounds like smoke and mirrors, doesn't it? Well, it is magic of a sort—the magic of compounding.

Albert Einstein, who knew a lot about math, is reported to have claimed that compounding was the greatest mathematical discovery of all time. And it certainly is true that compounding is a basic investing strategy—a concept that, when used correctly, can make an investor wealthy. Interest can be very interesting—and financially fantastic!

There are two ways to earn interest on money:

- Simple interest is a rate of interest applied only to principal (the amount of money originally invested). Any interest earned does not become part of the principal.
- Compound interest is interest earned on interest. It is calculated not only on the principal investment, but also on the interest that has been generated. This is the key to the magic of compounding because, over time, the interest on interest (also known as accumulated reinvested interest) adds tremendously to investment growth.

The key to success—start early and stay invested. The key to compounding is time. The longer you leave your investment alone, the more powerful the effect of compound interest. And the earlier you start your investment, the more you make from compound interest.

Source: "How to have a million-dollar baby," Investors Group Financial Services Inc. *The Guardian*, Charlottetown, P.E.I., August 20, 2005, p.B7. This column, written and published by Investors Group Financial Services Inc. (in Quebec – a Financial Services Firm), presents general information only and is not a solicitation to buy or sell any investments. For more information on this topic please contact your Investors Group Consultant.

QUESTIONS

1. If you invested \$7000 in a plan for sixty-five years, what is the rate of return required to reach the \$1 000 000 benchmark? Assume interest is compounded annually.
2. **a.** Assume \$1000 was initially invested at birth to age twenty-five years at a rate of 2.9% compounded quarterly. From age 26 to 65 years, what monthly payments are required to reach the \$1 000 000 benchmark? Assume a 6.6% interest compounded semi-annually.

   b. Calculate the effects of monthly payments made at the beginning of the month versus the end of the month on this calculation.

F. Mortgage statement

Currently, when financial institutions record monthly mortgage payments, they calculate interest for the exact number of days that have elapsed since the last payment. This is done by multiplying the effective monthly rate of interest by 12 to convert it into a simple annual rate of interest. The annual rate is then multiplied by the number of days expressed as a fraction of 365.

For example, $p = 0.6558\%$ becomes the simple annual interest rate $12(0.6558\%) = 7.86984\%$.

This approach takes into account that the number of days elapsed between payments fluctuates depending on the number of days in a particular month. It also allows for fluctuations in receiving payments, and permits semi-monthly, bi-weekly, or weekly payments for mortgages requiring contractual monthly payments.

EXAMPLE 14.4E

A credit union member made the contractual mortgage payment of $725 on May 31, leaving a mortgage loan balance of $75 411.79. The effective monthly fixed rate was 0.5345%. The member made the contractual payments on June 28, July 31, August 30, September 30, October 29, November 28, and December 30. The credit union agreed to convert the fixed-rate mortgage to a demand mortgage on October 29 at 5.25% compounded annually. This rate was changed to 4.75% on December 2. Determine the mortgage balance on December 30.

SOLUTION

The monthly effective rate $p = 0.5345\%$ is equivalent to the simple annual rate $12(0.5345\%) = 6.4136\%$.

Payment Date	Number of Days	Amount Paid	Interest Paid	Principal	Balance Repaid
May 31	rate is 6.4136%				75 411.79
June 28	28	725.00	371.03	353.97	75 057.82
July 31	33	725.00	435.23	289.77	74 768.05
August 30	30	725.00	394.14	330.86	74 437.19
September 30	31	725.00	405.47	319.53	74 117.66
October 29	29	725.00	377.69	347.31	73 770.35
October 29	rate becomes 5.25%				
November 28	30	725.00	318.32	406.68	73 363.67
December 2	rate becomes 4.75%				
December 30	32	725.00	309.54*	415.46	72 948.21

******Note:* Interest calculation for December is

4 days at 5.25% on $73 363.67	$ 42.21
28 days at 4.75% on $73 363.67	267.33
TOTAL	$309.54

EXAMPLE 14.4F

A mortgage of \$55 000 closed on April 12, amortized over 15 years at 8.50% compounded semi-annually for a five-year term. It requires contractual monthly payments rounded up to the nearest \$10. The lender agreed to accept bi-weekly payments of half the contractual monthly amount starting April 24. The mortgagor's second June payment was three days late.

(i) Determine the size of the contractual monthly payment.
(ii) Produce a mortgage statement to June 30.
(iii) Compute the accrued interest on June 30.

SOLUTION

(i) $PV_{nc} = 55\ 000.00; \quad n = 12(15) = 180; \quad i = 4.25; \quad c = \frac{1}{6}$

$$p = (1.0425)^{\frac{1}{6}} - 1 = 1.006961 - 1 = 0.006961\%$$

$$55\ 000.00 = PMT\left(\frac{1 - 1.006961^{-180}}{0.006961}\right)$$

$$55\ 000.00 = PMT(102.44)$$

$$PMT = \$536.89$$

The contractual monthly payment is \$540.

(ii) The bi-weekly payment is \$270.
The annual rate of interest is 12(0.6961) = 8.3533%.

Payment Date	Number of Days	Amount Paid	Interest Paid	Principal	Balance Repaid
April 12					55 000.00
April 24	12	270.00	151.05	118.95	54 881.05
May 8	14	270.00	175.84	94.16	54 786.89
May 22	14	270.00	175.54	94.46	54 692.43
June 5	14	270.00	175.24	94.76	54 597.67
June 22	17	270.00	212.42	57.58	54 540.09

The mortgage balance on June 30 is \$54 540.09.

(iii) On June 30 interest has accrued for 8 days.

$$\text{The amount of accrued interest} = 54\ 540.09(0.083533)\left(\frac{8}{365}\right) = \$99.86.$$

EXERCISE 14.4

EXCEL NOTES

If you choose, you can use Excel's **NPER, PMT, PV,** or **RATE** functions or **Template4** to answer the questions indicated below. Refer to the Spreadsheet Template Disk to find **Template4** or to learn how to use these Excel functions.

A. Answer each of the following questions.

1. A $90 000 mortgage is to be amortized by making monthly payments for 25 years. Interest is 8.5% compounded semi-annually for a five-year term.
   (a) Compute the size of the monthly payment.
   (b) Determine the balance at the end of the five-year term.
   (c) If the mortgage is renewed for a three-year term at 7% compounded semi-annually, what is the size of the monthly payment for the renewal term?

Reference Example 14.4C

2. A demand (variable-rate) mortgage of $150 000 is amortized over 20 years by equal monthly payments. After 18 months the original interest rate of 6% p.a. was raised to 6.6% p.a. Two years after the mortgage was taken out, it was renewed at the request of the mortgagor at a fixed rate of 7.5% compounded semi-annually for a four-year term.
   (a) Calculate the mortgage balance after 18 months.
   (b) Compute the size of the new monthly payment at the 6.6% rate of interest.
   (c) Determine the mortgage balance at the end of the four-year term.

3. A $40 000 mortgage is to be repaid over a ten-year period by monthly payments rounded up to the next-higher $50. Interest is 9% compounded semi-annually.
   (a) Determine the number of rounded payments required to repay the mortgage.
   (b) Determine the size of the last payment.
   (c) Calculate the amount of interest saved by rounding the payments up to the next-higher $50.

Reference Example 14.4D

4. A mortgage balance of $23 960 is to be repaid over a seven-year term by equal monthly payments at 11% compounded semi-annually. At the request of the mortgagor, the monthly payments were set at $440.
   (a) How many payments will the mortgagor have to make?
   (b) What is the size of the last payment?
   (c) Determine the difference between the total actual amount paid and the total amount required to amortize the mortgage by the contractual monthly payments.

5. A mortgage of $80 000 is amortized over 15 years by monthly payments of $826.58. What is the nominal annual rate of interest compounded semi-annually?

6. At what nominal annual rate of interest will a $195 000 demand (variable-rate) mortgage be amortized by monthly payments of $1606.87 over 20 years?

7. Interest for the initial four-year term of a $105 000 mortgage is 7.25% compounded semi-annually. The mortgage is to be repaid by equal monthly payments over 20 years. The mortgage contract permits lump-sum payments at each anniversary date up to 10% of the original principal.
   (a) What is the balance at the end of the four-year term if a lump-sum payment of $7000 is made at the end of the third year?

(**b**) How many more payments will be required after the four-year term if there is no change in the interest rate?

(**c**) What is the difference in the cost of the mortgage if no lump-sum payment is made?

8. The Berezins agreed to monthly payments rounded up to the nearest $100 on a mortgage of $36 000 amortized over ten years. Interest for the first five years was 8.75% compounded semi-annually. After 30 months, as permitted by the mortgage agreement, the Berezins increased the rounded monthly payment by 10%.

(**a**) Determine the mortgage balance at the end of the five-year term.

(**b**) If the interest rate remains unchanged over the remaining term, how many more of the increased payments will amortize the mortgage balance?

(**c**) How much did the Berezins save by exercising the increase-in-payment option?

9. A $40 000 mortgage taken out on June 1 is to be repaid by monthly payments rounded up to the nearest $10. The payments are due on the first day of each month starting July 1. The amortization period is 12 years and interest is 5.5% compounded semi-annually for a six-month term. Construct an amortization schedule for the six-month term. Reference Example 14.4E

10. For Question 9, produce the mortgage statement for the six-month term. Assume all payments have been made on time. Compare the balance to the balance in Question 9 and explain why there may be a difference.

11. For the mortgage in Question 9, develop a mortgage statement for the six-month term if semi-monthly payments equal to one-half of the monthly payment are made on the first day and the 16th day of each month. The first payment is due June 16. Compare the balance to the balances in Question 9 and Question 10. Explain why there are differences.

12. For the mortgage in Question 9, develop a mortgage statement for the six-month term if bi-weekly payments equal to one-half of the rounded monthly payments are made starting June 16. Compare the balance to the balances in Questions 9, 10, and 11. Explain why it differs significantly from the other three balances.

Review Exercise

1. Sylvie Cardinal bought a business for $45 000. She made a down payment of $10 000 and agreed to repay the balance by equal payments at the end of every three months for eight years. Interest is 8% compounded quarterly.

(a) What is the size of the quarterly payments?

(b) What will be the total cost of financing?

(c) How much will Sylvie owe after five years?

(d) How much interest will be included in the 20th payment?

(e) How much of the principal will be repaid by the 24th payment?

(f) Construct a partial amortization schedule showing details of the first three payments, Payments 10, 11, 12, the last three payments, and totals.

2. Angelo Lemay borrowed $8000 from his credit union. He agreed to repay the loan by making equal monthly payments for five years. Interest is 9% compounded monthly.

(a) What is the size of the monthly payments?

(b) How much will the loan cost him?

(c) How much will Angelo owe after eighteen months?

(d) How much interest will he pay in his 36th payment?

(e) How much of the principal will be repaid by the 48th payment?

(f) Prepare a partial amortization schedule showing details of the first three payments, Payments 24, 25, 26, the last three payments, and totals.

3. Comfort Swim Limited borrowed $40 000 for replacement of equipment. The debt is repaid in installments of $2000 made at the end of every three months.

(a) If interest is 7% compounded quarterly, how many payments are needed?

(b) How much will Comfort Swim owe after two years?

(c) How much of the 12th payment is interest?

(d) How much of the principal will be repaid by the 20th payment?

(e) Construct a partial amortization schedule showing details of the first three payments, the last three payments, and totals.

4. A $48 000 mortgage amortized by monthly payments over 35 years is renewable after five years. Interest is 9% compounded semi-annually.

(a) What is the size of the monthly payments?

(b) How much interest is paid during the first year?

(c) How much of the principal is repaid during the first five-year term?

(d) If the mortgage is renewed for a further five-year term at 8% compounded semi-annually, what will be the size of the monthly payments?

(e) Construct a partial amortization schedule showing details of the first three payments for each of the two five-year terms, the last three payments for the second five-year term, and totals at the end of the second five-year term.

5. Pelican Recreational Services owes $27 500 secured by a collateral mortgage. The mortgage is amortized over fifteen years by equal payments made at the end of every three months and is renewable after three years.

(a) If interest is 7% compounded annually, what is the size of the payments?

(b) How much of the principal is repaid by the fourth payment?

(c) What is the balance at the end of the three-year term?

(d) If the mortgage is renewed for a further four years but amortized over eight years and interest is 7.5% compounded semi-annually, what is the size of the quarterly payments for the renewal period?

(e) Construct a partial amortization schedule showing details of the first three payments for each of the two terms, the last three payments in the four-year term, and totals at the end of the four-year term.

6. A debt of $17 500 is repaid by payments of $2850 made at the end of each year. Interest is 8% compounded semi-annually.

(a) How many payments are needed to repay the debt?

(b) What is the cost of the debt for the first three years?

(c) What is the principal repaid in the fifth year?

(d) Construct an amortization schedule showing details of the first three payments, the last three payments, and totals.

7. A debt of $25 000 is repaid by payments of $3500 made at the end of every six months. Interest is 11% compounded semi-annually.

(a) How many payments are needed to repay the debt?

(b) What is the size of the final payment?

8. Jane Evans receives payments of $900 at the beginning of each month from a pension fund of $72 500. Interest earned by the fund is 6.30% compounded monthly.

(a) What is the number of payments Jane will receive?

(b) What is the size of the final payment?

9. A lease agreement valued at $33 000 requires payment of $4300 every three months in advance. The payments are deferred for three years and money is worth 10% compounded quarterly.

(a) How many lease payments are to be made under the contract?

(b) What is the size of the final lease payment?

10. A contract worth $52 000 provides benefits of $20 000 at the end of each year. The benefits are deferred for ten years and interest is 11% compounded quarterly.

(a) How many payments are to be made under the contract?

(b) What is the size of the last benefit payment?

11. A mortgage for $135 000 is amortized over 25 years. Interest is 8.7% p.a., compounded semi-annually, for a five-year term and payments are monthly.

(a) Compute the monthly payment.

(b) Compute the balance at the end of the five-year term.

(c) Compute the monthly payment if the mortgage is renewed for a three-year term at 7.8% compounded semi-annually.

12. A $180 000 mortgage is to be amortized by making monthly payments for 25 years. Interest is 7.9% compounded semi-annually for a four-year term.

(a) Compute the size of the monthly payment.

(b) Determine the balance at the end of the four-year term.

(c) If the mortgage is renewed for a five-year term at 8.8% compounded semi-annually, what is the size of the monthly payment for the renewal term?

13. An $80 000 mortgage is to be repaid over a 10-year period by monthly payments rounded up to the next-higher $50. Interest is 8.5% compounded semi-annually.

(a) What is the number of rounded payments required to repay the mortgage?

(b) What is the size of the last payment?

(c) How much interest was saved by rounding the payments up to the next-higher $50?

14. A $160 000 mortgage is to be repaid over a 20-year period by monthly payments rounded up to the next-higher $100. Interest is 9.2% compounded semi-annually.

(a) Determine the number of rounded payments required to repay the mortgage.

(b) Determine the size of the last payment.

(c) Calculate the amount of interest saved by rounding the payments up to the next-higher $100.

15. A debt of $6500 is repaid in equal monthly installments over four years. Interest is 9% compounded monthly.
   (a) What is the size of the monthly payments?
   (b) What will be the total cost of borrowing?
   (c) What is the outstanding balance after one year?
   (d) How much of the 30th payment is interest?
   (e) Construct a partial amortization schedule showing details of the first three payments, the last three payments, and totals.

16. Milton Investments borrowed $32 000 at 11% compounded semi-annually. The loan is repaid by payments of $4500 due at the end of every six months.
   (a) How many payments are needed?
   (b) How much of the principal will be repaid by the fifth payment?
   (c) Prepare a partial amortization schedule showing the details of the last three payments and totals.

17. A mortgage of $95 000 is amortized over 25 years by monthly payments of $748.06. What is the nominal annual rate of interest compounded semi-annually?

18. At what nominal annual rate of interest will a $135 000 mortgage be amortized by monthly payments of $1370.69 over 15 years?

19. A $28 000 mortgage is amortized by quarterly payments over twenty years. The mortgage is renewable after three years and interest is 6% compounded semi-annually.
   (a) What is the size of the quarterly payments?
   (b) How much interest will be paid during the first year?
   (c) What is the balance at the end of the three-year term?
   (d) If the mortgage is renewed for another three years at 7% compounded annually, what will be the size of the quarterly payments for the renewal period?

20. The Superior Tool Company is repaying a debt of $16 000 by payments of $1000 made at the end of every three months. Interest is 7.5% compounded monthly.
   (a) How many payments are needed to repay the debt?
   (b) What is the size of the final payment?

Self-Test

1. A $9000 loan is repaid by equal monthly payments over five years. What is the outstanding balance after two years if interest is 12% compounded monthly?

2. A loan of $15 000 is repaid by quarterly payments of $700 each at 8% compounded quarterly. What is the principal repaid by the 25th payment?

3. A $50 000 mortgage is amortized by monthly payments over twenty years. If interest is 9% compounded semi-annually, how much interest will be paid during the first three years?

4. A debt of $24 000 is repaid by quarterly payments of $1100. If interest is 6% compounded quarterly, what is the size of the final payment?

5. A \$190 000 mortgage is to be amortized by making monthly payments for 20 years. Interest is 6.5% compounded semi-annually for a three-year term.
   (a) Compute the size of the monthly payment.
   (b) Determine the balance at the end of the three-year term.
   (c) If the mortgage is renewed for a five-year term at 7.25% compounded semi-annually, what is the size of the monthly payment for the renewal term?

6. A \$140 000 mortgage is to be repaid over a 15-year period by monthly payments rounded up to the next-higher \$50. Interest is 8.25% compounded semi-annually.
   (a) Determine the number of rounded payments required to repay the mortgage.
   (b) Determine the size of the last payment.
   (c) Calculate the amount of interest saved by rounding the payments up to the next-higher \$50.

7. A mortgage of \$145 000 is amortized over 25 years by monthly payments of \$1297. What is the nominal annual rate of interest compounded semi-annually?

8. A loan of \$12 000 is amortized over ten years by equal monthly payments at 7.5% compounded monthly. Construct an amortization schedule showing details of the first three payments, the fortieth payment, the last three payments, and totals.

Challenge Problems

1. A debt is amortized by monthly payments of \$250. Interest is 8% compounded monthly. If the outstanding balance is \$3225.68 just after a particular payment (say, the xth payment), what was the balance just after the previous payment (i.e., the $(x - 1)$th payment)?

2. Captain Sinclair has been posted to Cold Lake, Alberta. He prefers to purchase a condo rather than live on the base. He knows that in four years he will be posted overseas. The condo he wishes to purchase will require a mortgage of \$130 000, and he has narrowed his choices to two lenders. Trust Company A is offering a five-year mortgage at 6.75% compounded semi-annually. This mortgage can be paid off at any time but there is a penalty clause in the agreement requiring two months' interest on the remaining principal. Trust Company B is offering a five-year mortgage for 7% compounded semi-annually. It can be paid off at any time without penalty. Both mortgages are amortized over 25 years and require monthly payments. Captain Sinclair will have to sell his condo in four years and pay off the mortgage at that time before moving overseas. Given that he expects to earn 3% compounded annually on his money over the next five years, which mortgage offer is cheaper? By how much is it cheaper?

Case Study 14.1 Managing a Mortgage

» Malcolm and Shannon purchased their first apartment with a \$180 000 mortgage. Their five-year mortgage had a 7.5% semi-annually compounded interest rate, and was amortized over 25 years. Payments were made monthly.

After three years, interest rates had fallen. Malcolm and Shannon considered that they should pay out the old mortgage (in spite of the interest penalties), and negotiate a new mortgage at the lower rate. They met with the loans officer at their bank, who laid out the options for them.

Interest on mortgages with a five-year term was 5.5% compounded semi-annually, the lowest rate in many years. The loans officer had informed Malcolm and Shannon that there is a penalty for renegotiating a mortgage early, before the end of the current term. According to their mortgage contract, the penalty for renegotiating the mortgage before the end of the five-year term is the greater of:

A. Three months' interest at the original rate of interest. (Banks generally calculate this as one month's interest on the mortgage principal remaining to be paid, multiplied by three.)

B. The interest differential over the remainder of the original term. (Banks generally calculate this as the difference between the interest the bank would have earned over the remainder of the original term at the original [higher] mortgage rate and at the renegotiated [lower] mortgage rate.)

The loans officer also explained that there are two options for paying the penalty amount: (1) you can pay the full amount of the penalty at the beginning of the new mortgage period or (2) the penalty amount can be added to the principal when the mortgage is renegotiated, allowing the penalty to be paid off over the term of the new mortgage.

Malcolm and Shannon agreed to look at their options before giving the loans officer their final decision.

QUESTIONS

1. Suppose there was no penalty for refinancing the mortgage after three years. How much would Malcolm and Shannon save per month by refinancing their mortgage for a five-year term at the new rate?

2. Suppose the couple choose to refinance their mortgage for a five-year term at the new interest rate.
(**a**) What is the amount of penalty A?
(**b**) What is the amount of penalty B?
(**c**) What penalty would Malcolm and Shannon have to pay in this situation?

3. If they pay the full amount of the penalty at the beginning of the new five-year term, what will Malcolm and Shannon's new monthly payment be?

4. If the penalty amount is added to the principal when the mortgage is renegotiated, what will the new monthly payment be?

Case Study 14.2 Steering the Business

» On March 1, 2006, Sandra and her friend Francisco arranged a loan to purchase two used black limousines for $28 000 and $35 000 respectively, and launched their new business, Classy Limousine Services. The loan was for four years at 9.5% compounded semi-annually. Payments were made quarterly beginning on March 1, 2006.

Business was brisk, especially for weddings. To meet the demand, the partners bought a new stretch limousine on August 1, 2006 for $90 000. They arranged a five-year loan for this amount at 8.8% interest compounded monthly. Payments were made monthly beginning on August 1, 2006.

On September 1, 2006, the partners were given an opportunity to buy a black super-stretch limousine for $120 000. They arranged a two-year loan for this amount at 7.8% interest compounded monthly. The monthly payments began on September 1, 2006.

Business continued to increase. Sandra and Francisco discussed the need for a new parking garage and office space they could own instead of rent. When an industrial warehouse large enough to house their expanding fleet became available, they decided to purchase it. The $475 000 mortgage had an interest rate of 8.9% compounded semi-annually for a five-year term. It was amortized over 20 years, and the end-of-month mortgage payments began on March 1, 2007.

QUESTIONS

1. What are the quarterly payments for the original loan obtained on March 1, 2005?
2. What are the monthly payments for the loan on the stretch limousine?
3. What are the monthly payments for the loan on the black super-stretch limousine?
4. **(a)** What are the monthly payments required for the mortgage on the warehouse?
   (b) What principal will remain to be paid at the end of the mortgage's five-year term?

SUMMARY OF FORMULAS

No new formulas were introduced in this chapter. However, some of the formulas introduced in Chapters 9 to 12 have been used, namely Formulas 9.1A, 11.2, 11.5, 12.1, 12.2, 12.3, and 12.5.

GLOSSARY

Amortization repayment of both interest and principal of interest-bearing debts by a series of equal payments made at equal intervals of time *(p. 570)*

Amortization schedule a schedule showing in detail how a debt is repaid *(p. 571)*

Canada Mortgage and Housing Corporation (CMHC) the corporation of the federal government that administers the National Housing Act (NHA) and provides mortgage insurance to lenders *(p. 609)*

Demand mortgage a mortgage for which the rate of interest changes as money market conditions change *(p. 608)*

Equity the difference between the price for which a property could be sold and the total debts registered against the property *(p. 608)*

First mortgage the first legal claim registered against a property; in the event of default by the borrower, first mortgagees are paid before all other claimants *(p. 608)*

Fixed-rate mortgage a mortgage for which the rate of interest is fixed for a specific period of time; it can be open or closed *(p. 608)*

Gross Debt Service (GDS) ratio the percent of gross annual income required to cover such housing costs as mortgage payments, property taxes, and heating costs *(p. 610)*

Mortgage contract a document specifying the obligations of the borrowers and the rights of the lender *(p. 608)*

Mortgagee the lender *(p. 608)*

Mortgagor the borrower *(p. 608)*

Prospective method a method for finding the outstanding debt balance that considers the payments that remain outstanding *(p. 577)*

Residential mortgage a claim to a residential property given by a borrower to a lender as security for the repayment of a loan *(p. 608)*

Retrospective method a method of finding the outstanding balance of a debt that considers the payments that have been made *(p. 577)*

Second mortgage the second legal claim registered against a property; in the event of default by the borrower, second-mortgage holders are paid only after first-mortgage holders have been paid *(p. 608)*

Total Debt Service (TDS) ratio the percent of gross annual income required to cover such housing costs as mortgage payments, property taxes, and heat, and all other debts and obligations *(p. 610)*

Variable-rate mortgage *see* **Demand mortgage**

USEFUL INTERNET SITES

www.cmhc-schl.gc.ca

Canada Mortgage and Housing Corporation (CMHC) As the Government of Canada's national housing agency, CMHC plays a major role in Canada's housing industry. CMHC develops new ways to finance home purchases.

www.tdcanadatrust.com

Mortgage Calculator Click on "Mortgages," then "How Much Can I Afford?" By entering values for the relevant variables in this tool on the TD Canada Trust site, you can calculate the payment, principal, or amortization period of a mortgage. You can also obtain mortgage rates and general mortgage information.

www.businessfinancemag.com

Business Finance Magazine Presents information on business management and technology issues for accountants and finance professionals, controllers, chief financial officers, and treasurers.

CHAPTER 15 Bond Valuation and Sinking Funds

OBJECTIVES

Upon completing this chapter, you will be able to do the following:

1. Determine the purchase price of bonds, redeemable at par or otherwise, bought on or between interest dates.
2. Calculate the premium or discount on the purchase of a bond.
3. Construct bond schedules showing the amortization of premiums or accumulation of discounts.
4. Calculate the yield rate for bonds bought on the market by the method of averages.
5. Make sinking fund computations when payments form simple annuities, including the size of the periodic payments, accumulated balance, interest earned, and increase in the fund.
6. Construct complete or partial sinking fund schedules.

Many financial planners recommend bonds as a part of a balanced investment portfolio. Historically, bonds represent a less risky investment than stocks. Companies and governments issue bonds to raise large sums of money. To have the funds to pay for the bonds when they mature, companies often create a *sinking fund* by making regular equal investments from the outset of the bond issue. Both individuals and companies use annuity formulas to decide about possible investments in bonds and sinking funds.

INTRODUCTION

Bonds are contracts used to borrow sizeable sums of money, usually from a large group of investors. The indenture, or contract, for most bonds provides for the repayment of the principal at a specified future date plus periodic payment of interest at a specified percent of the face value. Bonds are negotiable; that is, they can be freely bought and sold. The mathematical issues arising from the trading of bonds are the topic of this chapter.

15.1 PURCHASE PRICE OF BONDS

A. Basic concepts and terminology

Corporations and governments use bonds to borrow money, usually from a large group of lenders (investors). To deal with the expected large number of investors, the borrower prints up written contracts, called *bonds* or *debentures*, in advance.

The printed bonds specify the terms of the contract including

(a) the **face value** (or **par value** or **denomination**), which is the amount owed to the holder of the bond when it matures, usually a multiple of $100 such as $100, $1000, $5000, $10 000, $25 000, $100 000;

(b) the **bond rate** (or **coupon rate** or **nominal rate**), which is the rate of interest paid, usually semi-annually, based on the face value of the bond;

(c) the **maturity date** (or **redemption date** or **due date**), which is the date on which the principal of the bond is to be repaid;

(d) the **principal** (or **redemption value** or **maturity value**), which is the money paid by the issuer to the bondholder at the date of surrender of the bonds.

Most bonds are **redeemable at par**; that is, they are redeemable at their *face* value. However, some bonds have a redemption feature either to make the bonds more attractive to the investor or because they are callable, that is, because they can be redeemed *before* maturity. In either case, the bonds will be **redeemable at a premium**, that is, at a price *greater* than their face price. The redemption value in such cases is stated as a percent of the face value. For example, the redemption value of a $5000 bond redeemable at 104 is 104% of $5000, or $5200.

Investors in bonds expect to receive periodic interest payments during the term of the bond from the date of issue to the date of maturity and they expect to receive the principal at the date of maturity. The bond rate is used to determine the periodic interest payments.

To facilitate the payment of interest, some bonds have dated interest **coupons** attached that can be cashed on or after the stated interest payment date at any bank. For example, a twenty-year, $1000.00 bond bearing interest at 10% payable semi-annually will have attached to it at the date of issue forty coupons of $50 each. Each coupon represents the semi-annual interest due on each of the forty interest payment dates.

The issuer may or may not offer security such as real estate, plant, or equipment as a guarantee for the repayment of the principal. Bonds for which no security is offered are called **debentures**.

Bonds are marketable and may be freely bought and sold. When investors acquire bonds, they buy two promises:

1. a promise to be paid the principal of the bond at maturity;
2. a promise to be paid the periodic interest payments according to the rate of interest and the terms stated on the bond.

Two basic problems arise for investors when buying bonds:

1. What should be the purchase price of a bond to provide the investor with a given rate of return?
2. What is the rate of interest that a bond will yield if purchased at a given price?

In this section we will deal with the first of these two problems.

B. Purchase price of a bond bought on an interest date

EXAMPLE 15.1A A $1000 bond bearing interest at 6% payable semi-annually is due in four years. If money is worth 7% compounded semi-annually, what is the value of the bond if purchased today?

SOLUTION The buyer of the bond acquires two promises:

1. A promise of $1000 four years from now.
2. A promise of $30 interest due at the end of every six months. The annual interest is 6% and the periodic interest rate is 6%/2 = 3%. The interest amount paid is the periodic interest rate stated on the bond multiplied by the face value or maturity value of the bond. This interest will be paid semi-annually for four years, or eight times.

The two promises can be represented on a time graph as Figure 15.1 shows.

FIGURE 15.1 Graphical Representation of Method and Data

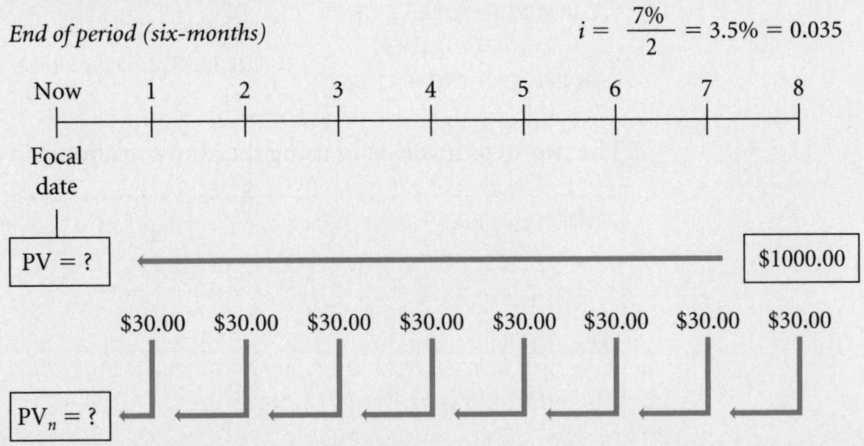

The focal date for evaluating the two promises is "now." The rate of interest to be used for the valuation at the focal date is the rate money is worth at that date. In this example, use the rate of 7% compounded semi-annually. The principal is the future value.

The value at the focal date of the principal of \$1000 is its present value.

$$FV = 1000.00; \; n = 4(2) = 8; \; P/Y = 2; \; C/Y = 2; \; I/Y = 7; \; i = \frac{7\%}{2} = 35\% = 0.035$$

$$\begin{aligned} PV &= 1000.00(1.035)^{-8} \quad \text{—— using Formula 9.1C} \\ &= 1000.00(0.759412) \\ &= \$759.41 \end{aligned}$$

Programmed Solution

("END" mode) (Set P/Y = 2; C/Y = 2) [2nd] (CLR TVM) 1000 [FV] 7 [I/Y]

8 [N] [CPT] [PV] [−759.411556]

The value "now" of the semi-annual interest payments is the present value of an ordinary annuity.

$$PMT = \frac{6\% \text{ of } 1000.00}{2} = 30.00; \; n = 8; \; i = 3.5\%$$

$$\begin{aligned} PV_n &= 30.00\left(\frac{1 - 1.035^{-8}}{0.035}\right) \quad \text{—— using Formula 11.2} \\ &= 30.00(6.873956) \\ &= \$206.22 \end{aligned}$$

Programmed Solution

0 [FV] 30 [PMT] 7 [I/Y] 8 [N] [CPT] [PV] [−206.218666]

The purchase price of the bond is the sum of the present values of the two promises

$= PV + PV_n$

$= 759.41 + 206.22 = \$965.63$

THE PURCHASE PRICE OF A BOND BOUGHT ON AN INTEREST PAYMENT DATE	=	THE PRESENT VALUE OF THE REDEMPTION PRICE	+	THE PRESENT VALUE OF THE INTEREST PAYMENTS

The two steps involved in using the above relationship can be combined.

$$\begin{aligned} \text{PURCHASE PRICE} &= P + A_n \\ &= S(1+i)^{-n} + R\left[\frac{1-(1+i)^{-n}}{i}\right] \end{aligned}$$

restated as —— **Formula 15.1**

$$\begin{aligned} \text{PURCHASE PRICE} &= PV + PV_n \\ &= FV(1+i)^{-n} + PMT\left[\frac{1-(1+i)^{-n}}{i}\right] \end{aligned}$$

where FV = the principal of the bond;
PMT = the periodic interest payment (coupon);
n = the number of outstanding interest payments (or compounding periods);
i = the yield rate per payment interval.

Note: It is important to recognize that two rates of interest are used in determining the purchase price:

1. the bond rate determines the size of the periodic interest payments (coupons);
2. the **yield rate** is used to determine the present values of the two promises.

EXAMPLE 15.1B

A $5000 bond bearing interest at 6.5% payable semi-annually matures in ten years. If it is bought to yield 5.8% compounded semi-annually, what is the purchase price of the bond?

SOLUTION

PRESENT VALUE OF THE PRINCIPAL + PRESENT VALUE OF THE PRINCIPAL COUPONS

$$= \text{PV} + \text{PV}_n$$
$$= 5000.00(1.029^{-20}) + 162.50\left(\frac{1 - 1.029^{-20}}{0.029}\right)$$
$$= 5000.00(0.564537) + 162.50(15.015961)$$
$$= 2822.69 + 2440.09$$
$$= \$5262.78$$

Programmed Solution

("END" mode) (Set P/Y = 2; C/Y = 2) [2nd] (CLR TVM) 5000 [FV] 5.8 [I/Y]

20 [N] [CPT] [PV] [−2822.685609]

0 [FV] 162.50 [PMT] 5.8 [I/Y] 20 [N] [CPT] [PV] [−2440.093714]

(These keystrokes can be eliminated, since they are still programmed in the calculator from the previous step.)

The purchase price is 2822.69 + 2440.09 = $5262.78.

Note: The calculator steps may be combined into one calculation by entering both the future value and the payment as positive numbers, then computing the present value. The present value will appear as a negative number.

EXAMPLE 15.1C

A municipality issues ten-year bonds in the amount of $1 000 000. Interest on the bonds is 10% payable annually. What is the issue price of the bonds if the bonds are sold to yield 11% compounded quarterly?

SOLUTION

The principal of the bonds FV = 1 000 000.00;
the annual interest payment PMT = 1 000 000.00(0.10) = $100 000.00.

Since the interest payment period (annual) is not equal in length to the yield rate conversion period (quarterly), the interest payments form an ordinary general annuity.

$n = 10$; P/Y = 1; C/Y = 4; $c = \frac{4}{1} = 4$; I/Y = 11; $i = \frac{11\%}{4} = 2.75\% = 0.0275$;

$p = 1.0275^4 - 1 = 1.114621 - 1 = 0.114621 = 11.4621\%$

The present value of the redemption price

$$\begin{aligned} PV &= 1\,000\,000.00(1.114621^{-10}) \\ &= 1\,000\,000.00(0.337852) \\ &= \$337\,852.22 \end{aligned}$$

The present value of the annual interest payments

$$\begin{aligned} PV_{nc} &= 100\,000.00\left[\frac{(1 - 1.114621^{-10}}{0.114621}\right] \quad \text{——— using Formula 12.3} \\ &= 100\,000.00(5.776832) \\ &= \$577\,683.22 \end{aligned}$$

Programmed Solution

("END" mode) (Set P/Y = 1; C/Y = 4) [2nd] (CLR TVM) 1 000 000 [FV] 11 [I/Y] 10 [N] [CPT] [PV] [-337852.2208]

0 [FV] 100 000 [PMT] 11 [I/Y] 10 [N] [CPT] [PV] [577683.2174]

The issue price is 337 852.22 + 577 683.22 = $915 535.44.

We can modify Formula 15.1 to allow for the general annuity case by using Formula 12.3.

$$\text{PURCHASE PRICE} = P + A_{nc} = S(1+p)^{-n} + R\left[\frac{1-(1+p)^{-n}}{p}\right]$$

restated as

$$\text{PURCHASE PRICE} = PV + PV_{nc} = FV(1+p)^{-n} + PMT\left[\frac{1-(1+p)^{-n}}{p}\right] \quad \text{——— Formula 15.2}$$

where $p = (1+i)^c - 1$

C. Purchase price of bonds between interest dates

Bonds are not just purchased and sold on interest payment dates. In practice, most bonds are traded between interest dates.

In such cases, we can compute the price of the bond on the date of purchase by first finding the purchase price on the interest date immediately preceding the date of purchase. The resulting value can then be accumulated using the future value formula for simple interest at the bond rate for the number of days elapsed between the interest payment date and the purchase date.

EXAMPLE 15.1D A bond with a face value of \$1000 bearing interest at 6% payable semi-annually matures on August 1, 2012. What is the purchase price of the bond on April 18, 2010 to yield 5.4% compounded semi-annually?

SOLUTION

STEP 1 Find the purchase price on the preceding interest date.

The principal FV = \$1000.00;

the semi-annual coupon $PMT = 1000.00\left(\frac{0.06}{2}\right) = \$30.00.$

Since the maturity date is August 1, the semi-annual interest dates are February 1 and August 1. The interest date preceding the date of purchase is February 1, 2010. The time period from February 1, 2010 to the date of maturity is 2.5 years.

$n = 2.5(2) = 5;\ P/Y = 2;\ C/Y = 2;\ I/Y = 5.4;\ i = \frac{5.4\%}{2} = 2.7\% = 0.027$

The purchase price of the bond on February 1, 2010

$$= 1000.00(1.027^{-5}) + 30.00\left(\frac{1 - 1.027^{-5}}{0.027}\right)$$

$$= 1000.00(0.875282) + 30.00(4.619201)$$

$$= 875.28 + 138.58$$

$$= \$1013.86$$

Programmed Solution

("END" mode) (Set P/Y = 2; C/Y = 2) [2nd] (CLR TVM) 1000 [FV]

5.4 [I/Y] 5 [N] [CPT] [PV] [-875.281566]

0 [FV] 30 [PMT] 5.4 [I/Y] 5 [N] [CPT] [PV] [−138.576038]

The purchase price is 875.28 + 138.58 = \$1013.86.

STEP 2 Accumulate the interest on February 1, 2010 at simple interest based on the bond rate.

The number of days from February 1, 2010 to April 18, 2010 is 76; the number of days in the interest interval February 1, 2010 to August 1, 2010 is 181.

$PV = 1000.00;\quad r = i = 0.03;\quad t = \frac{76}{181}$

$$\text{Interest} = 1000.00\left[0.03\left(\frac{76}{181}\right)\right] = \$12.60$$

The purchase price of the bond on April 18, 2010 is \$1013.86 + 12.60 = \$1026.46.

The bonds are offered for sale at the **market price**. In the example above, the market price is \$1013.86. The total purchase price of \$1026.46 is called the **cash price** or purchase price. This price includes interest that has accrued from February 1, 2010 to April 18, 2010 but will not be paid until August 1, 2010.

CASH PRICE = MARKET PRICE + ACCRUED INTEREST

EXAMPLE 15.1E

A $5000 bond redeemable at par in seven years and four months bearing interest at 6.5% payable semi-annually is bought to yield 7.5% compounded semi-annually. Determine

(i) the market price;
(ii) the accrued interest;
(iii) the cash price.

SOLUTION

(i) The redemption price FV = $5000.00;

the semi-annual coupon PMT $= 5000.00\left(\frac{0.065}{2}\right) = \$162.50$.

The interest date preceding the purchase date is 7.5 years before maturity.

$n = 7.5(2) = 15$; P/Y = 2; C/Y = 2; I/Y = 7.5; $i = \frac{7.5\%}{2} = 3.75\% = 0.0375$

The purchase price on the interest date preceding the date of purchase

$$= 5000.00(1.0375^{-15}) + 162.50\left(\frac{1 - 1.0375^{-15}}{0.0375}\right)$$

$$= 5000.00(0.575676) + 162.50(11.315296)$$
$$= 2878.38 + 1838.74$$
$$= \$4717.12$$

Programmed Solution

("END" mode) (Set P/Y = 2; C/Y = 2) [2nd] (CLR TVM) 5000 [FV]

7.5 [I/Y] 15 [N] [CPT] [PV] [-2878.381956]

0 [FV] 162.50 [PMT] 7.5 [I/Y] 15 [N] [CPT] [PV] [−1838.735638]

The purchase price is 2878.38 + 1838.74 = $4717.12.

(ii) The accrued interest two months later

PV = 5000.00; $r = i = 0.0325$; $t = \frac{2}{6}$;

$$\text{Interest} = 5000.00\left[0.0325\left(\frac{2}{6}\right)\right] = \$54.17$$

(iii) The cash price two months later is $4717.12 + 54.17 = 4771.29.

EXERCISE 15.1

EXCEL NOTES

Excel has a ***Bond Purchase Price (PRICE)*** function you can use to find the price per $100 face value of a security that pays periodic interest. If you choose, you can use this function to answer the questions in Part A and Part B below. Refer to **PRICE** on the Spreadsheet Template Disk to learn how to use this Excel function.

A. Determine the purchase price at the indicated time before maturity of each of the bonds redeemed at par shown in the table below.

	Par Value	Bond Rate Payable Semi-annually	Time Before Maturity	Yield Rate	Conversion Period
1.	$100 000	7%	5.5 years	7.5%	semi-annually
2.	5 000	8	12 years	7	semi-annually
3.	25 000	6	7 years	7	semi-annually
4.	1 000	8.5	12.5 years	8	semi-annually
5.	50 000	6.5	10 years	6	annually
6.	20 000	7.5	6.5 years	8	quarterly
7.	8 000	8	18.5 years	9	monthly
8.	3 000	6	20 years	8	quarterly

EXCEL NOTES

Excel has a number of functions you can choose to answer the questions in Part B below: ***Days Since Last Interest Date (COUPDAYBS)***, ***Total Number of Days in the Coupon Period (COUPDAYS)***, and ***Total Number of Remaining Coupon Periods (COUPNUM)***. Refer to **COUPDAYBS, COUPDAYS,** and **COUPNUM** on the Spreadsheet Template Disk to learn how to use these Excel functions.

B. Answer each of the following questions.

1. A $500 bond matures on March 1, 2014. Interest is 6% payable semi-annually. Find the purchase price of the bond on September 1, 2008 to yield 7.5% compounded semi-annually. Reference Example 15.1A

2. A $25 000, 10% bond is purchased twelve years before maturity to yield 7% compounded semi-annually. If the bond interest is payable semi-annually, what is the purchase price of the bond?

3. A $15 000, 7.5% bond is purchased six years and six months before maturity to yield 8% semi-annually. If the bond interest is payable semi-annually, what is the purchase price of the bond?

4. A $5000, 6% bond is purchased thirteen years before maturity to yield 6.5% semi-annually. If the bond interest is payable semi-annually, what is the purchase price of the bond?

5. A $10 000, 9% bond is purchased nine years and six months before maturity to yield 8.5% semi-annually. If the bond interest is payable semi-annually, what is the purchase price of the bond?

6. A $2000, 5.5% bond is purchased six years before maturity to yield 7.5% semi-annually. If the bond interest is payable semi-annually, what is the purchase price of the bond?

7. A 25-year bond issue of $5 000 000 and bearing interest at 7.25% payable annually is sold to yield 8.5% compounded semi-annually. What is the issue price of the bonds?

8. A $100 000 bond bearing interest at 6.75% payable semi-annually is bought eight years before maturity to yield 7.35% compounded annually. If the bond is redeemable at par, what is the purchase price?

9. Bonds with a maturity value of $40 000 in 7.5 years bearing interest at 8% payable quarterly are sold to yield 6.8% compounded semi-annually. Determine the purchase price of the bonds.

10. Six $1000 bonds with 7.4% coupons payable semi-annually are bought to yield 6.3% compounded monthly. If the bonds mature in eight years, what is the purchase price?

11. A $1000, 9% bond is purchased 8.5 years before maturity to yield 6.5% compounded semi-annually. If the bond interest is payable semi-annually, what is the purchase price of the bond?

12. A $100 000 bond is redeemable at par in fifteen years. If interest on the bond is 7.5% payable semi-annually, what is the purchase price to yield 8% compounded semi-annually?

13. A $25 000, 10% bond redeemable at par on December 1, 2021 is purchased on September 25, 2010 to yield 7.6% compounded semi-annually. Bond interest is payable semi-annually.
(a) What is the quoted price of the bond?
(b) What is the accrued interest?
(c) What is the cash price?

Reference Example 15.1D

14. A $100 000 bond redeemable at par on October 1, 2030 is purchased on January 15, 2009. Interest is 5.9% payable semi-annually and the yield is 9% compounded semi-annually.
(a) What is the quoted price of the bond?
(b) What is the accrued interest?
(c) What is the cash price?

15.2 PREMIUM AND DISCOUNT

A. Basic concepts—bond rate versus yield (or market) rate

A comparison of the redemption values with the purchase prices obtained in Examples 15.1A to 15.1E (see Table 15.1) shows that the purchase price is sometimes less than and sometimes more than the principal.

Table 15.1 **Comparison of Redemption Values with Purchase Prices for Examples 15.1A to 15.1E**

Example	Principal Value FV	Purchase Price PP	Comparison of FV and PP	Premium or Discount	Amount of Premium or Discount	Bond Rate b	Yield Rate i	b Versus i
15.1A	$ 1 000	$ 965.63	FV > PP	discount	$ 34.37	3%	3.5%	$b < i$
15.1B	5 000	5 262.78	PP > FV	premium	262.78	3.25	2.9	$b > i$
15.1C	1 000 000	915 535.44	FV > PP	discount	84 464.56	10	11.46	$b < i$
15.1D	1 000	1 013.86	PP > FV	premium	13.86	3	2.7	$b > i$
15.1E	5 000	4 717.12	FV > PP	discount	282.88	3.25	3.75	$b < i$

If the purchase price of a bond is greater than the principal, the bond is said to be bought at a premium and the difference between the purchase price and the principal is called the **premium.**

PREMIUM = PURCHASE PRICE − PRINCIPAL
where purchase price > principal

If the purchase price of a bond is less than the principal, the bond is said to be bought at a discount and the difference between the principal and the purchase price is called the **discount.**

DISCOUNT = PRINCIPAL − PURCHASE PRICE
where principal > purchase price

An examination of the size of the bond rate b relative to the size of the market rate i shows that this relationship determines whether there is a premium or discount.

The bond rate (or coupon rate) stated on the bond is the percent of the *face* value of the bond that will be paid at the end of each interest period to the bondholder. This rate is established at the time of issue of the bonds and remains the same throughout the term of the bond.

On the other hand, the rate at which lenders are willing to provide money fluctuates in response to economic conditions. The combination of factors at work in the capital market at any given time in conjunction with the perceived risk associated with a particular bond determines the yield rate (or market rate) for a bond and thus the price at which a bond will be bought or sold.

The bond rate and the market rate are usually *not* equal. However, if the two rates happen to be equal, then bonds that are redeemable at par will sell at their face value. If the bond rate is *less* than the market rate, the bond will sell at a price less than the face value, that is, at a *discount.* If the bond rate is *greater* than the market rate, the bond will sell at a price above its face value, that is, at a *premium.*

Conversely, if a bond is redeemable at par (i.e., at 100), purchasers will realize the bond rate if they pay 100. They will realize less than the bond rate if they buy at a premium and more than the bond rate if they buy at a discount.

At any time, one of three possible situations exists for any given bond:

(1) Bond rate = Market rate ($b = i$)	The bond sells at *par.*
(2) Bond rate < Market rate ($b < i$)	The bond sells at a *discount.*
(3) Bond rate > Market rate ($b > i$)	The bond sells at a *premium.*

EXAMPLE 15.2A

A $10 000 bond is redeemable at par and bears interest at 10% compounded semi-annually.

(i) What is the purchase price ten years before maturity if the market rate compounded semi-annually is
(a) 10%; (b) 12%; (c) 8%?

(ii) What is the purchase price five years before maturity if the market rate compounded semi-annually is
(a) 10%; (b) 12%; (c) 8%?

SOLUTION

(i) FV = 10 000.00; PMT = 10 000.00(0.05) = 500.00; $n = 10(2) = 20$; $b = 5\%$

(a) $i = \frac{10\%}{2} = 5\% = 0.05;\ (b = i)$

$$\text{Purchase price} = 10\,000.00(1.05^{-20}) + 500.00\left(\frac{1 - 1.05^{-20}}{0.05}\right)$$
$$= 10\,000.00(0.376889) + 500.00(12.46221)$$
$$= 3768.89 + 6231.11$$
$$= \$10\,000.00$$

Programmed Solution

("END" mode) (Set P/Y = 2; C/Y = 2) [2nd] (CLR TVM) 10 000 [FV]

10 [I/Y] 20 [N] [CPT] [PV] [-3768.894829]

0 [FV] 500 [PMT] 10 [I/Y] 20 [N] [CPT] [PV] [-6231.105171]

The purchase price is 3768.89 + 6231.11 = $10 000.00.
The bond sells at par.

(b) $i = \frac{12\%}{2} = 6\% = 0.06;\ (b < i)$

$$\text{Purchase price} = 10\,000.00(1.06^{-20}) + 500.00\left(\frac{1 - 1.06^{-20}}{0.06}\right)$$
$$= 10\,000.00(0.311805) + 500.00(11.469921)$$
$$= 3118.05 + 5734.96$$
$$= \$8853.01$$

Programmed Solution

("END" mode) (Set P/Y = 2; C/Y = 2) [2nd] (CLR TVM) 10 000 [FV]

12 [I/Y] 20 [N] [CPT] [PV] [-3118.047269]

0 [FV] 500 [PMT] 12 [I/Y] 20 [N] [CPT] [PV] [-5734.960609]

The purchase price is 3118.05 + 5734.96 = $8853.01.
The bond sells below par.
The discount is 10 000.00 − 8853.01 = $1146.99.

(c) $i = \frac{8\%}{2} = 4\% = 0.04; \quad (b > i)$

$$\text{Purchase price} = 10\,000.00(1.04^{-20}) + 500.00\left(\frac{1 - 1.04^{-20}}{0.04}\right)$$

$$= 10\,000.00(0.456387) + 500.00(13.590326)$$
$$= 4563.87 + 6795.16$$
$$= \$11\,359.03$$

Programmed Solution

("END" mode) (Set P/Y = 2; C/Y = 2) [2nd] (CLR TVM) 10 000 [FV]

8 [I/Y] 20 [N] [CPT] [PV] [–4563.869462]

0 [FV] 500 [PMT] 8 [I/Y] 20 [N] [CPT] [PV] [–6795.163172]

The purchase price 4563.87 + 6795.16 = $11 359.03.
The bond sells above par.
The premium 11 359.03 − 10 000.00 = $1359.03.

(ii) FV = 10 000.00; PMT = 500.00; $n = 5(2) = 10$; $b = 5\%$

(a) $i = 5\%$ ($b = \text{i}$)

$$\text{Purchase price} = 10\,000.00(1.05^{-10}) + 500.00\left(\frac{1 - 1.05^{-10}}{0.05}\right)$$

$$= 6139.13 + 3860.87$$
$$= \$10\,000.00$$

Programmed Solution

("END" mode) (Set P/Y = 2; C/Y = 2) [2nd] (CLR TVM) 10 000 [FV]

10 [I/Y] 10 [N] [CPT] [PV] [–6139.132535]

0 [FV] 500 [PMT] 10 [I/Y] 10 [N] [CPT] [PV] [–3860.867465]

The purchase price is 6139.13 + 3860.87 = $10 000.00.
The bond sells at par.

(b) $i = 6\%$; $(b < i)$

$$\text{Purchase price} = 10\,000.00(1.06^{-10}) + 500.00\left(\frac{1 - 1.06^{-10}}{0.06}\right)$$

$$= 5583.95 + 3680.04$$
$$= \$9263.99$$

Programmed Solution

("END" mode) (Set P/Y = 2; C/Y = 2) [2nd] (CLR TVM) 10 000 [FV]

12 [I/Y] 10 [N] [CPT] [PV] [-5583.947769]

0 [FV] 500 [PMT] 12 [I/Y] 10 [N] [CPT] [PV] [-3680.043526]

The purchase price is 5583.95 + 3680.04 = \$9263.99.

The bond sells below par.

The discount is 10 000.00 − 9263.99 = \$736.01. It is smaller than in part (i) because the time to maturity is shorter.

(c) $i = 4\%$; $(b > i)$

$$\text{Purchase price} = 10\,000.00(1.04^{-10}) + 500.00\left(\frac{1 - 1.04^{-10}}{0.04}\right)$$

$$= 6755.64 + 4055.45$$
$$= \$10\,811.09$$

Programmed Solution

("END" mode) (Set P/Y = 2; C/Y = 2) [2nd] (CLR TVM) 10 000 [FV]

8 [I/Y] 10 [N] [CPT] [PV] [-6755.641688]

0 [FV] 500 [PMT] 8 [I/Y] 10 [N] [CPT] [PV] [-4055.44789]

The purchase price is 6755.64 + 4055.45 = \$10 811.09.

The bond sells above par.

The premium is 10 811.09 – 10 000.00 = \$811.09. It is smaller than in part (i) because the time to maturity is shorter.

B. Direct method of computing the premium or discount—alternative method for finding the purchase price

EXAMPLE 15.2B

A \$5000, 7% bond with semi-annual interest coupons is bought six years before maturity to yield 5.6% compounded semi-annually. Determine the premium or discount.

SOLUTION

$FV = 5000.00$; $P/Y = 2$; $C/Y = 2$; $I/Y = 5.6$; $b = \frac{7\%}{2} = 3.5\% = 0.035$;

$PMT = 5000.00(0.035) = 175.00$; $i = \frac{5.6\%}{2} = 2.8\% = 0.028$; $n = 6(2) = 12$

Since $b > i$, the bond will sell at a premium.

$$\text{Purchase price} = 5000.00(1.028^{-12}) + 175.00\left(\frac{1 - 1.028^{-12}}{0.028}\right)$$

$$= 5000.00(0.717931) + 175.00(10.073898)$$
$$= 3589.65 + 1762.93$$
$$= \$5352.58$$

Programmed Solution

("END" mode) (Set P/Y = 2; C/Y = 2) [2nd] (CLR TVM) 5000 [FV] 5.6 [I/Y]

12 [N] [CPT] [PV] [-3589.65432]

0 [FV] 175 [PMT] 5.6 [I/Y] 12 [N] [CPT] [PV] [−1762.932101]

The purchase price is 3589.66 + 1762.93 = \$5352.59.

The premium is 5352.59 − 5000.00 = \$352.59.

While you can always determine the premium by the basic method using Formula 15.1, it is more convenient to determine the premium directly by considering the relationship between the bond rate b and the yield rate i.

As previously discussed, a premium results when $b > i$. When this is the case, the premium is paid because the periodic interest payments received exceed the periodic interest required according to the yield rate.

In Example 15.2B

The semi-annual interest payment	5000.00(0.035) = \$175.00
The required semi-annual interest based on the yield rate	5000.00(0.028) = 140.00
The excess of the actual interest received over the required interest to make the yield rate	= \$ 35.00

This excess is received at the end of every payment interval; thus it forms an ordinary annuity whose present value can be computed at the yield rate i.

PMT (the excess interest) = 35.00; $i = 2.8\%$; $n = 12$

$$PV_n = 35.00\left(\frac{1 - 1.028^{-12}}{0.028}\right)$$
$$= 35.00(10.073898)$$
$$= \$352.59$$

Programmed Solution

("END" mode) (Set P/Y = 2; C/Y = 2) 0 [FV] 35 [PMT] 5.6 [I/Y]

12 [N] [CPT] [PV] [−352.58642]

The premium is \$352.59.

The purchase price is 5000.00 + 352.59 = \$5352.59.

The premium is the present value of the ordinary annuity formed by the excess of the actual bond interest over the required interest based on the yield rate. We can obtain the purchase price by adding the premium to the principal.

$$\text{PREMIUM} = (\text{PERIODIC BOND INTEREST} - \text{REQUIRED INTEREST})\left[\frac{1-(1+i)^{-n}}{i}\right]$$

$$= (\text{FACE VALUE} \times b - \text{REDEMPTION PRICE} \times i)\left[\frac{1-(1+i)^{-n}}{i}\right]$$

EXAMPLE 15.2C

A $5000, 6% bond with semi-annual interest coupons is bought six years before maturity to yield 8% compounded semi-annually. Determine the premium or discount.

SOLUTION

$FV = 5000.00;\quad P/Y = 2;\quad C/Y = 2;\quad b = \frac{6\%}{2} = 3\% = 0.03;$

$PMT = 5000.00(0.03) = 150.00;\quad I/Y = 8;\quad i = \frac{8\%}{2} = 4\% = 0.04;$

$n = 6(2) = 12$

Since $b < i$, the bond will sell at a discount.

$$\begin{aligned}\text{Purchase price} &= 5000.00(1.04^{-12}) + 150.00\left(\frac{1-1.04^{-12}}{0.04}\right)\\ &= 5000.00(0.624597) + 150.00(9.385074)\\ &= 3122.99 + 1407.76\\ &= \$4530.75\end{aligned}$$

Programmed Solution

("END" mode) (Set P/Y = 2; C/Y = 2) [2nd] (CLR TVM) 5000 [FV]

8 [I/Y] 12 [N] [CPT] [PV] [-3122.985248]

0 [FV] 150 [PMT] 8 [I/Y] 12 [N] [CPT] [PV] [-1407.761064]

The purchase price is 3122.99 + 1407.76 = $4530.75.
The discount is 5000.00 − 4530.75 = $469.25.

As in the case of a premium, while you can always determine the discount by the basic method using Formula 15.1, it is more convenient to determine the discount directly.

When $b < i$, a discount results. The discount on a bond is received because the periodic interest payments are less than the periodic interest required to earn the yield rate.

In Example 15.2C

The semi-annual interest payment	5000.00(0.03) = $150.00
The required semi-annual interest based on the yield rate	5000.00(0.04) = 200.00
The shortage of the actual interest received compared to the required interest based on the yield rate	= $ 50.00

This shortage occurs at the end of every interest payment interval; it forms an ordinary annuity whose present value can be computed at the yield rate i.

$\text{PMT} = 50.00; \quad i = 4\%; \quad n = 12$

$$
\begin{aligned}
\text{PV}_n &= 50.00\left(\frac{1 - 1.04^{-12}}{0.04}\right) \\
&= 50.00(9.385074) \\
&= \$469.25
\end{aligned}
$$

Programmed Solution

("END" mode) (Set P/Y = 2; C/Y = 2) 0 FV 50 PMT 8 I/Y

12 N CPT PV -469.253686

The discount is \$469.25.

The purchase price is 5000.00 − 469.25 = \$4530.75.

The discount is the present value of the ordinary annuity formed by the shortage of the actual bond interest received as compared to the required interest based on the yield rate. We can obtain the purchase price by subtracting the discount from the principal.

$$
\begin{aligned}
\text{DISCOUNT} &= (\text{REQUIRED INTEREST} - \text{PERIODIC BOND INTEREST})\left[\frac{1-(1+i)^{-n}}{i}\right] \\
&= -(\text{PERIODIC BOND INTEREST} - \text{REQUIRED INTEREST})\left[\frac{1-(1+i)^{-n}}{i}\right] \\
&= -(\text{FACE VALUE} \times b - \text{REDEMPTION PRICE} \times i)\left[\frac{1-(1+i)^{-n}}{i}\right]
\end{aligned}
$$

Since in both cases the difference between the periodic bond interest and the required interest is involved, the premium or discount on the purchase of a bond can be obtained using the same relationship.

$$
\text{PREMIUM or DISCOUNT} = (b \times \text{FACE VALUE} - i \times \text{REDEMPTION PRICE})\left[\frac{1-(1+i)^{-n}}{i}\right]
$$

Formula 15.3

EXAMPLE 15.2D

A \$1000, 8.5% bond with semi-annual interest coupons redeemable at par in fifteen years is bought to yield 7% compounded semi-annually. Determine

(i) the premium or discount;

(ii) the purchase price.

SOLUTION

(i) $\text{FV} = 1000.00; \quad \text{P/Y} = 2; \quad \text{C/Y} = 2; \quad b = \frac{8.5\%}{2} = 4.25\% = 0.0425;$

$\text{PMT} = 1000.00(0.0425) = 42.50; \quad \text{I/Y} = 7; \quad i = \frac{7\%}{2} = 3.5\% = 0.035;$

$n = 15(2) = 30$

Since $b > i$, the bond will sell at a premium.

The required interest based on the yield rate is 1000.00(0.035) = 35.00; the excess interest is 42.50 − 35.00 = 7.50.

The premium is $7.50\left(\frac{1 - 1.035^{-30}}{0.035}\right) = 7.50(18.392045) = \$137.94$.

Programmed Solution

("END" mode) (Set P/Y = 2; C/Y = 2) 0 [FV] 7.50 [PMT] 7 [I/Y]

30 [N] [CPT] [PV] [−137.940341]

(ii) The purchase price is 1000.00 + 137.94 = $1137.94.

EXAMPLE 15.2E

A $50 000, 7.2% bond with quarterly interest coupons redeemable at par in ten years is purchased to yield 8% compounded quarterly.

(i) What is the premium or discount?

(ii) What is the purchase price?

SOLUTION

(i) FV = 50 000.00; P/Y = 4; C/Y = 4; $b = \frac{7.2\%}{4} = 1.8\% = 0.018$;

$n = 10(4) = 40$; I/Y = 8; $i = \frac{8\%}{4} = 2\% = 0.02$

Since $b < i$, the bond will sell at a discount.

$$\text{Discount} = (0.018 \times 50\,000.00 - 0.02 \times 50\,000.00)\left(\frac{1 - 1.02^{-40}}{0.02}\right)$$

using Formula 15.3

$$= (900.00 - 1000.00)(27.355479)$$
$$= (-100.00)(27.355479)$$
$$= -\$2735.55$$

the negative sign indicates a discount

Programmed Solution

("END" mode)

First compute PMT = (0.018 × 50 000) − (0.02 × 50 000) = −100.00

(Set P/Y = 4; C/Y = 4) 0 [FV] 100 [PMT] 8 [I/Y] 40

[N] [CPT] [PV] [−2735.547924]

(ii) The purchase price is 50 000.00 − 2735.55 = $47 264.45.

EXERCISE 15.2

EXCEL NOTES

If you choose, you can use these Excel functions to answer the questions indicated below: ***Bond Purchase Price (PRICE), Days Since Last Interest Date (COUPDAYBS), Total Number of Days in the Coupon Period (COUPDAYS),*** and ***Total Number of Remaining Coupon Periods (COUPNUM).*** Refer to **PRICE, COUPDAYBS, COUPDAYS,** and **COUPNUM** on the Spreadsheet Template Disk to learn how to use these Excel functions.

A. For each of the six bonds redeemed at par in the table below, use Formula 15.3 to determine
(a) the premium or discount;
(b) the purchase price.

	Par Value	Bond Rate Payable Semi-annually	Time Before Maturity	Yield Rate Compounded Semi-annually
1.	$25 000	6%	10 years	9%
2.	5 000	8.5	8 years	7
3.	10 000	9	15 years	11
4.	7 000	9	5 years	8.5

B. Answer each of the following questions.

1. A $100 000, 8% bond redeemable at par with quarterly coupons is purchased to yield 6.5% compounded quarterly. Find the premium or discount and the purchase price if the bond is purchased
(a) fifteen years before maturity;
(b) five years before maturity. Reference Example 15.2A

2. A $5000, 7.5% bond redeemable at par with semi-annual coupons is purchased to yield 6% compounded semi-annually. What is the premium or discount and the purchase price if the bond is bought
(a) ten years before maturity?
(b) six years before maturity?

3. A $25 000, 9% bond redeemable at par with interest payable annually is bought six years before maturity. Determine the premium or discount and the purchase price if the bond is purchased to yield
(a) 13.5% compounded annually;
(b) 6% compounded annually.

4. A $1000, 8% bond redeemable at par in seven years bears coupons payable annually. Compute the premium or discount and the purchase price if the yield, compounded annually, is
(a) 6.5%;
(b) 7.5%;
(c) 8.5%.

5. A $5 000 000 issue of ten-year bonds redeemable at par offers 7.25% coupons payable semi-annually. What is the issue price of the bonds to yield 8.4% compounded monthly? Reference Example 15.2D

6. A $3000 issue of nine-year bonds redeemable at par offers 7.5% coupons paid semi-annually. What is the issue price of the bonds to yield 10.5% semi-annually?
7. Twenty $5000 bonds redeemable at par bearing 8.4% coupons payable quarterly are sold eight years before maturity to yield 8.0% compounded annually. What is the purchase price of the bonds?
8. Sixty $1000 bonds redeemable at par bearing 7% coupons payable semi-annually are sold seven years before maturity to yield 9.5% compounded semi-annually. What is the purchase price of the bonds?

BUSINESS MATH NEWS BOX

Making It Last—Stretching Your Retirement Savings

Your retirement is here at last, and all those years of saving are over. The question now is, how much can you spend?

The answer hinges on how your resources match up against your ambitions. Begin by deciding on the lifestyle you would like. Will you travel? Take up gardening or another, more expensive, hobby? Perhaps you plan to downsize to a smaller home. Do you foresee major debts such as home renovation or medical bills? And do you plan on spending most of your hard-earned money, or will you save some of it for your heirs?

Write down all the expenses involved in the retirement you would like, including monthly payments on your mortgage and any other debts. No item should escape notice, including clothing, entertainment, and drug and dental expenses, if not covered by a pension plan. It may help to track your expenses for a few months, says Prime. "Carry a little book, and every time you spend something, write it down."

Now the big question: how much can you withdraw from your savings each year without reducing the value of your portfolio? Many retirees blithely assume that they will be able to draw out 10% or more a year of their assets—$50 000 a year, say, on a $500 000 portfolio.

Not so. A high withdrawal rate can quickly run down your savings if the stock market goes down and stays down for two or three years. Most studies show that you should count on withdrawing no more than 4% of your assets each year if you want your money to last through a typical 30-year retirement. More aggressive withdrawal strategies may approach 5%, but 6% is pushing it.

Source: Susanne Ruder, "Making It Last," *MoneySense* 7(6) (December 2005/January 2006), p. S34.

QUESTIONS

1. Calculate the number of years a $500 000 investment would last given a $50 000-per-year withdrawal. Assume interest on the investment averages 4.5% per annum, compounded monthly.
2. If you desired to withdraw from this $500 000 plan on a monthly basis, what amount could be withdrawn in order to satisfy a 30-year retirement? Assume a 4.5% interest compounded monthly.
3. You wish to live comfortably with an annual retirement income of $60 000 per year for 30 years. What monthly payments are required to develop this retirement plan over a 25-year period using a 3.8% interest rate compounded quarterly?
4. Given an initial investment of $75 000 and a retirement plan goal of $740 000 in 25 years, calculate the quarterly contributions required at 4.2% compounded quarterly.

15.3 BOND SCHEDULES

A. Amortization of premium

If a bond is purchased for more than the principal, the resulting premium is not recovered when the bond is redeemed at maturity, so it becomes a capital *loss*. To avoid the capital loss at maturity, the premium is written down or expensed gradually over the period from the date of purchase to the maturity date. The writing down of the premium gradually reduces the bond's book value until it equals the principal at the date of maturity.

The process of writing down the premium is called **amortization of the premium**. The most direct method of amortizing a premium assigns the difference between the interest received (coupon) and the interest required according to the yield rate to write down the premium. The details of writing down the premium are often shown in a tabulation referred to as a *schedule of amortization of premium*.

EXAMPLE 15.3A

A \$1000, 12% bond redeemable at par matures in three years. The coupons are payable semi-annually and the bond is bought to yield 10% compounded semi-annually.

(i) Compute the purchase price.

(ii) Construct a schedule of amortization of premium.

SOLUTION

(i) FV = 1000.00; $n = 3(2) = 6$; P/Y = 2; C/Y = 2;

$$b = \frac{12\%}{2} = 6\% = 0.06; \quad \text{I/Y} = 10; \quad i = \frac{10\%}{2} = 5\% = 0.05$$

Since $b > i$, the bond sells at a premium.

$$\begin{aligned}\text{Premium} &= (0.06 \times 1000.00) - (0.05 \times 1000.00)\left(\frac{1 - 1.05^{-6}}{0.05}\right)\\ &= (60.00 - 50.00)(5.075692)\\ &= (10.00)(5.075692)\\ &= \$50.76\end{aligned}$$

Programmed Solution

PMT = (0.06 × 1000.00) − (0.05 × 1000.00) = 10.00

("END" mode)

(Set P/Y = 2; C/Y = 2) 0 [FV] 10 [PMT] 10 [I/Y]

6 [N] [CPT] [PV] [−50.756921]

The purchase price is 1000.00 + 50.76 = \$1050.76.

(ii) ***Schedule of amortization of premium***

End of Interest Payment Interval	Bond Interest Recevied (Coupon) $b = 6\%$	Interest on Book Value at Yield Rate $i = 5\%$	Amount of Premium Amortized	Book Value of Bond	Remaining Premium
0				1050.76	50.76
1	60.00	52.54	7.46	1043.30	43.30
2	60.00	52.17	7.83	1035.47	35.47
3	60.00	51.77	8.23	1027.24	27.24
4	60.00	51.36	8.64	1018.60	18.60
5	60.00	50.93	9.07	1009.53	9.53
6	60.00	50.47	9.53	1000.00	0.00
TOTAL	360.00	309.24	50.76		

Explanations of schedule

1. The original book value shown is the purchase price of $1050.76.

2. At the end of the first interest payment interval, the interest received (coupon) is 1000.00(0.06) = $60.00; the interest required according to the yield rate is 1050.76(0.05) = $52.54; the difference 60.00 − 52.54 = 7.46 is used to write down the premium to $43.30 and reduces the book value from $1050.76 to $1043.30.

3. The coupon at the end of the second interest payment interval is again $60. The interest required according to the yield rate is 1043.30(0.05) = $52.17; the difference 60.00 − 52.17 = 7.83 reduces the premium to $35.47 and the book value of the bond to $1035.47.

4. Continue in a similar manner until the maturity date when the principal is reached. If a rounding error becomes apparent at the end of the final interest payment interval, adjust the final interest on the book value at the yield rate to make the premium zero and to obtain the exact principal as the book value.

5. The totals provide useful accounting information showing the total interest received ($360) and the net income realized ($309.24).

B. Accumulation of discount

If a bond is bought at less than the principal, there will be a gain at the time of redemption equal to the amount of discount. It is generally accepted accounting practice that this gain does not accrue in total to the accounting period in which the bond is redeemed. Instead, some of the gain accrues to each of the accounting periods from the date of purchase to the date of redemption.

To adhere to this practice, the discount is decreased gradually so that the book value of the bond increases gradually until, at the date of redemption, the discount is reduced to zero while the book value equals the principal. The process of reducing the discount so as to increase the book value is called **accumulation of discount.**

In the case of discount, the interest required according to the yield rate is greater than the actual interest received (the coupon). Similar to amortization of a premium, the most direct method of accumulating a discount assigns the difference between the interest required by the yield rate and the coupon to reduce the discount. The details of decreasing the discount while increasing the book value of a bond are often shown in a tabulation called a *schedule of accumulation of discount.*

EXAMPLE 15.3B

A $10 000 bond, redeemable at par in four years with 5.5% coupons payable semi-annually, is bought to yield 7% compounded semi-annually.

(i) Determine the discount and the purchase price.

(ii) Construct a schedule of accumulation of discount.

SOLUTION

(i) FV = 10 000.00; $n = 4(2) = 8$; P/Y = 2; C/Y = 2;

$b = \frac{5.5\%}{2} = 2.75\% = 0.0275$; I/Y = 7; $i = \frac{7\%}{2} = 3.5\% = 0.035$

Since $b < i$, the bond sells at a discount.

$$\text{Discount} = (0.0275 \times 10\,000.00) - (0.035 \times 10\,000.00)\left(\frac{1 - 1.035^{-8}}{0.035}\right)$$
$$= (275.00 - 350.00)(6.873956)$$
$$= (-75.00)(6.873956)$$
$$= -\$515.55$$

Programmed Solution

PMT = (0.0275 × 10 000) − (0.035 × 10 000) = 275.00

("END" mode)

(Set P/Y = 2; C/Y = 2) 0 [FV] 75 [PMT] 7 [I/Y]

8 [N] [CPT] [PV] [−515.546665]

The purchase price is 10 000.00 − 515.55 = $9484.45.

(ii) ***Schedule of accumulation of discount***

End of Interest Payment Interval	Coupon $b = 2.75\%$	Interest on Book Value at Yield Rate $i = 3.5\%$	Amount of Discount Accumulated	Book Value of Bond	Remaining Discount
0				9484.55	515.55
1	275.00	331.96	56.96	9541.41	458.59
2	275.00	333.95	58.95	9600.36	399.64
3	275.00	336.01	61.01	9661.37	338.63
4	275.00	338.15	63.15	9724.52	275.48
5	275.00	340.36	65.36	9789.88	210.12
6	275.00	342.65	67.65	9857.53	142.47
7	275.00	345.01	70.01	9927.54	72.46
8	275.00	347.46	72.46	10 000.00	0.00
TOTAL	2200.00	2715.55	515.55		

Explanations of schedule

1. The original book value shown is the purchase price of \$9484.55.
2. At the end of the first interest payment interval, the coupon is 10 000.00(0.0275) = \$275; the interest required according to the yield rate is 9484.55(0.035) = \$331.96; the difference used to reduce the discount and to increase the book value is 331.96 − 275.00 = \$56.96; the book value is 9484.55+ 56.96 = \$9541.41; and the remaining discount is 515.55 − 56.96 = \$458.59.
3. The coupon at the end of the second interest payment interval is again \$275; the interest required on the book value is 9541.41(0.035) = \$333.95; the difference is 333.95 − 275.00 = \$58.95; the book value is 9541.41 + 58.95 = \$9600.36; and the remaining discount is 458.59 − 58.95 = \$399.64.
4. Continue in a similar manner until the maturity date when the principal is reached. If a rounding error becomes apparent at the end of the final interest payment interval, adjust the final interest on the book value at the yield rate to make the remaining discount equal to zero and obtain the exact principal as the book value.
5. The totals provide useful accounting information showing the total interest received (\$2200) and the net income realized (\$2715.55).

C. Book value of a bond—finding the gain or loss on the sale of a bond

EXAMPLE 15.3C

A \$10 000, 8% bond redeemable at par with semi-annual coupons was purchased fifteen years before maturity to yield 6% compounded semi-annually. The bond was sold three years later at 101.25. Find the gain or loss on the sale of the bond.

SOLUTION

The market quotation of 101.25 indicates that the bond was sold at 101.25% of its face value. The proceeds from the sale of the bond are 10 000.00(1.0125) = \$10 125. To find the gain or loss on the sale of the bond, we need to know the book value of the bond at the date of sale. This we can do by determining the original purchase price, constructing a bond schedule, and reading the book value at the time of sale from the schedule.

$FV = 10\,000.00; \quad n = 15(2) = 30$

$P/Y = 2; \quad C/Y = 2; \quad I/Y = 6; \quad b = \frac{8\%}{2} = 4\% = 0.04; \quad i = \frac{6\%}{2} = 3\% = 0.03$

Since $b > i$, the bond was bought at a premium.

$$\begin{aligned}\text{Premium} &= (0.04 \times 10\,000.00) - (0.03 \times 10\,000.00)\left(\frac{1 - 1.03^{-30}}{0.03}\right)\\ &= (400.00 - 300.00)(19.600441)\\ &= (100.00)(19.600441)\\ &= \$1960.04\end{aligned}$$

Programmed Solution

PMT = (0.04 × 10 000) – (0.03 × 10 000) = 100.00

("END" mode)

(Set P/Y = 2; C/Y = 2) 0 [FV] 100 [PMT] 6 [I/Y] 30 [N]

[CPT] [PV] [−1960.044135]

The purchase price is 10 000.00 + 1960.04 = $11 960.04.

Schedule of amortization of premium

End of Interest Payment Interval	Coupon $b = 4\%$	Interest on Book Value at Yield Rate $i = 3\%$	Amount of Premium Amortized	Book Value of Bond	Remaining Premium
0				11 960.04	1960.04
1	400.00	358.80	41.20	11 918.84	1918.84
2	400.00	357.57	42.43	11 876.41	1876.41
3	400.00	356.29	43.71	11 832.70	1832.70
4	400.00	354.98	45.02	11 787.68	1787.68
5	400.00	353.63	46.37	11 741.31	1741.31
6	400.00	352.24	47.76	11 693.55	1693.55
	etc.				

The book value after three years (six semi-annual periods) is $11 693.55. Since the book value is greater than the proceeds, the loss on the sale of the bond is 11 693.55 – 10 125.00 = $1568.55.

We can solve this problem more quickly by computing the book value directly. The book value of a bond at a given time is the purchase price of the bond on that date. We can determine the book value of a bond without constructing a bond schedule by using Formula 15.1 or 15.3. This approach can also be used to verify book values in a bond schedule.

$FV = 10\,000.00;\ n = (15 - 3)(2) = 24;\ b = 4\%;\ i = 3\%$

$$\text{Premium} = (0.04 \times 10\,000.00) - (0.03 \times 10\,000.00)\left(\frac{1 - 1.03^{-24}}{0.03}\right)$$

$$= (100.00)(16.935542) = \$1693.55$$

Programmed Solution

PMT = (0.04 × 10 000) – (0.03 × 10 000) = 100.00

("END" mode)

(Set P/Y = 2; C/Y = 2) 0 [FV] 100 [PMT] 6 [I/Y]

24 [N] [CPT] [PV] [−1693.554212]

The purchase price is 10 000.00 + 1693.55 = $11 693.55.
The loss on the sale is 11 693.55 – 10 125.00 = $1568.55.

EXERCISE 15.3

If you choose, you can use these Excel functions to answer the questions indicated below: ***Bond Purchase Price (PRICE), Days Since Last Interest Date (COUPDAYBS), Total Number of Days in the Coupon Period (COUPDAYS),*** and ***Total Number of Remaining Coupon Periods (COUPNUM)***. Refer to **PRICE, COUPDAYBS, COUPDAYS,** and **COUPNUM** on the Spreadsheet Template Disk to learn how to use these Excel functions.

A. For each of the following bonds, compute the premium or discount and the purchase price, and construct the appropriate bond schedule.

1. A $5000, 6% bond redeemable at par in three-and-a-half years with semi-annual coupons is purchased to yield 6.5% compounded semi-annually. Reference Example 15.3B
2. A $25 000 bond with interest at 12.5% payable quarterly redeemable at par is bought two years before maturity to yield 11% compounded quarterly.
3. A $1000, 12% bond with semi-annual coupons redeemable at par on September 1, 2011 is bought on March 1, 2008 to yield 10% compounded semi-annually.
4. A $10 000, 7.75% bond with annual coupons redeemable at par in seven years is bought to yield 7.25% compounded annually.

B. Find the gain or loss on the sale of each of the following bonds without constructing a bond schedule.

1. A $25 000, 10.5% bond redeemable at par with semi-annual coupons bought ten years before maturity to yield 12% compounded semi-annually is sold four years before maturity at 99.25. Reference Example 15.3C
2. Four $5000, 8.5% bonds with interest payable semi-annually redeemable at par were bought twenty years before maturity to yield 7.5% compounded semi-annually. The bonds were sold three years later at 103.625.
3. A $5000 bond with 8% interest payable semi-annually redeemable at par on June 1, 2019 was bought on December 1, 2005 to yield 9% compounded semi-annually. The bond was sold on September 22, 2009 at 101.375.
4. Three $10 000, 10.5% bonds with quarterly coupons redeemable at par on August 1, 2015 were bought on May 1, 2001 to yield 12% compounded quarterly. The bonds were sold on January 16, 2009 at 93.5.

15.4 FINDING THE YIELD RATE

A. Quoted price of a bond—buying bonds on the market

Bonds are usually bought or sold through a bond exchange where agents trade bonds on behalf of their clients. To allow for the different denominations, bonds are offered at a market price stated as a percent of their face value.

It is understood that, if the bond is bought between interest dates, such a quoted price does not include any accrued interest. As explained in Section 15.1, the seller of a bond is entitled to the interest earned by the bond to the date of sale and the interest is added to the quoted price to obtain the cash price.

EXAMPLE 15.4A

A \$5000, 8% bond with semi-annual coupons payable April 1 and October 1 is purchased on August 25 at 104.75. What is the cash price of the bond?

SOLUTION

The quoted price is 5000.00(1.0475) = \$5237.50.
The time period April 1 to August 25 contains 146 days; the number of days in the interest payment interval April 1 to October 1 is 183.

$$PV = 5000.00; \quad r = i = \frac{8\%}{2} = 4\% = 0.04; \quad t = \frac{146}{183}$$

The accrued interest is $5000.00(0.04)\left(\frac{146}{183}\right) = \$159.56$.

The cash price is 5237.50 + 159.56 = \$5397.06.

B. Finding the yield rate—the average investment method

When bonds are bought on the market, the yield rate is not directly available; it needs to be determined. The simplest method in use is the so-called **method of averages**, which gives a reasonable approximation of the yield rate as the ratio of the average income per interest payment interval to the average book value.

$$\text{APPROXIMATE VALUE OF } i = \frac{\text{AVERAGE INCOME PER INTEREST PAYMENT INTERVAL}}{\text{AVERAGE BOOK VALUE}}$$

where

$$\text{AVERAGE BOOK VALUE} = \frac{1}{2}(\text{QUOTED PRICE} + \text{REDEMPTION PRICE})$$

and

$$\text{AVERAGE INCOME PER INTEREST PAYMENT INTERVAL} = \frac{\text{TOTAL INTEREST PAYMENTS} \begin{matrix} - \text{PREMIUM} \\ + \text{DISCOUNT} \end{matrix}}{\text{NUMBER OF INTEREST PAYMENT INTERVALS}}$$

Formula 15.4

EXAMPLE 15.4B

A \$25 000, 7.5% bond with semi-annual coupons redeemable at par in ten years is purchased at 103.5. What is the approximate yield rate?

SOLUTION

The quoted price (initial book value) is 25 000.00(1.035) = \$25 875.00; the principal is \$25 000.00.

The average book value is $\frac{1}{2}(25\,875.00 + 25\,000.00) = \$25\,437.50$.

The semi-annual interest payment is $25\,000.00\left(\frac{0.075}{2}\right) = \$937.50$;

the number of interest payments to maturity is 10(2) = 20;
the total interest payments are 20(937.50) = \$18 750.00;
the premium is 25 875.00 – 25 000.00 = \$875.00.

$$\text{Average income per interest payment interval} = \frac{18\,750.00 - 875.00}{20} = \$893.75$$

$$\text{Approximate value of } i = \frac{893.75}{25\,437.50} = 0.035135 = 3.51\%$$

The yield rate is 2(3.51) = 7.02%.

EXAMPLE 15.4C

Eight \$1000, 6% bonds with semi-annual coupons redeemable at par in seventeen years are purchased at 97.375. What is the approximate yield rate?

SOLUTION

The quoted price is 8000.00(0.97375) = \$7790.00;
the principal is \$8000.00;

$$\text{the average book value is } \frac{(7790.00 + 8000.00)}{2} = \$7895.00.$$

$$\text{The semi-annual interest payment is } 8000.00\left(\frac{0.06}{2}\right) = \$240.00;$$

the number of interest payments to maturity is 17(2) = 34;
the total interest payments are 34(240.00) = \$8160.00;
the bond discount is 8000.00 – 7790.00 = \$210.00.

$$\text{Average income per interest payment interval} = \frac{(8160.00 + 210.00)}{34} = \$246.18$$

$$\text{The approximate value of } i \text{ is } \frac{246.18}{7895.00} = 0.031182 = 3.12\%.$$

The approximate yield rate is 2(3.12%) = 6.24%.

EXAMPLE 15.4D

A \$5000, 10% bond with semi-annual coupons redeemable at par on July 15, 2018 is quoted on December 2, 2006 at 103.75. What is the approximate yield rate?

SOLUTION

To find the approximate yield rate for a bond purchased between interest dates, assume that the price was quoted on the nearest interest date. Since the interest dates are January 15 and July 15, the nearest interest date is January 15, 2007, which is 11.5 years before maturity.

The quoted price is 5000.00(1.0375) = \$5187.50;
the redemption price is \$5000.00;

$$\text{the average book value is } \frac{(5187.50 + 5000.00)}{2} = \$5093.75.$$

$$\text{The semi-annual interest is } 5000.00\left(\frac{0.10}{2}\right) = \$250.00;$$

the number of interest payments to maturity is 11.5(2) = 23;
the total interest payments are 23(250.00) = \$5750.00;
the premium is 5187.50 – 5000.00 = \$187.50.

The average income per interest payment interval $= \dfrac{(5750.00 - 187.50)}{23}$

$= \$241.85$

The approximate value of i is $\dfrac{241.85}{5093.75} = 0.047480 = 4.75\%$.

The approximate yield rate is $2(4.75\%) = 9.50\%$.

C. Finding the accurate yield rate by trial and error

EXCEL NOTES

A method of trial and error similar to the one used to find the nominal rate of interest may be used to obtain as precise an approximation to the yield rate as desired. The method is illustrated in Appendix B on the CD-ROM to this book.

EXERCISE 15.4

Use the method of averages to find the approximate yield rate for each of the six bonds shown in the table below. All are redeemed at par.

	Face Value	Bond Rate Payable Semi-annually	Time Before Maturity	Market Quotation
1.	\$10 000	6%	15 years	101.375
2.	5 000	10.5	7 years	94.75
3.	25 000	7.5	10 years	97.125
4.	1 000	8.5	8 years	101
5.	50 000	9	5 years, 4 months	98.875
6.	20 000	7	9 years, 8 months	109.25

15.5 SINKING FUNDS

A. Finding the size of the periodic payment

Sinking funds are interest-bearing accounts into which payments are made at periodic intervals to provide a desired sum of money at a specified future time. Such funds usually involve large sums of money used by both the private and the public sector to repay loans, redeem bonds, finance future capital acquisitions, provide for the replacement of depreciable plant and equipment, and recover investments in depletable natural resources.

The basic problem in dealing with sinking funds is to determine the *size of the periodic payments* that will accumulate to a known future amount. These payments form an annuity in which the accumulated value is known.

Depending on whether the periodic payments are made at the end or at the beginning of each payment period, the annuity formed is an ordinary annuity or an annuity due. Depending on whether or not the payment interval is equal in length to the interest conversion period, the annuity formed is a simple annuity or a general annuity. However, since sinking funds are normally set up so that the payment interval and the interest conversion period are equal in length, only the simple annuity cases are considered in this text.

(a) For sinking funds with payments at the beginning of each payment interval,

$$FV_n = PMT\left[\frac{(1+i)^n - 1}{i}\right] \qquad \text{Formula 11.1}$$

(b) For sinking funds with payments at the beginning of each payment interval,

$$FV_n(\text{due}) = PMT(1+i)\left[\frac{(1+i)^n - 1}{i}\right] \qquad \text{Formula 13.1}$$

EXAMPLE 15.5A

Western Oil plans to create a sinking fund of $20 000 by making equal deposits at the end of every six months for four years. Interest is 6% compounded semi-annually.

(i) What is the size of the semi-annual deposit into the fund?

(ii) What is the total amount deposited into the fund?

(iii) How much of the fund will be interest?

SOLUTION

(i) $FV_n = 20\,000.00$; P/Y = 2; C/Y = 2; $n = 4(2) = 8$; I/Y = 6; $i = \frac{6\%}{2} = 3\%$

$$20\,000.00 = PMT\left(\frac{1.03^8 - 1}{0.03}\right)$$

$$20\,000.00 = PMT(8.892336)$$

$$PMT = \$2249.13$$

Programmed Solution

("END" mode)

(Set P/Y = 2; C/Y = 2) 0 [PV] 20 000 [FV] 6 [I/Y]

8 [N] [CPT] [PMT] [−2249.127777]

The size of the semi-annual payment is $2249.13.

(ii) The total deposited into the sinking fund is 8(2249.13) = $17 993.04.

(iii) The amount of interest in the fund is 20 000.00 – 17 993.04 = $2006.96.

EXAMPLE 15.5B

Ace Machinery wants to provide for replacement of equipment seven years from now estimated to cost $60 000.00. To do so, the company set up a sinking fund into which it will pay equal sums of money at the beginning of each of the next seven years. Interest paid by the fund is 11.5% compounded annually.

(i) What is the size of the annual payment into the fund?

(ii) What is the total paid into the fund by Ace Machinery?

(iii) How much of the fund will be interest?

SOLUTION

(i) $FV_n(\text{due}) = 60\,000.00$; P/Y = 1; C/Y = 1; I/Y = 11.5; $n = 7$; $i = 11.5\%$

$$60\,000.00 = PMT(1.115)\left(\frac{1.115^7 - 1}{0.115}\right)$$

$$60\,000.00 = PMT(1.115)(9.934922)$$

$$PMT = \$5416.42$$

Programmed Solution

("BGN" mode)
(Set P/Y = 1; C/Y = 1) 0 [PV] 60 000 [FV] 11.5 [I/Y]

7 [N] [CPT] [PMT] [-5416.415057]

The size of the annual payment is $5416.42.

(ii) The total paid into the fund by Ace Machinery will be 7(5416.42) = $37 914.94.

(iii) The interest earned by the fund will be 60 000.00 – 37 914.94 = $22 085.06.

B. Constructing sinking fund schedules

The details of a sinking fund can be presented in the form of a schedule. Sinking fund schedules normally show the payment number (or payment date), the periodic payment into the fund, the interest earned by the fund, the increase in the fund, and the accumulated balance.

EXAMPLE 15.5C

Construct a sinking fund schedule for Example 15.5A.

SOLUTION

PMT = 2249.13; $n = 8$; $i = 3\% = 0.03$

Sinking fund schedule

Payment Interval Number	Periodic Payment	Interest for Payment Interval $i = 0.03$	Increase in Fund	Balance in Fund at End of Payment Interval
0				0.00
1	2 249.13	0.00	2 249.13	2 249.13
2	2 249.13	67.47	2 316.60	4 565.73
3	2 249.13	136.97	2 386.10	6 951.83
4	2 249.13	208.55	2 457.68	9 409.51
5	2 249.13	282.29	2 531.42	11 940.93
6	2 249.13	358.23	2 607.36	14 548.29
7	2 249.13	436.45	2 685.58	17 233.87
8	2 249.13	517.02	2 766.15	20 000.02
TOTAL	17 993.04	2006.98	20 000.02	

Explanations regarding the construction of the sinking fund schedule

1. The payment number 0 is used to introduce the beginning balance.
2. The first deposit is made at the end of the first payment interval. The interest earned by the fund during the first payment interval is \$0, the increase in the fund is \$2249.13, and the balance is \$2249.13.
3. The second deposit is added at the end of the second payment interval. The interest for the interval is 0.03(2249.13) = \$67.47. The increase in the fund is 2249.13 + 67.47 = \$2316.60, and the new balance in the fund is 2249.13 + 2316.60 = \$4565.73.
4. The third deposit is made at the end of the third payment interval. The interest for the interval is 0.03(4565.73) = \$136.97, the increase in the fund is 2249.13 + 136.97 = \$2386.10, and the new balance in the fund is 2386.10 + 4565.73 = \$6951.83.
5. Calculations for the remaining payment intervals are made in a similar manner.
6. The final balance in the sinking fund will probably be slightly different from the expected value. This difference is a result of rounding. The balance may be left as shown (\$20 000.02) or the exact balance of \$20 000.00 may be obtained by adjusting the last payment to \$2249.11.
7. The three totals shown are useful and should be obtained for each schedule. The total increase in the fund must be the same as the final balance. The total periodic payments are 8(2249.13) = 17 993.04. The total interest is the difference: 20 000.02 – 17 993.04 = \$2006.98.

EXAMPLE 15.5D

Construct a sinking fund schedule for Example 15.5B (an annuity due with payments at the beginning of each payment interval).

SOLUTION

PMT = 5416.42 (made at the beginning); $n = 7$; $i = 11.5\% = 0.115$

Sinking fund schedule

Payment Interval Number	Periodic Payment	Interest for Payment Interval $i = 0.115$	Increase in Fund	Balance in Fund at End of Payment Interval
0				0.00
1	5 416.42	622.89	6 039.31	6 039.31
2	5 416.42	1 317.41	6 733.83	12 773.14
3	5 416.42	2 091.80	7 508.22	20 281.36
4	5 416.42	2 955.24	8 371.66	28 653.02
5	5 416.42	3 917.99	9 334.41	37 987.43
6	5 416.42	4 991.44	10 407.86	48 395.29
7	5 416.42	6 188.35	11 604.77	60 000.06
TOTAL	37 914.94	22 085.12	60 000.06	

Explanations regarding the construction of the sinking fund schedule

1. The starting balance is \$0.
2. The first deposit is made at the beginning of the first payment interval and the interest earned by the fund during the first payment interval is 0.115(5416.42) = \$622.89. The increase in the fund is 5416.42 + 622.89 = \$6039.31 and the balance is \$6039.31.
3. The second deposit is made at the beginning of the second payment interval, the interest earned is 0.115(6039.31 + 5416.42) = \$1317.41, the increase is 5416.42 + 1317.41 = \$6733.83, and the balance is 6039.31 + 6733.83 = \$12 773.14.
4. The third deposit is made at the beginning of the third payment interval, the interest earned is 0.115(12 773.14 + 5416.42) = \$2091.80, the increase is 5416.42 + 2091.80 = \$7508.22, and the balance is 12 773.14 + 7508.22 = \$20 281.36.
5. Calculations for the remaining payment intervals are made in a similar manner. Be careful to add the deposit to the previous balance when computing the interest earned.
6. The final balance of \$60 000.06 is slightly different from the expected balance of \$60 000.00 due to rounding. The exact balance may be obtained by adjusting the last payment to \$5416.36.
7. The total increase in the fund must equal the final balance of \$60 000.06. The total periodic payments are 7(5416.42) = \$37 914.94. The total interest is 60 000.06 − 37 914.94 = \$22 085.12.

C. Finding the accumulated balance and interest earned or increase in a sinking fund for a payment interval; constructing partial sinking fund schedules

EXAMPLE 15.5E For Examples 15.5A and 15.5B, compute

(i) the accumulated value in the fund at the end of the third payment interval;

(ii) the interest earned by the fund in the fifth payment interval;

(iii) the increase in the fund in the fifth interval.

SOLUTION (i) The balance in a sinking fund at any time is the accumulated value of the payments made into the fund.

For Example 15.5A (when payments are made at the end of each payment interval)

$$\text{PMT} = 2249.13; \quad n = 3; \quad i = 3\%$$

$$\begin{aligned}\text{FV}_n &= 2249.13\left(\frac{1.03^3 - 1}{0.03}\right)\\ &= 2249.13(3.0909)\\ &= \$6951.83\end{aligned}$$

see sinking fund schedule, Example 15.5C

Programmed Solution

("END" mode)

(Set P/Y = 2; C/Y = 2) 0 [PV] 2249.13 [±] [PMT] 6 [I/Y]

3 [N] [CPT] [FV] [6951.835917]

For Example 15.5B (when payments are made at the beginning of each payment interval)

PMT = 5416.42; $n = 3$; $i = 11.5\%$

$$\begin{aligned} FV_n(\text{due}) &= 5416.42(1.115)\left(\frac{1.115^3 - 1}{0.115}\right) \\ &= 5416.42(1.115)(3.358225) \\ &= \$20\,281.36 \end{aligned}$$

see sinking fund schedule, Example 15.5D

Programmed Solution

("BGN" mode)

(Set P/Y = 1; C/Y = 1) 0 [PV] 5416.42 [±] [PMT]

11.5 [I/Y] 3 [N] [CPT] [FV] [20281.35612]

(ii) The interest earned during any given payment interval is based on the balance in the fund at the beginning of the interval. This figure is the same as the balance at the end of the previous payment interval.

For Example 15.5A
The balance at the end of the fourth payment interval

$$\begin{aligned} FV_4 &= 2249.13\left(\frac{1.03^4 - 1}{0.03}\right) \\ &= 2249.13(4.183627) \\ &= \$9409.52 \end{aligned}$$

Programmed Solution

("END" mode)

(Set P/Y = 2; C/Y = 2) 0 [PV] 2249.13 [±] [PMT]

6 [I/Y] 4 [N] [CPT] [FV] [9409.520995]

The interest earned by the fund in the fifth payment interval is 0.03(9409.52) = \$282.29.

For Example 15.5B
The balance in the fund at the end of the fourth payment interval

$$\begin{aligned} FV_4 &= 5416.42(1.115)\left(\frac{1.115^4 - 1}{0.115}\right) \\ &= 5416.42(1.115)(4.744421) \\ &= \$28\,653.02 \end{aligned}$$

Programmed Solution

("BGN" mode)

(Set P/Y = 1; C/Y = 1) 0 [PV] 5416.42 [±] [PMT]

11.5 [I/Y] 4 [N] [CPT] [FV] [28653.02037]

The interest earned by the fund in the fifth payment interval is
0.115(28 653.02 + 5416.42) = 0.115(34 069.44) = \$3917.99.

(iii) The increase in the sinking fund in any given payment interval is the interest earned by the fund during the payment interval plus the periodic payment.

For Example 15.5A
The increase in the fund during the fifth payment interval is
282.29 + 2249.13 = \$2531.42.

For Example 15.5B
The increase in the fund during the fifth payment interval is
3917.99 + 5416.42 = \$9334.41.

EXAMPLE 15.5F

The board of directors of National Credit Union decided to establish a building fund of \$130 000 by making equal deposits into a sinking fund at the end of every three months for seven years. Interest is 12% compounded quarterly.

(i) Compute the increase in the fund during the twelfth payment interval.

(ii) Construct a partial sinking fund schedule showing details of the first three deposits, the twelfth deposit, the last three deposits, and totals.

SOLUTION

Size of the quarterly deposit:

$FV_n = 130\,000.00$; P/Y = 4; C/Y = 4; I/Y = 12

$n = 7(4) = 28$; $i = \frac{12\%}{4} = 3\%$

$$\begin{aligned} 130\,000.00 &= PMT\left(\frac{1.03^{28} - 1}{0.03}\right) \\ 130\,000.00 &= PMT(42.930922) \\ PMT &= \$3028.12 \end{aligned}$$

Programmed Solution

("END" mode)

(Set P/Y = 4; C/Y = 4) 0 PV 130 000 FV 12 I/Y

28 N CPT PMT -3028.120347

(i) Balance in the fund at the end of the eleventh payment interval

$$FV_n = 3028.12\left(\frac{1.03^{11} - 1}{0.03}\right)$$
$$= 3028.12(12.807796)$$
$$= \$38\,783.54$$

Programmed Solution

("END" mode)

(Set P/Y = 4; C/Y = 4) 0 PV 3028.12 ± PMT

12 I/Y 11 N CPT FV 38783.54229

The interest earned by the fund during the twelfth payment interval is 0.03(38 783.54) = \$1163.51.

The increase in the fund during the twelfth payment interval is 1163.51 + 3028.12 = \$4191.63.

(ii) The last three payments are Payments 26, 27, and 28. To show details of these, we must know the accumulated value after 25 payment intervals.

$$FV_{25} = 3028.12\left(\frac{1.03^{25} - 1}{0.03}\right) = 3028.12(36.459264) = \$110\,403.03$$

Programmed Solution

("END" mode)

(Set P/Y = 4; C/Y = 4) 0 PV 3028.12 ± PMT

12 I/Y 25 N CPT FV 110403.0275

Partial sinking fund schedule

Payment Interval Number	Periodic Payment Made at End	Interest for Payment Interval $i = 0.03$	Increase in Fund	Balance in Fund at End of Payment Interval
0				0.00
1	3 028.12	0.00	3 028.12	3 028.12
2	3 028.12	90.84	3 118.96	6 147.08
3	3 028.12	184.41	3 212.53	9 359.61
•	•	•	•	•
•	•	•	•	•

Payment Interval Number	Periodic Payment Made at End	Interest for Payment Interval $i = 0.03$	Increase in Fund	Balance in Fund at End of Payment Interval
11	•	•	•	38 783.54
12	3 028.12	1 163.51	4 191.63	42 975.17
•	•	•	•	•
•	•	•	•	•
25	•	•	•	110 403.03
26	3 028.12	3 312.09	6 340.21	116 743.24
27	3 028.12	3 502.30	6 530.42	123 273.66
28	3 028.12	3 698.21	6 726.33	129 999.99
TOTAL	84 787.36	45 212.63	129 999.99	

EXAMPLE 15.5G

Laurin and Company want to build up a fund of $75 000 by making payments of $2000 at the beginning of every six months into a sinking fund earning 11% compounded semi-annually. Construct a partial sinking fund schedule showing details of the first three payments, the last three payments, and totals.

SOLUTION

To show details of the last three payments, we need to know the number of payments.

$FV_n(\text{due}) = 75\,000.00$; $PMT = 2000.00$; $P/Y = 2$; $C/Y = 2$; $I/Y = 11$; $i = \frac{11\%}{2} = 5.5\%$

$$75\,000.00 = 2000.00(1.055)\left(\frac{1.055^n - 1}{0.055}\right)$$

$$\begin{aligned} 1.055^n &= 2.954976 \\ n \ln 1.055 &= \ln 2.954976 \\ n\,(0.053541) &= 1.0834906 \\ n &= 20.236741 \end{aligned}$$

Programmed Solution

("BGN" mode)

(Set P/Y = 2; C/Y = 2) 0 [PV] 75 000 [FV] 2000 [±] [PMT]

11 [I/Y] [CPT] [N] [20.236741]

Twenty-one payments are needed. The last three payments are Payments 19, 20, and 21. The balance in the fund at the end of the 18th payment interval

$$\begin{aligned} FV_{18}(\text{due}) &= 2000.00(1.055)\left(\frac{1.055^{18} - 1}{0.055}\right) \\ &= 2000.00(1.055)(29.481205) \\ &= \$62\,205.34 \end{aligned}$$

Programmed Solution

("BGN" mode)

(Set P/Y = 2; C/Y = 2) 0 [PV] 2000 [±] [PMT]

11 [I/Y] 18 [N] [CPT] [FV] 62 205.3422

Partial sinking fund schedule

Payment Interval Number	Periodic Payment Made at Beginning	Interest for Payment Interval $i = 0.055$	Increase in Fund	Balance in Fund at End of Payment Interval
0				0.00
1	2 000.00	110.00	2 110.00	2 110.00
2	2 000.00	226.05	2 226.05	4 336.05
3	2 000.00	348.48	2 348.48	6 684.53
•	•	•	•	•
•	•	•	•	•
18	•	•	•	62 205.34
19	2 000.00	3 531.29	5 531.29	67 736.63
20	2 000.00	3 835.51	5 835.51	73 572.14
21	1 427.86	0.00	1 427.86	75 000.00
TOTAL	41 427.86	33 572.14	75 000.00	

Note: The desired balance in the sinking fund will be reached at the beginning of the 21st payment interval by depositing $1427.86.

D. Computer application—sinking fund schedule

EXCEL NOTES

The schedule in Example 15.5C displays the manual calculations for a sinking fund with an interest rate of 3% and eight periodic payments. Microsoft Excel and other spreadsheet programs can be used to create a file that will immediately display the results of a change in the interest rate, the increase in the fund, and the accumulated balance.

The following steps are general instructions for creating a file to calculate the sinking fund schedule in Example 15.5C. The formulas in the spreadsheet file were created using Excel; however, most spreadsheet software works similarly.

Although this exercise assumes a basic understanding of spreadsheet applications, someone without previous experience with spreadsheets will be able to complete it.

STEP 1 Enter the labels shown in Figure 15.2 in row 1 and in column A.

STEP 2 Enter the numbers shown in cells E2, F2, and F4. Do not type in a dollar sign or a comma.

STEP 3 Enter only the formulas shown in cells B3, C3, D3, and E3. Make sure that the formula entry includes the dollar ($) sign as shown in the figure.

STEP 4 The formulas entered in Step 3 can be copied through the remaining cells.

(a) Select and Copy the formulas in cells B3, C3, D3, and E3.

(b) Select cells B4 to B10 and then Paste.

(c) The formulas are now active in all the cells.

STEP 5 Enter the formula shown in cell B11, and then use Copy and Paste to enter the formula in cells C11 and D11.

STEP 6 To ensure readability of the spreadsheet, format the numbers to display in two decimal places, and widen the columns to display the full labels. This spreadsheet can now be used to reflect changes in aspects of the sinking fund and create a new schedule. Use cell F2 for new payment amounts and cell F4 for new interest rates.

Figure 15.2

Workbook 1

	A	B	C	D	E	F
1	Payment Interval	Periodic Payment	Interest	Increase in Fund	Balance at End	
2	0				0	2249.13
3	1	= F2	= F4*E2	= B3+C3	= E2+D3	
4	2	= F2	= F4*E3	= B4+C4	= E3+D4	= 0.03
5	3	= F2	= F4*E4	= B5+C5	= E4+D5	
6	4	= F2	= F4*E5	= B6+C6	= E5+D6	
7	5	= F2	= F4*E6	= B7+C7	= E6+D7	
8	6	= F2	= F4*E7	= B8+C8	= E7+D8	
9	7	= F2	= F4*E8	= B9+C9	= E8+D9	
10	8	= F2	= F4*E9	= B10+C10	= E9+D10	
11	Totals	= SUM(B3:B10)	= SUM(C3:C10)	= SUM(D3:D10)		

E. Debt retirement by the sinking fund method

When a sinking fund is created to retire a debt, the debt principal is repaid in total at the due date from the proceeds of the sinking fund while interest on the principal is paid periodically. The payments into the sinking fund are usually made at the same time as the interest payments are made. The sum of the two payments (debt interest payment plus payment into the sinking fund) is called the **periodic cost of the debt**. The difference between the debt principal and the sinking fund balance at any point is called the **book value of the debt**.

POINTERS AND PITFALLS

When a debt is retired by the sinking fund method, the borrower is, in effect, paying two separate annuities. Sinking fund installments are made to the fund's trustee, while periodic interest payments are made to the lender. Because of these two payment streams, two interest rates must be quoted in questions involving sinking fund debt retirement. One rate determines the *interest revenue* generated by the sinking fund, and the other rate determines the *interest penalty* paid by the borrower to the lender.

EXAMPLE 15.5H

The City Board of Education borrowed \$750 000 for twenty years at 13% compounded annually to finance construction of Hillview Elementary School. The board created a sinking fund to repay the debt at the end of twenty years. Equal payments are made into the sinking fund at the end of each year and interest earned by the fund is 10.5% compounded annually. Rounding all computations to the nearest dollar,

(i) determine the annual cost of the debt;

(ii) compute the book value of the debt at the end of ten years;

(iii) construct a partial sinking fund schedule showing the book value of the debt, the three first payments, the three last payments, and the totals.

SOLUTION

(i) The annual interest cost on the principal:

PV = 750 000; P/Y = 1; C/Y = 1; I/Y = 13; $i = 13\% = 0.13$;
I = 750 000(0.13) = \$97 500

The annual payment into the sinking fund

$FV_n = 750\,000$; $n = 20$; I/Y = 10.5; $i = 10.5\%$

$$750\,000 = \text{PMT}\left(\frac{1.105^{20} - 1}{0.105}\right)$$

$$750\,000 = \text{PMT}(60.630808)$$

$$\text{PMT} = \$12\,369.95$$

Programmed Solution

("END" mode)

(Set P/Y = 1; C/Y = 1) 0 [PV] 750 000 [FV] 10.5 [I/Y]

20 [N] [CPT] [PMT] [-12369.94895]

The annual cost of the debt is 97 500 + 12 370 = \$109 870.

(ii) The balance in the sinking fund after the tenth payment

$$FV_{10} = 12\,370\left(\frac{1.105^{10} - 1}{0.105}\right)$$

$$= 12\,370(16.324579)$$

$$= \$201\,935$$

Programmed Solution

("END" mode)

(Set P/Y = 1; C/Y = 1) 0 [PV] 12 370 [±] [PMT] 10.5 [I/Y]

10 [N] [CPT] [FV] [201935.0483]

The book value of the debt at the end of the tenth year is
750 000 – 201 935 = \$548 065.

(iii) The last three payments are Payments 18, 19, and 20. The balance in the sinking fund at the end of Year 17

$$FV_{17} = 12\,370\left(\frac{1.105^{17} - 1}{0.105}\right) = 12\,370(42.47213) = \$525\,380$$

Programmed Solution

("END" mode)

(Set P/Y = 1; C/Y = 1) 0 PV 12 370 ± PMT

10.5 I/Y 17 N CPT FV 525380.2441

Partial sinking fund schedule

Payment Interval Number	Periodic Payment Made at End	Interest for Payment Interval $i = 0.105$	Increase in Fund	Balance in Fund at End of Payment Interval	Book Value of Debt
0				0	750 000
1	12 370	0	12 370	12 370	737 630
2	12 370	1 299	13 669	26 039	723 961
3	12 370	2 734	15 104	41 143	708 857
•	•	•	•	•	•
•	•	•	•	•	•
17	•	•	•	525 380	224 620
18	12 370	55 165	67 535	592 915	157 085
19	12 370	62 256	74 626	667 541	82 459
20	12 367	70 092	82 459	750 000	0
TOTAL	247 397	502 603	750 000		

Note: The last payment has been adjusted to create a fund of exactly \$750 000.

EXERCISE 15.5

EXCEL NOTES

If you choose, you can use Excel's ***Periodic Payment Size (PMT)*** functions to answer the questions indicated below. Refer to **PMT** on the Spreadsheet Template Disk to learn how to use these Excel functions.

A. For each of the four sinking funds listed in the table below, compute (a) the size of the periodic payment; (b) the accumulated balance at the time indicated.

	Amount of Sinking Fund	Payment Interval	Payments Made At:	Term	Interest Rate	Conversion Period	Accumulated Balance Required After:
1.	$15 000	6 months	end	10 years	6%	semi-annually	10th payment
2.	9 600	1 month	end	8 years	12	monthly	36th payment
3.	8 400	1 month	beginning	15 years	9	monthly	96th payment
4.	21 000	3 months	beginning	20 years	8	quarterly	28th payment

B. Each of the four debts listed in the table below is retired by the sinking fund method. Interest payments on the debt are made at the end of each payment interval and the payments into the sinking fund are made at the same time. Determine

(a) the size of the periodic interest expense of the debt;
(b) the size of the periodic payment into the sinking fund;
(c) the periodic cost of the debt;
(d) the book value of the debt at the time indicated.

	Debt Principal	Term of Debt	Payment Interval	Interest Rate On Debt	Interest Rate On Fund	Conversion Period	Book Value Required After:
1.	$20 000	10 years	3 months	10%	12%	quarterly	6 years
2.	14 500	8 years	6 months	7	8.5	semi-annually	5 years
3.	10 000	5 years	1 month	7.5	6.0	monthly	4 years
4.	40 000	15 years	3 months	8.0	7.0	quarterly	10 years

C. Answer each of the following questions.

1. Hein Engineering expects to expand its plant facilities in six years at an estimated cost of $75 000. To provide for the expansion, a sinking fund has been established into which equal payments are made at the end of every three months. Interest is 5% compounded quarterly.
(a) What is the size of the quarterly payments?
(b) How much of the maturity value will be payments?
(c) How much interest will the fund contain?

2. To redeem a $100 000 promissory note due in ten years, Cobblestone Enterprises has set up a sinking fund earning 7.5% compounded semi-annually. Equal deposits are made at the beginning of every six months.
(a) What is the size of the semi-annual deposits?
(b) How much of the maturity value of the fund is deposits?
(c) How much is interest?

3. Equal deposits are made into a sinking fund at the end of each year for seven years. Interest is 5.5% compounded annually and the maturity value of the fund is $20 000. Find the size of the annual deposits and construct a sinking fund schedule showing totals.

4. A sinking fund amounting to $15 000 is to be created by making payments at the beginning of every six months for four years. Interest earned by the fund is

12.5% compounded semi-annually. Determine the size of the semi-annual payments and prepare a sinking fund schedule showing totals.

5. For Question 3, calculate the increase in the fund for the fourth year. Verify your answer by checking the sinking fund schedule.

6. For Question 4, compute the interest earned during the fifth payment interval. Verify your answer by checking the sinking fund schedule.

7. HY Industries Ltd. plans to replace a warehouse in twelve years at an anticipated cost of $45 000. To pay for the replacement, a sinking fund has been established into which equal payments are made at the end of every quarter. Interest is 10% compounded quarterly.
   (a) What is the size of the quarterly payments?
   (b) What is the accumulated balance just after the sixteenth payment?

8. To provide for expansion, Champlain Company has established a sinking fund earning 7% semi-annually. The fund is anticipated to reach a balance of $72 000 in fifteen years. Payments are made at the beginning of every six months.
   (a) What is the size of the semi-annual payment?
   (b) What is the accumulated balance at the end of the twentieth payment period?

9. Winooski Lamp Co. has borrowed $95 000 for capital expansion. The company must pay the interest on the loan at the end of every six months and make equal payments at the time of the interest payments into a sinking fund until the loan is retired in twenty years. Interest on the loan is 9% compounded semi-annually and interest on the sinking fund is 7% compounded semi-annually. (Round all answers to the nearest dollar.)
   (a) Determine the size of the periodic interest expense of the debt.
   (b) Determine the size of the periodic payment into the sinking fund.
   (c) What is the periodic cost of the debt?
   (d) What is the book value of the debt after fifteen years?

10. The City of Chatham has borrowed $80 000 to expand a community centre. The city must pay the interest on the loan at the end of every month and make equal payments at the time of the interest payments into a sinking fund until the loan is retired in twelve years. Interest on the loan is 6% compounded monthly and interest on the sinking fund is 7.5% compounded monthly. (Round all answers to the nearest dollar.)
    (a) Determine the size of the periodic interest expense of the debt.
    (b) Determine the size of the periodic payment into the sinking fund.
    (c) What is the periodic cost of the debt?
    (d) What is the book value of the debt after eight years?

11. Kirk, Klein & Co. requires $100 000 fifteen years from now to retire a debt. A sinking fund is established into which equal payments are made at the end of every month. Interest is 7.5% compounded monthly.
    (a) What is the size of the monthly payment?
    (b) What is the balance in the sinking fund after five years?

(c) How much interest will be earned by the fund in the 100th payment interval?
(d) By how much will the fund increase during the 150th payment interval?
(e) Construct a partial sinking fund schedule showing details of the first three payments, the last three payments, and totals.

12. The Town of Keewatin issued debentures worth $120 000 maturing in ten years to finance construction of water and sewer facilities. To redeem the debentures, the town council decided to make equal deposits into a sinking fund at the beginning of every three months. Interest earned by the sinking fund is 6% compounded quarterly.
(a) What is the size of the quarterly payment into the sinking fund?
(b) What is the balance in the fund after six years?
(c) How much interest is earned by the fund in the 28th payment interval?
(d) By how much will the fund increase in the 33rd payment interval?
(e) Prepare a partial sinking fund schedule showing details of the first three payments, the last three payments, and totals.

13. The Township of Langley borrowed $300 000 for road improvements. The debt agreement requires that the township pay the interest on the loan at the end of each year and make equal deposits at the time of the interest payments into a sinking fund until the loan is retired in twenty years. Interest on the loan is 8.25% compounded annually and interest earned by the sinking fund is 5.5% compounded annually. (Round all answers to the nearest dollar.)
(a) What is the annual interest expense?
(b) What is the size of the annual deposit into the sinking fund?
(c) What is the total annual cost of the debt?
(d) How much is the increase in the sinking fund in the tenth year?
(e) What is the book value of the debt after fifteen years?
(f) Construct a partial sinking fund schedule showing details, including the book value of the debt, for the first three years, the last three years, and totals.

14. Ontario Credit Union borrowed $225 000 at 13% compounded semi-annually from League Central to build an office complex. The loan agreement requires payment of interest at the end of every six months. In addition, the credit union is to make equal payments into a sinking fund so that the principal can be retired in total after fifteen years. Interest earned by the fund is 11% compounded semi-annually. (Round all answers to the nearest dollar.)
(a) What is the semi-annual interest payment on the debt?
(b) What is the size of the semi-annual deposits into the sinking fund?
(c) What is the total annual cost of the debt?
(d) What is the interest earned by the fund in the 20th payment interval?
(e) What is the book value of the debt after twelve years?
(f) Prepare a partial sinking fund schedule showing details, including the book value of the debt, for the first three years, the last three years, and totals.

Review Exercise

1. A $5000, 11.5% bond with interest payable semi-annually is redeemable at par in twelve years. What is the purchase price to yield
   (a) 10.5% compounded semi-annually?
   (b) 13% compounded semi-annually?

2. A $10 000, 6% bond with semi-annual coupons is redeemable at par. What is the purchase price to yield 7.5% compounded semi-annually
   (a) nine years before maturity?
   (b) fifteen years before maturity?

3. A $25 000, 9% bond with interest payable quarterly is redeemable at par in six years. What is the purchase price to yield 8.25% compounded annually?

4. A $1000, 9.5% bond with semi-annual coupons redeemable at par on March 1, 2018 was purchased on September 19, 2009 to yield 7% compounded semi-annually. What was the purchase price?

5. Four $5000, 7% bonds with semi-annual coupons are bought seven years before maturity to yield 6% compounded semi-annually. Find the premium or discount and the purchase price if the bonds are redeemable at par.

6. Nine $1000, 8% bonds with interest payable semi-annually and redeemable at par are purchased ten years before maturity. Find the premium or discount and the purchase price if the bonds are bought to yield
   (a) 6%;
   (b) 8%;
   (c) 10%.

7. A $100 000, 5% bond with interest payable semi-annually redeemable at par on July 15, 2020 was purchased on April 18, 2009 to yield 7% compounded semi-annually. Determine
   (a) the premium or discount;
   (b) the purchase price;
   (c) the cash price.

8. Four $10 000 bonds bearing interest at 6% payable quarterly and redeemable at par on September 1, 2022 were purchased on January 23, 2010 to yield 5% compounded quarterly. Determine
   (a) the premium or discount;
   (b) the purchase price;
   (c) the cash price.

9. A $5000, 8% bond with semi-annual coupons redeemable at par in ten years is purchased to yield 10% compounded semi-annually. What is the purchase price?

10. A $1000 bond bearing interest at 8% payable semi-annually redeemable at par on February 1, 2017 was purchased on October 12, 2010 to yield 7% compounded semi-annually. Determine the purchase price.

11. A $50 000, 11% bond with semi-annual coupons redeemable at par on April 15, 2015 was purchased on June 25, 2008 at 92.375. What was the approximate yield rate?

12. A $1000, 8.5% bond with interest payable annually is purchased six years before maturity to yield 10.5% compounded annually. Compute the premium or discount and the purchase price and construct the appropriate bond schedule.

13. A $5000, 12.25% bond with interest payable annually redeemable at par in seven years is purchased to yield 13.5% compounded annually. Find the premium or discount and the purchase price and construct the appropriate bond schedule.

14. Three $25 000, 11% bonds with semi-annual coupons redeemable at par were bought eight years before maturity to yield 12% compounded semi-annually. Determine the gain or loss if the bonds are sold at 89.375 five years later.

15. A $10 000 bond with 5% interest payable quarterly redeemable at par on November 15, 2020 was bought on July 2, 2004 to yield 9%

compounded quarterly. If the bond was sold at 92.75 on September 10, 2010, what was the gain or loss on the sale?

16. A $25 000, 9.5% bond with semi-annual coupons redeemable at par is bought sixteen years before maturity at 78.25. What was the approximate yield rate?

17. A $10 000, 7.5% bond with quarterly coupons redeemable at par on October 15, 2021 was purchased on May 5, 2009 at 98.75. What is the approximate yield rate?

18. What is the approximate yield realized if the bond in Question 17 was sold on August 7, 2014 at 92?

19. A 6.5% bond of $50 000 with interest payable quarterly is to be redeemable at par in twelve years.

(a) What is the purchase price to yield 8% compounded quarterly?

(b) What is the book value after nine years?

(c) What is the gain or loss if the bond is sold nine years after the date of purchase at 99.625?

20. A $5000, 14.5% bond with semi-annual coupons redeemable at par on August 1, 2022 was purchased on March 5, 2011 at 95.5. What was the approximate yield rate?

21. To provide for the purchase of heavy construction equipment estimated to cost $110 000, Valmar Construction is paying equal sums of money at the end of every six months for five years into a sinking fund earning 7.5% compounded semi-annually.

(a) What is the size of the semi-annual payment into the sinking fund?

(b) Compute the balance in the fund after the third payment.

(c) Compute the amount of interest earned during the sixth payment interval.

(d) Construct a sinking fund schedule showing totals. Check your answers to parts (b) and (c) with the values in the schedule.

22. Alpha Corporation is depositing equal sums of money at the beginning of every three months into a sinking fund to redeem a $65 000 promissory note due eight years from now. Interest earned by the fund is 12% compounded quarterly.

(a) Determine the size of the quarterly payments into the sinking fund.

(b) Compute the balance in the fund after three years.

(c) Compute the increase in the fund during the 24th payment interval.

(d) Construct a partial sinking fund schedule showing details of the first three deposits, the last three deposits, and totals.

23. The municipality of Kirkfield borrowed $100 000 to build a recreation centre. The debt principal is to be repaid in eight years and interest at 13.75% compounded annually is to be paid annually. To provide for the retirement of the debt, the municipal council set up a sinking fund into which equal payments are made at the time of the annual interest payments. Interest earned by the fund is 11.5% compounded annually.

(a) What is the annual interest payment?

(b) What is the size of the annual payment into the sinking fund?

(c) What is the total annual cost of the debt?

(d) Compute the book value of the debt after three years.

(e) Compute the interest earned by the fund in Year 6.

(f) Construct a sinking fund schedule showing the book value of the debt and totals. Verify your computations in parts (d) and (e) against the schedule.

24. The Harrow Board of Education financed the acquisition of a building site through a $300 000 long-term promissory note due in fifteen years. Interest on the promissory note is 9.25% compounded semi-annually and is payable at the end of every six months. To provide for the redemption of the note, the board agreed to make equal payments at the end of every six months into a sinking fund paying 8% compounded semi-annually. (Round all answers to the nearest dollar.)

(a) What is the semi-annual interest payment?

(b) What is the size of the semi-annual payment into the sinking fund?

(c) What is the annual cost of the debt?

(d) Compute the book value of the debt after five years.

(e) Compute the increase in the sinking fund in the 20th payment interval.

(f) Construct a partial sinking fund schedule showing details, including the book value of the debt, for the first three years, the last three years, and totals.

25. Northern Flying Service is preparing to buy an aircraft estimated to cost \$60 000 by making equal payments at the end of every three months into a sinking fund for five years. Interest earned by the fund is 8% compounded quarterly.

(a) What is the size of the quarterly payment made to the sinking fund?

(b) How much of the maturity value of the fund will be interest?

(c) What is the accumulated value of the fund after two years?

(d) How much interest will the fund earn in the 15th payment interval?

26. A sinking fund of \$10 000 is to be created by equal annual payments at the beginning of each year for seven years. Interest earned by the fund is 7.5% compounded annually.

(a) Compute the annual deposit into the fund.

(b) Construct a sinking fund schedule showing totals.

27. Joe Ngosa bought a retirement fund for \$15 000. Beginning twenty-five years from the date of purchase, he will receive payments of \$17 500 at the beginning of every six months. Interest earned by the fund is 12% compounded semi-annually.

(a) How many payments will Joe receive?

(b) What is the size of the last payment?

28. The town of Kildare bought firefighting equipment for \$96 000. The financing agreement provides for annual interest payments and equal payments into a sinking fund for ten years. After ten years the proceeds of the sinking fund will be used to retire the principal. Interest on the debt is 14.5% compounded annually and interest earned by the sinking fund is 13% compounded annually.

(a) What is the annual interest payment?

(b) What is the size of the annual payment into the sinking fund?

(c) What is the total annual cost of the debt?

(d) What is the book value of the debt after four years?

(e) Construct a partial sinking fund schedule showing details, including the book value of the debt, for the last three years and totals.

Self-Test

1. A \$10 000, 10% bond with quarterly coupons redeemable at par in fifteen years is purchased to yield 11% compounded quarterly. Determine the purchase price of the bond.

2. What is the purchase price of a \$1000, 7.5% bond with semi-annual coupons redeemable at par in ten years if the bond is bought to yield 6% compounded semi-annually?

3. A $5000, 8% bond with semi-annual coupons redeemable at par is bought six years before maturity to yield 6.5% compounded semi-annually. Determine the premium or discount.

4. A $20 000, 10% bond with semi-annual coupons redeemable at par March 1, 2017 was purchased on November 15, 2010 to yield 9% compounded semi-annually. What was the purchase price of the bond?

5. A $5000, 7% bond with semi-annual coupons redeemable at par on December 15, 2020 was purchased on November 9, 2009 to yield 8.5% compounded semi-annually. Determine the cash price.

6. A $5000, 11.5% bond with semi-annual coupons redeemable at par is bought four years before maturity to yield 13% compounded semi-annually. Construct a bond schedule.

7. A $100 000, 13% bond with semi-annual interest payments redeemable at par on July 15, 2018 is bought on September 10, 2011 at 102.625. What was the approximate yield rate?

8. A $25 000, 6% bond with semi-annual coupons redeemable at par in twenty years is purchased to yield 8% compounded semi-annually. Determine the gain or loss if the bond is sold seven years after the date of purchase at 98.25.

9. A $10 000, 12% bond with semi-annual coupons redeemable at par on December 1, 2020 was purchased on July 20, 2009 at 93.875. Compute the approximate yield rate.

10. Cottingham Pies made semi-annual payments into a sinking fund for ten years. If the fund had a balance of $100 000 after ten years and interest is 11% compounded semi-annually, what was the accumulated balance in the fund after seven years?

11. A fund of $165 000 is to be accumulated in six years by making equal payments at the beginning of each month. If interest is 7.5% compounded monthly, how much interest is earned by the fund in the 20th payment interval?

12. Gillian Armes invested $10 000 in an income fund at 13% compounded semi-annually for twenty years. After twenty years, she is to receive semi-annual payments of $10 000 at the end of every six-month period until the fund is exhausted. What is the size of the final payment?

13. A company financed a plant expansion of $750 000 at 9% compounded annually. The financing agreement requires annual payments of interest and the funding of the debt through equal annual payments for fifteen years into a sinking fund earning 7% compounded annually. What is the book value of the debt after five years?

14. Annual sinking fund payments made at the beginning of every year for six years earning 11.5% compounded annually amount to $25 000 at the end of six years. Construct a sinking fund schedule showing totals.

Challenge Problems

1. A $2000 bond with annual coupons is redeemable at par in five years. If the first coupon is $400, and subsequent annual coupons are worth 75% of the previous year's coupon, find the purchase price of the bond that would yield an interest rate of 10% compounded annually.

2. An issue of bonds, redeemable at par in *n* years, is to bear coupons at 9% compounded semi-annually. An investor offers to buy the entire issue at a premium of 15%. At the same time, the investor advises that if the coupon rate were raised to 10% compounded semi-annually, he would offer to buy the whole issue at a premium of 25%. At what yield rate compounded semi-annually are these two offers equivalent?

Case Study 15.1 Investing in Bonds

» Isabella recently attended a personal financial planning seminar, whereby the speaker discussed that bonds should be a component of a balanced investment portfolio. Currently, Isabella's RRSP contains mutual funds and a guaranteed investment certificate (GIC), but no bonds. She has decided to invest up to $6000 of her RRSP funds in bonds and has narrowed her choices to three.

- Bond A is a $1000, 4.3% bond with semi-annual coupons redeemable in six years. Isabella can purchase up to six of these bonds at 98.45.
- Bond B is a $1000, 5.4% bond with semi-annual coupons redeemable in seven years. She can purchase up to six of these bonds at 102.10.
- Bond C is a $1000, 6.2% bond with semi-annual coupons redeemable in eight years. Isabella can purchase up to four of these bonds at 103.85.

QUESTIONS

1. Suppose Isabella wants to invest in only one bond. Use the average investment method to answer the following questions.
   (a) What is the approximate yield of Bond A?
   (b) What is the approximate yield of Bond B?
   (c) What is the approximate yield of Bond C?
   (d) Assume Isabella is willing to hold the bond she chooses until it matures. Which bond has the highest yield?

2. Suppose Isabella decides to buy two $1000 denominations of Bond A. Bond A's semi-annual coupons are payable on January 1 and July 1. Suppose Isabella purchases these bonds on March 27.
   (a) What is the accrued interest on these two bonds up to the date of Isabella's purchase?
   (b) What is Isabella's cash price for these two bonds?

3. Suppose Isabella decides to buy three $1000 denominations of Bond B on April 17. Bond B's semi-annual coupons are payable on February 1 and August 1.
   (a) What is the accrued interest on these two bonds up to the date of Isabella's purchase?
   (b) What is Isabella's cash price for these two bonds?

Case Study 15.2 Raising Capital Through Bonds

» ScanSoft Development Company is developing a new process to manufacture optical discs. The development costs were higher than expected, so ScanSoft required an immediate cash inflow of $5 200 000. To raise the required capital, the company decided to issue bonds. Since ScanSoft had no expertise in issuing and selling bonds, the company decided to work with an investment dealer. The investment dealer bought the company's entire bond issue at a discount, and then sold the bonds to the public at face value or the current market value. To ensure it would raise the $5 200 000 it required, ScanSoft issued 5400 bonds with a face value of $1000 each on January 20, 2005. Interest is paid semi-annually on July 20 and January 20, beginning July 20, 2005. The bonds pay interest at 5.5% compounded semi-annually.

ScanSoft directors realize that when the bonds mature on January 20, 2025, there must be $5 200 000 available to repay the bondholders. To have enough money on hand to meet this obligation, the directors set up a sinking fund using a specially designated savings account. The company earns interest of 3.2% compounded semi-annually on this sinking fund account. The directors began making semi-annual payments to the sinking fund on July 20, 2005.

ScanSoft Development Company issued the bonds, sold them all to the investment dealer, and used the money raised to continue its research and development.

QUESTIONS

1. How much would an investor have to pay for one of these bonds to earn 6.6% compounded semi-annually?

2. (a) What is the size of the sinking fund payment?
   (b) What will be the total amount deposited into the sinking fund account?
   (c) How much of the sinking fund will be interest?

3. Suppose ScanSoft discovers on January 20, 2015 that it can earn 4.8% interest compounded semi-annually on its sinking fund account.
   (a) What is the balance in the sinking fund after the January 20, 2015 sinking fund payment?
   (b) What is the new sinking fund payment if the fund begins to earn 4.8% on January 21, 2015?
   (c) What will be the total amount deposited into the sinking fund account over the life of the bonds?
   (d) How much of the sinking fund will then be interest?

SUMMARY OF FORMULAS

Formula 15.1

$$PP = FV(1+i)^{-n} + PMT\left[\frac{1-(1+i)^{-n}}{i}\right]$$

Basic formula for finding the purchase price of a bond when the interest payment interval and the yield rate conversion period are equal

Formula 15.2

$$PP = FV(1+p)^{-n} + PMT\left[\frac{1-(1+p)^{-n}}{p}\right]$$

where $p = (1+i)^c - 1$

Basic formula for finding the purchase price of a bond when the interest payment interval and the yield rate conversion period are different

Formula 15.3

Direct formula for finding the premium or discount of a bond (a negative answer indicates a discount)

$$\text{PREMIUM OR DISCOUNT} = (b \times \text{FACE VALUE} - i \times \text{REDEMPTION PRICE})\left[\frac{1-(1+i)^{-n}}{i}\right]$$

Formula 15.4

Basic formula for finding the yield rate using the method of averages

$$\text{APPROXIMATE VALUE OF } i = \frac{\text{AVERAGE INCOME PER INTEREST PAYMENT INTERVAL}}{\text{AVERAGE BOOK VALUE}}$$

where

$$\text{AVERAGE BOOK VALUE} = \frac{1}{2}(\text{QUOTED PRICE} + \text{REDEMPTION PRICE})$$

and

$$\text{AVERAGE INCOME PER INTEREST PAYMENT INTERVAL} = \frac{\text{TOTAL INTEREST PAYMENTS} \begin{array}{l} - \text{PREMIUM} \\ + \text{DISCOUNT} \end{array}}{\text{NUMBER OF INTEREST PAYMENT INTERVALS}}$$

In addition, Formulas 9.1C, 11.1, 11.2, 12.3, and 13.1 were used in this chapter.

GLOSSARY

Accumulation of discount the process of reducing a bond discount *(p. 650)*

Amortization of the premium the process of writing down a bond premium *(p. 649)*

Bond rate the rate of interest paid by a bond, stated as a percent of the face value *(p. 630)*

Book value of a debt the difference at any time between the debt principal and the associated sinking fund balance *(p. 667)*

Cash price the total purchase price of a bond (including any accrued interest) *(p. 635)*

Coupon a voucher attached to a bond to facilitate the collection of interest by the bondholder *(p. 630)*

Coupon rate *see* **Bond rate**

Debentures bonds for which no security is offered *(p. 630)*

Denomination *see* **Face value**

Discount the difference between the purchase price of a bond and its principal when the purchase price is less than the principal *(p. 639)*

Due date *see* **Redemption date**

Face value the amount owed by the issuer of the bond to the bondholder *(p. 630)*

Market price *see* **Quoted price**

Maturity date *see* **Redemption date**

Maturity value *see* **Redemption value**

Method of averages a method for finding the approximate yield rate *(p. 655)*

Nominal rate *see* **Bond rate**

Par value *see* **Face value**

Periodic cost of a debt the sum of the interest paid and the payment into the sinking fund when a debt is retired by the sinking fund method *(p. 667)*

Premium the difference between the purchase price of a bond and its principal when the purchase price is greater than the principal *(p. 639)*

Principal value *see* **Redemption value**

Quoted price the net price (without accrued interest) at which a bond is offered for sale *(p. 635)*

Redeemable at a premium bonds whose principal is greater than the face value *(p. 630)*

Redeemable at par bonds that are redeemed at their face value *(p. 630)*

Redemption date the date at which the bond principal is repaid *(p. 630)*

Redemption value the amount that the issuer of the bond pays to the bondholder upon surrender of the bond on or after the date of maturity *(p. 630)*

Sinking fund a fund into which payments are made to provide a specific sum of money at a future time; usually set up for the purpose of meeting some future obligation *(p. 657)*

Yield rate the rate of interest that an investor earns on his or her investment in a bond *(p. 633)*

USEFUL INTERNET SITES

www.cis-pec.gc.ca

Canada Investment and Savings **(CIS)** CIS is a special operating agency of the Department of Finance that markets and manages savings and investment products for Canadians. This Website provides information on products, including Canada Savings Bonds and Canada Premium Bonds.

www.bankofcanada.ca/en

Bond Market Rates Click on "Rates and Statistics." The current Government of Canada bond yields and marketable bond average yields are found at this site. The site also provides links to selected historical interest rates.

www.carswell.com

The Payroll Community This site, hosted by Carswell publishers, provides information about payroll, FAQs, new products, payroll publications, and links to relevant sites.

www.benefitscanada.com

Benefits Canada This magazine deals with employee benefits and pension investments.

CHAPTER 16 Investment Decision Applications

OBJECTIVES

Upon completing this chapter, you will be able to do the following:

1. Determine the discounted value of cash flows and choose between alternative investments on the basis of the discounted cash flow criterion.
2. Determine the net present value of a capital investment project and infer from the net present value whether a project is feasible or not.
3. Compute the rate of return on investment.

Choices among different investment opportunities must be made often by both individuals and companies. Whether one is deciding between buying and leasing a car or how to increase plant capacity, an understanding of the time value of money is critical. When comparing different ways of achieving the same goal, we should always examine cash flows at the same point in the time—usually at the beginning when a decision must be made. Only then can we know whether it is better to buy or lease that car, or to expand the plant now or to wait.

INTRODUCTION

When making investment decisions, all decision makers must consider the comparative effects of alternative courses of action on the cash flows of a business or of an individual. Since cash flow analysis needs to take into account the time value of money (interest), present value concepts are useful.

When only cash inflows are considered, the value of the discounted cash flows is helpful in guiding management toward a rational decision. If outlays as well as inflows are considered, the net present value concept is applicable in evaluating projects.

The net present value method indicates whether or not a project will yield a specified rate of return. To be a worthwhile investment, the rate of return on a capital project must be attractive or meet a desired minimum target. Required rates of return tend to be high to be attractive. Knowing the actual rate of return provides useful information to the decision maker. It may be computed using the net present value concept.

16.1 DISCOUNTED CASH FLOW

A. Evaluation of capital expenditures—basic concepts

Projects expected to generate benefits over a period of time longer than one year are called capital investment projects, and they result in capital expenditures. The benefits resulting from these projects may be in either monetary or non-monetary form. The methods of analysis considered in this chapter will deal only with investment projects generating cash flows in monetary form.

While capital expenditures normally result in the acquisition of assets, the primary purpose of investing in capital expenditures is to acquire a future stream of benefits in the form of an inflow of cash. When an investment is being considered, analysis of the anticipated future cash flows aids in the decision to acquire or replace assets, and whether to buy or lease them.

The analysis generally uses the technique of discounted cash flow. This technique involves estimating all anticipated future cash flows flowing from an investment or project, projecting an interest rate, and calculating the present value of these cash flows. It is important that the present value be calculated, not the future value, due to the need to make a decision on the investment in the beginning, or in the present, before cash or other resources are invested. The decision to be made might involve determining whether to invest in a project, or choosing which project to invest in.

In some situations, the cash flows estimated may not be certain, or there may be other, non-financial concerns. The analysis techniques considered in this text are concerned only with the amount and the timing of cash receipts and cash payments under the assumption that the amount and timing of the cash flow are certain.

From the mathematical point of view, the major issue in evaluating capital expenditure projects is the time value of money. This value prevents direct comparison of cash received and cash payments made at different times. The concept of present value, as introduced in Chapter 9 and subsequent chapters, provides the vehicle for making sums of money received or paid at different times comparable at a given time.

B. Discounted cash flow

Discounted cash flow is the present value of all cash payments. When using the discounting technique to evaluate alternatives, two fundamental principles serve as decision criteria:

1. *The bird-in-the-hand principle.* Given that all other factors are equal, earlier benefits are preferable to later benefits.
2. *The the-bigger-the-better principle.* Given that all other factors are equal, bigger benefits are preferable to smaller benefits.

EXAMPLE 16.1A

Suppose you are offered a choice of receiving \$1000 today or receiving \$1000 three years from now. What is the preferred choice?

SOLUTION

Accepting the bird-in-the-hand principle, you should prefer to receive \$1000 today rather than three years from now. The rationale is that \$1000 can be invested to earn interest and will accumulate in three years to a sum of money greater than \$1000. Stated another way, the present value of \$1000 to be received in three years is less than \$1000 today.

EXAMPLE 16.1B

Consider a choice of \$2000 today or \$3221 five years from now. Which alternative is preferable?

SOLUTION

No definite answer is possible without considering interest. A rational choice must consider the time value of money; that is, we need to know the rate of interest. Once a rate of interest is established, we can make the proper choice by considering the present value of the two sums of money and applying the principle of the-bigger-the-better.

If you choose "now" as the focal date, three outcomes are possible.

1. The present value of \$3221 is greater than \$2000. In this case, the preferred choice is \$3221 five years from now.
2. The present value of \$3221 is less than \$2000. In this case, the preferred choice is \$2000 now.
3. The present value of \$3221 equals \$2000. In this case, either choice is equally acceptable.

(a) *Suppose the rate of interest is 8%.*
$FV = 3221.00; \quad i = 8\% = 0.08; \quad n = 5$
$PV = 3221.00(1.08^{-5}) = 3221.00(0.680583) = \$2192.16$
Since at 8% the discounted value of \$3221 is greater than \$2000, the preferred choice at 8% is \$3221 five years from now.

(b) *Suppose the rate of interest is 12%.*
FV = 3221.00; $i = 12\% = 0.12$; $n = 5$
$PV = 3221.00(1.12^{-5}) = 3221.00(0.567427) = \$1827.68$
Since at 12% the discounted value is less than \$2000, the preferred choice is \$2000 now.

(c) *Suppose the rate of interest is 10%.*
FV = 3221.00; $i = 10\% = 0.10$; $n = 5$
$PV = 3221.00(1.10^{-5}) = 3221.00(0.620921) = \$1999.99$
Since at 10% the discounted value is equal to \$2000, the two choices are equally acceptable.

Programmed Solution

("END" mode)

(Set P/Y = 1; C/Y = 1)

(a) [2nd] (CLR TVM) 3221 [FV] 8 [I/Y] 5 [N] [CPT] [PV] [-2192.158478]

(b) [2nd] (CLR TVM) 3221 [FV] 12 [I/Y] 5 [N] [CPT] [PV] [-1827.681902]

(c) [2nd] (CLR TVM) 3221 [FV] 10 [I/Y] 5 [N] [CPT] [PV] [-1999.987582]

EXAMPLE 16.1C

Two investment alternatives are available. Alternative A yields a return of \$6000 in two years and \$10 000 in five years. Alternative B yields a return of \$7000 now and \$7000 in seven years. Which alternative is preferable if money is worth

(i) 11%? (ii) 15%?

SOLUTION

To determine which alternative is preferable, we need to compute the present value of each alternative and choose the alternative with the higher present value.

Since the decision is to be made immediately, choose a focal point of "now."

(i) For $i = 11\%$

Alternative A

The present value of Alternative A is the sum of the present values of \$6000 in two years and \$10 000 in five years.

Present value of \$6000 in two years		
$= 6000(1.11^{-2}) = 6000(0.811622)$	=	\$ 4 870
Present value of \$10 000 in five years		
$= 10\ 000(1.11^{-5}) = 10\ 000(0.593451)$	=	5 935
The present value of Alternative A	=	\$10 805

Alternative B

The present value of Alternative B is the sum of the present values of \$7000 now and \$7000 in seven years.

Present value of \$7000 now	=	\$ 7 000
Present value of \$7000 in seven years $= 7000(1.11^{-7}) = 7000(0.481658)$	=	3 372
The present value of Alternative B	=	\$10 372

Programmed Solution

Alternative A

("END" mode)

(Set P/Y = 1; C/Y = 1)

2nd (CLR TVM) 6000 FV 11 I/Y 2 N CPT PV –4869.734599

2nd (CLR TVM) 10 000 FV 11 I/Y 5 N CPT PV -5934.513281

\$4870 + \$5935 = \$10 805

Alternative B

2nd (CLR TVM) 7000 FV 11 I/Y 7 N CPT PV -3371.608876

\$3372 + \$7000 = \$10 372

Since at 11% the present value of Alternative A is greater than the present value of Alternative B, Alternative A is preferable.

(ii) For $i = 15\%$

Alternative A

Present value of \$6000 in two years $= 6000(1.15^{-2}) = 6000(0.756144)$	=	\$4537
Present value of \$10 000 in five years $= 10\,000(1.15^{-5}) = 10\,000(0.497177)$	=	4972
The present value of Alternative A	=	\$9509

Alternative B

Present value of \$7000 now	=	\$7000
Present value of \$7000 in seven years $= 7000(1.15^{-7}) = 7000(0.375937)$	=	2632
The present value of Alternative B	=	\$9632

Programmed Solution

Alternative A

("END" mode)

(Set P/Y = 1; C/Y = 1)

2nd (CLR TVM) 6000 FV 15 I/Y 2 N CPT PV −4536.862004

2nd (CLR TVM) 10 000 FV 15 I/Y 5 N CPT PV −4971.767353

$\$4537 + \$4972 = \$9509$

Alternative B

2nd (CLR TVM) 7000 FV 15 I/Y 7 N CPT PV −2631.559279

$\$2632 + \$7000 = \$9632$

Since at 15% the present value of Alternative B is greater than the present value of Alternative A, Alternative B is preferable.

Note: Applying present value techniques to capital investment problems usually involves estimates. For this reason, dollar amounts in the preceding example and all following examples may be rounded to the nearest dollar. We suggest that you do the same when working on problems of this nature.

EXAMPLE 16.1D

An insurance company offers to settle a claim either by making a payment of $50 000 immediately or by making payments of $8000 at the end of each year for ten years. What offer is preferable if interest is 8% compounded annually?

SOLUTION

Present value of $8000 at the end of each year for ten years is the present value of an ordinary annuity in which PMT = 8000, $n = 10$, and $i = 8\%$.

$$PV_n = 8000\left(\frac{1 - 1.08^{-10}}{0.08}\right) = 8000(6.710081) = \$53\,681$$

Programmed Solution

("END" mode)

(Set P/Y = 1; C/Y = 1)

0 FV 8000 PMT 10 N 8 I/Y CPT PV −53680.65119

Since the immediate payment is smaller than the present value of the annual payments of $8000, the annual payments of $8000 are preferable.

EXAMPLE 16.1E

National Credit Union needs to decide whether to buy a high-speed scanner for \$6000 and enter a service contract requiring the payment of \$45 at the end of every three months for five years, or to enter a five-year lease requiring the payment of \$435 at the beginning of every three months. If leased, the scanner can be bought after five years for \$600. At 9% compounded quarterly, should the credit union buy or lease?

SOLUTION

To make a rational decision, the credit union should compare the present value of the cash outlays if buying the scanner with the present value of the cash outlays if leasing the scanner.

Present value of the decision to buy

Present value of cash payment for the scanner = \$6000

Present value of the service contract involves an ordinary annuity in which PMT = 45, $n = 20$, P/Y = 4; C/Y = 4; I/Y = 9; $i = 2.25\%$

$$= 45\left(\frac{1 - 1.0225^{-20}}{0.0225}\right) = 45(15.963712) \quad = \quad 718$$

Present value of decision to buy = \$6718

Present value of the decision to lease

Present value of the quarterly lease payments involves an annuity due: PMT = 435, $n = 20$, $i = 2.25\%$

$$= 435(1.0225)\left(\frac{1 - 1.0225^{-20}}{0.0225}\right) = 435(1.0225)(15.963712) \quad = \quad \$7100$$

Present value of purchase price after five years

$= 600(1.0225^{-20}) = 600(0.640816)$ = 384

Present value of decision to lease = \$7484

Programmed Solution

Present value of the decision to buy

Present value of cash payment for the scanner = \$6000

Present value of the service contract

("END" mode)

(Set P/Y = 4; C/Y = 4)

0 FV 45 PMT 20 N 9 I/Y CPT PV −718.367057

Present value of decision to buy is \$6000 + 718 = \$6718.

Present value of the decision to lease

Present value of the quarterly lease payments:

("BGN" mode)

0 FV 435 PMT 20 N 9 I/Y CPT PV −7100.459716

Present value of purchase price after five years:

0 PMT 600 FV 20 N 9 I/Y CPT PV −384.489883

Present value of the decision to lease is \$7100 + 384 = \$7484.

In the case of costs, the selection criterion follows the principle of the-*smaller-the-better*. Since the present value of the decision to buy is smaller than the present value of the decision to lease, the credit union should buy the scanner.

EXAMPLE 16.1F

Hans Machine Service needs a brake machine. The machine can be purchased for \$4600 and after five years will have a salvage value of \$490, or the machine can be leased for five years by making monthly payments of \$111 at the beginning of each month. If money is worth 10% compounded annually, should Hans Machine Service buy or lease?

SOLUTION

Alternative 1: Buy machine

Present value of cash price	=	\$4600
Less: Present value of salvage value		
$= 490(1.10^{-5}) = 490(0.620921)$	=	304
Present value of decision to buy	=	\$4296

Alternative 2: Lease machine

The monthly lease payments form a general annuity due in which

PMT = 111; P/Y = 12; C/Y = 1; I/Y = 10; $c = \frac{1}{12}$; $n = 60$; $i = 10\%$;
$p = 1.10^{\frac{1}{12}} - 1 = 1.007974 - 1 = 0.7974\%$

Present value of the monthly lease payments

$$= 111(1.007974)\left(\frac{1 - 1.007974^{-60}}{0.007974}\right)$$

$$= 111(1.007974)(47.538500)$$

$$= \$5319$$

The present value of the decision to lease is \$5319.

Programmed Solution

Alternative 1: Buy machine

Present value of cash price	=	\$4600
Less: Present value of salvage value		

("END" mode)

(Set P/Y = 12; C/Y = 1)

2nd (CLR TVM) 490 FV 60 N 10 I/Y CPT PV −304.251448

Present value of decision to buy is \$4600 − 304 = \$4296.

Alternative 2: Lease machine

Present value of the monthly lease payments

("BGN" mode) (Set P/Y = 12; C/Y = 1) 0 FV 111 PMT

60 N 10 I/Y CPT PV −5318.851263

Since the present value of the decision to buy is smaller than the present value of the decision to lease, Hans Machine Service should buy the machine.

EXERCISE 16.1

EXCEL NOTES

You can use Excel's Net Present Value (NPV) function to answer the questions below. Refer to **NPV** on the Spreadsheet Template Disk to learn how to use this function.

A. For each of the following, compute the present value of each alternative and determine the preferred alternative according to the discounted cash flow criterion.

1. The D Company must make a choice between two investment alternatives. Alternative 1 will return the company $20 000 at the end of three years and $60 000 at the end of six years. Alternative 2 will return the company $13 000 at the end of each of the next six years. The D Company normally expects to earn a rate of return of 12% on funds invested.

2. The B Company has a policy of requiring a rate of return on investment of 16%. Two investment alternatives are available but the company may choose only one. Alternative 1 offers a return of $50 000 after four years, $40 000 after seven years, and $30 000 after ten years. Alternative 2 will return the company $750 at the end of each month for ten years.

3. An obligation can be settled by making a payment of $10 000 now and a final payment of $20 000 in five years. Alternatively, the obligation can be settled by payments of $1500 at the end of every three months for five years. Interest is 10% compounded quarterly.

4. An unavoidable cost may be met by outlays of $10 000 now and $2000 at the end of every six months for seven years or by making monthly payments of $500 in advance for seven years. Interest is 7% compounded annually.

5. A company must purchase new equipment costing $2000. The company can pay cash on the basis of the purchase price or make payments of $108 at the end of each month for 24 months. Interest is 7.8% compounded monthly. Should the company purchase the new equipment with cash or make payments on the installment plan?

6. For less than a dollar a day, Jerri can join a fitness club. She would have to pay $24.99 at the end of each month for 30 months, or she can pay a lump sum of $549 at the beginning. Interest is 16.2% compounded monthly. Should Jerri pay a lump sum or use the monthly payment feature?

B. Answer each of the following questions.

1. A contract offers $25 000 immediately and $50 000 in five years or $10 000 at the end of each year for ten years. If money is worth 6%, which offer is preferable?

2. A professional sports contract offers $400 000 per year paid at the end of each of six years or $100 000 paid now, $200 000 paid at the end of each of the second and third years, and $800 000 paid at the end of each of the last three years. If money is worth 7.3%, which offer is preferable?

3. Bruce and Carol want to sell their business. They have received two offers. If they accept Offer A, they will receive $15 000 immediately and $20 000 in three years. If they accept Offer B, they will receive $3000 now and $3000 at the end of every six months for six years. If interest is 10%, which offer is preferable?

4. When Peter decided to sell his farm, he received two offers. If he accepts the first offer, he would receive \$250 000 now, \$750 000 one year from now, and \$500 000 two years from now. If he accepts the second offer, he would receive \$600 000 now, \$300 000 one year from now, and \$600 000 two years from now. If money is worth 9.8%, which offer should he accept?

5. A warehouse can be purchased for \$90 000. After twenty years the property will have a residual value of \$30 000. Alternatively, the warehouse can be leased for twenty years at an annual rent of \$10 000 payable in advance. If money is worth 8%, should the warehouse be purchased or leased?

6. A car costs \$9500. Alternatively, the car can be leased for three years by making payments of \$240 at the beginning of each month and can be bought at the end of the lease for \$4750. If interest is 9% compounded semi-annually, which alternative is preferable?

16.2 NET PRESENT VALUE METHOD

A. Introductory examples

EXAMPLE 16.2A Net cash inflows from two ventures are as follows:

End of Year:	1	2	3	4	5	Total
Venture A	12 000	14 400	17 280	20 736	24 883	89 299
Venture B	17 000	17 000	17 000	17 000	17 000	85 000

Which venture is preferable if the required yield is 20%?

SOLUTION

Present value of Venture A

$$\begin{aligned}&= 12\,000(1.20^{-1}) + 14\,400(1.20^{-2}) + 17\,280(1.20^{-3})\\&\quad + 20\,736(1.20^{-4}) + 24\,883(1.20^{-5})\\&= 12\,000(0.833333) + 14\,400(0.694444) + 17\,280(0.578704)\\&\quad + 20\,736(0.482253) + 24\,883(0.401878)\\&= 10\,000 + 10\,000 + 10\,000 + 10\,000 + 10\,000\\&= \$50\,000\end{aligned}$$

Present value of Venture B

$$= 17\,000\left(\frac{1 - 1.20^{-5}}{0.20}\right) = 17\,000(2.990612) = \$50\,840$$

Programmed Solution

Present value of Venture A

("END" mode)

(Set P/Y = 1; C/Y = 1)

[2nd] (CLR TVM) 12 000 [FV] 20 [I/Y] 1 [N] [CPT] [PV] [−10000]

[2nd] (CLR TVM) 14 400 [FV] 20 [I/Y] 2 [N] [CPT] [PV] [−10000]

2nd (CLR TVM) 17 280 FV 20 I/Y 3 N CPT PV −10000

2nd (CLR TVM) 20 736 FV 20 I/Y 4 N CPT PV −10000

2nd (CLR TVM) 24 883 FV 20 I/Y 5 N CPT PV −10000

The present value of Venture A is \$10 000 + 10 000 + 10 000 + 10 000 + 10 000 = \$50 000.

Present value of Venture B

0 FV 17 000 ± PMT 20 I/Y 5 N CPT PV −50840.40638

The present value of Venture B is \$50 840.

Since at 20% the present value of Venture B is greater than the present value of Venture A, Venture B is preferable to Venture A.

EXAMPLE 16.2B

Assume for Example 16.2A that Venture A requires an immediate non-recoverable outlay of \$9000 while Venture B requires a non-recoverable outlay of \$11 000. At 20%, which venture is preferable?

SOLUTION

	Venture A	Venture B
Present value of cash inflows	\$50 000	\$50 840
Present value of immediate outlay	9000	11 000
Net present value	\$41 000	\$39 840

Since the net present value of Venture A is greater than the net present value of Venture B, Venture A is preferable.

B. The net present value concept

When the present value of the cash outlays is subtracted from the present value of cash inflows, the resulting difference is called the **net present value.** In Example 16.2A, Venture B was preferable, where only the cash inflows were considered. In Example 16.2B, the present value of the outlays as well as the present value of the cash inflows resulted in the net present value being calculated. This approach is necessary when the cash outlays are different.

$$\text{NET PRESENT VALUE (NPV)} = \text{PRESENT VALUE OF INFLOWS} - \text{PRESENT VALUE OF OUTLAYS}$$

Formula 16.1

Since the net present value involves the difference between the present value of the inflows and the present value of the outlays, three outcomes are possible:

1. If the present value of the inflows is greater than the present value of the outlays, then the net present value is greater than zero.

2. If the present value of the inflows is smaller than the present value of the outlays, then the net present value is smaller than zero.

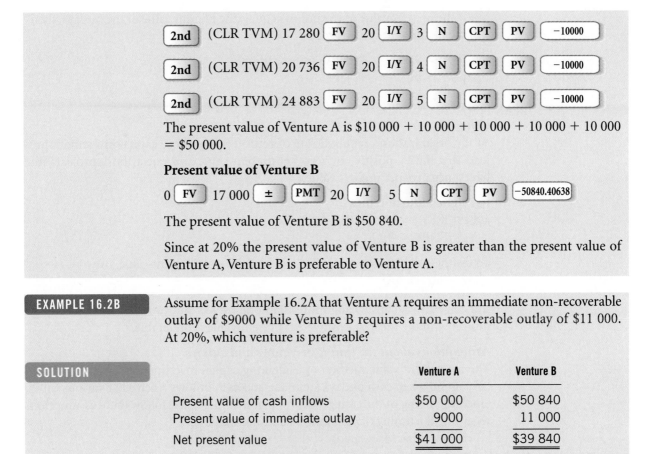

3. If the present value of the inflows equals the present value of the outlays, then the net present value is zero.

$PV_{IN} > PV_{OUT} \longrightarrow NPV > 0$ (positive)
$PV_{IN} = PV_{OUT} \longrightarrow NPV = 0$
$PV_{IN} < PV_{OUT} \longrightarrow NPV < 0$ (negative)

Criterion rule
At the organization's required rate of return, accept those capital investment projects that have a positive or zero net present value and reject those projects that have a negative net present value.

For a given rate of return:
ACCEPT if $NPV > 0$ or $NPV = 0$;
REJECT if $NPV < 0$.

To distinguish between a negative and a positive net present value, use
$NPV = PV_{IN} - PV_{OUT}$.

If a company is considering more than one project but can choose only one, the project with the greatest positive net present value is preferable.

Assumptions about the timing of inflows and outlays
The net present value method of evaluating capital investment projects is particularly useful when cash outlays are made and cash inflows received at various times. Since the timing of the cash flows is of prime importance, follow these assumptions regarding the timing of cash inflows and cash outlays.

Unless otherwise stated:

1. All cash inflows (benefits) are assumed to be received at the end of a period.
2. All cash outlays (costs) are assumed to be made at the beginning of a period.

C. Applications

EXAMPLE 16.2C

A company is offered a contract promising annual net returns of \$36 000 for seven years. If it accepts the contract, the company must spend \$150 000 immediately to expand its plant. After seven years, no further benefits are available from the contract and the plant expansion undertaken will have no residual value. Should the company accept the contract if the required rate of return is

(i) 12%? (ii) 18%? (iii) 15%?

SOLUTION

The net inflows and outlays can be represented on a time graph.

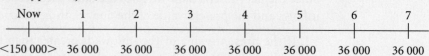

End of period (year)

Now	1	2	3	4	5	6	7
<150 000>	36 000	36 000	36 000	36 000	36 000	36 000	36 000

Note: Cash outlays (costs) are identified in such diagrams by a minus sign or by using accounting brackets.

(i) For $i = 12\%$

Since we assume the annual net returns (benefits) are received at the end of a period unless otherwise stated, they form an ordinary annuity in which

PMT = 36 000; $n = 7$; $i = 12\%$

$$PV_{IN} = 36\,000\left(\frac{1 - 1.12^{-7}}{0.12}\right) = 36\,000(4.563756) = \$164\,295$$

$$PV_{OUT} = \text{Present value of 150 000 now} = 150\,000$$

$$\text{The net present value (NPV)} = 164\,295 - 150\,000 = \$\ 14\,295$$

Since at 12% the net present value is greater than zero, the contract should be accepted. The fact that the net present value at 12% is positive means that the contract offers a return on investment of more than 12%.

(ii) For $i = 18\%$

$$PV_{IN} = 36\,000\left(\frac{1 - 1.18^{-7}}{0.18}\right) = 36\,000(3.811528) = \$137\,215$$

$$PV_{OUT} = 150\,000$$

$$NPV = 137\,215 - 150\,000 = -\$\ 12\,785$$

Since at 18% the net present value is less than zero, the contract should not be accepted. The contract does not offer the required rate of return on investment of 18%.

(iii) For $i = 15\%$

$$PV_{IN} = 36\,000\left(\frac{1 - 1.15^{-7}}{0.15}\right) = 36\,000(4.16042) = \$149\,775$$

$$PV_{OUT} = 150\,000$$

$$NPV = 149\,775 - 150\,000 = -\$\quad 225$$

The net present value is slightly negative, which means that the net present value method does not provide a clear signal as to whether to accept or reject the contract. The rate of return offered by the contract is almost 15%.

Programmed Solution

(i) For $i = 12\%$

("END" mode)

PV_{IN}: (Set P/Y = 1; C/Y = 1) 0 [FV] 36 000 [PMT] 7 [N]

12 [I/Y] [CPT] [PV] [−164295.2354]

PV_{OUT} = Present value of 150 000 now = \$150 000

The net present value (NPV) = \$164 295 − 150 000 = \$14 295.

(ii) For $i = 18\%$

("END" mode)

PV_{IN}: (Set P/Y = 1; C/Y = 1) 0 [FV] 36 000 [PMT] 7 [N]

18 [I/Y] [CPT] [PV] [−137214.9934]

$PV_{OUT} = \$150\,000$

$NPV = 137\,215 - 150\,000 = -\$12\,785$

(iii) For $i = 15\%$

("END" mode)

PV_{IN}: (Set P/Y = 1; C/Y = 1) 0 [FV] 36 000 [PMT] 7 [N]

15 [I/Y] [CPT] [PV] [−149775.1104]

$PV_{OUT} = \$150\,000$

$NPV = \$149\,775 - 150\,000 = -\$225$

EXAMPLE 16.2D

A project requires an initial investment of \$80 000 with a residual value of \$15 000 after six years. It is estimated to yield annual net returns of \$21 000 for six years. Should the project be undertaken at 16%?

SOLUTION

The cash flows are represented in the diagram below.

End of period(year) $i = 16\%$

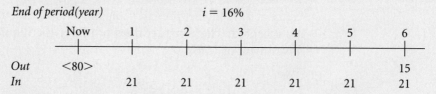

	Now	1	2	3	4	5	6
Out	<80>						15
In		21	21	21	21	21	21

Note: The residual value of \$15 000 is considered to be a reduction in outlays. Its present value should be subtracted from the present value of other outlays.

$$PV_{IN} = 21\,000\left(\frac{1 - 1.16^{-6}}{0.16}\right) = 21\,000(3.684736) = \$77\,379$$

$$\begin{aligned} PV_{OUT} &= 80\,000 - 15\,000(1.16^{-6}) \\ &= 80\,000 - 15\,000(0.410422) = 80\,000 - 6157 = 73\,843 \\ &= \text{Net present value (NPV)} = \$\,3\,536 \end{aligned}$$

Programmed Solution

("END" mode)

PV_{IN}: (Set P/Y = 1; C/Y = 1) 0 [FV] 21 000 [PMT] 6 [N]

16 [I/Y] [CPT] [PV] [−77379.45407]

PV_{OUT}: 0 [PMT] 15 000 [FV] 6 [N] 16 [I/Y] [CPT] [PV] [−6156.63382]

$NPV = \$77\,379 - (80\,000 - 6157) = \$3536$

Since the net present value is positive (the present value of the benefits is greater than the present value of the costs), the rate of return on the investment is greater than 16%. The project should be undertaken.

EXAMPLE 16.2E

The UBA Corporation is considering developing a new product. If undertaken, the project requires the outlay of \$100 000 per year for three years. Net returns beginning in Year 4 are estimated at \$65 000 per year for twelve years. The residual value of the outlays after fifteen years is \$30 000. If the corporation requires a return on investment of 14%, should it develop the new product?

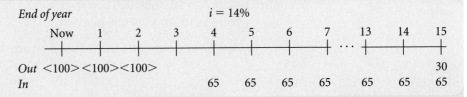

End of year $i = 14\%$

	Now	1	2	3	4	5	6	7	…	13	14	15
Out	<100>	<100>	<100>									30
In					65	65	65	65		65	65	65

SOLUTION

The net returns, due at the end of Year 4 to Year 15 respectively, form an ordinary annuity deferred for *three* years in which PMT = 65 000, $n = 12$, $d = 3$, $i = 14\%$.

$$PV_{IN} = 65\,000\left(\frac{1 - 1.14^{-12}}{0.14}\right)(1.14^{-3})$$
$$= 65\,000(5.660292)(0.674972)$$
$$= \$248\,335$$

The outlays, assumed to be made at the beginning of each year, form an annuity due in which PMT = 100 000, $n = 3$, $i = 14\%$.

$$PV_{OUT} = 100\,000(1.14)\left(\frac{1 - 1.14^{-3}}{0.14}\right) - 30\,000(1.14^{-15})$$
$$= 100\,000(1.14)(2.321632) - 30\,000(0.140096)$$
$$= 264\,666 - 4203$$
$$= \$260\,463$$
$$NPV = 248\,335 - 260\,463 = <\$12\,128>$$

Programmed Solution

("END" mode)

PV_{IN}: (Set P/Y = 1; C/Y = 1) 0 [FV] 65 000 [PMT] 12 [N]

14 [I/Y] [CPT] [PV] [−367918.9882]

0 [PMT] 367 919 [FV] 3 [N] 14 [I/Y] [CPT] [PV] [−248334.853]

("BGN" mode)

PV_{OUT}: 0 [FV] 100 000 [PMT] 3 [N] 14 [I/Y] [CPT] [PV] [−264666.0511]

0 [PMT] 30 000 [FV] 15 [N] 14 [I/Y] [CPT] [PV] [−4202.894462]

NPV = \$248 335 − (264 666 − 4203) = −\$12 128

Since the net present value is negative, the investment does not offer a 14% return. The corporation should not develop the product.

EXAMPLE 16.2F A feasibility study concerning a contemplated venture yielded the following estimates:

Initial cost outlay: \$1 300 000;
further outlays in Years 2 to 5: \$225 000 per year;
residual value after 20 years: \$625 000;
net returns: Years 5 to 10: \$600 000 per year;
Years 11 to 20: \$500 000 per year.

Should the venture be undertaken if the required return on investment is 15%?

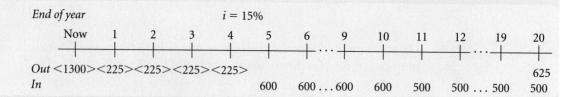

End of year $i = 15\%$

	Now	1	2	3	4	5	6	9	10	11	12	19	20
Out	<1300>	<225>	<225>	<225>	<225>								625
In						600	600 ...	600	600	500	500 ...	500	500

SOLUTION

$$PV_{IN} = 600\,000\left(\frac{1 - 1.15^{-6}}{0.15}\right)(1.15^{-4}) + 500\,000\left(\frac{1 - 1.15^{-10}}{0.15}\right)(1.15^{-10})$$
$$= 600\,000(3.784483)(0.571753) + 500\,000(5.018769)(0.247185)$$
$$= \$1\,298\,274 + 620\,281$$
$$= \$1\,918\,555$$

$$PV_{OUT} = 1\,300\,000 + 225\,000\left(\frac{1 - 1.15^{-4}}{0.15}\right) - 625\,000(1.15^{-20})$$
$$= 1\,300\,000 + 225\,000(2.854978) - 625\,000(0.061100)$$
$$= \$1\,300\,0000 + 642\,370 - 38\,188$$
$$= \$1\,904\,182$$
$$NPV = 1\,918\,555 - 1\,904\,182 = \$14\,373$$

Programmed Solution

("END" mode)

PV_{IN}: (Set P/Y = 1; C/Y = 1)

0 [FV] 600 000 [PMT] 15 [I/Y] 6 [N] [CPT] [PV] -2270689.616

0 [PMT] 2 270 689 [FV] 15 [I/Y] 4 [N] [CPT] [PV] -1298273.805

0 [FV] 500 000 [PMT] 15 [I/Y] 10 [N] [CPT] [PV] -2509384.313

0 [PMT] 2 509 384 [FV] 15 [I/Y] 10 [N] [CPT] [PV] -620281.3466

$PV_{IN} = \$1\,298\,274 + 620\,281 = \$1\,918\,555$

PV_{OUT} 0 [FV] 225 000 [PMT] 15 [I/Y] 4 [N] [CPT] [PV] -642370.1316

0 [PMT] 625 000 [FV] 15 [I/Y] 20 [N] [CPT] [PV] -38187.67434

$PV_{OUT} = \$1\ 300\ 000 + 642\ 370 - 38\ 188 = \$1\ 904\ 182$

$NPV = \$1\ 918\ 555 - 1\ 904\ 182 = \$14\ 373$

Since the net present value is positive, the rate of return on investment is greater than 15%. The venture should be undertaken.

Net present value can be determined by using a preprogrammed financial calculator.

EXERCISE 16.2

EXCEL NOTES

If you choose, you can use Excel's ***Net Present Value (NPV)*** function to answer the questions in Part A and Part B below. Refer to **NPV** on the Spreadsheet Template Disk to learn how to use this Excel function.

A. For each of the following six investment choices, compute the net present value. Determine which investment should be accepted or rejected according to the net present value criterion.

1. A contract is estimated to yield net returns of $3500 quarterly for seven years. To secure the contract, an immediate outlay of $50 000 and a further outlay of $30 000 three years from now are required. Interest is 12% compounded quarterly.

2. Replacing old equipment at an immediate cost of $50 000 and an additional outlay of $30 000 six years from now will result in savings of $3000 per quarter for twelve years. The required rate of return is 10% compounded annually.

3. A business has two investment choices. Alternative 1 requires an immediate outlay of $2000 and offers a return of $7000 after seven years. Alternative 2 requires an immediate outlay of $1800 in return for which $250 will be received at the end of every six months for the next seven years. The required rate of return on investment is 17% compounded semi-annually.

4. Suppose you are offered two investment alternatives. If you choose Alternative 1, you will have to make an immediate outlay of $9000. In return, you will receive $500 at the end of every three months for the next ten years. If you choose Alternative 2, you will have to make an outlay of $4000 now and $5000 in two years. In return, you will receive $30 000 ten years from now. Interest is 12% compounded semi-annually.

5. You have two investment alternatives. Alternative 1 requires an immediate outlay of $8000. In return, you will receive $900 at the end of every quarter for the next three years. Alternative 2 requires an immediate outlay of $2000, and an outlay of $1000 in two years. In return, you will receive $300 at the end of every quarter for the next three years. Interest is 7% compounded quarterly. Which alternative would you choose? Why?

6. Your old car costs you $300 per month in gas and repairs. If you replace it, you could sell the old car immediately for $2000. To buy a new car that would last five years, you need to pay out $10 000 immediately. Gas and repairs would cost you only $120 per month on the new car. Interest is 9% compounded monthly. Should you buy a new car? Why?

B. Answer each of the following questions.

1. Teck Engineering normally expects a rate of return of 12% on investments. Two projects are available but only one can be chosen. Project A requires an immediate investment of $4000. In return, a revenue payment of $4000 will be received in four years and a payment of $9000 in nine years. Project B requires an investment of $4000 now and another $2000 in three years. In return, revenue payments will be received in the amount of $1500 per year for nine years. Which project is preferable?

2. The owner of a business is presented with two alternative projects. The first project involves the investment of $5000 now. In return the business will receive a payment of $8000 in four years and a payment of $8000 in ten years. The second project involves an investment of $5000 now and another $5000 three years from now. The returns will be semi-annual payments of $950 for ten years. Which project is preferable if the required rate of return is 14% compounded annually?

3. Northern Track is developing a special vehicle for Arctic exploration. The development requires investments of $60 000, $50 000, and $40 000 for the next three years respectively. Net returns beginning in Year 4 are expected to be $33 000 per year for twelve years. If the company requires a rate of return of 14%, compute the net present value of the project and determine whether the company should undertake the project.

4. The Kellog Company has to make a decision about expanding its production facilities. Research indicates that the desired expansion would require an immediate outlay of $60 000 and an outlay of a further $60 000 in five years. Net returns are estimated to be $15 000 per year for the first five years and $10 000 per year for the following ten years. Find the net present value of the project. Should the expansion project be undertaken if the required rate of return is 12%?

5. Agate Marketing Inc. intends to distribute a new product. It is expected to produce net returns of $15 000 per year for the first four years and $10 000 per year for the following three years. The facilities required to distribute the product will cost $36 000 with a disposal value of $9000 after seven years. The facilities will require a major facelift costing $10 000 each after three and after five years respectively. If Agate requires a return on investment of 20%, should the company distribute the new product?

6. A company is considering a project that will require a cost outlay of $15 000 per year for four years. At the end of the project the salvage value will be $10 000. The project will yield returns of $60 000 in Year 4 and $20 000 in Year 5. There are no returns after Year 5. Alternative investments are available that will yield a return of 16%. Should the company undertake the project?

7. Demand for a product manufactured by Eagle Manufacturing is expected to be 15 000 units per year during the next ten years. The net return per unit is \$2. The manufacturing process requires the purchase of a machine costing \$140 000. The machine has an economic life of ten years and a salvage value of \$20 000 after ten years. Major overhauls of the machine require outlays of \$20 000 after four years and \$40 000 after seven years. Should Eagle invest in the machine if it requires a return of 12% on its investments?

8. Magnum Electronics Company expects a demand of 20 000 units per year for a special purpose component during the next six years. Net return per unit is \$4. To produce the component, Magnum must buy a machine costing \$250 000 with a life of six years and a salvage value of \$40 000 after six years. The company estimates that repair costs will be \$20 000 per year during Years 2 to 6. If Magnum requires a return on investment of 18%, should it market the component?

BUSINESS MATH NEWS BOX

General Motors Planning Its Comeback

Corvette! Cadillac! Buick! These words remind most people of performance and luxury automobiles made by automobile giant General Motors. Founded in 1908, GM prides itself on being the world's largest automobile maker. However, this distinction may not last much longer.

To say GM's Chief Executive Officer Rick Wagoner has been busy is an understatement. He has been closing production facilities, selling \$17 billion worth of assets, and reorganizing the company ever since GM posted a massive \$10.6 billion loss.

Changing consumer preference has transformed the automobile industry; buyers focus on quality and price, and are no longer concerned with brand loyalty when purchasing their next vehicle. With fierce competition from Japanese manufacturer Toyota and Korean automaker Hyundai, GM has seen its market share peak at 51% in 1962 and fall to 24.7% in August 2006.

To entice buyers, GM and other domestic automobile manufacturers such as Ford and DaimlerChrysler offered extremely generous incentives such as zero-interest loans and additional price cuts. Although these enticements may have increased GM's total sales, the cost of selling some of the vehicles was equal to or greater than the selling price of the vehicle. This marketing strategy has changed the way investors look at General Motors. GM is a public company trading its shares on the New York Stock Exchange. Over the past 10 years, the company's shares have declined significantly. In addition, GM's bond rating has deteriorated to "junk bond" status. This decline in credit rating means that investors require GM to pay a higher rate of interest because of the risk associated with borrowing money. GM's debt is rated B by Standard & Poor's and Caa1 by Moody's.

Sources: Mark Pittman and Aparajita Saha-Bubna. Bloomberg News. "GM May Sell First Bonds Since 2004 as Debt Rallies." September 11, 2006. (New York); *Bonds Online* website. Downloaded February 13, 2007. www.bondsonline.com/asp/research/bondratings.asp; *Wikipedia—The Free Encyclopedia* website. Downloaded February 13, 2007. http://en.wikipedia.org/wiki/General_Motors_Corporation; CNW Group website, Auto Sales, Downloaded February 13, 2007. "GM's U.S. Divisions Deliver 301,317 Vehicles in October." www.newswire.ca/en/releases/archive/November2006/01/c7268.html.

QUESTIONS:

1. Calculate the average annual decline of GM's market share from 1962 to 2006.
2. Research Standard & Poor's and Moody's bond ratings. Focus your search on the Internet.
3. Examine the relationship between bond price and bond yield. Focus your search on the Internet.
4. GM sold 9.17 million vehicles in 2005. If the average discount provided to customers was $1500, calculate the potential revenue lost as a result of the discount.
5. The average selling price of a GM vehicle is $21 000. If GM offers a zero-interest loan on a 5-year monthly loan, determine the potential revenue lost per vehicle when compared to an interest rate of 6% compounded monthly.

16.3 FINDING THE RATE OF RETURN ON INVESTMENT

A. Net present value, profitability index, rate of return

The **rate of return** on investment (R.O.I.) is widely used to measure the value of an investment. This rate of return is often referred to as the **internal rate of return** (I.R.R.). Since it takes interest into account, knowing the rate of return that results from a capital investment project provides useful information when evaluating a project.

The method of finding the rate of return that is explained and illustrated in this section uses the net present value concept introduced in Section 16.2. However, instead of being primarily concerned with a specific discount rate and with comparing the present value of the cash inflows and the present value of the cash outlays, this method is designed to determine the rate of return on the investment.

As explained in Section 16.2, three outcomes are possible when using Formula 16.1. These three outcomes indicate whether the rate of return is greater than, less than, or equal to the discount rate used in finding the net present value.

1. If the net present value is greater than zero (positive), then the rate of return is greater than the discount rate used to determine the net present value.
2. If the net present value is less than zero (negative), then the rate of return is less than the discount rate used.
3. If the net present value is equal to zero, then the rate of return is equal to the discount rate used.

If NPV > 0 (POSITIVE)	R.O.I. $> i$
If NPV < 0 (NEGATIVE)	R.O.I. $< i$
If NPV $= 0$	R.O.I. $= i$

It follows, then, that the rate of return on investment (R.O.I.) is that rate of discount for which the NPV = 0, that is, for which $PV_{IN} = PV_{OUT}$.

The above definition of the rate of return and the relationship between the net present value, the rate of discount used to compute the net present value, and the rate of return are useful in developing a method of finding the rate of return.

However, before computing the rate of return, it is useful to consider a ratio known as the **profitability index** or **discounted benefit–cost ratio.** It is defined as the ratio that results when comparing the present value of the cash inflows with the present value of the cash outlays.

$$\text{PROFITABILITY INDEX (or DISCOUNTED BENEFIT-COST RATIO)} = \frac{PV_{IN}}{PV_{OUT}}$$ Formula 16.2

Since a division is involved, three outcomes are possible when computing this ratio. Each of these outcomes gives an indication of the rate of return.

1. If the numerator (PV_{IN}) is greater than the denominator (PV_{OUT}), then the profitability index is greater than one, and the rate of return is greater than the discount rate used.
2. If the numerator (PV_{IN}) is less than the denominator (PV_{OUT}), then the profitability index is less than one, and the rate of return is less than the discount rate used.
3. If the numerator (PV_{IN}) is equal to the denominator (PV_{OUT}), then the profitability index is equal to one, and the rate of return equals the discount rate used.

The relationship between the present value of the inflows, the present value of the outlays, the net present value, the profitability index, and the rate of return at a given rate of discount *i* is summarized below.

PV_{IN} Versus PV_{OUT}	Net Present Value (NPV)	Profitability Index	Rate of Return (R.O.I.)
$PV_{IN} > PV_{OUT}$	NPV > 0	> 1	$> i$
$PV_{IN} = PV_{OUT}$	NPV $= 0$	$= 1$	$= i$
$PV_{IN} < PV_{OUT}$	NPV < 0	< 1	$< i$

B. Procedure for finding the rate of return by trial and error

From the relationships noted above, the rate of return on investment can be defined as the rate of discount for which the present value of the inflows (benefits) equals the present value of the outlays (costs). This definition implies that the rate of return is the rate of discount for which the net present value equals zero or for which the profitability index (benefit–cost ratio) equals 1. This conclusion permits us to determine the rate of return by trial and error.

STEP 1 Arbitrarily select a discount rate and compute the net present value at that rate.

STEP 2 From the outcome of Step 1, draw one of the three conclusions.

(a) If NPV $= 0$, infer that the R.O.I. $= i$.
(b) If NPV > 0, infer that the R.O.I. $> i$.
(c) If NPV < 0, infer that the R.O.I. $< i$.

STEP 3 **(a)** If, in Step 1, NPV $= 0$, then R.O.I. $= i$ and the problem is solved.
(b) If, in Step 1, NPV > 0 (positive), then we know that R.O.I. $> i$. A second attempt is needed. This second try requires choosing a discount rate greater

than the rate used in Step 1 and computing the net present value using the higher rate.

If the resulting net present value is still positive, choose a still higher rate of discount and compute the net present value for that rate. Repeat this procedure until the selected rate of discount yields a negative net present value.

(c) If, in Step 1, NPV < 0 (negative), then we know that R.O.I. $< i$. The second try requires choosing a discount rate less than the rate used in Step 1 and computing the net present value using the lower rate.

If the resulting net present value is still negative, choose a still lower rate of discount and compute the net present value for that rate. Repeat this procedure until the selected rate of discount yields a positive net present value.

STEP 4 The basic aim of Step 3 is to find one rate of discount for which the net present value is positive and a second rate for which the net present value is negative. Once this has been accomplished, the rate of return must be a rate between the two rates used to generate a positive and a negative net present value.

You can now obtain a reasonably accurate value of the rate of return by using linear interpolation. To ensure sufficient accuracy in the answer, we recommend that the two rates of discount used when interpolating be no more than two percentage points apart. The worked examples in this section have been solved using successive even rates of discounts when interpolating.

STEP 5 (Optional) You can check the accuracy of the method of interpolation when using an electronic calculator by computing the net present value. Use as the discount rate the rate of return determined in Step 4. Expect the rate in Step 4 to be slightly too high. You can obtain a still more precise answer by further trials.

C. Selecting the rate of discount—using the profitability index

While the selection of a discount rate in Step 1 of the procedure is arbitrary, a sensible choice is one that is neither too high nor too low. Since the negative net present value immediately establishes a range between zero and the rate used, it is preferable to be on the high side. Choosing a rate of discount within the range 12% to 24% usually leads to quick solutions.

While the initial choice of rate is a shot in the dark, the resulting knowledge about the size of the rate of return combined with the use of the profitability index should ensure the selection of a second rate that is fairly close to the actual rate of return.

In making the second choice, use the profitability index.

1. Compute the index for the first rate chosen and convert the index into a percent.
2. Deduct 100% from the index and divide the difference by 4.
3. If the index is greater than 1, add the above result to obtain the rate that you should use for the second attempt. If, however, the index is smaller than 1, deduct the above result from the rate of discount initially used.

To illustrate, assume that the rate of discount initially selected is 16%. The resulting $PV_{IN} = 150$ and the $PV_{OUT} = 120$.

1. The profitability index is $\frac{150}{120} = 1.25 = 1.25\%$.
2. The difference $(125\% - 100\%)$ divided by $4 = 6.25\%$.
3. Since the index is greater than 1, add 6.25% to the initial rate of 16%; the recommended choice is 22%.

Assume that the rate of discount initially selected is 20%. The resulting $PV_{IN} = 200$ and the $PV_{OUT} = 250$.

1. The profitability index is $\frac{200}{250} = 0.80 = 80\%$.
2. The difference $(80\% - 100\%)$ divided by $4 = -5\%$.
3. Since the index is less than 1, subtract 5% from the initial rate of 20%; the recommended choice is 15%. (If, as in this text, you are using only even rates, try either 14% or 16%.)

D. Using linear interpolation

The method of linear interpolation used in Step 4 of the suggested procedure is illustrated in Example 16.3A below.

EXAMPLE 16.3A

Assume that the net present value of a project is \$420 at 14% and −\$280 at 16%. Use linear interpolation to compute the rate of return correct to the nearest tenth of a percent.

SOLUTION

The data can be represented on a line diagram.

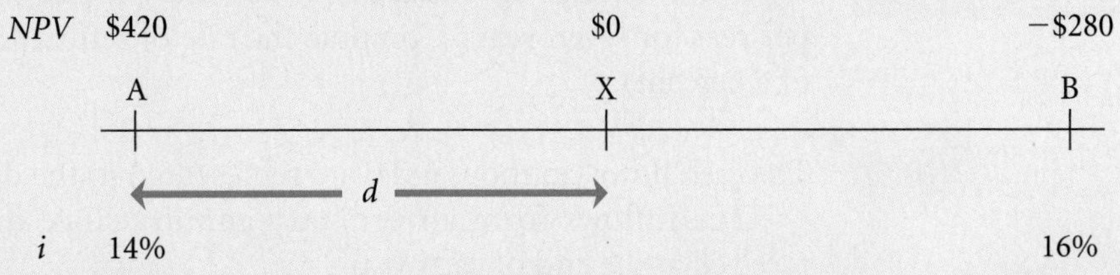

The line segment AB represents the distance between the two rates of discount that are associated with a positive and a negative net present value respectively.

At Point A, where $i = 14\%$, the NPV = 420;
at Point B, where $i = 16\%$, the NPV = −280;
at Point X, where i is unknown, the NPV = 0.

By definition, the rate of return is that rate of discount for which the net present value is zero. Since 0 is a number between 420 and −280, the NPV = 0 is located at a point on AB. This point is marked X.

We can obtain two useful ratios by considering the line segment from the two points of view shown in the diagram.

(i) In terms of the discount rate i,

AB = 2% ———————— 16% − 14%

AX = d% ———————— the unknown percent that must be added to 14% to obtain the rate of discount at which the NPV = 0

$$\frac{AX}{AB} = \frac{d\%}{2\%}$$

(ii) In terms of the net present value figures,

AB = 700 ———————— 420 + 280

AX = 420

$$\frac{AX}{AB} = \frac{420}{700}$$

Since the ratio AX:AB is written twice, we can derive a proportion statement.

$$\frac{d\%}{2\%} = \frac{420}{700}$$

$$d\% = \frac{420}{700} \times 2\%$$

$$d\% = 1.2\%$$

Therefore, the rate at which the net present value is equal to zero is 14% + 1.2% = 15.2%. The rate of return on investment is 15.2%.

E. Computing the rate of return

EXAMPLE 16.3B A project requires an initial outlay of \$25 000. The estimated returns are \$7000 per year for seven years. Compute the rate of return (correct to the nearest tenth of a percent).

SOLUTION The cash flows (in thousands) are represented in the diagram below.

The inflows form an ordinary annuity since inflows are assumed to be received at the end of each year.

End of year	Now	1	2	3	4	5	6	7
Out	<25>							
In		7	7	7	7	7	7	7

$$PV_{IN} = 7000\left[\frac{1 - (1 + i)^{-7}}{i}\right]$$

The outlays consist of an immediate payment.

$PV_{OUT} = 25\ 000$

To determine the rate of return, we will choose a rate of discount, compute the net present value, and try further rates until we find two successive even rates. For one, the NPV > 0 (positive) and, for the other, NPV < 0 (negative).

STEP 1 Try $i = 12\%$.

$$PV_{IN} = 7000\left(\frac{1 - 1.12^{-7}}{0.12}\right) = 7000(4.563757) = \$31\ 946$$

$$PV_{OUT} = 25\ 000$$

$$\text{NPV at } 12\% = \$\ 6\ 946$$

Since the NPV > 0, R.O.I. > 12%.

STEP 2 Compute the profitability index to estimate what rate should be used next.

$$\text{INDEX} = \frac{PV_{IN}}{PV_{OUT}} = \frac{31\ 946}{25\ 000} = 1.278 = 127.8\%$$

Since at $i = 12\%$, the profitability index is 27.8% more than 100%, the rate of discount should be increased by $\frac{27.8\%}{4} = 7\%$ approximately. To obtain another even rate, the increase should be either 6% or 8%. In line with the suggestion that it is better to go too high, increase the previous rate by 8% and try $i = 20\%$.

STEP 3 Try $i = 20\%$.

$$PV_{IN} = 7000\left(\frac{1 - 1.20^{-7}}{0.20}\right) = 7000(3.604592) = \$25\ 232$$

$$PV_{OUT} = 25\ 000$$

$$\text{NPV at } 20\% = \$\ 232$$

Since the NPV > 0, R.O.I. > 20%.

STEP 4 Since the net present value is still positive, a rate higher than 20% is needed. The profitability index at 20% is $\frac{25\ 232}{25\ 000} = 1.009 = 100.9\%$. The index exceeds 100% by 0.9%; division by 4 suggests an increase of 0.2%. For interpolation, the recommended minimum increase or decrease is 2%. The next try should use $i = 22\%$.

STEP 5 Try $i = 22\%$.

$$PV_{IN} = 7000\left(\frac{1 - 1.22^{-7}}{0.22}\right) = 7000(3.415506) = \$23\ 909$$

$$PV_{OUT} = -\$25\ 000$$

$$\text{NPV at } 22\% = -\$\ 1\ 091$$

Since the NPV < 0, R.O.I. < 22%.
Therefore, 20% < R.O.I. < 22%.

STEP 6 Now that the rate of return has been located between two sufficiently close rates of discount, linear interpolation can be used as illustrated in Example 16.3A.

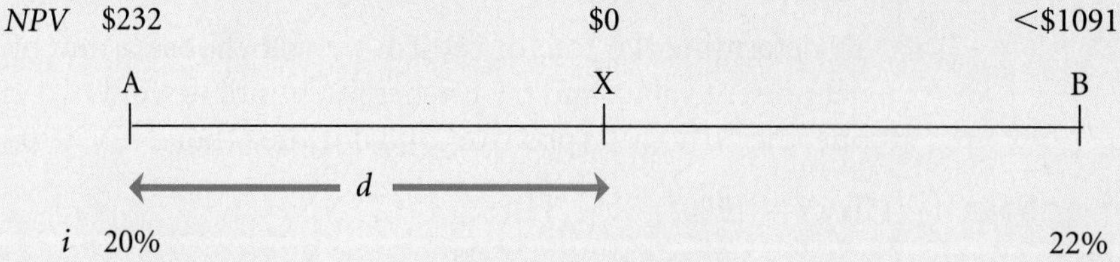

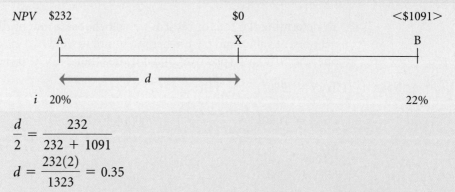

$$\frac{d}{2} = \frac{232}{232 + 1091}$$

$$d = \frac{232(2)}{1323} = 0.35$$

The rate of discount for which the NPV = 0 is approximately 20% + 0.35% = 20.35%. The rate of return is approximately 20.3%. (A more precisely computed value is 20.3382%.)

Note: Three attempts were needed to locate the R.O.I. between 20% and 22%. Three is the usual number of tries necessary. The minimum number is two attempts. Occasionally four attempts may be needed. To produce a more concise solution, organize the computation as shown below. Since estimates are involved, it is sufficient to use present value factors with only three decimal positions. In the following examples, all factors are rounded to three decimals.

Present Value of Amounts in General Form	Attempts					
	$i = 12\%$		$i = 20\%$		$i = 22\%$	
PV_{IN}	Factor	$	Factor	$	Factor	$
$7000\left[\frac{1-(1+i)^{-7}}{i}\right]$	4.563757	31 946	3.604592	25 232	3.415506	23 909
PV_{OUT} 25 000 now		25 000		25 000		25 000
NPV		6 946		232		<1 091>

Programmed Solution

(Set P/Y = 1; C/Y = 1)

Present Value of Amounts in General Form	Attempts					
	$i = 12\%$	$i = 20\%$	$i = 22\%$	$i = 20.5\%$	$i = 20.3\%$	$i = 20.34\%$
PV_{IN}	0 FV	0 FV	0 FV	0 FV	0 FV	0 FV
$7000\left[\frac{1-(1+i)^{-7}}{i}\right]$	−7000 PMT	−7000 PMT	−7000 PMT	−7000 PMT	−7000 PMT	−7000 PMT
	7 N	7 N	7 N	7 N	7 N	7 N

Present Value of Amounts in General Form	Attempts					
	$i = 12\%$	$i = 20\%$	$i = 22\%$	$i = 20.5\%$	$i = 20.3\%$	$i = 20.34\%$
	12 I/Y CPT PV	20 I/Y CPT PV	22 I/Y CPT PV	20.5 I/Y CPT PV	20.3 I/Y CPT PV	20.34 I/Y CPT PV
PV_{IN}	31 946	25 232	23 909	24 890	25 026	24 999
PV_{OUT} 25 000 now	25 000	25 000	25 000	25 000	25 000	25 000
NPV	6946	232	−1091	−110	26	−1
R.O.I.	$> 12\%$	$> 20\%$	$< 22\%$	$< 20.5\%$	$> 20.3\%$	$= 20.34\%$

EXAMPLE 16.3C

A venture that requires an immediate outlay of $320 000 and an outlay of $96 000 after five years has a residual value of $70 000 after ten years. Net returns are estimated to be $64 000 per year for ten years. Compute the rate of return.

SOLUTION

The cash flow is represented in the diagram below (in thousands).

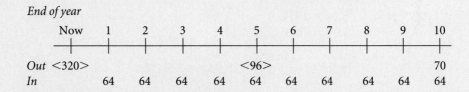

End of year

	Now	1	2	3	4	5	6	7	8	9	10
Out	<320>					<96>					70
In		64	64	64	64	64	64	64	64	64	64

The computations are organized in a chart; explanations regarding the computations follow.

Present Value of Amounts in General Form	Attempts					
	$i = 20\%$		$i = 14\%$		$i = 12\%$	
PV of benefits	Factor	$	Factor	$	Factor	$
$64\,000\left[\frac{1-(1+i)^{-10}}{i}\right]$	4.192	268 288	5.216	333 824	5.650	361 600
PV of costs:						
320 000 now		320 000		320 000		320 000
$96\,000(1+i)^{-5}$	0.402	38 592	0.519	49 824	0.567	54 432
<$70\,000(1+i)^{-10}$>	0.162	<11 340>	0.270	<18 900>	0.322	<22 540>
TOTAL		347 252		350 924		351 892
NPV		<78 964>		<17 100>		9 708

Explanations for computations

STEP 1 Try $i = 20\%$.
Since $\text{NPV} < 0$, $\text{R.O.I.} < 20\%$

$$\text{Index at } 20\% = \frac{268\,288}{347\,252} = 0.773 = 77.3\%$$

$$\text{Reduction in rate} = \frac{22.7\%}{4} = 5.7\% \longrightarrow 6\%$$

STEP 2 Try $i = 14\%$.
$\text{NPV} < 0$, $\text{R.O.I.} < 14\%$

$$\text{Index} = \frac{333\,824}{350\,924} = 0.951 = 95.1\%$$

$$\text{Reduction in rate} = \frac{4.9\%}{4} = 1.2\% \longrightarrow 2\%$$

STEP 3 Try $i = 12\%$
$\text{NPV} > 0$; $\text{R.O.I.} > 12\%$
$12\% < \text{R.O.I.} < 14\%$

STEP 4 $$\frac{d}{2} = \frac{9708}{9708 + 17\,100} = \frac{9708}{26\,808} = 0.362131$$

$$d = 2(0.362131) = 0.724$$

The rate of discount at which the net present value is zero is 12% + 0.72% = 12.72%. The rate of return is 12.7%.

Programmed Solution

(Set P/Y = 1; C/Y = 1)

Present Value of Amounts in General Form	Attempts				
	$i = 20\%$	$i = 14\%$	$i = 12\%$	$i = 12.7\%$	$i = 12.68\%$
PV of benefits	0 FV	0 FV	0 FV	0 FV	0 FV
$64\,000\left[\frac{1-(1+i)^{-10}}{i}\right]$	−64 000 PMT	−64 000 PMT	−64 000 PMT	−64 000 PMT	−64 000 PMT
	10 N	10 N	10 N	10 N	10 N
	20 I/Y	14 I/Y	12 I/Y	12.7 I/Y	12.68 I/Y
	CPT	CPT	CPT	CPT	CPT
	PV	PV	PV	PV	PV
PV_{IN}	268 318	333 831	361 614	351 484	351 767
PV of costs					
320 000 now	320 000	320 000	320 000	320 000	320 000
$96\,000(1+i)^{-5}$	0 PMT	0 PMT	0 PMT	0 PMT	0 PMT
	96 000 FV	96 000 FV	96 000 FV	96 000 FV	96 000 FV
	5 N	5 N	5 N	5 N	5 N
	20 I/Y	14 I/Y	12 I/Y	12.7 I/Y	12.68 I/Y
	CPT	CPT	CPT	CPT	CPT
	PV	PV	PV	PV	PV
Outflow	−38 580	−49 859	−54 473	−52 802	−52 849
<70 000$(1+i)^{-10}$>	70 000 FV	70 000 FV	70 000 FV	70 000 FV	70 000 FV
	10 N	10 N	10 N	10 N	10 N
	20 I/Y	14 I/Y	12 I/Y	12.7 I/Y	12.68 I/Y
	CPT	CPT	CPT	CPT	CPT
	PV	PV	PV	PV	PV
<inflow>	<11 305>	<18 882>	<22 538>	<21 177>	<21 214>
PV_{OUT}	347 275	350 977	351 935	351 625	351 635
NPV	<78 957>	<17 146>	9 679	<141>	132
R.O.I.	<20%	<14%	>12%	<12.7%	>12.68%

EXAMPLE 16.3D

A project requires an immediate investment of \$33 000 with a residual value of \$7000 at the end of the project. It is expected to yield a net return of \$7000 in Year 1, \$8000 in Year 2, \$11 000 per year for the following six years, and \$9000 per year for the remaining four years. Find the rate of return.

SOLUTION

The cash flows for the project (in thousands) are represented in the diagram below.

End of year

	Now	1	2	3	4	5	6	7	8	9	10	11	12
Out	<33>												7
In		7	8	11	11	11	11	11	11	9	9	9	9

The computations are organized in the chart that follows.

Present Value of Amounts in General Form	Attempts $i = 20\%$		$i = 28\%$		$i = 26\%$	
PV of returns	Factor	\$	Factor	\$	Factor	\$
$7000(1+i)^{-1}$	0.833	5 831	0.781	5 467	0.794	5 558
$8000(1+i)^{-2}$	0.694	5 552	0.610	4 880	0.630	5 040
$11\,000\left[\frac{1-(1+i)^{-6}}{i}\right]$	3.326		2.759		2.885	
	×	25 391	×	18 513	×	19 993
$\times (1+i)^{-2}$	0.694		0.610		0.630	
$9000\left[\frac{1-(1+i)^{-4}}{i}\right]$	2.589		2.241		2.320	
	×	5 429	×	2 803	×	3 278
$\times (1+i)^{-8}$	0.233		0.139		0.157	
TOTAL PV_{IN}		42 203		31 663		33 869
PV of costs 33 000 now		33 000		33 000		33 000
<$7000(1+i)^{-12}$>	0.112	<784>	0.052	<364>	0.062	<434>
TOTAL PV_{OUT}		32 216		32 636		32 566
NPV		9 987		<973>		1 303

Explanations for computations

STEP 1 The present value of the returns consists of \$7000 discounted for one year, \$8000 discounted for two years, the present value of an ordinary annuity of six payments of \$11 000 deferred for two years, and the present value of an ordinary annuity of four payments of \$9000 deferred for eight years. The present value of the costs consists of the lump sum of \$33 000 less the salvage value of \$7000 discounted for twelve years.

STEP 2 The rate of discount chosen for the first attempt is 20%.
For $i = 20\%$, NPV > 0; R.O.I. $> 20\%$

$$\text{Index} = \frac{42\,203}{32\,216} = 1.310 = 131.0\%$$

$$\text{Increase in rate} = \frac{31.0}{4} = 7.75\% \text{ or } 8\%$$

STEP 3 For $i = 28\%$, NPV < 0; R.O.I $< 28\%$

$$\text{Index} = \frac{31\,663}{32\,636} = 0.970 = 97.0\%$$

$$\text{Decrease in rate} = \frac{3}{4} = 0.75\% \text{ or } 2\% \text{ (rounded up)}$$

STEP 4 For $i = 26\%$, NPV > 0; R.O.I. $> 26\%$
$26\% <$ R.O.I. $< 28\%$

STEP 5

$$d = \frac{1303}{1303 + 973} \times 2 = \frac{2606}{2276} = 1.14499$$

The rate of discount for which the net present value is zero is approximately 26% + 1.14% = 27.14%. The rate of return, correct to the nearest tenth of a percent, is 27.1%.

POINTERS AND PITFALLS

Investors should always be aware of the fact that higher rates of return (yield) are accompanied typically by higher levels of investment risk. For the most daring investors, high-risk/high-yield investments include derivatives, commodities, precious metals, gemstones, collectible items, common stocks, and growth stocks. For investors more comfortable with moderate-risk/moderate-yield, investment choices include mutual funds, real estate, corporate bonds, and preferred stocks. Low-risk/low-yield options such as savings accounts, term deposits, guaranteed investment certificates (GICs), and Canada Savings Bonds (CSBs) are designed to appeal to the most conservative investors.

Internal rate of return can be determined by using a preprogrammed financial calculator.

EXERCISE 16.3

EXCEL NOTES

If you choose, you can use Excel's ***Internal Rate of Return (IRR)*** function to answer the questions in Part B below. Refer to **IRR** on the Spreadsheet Template Disk to learn how to use this Excel function.

A. Use linear interpolation to find the approximate value of the rate of return for each of the projects below. State your answer correct to the nearest tenth of a percent.

	Positive NPV at *i*	Negative NPV at *i*
1.	\$2350 at 24%	−\$1270 at 26%
2.	\$850 at 8%	−\$370 at 10%
3.	\$135 at 20%	−\$240 at 22%
4.	\$56 at 16%	−\$70 at 18%

B. Find the rate of return for each of the six situations below (correct to the nearest tenth of a percent).

1. The proposed expansion of CIV Electronics' plant facilities requires the immediate outlay of \$100 000. Expected net returns are

Year 1: Nil	Year 2: \$30 000	Year 3: \$40 000
Year 4: \$60 000	Year 5: \$50 000	Year 6: \$20 000

2. The introduction of a new product requires an initial outlay of \$60 000. The anticipated net returns from the marketing of the product are expected to be \$12 000 per year for ten years.

3. Your firm is considering introducing a new product for which net returns are expected to be

Year 1 to Year 3 inclusive:	\$2000 per year
Year 4 to Year 8 inclusive:	\$5000 per year
Year 9 to Year 12 inclusive:	\$3000 per year

The introduction of the product requires an immediate outlay of \$15 000 for equipment estimated to have a salvage value of \$2000 after twelve years.

4. A project requiring an immediate investment of \$150 000 and a further outlay of \$40 000 after four years has a residual value of \$30 000 after nine years. The project yields a negative net return of \$10 000 in Year 1, a zero net return in Year 2, \$50 000 per year for the following four years, and \$70 000 per year for the last three years.

5. You are thinking of starting a hot dog business that requires an initial investment of \$16 000 and a major replacement of equipment after ten years amounting to \$8000. From competitive experience, you expect to have a net loss of \$2000 the first year, a net profit of \$2000 the second year, and, for the remaining years of the first fifteen years of operations, net returns of \$6000 per year. After fifteen years, the net returns will gradually decline and will be zero at the end of twenty-five years (assume returns of \$3000 per year for that period).

After twenty-five years, your lease will expire. The salvage value of equipment at that time is expected to be just sufficient to cover the cost of closing the business.

6. The Blue Sky Ski Resort plans to install a new chair lift. Construction is estimated to require an immediate outlay of $220 000. The life of the lift is estimated to be fifteen years with a salvage value of $80 000. Cost of clearing and grooming the new area is expected to be $30 000 for each of the first three years of operation. Net cash inflows from the lift are expected to be $40 000 for each of the first five years and $70 000 for each of the following ten years.

Review Exercise

1. Wells Inc. has to choose between two investment alternatives. Alternative A will return the company $20 000 after three years, $60 000 after six years, and $40 000 after ten years. Alternative B will bring returns of $10 000 per year for ten years. If the company expects a return of 14% on investments, which alternative should it choose?

2. A piece of property may be acquired by making an immediate payment of $25 000 and payments of $37 500 and $50 000 three and five years from now respectively. Alternatively, the property may be purchased by making quarterly payments of $5150 in advance for five years. Which alternative is preferable if money is worth 15% compounded semi-annually?

3. An investor has two investment alternatives. If he chooses Alternative 1, he will have to make an immediate outlay of $7000 and will receive $500 every three months for the next nine years. If he chooses Alternative 2, he will have to make an immediate outlay of $6500 and will receive $26 000 after eight years. If interest is 12% compounded quarterly, which alternative should the investor choose on the basis of the net present value criterion?

4. Replacing old equipment at an immediate cost of $65 000 and $40 000 five years from now will result in a savings of $8000 semi-annually for ten years. At 14% compounded annually, should the old equipment be replaced?

5. A real estate development project requires annual outlays of $75 000 for eight years. Net cash inflows beginning in Year 9 are expected to be $250 000 per year for fifteen years. If the developer requires a rate of return of 18%, compute the net present value of the project.

6. A company is considering a project that will require a cost outlay of $30 000 per year for four years. At the end of the project, the company expects to salvage the physical assets for $30 000. The project is estimated to yield net returns of $60 000 in Year 4, $40 000 in Year 5, and $20 000 for each of the following five years. Alternative investments are available yielding a rate of return of 14%. Compute the net present value of the project.

7. An investment requires an initial outlay of $45 000. Net returns are estimated to be $14 000 per year for eight years. Determine the rate of return.

8. A project requires an initial outlay of $10 000 and promises net returns of $2000 per year over a twelve-year period. If the project has a residual value of $4000 after twelve years, what is the rate of return?

9. Compute the rate of return for Question 5.

10. Compute the rate of return for Question 6.

11. Superior Jig Co. has developed a new jig for which it expects net returns as follows.

Year 1:	$8 000
Years 2 to 6 inclusive:	$12 000 per year
Years 7 to 10 inclusive:	$6 000 per year

The initial investment of $36 000 has a residual value of $9000 after ten years. Compute the rate of return.

12. The owner of a sporting goods store is considering remodelling the store in order to carry a larger inventory. The cost of remodelling and additional inventory is $60 000. The expected increase in net profit is $8000 per year for the next four years and $10 000 each year for the following six years. After ten years, the owner plans to retire and sell the business. She expects to recover the additional $40 000 invested in inventory but not the $20 000 invested in remodelling. Compute the rate of return.

13. Outway Ventures evaluates potential investment projects at 20%. Two alternative projects are available. Project A will return the company $5800 per year for eight years. Project B will return the company $13 600 after one year, $17 000 after five years, and $20 400 after eight years. Which alternative should the company choose according to the discounted cash flow criterion?

14. Project A requires an immediate investment of $8000 and another $6000 in three years. Net returns are $4000 after two years, $12 000 after four years, and $8000 after six years. Project B requires an immediate investment of $4000, another $6000 after two years, and $4000 after four years. Net returns are $3400 per year for seven years. Determine the net present value at 10%. Which project is preferable according to the net present value criterion?

15. Net returns from an investment are estimated to be $13 000 per year for twelve years. The investment involves an immediate outlay of $50 000 and a further outlay of $30 000 after six years. The investments are estimated to have a residual value of $10 000 after twelve years. Find the net present value at 20%.

16. The introduction of a new product requires an immediate outlay of $45 000. Anticipated net returns from the marketing of the product are expected to be $12 500 per year for ten years. What is the rate of return on the investment (correct to the nearest tenth of a percent)?

17. Games Inc. has developed a new electronic game and compiled the following product information.

	Production Cost	Promotion Cost	Sales Revenue
Year 1	$32 000	—	—
Year 2	32 000	$64 000	$ 64 000
Year 3	32 000	96 000	256 000
Year 4	32 000	32 000	128 000
Year 5	32 000		32 000

Should the product be marketed if the company requires a return of 16%?

18. Farmer Jones wants to convert his farm into a golf course. He asked you to determine his rate of return on the basis of the following estimates: development cost for each of the first three years, $80 000; construction of a clubhouse in Year 4, $240 000; upon his retirement in fifteen years, improvements in the property will yield him $200 000; net returns from the operation of the golf course will be nil for the first three years and $100 000 per year afterwards until his retirement.

Self-Test

1. Opportunities Inc. requires a minimum rate of return of 15% on investment proposals. Two proposals are under consideration but only one may be chosen. Alternative A offers a net return of $2500 per year for twelve years. Alternative B offers a net return of $10 000 each year after four, eight, and twelve years respectively. Determine the preferred alternative according to the discounted cash flow criterion.

2. A natural resources development project requires an immediate outlay of $100 000 and $50 000 at the end of each year for four years. Net returns are nil for the first two years and $60 000 per year thereafter for fourteen years. What is the net present value of the project at 16%?

3. An investment of $100 000 yields annual net returns of $20 000 for ten years. If the residual value of the investment after ten years is $30 000, what is the rate of return on the investment (correct to the nearest tenth of a percent)?

4. A telephone system with a disposable value of $1200 after five years can be purchased for $6600. Alternatively, a leasing agreement is available that requires an immediate payment of $1500 plus payments of $100 at the beginning of each month for five years. If money is worth 12% compounded monthly, should the telephone system be leased or purchased?

5. A choice has to be made between two investment proposals. Proposal A requires an immediate outlay of $60 000 and a further outlay of $40 000 after three years. Net returns are $20 000 per year for ten years. The investment has no residual value after ten years. Proposal B requires outlays of $29 000 in each of the first four years. Net returns starting in Year 4 are $40 000 per year. The residual value of the investment after ten years is $50 000. Which proposal is preferable at 20%?

6. Introducing a new product requires an immediate investment in plant facilities of $180 000 with a disposal value of $45 000 after seven years. The facilities will require additional capital outlays of $50 000 each after three and five years respectively. Net returns on the investment are estimated to be $75 000 per year for each of the first four years and $50 000 per year for the remaining three years. Determine the rate of return on investment (correct to the nearest tenth of a percent).

Challenge Problems

1. The owners of a vegetable processing plant can buy a new conveyor system for $85 000. They estimate they can save $17 000 per year on labour and maintenance costs. They can purchase the same conveyor system with an automatic loader for $114 000, and estimate they can save $22 000 per year with that system. If the owners expect both systems to last ten years and they require at least 14% return per year, should they buy the system with the automatic loader?

2. CheeseWorks owns four dairies in your province and has planned upgrades for all locations. The owners are considering four projects, each of which is independent of the other three projects. The details of each project—A, B, C, and D—are shown below.

Project	Cost at Beginning of Year 1	Revenues and Cost Savings at End of: Year 1	Year 2	Year 3	Year 4	Year 5
A	300 000	150 000	120 000	120 000	0	0
B	360 000	0	40 000	200 000	200 000	200 000
C	210 000	10 000	10 000	100 000	120 000	120 000
D	125 000	30 000	40 000	40 000	40 000	40 000

The owners of CheeseWorks have $700 000 to invest in these projects. They expect at least 12% return on all of their projects. In which projects should the owners of CheeseWorks invest to maximize the return on their investment?

Case Study 16.1 To Lease or Not to Lease?

» To travel to her new job, Dharshana required a car. Reading the newspaper, she noticed an ad for an Acura TSX. It was just the vehicle she wanted.

The ad quoted both a cash purchase price of $37 500 and a monthly lease payment option. Since she did not have enough money to pay for a car, she would have to finance it from Honda by paying interest of 7.8% compounded monthly on the loan.

The lease option required payments of $594 a month for 48 months with a $1330 down payment or equivalent trade. Freight and air tax was included. Dharshana did not have a vehicle to offer as a trade-in. If the vehicle was leased, then after 48 months it could be purchased for $16 155. The lease was based on a finance interest rate of 3.8%. During the term of the lease, kilometres were limited to 24 000 per year, and an additional charge of $0.08 per kilometre for excess kilometres. The costs included freight, but excluded taxes, registration, licence, and dealer administration charges. Dharshana was particularly impressed with the "four-years or 100 000 kilometre" warranty on the engine and transmission. The manufacturer also offered 24-hour roadside assistance.

Dharshana must decide whether to buy or lease this car. She lives in a province with a 7% PST and 6% GST tax rate. She realizes that the costs of licence and insurance must be paid, but she will ignore these in her calculations.

QUESTIONS

1. If Dharshana buys the car, what is the total purchase price, including taxes?
2. Since Dharshana has no down payment, she must finance the car if she purchases it.
   (a) Is it cheaper to borrow the money from the bank or to lease?
   (b) The bank is offering a vehicle loan rate of 8% compounded annually. Is it better to buy or to lease the car at this rate?
3. Suppose Dharshana has a $4000 down payment for this car.
   (a) What is the purchase price of the car if she pays cash for it? Assume the down payment is subtracted from the price of the car including tax.
   (b) If the monthly lease payment is $594, is it cheaper to lease or buy the car if Dharshana can get the special dealer rate of 3.8%?

Case Study 16.2 Building a Business

» Advanced Manufacturing Ltd. has demolished an old warehouse to make room for additional manufacturing capacity. The company has decided to construct a new building, but must decide on how to proceed. There are two alternatives for the new building, both of which will create a building with an expected life of sixty years. The residual value is unknown but will be the same for either alternative.

Alternative A is to construct a new building that would have 210 000 square metres. Construction costs will initially total $2 800 000 at the start. Maintenance costs are expected to be $18 000 per year. The building will need to be repainted every ten years (starting in ten years) at an estimated cost of $15 000.

Alternative B is to construct the building in two stages: build 100 000 square metres now; and add 110 000 square metres in ten years. Construction costs for the first stage will be $1 900 000 at the start of the project. Construction costs for the second stage will be $1 000 000 when the addition is completed at the end of Year 10. Maintenance costs are expected to be $12 000 per year for the first ten years, then $21 000 per year after that. The building and the addition will have to be painted every ten years, beginning in Year 20, at an estimated cost of $15 000.

QUESTIONS

1. Suppose the company's required rate of return is 12%.
   (a) What is the present value of Alternative A?
   (b) What is the present value of Alternative B?
   (c) Which alternative would you recommend on the basis of your discounted cash flow analysis?

2. Which alternative would you recommend if the company's required rate of return was 18%? Show all calculations.

3. Suppose the company could rent a portion of its building for $55 000 per year for the first ten years if it chose Alternative A.
   (a) If the company's required rate of return is 12%, what is the net present value of Alternative A?
   (b) On the basis of the new information, would you recommend Alternative A or Alternative B if the company's required rate of return is 18%?

SUMMARY OF FORMULAS

Formula 16.1

$$\underset{\text{(NPV)}}{\text{NET PRESENT VALUE}} = \underset{\text{OF INFLOWS}}{\text{PRESENT VALUE}} - \underset{\text{OF OUTLAYS}}{\text{PRESENT VALUE}}$$

Formula for finding the difference between the present value of cash inflows and the present value of cash outflows, known as the net present value

Formula 16.2

$$\text{PROFITABILITY INDEX} = \frac{\text{PRESENT VALUE OF INFLOWS}}{\text{PRESENT VALUE OF OUTLAYS}} = \frac{PV_{IN}}{PV_{OUT}}$$

Formula for finding the relationship by dividing the present value of cash inflows by the present value of cash outflows, known as the profitability index

In addition, Formulas 9.1B, 9.1C, 11.2, 12.3, 13.2, and 13.4 were used in this chapter.

GLOSSARY

Discounted benefit–cost ratio *see* **Profitability index**

Discounted cash flow the present value of cash payments *(p. 700)*

Internal rate of return *see* **Rate of return**

Net present value the difference between the present value of the inflows (benefits) and the present value of the outlays (costs) of a capital investment project *(p. 691)*

Profitability index the ratio of the present value of the inflows (benefits) to the present value of the outlays (costs) of a capital investment project *(p. 700)*

Rate of return the rate of discount for which the net present value of a capital investment project is equal to zero *(p. 700)*

USEFUL INTERNET SITES

www.tsx.com
TSX Group Visit this site for information on all the companies that are traded on the Toronto Stock Exchange (TSX).

www.investorwords.com
InvestorWords.com A comprehensive financial glossary with definitions and related terms.

http://finance.yahoo.com
Yahoo! Finance A full education site that also contains quotes, charts, historical analysis, and reports.

APPENDIX I

Further Review of Basic Algebra

I.1 BASIC LAWS, RULES, AND DEFINITIONS

A. The fundamental operations

The fundamental operations of algebra are *addition*, *subtraction*, *multiplication*, and *division*. The symbols used to show these operations are the same as the symbols used in arithmetic.

For any two numbers a and b, the fundamental operations are as follows.

1. *Addition* is denoted by $a + b$ and referred to as the sum of a and b.
If $a = 7$ and $b = 4$, then $a + b = 7 + 4 = 11$.

2. *Subtraction* is denoted by $a - b$ and referred to as the difference between a and b.
If $a = 7$ and $b = 4$, then $a - b = 7 - 4 = 3$.

3. *Multiplication* is denoted by $a \times b$ or $(a)(b)$ or ab. a and b are called *factors* and ab is referred to as the product of a and b.
If $a = 7$ and $b = 4$, then $ab = (7)(4) = 28$.

4. *Division* is denoted by $a{:}b$ or $\frac{a}{b}$ or a/b. a is the dividend, b is the divisor, and $\frac{a}{b}$ is the quotient.
If $a = 7$ and $b = 4$, then $\frac{a}{b} = \frac{7}{4}$.

B. Basic laws

The basic laws governing algebraic operations are the same as those used for arithmetic operations.

1. The Commutative Laws for Addition and Multiplication

(a) When adding two numbers, the two numbers (addends) may be interchanged.

$$a + b = b + a$$ —— **Formula I.1**

If $a = 7$ and $b = 4$, then $7 + 4 = 4 + 7 = 11$.

(b) When multiplying two numbers, the two factors may be interchanged.

$$ab = ba$$ —— Formula I.2

If $a = 7$ and $b = 4$, then $(7)(4) = (4)(7) = 28$.

2. The Associative Laws for Addition and Multiplication

(a) When adding three or more numbers, the numbers (addends) may be combined in any order.

$$a + b + c = (a + b) + c = a + (b + c) = b + (a + c)$$ —— Formula I.3

If $a = 7$, $b = 4$, and $c = 2$, then $7 + 4 + 2 = (7 + 4) + 2 = 7 + (4 + 2) = 4 + (7 + 2) = 13$.

(b) When multiplying three or more numbers, the numbers (factors) may be combined in any order.

$$abc = (ab)c = a(bc) = b(ac)$$ —— Formula I.4

If $a = 7$, $b = 4$, and $c = 2$, then $7 \times 4 \times 2 = (7 \times 4) \times 2 = 7 \times (4 \times 2) = 4 \times (7 \times 2) = 56$.

3. The Distributive Law of Multiplication over Addition

The product of a times the sum of b and c is equal to the sum of the products ab and ac.

$$a(b + c) = ab + ac$$ —— Formula I.5

If $a = 7$, $b = 4$, and $c = 2$, then $7(4 + 2) = 7 \times 4 + 7 \times 2 = 42$.

4. Special Properties of 1

(a) $a \times 1 = 1 \times a = a$

When any number a is multiplied by 1, the product is the number a.

If $a = 5$, then $5 \times 1 = 1 \times 5 = 5$.

(b) $\frac{a}{1} = a$

When any number a is divided by 1, the quotient is the number a.

If $a = 5$, then $\frac{5}{1} = 5$.

(c) $\frac{a}{a} = 1$

When any number a is divided by itself, the quotient is 1.

If $a = 5$, then $\frac{5}{5} = 1$.

5. Special Properties of 0

(a) *Addition with 0*

$\boxed{a + 0 = 0 + a = a}$

When 0 is added to any number *a*, the sum is the number *a*.

If $a = 5$, then $5 + 0 = 0 + 5 = 5$.

(b) *Subtraction with 0*

(i) $\boxed{a - 0 = a}$

When 0 is subtracted from any number *a*, the difference is the number *a*.

If $a = 5$, then $5 - 0 = 5$.

(ii) $\boxed{0 - a = -a}$

When any number *a* is subtracted from 0, the difference is the inverse value of *a*, that is, *a* with the sign changed.

If $a = 5$, then $0 - 5 = -5$.

(c) *Multiplication with 0*

$\boxed{a \times 0 = 0 \times a = 0}$

When 0 is multiplied by any number *a*, the product is 0.

If $a = 5$, then $5 \times 0 = 0 \times 5 = 0$.

(d) *Division with 0*

(i) $\frac{0}{a} = 0$

When 0 is divided by any number *a* other than 0, the quotient is 0.

(ii) $\frac{a}{0} = \text{undefined}$

Division by 0 has no meaning.

If $a = 5$, then $\frac{5}{0} = \text{undefined}$.

C. Definitions

1. An **algebraic expression** is a combination of numbers, variables representing numbers, and symbols indicating an algebraic operation.

   $7ab$, $3a - 5b$, $x^2 - 3x + 4$, $\frac{3}{4}x - \frac{1}{5}y$ are algebraic expressions.

2. A **term** is a part of an algebraic expression separated from other parts by a positive (+) sign or by a negative (−) sign. The preceding (+) sign or (−) sign is part of the term.

   The terms for the algebraic expressions listed in part (1) are

   $7ab$; $3a$ and $-5b$; x^2, $-3x$, and $+4$; $\frac{3}{4}x$ and $-\frac{1}{5}y$

3. A **monomial** is an algebraic expression consisting of *one* term, such as $7ab$.
   A **binomial** is an algebraic expression consisting of *two* terms, such as $3a - 5b$ or $\frac{3}{4}x - \frac{1}{5}y$.
   A **trinomial** is an algebraic expression consisting of *three* terms, such as $x^2 - 3x + 4$.
   A **polynomial** is an algebraic expression consisting of *more than one* term.

4. A **factor** is one of the numbers that when multiplied by another number or other numbers yields a given product.

   The factors of the term $7ab$ are 7, a, and b.

5. A *factor of a term* is called the *coefficient* of the rest of the term.

   In the term $7ab$, 7 is the coefficient of ab,
   $7a$ is the coefficient of b,
   $7b$ is the coefficient of a.

6. The **numerical coefficient** is the part of a term formed by *numerals.*

   In the term $7ab$, the numerical coefficient is 7;
   in the term x^2, the numerical coefficient is *understood* to be 1 (1 is usually not written);
   in the term $-\frac{1}{5}y$, the numerical coefficient is $-\frac{1}{5}$ (the sign is considered to be part of the numerical coefficient).

7. The **literal coefficient** of a term is the part of the term formed with *letter* symbols.

   In the term $7ab$, ab is the literal coefficient;
   in the term $3x^2$, x^2 is the literal coefficient.

8. **Like terms** are terms having the *same* literal coefficients.

   $7a, -3a, a, -\frac{1}{3}a$ are like terms;

   $x^2, -2x^2, -\frac{1}{2}x^2, 5x^2$ are like terms.

9. **Combining like terms** or **collecting like terms** means *adding* like terms. Only like terms can be added.

10. **Signed numbers** are numbers preceded by a positive (+) or a negative (−) sign. Numbers preceded by a positive (+) sign are called **positive numbers,** while numbers preceded by a negative (−) sign are called **negative numbers**.

11. **Like signed numbers** are numbers that have the *same* sign, while numbers with *different* signs are called **unlike signed numbers.**

    $+7$ and $+8$ are like signed numbers;
    -7 and -8 are like signed numbers;
    $+7$ and -8 are unlike signed numbers;
    -7 and 8 are unlike signed numbers.

    Note: If no sign is written in front of a number, a plus (+) sign is understood to precede the number.

    6 means $+6$.

12. The **absolute value** of a signed number is the value of the number *without* the sign and is denoted by the symbol | | surrounding the number.

    The absolute value of $+5 = |+5| = 5$;
    the absolute value of $-5 = |-5| = 5$.

EXERCISE I.1

A. Answer each of the following questions.

1. List the terms contained in each of the following expressions.

(a) $-3xy$ **(b)** $4a - 5c - 2d$

(c) $x^2 - \frac{1}{2}x - 2$ **(d)** $1.2x - 0.5xy + 0.9y - 0.3$

2. Name the numerical coefficient of each of the following terms.

(a) $-3b$ **(b)** $7c$ **(c)** $-a$ **(d)** x

(e) $12a^2b$ **(f)** $-3ax$ **(g)** $-\frac{1}{2}x^2$ **(h)** $\frac{x}{5}$

3. Name the literal coefficient of each of the following.

(a) $3x$ **(b)** ab **(c)** $-4y$ **(d)** $-xy$

(e) $-15x^2y^2$ **(f)** $3.5abx$ **(g)** $\frac{4}{3}x^3$ **(h)** $\frac{by}{6}$

I.2 FUNDAMENTAL OPERATIONS WITH SIGNED NUMBERS

A. Additions with signed numbers

1. *Addition of like signed numbers*
To add like signed numbers,

(i) add their absolute values, and
(ii) prefix the common sign.

EXAMPLE 1.2A Add each of the following.

(i) -6 and -8

SOLUTION The absolute values are 6 and 8;
the sum of 6 and 8 is 14;
the common sign is $(-)$.
$(-6) + (-8) = -6 - 8 = -14$

(ii) $+6$, $+5$, and $+12$

SOLUTION The absolute values are 6, 5, and 12;
the sum of 6, 5, and 12 is 23;
the common sign is $(+)$.
$(+6) + (+5) + (+12) = +6 + 5 + 12 = +23$, or 23

SOLUTION

(iii) $-9, -3, -1$, and -15

The absolute values are 9, 3, 1, and 15;
the sum of the four numbers is 28;
the common sign is $(-)$.
$(-9) + (-3) + (-1) + (-15) = -9 - 3 - 1 - 15 = -28$

2. *Addition of unlike signed numbers*
To add unlike signed numbers,
   (i) subtract the smaller absolute value from the larger absolute value, and
   (ii) prefix the sign of the *larger* absolute value.

EXAMPLE 1.2B

Add each of the following.

(i) 8 and -5

SOLUTION

The absolute values are 8 and 5;
the difference between the absolute values is 3;
the sign of the larger absolute value is $(+)$.
$(+8) + (-5) = +8 - 5 = +3$, or 3

(ii) 4 and -9

The absolute values are 4 and 9;
the difference between the absolute values is 5;
the sign of the larger absolute value is $(-)$.
$(+4) + (-9) = 4 - 9 = -5$

(iii) $-6, +8, +3, -4$, and -5

When more than two numbers are involved and unlike signs appear, two approaches are available.

METHOD 1 Add the first two numbers and then add the sum to the next number and so on.

$(-6) + (+8) + (+3) + (-4) + (-5)$
$= -6 + 8 + 3 - 4 - 5$
$= +2 + 3 - 4 - 5$ ——— add -6 and $+8$, which equals $+2$
$= +5 - 4 - 5$ ——— add $+2$ and $+3$, which equals $+5$
$= +1 - 5$ ——— add $+5$ and -4, which equals $+1$
$= -4$ ——— add $+1$ and -5, which equals -4

METHOD 2 First add the numbers having like signs and then add the two resulting unlike signed numbers.

$(-6) + (+8) + (+3) + (-4) + (-5)$
$= -6 + 8 + 3 - 4 - 5$
$= (-6 - 4 - 5) + (+8 + 3)$
$= (-15) + (+11)$
$= -15 + 11$
$= -4$

B. Subtraction with signed numbers

The subtraction of signed numbers is changed to addition by using the inverse of the *subtrahend*. Thus, to subtract with signed numbers, change the sign of the subtrahend and add.

EXAMPLE 1.2C Perform each of the following subtractions.

(i) (+6) from (4)

SOLUTION

$(+4) - (+6)$

$= (+4) + (-6)$ — change the subtrahend (+6) to (−6) and change the subtraction to an addition

$= +4 - 6$

$= -2$ — use the rules of addition to add +4 and −6

(ii) (−12) from (+7)

$(+7) - (-12)$

$= (+7) - (+12)$ — change the subtrahend (−12) to (+12) and add

$= +7 + 12$

$= 19$

(iii) (+9) from (−6)

$(-6) - (+9)$

$= (-6) + (-9)$

$= -6 - 9$

$= -15$

C. Multiplication with signed numbers

The product of two signed numbers is positive or negative according to the following rules.

(a) If the signs of the two numbers are *like*, the product is *positive*.

$(+)(+) = (+)$

$(-)(-) = (+)$

(b) If the signs of the two numbers are *unlike*, the product is *negative*.

$(+)(-) = (-)$

$(-)(+) = (-)$

EXAMPLE 1.2D

(i) $(+7)(+4) = 28$ — the signs are like (both positive); the product is positive

(ii) $(-9)(-3) = 27$ — the signs are like (both negative); the product is positive

(iii) $(-8)(3) = -24$ — the signs are unlike; the product is negative

(iv) $(7)(-1) = -7$ — the signs are unlike; the product is negative

(v) $(-8)(0) = 0$ — the product of any number and 0 is 0

(vi) $(-7)(3)(-4) = (-21)(-4)$ — (-7) times (3) is (-21)
$= -84$

(vii) $(-2)(-1)(-4)(3) = (2)(-4)(3) = (-8)(3) = -24$

Note: Brackets around one or both numbers indicate multiplication.

D. Division with signed numbers

The quotient of two signed numbers is positive or negative according to the following rules.

(a) If the signs are *like*, the quotient is *positive*.
$(+) \div (+) = (+)$
$(-) \div (-) = (+)$

(b) If the signs are *unlike*, the quotient is *negative*.
$(+) \div (-) = (-)$
$(-) \div (+) = (-)$

EXAMPLE 1.2E

(i) $15 \div (+5) = 3$ — the signs are like; the quotient is positive

(ii) $(-24) \div (-4) = 6$ — the signs are like; the quotient is positive

(iii) $(-18) \div 2 = -9$ — the signs are unlike; the quotient is negative

(iv) $(12) \div (-1) = -12$ — the signs are unlike; the quotient is negative

(v) $0 \div (-10) = 0$ — 0 divided by any number is 0

(vi) $(-16) \div 0 =$ undefined — division by 0 has no meaning

E. Absolute value of signed numbers

The absolute value of signed numbers, denoted by $|\ |$, is the value of the numbers without the signs.

EXAMPLE 1.2F

(i) $|-7| = 7$

(ii) $|-3 + 8| = |+5| = 5$

(iii) $|4 - 9| = |-5| = 5$

(iv) $|-9 - 4| = |-13| = 13$

(v) $|4(-7)| = |-28| = 28$

(vi) $|(-9)(-3)| = |27| = 27$

(vii) $|(-12) \div (4)| = |-3| = 3$

(viii) $|(-30) \div (-5)| = |+6| = 6$

EXERCISE I.2

A. Simplify.

1. $(+3) + (+7)$ **2.** $(+12) + (+6)$ **3.** $(-5) + (-9)$

4. $(-15) + (-12)$ **5.** $4 + (+5)$ **6.** $(+6) + 8$

7. $-8 + (-7)$ **8.** $(-18) - 7$ **9.** $+3 + 14$

10. $+12 + 1$ **11.** $-6 - 9$ **12.** $-14 - 3$

13. $-8 + 3$ **14.** $-12 + 16$ **15.** $8 - 12$

16. $0 - 9$ **17.** $1 - 0.6$ **18.** $1 - 0.02$

19. $(-4) + (6) + (-3) + (+2)$ **20.** $12 + (-15) + (+8) + (-10)$

21. $-3 - 7 + 9 + 6 - 5$ **22.** $10 - 8 - 12 + 3 - 7$

B. Simplify.

1. $(+9) - (+8)$ **2.** $(+11) - (+14)$ **3.** $(+6) - (-6)$

4. $(+11) - (-12)$ **5.** $(-8) - (-7)$ **6.** $(-9) - (-13)$

7. $(-4) - (+6)$ **8.** $(-15) - (+3)$ **9.** $0 - (-9)$

10. $1 - (-0.4)$ **11.** $1 - (-0.03)$ **12.** $0 - (+15)$

13. $6 - (-5) + (-8) - (+3) + (-2)$

14. $-12 - (-6) - (+9) + (-4) - 7$

C. Simplify.

1. $(+5)(+4)$ **2.** $11(+3)$ **3.** $(-4)(-6)$

4. $-7(-3)$ **5.** $(+7)(-1)$ **6.** $10(-5)$

7. $-3(12)$ **8.** $-9(1)$ **9.** $0(-6)$

10. $-12(0)$ **11.** $6(-4)(-3)(2)$ **12.** $-3(5)(-2)(-1)$

D. Simplify.

1. $(+18) \div (+3)$ **2.** $(32) \div (+4)$ **3.** $(+45) \div (-9)$

4. $(63) \div (-3)$ **5.** $(-28) \div (+7)$ **6.** $(-36) \div (+12)$

7. $(-16) \div (-1)$ **8.** $(-48) \div (-8)$ **9.** $0 \div (-5)$

10. $0 \div 10$ **11.** $(+4) \div 0$ **12.** $(-12) \div 0$

E. Simplify.

1. $|-9|$ **2.** $|+4|$ **3.** $|6 - 10|$ **4.** $|-5 + 12|$

5. $|-7 - 8|$ **6.** $|0 - 3|$ **7.** $|(-3) \times 3|$ **8.** $|4 \times (-5)|$

9. $|20 \div (-5)|$ **10.** $|(-35) \div (7)|$

I.3 COMMON FACTORING

A. Basic concept

In arithmetic, certain computations, such as multiplication and division involving common fractions, are helped by factoring. Similarly, algebraic manipulation can be made easier by the process of finding the factors that make up an algebraic expression.

Factoring an algebraic expression means writing the expression as a product in component form. Depending on the type of factors contained in the expression, the process of factoring takes a variety of forms. Only the simplest type of factoring applies to the subject matter dealt with in this text. Accordingly only this type, called *common factoring*, is explained in this section.

A **common factor** is one that is divisible without remainder into each term of an algebraic expression. The factor that is common to each term is usually found by inspection; the remaining factor is then obtained by dividing the expression by the common factor.

B. Examples

EXAMPLE I.3A

Factor $14a + 21b$.

SOLUTION

By inspection, recognize that the two terms $14a$ and $21b$ are both divisible by 7.

The common factor is 7.
The second factor is now found by dividing the expression by 7.

$$\frac{14a + 21b}{7} = \frac{14a}{7} + \frac{21b}{7} = 2a + 3b$$

Thus the factors of $14a + 21b$ are 7 and $2a + 3b$.

$$14a + 21b = 7(2a + 3b)$$

EXAMPLE I.3B

Factor $18a - 45$.

SOLUTION

By inspection, the highest common factor is 9;

the second factor is $\dfrac{18a - 45}{9} = 2a - 5$.

$$18a - 45 = 9(2a - 5)$$

Note: If 3 is used as the common factor, the second factor, $6a - 15$, contains a common factor 3 and can be factored into $3(2a - 5)$.

$$\begin{aligned} \text{Thus, } 18a - 45 &= 3[6a - 15] \\ &= 3[3(2a - 5)] \\ &= 9(2a - 5) \end{aligned}$$

When factoring, the accepted procedure is to always take out the *highest* common factor.

EXAMPLE 1.3C Factor $mx - my$.

SOLUTION The common factor is m;

the second factor is $\dfrac{mx - my}{m} = x - y$.

$mx - my = m(x - y)$

EXAMPLE 1.3D Factor $15x^3 - 25x^2 - 20x$.

SOLUTION The common factor is $5x$.

The second factor is $\dfrac{15x^3 - 25x^2 - 20x}{5x} = 3x^2 - 5x - 4$.

$15x^3 - 25x^2 - 20x = 5x\,(3x^2 - 5x - 4)$

EXAMPLE 1.3E Factor $\mathrm{P} + \mathrm{P}rt$.

SOLUTION The common factor is P.

The second factor is $\dfrac{\mathrm{P} + \mathrm{P}rt}{\mathrm{P}} = \dfrac{\mathrm{P}}{\mathrm{P}} + \dfrac{\mathrm{P}rt}{\mathrm{P}} + 1 + rt$.

$\mathrm{P} + \mathrm{P}rt = \mathrm{P}(1 + rt)$

EXAMPLE 1.3F Factor $a(x + y) - b(x + y)$.

SOLUTION The common factor is $(x + y)$.

The second factor is $\dfrac{a(x + y) - b(x + y)}{x + y} = \dfrac{a(x + y)}{x + y} - \dfrac{b(x + y)}{x + y} = a - b$.

$a(x + y) - b(x + y) = (x + y)(a - b)$

EXAMPLE 1.3G Factor $(1 + i) + (1 + i)^2 + (1 + i)^3$.

SOLUTION The common factor is $(1 + i)$.

The second factor is $\dfrac{(1 + i) + (1 + i)^2 + (1 + i)^3}{(1 + i)}$

$$= \frac{(1+i)}{(1+i)} + \frac{(1+i)^2}{(1+i)} + \frac{(1+i)^3}{(1+i)}$$

$$= 1 + (1+i) + (1+i)^2$$

$$(1+i) + (1+i)^2 + (1+i)^3 = (1+i)[1 + (1+i) + (1+i)^2]$$

EXERCISE I.3

A. Factor each of the following.

1. $8x - 12$

2. $27 - 36a$

3. $4n^2 - 8n$

4. $9x^2 - 21x$

5. $5ax - 10ay - 20a$

6. $4ma - 12mb + 24mab$

B. Factor each of the following.

1. $mx + my$

2. $xa - xb$

3. $m(a-b)+n(a-b)$

4. $k(x-1)-3(x-1)$

5. $P + Pi$

6. $A - Adt$

7. $r - r^2 - r^3$

8. $(1+i)^4 + (1+i)^3 + (1+i)^2$

I.4 GRAPHING INEQUALITIES

A. Basic concepts and method

A straight line drawn in a plane divides the plane into two regions:

(a) the region to the left of the line drawn in the plane;
(b) the region to the right of the line drawn in the plane.

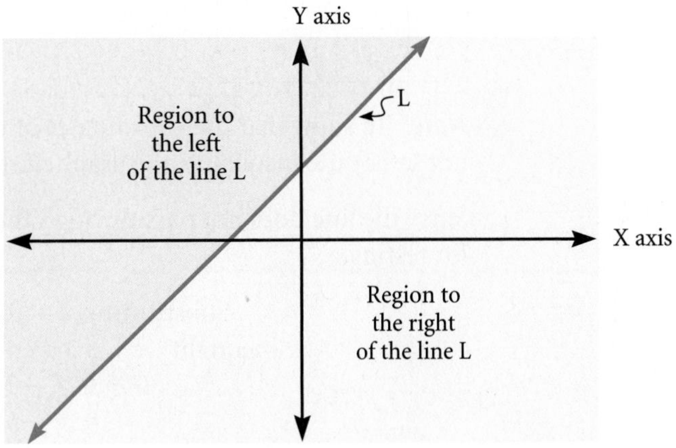

When a system of axes is introduced into the plane, each region consists of a set of points that may be represented by ordered pairs (x, y). Relative to the dividing line, the two sets of ordered pairs (x, y) that represent the points in the regions are defined by the two **inequalities** associated with the equation of the dividing line.

For the equation $x = 5$, the associated inequalities are $x < 5$ (x is less than 5) and $x > 5$ (x is greater than 5). For the equation $y = -3$, the associated inequalities are $y < -3$ and $y > -3$. For the equation $2x + 3y = 6$, the associated inequalities are $2x + 3y < 6$ and $2x + 3y > 6$.

Graphing an inequality means identifying the region that consists of the set of points whose coordinates satisfy the given inequality. To identify this region, use the following method.

1. *Draw* the graph of the equation associated with the inequality.
2. *Test* an arbitrarily selected point that is not a point on the line by substituting its coordinates in the inequality. The preferred point for testing is (0, 0). If (0, 0) is not available because the line passes through the origin, try the points (0, 1) or (1, 0).
3. **(a)** If substituting the coordinates of the selected point in the inequality yields a mathematical statement that is true, the selected point is a point in the region defined by the inequality. Thus, the region is identified as the area containing the selected point.

   (b) If substituting the coordinates of the selected point in the inequality yields a mathematical statement that is false, the selected point is not a point in the region defined by the inequality. Thus, the region defined by the inequality is the area that does not contain the point tested.

B. Graphing inequalities of the form $ax + by > c$ and $ax + by < c$

EXAMPLE 1.4A Graph each of the following inequalities.

(i) $x - y > -3$ (ii) $3x + 2y < -8$

SOLUTION (i) The equation associated with the inequality $x - y > -3$ is $x - y = -3$.

Table of values

x	0	−3	2
y	3	0	5

Note: To show that the coordinates of the points on the line $x - y = -3$ do not satisfy the inequality, the graph of the equation is drawn as a broken line.

Since the line does not pass through the origin, the point (0, 0) may be used for testing.

Substituting $x = 0$ and $y = 0$ in the inequality $x - y > -3$ yields the statement

$$0 - 0 > -3$$

$$0 > -3$$

Since the statement $0 > -3$ is true, the point (0, 0) is a point in the region. The region defined by the inequality $x - y > -3$ is the area to the right of the line as shown in the diagram below.

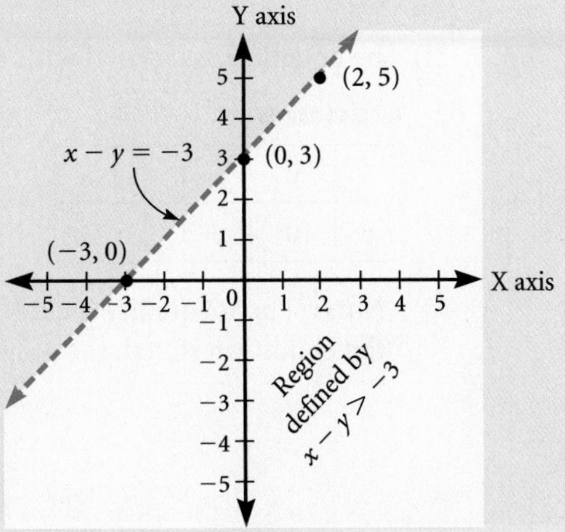

(ii) The equation associated with the inequality $3x + 2y < -8$ is $3x + 2y = -8$.

Table of values

x	0	−2	−4
y	−4	−1	2

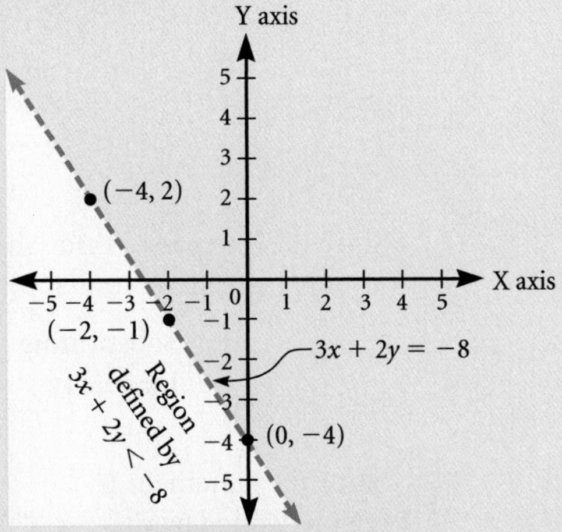

Testing the point (0, 0)

$$3(0) + 2(0) < -8$$
$$0 + 0 < -8$$
$$0 < -8$$

Since the statement $0 < -8$ is false, the point (0, 0) is not a point in the region defined by $3x + 2y < -8$. The region defined by the inequality is the area to the left of the line as shown.

C. Graphing inequalities of the form $ax > by$ or $ax < by$

EXAMPLE 1.4B Graph each of the following inequalities.

(i) $y \leq -x$ (ii) $3x < 2y$

SOLUTION (i) The equation associated with the inequality $y \leq -x$ is $y = -x$.

Table of values

x	0	3	−3
y	0	−3	3

Note: The inequality includes $y = -x$. Because the points on the line meet the condition stated, the graph of the equation is drawn as a solid line.

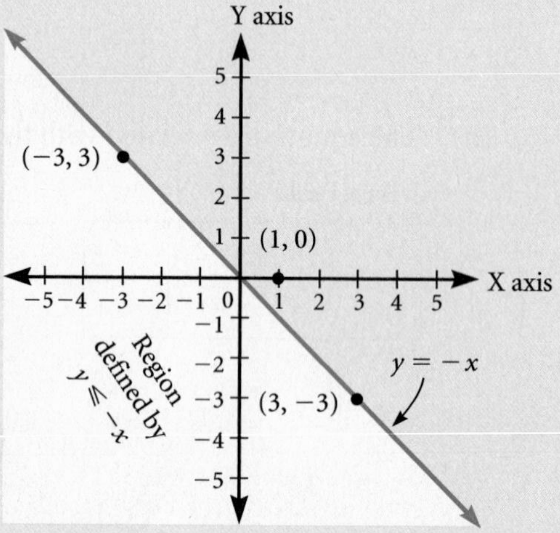

Since the line passes through the origin, the point (0, 0) cannot be used for testing. Instead, we test (1, 0).

Substituting $x = 1, y = 0$ in the inequality $y < -x$ yields the statement $0 < -1$.

Since the statement $0 < -1$ is false, the point (1, 0) is not a point in the region defined by $y \leq -x$. The region defined by the inequality is the area to the left of the line *including* the line.

(ii) The equation associated with the inequality $3x < 2y$ is $3x = 2y$.

Table of values

x	0	2	−2
y	0	3	−3

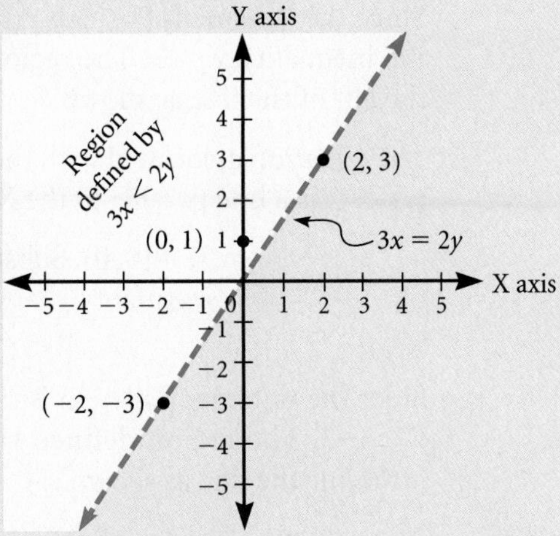

Since (0, 0) is on the line, test (0, 1).
Substituting $x = 0, y = 1$ in the inequality $3x < 2y$ yields the statement

$$0 < 2.$$

Since the statement $0 < 2$ is true, the point (0, 1) is a point in the region defined by $3x < 2y$. The region defined by the inequality is the area to the left of the line as shown.

D. Graphing inequalities involving lines parallel to the axes

EXAMPLE 1.4C Graph each of the following inequalities.

(i) $x < 3$ (ii) $y \geq -3$

SOLUTION (i) The equation associated with the inequality $x < 3$ is $x = 3$. The graph of $x = 3$ is a line parallel to the Y axis three units to the right.

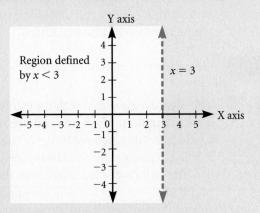

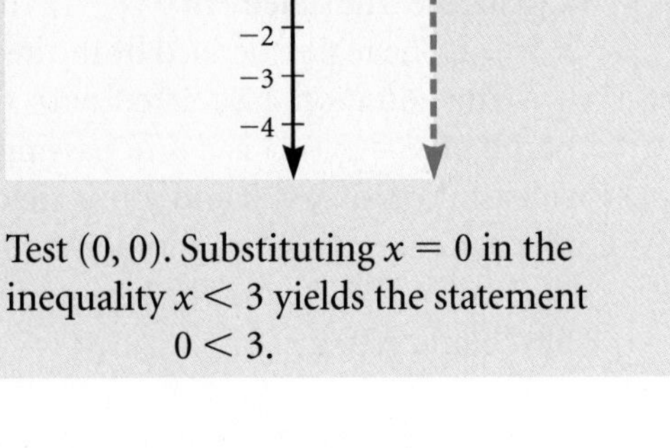

Test (0, 0). Substituting $x = 0$ in the inequality $x < 3$ yields the statement

$$0 < 3.$$

Since the statement $0 < 3$ is true, $(0, 0)$ is a point in the region defined by the inequality $x < 3$. The region defined by the inequality is the region to the left of the line as shown.

(ii) The equation associated with the inequality $y \geq -3$ is $y = -3$. The graph of $y = -3$ is a line parallel to the X axis three units below it.

Test $(0, 0)$. Substituting $y = 0$ in the inequality $y > -3$ yields the statement

$$0 > -3.$$

Since the statement $0 > -3$ is true, $(0, 0)$ is a point in the region defined by $y \geq -3$. The region defined by the inequality is the area above the line *including* the line as shown.

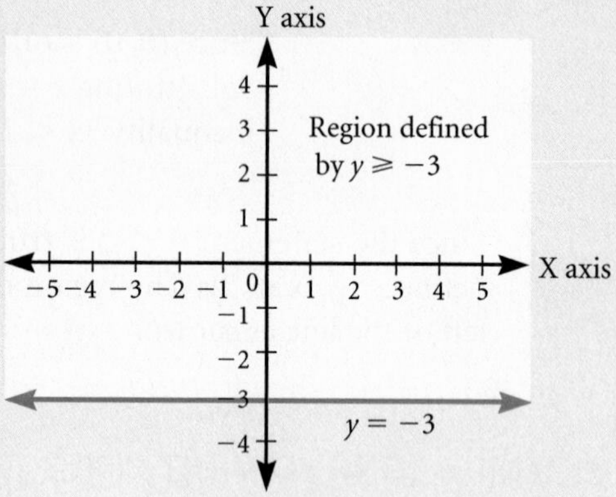

E. Graphing systems of linear inequalities

Systems consisting of two or more linear inequalities in two variables can be drawn by graphing each of the inequalities in the system. The graph of the system is the region *common* to all inequalities.

EXAMPLE 1.4D Graph the region defined by $x > -2$ and $y > x - 3$.

SOLUTION The equation associated with the inequality $x > -2$ is $x = -2$. The graph of $x = -2$ is a line parallel to the Y axis and two units to the left of it. The substitution of 0 for x yields the true statement $0 > -2$. The point $(0, 0)$ is a point in the region defined by $x > -2$. The region defined by the inequality is the area to the right of the line.

The equation associated with the inequality $y > x - 3$ is $y = x - 3$. The graph of $y = x - 3$ is a line passing through the points $(3, 0)$ and $(0, -3)$. The substitution of $x = 0$ and $y = 0$ yields the statement $0 > 0 - 3$, or $0 > -3$. Since this statement is true, the point $(0, 0)$ is a point in the region defined by the inequality $y > x - 3$. The region defined by the inequality is the area to the left of the line $y = x - 3$.

The region defined by the two inequalities is the area formed by the intersection of the two regions. The common region is shown in the diagram.

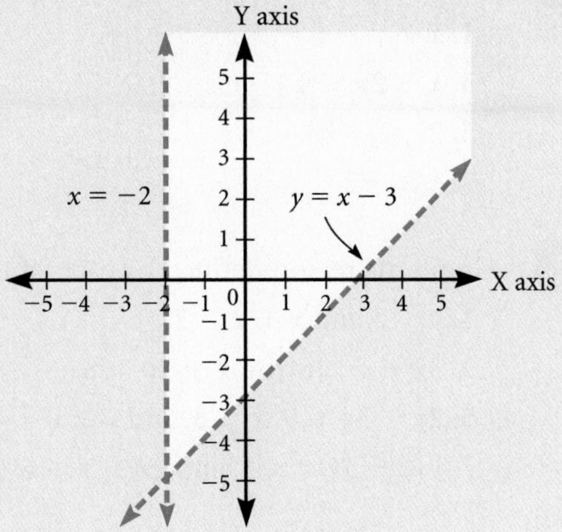

EXAMPLE 1.4E

Graph the region defined by $y \geq 0$, $4x + 5y \leq 20$, and $4x - 3y \geq -12$.

SOLUTION

The equation associated with the inequality $y \geq 0$ is $y = 0$. The graph of $y = 0$ is the X axis. The region defined by the inequality $y \geq 0$ is the area above the X axis and includes the points forming the X axis.

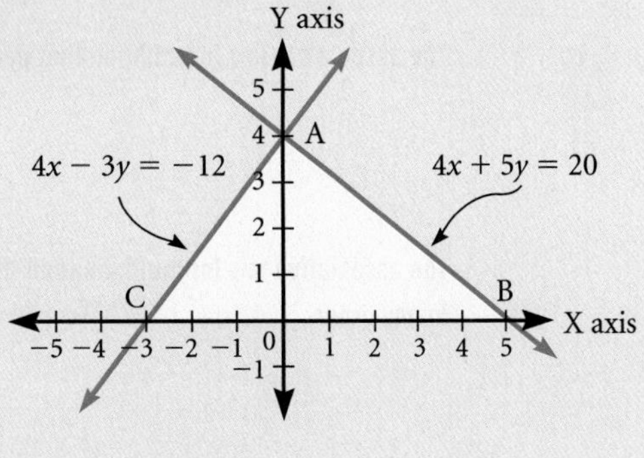

The equation associated with the inequality $4x + 5y \leq 20$ is $4x + 5y = 20$. The graph of the equation is the line passing through the points A(0, 4) and B(5, 0). The true statement $0 < 20$ shows that the origin is a point in the region defined by the inequality. The region defined by $4x + 5y \leq 20$ is the area to the left of the line and includes the line itself.

The equation associated with the inequality $4x - 3y \geq -12$ is $4x - 3y = -12$. The graph of this equation is the line passing through the points A(0, 4) and C(−3, 0). The true statement $0 > -12$ shows that the origin is a point in the region defined by the inequality. The region defined by $4x - 3y \geq -12$ is the area to the right of the line, including the line itself.

The region defined by the three inequalities is the area formed by the intersection of the three regions. It is the triangle ABC shown in the diagram.

EXERCISE I.4

A. Graph each of the following inequalities.

1. $x + y > 4$ **2.** $x - y < -2$

3. $x - 2y \leq 4$ **4.** $3x - 2y \geq -10$

5. $2x < -3y$ **6.** $4y \geq 3x$

7. $x \geq -2$ **8.** $y < 5$

B. Graph the region defined by each of the following linear systems.

1. $y < 3$ and $x + y > 2$ **2.** $x - 2y < 4$ and $x > -3$

3. $3x - y \leq 6$ and $x + 2y > 8$ **4.** $5x > -3y$ and $2x - 5y \geq 10$

5. $2y - 3x \leq 9, x \leq 3$, and $y \geq 0$ **6.** $2x + y \leq 6, x \geq 0$, and $y \geq 0$

7. $y \geq -3x, y \leq 3$, and $2x - y \leq 6$ **8.** $2x \leq y, x \geq -3y$, and $x - 2y \geq -6$

SUMMARY OF FORMULAS (LAWS)

Formula I.1

$a + b = b + a$ **The commutative law for addition that permits the addition of two numbers in any order**

Formula I.2

$ab = ba$ **The commutative law for multiplication that permits the multiplication of two numbers in any order**

Formula I.3

$$a + b + c = (a + b) + c = a + (b + c) = b + (a + c)$$

The associative law for addition that permits the addition of three or more numbers in any order

Formula I.4

$$abc = (ab)c = a(bc) = b(ac)$$

The associative law for multiplication that permits the multiplication of three or more numbers in any order

Formula I.5

$a(b + c) = ab + ac$ **The distributive law of multiplication over addition that provides the basis for the multiplication of algebraic expressions**

GLOSSARY

Absolute value the value of a number without its sign *(p. 723)*

Algebraic expression a combination of numbers, variables representing numbers, and symbols indicating an algebraic operation *(p. 722)*

Binomial an algebraic expression consisting of two terms *(p. 722)*

Collecting like terms adding like terms *(p. 723)*

Combining like terms *see* **Collecting like terms**

Common factor a factor that is divisible without remainder into each term of an algebraic expression *(p. 729)*

Factor one of the numbers that when multiplied with the other number or numbers yields a given product *(p. 723)*

Inequality a mathematical statement involving relationships between variables described as "greater than" or "less than" *(p. 732)*

Like signed numbers numbers having the same sign *(p. 723)*

Like terms terms having the same literal coefficient *(p. 723)*

Literal coefficient the part of a term formed with letter symbols *(p. 723)*

Monomial an algebraic expression consisting of one term *(p. 722)*

Negative numbers signed numbers preceded by a minus (−) sign *(p. 723)*

Numerical coefficient the part of a term formed with numerals *(p. 723)*

Polynomial an algebraic expression consisting of more than one term *(p. 722)*

Positive numbers signed numbers preceded by a plus (+) sign *(p. 723)*

Signed numbers numbers preceded by a plus (+) or by a minus (−) sign *(p. 723)*

Term a part of an algebraic expression separated from other parts by a plus (+) sign or by a minus (−) sign *(p. 722)*

Trinomial an algebraic expression consisting of three terms *(p. 722)*

Unlike signed numbers numbers having different signs *(p. 723)*

APPENDIX II

Instructions and Tips for Three Preprogrammed Financial Calculator Models

Different models of financial calculators vary in their operation and labelling of the function keys and face plate. This appendix provides you with instructions and tips for solving compound interest and annuity problems with these financial calculators: Texas Instruments BAII Plus, Sharp EL-733A, and Hewlett-Packard 10B. The specific operational details for each of these calculators are given using the following framework:

A. Basic Operations

1. Turning the calculator on and off
2. Operating modes
3. Using the Second function
4. Clearing operations
5. Displaying numbers and display formats
6. Order of operations
7. Memory capacity and operations
8. Operating errors and calculator dysfunction

B. Pre-Calculation Phase (Initial Set-up)

1. Setting to the financial mode, if required
2. Adjusting the calculator's interest key to match the text presentation, if required
3. Setting to the floating-decimal-point format, if required
4. Setting up order of operations, if required

C. Calculation Phase

1. Clearing preprogrammed registers
2. Adjusting for annuities (beginning and end of period), if required
3. Entering data using cash flow sign conventions and correcting entry errors
4. Calculating the unknown variable

D. Example Calculations

1. Compound interest
2. Annuities

E. Checklist for Resolving Common Errors

Go to the section of this appendix that pertains to your calculator. You may want to flag those pages for easy future reference.

II. 1. Texas Instruments BAII Plus Advanced Business Analyst, page 741
II. 2. Sharp Business/Financial Calculator EL-733A, page 745
II. 3. Hewlett-Packard 10B Business, page 748

II.1 TEXAS INSTRUMENTS BAII PLUS

A. Basic operations

1. Turning the calculator on and off

The calculator is turned on by pressing [ON/OFF]. If the calculator was turned off using this key, the calculator returns in the standard-calculator mode. If the Automatic Power Down (APD) feature turned the calculator off, the calculator will return exactly as you left it—errors and all, if that was the case. The calculator can be turned off either by pressing [ON/OFF] again or by not pressing any key for approximately 10 minutes, which will activate the APD feature.

2. Operating modes

The calculator has two modes: the standard-calculation mode and the prompted-worksheet mode. In the standard-calculation mode, you can perform standard math operations and all of the financial calculations presented in this text. This is the default mode for your calculator. Refer to your calculator's *Guidebook* to learn more about the worksheet mode, since it is not addressed in this appendix.

3. Using the Second function

The primary function of a key is indicated by a symbol on its face. Second functions are marked on the face plate directly above the keys. To access the Second function of a key, press [2nd] ("2nd" will appear in the upper-left corner of the display) and then press the key directly under the symbol on the face plate ("2nd" will then disappear from the display).

4. Clearing operations

[→] clears one character at a time from the display, including decimal points.

[CE/C] clears an incorrect entry, an error condition, or an error message from the display.

[2nd] (QUIT) clears all pending operations in the standard-calculation mode and returns the display to 0.

[CE/C] [CE/C] clears any calculation you have started but not yet completed.

[2nd] (CLR TVM) sets the financial function registers to 0 and returns to standard-calculation mode.

5. Displaying numbers and display formats

The display shows entries and results up to 10 digits but internally stores numeric values to an accuracy of 13 digits. The default setting in the calculator is 2 decimal places. To change the number of fixed decimal places, press **2nd** (FORMAT) along with a number key for the decimal places desired. Then press **ENTER** to complete the installation. For a floating-decimal-point format, press **2nd** (FORMAT) **9** **ENTER**. Return to standard-calculation mode by pressing **2nd** (QUIT).

6. Order of operations

The default for the BAII Plus is Chn. To change to AOS, which will have the calculator do all mathematical calculations in the proper order according to the rules of mathematics, press **2nd** (FORMAT), arrow down four times, and with display on Chn press **2nd** **SET**. Press **2nd** (QUIT) to go back to the standard-calculation mode.

7. Memory capacity and operations

The calculator has ten memory addresses available, numbered 0 through 9. To store a displayed value in a memory address (0 through 9), press **STO** and a digit key **0** through **9**. To recall a value from memory and display it, press **RCL** and a digit key **0** through **9**. The numeric value is displayed but is also retained in that memory address.

To clear each memory address individually, store "0" in each selected memory. To clear all of the addresses at the same time, press **2nd** (MEM) **2nd** (CLR WORK).

Memory arithmetic allows you to perform a calculation with a stored value and then store the result with a single operation. You may add, subtract, multiply, divide, or apply an exponent to the value in the memory. Use this key sequence:

(number in display) **STO** **+** (or **−** or **×** or **÷** or **x^{-1}**) and a digit key **0** to **9** for the memory address.

8. Operating errors and calculator dysfunction

The calculator reports error conditions by displaying the message "Error n," where n is a number that corresponds to a particular error discussed in the calculator's *Guidebook* on pages 80–82. Errors 4, 5, 7, and 8 are the most common financial calculation errors. A list of possible solutions to calculator dysfunction is given on page 87 of the *Guidebook*. Generally, if you experience difficulties operating the calculator, press **2nd** (RESET) **ENTER** to clear the calculator, and repeat your calculations.

B. Compound interest and annuity calculations

The BAII Plus calculator can be used for virtually all compound interest calculations using the third row of the calculator *after* the payment and interest schedules have been set up in the Second function area of the calculator. Each key represents one of the variables in the formula. The variables are:

- N—Represents time. The value is arrived at by taking the number of *years* involved in the transaction and multiplying it by the value set up in P/Y.
- I/Y—The stated or nominal yearly interest rate.
- PV—The amount of money one has at the beginning of the transaction.
- PMT—The amount of money paid on a regular basis.
- FV—The amount of money one has at the end of the transaction.

To perform compound interest or annuity calculations, the process will be to input the variables that are known and to compute the unknown variable.

For compound interest, the process will be:

1. Set up the payment and interest schedules in the Second function of the calculator. This is done by pressing 2nd (P/Y) and inputting the payment and interest schedules as prompted. Since the transaction will not have any payments, simply make the payment and interest schedules the same. For example, if there are no payments and interest is compounded quarterly, the process would be 2nd (P/Y), 4, Enter 2nd (QUIT). This will set up the proper schedules in both P/Y and C/Y and take you back to the calculator mode.
2. Clear out any old information with 2nd (CLR TVM).
3. Input the variables you know.
4. Compute the variable you need to find.

For annuity calculations, the process will be:

1. Set up the calculator for either an ordinary annuity (payments made at the end) or an annuity due (payments made at the beginning). This is done by hitting 2nd (BGN) and then setting up the display to END or BGN. 2nd (SET) will allow you to switch between the two options. 2nd (QUIT) will take you back to the calculcator. Note: if the calculator is in END mode, the display will be clear in the upper-right-hand corner of the display; if it is in BGN mode, the letters BGN will appear in the upper-right-hand corner.
2. Set up the payment and interest schedules in the Second function of the calculator. This is done by pressing 2nd (P/Y) and inputting the payment and interest schedules as prompted. For example, if the transaction had monthly payments with quarterly compounding, the process would be 2nd (P/Y) 12, Enter, ↓, 4, Enter, 2nd (QUIT). This would set up monthly payments with interest compounded quarterly.
3. Clear out the old information with 2nd (CLR TVM).
4. Input the variables you know.
5. Compute the variable you need to find.

C. Calculation phase

1, 2. The steps required to perform calculations and an example calculation appear on pages 339–341 in Chapter 9. The steps required for annuities and sample annuity calculations appear on pages 477–478 in Chapter 12.

3. Entering data using cash flow sign conventions and correcting entry errors

Data can be entered in any order, but you *must* observe the cash flow sign conventions. For compound interest calculations, always enter PV as a negative number and all other values (N, I/Y, FV) as positive numbers. An error message will be displayed when calculating I/Y or N if both FV and PV are entered using the same sign. For annuity calculations, enter either PV or PMT as negative numbers and all other values (N, I/Y, FV) as positive numbers. When PV = 0, designate PMT as the negative number and all other values (N, I/Y, FV) as positive numbers. Failure to observe this sign convention will result in either an error message in the display when calculating I/Y values or an incorrect negative number when calculating values of N.

Data entry errors can be corrected one character at a time by using [→] or the entry, and error messages can be cleared from the display by using [CE/C]

4. Calculating the unknown variable

Press [CPT] and the financial key representing the unknown variable after all the known variable data are entered (including 0 for PV or FV if required). Successive calculations are possible because numerical values stored in the function key registers remain there until cleared or replaced. The value stored in any of the function key registers can be determined without altering its value by pressing [RCL] and the function key.

D. Example calculations

1. Compound interest

See pages 339–341 in Chapter 9 for an example of a compound interest calculation using this calculator.

2. Annuities

See pages 478 and 481 in Chapter 11 for examples of annuity calculations using this calculator.

E. Checklist for resolving common errors

1. Confirm that the P/Y and C/Y are properly set.
2. Confirm that the decimal place format is set to a floating decimal point.
3. If attempting annuity calculations, check to see that the calculator is in the appropriate payment mode ("END" or "BGN").
4. Clear all function key registers before entering your data.

5. Be sure to enter a numerical value, using the cash flow sign convention, for all known variables before solving for the unknown variable, even if one of the variables is 0.

II.2 SHARP EL-733A BUSINESS/FINANCIAL CALCULATOR

A. Basic operations

1. Turning the calculator on and off

C·CE turns the calculator on. OFF turns the calculator off. To conserve battery life, the calculator will turn itself off automatically 9 to 13 minutes after the last key operation.

2. Operating modes

The available operational modes are financial (FIN), statistical (STAT), and Normal (no message). The message FIN, STAT, or no message appears in the upper right corner of the display to indicate the current mode. Change the mode by pressing 2nd F (MODE) until the desired mode is displayed.

3. Using the Second function

The primary function of a key is indicated by a symbol on the face of the key. Second functions are marked on the face plate directly above the keys. To access the Second function of a key, press 2nd F ("2ndF" will appear in the upper-left corner of the display), and then press the key directly under the symbol on the face plate ("2ndF" will then disappear from the display).

4. Clearing operations

2nd F (CA) clears the numerical values and calculation commands including data for financial calculations. The contents of memory register storage are not affected.

C·CE x→M clears the memory.

C·CE clears the last entry.

C·CE C·CE clears the calculator of all data *except* the data for financial calculations.

→ clears the last digit entered.

5. Displaying numbers and display formats

The display shows entries and results up to 10 digits. The default setting in the calculator is the floating decimal. To change the number of fixed decimal places, press 2nd F (TAB) along with a number key for the decimal places desired. For a floating-decimal-point format, press 2nd F (TAB) •. The number of decimal places is retained even when the power is turned off.

Various messages can appear in the display from time to time. Refer to page 73 of the *Operation Manual and Application Manual* for a complete list.

6. Memory capacity and operations

This calculator has one memory address. To store a displayed value in memory, press x→M.

To clear the memory of values other than zero, press C·CE x→M.

To recall a value from memory and display it, press RM.

To add a displayed amount to the value in the memory, press M+. To subtract a displayed amount to the value in the memory, press ± M+.

7. Operating errors and calculator dysfunction

Operational errors are indicated by the symbol **E** in the lower-left corner of the display. See pages 74–77 of the *Operation Manual and Application Manual* for a complete description of errors and error conditions that may affect the operation and functioning of your calculator. The error symbol is cleared from the display by pressing C·CE.

B. Pre-calculation phase

With the calculator on, set the financial mode by pressing 2nd F (MODE) until the FIN message appears in the upper-right corner of the display. The calculator requires no change to a register or mode in order to match the text presentation. To set the calculator to the floating-decimal-point format, press 2nd F (TAB) •.

C. Calculation phase

1. Clearing preprogrammed registers

2nd F (CA) clears the preprogrammed registers of numerical values and sets them to 0 for financial calculations.

2. Adjusting for annuities (beginning and end of period)

The default mode for annuity calculations is "end of period." If "beginning of period" calculations are required, press BGN. "BGN" will appear in the upper-right corner of the display. To return to "end of period" mode, press BGN again. "BGN" will disappear from the display.

3. Entering data using cash flow sign conventions and correcting entry errors

Data can be entered in any order but you must observe the cash flow sign conventions to avoid operational errors and incorrect answers. For compound interest calculations, *always* designate PV as a negative number and all other values (N, *i*, FV) as positive numbers. If you do not observe this sign convention when you enter data, your answer will be the same numerical value but the opposite sign of the answer in the text. An error message will be displayed when calculating *i* or N if both FV and PV are entered using the same sign. For annuity calculations, when FV = 0, designate PV as a negative number and all other values (N, *i*, PMT) as positive numbers. When PV = 0, designate PMT as the negative number and all other values (N, *i*, FV) as positive numbers. Failure to observe this sign convention will result in either an error message in the display when calculating *i* values or an incorrect negative number when calculating values of N.

4. Calculating the unknown variable

Press COMP and the financial key representing the unknown variable after all the known variable data are entered (including 0 for PV or FV if required). Successive calculations are possible because numerical values stored in the function key registers remain there until cleared or replaced. The value stored in any of the function key registers can be determined without altering its value by pressing 2nd F (RCL) and the function key.

D. Example calculations

1. Compound interest (Example 9.2A, page 337)

Key in	*Press*	*Display* shows	
	2nd F (CA)	no change	clears all registers
6000	± PV	−6000	this enters the present value P (principal) with the correct sign convention
2.5	i	2.5	this enters the periodic interest rate *i* as a percent
20	N	20	this enters the number of compounding periods *n*
	COMP FV	9831.698642	this computes and displays the unknown future value S

2. Annuities (Example 11.2D, pages 428–429)

Key in	*Press*	*Display shows*	
0	PV	0	a precaution to avoid incorrect answers
10	± PMT	−10	this enters the periodic payment R
0.5	*i*	0.5	this enters the conversion rate *i* as a percent
60	N	60	this enters the number of payments *n*
	COMP FV	697.7003051	this computes the unknown future value S_n

E. Checklist for resolving common errors

1. Check to see that your calculator is in the financial (FIN) mode.
2. Check to see that the calculator is in the appropriate payment mode (BGN or end mode).
3. Clear all registers before entering your data by pressing 2nd F (CA).
4. Be sure to enter values for all variables except the unknown variable, before solving for the unknown variable, even if one of the variables is 0.
5. Observe the cash flow sign conventions (discussed above) when entering the data to avoid unwanted negative signs, display errors, or incorrect answers.

II.3 HEWLETT-PACKARD 10B II BUSINESS CALCULATOR

A. Basic operations

1. Turning the calculator on and off

Turn the calculator on by pressing ON. Turn the calculator off by pressing the [ ] (SHIFT) OFF.

To conserve energy, the calculator turns itself off automatically approximately 10 minutes after you stop using it. The calculator has a continuous memory, so turning it off does not affect the information you have stored in the memory.

2. Operating modes

You can perform all of the financial calculations presented in this text as soon as you turn on the calculator. No mode adjustment is required for financial-, statistical-, or standard-mode calculations.

3. Using the SHIFT function

The primary function of a key is indicated by a symbol on the top face of the key. SHIFT functions are marked on the bottom face of the key. To access the SHIFT function of a key, press [ ] (SHIFT) ("SHIFT" will appear in the lower-left corner of the display), and then press the key with the symbol on the lower face of the key ("SHIFT" will then disappear from the display).

4. Clearing operations

[ON] [N] [FV], all held down at the same time, clears all memory and resets all modes.

[ ] [C ALL] (CLEAR ALL) clears all memory, but does not reset the modes.

[←] [C] clears the message and restores the original constants.

[C] clears the entered number to 0.

[←] clears the last digit entered.

5. Displaying numbers and display formats

The display shows entries and results up to 12 digits. Brightness is controlled by holding down [ON] and then pressing [+] or [−]. The default setting is 2 decimal places. Regardless of the display format, each number entered is stored with a signed 12-digit number and a signed 3-digit exponent. To change the number of fixed decimal places, press [ ] [DISP] and a number key for the number of decimal places desired. For a floating decimal point, press [ ] [DISP] [•]. To temporarily view all 12 digits, press [ ] [DISP] and hold [=].

Graphics in the display are used to indicate various settings, operating modes, error conditions, and calculator dysfunctions. Refer to the *Owner's Manual*, pages 137–138, for a complete list.

6. Memory capacity and operations

This calculator has 10 numbered registers available to store numbers, as well as a single storage register called the M register.

To store a number in the M register, press [→M].

To recall a value from the M register and display it, press [RM].

To add a displayed amount to the value in the M register, press [M+]. To subtract a displayed amount to the value in the memory, press [±] [M+].

To store a displayed value in a numbered memory register (numbered 0 to 9), press [ ] [STO] and a digit key [0] through [9].

To recall a number from a numbered memory register, press [RCL] and the digit key for the memory register number.

7. Operating errors and calculator dysfunction

Operational errors are indicated by an error message appearing in the display. For a complete description of the error messages, refer to pages 137–138 of the *Owner's*

Manual. For calculator dysfunctions, refer to pages 121–122 of the *Owner's Manual.*

No additional adjustment is required to set the calculator to the financial mode. Begin calculations as soon as you turn on your calculator.

B. Calculation phase

1. Clearing preprogrammed registers

[ ] [C ALL] sets all key numerical registers to 0 and momentarily displays the P/YR value.

2. Adjusting for annuities (beginning and end of period)

The default mode for annuity calculations is "end of period." If "beginning of period" calculations are required, press [ ] [BEG/END]. "BEGIN" will appear in the lower middle portion of the display. To return to "end of period" mode, press [ ] [BEG/END] again. "BEGIN" will disappear from the display.

3. Entering data using cash flow sign conventions and correcting entry errors

Data can be entered in any order using the financial function keys. To confirm the values already in the registers or to validate your data entry, press [RCL] and the desired function key.

You must observe the cash flow sign conventions to avoid errors like "no solution" or incorrect answers when calculating N. For compound interest calculations, *always* enter PV as a negative number and the other variables as positive numbers. For annuity calculations, when FV = 0, enter PV as a negative number and all other values (N, I/YR, PMT) as positive numbers. However, when PV = 0, enter PMT as a negative number and all other values (N, I/YR, FV) as positive numbers. If you do not observe the sign convention, the numerical value you calculate will be identical to that of this text except when calculating N (your answer will be incorrect) or when calculating I/YR (an error message may appear in the display).

Data entry errors can be corrected character by character by pressing [←] or the entry can be cleared from the display by pressing [C].

4. Calculating the unknown variable

Press the financial key representing the unknown variable after all the known variable data are entered (including 0 for PV or FV if required). Successive calculations are possible because numerical values stored in the function key registers remain there until cleared or replaced. The value stored in any of the function key registers can be determined without altering its value by pressing [RCL] and the function key.

C. Example calculations

1. Compound interest (Example 9.2A, page 337)

Key in	*Press*	*Display shows*	
	[ ] [C ALL]	0	clears the function key registers and confirms the value in the P/YR register
6000	[±] [PV]	−6000	this enters the present value P (principal) with the correct sign convention
10	[I/YR]	10	this enters the periodic interest rate *i* as a percent
4	[ ] [P/YR]	4	
20	[N]	20	this enters the number of compounding periods *n*
	[FV]	9831.698642	this computes and displays the unknown future value S

2. Annuities (Example 11.2D, pages 428–429)

Key in	*Press*	*Display shows*	
0	[PV]	0	a precaution to avoid incorrect answers
10	[±] [PMT]	-10	this enters the periodic payment R
6	[I/YR]	6	this enters the conversion rate *i* as a percent
12	[ ] [P/YR]	12	
60	[N]	60	this enters the number of payments *n*
	[FV]	697.700305	this computes the unknown future value S_n

D. Checklist for resolving common errors

1. Confirm that P/YR is properly set.
2. Clear all registers before entering your data by pressing [ ] [C ALL].
3. Check to see that the calculator is in the appropriate payment mode (BEGIN or END mode).
4. Be sure to enter values for all variables except the unknown variable, before solving for the unknown variable, even if one of the variables is 0.
5. Observe the cash flow sign conventions (discussed above) when entering the data to avoid unwanted negative signs, display errors, or incorrect answers.

Answers to Odd-Numbered Problems, Review Exercises, and Self-Tests

CHAPTER 1

Exercise 1.1

A. **1.** 14
3. 9
5. 53
7. 23
9. 4
11. 24
13. 1.3333333
15. 1

Exercise 1.2

A. **1.** $\frac{2}{3}$
3. $\frac{7}{12}$
5. $\frac{8}{5}$
7. $\frac{2}{5}$
9. $\frac{5}{73}$
11. $\frac{5}{1}$

B. **1.** 1.375
3. $1.\dot{6}$
5. $1.8\dot{3}$
7. $1.08\dot{3}$

C. **1.** 3.375
3. 8.333333
5. 33.333333
7. 7.777778

D. **1.** 5.63
3. 18.00
5. 57.70
7. 13.00

E. **1.** 730
3. 630.70
5. 1913.59
7. 220 364.90
9. 3991.47

Exercise 1.3

A. **1.** .64
3. 0.025
5. 0.005
7. 2.5
9. 4.5
11. 0.009
13. 0.0625
15. 0.99
17. 0.0005
19. 0.005
21. 0.09375
23. 1.625
25. 0.0025
27. 0.0175
29. 1.375
31. 0.00875
33. $0.\dot{3}$
35. $0.1\dot{6}$
37. $1.8\dot{3}$
39. $1.\dot{3}$

B. **1.** $\frac{1}{4}$
3. $\frac{7}{4}$
5. $\frac{3}{8}$
7. $\frac{1}{25}$
9. $\frac{2}{25}$
11. $\frac{2}{5}$
13. $\frac{5}{2}$
15. $\frac{1}{8}$
17. $\frac{9}{400}$
19. $\frac{1}{800}$
21. $\frac{3}{400}$
23. $\frac{1}{16}$
25. $\frac{1}{6}$
27. $\frac{3}{400}$
29. $\frac{1}{1000}$
31. $\frac{5}{6}$
33. $\frac{4}{3}$
35. $\frac{5}{3}$

C. **1.** 350%
3. 0.5%
5. 2.5%
7. 12.5%
9. 22.5%
11. 145%
13. 0.25%
15. 9%
17. 75%
19. 166.67%
21. 4.5%
23. 0.75%
25. 1.125%
27. 37.5%
29. 133.33%
31. 65%

Exercise 1.4

A. **1.** $409 062.50
3. $1147.50
5. $176.00

B. **1.** $0.41
3. 2.9
5. **(a)** $10.45
(b) $115.899
(c) $10.35
(d) $1379.20

Exercise 1.5

A. **1.** **(a)** $955.50
(b) $12.25
(c) $1157.63
3. **(a)** $7.26
(b) $1185.50
5. **(a)** $16.47
(b) $875.94
7. $1568.06
9. **(a)** $225.00
(b) $332.25
11. 9.25%
13. $19 680
15. $425.21
17. $7.26

Exercise 1.6

A. **1.** $33 274.20
3. $0.09
5. $0.80
7. $2843.88
9. 14.49786

Review Exercise

1. **(a)** 29
(b) −8
(c) 11
(d) 8
(e) 1520.83
(f) 0.15
(g) 339.73
(h) 950.68
(i) 625.45
(j) 1250
3. **(a)** $\frac{1}{2}$
(b) $\frac{3}{8}$
(c) $\frac{1}{6}$
(d) $\frac{5}{3}$
(e) $\frac{1}{200}$
(f) $\frac{3}{40}$
(g) $\frac{3}{400}$
(h) $\frac{1}{160}$
5. **(a)** 20.208333 kg
(b) $24.25
(c) 5.05 kg
(d) $6.06
7. **(a)** $11.19
(b) $9.60
9. $13 680
11. **(a)** $1456.00
(b) $9.60
(c) 16.5
13. **(a)** $367.50
(b) $8.55
15. $1924.25
17. 4.25%
19. $8.44
21. $5945.00
23. 41.5
25. $4581.00
27. 14.48%

29. **(a)** 46.71143
(b) \$1634.90
(c) 2.05023
(d) \$71.76

Self-Test

1. **(a)** 4415.87
(b) 93.21
(c) 2610.15
(d) 4623.33
(e) 4804.16
3. **(a)** $\frac{1}{40}$
(b) $\frac{50}{300}$
5. \$7080
7. \$7.35
9. \$650
11. \$2382.41
13. \$8.90
15. \$9.00
17. \$45 500.00

CHAPTER 2

Exercise 2.1

A. **1.** $19a$
3. $27a - 10$
5. $-2x - 4y$
7. $14f - 4v$
9. $0.8x$
11. $1.4x$
13. $2.79x$
15. $-x^2 - x - 8$
17. $x - 7y$
19. $4b + 2c + 2$
21. $-m^2 + 6m + 1$
23. $10a - 14b$

B. **1.** $-12x$
3. $-10ax$
5. $-2x^2$
7. $60xy$
9. $-2x + 4y$
11. $2ax^2 - 3ax - a$
13. $35x - 30$
15. $-20ax + 5a$
17. $3x^2 + 5x - 2$
19. $x^3 + y^3$
21. $7x^2 + 3x + 39$
23. $4ab$
25. $4x$
27. $10m - 4$
29. $-2x^2 + 3x + 6$

C. **1.** -5
3. 5500
5. 0.58604
7. 378
9. 3000
11. 901.99
13. 1366.74

Exercise 2.2

A. **1.** 81
3. 16
5. $\frac{16}{81}$
7. $\frac{1}{-64}$
9. 0.25
11. -0.001
13. 1
15. $\frac{1}{9}$
17. $-\frac{1}{125}$
19. 125
21. $\frac{1}{1.01}$

B. **1.** 2^8
3. 4^3
5. 2^{15}
7. a^{14}
9. 3^{11}
11. 6
13. $\frac{3^{11}}{5^{11}}$
15. $\frac{(-3^{11})}{2^{11}}$
17. 1.025^{150}
19. 1.04^{80}
21. $(1 + i)^{200}$
23. $(1 + i)^{160}$
25. a^5b^5
27. $m^{24}n^8$
29. 2^4
31. $\frac{b^8}{a^8}$

Exercise 2.3

A. **1.** 72
3. 3
5. 1.0758857
7. 1.0132999

B. **1.** 55
3. 12.25
5. 1.0711221
7. 0.6299605
9. 163.0534333
11. 2.158925
13. 1630.176673
15. 1139.915716
17. 5000.00
19. 3%

Exercise 2.4

A. **1.** $9 = \log_2 512$
3. $-3 = \log_5 \frac{1}{125}$
5. $2j = \log_e 18$
or $2j = \ln 18$

B. **1.** $2^5 = 32$
3. $10^1 = 10$

C. **1.** 0.6931472
3. -2.2537949
5. 6.8253032

Exercise 2.5

A. **1.** 3
3. 80
5. 18
7. -35
9. -4
11. -8
13. 5
15. 20
17. 200

B. **1.** $x = 4$;
LS = 17 = RS
3. $x = 0$;
LS = -7 = RS
5. $x = 5$
LS = 29 = RS
7. $x = 21$
LS = 92 = RS

Exercise 2.6

A. **1.** $x = -10$;
LS = 320 = RS
3. $x = -3$;
LS = -15 = RS
5. $x = 3$
LS = 18 = RS
7. $x = 14$
LS = 32 = RS

B. **1.** 20
3. -1
5. $\frac{1}{2}$

C. **1.** -1
3. $\frac{5}{6}$

D. **1.** $h = \frac{2A}{b}$
3. $c = \frac{5}{9}(F - 32)$
5. $r = \frac{A-P}{Pt}$

Exercise 2.7

A. **1.** \$28.28
3. \$35.00
5. 192
7. \$670
9. \$89.00
11. 1300
13. 20 units
15. 30 \$ 12 tickets
100 \$ 8 tickets
21 \$ 15 tickets

Review Exercise

1. **(a)** $-2x - 7y$
(b) $1.97x$
(c) $6a - 7$
(d) $x + 3y$
(e) $9a^2 - 4b - 4c$
(f) $-x^2 + 3x + 1$
3. **(a)** -47
(b) $6\frac{1}{3}$
(c) 0.16
(d) 200
(e) 644.40
(f) 2500

5. **(a)** 0.96
(b) 1.0121264
(c) 1.07
(d) 0.9684416
(e) 1.0986123
(f) -2.9957323

(g) 7.0875402
(h) 9.8716464

7. **(a)** $x = -7$;
LS $= -203 =$ RS
(b) $x = 5$
LS $= -32 =$ RS
(c) $x = -3$;
LS $= -\frac{23}{14} =$ RS
(d) $x = -\frac{7}{12}$
LS $= \frac{11}{9} =$ RS
(e) $x = 7$
LS $= 25 =$ RS
(f) $x = -\frac{1}{3}$
LS $= -1 =$ RS
(g) $x = -\frac{1}{2}$
LS $= -\frac{31}{6} =$ RS

9. **(a)** 138
(b) \$63 350
(c) \$117
(d) \$44 500
(e) heat = \$814
power = \$1056
water = \$341
(f) \$37 500
(g) Machine C,
35 minutes
(h) superlight, 27;
ordinary, 45
(i) 164

Self-Test

1. **(a)** $-2 - 8x$
(b) $-2x - 9$
(c) $-16a - 7$
(d) $-6x^2 + 6x + 12$

3. **(a)** -8
(b) $\frac{4}{9}$
(c) 1
(d) 2187
(e) $\frac{9}{16}$
(f) $-x^{15}$

5. **(a)** $n = 6$
(b) $n = 5$

7. **(a)** $P = \frac{I}{rt}$
(b) $d = \frac{S - P}{St}$

CHAPTER 3

Exercise 3.1

A. **1.** **(a)** 3:8
(b) 3:2
(c) 5:8:13
(d) 3:6:13
3. **(a)** $\frac{5}{16}$
(b) $\frac{2}{7}$
(c) 2:7:11
(d) 23:14:5
(e) 5:4
(f) 25:21
(g) 9:16:18
(h) 28:40:25
(i) 32:60:25
(j) 9:7:17
(k) 69:89
(l) 28:55
(m) 8:15
(n) 9:10

B. **1.** $\frac{8}{7}$
3. 2:3:12
5. $\frac{29}{1}$

C. **1.** \$2295; \$510; \$255
3. \$5250; \$2800; \$1400
5. \$4400000; \$2200000;
\$4950000

Exercise 3.2

1. 4
3. 56
5. 7.4
7. 2.4
9. $\frac{7}{10}$
11. 1

B. **1.** 21 months
3. 600 km
5. **(a)** \$3600
(b) \$9000
7. \$100 800

Exercise 3.3

A. **1.** 36
3. 300
5. 18
7. 6
9. 0.5
11. 2
13. 7.5
15. 17.5

B. **1.** \$16
3. \$1950
5. \$9
7. \$200
9. \$600
11. \$49
13. \$135
15. \$60

C. **1.** 60%
3. 115%
5. 5%
7. 600%
9. $166\frac{2}{3}$%

D. **1.** \$200
3. \$3.60
5. \$3.06
7. 200
9. \$1.10
11. \$240
13. \$300

E. **1.** \$28
3. \$1500
5. \$45 000
7. \$60 000
9. \$6

Exercise 3.4

A. **1.** 168
3. \$1140
5. 88

B. **1.** 50%
3. 200%
5. 2%

C. **1.** 20
3. 440
5. 36
7. 30

D. **1.** 32
3. \$130
5. \$4.40

Exercis

A. **1.** 2
3. 1
5. \$
7. **(a**
(b) \$225 000

B. **1.** \$14.52
3. \$130
5. \$84.36
7. \$5000
9. $83\frac{1}{3}$%
11. 325%
13. \$96.69
15. \$680
17. \$44 800
19. \$900

Exercise 3.6

A. **1.** \$674.95 U.S.
3. \$335.96 Cdn

B. **1.** \$390.25 Cdn
3. 213.92 Swiss francs
5. \$783.53 Cdn

Exercise 3.7

A. **1.** 3.36%, 4.76%,
5.08%

B. **1.** **(a)** \$0.881, \$0.8026
(b) \$0.9109
3. \$40 656.43

Exercise 3.8

A. **1.** \$8332.84
3. \$6390.24

Review Exercise

1. **(a)** 5:6
(b) 6:1
(c) 9:40
(d) 6:1
(e) 240:20:1
(f) 15:4:3
3. **(a)** 210
(b) 7.2
(c) 195
(d) 3.6

5. **(a)** \$6.66
(b) \$8.30
(c) \$90.00
(d) \$27.72

7. **(a)** \$18
(b) \$1955
(c) $16\frac{2}{3}\%$
(d) 550%
(e) \$56
(f) \$340
(g) \$140

9. \$2400; \$4200; \$4800

11. \$75 000; \$50 000; \$60 000

13. \$182 000

15. 540

17. Bonds \$56 250
Common stock \$84 375
Preferred Shares \$9375

19. **(a)** \$400 000
(b) \$280 000

21. **(a)** 7.5%
(b) $16\frac{2}{3}\%$

23. **(a)** $166\frac{2}{3}\%$
(b) $266\frac{2}{3}\%$

25. \$165

27. \$15 000

29. **(a)** \$80 000
(b) \$250 000
(c) 312.5%

31. \$187.83 U.S.

33. \$16 240.44

Self-Test

1. **(a)** \$350
(b) \$76.05
(c) \$145.00
(d) \$13.20

3. 45%

5. \$10 000

7. \$16 875; \$11 250; \$6 750; \$5 625

9. \$37.50

11. 180

13. **(a)** 1.1084 Australian dollars
(b) 554.2 Australian dollars

15. \$0.88

CHAPTER 4

Exercise 4.1

A. **1.** $x = -8, y = -1$
3. $x = 10, y = 12$
5. $x = -3, y = 3$

B. **1.** $x = -4, y = 3$
3. $x = -1, y = 3$
5. $x = 4, y = 3$

C. **1.** $x = 12, y = 8$
3. $x = 1.5, y = 2.5$
5. $x = 6, y = 10$
7. $x = \frac{1}{2}, y = \frac{3}{4}$

Exercise 4.2

A. **1.** A $(-4, -3)$
B $(0, -4)$
C $(3, -4)$
D $(2, 0)$
E $(4, 3)$
F $(0, 3)$
G $(-4, 4)$
H $(-5, 0)$

3. **(a)**

x	−5	−4	−3	−2	−1	0	1	2	3
y	−3	−2	−1	0	1	2	3	4	5

(b)

x	3	2	1	0	−1	−2
y	5	3	1	−1	−3	−5

(c)

x	3	2	1	0	−1	−2	−3
y	6	4	2	0	−2	−4	−6

(d)

x	−5	−4	−3	−2	−1	0	1	2	3	4	5
y	5	4	3	2	1	0	−1	−2	−3	−4	−5

B. **1.**

x	0	3	2
y	−3	0	−1

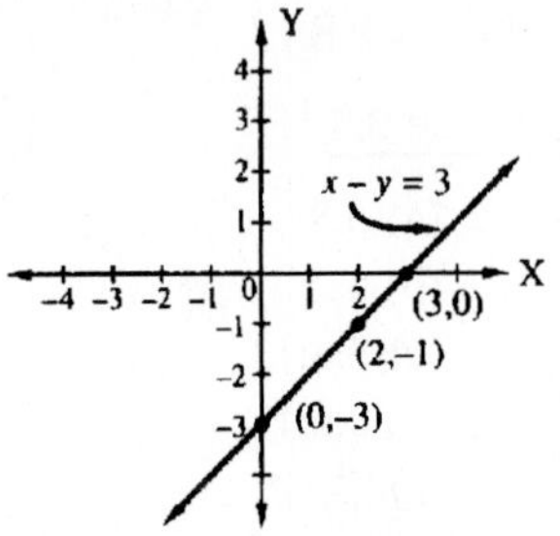

3.

x	0	−2	2
y	0	2	−2

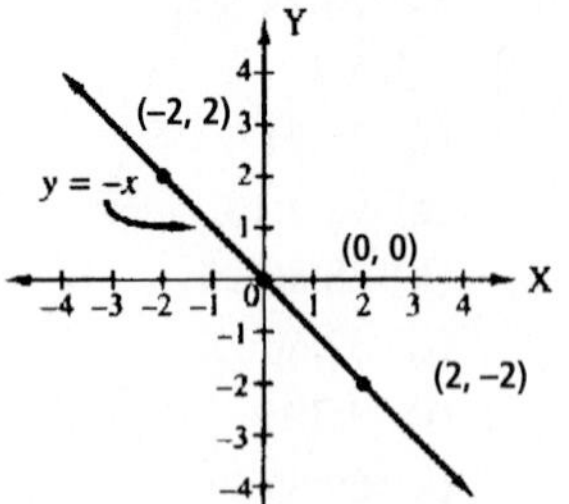

5.

x	0	4	−4
y	−3	0	−6

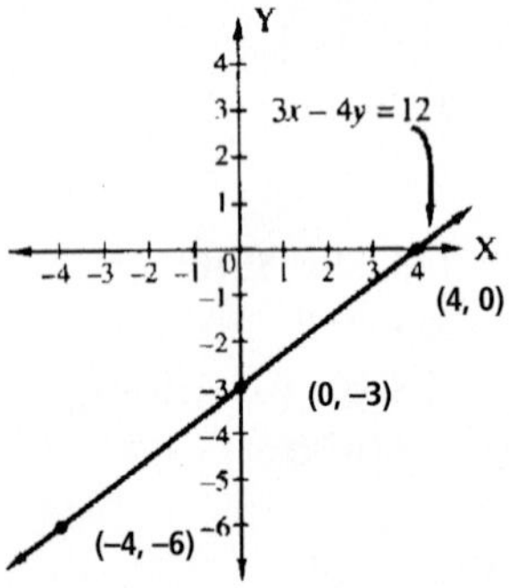

7.

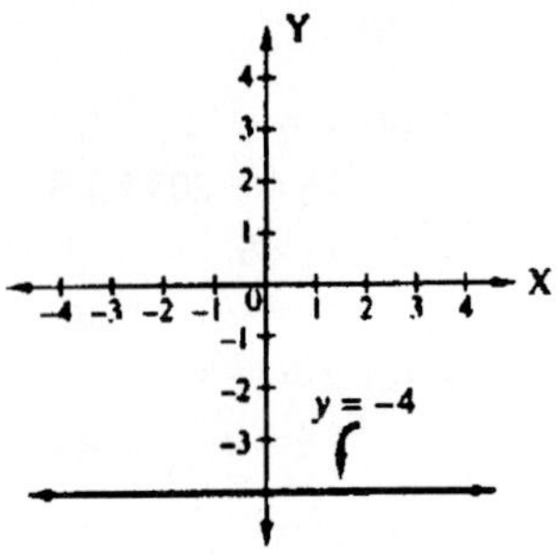

9. For
$y = 2x - 3$
slope, $m = 2$
y-intercept, $b = -3$

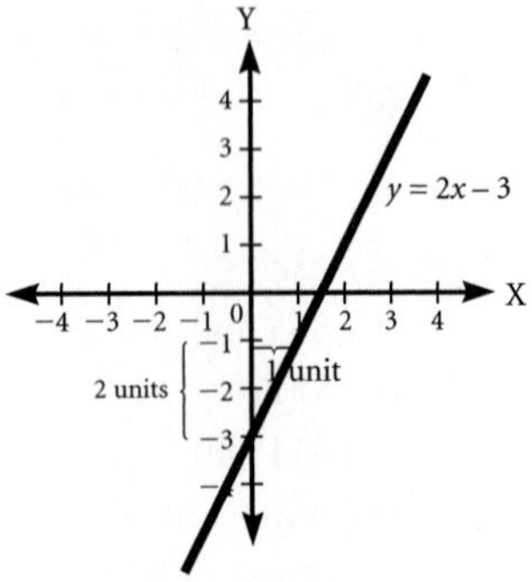

C. **1.** For $y = 3x + 20$
For $x = 0$
to $x = 40$

x	0	20	40	
y	20	80	140	

or $m = 3$
$b = 20$

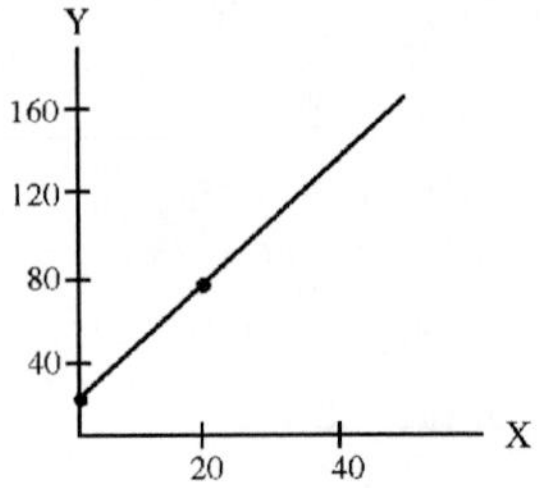

3. For $3x + 4y = 1200$
For $x = 0$
to $x = 40$

x	0	200	400	
y	300	150	0	

or $m = -\frac{3}{4}$
$b = 300$

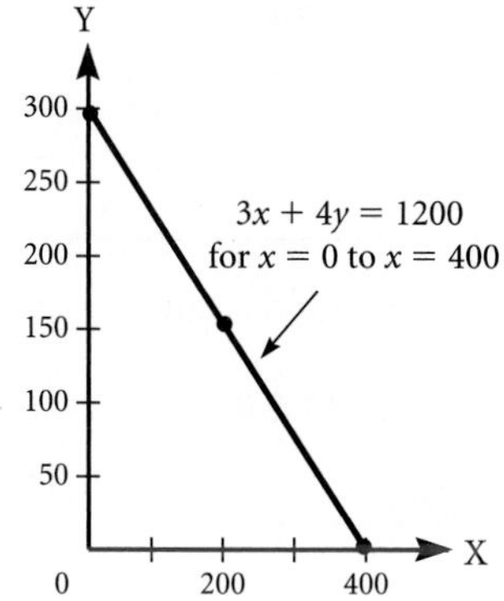

Exercise 4.3

A. 1.

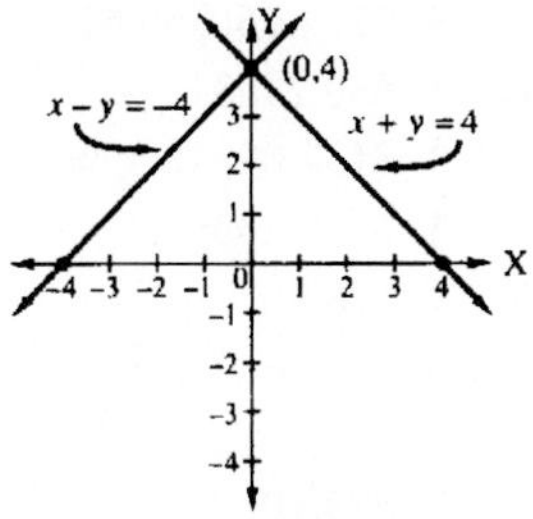

(0, 4) is the solution.

3. $x = 2y - 1$

x	3	−1	−5
y	2	0	−2

$y = 4 - 3x$

x	0	2	1
y	4	−2	1

(1,1) is the solution.

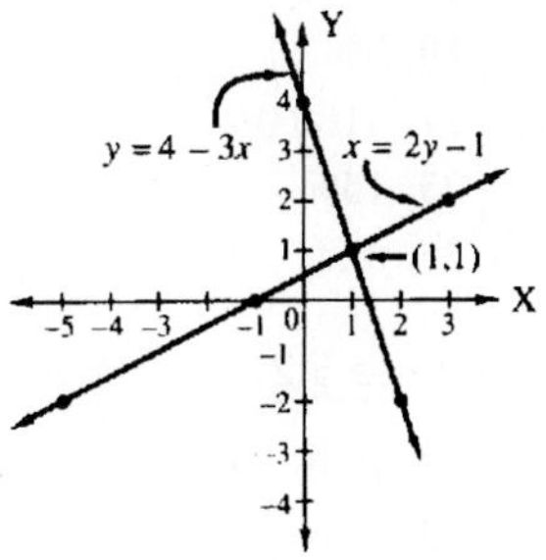

5. $3x - 4y = 18$

x	6	2	−2
y	0	−3	−6

$2y = -3x$

x	0	2	−2
y	0	−3	3

(2,−3) is the solution.

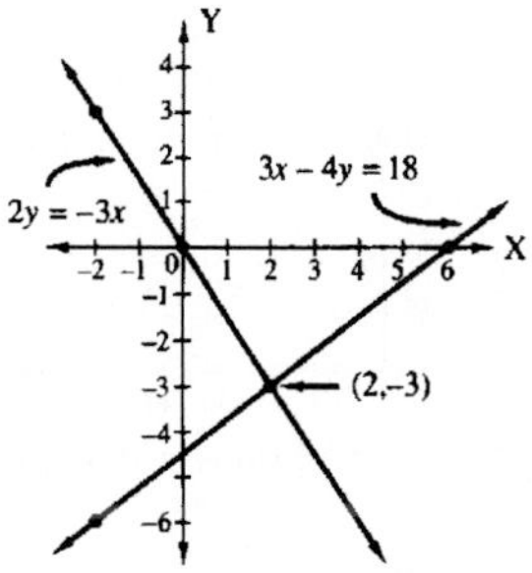

7. $5x = 2y = 20$

x	4	2	6
y	0	−5	5

(6, 5) is the solution.

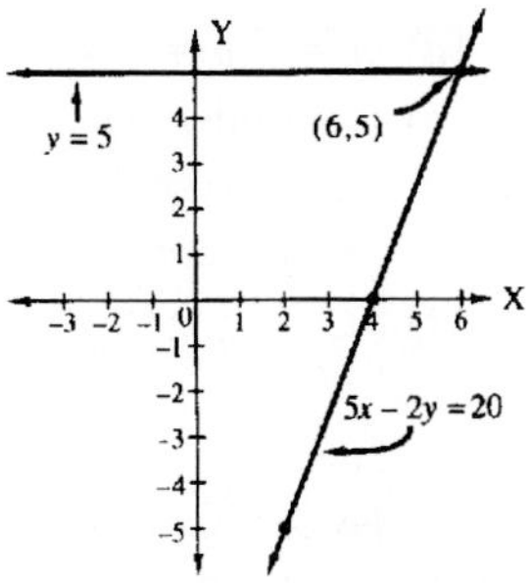

B. 1. For $y - 4x = 0$
For x = 0
to x = 10 0000

x	0	5000	10 000
y	0	20 000	40 000

For $y - 2x - 10\,000 = 0$
For $x = 0$ to $x = 10\,0000$

x	0	5000	10 000
y	10 000	20 000	30 000

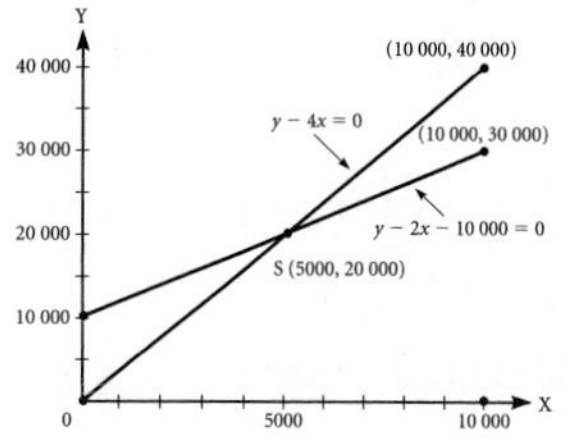

3. For
$3x + 3y = 2400$
For $x = 0$ to $x = 800$

x	0	400	800
y	800	400	0

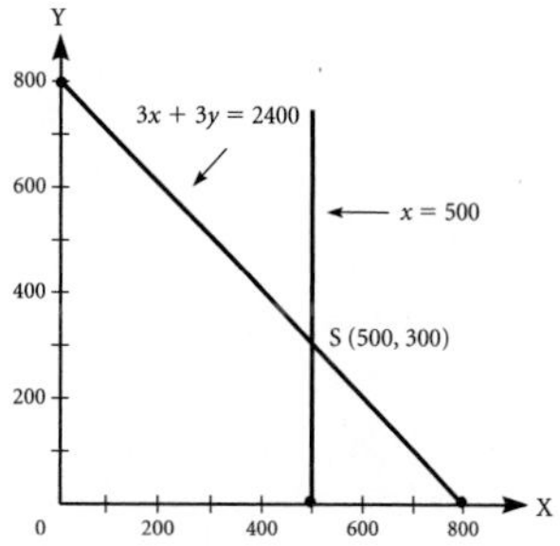

Exercise 4.4

A. 1.

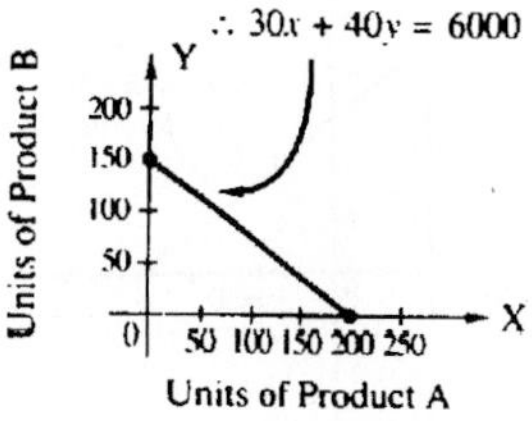

3.

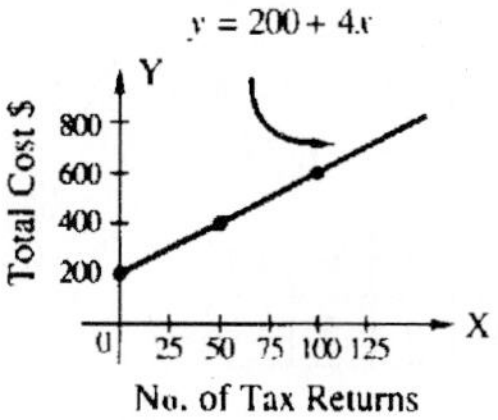

B. 1. 15; 9
3. Brand X, 90; No-Name, 50
5. Kaya, \$31 500; Fred, \$23 500
7. Type A, 42; Type B, 18
9. 55 quarters; 72 loonies

Re

1. (a

(b

(c) $\frac{}{2}, b = 4$

(d) $m = -6, b = 10$

(e) m is undefined, there is no y-intercept

(f) $m = \frac{1}{3}, b = -3$

(g) $m = \frac{1}{4}, b = -1$

(h) $m = 0, b = 5$

3. (a) $3x + y = 6$ and $x - y = 2$

x	0	2	4
y	6	0	−6

x	0	2	4
y	−2	0	2

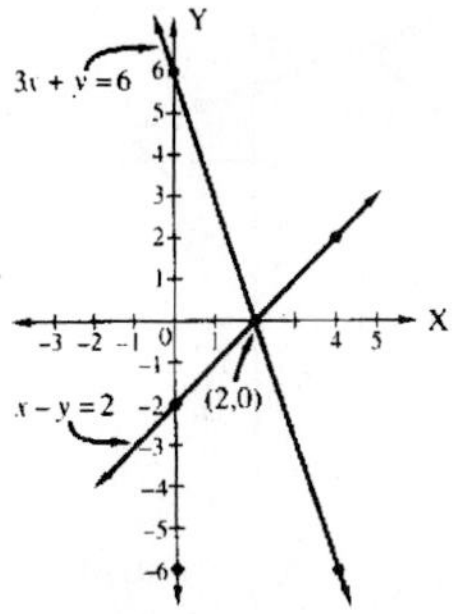

(b) $x + 4y = -8$ and $3x + 4y = 0$

x	0	4	−4
y	−2	−3	−1

x	0	4	−4
y	0	−3	3

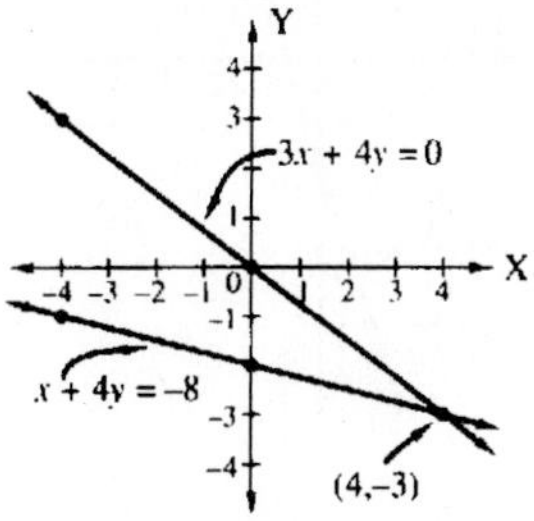

(c) $5x = 3y$ and
$y = -5$

x	0	3	-3
y	0	5	-5

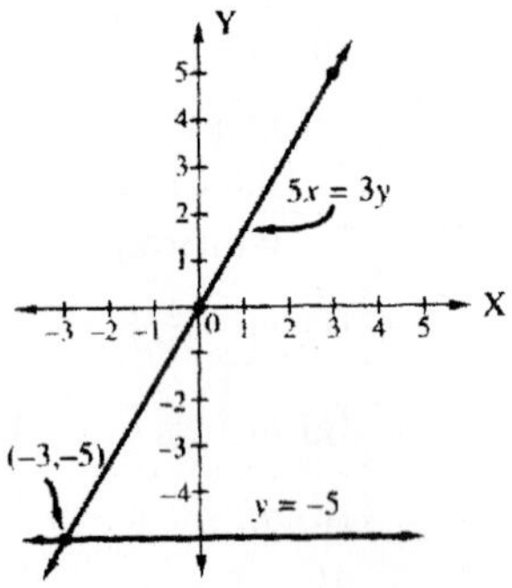

(d) $2x + 6y = 8$ and
$x = -2$

x	4	-2	1
y	0	2	1

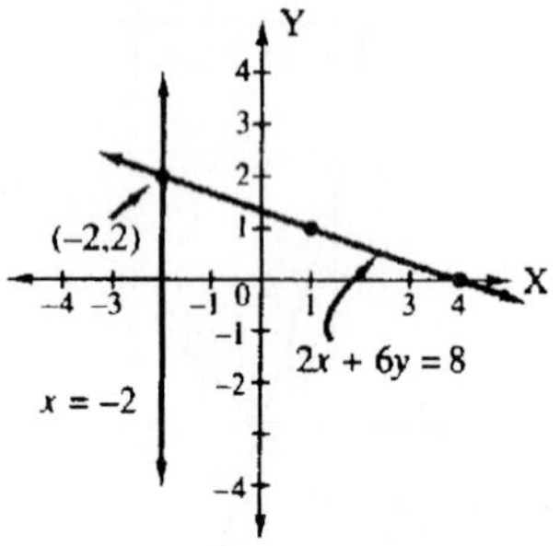

(e) $y = 3x - 2$ and
$y = 3$

x	0	$\frac{5}{3}$	-1
y	-2	3	-5

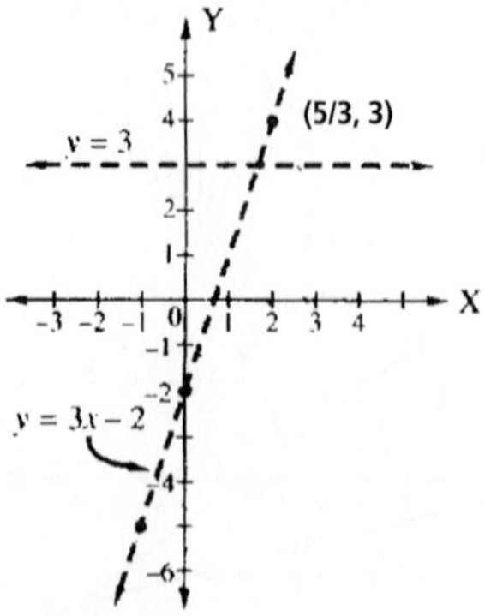

(f) $y = -2x$ and
$x = 4$

x	0	4	-2
y	0	-8	4

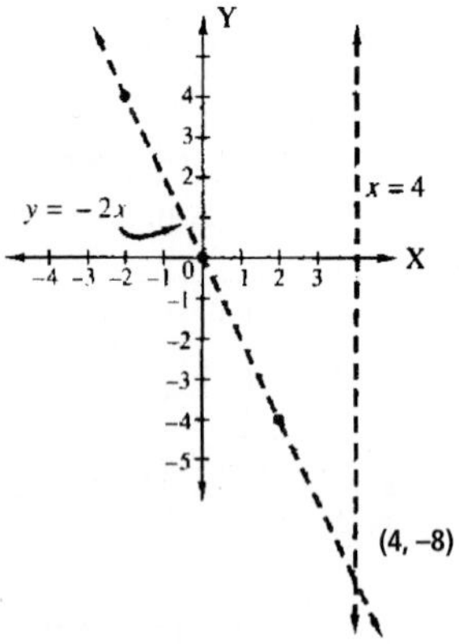

(g) $x = -2$,
$y = 0$, and
$3x + 4y = 12$

x	0	-2	4
y	3	4.5	0

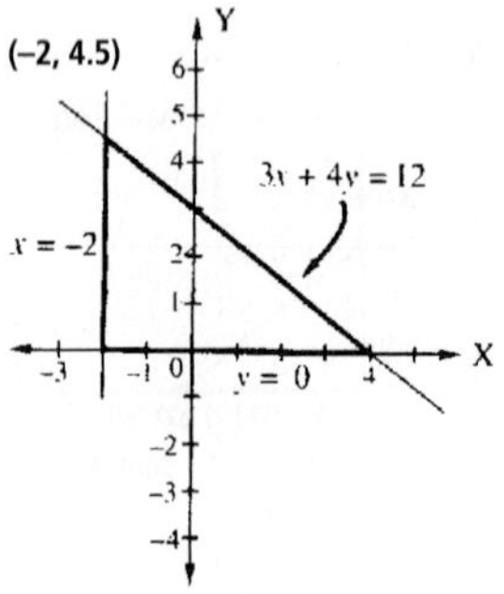

(h) $y = -2$ and
$5x + 3y = 15$

x	3	0	4.2
y	0	5	-2

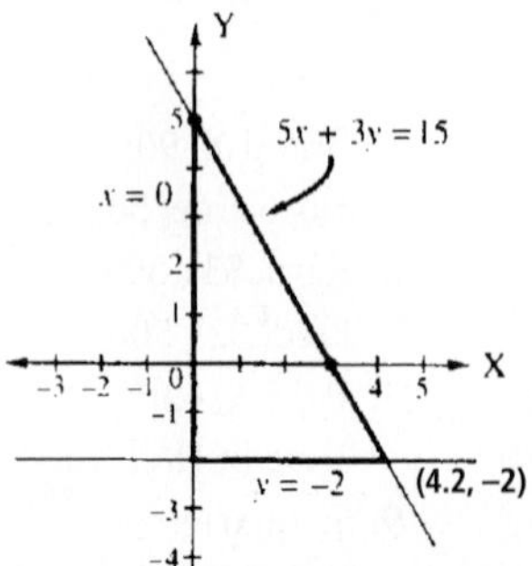

5. (a)

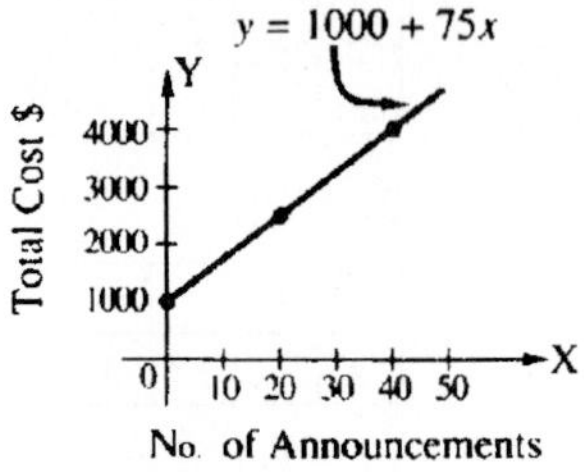

(b)

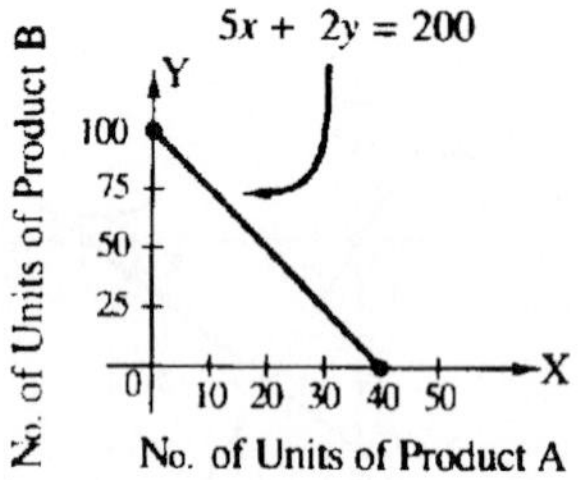

Self-Test

1. (a) $m = 0$,
   $b = -\frac{11}{3}$
   (b) $m = 6$,
   $b = -9$
   (c) $m = -\frac{1}{3}$,
   $b = 0$
   (d) $m = 0, b = -3$
   (e) m is undefined, there is no y-intercept
   (f) $m = -\frac{a}{b}, b = \frac{c}{b}$

3. (a) For $-x = -55 + y$
   For $x = 0$ to $x = 55$

x	0	25	55
y	55	30	0

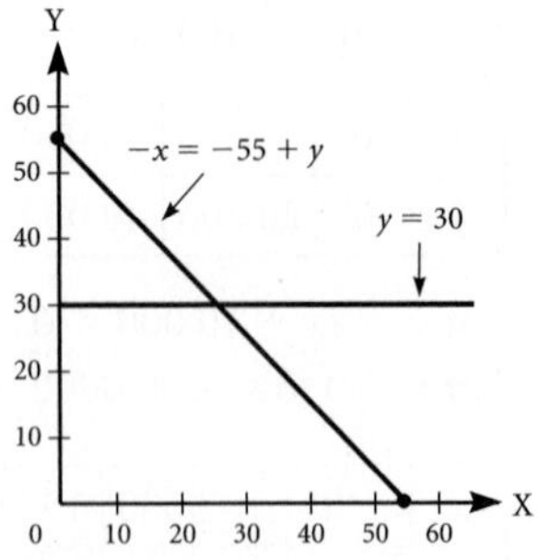

(b) For
$3x + 2y + 600 = 0$
for $x = 0$ to $x = 200$

x	0	100	200
y	-300	-450	-600

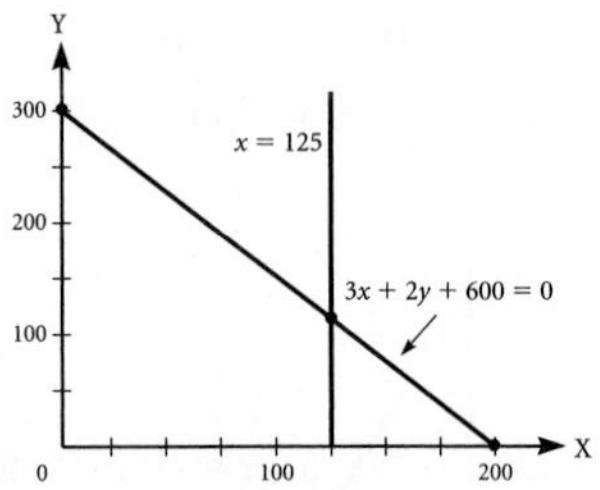

5. \$8000; \$4000

CHAPTER 5

Exercise 5.1

A. 1. \$11.07; \$13.53
3. $33\frac{1}{3}$%; \$25.65
5. 15%; \$252.60
7. \$133.36; \$50.01
9. \$134.96; \$50.61

B. 1. \$30.24; 32.5%
3. \$137.89; 48.55%
5. \$1583.33; 61%

C. 1. \$78.25
3. 15.9%
5. \$3200
7. \$74.10
9. \$4.26
11. (a) 38.75%
(b) 48.26%
13. (a) \$318.67
(b) \$280.33
(c) 46.8%
15. (a) \$443.79
(b) \$342.41
(c) 43.552%
17. 15%
19. 5%
21. \$180.00
23. 15%
25. 8.7%

Exercise 5.2

A. 1. \$640.00
3. \$776.11

5. $1136.80
7. $4581.50

B. 1. $582.00; $850.00
3. $564.50; $536.28
5. $810.00; $810.00

C. 1. (a) May 23
(b) $2449.02
3. (a) $799.90
(b) $825.16
(c) $842.00
5. $2507.19
7. $2184.00
9. (a) September 10
(b) $5276.85
(c) $103.20
11. (a) $1164.00
(b) $733.54
(c) Amount paid on October 25 is $600.00.
13. (a) $1925.00
(b) $3400.00
15. (i) $1.96
(ii) 3.5%

Exercise 5.3

A. 1. (a) $6.00
(b) $3.84
(c) $2.16
(d) 25%
(e) 20%
3. (a) $35.00
(b) $31.50
(c) $3.50
(d) $66\frac{2}{3}\%$
(e) 40%
5. (a) $10.50
(b) $12.75
(c) ($2.25)
(d) $38\frac{8}{9}\%$
(e) 28%

B. 1. $6.25; 25%; 20%
3. $102.40; 60%; 37.5%
5. $75.95; $21.70; 28.6%
7. 44.24; $22.12; $33\frac{1}{3}\%$
9. $78.10; $46.86; 150%
11. $111.30; $133.56; 20%

C. 1. $13.60
3. $3.00
5. $102.08
7. (a) 150%
(b) 60%
9. (a) $36.50
(b) $29.93
(c) 21.95%
11. (a) $1.65
(b) $66\frac{2}{3}\%$
13. (a) $234.20
(b) 47.37%
15. (a) $140.00
(b) $66\frac{2}{3}\%$
17. (a) $16.80
(b) 27.3%

Exercise 5.4

A. 1. $51.00; $59.00; ($8.00)
3. $96.40; $30.65; $7.91
5. $160.00; $19.20; 12%

B. 1. (a) $21.99
(b) $17.59
(c) $4.62
3. 20%
5. 16%
7. (a) $7.00
(b) 21.21%
9. (a) $17.79
(b) $25.44
(c) 12.28%
(d) 38.66%

Exercise 5.5

A. 1. (a) $228.69
(b) 54%
3. (a) 40%
(b) ($8.00)
(c) 10.3%
(d) $9\frac{1}{3}\%$
5. ($2.23)
7. (a) normal quality = $14.85
seconds = $9.92
substandard = $6.60
(b) $957.00
(c) 34.5%
9. (a) $72.00
(b) $54.00
(c) 25%
11. ($6.50)
13. ($97.50)
15. ($82.50)

Review Exercise

1. (a) $31.92
(b) $24.08
(c) $43%
3. 45.66%
5. 15%
7. $30.00
9. September 12; $25 117.40
11. (a) $1940.00
(b) $2813.00
13. (a) $1645.00
(b) $1500.00
15. (a) $90.00
(b) $58.50
(c) 53.85%
(d) $74.88
(e) −$6.48
17. (a) $77.50
(b) 42.86%
19. $240.00
21. (a) −$0.60
(b) 26.98%
23. (a) −$13.20
(b) 25%
25. (a) $189.00
(b) 21.25%
(c) $133\frac{1}{3}\%$
27. (a) $2152.40
(b) 69.43%
(c) 40.98%

Self-Test

1. $295.77
3. 50.5%
5. $1635.04
7. $
9. $
11. $
13. 1
15. 2
17. −$660.45

CHAPTER 6

Exercise 6.1

A. 1. (a)
(i) Revenue = 120x
(ii) Cost = 2800 + 50x
where x represents the number of units per period
(b) (i) 40
(ii) $4800
(iii) 40%
3. (a) (i) Revenue = 6.95x
(ii) Total cost = 1800 + 3.95x
(b) (i) not applicable
(ii) $4170.00
(iii) 60%

B. 1. 45
3. $18 000
5. $9.95
7. (a) $1600
(b) 900
9. (a) 28
(b) $2.44

Exercise 6.2

A. 1. (a) $72
(b) 48%
(c) 82
(d) $12 300
3. (a) $46
(b) 46.5% (rounded)
(c) 11
(d) $1089
5. (a) $438 600
(b) 43%
(c) 372 093
(d) $372 093

1. 27 units (rounded)
3. 169 units
5. $1610.00
7. 400 000 units

Exercise 6.3

1.

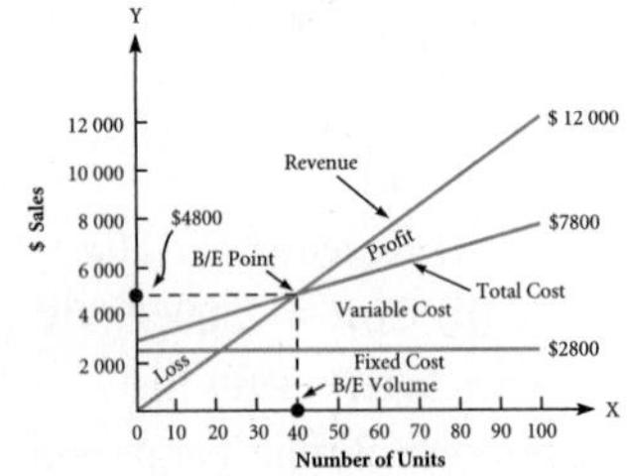

3.

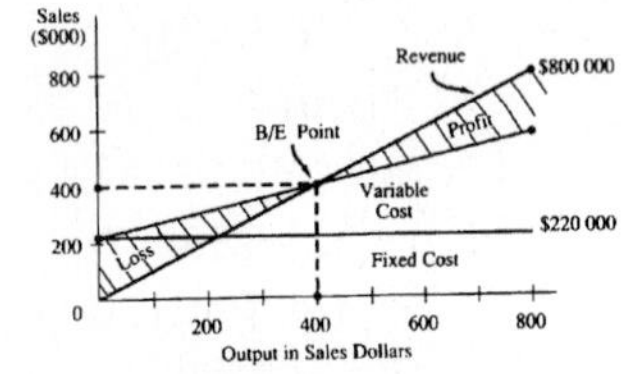

Exercise 6.4

1. (a) 164
   (b) 246
   (c) 250
   (d) $13
3. (a) 975
   (b) 1034
   (c) $2094
   (d) 1338 (rounded)

Review Exercise

1. (a) (i) $28.00
   (ii) 15.135%
   (b) (i) 112
   (ii) 35%
   (iii) $20 720
   (c) Revenue =
   Total cost =185x;
   3136 + 157x

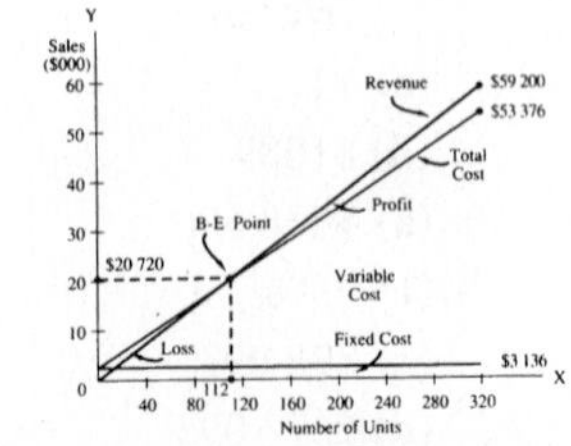

(d) (i) 30%
   (ii) 38.75%
   (iii) 70%
3. (a) (i) 140 000
   (ii) 35%
   (b) (i) 60%
   (ii) $300 000
   (c) Total cost =
   10 5000 + 0.65x

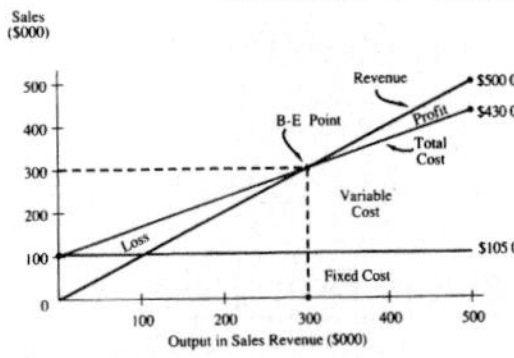

(d) $335 000
5. 802

Self-Test

1. (a) (i) $3.00
   (ii) 30%
   (b) (i) 6000 CDs
   (ii) $60 000
   (iii) 40%
   (c) Revenue = 10x
   Cost = 18 000
   + 7.00x

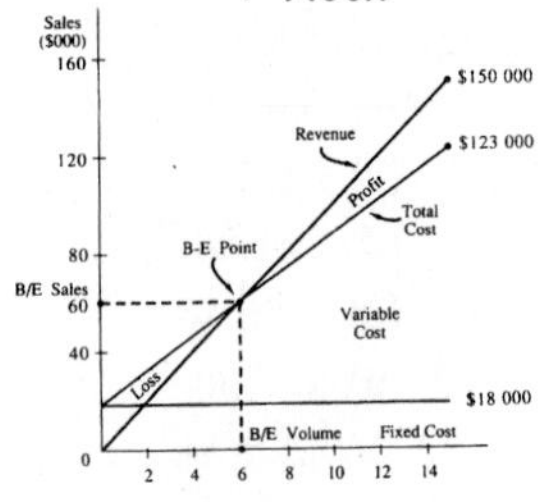

(d) 5600
(e) 5500

CHAPTER 7

Exercise 7.1

A. 1. 0.035; 1.25
   3. 0.0825; $\frac{183}{365}$
B. 1. $1096.88
   3. $95.21
   5. $75.34
   7. $10.87
   9. $21.76
   11. $26.44
C. 1. $88.77
   3. $48.63

Exercise 7.2

A. 1. $1224.00
   3. 10.75%
   5. 14 months
   7. 144 days
B. 1. $3296.00
   3. 9.5%
   5. 8.4%
   7. 11
   9. 126
   11. $876.00
   13. $400 000
   15. 9%
   17. 41

Exercise 7.3

A. 1. $490.13
   3. $768.75
   5. $849.21
   7. $1298.00
B. 1. $2542.53
   3. $13 800.00
   5. $26 954.84
   7. $13 864.50
   9. (a) $51 975
   (b) $51 943.53
   (c) 3.887%

Exercise 7.4

A. 1. $266.00; $13.30
   3. $517.50; $547.17
   5. $2025.00; 292 days
B. 1. $1222.00
   3. $1704.60
   5. $644.00
   7. $6947.60
   9. $23 000.00

Exercise 7.5

A. 1. $829.33
   3. $617.50
   5. $1103.37
   7. $856.47
   9. $777.81
   11. $1070.39
B. 1. $1156.80
   3. $2248.66
   5. $1722.00
   7. $519.48
   9. $569.45
   11. $421.97
   13. $811.93
   15. $1408.21
   17. $1599.35

Review Exercise

1. (a) 172
   (b) 214
3. (a) $1160.00
   (b) $601.77
5. (a) $750.00
   (b) $5709.97
7. $3000.17
9. 8.25%
11. 196 days
13. $1601.89
15. $3200.00
17. $1736.47
19. $2664.00
21. $3404.32
23. $1614.74
25. $961.50
27. $1587.06

Self-Test

1. $21.40
3. 6.5%
5. $6187.50
7. $4306.81
9. 359 days
11. $7432.80
13. $1163.85
15. $1799.23

CHAPTER 8

Exercise 8.1

A. 1. December 30, 2010
   3. $530.00
   5. 154 days
   7. $544.54
B. 1. (a) March 3, 2012
   (b) 155 days
   (c) $21.40
   (d) $861.40
   3. (a) April 3, 2008
   (b) 63 days
   (c) $14.02
   (d) $1264.02

Exercise 8.2

A. 1. $631.24
3. $837.19
5. $856.35
7. $10 413.71

Exercise 8.3

A. 1. $500.00
B. 1. $1471.28
3. $1615.56
C. 1. $99 054.15
3. 2.73%
5. (a) 2.72%
(b) $99 636.18
(c) 2.706%

Exercise 8.4

A. 1. $37.50
3. $22.50
5. $307.56
B. 1. $3785.67
3. $1825.63
5. $178.66

Exercise 8.5

A. 1. (a) $0.16
(b) $4.16
(c) $1.24
(d) $10.00
(e) −$956.34

Exercise 8.6

A. 1. Totals are $1233.69; $33.69; $1200.00
3. Totals are $922.36; $22.36; $900

Review Exercise

1. (a) November 2
(b) $35.62
(c) $1635.62
3. $1500.00
5. $5125.75
7. $814.17
9. $1269.57
11. 6.1493%
13. $449.12
15. (a) $54.57; $62.49; $70.82; $69.86; $70.75
(b) −$10 623.49

Self-Test

1. $19.79
3. $1160.00
5. $1664.66
7. (a) $98 116.43
(b) 3.680%
9. $340.26
11. Totals are $4070.41; $70.41; $4000.00

CHAPTER 9

Exercise 9.1

A. 1. 1; 0.12; 5
3. 4; 0.01375; 36
5. 2; 0.0575; 27
7. 12; 0.0066667; 150
9. 2; 0.06125; 9
B. 1. 1.7623417
3. 1.6349754
5. 4.5244954
7. 2.7092894
9. 1.7074946
C. 1. (a) 48
(b) 2.5%
(c) 1.025^{48}
(d) 3.2714896

Exercise 9.2

A. 1. $713.39
3. $2233.21
5. $5468.38
7. $6639.51
9. $662.02
11. $4152.58
13. $2052.74
B. 1. $6884.47; $1884.47
3. $1441.71
5. (a) $199.26
(b) $202.24
(c) $203.81
(d) $204.89
7. (a) $148.59; $48.59
(b) $220.80; 120.80
(c) $487.54; 387.54
9. $8712.50
11. $761.75
13. $17 116.96
15. 162.81
17. (a) Bank; $6968.27; $6914.09
(b) $54.18
C. 1. $2372.65
3. $1452.79
5. $3956.97
7. $1102.13
9. $1444.24
11. $10 526.69

Exercise 9.3

A. 1. $574.37
3. $371.86
5. $409.16
7. $500.24
9. $749.91
11. $4344.21
B. 1. $1338.81; $261.19
3. $762.84
5. $3129.97
7. $1398.85
9. two payments; $4835.49
11. two payments

Exercise 9.4

A. 1. $1767.71; $232.29
3. $3981.87; $1018.13
5. $2642.50; $557.50
7. $1012.96; $671.00
9. $2310.82; $720.62
11. $2036.86; $540.42
13. $1332.82; $261.78
B. 1. $4589.47
3. $1345.06
5. $3800.24
7. $1561.49
C. 1. $8452.52
3. $2346.36
5. $3488.29
7. $1074.71
9. $1972.80
11. $1492.15

Exercise 9.5

A. 1. $5983.40
3. $2537.13
5. $1673.49
7. $641.36
B. 1. $3426.73
3. $2464.35
5. $1536.03
7. $987.93
C. 1. (a) $2851.94
(b) $3265.19
(c) $4000.00
(d) $5610.21
3. $6805.31
5. $655.02
7. $2464.35
9. $1955.51
11. $1231.82
13. (a) $646.41
(b) $946.41
15. $3076.33
17. $987.93

Review Exercise

1. (a) $1198.28
(b) $1221.61
(c) $1227.05
3. (a) $2890.09
(b) $890.09
5. (a) $6144.45; $4344.45
(b) $3305.27; $2055.27
7. $10 681.77
9. $11 102.50
11. $4194.33
13. $9791.31
15. $2830.68; $3190.63
17. $9294.85
19. $1035.70
21. $2838.62
23. $2079.94
25. $110 440.03
27. $26 048.42
29. (a) $2742.41
(b) $2911.55
(c) $3281.79
31. $4857.56

33. $1820.32
35. $3574.57

Self-Test

1. $2129.97
3. 2.7118780
5. $6919.05
7. $14 711.80
9. $4504.29
11. $10 138.19
13. $2661.85
15. $848.88

CHAPTER 10

Exercise 10.1

A. **1.** **(a)** 13.4 years
(b) 28 quarters
(c) 117.8 months
(d) 8 half-years
(e) 37.313 quarters
(f) 37.167 half-years

B. **1.** 9.329 years
3. 17.501 years
5. 5.622 years
7. November 1, 2011
9. 21 months
11. 2 years, 298 days
13. 3 years, 230 days

Exercise 10.2

A. **1.** 4.5%
3. 9.6%
5. 9.778%

B. **1.** 9.237%
3. **(a)** 10.402%
(b) 7.585%
5. 3.5%
7. 4.771%

Exercise 10.3

A. **1.** **(a)** 12.891%
(b) 6.168%
(c) 7.397%
(d) 10.691%
3. **(a)** 8.9%
(b) 6.465%
(c) 7.385%
(d) 4.273%

B. **1.** 6.991%
3. 4.656%
5. 8.945%
7. 6.2196%
9. 7.385%
11. **(a)** $714.57
(b) $114.57
(c) 3.5567%
13. **(a)** $1831.40
(b) $631.40
(c) 4.3182%

Review Exercise

1. 5.592%
3. 1 year, 231 days
5. 22.517085 half-years (11 years, 95 days)
7. 6.03%
9. **(a)** 5.92%
(b) 14.35%
(c) 8.833%
(d) 8.24%
11. **(a)** 4.59%
(b) 5.96%
13. 8.44%
15. **(a)** 4.0%
(b) 3.7852%
(c) 3.5462%
(d) 3.2989%
17. 1.831663 years (1 year, 304 days)
19. 1.5677878 years (1 year, 208 days)
21. 6.8287904 years (6 years, 303 days–2007-09-30)

Self-Test

1. 10.50 half-years (63 months)
3. 5.535675%
5. 7.352%
7. 10.0%
9. 7.5%

CHAPTER 11

Exercise 11.1

A. **1.** **(a)** annuity certain
(b) annuity due
(c) general annuity
3. **(a)** perpetuity
(b) deferred annuity
(c) general annuity
5. **(a)** annuity certain
(b) deferred annuity due
(c) simple annuity

Exercise 11.2

A. **1.** $54 193.60
3. $59 185.19
5. $17 915.08

B. **1.** $13 045.68
3. $32 434.02
5. **(a)** $8531.12
(b) $4500.00
(c) $4031.12
7. **(a)** $20090.19
(b) $15 000.00
(c) $5090.19
9. $62177.25

Exercise 11.3

A. **1.** $9515.19
3. $30 941.11
5. $10 544.91

B. **1.** $6897.02
3. **(a)** $9906.20
(b) $2093.80
5. **(a)** $2523.82
(b) $372.06
7. $12 710.96
9. Joel, $280.28

Exercise 11.4

A. **1.** $821.39
3. $1117.37
5. $272.73
7. $232.54
9. $1653.70

B. **1.** $207.87
3. $591.66
5. $320.61
7. $410.00
9. $557.65
11. $317.49
13. $229.33
15. $62.61
17. $8567.28
19. $10 017.56
21. $438.10

Exercise 11.5

A. **1.** 14.6023573 years (14 years, 8 months)
3. 93.0687373 months (7 years, 10 months)
5. 15.5775778 half-years (7 years, 10 months)
7. 15.395937 semi-annual periods (7 years, 9 months)
9. 71.517450 months (6 years)

B. **1.** 74.498331 months (6 years, 3 months)
3. 22 deposits
5. 45.648036 months (3 years, 10 months)
7. 27.973645 months (2 years, 4 months)
9. 47.999053 months (4 years)
11. 12.384875 semi-annual periods (6.192437 years)
13. 9 months

Exercise 11.6

A. **1.** 5.0%
3. 9.0%
5. 7.6%
7. 11.37%

B. **1.** 12.5%
3. 3.04%
5. 7.2%
7. 9.50%
9. 7.685%

Review Exercise

1. (a) $26 734.60
   (b) $17 280.00
   (c) $9454.60
3. $722.62
5. 12.575297 years (12 years, 7 months)
7. $411.57
9. $101 517.64
11. 10.524175 half-years (5 years, 4 months)
13. 7.25%
15. $34 031.63
17. 8.583884 half-years (9 semi-annual payments)
19. $16 102.46

Self-Test

1. $35 786.08
3. 10.9%
5. 28.06 quarters (84 months)
7. $40 385.39
9. $3268.62

CHAPTER 12

Exercise 12.1

A. 1. $45 855.46
   3. $16 317.77
   5. $63 686.72
   7. $32 876.06

B. 1. $23 268.52
   3. $2326.66
   5. (a) $13 265.50
      (b) $3265.50
   7. $31 293.63
   9. $1592.095784

Exercise 12.2

A. 1. $47 583.23
   3. $42 505.51
   5. $5106.97
   7. $34 627.97

B. 1. $10 041.88
   3. $31 736.57
   5. (a) $29 829.03
      (b) $5170.97
   7. $80 000.02
   9. $52 937.17
   11. $223.27

Exercise 12.3

A. 1. $823.60
   3. $1121.26
   5. $273.20
   7. $1426.84
   9. $271.68

B. 1. $124.41
   3. $799.39
   5. $330.63
   7. $117.26
   9. $26.63

Exercise 12.4

A. 1. 14.51 years (14 years, 6 months)
   3. 92.97 months (7 years, 9 months)
   5. 15.64 semi-annual periods (7 years, 10 months)
   7. 15.43 half-years (7 years, 9 months)
   9. 71.57 months (6 years)

B. 1. 44.76 months (3 years, 9 months)
   3. 39.42 months (3 years, 4 months)
   5. 13 years, 7.3 months
   7. 21.27 months
   9. 40 deposits

Exercise 12.5

A. 1. 6.01%
   3. 6.86%
   5. 12.41%
   7. 4.40%

B. 1. 5.09%
   3. 7.31%
   5. 8.82%
   7. 10.778%
   9. 7.86%
   11. 9.24%

Exercise 12.6

A. 1. (a) 1016.40
      (b) 18 229.63
   3. (a) 27 748.40
      (b) 35 011.37
      (c) 1413.54
      (d) 7262.97

B. 1. 17 790.55
   3. 107 789.17

Review Exercise

1. $13 509.62
3. $64 125.87
5. $75 962.59
7. (a) $101.81
   (b) $1714.37
9. (a) 30.62 quarters (7 years, 8 months)
   (b) 27.84 semi-annual periods (13 years, 11 months)
11. (a) 12.46 months (6 years, 3 months)
    (b) 23.24 months (1 year, 11 months)
13. 16.33 quarters (4 years, 1 month)
15. 8.30 quarters (2 years, 1 month)
17. (a) $13 719.16
    (b) $3951.16
    (c) $382.25
    (d) $8580.00
19. 96.82 months (8 years, 1 month)
21. $160 296.97

Self-Test

1. $55 246.47
3. 17.34 quarters (4 years, 4 months)
5. $3003.81
7. 32 quarters (8 years)
9. $13 355.86; $96.29
11. $302 131.40

CHAPTER 13

Exercise 13.1

A. 1. $135 334.71; $71 813.10
   3. $69 033.69; $35 581.67
   5. $43 738.24 $7278.61

B. 1. $204.80
   3. $909.95

C. 1. n = 113 months (9 years, 5 months)
   3. n = 8 years

D. 1. nominal annual rate = 7.125%
   3. nominal annual rate = 12.498%

E. 1. $31 378.29
   3. (a) $29 513.14
      (b) $10 313.14
   5. $33 338.44
   7. (a) $1238.56
      (b) $1575.00
      (c) $336.44
   9. $2150.38
   11. (a) $77 820.42
       (b) $55 800.00
       (c) $22 020.42
   13. $659.95
   15. $300.36
   17. $1046.16
   19. 11 years, 11 months
   21. 4 years, 4 months
   23. 7.0%
   25. 8.58%

Exercise 13.2

A. 1. $39 342.74
   3. $11 304.97

B. 1. $1316.98
   3. $903.61

C. 1. n = 35 half-years (17.5 years)
   3. n = 18 quarters (4.5 years)

D. **1.** nominal annual rate = 11.28%
3. nominal annual rate = 4.89%

E. **1.** $59 113.10
3. $24 111.08
5. $459.47
7. n = 37 quarters (9 years, 3 months)
9. nominal annual rate = 9.18%

Exercise 13.3

A. **1.** $1403.20
3. $3058.17
5. $45 376.41

B. **1.** $126 738.19
3. **(a)** –$147 329.91
(b) $272 000.00
(c) $124 670.09
5. $1651.45
7. $1984.62
9. n = 36 months (3 years)
11. n = 26.712 months
15. $88 092.69
17. 37.78
19. n = 14.75
21. $147.55

Exercise 13.4

A. **1.** $5048.75
3. $3058.17
5. $3135.48

B. **1.** $21831.32
3. **(a)** $32 277.80
(b) $38 400.00
(c) $6122.20
5. $576.10
7. $3259.68
9. 16 quarters (4 years)
11. 13.660591 quarters
13. $27 246.85
15. $42 162.27
17. $1972.34
19. $11 499.21
21. 71.862 months (72 months)
23. n = 6.861579 years

Exercise 13.5

A. **1.** $73 529.41
3. $91 027.01
5. $44 762.78
7. $96 992.34

B. **1.** $214.60
3. $850.87
5. $210 240.91
7. $41 854.67
9. $166.70

Review Exercise

1. **(a)** S_n = $11 223.39
A_n = $5799.35
(b) S_n(due) = $11 728.44
A_n(due) = $6060.32
3. $19 153.93
5. **(a)** $2638.84
(b) $3444.00
(c) $805.16
7. n = 109 months
9. n = 28 months
11. nominal annual rate = 5.51%
13. **(a)** $411.57
(b) $403.50
15. **(a)** $15 749.42
(b) $3149.42
(c) $432.91
(d) $8179.68
17. n = 51 months
19. n = 49 months
21. **(a)** $28 435.38
(b) $28 552.64
23. $42 092.99
25. $2736.49
27. **(a)** $503.87
(b) $1437.96
(c) –$275.12
(d) $1782.29
(e) $89.52
(f) $1037.88
29. n = 29 years
31. **(a)** n = 6.78 half-years
(b) n = 7.51 years
(c) n = 10.111884 quarters
(d) n = 8.86133 half-years
33. **(a)** $16 102.46
(b) $3120.21
(c) $17 860.97
(d) $120.21
35. $301.80
37. $910.15
39. n = 26 quarters (6 years, 6 months)
41. $20 964.79
43. $34 543.54
45. $8908.36
47. n = 28.605079 quarters
49. **(a)** $60 229.26
(b) $49 312.99
(c) $29 620.76
(d) $36 229.73
(e) $86 633.66
(f) $90 133.66
51. $318 181.82
53. $105.30
55. $28 089.24

Self-Test

1. $84 209.75
3. $1258.38
5. $357.34
7. Nominal Annual Rate = 8.185%
9. $43 246.07
11. $1170.69
13. $6056.04
15. $21.97
17. $122 263.84

CHAPTER 14

Exercise 14.1

A. **1.** **(a)** $549.22
(b) $5633.77
(c) $140.84
(d) $408.38
3. **(a)** $1103.73
(b) $4913.61
(c) $196.54
(d) $907.19

B. **1.** **(a)** n = 19.48 payments
(b) $2493.97
3. **(a)** n = 14.53
(b) $8035.94

C. **1.** **(a)** $920.57
(b) $15 052.64
(c) $59 234.20
(d) $23 234.20
3. **(a)** $136.87
(b) $4199.54
(c) $31.50
(d) $105.37
5. $2054.05; totals are $14 378.41; $4378.41; $10 000.00
7. totals are $14 943.16; $5743.16; $9200.00
9. $651.11
11. $1160.09
13. **(a)** $3621.90
(b) $1035.27
(c) $2799.85
(d) $10 445.14; totals are $115 900.80; $30 900.80; $8500.00
15. **(a)** n = 14.022508
(b) $957.79
(c) $1910.53
(d) $4664.98; totals are $35 057.75; $11 057.75; $24 000.00

Exercise 14.2

A. **1.** **(a)** $1829.69
(b) $20 286.42

(c) $819.57
(d) $1010.12
3. (a) $164.04
(b) $4563.53
(c) $22.54
(d) $141.50

B. 1. (a) $n = 17.13$
(b) $2685.85
3. (a) $n = 14.894762$
(b) $1584.96

C. 1. (a) $2790.38
(b) $34 892.23
(c) $1599.89
(d) $1190.49
3. (a) $252.15
(b) $34 200.11
(c) $7277.51
(d) $294.24
5. (a) $n = 15.413529$
(b) $2911.17
(c) $4311.17
7. $3212.01; totals are $22 484.09; $6484.09; $16 000.00
9. $752.68
11. (a) $318.15
(b) $3323.27
(c) $263.14
(d) $364.44
(e)

Partial Amortization Schedule

Payment number	*Amount paid*	*Interest paid*	*Principal repaid*	*Outstanding principal*
0				40 000.00
1	318.15	278.44	39.71	39 960.29
2	318.15	278.17	39.98	39 920.31
3	318.15	277.89	40.26	39 880.05
:	:	:	:	:
:	:	:	:	:
60	:	:	:	37 056.28
61	364.44	317.37	47.07	37 009.21
62	364.44	316.97	47.47	36 961.74
63	364.44	316.56	47.88	36 913.86
:	:	:	:	:

Exercise 14.3

A. 1. $1006.24
3. $348.26
5. $306.39

B. 1. (a) $n = 29.434057$
(b) $157.46
3. (a) $n = 47.779687$
(b) $722.00
5. $234.53
7. $301.45
9. $1152.87
11. (a) $n = 61.523813$
(b) $724.48
(c) $84 599.48
(d) $68 599.48

Exercise 14.4

A. 1. (a) $715.83
(b) $83 375.45
(c) $641.41
3. (a) $503.15 rounded to $550.00; $n = 104.522813$ months
(b) $288.05
(c) $2889.95
5. nominal annual rate compounded semi-annually = 9.50%
7. (a) $86 514.51
(b) $n = 165.56125$ months
(c) $54 269.19
9. $380.00; balance $38 794.01
11. Balance December 1 = $38 795.58

Review Exercise

1. (a) $1491.37
(b) $12 723.84
(c) $15 771.75
(d) $338.49
(e) $1247.91
(f) $4300.94; totals are $47 723.84; $12 723.84; $35 000.00
3. (a) $n = 24.830989$
(b) $28 940.29
(c) $426.66
(d) $1807.58
(e) $5477.40; totals are $49 664.41; $9664.41; 40 000.00
5. (a) $735.80
(b) $280.57
(c) $23 981.92
(d) $1000.88
(e) $15 900.11; totals are $24 843.68; $11 087.74; $13 755.94
7. (a) $n = 9.3198366$
(b) $1139.88
9. (a) $n = 11.744464$
(b) $3211.27
11. (a) $1091.28
(b) $125 324.69
(c) $1023.15
13. (a) $n = 117.33202$ months
(b) $332.79
(c) $118 274.40; $117 332.79; $941.61
15. (a) $161.75
(b) $1264.00
(c) $5086.52
(d) $21.41
(e) $478.06; totals are $7764.00; $1264.00; $6500.00
17. 8.38%
19. (a) $601.20
(b) $1651.04
(c) $25 598.05
(d) $638.94

Self-Test

1. $6027.52
3. $12 866.98
5. (a) $1406.95
(b) $174 506.12
(c) $1479.66
7. 10.0%

CHAPTER 15

Exercise 15.1

A. 1. $97 780.05
3. $23 634.93
5. $52 193.61
7. $7173.32

B. 1. $466.70
3. $14 625.54
5. $10 321.48
7. $4 278 801.75
9. $42 940.38
11. $1161.31
13. (a) $29 546.64
(b) $792.35
(c) $30 338.99
15. $5450.07

Exercise 15.2

A. 1. (a) $4877.98
(b) $20 122.02
3. (a) $1453.37
(b) $8546.63

B. **1.** **(a)** $14 304.00; $114 304.00
(b) $6359.60; $106 359.60
3. **(a)** $–4435.32; $20 564.68
(b) $3687.99; $28 687.99
5. $4 569 384.48
7. $103 723.59

Exercise 15.3

A. **1.** –$77.15; $4922.85

Schedule of Accumulation of Discount

Payment interval	*coupon b = 3%*	*Interest on book i = 3.25%*	*Discount accumulated*	*Book value*	*Discount balance*
0				4922.85	77.15
1	150.00	159.99	9.99	4932.84	67.16
2	150.00	160.32	10.32	4943.16	56.84
3	150.00	160.65	10.65	4953.81	46.19
4	150.00	161.00	11.00	4964.81	35.19
5	150.00	161.36	11.36	4976.17	23.83
6	150.00	161.73	11.73	4987.90	12.10
7	150.00	162.10	12.10	5000.00	—
Total	1050.00	1127.15	77.15		

3. 57.86; 1057.86

Schedule of Amortization of Premium

Payment interval	*Coupon b = 6%*	*Interest on book i = 5%*	*Premium amortized*	*Book value*	*Premium balance*
0				1057.86	57.86
1	60.00	52.89	7.11	1050.75	50.75
2	60.00	52.54	7.46	1043.29	43.29
3	60.00	52.16	7.84	1035.45	35.45
4	60.00	51.77	8.23	1027.22	27.22
5	60.00	51.36	8.64	1018.58	18.58
6	60.00	50.93	9.07	1009.51	9.51
7	60.00	50.49	9.51	1000.00	—
Total	420.00	362.14	57.86		

B. **1.** $976.84
3. $387.55

Exercise 15.4

1. 5.868%
3. 7.9%
5. 9.26%

Exercise 15.5

A. **1.** **(a)** $558.24
(b) $6399.60
3. **(a)** $22.03
(b) $3104.14

B. **1.** **(a)** $500.00
(b) $265.25
(c) $765.25
(d) $10 868.38
3. **(a)** $62.50
(b) $143.33
(c) $205.83
(d) $2246.16

C. **1.** **(a)** $2699.00
(b) $64 776.00
(c) $10 224.00
3. $2419.29; totals are $16 935.03; $3064.99; $20 000.02
5. $2840.83
7. **(a)** $495.27
(b) $9598.44
9. **(a)** $4275.00
(b) $1124.00
(c) $5399.00
(d) $36 976.00
11. **(a)** $302.01
(b) $21 903.91
(c) $257.62
(d) $764.19
(e) $97 252.61; totals are $54 361.80; $45 637.43; $99 999.23
13. **(a)** $24 750.00
(b) $8604.00
(c) $33 354.00
(d) $13 931.00
(e) $107 196.00
(f) $232 277.00; totals are $172 073.00; $127 921.00; $300 000.00

Review Exercise

1. **(a)** $5336.73
(b) $4550.35
3. $26 174.35
5. $1129.61; $21 129.61
7. **(a)** $15 620.41
(b) $84 379.59
(c) $85 664.12
9. $4527.64
11. **(a)** $12.56%
13. $272.16; $4727.84
15. gain of $1899.18
17. $7.65%
19. **(a)** $44 248.79
(b) $48 017.12
(c) $1795.38
21. **(a)** $9268.75
(b) $28 862.02
(c) $1873.21
(d) Totals are $92 687.50; $17 312.54; $110 000.04
23. **(a)** $13 750.00
(b) $8279.90
(c) $22 029.90
(d) $72 194.23
(e) $5989.29
(f) Totals are $66 239.23; $33 760.77; $100 000.00
25. **(a)** $2469.40
(b) $10 612.00
(c) $21 194.78
(d) $788.92
27. **(a)** $n = 38.468063$
(b) $8318.12

Self-Test

1. $9269.44
3. $367.77 (premium)
5. $4596.98
7. 12.46%
9. 12.94%
11. $240.24
13. $603 102.20

CHAPTER 16

Exercise 16.1

A. 1. Alternative 2; PV \$44 634; \$53 448
3. Alternative 1; PV \$22 205; \$23 384
5. Alternative 1 PV \$2000; \$2392.76

B. 1. Alternative 2; PV \$62 363; \$73 601
3. Offer A; PV \$30 026; \$29 769
5. Buy; Cost of buying = \$83 564; leasing = \$106 036

Exercise 16.2

A. 1. Reject; NPV is −\$5367
3. Alternative 1; NPV \$234; \$203
5. Alternative 1; NPV \$1666; \$352

B. 1. Project B; NPV \$2568; \$1787
3. No; NPV is −\$8561
5. Yes; NPV \$5696
7. Yes; NPV \$5142

Exercise 16.3

A. 1. 25.3%
3. 20.7%

B. 1. at 18%, NPV = \$6102; at 20%, NPV = −\$292; R.O.I. = 19.9%
3. at 18%, NPV = \$1286; at 20%, NPV = −\$104; R.O.I. = 19.9%
5. at 22%, NPV = \$148; at 24%, NPV = −\$1538; R.O.I. = 22.2%

Review Exercise

1. Alternative B; PV \$51 624; \$52 161
3. Alternative 1; NPV \$3916; \$3597
5. −\$22 226
7. at 26%, NPV = \$370; at 28%, NPV = −\$1939; R.O.I. = 26.3%
9. at 16%, NPV = \$47 272; at 18%, NPV = −\$22 226; R.O.I = 17.4%
11. at 24%, NVP = \$2035; at 26%, NVP = −\$184; R.O.I = 25.8%
13. Project B; PV \$22 256, \$22 909
15. −\$1215
17. Yes; NPV = \$28 940

Self-Test

1. Alternative A; PV \$13 552; \$10 856
3. at 16%, NPV = \$3466; at 18%, NPV =−\$4386; R.O.I. = 16.9%
5. Proposal B; NPV \$701; \$1427

Index

A

B

C

Q

R

S

T

"AS IS" LICENSE AGREEMENT AND LIMITED WARRANTY

READ THIS LICENSE CAREFULLY BEFORE OPENING THIS PACKAGE. BY OPENING THIS PACKAGE, YOU ARE AGREEING TO THE TERMS AND CONDITIONS OF THIS LICENSE. IF YOU DO NOT AGREE, DO NOT OPEN THE PACKAGE. PROMPTLY RETURN THE UNOPENED PACKAGE AND ALL ACCOMPANYING ITEMS TO THE PLACE YOU OBTAINED THEM. THESE TERMS APPLY TO ALL LICENSED SOFTWARE ON THE DISK EXCEPT THAT THE TERMS FOR USE OF ANY SHAREWARE OR FREEWARE ON THE DISKETTES ARE AS SET FORTH IN THE ELECTRONIC LICENSE LOCATED ON THE DISK:

1. GRANT OF LICENSE and OWNERSHIP: The enclosed computer programs and any data ("Software") are licensed, not sold, to you by Pearson Canada Inc. ("We" or the "Company") in consideration of your adoption of the accompanying Company textbooks and/or other materials, and your agreement to these terms. You own only the disk(s) but we and/or our licensors own the Software itself. This license allows instructors and students enrolled in the course using the Company textbook that accompanies this Software (the "Course") to use and display the enclosed copy of the Software for academic use only, so long as you comply with the terms of this Agreement. You may make one copy for back up only. We reserve any rights not granted to you.
2. USE RESTRICTIONS: You may not sell or license copies of the Software or the Documentation to others. You may not transfer, distribute or make available the Software or the Documentation, except to instructors and students in your school who are users of the adopted Company textbook that accompanies this Software in connection with the course for which the textbook was adopted. You may not reverse engineer, disassemble, decompile, modify, adapt, translate or create derivative works based on the Software or the Documentation. You may be held legally responsible for any copying or copyright infringement that is caused by your failure to abide by the terms of these restrictions.
3. TERMINATION: This license is effective until terminated. This license will terminate automatically without notice from the Company if you fail to comply with any provisions or limitations of this license. Upon termination, you shall destroy the Documentation and all copies of the Software. All provisions of this Agreement as to limitation and disclaimer of warranties, limitation of liability, remedies or damages, and our ownership rights shall survive termination.
4. DISCLAIMER OF WARRANTY: THE COMPANY AND ITS LICENSORS MAKE NO WARRANTIES ABOUT THE SOFTWARE, WHICH IS PROVIDED "AS-IS." IF THE DISK IS DEFECTIVE IN MATERIALS OR WORKMANSHIP, YOUR ONLY REMEDY IS TO RETURN IT TO THE COMPANY WITHIN 30 DAYS FOR REPLACEMENT UNLESS THE COMPANY DETERMINES IN GOOD FAITH THAT THE DISK HAS BEEN MISUSED OR IMPROPERLY INSTALLED, REPAIRED, ALTERED OR DAMAGED. THE COMPANY DISCLAIMS ALL WARRANTIES, EXPRESS OR IMPLIED, INCLUDING WITHOUT LIMITATION, THE IMPLIED WARRANTIES OF MERCHANTABILITY AND FITNESS FOR A PARTICULAR PURPOSE. THE COMPANY DOES NOT WARRANT, GUARANTEE OR MAKE ANY REPRESENTATION REGARDING THE ACCURACY, RELIABILITY, CURRENTNESS, USE, OR RESULTS OF USE, OF THE SOFTWARE.
5. LIMITATION OF REMEDIES AND DAMAGES: IN NO EVENT, SHALL THE COMPANY OR ITS EMPLOYEES, AGENTS, LICENSORS OR CONTRACTORS BE LIABLE FOR ANY INCIDENTAL, INDIRECT, SPECIAL OR CONSEQUENTIAL DAMAGES ARISING OUT OF OR IN CONNECTION WITH THIS LICENSE OR THE SOFTWARE, INCLUDING, WITHOUT LIMITATION, LOSS OF USE, LOSS OF DATA, LOSS OF INCOME OR PROFIT, OR OTHER LOSSES SUSTAINED AS A RESULT OF INJURY TO ANY PERSON, OR LOSS OF OR DAMAGE TO PROPERTY, OR CLAIMS OF THIRD PARTIES, EVEN IF THE COMPANY OR AN AUTHORIZED REPRESENTATIVE OF THE COMPANY HAS BEEN ADVISED OF THE POSSIBILITY OF SUCH DAMAGES. SOME JURISDICTIONS DO NOT ALLOW THE LIMITATION OF DAMAGES IN CERTAIN CIRCUMSTANCES, SO THE ABOVE LIMITATIONS MAY NOT ALWAYS APPLY.
6. GENERAL: THIS AGREEMENT SHALL BE CONSTRUED AND INTERPRETED ACCORDING TO THE LAWS OF THE PROVINCE OF ONTARIO. This Agreement is the complete and exclusive statement of the agreement between you and the Company and supersedes all proposals, prior agreements, oral or written, and any other communications between you and the company or any of its representatives relating to the subject matter.

Should you have any questions concerning this agreement or if you wish to contact the Company for any reason, please contact in writing: Permissions, Pearson Education Canada, a division of Pearson Canada Inc., 26 Prince Andrew Place, Toronto, Ontario M3C 2T8.